Bradshaw's Railway Manual
Shareholders' Guide and Directory
1869

Bradshaw's
Railway Manual
Shareholders' Guide and Directory
1869

A new edition of Bradshaw's Railway Manual,
Shareholders' Guide and Official Directory for 1869
with enlarged type and an introduction by
C. R. Clinker

DAVID & CHARLES REPRINTS

This book is a new edition with enlarged
type of the 1869 issue of Bradshaw's Railway Manual,
Shareholders' Guide and Official Directory
published by W. J. Adams London and Bradshaw & Blacklock Manchester
Introduction © C. R. Clinker 1969

This edition first published 1969

Printed in Great Britain for
David & Charles (Publishers) Limited
South Devon House Newton Abbot
by Latimer Trend & Company Limited
Whitstable

INTRODUCTION

The name 'Bradshaw' is inevitably associated with the famous railway timetable which *Punch,* poking fun at its complications in a series of articles in 1865, turned into a national institution. But, amongst lesser known works, George Bradshaw and his firm also published exquisite railway maps, descriptive guides and itineraries, and a handbook to canals and navigable rivers.

Bradshaw's Railway Manual, Shareholders' Guide and Official Directory (the title finally adopted in 1863) was started in 1848 and issued annually up to 1923, inclusive. As will be obvious from the title, this serial publication was primarily for the benefit of people having a financial interest in railways and, especially, those whose concern extended rather beyond the mere return on their money to attendance at company meetings, criticism of management, writing letters to the railway press, and so on. In short, a practical interest which required a fairly extensive knowledge of railway companies and their activities.

The *Manual* set out to meet this need by building up and maintaining, year after year, a detailed annual record of the history and contemporary position of every railway company in the British Isles, to which were added foreign and colonial railways financed by British money or under British management, canals and sundry auxiliary firms engaged in rolling stock construction and similar business. Some idea of the magnitude of the work may be gained from knowledge of the fact that the number of railway companies in the British Isles alone rose steadily to a peak of 476 in 1867, after which it slowly declined by amalgamation and abandonment.

In addition to the record of individual companies, the *Manual* contains a comprehensive selection of other information of a more general nature, including statistics, some bringing together data not easily obtainable elsewhere. The information given has varied considerably at different periods, but has usually included reproduction *in toto* of important general Acts of Parliament passed in the preceding session and tables of local Acts passed, withdrawn and rejected. A number of tables are devoted to new capital authorised, debenture debts, bank rate changes since 1836, traffic receipts, fluctuations in share prices of the principal companies and a useful section setting out the dividend rates of the larger companies in each half year since their inception. The Railway Directory lists directors with seats in Parliament and provides an index to directors and senior railway officers with the companies they serve. Among miscellanea, there are useful extracts from companies' half-yearly and annual reports, engineers' reports on the progress of new works currently in hand, full texts of the more important inter-company agreements (many concerning limitation of competition and pooling of receipts) and particulars of lines opened during the preceding year.

The principal present-day value of the *Manual* is as a contemporary source of information for railway historians. But the inexperienced user, generally more fastidious in the matter of accuracy than the investors of the last century, should beware of pitfalls. As with Bradshaw's timetable, the large volume of intelligence packed into each issue was supplied by the railway companies themselves and printed more or less as received. Here and there may be detected the reticence of a moribund or ailing concern and a reluctance to revise its information yearly, probably for fear of giving away its true position or, for the same reason, supplying the barest of statistics. Misprints in figures are not numerous and usually obvious.

It it tempting to the casual or less experienced user to treat the lists of lines opened in the previous year as a ready-to-use source. However, these require particular care and it is strongly recommended that the information given, especially the dates, be checked with at least one other contemporary source. The dates quoted in the lists are frequently at variance with those for the same event mentioned in the section dealing with the company concerned. After January 1892, when Bradshaw's timetable commenced to show the opening dates of new lines, an additional variant is introduced, with a tendency to date many lines as opened on the first of the month (the date on which the timetable came into force), whereas some had been opened during the preceding weeks.

The *Manual* has long been recognised by railway historians as a valuable source book, used with care. This reprint will make it available to many more, to some of whom it may be unexplored, or even unknown. They, too, should be cautious.

C. R. CLINKER

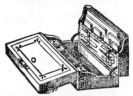

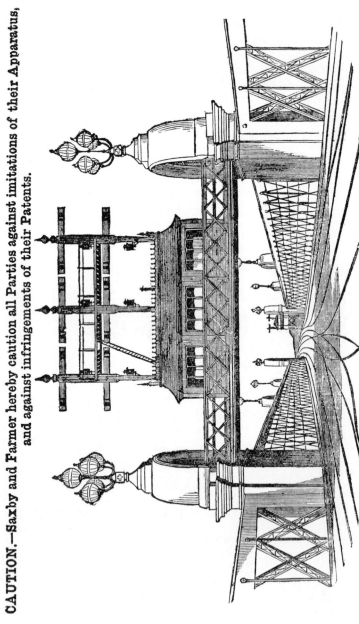

THE LONDON
𝔚arming and 𝔙entilating ℭompany
(LIMITED),

ABINGDON CHAMBERS, 12, ABINGDON STREET,
Westminster, S.W.

MANAGING DIRECTOR AND SECRETARY, MR. WOODCOCK.

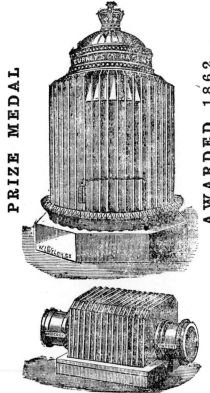

PRIZE MEDAL

AWARDED 1862.

Churches, Greenhouses, Offices, and Buildings of every description warmed by means of a modification of the plan successfully used by Sir Goldsworthy Gurney in both Houses of Parliament.

Steam, Hot Water, Gas, and in open or enclosed Fire-places, Coal and Coke are equally available for the process.

The cost is less and the effect greater than that of any other known means.

For ordinary Sitting Rooms a patent fresh air grate is made use of.

The Horticulturist will find herein an instrument of new and important powers.

The apparatus may be seen at work in the *Houses of Parliament*, the offices of the department of *Science and Art*, in St. Paul's, *York Minster*, and 14 other *Cathedrals*, besides 1,000 *Churches* in England, and Government and other Public and Private Buildings, too numerous to name in an advertisement. Particulars and testimonials forwarded on application.

N.B.—In order to meet constant applications for the heating of smaller rooms, a small Coke Stove has since last season been produced, suitable for Sitting Rooms, Bed Rooms, small Halls, Offices, and Conservatories. Prices, from 34s. and upwards. [38-Lo.

THE
NEW REGISTERED PORTMANTEAU,

Registered and Manufactured by

JOHN SOUTHGATE,

75 & 76, WATLING STREET, LONDON, E.C.

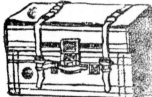

THIS PORTMANTEAU is admitted by all who have used it to be the most PERFECT and USEFUL of any yet invented, and to combine all the advantages so long desired by all who travel.

The peculiar conveniences of this Portmanteau are, that it contains *separate compartments* for each description of Clothes, Boots, &c.; each division is kept entirely distinct, and is immediately accessible on opening the Portmanteau without lifting or disturbing anything else. Every article is packed perfectly flat, and remains so during the whole of the journey.

It may be obtained of MESSRS. MOORE and Co., 14, St. James's Street, London; of Mr. BAYS, Hatter, Cambridge; of Messrs. ELLENGER and Co., Moseley Street, Newcastle-on-Tyne; Mr. MULBY, Trunk Maker, Manchester; Mr. NICHOLSON, Saddler, Manchester; Mr. LOVE, Trunk Maker, Hull; Mr. NORTHAM, Trunk Maker, opposite St. Sidwell's Church, Exeter; of most Outfitters and Saddlers throughout the kingdom; and of

JOHN SOUTHGATE,

MANUFACTURER OF EVERY DESCRIPTION OF

PORTMANTEAUS AND TRAVELLING EQUIPAGES,

75 and 76, WATLING STREET, CITY, E.C.

[42.-Lo.

BRADSHAW'S
RAILWAY MANUAL,
SHAREHOLDERS' GUIDE,
AND
OFFICIAL DIRECTORY for 1869;

CONTAINING THE

HISTORY AND FINANCIAL POSITION OF EVERY COMPANY,

BRITISH, FOREIGN, AND COLONIAL;

STATISTICS, POWERS, AND OTHER DATA TO THE CLOSE OF THE YEAR;

THE RAILWAY INTEREST IN PARLIAMENT, ETC.,

ACCOMPANIED BY AN

ALPHABETICAL ARRANGEMENT OF THE WHOLE ADMINISTRATIVE

AND EXECUTIVE STAFFS IN THE THREE KINGDOMS;

ILLUSTRATED WITH ELABORATE

STEEL-ENGRAVED RAILWAY MAPS

OF THE

BRITISH ISLES AND THE CONTINENT OF EUROPE, INDIA, &c.

VOL. XXI.

London:
PUBLISHED BY W. J. ADAMS,

BRADSHAW'S GENERAL RAILWAY PUBLICATION OFFICES, 59, FLEET STREET, E.C.;
EFFINGHAM WILSON, 11, ROYAL EXCHANGE, E.C.

Manchester:
BRADSHAW & BLACKLOCK, ALBERT SQUARE,

ALSO AT

BRADSHAW'S PUBLICATION OFFICES, 13, CANNING PLACE, LIVERPOOL;
52, BULL STREET, BIRMINGHAM; 21, BOW STREET, SHEFFIELD;
HANOVER STREET, EDINBURGH; 144, ARGYLE STREET, GLASGOW;
51, GRAFTON STREET (CORNER OF STEPHEN'S GREEN), DUBLIN;
AND OF ALL BOOKSELLERS.

1869.

PREFACE TO VOLUME XXI.

There cannot be much of freshness in a series of prefaces extending over a period of twenty-one years. Up to 1867 there had been a progressive increase, not merely in the extent of mileage brought into operation, but in the number of companies owning the properties. The highest number of separate undertakings in the three kingdoms we have had to record (in the volume commencing 1867) was 476, but in that year the number, by amalgamations, had decreased to 463; and a further diminution, not merely by amalgamation but by abandonments during 1868, reduces the number of separate companies of which we can take cognisance to 455. A still greater reduction may be anticipated for 1869, not alone in consequence of the paucity of new companies for the current year, but also on account of abandonments and amalgamations which are to be brought before Parliament during the forthcoming session.

But, although the number of separate undertakings gives promise to be annually on the decrease, the actual mileage brought under traffic is making steady progress. In 1866 the number of miles in operation extended to 13,854, of which 7,711 were double lines, and 6,143 single. During 1867 this mileage had increased to 14,247, of which 7,844 were double and 6,403 single. The increase for the latter year was therefore 133 of double lines, and 260 of single, making a total of 393 additional miles. Of this increase of 393 miles, there were in England 114 of double and 222 of single, making 336 out of the 393. In Scotland the extensions were confined to 19 miles of double and 19 miles of single, while in Ireland, curiously enough, the extension was also 19 miles, but wholly of single line.

It will be observed from our customary compilation of new mileage brought under traffic during 1868, that the openings extend to 315 miles, of which at least one half may be regarded as composed of single lines.

Thus far the decrease in separate undertakings and the advance of mileage in operation.

The growth of capital, notwithstanding the enormous financial difficulties which companies have had to encounter, has still been comparatively enormous. In our preface for last year we gave an outline of the growth of capital and revenue since 1855. For that year and for 1865, the progress of ten years was thus exemplified :—

	Capital.	Revenue.
1855	£297,584,709	£21,507,599
1865	455,478,143	35,751,655
Increase	£157,893,434	£14,244,056

For ten years, therefore, the average increase of capital had been at the rate of £15,789,343, and of revenue £1,424,405. Matters have since proceeded in more sober fashion, the statistics for 1866 and 1867 having been as follow :—

AUTHORISED.		Shares. £	Loans. £	Total. £
ENGLAND and WALES	1866	388,605,689	129,762,809	518,368,498
	1867	400,073,180	135,982,971	536,056,151
Increase in 1867...............................£		11,467,491	6,220,162	17,687,653
SCOTLAND	1866	50,104,794	17,024,623	67,129,417
	1867	52,915,650	17,447,356	70,363,006
Increase in 1867...............................£		2,810,856	422,733	3,233,589
IRELAND	1866	27,141,150	7,625,341	35,066,491
	1867	28,458,610	7,975,641	36,434,251
Increase in 1867...............................£		1,017,460	350,300	1,367,769
UNITED KINGDOM	1866	466,151,633	154,412,773	620,564,406
	1867	481,447,440	161,405,968	642,853,408
Increase in 1867...............................£		15,295,807	6,993,195	22,289,002

PAID UP.		Ordinary. £	Preferential. £	Debentures. £	Total. £
ENGLAND and WALES	1866	193,674,973	109,322,884	12,566,697	315,564,554
	1867	197,369,264	115,873,397	14,007,908	327,250,569
Increase in 1867 ....£		3,694,291	6,550,513	1,441,211	11,686,015
SCOTLAND	1866	19,797,076	19,460,908	1,254,732	40,512,716
	1867	20,430,938	21,482,910	1,246,972	43,160,820
Increase in 1867 ....£		633,862	2,022,002	Dec. 7,760	2,648,104
IRELAND	1866	14,773,580	5,671,306	284,165	20,729,051
	1867	15,223,652	5,853,050	382,237	21,458,939
Increase in 1867 ....£		450,072	181,744	98,072	729,888
UNITED KINGDOM	1866	228,245,629	134,455,098	14,105,594	376,806,321
	1867	233,023,854	143,205,357	15,637,117	391,870,328
Increase in 1867 ....£		4,778,225	8,754,259	1,531,523	15,064,007

It is only proper to add that a number of companies, incorporated in 1864 and 1865, had not raised any of their capital—a position in which they continue to be placed, and from among whom the propositions for abandonment continue to issue.

The compilations of revenue for 1866 and 1867 are given by the
Board of Trade as under:—

Year.	Receipts.	Per Mile.	Expenditure.	Per Cent.	Net.	Per Cent. to Capital.
1866......	£38,164,354	£2,755	£18,811,673	49	£19,352,681	4·01
1867......	39,479,999	2,770	19,848,952	50	19,631,017	3·91

Such are a few of the distinctive materials with which the Manual
has to deal from year to year, apart from and in addition to the
details of traffic, the distributions in dividend, and the alliances,
more or less intimate, that are continually being formed between
companies that had in former periods evinced so much antagonism
towards each other. For all these details, and for warrant of their
authenticity, we continue indebted to the prompt kindness of the
official staff of the United Kingdom. It has become with them a
" household word " to contribute to the sufficiency and the accuracy
of BRADSHAW'S MANUAL, for which evidence of regard the Proprietors, the Publishers, and the Compilers alike tender their annual
acknowledgments.

We here simply add, almost as a matter of routine, that the
APPENDIX to the present Volume is enriched, in common with its
predecessors, by a number of valuable and useful documents that are
not to be found in any extant publication ;—that the MAPS which
customarily accompany our annual issue are corrected and extended
to the latest moment; and also that the OFFICIAL DIRECTORY maintains that claim for completeness and accuracy which has been
unreservedly accorded to it for so many years.

Manchester, February, 1869.

CONTENTS.

CONTINENTAL, &c.

AFRICA.

AUSTRALASIA.

ADDENDA.

APPENDIX.

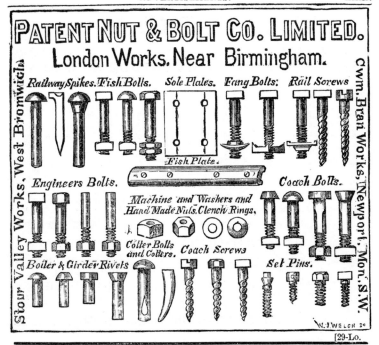
GOADSBY AND CO.,

MANUFACTURERS OF

COLOURS, WHITE LEAD, PAINTS,

AND VARNISHES,

ALSO OF

RAILWAY, COLLIERY, AND WAGON GREASE.

MAKERS OF OXIDE OF IRON PAINT.

G. & Co. have the testimony of many of the largest Engineers in the North of England as to the superiority of their Manufacture of this Article.

COLOURS, PAINTS, and VARNISHES packed in strong and appropriate Packages for Export, suitable for every Market in the world.

Messrs. G. & Co. can refer with pleasure to several of the large Railway Companies (both British and Continental) with whom they have had, and still hold, Contracts as to the satisfactory manner in which they have been executed.

Manufactory—NEWTON HEATH,   } MANCHESTER.
Offices—2, 4, and 6, ALBERT BRIDGE,

London Offices: 187, BISHOPSGATE STREET WITHOUT.

[9-z.

BRADSHAW'S
MANUAL AND DIRECTORY.

INTRODUCTION.

THIS MANUAL is divided into four departments, viz., United Kingdom; Continental; Indian, American, and Colonial; and Auxiliary Associations, which may be more or less connected with the railway interest. The Appendix contains Parliamentary Documents, Agreements, &c., and is accompanied by an Alphabetical Arrangement of the whole Administrative and Executive Staff in the Three Kingdoms.

Schemes passed since 1853 have their deposits retained until the line is completed, unless a bond to twice the amount is lodged, or one-half the capital expended on authorised purposes. Companies promoting extensions are debarred paying dividends on ordinary stock when the fixed periods expire, unless the branches are opened under certificate of Board of Trade.

A general clause is also inserted in Acts passed since 1856, in these terms:—"That this Act, or anything therein, shall not exempt the railway from the provisions of any general Act relating to the recited Acts, or this Act, or of any general Act relating to railways, or to the better or more impartial audit of the accounts of railway companies now in force, or which may hereafter pass during this or any other session of Parliament, or from any future revision or alteration under the authority of Parliament, of the maximum rates of fares and charges by the recited Acts, or the maximum rates of small parcels, thereby respectively authorised."

By a clause inserted in the Acts passed since 1859, arrears of interest on "preference shares," created on and after that date, are not to accumulate. Should the profits in any one year not be sufficient to pay preference dividends, it is expressly stipulated that "no part of the deficiency shall be made good out of the profits of any subsequent year, or out of any other funds of the company."

The subjoined stringent standing order was adopted in the session of 1863:—"In every Railway Bill in which new works are authorised the committee shall make provision for insuring the completion of the line by impounding the deposit, or by providing that after the expiration of a period to be limited to such Bill, not exceeding five years from the passing of the Act in the case of a new line, and three years in case of the extension of time for completing the line, the company shall be liable to a penalty of not less than 20l. and not exceeding 50l. per day, to be recoverable as a debt due to the Crown, for every day after the period so limited, until such line shall be completed and open for public traffic; but no penalty shall accrue in respect of any time during which it shall appear by a certificate to be obtained from the Board of Trade, that the company was prevented from completing or opening such line by unforeseen accident or circumstances beyond their control; but the want of sufficient funds shall not be held to be a circumstance beyond their control."

Another general rule was imported into the legislation of 1864, namely:—"That it shall not be lawful for any company to issue any share, nor shall any share vest in the person accepting the same, unless and until a sum not being less than one-fifth part of the amount of such share shall have been paid up in respect thereof."

The scale of voting is thus regulated by the Consolidation Act (8 Vic., cap. 16, 1845),—"Section 75. At all general meetings every shareholder shall be entitled to vote according to the prescribed scale of voting, and where no scale shall be prescribed every shareholder shall have one vote for every share up to 10, and shall have an additional vote for every five beyond the first 10 shares held by him up to 100, and an additional vote for every 10 shares held by him beyond the first 100 shares: provided always, that no shareholder be entitled to vote unless he shall have paid the calls then due upon the shares held by him."

I.—UNITED KINGDOM.

1.—ABERDARE.

Incorporated by 8 and 9 Vic., cap. 159 (July 31st, 1845), for making a line from the Taff Vale Railway to a certain tramroad leading from the Hirwain Iron Works to the Aberdare Canal, in the parish of Aberdare, Glamorganshire. Length, 8¼ miles, and leased under the Aberdare Incorporation Act, to the Taff Vale, at 10 per cent.

CAPITAL.—50,000l., in 1,000 shares of 50l. each, called up; loans, 16,000l. From this sum is deducted one shilling per cent. for management.

DIRECTORS:

Chairman—JAMES POOLE, Esq., Wick House, Durdham Down, Bristol.

Philip Henry Vaughan, Esq., Redland, near Bristol.

Charles Mallard, Esq., Dundonald House, Tyndalls Park, Bristol.

Henry Jones Evans, Esq., Brecon Old Bank, Cardiff.

Richard Vaughan, Esq., Bath Street, Bristol.

*John Jones, Esq., Rownham Wharf, Bristol.

*A. George Downside, Esq., Stoke Bishop. near Bristol.

* Retire in February, 1869.

Secretary, John Curtis.

Offices—Exchange Buildings, Bristol.

2.—ABERDARE AND CENTRAL WALES JUNCTION.

Incorporated by 29 and 30 Vic., cap. 304 (30th July, 1866), to construct a line from the Taff Vale at Aberdare to the Neath and Brecon, with a branch to the Taff Vale. Length, 13¼ miles. Capital, 210,000l. in 10l. shares, and 70,000l. on loan. Arrangements with Central Wales and Neath and Brecon, which may subscribe 50,000l. each.

No. of Directors—5; minimum, 3; quorum, 3 and 2. *Qualification*, 300l.

DIRECTORS:

Sir Charles Henry Rouse Boughton, Bart., Downton Hall, Ludlow.

John Robertson, Esq., Llangollen.

Richard Green Price, Esq., M.P., Norton Manor, Presteign, and 3, Suffolk Place S.W.

3.—ABERGAVENNY AND MONMOUTH.

Incorporated by 28 and 29 Vic., cap. 276 (5th July, 1865), to construct a line from the West Midland, at Abergavenny, to the Coleford Monmouth Usk and Pontypool. Length, 19¾ miles. Capital, 150,000l. in shares, and 49,900l. on loan. Facilities over Coleford and Monmouth, and part of West Midland, and Merthyr and Tredegar. Arrangements with London and North Western and Vale of Crickhowell.

By 31 and 32 Vic., cap. 102 (13th July, 1868), an extension of time till 1873 for completion of works was obtained.

No. of Directors—6; minimum, 4; quorum, 3. *Qualification*, 500l.

DIRECTORS:

Crawshay Bailey, Esq., Nant-y-Glo, near Newport, Monmouthshire, and 16, New Street, Spring Gardens, S.W.

Abraham Darby, Esq., Ebbw Vale, Monmouthshire.

Colonel Henry Morgan Clifford,

Frederick Levick, Esq., Newport, Monmouthshire.

John Allen Rolls, Esq.

4.—ABINGDON.

Incorporated by 18 Vic., cap. 69 (June 15th, 1855), to make a railway from the Oxford Branch of the Great Western to Abingdon. Length, 1¾ mile. Broad gauge. Power is given by the Act to lay an additional rail, so as to admit the passage thereon of engines and carriages adapted for the narrow gauge. Opened 2nd June, 1856. Worked by the Great Western, by which the line is rented for 60 per cent. of goods traffic receipts.

By 25 and 26 Vic., cap. 216 (7th August, 1862), the company was authorised to raise additional capital to the extent of 5,000l. at 5 per cent., to cancel and re-issue forfeited shares, and to create debenture stock in lieu of loans.

No. of Directors—7; minimum, 6; quorum, 3. *Qualification*, 20 shares.

DIRECTORS;

Chairman—JOHN HYDE, Jun., Esq., Abingdon.

Georges Bowes Morland, Esq., Abingdon. | James Williams, Esq., Abingdon.
James Badcock Sedgefield, Esq., Abingdon. | Geo. Reed, Esq., Burnham, Bridgwater.
John Creemer Clarke, Esq., Abindon.

OFFICERS.—Sec., W. J. Sedgefield; Auditors, E. S. Copeland and Bromley Challenor.

5.—ABOYNE AND BRAEMAR.

Incorporated by 28 and 29 Vic., cap. 279 (5th July, 1865), to construct a line from the Deeside Extension, at Aboyne, to Bridge of Gairn. Length, 11 miles. Capital, 66,000l. in shares, and 22,000l. on loan. Deeside, which works the line, subscribed 10,000l. Opened to Ballater, 17th October, 1866.

REVENUE.—The receipts for the half-year ending 31st December were 1,733l., the working expenditure 549l., leaving a net revenue of 1,184l. Interest on debentures, &c., left 654l., which, with 331l. accrued to revenue from the opening of the line. It was resolved in March, that, as there had not been a sufficient amount of capital raised to meet all the necessary expenditure on the line, works, &c., the sum of 785l. be transferred to the credit of capital account instead of being paid in dividend.

CAPITAL.—The expenditure to 31st July amounted to 65,820l. The receipts from shares were 40,096l., and from loans on debenture 21,999l., making a total of 62,095l., and showing a balance against receipts of 3,730l.

The report for September stated that the receipts for the half-year amounted to 1,536l., and the working expenses to 478l., leaving 1,058l. net. Out of this was deducted 549l. for interest on debentures, leaving 519l. The total free revenue from the opening of the line now amounted to 923l. The net balance, after payment of interest on debentures, was 519l., and interest on bank accounts and other sums due by the Company properly chargeable to the half-year amounted to 196l., leaving a free balance of 324l. This would be sufficient to pay a dividend at the rate of 2 per cent. per annum on the paid-up ordinary capital, but the directors recommended that it be retained until arrangements could be completed to pay off the balances due on capital account.

No. of Directors—6; quorum, 3. *Qualification*, 300l.

DIRECTORS:

Chairman—Lieut.-Col. JAMES ROSS FARQUHARSON, of Invercauld.

Deputy-Chairman—*JOHN DUNCAN, Esq., Advocate, Aberdeen.

William Brown, Esq., Factor, Invercauld. | *Thomas Ruxton, Esq., Advocate, Aberdeen.
John Hickie, Esq., Merchant, London. | deen.
* Representing Deeside. | *AlexanderBurnettWhyte,Esq.,Aberdeen.

OFFICERS.—Sec., W. B. Ferguson, Aberdeen; Gen. Man., Robert Milne, Aberdeen; Eng., Patrick M. Barnett; Auditors, Robert Fletcher, Aberdeen, and James Meston, Aberdeen.
Offices—Aberdeen.

6.—ACTON AND BRENTFORD.

Incorporated by 28 and 29 Vic., cap. 320 (5th July, 1865), to construct a line from the Great Western, at Acton, to Brentford, on the Great Western and Brentford. Length, 3¼ miles. Capital, 90,000l. in shares, and 30,000l. on loan. Arrangements with Great Western and Great Western and Brentford. Mixed gauge.

By 31 and and 32 Vic., cap. 52 (25th June, 1868), an extension of time for completion of works till 1871 was obtained.

No. of Directors—5; quorum, 3. *Qualification*, 200l.

DIRECTORS:

Peter Davey, Esq., Horton, Slough, Bucks. | A. S. Davey, Esq., Blackfriars.
Capt. Bulkeley, G. W. R., Paddington. | George Wyatt, Esq., Highbury.
Secretary, Charles Eley.

Offices—5, Westminster Chambers, Victoria Street, Westminster, S.W.

7.—AFON VALLEY.

Incorporated by 28 and 29 Vic., cap. 376 (6th July, 1865), to construct a line from Port Talbot on the South Wales, to Llangynwyd. Length, 10¾ miles. Capital, 130,000*l.* in shares, and 43,000*l.* on loan. Arrangements with Great Western.

By 29 Vic., cap. 45 (18th May, 1866), the company was authorised to divide its capital into preferred and deferred half-shares, the dividends on the former to be paid out of the profits of the year only.

*No. of Directors—*5; quorum, 3. *Qualification,* 200*l.*

DIRECTORS:

Richard Hanbury Miers, Esq., Newnham, Gloucestershire.
Captain Charles Miller Layton, Glasbury.

William Laurence Banks, Esq., F.S.A. . Watton House, Brecon.
George Grant Francis, Esq.

8.—ALDBOROUGH PIER.

Incorporated by 27 and 28 Vic., cap. 326 (29th July, 1864), to construct a pier at Aldborough, with a railway to the Great Eastern at that place, and a branch to Slaughden. Length, 1½ mile. Capital, 20,000*l.* in 10*l.* shares, and 6,660*l.* on loan. Arrangements with Great Eastern. Meetings in February and August. Works in progress.

*No. of Directors—*5; minimum, 3; quorum, 3 and 2. *Qualification,* 200*l.*

DIRECTORS:

G. T. W. Ferrand. Esq.
Newson Garret, Esq.
Frederick Nash, Esq.

Lieut.-Col. A. J. B. Thélluson.
Rev. William Tate.

OFFICERS.—Sec., Theodore Grant Cresy; Eng., Peter S. Bruff.

9.—ALFORD AND MABLETHORPE.

Incorporated by 27 and 28 Vic., cap. 283 (29th July, 1864), to construct a railway from Alford to Mablethorpe. Length, 8 miles. Capital, 60,000*l.* in 10*l.* shares, and 20,000*l.* on loan. Arrangements with Great Northern.

*No. of Directors—*4; Quorum, 2. *Qualification,* 200*l.*

DIRECTORS:

John Everett, Esq.
Archibald Park, Esq.

Edmund Reeves, Esq.
Thomas Smith, Esq.

10.—ALYTH.

Incorporated by 21 Vic., cap. 43 (14th June, 1868), to make a railway from the Meigle Station of the Scottish North Eastern to the town of Alyth. Capital, in 10*l.* shares, 33,000*l.*; on loan, 11,000*l.* Length, 5¼ miles. Opened September 2nd, 1861.

By 27 and 28 Vic., cap. 82 (23rd June, 1864), the Alyth was leased in perpetuity to the Scottish North Eastern, at an annual rent of 45 per cent. of gross receipts. Power was also given by the the same act to raise new capital in shares to the extent of 3,000*l.*, all of which may be held by the Scottish North Eastern.

REVENUE.—The report for the half-year ending 31st January, stated that, as compared with the corresponding period of last year, the excess was not less than 257*l.* on the receipts and 120*l.* on the free revenue. For the half-year ended 31st December, 1866, the goods traffic was 561*l.*, but for the half-year ended 31st December, 1867, it produced 727*l.* At the same time the increase on the passenger traffic was upwards of 100*l.*

The revenue for the half-year ending 31st July, furnished a dividend equal to 5 per cent. per annum on the preference shares, and of 20s. on the ordinary stock. The chairman remarked it was very gratifying that at last they had for the first time been enabled to declare a dividend, and thus to have fairly turned the corner in the affairs of the company. He also thought that should things continue, as they had every reason to believe they would, they would soon be enabled to declare a dividend equal to that of the parent company. They had, he thought, taken a wise and prudent course in not declaring any dividend until they were enabled to do so on the ordinary as well as the preference stock.

DIRECTORS:
Chairman—GEORGE KINLOCH, Esq., of Kinloch.

Right Hon. The Earl of Airlie, Airlie Lodge, Camden Hill, W.	David Matthewson, Esq., Alyth. David Hean, Esq., Dundee.
Sir George Ramsay, Banff.	David Jobson, Esq., Dundee.

11.—ANGLESEA CENTRAL.

Incorporated by 26 and 27 Vic., cap. 128 (13th July, 1863), to construct a line from the Gaerwen Station of the Chester and Holyhead to the port of Amlwch. Length, 18¾ miles. Capital, 120,000*l.* in 10*l.* shares, and 40,000*l.* on loan. Arrangements with London and North Western. Opened throughout on June 3rd, 1867.

By 27 Vic., cap. 34 (13th May, 1864), the company was authorised to make a deviation of about 3 miles.

By 29 and 30 Vic., cap. — (6th August 1866) the company was authorised to lease or transfer the line to the London and North Western. Also to raise new capital to the extent of 20,000*l.* in shares, 6,600*l.* on loan.

DIRECTORS:

Chairman—WILLIAM BULKELEY HUGHES, Esq., Plâs Côch.

Vice-Chairman—HENRY BRAZIER MITCHELL, Esq., Llaniog, Beaumaris.

Major-General Robert George Hughes, Brynddu, Bangor.	The Rt. Hon. Lord Clarence Paget, Plas Llanfair.
Wm. Laurence Banks, Esq., Pont-y-wal Hall, Brecon.	Edward Richards, Esq., Ynys, Llanerchymedd.
Henry Pritchard, Esq., Trescawen.	Benjamin Roose, Esq., Vrondeg, Almwch, Anglesey.

OFFICERS.—Sec., W. Dew, Bangor; Man., R. T. Phillips; Eng., Robert Algeo; Solicitors, Richard Montagu Preston, Chester, and Samuel Dew, Llangefni; Bankers, National Provincial Bank of England, Amlwch; Auditors, D. Howell Morgan, Westminster Chambers, Victoria Street, London, S.W.

12.—ARBROATH AND FORFAR.

Incorporated by 6 and 7 Wm. IV., cap. 34 (17th May, 1836), for construction of a line commencing on the west at Forfar, in conjunction with the Scottish Midland, and terminating on the east of Arbroath harbour, 15¼ miles. Worked by and leased to, the Scottish North Eastern, from 1st February, 1848. The dividend continues to be equal to 6 per cent. per annum.

CALEDONIAN.—The following clause was inserted in the Act by which the Scottish North Eastern is leased to the Caledonian:—Nothing in this Act contained shall in any way alter, diminish, prejudice, or affect any right, interest, power, preference, or privilege belonging to or vested in the Arbroath and Forfar, under or by virtue of the Arbroath and Forfar Act, 1846, and the Arbroath aud Forfar Act, 1848, or the rent agreed and payable to the Arbroath and Forfar by the Aberdeen, under or in virtue of the same Acts, or shall in any way alter, diminish, prejudice, or affect the nature of the rent-charge, real burden, and priority created by such Acts in respect of the said rent or the right to levy and recover any such rent under and in terms of such Acts; it being hereby expressly provided and declared that all such rights, interest, powers, priority, privileges, rents, rent-charge, and real burden are to remain the same in all respects as if this Act had not been passed, with this exception, that where any obligations were conferred or imposed with reference thereto upon the Aberdeen, the same shall, after the passing of this Act, be performed by, and may be enforced against, the company in the same way and manner, and to the same extent and effect as the same, but for the passing of this Act ought to be performed by, or might have been enforced against, the Scottish North Eastern, under the Scottish North Eastern Act, 1856, and the Scottish North Eastern Act, 1863.

CAPITAL.—The receipts and expenditure on this account, as detailed to the annual meeting in March last, were as follow:—

Received.		Expended.	
Original stock, 2,800 shares, at 25l.	£70,000	Construction of the railway and works, including working plant	£230,350
Guaranteed, 3,200 shares, at 12l. 10s.	40,000	Account for balance of income-tax allowed the Caledonian on	
Unguaranteed, 800 shares at 12l. 10s.	10,000	Guaranteed rent for the year ending 31st January, 1868, to	
Additional stock, 3,200 shares at 12l. 10s.	40,000	be retained from dividends payable to shareholder	204
Liquidation stock, 5,525 shares, at 6l. 5s.	34,531	British Linen Banking Company —balance in their hands	13,247
New additional stock (fifths), 5,862 shares, at 5l.	29,310		
	£223,841		
Loans on mortgage	5,600		
Other debts and liabilities, including unpaid dividends, &c.	358		
Revenue account for balance	14,001		
	£243,801		£243,801

The directors had during the year exercised the power which has been given at several of the annual meetings, to sell part of the liquidation stock held in respect of the reserve fund. The stock sold amounted to 48 shares, and the price received was at the rate of 32l. 15s. per original share of 25l. The premium, being 93l., was carried to credit of revenue.

Directors' Qualification—4 shares of 25l. each.

COMMITTEE OF MANAGEMENT.

Chairman—ROBERT MILN, Esq., of Viewfield, Arbroath.

John Mudie, Esq., of Pitmuies, Arbroath.
James Powrie, Esq., Reswallie, Forfar.
Donald Lindsay, Esq., Ardargie, Bridge of Earn.

Alexander Gordon, Esq., of Ashludie, Arbroath.
William Roberts, Esq., Forfar.
John Trail, Esq., Arbroath.

Three rotate, in order required by Act, every year, and are eligible for re-election.

OFFICERS.—Sec., W. K. Macdonald, Arbroath; Treasurer, William Rollo, Banker, Arbroath.

Head Offices—Arbroath, N. B.

13.—ATHENRY AND ENNIS JUNCTION.

Incorporated by 23 and 24 Vic., cap. 200 (20th August, 1860), to construct a line from the Midland Great Western, at Athenry, to Limerick and Ennis, at the latter place. Length, 36 miles. Capital, 200,000l., in 10l. shares; loans, 66,000l. Works in progress.

By 26 and 27 Vic., cap. 133 (13th July, 1863), an extension of time for compulsory purchase of land to 20th August, 1865, and for construction of works to 20th August, 1867, was obtained. This bill also includes a working agreement for 20 years with the Waterford and Limerick who subscribe 9,000l.

By 28 Vic., cap. 18 (26th May, 1864), the company was authorised to cancel 100,000l. of the original capital of the company, and issue, in lieu and in addition thereto, preference share capital amounting to 130,000l., bearing a dividend of 5 per cent.; and the borrowing powers have been increased from 66,000l., under previous Acts, to 76,000l. Power is also given to issue debenture stock for the last amount in lieu of bonds.

By 30 Vic., cap. 74 (17th June, 1867), the company obtained an extension of time for completion of works to 20th August, 1869, and also running powers over the Midland Great Western, and Limerick and Ennis. Reciprocal facilities with the Waterford and Limerick, and power to abandon former agreement with latter company.

By 31 and 32 Vic., cap. 144 (13th July, 1868), the company was authorised to cancel 35,000l. of its preference shares at 5 per cent., and to issue in lieu thereof 15,000l. of debentures at the same rate, thus obtaining a higher class of security at a saving of 1,000l. annually to revenue; also to lease the Athenry and Tuam on surrender of the existing lease to the Midland Great Western.

It was reported in July that the works were advancing rapidly, and every advantage taken of an unusually fine season in pressing on the line to completion; this advance will be best understood by stating that a sum of 39,000l. had been laid out on works within the past six months. The line is expected to be opened early in the year, the whole of the government loan having been obtained.

CAPITAL.—The expenditure to 30th June amounted to 243,980l., leaving a balance in hand of 5,014l. The receipts on this account were given as follow:—

Ordinary share capital—on calls—

1st call, 1st instant	October, 22, 1860			£9,581
„ 2nd „	January 22, 1861			9,566
2nd „ 1st „	December 1, 1861			9,561
„ 2nd „	March 1, 1862			9,561
3rd „	March 16, 1863			19,084
4th „	December 1, 1863			18,997
5th „	May 2, 1864			18,889
Interest on calls				268
Preference—Class A, paid up in full				65,790
„ B, „				20,000
Loans on debentures—Public Works Loan Commissioners...				40,000
Debentures, ordinary				16,600
Temporary loans				2,246
„ under arrangement to exchange for preference shares			8,850	=248,995

Accounts to 31st December and 30th June. Meetings in January or February, and August or September.

No. of Directors.—Maximum, 9; minimum, 6. Qualification, 500l. Directors retire and are elected in accordance with the Companies Clauses Act.

DIRECTORS:

Chairman—2 Sir COLMAN M. O'LOGHLEN, Bart., M.P., Merrion Square, Dublin, and Drumconora, County Clare.

1 James Fitzgerald Lombard, Esq., J. P., Rathmines, Dublin.
2 David Coffey, Esq., Belvidere House, Drumcondra, County Dublin.
1 William Henry Gregory, Esq., M. P., Coole Park, Gort, County Galway.
1 Joseph Wm. Holland, Esq., Birley House, Sydenham, London.

3 Denis Kirwan, Esq., D.L., Castle Hacket, Tuam.
3 Thomas Redington Roche, Esq., Ryehill, Monivea.
2 Abraham Stephens, Esq., Duncannon, County Wexford.
1, Retire in February,1869; 2, 1870; 3, 1871.

OFFICERS.—Sec., John Fowler Nicoll; Eng.-in-Chief; George Willoughby Hemans. 13, Queen's Square, Westminster, S. W.; Auditors, 1 Michael MacNamara, Ennis, and 2 Thos. Greene, J. P., Ennis; Solicitors, William H. M'Grath and Co.

Offices—53, Lower Dominick Street, Dublin.

14.—ATHENRY AND TUAM.

Incorporated by 21 and 22 Vic., cap. 112 (23rd July, 1858), to construct a line from the Midland Great Western at Athenry to the town of Tuam. Capital, 90,000l , in 10l. shares; loans, 30,000l. Length, 15¼ miles. Estimate, 90,000l., actual cost, 94,500l. Single line, opened 27th September, 1860. A special agreement, dated 26th April, 1859, was entered into with the Midland Great Western to lease the line from date of completion for ten years, at a clear annual fixed rental of 4,000l., the Midland further agreeing to keep the permanent way, stations, and other works and plant in perfect repair during the lease, but allowing for reasonable wear and tear. Power is given both companies to renew this agreement at the termination of the first lease, the terms of such renewal to be subject to the approval of the Board of Trade.

An Act, 23 and 24 Vic., cap. 182, was obtained during the session 1859-60, giving effect to the foregoing agreements, and thus rendering the stock of the company a guaranteed security.

By 31 and 32 Vic., cap. 144 (13th July, 1868) the Athenry and Ennis was authorised to take a lease of the Athenry and Tuam on surrender of the existing lease of the Midland Great Western.

Notice of an application to Parliament in session of 1868-69 has been made to extend the Tuam line to join the Great Northern and Western of Ireland at Claremorris, a distance of 15 miles. This gap, when filled up, will complete the railway system from Waterford through the counties of Limerick, Clare, and Galway to the remotest portions of Mayo and the north-west of Ireland. The application is made under the auspices of the Athenry and Tuam company, and has the support of the southern companies running into that company at Athenry.

The dividends during the year have been at the rate of 3 per cent., the balance from the half-year ending 29th September being 198*l.*

With regard to the advance of 30,000*l.* from the Loan Commissioners, the period for the repayment of which was extended to 31st July last, an Act was passed during the past session, further extending the period of such loans for another year, and the opinion is now confidently entertained, that, before the expiry of that time, Government will have made arrangements either for the purchase of the Irish railways, or for permanent advances, upon fixed terms, of such loans as that obtained by this company.

CAPITAL.—The expenditure on this account to 29th September, 1868, amounted to 95,458*l.*, leaving a balance against the company of 1,221*l.* The receipts have been as under:—

Shares	£61,818
Loans	30,000
Interest, &c.	625
On shares forfeited	30
Transfer from revenue to credit of capital	1,803
	£94,277
Balance	1,221=£95,498

Accounts made up to 25th March and 29th September. Meetings in April and October. *No. of Directors.*—Maximum, 8; minimum, 6; quorum, 3. Directors retire, and are elected in accordance with the Companies Clauses Act. *Qualification*, 50 shares.

DIRECTORS:

3 Chairman— DENIS KIRWAN, Esq., D.L., Castle Hacket, Tuam.

1 Robt. Bodkin, Esq., Annagh, Ballyglunin.	2 Robert Henry, Esq., Tohermore, Tuam.
2 Charles Blake, Esq., Tuam.	1 David Rutledge, Esq., Barbersfort,
2 John William Cannon, Esq., Castlegrove, Tuam.	Ballyglunin.

1, Retire October, 1869; 2, 1870; 3, 1871.

OFFICERS.—Sec., John Fowler Nicoll; Auditors, 1, Laurence Mullen and 2, John Cannon Evans; Eng.-in-Chief, George Willoughby Hemans, 13, Queen Square, Westminster, S.W.; Acting Eng., Henry Brett; Joint Solicitors, James Dillon Meldon and Thomas Higgins.

Head Office—53, Lower Dominick Street, Dublin.

15.—AYLESBURY AND BUCKINGHAM.

Incorporated by 23 and 24 Vic., cap. 192 (6th August, 1860), to construct a line from the town of Aylesbury to join the Buckinghamshire at Claydon Junction. Length, 12¼ miles. Capital, 98,000*l.*, in 25*l.* shares. Loans, 32,500*l.* Working arrangements under usual restrictions, with London and North Western and Buckinghamshire. Opened for traffic September 23rd, 1868.

By 27 and 28 Vic., cap. 217 (25th July, 1864), the company was authorised to raise additional capital to the extent of 12,000*l.* in shares, and 4,000*l.* by loan.

By 28 Vic., cap. 93 (19th June, 1864), the company was authorised to raise additional capital to the extent of 110,000*l.* in shares, and 35,000*l.* on loan. Also to extend the time for completing the undertaking until 2 years after passing of this Act.

By resolution of a special meeting held 18th June, 1866, the directors were authorised to issue preference shares to the extent of 15,000*l.*

By a resolution passed 26th May, 1868, the directors were authorised to issue 15,000*l.* additional preference shares; total, 30,000*l.*

No. of Directors—9; minimum, 3; quorum, 4; and 2 when reduced to 3. *Qualification*, 250*l.*

DIRECTORS:

Chairman—His Grace the DUKE OF BUCKINGHAM and CHANDOS, Wotton, Aylesbury; Stowe, Buckingham; and Chandos House, Cavendish Square, W.

Deputy-Chairman—Sir HARRY VERNEY, Bart., M P., Claydon House, Winslow, Bucks, and 32, South Street, Park Lane, W.

Captain Edmund Hope Verney, Claydon House, Winslow, Bucks.	John Kersley Fowler, Esq., Aylesbury.
Lieut-Colonel Philip Smith, The Guards' Club, Pall Mall, and Wendover, Bucks.	Acton Tindal, Esq., The Manor House, Aylesbury.
Timothy Rhodes Cobb, Esq., Banbury.	J. W. Williamson, Esq., 4, Stone Buildings, Lincoln's Inn, W.C.

OFFICERS.—Sec., J G. Rowe; Eng., Wm. Wilson, 4, Victoria Street, Westminster, S.W.; Auditors, John Edward Bartlett, Aylesbury, and Henry Hearn, Buckingham ; Solicitors, Jennings, White, and Buckston, Whitehall Place, Westminster, S.W

Offices—5, Queen Square, Westminster, S.W.

16.—AYR AND MAYBOLE JUNCTION.

Incorporated by 17 and 18 Vic., cap. 146 (1854) ; length, 5¾ miles ; capital, 33,000l., in 10l. shares, with 10,000l. by loan. Worked, maintained, and renewed under an Act obtained in 1863 by the Glasgow and South Western, at 45 per cent.; to be gradually reduced to 39 per cent. when the yearly receipts amount to 3,000l.

The directors, in terms of the Company's Powers Act, 1864, obtained authority by certificate from the Board of Trade to raise 2,000l. of additional capital, partly in shares and partly on mortgage.

REVENUE.—It was reported in March that the directors having become dissatisfied with the mode in which the Glasgow and South Western had been allocating the revenue of the line, appointed a qualified person to investigate the accounts, and, his report having confirmed that of the directors, they resolved to fix a table of rates for themselves.

It was reported in September that the company was entirely free from liabilities, excepting the mortgage debt. A dividend equal to 5 per cent. was declared.

Meetings in February or March, and in August or September.

No. of Directors.—Maximum, 7; minimum, 4 ; quorum, 3. *Qualification*, 250l.

DIRECTORS :

Chairman—THOMAS DYKES, Esq., The Castle, Maybole.

Deputy-Chairman—WILLIAM B. CUTHBERTSON, Esq., Merchant, Ayr.

James Murdoch, Esq., Manufacturer, Maybole.	John Ross, Jun., Esq., Merchant, Glasgow. Andrew Paterson, Esq., of Carston, Ayr.
David Brown, Esq., Banker, Maybole.	G. M. Bone, Esq,, Maybole.

OFFICERS. — Sec. and Treasurer, Wm. Pollock, Banker, Ayr; Auditors, G.. Gemmell and Wm. Bone.

17.—BALA AND DOLGELLY.

Incorporated by 25 and 26 Vic., cap. 109 (30th June, 1862), to construct a line from Bala to Dolgelly. Length, 18½ miles ; capital, 112,000l. in 10l. shares, and 37,000l. on loan.

By 26 and 27 Vic., cap. 179 (21st July, 1863), the company was authorised to construct several new works and junctions at Dolgelly, and to enter into arrangements with the Aberystwyth and Welsh Coast. Length, 3¼ miles. New capital, 38,000l. in shares, and 11,900l. on loan.

By 28 Vic., cap. 81 (19th June, 1865), the Bala and Dolgelly was authorised to abandon a portion of its original line, and to participate in an extension from the Corwen and Bala, with joint station at the latter place. Opened 4th August, 1868.

Arrangements with Great Western, which works the line, with mutual use of lines between the Bala and Dolgelly, and the Denbigh Ruthin and Corwen.

CAPITAL.—Received on shares, 180,000l.; on loans, 58,900l. Total, 238,900l.

Meetings in February and August.

*No. of Directors—*5 ; minimum, 3 ; quorum, 3. *Qualification*, 500l.

DIRECTORS :

Chairman—WILLIAM FENTON, Esq., Beaumonds, near Rochdale.

William Wagstaff, Esq., The Rhûg, Corwen.	A. C. Sherriff, Esq., M.P., Perdiswell Hall, Worcester, and 10, Dean's Yard,
Captain Bulkeley, Clewer Lodge, Windsor.	Westminster, S.W.
Charles Edwards, Esq., Dolserau, Dolgelly.	

OFFICERS.—Sec., Stephen Woodley, Shrub Hill, Worcester; Eng., Edward Wilson, C.E., Shrub Hill, Worcester, and 9, Dean's Yard, Westminster, S.W.; Solicitors, Messrs. Burchells, 5, Broad Sanctuary, Westminster, S.W.

18.—BARNOLDSWICK.

Incorporated by 30 and 31 Vic., cap. 181 (12th August, 1867), to construct a line from Barnoldswick to the Leeds and Bradford Extension of the Midland. Length, 2 miles. Capital, 40,000l. in 10l. shares, and 13,300l. on loan.
Arrangements with Midland, which is to work the line.
First meeting to be held within twelve months after passing of the Act.
No. of Directors—5;. minimum,.3 ; quorum, 3. Qualification, 250l.

DIRECTORS :

Thomas Bennett, Esq.
William Bracewell, Esq.
Henry Dean, Esq.

William Boothman, Esq.
Thomas Wilkinson Smith, Esq.

19.—BANBRIDGE EXTENSION.

Incorporated by 24 and 25 Vic., cap. 89 (28th June, 1861), to construct a line from Banbridge to Ballyroney, with a branch to Rathfriland. Length, 12 miles. Capital, 90,000l. in 10l. shares; loans, 30,000l. Working arrangements with Ulster, the Dublin and Belfast, the Banbridge and Lisburn, and the Banbridge Junction.
This undertaking is in bankruptcy, the works having been stopped for several years.
No. of Directors—6 ; minimum, 3 ; quorum, 3. Qualification, 200l.

DIRECTORS :

Chairman—SAMUEL MURLAND, Esq., Castlewellan.

George Shaw, Esq., Castlewellan.
Benjamin Dickson, Esq., Gilford.

J. F. Ruxton, Esq., Hilltown.

OFFICERS.— Sec., John Simms ; Eng., W. H. Coddington, Howard Street, Belfast ; Solicitors, James Murland, Downpatrick, and Joseph Dickson, Dromore ; Auditors, Reuben Simms and Richard Waite.

Offices—5, Donegal Square South, Belfast.

20.—BANBRIDGE JUNCTION.

Incorporated by 16 and 17 Vic., cap. 208 (August 20th, 1853). for a line from Banbridge to a junction with the Dublin and Belfast Junction, near Scarva, and opening up communication with the ports of Newry, Dublin, and Belfast. Length, 6¾ miles. Opened April, 1859. Worked by Dublin and Belfast Junction, which includes Banbridge receipts in its traffic returns.
By 19 and 20 Vic., cap. 54 (23rd June, 1856), the name of the company was altered from "Banbridge, Newry, Dublin, and Belfast Junction," to "Banbridge Junction." The capital was fixed at 60,000l. in 20l. shares; loans 20,000l. Calls 5l., with intervals of three months. The New shares (equal to 20,000l.) might be issued with a preference attached 7l. 10s. per cent.
By 23 Vic., cap. 59 (25th May, 1860), the Banbridge Junction is leased to the Dublin and Belfast; at a rental of 2,000l. per annum.
No dividend was declared in March on the ordinary stock, while that for September was at the rate of 2 per cent. per annum.
CAPITAL.—The receipts on this account have been 22,128l. in ordinary stock ; 17 800l. in preference at 5 per cent., and 17,350l on mortgage. This total of 57,278l. has been expended excepting a balance of 239l.
Meetings in March, and September, at Banbridge. Quorum, 10 shareholders, in person or by proxy, if representing 3,000l. Ten shareholders holding the same amount may require a special meeting.
No. of Directors—6 ; one of whom to represent Dublin and Belfast Juntion ; quorum, 3. Qualification, 200l.

DIRECTORS :

Chairman—JOHN TEMPLE REILLY, Esq., D.L., J.P., Scarvagh House, Scarvagh, County Down.
Deputy-Chairman—THOMAS CRAWFORD, Esq., J.P., Ballyvally House, Banbridge.

James Birch Kennedy, Esq., J.P., 50, Dame Street, Dublin, and Marybrook, Dromore, County Down.
Samuel Law, Esq., J.P., Kilbarrack House, Raheny, County Dublin (Delegate from Dublin and Belfast Junction).

Samuel Hill, Esq., Solitude House, Banbridge.
Robert Mc. Clelland, Esq., Bellemount, Banbridge.

OFFICERS.—Sec., William Mackay, Banbridge ; Auditors, William Waugh, Banbridge, and John Smith, Banbridge ; Eng., James Barton, Dundalk.

21.—BANBRIDGE, LISBURN, AND BELFAST.

, Incorporated by 21 Vic., cap. 46 (14th June, 1858), to construct a line from Banbridge to Lisburn. Capital, 150,000*l.*, in 10*l.* shares; loans, 49,000*l.* Main line from Banbridge to junction with the Ulster, near Lisburn, 15 miles; junction from Banbridge to Banbridge Junction, 17 chains. Opened 13th July, 1863. Worked by Ulster at 66 per cent.

By 25 and 26 Vic., cap. 107 (30th June, 1862), the line was authorised to be leased to the Ulster for 21 years from the date of completion; and for a further period of 10 years, on terms to be agreed upon (if necessary, by arbitration), on Ulster taking 25,000*l.* stock, guaranteed 4 per cent,

By 23 Vic., cap. 6 (3rd April, 1860), the Ulster was authorised to hold 25,000*l.* in the stock of the company, at a pre-preference of 4 per cent.; the company also authorised to issue 1,500 shares at a preference of 5 per cent.

REVENUE.—The following is a statement of the revenue account for three years:—

Year.	Gross Receipts.	Per mile per week.	Banbridge proportion.	Per centage.
1864.	£6,786	£8	£1,919	28
1865.	6,897	8	1,965	28
1866.	7,835	10	2,693	34¼

Accounts made up to 31st December and 30th June.

No. of Directors—9; minimum, 3; quorum, 3. *Qualification*, 200*l.*

DIRECTORS:

Chairman—FITZHERBERT FILGATE, Lsq., Hillsborough,

George Brush, Esq., Gillhall, Dromore.
Thomas Ferguson, Esq., Edenderry, Banbridge.
Wm. Malcomson, Esq., Portlaw.
William Waugh, Esq., Banbridge.

Charles Murland, Esq., Ardnabannon-Castlewellan.
James Gray, Esq., Woodbank, Whiteabbey, Belfast.

OFFICERS.—Sec., John Innis, 5, Donegal Square South, Belfast; Eng., W. H Coddington, Howard Street, Belfast; Auditors, Reuben Simms and Alexander Finlay, Belfast; Solicitors, James Murland, Downpatrick, and Joseph Dickson, Belfast.

22.—BARRY.

Incorporated by 28 and 29 Vic., cap. 234 (5th July, 1865), to construct a line from Peterston, on the South Wales, to Barry, with a Branch to Sully. Length, 7¾ miles. Capital, 70,000*l.* in shares, and 23,000*l.* on loan. Mixed gauge. Arrangements with Great Western.

By 29 Vic., cap. 92 (11th June, 1866), the company was authorised to effect an alteration in the line and levels; to abandon some portion of the work and to construct others in lieu thereof. Also to raise additional capital to the extent of 21,000*l* in 10*l.* shares, and 7,000*l.* on mortgage.

By 29 and 30 Vic., cap. 333 (6th August, 1866), the company was authorised to establish a connection with the Penarth; length, 3½ mies. Capital, 45,000*l.*, in 10*l.* shares, and 15,000*l.* on loan.

By the Barry Harbour Act of 1866, the railway company was authorised to subscribe 10,000*l.* to that undertaking.

By 31 and 32 Vic., cap 97 (13th July, 1868), an extension of time for completion of works till 1871 was obtained.

No. of Directors—6; minimum, 3; quorum, 3 and 2. *Qualification*, 300*l.*

DIRECTORS:

Robert Francis Lascelles Jenner, Esq., Wenvoe Castle, Glamorganshire.
Sir Ivor Bertie Guest, Bart., Canford Manor, Dorset.

J. J. W. Fredricks, Esq., Abermellte, Glyn Neath, Glamorganshire.
Samuel F. Bolden, Esq., Lancaster.

OFFICERS.—Sec., Robert Smith; Eng., Henry Bolden, 12, Abingdon Street, Westminster, S.W.; Solicitor, Edward Reddish, 12, Abingdon Street, Westminster, S.W.

Offices—12, Abingdon Street, Westminster, S.W.

23.—BEDDGELERT.

Incorporated by 28 and 29 Vic., cap. 322 (5th July, 1865), to construct a line from Beddgelert to Port Madoc, on the Cambrian. Length, 9 miles. Capital, 100,000*l.* in shares of 10*l.* each, and 33,000*l.* on loan. Arrangements with the Cambrian. Works in progress.

By 29 and 30 Vic., cap. 183 (16th July, 1866), the company was authorised to construct an extension to Llyn Gwynant, and also to make a deviation in the line of 1865. Length, 2¼ miles. New capital, 40,000*l.*, in shares (deferred and preferred), and 13,300*l.* on loan.

No. of Directors—6; quorum, 3. *Qualification*, 1,000*l.*

DIRECTORS:

Chairman—DAVID WILLIAMS, Esq., Deudraeth Castle, Port Madoc.

Deputy Chairman—J. W. JOHNS, Esq., Wolverton Park, Newbury, Hants.

David Hart, Esq., 42, Trinity Square, Tower Hill, London, E.C. | J. Williams Jones, Esq., 4, Duke Street, St. James's, London, S.W.

OFFICERS.—Sec., W. Roberts; Engs., Ordish and Le Feuvre, Great George Street, Westminster, S.W.; Solicitors, R. H. Wyatt, Parliament Street, London, S.W., and Edward Breese, Port Madoc; Auditors, A. Howell, Welshpool, and George Lea, 54, Chancery Lane, W.C.

Offices—7, Bank Buildings, Lothbury, E.C.

24.—BEDFORD AND NORTHAMPTON.

Incorporated by 28 and 29 Vic., cap. 355 (5th July, 1865), to construct a line from Bedford, on the Midland, to Northampton. Length, 26 miles. Capital, 400,000*l.* in shares, and 133,000*l.* on loan. Arrangements with Midland.

By 29 and 30 Vic., cap. 240 (23rd July, 1866), the company was authorised to construct several new lines in lieu of others abandoned. Also to divide the shares into deferred and preferred.

By 30 and 31 Vic., cap. 123 (15th July, 1867), the company was authorised to construct several deviations in substitution of lines to be abandoned. Application is being made to the Board of Trade for another extension of time.

No. of Directors—7; quorum, 3. *Qualification*, 500*l.*

DIRECTORS:

Lieut.-Col. Wm. Bartholomew Higgins, Picts Hill, Bedford. | Thomas Pain, Esq., 22, Great George Street, Westminster, S.W.
Joseph Palmer, Esq., Olney, Bucks. |

OFFICERS.—Sec., Arthur Lankester; Eng., Charles Liddell, 24, Abingdon Street, Westminster, S.W.; Auditors, Henry Wilkes Notman, 2, Leadenhall Street, E.C., and S. Price, 3, Prince's Street, Westminster, S.W.; Solicitors, Hodding, Townsend, and Co., 3, Prince's Street, Westminster, S. W.

Offices—2, Westminster Chambers, Victoria Street, S.W.

25.—BELFAST CENTRAL.

Incorporated by 27 and 28 Vic., cap. 254 (25th July, 1864), to connect the several railways in the town of Belfast, and construct a central station therein. Capital, 300,000*l.* in 10*l.* shares; loans, 100,000*l.* Length, 5¾ miles. Works in progress, and line expected to be opened at the end of 1869.

By 28 and 29 Vic., cap. 220 (5th July, 1865), the company was authorised to execute further works in lieu of alterations, and to enter into arrangements with the Belfast Harbour commissioners. Length, 2¾ miles. No new capital.

By 31 and 32 Vic., cap. 166 (31st July, 1868), the Belfast Central was authorised to construct new lines and tramways, 2½ miles, and a central station; also to abandon portions of the previously authorised undertaking, and to raise new capital to the extent of 150,000*l.* in divided shares, and 50,000*l.* on mortgage. Extension of time for previous works to 1873, with power to Ulster, Belfast and County Down, and Belfast Holywood and Bangor to use parts of Belfast Central.

No. of Directors—6; maximum, 8; quorum, 3. *Qualification*, 500*l.*

DIRECTORS:

John Taylor, Esq., Warwick Terrace, Kensington, London.

James Thornton, Esq., Theobalds, Herts.

James Dickson, Esq., 16, New Broad Street, London, E.C.

G. Lathom Browne, Esq., Gresham House, London.

Edmund Etlinger, Esq., Gower Street, London, W.C.

John Everitt, Esq., Allhallows Chambers, Lombard Street, London, E.C.

OFFICERS.—Sec., James Hutt; Engs., Sir John MacNeill, and Telford MacNeill; Solicitors, Messrs. Tahourdens, 1, Victoria Street, Westminster, S.W., and Robert Cassidy, Belfast.

Offices—2, Westminster Chambers, Victoria Street, London, S.W.

26.—BELFAST AND COUNTY DOWN.

Incorporated by 10 Vic., cap. 87 (20th June, 1846), for a line from Belfast to Downpatrick, with branches to Holywood, Donaghadee, and Bangor; total, 45 miles. The branch to Holywood, 4½ miles, was opened on 2nd of August, 1848; from Belfast to Newtownards, 12½ miles, on 6th May, 1850; from Comber to Ballynahinch, on 10th September, 1858, 13 miles; to Downpatrick, 9 miles, on 23rd March, 1859; and the line completed by the opening of the branch from Newtownards to Donaghadee, on 3rd June, 1861, 10 miles.

By Act 18 Vic., cap. 18 (May 25th, 1855), the capital is fixed at 500,000l. of which 20,000l. received for forfeited shares is not liable to dividend; new shares in place of those forfeited, and all shares then unissued may be issued at a preference not exceeding 5 per cent. The borrowing powers were restricted to 166,666l. By this Act the line was authorised to be extended to Ballynahinch, 3¼ miles further.

By 21 and 22 Vic., cap. 78 (12th July, 1858), an extension of time for purchase of land under Act 1855, was granted till July, 1859.

By 20 and 21 Vic., cap. 149 (10th August, 1857), powers were granted to subscribe 15,000l. to the Portpatrick, and to issue shares to that amount, bearing a preferential dividend not exceeding 5 per cent.

By 21 and 22 Vic., cap. 78 (1858), a further extension of time for making the Donaghadee branch was granted till August, 1861; and also powers to abandon the branch to Bangor.

By Act of 24 and 25 Vic., cap. 64 (Downpatrick and Newry Act, 1861), powers were granted to subscribe 20,000l. to the Downpatrick and Newry, and to issue preference shares to that amount not exceeding 5 per cent.

By 28 and 29 Vic., cap. 198 (29th June, 1865), the Holywood branch was transferred to the Belfast Holywood and Bangor, at a charge of 50,000l. in cash, with an annual rent of 5,000l. in monthly instalments, but redeemable within ten years by gradual payment of 100l. for 4½ of the said rent.

REVENUE.—The receipts, for the half-year ending 30th January, amounted to 21,869l., being an increase of 1,617l. over corresponding period of the previous year, of which 984l. is referrible to the passenger traffic, 574l. to goods, and 58l. to other sources. This additional traffic had been carried at the comparatively small increase of 205l. in the working expenses. After making provision for payment of interest on loans, amounting to 4,957l. there remained a balance available for dividends of 6,624l., which was disposed of as follows, viz.:—

Dividends on A, B, C, and D preference shares, at the rate of 5 per cent. per annum, 4,585l.; balance of arrears of dividends due on said shares, 840l.; dividends on the E preference shares, at the rate of 4¼ per cent. per annum. 234l.; balance of arrears of dividends due on said E shares, 454l.; carried forward, 509l.

The directors congratulated the proprietors on having cleared off all the accumulative arrears of dividends on the preference shares, thereby opening the way for future dividends on the ordinary stock.

The receipts for the six months ending 31st July, amounted to 22,982l., against 21,309l. for the corresponding period of last year, showing an increase of 1,672l. The working expenses were 11,976l. against 10,832l., showing an increase of 1,143l.

After making provision for payment of interest on loans, the balance available for division among the proprietors was 6,865l., viz.:—4,835l. dividends at the rate of 5 per cent. per annum, on the A, B, C, and D preference shares; 234l. dividend at the rate of 4¼ per cent. per annum, on the E preference shares; 1,194l. dividend of 1 per cent. per annum, on the ordinary shares; 600l. carried forward to next half-year's account.

It was reported in August that the Act of Parliament obtained by the Government at the close of last session, authorised a loan to this company of 166,000*l.* (being the amount of the debenture debt), at 3½ per cent. for a term of 35 years, by way of compensation for the non-fulfilment of the agreement in reference to the postal service between Donaghadee and Portpatrick. This loan when completed will be a present saving to the company of at least 2,000*l.* per annum.

CAPITAL.—The expenditure on this account, including the Donaghadee Extension, amounted on 31st July to 717,672*l.* The receipts were reported to have been as follow:—

Original shares..				£266,004
50*l.* per share on 1,405 50*l.* A, 5 per cent. preference......	£70,250			
10*l.*	„	2,463 10*l.* B, 5 per cent.	„ 24,630	
15*l.*	„	2,463 15*l.* C, 5 per cent.	„ 36,945	
25*l.*	„	2,463 25*l.* D, 5 per cent.	„ 61,575	
10*l.*	„	1,105 10*l.* E, 4¼ per cent.	„ ...... 11,050=	204,450
Loans on Mortgage..				166,666
				£637,120

Received from Belfast Holywood and Bangor, on account of the purchase of the Holywood Branch, under Belfast Holywood and Bangor Act of 1865	£50,000	
Less agreed to be deducted for station accommodation at Belfast	400 =	49,600=£686,720

Scale of Voting.—One vote for every share up to 10; one for every five shares from 10 to 100; and one for every 10 above 100.

Certificates are required for transfers. Registration fee 2*s.* 6*d.* each deed and seller. *No. of Directors.*—Maximum, 12; minimum, 8. *Qualification*, 1,000*l.*

DIRECTORS:

Chairman—2 WM. R. ANKETELL, Esq., J.P., Ardtulla, Holywood.

2 John Cleland, Esq., Downpatrick.
1 Wm. Valentine, Esq., J.P., Whiteabbey.
1 J. M. Pirrie, Esq., M D., Belfast.
2 Robert Gray, Esq., Belfast.

3 Henry Murney, Esq., Holywood.
3 James Ireland, Esq., Oakley, Holywood.
1 James Heron, Esq., J.P., Belfast.

1 Retire in February, 1869; 2, in 1870; 3, in 1871.

OFFICERS.—Sec., John Milliken. Belfast; Gen. Man., T. C. Haines, Belfast; Res. Eng. and Supt. of Loco. Dept., C. K. Domville, Belfast; Auditors, W. B. Caughey, Belfast, and John G. McGee, Belfast.

Head Offices—Queen's Quay, Belfast.

27.—BELFAST, HOLYWOOD, AND BANGOR.

Incorporated by 23 Vic., cap. 61 (25th May, 1860), to construct a railway from the Holywood branch of the County Down to the town of Bangor; length, 7¼ miles; capital, 115,000*l.*, in 10*l.* shares; loans, 38,000*l.* Traffic arrangements with Belfast and County Down.

By 26 and 27 Vic., cap. 123 (13th July, 1863), the period for the completion of works was extended to 13th February, 1865. The company was also authorised to raise additional capital, to the extent of 35,000*l.* in shares, and 11,000*l.* on mortgage, with power to contribute to the erection of a quay and hotel at Bangor. Opened from Holywood to Bangor, 7½ miles, on 1st May. On 22nd August, the company purchased the line from Belfast to Holywood (6¾ miles) from the Belfast and County Down.

By 28 and 29 Vic., cap. 108 (29th June, 1865), the Holywood branch of the Belfast and County Down was transferred to the Holywood and Bangor, at a charge of 50,000*l.* in cash, with an annual rent 5,000*l.* in monthly instalments, but redeemable within 10 years by gradual payments of 100*l.* for each 4*l.* 10*s.* of said rent.

REVENUE.—The receipts for the half-year ending the 31st of December showed an increase over the corresponding period of 1866 of more than 1,000*l.*; and that, too, during a period of great commercial depression, and when the mills had been worked short time. The working expenses were about 45 per cent. The receiver appointed by the Court of Chancery had a large sum of money in hand, and an application was about being heard by the Master with reference to its division. The income from gross traffic amounted in 1866 to 14,111*l.*, and in 1867 to 16,000*l.* The expenses in 1866 amounted to 8,171l., and in 1867 to 7,874l., showing a balance on the working in favour of 1866 of 5,940l., and in favour of 1867 of 8,126l. The revenue for the half-year ending 30th June showed that 7,251l. had been received for traffic, which, added to the balance of 980l. from the preceding half-year, made a total of 8,231l. From this was deducted 950l. for interest on mortgages, 2,500l. for rent of Holywood branch, 3,232l. for working the line, 685l. for expenses of management, salaries, &c., and 12l. 10s. rebate for tickets, leaving a balance of 850l. The funds paid into the hands of the receiver were distributed by him under the order of the Court, but the board could not concur in the mode in which the funds were distributed.

An application was actually made to the Court, at the instance of the Belfast and County Down, and other parties, to divide the funds wholly regardless of the claims and first charges of the holders of the mortgage debentures; thus it became necessary for such debenture holders to take legal proceedings, and to follow up the appeal of the directors, to protect the rights secured to them under Acts of Parliament. The directors have given, and will continue to give, their cordial assistance to the mortgagees.

CAPITAL.—This account to 30th June showed that 286,783l. had been expended, leaving a balance against that account of 35,732l. The receipts had been derived as under:—

On account of capital..£249,528
Borrowed from revenue 1,522
Balance carried forward .... 35,731=£286,783

Meetings in February and August.

No. of Directors—5 ; minimum, 3; quorum, 3, and on reduction, 2. *Qualification, 250l*

DIRECTORS:

Chairman—J. B. DUNN, Esq.

Sir Charles Lanyon, Belfast.
John Alldin Moore, Esq., 4, Hare Court, Temple, E.C.

Henry Grissell, 17, Montague Square, W.
Samuel Frederick Noyes, Esq., 1, Broad Sanctuary, Westminster, S.W.

OFFICERS.—Gen. Man., John Dodds, Belfast; Sec., F. Pembroke Jones; Solicitors, Elmslie, Forsythe, and Sedgwick, London, and Longfield, Davidson, and Kelly, 47, Sackville street, Dublin.

Offices—Ethelburga House, Bishopsgate, London, E. C.

28.—BELFAST AND NORTHERN COUNTIES.

BELFAST AND BALLYMENA.—Incorporated by 8 and 9 Vic., cap. 81 (21st July, 1845), for a railway from Belfast to Ballymena, with branches to Carrickfergus and Randalstown. Opened 11th April, 1848.

Under Act 17 Vic., cap 68 (1853), an extension from Randalstown, through Toome, Castle Dawson, Magherafelt, and Moneymore, to Cookstown, was obtained. 27 miles. Single line. Opened 10th November, 1856. The capital for this branch was created on the 30th May, 1856, viz. 192,500l. in 25l. shares, the whole of which were taken by holders of original stock. By 23 Vic., cap. 46 (15th May, 1860), the name of the company was changed to "Belfast and Northern Counties," and the capital increased by 70,000l., which may be raised in shares, or by borrowing. The company was also authorised to purchase the Coleraine Junction from the Ballymena Ballymoney and Portrush.

By 27 and 28 Vic., cap. 106 (23rd June, 1864), the company was authorised to construct an extension or tramroad at Portrush, and to purchase additional land. New capital, 100,000l. in shares, and 33,000l. on loan. Length, 34 chains. Completion of works, two years.

BALLYMENA, BALLYMONEY, COLERAINE, AND PORTRUSH JUNCTION.—Incorporated by 16 and 17 Vic., cap. 80 (8th July, 1853), for a line from Ballymena by Ballymoney and Coleraine to Portrush, (35 statute miles), to complete the chain from Dublin to Derry (north-west), and with the Coleraine and Portrush (north), and the great trunk from the north to the south of Ireland, and between Portrush Harbour and Glasgow, steamers opening up the beauties of the north, &c. Single line, but company bound to acquire land, and to lay down double when required by Board of Trade. Opened 7th

November, 1855. By 21 and 22 Vic., cap. 53 (28th June, 1858), power was given to dispose of the line and works to the Belfast and Ballymena. By 22 Vic., cap. 31 (19th April, 1859), the company was authorised to make a Junction at Coleraine with the Londonderry and Coleraine. New capital, 15,000l., in shares at 5 per cent. preference, and 2,000l. on loan. By 23 Vic., cap. 46 (15th May, 1860), this junction was authorised to be purchased by the Belfast and Northern Counties, which obtained possession on January 1st, 1861, since which it has been worked as part of the railway The purchase money consisted of 160,000l. in preference shares, bearing interest at 4 per cent., the Belfast assuming the Portrush bonded debt of 60,000l., making together a tota payment of 220,000l.

LONDONDERRY AND COLERAINE.—This line is worked by the Belfast and Northern Counties at a mileage per centage.

MILEAGE.—Belfast and Northern Counties, 99¾; Londonderry and Coleraine, 36 Carrickfergus and Larne, 14. Total, 149¾.

REVENUE.—The receipts for the half-year ending 31st December amounted to 64,300l., and the working expenses, including interest, rates, taxes, &c., to 34,400l. Of the balance of 29,900l. there were expended on renewals, 5,583l. After payment of dividend on the preference shares, and 2½ per cent. for the half-year on the ordinary stock, 4,567l. was left to next account. The receipts for the half-year ending the 30th of June amounted to 55,685l., the expenditure to 32,421l., and the balance to 23,264l., out of which 6,473l. was deducted for interest on bonded debt, and 138l. for rent of Carrickfergus station, leaving 21,491l., out of which dividend, at the rate of 5 per cent per annum, left 1,170l. for next account.

CAPITAL.—The expenditure on this account to 30th June amounted to 1,151,978l., the receipts for which were as follow :—

Shares	£557,202
Preference shares, 4 per cent.	160,000
Do. 4½ per cent.............................	95,100
Loans on Debentures..	289,769
Debenture stock, 4 per cent.................................	110
Balance	49,796=£1,151,978

DIRECTORS:

Chairman—2 GEORGE J. CLARKE, Esq., Steeple, Antrim.

Deputy-Chairman—3 SIR CHARLES LANYON, The Abbey, Whiteabbey.

Godfrey Lyle, Esq., Bangor.
1 John Thomson, Esq., Low Wood, Belfast.
1 George Gray, Esq., Graymount, Belfast.
1 Edward C. Knox, Esq., Dungannon.
1 Thomas M. Hamilton-Jones, Esq., Moneyglass, Toome.
1 James Cramsie, Esq., Ballymoney.
3 John Young, Esq., Galgorm Castle, Ballymena.

3 William Valentine, Esq., Belfast.
3 Henry Hugh M'Neile, Esq., Parkmount, Belfast.
3 Edmund M'Neill, Esq., Ballycastle.
2 Benjamin C. Adair, Esq., Loughanmore, Parkgate, County Antrim.
2 Thomas Verner, Esq., Belfast,
2 The Right Hon. Viscount Templetown. Castle Upton, Templepatrick.

The figures opposite the names indicate the order of retirement; No. 1 retiring in August, 1869; when a ballot of shareholders will fill up the vacancies. All re-eligible.

OFFICERS.—Sec., Charles Stewart; Gen. Man., Edward J. Cotton; Res. Eng., Phineas Howell, C. E.; Supt. of Loco. Dept., Edward Leigh; Accountant, Francis J. Hopkirk; Treas., Belfast Banking Company; Public Accountant, H. H. Boyd, Belfast, Auditors, John Pim and William C. Cunningham, Belfast; Solicitor, James Torrens, Belfast.

Head Offices—Terminus, York Street, Belfast.

29.—BEMBRIDGE.

Incorporated by 27 and 28 Vic., cap. 327 (29th July, 1864), to construct a line from Yar Bridge to Bembridge Point, with Pier, landing place, and tramway, Length, 2 miles. Capital 50,000l., in 10l. shares, and 16,000l. on loan. Arrangements with the Isle of Wight. In abeyance.

No. of Directors—6; quorum, 3. *Qualification*, 200l.

30.—BERKS AND HANTS.

Incorporated by 22 and 23 Vic., cap. 105 (13th August, 1859), to construct a line from Hungerford to Devizes. Broad gauge. Length, 25 miles. Capital, 298,000*l*., in 10*l*. shares; loans, 99,000*l*. Arrangements with Great Western, which works the line. Opened 11th November, 1862.

By 36 Vic., cap. 3 (4th May, 1863), the company was authorised to cancel 50,000*l* forfeited or unissued shares, and to create in lieu thereof preference stock. Also to subscribe 1,000*l*. to the Marlborough.

By 29 and 30 Vic., cap. 154 (28th June, 1866), the company was authorised to extend the line to the Wilts Somerset and Weymouth, at Westbury. Length, 13 miles. New Capital, 200,000*l*., in shares, which may be issued at 6 per cent. preference, or in half-shares, and 66,000*l*. on loan.

The dividends declared during the year have been at the rate of 1½ per cent. per annum.

CAPITAL—The expenditure on this account, to 30th June, was stated at 248,431*l*.

Receipts.		Expenditure.	
Share capital—deposits and calls..	£108,725	Preliminary expenses	£6,894
Preference share capital	14,360	Parliamentary Act, 1863	420
Temporary loans	26,400	Parliamentary—Stert and Westbury Extension Act, 1866	605
Debenture loans......................	97,900	Land purchase and tenants' compensation.............................	44,293
Balance	1,046	Rent charges	546
		Rates, tithes, and taxes	151
		Construction—Engineer	7,944
		„ Contractors.........	167,104
		Station contracts	9,865
		Level crossing lodges	597
		Electric telegraph	1,042
		Interest on loans	6,029
		Auditors	73
		Salaries, rents, &c....................	2,862
	£248,431		£248,431

Meetings in February or March, and in August or September.

No. of Directors—8; minimum 5; quorum, 3. *Qualification*, 1,000*l*.

DIRECTORS :

Chairman—MARQUIS OF AILESBURY, Savernake Forest, Marlbro', and 78, Pall Mall, S.W.

The Right Hon. Lord Ernest Bruce, M.P., 6, St. George's Place, Hyde Park, S.W.
Colonel G. W. Wroughton, Stowell Lodge, Pewsey.
W. E. Tugwell, Esq., Devizes, Hants.
C. Darby Griffith, Esq., Padworth House, Reading.

Head P. Best, Esq., Donnington Grove, Newbury.
Richard Benyon, Esq., M.P., Englefield House, Reading, and 34, Grosvenor Square, W.
William Ewart, Esq., Broadleas, Devizes.

OFFICERS.—Sec., Charles F. Hart; Eng., R. J. Ward, 11, Great Queen Street, Westminster, S.W.; Auditors, Edmund Harvey and John James Fox; Solicitors, Jackson and Lush, Devizes, Merriman and Co., Marlbro', and Baxter, Rose, and Norton, 6, Victoria Street, Westminster, S.W.

Offices—Devizes.

31—BERWICKSHIRE.

Incorporated by 25 and 26 Vic., cap. 142 (7th July, 1862), to construct a line from the St. Boswell's station of the North British to Dunse. Length 20½ miles. Capital, 190,000*l*., in 10*l*. shares; loans, 33,300*l*. Arrangements with North British, which subscribes 50,000*l*. and works the line. Opened from Dunse to Earlston on the 16th November, 1863. The remainder, from Earlston to North British at Newtown St. Boswell's (4 miles), was opened on 2nd October, 1865.

By 29 and 30 Vic., cap. 278 (30th July, 1866), the company was authorised to raise additional capital to the extent of 30,000l. in shares, and 10,000l. on mortgage. The North British were by the same Act authorised to subscribe the sum of 30,000l. towards completion of the Berwickshire.

REVENUE.—It was reported for the half-year ending 31st January, that the receipts had been 1,930l., and the expenditure 997l., the balance of 932l. with 1,158 on hand, made a total of 2,090l., out of which a dividend of 15s. for the half year and payment of 371l. to the North British, left a balance of 219l. to next account.

The receipts for the half-year ending 31st July were 1,802l., the expenditure amounted to 977l., which left a balance of 825l. Adding 219l. from previous six months a sum of 1,044l. was carried to next account. The chairman said that while the accounts showed an improvement in the receipts for the half-year, still the increase was not such as to give the satisfaction expected. He hoped, however, to lay before the shareholders a more satisfactory report when they next met in the spring.

Meetings in February or March, and in August or September.

Scale of Voting—5 to 10 shares, 1 vote; additional vote for every 10 shares to 100; extra vote for every 20 shares beyond.

Number of Directors—5; quorum, 3.   *Qualification*, 300l.

DIRECTORS:

1 Chairman—Sir HUGH HUME CAMPBELL, Bart.

2 Geo. Cranstoun Trotter Cranstoun, Esq.
3 James Dalrymple, Esq., Greenknowe.
* John Ronald, Esq., S.S.C., Edinburgh.

* George Robertson, Esq., W.S., Royal Circus, Edinburgh.

1, Retires in 1869; 2, in 1870; 3, in 1871.—All eligible for re-election.

* Representing North British.

OFFICERS.—Sec., James Turnbull, W.S., Edinburgh; Auditors, Allan Purves, Greenlaw, and William Stevenson, Dunse; Agents, J. and J. Turnbull, W.S.

Offices—Edinburgh.

32.—BIDEFORD, APPLEDORE, AND WESTWARD HO.

Incorporated by 29 and 30 Vic., cap. 224 (16th July, 1866), to construct a line from Bideford to Appledore, with a branch to Westward Ho. Length, 4 miles. Capital 60,000l. in 10l. shares, and 20,000l. on loan.

No. of Directors—5; minimum, 3; quorum, 3 and 2.   *Qualification*, 500l.

DIRECTORS:

William Nelson Hutchinson, Esq.
George M. F. Molesworth, Esq.

Edward Parry, Esq.
Robert Edward Diggles, Esq.

33.—BIRKENHEAD.

An amalgamation of a company incorporated under the title of the BIRKENHEAD LANCASHIRE AND CHESHIRE JUNCTION, and of the CHESTER AND BIRKENHEAD, under Act 11 Vic., cap. 222 (1847). By an Act passed 1st July, 1852, 16 Vic., cap. 167, this undertaking became dissolved and incorporated anew, under the same title. It enacts that the company shall be limited to the works at the time vested in the dissolved company, or authorised, viz.: 1st, a main line from Chester to Grange Lane; 2nd, Grange Lane to Monk's Ferry; 3rd, Grange Lane to Bridge End, all at Birkenhead; 4th, share in Chester Station; a railway from L. & N. W. at Chester to L. & N. W. at Lower Walton, Runcorn. Productive mileage, 48 miles.

By 22 and 23 Vic., cap. 74 (1st August, 1859), the company was authorised to change its name to "Birkenhead" to make a branch from Hooton to Helsby, and a branch to Tranmere Pool. Length of the line from Hooton to Helsby, 8¾ miles. Opened 1st July, 1863.

By 24 and 25 Vic., cap 134, the line is vested in the London and North Western and Great Western, the Birkenhead register being kept by the former.

By 25 and 26 Vic., cap. 198 (17th July, 1862), the leasing companies were authorised to construct a line from Hooton to Parkgate. Length, 5 miles. Opened, 1st Oct., 1866.

The 4½ per cent. preference shares have been issued to the extent of 220,200l.

DIRECTORS:

Line managed by a joint committee, representing the Great Western and the London and North Western, namely:—

Great Western.

Sir D. Gooch, Bart, M.P., Fulthorpe House, London.
C. A. Wood, Esq., 25, Chesham Place, London, S.W.
Hon. F. G. B. Ponsonby, 3, Mount Street, Grosvenor Square, London.
Capt. Bulkeley, Clewer Lodge, Windsor.
C. G. Mott, Esq., Sunnyside, Birkenhead Park, Birkenhead.

London and North Western.

R. Moon, Esq., Bevere, Worcester.
J. P. Brown-Westhead, Esq., M.P., 13, Eaton Square, S.W.
J. Bancroft, Esq., 5, Police Street, Manchester.
O. L. Stephen, Esq., Bardon Hall, Leicester.
J. P. Bickersteth, Esq., Southcot, Leighton, Beds.

JOINT-OFFICERS.—Sec., J. Wait, Birkenhead; Supt., W. Patchett, Shrewsbury; Eng., R. E. Johnston, Birkenhead.
Secretary's Offices—Cathcart Street, Birkenhead.

34.—BIRMINGHAM AND SUTTON COLDFIELD EXTENSION.

Incorporated by 26 and 27 Vic., cap. 174 (21st July, 1863), to construct a line from Sutton Coldfield, on the London and North Western Branch of that name to Lichfield on the South Staffordshire. Length, 7¾ miles. Capital, 100,000*l.* in 10*l.* shares, and 33,000*l.* on loan. Works in progress.

No. of Directors.—Maximum, 6; minimum, 4; quorum, 3. *Qualification*, 150*l.*

DIRECTORS:

Chairman—JOHN EDWARD CAMPBELL KOCH, Esq., Threadneedle Street, London, E.C.

John Foster Vesey Fitzgerald, Esq., 11, Chester Square, S.W.
Frederick Pembroke Jones, Esq., Longton Grove, Sydenham.

Richard Henegan Lawrie, Esq., The Temple, London, E.C.
Augustus Samuel Wildy, Esq., 11, Queen's Terrace, Regent's Park, N.W.

Two directors go out of office by rotation, at the next half-yearly meeting, but are eligible for re-election.

OFFICERS.—Sec., Thomas Edward Watkins; Eng., Julian Horn Tolmé, 1, Victoria Street, Westminster, S.W.; Solicitor, Samuel Frederick Noyes, 1, Broad Sanctuary, Westminster, S.W.; Auditors, Thomas Paris, Greenwood, near Barnet, and George Augustus Addison, 27, Regent Street.
Offices—16, Abingdon Street, Westminster, S.W.

35.—BISHOP'S CASTLE.

Incorporated by 24 and 25 Vic., cap. 103 (28th June, 1861), for making railways from the Oswestry and Newtown, near Montgomery, to the Shrewsbury and Hereford at Winstantow, and to Bishop's Castle, in the county of Salop. Length, 19¼ miles. Capital, 180,000*l.* in 10*l.* shares; loans, 60,000*l.* Opened from Craven Arms to Bishop's Castle (9 miles) on 1st February, 1866. No traffic returns or revenue statements are issued.

By 27 and 28 Vic., cap. 161 (14th July, 1864), the Oswestry and Newtown was authorised to subscribe 50,000*l.* to the Bishop's Castle.

By 28 and 29 Vic., cap. 173 (29th June, 1865), the company was authorised to extend the line from Chirbury to the Minsterley branch of the Shrewsbury and Welshpool Length, 9¼ miles. New capital, 100,000*l.* in shares, and 33,000*l.* by loan. Preference shares are not to be issued until the line is opened from Montgomery to Bishop's Castle.

By 28 and 29 Vic., cap. 241 (5th July, 1865), the company was authorised to extend the line to Craven Arms, and to effect other alterations. Length, 4 miles. Capital, 12,000*l.* in shares, but not by preference until the original line between Montgomery and Bishop's Castle is completed. Also 4,000*l.* on loan.

By 28 and 29 Vic., cap. 323 (5th July, 1865), the company was authorised to make certain deviations, and to substitute other lines, and to raise new capital to the extent of 90,000*l.* in shares, and 30,000*l.* on loan.

The line was closed in the beginning of 1867, the rolling stock having been seized by judgment creditors. The traffic is now conducted by a receiver appointed by the Court of Chancery, but no accounts of receipts or working expenses appear to be issued.

DIRECTORS:
Chairman—G. H. WHALLEY, Esq., M.P., Plâs Madoc, Ruabon.

Richard Kyrke Penson, Esq., Ludlow. | William Lefeaux, Esq., Landidloes, Mont-
G. Farmer, Esq., Montgomery. | gomeryshire.
OFFICERS.—Sec., William Wilding; Manager, John Craston, Bishop's Castle;
Solicitors, Thomas Griffiths, Bishop's Castle, and William Wilding, Montgomery;
Bankers, The North and South Wales Bank, Bishop's Castle, and Messrs. Beck & Co.,
Welshpool.
Offices—Montgomery.

36.—BISHOP'S WALTHAM.

Incorporated by 25 and 26 Vic., cap. 143 (17th July, 1862), to construct a line from
Bishop's Waltham to Botley, on the South Western. Length, 3½ miles. Capital,
16,000l. in 10l. shares, and 5,000l. on loan. Opened 6th June, 1863. Traffic and
working agreements with South Western, which works the line at 45 per cent.
By 26 and 27 Vic., cap. 85, the company was authorised to raise new capital to the
extent of 8,000l. in shares of 5 per cent., and 2,600l. on loan.
Meetings in February and August.
No. of Directors—5; quorum, 3. *Qualification*, 250l.
DIRECTORS:
Chairman—WILLIAM HENRY STONE, Esq., M.P., Leigh Park, Havant
and Dulwich Hill, S.
Deputy-Chairman—THEODORE MARTIN, Esq., Abingdon Street,
Westminster, S.W.
John Alldin Moore, Esq., 4, Hare Court, | Alexander Williams, Esq., New Street,
Temple, E.C. | Spring Gardens.
Arthur Helps, Esq., Croydon.
OFFICERS.—Solicitor, Samuel Cook Frankish, 23, Parliament Street, Westminster,
S.W.; Auditors, Charles James Gunner and Francis Clark, Bishop's Waltham; Bankers
Cocks, Biddulph, and Co., 43, Charing Cross.
Offices—23, Parliament Street, Westminster, S.W.

37.—BLACKPOOL AND LYTHAM.

Incorporated by 24 Vic., cap. 9 (17th May, 1861), to construct a line from Blackpool
to Lytham, both in the county of Lancaster. Length, 7 miles. Capital, 45,000l., in
10l. shares; loans, 15,000l. Opened 6th April, 1863.
REVENUE.—The receipts for the half-year ending 31st December, were 2,874l.; and
the working expenses, including local and Government taxes, and passenger duty
1,096l.; leaving a gross profit of 1,777l.; from this sum were deducted for interest on
loans, 644l., leaving net balance 1,133l.; which with that brought forward, made a
total sum of 1,289l. available for dividend, at the rate of 3 per cent. per annum on the
45,000l. subscribed capital, which absorbed 663l., and left 625l. to next account.
No. of Directors—6; maximum, 8; minimum, 4; quorum, 5 and 2. *Qualification*, 500l.
DIRECTORS:
Chairman—THOMAS LANGTON BIRLEY, Esq., Kirkham.
John Roscoe Allen, Esq., Preston. | Colonel Clifton, Lytham Hall, Lytham.
Charles Birley, Esq., Bartle Hall, near | Thomas Fair, Esq., Lytham.
Preston. | Charles Low Swainson, Esq., Manchester.
OFFICERS.—Sec., Thomas Cowgill; Auditors, Richard Cookson, Layton Hawes
Blackpool, and G. T. Tully, Preston Banking Company, Preston.
Offices—Lytham.

38.—BLANE VALLEY.

Incorporated by 24 and 25 Vic., cap. 248 (6th August, 1861), to construct a line from
Lennoxtown, on the Edinburgh and Glasgow, to Strathblane, with a branch to Letter-
mill, in the county of Stirling. Length, 8½ miles. Capital, 51,000l., in 10l. shares, and
17,000l. on loan. Arrangements with North British, which subscribed 17,000l. Opened
for goods on 19th October, 1866, and for passengers on 1st July, 1867.
By 28 and 29 Vic., cap. 356 (5th July, 1855), the company was authorised to construct
an extension to the Forth and Clyde. Length, 2¾ miles. Original capital restricted to
33,000l. in shares, and 11,000l. on loan. New capital 42,000l. in shares with 14,000l.
on loan.
It was reported in September that the whole of the land settlements upon the

original line had been completed, and its liabilities reduced to about 8,000*l.* The directors considered it proper to charge against revenue the whole interest accruing upon the liabilities since the line was opened, which prevented them from declaring any dividend. The powers of constructing the authorised extension to the Forth and Clyde expired on 5th July, 1868, and an application was made to the Board of Trade for an extension of these powers for two years. Colonel Rich, of the Board of Trade, on the 22nd of August, expressed himself satisfied, and it was expected that the desired extension of time would be granted.

CAPITAL.—The expenditure on this account to 31st July, amounted to 76,806*l.* ; the receipts having been as under :—

Share capital	£32,990
Interest account	715
Preference stock	30,210
Mortgages—5 per cent.	3,200
Forfeited deposits	184
Balance	£9,506 = £76,806

Meetings in February or March, and August or September.

No. of Directors—6; minimum, 5; quorum, 3. *Qualification*, 250*l.*

DIRECTORS:

Chairman—FRANCIS MAXWELL, Esq., Insurance Broker, Glasgow.

Deputy-Chairman—ROBERT SHARP MUIR, Esq., Merchant, Glasgow.

Alex. Harvie, Esq., Merchant, Glasgow.
Major Charles Campbell Graham Stirling, of Craigbarnet, Strathblane.

Robert Young, Esq., 107, Buchanan Street, Glasgow.
Robert Kaye, Esq., of Fountain Bank, Patrick.

OFFICERS.—Sec., James Keyden; Engs., Forman and Mc.Call; Auditors, Alexr. James Watson and Robert Strang; Solicitors, Keyden, Strang, and Keyden.
Office—186, West George Street, Glasgow.

39.—BLYTH AND TYNE.

Incorporated by 16 Vic., cap. 122 (1852), for a line from Blyth, through a coal and mineral district, to Hayhole Tyne, for coal, and to Percy Main, on North Shields line of York Newcastle and Berwick, for passengers and goods. Length, 20 miles. The company also possess several coal staiths, &c.

By 17 Vic., cap. 172 (1853), the company was authorised to construct a branch from Seaton Delaval, Earsdon, for 1¾ mile of Tynemouth Branch, to Dairy-house; also a branch from Newsham and South Blyth, Earsdon, to York Newcastle and Berwick, near Morpeth. This branch, 6 miles, was opened on 31st October, 1860.

By 20 and 21 Vic., cap. 114 (10th August, 1857), the company was authorised to make certain deviations and extensions. New capital, 110,000*l.* raised by preference, and is the amount of the estimated cost of new works, after deducting 23,000*l.* to be saved by the relinquishment of the Longhirst extension, the powers for the construction of which are repealed. The length of the Warkworth extension is 13¾ miles, and of the branch to Blyth Docks, 1 mile 1 furlong and 5½ chains.

By 24 and 25 Vic., cap. 98 (28 June, 1861), the company was empowered to extend their main line to Newcastle, and to construct certain branches. Length, 25 miles. New capital, 210,000*l.* in shares at 5 per cent., and 70,000*l.* on loan. Opened to Newcastle (9¼ miles) on 1st June, 1864. In operation 34 miles.

By 27 and 28 Vic., cap. 244 (25th July, 1864), the company was authorised to raise new capital to the extent of 50,000*l.* in shares, and 16,000*l.* on loans, with an extension of time for three years for completion of certain works.

By 30 and 31 Vic , cap. 203 (15th August, 1867), the Blyth and Tyne obtained power to construct new lines, called the North Shields, the Camboise, the Walbottle, the Newbiggin, the Tynemouth Branches, and the Warkworth Extension. Length, 24 miles. New capital, 350,000*l.* in shares, and 27,500*l.* on loan. Also to purchase certain lands, way-leaves, and other rents, &c.

AGREEMENTS.—Traffic arrangements have been made with the Wansbeck Valley, the North British, the Port Carlisle, and Silloth Bay.

REVENUE.—The gross revenue for the half-year ending 31st December amounted to 71,883*l.*, and the expenditure, including way-leaves and interest to 49,776*l.*, leaving a balance of 22,106*l.* applicable to dividend, at the rate of 10 per cent. per annum.

The receipts for the half-year ending 30th June, were 66,387*l.*; and the expenditure, including way-leaves and interest, 44,411*l.*; leaving a balance of 21,976*l.* applicable to dividend, at the rate of 10 per cent.

CAPITAL.—The expenditure on this account to 30th June amounted to 696,105*l*
The receipts have been as follow :—

10 per cent. Preference Stock				£50,000
5 per cent.	do.			110,000
5 per cent.	do.	1867		102,980
Ordinary Stock				210,000
10,500 Ordinary Shares (6*l*. 10*s*. paid)			£68,250	
Prepaid	do.		6,129=	74,379
Balance				148,746
				£696,103

Directors, Meetings, &c.—Company subject to C. C. C. Act.

DIRECTORS:

Chairman—JOSEPH LAYCOCK, Esq., Gosforth, Newcastle.

Collingwood Foster Jackson, Esq., Jesmond House, Newcastle.
Joseph Davison, Esq., Greencroft, Durham.

I. F. Ayton, Esq., Hendley, Stocksfield.
John Peter Mulcaster, Esq., Benwell, Newcastle.

OFFICERS.—Man., Joseph Cabry; Sec., George Armstrong, Newcastle; Eng., John F. Tone, Newcastle; Loco. Supt., William Kendall; Accountant, John Anderson; Auditors, D. D. Main and Thomas Hedley, Newcastle; Solicitor, R. P. Phillipson, Newcastle.

Offices—Newcastle-on-Tyne.

40.—BODMIN.

Incorporated by 27 and 28 Vic., cap. 170 (14th July, 1864), to construct a line from the Cornwall to Bodmin. Capital, 36,000*l*. in 20*l*. shares, and 12,000*l*. on loan. Length, 3 miles; completion of works, three years; broad gauge. Arrangements with Cornwall.

By 28 Vic., cap. 53 (2nd June, 1865), the company was authorised to extend its line to the Bodmin and Wadebridge. Length, 1 mile; broad gauge, and to raise further capital to the extent of 25,000*l*. in shares, and 8,300*l*. on mortgage.

By 30 and 31 Vic., cap. 119 (15th July, 1867), the company obtained power to make certain deviations; to divide the shares into preferred and deferred.

It was reported in October that the directors had not yet succeeded in clearing the contractor who commenced the works, but having recently obtained a report from an eminent engineer as to the practicability of raising the required capital, by guaranteeing the interest of such capital, it was advisable to adjourn the meeting until 30th November.

No. of Directors —6; minimum, 3; quorum, 3 and 2. *Qualification*, 100*l*.

DIRECTORS:

Chairman—THOMAS FREDERICK HILL ALMS, Esq.

Hon. Edward Frederick Leveson Gower, M.P., 14, South Audley Street, W.
James Wyld, Esq., 51, Gloucester Road, Regent's Park, N.W.

John Hichens, Esq.
George Pentyre Parkyn, Esq.
John Crang, Esq.

41.—BODMIN AND WADEBRIDGE.

Incorporated by 2 and 3 Wm. IV., cap. 47, for the purposes of mineral traffic. Capital, 27,500*l*. in shares, and 8,010*l*. on loan. Reconstructed by 28 and 29 Vic., cap. 370 (5th July, 1865). New capital, 75,000*l*. in shares, and 25,000*l*. on loan. Length, 15 miles. Arrangements with Launceston, Bodmin, and Devon and Cornwall.

DIRECTORS:

Chairman—Capt. CHARLES E. MANGLES, Poyle Park, Farnham, Surrey.

Deputy-Chairman—CHARLES CASTLEMAN, Esq., Glasshayes, Lyndhurst, Hants.

Hon. R. H. Dutton, Timsbury Manor, Romsey, Hants.
The Count Eyre, 7, Hind Street, Manchester Square, W.
Mr. Sergeant Gaselee, 2, Cambridge Square, Hyde Park, W.
Edward J. Hutchins, Esq., Beenham House, Reading.

Lieut.-Col. Luard, Farnham, Surrey.
Capt. Johnston, 8, York Terrace, Regent's Park, N.W.
H. C. Lacy, Esq., With-Deane Hall, near Brighton.
C. S. Mortimer, Esq., Morden Park, Surrey, S.
William P. Snell, Esq., Belmont, near Havant, Hants.

Secretary, Frederick Clarke, Waterloo Bridge Station, London, S.

42.—BO'NESS AND GRANGEMOUTH.

Incorporated by 29 and 30 Vic., cap. 341 (6th August, 1866), to construct a line from the North British, near Abercorn, to Bo'ness and Grangemouth. Length, 9½ miles. Capital, 85,000*l.*, in 10*l.* shares, and 28,500*l.* on loan. Arrangements with the North British.

*No. of Directors—*6; minimum, 4; quorum, 3. *Qualification,* 200*l.*

DIRECTORS:

Henry Cadell, Esq.	John Anderson, Esq.
John Begg, Esq.	John Marshall, Esq.
John Nimmo, Esq.	James Gowans, Esq.

43.—BOURTON-ON-THE-WATER.

Incorporated by 23 Vic., cap. 82 (14th June, 1860), to construct a line from the Great Western (West Midland Section), at the Chipping Norton Junction, to Bourton-on-the-Water. Length, 6¾ miles. Capital, 50,000*l.*, in 10*l.* shares. Loans, 10,000*l.* Opened 1st March, 1852. Working and traffic arrangements with Great Western (West Midland), which subscribed 3,000*l.* The traffic returns are included in those of the Great Western.

By 27 and 28 Vic., cap. 210 (25th July, 1864), the company was authorised to extend the line towards Cheltenham, and to raise 220,000*l.* in shares, and 73,000*l.* on loan. Length, 15¾ miles; but by 30 and 31 Vic., cap. 193 (12th August, 1867), the company was authorised to abandon this extension to Cheltenham, and to refrain from raising the capital so required.

CAPITAL.—The receipts on calls have been 29,907*l.*; on debentures, 9,770*l.*; and interest, 132*l.* The expenditure amounted to 39,817*l.*

The dividends declared during the year have been at the rate of 2¼ per cent. per annum.

Meetings in February or March, and August or September.

*No. of Directors—*6; minimum, 3 (two appointed by Great Western); quorum, 3, on reduction, 2. *Qualification,* 200*l.*

DIRECTORS:

Chairman—A. C. SHERRIFF, Esq., M.P., Perdiswell Hall, Worcester, and 10, Dean's Yard, Westminster, S.W.

W. Bliss, Esq., Chipping Norton, Oxon.	J. Waddingham, Esq., Guyting Grange, near Winchcomb,
C. S. Whitmore, Esq., Rutland Gate, Hyde Park, London.	J. Bennett, Esq., Little Rissington, Stow-on-the-Wold.

OFFICERS.—Sec., W. T. Adcock, Worcester; Eng., E. Wilson, Worcester; Auditors, A. Ransford and W. Garne; Solicitors, Messrs. Burchell, 5, Broad Sanctuary, Westminster, S.W..

44.—BRADFORD, ECCLESHILL, AND IDLE.

Incorporated by 29 and 30 Vic., cap. 114 (28th June, 1866), to construct a line from Bradford, through Eccleshill, to Idle. Length, 3¼ miles. Capital, 65,000*l.* in 10*l.* shares, and 21,600*l.* on loan. Great Northern may subscribe 50,000*l.*, and enter into arrangements for working the traffic.

*No. of Directors—*5; quorum, 3. *Qualification,* 1,000*l.*

DIRECTORS:

Chairman—Colonel GEORGE HUSSEY PACKE, Caythorpe Hall, near Grantham.

Colonel the Hon. Octavius Duncombe, M.P., Waresley Park, St. Neots, and 84, Eaton Square, S.W.	Robert Tennant, Esq., Scarcroft Lodge, Shadwell, Leeds.
Wm. Firth, Esq., Burley Wood House, Leeds.	Samuel Waterhouse, Esq., M.P., Hope Hall, Halifax, and 66, Pall Mall, S.W.

45.—BRAMPTON AND LONGTOWN.

Incorporated by 29 and 30 Vic., cap. 349 (10th August, 1866), to construct a line from the North British, at Longtown, to Brampton. Length, 12½ miles. Capital, 120,000*l.* in 10*l.* shares, and 40,000*l.* on loan. Arrangements with North British and Glasgow and South Western, which may subscribe 30,000*l.* each.

*No. of Directors—*5; minimum, 3; quorum, 3 and 2. *Qualification,* 200*l.*

DIRECTORS:

Joseph Dacre, Esq.	Thomas Graham, Esq.
George Africanus Thompson, Esq.	Edward Waugh, Esq.
John Sutton, Esq.	

46.—BRAY AND ENNISKERRY.

Incorporated by 29 and 30 Vic., cap. 321 (6th August, 1866), to construct a line from the Dublin Wicklow and Wexford, near Bray, to the town of Enniskerry. Length, 3½ miles. Capital, 36,000*l* in 10*l*. shares, and 12,000*l*. on loan. Arrangements with Dublin Wicklow and Wexford, which may subscribe 15,000*l*. Works not commenced. *No. of Directors*—6; minimum, 4; quorum, 3. *Qualification*, 300*l*.

DIRECTORS:

Viscount Powerscourt, 37, Grosvenor Square, W.
George Posnett, Esq.

Richard Marten, Esq.
Edward Barrington, Esq.
Edward Breslin, Esq.

47.—BREAN DOWN HARBOUR.

The Harbour Company was incorporated in 1862, under 25 and 26 Vic., cap. 29, 75,000*l*. in shares, and 25,000*l*. on loan; and by 28 Vic., cap. 122 (19th June, 1865), the company was further empowered to construct a railway to connect the harbour with the Bristol and Exeter, at Bleadon. Length, 3¼ miles. New capital, 51,000*l*. in shares, and 17,000*l*. by mortgage. Mixed gauge. Arrangements with Bristol and Exeter, to which the construction of the railway is now transferred, with power to work the railway traffic.

By 31 and 32 Vic., cap. 65 (25th June, 1868), an extension of time for completion of the railway works till 1871 was obtained, and for further extension or suspension contingent upon progress in the harbour works.

By Act of 29 and 30 Vic., cap. 228 (the Brean Down Dock Act, 1866), the Harbour Company was authorised also to construct Docks on the river Axe, and a road and bridge and other works in connection therewith.

48.—BRECON AND LLANDOVERY JUNCTION.

Incorporated by 26 and 27 Vic., cap. 201 (28th July, 1863), to construct a line from the Vale of Towy and the Central Wales at Llandovery to the Neath and Brecon at Devynnock. Length, 12 miles. Capital, 120,000*l*. in 10*l*. shares; loans, 40,000*l*. Works in progress.

By 28 and 29 Vic., cap. 284 (5th July, 1865), certain deviations were authorised, as well as division of shares into deferred and preferred.

By 29 and 30 Vic., cap. 306 (30th July, 1866), the company was authorised to make use of certain portions of the Brecon and Merthyr Tydfil Junction, reciprocal facilities being granted to the latter company.

No. of Directors—7; minimum, 3; quorum, 3. *Qualification*, 200*l*.

DIRECTORS:

Chairman—EDWARD PARKER, Esq., Barnsley.

William Laurence Banks, Esq., F.S.A., Watton House, Brecon.
Samuel Hawksley Burbury, Esq., 1, New Square, Lincoln's Inn Fields, W.C,

Chas. Kemp Dyer, Esq., Lloyd's, London.
John Townsend Kirkwood, Esq., Yeo Vale, near Bideford.

OFFICERS.—Sec., John Wade, 75, Ethelburga House, Bishopsgate Street, London, E.C.; Engs., R. and B. Piercy, 19, Duke Street, Westminster, S.W.; Solicitors, Tilleard, Son, Godden, and Holme, 34, Old Jewry, London, E.C., and Rixon and Son, 38, Cannon Street, London; Auditor; J. T. Morgan, St. John's Park, Holloway, N.; Bankers, The Consolidated Bank (Limited), Threadneedle Street, London, E.C.

49.—BRECON AND MERTHYR TYDFIL JUNCTION.

Incorporated by 22 and 23 Vic., cap. 68 (1st August, 1859), for constructing railways in the district between Brecon and Merthyr Tydfil. Share capital, 80,000*l*., in 10*l*. shares; loans, 26,000*l*. Calls, 2*l*. per share, with intervals of three months. The length of the first line is 12 miles 5 furlongs and 7¾ chains, which commences upon the Brecknock and Abergavenny Canal, in the parish of Llanthetty, and terminates in Merthyr Tydfil; the length of the second line is 1 mile 3 furlongs and 1 chain, which commences in Merthyr Tydfil at the termination of the first line, forming therewith one continuous line, and terminates in the same parish by a junction with the Dowlais, which communicates with the Taff Vale.

By 23 Vic., cap. 17 (15th May, 1860), the company was authorised to extend their line from Tal-y-bont to Brecon. By the Mid-Wales, with whom traffic arrangements may be made, a route is thus opened to Liverpool, Birkenhead, and Manchester, by way of Oswestry, Newtown, Llanidloes, and the Valley of the Wye, to Swansea, Cardiff, and Merthyr Tydfil. New capital, 50,000*l*. in shares, to which the Taff Vale may subscribe 30,000*l*. Loans, 16,000*l*. Works for a double line. Mr. Savin, on condition that those capabilities be secured, has agreed to complete the line, to provide rolling stock, working plant, and capital, and to become lessee of the whole for ten years from its completion from Merthyr to Tal-y-bont, paying to the shareholders 5 per cent. Opened from Dowlais to Brecon, 20 miles, 1st May, 1863. Four miles have since been opened for coal traffic.

By 24 Vic., cap. 10 (17th May, 1861), the company was empowered to raise additional capital, to the extent of 63,000*l*., in preference shares, at 5 per cent., and 21,000*l*. on loan.

By 24 and 25 Vic., cap. 235 (6th August, 1861), the company was also authorised to construct an extension from the main line, at Pant-coed-ifor, to Aberbargoed station, on the main line of the Rhymney. Length, 8 miles. New capital, 130,000*l*. in 10*l*. shares, and 43,300*l*. on loan. Compulsory purchase of land, two years; completion of works five years. The same Act confers powers for obtaining immediate possession of the portion of the Hay tram-road required for construction of the line into the town of Brecon.

By 25 and 26 Vic., cap. 184 (28th July, 1862), the company was authorised to construct new lines and deviations. Length, 10½ miles. Capital, 177,000*l*. in shares, and 58,000*l*. on loan. Extensions to be leased as above. Mutual facilities with Merthyr Tredegar and Abergavenny.

By 26 and 27 Vic., cap. 196 (21st July, 1863), the company was authorised to make a deviation in one of the lines of 1862, and to improve the access to the Brecon station. New capital, 50,000*l*. in shares, at 5 per cent., and 16,500*l*. on loan.

By 26 and 27 Vic., cap. 202 (28th July, 1863), the company was authorised to construct an extension to the Rumney. Length, 8 miles. Capital, 60,000*l*. in shares, and 20,000*l*. on loan. The Brecon also obtained power to acquire the Rumney, as well as special privileges over the Rhymney.

By 27 and 28 Vic., cap. 265 (25th July, 1864), the company was authorised to construct certain deviations, and to form a junction (1¾ mile) with the Rhymney, as well as to exercise the powers of the Vale of Neath in regard to the Merthyr Curve. New capital, 11,000*l*. in shares, and 3,660*l*. on loan.

By 27 and 28 Vic., cap. 304 (29th July, 1864), the company was authorised to construct new lines to the Rhymney, also to connect with and adopt the Rumney, which was shortly afterwards effected as part of the separate undertaking. Length of Rumney, 26 miles. New capital, 200,000*l*. in shares, and 66,600*l*. on loan.

By 28 and 29 Vic., cap. 285 (5th July, 1865), the company was authorised to construct branches to Dowlais and Ivor. Length, 7 miles. The company also obtained an extension of time for fifteen months for construction of the Cyfarthfa branch. The Act also authorises amalgamation of the general and separate undertakings, which was shortly afterwards carried into effect, and the raising of new capital to the extent of 255,000*l*., in shares, and 85,000*l*. on loan, for rolling stock and other purposes.

By 30 and 31 Vic., cap. 177 (12th August, 1867), the Brecon and Merthyr was authorised to make a deviation in the Rumney West Fork, and to construct a new line called the Rumney New Junction, 1 furlong 9 chains in length, but only in event of the London and North Western not proceeding, in the course of two years, to construct its Dowlais Extension. By the same Act running powers were conceded to the Rhymney, over the above-mentioned lines, if constructed. The Brecon and Merthyr was also authorised, under certificate of the Board of Trade, to borrow 190,000*l*., in proportions of 16,600*l*. on each 50,000*l*. share capital paid up on the sum of 570,500*l*. and also 24,000*l*. on the residue of 70,500*l*. being paid up.

By 30 and 31 Vic., cap. 142 (13th July, 1868), the company obtained a suspension o legal proceedings against it for ten years, and also several other privileges, including conversion of mortgage and other debts into debenture stock. Completion of lines, regulation of capital, constitution of new board, &c. The preference shareholders, acquired the right of voting, while the mortgage holders are to meet by themselves. By the same Act the agreement to amalgamate with the Hereford Hay and Brecon, was declared to be void, and that company to resume the whole of its privileges and independent course of action, including traffic arrangements with the Brecon and Merthyr.

RUMNEY.—Re-incorporated by 24 and 25 Vic., cap. 227 (1st August, 1861), to alter line and level of tram-road, and to make a new railway from Machen Upper to the Caerphilly branch of the Rhymney. Length, 4¼ miles. Capital, 100,000*l*. in 100*l* shares and 33,300*l*. on loan.

REVENUE.—The receipts for the half-year ending 30th June were 28,771*l.*, and the working expenditure 21,241*l.*; which was increased by other charges to 23,859*l.* The accumulated balance on hand is now 30,832*l.* The general balance sheet to the same date, furnished the subjoined particulars:—

Debtor—Balance of Revenue Account £30,832
Due to Railway Clearing House 2,330
Sundry Creditors .... 15,228 = £48,390
Creditor—Balance of Capital Account £26,664
Sundry Debtors, for freights, &c. 12.389
Balance due from Savin and Ward's Estate (irrespective of other liabilities arising from their failure as Contractors and Lessees) subject to realization 1,747
Stores on hand.. 2,788
Stationery on hand... 264
Receiver's balance to 31st December, 1867, paid into the Court of Chancery 426
Balance at Bankers, including amounts reserved towards payment of capital outlay authorised by Court of Chancery .... 4,109 = £48,390

The following special report was intended to have been submitted to three separate meetings—shareholders, holders of Lloyd's bonds, and of debenture holders—on 23rd September, but no quorum of either of the parties could be formed :—

" Consequent on the recent reconstruction of the board, the directors ask the forbearance of the proprietors if in their first report they do not enter so fully into details as to the company's position as they would otherwise have done.

" As the proprietors are aware, the company obtained a most important Act in the past Session of Parliament (Brecon and Merthyr Railway Arrangement Act, 1868), under which the board now consists of 8 directors, 4 being elected by the shareholders, 3 by the debenture holders, and 1 by the Lloyd's bond (or C debenture) holders.

" The following are the most important changes authorised by the Act:—

" 1. Power is given to the company to issue 100,000*l.* A preferential debenture stock, to be applied in discharge of all debenture interest up to 31st July, 1869, and for other purposes.

" 2. The whole of the debentures of the company are capitalised as B debenture stock.

" 3. The entire Lloyd's bond debt of the company, with the accumulated interest to the date of the Act, namely—13th July, 1868, is capitalised as C debenture stock.

" 4. The receiver in chancery is discharged as from the date of the Act.

" 5. The receipts of the company from the 13th July, 1868, until the 31st July, 1869, are to be applied in a certain order of appropriation defined by the Act, and

" 6. The union hitherto existing with the Hereford Hay and Brecon is annulled, and the line from Three Cocks to Hereford (about 26 miles in length) together with the capital and the liabilities attaching thereto, are re-transferred to that company."

" This company will continue to work the Hereford, until 1st October next, in order to prevent inconvenience to that company. The accounts between the two companies are now being prepared with a view to their speedy adjustment.

" The accounts are submitted in the form hitherto adopted, but the directors hope to submit them hereafter in a form calculated to furnish the proprietors with fuller particulars as to the working of the company's affairs.

" The falling off in the traffic is a subject of great regret, but is doubtless due to exceptional causes, more especially to the colliers' strike, now happily brought to a close : the depression in the iron trade, and the general stagnation in the district consequent thereon. It is to be hoped that the turning point has now been reached, and that the future receipts will show a steady improvement.

" The expenses of the company have been large, in consequence of the proceedings in Chancery and in Parliament, and of the losses attendant on two most unfortunate cases of collision, at Torpantau and Talybont. These items have, as yet, been but partially provided for, and further sums will come into the accounts for the present half-year. It is hoped that these exceptional items may be avoided in the future. But the directors think it right at the same time to state that no provision has heretofore been made for depreciation and renewal of rolling stock and permanent way, except to the extent of the actual expenditure on repairs.

"The line between Fochriew and Deri Junction, which completes the through communication between Brecon and Newport, was opened on the 1st inst., and the line nto Merthyr on the 1st August, making a total addition of nearly 6 miles to the company's lines.

"The construction of the Ivor and Dowlais extension and the erection of the Engine Shed at Talyllyn are being proceeded with, and will be completed with every despatch

"The Policy of the Board will be to cultivate the most friendly relations with neighbouring companies; to concentrate their energies on the development of their own traffic; to do everything in their power to reduce expenses; and they look confidently to the shareholders for support in their endeavours to raise the company into a strong financial position.

"The accounts have been audited by one auditor only. This has arisen from the circumstance that Mr. Fraser, who was elected as the second auditor, at the meeting of 31st March last, has subsequently been appointed secretary and receiver of the Hereford Hay and Brecon, with whom this company have to adjust some complicated matters of account. The directors have not, therefore, thought it necessary to call upon Mr. Fraser to act on this occasion."

CAPITAL.—The account to the 30th June, 1868, furnished the subjoined details:—

Receipts.		Expenditure.	
Ordinary shares and stock	£265,340	Brecon and Newport Section:—	
Preference shares and stock	1,203,217	Works, land, &c.	£1,272,905
Debentures	508,890	Extra works	126,·20
Suspense account	507	Rumney liabilities	86,200
Interest	499	Hereford Section:—	
Transfer fees	81	Works, &c.	424,990
Balance	26,664	Extra works	29,000
		Payments for and on account of rolling stock	* 65,884
	£2,005,200		£2,005,200

The above figures do not include existing liabilities on Lloyd's bonds, and for land and other matters.

Under the Act of last session, the capital of the Hereford Section is re-transferred to the Hereford Hay and Brecon, as stated in the report.

* Note.—Rolling stock, standing the company in their books in 34,769l., is held by certain creditors as against their claims amounting to 18,156l., but under an agreement by which this company will, on payment of the latter sum on or before 5th April, 1870, with rent in the meanwhile as agreed, have the stock re-transferred to them. The company have also to pay the balance of instalments on their rolling stock, amounting to 14,45ul.

Meetings, last week in February and August.

No. of Directors—8; quorum 3. Qualification, 500l.

DIRECTORS:

1 Chairman—A. H. PHILPOTTS, Esq., Carshalton, Surrey.

1 Deputy-Chairman—WILLIAM DE WINTON, Esq., Maesderwen.

1 James A. Mann, Esq., Brecon.
2 Thomas A. Bushby, Esq., 38, Brown's Buildings, Liverpool.
2 S. Robinson, Esq., The Moor, Kington, Herefordshire.
2 T. Salt, Esq., Jun., Walton-on-the-Hill, Stafford.
3 F Francis, Esq., Ramsdon Hall, Billericay, Essex.

1, Share Directors; 2, Debenture Directors; 3, C. Debenture Director.

OFFICERS.—Sec., W. Roberts, Brecon; Consulting Eng., Henry Conybeare, 20, Duke Street, Westminster, S.W.; Resident Eng., T. D. Roberts, Brecon; Traffic Man., Alfred Henshaw, Brecon; Loco. Supts., Andrew Baxter and Thomas Simpson; Audit Clerk, John Gall; Auditors, Wm. Edwards, and Alfred Augustus James, 18, King Street, London, E.C.; Solicitor, J. R. Cobb, Brecon; Bankers, Wilkins and Co., Brecon, Merthyr, and Cardiff, and London and County.

Offices—Free Street, Brecon.

50.--BRIDGNORTH, WOLVERHAMPTON, AND STAFFORDSHIRE.

Incorporated by 29 and 30 Vic., cap. 129, (28th June, 1866), to construct a line from Bridgnorth to Wolverhampton, and other places in Staffordshire. Length, 21 miles. Capital, 270,000*l.* in 10*l.* shares, and 90,000*l.* on loan. Arrangements with Great Western. *No. of Directors*—7 ; minimum, 5; quorum, 3. *Qualification*, 500*l.*

DIRECTORS:

Chairman—SIR JOHN D'ALBERG ACTON, Bart., Aldenham, Bridgnorth.

John Everitt, Esq., Allhallows Chambers, Lombard Street, London.

William Watkin, Esq., Swindon Iron Works, Stourbridge.

Frederick Charles Perry, Esq., Dunston, near Penkridge, Staffordshire.

Hall W. Keary, Esq., Oldbury, near Bridgnorth.

William Wyley, Esq., Dothill Park, near Bridgnorth.

OFFICERS.—Sec., W. Roberts; Eng., Joseph Fogerty, 1, Westminster Chambers, Victoria Street, Westminster, S.W.; Solicitors, Crawley, Arnold, and Green, 20, Whitehall Place, London, S.W., R. O. Backhouse, Bridgnorth, and Underhill, Corser, and Fowler, Wolverhampton.

Registered Offices—7, Bank Buildings, Lothbury, London, E.C.

51.--BRIDPORT.

Incorporated by 18 Vic , cap. 11 (May 5th, 1855), for constructing a railway from Bridport to Maiden Newton, to the Wilts Somerset and Weymouth. Broad gauge. Length, 9¾ miles. Opened November 12th, 1857. Worked by Great Western at 52½ per cent. of gross receipts.

By 22 and 23 Vic., cap. 120 (13th August, 1859), the company is authorised to lease the line to the Great Western, and to raise additional capital to complete the undertaking. New capital, 20,000*l.* Preference interest not to exceed 6 per cent. Cancelled shares may also be issued at same preference.

REVENUE.—It was announced in March that for the December half-year the available balance of revenue, 610*l.*, was insufficient for any dividend, except on the preference shares, at the rate of 6 per cent. per annum. The directors called attention to the unsatisfactory relationship of the company to the Great Western, and expressed an opinion that the time had arrived for collecting the views and opinions of the shareholders thereon. The directors stated that when the working agreement was negotiated between the two companies it was distinctly understood that the Bridport were to receive a clear 47½ per cent. of the gross receipts, and that the remaining 52½ was to cover all expenses whatever of the Great Western, or they would not have agreed to such terms. The Bridport directors, therefore, contended that nothing should be deducted for cartage or anything else previously to a division of gross receipts.

The meetings are to be held in February or March, and in August or September; all ordinary meetings to be held in Bridport; quorum of shareholders, 15, representing at least 6,000*l.*

No. of Directors—6; quorum, 3. *Qualification*, 50 shares.

DIRECTORS :

Chairman--THOMAS LEGG, Esq., Arlington, Bridport.

Thos. Alex. Mitchell, Esq., 50, Charles Street, Berkley Square, W.

William Smith, Esq., Bridport.

William Swatridge, Esq., Maiden Newton.

Kirkman Daniel Hodgson, Esq., 36, Brook Street, W.

John Pike Stephens, Esq., Bothenhampton.

OFFICERS.—Sec. and Solicitor, E. G. Flight ; Eng., M. Lane; Auditors, James Williams and Frederick Good.

Offices—Bridport.

52.--BRISTOL AND EXETER.

Incorporated by 6 Wm. IV., cap. 36 (19th May, 1836), for making a broad gauge line from Bristol to Exeter, with branches; the main line starting from Bristol, where it joins the Great Western line from London, and terminating at Exeter, where it is joined by the South Devon, which runs to Plymouth. In operation, 134¼ miles.

By 26 Vic., cap. 60 (1863), the company was authorised to purchase additional lands, to construct the Chard and Taunton line (length, 15½ miles) as part of their own undertaking (the Chard and Taunton company being dissolved), and to lease or purchase the West Somerset (14½ miles), already worked by the Bristol and Exeter. Under the Act of 1867 (30 and 31 Vic., cap. 130), the Chard Canal, running from Chard to Taunton, was transferred to the Bristol and Exeter, and has been closed, and the lands are in course of sale.

GRAND WESTERN CANAL.—Under 27 and 28 Vic., cap. 184 (14th July, 1864), this canal has been transferred to and vested in the Bristol and Exeter, which was authorised to raise capital for the purchase. A considerable portion of the canal was authorised to be abandoned, and has since been closed and the land sold.

CHEDDAR VALLEY AND YATTON.—By 27 and 28 Vic., cap. 181 (14th July, 1864), the company was authorised to contribute to the construction of this line, from Yatton to Wells, and it has since been altogether transferred to the Bristol and Exeter by whom it is being made as a part of their own undertaking, under 28 Vic., cap. 97 (19th June, 1865), by which capital was authorised to be raised for the purpose. Length, 17¾ miles.

BRIDGWATER AND TAUNTON CANAL.—By 29 and 30 Vic., cap. 96 (28th June, 1866), the Bristol and Exeter was authorised to accept a transfer of the Bridgwater and Taunton canal and Stolford railway and harbour, and to raise the requisite capital for purchase thereof. The Canal is now worked by the Bristol and Exeter.

By 29 and 30 Vic., cap. 115 (28th June, 1866), the company was authorised to raise capital and construct new lines and works of about half-a-mile in length, in the county of Somerset, and to take upon itself the powers of constructing the Brean Down Railway from the main line to Brean Down Harbour, for which an extension of time has since been obtained. Also to lay down the narrow gauge on the Bristol and Exeter from Highbridge, at the junction of the Somerset and Dorset, to Bridgwater, and likewise upon the Yeovil branch, within two years from passing of the Act, which has been done, and the narrow gauge is now worked there.

By 30 and 31 Vic., cap. 130 (15th July, 1867), the Bristol and Exeter to make certain deviations in the Cheddar line, and also a railway (4 furlongs in length) from the main line in the Puriton cutting and terminating on the north bank of the river Parret, at Dunball.

OTHER LINES.—The company has been authorised to contribute to the South Devon, the Cornwall, the Exeter and Crediton, the North Devon, and the Somerset Central lines; and also to the Plymouth Great Western Docks.

THE TIVERTON AND NORTH DEVON, to which they were authorised to contribute, has been abandoned, under 31 and 32 Vic., cap. 65 (25th June, 1868).

WEST CORNWALL.—Under an Act of 5th July, 1865 (28 and 29 Vic., cap. 219), this line has been leased to the Bristol and Exeter, the Great Western, and the South Devon jointly, by whom it is now worked, with powers for an ultimate purchase.

Various other powers conferred from time to time have expired or been superseded: and the arrangements under which the company leased or worked the Exeter and Crediton, and the Somerset Central, have terminated. The Bristol and Exeter, however, by agreement, run a broad gauge train daily, each way, for goods over the Exeter and Crediton (5¾ miles).

SOUTH WESTERN.—Pursuant to Act, station arrangements have been made with this company at Yeovil and Exeter; a joint station for the two companies having been erected and opened at Yeovil; and a new station has been erected by the Bristol and Exeter, at St. David's, Exeter, to which the South Western, which now works the Exeter and Crediton and the North Devon, is admitted, as well as the South Devon.

WEST SOMERSET.—This line (from Taunton Junction to Watchet), 14½ miles, is worked under a lease for 999 years, the Bristol and Exeter paying to the West Somerset a minimum rent of 4,500l. a-year (less income tax), or 55 per cent. of gross receipts whenever in any year such per centage would exceed that amount.

MINEHEAD.—By an Act of 5th July, 1865 (29 and 30 Vic., cap. 317), a line is authorised to be constructed by an independent company from Watchet to Minehead, with power to the Bristol and Exeter to work it by agreement.

DEVON AND SOMERSET.—This line, from Taunton to Barnstaple, is authorised by an Act of 1864 to be constructed on the broad gauge, by an independent company, the Bristol and Exeter agreeing to work the line when made at 50 per cent. of the receipts.

The agreement was confirmed by Act 28 Vic., cap. 42 (26th May, 1865). An Act also received the royal assent on 25th July, 1864, amended by 28 Vic., cap. 71 (2nd June, 1865), for a line from Barnstaple to Ilfracombe, with powers to make it of both broad and narrow gauges, joint ownership and control over the line being given to the Devon and Somerset and the London and South Western, on their entering into arrangements for that purpose, each of the two companies providing half the share capital. This, however, was declined at a meeting of the Devon and Somerset, in August, 1865, and an Act has since been passed making other provision in reference to the Ilfracombe undertaking.

BRISTOL AND PORTISHEAD.—This line (9½ miles), belonging to the Bristol and Portishead Pier and Railway Company was opened on the 18th April, 1867, and is worked for that company by the Bristol and Exeter at cost price, under a temporary arrangement until the pier is made, when the permanent working agreement takes effect. The mileage and traffic of this line are not at present included in the Bristol and Exeter returns.

BRISTOL JOINT STATION.—By 28 Vic., cap. 91 (19th June, 1865), the Bristol and Exeter, in conjunction with the Great Western and the Midland, undertook to provide its quota towards construction of a joint station at Bristol, the new capital for which is restricted to a total of 150,000*l.* in shares and 35,000*l.* on loan, for the three companies.

BRISTOL HARBOUR.—Under an Act of 1866 (29 and 30 Vic., cap. 148), the Bristol and Exeter and the Great Western jointly, in concert with the Municipal Corporation of Bristol, are authorised to make a railway to connect their existing railways with the Floating Harbour, and to provide a wharf, depôt, and wharfage accommodation at the harbour. The corporation have exercised their power of electing to construct the wharf, depôt, and wharfage accommodation, at a cost of 50,000*l.*, to be provided by the city, leaving 115,000*l.* to be raised by the two companies jointly in share capital, with borrowing power for one-third of that amount. This share capital has been raised in 5 per cent. stock, guaranteed under the seals of the two companies.

CAPITAL.—Under the various Acts of the company, the capital authorised from time to time and raised has been as stated below. By an Act of 25th June, 1868 (31 and 32 Vic., cap. 65, the Bristol and Exeter Railway Act, 1868), the capital was rearranged and consolidated, power obtained to issue debenture stock in lieu of debentures, to exchange the inconvertible stock into debenture stock of equal rate of interest, to abandon any further issue of the 4 per cent. preference stock (the unissued portion of which was issuable in debentures until it should be taken up as preference stock), and to consolidate the two terminable 4½ per cent. stocks (repayable at the end of 1870) into one stock of the same amount. The Act also gives power to exchange any preference stock of the company being interest at 4½ per cent. or upwards, for original stock. By these provisions, the various classes of securities are reduced from seven to five in number, the total capital remaining the same.

The future authorised capital of the company is as follows, in order of priority, under the Bristol and Exeter Act, 1868:—

1. Debentures or Debenture Stock : namely,

Amount already issuable under Act of 1855 in debentures, (being the difference between £4,000,000 and £3,198,189 permanent stocks issued under that Act) £801,811

Borrowing powers under subsequent Acts passed 219,500

Total present borrowing powers (subject to conversion into debenture stock) £1,021,311

Inconvertible 4 per cent. stock, exchangeable into debenture stock under Act of 1868 51,915

Total issuable in debentures or debenture stock £1,073,226

2. Perpetual 4 per cent. stock 1,123,814

3. Present terminable 4½ per cent. stocks, and stock to be created in lieu thereof 566,000

4. Perpetual 5 per cent. preference stock, created in 1867 219,000

5. Ordinary stock (subject to increase by exchange and corresponding decrease of preference stocks under Act of 1868) 2,022,460

Total loan and share capital of Bristol and Exeter £5,004,500

To carry out these arrangements, it was accordingly resolved at the half-yearly meeting in August after the passing of the Act:—

"That the directors be and are hereby authorised to raise all or any part of the money wh'ch they are authorised to raise on mortgage or bond, by the issue of debenture stock in lieu thereof, in conformity with the Acts relating to such stock ; provided that the amount of debentures and debenture stock together shall not at any time exceed the amount authorised by the company's Acts to be from time to time so raised or borrowed.

"That the directors be authorised to exercise the remaining borrowing powers of the company, as soon as the statutory requirements in that behalf are complied with, or in lieu of borrowing to issue debenture stock in conformity with the Bristol and Exeter Railway Act, 1868.

"That the company hereby create, and the directors are hereby authorised to issue, at such times and on such terms as they may see fit, preference stock not exceeding 566,000l., in conformity with the Bristol and Exeter Railway Act, 1868, in lieu of and to pay off or replace the 4½ per cent. preference stocks terminable at 31st December, 1870."

CAPITAL.—The receipts and expenditure to 30th June were detailed as follows :—

Receipts.—Consolidated original stock	............£2,022,460		
Perpetual 4 per cent. preference stock	 1,175,729	=£3,198,189	
Terminable 4½ per cent. preference stock, created 1863	....	336,000	
Do. do. created 1865	....	230,000	
Perpetual 5 per cent. preference stock	....	141,000	= £3,905,189
Debentures (as in annexed debenture account)	....		891,200

£4,796,389

Expenditure.—From last account	....£4,111,103
Half-year ended 30th June, 1868 :—	
Main line	 6,869
Laying narrow gauge lines, between Highbridge and Yeovil	 3,829
Yeovil branch	 249
Weston branch	 105
Tiverton branch	 5
West Somerset branch	 23
Chard branch	 349
Cheddar branch	 46,183
Brean Down Railway	 151
Grand Western Canal	 227
Bridgwater and Taunton Canal	 64
Chard Canal purchase	 5,945
Plant	 15,753
Telegraph, main line and branches	 74
Law and parliamentary expenses	 353

Expended to 30th June, 1868 .... £4,191,296

Investments: In 3 per cent. consols in name of County Treasurer of Somerset	....	£1,000
South Devon, original stock and annuities	....	300,000
„ Additional preference shares	....	20,000
Exeter and Crediton, 1,031 shares, cost	....	28,153
„ „ 400 preference shares	....	8,000
South Western, 784l. ordinary stock in exchange for 100 North Devon shares	....	1,600
Plymouth Great Western Dock, 375 shares	....	7,500
„ „ „ 500 preference shares*	....	5,000
„ „ „ debentures	....	13,082
Somerset Central, 400 shares (in exchange for Glastonbury Canal), cost	....	7,392
„ 100 shares	....	2,000
Cornwall, 4,500 shares	....	90,000
Tiverton and North Devon	....	3,000 = £486,729

Total expenditure	.... £4,678,025
Balance	 118,363

Total.. £4,796,389

*And in addition, 4,530l. or 453 10l. 5 per cent. preference shares of Plymouth Great Western Dock Company, as composition for overdue debenture and preference interest : *see* Report of Feb. 1868.

JOINT UNDERTAKINGS:—CAPITAL AUTHORISED.

Bristol Harbour Railway; joint undertaking by the Great Western and the Bristol and Exeter:—

Share capital raised by the two companies, under Act of
1866 (exclusive of 50,000*l.* for wharf depôt to be provided
by Municipal Corporation) £115,000

Borrowing powers in respect of same .... 38,333=£153,333

Bristol Joint Station; joint undertaking by the Great Western,
the Bristol and Exeter, and the Midland Railway Companies:—

Share capital to be raised under Act of 1865 by the three
companies, in proportions not yet .determined, not ex-
ceeding a total of 150,000

Borrowing powers in respect of same, not exceeding one-
fourth of each company's proportion of share capital ...... 37,500= 187,500

Total capital of joint undertakings, the Bristol and
Exeter proportion thereof not being yet ascertained................ £340,833

REVENUE.—The traffic receipts for the half-year ending 31st December were 207,247*l.*,
or 1,543*l.* 14*s* 10*d.* per mile, as against 195,252*l.*, or 1,454*l.* 7*s.* 10*d.* per mile for 1866,
showing an increase of 11,955*l.*, and of 89*l.* 7*s.* per mile. The particulars exhibited an
increase of 8,342*l.* for passengers, of 2,495*l.* for goods and cattle, of 1,108*l.* for parcels,
horses, &c., and 285*l.* on interchange of carriage stock. Under the head of mails
and expresses there was a decrease of 176*l.* and the toll at Exeter, 62*l.* While the
traffic receipts thus showed a net increase of 11,995*l.*, the working expenses exhibited
a net decrease of 423*l.* The total revenue receipts from all sources amounted to
216,961*l.*, as against 206,316*l.*, showing an increase of 10,605*l.*, and the total expenditure
was 111,650*l.*, as against 108,380*l.*, showing an increase of 3,270*l.*, and giving (with
the balance from previous half-year) a profit of 105,860*l.*, out of which 56,662*l.* was
paid for debenture and preference interest; and the available balance of 49,198*l.*
authorised a dividend for the half-year, at the rate of 4¾ per cent. per annum. This
dividend amounted to 48,033*l.*, leaving a balance of 1,165*l.* to next account. The dividend for 31st December, 1866, was at the rate of 4½ per cent., with a balance of 2,474*l.*,
the mileage at the two dates being the same (134¼ miles open).

The traffic receipts for the June half-year amounted to 190,613*l.*, showing an increase
of 11,300*l.* on the corresponding period of 1867. The working expenses showed an increase of 5,259*l.* The revenue receipts from all sources amounted to 204,957*l.*, as against
193,081*l.*, showing an increase of 11,876*l.* The expenditure amounted to 107,124*l.*
The profit on the working (including balance brought forward) amounted to 98,998*l.*,
out of which 60,368*l.* were charged for debenture and preference interest, leaving an
available balance of 38,630*l.*, out of which a dividend at the rate of 3¾ per cent. per
annum, left a balance of 709*l.* for next account.

Accounts made up to the 30th June and 31st December in each year. Statutory
meetings at Bristol, within 20 days after the second week in February and August.

Scale of Voting.—1 for every 100*l.* up to 2,000*l.*; then 1 for every 500*l.* Proxies to be
lodged with secretary five days before meeting.

Transfer fees, 2*s.* 6*d.* each deed; certificates or coupons must accompany transfer
deeds. Stocks may be transferred in any amounts not less than a pound sterling.

Directors.—Maximum, 16; minimum, 12; present number, 12. One-fourth retire
annually, but are re-eligible. *Qualification*, 1,000*l.* Allowance, 1,800*l.* a year.

DIRECTORS:

Chairman—3 The EARL OF DEVON, Powderham Castle, Exeter.

Deputy-Chairman—1 MICHAEL CASTLE, Esq., Clifton, Bristol.

3 Wm. Thos. Poole King, Esq., Bristol.
4 Francis Fry, Esq., Cotham, Bristol.
2 Robt. Phippen, Esq., Bedminster, Bristol.
4 Wm. Adair Bruce, Esq., Ashley, Chippenham.
3 Richard K. Meade King, Esq., Walford,
Taunton.
1 James Poole, Esq., Wick House, Durdham Park, Bristol.

2 William Barnes, Esq., Great Duryard,
Exeter.
1 John Walrond Walrond, Esq., Brad-
field, Cullompton, and 12, Wimpole
Street, W.
2 William Henry Wills, Esq., Clifton
Down, Bristol.
4 Henry S. Ellis, Esq., Fair Park,
Exeter.

1 Retire in February 1869; 2, in 1870; 3, in 1871; 4, in 1872; all eligible for re-election

OFFICERS.—Sec., Arthur Moore, Cradley House, Clifton; Traffic Supt., Henry Dykes; Eng., Francis Fox; Loco. Supt., James Pearson; Carriage Supt., Henry Bridges, Bridgwater; Chief Accountant. John B. Marwood; Storekeeper, Wm. Pyke; Solicitors, Messrs. Fussell and Prichard, Bristol; Auditors, George Thomas and Wilberforce Tribe, Public Accountants, Bristol; Goods Agent, J. C. Wall, Bristol.

Head Offices—Temple Mead, Bristol.

53,—BRISTOL HARBOUR.

Powers were given by 29 and 30 Vic., cap. 148 (28th June, 1866), to construct a wharf and depôt at Wapping, in Bristol, and a railway to connect the existing railways with the Floating Harbour. Length, ¾ mile. Capital 165,000l., of which 50,000l. is to be provided by the Bristol Municipal Corporation, for making the wharf and depôt, leaving 115,000l. to be raised in shares by the Great Western and the Bristol and Exeter, in such manner or proportions as they may agree, and with power to borrow one-third of the amount raised by them in shares. The 115,000l. has since been all raised by the Great Western and the Bristol and Exeter jointly, as a 5 per cent. stock guaranteed by the two companies, and called Bristol Harbour Railway Stock.

The works are in progress, and the railway is under the management of a Joint Committee, appointed by the Great Western and the Bristol and Exeter from their own boards.

Arrangements with Bristol Corporation, and facilities to Bristol and North Somerset.

54.—BRISTOL AND NORTH SOMERSET.

Incorporated by 26 and 27 Vic., cap. 168 (21st July, 1863), to construct a line from the Great Western, at Bristol, to Radstock, with a branch to Camerton. Length, 20 miles. Capital, 275,000l., in 20l. shares, and 91,000l. on loan. Mixed gauge.

By 29 and 30 Vic., cap. 262 (23rd July, 1866), the company was authorised to raise additional capital to the extent of 100,000l. in shares, and 33,500l. on loan.

By 31 and 32 Vic., cap. 178 (31st July, 1868), the company was authorised to make several deviations, and to form a junction with the Great Western at Bristol. An extension of time for completion of works till July, 1871, was also secured.

*No. of Directors—*8 ; minimum, 6; quorum, 5 and 3. *Qualification,* 400l.

DIRECTORS:

Chairman—GWINNETT TYLER, Esq , Worcester Terrace, Clifton.

Captain Bulkeley, Clewer Lodge, Windsor. | Frederick Patey Chappell, Esq., 26, Golden
John William Miles, Esq., King's Weston, | Square, London.
Bristol. | James William Dawson, Esq., 28, Lincoln's Inn Fields, W.C.

Three vacancies.

OFFICERS.—Sec., George Edgar Frere; Eng., John Furness Tone, Newcastle; Bankers, Baillie, Cave, Baillie, and Co., Bristol, and the Union Bank of London, Chancery Lane, W.C.

Offices—52, Queen's Square, Bristol.

55.—BRISTOL PORT AND PIER.

Incorporated by 25 and 26 Vic., cap. 159 (17th July, 1862), to construct a railway from the port of Bristol to the old channel at the mouth of the Avon, with pier, &c. Length, 5¾ miles. Capital, 125,000l., in 10l. shares, and 45,000l. on loan. Corporation of Bristol may purchase undertaking under parliamentary authority, within ten years from incorporation. Opened on 6th March, and pier on 3rd June, 1865.

By 28 and 29 Vic., cap 155 (29th June, 1865), the mortgage debt of the company was specially defined and consolidated, as well as extended over the whole of the undertaking, instead of portions on each.

By 30 and 31 Vic., cap. 204, the company was authorised to construct new lines to form a connection with the South Wales Union and the Bristol and Birmingham line of the Midland. Length, 4 miles. New capital, 132,000l. in shares, and 43,900l. on loan. Arrangements with Great Western and Midland.

Messrs. Waring work the line for six years from 1865, at a rate calculated to pay a dividend commencing at 2½ per cent. and increasing to 5 per cent. Dividends were declared at the rate of 3 per cent. for the December and 4 per cent. for the June half-years.

No. of Directors—4; quorum, 3. *Qualification*, 500*l.*

DIRECTORS:

Chairman—PHILIP W. S. MILES, Esq.

The Right Hon. Viscount Gort, Warwick Square, London, S.W.
Henry Hurry Goodeve, Esq., Clifton.

Henry Danby Seymour, Esq., Knoyle, Hindon, Wilts.

OFFICERS.—Sec., Hew Dalrymple; Solicitor, James Wheeler, 4, Victoria Street, Westminster, S.W.; Auditors, Thomas T. Taylor and William Terrell.

Offices—Royal Insurance Buildings, Bristol.

56.–BRISTOL AND PORTISHEAD.

Incorporated by 26 and 27 Vic., cap. 107 (29th June, 1863), to construct a pier at Portbury, and a railway therefrom to the Bristol and Exeter, with a branch to Portishead. Length, 10 miles. Broad gauge. Capital, 200,000*l.* in 25*l.* shares; loans, 66,600*l.* Opened 12th April, 1867.

Agreements with the Bristol and Exeter, by which that company provided the necessary rolling stock, and worked the line in connection with their system, at 40 per cent. when they shall have reached 10,000*l.* per annum.

By 29 Vic., cap. 88 (11th June, 1866), the company was authorised to alter the pier at Portishead, to construct other works, and also to extend the time for their completion till 1870. New capital, 60,000*l.* in shares, and 20,000*l.* on loan.

REVENUE.—It was reported in August that the pier and jetty were completed, and would contribute materially to the revenue of the company during the time the works now being extended into deeper water were being constructed. The receipts had been sufficient to cover all the expenses of the line, and to leave a profit applicable to payment of interest. The number of passengers had been 188,404, exclusive of season ticket holders.

Meetings in February and August.

No. of Directors—7; minimum, 5; quorum, 3 and 5. *Qualification*, 500*l.*

DIRECTORS:

Chairman—JAMES FORD, Esq., Clarence Villa, Clifton.

Deputy-Chairman—GEORGE ROCKE WOODWARD, Esq., Cornwallis Grove, Clifton.

Richard Fry, Esq., Cotham Lawn, Bristol.
Richard Robinson, Esq., Richmond Cottage, Clifton.
Lewis Fry, Esq., Clifton Hill.

Richard Fuidge, Esq., Victoria Square, Clifton.
Frederick Weatherly, Esq., Hillside, Portishead.

OFFICERS.—Sec., J. F. R. Daniel; Engs., McClean and Stileman, 23, Great George Street, Westminster, S.W.; Solicitors, Isaac Cooke and Sons, Bristol; Auditors, J. T. Pike and W. Tribe.

Offices—6, Clare Street, Bristol.

57.–BRISTOL AND SOUTH WALES UNION.

Incorporated by 20 and 21 Vic., cap. 54 (27th July, 1857), to construct railways between the city of Bristol and the South Wales, in the county of Monmouth, with a steam ferry across the river Severn in connection therewith. Capital, 300,000*l.* in 25*l.* shares; loans, 98,000*l.*; calls, 5*l.* per share, with intervals of three months. Length on Gloucestershire side of Severn, 11½ miles; on the Monmouthshire side there are two lines connecting the ferry with the South Wales, of the respective lengths of 7 furlongs 2½ chains, and 3 furlongs 2 chains. Broad gauge. The Act also provides that the company may purchase an existing ferry across the Severn, called New Passage Ferry, and acquire and use steamboats for conveyance of passengers and goods. Arrangements with Great Western, which works the traffic. Opened 9th September, 1863.

By 24 Vic., cap. 2 (17th May, 1861), the period for completion of works was extended to May, 1864. Forfeited shares to be cancelled, and new capital created by preference shares, but the aggregate amount not to exceed that limited by Act of 1857.

By 25 and 26 Vic., cap. 149 (17th July, 1862), the company was authorised to construct a branch to the pier and the mouth of the river Avon. Length, 7 miles. New capital, 40,000*l.* in 25*l.* shares, and 9,800*l.* on loan.

By 27 and 28 Vic., cap. 136 (30th June, 1864), an extension of time for one year was conceded for completion of works on the extension to the river Avon.

By the Great Western Act, 1868, the British and South Wales Union is merged into and amalgamated with the Great Western, the latter taking upon itself the following liabilities:—

1. The debenture debt of the Union Company, bearing interest at not exceeding 5 per cent. £98,000

2. The preference share capital of the Union Company bearing interest in perpetuity at 5 per cent. on and from 1st February, 1870, these shares are to be coverted into Great Western (South Wales Union) guaranteed 5 per cent. preference stock 120,450

3. The ordinary share capital of the Union Company, on and from 1st February, 1870, these shares are to be converted into and rank with Great Western ordinary stock 168,225

The Great Western became possessed of the property of the Union Company from 1st August, 1868, and receive all tolls, &c.

DIRECTORS:

Chairman—CHRISTOPHER JAMES THOMAS, Esq., Durdham Park, Bristol.

Deputy-Chairman—FRANCIS TOTHILL, Esq., 7, Laurence Pountney Hill, London.

Thomas William Booker, Esq., Melin Griffith, near Cardiff.

William Henry G. Langton, Esq., 2, Princess Gate, Hyde Park, London, W.

John William Miles, Esq., King's Weston, near Bristol.

Thomas Wright Rankin, Esq., Clifton.

John Ravenhill, Esq., Ashton, near Heytesbury, Wilts.

Christopher Rice Mansel Talbot, Esq., M.P., Margam Park, Taibach, Glamorganshire, and 3, Cavendish Square, W.

Gwinnett Tyler, Esq., Clifton.

George Wills, Esq., Bristol.

OFFICERS.—Sec., Leonard Bruton; Engineers, R. P. Brereton, 18, Duke Street, Westminster, S.W., and Charles Richardson, Almondsbury, near Bristol; Auditors, George Thomas and John Shute; Solicitors, Fussell and Prichard, Bristol.

Offices—52, Queen Square, Bristol.

58.—BROXBURN.

Incorporated by 30 and 31 Vic., cap. 175 (12th August, 1867), to construct a line from the Edinburgh and Glasgow at Kirkliston to Broxburn. Length, 1¼ mile. Capital, 8,000l. in 10l. shares, and 2,600l. on loan. Arrangements with North British.

No. of Directors—3; quorum, 2. *Qualification*, 100l.

DIRECTORS:

Walter Maclellan, Esq.
George Auldjo Jamieson, Esq.

Robert Bell, Esq.

59.—BRYNMAWR AND BLAENAVON.

Incorporated by 29 and 30 Vic., cap. 209 (16th July, 1866), to construct a line from the Merthyr Tredegar and Abergavenny, near the Brynmawr station, to Blaenavon. Length, 4¾ miles. Capital. 60,000l., in 10l. shares (deferred and preferred), and 20,000l. on loan. Arrangements with London and North Western, which may subscribe 25,000l.

No. of Directors—5; quorum, 3. *Qualification*, 500l.

DIRECTORS:

*George Skirrow Beecroft, Esq., Abbey House, Kirkstall, Leeds.

*William Tipping, Esq., M.P., Arques, near Dieppe.

*Oscar Leslie Stephen, Esq., Bardon Hall, Leicester.

George Frederick Finch, Esq.

John Jayne, Esq.

* Represent L. and N. W.

60.—BUCKFASTLEIGH, TOTNES, AND SOUTH DEVON.

Incorporated by 27 and 28 Vic , cap. 258 (25th July, 1864), to construct a line from the South Devon, at Littlehemstone, to Buckfastleigh, and a branch to Totnes. Broad gauge. Length. 7¾ miles. Capital, 48,000l., in 10l. shares, and 16,000l. on loan. Arrangements with South Devon. Works in progress.

By 28 Vic., cap. 41 (26th May, 1865), the company was authorised to extend its line to Ashburton. Length, 2¼ miles. New capital, 48,000l. in shares, and 16,000l. on loan.

By 31 Vic., cap. 14 (29th May, 1868), an extension of time for completion of works till 1871 was obtained.

It was reported in March and August that ineffectual negotiations had taken place between the directors and the contractor, with the view of getting him to complete his contract, and they were convinced that the works would remain at a standstill until another contractor was obtained.

CAPITAL.—The receipts from calls amounted to 17,641l., of which 13,375l. had been expended in constructing the line, 2,376l. had been paid for land, and 1,624l. in Parliamentary expenses. The balance against receipts is now 176l.

No. of Directors—6; minimum, 3; quorum, 3 and 2. *Qualification*, 250l.

DIRECTORS:

John Bowden, Esq., Totnes.
John Hamlyn, Esq., Buckfastleigh.
* Samuel Huxham, Esq., Totnes.

* John Winterbotham Batten, Esq., 10, Causland Place, Kensington, W.
* Retiring directors, 1869.

OFFICERS.—Sec., Alexander E. Lhoyd, Newton Abbott; Eng., P. J. Margary, Plymouth; Solicitors, J. B. Batten, 32, Great George Street, Westminster, S.W., and H. Michelmore, Newton Abbott; Auditors, John Barns and †Robert Bourne. †Retireing auditor, 1869.

61.—BUCKINGHAMSHIRE.

An amalgamation of the BUCKINGHAM AND BRACKLEY, incorporated by 9 and 10 Vic., cap. 233 (1846), and of the OXFORD AND BLETCHLEY, incorporated by 9 and 10 Vic., cap. 82 (1846), under the present title by 10 and 11 Vic., cap. 336 (1847), with further powers or an extension of the former scheme north to Banbury: Bletchley to Oxford, 31⅓ miles, with a line from Claydon to a junction with the Great Western. Oxford and Rugby, at Banbury—21½ miles. Total, 53 miles. The amount authorised by the Extension Act of 1847 (450,000l.) was provided by the London and North Western. An Act was obtained in 1853 to authorise a junction with the Oxford Worcester and Wolverhampton, near Oxford. The whole undertaking is leased from 1st July, 1851, for 999 years, under Act 11 and 12 Vic., cap. 236, to the London and North Western, at 4 per cent. per annum, with half surplus profits.

Meetings are held in London, in February and August.

Scale of Voting.—C. C. C. Act, sec. 75.

Certificates must accompany transfer stock. Registration fee, 2s. 6d. each deed. The company will transfer 10s. of stock.

Director's Qualification, 50 shares—875l. stock.

DIRECTORS:

Chairman—Sir HARRY VERNEY, Bart., M.P.. 32, South Street, Park Lane, W., and Claydon House, Buckinghamshire.

Robert Benson, Esq., Craven Hill Gardens, Hyde Park, W.
His Grace the Duke of Buckingham, Stowe, Buckinghamshire.
The Earl of Caithness, 17, Hill Street, Berkeley Square, W.
Timothy Rhodes Cobb, Esq., Banbury.

Richard Ryder Dean, Esq., Gloucester Place, Portman Square, W.
The Hon. Arthur Fitzgerald Kinnaird, M.P., 2, Pall Mall East, S.W.
Matthew Lyon, Esq , Leamington.
William Tipping, Esq., M.P., Arques, near Dieppe.

The directors retire from office in rotation, in the alphabetical order of their names. All eligible for re-election.

OFFICERS.—Sec., William Long; Auditors, Henry Crosfield, Liverpool, and Richard Carter, Buckingham.

Offices—Euston Station, London, N.W.

62.—BUCKLEY.

Incorporated by 23 Vic., cap. 89 (14th June, 1860), to construct a line from Buckley to Connah's Quay, Flintshire. Length, 5 miles. Capital, 30,000l. in 10l. shares; loans, 10,000l. The line is purely of a mineral character, and the shares are held by traders and others connected with the district.

By 26 and 27 Vic., cap. 104 (29th June, 1863), the company was authorised to raise new capital to the extent of 30,000l. at such preference as the proprietors might think fit, and 10,000l. on mortgage.

By 29 Vic., cap. 41 (18th May, 1866), the company was authorised to carry passengers on the line, and also to create new capital to the extent of 30,000l. in shares, and 10,000l. on loan.

By 29 and 30 Vic., cap. 270 (23rd July, 1866), certain articles of agreement between this company and the Wrexham Mold and Connah's Quay, obtained parliamentary sanction. They chiefly related to joint-working or amalgamation at a period to be afterwards determined.

By this agreement the Wrexham Mold and Connah's Quay work the line, and guarantee 5 per cent. on the ordinary and preference shares, and interest on debentures.

No. of Directors.—Maximum, 7; minimum, 5; quorum, 3. *Qualification*, 200l.

DIRECTORS:

Chairman—WM. REYNOLDS, Esq., M.D., Coed Dû, near Mold.

Deputy-Chairman—C. B. CLOUGH, Esq., Llwyn Offa, near Mold.

Charles Davison, Esq., Celyn Northop, Flint.

G. M. Dixon, Esq., Bucknowle House, Wareham, Dorset.

James Richardson Barnes, Esq., Brookside, Chirk, North Wales.

W. B. Buddicom, Esq., Penbedu Hall, near Mold.

Richard Kyrke Penson, Esq., Ferryside, Kidwelly.

OFFICERS.—Sec., George Lewis, the Grange, Frankton, near Oswestry; Eng., Geo. Bellis, Mold; Auditor, Robt. Williams; Solicitors, Roberts, Kelly, and Keene, Mold; Bankers, The North and South Wales Bank, Mold.

Offices—Oswald Chambers, Oswestry.

63.—BUDE CANAL AND LAUNCESTON JUNCTION.

Incorporated by 28 and 29 Vic., cap. 263 (5th July, 1865), to construct a line from the Bude Canal, in the parish of Werrington, Devonshire, to the Launceston and South Devon. Length, 2¾ miles. Capital, 20,000l. in shares, and 6,600l. in loans. Arrangements with Launceston and South Devon.

No. of Directors—5; minimum, 3; quorum, 3 and 2. *Qualification*, 100l.

DIRECTORS:

George Alfred Hillier, Esq., Gresham House, London, E. C.

Daniel Shilson, Esq., Launceston, John Ching, Esq., Launceston.

64.—BURNHAM TIDAL HARBOUR AND RAILWAY.

Incorporated by 23 and 24 Vic , cap. 191 (6th August, 1860), to convert part of the river Brue into a tidal harbour, for making a quay or landing place at Burnham, and lines as sidings in connection with Somerset and Dorset, with power for the company to work steam vessels between Burnham and any place on the South Wales Coast, or in the Bristol Channel. Capital, 37,000l. in 10l. shares (of which 7,000l. is to be for purposes of the railway). Loans, 12,300l. Length, 18 miles. The Somerset and Dorset subscribed for 12,000l. The Act also authorises the company to enter into agreement with the Somerset and Dorset, with respect to construction, working, and traffic.

By 28 and 29 Vic., cap. 188 (29th June, 1865), the number of directors was reduced to seven, and new capital authorised to the extent of 225,000l. in shares, and 75,000l. on mortgage. Also to construct new docks at Burnham, and to alter the channel of the river.

No. of Directors—5; quorum, 3. *Qualification*, 500l.

DIRECTORS:

George Reed, Esq., Burnham, Somerset.

George Warry, Esq., Shapwick House, Somerset.

Sir Edward Baker Baker, Bart., Ranston, near Blandford, Dorset.

OFFICERS.—Sec. and Gen. Man., Robert A. Read; Goods Man., Henry Briscoe.

Chief Offices—Glastonbury, Somerset; Offices in Cardiff, —5 Stuart Street, Bute Docks.

65.—BURY ST. EDMUNDS AND THETFORD.

Incorporated by 28 and 29 Vic., cap. 348 (5th July, 1865), to construct a line from Bury St. Edmunds to Thetford, to and from the Great Eastern at these places. Length, 13¼ miles. Capital, 120,000*l.* in shares, and 40,000*l.* on loan. Arrangements with Great Eastern. Works in progress.

It was reported in March that matters had been adjusted with the original contractors, and that the works had been commenced by new contractors and were progressing satisfactorily. The directors believed that if a policy of executing the line in small contracts at cash prices were adhered to the lines would eventually prove remunerative to the shareholders.

It was further stated in August that the undertaking was being prosecuted with the greatest economy, and the chairman entertained sanguine hopes as to its future prospects. The next contract which would be let was for the section between Ingham and Bury.

CAPITAL.—The receipts to 30th June had been 7,508*l.*, while an expenditure of 7,861*l.* left a balance against the company of 263*l.*

No. of Directors—5; quorum, 3. *Qualification*, 200*l.*

DIRECTORS:

Chairman—EDWARD GREENE, Esq., M,P., The Abbey, Ixworth, and Palace Hotel, Buckingham Gate, S.W.

Deputy-Chairman—ROBERT ROBY, Esq., Ironmonger, Bury St. Edmunds.

Hunter Rodwell, Esq., Q. C., Ampton Park, Bury St. Edmunds.

Fuller Maitland Wilson, Esq., Stowlangtoft Hall.

James Henry Porteus Oakes, Esq., Nowton Court, Bury St. Edmunds.

All eligible for re-election.

OFFICERS.—Sec., John W. Ion, Solicitor, Bury St. Edmunds; Eng., Peter Bruff, C.E., 16, Charing Cross, London; Solicitors, Partridge and Greene, Bury St. Edmunds, and Messrs. Tahourdin, 1, Victoria Street, Westminster, S.W.; Auditors, Eld Edmund Clayton, Draper, Bury St. Edmunds, and George John Oliver, Grocer, Bury St. Edmunds; Brokers, Partridge and Greenfield, 21, Throgmorton Street, London.

66.—BURRY PORT AND GWENDRAETH VALLEY
(LATE KIDWELLY AND BURRY PORT).

Incorporated by 28 and 29 Vic., cap. 218 (5th July, 1865), to convert the canal into a railway from Burry Port to the Mountain Branch of the Llanelly, with several branches. Length, 18½ miles. Capital, 120,000*l.*, in shares, and 18,000*l.* on loan. Of the shares, 72,100*l.* represent the old canal property, and 47,900*l.* that required for the conversion. The works were announced in November as about to be commenced.

By 29 Vic., cap. 5 (30th April, 1866), the Burry Port and Gwendraeth Valley was amalgamated with the Kidwelly, the share capital of which is 85,000*l.*

By 30 Vic., cap. 1 (29th May, 1868), an extension of time for completion of works till 1st August 1871 was obtained.

No. of Directors—5; minimum, 3; quorum, 3 and 2. *Qualification*, 500*l.*

67.—BUSBY.

Incorporated by 26 Vic., cap. 26 (11th May, 1863), to construct a line from the Glasgow Barrhead and Neilston, to Busby, with a branch to printworks. Length, 4¼ miles. Capital, 60,000*l.* in 10*l.* shares; and 20,000*l.* on loan. Arrangements with Caledonian, which subscribes 15,000*l.*, and works the line at 50 per cent. of gross receipts.

By 28 and 29 Vic., cap. 229 (5th July, 1865), the company was authorised to extend the line to East Kilbride. Length, 4¼ miles. New capital, 45,000*l.* in shares, and 15,000*l.* on loan; Caledonian subscribes 15,000*l.* in shares.

Meetings in February or March, and August or September.

No. of Directors—4 ; minimum, 3 ; quorum, 2. *Qualification, 250l.*

DIRECTORS :

Chairman—JOSEPH COLIN WAKEFIELD, Esq,, Eastwood Park.

Deputy-Chairman—ROBERT OSBORNE, Esq., ot Thornton Hall.

Robert Paterson, Esq., of Birthwood. | Michael James Jamieson, Esq., of Arngomery.

OFFICERS.—Sec., James Keyden ; Auditors, Walter Mackenzie and William Anderson ; Engs., Forman and M'Call ; Solicitors, Keyden, Straug, and Keyden.

Offices—186, West George Street, Glasgow.

68.—CAITHNESS.

Incorporated by 29 and 30 Vic., cap. 292 (30th July, 1866), to construct a line between Wick and Thurso, with a view to its further extension to join the Sutherland. Length, 21¾ miles. Capital, 130,000l. in 10l. shares, and 43,000l. on loan. Arrangements with Highland, which may subscribe 10,000l. Works not commenced.

No. of Directors—6 ; minimum, 3 ; quorum, 3 and 2. *Qualification, 200l.*

DIRECTORS :

Chairman—Right Hon. the EARL OF-CAITHNESS, 17, Hill Street, Berkeley Square, W.

Sir Robert Anstruther, Bart., M.P., 3, Onslow Gardens, S.W.	James Horne, Esq.
	Alexander Adams, Esq.
Samuel Laing, Esq., 6, Kensington Gardens Terrace, W.	Thomas Brassey, Esq.

69.—CALEDONIAN.

Incorporated by 8 and 9 Vic., cap. 162, for a line from Carlisle to a junction with the Scottish Central, at Castlecary, with branches diverging therefrom at Carstairs, to Edinburgh and Glasgow. Under powers of various Acts, this company at a time of great excitement and much uncertainty as regards the real profits made out of railway undertakings, became involved in engagements which were subsequently found to be beyond its resources. After protracted negotiations with the conflicting interests involved in questions arising out of the leases (the position of the preference shares, as to priority, being a particularly difficult point), before the close of the session of 1851, and inquiries in parliament as to return of capital, &c., giving the early history of the transactions, &c., an agreement was finally arrived at, and the result is the "*Arrangements Act*," 14 and 15 Vic., cap. 134 (1851), of which an ample synopsis is given in the MANUAL for 1854. Productive, 573½ miles, including Scottish Central and Scottish North Eastern.

By 18 and 19 Vic., cap. 96 (June 26th, 1855), the company was authorised to raise additional capital to the extent of 375,000l., at a preferential dividend not exceeding 5 per cent. Borrowing powers, in addition to those already possessed, are conferred by same Act, to the extent of 124,900l. Debenture stock to be issued in lieu of mortgage debt.

GRANTON.—By 20 and 21 Vic., cap. 123 (10th August, 1857), an arrangement is authorised with the promoters of this line. The capital created is 60,000l., one half of which was provided by the Duke of Buccleuch. The loans extend to 20,000l. The length of the line is 3¼ miles, and of the branch to Granton western breakwater 9 furlongs 4 chains 30 links. Opened July, 1861. By 26 Vic., cap. 38, the Granton branches were merged into the Caledonian, and the Duke of Buccleuch bought out.

LEITH BRANCHES.—By 25 and 26 Vic., cap. 137 (7th July, 1862), the company were authorised to construct an extension from Granton Branch to Leith, length, 3½ miles, and to raise new capital to the extent of 150,000l. in shares of 5 per cent., and 49,950l. on loan.

DALMARNOCK.—By 21 Vic., cap. 13 (21st May, 1858), the Caledonian was authorised to construct a branch of one mile to Dalmarnock. New capital, shares 37,000l. ; loans, 12,300l. Opened 24th June, 1861.

PORT CARLISLE.—By 21 and 22 Vic., cap. 66 (28th June, 1858), the Caledonian was authorised to construct a branch half a mile in length, to join the Port Carlisle. New capital, shares 10,000l. ; loans, 3,300l. Estimate, 10,000l. Opened.

WILSONTOWN.—By 22 and 23 Vic., cap. 3 (21st July, 1859), the company's powers to construct a branch to the mineral coalfields at Wilsontown were revived. The length of the branch is 2⅜ miles, with a connecting branch of 1 furlong and 6 chains. Commences with a junction to the Caledonian at a point in the parish of Carnwath, about 80¼ miles from Carlisle, and terminates at Wilsontown, with a short connecting branch, commencing by a junction with the Caledonian at a point about 80 miles from Carlisle, and terminating by a junction with the first-mentioned branch, about 1½ furlong north-westward of the last-mentioned point of junction with the Caledonian. Estimate, 22,500l. Extra land, 10 acres; compulsory purchase, two years; completion of works, four years. New capital, not exceeding 22,500l., to be raised by 5 per cent. preference stock, and 7,500l. on mortgage may be raised.

SYMINGTON, BIGGAR, AND BROUGHTON.—Incorporated by 21 Vic., cap. 15 (21st May, 1858), to construct a railway from the Caledonian, near Symington, to Biggar and Broughton. Capital, 36,000l. (of which 7,500l. is furnished by Caledonian), in 10l. shares. Loans, 12,000l. Length, 8 miles. Estimate, 34,800l. Opened 5th November, 1860. By 23 and 24 Vic., cap. 120 (3rd July, 1860), the company was authorised to construct an extension to Peebles; length, 11¼ miles. New capital, 75,000l. in shares; and 24,900l. by mortgage. Caledonian subscribed 15,000l., and authorised to contribute any amount up to 30,000l. By 24 and 25 Vic., cap. 201 (1st August, 1861), the Symington was amalgamated with the Caledonian. New capital was also authorised to the extent of 39,500l. in shares, and 24,900l. on loan.

LESMAHAGOW.—By 23 Vic., cap. 97 (14th June, 1860), these branches were incorporated with the Caledonian, the capital thereof having hitherto been kept separate, but is not guaranteed in same manner as the other undertakings held by the Caledonian, although the proprietors therein retain a separate existence. The guarantee to the Lesmahagow shareholders extends to 5,885l. per annum. By the same Act the Caledonian was authorised to raise additional capital to the extent of 44,300l., in shares of 5 per cent., and 30,000l. on loans, to be applied solely to the purposes of the Lesmahagow. By 26 Vic., cap. 25, the Caledonian was authorised to effect certain improvements, deviations, &c., to enlarge stations, and to acquire new lands, &c. New capital, 120,000l., at 5 per cent., and 40,000l. on mortgage.

LANARK.—By 23 and 24 Vic., cap. 144 (23rd July, 1860), the Caledonian was authorised to construct certain branches to Lanark and to the Douglas coalfield. New capital, 100,000l., in shares of 5 per cent., and 33,300l. on loan.

CARLISLE CITADEL STATION.—By 24 and 25 Vic., cap. 166 (22nd July, 1861), the Caledonian and London and North Western obtained powers for the better regulation of this important station. Its management is placed under the direction of a joint committee, consisting of two representatives from each board, and the agreements respectively made with the Maryport, the Glasgow and South Western, and the North British, were confirmed. New works were also authorised, and further purchase of lands permitted. The Caledonian under this Act, and for its purposes, was authorised to raise new capital to the extent of 25,000l., in shares of 5 per cent. preference, and 8,300l. on loan.

CLELAND AND MORNINGSIDE.—By 24 and 25 Vic., cap. 229 (1st August, 1861), the company was authorised to extend the Cleland Branch to Morningside, and to construct some other small branches. Length, 11 miles. Capital, 160,000l., in shares of 5 per cent., and 53,300l. on loan; completion of works five years. Certain deviations were authorised by the Act of 7th July, 1862. Opened 1st November, 1864.

RUTHERGLEN AND COATBRIDGE.—By 24 and 25 Vic., cap. 202 (1st August, 1861), the company construct this branch, with another to Whifflet. Length, 8⅛ miles; capital, 180,000l., in shares at 5 per cent., and 60,000l. on loan. By 26 Vic., cap. 10, several deviations were authorised to be completed by 1st August, 1866. Opened November, 1865.

STONEHOUSE.—By 24 and 25 Vic., cap. 228 (1st August, 1861), the company was authorised to construct a branch from the Lesmahagow to Stonehouse; to extend the Southfield branch of the Lesmahagow; to enlarge the station at Symington, &c. Length, 4½ miles. Capital, 800,000l., in shares at 5 per cent., and 26,000l. on loan; completion of works, four years.

CARSTAIRS AND DOLPHINTON.—By 26 Vic., cap. 24, the Caledonian was authorised to construct a branch from Carstairs to join the Leadburn Linton and Dolphinton. Length, 11 miles. New capital, 105,000l. in shares at 5 per cent., and 35,000l. on loan Completion of works, five years.

DUMBARTON AND HELENSBURGH.—On the opening of this line in May, 1858, a ten years' agreement was concluded with the Dumbartonshire companies to regulate the management of the traffic, and to save undue competition between Glasgow and those places on the coast accessible by either route.

JOINT LINE.—By 27 and 28 Vic., cap. 132 (30th June, 1864), the Coledonian and the Glasgow and South Western were authorised to construct branches and alter works in connection with their joint line between Glasgow and Paisley. Length, 2 miles. Capital, 70,000l. in shares, and 22,000l. on loan, in equal proportions.

GLASGOW HARBOUR.—By 27 and 28 Vic., cap. 271 (25th July, 1864), an agreement was ratified with the Edinburgh and Glasgow, by which running powers over the Glasgow Harbour branches were obtained, with power to erect separate and joint stations. New capital, 150,000l. in shares, and 50,000l. on loan.

HAMILTON AND STRATHAVEN.—An agreement had been concluded for the acquisition of this railway; the liability of the Caledonian restricted to 36,500l., in addition to the share capital of 70,000l. Ratified by 27 and 28 Vic., cap. 250 (25th July, 1864).

BREDISHOLM AND TENNOCHSIDE.—By 27 and 28 Vic., cap. 60 (23rd June, 1864), the Caledonian was authorised to construct a branch to Tennochside. New capital, 25,000l. in shares, and 8,300l. on loan. Length, 1¼ mile.

BARRHEAD.—By 28 and 29 Vic., cap. 135 (29th June, 1865), the company was authorised to construct a line from Barrhead to Paisley, and to improve the line between Barrhead and Crofthead. Length, 7¼ miles. New captal, 130,000l. in shares, and 43,300l. on loan.

SHIELHILL.—By 28 and 29 Vic., cap. 136 (29th June, 1865), the company was authorised to construct a branch from Dalmakeddar to Shielhill, on the Dumfries Lochmaben and Lockerbie. Length, 7 miles. New capital, 116,000l. in shares, and 36,000l. on loan.

BALERNO.—By 28 and 29 Vic., cap. 161 (29th June, 1865), the compauy was authorised to construct a branch from Slateford to Balerno. Length, 7 miles. Capital, 150,000l. in shares, and 50,000l. on loan.

BANGHOLM JUNCTION.—By 28 and 29 Vic., cap. 202 (29th June, 1865),·the company was authorised to construct a junction to Bangholm, to connect with the Leith Branch of the North British. Length, ¼ mile. Capital, 15,300l. in shares, and 5,000l. on loan.

CROFTHEAD AND KILMARNOCK.—By 28 and 29 Vic., cap. 139 (29th June, 1865), the Caledonian was authorised to contribute 140,000l. to the Crofthead and Kilmarnock, and to work the line.

GENERAL TERMINUS AND GLASGOW HARBOUR.—By 28 and 29 Vic., cap. 167 (29th June, 1865), this undertaking was amalgamated with the Caledonian, which issued stock in new and old capital, to the extent of 160,000l. guaranteed 4 per cent. till 31st January, 1867, and thereafter, 4½ per cent. The liabilities of the General Terminus are restricted to 54,000l., in addition to 160,000l., the amount of the ordinary stock.

ADDITIONAL POWERS.—By 28 and 29 Vic., cap. 288 (5th July, 1865), the Caledonian was authorised to construct several short branches, to improve stations, and purchase additional lands. Length, 7½ miles. New capital, 235,000l. in shares, and 78,300l. by mortgage.

CLELAND AND MIDCALDER.—By 28 and 29 Vic., cap. 289 (5th July, 1865), the Caledonian was authorised to construct a connecting link from Cleland to Midcalder, so as to shorten the route between Edinburgh and Glasgow, with branches to certain mineral fields. Length, 31 miles. Capital, 450,000l. in shares, and 150,000l. on loan.

MUIRKIRK.—By 28 and 29 Vic., cap. 290 (5th July, 1865), the company was authorised to extend the Douglas branch to Muirkirk. Length, 7 miles. Capital, 160,000l. in shares, and 53,000l. on loan.

DUMFRIES, LOCHMABEN, AND LOCKERBIE.—Incorporated by 23 Vic., cap. 83 (14th June, 1860), to construct a line from the Glasgow and Soutlr Western at Dumfries, to a junction with the Caledonian at Lockerbie. Length, 14¼ miles. Capital, 85,000l. in 10l. shares; loans, 28,300l. By 24 and 25 Vic., cap. 163 (22nd July, 1861), the company was authorised to make a deviation in the line, and to raise new capital to the amount of 5,000l. in shares. Opened 1st September, 1863. Dividends at the rate of 4 per cent. were declared in February and in August. By 28 and 29 Vic., cap. 297 (5th July, 1865), the line was amalgamated with the Caledonian at 6 per cent. in perpetuity. Running powers to London and North Western between Carlisle, Lockerbie, and Duinfries.

GREENOCK AND GOUROCK EXTENSIONS.—By 29 and 30 Vic., cap. 246 (23rd July, 1866), the Caledonian was authorised to construct lines to the Albert Harbour, at Greenock and to Gourock, &c. Length, 4 miles. Capital, 410,000l. in shares, and 136,600l. on loan.

EDINBURGH STATION.—By 29 and 30 Vic., cap. 325 (6th August, 1866), the company was authorised to alter the terminus in Edinburgh, to improve the station and to erect a hotel in connection therewith. New capital, 250,000l. in shares, and 83,300l. on loan.

LANARKSHIRE AND MIDLOTHIAN BRANCHES.—By 29 and 30 Vic., cap. 342 (6th August, 1866), the company obtained power to construct ten branches in the counties of Lanark and Midlothian. Length, 21 miles. New capital, 370,000l. in shares, and 123,300l. on loan. By 30 Vic., cap. 60 (31st May, 1867), the company was authorised to construct certain additional branches in connection with these lines as well as to acquire additional station ground at Carlisle. Length, 10¼ miles. New capital, 140,000l. in shares, and 46,600l. on loan.

FORTH AND CLYDE NAVIGATION.—By 30 and 31 Vic., cap. 106 (20th June, 1867), the Forth and Clyde Navigation became vested in the Caledonian. Capital, 1,141,333l. Annuity, 71,333l. For arrangement with North British, see APPENDIX to volume XX.

FORFARSHIRE.—By 30 and 31 Vic., cap. 176 (12th August, 1867), the company was authorised to erect a sea-wall of more than ½ a mile in length at Dundee, and also to construct new lines (7¼ miles) in substitution of a portion of the Dundee and Forfar, and of the Newtyle and Meigle branch. New capital, 260,000l. in shares, and 86,600l. on loan.

SCOTTISH CENTRAL.—Incorporated by 8 and 9 Vic., cap. 161 (31st July, 1845), for a line from Falkirk (junction with the Edinburgh and Glasgow) and a junction with the Caledonian (Castlecary branch) to the general station in Perth, in conjunction with the Scottish Midland and Dundee Perth and Aberdeen Junction. This company has also acquired by purchase the Tay Ferries. By 19 and 20 Vic., cap. 139 (July, 1856), the company was authorised to construct a line to Denny, and by 20 and 21 Vic., cap. 81 (27th July, 1857), certain extensions of about three miles were sanctioned. By 22 and 23 Vic., cap. 83 (8th August, 1859), the Acts of the company were consolidated, the general station at Perth regulated, and other powers granted. By 26 and 27 Vic., cap. 149 (13th July, 1863), the company was authorised to construct a line to Plean Mineral Fields. Length, 2 miles. New capital, 20,000l. for branch, and 30,000l. for general purposes. Loans, 16,650l. By 26 and 27 Vic., cap. 223 (28th July, 1863), the Dundee Perth and Aberdeen, and Dundee and Newtyle were vested in the Scottish Central, subject to an obligation to discharge all debts — to satisfy the claims of preference shareholders—and to pay to the ordinary shareholders a dividend on their shares for the year ending 31st July, 1864, at the rate of 2 per cent.—for the year ending 31st July, 1865, at the rate of 2½ per cent.—and thereafter at the rate of 3 per cent. per annum, with right after 1866 to share the surplus profits on the transferred lines. By 27 and 28 Vic., cap. 292 (29th July, 1864), the company obtained powers to extend the stations at Perth and Dundee and to execute other works in the counties of Perth, Forfar, and Stirling. Capital, 90,000l. in shares, and 30,000l. on loan. By 28 and 29 Vic., cap. 287 (5th July, 1865), the Scottish Central was amalgamated with the Caledonian, a full detail of the enactments respecting which being given in the APPENDIX to the volume for 1866.

DUNDEE AND PERTH AND ABERDEEN JUNCTION.—This company's line commences at Perth (in conjunction with the Scottish Central, Scottish North Eastern, and Edinburgh Perth and Dundee), proceeding thence along the banks of the Tay to Dundee, where the Newtyle diverges at a right angle to a point of junction with the Scottish North Eastern at Newtyle. The connection formerly subsisting with the Dundee and Arbroath was dissolved from 9th March, 1850, and an Act repealing the Act of Amalgamation, was obtained in 1850 (14 Vic., cap. 39), subject to the payment by this company of 25,639l. The various Acts of the company were consolidated by 18 Vic., cap. 56 (June 15th, 1865). The leading provisions of this enactment authorise raising further moneys for the payment of debts by creation of first-class preference shares. By 22 and 23 Vic., cap. 18 (21st July, 1859), the company was authorised to improve the Dundee and Newtyle, and to raise 70,000l. at 5 per cent. preference for that purpose. Length of new portion of railway 7 miles 6 furlongs 24 yards. Opened 10th June, 1859. At a meeting on 17th October, 1859, it was resolved that 70,000l. of stock be created in 7,000 shares at 10l. each, with all the priorities and privileges conferred by the Dundee and Newtyle Act of 1859. By 25 Vic., cap. 35 (3rd June, 1862), the company was authorised to raise additional capital to the extent of 60,000l. at 5 per cent. in shares and 20,000l. on loan, for the Dundee and Perth ; and 19,000l. at 5 per cent. in shares, and 4,900l. on loan, for the Dundee and Newtyle. By 26 and 27 Vic., cap.

223 (26th July, 1863), the whole undertaking of Dundee and Perth was vested in the Scottish Central. By 27 and 28 Vic., cap. 214 (25th July, 1864), power was given to improve and extend the Dundee and Newtyle 4½ miles, and to raise new capital to the extent of 30,000l. in shares, and 10,000l. on loan. Through-booking arrangements with the Scottish North Eastern.

CRIEFF JUNCTION.—Incorporated 15th August, 1853, for a line from the Scottish Central, near Loaninghead, to Crieff. Length, 9 miles. Opened 16th March, 1856. An agreement was made in 1853, with the Scottish Central, to work the line at cost price ; to supply the necessary plant, and to allow this company, for ten years from opening, a third of the free revenue of the additional traffic brought on the Central by the Crieff Junction. By 28 and 29 Vic., cap. 134 (29th June, 1865, the Crieff Junction was amalgamated with the Scottish Central as from 1st August, 1864. Capital, 45.000l. at par.

CRIEFF AND METHVEN JUNCTION.—Incorporated by 27 and 28 Vic., cap. 189 (14th July, 1864), to form a Junction between the Perth Almond Valley and Methven and the Crieff Junction. Length, 11⅛ miles. Capital, 50,000l. in 10l. shares, and 16,600l. on loan.

CALLANDER AND OBAN.—The Scottish Central are also authorised to contribute 200,000l. towards the capital of the Oban, and to work and maintain the line in perpetuity, at the rate of 50 per cent. of gross receipts. They were also empowered by the Crieff and Comrie Act to subscribe 20,000l. towards the capital of the extension to Comrie, and to work the line. These provisions now apply to the Caledonian.

DUNBLANE, DOUNE, AND CALLANDER.—Incorporated by 19 and 20 Vic., cap. 113 (21st July, 1856), to construct a line from the Scottish Central at Dunblane, to the town of Callander. Capital, 60,000l. in 10l. shares; loans, 20,000l., calls, 2l. per share, with intervals of two months. Length, 11 miles. Opened 1st July, 1858. By 24 and 25 Vic., cap. 96 (28th June, 1861), the company was authorised to cancel unissued share capital (15,000l.), so as to reduce ordinary shares to 45,000l., and to create preference shares, to the extent of 25l. at 5 per cent. Also to convert debentures into stock. By 28 and 29 Vic., cap. 133 (29th June, 1865), the company was amalgamated with the Scottish Central, and thence transferred to the Caledonian. Substituted stock to ordinary shareholders to be equal to three-fourths of amount paid, and to rank thereafter with Scottish Central stock as guaranteed by the Caledonian. The Dunblane Doune and Callander ordinary stock is exchanged for 23,070l. of Central stock, being three-fourths of the ordinary share capital issued by the Dunblane.

SCOTTISH NORTH EASTERN.—This line, amalgamated with the Caledonian by 29 and 30 Vic., cap. 350 (10th August, 1865), is an amalgamation (by 19 and 20 Vic., cap. 134, 29th July, 1866) of the Aberdeen and Scottish Midland Junction.

ABERDEEN.—Incorporated by 8 and 9 Vic., cap. 153 (31st July, 1845), for a line from Guthrie (Arbroath and Forfar) to Aberdeen; with branches from the trunk line to Brechin and Montrose. Length, 72 miles, including the leased line, Arbroath and Forfar.

SCOTTISH MIDLAND JUNCTION. — Incorporated by 8 and 9 Vic., cap. 170 (31st July, 1845), for a line commencing in conjunction with the Scottish Central, at Perth, and terminating by a junction with the Aberdeen and Forfar, with some small branches ; the main line, 32¼ miles, was opened throughout, 11th September, 1848, for goods and passengers, and a branch to connect this with the Newtyle, has since been made. Branches authorised, 1853 :--Coupar Angus to Blairgowrie ; Drungley to Kirriemuir ; and extend works near southern terminus, and the general station at Perth. The company had obtained powers in 1846 to make these branches, but these expired in 1852. By Act 17 Vic., cap. 82 (8th July, 1853), power was also granted to make the said two branches, 4¾ and 3⅛ miles, cost, 50,000l., out of existing powers ; time, five years. Also for improvements and extension of south terminus into Perth ; create in lieu of ordinary shares in company's hands, bond or debenture debts, or annuity bonds, or funded debt, and therewith to discharge the existing bond or other debts not exceeding 200,000l. The branch at Kirriemuir, 3¾ miles, was opened in November, 1854 ; the branch to Blairgowrie, 4¼ miles, in August 1855. Productive 41¾ miles.

By 25 and 26 Vic., cap. 64 (30th June, 1862), additional capital was authorised to the extent of 350,000l. in shares, dividend not to exceed 5 per cent. per annum, and 50,000l. on loan.

ARBROATH AND FORFAR.—By the leasing Act of 1846, the Scottish North Eastern was empowered to have the surplus profits payable to the Arbroath and Forfar, under that Act, fixed for the future on the average of the surplus profits paid for the first five years after the opening throughout of the Aberdeen. The directors have succeeded in making an agreement with the Arbroath and Forfar, whereby the amount of surplus profits is fixed for the time coming, and the expense of keeping a separate set of books, and paying the Arbroath and Forfar, is saved to the Scottish North Eastern.

DUNDEE AND ARBROATH.—By agreement with this company, the two companies were held as amalgamated from 31st January, 1862, the same being ratified by 26 and 27 Vic., cap. 231 (28th July, 1863), the company was incorporated by 6 Wm. IV., cap. 32 (1836), for a line from Dundee to Arbroath, a junction with the Arbroath and Forfar (17 miles and 7 chains). Opened 1st April, 1840. Further powers were granted by 5 Vic., cap. 83; 10 Vic., cap. 133; and 12 Vic , cap. 129.

DENBURN VALLEY.—By 27 and 28 Vic., cap. 111 (23rd June, 1864), the Scottish North Eastern was authorised to construct a line through the city of Aberdeen, to connect with the Great North of Scotland. Length, 1¾ mile. The capital of 190,000l., in shares is provided by subscription from the Great North of Scotland of 125,000l., and 70,000l. by the Scottish North Eastern, the obligation incurred by the former company, in 1863, to construct the "Aberdeen Junction" being repealed. Through booking and mutual facilities between the companies. Borrowing powers, 63,000l. Works in progress.

ALYTH.—By 27 and 28 Vic. cap. 82 (23rd June, 1864), the Alyth was vested in the Scottish North Eastern at an annual rent of 45 per cent. gross receipts, and power also given to raise new capital to the extent of 3,000l., in shares, all of which may be held by the Caledonian, as representing the Scottish North Eastern.

PERTH, ALMOND VALLEY, AND METHVEN.—Incorporated by 19 and 20 Vic., cap. 136 (29th July 1856), to make a railway from the Scottish Midland, near Dunkeld Road, to Methven, county of Perth. Capital, 25,000l., in 10l. shares. Loans, 8,000l. Length, 6 miles. By 27 and 28 Vic., cap. 83 (23rd June, 1864), this company was leased to the Scottish North Eastern, at the rate of 4 per cent., as from 1st January, 1864.

NEWTYLE AND MEIGLE JUNCTION.—By 27 and 28 Vic., cap. 115 (23rd June, 1864), the Scottish North Eastern was authorised to construct a line from Newtyle to its station at Meigle. Length, 2¼ miles. Capital, 8,000l. in shares, and 2,600l. on loan. Through booking with Scottish Central.

DUNDEE AND FORFAR.—By 27 and 28 Vic., cap. 173 (14th July, 1864), the Scottish North Eastern was authorised to construct a new line between Dundee and Forfar. Length, 17¼ miles. Capital, 125,000l. in shares, and 40,000l. on loan.

CARMYLLIE.—By 28 Vic., cap. 83 (19th June, 1865), this private railway was vested in the Scottish North Eastern. New capital, 25,000l. in shares, and 4,550l. on loan.

MONTROSE AND BERVIE.—This line of 12 miles, opened on 1st November, 1865, is worked by the Caledonian, the Scottish North Eastern having contributed 15,000l. towards its construction.

AMALGAMATION.—The Bill for amalgamation with the Caledonian received the royal assent on the 10th August, 1866. The Scottish North Eastern was dissolved on the 31st July, and only existed for payment of dividend for the half-year ending on that day, and winding up the revenue accounts. The following are the principal "Heads of Agreement" between the companies:—"The undertaking of the Scottish North Eastern, and the whole lands, works, plant, property, moneys, estate, and effects of the said company (except the balances due to the said company on revenue account at and prior to the 1st August, 1866, and the revenue stores on hand at that date, which shall be taken over by the Caledonian after being verified and valued) shall be transferred to and vested in the Caledonian, as at the said 1st August, 1866. The Caledonian to undertake all liabilities on capital account of the Scottish North Eastern, including the suspense permanent way renewal account, as at the 1st August, 1866, and the cost of the engines and wagons already contracted for by the Scottish North Eastern, and to relieve the Scottish North Eastern of the same ; but the said last-mentioned company shall charge to renewal a sum not exceeding 12,000l. half-yearly for said renewals and maintenance of permanent way and works. The Scottish North Eastern to have right to all sums due on account of revenue at and prior to 31st July, 1866 (including the value of the revenue stores, including insurance fund as aforesaid), and to free the Caledonian from all liabilities on revenue account at and prior to the said last-mentioned date. The amalgamated company shall pay to the holders of the ordinary Aberdeen capital stock, amounting to 830,000l., the following guaranteed minimum dividends, viz.:—From 31st July, 1866, to 31st January, 1867, a dividend at the rate of 3 per cent. per annum. From 31st January to 31st July, 1867, 3¼ per cent. per annum. From 31st July, 1867, to 31st January, 1868, 3½ per cent. per annum. From 31st January, 1868, to 31st July, 1868, 3¾ per cent. per annum. From 31st July, 1868, to 31st January, 1869, 4 per cent. per annum, and at the same minimum rate in all time thereafter ; but in case the Caledonian shall, after 31st January, 1869, in any half-year, pay a dividend on their ordinary capital stock at a rate exceeding 7 per cent. per annum, then the holders of ordinary Aberdeen capital stock shall receive a corresponding increase on their dividends—keeping always 3 per cent. per annum below the dividend payable on the Caledonian ordinary stock for the time. The holders of the Scottish Midland ordinary stock, amounting to 600,000l., and the holders of the Dundee and Arbroath ordinary stock, amounting to 200,000l., shall be entitled to receive the rateable increased dividends which they would have received had the increased dividends before-mentioned been received by the holders of Aberdeen ordinary stock, had the Scottish North Eastern remained, as at present, a separate and independent company; but the holders of other stocks or shares of the Scottish North Eastern shall not participate in or be entitled to receive any increased dividend under this agreement. The Scottish North Eastern shall not be entitled to increase their capital account, or to carry any sums to capital after the date of this agreement, without the consent of the directors of the Caledonian, except only such sums as may be expended on new works, for which they have already obtained statutory powers. The holders of stock in the Scottish North Eastern shall not be entitled to have any future allocations of stock of the amalgamated company, nor to interfere with the mode or conditions on which such future allocations shall be made until 1869, when they shall be entitled to participate in the allocations of stock thereafter raised under powers obtained after August, 1869."

ABANDONMENT, &c.—By 31 and 32 Vic., cap. 105 (13th July, 1868), the company was authorised to abandon (1st) the connecting branch between the Scottish Central and the Crieff Junction. 2nd. The line from the Glasgow and Barrhead to the Glasgow and Paisley. 3rd. The branch from the main line at Applegarth to the Dumfries Lochmaben and Lockerbie; and 4th, the branch at Leith to the North British at the same place. The power to raise money for these works was also repealed. Completion of works on the Muirkirk branch was extended for two years and six months. The company was also authorised to raise new capital for the general purposes of the undertaking to the extent of 600,000l. in shares, and 200,000l. on loan.

REVENUE.—It was reported in March that the revenue of the united undertaking for the half-year amounted to 902,541l., and the working expenses to 410,337l., or 45½ per cent., leaving a balance of 492,204l. The balance of net revenue for the half-year ending 31st January amounted to 247,598l., and the surplus from the previous half-year to 5,503l., making 253,102l. After payment of dividends on the preference stocks, including those of the Scottish Central and the Scottish North Eastern, amounting to 191,995l., there remained 61,107l., out of which a dividend on the ordinary stock at the rate of 2½ per cent. per annum, amounting to 46,805l., left 14,301l. to next half-year. This balance was sufficient for an additional rate of 15s. per cent. per annum ; but it was thought better not to divide it until the sanction of the Legislature had been obtained to the bill now before Parliament, to charge to capital the extraordinary expenditure on the Scottish North Eastern. The auditors reported that the excess of expenditure on capital account over receipts, at the 31st January last, amounted to 412,232l. They certify that the half-yearly accounts contain a full and true statement of the financial condition of the company, as shown in the books, and that the dividend proposed to be declared on the ordinary stock of the company (exclusive of the stock raised under the Cleland and Mid-Calder branches, and other Acts of 1865, proposed to be paid as heretofore out of premium account, in accordance with the resolution of the shareholders, was bonâ fide due thereon, after charging the revenue of the half-year with all expenses, which, in their judgment, ought to be paid thereout.

It was reported in September that the sum available for dividend was 232,451l., including 3,190l. from previous half-year. The dividend on the ordinary stock was reduced to 15s. for the half-year. For legal proceedings in respect to interdict against payment of this dividend, see APPENDIX.

The revenue and working expenses of the united undertaking, including the canal, were as follow, viz.:—

	Revenue.	Expenses.	Per cent.
Railway	£837,915	£385,475	£46 0 1
Canal	47,899	13,039	27 4 5
Together	£855,814	£398,514	£44 19 9

NORTH BRITISH.—It was reported in September that the proportion of the joint traffic receipts of the North British and Caledonian to be drawn by each company under the joint purse agreement of 16th January last has not yet been finally ascertained, but it is in course of adjustment. In the meantime, by agreement between the two boards, the actual receipts earned on each line for the half-year to 31st July last are given in the respective revenue accounts; but it is understood that neither company shall be in the slightest degree prejudiced by this interim arrangement when the provisions of the agreement come to be applied. Under the direction of the joint committee, and by the united action and good mutual understanding of the companies' officers, the traffic is being satisfactorily conducted. Unless the shareholders of either company desire otherwise, it is proposed to postpone to a future session application to

Parliament for sanction of the joint-working agreement. The directors of both companies concur in recommending the postponement.

FURTHER ABANDONMENTS.—The directors propose to introduce a bill in the coming session for the abandonment of other branches, which may now, it is hoped, be dispensed with. The branches referred to are—the Balerno; Greenock and Gourock Extension; Waterland to Shotts; Castlehill Ironworks; Climpy to Shotts; Mauldslie; Hallcraig; Harburnhead; East Kilbride and Blantyre; and Heywood and Addiewell.

CAPITAL.—The expenditure during the half-year ending 31st July, 1868 (including 5,900*l*. transferred from the Scottish North Eastern suspense account), has been 281,056*l*. 10*s*. 11¼*d*., falling short of the estimate given in last report by.........£143,228

In addition to this, the expenditure during the half-year to 31st January, 1868, was estimated as follows:—

1. On account of works referred to as in progress in March last £100,320
2. On account of necessary works in addition to those in progress* 13,230
3. On account of subscriptions for the Callander and Oban and Crofthead and Kilmarnock .... 55,000 = £169,150

Total estimated expenditure of capital during the half-year to January 31st, 1869 ....£312,378

The total expenditure from capital to 31st July, 1868, was stated at 21,905,297*l*., which left a balance against the company of 262,122*l*. The receipts were acknowledged as under:—

AUTHORISED AND RAISED.	Authorised	Unissued and In Arrears.	Raised.
I. Share capital—			
Caledonian ordinary	£4,734,434	....	£4,734,434
Scottish Central ordinary	£1,113,070	£948	£1,112,122
Aberdeen ordinary	£830,000	....	£830,000
Scottish Midland ordinary	600,000	....	600,000
Dundee and Arbroath ordinary	200,000	....	200,000
	£1,630,000	....	£1,630,000
Caledonian preference shares and stocks—			
4½ per cent. (Caledonian original)...............	£745,180	....	£745,180
4½ per cent. (Scottish Central No. 1)	343,400	....	343,400
4 per cent. (Caledonian)	40,000	....	40,000
5 per cent. (Caledonian No. 1)..................	135,000	....	135,000
5 per cent. (Caledonian No. 2)..................	375,000	....	375,000
Granton guaranteed stock	30,000	....	30,000
4½ per cent. (Caledonian No. 2).................	77,000	....	77,000
4½ per cent. (Caledonian No. 3).................	189,300	....	189,300
4½ per cent. (Caledonian No. 4).................	484,550	....	484,550
4½ per cent. (Scottish Central No. 2)	145,300	....	145,300
Hamilton and Strathaven	53,090	£251	52,838
4½ per cent. (Scottish Central No. 3)	120,000	53,909	66,090
4½ per cent. (Caledonian No. 5).................	226,910	....	226,910
Dunblane Doune and Callander 5 per cent......	15,000	....	15,000
General Terminus guaranteed	160,000	631	159,368
Lockerbie guaranteed............................	90,000	843	89,157
5 per cent. (Caledonian No. 3)..................	620,000	155,441	464,559
Caledonian 4 per cent. (Convertible), 1868—			
By 28 and 29 Vic. c. 226, Callander and Oban Act, 1865 ....£200,000			
By 30 and 31 Vic., c. 116, Solway Junction Act, 1867 60,000			
By 30 and 31 Vic., c. 176, Caledonian (Forfarshire Works) Act, 1867 260,000			
£520,000			
Authorised by resolution of Meeting held at Glasgow, 5th March, 1868, to be issued at discount of 20 per cent.. 104,000 =	416,000	24,565	391,434
Caledonian Preference.................	£4,265,730	£235,641	£4,030,088

* This amount is on account of additional works, estimated to cost in all 266,650*l*.

AUTHORISED AND RAISED.	Authorised	Unissued and In Arrears.	Raised.
Scottish North Eastern preference—			
Dundee and Arbroath 5 per cent.	£66,700	....	£66,700
Aberdeen 3½ per cent.	73,174	....	73,174
Aberdeen 6 per cent.	276,666	323	276,342
Aberdeen 3½ per cent. No. 2	63,650	....	63,650
Aberdeen No. 2 7 per cent.	150,000	....	150,000
Scottish North Eastern 4½ per cent. authorised ...£350,000			
Issued by the Scottish North Eastern .. 199,579	199,579	....	199,579
Remaining...£150,421			
Scottish North Eastern 5 per cent. authorised ...£213,000			
Issued by Scottish North Eastern 188,900	188,900	80	188,820
Remaining... £24,100			
Scottish North Eastern preference ..	£1,018,671	£403	£1,018,267
Total preference	£5,284,401	£236,045	£5,048,355
II. Guaranteed—			
Garnkirk........	£156,355	....	£156,355
Clydesdale Junction	450,000	....	450,000
Greenock ordinary ...£500,000			
Do. preference ...... 150,000 =	650,000	£441	649,558
Wishaw........	240,000	....	240,000
Barrhead, old shares ...£150,000			
Do. new shares... 125,000 =	275,000	....	275,000
Lesmahagow, A shares... 60,000			
Do. B shares... 45,700 =	105,700	....	105,700
Dundee and Perth ordinary 299,700			
Do. pref. 1st class..£120,000			
Do. quarter shares.. 150,000			
Do. shares, 1862.... 60,000=330,000			
Dundee and Newtyle preference....... 70,000 =	699,700	....	699,700
Forth and Clyde Navigation	1,141,333	....	1,141,333
Total guaranteed companies capital......	£3,718,088	£441	£3,717,647
III. Loan capital and debenture stock—			
Authorised. Raised.			
At 31st January, 1868....£5,485,991 £5,337,669			
By 30 and 31 Vic., cap. 176, Caledonian(Forfarshire Works) Act, 1867, being part of 86,600l. 69,266			
£5,555,257			
Paid off or renewed since 31st January, 1868 524,685			
£4,812,984			
Issued since ditto 556,634			
£5,369,618	5,555,257	185,638	5,369,618
Total loan capital and debenture stock....	£5,555,257	£185,638	£5,369,618
Total capital......................	£22,035,251	£423,073	£21,612,178
IV. Shares cancelled, and abated—amount applicable thereto unappropriated—			
Amount applicable to 137 Caledonian£50 shares-cancelled£1,760			
Do. do. 11,800 do. 12 10 do. 21,547=£23,307			
Amount applicable to Dunblane Doune and Callander ordinary stock, abated per Scottish Central and Dunblane Doune and Callander, and Caledonian and Scottish Central Amalgamation Acts, 1865 .... 7,690 =			30,997
Total................................			£21,643,175

The accounts are made up to 31st January and 31st July in every year; and the statutory meetings held in Glasgow in March or September following.

Scale of Voting.—C. C. C. Act (Scotland), sec. 75.

Certificates must accompany transfer deed. In transferring stock, 10s. is the only part of a pound sterling which can be transferred. Registration fee 2s. 6d. each seller. Transfer books close 15 days before meetings.

No. of Directors.—Maximum, 18 ; minimum, 9. *Qualification*, 2,000l. stock.

DIRECTORS :

Chairman—THOMAS HILL, Esq., Merrylee, Glasgow.

Lieut.-Col. Salkeld, Holm Hill, Carlisle.
Daniel Ainslie, Esq., the Gart, Callander, and 48, Moray Place, Edinburgh.
James F. Wyllie, Esq., Bolfracks, Aberfeldy.
John Wilson, Esq., Hill Park, Bannockburn.
Lieut.-Col. Gandy, Heaves, Milnthorpe.
Andrew Buchanan, Esq., Auchentorlie, Dumbartonshire.

J. C. Bolton, Esq., Glasgow.
Robert Fergusson, Esq., Merchant, Dundee.
James Clerk, Esq., Glasgow.
James Taylor, Esq., Starley Hall, Burntisland.
John Cowan, Esq., Glasgow.
Andrew Davidson, Esq., Perth.
Sir Thomas Gladstone, Bart., of Fasque, Laurencekirk.

OFFICERS.—Gen. Man., James Smithells ; Sec., Archibald Gibson ; Gen. Goods Man., William Mathison ; Eng., George Graham, C.E.; Gen. Supt. of the Line, Henry Ward ; Loco. Supt., Benjamin Conner ; Treas., Alexander Fergusson ; Accountant, George Galbraith ; Registrar, Henry William Murgatroyd ; Traffic Auditor, Alexander Murray ; Store Supt., John Fyfe, Auditors, John Young, Accountant, London, and John Graham, C.A., Glasgow ; Solicitors, Hope and Mackay, W.S., Edinburgh, and Sheill and Small, Dundee.

Head Offices—302, Buchanan Street, Glasgow.

70.—CALLANDER AND OBAN.

Incorporated by 28 and 29 Vic., cap. 266 (5th July, 1865), to construct a line from the town of Oban to the Dunblane Doune and Callander. Length, 70¾ miles. Capital, 600,000l. in shares, and 200,000l. on loan. Arrangements with Scottish Central (Caledonian), which subscribes 200,000l., and is to work the line at 50 per cent. Works in progress.

CALEDONIAN.—The following resolution was passed at the meeting of the Caledonian, on 29th September, 1868 :—" That the directors be instructed not to expend any further money upon the Oban line, beyond the completion of the works already contracted for, until the proprietors and other subscribers to the undertaking have subscribed such a sum as will, along with the amount for which the company are still liable, be sufficient to construct the line to Oban."

CAPITAL.—The receipts on this account to 31st July, including subscription from Caledonian amounted to 161,745l., and the expenditure to 108,689l.

No. of Directors—9 ; quorum, 3. *Qualification*, 500l.

DIRECTORS :

* Chairman—J. C. BOLTON, Esq., West George Street, Glasgow, and Carbrook, near Stirling.

* Deputy-Chairman—Daniel Ainslie, Esq., 48, Moray Place, Edinburgh, and The Gart, Callander.

1 John Wingfield Malcolm, Esq., M.P., 7, Great Stanhope Street, W., and Inverliver, Killinartin, Argyleshire.
2 Robert Macfie, Esq., of Airds, Fort William.
3 Captain Farquhar Campbell, of Aros, Mull.

3 Robert Tennant, Esq., of Ballachulish, Leeds.
* James F. Wyllie, Esq., Bolfracks, Aberfeldy.
* John Wilson, Esq., Hill Park, Bannockburn.
* James Clerk, Esq., Park Circus, Glasgow.
* Represent the Caledonian.

1 Retire in 1869 ; 2 in 1870 ; 3 in 1871.

OFFICERS.—Sec., John Anderson ; Engs., B. and E. Blyth, Edinburgh ; Auditors, Henry Kerr and John Graham, Accountants, Glasgow ; Solicitors, Sheill and Small, Dundee.

Offices—48, Dundas Street, Glasgow.

71. CALNE.

Incorporated by 23 Vic., cap. 11 (15th May, 1860), to construct a line from the Great Western, at Chippenham, to Calne. Length, 5¼ miles. Capital, 35,000*l.*, in 10*l.* shares; loans, 11,600*l.* Working and other agreements with Great Western. Opened 3rd November, 1863.

By 27 Vic., cap. 16 (28th April, 1864), the company was authorised to raise additional capital to the extent of 14,000*l.* in shares, and 4,000*l.* on loan.

Meetings in February or March, and August or September.

No. of Directors—5; quorum, 3. *Qualification*, 300*l.*

DIRECTORS:

2 Chairman—THOMAS LARGE HENLY, Esq., Calne.

4 George Harris, Esq., Calne.	3 Charles Harris, Esq., Calne.
1 Thomas Harris, Esq., Calne.	5 Robert Henly, Jun., Esq., Calne.

Retire by rotation as numbered.   All eligible for re-election.

OFFICERS.—Sec., William Martin Vizard; Auditors, John Spencer and [John Dolman Bailey; Solicitor, F. R. Ward, 1, Grey's Inn Square, London, W.C. Offices—Calne.

72.-CAMBRIAN.

Incorporated by 27 and 28 Vic., cap. 262 (25th July, 1864), and formed out of the following undertakings:—

I. OSWESTRY AND NEWTOWN.—Incorporated by 18 and 19 Vic., cap. 86 (June 26th, 1855), for the construction of a railway from Oswestry to Welshpool and Newtown. Length, 30 miles. Capital, 250,000*l.*, in 10*l.* shares. Loans, 83,000*l.* Opened from Oswestry to Pool Quay station (16 miles), 1st May, 1860; from Newtown to Abermule (5 miles), in August, 1860; and the intervening section (9 miles) on 19th June, 1861.

By 23 and 24 Vic., cap. 101 (3rd July, 1860), the line was leased to Messrs. Davies and Savin for ten years. The same Act authorised additional capital to be raised, to the extent of 100,000*l.*, as well as the re-issue of cancelled shares at a preference of 5½ per cent.; also to borrow 25,000*l.* on mortgage in lieu of raising such amount by shares. Arrangements with London and North Western.

By 23 and 24 Vic., cap. 139 (3rd July, 1860), the company was authorised to construct a branch from Llynclys to Porthywaen lime rocks. Length, 1¼ mile. New capital, 10,000*l.* in shares, and 3,000*l.* on loan.

By 24 Vic., cap. 17 (17th May, 1861), the company was authorised to construct branches to Llanfyllin and to Kerry. Length, 15 miles. Capital, 90,000*l.* in 10*l.* shares, at 5 per cent., and 30,000*l.* on loan. Opened 11th July, 1863.

By 26 and 27 Vic., cap. 96 (29th June, 1863), the company was authorised to construct a branch from Cilgurgan to Aberbechan. Length, 4½ miles. New capital, 200,000*l.*, in shares at 5 per cent., and 66,000*l.* on loan.

By the Oswestry Ellesmere and Whitchurch Act, 1861, the Oswestry and Newtown subscribed 30,000*l.* to that undertaking.

Under the Aberystwyth and Welsh Coast Act, October, 1861, this company subscribed 75,000*l.* to that undertaking.

By 27 and 28 Vic., cap. 161 (14th July, 1864), the Oswestry and Newtown was authorised to raise new capital to the extent of 50,000*l.*, to aid the Bishop's Castle, and 100,000*l.* to double the original line. Loans, 33,000*l.*

II. LLANIDLOES AND NEWTOWN.—Incorporated by 16 and 17 Vic., cap. 143 (4th August, 1853), for a line from Llanidloes to Newtown. Length, 12¼ miles. Capital, 60,000*l.* in 10*l.* shares, and 20,000*l.* on loan.

By 19 Vic., cap. 22 (5th June, 1856), certain deviations were permitted, by which considerable saving would be effected in the cost of the works.

By 22 and 23 Vic., cap. 30 (21st July, 1859), the company was authorised to construct a tramway from Newtown to the Shropshire Canal, to be worked by horse-power; compulsory purchase of land, one year; completion of works, two years. By the same Act completion of one of the deviations conceded in 1856 was permitted to be delayed for one year. The authorised line was also by the same authority to be leased to Messrs. Davies and Savin, by three-fifths of the shareholders.

By 24 and 25 Vic., cap. 90 (28th June, 1861), the company was authorised to raise new capital to the extent of 25,000*l.* at 5 per cent. Completion of works was also extended for two years.

By 25 and 26 Vic., cap. 162 (17th July, 1862), the Llanidloes and Newtown was authorised to construct a joint line from Llanidloes to Penpontbren, to be completed in twelve months, with powers of user to the Mid-Wales and Manchester and Milford, which had each power to construct a line in the same direction. Arrangements were also authorised with these companies respecting occupation of a joint station at Llanidloes, interest on one-third of outlay on which is to be borne by each of the parties. The Llanidloes and Newtown was also authorised to raise additional capital to the extent of 25,000*l.* in shares at 5 per cent. and 8,000*l.* on loan.

By 27 Vic., cap. 22 (13th May, 1864), the Llanidloes and Newtown was allowed further time for the purchase of certain lands, and also to raise new capital to the extent of 25,000*l.* in shares, and 13,300*l.* on loan.

III. NEWTOWN AND MACHYNLLETH.—Incorporated by 20 and 21 Vic., cap. 106 (27th July, 1857), to construct a line from Llanidloes and Newtown, near Llandinam, to Machynlleth, Montgomeryshire. Length. 23 miles. Capital, 150,000*l.* in 10*l.* shares ; loans, 50,000*l.* Agreements under usual restrictions, with Llanidloes and Newtown, Oswestry and Newtown, Shrewsbury and Welshpool, Great Western, London and North Western, and Shropshire Union, or any of them. Opened 3rd January, 1863.

By 26 Vic., cap. 40 (8th June, 1863), the company was authorised to create new capital to the extent of 40,000*l.* in preference shares at 5 per cent., and to re-issue forfeited shares at a like preference.

IV. OSWESTRY, ELLESMERE, AND WHITCHURCH.—Incorporated by 24 and 25 Vic., cap. 223 (1st August, 1861), to construct a line from the Oswestry and Newtown, by Ellesmere to Whitchurch. Length, 20 miles. Capital, 150,000*l.* in 10*l.* shares, 50,000*l.* on loan. Extra land, 10 acres ; compulsory purchase, three years ; completion of works, five years. Opened from Whitchurch to Ellesmere (11 miles) on 4th May, 1863, and to Oswestry (8 miles) on 27th July, 1864. Arrangements with London and North Western and Oswestry and Newtown which each subscribed 30,000*l.*

By 25 and 26 Vic., cap. 218 (7th August, 1862), the company was authorised to construct a line from Elesmere to Wem, on the London and North Western. Length, 6¼ miles. Capital, 60,000*l.* in shares, and 20,000*l.* on loan.

By 27 and 28 Vic., cap. 97 (23rd June, 1864), the Oswestry Ellesmere and Whitchurch was authorised to raise new capital to the extent of 100,000*l.* in shares, and 33,000*l.* on loan.

By 28 and 29 Vic., cap. 277 (5th July, 1865), the Cambrian was authorised to abandon the branch to Wem, and also to transfer its agreement to work the Aberystwyth and Welsh Coast to its lessee, Mr. Thomas Savin.

V.—ABERYSTWYTH AND WELSH COAST.—Incorporated by 24 and 25 Vic., cap. 181 (22nd July, 1861), to construct various lines from Aberystwyth, namely:—

1st, From Aberystwyth to Penmochno Embankment, parish of Llancynfelyn ; 2nd, a junction from No. 1 to Towyn, Merionethshire ; 3rd, from Towyn to Barmouth ; 4th, from Barmouth to Port Madoc ; and 5th, a Junction from No. 1, at Llancynfelyn, to Machynlleth, to join the Newtown and Machynlleth. Length, 86 miles. Capital, 400,000*l.* in 10*l.* shares, and 133,000*l.* on loan. Opened from Machynlleth to Borth (12 miles), on 1st July, 1863 ; from Aberdovey to Llwyngwril (12 miles), in November, 1863, and from Borth to Aberystwyth (8½ miles), on 1st August, 1864. The Oswestry and Newtown subscribed 75,000*l.*, and Llanidloes, 25,000*l.*, by creation of 5 per cent. preference shares.

By 25 and 26 Vic., cap. 176 (29th July, 1862), the company was authorised to extend the line from Port Madoc to Porthdynllaen, and from Barmouth to Dolgelly. Length, 30½ miles. Also to reclaim certain lands on the coast. New capital, 250,000*l.* in shares, and 83,300*l.* on loan.

By 26 and 27 Vic., cap. 141 (13th July, 1863), the company was authorised to construct several small branches and tramways. Length, 10½ miles. New capital, 150,000*l.* in shares, and 50,000*l.* on loan.

By 27 and 28 Vic., cap. 147(30th June, 1864), the company was authorised to acquire additional land and to raise 330,000*l.* in shares, and 110,000*l.* on loan. The Oswestry and Newtown was also authorised by the same Act to increase its subscription to the Aberystwyth by the sum of 100,000*l.*

By 28 and 29 Vic., cap. 283 (5th July, 1865), the Aberystwyth and Welsh Coast was authorised to make certain deviations, and to construct some small extensions. Length, 3 miles. New capital, 120,000*l.* in shares, and 40,000*l* on loan.

By 28 and 29 Vic., cap. 291 (5th July, 1865), the Aberystwyth and Welsh Coast was vested in the Cambrian, by amalgamation, as from 5th August, 1865. Separate accounts to be kept of revenue, and facilities extended to Great Western and London and North Western. The Coast ordinary capital to be ordinary capital of the amalgamated company on consent of shareholders in general meeting, which was formally granted at meetings held 29th August and 6th October, 1865, respectively. (See clause 11 of the Coast Amalgamation Act.)

By 29 and 30 Vic., cap. 334 (6th August, 1866), the company was authorised to make a deviation, to construct a variety of new works, and to raise capital to the extent of 142,000*l.* in shares for the Cambrian, and 300,000*l.* for the Aberystwyth and Welsh Coast, and 147,300*l.* on loan.

By 30 and 31 Vic., cap. 137 (15th July, 1867), the company obtained various facilities by which to raise part of the loan capital, and also an extension of time for one year for completion of works.

AGREEMENTS.—By 27 and 28 Vic., cap. 263, the Cambrian was authorised to enter into agreements with regard to traffic, and rebate with the London and North Western, the Hereford Hay and Brecon, and the Brecon and Merthyr Tydfil. Traffic facilities were also authorised with the Mid-Wales.

ARRANGEMENTS ACT.—By 31 and 32 Vic., cap. 177 (31st July, 1868), it was enacted that as from 1st July, 1868, that the revenue from all the undertakings of the company should form one common fund, and that after deduction of the working expenses, the surplus should be divided between the Coast and Inland, in proportions to be determined. That a provisional period of ten years should be established for this division, separate accounts of receipts and payments being kept, and the net surplus of each section being carried to a distinct fund. During this provisional period of ten years the board shall consist of ten directors, four appointed by the Coast section, and four by the Inland section. Arbitrators and umpire are to be appointed to decide on the proportions of surplus to be assigned to each section, and their award may be revised three times within the provisional period of ten years. From and after the termination of this provisional period the division of the net surplus shall continue for ever as determined by the arbitrators.

By the same Act power was given to the company to create debenture stock, and also certain regulations enforced in respect to the raising of the mortgage sums of 100,000*l.* and 47,300*l.* The first amount is to be paid to the landowners on the Coast section, in payment of lawsuits in respect to the same, in completing the railway and works, and in recouping to income the sums paid therefrom to capital. The 47,300*l.* to be offered in the same manner and for the like purposes in the Inland section.

The right of voting on preference stock was also conferred, subject only to the same conditions as relate to the possession of ordinary stock.

It was reported in September that the traffic had increased, notwithstanding the general depression of trade, to an extent which afforded ample grounds for confidence that with the revival of trade, the complete equipment of the line, and a reorganization of the company, the proprietors might look forward to an improvement of their property. The applications for relief to the Court of Chancery failed mainly in consequence of the defect of the general Act of 1867, which was passed at the end of that session in a hurried manner, the object being to enable the Court of Chancery to deal with companies in embarrassed circumstances; the provisions of the Act, however, proved insufficient for that purpose, the Court having power only to sanction or reject any scheme laid before it, and not to alter or amend. Under those circumstances the Board applied to Parliament for relief, and it was known that certain proprietors deposited an independent bill, the object of which was to repeal the union of the Inland and Coast sections. The Board opposed this bill, which was rejected by the committee of the House of Lords, and the bill which the proprietors at their general meeting sanctioned was passed by the committee. In the committee of the House of Commons a scheme was presented by parties in connection with the Inland and Coast sections. The scheme as a whole was inadmissible; but the Board having stated before the committee that while they could not accept the machinery, they did not object to the principle of the scheme, the committee passed the bill, omitting the machinery. Other important provisions were added, the assents required had been obtained, and at an extraordinary meeting to be held upon the close of the ordinary half-yearly meeting the shareholders would be called upon to take the necessary steps to put the Act into operation—viz., the Coast proprietors to appoint two directors and an arbitrator, and the Inland to appoint another arbitrator.

CAPITAL.—The expenditure to 30th June, 1868, amounted to 3,482,429*l.*, the receipts to meet which have been as follow:—

Ordinary capital	£824,205	
Preference	1,760,170	
Debentures	849,876	
Rent charges capitalised	29,625= £3,463,876	
Balance (being expenditure in excess of receipts)	18,553= £3,482,429	

The general balance sheet, to the same date, furnished the subjoined particulars in its debtor and creditor accounts:—

Debtor.—Balance of loan on security of property belonging to

Mr. Savin		£6,923	
Sundry credit balances		26,057	
Inspectors of Mr. Savin's estate		602	

Interest due and accrued to date, viz.:—

	Inland.	Coast.	
On debentures	£8,647	£40,456	
On certificates of indebtedness	7,519	12,409	
Rent-charges	641	640	

	£16,807	£53,505=	70,312
Inland section—Balance from general revenue account			21,324= £125,218

Creditor.—Cash at bankers' and in hand	£633	
Cash in hands of receiver	10,396=£11,029	
Outstanding traffic		11,588
Sundry debit balances		43,364
Denbigh Ruthin and Corwen, due for hire of rolling stock, &c.		949

Inspectors of Mr. Savin's estate, viz.:—

Due for hire	£3,162	
Due for freight	8,208=	11,370

Capital account—Expenditure in excess of receipts:—

Inland section	£13,081	
Coast section	5,472=	18,553
Coast section—Balance from general revenue account		28,365= £125,218

Meetings in February and August.

No. of Directors—10; quorum, 3. *Qualification*, 500*l.*

DIRECTORS:

Chairman—The Right Hon. The EARL VANE, Plas, Machynlleth, Montgomeryshire.

Deputy-Chairman—3 ROBERT DAVIES PRYCE, Esq., Cyfronydd, Welshpool.

3 Henry Gartside, Esq., Wharmton Tower, Greenfield, near Manchester.

2 David Davies, Esq., Vroneiron, Llandinam, Montgomeryshire.

2 James Falshaw, Esq., 26, Castle Street, Edinburgh.

Hon. R. C. Herbert, Orleton, Wellington, Salop.

1 J. W. Johns, Esq., Wolverton Park, near Newbury, Hants.

3 J. A. Mann, Esq., Brecon.

3 A. H. Phillpotts, Esq., Carshalton, Surrey.

1 David Williams, Esq., M.P., Deudraeth Castle, Merionethshire.

1 Retire in 1869; 2, in 1870; 3, in 1871.

OFFICERS.—Sec., George Lewis, Oswestry; Traffic Man., Elijah Elias, Oswestry; Eng., George Owen, Oswestry; Auditors, John Young, 16, Tokenhouse Yard, London, E.C., and W. E. Revell, 43, Charing Cross, London; Solicitor, Abraham Howell, Welshpool; Bankers, The North and South Wales Bank, Oswestry, and the London and South Western Bank, 27, Regent Street, London, S.W.

Offices—Oswestry, Salop.

73.—CANNOCK CHASE EXTENSION.

Incorporated by 25 and 26 Vic., cap. 194 (29th June, 1862), to construct a line from the Norton Branch of the South Staffordshire to the Eastern terminus of the Cannock Chase. Length, 4¼ miles. Capital, 30,000*l.* in 10*l.* shares; loans, 10,000*l.* Line not to be used for passengers without further authority from Parliament.

No. of Directors—5; quorum, 3. *Qualification*, 200*l.*

DIRECTORS:

Chairman—EARL OF UXBRIDGE.

Edward Tredcroft, Esq.

Thomas Landor, Esq.

John Thomas Woodhouse, Esq.

74.—CANNOCK CHASE AND WOLVERHAMPTON.

Incorporated by 27 and 28 Vic., cap. 312 (29th July, 1864), to construct a line between Cannock Chase and Wolverhampton, on the Great Western. Length, 10½ miles. Capital, 100,000*l.* in 10*l.* shares, and 33,000*l.* on loan.

By 29 and 30 Vic., cap. 196 (16th July, 1866), the company was authorised to extend the line to Hednesford and to the South Staffordshire. Length, 5¼ miles. New capital, 60,000*l.* in shares, and 20,000*l.* on loan.

Meetings in February and August.

No. of Directors—6; minimum, 5; quorum, 4 and 3. *Qualification*, 500*l.*

DIRECTORS:

Right Hon. Earl of Uxbridge.
Richard Croft Chawner, Esq.
William Bealey Harrison, Esq.

John Narthall Brown, Esq.
Charles Manley, Esq.
George Elliott, Esq.

75.—CANNOCK MINERAL.

Originally incorporated in 1847 (as DERBYSHIRE, WORCESTERSHIRE, AND STAFFORDSHIRE JUNCTION), re-incorporated by 18 and 19 Vic., cap. 194 (14th August, 1855), Capital, 160,000*l.* in 10*l.* shares; loans, 40,000*l.* Commences on South Staffordshire at Cannock, and proceeds to Rugeley station of the Trent Valley. With the view of saving a cost of a duplicate station at Cannock, arrangements are made for the use of the South Staffordshire station at that place. Opened November, 1859. Leased to London and North Western at a rent of 5,500*l.* a year; being at the rate of 3¼ per cent. per annum.

LONDON AND NORTH WESTERN.—The arrangements with this company involve the following, in addition to minor stipulations:—The North Western to have all the privileges, and to be subject to all the liabilities of lessees, as referred to in the 112th and 113th sections of the Consolidation Act, 1845, save as regards any extraordinary expenses of maintenance, arising from subsidence caused by mining operations, where the Cannock Mineral have failed to purchase the minerals; and in the event of difference between the lessors or lessees, as to such extraordinary expenses, and the mode in which they shall be provided for, such difference shall be settled by an arbitrator to be appointed under the provisions of the Clauses Consolidation Act, 1845. The Board of the Cannock to consist of nine directors, of whom five shall be approved by the North Western. In the event of the construction of any other railway forming a communication between Colwich and the South Staffordshire at or near Cannock, the rent thereafter to be reduced to 5,000*l.* per annum. This arrangement was sanctioned by Parliament in 1855 and 1862.

The dividends are equal to about 6*s.* 6*d.* per share—3¼ per cent. per annum.

No. of Directors—9; minimum, 6; quorum, 3. *Qualification*, 25 shares.

DIRECTORS:

Chairman—Lieutenant-Colonel T. E. BIGGE, Bryanstone Square, London, W.

H. J. W. H. Foley, Esq., Prestwood, Stourbridge.
Matthew Lyon, Esq., Leamington.
Michael L. Melville, Esq., Tunbridge Wells.

Oscar L. Stephen, Esq., Bardon Hall, Leicester.
Edward Tootal, Esq., The Weaste, near Manchester.
W. Wagstaff, Esq., 4, Gt. George Street, Westminster, S.W.

OFFICERS.—Sec., F. Harley, Cannock Mineral Railway, Euston Station, London, N.W.; Supt. of Goods Dept., Edward Huntley, Queen Street, Wolverhampton; Bankers, Glyn, Mills, and Co.

76.—CARLISLE AND SILLOTH BAY.

Incorporated by 18 and 19 Vic., cap, 153 (July 16th, 1855), to make a railway from the Port Carlisle, at Drumburgh, to the Coat lighthouse in Silloth Bay, and a dock and jetty at the latter place. Length, 12¾ miles; opened 4th September, 1856. The dock at Silloth was opened on 3rd August, 1859. It measures 600 feet in length and 300 in width, giving an area of water surface of upwards of four acres, with a width at the entrance gate of 60 feet.

By 25 Vic., cap. 45 (3rd June, 1862), the company was authorised to raise additional capital to the extent of 75,000*l.* at 6 per cent. in preference shares, and 25,000*l.* on loan. The whole of these shares have been paid up.

By 25 Vic., cap. 47 (June 3rd, 1862), the Carlisle and Silloth is leased to the North British for 999 years, at an annual rental of 2,000*l.*, with any addition requisite to make the Silloth dividend equal to that of the North British.

It was reported in October that the directors could not recommend the payment of any dividend, but that the balance should be carried forward to the next half-year, when they hoped to distribute the same amount among the holders of preference stock as was paid in April, viz.,—15*s.* for the half-year.

DIRECTORS:

Chairman—PETER JAMES DIXON, Esq., Houghton Hall.

Deputy-Chairman—JOHN IRVING, Esq., Carlisle.

J. D. Carr, Esq., Coledale Hall, Carlisle. | Robert Ferguson, Esq., Morton, Carlisle.
Joseph Hope, Esq., Whoof House, Carlisle. | R. S. Dixon, Esq., Knells.
Robert Creighton, Esq., Carlisle.

OFFICERS.—Sec., John Laver; Auditors, Isaac Cartmell and Joseph Forster; Solicitor, John Nanson, Carlisle.

Offices—Carlisle.

77.—CARMARTHEN AND CARDIGAN.

Incorporated by 17 and 18 Vic., cap. 218 (1854). Capital. 300,000*l.* in 10*l.* shares. Borrowing powers, 80,000*l.* Arrangements with South Wales.

A deviation and extension of time (viz., for four years from 30th June, 1856), was conceded by 19 and 20 Vic., cap. 68 (1st July, 1856). The same Act permits a preference of 6 per cent. to be attached to unissued shares.

By 25 and 26 Vic., cap. 172 (29th July, 1862), the company was authorised to extend the line from Llangeler to Newcastle Emlyn. Length, 7¼ miles. New capital, 174,000*l.* at 6 per cent. and 58,000*l.* on loan.

By 26 and 27 Vic., cap. 166 (1st July, 1863), the company was authorised to extend the line from Newcastle Emlyn to Cardigan. Length, 12¾ miles. Opened in March, from Conwil to Pencader, 8 miles; to Llandyssil, in May, 1864, 3½ miles. Omnibus traffic to Newcastle Emlyn and Cardigan, commenced in June, 1864. Productive 19 miles.

By 27 Vic., cap. 13 (28th April, 1864), the company was authorised to construct a branch from the South Wales at Kidwelly to Velindre. Capital (to be kept separate), 100,000*l.* in shares, and 33,000*l.* on loan. Length, 6½ miles. This line is to be constructed solely for the purpose of procuring the lime from the Kidwelly range for conveyance over the main line.

By 28 Vic., cap. 37 (26th May, 1865), the capital authorised in 1862 and 1863 was divided into two separate sections, namely, Newcastle Emlyn, 74,000*l.*, and Cardigan Extension, 160,000*l.*, which are to be kept distinct from the general capital of the company, such amount being offered to its own section exclusively. An extension of time for three years was also conceded to the works authorised in 1862, and of five years for those sanctioned in 1863.

By 28 and 29 Vic., cap. 170 (29th June, 1865), the company was authorised to construct an extension to Kidwelly. Length, 7½ miles. Capital, 70,000*l.* in shares, and 23,000*l.* on mortgage.

By 29 and 30 Vic., cap. 297 (30th July, 1866), this extension to Kidwelly was erected into a separate undertaking under the title of "Gwendraeth," which see.

The company is in Chancery, and in considerable financial difficulty, without any apparent probability of extrication.

No. of Directors.—Maximum, 9; minimum, 6; quorum, 3. *Qualification*, 50 shares.

DIRECTORS:

Chairman—JOHN EVERITT, Esq., Allhallows Chambers, 49, Lombard Street, E.C.

Robert Collum, Esq., M.D., Cray, Surbiton. | John M. Knight, Esq., Northfleet.
James H. Crawford, Esq., Whitebarns, | Joseph Ivimey, Esq., 8, Staple Inn, W.C.
  Buntingford. | Philip E. Sewell, Norwich.
Gwynnet Tyler, Esq., 12, Worcester | J. Lumsden Propert, Esq., 100, Gloucester
  Terrace, Clifton, and Mount Gernos, | Place, Portman Square, W.
  Newcastle Emlyn. | William Parsons, Esq., Nottingham.

OFFICERS.—Sec., A. Young; Eng., John Wright; Auditors, Edmund Harvey and Gustavus Jordan; Solicitor, Henry Ivimey, 8, Staple Inn.

78.—CARMARTHENSHIRE.

Incorporated by 27 and 28 Vic., cap. 224 (25th July, 1864), to construct three lines in conjunction with the Llanelly. Length, 20¾ miles. Capital, 125,000*l.*, in 10*l.* shares, and 41,600*l.* on loan. Arrangements with Llanelly. Completion of works, five years.

By 28 and 29 Vic., cap. 352 (5th July, 1865), a portion of the line was transferred to the Llanelly, by which a reduction of the capital of the Carmarthenshire takes place to the extent of 15,000*l.* in shares, and 5,000*l.* on loan. Power was also conferred upon the company to divide the shares under certain circumstances into two equal parts, and to give one moiety a preferential claim to dividends to an amount not exceeding 5 per cent.

An agreement has been made with the Llanelly, and confirmed by Parliament, conferring upon the two companies mutual running powers, by which the trains of the Carmarthen would be able to gain direct access to the docks.

OFFICERS.—Engs., Lane and Bagot, 34, Great George Street, Westminster, S.W., and Llanelly, Carmarthenshire; Solicitors, Rixton and Son, 38, Cannon Street, E.C.

79.—CARNARVON AND LLANBERIS.

Incorporated by 27 and 28 Vic., cap. 186 (14th July, 1864), to construct a line from Carnarvon to Llanberis. Length, 9 miles. Capital, 110,000*l.* in 10*l.* shares and 36,600*l.* on loan. Arrangements with London and North Western, which is to work the line at 55 per cent. Works in progress.

By 28 and 29 Vic., cap 326 (5th July, 1865), the company was authorised to construct an extension to the Bangor and Carnarvon line of the London and North Western, with a branch into the Bettws Garmon Valley. Length, 10¾ miles. Capital, 138,000*l.* in shares, and 46,000*l.* on loan.

By 30 and 31 Vic., cap. 151 (25th July, 1867), an agreement was confirmed by which the London and North Western was admitted as joint owners of the line extending 5 miles beyond Llanberis, at which point the London and North Western may construct a junction with the Bangor and Carnarvon. By the same Act the Carnarvon and Llanberis were authorised to attach a preference to unissued shares.

By 31 Vic., cap. 21 (29th May, 1868), the company obtained power to construct several new works, and to abandon other portions of the line, to be completed in 1872. The London and North Western was authorised to contribute 50,000*l.* of new capital, and to work the line at 55 per cent.

Meetings in February or March, and in August or September.

No. of Directors—7; minimum, 3; quorum, 3. *Qualification,* 250*l.*

DIRECTORS:

Chairman—JAMES BANCROFT, Esq., Manchester.

Deputy-Chairman—JAMES OLIVER MASON, Esq., 44, Denbigh Street, Warwick Square, S.W.

Henry Crosfield, Esq., Liverpool.	Thomas Turner, Esq , Plas Brereton, Carnarvon.
Richard Ryder Dean, Esq., 97, Gloucester Place, Portman Square, W.	William Bailey Hawkins, Esq., Reigate, Surrey.

OFFICERS.—Sec., John Wilson Theobald; Eng., Edwin Clark, 5, Westminster Chambers, Victoria Street, Westminster, S.W.; Solicitors, Eady and Champion, 18, Park Street, Westminster, S.W.; Bankers, Ransom, Bouverie, and Co., Pall Mall East. S.W.

Offices—6, Victoria Street, Westminster, S.W.

80.—CARNARVONSHIRE.

Incorporated by 25 and 26 Vic., cap. 202 (22nd July, 1862), to construct a line from the Bangor and Carnarvon Branch of the London and North Western to Port Madoc. Length, 77¾ miles. Capital, 200,000*l.*, in 10*l.* shares; loans. 65,500*l.* Arrangements with London and North Western and Aberystwyth and Welsh Coast. Opened 2nd September, 1867.

By 28 and 29 Vic., cap. 175 (29th June, 1865), the company obtained an extension of time till June, 1867, for completion of its works.

By 30 and 31 Vic., cap. 152 (25th July, 1867), the Carnarvonshire was authorised to make certain deviations, to be completed within two years, and also to exercise running powers over the Cambrian between Pwilheli and Port Madoc.

NANTLLE.—Incorporated by 6 Geo. IV., cap. 63, for making a tramroad from Llandwrog to Carnarvon. Capital, 20,000*l.* By Act of 1827, the company obtained power to borrow 20,000*l.* By 28 and 29 Vic., cap. 337 (5th July, 1865), the company was authorised to widen and extend the line. Length, 17½ miles. Capital, 120,000*l.* in shares, and 40,000*l.* on loan.

By 30 and 31 Vic., cap. 152 (25th July, 1867), the Nantlle was vested in the Carnarvonshire, the whole of the capital of the former being cancelled, and 1,000 preference shares at 5 per cent. issued to the Nantlle shareholders instead. By new Act the capital of the united undertaking consists of :—

Ordinary shares	£190,000
Preference shares	10,000
Debentures	126,500

The above Act also gives power to convert 80,000*l.* (at present unissued) of the ordinary shares into 5 per cent. preference shares.

The line was opened throughout from Pant Station, Carnarvon, to Afonwen (a station on the Cambrian), in September, 1867. The locomotive line is 17 miles in length, there being about 2½ miles of tramway, leading to the Nantlle slate quarries, in addition.

No. of Directors—minimum, 4 ; quorum, 3. *Qualification*, 200*l.*

DIRECTORS :

Chairman—DAVID WILLIAMS, Esq., M.P., Deudraeth Castle, Port Madoc.

Deputy-Chairman—JASPER WILSON JOHNS, Esq., Wolverton Park, Newbury, Hants.

William Smith, Esq., 53, Coleman Street, London.

Augustus S. Wildy, 116, Regent's Park Road, London.

OFFICERS.—Sec.. James Fraser, 7, Bank Buildings, Lothbury, London, E.C.; Eng., C. E. Spooner, C.E., Bron-y-garth, Port Madoc; Auditors, Hugh Owen, 21, Richmond Crescent, Barnsbury, N., and Charles Morrison, 7, Bank Buildings, Lothbury, London ; Solicitor, R. W. Wyatt, Parliament Street, Westminster, S.W., and Edward Breese, Port Madoc.

Offices—7, Bank Buildings, Lothbury, London, E.C.

81.—CARRICKFERGUS AND LARNE.

Incorporated by 23 Vic., cap. 54 (15th May, 1860), for constructing a railway from the Belfast and Northern Counties at Carrickfergus to Larne. Length, 14½ miles. Capital, 125,000*l.* in 25*l.* shares. Loans, which may be converted into debenture stock, 41,500*l.* Opened 1st October, 1863. The Belfast and Northern Counties subscribed 20,000*l.*, and works the line for seven years, from 1st November, 1865.

REVENUE.—The receipts for the half-year ending 31st December, amounted to 2,680*l.*, and the working expenses, including interest, and payment of an old balance to credit of revenue to the same amount. The receipts for the June half-year were 2,872*l.*, the working and other charges leaving a balance to the credit of revenue of 203*l.*

CAPITAL.—The expenditure on this account to 30th June amounted to 120,385*l.*, which left a balance against receipts of 2,043*l.*

DIRECTORS :

Chairman—LORD TEMPLETOWN, Castle Upton, Templepatrick, and Grosvenor Hotel, Pimlico, S. W.

Deputy-Chairman—HENRY H. M'NIELE, Esq., Parkmount, Belfast.

Sir Edward Coey, Merville, Belfast.
John Ross, Esq., Larne.
Charles M'Garel, Esq., Belgrave Square, London.
John Thomson, Esq., Low Wood, Belfast.
E. M'G. Casement, Esq., Larne.

George B. Johnston, Esq., Glynn, Larne.
James Macaulay, Esq., Belfast.
R. M'Calmont, Esq., Eaton Square, London, S.W.
James Agnew, Esq., Cheltenham.
James Chaine, Esq., Antrim.

OFFICERS.—Sec., Charles Stewart ; Eng., Sir Charles Lanyon, Wellington Place, Belfast; Auditors, Thomas Smyth and J. M. Mc.Cormick, of Larne; Solicitor, James Torrens, Wellington Place, Belfast.

Offices—York Street, Belfast.

82.—CENTRAL CORNWALL.

(LATE LAUNCESTON, BODMIN, AND WADEBRIDGE JUNCTION.)

Incorporated by 27 and 28 Vic., cap. 289 (29th July, 1864), to construct a railway from the Launceston and South Devon to the Bodmin and Wadebridge. Length, 21 miles. Capital, 250,000*l.* in 10*l.* shares, and 83,000*l.* on loan. Arrangements with Devon and Cornwall.

By 28 and 29 Vic., cap. 374 (6th July, 1865), the company was authorised to construct an extension from Ruthern to the Cornwall at Truro. Length, 23 miles. Capital, 320,000*l.* in shares, and 106,600*l.* on loan, to be kept separate from original capital. By the same Act the name of the company was changed to " Cornwall Central." Facilities to South Western and other narrow gauge companies on the route.

By 30 and 31 Vic., cap. 199 (15th August, 1867), the Central Cornwall was authorised to divide its shares into deferred and preferred, and also obtained an extension of time for three years for completion of works.

Meetings in February and August.

No. of Directors—5 ; quorum, 3.   *Qualification*, 500*l.*

DIRECTORS:

Francis Rodd, Esq., Trebartha Hall, Launceston.	Thomas Martyn, Esq., Wadebridge.
J. C. B. Lethbridge, Esq.	George Browne Collins, Esq., Caloggas, St. Columb.
John Ching, Esq., Launceston.	

83.—CENTRAL IRELAND.

Incorporated by 29 and 30 Vic., cap. 257 (23rd July, 1866), to construct lines from the Kilkenny Junction at Maryborough to Mullingar on the Midland Great Western, with two branches to the Great Southern and Western. Length, 36 miles. Capital, 220,000*l.* in shares, and 72,000*l.* on loan. These sums are to be raised respectively by the Waterford and Kilkenny and the Kilkenny Junction, in which companies the construction and management of the Central Ireland are placed. Joint committee of eight members to be appointed. No progress appears to have yet been made with this undertaking.

84.—CHESTER AND WEST CHESHIRE JUNCTION.

Incorporated by 28 and 29 Vic., cap. 292 (5th July, 1865), to construct a railway from the West Cheshire, at Mouldsworth, to the Birkenhead, at Mickle Trafford, and to Chester. Length, 8 miles. Capital, 150,000*l.* in shares, and 50,000*l.* on loan. Arrangements with Great Northern and Manchester and Sheffield. Facilities to London and North Western and Great Western. In abeyance.

By 30 Vic., cap. 26 (29th May, 1868), an extension of time for purchase of lands till 1870 was obtained.

No. of Directors—9 ; minimum, 5.   *Qualification*, 200*l.*

DIRECTORS:

Charles Townshend, Esq.	Alfred Barry, Esq.
John Jones, Esq.	Thomas M. Crowder, Esq.
F. L. Bagnall, Esq.	

85.—CHICHESTER AND MIDHURST.

Incorporated by 27 and 28 Vic., cap. 75 (23rd June, 1864), to construct a line from the Brighton at Chichester, to join the Mid-Sussex and Midhurst, and Petersfield. Length, 11½ miles. Capital, 190,000*l.* in 10*l.* shares, and 63,000*l.* on loan.

By 28 and 29 Vic., cap. 354 (5th July, 1865), the company was authorised to construct an extension to Haslemere. Length, 9¾ miles. New capital, 180,000*l.* in shares, and 60,000*l.* on loan ; but by 31 and 32 Vic., cap. 162 (31st July, 1868), the extension was authorised to be abandoned. The undertaking is practically embodied in the London Brighton and South Coast.

Meetings in February or March, and in August or September.

No. of Directors—5 ; quorum, 3.   *Qualification*, 250*l.*

DIRECTORS:

Chairman—WILLIAM FRANCIS DOBSON, Esq., Bearsted House, near Maidstone, Kent.

George Henty, Esq., J.P., Northlands, Chichester.

George Battcock, Esq., 4, Carlton Street, Regent Street, S.W.

James Goodson, Esq., 32, Kensington Gardens Square, W.

Sir Charles Taylor, Bart., Hollycombe, Sussex.

John T. Pagan, Esq., J.P., Rochdale, and Oak Lodge, Guildford.

OFFICERS.—Sec., John Widdecombe; Eng., Edward Woods, 3, Storey's Gate, Great George Street, Westminster, S.W.; Auditors, James Johnstone, 5A, Lothbury, E.C., and James Hutt, Westminster Chambers, Victoria Street, Westminster, S.W.; Solicitors, W. and H. P. Sharp, 92, Gresham House, Old Broad Street, London, E.C.

Offices—3, Bridge Street, Westminster, S.W.

86.—CITY OF GLASGOW UNION.

Incorporated by 27 and 28 Vic., cap. 286. Capital, 900,000l. in 10l. shares, and 300,000l. on loan. Length, 6¾ miles. By 28 and 29 Vic., cap. 247, company empowered to deviate their line and to form a railway to the Harbour of Glasgow, also to raise further capital to the extent of 150,000l. in shares, and 50,000l. on loan. By the latter Act the Glasgow and South Western become shareholders to the extent of 300,000l., and the North British also shareholders to the extent of 300,000l.

The railway forms a junction with the North British at Sighthill, and also with the Caledonian, and is then carried chiefly on arches through the City of Glasgow and across the river Clyde, onwards until it joins the Glasgow and South Western and the Caledonian (southside branches), on the south side of the City. It therefore connects all the existing lines of railway around Glasgow. It will also afford a large central station at St. Enoch's Square, adjoining Argyle and Buchanan Streets, in the most central situation of Glasgow, affording accommodation for the traffic of all the lines running into Glasgow.

By 30 and 31 Vic., cap. 166 (25th July, 1867), the company was authorised to make certain deviations and to construct a junction with the Glasgow and Coatbridge. Length, 1 mile. New capital, 60,000l. in shares and 20,000l. on loan. The Glasgow and South Western were empowered to subscribe 140,000l. in addition to previous sums. Shares to the extent of 300,000l., held individually, to become preference, and the residue as subscribed by the North British and the Glasgow and South Western to rank as ordinary. Extension of time for completion of works till 29th July, 1870.

For new arrangements with the North British and Glasgow and South Western, as well as with the contractors, see APPENDIX to the present Volume.

It was reported in September, that the contractors had confined their operations almost entirely to the formation of the bridge carrying the Shields road over the railway at Pollockshields Junction, and to the completion of the diversion of the canal and works in that neighbourhood. The directors, however, were now empowered by the approval of the recent meetings both of this and the other two contributing companies to carry out the scheme then approved, and the works on the north side of the Clyde necessary for effecting a junction with the Coatbridge would at once be resumed. In terms of the Act of 1867, the shares raised under the original Act, other than those subscribed for by the North British and Glasgow and South Western, had been converted into preference stock, the proceeds of which were devoted to the construction of the stations at Dunlop-street and the College.

It was also resolved to apply to the Board of Trade for an extension of time for completion of works.

Meetings in March or April, and in September or October.

*No. of Directors—*9; minimum, 7; quorum, 3. *Qualification,* 1,000l.

DIRECTORS:

Chairman—JAMES KING, Esq., Glasgow.

Walter Macfarlane, Esq., Glasgow.
*Sir Andrew Orr, of Harviestoun.
*Peter Clouston, Esq., Glasgow.
*James Rodger, Esq., Glasgow.

† John Stirling, Esq., of Kippendavie, Dunblane, Perthshire.
† Robert Young, Esq., Glasgow.
† Francis Maxwell, Esq., St. Vincent Place, Glasgow.

* Represent Glasgow and South Western.   † Represent North British.

OFFICERS.—Sec., George Tawse; Engs., John Fowler, Queen Square Place, Westminster, S.W., and James F. Blair, Hope Street, Glasgow; Solicitors, M'Grigor, Stevenson, and Fleming, 136, St. Vincent Street, Glasgow; Bankers, Union Bank of Scotland, Glasgow; Auditors, Henry Kerr and L. R. Robertson, Accountants, Glasgow.

Offices—146, West George Street, Glasgow.

87.—CLONMEL, LISMORE, AND DUNGARVAN.

Incorporated by 28 and 29 Vic., cap. 264 (5th July, 1865), to construct a line from the Waterford and Limerick, at Clonmel, to Lismore and Dungarvan. Length, 37¾ miles. Capital, 300,000l. in shares, and 100,000l, on loan. Arrangements with Waterford and Limerick.

By 30 and 31 Vic., cap. 93 (13th July, 1868), an extension of time for completion of works till 1871 was obtained.

CAPITAL —The balance sheet to 30th June, 1868, presented the subjoined detail of income and expenditure:—

Received.	Expended.	
On share capital, including a sum of 200l. received towards preliminary expenses £5,779	General expenditure......£7,468	
	Engineer	450
Directors' advances per London and Westminster Bank 2,200	Bank charges......	53
	Balance in hand......	6
£7,979	£7,979	

No. of Directors—10; minimum, 3; quorum, 3 and 2. Qualification, 300l.

DIRECTORS:

Chairman—His Grace The DUKE OF DEVONSHIRE, K.G., &c., Devonshire House, Piccadilly; Lismore Castle, County Waterford, &c.

Lord Stuart De Decies, Dromana, County Waterford, and 6, Clifford Street, W.
Sir Richard Musgrave, Bart., Tourin, County Waterford.
John Bagwell, Esq., M.P.. Marlfield, Clonmel, and 83, Ebury Street. S.W.
William Currey, Esq., 14, Great George Street, Westminster, S.W.
Francis Edmund Currey, Esq., Lismore Castle.
George Le Hunte, Esq., Artramont, County Wexford.

OFFICERS.—Sec., W. B. Lewis, 11, Great Queen Street, Westminster, S.W.; Eng.-in-Chief, W. Purdon, 11, Great Queen Street, Westminster, S.W.; Local Engs., C. Tarrant, Waterford, and O. C. Edwards, Cork; Auditors, Joseph Atwell, 72, Bedford Gardens, W., and Alfred Bennett, 35, Craven Street, Strand. W.C.; Solicitor, Edmund Power, Clonmel, and 35, Upper Ormond Quay, Dublin; Bankers, the National Bank.

Offices—11, Great Queen Street, Westminster, S.W.

88.—COCKERMOUTH, KESWICK, AND PENRITH.

Incorporated by 24 and 25 Vic., cap. 203 (1st August, 1861), to construct a line from the Cockermouth and Workington to Penrith, on the Lancaster and Carlisle. Length, 31½ miles. Capital, 200,000l. in 20l. shares, and 66,000l. on loan. Arrangements with Cockermouth and Workington. Opened for minerals on 1st November, 1864, and for passengers on 2nd January, 1865.

By 26 and 27 Vic., cap. 108 (29th June, 1864), several new works were authorised. Certain shares were cancelled and a preference issue of 5 per cent. allowed instead. The London and North Western and the Stockton and Darlington were permitted to subscribe 25,000l. each to the undertaking and to enter into working agreements.

REVENUE.—For the half-year ending 31st January the receipts exhibited an increase of 3,157l. The directors recommended that out of the gross receipts 2½ per cent. be set aside half-yearly to form the nucleus of a reserve fund. After making this deduction, which amounted to 358l., there remained 2,722l., out of which a dividend at the rate of 2l. 5s. per cent. per annum, left a balance of 89l.

The receipts for the June half-year were 13,529l., showing a diminution of 50l. There had been an increase of 359l. in working expenses, chiefly arising from increased cost of Penrith joint station. The working expenses amounted to 8,553l., leaving a balance of 4,976l.; an amount equal to 2½ per cent. of the gross receipts was carried to a reserve fund, and 2,365l. remained for divisions among the shareholders, out of which a dividend at the rate of 2 per cent. per annum was declared.

CAPITAL —This account showed that 337,478l. had been expended to 30th June, leaving a balance of 13,075l. against the company.

DIRECTORS:

Chairman—ISAAC FLETCHER, Esq., M.P., Tarn Bank, Workington.

Deputy-Chairman—JOHN JAMESON, Esq., J.P., Moorhouses, Penrith.

Capt. Henry Gandy, of Eden Grove, Penrith.
Isaac Lowthian, Esq., Penrith.
*Thomas McGlasson, Esq., Penrith.
John Simpson, Esq., Penrith.
*John James Spedding, Esq., J.P., Greta Bank, Keswick.
*Arthur Dover, Esq., Skiddaw Bank, Keswick.

†William Nicholson Hodgson, Esq., M.P., Newby Grange, Carlisle, and Carlton Club, S.W.
†Major Andrew Green Thompson, J.P., The Hollies, Keswick.
‡Henry Pease, Esq., Pierremont, Darlington.
‡Isaac Wilson, Esq., J.P., Middlesbro'-on-Tees.

*Retire by rotation in August, 1869, but are eligible for re-election.   †Nominated by the London and North Western.   ‡Nominated by the North Eastern.

OFFICERS.—Sec. and Man., Henry Cattle; Eng., John Wood, C.E., Keswick; Accountant, Peter Thompson; Solicitor, Edward Waugh, Cockermouth; Auditors, *John F. Crosthwaite, Keswick, and Lieut.-Col. C. H. Wake, of Ormathwaite House, Keswick.

Offices—Keswick.

89.—COLCHESTER, STOUR VALLEY, SUDBURY, AND HALSTEAD,

Incorporated by 9 and 10 Vic., cap. 76 (1846).   Reconstituted by 18 Vic., cap. 19 (May 25th, 1855).   The rent by the Great Eastern being regularly paid, the directors are chiefly occupied in distributing the proceeds.   The dividends declared for the year ending 30th June, 1868, were equal to 2l. 6s. per cent.

DIRECTORS:

Chairman—THOMAS L'ESTRANGE EWEN, Esq., Dedham, near Colchester, Essex.

John Garrad, Esq., Bures St. Mary, near Colchester, Essex.
James Dalton, Esq., Bures St. Mary, near Colchester, Essex.

William Quilter, Esq., Moorgate Street, E.C.
Charles Henry Hawkins, Esq., Colchester, Essex.

OFFICERS.—Sec., Frederick Blomfield Philbrick, Solicitor, Colchester; Auditors, John Ward, Head Street, Colchester, and Charles Frederick Fenton, of Colchester.

Offices—Church Lane, Colchester.

90.—COLEFORD, MONMOUTH, USK, AND PONTYPOOL.

Incorporated by 17 Vic., cap. 217 (20th August, 1853), for a central line through Monmouthshire, to develope the mineral resources, from Llanfihangel (Pontemoyle junction with the Newport and Hereford) to Coleford, Gloucestershire; branch, Dixton to Monmouth gas works.   Connection established with the Newport and Pontypool which communicates with Taff Vale Extension and Monmouthshire lines.   Designed to go through the Forest of Dean to the South Wales, and effect communication with Gloucester and London.   Length, main line, 21⅜ miles; branch, ½ mile.   Narrow gauge.

By 24 and 25 Vic., cap. 197 (22nd July, 1861), the company was authorised to lease the undertaking to the West Midland, at the rent of 4,680l. for the first year; 5,616l. for the second; 7,020l. for the third, fourth, fifth, and sixth; 8,190l. for the seventh; 9,360l. for the eighth; 10,062l. for the ninth; and thereafter, 10,764l. per annum.   This lease has been carried into effect; and the traffic returns appear in those of the Great Western.

Dividends equal to 3¼ per cent. per annum have been declared half yearly for 1868.

No. of Directors.—Maximum, 12; minimum, 9; quorum, 4.   *Qualification, 25 sui juris*

Committee of Directors, 3 to 5; quorum, 3.

DIRECTORS:

Chairman—CRAWSHAY BAILEY, Esq., Llanfoist House, Monmouthshire.

Deputy-Chairman—THOMAS BROWN, Esq., Lower Hardwick, Chepstow, Monmouthshire.

George Cave, Esq., Westbury-on-Trym, Gloucestershire.

Thomas Gratrex, Esq., King's Hill House, Newport, Monmouthshire.

Henry Dyke, Esq., Monmouth.

George Relph Greenhow Relph, Esq., Beech Hill, near Usk.

Osmond A. Wyatt, Esq., Troy House, near Monmouth.

John Russell, Esq., Terhill House, Cheltenham.

Thomas Powell, Esq., Coldra, near Newport.

Solicitor and Secretary, A. Waddington, Usk.

Offices—Usk.

91.—COLNBROOK.

Incorporated by 29 and 30 Vic., cap. 343 (6th August, 1866), to construct a line from West Drayton, on the Great Western, to Colnbrook, with a branch to the South Western at Staines. Length, 5¾ miles. Capital, 60,000*l.*, in 10*l.* shares, and 20,000*l.* on loan, Arrangements with Great Western and South Western.

No. of Directors—6; minimum, 3; quorum, 3 and 2. *Qualification*, 200*l.*

DIRECTORS:

Charles Edward Barlow, Esq.

Matthew Hale, Esq.

Edward V. Hemingway, Esq.

Percy Grove Ibotson, Jun., Esq.

John Frederick Robinson, Esq.

John Scott Smith, Esq.

92.—COLNE VALLEY AND HALSTEAD.

Incorporated by 19 and 20 Vic., cap. 61 (30th June, 1856), to make a railway from the Chappel station of the Colchester and Stour Valley to the town of Halstead, in the county of Essex. Capital, 40,000*l.*, in 10*l.* shares; loans, 13,333*l.*

Agreement may be made with the Colchester and Stour Valley and Great Eastern. Length, 6¼ miles, forming a junction with Colchester and Stour Valley. Opened 16th April, 1860.

By 22 and 23 Vic., cap. 122 (13th August, 1859), the company was authorised to extend the line from Halstead to Haverhill. New capital, 80,000*l.* in shares, and 27,000*l.* on loan. Open to Castle Hedingham, 3½ miles, 1st July, 1851; to Yeldham, 2½ miles, on 29th May, 1862; to Haverhill, 10th May, 1863. In operation, 20 miles.

By 24 and 25 Vic., cap 237 (6th August, 1861), the company was authorised to raise additional capital to the extent of 30,000*l.* in shares, and 10,000*l.* on loan.

By the Amalgamation Act of 1862, the Great Eastern is bound to take and work the Colne Valley, if the company call upon them to do so, on the terms of paying over 50 per cent. of the earnings. Facilities are also given for transmission and receipt of traffic between the Colne Valley and the Great Eastern, by through booking and through rates, in case the former company should prefer to work its own line.

By 26 and 27 Vic., cap. 186 (21st July, 1863), the company was authorised to increase its capital by 28,000*l.*, in shares at 5 per cent., and 9,000*l.* on loan. An agreement for joint use of the Great Eastern station at Haverhill, with running powers thereto, was also sanctioned.

By 28 Vic. cap. 1 (7th April, 1865), the company was authorised to raise new capital to the extent of 40,000*l.* in shares, and 13,300*l.* on loan.

REVENUE.—It was reported in March, that the receipts for the December half-year had been sufficient only to meet the working expenses. Differences were still outstanding with the Great Eastern and with Mr. Sperling, who had been working the line. The directors proposed to expend the profits of the current half-year upon the permanent way. It was reported in August that the working expenses had been reduced, but the traffic had not increased. The receipts on revenue account for the half-year amounted to 3,217*l.*, and the expenditure to 3,102*l.*, leaving a balance of 115*l.*

CAPITAL.—The expenditure on this account extends to 264,804*l.* which has been provided for as follows:—

Ordinary Shares—Original line	£25,948	
Extension line	36,970=	£62,918
Preference shares	89,260	
Less rebate	23,680=	£65,580
Debentures	56,714	
Construction bonds	76,200	
Balance	3,391=	£264,804

Meetings in February and August.

No. of Directors—6; minimum, 3; quorum, 3. *Qualification*, 250*l.*

DIRECTORS:

Chairman—JAMES BREWSTER, Esq., J.P., Ashford Lodge, Halstead, Essex.

Robt. Chas. Hanam, Esq., 1, Alderman's Walk, Bishopsgate Street, London, E.C.
G. J. Mayhew, Esq., Great George Street, Westminster, S.W.

Edgar Corrie, Esq., 26, Lombard Street, London, E.C.
Fred. Payne, Esq., Wixoe, Haverhill.

OFFICERS—Gen. Man. and Lessee, Robert Johnston Watt, Halstead, Essex; Sec., Edmund Harvey, 6, Victoria Street, Westminster, S.W.; Eng., Joseph Cubitt, C.E., 6, Great George Street, Westminster, S.W.; Auditors, W. H. Wilson, 6, Victoria Street, Westminster, S.W., and Jas. Cardinall, Halstead, Essex; Solicitors, Baxter, Rose, and Norton, 6, Victoria Street, Westminster, S.W.

Offices—6, Victoria Street, Westminster, S.W.

93.—CORK AND BANDON.

Incorporated by 9 Vic., cap. 122 (July, 1845), for a line from Cork to Bandon. By 11 Vic., cap. 194, a deviation and extension into Cork authorised. Length, 20 miles. Irish gauge (5 feet 3 inches). Open from Bandon to Ballinhassig, 9¾ miles, 1st August, 1849, the remainder December 8th, 1851.

By 15 Vic., cap. 35 (28th May, 1852), this company has been further authorised to raise an additional capital of 48,000*l.*; to issue new shares for the additional capital authorised and in lieu of shares forfeited, cancelled, or surrendered, with guaranteed interest not exceeding 6 per cent. per annum, under sanction of three-fifths of special meeting; also to create "debenture shares," in lieu of loans under first Act, with interest not exceeding 5 per cent. per annum.

By Act of 1854 the company were entitled to create 6,000 shares of 5*l.* each, at 6 per cent. dividend till 31st December, 1863; 4 per cent. in perpetuity thereafter. These were issued on 7th August, 1854, and 12th February, 1856.

REVENUE.—The following is a statement of the traffic receipts for twelve years ending 31st December, 1867:—

1856	£13,302	1862	£17,562
1857	14,548	1863	18,634
1858	15,293	1864	19,483
1859	15,855	1865	20,382
1860	17,762	1866	22,474
1861	17,610	1867	22,845

The revenue balance for June, 1868, showed a surplus of 8,630*l.* after providing for the half-year's debenture interest, outstanding dividends, and accounts due, out of which dividends were paid on the No. 1 preference shares, at the rate of 5½ per cent. per annum, and on the No. 2 preference shares, at the rate of 4 per cent. amounting to 1,912*l.*, and leaving a balance of 6,718*l.*

CAPITAL.—The disbursements on this account to 30th June were stated at 347,485*l.* the receipts being detailed as follow:—

Original stock	£175,241	
No. 1 and 2 preference shares	77,592	
Loans on debentures	£62,878	
Debenture shares	8,310	
Loan from P.W.C. Commissioners	6,529 =	77,717
Interest, sale of old materials, &c.		6,762
Loan from revenue	7,779	
Do. this half-year	110 =	7,889
Royal Bank, paid on debenture bonds		2,232 = £347,485

The accounts are made up to the 31st December and 30th June; and the statutory meetings held second Wednesday in February and August.

Scale of Voting.—1 to 5 shares, 1 vote; 6 to 10 shares, 2 votes; and one vote additional for every 10 shares, under Companies Clauses Consolidation Act. Proxies, 48 hours at least before each meeting.

Certificates must accompany transfer deeds. Transfer books close 14 days before each meeting. Transfer fee, 2s. 6d. each, in cash or stamps.

No. of Directors.—Maximum 12; minimum, 6; quorum, 3. *Qualification,* 1,000l. stock, except debenture stock. Committee of Directors, 3 to 7; quorum, 3.

DIRECTORS:

Chairman—VALENTINE O'BRIEN O'CONNOR, Esq., Deputy-Lieut., 3, Beresford Place, Dublin.

Alexander Findlater, Esq., The Slopes, Kingstown.
William J. Maynard, Esq., Crosthwaite Park, Kingstown.

Robert G. Collis, Esq., Leeson Park, Dublin.

LOCAL COMMITTEE AT CORK.

Wm. Lumley Perrier, Esq., Cork.
David Barry, Esq., Cork.

Thomas Clarke, Esq., J.P., Rocksavage, Cork.

OFFICERS.—Sec, James H. Connell; Engineers-in-Chief, Cotton and Flemyng; Traffic Supt., Richard Coghlan; Solicitors, Barrington, Son, and Jeffers; Auditors, Charles Copland and Maurice Leonard; Bankers, National Bank, Old Broad Street, London, E.C., Royal Bank, Foster Place, Dublin, and National Bank, Cork.

Offices—45, Talbot Street, Dublin.

94.—CORK, BLACKROCK, AND PASSAGE.

Incorporated by 9 and 10 Vic., cap. 148 (July, 1846)), for a line—Cork to Passage West—6¼ miles. In 1847 an extension was granted to Monkstown Baths, 1½ mile. From Cork to Passage West, 6¼ miles, opened on 8th June, 1850.

The dividend for half-year ending 31st October, 1867, was equal to 5s. per share, or 2½ per cent. per annum. The balance on hand at 30th April amounted to 373l.

CAPITAL.—The receipts to 30th April, 1868, were 168,392l., which left a balance on expenditure of 85l.

The accounts are made up to 30th April and 31st October; and the statutory meetings held at Cork in May and November. Certificates must accompany transfer deeds. Transfer fee, 2s. 8d.

Scale of Voting.—1 to 5 shares, 1 vote; 6 to 10 shares, 2 votes; and 1 additional vote for every 10 shares.

No. of Directors.—Maximum, 15; minimum, 12; present number, 12. *Qualification,* 20 shares.

DIRECTORS:

Chairman—ROBERT HALL, Esq., South Mall, Cork.

Deputy-Chairman—MICHAEL HAYES, Esq., Summer Hill, Cork.

John H. Sugrue, Esq., Cork.
William Thomas Barrett, Esq., Upper Glanmire Road, Cork.
John Chinnery Armstrong, Esq., B.L., Grenville Street, Dublin.
Timothy Mahony, Esq., J.P., Camden Place, Cork.
Nicholas King, Esq., M.D., Dublin.
Edmund Burke, Esq., D.L., Prospect, Cork.

Sir William B. Hackett, J.P., Merchant, Lota, Cork.
Alexander Findlater, Esq., Upper Sackville Street, Dublin.
Joseph H. Carroll, Esq, Strand Crescent, Lower Road, Cork.
Patrick David Jeffers, Esq,, Ely Place, Dublin.

OFFICERS.—Sec., John Hackett; Loco. and Traffic Supt., James Barber; Auditors, Dennis M'Carthy Mahony and Thomas Exham; Solicitor, David Hall.

Head Office—Victoria Road, Cork.

95.—CORK AND KINSALE JUNCTION.

Incorporated by 22 Vic., cap. 23 (19th April, 1859), to construct a line from the Cork and Bandon to Kinsale, with a branch or tramway to Kinsale Harbour. Capital, 45,000*l.*, in 10*l.* shares; loans, 15,000*l.* The line commences 13¼ miles from Cork, and terminates near the military barracks in Kinsale. Length from junction of line with Cork and Bandon to the deep water of Kinsale Harbour, 11 miles. Opened, 27th June, 1863.

By 26 Vic., cap. 56 (8th June, 1863), the company was authorised to raise new capital to the extent of 20,000*l.* at 6 per cent., and 6,600*l.* on loan, which has been so raised and created at a special meeting held 21st November, 1863, and some unissued original shares were cancelled and preference substituted therefore on the same terms.

CORK AND BANDON.—This company is to work the Kinsale Junction for five years, and provide the necessary rolling stock; defray all charges for locomotives, wages, carriages, clothing, coke, coals, water, oil, grease, tallow, maintenance and renewal of works, repairs of rolling stock, salaries, &c., for 30 per cent. of the gross traffic receipts of the line; the Cork and Kinsale to have the privilege of working its through traffic over two miles of the Cork and Bandon free of expense.

*No. of Directors—*7; minimum, 5; quorum, 3. *Qualification,* 250*l.*

DIRECTORS:

William James Shaw, Esq., M.P., J.P., Kilnap Glen, Cork.
Lieut.-Col. N. Ludlow Beamish, K.H., Queenstown, Cork.
Sir John Benson, Montenotte, Cork.
F. W. Sedgwick, Esq., Lewisham Park, Lewisham, S.E.
William Parsons, Esq. St. Luke's, Cork.

OFFICERS.—Sec., H. Williams Wood; Solicitors, Radcliffe and Davis, Craven Street, London, and Thomas Babington, Cork; Bankers, National Bank, London, Dublin, and Cork.

Offices—6, Westminster Chambers, Victoria Street, Westminster, S.W.

96.—CORK AND LIMERICK DIRECT.

Incorporated by 23 and 24 Vic., cap. 100 (3rd July, 1860), to construct a line from the Great Southern and Western, near Charleville, to the Limerick and Foynes, near Patrick's Well. Also a short line at Limerick. Length, 25 miles. Capital, 100,000*l.* in 10*l.* shares. Loans, 33,000*l.* Opened 1st August, 1862.

By 28 and 29 Vic., cap., 156, the company was authorised to issue preference shares in lieu of those cancelled, and also to create debenture stock.

Portions of Great Southern and Limerick and Foynes are used by agreement. Traffic arrangements with those companies under the usual restrictions, during continuance of which the entire system to be considered as one. The Cork and Limerick is also authorised to subscribe 5,000*l.* to the Rathkeale and Newcastle Junction. The line is worked by the Great Southern and Western at 40 per cent., and the Cork and Limerick pays 1,400*l.* a-year for the use of eight miles on the Foynes into Limerick.

REVENUE.—The receipts for the six months ending 31st December, were 8,813*l.*, and the net profits 1,826*l.* After payment of 294*l.* for interest on preference shares, a dividend at the rate of 4 per cent. per annum left 105*l.* to next account.

The receipts for the June half-year amounted to 8,157*l.* The net profits were 1,368*l.*, so that a dividend at the rate of 3 per cent. per annum left a balance of 1,069*l.* to next account.

CAPITAL.—The expenditure on this account to 30th June amounted to 120,894*l.*, which left a balance against the account of 3,164*l.*

*Scale of Voting.—*One vote for every share held.

*No. of Directors—*7; minimum, 3; quorum, 4. *Qualification,* 500*l.*

DIRECTORS:

1 Chairman—EBENEZER PIKE, Esq., Besborough, Cork.

4 William W. Leycester, Esq., East View, Cork.
5 Henry Lyons, Esq., J.P., Croom House, Croom, County Limerick.
2 Nicolas Daniel Murphy, Esq., M.P., Lauriston, Cork.
3 Francis Lyons, Esq., Montenotte, Cork.
6 George Cotter Beale, Esq., Valebrook, Ballyoolane, Cork.
7 Michael Ryan, Esq., J.P., Bruree, County Limerick.

The figures show the order of retirement.

OFFICERS.—Sec., David John Madden; Eng. Sir John Benson; Solicitors, Tracy and Nagle; Bankers, National Bank; Auditors, Michael M'Namara, J.P., and John Henry Sugrue, J.P

Officers—35, South Mall, Cork.

97.—CORK AND MACROOM DIRECT.

Incorporated by 24 and 25 Vic., cap. 207 (1st August, 1861 , to construct a line from the Cork and Bandon, near Cork, to the town of Macroom. Length, 24¾ miles, Capital, 120,000*l*. in 10*l*. shares; loans, 40,000*l*. Opened 12th May, 1866.

By 31 and 32 Vic., cap. 180 (31st July, 1868), the company was authorised to issue 50,000*l*. in preference shares, at 6 per cent., with powers to borrow an additional sum of 10,000*l*. on mortgage, and to create debenture stock at 6 per cent.

REVENUE.—It was reported in February, 1867, the receipts for the six months ending 31st December, were 5,529*l*., which added to 1,325*l*., receipts for the period from the opening on 12th May, to June 30th, made a gross total of 6,854*l*., being an average of 208*l*. per week for the first seven weeks, and 212*l*. per week for the half-year.

After providing for working expenses, maintenance, rent and tolls to Cork and Bandon, interest on debentures, and all other items chargeable to revenue, the net realised profit amounted to 1,715*l*., being over 4 per cent. per annum on the subscribed capital, from the day the line opened, or 5 per cent. per annum for the six months.

The net profits for the half-year ending 30th June, 1868, however (after providing for interest on debentures, loans, &c., and all outstanding liabilities on revenue account), amounted only to 883*l*., which, added to the credit balance of last account, gave a gross balance of 3,798*l*.

CAPITAL.—The receipts on this account to 30th June, 1868, amounted to 152,159*l*., the whole of which (including 578*l*. "share debits"), had been expended.

No. of Directors —8; minimum, 5; quorum, 3. *Qualification*, 500*l*.

DIRECTORS:

Chairman—Sir JOHN ARNOTT, D.L., Woodlands, Cork.

Vice-Chairman—Sir GEORGE C. COLTHURST, Bart., M.P., Ardrum, Cork, and 36, Wilton Crescent, S.W.

Capt. R. T. Rye, D.L., Ryecourt.	Timothy Mahony, Esq.; J.P., Ardsulla.
W. Massy H. Massy, Esq., J.P., Massytown, Macroom.	S. M. Hussey, Esq., J.P., Cork.
	James Harding, Esq., Cork.
James Morton, Esq., J.P., Apsley House.	Sir Augustus Warren, Bart.
William Clark, Esq., Farran.	

OFFICERS.—Sec., George Purcell ; Manager, F. L. Lyster.

Offices—91, South Mall, Cork.

98.—CORNWALL.

Incorporated by 9 and 10 Vic., cap. 335 (August, 1846, for a line in connection with the South Devon at Plymouth to Falmouth. Opened, 4th May, 1859). In operation, 65½ miles.

By the Act of incorporation each of the following companies were authorised to subscribe, viz., the Great Western, for 75,000*l*.; Bristol and Exeter for 112,000*l*.; and South Devon, for 150,000*l*.; and the line may be leased or sold to those three companies, or any of them. By subsequent authority of Board of Trade, the Great Western subscribe 60,000*l*.; Bristol and Exeter, 90,000*l*. ; South Devon, 52,000*l*.; instead of the above amounts.

Until 1853 the entire undertaking had been in abeyance. After various financial schemes had been tried, with only partial success, it was at last determined to divide the shares into A and B. stock, similar to the plans adopted with so much success by the Great Northern. An agreement was also ratified between the Cornwall on the one hand, and the Great Western, the Bristol and Exeter, and the South Devon, which, in fixed proportions between themselves, guarantee interest on debenture debt.

By 20 Vic., cap. 1 (21st March, 1857), an extension of time for completion of works till 23rd June, 1860, was obtained. The same Act authorised creation and issue of preference shares to the amount of 300,000*l*., with a further power, at the option of the associated companies, to create such further number of shares, not exceeding 100,000*l*. in amount, as may be needful for completing the line from Plymouth to Truro. The associated companies guarantee 5 per cent. on these shares. This stock is redeemable at par at the end of seven years after last call is made, on Cornwall giving six months' notice.

By 21 and 22 Vic., cap. 88 (12th July, 1858), an extension of time for completing the line between Truro and Falmouth was obtained; and by 24 and 25 Vic., cap. 215 (1st August, 1861), the various Acts of the company were consolidated, a deviation was allowed, and the period for completion of the Falmouth Extension (11¾ miles) fixed for 3rd August, 1864. Opened 24th August, 1863.

With the concurrence of all the parties interested, it has been agreed that with regard to locomotives, the South Devon, the Cornwall, and the West Cornwall railways should be worked as one system, and that, after making due allowance, for interest on capital, the locomotive expenditure should be carried to one account and divided between the three companies in proportion to the number of miles run on each section.

REVENUE.—The report for the half year ending 30th June stated that by the result of the half-year's working the associated companies had to provide 6,327l. to cover their guarantees, being a reduction of 1,655l. as compared with the corresponding half-year of 1867. The receipts compare with the six months to 30th June, 1867, as follows :—

	1867.		1868.		Increase.		Decrease.
Passengers	£23,265	...	£25,438	...	£2,173	...	...
Parcels and fish	5,047	...	6,300	...	1,253	...	...
Merchandise and minerals	14,101	...	15,797	...	1,696	...	...
Mails and sundries	3,340	...	3,279	...	...	...	£61
	£45,753	...	£50,814	...	£5,122	...	£61
Expenditure	£21,563	...	£24,137	...	£2,574	...	...

CAPITAL.—This account to 30th June showed that 1,829,258l. had been expended, the receipts having been—

To 31st December.

Original 20l. shares	£297,786	
£10 A. shares	137,820	
£10 B. shares	136,876 =	£572,482
£20 guaranteed 5 per cent. redeemable preference shares	399,500	
£20 guaranteed 4½ per cent. perpetual preference shares	250,000	
£20 6 per cent. preference shares, being portion of the 149,600l. advanced by the associated companies	54,180	
4½ per cent. guaranteed perpetual preference stock	95,420	
Debentures	447,944=	£1,247,044
		£1,819,527

To 30th June, 1868.

Original 20l. shares	732	
£10 B. shares	96 =	828
		£1,820,355
4½ per cent. guaranteed perpetual preference stock	100	
Less 20l. 6 per cent. preference shares paid off	100	
Debentures paid off	90,112	
Less debentures issued	70,242 =	19,870
		£1,800,485
Balance		28,773
		£1,829,258

The accounts are made up to 30th June and 31st December; and the statutory meetings held in February or March, and August or September in every year.

Scale of Voting.—C. C. C. Act, sec. 75. The subscribing companies have one vote for every two shares.

Transfer books close usually 14 days. Transfer fee, 2s. 6d. each deed. Certificates not required.

No of Directors.—Present board, 12; 2 rotate in Feb. or March. *Qualification*, 50 shares.

DIRECTORS.
3 Chairman—ROBERT TWEEDY, Esq., Tregolls, Truro.
Deputy-Chairman—‡ THOMAS WOOLLCOMBE, Esq., Ker Street, Devonport.

4 H. Borrow, Esq., Truro.
4 R. R. Broad, Esq., K.N.L. and K.S.M., Falmouth.
2 John Carlyon, Esq., Truro.
2 John Claude Daubuz, Esq., Killiow, Truro.
1 Major S. M. Grylls, of Glynn, near Bodmin.

*Richard Bassett, Esq. Bonvilstone, Cardiff
1 T. J. A. Robartes, Esq., Lanhydrock.
3 Frederick Martin Williams, Esq., M.P., Goonvrea, and 9, Portugal Street, W.
†W. A. Bruce, Esq., Ashley, Chippenham.
†Michael Castle, Esq., Clifton, Bristol.

1 retire in 1869 : 2, in 1870 ; 3, in 1871 ; 4, in 1872—all eligible for re-election.

*Representative of Great Western ; †Bristol and Exeter ; ‡South Devon Railway.

OFFICERS.—Sec., J. H. Matthews. Joint Committee Officers—Sec., L. J. Seargeant ; Eng., P. J. Margary ; Supt., C. E. Crompton ; Goods Man., W. H. Avery ; Chief Accountant, J. H. Matthews ; Auditors, Alfred Fox and Reginald Rogers ; Solicitors, Smith, Roberts, and Paul, Truro.

Head Offices—Plymouth.

99.—CORRIS.
Incorporated for making a railway or tramroad from the Aberllefenny and Corris Slate Quarries, in the parish of Talyllyn, in the county of Merioneth, to Llandyrnog, on the river Dovey, in the parish of Towyn, with branches therefrom, and for other purposes. Length, 15 miles. Capital, 15,000l. in shares, and 5,000l. debentures. Gauge, 2ft. 3in.

By 27 and 28 Vic., cap. 225 (25th July, 1864), authorised to make a railway from existing line at Corris to the iron ore quarries at Garthgynfawr, in the parish of Dolgelly. Length, about 6 miles. Gauge, 2ft. 3in., and to use locomotives for mineral and goods traffic. Power to raise 24,000l. additional share capital, and 8,000l. by borrowing. Capital: shares, 39,000l.; debentures, 13,000l. Power to enter into working agreements with the Cambrian.

DIRECTORS:
William Laurence Banks, Esq., F.S.A., Watton House, Brecon.
Capt. C. M. Layton, Glasbury.

John Rowlands, Esq.
John William Rowlands, Esq., Corris, Machynlleth.

OFFICERS.—Sec., James Fraser, 7, Bank Buildings, E.C.; Eng., Geo. Owen, Oswestry ; Solicitors, Howell and Morgan, Machynlleth.

Offices—7, Bank Buildings, Lothbury, E.C.

100.—CORWEN AND BALA.
Incorporated by 25 and 26 Vic., cap. 110 (30th June, 1862), to construct a line from Corwen to Bala. Length, 13½ miles. Capital, 120,000l. in 10l. shares; and 40,000l. on loan. Arrangements with Great Western, Vale of Llangollen, and Llangollen and Corwen. The first may subscribe 40,000l., and the second 10,000l.

By 28 Vic., cap. 81 (19th June, 1865), the company was authorised to construct an extension to the Bala and Dolgelly, and the latter to abandon a portion of its line. Joint station at Bala. No new capital. Opened 1st April, 1868.

A dividend at the rate of 1½ per cent. per annum was declared in September, when it was announced that the railways from Ruabon to Dolgelly were worked by the Great Western, as a through route in connection with their system, and that the result of the opening of the railway to Dolgelly exhibits a satisfactory increase in the traffic.

Meetings in February or March, and August or September.

No. of Directors—6 ; minimum, 3 ; quorum, 3. Qualification, 50 shares.

DIRECTORS:
Chairman—CHARLES JOHN TOTTENHAM, Esq., Plas Berwyn, Corwen.

William Price Jones, Esq., Bedweni, Bala.
R. J. D. Price, Esq., Rhiwlas, Bala.

William Wagstaff, Esq., Rûg, Corwen.
John Robertson, Esq., Llangollen.

OFFICERS.—Sec., John Jones, Solicitor, Oswestry ; Eng., Henry Robertson ; Solicitors, Longueville, Williams, Jones, and Williams, Oswestry.

101.—COVENTRY AND GREAT WESTERN JUNCTION.

Incorporated by 28 and 29 Vic., cap. 293 (5th July, 1865), to construct a line from Coventry to the Southam. Length, 10 miles. Capital, 200,000l. in shares, and 66,600l. on loan. Arrangements with Great Western and facilities to London and North Western. Mixed gauge.

No. of Directors—7; minimum, 3; quorum, 3 and 2. *Qualification, 500l.*

DIRECTORS:

Francis Wyley, Esq., Coventry.	Henry Soden, Esq., Coventry.
Andrew Hughes, Esq., Coventry.	Richard Hands, Esq., Coventry.
Richard Robbins, Esq., Coventry.	James Marriott, Esq., Coventry.

Solicitor, Edward Poole, Southam, near Rugby.

102.—COWBRIDGE.

Incorporated by 25 and 26 Vic., cap. 179 (29th July, 1862), for making railways from Cowbridge, in the county of Glamorgan, to join the Llantrissant and Taff Vale Junction, and the South Wales at the Llantrissant station. Length, 6 miles. Capital, 35,000l., in 3,500 shares of 10l. each; power to borrow on mortgage, 11,600l. Opened 18th September, 1865, and worked by Taff Vale.

REVENUE.—It was reported in March that there had been a considerable increase in the traffic during the past half-year, and that there was a probability that ultimately there would be some return to the shareholders on the capital expended.

DIRECTORS:

Chairman—ROBERT CHARLES NICHOLL CARNE, Esq., Nash Manor,
near Cowbridge.
Deputy-Chairman—JOHN WHITLOCK NICHOLL CARNE, Esq., D.C.L., Dimland
Castle, near Cowbridge.

Rowland Fothergill, Esq., M.P., Hensol Castle, near Cowbridge.	Hubert Churchill Gould, Esq.
John Homfray, Esq., Penlline Castle, near Cowbridge.	Gwilym Williams, Esq., Miscyn Manor, near Cardiff.

OFFICERS.—Sec., John Stockwood, Solicitor, Cowbridge; Eng., Alex. Bassett; Accountant, David Roberts.

Offices—Cowbridge.

103.—COWES AND NEWPORT (Isle of Wight).

Incorporated by 22 and 23 Vic., cap. 94 (8th August, 1859), for making a railway from West Cowes to Newport, in the Isle of Wight. Length, 5 miles. Capital, 30,000l. in 10l. shares; loans, 10,000l. Opened 1st July, 1862.

By 26 and 27 Vic., cap. 50 (August, 1863), the company was authorised to raise new capital to the extent of 20,000l. in shares, 5¼ per cent., and 6,500l. on loan.

By 27 and 28 Vic , cap. 58 (23rd June, 1864), several branches and extensions were authorised. Length, ½ mile. Capital, 12,000l, in shares, and 4,000l. on loan.

REVENUE.—It was reported in March that the earnings of the line for the half-year did not show any improvement, owing to the falling off of the through traffic, which previously to the opening of the Isle of Wight, passed through Newport. A slight increase, however, was reported for the six months ending 30th June.

Meetings in February and August, in London, or Newport, or Cowes, I.W.

No. of Directors—5; reduced to 3. *Qualification, 300l.*

DIRECTORS:

Chairman—The Hon. H. W. PETRE, Chelmsford, Essex.

H. J. Castle, Esq., 5, Chancery Lane, W.C.	George Hay Donaldson, Esq., Austin Friars, London. E.C.

OFFICERS.—Sec., Edward Lincoln, 2, Winchester Buildings, Great Winchester Street, London, E.C.; Eng., Henry Martin, 18, Abingdon Street, Westminster S.W.; Auditor, James Binfield Bird, West Cowes, Isle of Wight; Bankers, the National Provincial Bank of England.

104.—CRIEFF AND COMRIE.

Incorporated by 28 and 29 Vic., cap. 294 (5th July, 1865), to construct a line from Comrie to a junction with the Crieff and Methven. Length, 6½ miles. Capital, 40,000*l*. in shares, and 13,300*l*. on loan. Arrangements with Scottish Central, which subscribes 20,000*l*. and appoints one director. Running powers to Scottish North Eastern.

No. of Directors—6; minimum, 4; quorum, 3. *Qualification*, 250*l*.

DIRECTORS:

Sir Patrick Keith Murray, Bart.
Peter Drummond, Esq.
Daniel Ainslie, Esq., of the Gart, 48, Moray Place, Edinburgh.

Allan Cunningham Pagan, Esq.
James F. Wyllie, Esq., Bolfracks, Aberfeldy.
John Wilson, Esq., Hill Park, Bannockburn.

105.—CROESOR AND PORT MADOC.

Incorporated by 28 and 29 Vic., cap. 295 (5th July, 1865), to maintain an existing line from Carreg Hylldrem to Port Madoc, and to construct an extension to Borth-y-gest. Length, 1¼ mile. Capital, 25,000*l*. in shares, and 8,300*l*. on loan. Arrangements with Cambrian. In abeyance.

No. of Directors—5; quorum, 2. *Qualification*, 200*l*.

DIRECTORS:

Hugh Beaver Roberts, Esq.
Hugh A. Mackie, Esq.
Arthur T. Roberts, Esq.
Offices—Carnarvon.

Richard M. Preston, Esq.
John Ormiston, Esq.

106.—CROFTHEAD AND KILMARNOCK EXTENSION.

Incorporated by 28 and 29 Vic., cap. 139 (29th June, 1865), to construct a line from Crofthead to Kilmarnock, with a branch to Beith. Length, 20¼ miles. Capital, 240,000*l*. in shares, and 80,000*l*. by mortgage. Arrangements with Caledonian, which is to work the line and subscribe 140,000*l*. Works in progress.

By 29 and 30 Vic., cap. 108 (28th June, 1866), certain deviations were authorised to be made within four years from passing of the Act.

It was reported in September that, as considerable delay in the completion of the undertaking was unavoidable, the directors had made application to the Board of Trade for an extension of time for two years. The Board had ordered an inquiry into the financial position of the company preparatory to granting the desired extension. From the engineer's report it appeared that the whole works between Crofthead and Stewarton were proceeding in a satisfactory manner.

CAPITAL.—The receipts to 31st July, 1868, amounted to 155,516*l*., and the expenditure left a balance in hand of 14*l*. The receipts were detailed as under:—

Share capital	£119,489
Commercial Bank	8,941
„ „ Account No. 2.	19,200
„ „ Account No. 3.	4,800
Transfer fees	2
Surplus lands and houses	124
Interest account	2,959=£155,516

Meetings in February or March, and August or September.

No. of Directors—10; minimum, 6; quorum, 3. *Qualification*, 500*l*.

DIRECTORS:

Chairman—Lieut.-Colonel WILLIAM MURE, of Caldwell.

FOR THE CALEDONIAN RAILWAY.

Thomas Hill, Esq., of Merrylee.
John Cowan, Esq., 2, Park Circus Place, Glasgow.
James Clerk, Esq., 27, Park Circus, Glasgow

Andrew Buchanan, Esq., of Auchtentorlie.
J. C. Bolton, Esq., 27, West George Street. Glasgow.

FOR THE ORDINARY SHAREHOLDERS.

Lieut.-Colonel William Mure, of Caldwell.
Hugh Crawford, Esq., of Barr.
John Heys, Esq., of South Athurlie.

Peter Sturrock, Esq., Coalmaster, Kilmarnock.
William Ralston Patrick, Esq., of Roughwood.

OFFICERS.—Sec., James Keyden; Auditors, Robert Strang and Andrew Banna-tyne, Jun.; Eng., George Cunningham, C.E., Edinburgh; Solicitors, Keyden, Strang, and Keyden, Glasgow.

Office—186, West George Street, Glasgow.

107—CROMFORD AND HIGH PEAK.

(LEASED IN PERPETUITY TO THE LONDON AND NORTH WESTERN.)

This old-established canal and tramway (6th Geo. IV., cap. 30) was re-incorporated by Act 18 and 19 Vic., cap. 75 (June 26th, 1855). The undertaking consists of a railway from Peak Forest Canal to the Cromford Canal, and to a junction with the Manchester Buxton Matlock and Midlands Junction. The Cromford subscribes 3,750l. to the Stockport Disley and Whaley Bridge.

By 21 and 22 Vic., cap. 61 (28th June, 1858), the company was authorised to issue additional capital to the extent of 60,000l. at 6 per cent., on an equality with existing preference shares, and by borrowing to the extent of one-third of additional share capital.

By 25 and 26 Vic., cap. 66 (30th June, 1862), a lease to the London and North Western was authorised, and the capital re-arranged. This lease took effect on 25th March, 1861, at a rent of 3,500l. for the first year, and 4,000l. subsequently.

The meetings may be held in Derby twice a-year, or at such times and places as the directors appoint. Quorum of shareholders, 5; qualification, 10,000l.

*No. of Directors—*10; minimum, 5; quorum, 3. *Qualification,* 500l.

DIRECTORS :

Chairman—FRANCIS WRIGHT, Esq., of Osmaston Manor, near Derby.

Robert Broom, Esq., Burbage, near Buxton. | John Wright, Esq., Osmaston Manor, near
Philip Hubbersty, Esq., Wirksworth. | Derby.
William Jessop, Esq., Butterley Hall, near | James Charles Arkwright, Esq., Cromford.
Alfreton. |

OFFICERS.—Sec., Edward Lacey, Burbage, near Buxton; Auditors, Nathaniel Wheatcroft, Jun., Cromford, and George Staley, Butterley.

Office—Burbage, Buxton.

108.—CRYSTAL PALACE AND SOUTH LONDON JUNCTION.

Incorporated by 25 and 26 Vic., cap. 144 (17th July, 1862), with a view to effect railway communication from the Metropolitan Extension of the London Chatham and Dover, to the Crystal Palace at Sydenham. Length, 6¼ miles. Capital, 675,000l. in 10l. shares, in preferred and deferred half-shares, and 225,000l. on loan. Agreement with London Chatham and Dover, by which the Crystal Palace and South London receive out of the gross receipts from traffic booked between the Metropolitan Extension of the Chatham and Dover, and the Crystal Palace, as well as the traffic on that line, after deducting working expenses, in no case to exceed 60 per cent., the sum of 34,000l. per annum ; any excess in receipts above that sum to be divided equally between the two companies. Opened 1st August, 1865.

By 27 and 28 Vic., cap. 94 (23rd June, 1864), the company was authorised to connect the line with the Greenwich branch of the Chatham and Dover; also to let or transfer the undertaking to that company. Length, 1¼ mile. No new capital.

The directors reported in August that the capital had been raised under a prospectus wherein it was stated that an arrangement had been made with the London Chatham and Dover for working the line on certain advantageous terms. Though that arrangement was publicly represented as an accomplished fact the formalities required to render it legally binding were never completed : the London Chatham and Dover, however, entered upon and still retain possession of the line, alleging that they are working it " by request of, and at the cost of" this company. This statement is not in accordance with the facts of the case, and a suit has been instituted by a debenture holder, with the full concurrence of the Board, which will determine the occupation, and decide what payment this company shall receive for the use of the line. Although the circumstances under which the traffic is worked remain unaltered, the directors had much satisfaction in stating that the weekly returns prepared by the London Chatham and Dover indicated a very considerable growth in the receipts. The mileage proportion of receipts attributed to this Company for the 26 weeks ending 28th June last, is 6,505l. against 4,880l. for the corresponding period of last year, being an increase of 33 per cent.

CAPITAL.—The expenditure to 30th June, including arrears of interest on debentures (30,584*l.*), amounted to 861,368*l.*, which was represented by the subjoined statement of receipts:—

A Shares	337,500	
Less in hands of company	54,380=	£283,120
B Shares	337,500	
Less in hands of company and calls in arrear	4,425=	333,075
Debentures—Parliamentary limit	225,000	
Amount not borrowed	410=	224,590
Balance	20,583=	£861,368

DIRECTORS:

Chairman—J. E. LEVESON-GOWER, Esq., Finchampstead, Wokingham, Berks.

A. T. Hotham, Esq., Calverley Park, Tunbridge Wells.

Edwin Humby, Esq., Hamilton Terrace, St. John's Wood, N.W.

M. S. Lynch-Staunton, Esq., Athenæum Club.

OFFICERS.—Sec., W. E. Johnson ; Eng., F. T. Turner, 15, Parliament Street, Westminster, S.W.; Solicitors, Maynard and Co., Coleman Street, E.C.; Bankers, Barclay, Bevan, and Co., Lombard Street, E.C.; Auditors, J. Weise and Charles Banks.

Offices—2, Great Winchester Street Buildings, E.C.

109.—DARE VALLEY.

Incorporated by 26 and 27 Vic., cap. 171 (21st July, 1863), to construct a line from certain collieries to the Aberdare, with a branch to Hirwain. Length, 2½ miles. Capital, 35,000*l.* in 10*l.* shares, and 11,500*l.* on mortgage. Leased to Taff Vale for 21 years, at 5 per cent. upon cost of construction, the rent commencing in July, 1866. The traffic is reported to be gradually improving, and that the works are well maintained by the Taff Vale.

CAPITAL.—The expenditure on this account to 30th June, 1868, was stated at 47,892*l.* the receipts having been as under :—

Capital 10*l.* shares	£35,000	
Mortgage debentures	11,500	
Balance	1,392=	£47,892

No. of Directors—4 ; maximum, 6 ; quorum, 3. *Qualification*, 300*l.*

DIRECTORS :

Chairman—JAMES POOLE, Esq., Wick House, Durdham Down, Bristol.

Deputy-Chairman—WILLIAM DONE BUSHELL, Esq., Cardiff.

John J. Mogg, Esq., West Clifton, Bristol.

Ebenezer Lewis, Esq., Brocastle, Bridgend.

OFFICERS.—Sec., David Roberts, Cardiff; Eng., George Fisher, C.E., Cardiff.
Officers—Taff Vale Railway Office, Cardiff.

110.—DARTMOUTH AND TORBAY.

Incorporated by 20 and 21 Vic., cap. 103 (27th July, 1857), to make a railway from Torquay branch of South Devon to or near the town of Dartmouth. Capital, 90,000*l.* in 25*l.* shares; loans 30,000*l.* Length, 9 miles. Broad gauge. The Act contains powers to establish and maintain a ferry or steam communication between the proposed terminus, across the river Dart, to any pier or landing place in the borough of Dartmouth, and in any other place in or adjoining to the said river within half a mile on either side of the Dartmouth terminus; and for the purpose of such ferry, to purchase or hire and use steam vessels, and to make, on any lands belonging to the company, conveniences for the transit of traffic across such ferry. The Act also contians a power to purchase, maintain, and use the undertaking of the Dartmouth Floating Bridge Company. The first section to Paignton was opened for passenger traffic on the 2nd August, 1859. The second section to Brixham Road, 3 miles, was opened for passengers on 14th March, and for goods on 1st April, 1861, and the remainder on the 16th August, 1864. Worked by South Devon.

By 24 Vic., cap. 46 (7th June, 1861), the company was authorised to raise additional capital, to the extent of 32,000*l.*, at 6 per cent., and 10,800*l.* on mortgage. Also to cancel forfeited shares and to create debenture stock.

By 25 and 26 Vic., cap. 132 (7th July, 1862), the company obtained an extension of time to 1865, for completion of their works between Churston Ferrers and Brixham. Also to raise 52,500*l.*, at 6 per cent., in shares, and 17,500*l.* by mortgage.

SOUTH DEVON.—The agreement with this company, which took effect on 1st January, 1866, provides for the following annual payments to the Dartmouth:—

1866	£6,150	1868	£8,150
1867	7,150	1869	9,150

and during the 5th, and every subsequent year, of such a sum as will cover the interest on the debenture debt and preferential capital, not exceeding together 200,000*l.* The agreement further provides that the South Devon shall keep an account of the receipts of the Dartmouth for 10 years, and that deducting therefrom 50 per cent. for working expenses, there shall be paid to this company in perpetuity such an annual sum, in addition to that referred to in the preceding paragraph, as the net earnings on the average of the 8th, 9th, and 10th years, shall exceed the amount of the dividends and interest payable on the preference capital and debenture debt on the average of those years, and also for eventual amalgamation of the two companies, on equivalent terms.

REVENUE.—This account for the half-year ending 31st December showed a balance against the company of 8,070*l.* The revenue account for the half-year ending 30th June, embodied the following information:—

Debtor.		Creditor.	
Balance from December, 1867	£8,070	Half-year's rent from South Devon	£4,075
Income tax on rent for year, 1867.	148	Balance carried on	8,994
Do. on rent to June, 1868	101		
Half-year's interest on debentures	1,352		
Interest &c., on loans	3,200		
Salaries, office expenses, &c.	195		
	£13,069		£13,069

CAPITAL —The expenditure on this account to 30th June, amounted to 264,674*l.*, which had been thus provided for:—

Ordinary shares	£71,176
Debentures	54,800
Preference shares (No. 1.)	32,500
Do. do (No. 2.)	52,500
Temporary loans	53,697=£264,674

Meetings in February and August,

No. of Directors—6; minimum, 3; quorum, 3. *Qualification,* twenty 25*l.* shares.

DIRECTORS:

Chairman—CHARLES SEALE HAYNE, Esq., Kingswear, Dartmouth,
*John Belfield, Esq., Primley, Paignton. | *Henry Carew Hunt, Esq., Maisonette, Stoke Gabriel, Totness.
Henry Studdy, Esq., Waddeton Court, Stoke Gabriel, Torquay. | George Knight, Esq., 1, Great George Street, Westminster, S.W.
W. Froude, Esq., Chelston Cross, Torquay. |
* Retiring Directors, 1869.
Two of the directors retire annually, but are eligible for re-election.

OFFICERS.—Sec., A. E. Lhoyd; Eng., R. P. Brereton, 18, Duke Street, Westminster, S.W.; Auditors, †Percy Hockin, Solicitor, and Charles Vincent; Solicitor, J. H. Mackenzie, 1, Crown Court, Old Broad Street, London, E.C.; Bankers, the Devon and Cornwall Banking Company, Plymouth; Vivian, Kitson, and Kitson, Torquay.
† Retiring Auditor, 1869.

Offices—Newton Abbott.

111.—DAVENTRY.

Incorporated by 25 and 26 Vic., cap. 55 (30th June, 1862), to construct a line from Daventry to the Weedon station of the London and North Western. Length, 3¾ miles.
CAPITAL.—30,000*l.*, in 10*l.* shares; loans, 10,000*l.* Arrangements with London and North Western.

No. of Directors—6; minimum, 4; quorum, 3 and 2. *Qualification,* 100*l.*

DIRECTORS:

David Joseph Henry, Esq., 55, Kensington Gardens Square, W. | Henry Kingsford, Esq., 6, Queen's Gate Gardens, W.
Alfred Beeston, Esq., 4, Regent's Park Terrace, N.W. | Colonel Cole, 12, Lansdowne Road, Wimbledon, S.W.
George Tate, Esq., M.D., 65, Camden Road Villas, N.W. |

OFFICERS.—Secretary, Richard Stephens, Hampstead; Eng., George Willoughby Hemans, 13, Queen Square, Westminster, S.W.

Offices—1, Poet's Corner, Westminster Abbey, S.W.

112.—DEAL AND DOVER.

Incorporated by 28 and 29 Vic., cap. 296 (5th July, 1865), to construct lines from the Chatham to connect Deal and Walmer with Dover. Length, 9¼ miles. Capital, 150,000*l*. in shares, and 50,000*l*. on loan. The Deal Extension of the Chatham repealed, and arrangements made with that company to work the line. No progress has been made in this undertaking.

No. of Directors—6; quorum, 2. *Qualification*, 200*l*.

DIRECTORS:

Frederick Leith, Esq. | Archibald Park, Esq.
Walter Leith, Esq.

113.—DEESIDE.

Incorporated by 9 and 10 Vic., cap. 158 (16th July, 1846), for a line along the left bank of the Dee, by a junction with the Aberdéen. The capital was 220,000*l*., in 4,400 shares of 50*l*. Shares issued, 4,315, on which a deposit of 5*l*. per share was paid, amounting to 21,575*l*. Expenses of first Act, &c., 5,750*l*. Re-incorporated by an Act passed 28th May, 1852 (15 Vic., cap. 61), which repeals the original Act, and defines the present undertaking as commencing from the same point of junction with the Aberdeen, and terminating at Banchory; the remainder of the original scheme being abandoned. Length, 17 miles. Opened, 8th September, 1853.

EXTENSION TO ABOYNE.—By 20 and 21 Vic., cap. 49 (27th July, 1847), an extension from Banchory to Aboyne was authorised, the capital being furnished by a new list of original subscribers, and kept separate from that of old company. Capital 80,000*l*. in 10*l*. shares; loans, 26,000*l*. Length, 15¾ miles. Opened 3rd December, 1859. The new subscribers elect two directors to the Deeside Board, and vote separately on questions of dividend. The Deeside subscribes 5,000*l*., and furnishes rolling stock at cost price. When dividends are equal the stock may be united, and the two proprietaries become one. In operation 32½ miles.

By 25 and 26 Vic., cap. 88 (30th June, 1862), the Deeside was authorised to raise additional capital to the extent of 23,000*l*., at 5*l*. per cent., and 8,000*l*. on loan; also to maintain that portion of the extension which had been constructed beyond the authorised limits.

GREAT NORTH OF SCOTLAND.—By Act of 1866 the Deeside is leased to this company. The ordinary capital is guaranteed a minimum dividend of 7½ per cent., and the extension shares a minimum dividend of 3 per cent. for the first year, and 3¼ per cent., thereafter. When the gross earnings of the leased undertakings exceed 27,000*l*., one half of the excess to be appropriated among the holders of the original and extension shares in certain proportions, in addition to the minimum dividends above stated.

ABOYNE AND BRAEMAR.—Under the powers of this Act, the Deeside was authorised to issue new shares in either capital or both of the original capitals to the amount subscribed to that line.

REVENUE.—The following is the statement of traffic for the year ending 31st August, 1868, as certified by the auditors:—

DEESIDE.

Passenger traffic	£9,493	
Carriages, horses, dogs, and parcels	628	
Mails	125	=£10,246
Goods and minerals	7,220	
Less cartages and expenses of collection and delivery	394	
	£6,825	
Live stock	141 =	6,967
Miscellaneous receipts		207
		£17,422

EXTENSION.

Passenger traffic	£3,539	
Carriage, horses, dogs, and parcels......................	412	=£4,065
Mails	114	
Goods and minerals	2,616	
Live stock	69	= 2,685
Miscellaneous receipts	17	=£6,767

£24,190

The debenture and other interests and the guaranteed dividends
for the year amount to 14,884

Leaving a surplus for rents, taxes, and working expenses to Great
North of Scotland of... £9,306

The gross receipts had been regularly consigned in bank to the credit of the joint
committee nominated under the leasing agreement, in terms of its provisions to that
effect; and they retained thereout a sum sufficient to secure the regular payment of
the interests and dividends guaranteed under the lease. The accounts showed that,
after meeting all claims, there remained a surplus revenue of 9,306l.

CAPITAL.—The receipts on the Deeside have been 186,401l. and the expenditure
187,528l., showing a balance against the account, of 1,226l. The receipts on the Extension line have been 103,946l., and the expenditure 104,804l., exhibiting a balance against
receipts of 858l.

No. of Directors.—Maximum, 6; minimum, 3. *Qualification*, 50 shares.

DIRECTORS:

Chairman—JOHN DUNCAN, Esq., Advocate, Aberdeen.

Deputy-Chairman—PATRICK DAVIDSON, Esq., of Inchmarlo.

Alexander Burnett Whyte, Esq., Merchant, Aberdeen. | Francis Aberdein, Esq., of Keithock, Montrose.
*Thomas Ruxton, Esq., Advocate, Aberdeen. | *Alexander Davidson, Esq., of Desswood.

* Elected by Extension Shareholders.

OFFICERS.—Sec., William B. Ferguson, Aberdeen; Gen. Man., Robert Milne,
Aberdeen; Eng., Patrick M. Barnett, Aberdeen; Auditors, George Marquis and James
Augustus Sinclair, Aberdeen.
Offices—Aberdeen.

114.—DELABOLE AND BOSSINEY.

Incorporated by 29 and 30 Vic., cap. 347 (6th August, 1856), to construct a railway
from Delabole to Bossiney, with an extension to Bossiney Harbour, and a branch to
Trewarmet, in Cornwall. Length, 4½ miles. Capital, 80,000l. in 10l. shares, and
26,500l. on loan.

No. of Directors—5; minimum, 3; quorum, 3 and 2. *Qualification*, 500l.

DIRECTORS:

Samuel Grahame Bake, Esq. | William Ponsonby Llewellyn, Esq.
Edward Parry, Esq. | Henry Wakefield, Esq.
Thomas Parker, Esq. |

115.—DENBIGH, RUTHIN, AND CORWEN.

Incorporated by 23 and 24 Vic., cap. 164 (July 23rd, 1860), to construct a line from
the Vale of Clwyd, at Denbigh, to Corwen, by a junction by the Llangollen and Corwen. Length, 17 miles. Capital, 150,000l. in 10l. shares; loans, 50,000l. Opened to
Ruthin, 6½ miles, on 1st March, 1862; to Corwen, 11¾ miles, October, 1864.

By 25 and 26 Vic., cap. 60 (30th June, 1862), the company was authorised to attach
a preference of 5 per cent. to any amount of forfeited shares which could not be sold
at a price equal to the arrears of calls due thereon. These ordinary shares have been
cancelled and 48,000l. preference 10l. shares have been issued.

By 28 and 29 Vic., cap. 190 (29th June, 1865), the company was authorised to raise
additional capital to the extent of 22,500l. in shares, and 7,500l. on loan. Also to
create debenture stock. Interchange of facilities with Vale of Clwyd.

It was reported at the half-yearly meeting held in October that a scheme was being prepared by the board to raise a sum sufficient to meet the liabilities and to recoup to revenue the sum applied therefrom for capital purposes. In the event of the scheme not receiving the sanction of the court, it was intended to give notice of application to Parliament for a bill during the next session to enable the board to raise the required amount. They hoped soon to be able to resume payment of the rent-charges and debenture interest. The traffic had been worked without the slightest accident to passengers. The revenue for the June half-year was 4,710l., being an increase of 150l. over that of the corresponding period of 1867. The receipts from all sources were 4,771l., and the working expenses 3,321l., including rates and taxes and repairs.

CAPITAL.—The receipts and expenditure on this account to 30th June, 1868, were detailed as follow:—

Received.		Expended.	
Ordinary shares	£88,604	On works, &c.	£183,729
Preference shares	53,160	Land (rent charges capitalised	
Debentures (less 900l., paid off)..	49,100	per contra)	29,623
Rent charges capitalised	29,623	Rolling stock	4,520
This capitalised value is the actual amount of the purchase money of land, and is represented by an annual charge of £1,445 13s. 2d.		Parliamentary expenses(Act 1865)	1,490
		Law charges (in pref. shares)	760
		Directors' fees 1865 (in pref. shares)	1,000
Bank interest (less commission)..	146	Deposit on Rhug estate	1,700
Balance	2,799	Nantclwyd tramway	610
	£223,434		£223,434

The general balance sheet to the same date furnished the subjoined particulars:—

Debtor.		Creditor.	
Clearing house	£475	Cash in hand and at the North and	
Station rent and engine hire	2,048	South Wales Bank	£654
Sundry creditors for stores, work work done, &c	507	Ditto in the hands of the Accountant-General	312
Debenture interest (arrears up to 30th June)	3,791	Sundry debtors for freights, stores, &c.	486
To rent charges (ditto)	2,028	Stores in hand	148
			£1,602
		Balance of capital account	2,799
		Balance of revenue account	4,449
	£8,850		£8,850

No. of Directors.—Maximum, 9; minimum, 6; quorum, 3. Qualification, twenty 10l. shares.

Election by shareholders agreeably to the provisions contained in "The Companies Clauses Consolidation Act, 1845."

DIRECTORS:

Chairman—JAMES ASHBURY, Esq., 9, Sussex Place, Hyde Park Gardens.

Deputy-Chairman—HENRY GARTSIDE, Esq., Wharmton Towers, Greenfield, near Manchester.

Spencer Henry Bickham, Esq., Gorsefield, Bowdon, near Manchester. | James Kershaw, Esq., Delamere Place, Ashton-under-Lyne.
Frederick Adolphus Fynney, Esq., Queen's Chambers, Manchester.

OFFICERS.—Traffic Man., Thomas Cartwright ; Sec., John Lloyd ; Eng., George Owen; Solicitor, S. F. Noyes, 1, Broad Sanctuary, Westminster, S.W.; Auditors, William Green and John Pierce, Ruthin.

Offices—7, Bank Buildings, Lothbury, E.C.

116.—DEVON AND CORNWALL.

Incorporated by 25 and 26 Vic., cap. 165 (17th July, 1862), to construct a line from the North Devon at Colebrook, to Okehampton. Length, 13 miles. Capital, 130,000l., in 20l. shares; loans, 43,000l. Arrangements with South Western. Opened to North Tawton on 1st November, 1865, and to Okehampton 8th January, 1867. In operation 10 miles.

By 26 and 27 Vic., cap. 129 (13th July, 1863), the company was authorised to extend the line from Okehampton to Lidford, on the Launceston and South Devon. Length, 10¾ miles. New capital, 160,000*l.* and 53,333*l.* on loan.

By 27 aad 28 Vic., cap. 114 (23rd June, 1864), the company was authorised to make certain deviations.

By 28 and 29 Vic., cap. 149 (29th June, 1865), the company was authorised to construct extensions to Bude and to Great Torrington, in connection with South Western. Length, 41¼ miles. Capital, 350,000*l.* in shares, and 116,600*l.* on loan. By the same Act the name cf the company was changed to " Devon and Cornwall."

By 30 and 31 Vic., cap. 125 (15th July, 1867), the Bude and Torrington Extensions were divided into four sections, each with separate capital. The shares of any portion of the company were also authorised to be divided into " preferred" and "deferred."

By 31 and 32 Vic., cap. 174 (31st July, 1868), the company obtained power to alter its line and levels, as also an extension of time till July, 1871, for completion of the Okehampton and Lidford Extensions.

Meetings in February or March, and in August or September.

No. of Directors.—Maximum, 10; quorum, 3. *Qualification*, 500*l.*

DIRECTORS :

Chairman—The Right Hon. THE EARL OF PORTSMOUTH, Eggesford House, North Devon, and Brooks's Club, S.W.

Deputy-Chairman—SHILSTON CALMADY HAMLYN, Esq., Paschoe House, Bow, North Devon.

George A. Hillier, Esq., Gresham House, Old Broad Street, E C.

James Hunt Holley, Esq., Oaklands, Okehampton, Devon.

The Hon. Mark G. Kerr Rolle, Stevenstone House, North Devon

Jno. Chapman, Esq , 2, Leadenhall St., E.C.

Francis John Thynne, Esq., Haynes Park, Bedford.

OFFICERS.—Sec.. Arthur Lankester, 2, Westminster Chambers, Westminster, S.W.; Eng., W. R. Galbraith, 1, Victoria Street, Westminster, S.W. ; Solicitors, Hodding, Townsend, and Co., 3, Princess Street, Westminster, S.W.

Offices—2, Westminster Chambers, Victoria Street, Westminster, S.W.

117.—DEVON AND SOMERSET.

Incorporated by 27 and 28 Vic., cap. 307 (29th July, 1864), to construct a line from the Bristol and Exeter, at Taunton, to Barnstaple. Broad gauge. Length, 43 miles. Capital, 500,000*l.* in 25*l.* shares, and 166,000*l.* on loan. Arrangements with Bristol and Exeter. Works in abeyance.

By 28 Vic., cap. 42 (26th May, 1865), an agreement with the Bristol and Exeter was confirmed by which that company is to work and maintain the Devon and Somerset in perpetuity.

By 29 Vic., cap. 17 (18th May, 1866), the company was authorised to effect various arrangements in its capital account; to cancel certain shares and to issue others in lieu thereof, in classes A. and B.; the former with a preference dividend of 5 per cent.

By 30 and 31 Vic., cap. 147 (15th July, 1867), the company was authorised to make certain deviations and to construct a junction with the Tiverton and North Devon.

By 30 and 31 Vic., cap. 182 (12th August, 1867), the company was authorised to extend the line at Barnstaple, by 1 mile in length, and to increase the capital of the company by 30,000*l.* in shares, and 10,000*l.* on loan.

By 30 and 31 Vic., cap. 172 (12th August, 1867), the Devon and Somerset was released from its obligations to contribute to the construction of the Ilfracombe.

It was reported in August that a scheme of arrangement had been filed in the Court of Chancery, as the only means of relieving the company from its difficulties and of enabling it to prosecute the works to completion of the undertaking. One of the principal provisions of the scheme gave power to create and issue a new stock to be called " A" debenture stock, to the amount of 270,000*l.*, being a first charge on the entire undertaking. It is to be irredeemable, and to carry interest at a rate not exceeding 6 per cent. Another provision of the scheme was that the future board of directors should consist of not less than six nor more than eight, of whom two should represent the holders of "A" debenture stock, and two the holders of "B" debenture stock, the remaining two or four, as the case might be, to represent the ordinary shareholders. The debenture "A" stock being a first charge upon the undertaking, induced the directors to entertain little doubt of being able to place out that stock; and, in this assurance, they had been in communication with Messrs. Brassey and Wythes for completion of the works from Taunton to Barnstaple, deterring for the present making the extension into the latter town. The "B" debentures would carry interest at the rate of 5 per cent., and would take precedence of all the other securities excepting the "A" debentures.

No. of Directors—9; minimum, 6; quorum, 3. *Qualification, 500l.*

DIRECTORS:

Chairman—The Right Hon. LORD POLTIMORE, Poltimore Park, Exeter,
Court Hall, Northmolton, Devon, and Brooks's Club, S.W.

Vice-Chairman—JOHN ARTHUR LOCKE, Esq., Northmore House,
Dulverton, Somerset.

Sir William Throckmorton, Bart., Coughton Court, Bromsgrove, Worcester.
John Thomas Nash, Esq., Elm Cottage, Southmolton, North Devon.

Thomas C. Sandars, Esq., Mitchenden Lodge, Southgate, N.
Henry Gorges Moysey, Esq., Bashealton Court, Somerset.

OFFICERS. — Sec., John M'Millan ; Eng., E. Birch, M.I.C.E., 7, Westminster Chambers, Victoria Street, S.W.; Solicitors, Riccard and Son, Southmolton, Devon; Bankers, the West of England and South Wales District Bank, Southmolton.

Offices—7, Westminster Chambers, S.W.

118.—DEVON VALLEY.

Incorporated by 21 and 22 Vic., cap. 122 (23rd July, 1858), to construct a line from Tillicoultry station of Stirling and Dunfermline, to the Fife and Kinross at Hopefield. Capital, 90,000l., in 10l. shares, and 30,000l. by loan. Length, 13¼ miles. Opened from Kinross to Rumbling Bridge, 7 miles, on 1st May, 1863.

By 24 and 25 Vic., cap. 200 (1st August, 1861), certain deviations and alterations of levels were allowed.

By 26 and 27 Vic., cap. 124 (13th July, 1863), the company was authorised to create preference shares in lieu of certain shares cancelled, and to reduce the capital from 90,000l. to 80,000l.

By 29 and 30 Vic., cap. 277 (30th July, 1866), the company was authorised to construct branches into the mineral districts of Fife and Clackmannan. Length, 16¼ miles. Capital, 95,000l. in shares, and 31,600l, on loan.

By 29 and 30 Vic., cap. 326 (6th August, 1866), the Devon Valley was authorised to raise additional capital to the extent of 20,000l. in shares, when agreement in relation to future amalgamation with, or lease to, the North British was comprised by the same Act, the latter company obtaining power to subscribe 60,000l. in B shares.

Meetings in March and September. Accounts made up to 31st January and 31st July.

No. of Directors—6 ; quorum, 3. *Qualification, 200l.*; certificate to accompany deed of transfer.

DIRECTORS:

Chairman—W. P. ADAM, Esq., M.P., of Blairadam, and 2, Ennismore Place,
Princess Gate, S.W.

Deputy-Chairman—HARRY YOUNG, Esq., of Cleish.

* George Robertson, Esq., W.S., Edinburgh.
Robert Scott Moncrieff, Esq., of Fossoway, Dalkeith Park.

*Alexander Crombie Matthew, Esq., M.D., Aberdeen.
*George Harrison, Esq., Merchant, Edinburgh.

* Represent the North British.

OFFICERS.—Sec., Alexander Patrick Lorimer ; Eng., Charles Jopp, C.E., Edinburgh ; Solicitor, A. J. Dickson, Edinburgh ; Auditors, George Bogie, Banker, Kinross, and Henry West Walker, Banker, Auchtermuchty ; Bankers, Royal Bank of Scotland

Offices—Tillicoultry.

119.—DINGWALL AND SKYE.

Incorporated by 28 and 29 Vic., cap. 223 (5th July, 1865), to construct a line from Dingwall to Kyle of Lochalsh, with a pier thereat. Length, 63½ miles. Capital, 450,000l. in shares, and 150,000l. on loan. Arrangements with Highland, which is to contribute 50,000l., and with Caledonian, which is to subscribe 100,000l. Works in progress, and line expected to be open early in 1870.

By 31 Vic., cap. 19 (29th May, 1868), the company was authorised to make several deviations, and also to reduce the capital to 400,000l. in shares, and 133,300l. on mortgage.

HIGHLAND.—For working arrangement with this company see "Highland."

CAPITAL.—This account at 31st August, 1868, exhibited the income and expenditure as follows;—

Received.		*Expended.*	
Deposit	£13,900	Preliminary and Parliamentary ...	£10,970
Calls paid in advance	426	General expenses	1,028
		Interest	263
			£12,262
		Balance	2,064
	£14,326		£14,326

No. of Directors—8; minimum, 5; quorum, 3. *Qualification*, 1,000l.

DIRECTORS:

Chairman—ALEX. MATHESON, Esq., M.P., of Ardross and Lochalsh, Ardross Castle, Ross-shire, and 38, South Street, W.

Deputy-Chairman—Sir JOHN STUART, of Lochcarron, Ross-shire.

The Right Hon. Lord Middleton, Applecross, Ross-shire, and 32, Albemarle Street, W.
The Hon. the Master of Lovat, Beaufort Castle, Beauly.
MacLeod of MacLeod, Dunvegan Castle, Skye, and South Kensington Museum, London.

Alex. G. Dallas, Esq., Hudson's Bay Co., London.
Eneas W. Mackintosh, Esq., M.P., of Raigmore, Inverness.
John Fowler, Esq., of Braemore, Ross-shire, and 2, Queen's Square Place, Westminster, S.W.

OFFICERS.—Sec., Andrew Dougall; Eng., Murdoch Paterson; Accountant, Wm. Gowenlock; Auditors, A. Penrose Hay and Robert Davidson, Inverness; Solicitors, Stewart and Rule, Inverness; H. and A. Inglis, W.S., Edinburgh; and Martin and Leslie, London.
Head Offices—Inverness.

120.—DOWNPATRICK, DUNDRUM, AND NEWCASTLE.

Incorporated by 29 and 30 Vic., cap. 362 (10th August, 1866), to construct a railway from Downpatrick through Dundrum, to Newcastle, County Down. Length, 11½ miles. Capital, 75,000l. in 10l. shares, and 25,000l. on loan.

By 31 and 32 Vic., cap. 68 (25th June, 1868), the company was authorised to reduce its capital to 60,000ll. in shares, and 20,000l. on mortgage. The Belfast and County Down was authorised to subscribe 10,000l. to the undertaking, and to enter into traffic arrangements. Opened in November, 1868.

CAPITAL.—The expenditure to 31st July, 1868, was stated at 20,662l., which has been thus provided for:—

Deposit on shares	£1,322
1st call	2,694
2nd call	2,314
3rd call	1,014
4th call	1,564
5th call	250
On account of calls paid after due date	24
Profit on re-sale of 5,700l new 3 per cent. consols, lodged with Accountant-General in Court of Chancery for deposit on bill	15
Northern Bank, balance due to them	10,464=£20,662

No. of Directors—5; quorum, 3. *Qualification*, 1,000l.

DIRECTORS:

William R. Anketell, Esq., J.P., Ardtulla, Belfast.
James T. Bristow, Esq., Wilmont, Belfast.
William Ewart, Esq., Jun., Glenmachan, Belfast.

James Hind, Esq., Lismara, Belfast.
Joseph J. Murphy, Esq., Oldforge, Belfast.
John Cleland, Esq., Vianstown, Downpatrick.
Charles Murland, Esq., Castlewellan.

OFFICERS.—Sec., Silas Evans; Engs., Sir John MacNeill and William Lewis; Solicitors, Hugh Wallace & Co., Belfast and Downpatrick; Auditors, John Lytle and Henry J M'Cance; Bankers, The Northern Banking Company, Belfast.
Offices—15, Waring Street, Belfast.

121.—DUBLIN AND ANTRIM JUNCTION.

Incorporated by 24 and 25 Vic., cap. 122 (11th July, 1861), to construct a line from the Ulster, at Lisburn, to the Belfast and Northern Counties, at Antrim. Length, 18½ miles. Capital, 120,000l. in 10l. shares; loans, 40,000l. Works in progress.

By 28 Vic., cap. 114 (19th June, 1865), the company was authorised to create preference shares in lieu of those unissued, surrendered, or forfeited, at a rate not exceeding 6 per cent.

By 29 and 30 Vic., cap. 179 (16th July, 1866), an extension of time for three years was obtained for completion of works; certain shares were authorised to be issued at a preference; and the Belfast and Northern Counties, or the Ulster, were permitted to lease the undertaking.

No. of Directors—6; minimum, 3; quorum, 3. *Qualification*, 400l.

DIRECTORS:
Chairman—The Rev. ARTHUR H. PAKENHAM, J.P., Langford Lodge, Crumlin, County Antrim.

Deputy-Chairman—WALTER T. STANNUS, Esq., J.P., Lisburn.

James Hunter, Esq., J.P., Dunmurry House, Dunmurry, County Antrim.
The Very Rev. The Dean of Ross, Lisburn.

Thomas Walkington, Esq., J.P., Ballinderry, County Antrim.

OFFICERS.—Sec., William Mackay, Belfast; Eng., John Bower, 60, Upper Sackville Street, Dublin; Solicitor, George K. Smith, The Castle, Belfast.
Offices—8 and 9, Donegall Place Buildings, Belfast.

122.—DUBLIN AND BALTINGLASS JUNCTION.

Incorporated by 27 and 28 Vic., cap. 329 (29th July, 1864), to construct a line from the Great Southern and Western, at Naas, to the town of Baltinglass. Length, 23¼ miles. Capital, 180,000l. in 10l. shares, and 60,000l. on loan.

Meetings in February and August.

No. of Directors—7; minimum, 5; quorum, 3. *Qualification*, 200l.

DIRECTORS:

Chairman—THOMAS PIM, Esq., Junior, William Street, Dublin.
William Jones Westby, Esq., High Park, Kittegan.

David Mahony, Esq., Grange Con, Athy.
Abraham Shackleton, Esq., Ballytore.

OFFICERS.—Sec., H. W. Kelly; Chief Eng., George W. Hemans; Resident Eng., James Dillon; Solicitors, Newtons and Armstrong.
Offices—62, Upper Sackville Street, Dublin.

123.—DUBLIN AND BELFAST JUNCTION.

Incorporated by 8 and Vic., cap. 130 (21st July, 1845), for a line from Drogheda to Newry, and thence to a junction with the Ulster, at Portadown, and to Navan. Productive mileage, including Banbridge Junction, 63 miles.

On 11th July, 1853, a special meeting authorised the directors to subscribe 5,000l. for shares in the Banbridge Junction.

By 11 Vic., cap. 100 (1847), amalgamation with the Drogheda, the Enniskillen, or the Ulster, is authorised.

By 27 Vic., cap. 12 (28th April, 1864), the capital and borrowing powers of the company were regulated, forfeited shares were cancelled, and the share capital reduced from 950,000l. to 873,500l. and the borrowing powers enlarged from 135,000l. to 291,150l.

BANBRIDGE.—This line (7 miles) was opened on the 23rd of March, 1859, and has since been worked by the Dublin and Belfast, to which it is leased, the traffic being returned on the united mileage—namely, 63 miles.

IRISH NORTH WESTERN.—By 22 and 23 Vic., cap. 41 (1st August, 1859), the Dublin and Belfast, as well as the Drogheda and Ulster, contributed 20,000l. to the line from Clones to Cavan. In return for its contribution this company receives preference shares of the Irish North Western, bearing interest at 4 per cent. per annum or such higher rate as may at any time be divided on the shares of that company.

REVENUE.—The receipts for the half-year ending 31st December amounted to 41,335l., against 42,293l., showing a decrease of 963l. The income of the company amounted to 42,103l. and the working expenses and taxes to 17,444l., the interest on loans to 5,915l., and the rent of the Banbridge to 1,000l., leaving 17,743l., to which was added 613l. from preceding half-year, making a disposable sum of 18,356l., from which a dividend at the rate of 4 per cent. per annum on the ordinary stock, left a balance of 887l.

The receipts for the half-year ending the 30th June amounted to 38,766l. The total income amounted to 39,640l., and the working expenses, rates, and taxes, to 15,887l., —leaving 23,753l. out of which 5,825l. was deducted for interest on loans and 1,000l. for rent of the Banbridge Junction, leaving 16,927l., to which was added 887l. balance from last account, making together 17,814l. A dividend at the rate of 4 per cent. per annum left 780l. for next account.

AMALGAMATION.—The question of the Amalgamation of the three lines between Dublin and Belfast, which had so frequently occupied the attention of the directors, with an anxious desire to carry out so desirable an arrangement, seemed now in a fair way of being settled. At a conference of members of the Dublin and Drogheda, Dublin and Belfast Junction, and Ulster Boards recently held, it was resolved to recommend to their respective shareholders that the three companies be amalgamated, on terms to be settled in case of difference by arbitration; and, further, that the companies should enter into a joint purse agreement with the Irish North Western, if the latter were so disposed, and thus to enable them to participate in the benefits to be derived from amalgamation.

CAPITAL.—This account showed that 1,128,696l. had been expended, leaving a balance against the account of 9,266l.

DIRECTORS:

Chairman—JOHN BARLOW, Esq., Sibyl Hill, Raheny, County Dublin.

Deputy-Chairman—WILLIAM DIGGES LA TOUCHE, Esq., 34, St. Stephen's Green, Dublin.

Samuel Law, Esq., Kilbarrack House, Raheny, County Dublin

James Hawkins, Esq., 20, Middle Gardiner Street, Dublin.

Henry Hutton, Esq., Edenfield, Dundrum, County Dublin.

Thomas Hone, Esq., Yapton, Monkstown, County Dublin.

Robert Culley, Esq., Tudor Hall, Monkstown, County Dublin.

Francis Donagh, Esq., Newtown, Drogheda.

John T. Reilly, Esq., Scarvagh House, Scarvagh, County Down.

James C. Colvill, Esq., Coolock House, Coolock, County Dublin.

Directors all eligible for re-election.

OFFICERS.—Sec., Geo. Wm. Greene; Eng., Wm. Mc. Cartan; Consulting Eng., James Barton; Traffic Supt., Thomas Cowan; Loc. Sup., Henry Harden; Cashier and Accountant, Thomas Mac Blain; Audit Accountant, J. Alfred Leadbetter; Auditors, Robert Warren, Junior, 40, Rutland Square, Dublin, and Samuel Bewley, Dame Street, Dublin; Solicitor, R. D. Kane, 89, Talbot Street, Dublin.

Head Offices—83, Talbot Street, Dublin; Engineer's and Traffic and Locomotive Superintendent's Offices—Dundalk.

124.—DUBLIN AND DROGHEDA.

Incorporated by 7 Wm. IV., cap. 132 (August, 1836), for a line connecting those towns (31¾ miles), opened 26th May, 1844, with a branch to Howth (3¾), opened 30th July, 1846. The company also obtained (by 2 Vic., cap. 186), a transfer of the Navan branch, constructed by the Dublin and Belfast Junction, at a cost of 183,433l., with power to extend the same to Kells.

By 22 and 23 Vic., cap. 37 (1st August, 1859), the company was authorised to create debenture stock, at 5 per cent., to pay off existing mortgages, and to create new shares for the purpose of redeeming existing preference stock. The station at Dublin was also allowed to be enlarged, and certain streets stopped up.

By 23 and 24 Vic., cap. 114 (3rd July, 1860), an extension from Kells to Oldcastle (12¼ miles) was authorised. Opened 17th March, 1863. Miles in operation, 75.

IRISH NORTH WESTERN.—Under this company's Act of 1859 the Dublin and Drogheda subscribes 20,000*l.* to that undertaking.

REVENUE.—The receipts for the half-year ending 31st December were 52,231*l.*, out of which, after payment of all prior charges, a dividend of 2*l.* 7*s.* 6*d.* for the half-year, left a balance of 3,084*l.* Of this sum 500*l.* was credited to the renewal of bridges, and the remainder carried to next account..

The receipts for the half-year ending 30th June, amounted to 46,254, and for the half-year ending 30th June, 1868, to 47,826*l.*, showing an increase of 1,572*l.* The net surplus, after providing for current expenses, interest on loans, and dividends on preference shares and stocks, was 17,244*l.*, out of which a dividend on the ordinary stock at the rate of 5 per cent. left a balance of 1,124*l.* There was an increase of 1,795*l.* in the passenger traffic, and of 612*l* for the conveyance of mails; but there was a falling off in the receipts for goods of 824*l.*

AMALGAMATION.—The August report stated that the question of the amalgamation of the three companies owning the railways between Dublin and Belfast had been considered by the several boards, and it had been resolved by them to recommend to their respective shareholders that the Dublin and Drogheda, the Dublin and Belfast Junction, and the Ulster be amalgamated on terms to be settled, in case of difference, by arbitration; and also that the companies shall enter into a joint purse agreement with the Irish North Western, should that company be so disposed, so as to enable it to participate in the benefit to be derived from amalgamation.

NEW CAPITAL.—At a special meeting held on 27th February, 1868, it was resolved:— "That for the purpose of redeeming a portion of the five per cent. preference shares of the company, created on the 20th August, 1852, and the 2nd October, 1857, being 5,031 shares of twenty-five pounds each, and numbered 1,770 to 6,800, both inclusive, there be now raised, pursuant to the provisions of the Dublin and Drogheda Act, 1859, and the several other Acts of the company, the sum of 5,775*l.*, by the creation of stock, to be called 'Guaranteed 4 per cent. stock,' which shall bear a fixed dividend of 4*l.* per centum per annum in perpetuity, and the further sum of 120,000*l.*, by the creation of stock, to be called 'Guaranteed 4½ per cent. stock,' which shall bear a fixed dividend of 4*l.* 10*s.* per centum per annum in perpetuity, and that such several dividends of 4 per cent. per annum and 4½ per cent. per annum shall become due in half-yearly portions, on the 1st day of April and 1st day of October in every year, to the then registered proprietors of said stocks, and to be payable in ten days after the same shall have become due as aforesaid, and which said 4 per cent. stock and 4½ per cent. stock shall have attached thereto such privileges by way of preference or priority in payment of dividends over other shares or stock of the company as the said preference 5 per cent. shares now have over such other shares or stock, and that no person shall hold less of either of the said 4 per cent. and 4½ per cent. stocks than 25*l.* at any one time, and that no transfer thereof shall convey any fractional part of 1*l.* sterling, and that the directors be, and they are hereby authorised to allot and dispose of the said 4 per cent. and 4½ per cent. stocks, respectively, in such manner and subject to such terms and conditions as the directors shall, from time to time, fix and determine."

CAPITAL.—The receipts and disbursements on this account to 30th June, 1868, were detailed as follows:—

Received.		Expended.	
Capital stock	£637,922	Main line	£714,470
Guaranteed 4*l.* per cent. stock, perpetual	94,225	Ulster gauge (alteration of)	3,367
Preference 5*l.* per cent. shares, redeemable, 6,231 @ 25*l.*	155,775	Howth branch	35,644
		Navan branch	184,325
	£887,922	Kells extension	46,034
		Oldcastle extension	75,249
Debenture stock:—			£1,059,091
4*l.* per cent. perpetual	43,722	Rolling stock:—	
Loans on mortgage	252,698	Carriages, wagons, &c.	60,510
	£1,184,342	Locomotives	50,508
Balance	4,313	Irish North Western Co., paid on account of Clones Extension	18,546
	£1,188,656		£1,188,656

The accounts made up to 30th June and 31st December; and the statutory meetings are held in Dublin, in February or March, and August or September.

Scale of Voting—1 vote for each 75*l*. stock as far as 20 ; and one additional vote for every 375*l*. above 20.

Certificate must accompany transfer deed.   Registration fee, 2*s*. 6*d*. each deed, whether a bond or share be conveyed, but only one class of share can be put on a deed.

No. of Directors.—Maximum, 12; minimum, 3. *Qualification*, 750*l*.

DIRECTORS :

Chairman—JAMES WILLIAM MURLAND, Esq., 25, Fitzwilliam Square, Dublin.

Deputy-Chairman—WILLIAM EVANS, Esq., 38, Gordon Square, W.C.

T. M. Gresham, Esq., Raheny Park, near Dublin.	Peter Eckersley, Esq., Manchester.
J. F. Meade, Esq., 37, Eccles Street, Dublin.	Nich. Jas. Lalor, Esq., Dublin.
Hugh Law, Esq., Dublin.	Luke John M'Donnell, Esq., Dublin.
H. T. Vickers, Esq., Dublin.	Lucius O. Hutton, Esq., Dublin.
	Peter Verdon, Esq., Drogheda.

OFFICERS.—Sec. and Gen. Man., Joseph Pope Culverwell; Res. Eng., Marcus Harty ; Auditors, Robert Warren, Jun., and Samuel H. Close; Solicitor, Richard D. Kane, 89, Talbot Street, Dublin; Accountant, William Thompson.

Head Offices—Amiens Street, Dublin.

125.—DUBLIN AND KINGSTOWN.

Incorporated by 1 and 2 William IV., cap. 69, for a line from Dublin to Kingstown, open since 17th December, 1834 (6 miles) ; subsequently an extension of 1¾ mile was made, on the atmospheric system, to Dalkey, altered in 1856 to a locomotive branch, in connection with the Dublin and Wicklow.

In 1846 an Act was obtained for an extension to Bray (7½ miles), which, under the Act incorporating the Dublin and Wicklow, has been transferred to that company, including the Dalkey branch.

The whole of the Kingstown is now in the hands of the Dublin Wicklow and Wexford.   The dividends for the year have been at the rate of 9½ per cent.

CAPITAL.—The receipts in stock have been 350,000*l*., and on debentures, at 4 per cent, 70,000*l*.   The expenditure to 31st August, 1868, left a balance in hand of 1,446*l*.

Certificates are required to accompany transfer deed. Registration fee, 1*s*. per 100*l*. stock, but not exceeding 5*s*. on any one deed.

No. of Directors—9. *Qualification*, 1,000*l*.

DIRECTORS :

Chairman—*ALEXANDER FINDLATER, Esq., Kingstown.

Deputy-Chairman—*THOMAS HONE, Esq., Monkstown.

George Pim, Esq., Brennanstown, Cabinteely.	Jonathan Pim, Esq. M.P., Monkstown, and 115, Jermyn Street, S.W.
William Haughton, Esq., Roebuck.	Henry Pim, Esq., Lower Baggot Street, Dublin.
Joseph Kincaid, Esq., Herbert Street, Dublin.	Robert Samuel Palmer, Esq., Merrion Square, Dublin.
*Alexander Boyle, Esq., Killiney.	

* Retire in March next, but re-eligible.

OFFICERS.—Sec., Joseph B. Pim ; Solicitor, Joseph Hone, Foster Place, Dublin.

Office—35, Westland Row, Dublin.

126.—DUBLIN AND MEATH.

Incorporated by 21 and 22 Vic., cap. 119 (23rd July, 1858), to construct a line from a junction with the Midland Great Western at Clonsilla, to a junction at Navan, with the Navan and Kells branch of the Dublin and Drogheda (over which branch, running powers are secured), with a branch from Kilmessan to Trim and Athboy.   Length, 23 miles ; branch, 12 miles.   Opened from Clonsilla to Navan, 23 miles, 29th August, 1862 ; branch to Athboy, 26th February, 1864.   In operation, 35 miles.

By 25 Vic., cap. 39 (3rd June, 1862), the company was authorised to raise additional capital to the extent of 45,000*l*., preference interest not to exceed 6 per cent.; and 15 000*l*. on loan.   Also to cancel and re-issue forfeited shares at like preference.

By 27 Vic., cap. 28 (23rd May, 1864), the company was authorised to raise new capital to the extent of 75,000*l*. in shares, and not exceeding 6 per cent. preference, and 25,000*l*. on loan.

The Dublin and Meath subscribes 40,000l. to the Navan and Kingscourt, which see.

The receipts for the half-year ending 30th June, amounted to 7,548l. as compared with 6,566l. The working expenses had been reduced by 5 per cent., while for renewals and repairs the outlay was somewhat in excess of the corresponding period in 1867. Credit was due to the management of the receiver, but the directors were of opinion that the interests of the company would be best served by their resumption of the control of the undertaking at the earliest possible date.

No. of Directors—7 ; quorum, 3. *Qualification*, 1,000l.

DIRECTORS:

Chairman—SAMUEL GURNEY SHEPHARD, Esq., Threadneedle Street, E.C.

William Blackmore, Esq., Founders Court, Lothbury, E.C. | James Coates, Esq., Gresham Street, E.C.
William Montagu Baillie, Esq., Bristol.

OFFICERS.—Sec., William Huxley ; Manager, John Dowd; Bankers, Provincial Bank of Ireland and the Union Bank of London.

Offices—10, Angel Court, Throgmorton Street, E.C.

127.—DUBLIN METROPOLITAN JUNCTIONS.

Incorporated by 28 and 29 Vic., cap. 382 (6th July, 1865), to construct several lines in or near Dublin, connecting the Rathmines with the Wicklow and Wexford, and the Great Southern and Western. Length, 5½ miles. Capital, 160,000l. in shares, and 53,000l. on loan. Arrangements with Wicklow and Wexford. Works not commenced

No. of Directors—6 ; quorum, 3. *Qualification*, 500l.

DIRECTORS:

Sir Percy Nugent, Bart., D.L.,J.P.,Donore, Multifarnham, Westmeath, and 42, Upper Sackville Street, Dublin.
Sir John Gray, M.P., J.P., Charleville House, Rathmines; Prince's Street, Dublin ; and Whitehall Club, S.W. | Joseph Kincaid, Esq., 3, Herbert Street, Dublin.
Daniel Treacy, Esq., 48, Pembroke Road, Dublin.
Major Lawrence Edward Knox, M.P., 53, Fitzwilliam Square North, Dublin.

OFFICERS.—Sec., R. Crofton Lawrenson, 41, Grosvenor Square, Rathmines, Dublin ; Con. Eng., Charles Vignoles, F.R.S., &c., 41, Duke Street, Westminster, London, S.W.; Engs.-in-Chief, Joseph Kincaid, C.E., 20, Spring Gardens, London, S.W., and Henry Brett, C.E., 8, Harrington Street, Dublin ; Auditors, Henry Robert Perry, 9, Burgh Quay, Dublin, and James Lynch Byrne, 19, Lower Pembroke Street, Dublin; Solicitors, James Dillon Meldon and Son, 14, Upper Ormond Quay, Dublin ; Architect, Edward Henry Carson, C.E., F.R.I.A.I., 25, Harcourt Street, Dublin ; Brokers, Edward Fox, Dame Street, and Smyth and Du Bedat, College Green, Dublin ; Bankers, The Royal Bank, Dublin, The Hibernian Bank, Dublin, and its branches, The National Bank, London and Dublin, and its branches.

Offices—136, St. Stephen's Green West, Dublin.

128.—DUBLIN, RATHMINES, RATHGAR, ROUNDTOWN, RATHFARNHAM, AND RATHCOOLE.

Incorporated by 27 and 28 Vic., cap. 281 (29th July, 1864), to construct lines from the Dublin Wicklow and Wexford to the place mentioned. Length, 14¾ miles. Capital, 200,000l., in 10l. shares, and 83,000l. on loan. Arrangements with Dublin Wicklow and Wexford.

By 28 and 29 Vic., cap. 265 (5th July, 1865), the company was authorised to extend the line to Blessington, and in Dublin. Length, 9¼ miles. Capital, 200,000l. in shares, and 66,000l. on loan. Works not commenced.

DIRECTORS:

Sir Percy Nugent, Bart., D.L., J.P., Donore, Multifarnham, Westmeath, and 42, Upper Sackville Street, Dublin.
Sir John Gray, M.P., J.P., Charleville House, Rathmines; Prince's Street, Dublin; and Whitehall Club, S.W. | Daniel Treacy, Esq., 48, Pembroke Road, Dublin.
Major Lawrence Edward Knox, M.P., 53, Fitzwilliam Square North, Dublin.
Joseph Kincaid, Esq., 3, Herbert Street, Dublin.

OFFICERS.—Sec., R. Crofton Lawrenson, 41, Grosvenor Square, Rathmines, Dublin; Con. Eng., Charles Vignoles, F.R.S., &c., 21, Duke Street, Westminster, London, S.W.; Engs.-in-Chief, Joseph Kincaid, C.E., 20, Spring Gardens, London, S.W., and Henry Brett, C.E., 8, Harrington Street, Dublin; Solicitors, James Dillon Meldon and Son, 14, Upper Ormond Quay, Dublin; Architect, Edward Henry Carson, C.E., F.R.I.A.I., 25, Harcourt Street, Dublin; Brokers, Edward Fox, Dame Street, and Smyth and Du Bedat, College Green, Dublin; Bankers, The Royal Bank, Dublin, The Hibernian Bank, Dublin, and its branches, The National Bank, London and Dublin, and its branches.

Offices—136, St. Stephen's Green West, Dublin.

129.—DUBLIN TRUNK CONNECTING.

Incorporated by 27 and 28 Vic., cap. 321 (29th July, 1864), to construct railways and tramways in and near the city of Dublin, so as to connect the whole of the lines having stations in that city.   Length, 8½ miles.   Capital, 255,000l. in 10l. shares, and 85,000l. on loan. In abeyance.

By 28 and 29 Vic., cap. 221 (5th July, 1865), the company was authorised to make several junctions and deviations.   New capital, 24,000l. in shares, and 8,000l. on loan. Half-shares may be issued in lieu of cancelled or unissued shares.

By 30 and 31 Vic., cap. 205 (15th August, 1867), the company obtained an extension of time till 15th August, 1870, for the completion of works.

It was reported in August, that in the previous half-year's accounts the sum of 72,581l. was shown as the arrears of calls due.   That amount included the arrears on the shares added to the register at the last half-yearly meeting; but, acting on the authority of the judgment delivered by Vice-Chancellor Giffard, in the case of A. Eustace, one of the allottees, who disputed his liability, the directors have corrected the register, by removing therefrom all the additional shareholders added under like circumstances at such half-yearly meeting, and the arrears shown on the books on such shares have been written off the capital account, reducing the arrears of calls to 37,579l., as stated. Since the last half-yearly meeting judgment has been recovered against the late secretary for the amount of calls claimed in the action against him.   Further, the bills of costs to the amount of 2,579l. have been rendered by the late solicitors, Messrs. Kernaghan and Saunders, who have commenced proceedings for the recovery of the amount. The action against Kernaghan and Saunders is still pending. Mr. Kernaghan has applied for and obtained an injunction of the Master of the Rolls against the directors applying any funds of the company in the suit of "Williams v. O'Meara," consequent upon the resolutions passed at the special meeting. The contractors' plant and materials, which cost many thousands of pounds, realised only 1,357l., which is subject to further reduction for expenses.

No. of Directors—7; minimum, 4; quorum, 3.   *Qualification*, 250l.

DIRECTORS:

Chairman—S. D. WILLIAMS, Jun., Esq., Edgbaston, Birmingham.
Vice-Chairman—W. B. PATRICK, Esq., Upper Clapton, N.E.

F. R. Bluett, Esq., Stanhope Villa, Bromley, Kent.	John Gethen, Esq., 29, Carlton Road, Westbourne Park, W.
Jos. Wright, Esq., Oak Villa, Surbiton, S.W.	

OFFICERS.—Sec., James Hutt; Solicitors, Hayes, Twisden, and Co., 60, Russell Square, London.

Offices—Messrs. Hutt and Browne's, Public Accountants, 2, Westminster Chambers, Westminster, S.W.

130.—DUBLIN, WICKLOW, AND WEXFORD.

Originally incorporated as the WATERFORD WEXFORD WICKLOW AND DUBLIN by Act 9 and 10 Vic., cap. 208 (16th July, 1846), for the construction of a line from Dundrum, near Dublin, to Waterford, and a branch from Kingstown (where it joins the Dublin and Kingstown) to Bray, forming a junction near Bray with the former or main line. Powers also over a line from Dundrum to Dublin, which was afterwards purchased up from the Dublin Dundrum and Rathfarnham; the latter company has since been formally dissolved, by 20 and 21 Vic., cap. 29 (3rd July, 1857), and merged with the undertaking in the Dublin and Wicklow. Several Acts had been obtained between 1846 and 1857; and by 14 and 15 Vic., cap. 108 (24th July, 1851), the undertaking was re-constructed, the original capital reduced to 500,000l., with borrowing powers for 166,666l., the portions of the original line beyond Wicklow to Wexford and Waterford abandoned, and the name of the company changed to the Dublin and Wicklow. Additional capital authorised by the above Act of 1857, 200,000l., which has been raised in 10*l.* shares at 6 per cent. perpetual preference, with borrowing powers for 66,666*l.* These, and the original shares, have since been converted into stock.

By 22 and 23 Vic., cap. 80 (8th August, 1859), the company was authorised to extend its line from Wicklow to Gorey, in county Wexford. Length, 31 miles. New capital, 200,000*l.*, with 66,000*l.* on mortgage.

By 23 Vic., cap. 47 (15th May, 1850), the name of the company was again changed as above, and an extension from Gorey to Enniscorthy in the same county (18 miles) authorised. Additional share capital, 100,000*l.*, borrowing power, 33,300*l.*

By 24 Vic., cap. 11 (17th May, 1861), the company obtained powers to make deviation in the line of the Gorey Extension, to be completed within four years. Opened to Enniscorthy, 34 miles, 16th November, 1863.

By 26 and 27 Vic., cap. 86 (22nd June, 1863), the company was authorised to purchase additional lands, to construct a branch (16½ miles) to Shillelagh; and to raise new capital to the extent of 145,000*l.* in shares, and 48,300*l.* on loan. Opened 22nd May, 1865.

By 27 and 28 Vic., cap. 126 (23rd June, 1864), several deviations and extensions were authorised. Length of new line, 16 miles. New capital, 150,000*l.* in shares and 50,000*l.* on loan.

By 28 and 29 Vic., cap. 222 (5th July, 1865), the company was authorised to construct a connection with the Dublin and Kingstown. Length, 2¾ miles. Capital, 150,000*l.* in shares, and 50,000*l.* on loan.

The Dublin and Kingstown is also in the hands of the Dublin and Wicklow, under lease of 30th June, 1856, which took effect on and from 1st July, 1856, for 35 years, with a clause of renewal for a second term of 35 years (see Dublin and Kingstown). In operation, 106 miles.

By 31 and 32 Vic., cap 62 (25th June, 1868), the company obtained an extension of time till 1873, for the construction of the Wexford branch, and the Kingstown connecting branches. Also to consolidate the whole of the preferential stocks of the company into one 5 per cent. preferential.

REVENUE.—The receipts for the half-year ending 31st December, amounted to 90,005*l.*, showing an increase of 1,572*l.* The depression in the sulpher ore trade had caused a decrease in the quantity of minerals carried over the line during the half-year of 5,792 tons, as compared with the corresponding period of 1866. The balance of revenue available for dividend was 21,655*l.*, out of which the dividends upon the preference shares left a balance of 2,654*l.* to next account.

The receipts for the half-year ending 30th June were 82,287*l.*, showing an increase of 3,835*l.* The working expenses had been increased by 4,166*l.*, in consequence of 5,383*l.* being charged on account of the accident at Bray.

The balance on revenue account amounted to 16,843*l.*, out of which payment of the dividend of the preference stocks, together with the 2 per cent. of arrears left due on the half-year ending 31st December, 1867, absorbed 16,500*l.*, and left 343*l.* to next account.

CAPITAL.—The gross expenditure to 30th June, 1868, amounted to 1,808,576*l.*, which left a balance against the account of 59,204*l.*

Meetings half-yearly, in February and August, in Dublin. Accounts made up to 31st December and 30th June.

Transfer fee, 2*s.* 6*d.* each deed. Certificates for stock must accompany transfer deed. Transfer books close 21 days before meetings. Proxies, 48 hours at least.

DIRECTORS:

Chairman—LAURENCE WALDRON, Esq., Ballybrack, Dalkey, County Dublin, Killenaule, Thurles, County Tipperary, and 38, Rutland Square West, Dublin.

Deputy-Chairman—Sir JAMES POWER, Bart., M.P., 27, Merrion Square North, Dublin, Edermine, Enniscorthy, County Wexford, and Hatchett's Hotel, Piccadilly, W.

Hon. Frederick G. B. Ponsonby, 3, Mount Street, Grosvenor Square, London, W., and Coollattin, Carnew, County Wicklow.

John Francis Waller, Esq., LL.D., 4, Herbert Street, Dublin.

Thomas Vance, Esq., J.P., Blackrock House, Blackrock, County Dublin.

Richard Martin, Esq., 7, Merrion Square, South, and 33, Rogerson's Quay, Dublin.

Wm. Foot, Esq., 23, Rutland Square North, Dublin.

Alexander Parker, Esq., 46, Rathmines Upper, County Dublin.

Robert Gray, Esq., Temple Hill, Blackrock, County Dublin.

Joseph Boyce, Esq., 52, Upper Mount Street, Dublin.

Valentine O'Brien O'Connor, Esq., 3, Beresford Place, Dublin, and Rockfield House, Newtownpark Avenue, Blackrock, County Dublin.

OFFICERS.—Sec., E. William Maunsell, 14, Montpellier Parade, Monkstown, County Dublin; Eng., John Chaloner Smith, C.E., Bray; Traffic-Man., W. L. Payne, Harcourt Street Terminus, Dublin; Loc.-Supt., John Wakefield, Grand Canal Street, Dublin; Auditors, R. J. Devitt, Commercial Buildings, Dublin, and Robert Hoey, Jun.. Chapelizod Mills, County Dublin; Solicitor, George Keogh, 50, Westland Row, Dublin. Offices—48, Westland Row, Dublin.

131.—DUNDALK AND GREENORE.

Incorporated by 26 and 27 Vic., cap. 233 (28th July, 1863), to construct a line from the Irish North Western, at Dundalk, to Greenore. Length, 18 miles. Capital, 110,000l. in 25l. shares, and 36,600l. on loan.

By 30 and 31 Vic., cap. 183 (12th August, 1867), the company obtained an extension of time till 12th August, 1870, for completion of the works on hand and also to construct an extension at Dundalk, as well as to complete the joint works authorised by the Newry and Greenore Act 1863. Length, ¾ of a mile. New capital, 50,000l. in shares, and 16,600l. on loan. Also to issue debenture stock at 5 per cent. Arrangements with Irish North Western and London and North Western (which latter may subscribe 130,000l.), and facilities to Ulster and Midland Great Western.

No. of Directors—8; minimum, 10; quorum, 3. *Qualification*, 500l.

DIRECTORS:

The Earl of Erne, Crom Castle, Newtown Butler, and 95, Eaton Square, S.W.

Samuel Robert Graves, Esq., M.P., Liverpool.

Richard Allen Minnett, Esq., Derrygooney Lodge, Cortubber, Ballybay.

Lord Alfred Paget, 56, Queen Anne Street, Cavendish Square, W.

George Sheward, Esq., 17, Leinster Square, Bayswater, W.C.

Oscar L. Stephen, Esq., Bardon Hall, Leicester.

Patrick James Byrne, Esq., Lisnawilly, Dundalk.

Robert Haig, Esq., Fane Valley, Dundalk.

OFFICERS.—Sec., Stephen Reay, Euston Station, London; Eng.-in-Chief, James Barton, Dundalk; Auditors, William Robson, Dundalk, and Samuel Bradford, Jun., Carnbeg, Dundalk; Solicitors, Macrory and Co., Rutland Square West, Dublin, and Belfast.

132.—EAST GLOUCESTERSHIRE.

Incorporated by 27 and 28 Vic., cap. 285 (29th July, 1864), to construct lines from Cheltenham to Witney, and to Faringdon. Length, 50 miles; mixed or narrow gauge. Capital, 600,000l. in 10l. shares, and 200,000l. on loan. Arrangements with Midland and Bourton-on-the-Water. It was reported in September, 1865, that the rejection by parliament of the proposition to enable the Midland to subscribe 100,000l. towards the capital of the East Gloucestershire had placed the directors in a position of considerable difficulty, preventing the signing of the contract for the construction of the line. Subsequent communication took place, which resulted in a resolution of the Midland Board authorising an agreement by which they were to work the East Gloucestershire when completed, upon terms which would secure payment of 5 per cent. upon 300,000l. of A or preferred stock, and 200,000l. of debentures, and the application of the additional earnings (after payment of the working expenses) to the payment of dividend on the deferred capital. The Great Western, however, disputed the right of the Midland even to enter into an agreement for that purpose, and the question was accordingly referred to the arbitration of Captain Galton, who decided that the Midland might work the local line with Cheltenham (3 miles), but that it ought not to work the main line (47 miles in length).

By 29 and 30 Vic., cap. 214 (18th July, 1866), certain deviations were allowed to be completed within three years.

By 30 and 31 Vic., cap. 143 (15th July, 1867), the company obtained till 1st October, 1871, wherein to complete its works, and was also authorised to enter into arrangements with the Great Western.

It was reported in September, that the directors had been engaged in making the necessary preliminary arrangements for carrying out the proposed contract for the construction of a portion of the railway between Witney and Fairfield. In their negotiations for the acquisition of land the directors have been eminently successful, no contest as to value having occurred. Nearly the whole of the additional provisional subscription had been obtained in the district, and the directors confidently anticipated that the section would be completed and open for traffic in the course of next year.

CAPITAL.—From the financial statement it appeared that the amount received on account of calls was 60,213*l.*
Meetings in February or March, and in August or September.
No. of Directors—8; minimum, 6; quorum, 3. *Qualification*, 2,000*l.*

DIRECTORS:

Chairman—Colonel Sir WILLIAM RUSSELL, Bart., C.B., M.P., Charlton Park, Charlton Kings, Cheltenham, and 10, James Street, Buckingham Gate, S.W.
Vice-Chairman — J. R. RAYMOND BARKER, Esq., Fairford Park, Fairford, Gloucestershire.

Sir Michael E. Hicks Beach, Bart., M.P., Williamstrip Park, Fairford, Gloucestershire.	Hon. and Rev. G. G. C. Talbot, Withington, Cheltenham.
Walter Strickland, Esq., Cokethorpe Park, Witney, Oxon.	Henry Akers, Esq., Black Bourton, Faringdon, Berks.
	G. C. Taylor, Esq., 42, Elvaston Place, South Kensington, W.

OFFICERS.—Sec., George Broom, Jun., 80, Coleman Street, E.C.; Engs., Chas. Liddell and E. Richards, 24, Abingdon Street, Westminster, S.W.; Auditors, G. C. Ring, Great Knight Rider Street, Doctors Commons, E.C., and R. B. Hays, 80, Coleman Street, E.C.; Solicitors, Johnston, Farquhar, and Leech, 65, Moorgate Street, E.C., and Sewell and Newmarch, Cirencester, Gloucestershire.

133.—EAST LINCOLNSHIRE.

Incorporated by 10 Vic., cap 88 (26th July, 1846). Commences (in conjunction with the Great Northern loop) at Boston, and terminates (in conjunction with the Manchester, Sheffield, and Lincolnshire) at Great Grimsby—18 miles; opened from Grimsby to Louth, 14 miles, 1st March; from Louth to Firsby, 12 miles, 3rd September; and the remainder from Firsby to Boston Junction, 15 miles, 1st October, 1848.

This company has also by 10 and 11 Vic., cap. 113, and under the sanction of the lessees, who are now the responsible parties, purchased the unexpired interest of Messrs. F. and G. Chaplin, in the lease held by them for 48 years, commencing 28th August, 1828, in the Louth Navigation; also of the unexpired lease of a piece of land, known as " Mallard Ings " held by Mr. Thomas Chaplin for 99 years, commencing from 9th April, 1800, the consideration paid being an annuity of 1,500*l.* for the unexpired term and an assumption of the bond debt of the canal, supposed to be about 1,500*l.* per annum more.

By 11 Vic., cap. 125, power was given to make the Great Grimsby branch and Sheffield Junction half a mile additional length.

Under 11 Vic., cap. 148 (1847), this line has been leased in perpetuity to the Great Northern, at a fixed rental of 36,000*l.* per annum, equal to 6 per cent. per annum on the share capital (fixed capital of 600,000*l.*) from 1st October, 1848; the G. N. providing all extra cost of construction, and assuming the loan debt. Lease is dated February 21st, 1849, and the terms are repeated in sec. 34 of 13 Vic., cap. 84, which gives this company right to repossess, on non payment of the rent for seven months, from 1st April and 1st October. Meantime the G. N. pay all expenses connected with the registration of transfers, the distribution of dividend, and all other administrative charges attending the same.

134.—EAST LONDON.

Incorporated by 28 Vic., cap. 51 (26th May, 1865), to connect by means of the Thames Tunnel the railways on the north and south of the Thames. Length, about 8 miles. Capital, 1,400,000*l.* in shares, and 466,600*l.* on mortgage.

By 29 and 30 Vic., cap. 180 (16th July, 1866), the company was authorised to construct several short branches and alter new works. Length, ¾ mile. No new capital.

By 31 and 32 Vic., cap. 163 (31st July, 1868), the company obtained various additional powers, including certain deviations and altered lines; an extension of time till 1873, for completion of works; and confirmation of agreement with Brighton, for which, see APPENDIX to present volume.

This line commences by junctions with the Brighton, South London, South Eastern, and North Kent Railways, near New Cross, accommodating in its course the Surrey and Commercial Docks, the London Docks, and the East of London, terminates in the city, at a great terminal station in Liverpool street. There is to be a branch to the Great Eastern, and the line will pass through and accommodate the districts of New Cross, Deptford, Rotherhithe, Wapping, St. Georges-in-the-East, Limehouse, Stepney, Whitechapel, Bethnal-green, Bishopsgate, and Shoreditch. Works in progress.

CAPITAL.—The receipts and expenditure on this account to 30th June, 1868, have been as follow:—

Received.		*Expended.*	
Capital, 1,400,000l., in 70,000 shares of 20l. each	£1,170,342	As per last account	£1,001,960
Interest...................	12,861	Land	8,357
Sale of surplus property	7,724	Construction	63,534
Transfer fees	26	Office rent, salaries, printing, and stationery, &c..............	997
		Directors and auditors ....,.	1,070
		Law charges	1,846
		Parliamentary expenses	850
		Discount on shares..................	92,685
		Commission.........................	123
			£1,171,425
		Cash and securities	19,528
	£1,190,954		£1,190,954

No. of Directors—12; minimum, 6; quorum, 3. *Qualification,* 50 shares of 20l. each.

DIRECTORS;

Chairman—WILLIAM HAWES, Esq., 17, Montague Place, Russel Square, W.C.

Lawford Ackland, Esq., Langdown Lawn, Hythe, Southampton.

Major-Gen. J. S. Brownrigg, C.B., 91, Victoria Street, Westminster, S.W.

John Sale Barker, Esq., 11, Palace Gardens Terrace, Kensington, W.

James Childs, Esq., Summerfield, Putney Park Lane, Roehampton, S.W.

Peter Graham, Esq., Queen's Road, Regent's Park, N.W.

Alfred Smee, Esq., F.R.S., Finsbury Circus, London, E.C.

OFFICERS.—Sec., G. E. Cooper; Eng., John Hawkshaw, C.E.; Auditors, H. M. Brownrigg and H. H. Stansfeld; Solicitors, Wilson, Bristows, and Carpmael, 1, Copthall Buildings; Surveyor and Valuer, E. N. Clifton; Bankers, The London and Westminster Bank.

Offices—3, Great Winchester Street Buildings, E.C.

135.—EAST NORFOLK.

Incorporated by 27 and 28 Vic., cap. 122 (23rd June, 1864), to construct a line from the Great Eastern, near Norwich, to the town of Walsham. Length, 14 miles. Capital, 88,000l. in 10l. shares, and 29,300l. on loan. Arrangements with Great Eastern, which subscribes 29,300l. Works in progress.

No. of Directors—9; quorum, 3. *Qualification,* 500l.

DIRECTORS:

Chairman—The Right Hon. LORD SUFFIELD, Gunton Park, North Walsham, and 4, Upper Brook Street, W.

Sir J. H. Preston, Bart.
William Henry Trafford, Esq.
Robert Blake Humfrey, Esq.

Edward Leathes, Esq.
H. Chamberlin, Esq.

136.—EAST SOMERSET.

Incorporated by 19 and 20 Vic., cap. 16 (5th June, 1856), to make a railway from the Wilts Somerset and Weymouth, near Frome, to Shepton Mallet. Broad gauge. Capital, 75,000l.; loans, 25,000l. Agreements with Great Western, which works the line. Length, 9½ miles; opened 9th November, 1858.

By 20 and 21 Vic., cap. 165 (27th July, 1857), an extension to Wells was authorised, the new capital consisting of 40,000l. in shares; 13,000l. on loan. Length, 5 miles 2 chains.

By 23 Vic., cap. 73 (14th June, 1860), certain deviations were authorised, and the line originally contemplated to Wells was allowed to be abandoned. The deviated extension (5 miles) was opened on 1st March, 1862. By the same Act the company was authorised to cancel and re-issue forfeited shares, as well as to raise additional capital to the extent of 65,000l., making the total share capital, 135,000l. New shares may be issued at 5 per cent. preference. The borrowing powers were extended to 38,000l. Agreements with Great Western, under usual restrictions, as to maintenance, working, &c.

It was reported in September that, notwithstanding the extreme depression of trade during the haf-year ending June 30, the returns showed a slight increase over the corresponding period of 1867. The gross earnings for the half-year amounted to 3,582*l.*, which after paying 1,033*l.* for interest on debenture debt and rent charges, left 1,530*l.* or 60 per cent. of the balance, to the Great Western for working, and 1,020*l.*, or 40 per cent., to the company. Dividends on the preference shares at the rate of 3½ per cent. per annum were declared.

CAPITAL.—The expenditure on this account to 30th June amounted to 159,825*l.*, leaving a balance in hand of 3*l.* The receipts have been as follow :—

Ordinary share capital £69,850
Deduct in arrear £360
   „   Amount unpaid on forfeited shares .... 916 = 1,276 £68,573
Preference share capital as in last statement............................ 51,630
Debentures.. 38,300
Incidental receipts .... 1,325 = £159,828

Meetings in February or March, and August or September, in London or Shepton Mallet.

No. of Directors—8; minimum, 3; quorum, 3. *Qualification*, 300*l.*

DIRECTORS :

Chairman—*The MARQUIS OF BATH, Longleat, Wilts, and 55, Portland Place, S.W.
Deputy-Chairman—JAMES CURTIS SOMERVILLE, Esq., Dinder House, near Wells.

*Edward Charles Chetham Strode, Esq., Southill, near Shepton Mallet.
Edmund Hugh Clerk, Esq., Burford House, near Shepton Mallet.
*Mr. Thomas Somerton Foxwell, Shepton Mallet.

Richard Horner Paget, Esq., M.P., 13, Stratton Street, W., and Cranmore Hall, near Shepton Mallet.
Mr. William Chester Berryman, Wells.
Mr. John Gifford Everett, Wells.

* Retire by rotation, but are eligible for re-election.

OFFICERS.—Sec., George Mackenzie Mackay, Shepton Mallet ; Auditors, William Clarke, Shepton Mallet, and John Willmott, Wells ; Solicitors, Cope, Rose, and Pearson, 26, Great George Street, Westminster, S.W., and George Mackenzie Mackay, Shepton Mallet.

Offices—Shepton Mallet.

137.—EAST AND WEST JUNCTION.

Incorporated by 27 and 28 Vic., cap. 76 (23rd June, 1864), to construct a line from Towcester, on the Northampton and Banbury, to Old Stratford, on the Honeybourne branch of the Great Western. Length, 40½ miles. Capital, 300,000*l.*, in 20*l.* shares, and 100,000*l.* on loan.

By 29 and 30 Vic., cap. 142 (28th June, 1866), the company was authorised to raise additional capital to the extent of 300,000*l.* in shares at 5 per cent. preference, and 100,000*l.* on loan. Also to create and issue debenture stock.

By 29 and 30 Vic., cap. 239 (23rd July, 1866), the company obtained power to divert and stop up certain roads in the parish of Alderminster.

Meetings in April and October.

No. of Directors—9; minimum, 3; quorum, 3. *Qualification*, 500*l.*

DIRECTORS :

Sir Charles Mordaunt, Bart. 15, Chesham Street, S.W.

William Malcolm, Esq.
William John Addison, Esq.

138.—EASTON AND CHURCH HOPE.

Incorporated by 30 and 31 Vic., cap. 167 (25th July, 1867), to construct a railway from Easton, in the Isle of Portland, to Church Hope Cove, with a pier in connection therewith. Length, 1½ mile. Capital, 30,000*l.* in 20*l.* shares, and 20,000*l.* on loan, which may be converted into debenture stock. Broad gauge.

First meeting to be held within six months after passing of Act.

No. of Directors—5; minimum, 3; quorum, 3 and 2. *Qualification*, 200*l.* in shares.

DIRECTORS :

Robert Amadeus Heath, Esq., 31, Old Jewry, E.C.
Walter Amos Michael, Esq.

Lachlan Mackintosh Rate, Esq., King's Arms Yard, E.C.

139,—EDINBURGH AND BATHGATE.

Incorporated by 10 Vic., cap. 332 (3rd August, 1846), amended by subsequent Acts, for a line from the Edinburgh and Glasgow, near Ratho Station, to Bathgate. Completed and open, 11 miles; in abeyance, 12 miles. This railway was leased to the Edinburgh and Glasgow for 999 years, at 4 per cent., and one-half surplus profits in addition; working charges to be estimated at 33 per cent. on gross receipts.

The dividends declared for the year ending 30th June, were at the rate of 5s. 6d. per share, with 4 per cent. on sums paid in anticipation of calls.

It was reported in August that the directors had been unremitting in their endeavours to obtain from the North British detailed accounts of the traffic, to enable the auditors to prepare an accurate statement of the amount of surplus rents due to this company during bye-gone years, in accordance with the findings of the decree-arbitral in the submission between the North British and the company. The directors were glad to report that they had at length been furnished with accounts for the years ending 31st January, 1867 and 1868, both of which showed a considerable balance due to this company, which will no doubt be considerably augmented when the accounts for the preceding years have been rendered and adjusted, and upon which, interest will fall to be paid by the North British from the respective years in which surplus arose, until settled. Owing to a difference of opinion, however, between the directors and the North British Board as to the correct reading of various findings in the arbiters' award, and points connected with the mineral traffic, the directors did not feel warranted in stating the amount of arrears of surplus rents; but they will continue to press this matter to a final issue, that the arrears may be paid over to this company.

CAPITAL.—The expenditure on this account to 31st July, amounted to 253,991l., the receipts being acknowledged as under;—

Deposit			£25,000
Received on account of 1st call			25,000
,,	,,	2nd call	24,992
,,	,,	3rd call	24,910
,,	,,	4th call	24,902
,,	,,	5th call	24,890
,,	,,	6th call	11,198
,,	,,	7th call	18,656
Sums paid in anticipation of future calls			9,436
Interest on arrears of calls			288
Amount transferred from unclaimed dividend account			91
Balance at debit with bank			675
Amount of debenture debt			63,950 = £253,991

DIRECTORS:

Chairman—THOMAS HILL, Esq., Merrylee, Glasgow.

Robert Hutchinson, Esq., of Carlowrie, Kirliston.
George F. Barbour, Esq., of Bonskeid, 11, George Square, Edinburgh.

John Fulton, Esq., Brewer, Edinburgh.
John Walker, Esq., W.S., 2, Queen Street, Edinburgh.
All eligible for re-election.

OFFICERS.—Sec., Alexander Jamieson; Auditors, Frederick Hayne Carter, C.A., and Wm. Moncrieff, C.A., Edinburgh; Solicitor, Wm. Waddell, W.S.

Offices—8, South Charlotte Street, Edinburgh.

140.—ELHAM VALLEY.

Incorporated by 29 and 30 Vic., cap. 316 (6th August, 1866), to construct a railway from Canterbury to Hythe, with branches to the Chatham and Dover and South Eastern. Length, 19 miles. Capital, 300,000l. in 10l. shares, and 100,000l. on loan. Arrangements with South Eastern and London Chatham and Dover.

*No. of Directors—*5; quorum, 3. *Qualification,* 500l.

DIRECTORS:

William Alexander Mackinnon, Jun., Esq., Acres Park, Kent.
Major Alexander George Dickson, M.P., Waldershaw Park, Kent, and 3A, King Street, St. James's, S.W.
Joseph Cary, Esq., 49, Pall Mall, S.W.

Robert John Biron, Esq., Recorder of Hythe, 2, Dr. Johnson's Buildings, Temple, E.C.
Thomas Knox Holmes, Esq., 18, Abingdon Street, S.W.

OFFICERS.—Sec., E. Bannister Callow; Eng., J. H. Tolmé, 1, Victoria Street, Westminster, S.W.; Solicitors, Messrs. Burchells, 5, Broad Sanctuary, Westminster, S.W.; Bankers, Glyn, Mills, Currie, and Co, Lombard Street, and National Provincial Bank of England, Folkestone.

Offices—Sandgate, Kent.

141.—ELLESMERE AND GLYN VALLEY.

Incorporated by 29 and 30 Vic., cap. 335 (6th August, 1866), to construct a railway, from the Cambrian at Ellesmere to Llansaintffraid Glyn Cerriog. Length, 15 miles. Capital, 120,000l., in 10l. shares, and 40,000l. on loan. Mutual facilities and arrangements with Great Western and Cambrian.

No. of Directors—5; minimum, 3; quorum, 3 and 2.   *Qualification, 500l.*

DIRECTORS:

Lord Arthur E. H. Trevor, M.P., 24, Rutland Gate, S.W.
Richard George Jebb, Esq.

Robert Myddleton Biddulph, Esq., 35, Grosvenor Place, S.W.
Richard Steele Perkins, Esq.

142.—ELY, HADDENHAM, AND SUTTON.

Incorporated by 27 and 28 Vic., cap. 86 (23rd June, 1864), to construct a line from Ely, through Haddenham, to Sutton. Length, 6¾ miles. Capital, 36,000l. in 10l. shares, and 12,000l. on loan. Arrangements with Great Eastern which subscribes 12,000l.

Meetings in February or March, and in August or September.

No. of Directors—5; minimum, 3; quorum, 3 and 2.   *Qualification, 250l.*

DIRECTORS:

Chairman—OLIVER CLAUDE PELL, Esq., Manor House, Wilburton.

Frederick Camps, Esq., Haddenham, Ely.

J. S. Valentine, Esq., 11, Park Street, Westminster, S.W.

OFFICERS.—Sec., T. P. Bond, 5, Great Queen Street, Westminster, S.W.; Eng., J. S. Valentine, 11, Park Street, Westminster, S.W.; Solicitor, James Wheeler, 4, Victoria Street, Westminster, S.W.

143.—ELY VALLEY.

Incorporated by 20 and 21 Vic., cap. 41 (13th July, 1857), to construct a line from the Llantrissant station of the South Wales to Penrhiwfer, Glamorganshire, with branches to Glanmychydd and Mynydd Gellyrhaidd. Capital, 70,000l. in 10l. shares, and 23,000l. on loan. Length, 8¼ miles; broad gauge.

By 21 Vic., cap. 30 (14th June, 1858), the company is authorised to construct a branch to Mwyndy; length, 2 miles. New capital, 13,000l. in shares, and 4,300l. by loan. The steepest gradient is 1 to 121. Completion of works, three years.

An agreement for lease to the Great Western for 999 years, confirmed by 25 Vic., cap. 196 (29th July, 1862), came into operation as from 1st January, 1861. The Great Western hold 35,000l. of Ely Valley stock, and pay Ely Valley a rent of 4,000l., which pays 5l. per cent. on Ely Valley stock and debenture debt.

Half-yearly meetings in February and August, or such other months as the directors may appoint.

No. of Directors—9; minimum, 4; quorum, 3.   *Qualification, fifty 10l. shares.*

DIRECTORS:

Sir I. B. Guest, Bart., Canford Manor, Dorset.
John Samuel Gibbon, Esq., Newton House, Glamorganshire.

Henry Lewis, Esq., Green Meadow, Glamorganshire.
Richard Bassett, Esq., Bouvilstone, Glamorganshire.

Solicitor, Richard Wyndham Williams, Cardiff.

144.—ENNISKILLEN, BUNDORAN, AND SLIGO.

Incorporated by 24 and 25 Vic., cap. 138 (11th July, 1861), to construct a line from the Londonderry and Enniskillen, near Lowtherstown, to Bundoran, County Donegal. Length, 36 miles. Capital, 20),000*l.* in 10*l.* shares; loans, 66,600*l.* Arrangements with Irish North Western.

By 25 and 26 Vic., cap. 114 (30th June, 1862), the company was authorised to extend the line to the Midland Great Western at Sligo (23 miles), and to raise capital to the extent of 150,000*l.* in shares, and 50,000*l.* on loan.

By 28 Vic., cap. 113 (19th June, 1865), the company was authorised to raise new capital to the extent of 100,000*l.* in preference shares, at not exceeding 6 per cent. for the first ten years, and 5 per cent. in perpetuity thereafter. Also to raise 33,300*l.* on loan. An extension of time for three years was conceded to the Sligo Extension.

It was reported in October that the receipts for the half-year were slightly in excess of those for the corresponding period. The great want of hotel lodging accommodation at Bundoran partly accounted for the decreased number of passengers. The heavy rate of mileage charged by the Irish North Western pressed severely on the interests of the company, being at present equal to 75 per cent. of the gross receipts. The balance of profit was so small that the company could not pay the full interest on their debentures. One great object was to obtain the extension of the line into Sligo, as it was much wanted for the development of traffic between Belfast and Sligo.

IRISH NORTH WESTERN.—At a meeting of this company on 4th May, 1865, it was stated that the great change in the agreement that affected the North Western was their getting 2*s.* per working train mile, instead of 1*s.* 6*d.*; and receiving a sum of 15,000*l.* from Messrs. Brassey and Field for the purchase of rolling stock. Until they receive that 15,000*l.*, which was the subject of a separate agreement, they could not add the seal of the company to the working agreement. The solicitor of the Enniskillen and Bundoran had signed the following:—"The Irish North Western having approved of the working agreement entered into between them and the Enniskillen Bundoran and Sligo, conditioned upon the advance of 15,000*l.* for the purchase of rolling stock, I hereby agree, on the part of the Bundoran company, that unless and until the said 15,000*l.* be advanced, the agreement so sanctioned shall not be binding in any way upon the Irish North Western."

Meetings in April and October.

No. of Directors—9; minimum, 6; quorum, 3. *Qualification*, 1,000*l.*

DIRECTORS:

Chairman—THOMAS CONOLLY, Esq., M.P., Cliff, County Donegal, and Langham Hotel, Portland Place, W.

Deputy-Chairman—DAVID Mc.BIRNEY, Esq., J.P., Astons Quay, Dublin.

Henry M. Darcy Irvine, Esq., Castle Irvine, County Fermanagh.
John C. Bloomfield, Esq., D.L., Castle-caldwell, County Fermanagh,
Rev. George N. Tredennick, Kildoney, Ballyshannon.
Thomas Bailey, Esq., J.P., Herbert Place, Dublin.

James Peebles, Esq., LL.D., Eccles Street, Dublin.
John Taylor, Esq., Warwick Crescent, London, W.
Major F. D'Arcy, Prospect House, Enniskillen.

OFFICERS.—Sec., James H. Connell; Eng., Geo. W. Hemans; Solicitors, John Collum and Son; Auditors, Allan Taylor and James B. Kennedy.

145.—ESK VALLEY.

Incorporated by 26 and 27 Vic., cap. 195 (21st July, 1863), to construct a line from the Hawick branch of the North British, at Eskbank station, to Springfield. Length, 2½ miles. Capital, 27,000*l.* in 10*l.* shares, and 9,000*l.* on loan. Arrangements with North British, which by 29 and 30 Vic., cap. 200 (16th July, 1866), leases the line on the following conditions:—

"1. The North British pay 1,350*l.* yearly of rent, being 5 per cent. on the share capital, commencing the first half-year's payment of 675*l.* six months after the date of the line being opened for public traffic.

"2. The North British pays in addition the interest on so much of the loan capital, not exceeding 9,000*l.*, as it may be found necessary to raise for the purpose of completing the undertaking; or in the option of the North British, the money required to be raised on mortgage shall be raised by the North British, who shall pay all expenses thereof, and of renewals of such mortgages.

" 3. The North British shall pay all public and parish burdens, including poor-rates, prison assessments, and taxes generally, that may be charged against the Esk Valley, or in respect of the line and works, and also the Government duty on passengers.

"4. From and after the commencement of the lease, the Esk Valley and works and conveniences thereof shall be maintained in an efficient working condition by the North British in all time coming."

The line was opened on 15th April, 1866, when the North British entered into possession of perpetual lease. The line is not amalgamated with the North British, but simply leased at a fixed rent in the same way as the Peebles.

It was reported in September that the directors had requested the auditors to make a special report on the whole accounts and general position of the company. From that report the shareholders would see that the sum expended on the line and works beyond the share and loan capital amounted to 5,889*l.* The auditors submitted two proposals for consideration of the shareholders—one being that the rent of 1,350*l.*, payable by the North British, be retained and applied in extinction of the 5,889*l.*, and in a short time the company would be free of debt, and in receipt of 5 per cent. per annum on the stock in perpetuity; and the other, that that sum owing be borrowed as a permanent loan, and, besides meeting the interest thereon, the shareholders could at once be paid a dividend of 4 per cent.

Meetings in March or April, and August or September.

No. of Directors—5; minimum, 4; quorum, 3. *Qualification*, 200*l.*

DIRECTORS:

Chairman—ARCHIBALD FULLERTON SOMERVILLE, Esq., Kevock, Lasswade.

James Hunter Annandale, Esq., Polton, Lasswade.	William Tod, Jun., Esq., Glenesk House, Lasswade.
Henry Widnell, Jun., Esq., St. Ann's, Lasswade.	James Cowan, Esq., Paper Maker, Edinburgh.

Secretary, William White Millar.

Offices—8, Bank Street, Edinburgh.

146.—EVESHAM AND REDDITCH.

Incorporated by 26 and 27 Vic., cap. 114 (13th July, 1863), to construct a line from Evesham, on the West Midland, to Redditch. Length, 17¼ miles. Capital, 140,000*l.* in 10*l.* shares; loans, 49,600*l.* Arrangements with Midland, and facilities to Great Western.

It was reported in September that the engineer had given his certificate for payment of a further sum of 40,000*l.* on account of works; and, in payment thereof, and of 400*l.* previously due, 4,392*l.* had been paid to the contractors by writing up 9*l.* per share on 2,244 shares standing in the name of Thomas Brassey, and a like amount on 2,244 shares, standing in the name of Stephen Ballard, leaving a balance of 8*l.* due to the contractors. The directors had every reason to expect that the remaining portion of the railway between Alcester and Redditch would be completed in the course of the current year.

Meetings in February or March, and in August or September.

No. of Directors—6; quorum, 3. *Qualification*, 200*l.*

DIRECTORS:

Edward Holland, Esq., Union Club, S.W.	William Smith, Esq.
Benjamin Bomford, Esq.	John Edward Clift, Esq., Birmingham.
	Alan Lambert, Esq., 2, Portugal Street, W.

Offices—Shrewsbury.

147.—EXETER AND CREDITON.

Incorporated by 8 and 9 Vic., cap. 88 (1st July, 1845), for the construction of a line from the Cowley Bridge station of the Bristol and Exeter, and terminating by a junction with the North Devon at Crediton. Length, 5¾ miles. Worked under lease by the South Western.

The dividend declared in February, 1868, was at the rate of 5 per cent., and in August, 4 per cent. per annum.

CAPITAL.—The receipts on this account have been as under:—

Original share capital £70,000
5l. per cent. per preference shares 20,000
Debenture and temporary loans .... 22,950= £112,950
the balance on hand being 380l.

The accounts are made up to 31st June and 31st December, and the statutory meetings held in February and August.

Certificates are not required to accompany transfer deeds. Fee charged for each transfer, 2s. 6d.

No. of Directors.—Maximum, 10 ; minimum, 6. *Qualification*, 20 shares.

DIRECTORS :

Chairman—2 The Hon. RALPH H. DUTTON, Timsbury Manor, Romsey, Hants.

3 Charles Castleman, Esq., Glasshayes, Lyndhurst, Hants.
1 The Count Eyre, 7, Hinde Street, Manchester Square, W.
1 Serjeant Gaselee, 2, Cambridge Square, Hyde Park, W.

2 Captain James G. Johnston, 8, York Terrace, Regent's Park, N.W.
3 Captain Charles Edward Mangles, Poyle Park, Farnham.

1, retire in 1869; 2, in 1870 ; 3, 1871; all eligible for re-election.

OFFICERS.—Sec., George Henry Harris ; Solicitors, Bircham, Dalrymple, and Drake ; Auditors, William Kennaway and William Cann.

Head Office—12, Bishopgate Street Within, London, E.C.

148.—FAREHAM AND NETLEY.

Incorporated by 28 and 29 Vic., cap. 153 (29th June, 1865), to construct a line from the Southampton and Netley to Fareham, with two small branches. Length, 8 miles. Capital, 105,000l., in 10l. shares, and 35,000l. on loan. Arrangements with South Western.

By 31 and 32 Vic., cap. 159 (31st July, 1868), an extension of time and revival of powers for cumpulsory purchase of land was conceded to the company, the period for completion of works being fixed for 29th June, 1871.

149.—FARINGDON.

Incorporated by 23 and 24 Vic., cap. 196 (13th August, 1860), to construct a line from Balking, on the Great Western, to the town of Faringdon. Length, 3¾ miles ; broad gauge. Capital, 22,500l., in 10l. shares ; loans, 7,500l. Working and other agreements with Great Western under usual restrictions.

By 25 Vic., cap. 10 (16th May, 1862), the company was authorised to attach a preference of 5½ per cent. to any portion of the unissued capital.

Accounts made up to 30th June and 31st December. Meetings in March or April, and in August or September.

No. of Directors—7 ; minimum, 4 ; quorum, 3. *Qualification*, 100l.

DIRECTORS :

Daniel Bennett, Esq., Faringdon House.
Robert Campbell, Esq., Buscot Park.
Joseph Clarke, Esq., Faringdon.
Mr. Robert Charlwood, Faringdon.

Mr. Richard Smith, Colleymore Farm.
Mr. John Anns, Faringdon.
Mr. John Dyke, Faringdon.

Secretaries—Geo. J. Haines and George F. Crowdy, Faringdon.

150.—FINDHORN.

Incorporated by 22 Vic., cap. 8 (19th April, 1859), to construct a line from the Inverness and Aberdeen Junction, near Kinloss, to the town of Findhorn. Capital, 9,000l., in 10l. shares ; loans, 3,000l. Length, 3 miles and 5 chains. Opened 18th April, 1860, and worked by the Highland as a branch.

Meetings annual, in September or October.

No. of Directors—7 ; minimum, 3 ; quorum, 3. *Qualification*, 100l.

DIRECTORS:

Chairman—JAMES FORBES, Esq., Novar.

James Michie, Esq., Forres.	Robert Mackessack, Esq., Waterford.
Felix Calvert Mackenzie, Esq., Forres.	Thomas Davidson, Esq., Forres.
Robert Davidson, Esq., Mayfield.	John Kynock, Esq., Forres.

OFFICERS.—Sec., John D. Davidson; Auditors, Robert Urquhart, town clerk, and William Sclanders, writer.

Offices—Forres.

151.—FINN VALLEY.

Incorporated by 23 Vic., cap. 40 (15th May, 1860), to make a railway from Stranorlar. county Donegal, to Strabane, on the Londonderry and Enniskillen. Length, 13¼ miles. Capital, 68,000l. in 10l. shares. Loans, 20,000l. Opened 7th September, 1863.

IRISH NORTH WESTERN.—An agreement has been effected with this company, under which the Finn Valley is to be worked for 35 per cent. of the traffic receipts, with a new clause fixing at 375l. a year, from 1st July, 1865, the rent to be paid for station accommodation at Strabane, and the half mile of line.

REVENUE.—The receipts for the half-years ending 31st December have been as under:—

1863.	1864.	1865.	1866.	1867.
£1,112	£1,630	£1,827	£1,993	£2,058
Increase per cent..........		12	22¼	26¼

For the June half-years the progressive increase of traffic is shown as follows:—

1864.	1865.	1866.	1867.	1868.
£1,809	£1,721	£1,952	£2,171	£2,118
Increase per cent..........		7·20	20·01	17·07

It was reported in October that the modified terms which the directors obtained from the treasury, in relation to the 20,000l. borrowed from the Public Works Loan Commissioners (to take effect on the payment of arrears of interest due), had been in operation since 13th June. The option is of repaying the loan in 18 years from September, 1865, with 5 per cent. interest; or of repaying it in 22 years from June 1868, with 3½ per cent. interest; or in 2⅗ years from the latter date with 4 per cent. interest. Exercise of either option was left to the discretion of the board.

CAPITAL.—The expenditure on this account to 30th June amounted to 76,186l., the receipts being detailed as under:—

Original shares..		£43,635
4,775 shares, 10l each	£47,750	
Amount to be received	£32	
Loss on sale of 123 forfeited shares	4,082	4,114
		£43,635
Preference shares		6,530
Public Works Loan Commissioners		20,000
		£70,165
Balance, viz:—		6,021
Cash borrowed from revenue, and expended in excess of receipts on capital account to 31st December, 1867....................	£7,176	
Less repaid since 31st December, 1867	2,410	
	£4,765	
Liabilities due by the company, charged to expenditure £2,817		
Less amounts due to the company....................	1,561	1,255
		£6,021
		£76,186

Accounts made up to 30th June and 31st December. Meetings in April and October.

No. of Directors—8 ; minimum, 5; quorum, 3. Qualification, 300l.

DIRECTORS:

Chairman—THE RIGHT HON. VISCOUNT LIFFORD, Meen Glas, Stranorlar, County Donegal, and Cecil House, Wimbledon, S.W.

Vice-Chairman—JAMES THOMPSON MACKY, Esq., J. P., Bank of Ireland, and Belmont, Londonderry.

James B. Delap, Esq., Monellun, Killygordon, County Donegal.

Edward Hunter, Esq., D. L., J. P., The Glebe, Blackheath, Kent.

James Cochran, Esq., Croghan House, Lifford.

Lord Francis Conyngham, The Hall, Mountcharles, County Donegal.

Robert Russell, Esq., J. P., Salthill, Mountcharles, County Donegal.

Benjamin Briggs Popplewell, Esq., Beacon Hill, Addingham, Yorkshire.

OFFICERS.—Sec., James Alex. Ledlie, Stranorlar; Auditors, John 'Craig, Killygordon, and John Gunning, Stranorlar; Bankers, Northern Banking Company. Offices—Stranorlar.

152.—FISHGUARD.

Incorporated by 28 and 29 Vic., cap. 380 (6th July, 1865), to construct a line from Pembroke on the South Wales, to Fishguard, and also to construct a harbour and other works at the latter place. Length, 15¼ miles. Capital, 250,000l. in shares, and 83,000l. on loan. Arrangements with Great Western.

No. of Directors—7; minimum, 5; quorum, 3. *Qualification*, 300l.

DIRECTORS:

Sir Richard Musgrave, Bart.

George Le Hunte, Esq.

Lewis Mathias, Esq,

Charles Henry Barham, Esq.

William John Sharpe, Esq.

William Montagu Baillie, Esq.

John Chapman, Esq.

OFFICERS.—Solicitors, Edwards and Co., 8, Delahay Street, Westminster, S.W.

153.—FLEETWOOD, PRESTON, & WEST RIDING JUNCTION.

Incorporated by 9 and 10 Vic., cap. 246 (27th July, 1864), for a line from Preston to Clitheroe, to join the Blackburn. This company purchased the Preston and Longridge for 48,000l., and an Act 19 and 20 Vic., cap. 44 (23rd June, 1856), prescribes that there shall be no revival of powers to construct any further portion of the line. Capital, restricted to 27,000l. Shares may be divided, and dividend guaranteed on second portion when firct half is paid up. Borrowing powers 50,000l. The purchase money of Preston and Longridge was paid in instalments of 6,000l. on 31st of August of each year, commencing in 1856, and completed on 30th June, 1860. Length of line opened and worked, inclusive of Longridge, 8½ miles.

By 30 Vic., cap. 95 (17th June, 1867), the Fleetwood is vested jointly in the London and North Western and the Lancashire and Yorkshire, on terms of the following agreement dated 12th May, 1866:—

"1. The purchasers to pay 8l. net for each paid up share in the undertaking, within two years from 1st July next, three months' notice of payment to be given, and interest at the rate of 5 per cent. per annum is to be paid on the purchase money from the 1st of July next, until the date of payment.

"2. The mortgage debt and liabilities on capital account to be taken by the purchasers.

"3. The sellers to pay and receive their own simple contract debts and credits including parliamentary expenses, up to 1st of July next, when the transfer is to take effect.

"4. The current half-year's revenue account of the sellers is to be made out upon the same principle as heretofore.

"5. The purchasers are to pay 1,000l. to the sellers, towards their parliamentary expenses.

"6. The purchasers to pay the expenses of any parliamentary authority that may be necessary for carrying out the purchase."

DIRECTORS:

2 Chairman—T. B. ADDISON, Esq., Preston.

3 J. B. Booth, Esq., Preston.

3 W. D. Whitehead, Esq., Manchester.

1 Richard Calverley, Esq., Preston.

1 William Birley, Esq., Preston.

1 John Rawclifle, Esq., Preston.

2 Evan Makinson, Esq., Preston.

1, retire in 1868; 2, in 1869; 3, in 1870. All eligible for re-election.

OFFICERS.—Sec. and Man., B. Walmsley, Preston; Solicitors, Bray and Gilbertson, Preston; Auditors, Richard Pedder aud William Thornborrow.

154.—FORCETT.

Incorporated by 28 Vic., cap. 61 (2nd June, 1865), to construct a line from the Darlington and Barnard Castle and Forcett. Length, 8 miles. Capital, 30,000*l.*, in shares, and 10,000*l.* on mortgage. Arrangements with North Eastern. The line has been opened for goods and minerals, but is not yet employed in the conveyance of passengers.

No. of Directors—7 ; quorum, 3. *Qualification*, 400*l.*

DIRECTORS:

Chairman—CARL F. H. BOLCKOW, Esq., of Middlesbro'.

Thomas Light Elwon, Esq., Middlesbro'.	James Bowron, Esq., Forest Hall, New-
Thomas Vaughan, Esq., Middlesbro'.	castle-on-Tyne.
J. G. Swan, Esq., Middlesbro'.	Thomas Snowdon, Esq., Stockton.
	R. T. Richardson, Esq., Barnard Castle.

OFFICERS. — Sec. and Solicitor, W. T. Richardson, Barnard Castle ; Eng., Wm. Bryson, C.E., Darlington; Auditors, J. C. MacNay, Darlington, and J. Bowron, Jun., South Stockton.

Offices—Barnard Castle.

155.—FOREST OF DEAN CENTRAL.

Incorporated by 19 and 20 Vic., cap. 100 (11th July, 1856), to make a railway from the South Wales, near Brimspill, to Howbeach Valley, in the Forest of Dean (broad gauge). Capital, 65,000*l.*, in 10*l.* shares; loans, 21,660*l.* The Woods and Forests advance 20,000*l.*, secured by prior claim of 5 per cent. Length of main line, 4¼ miles ; of Fox Bridge branch, 2¾ miles ; and of the branch which terminates by a junction with that railway, 4 furlongs 7¼ chains.

By 23 and 24 Vic., cap. 199 (20th August, 1860), an extension of time for completion of works was conceded till 14th July, 1862. Agreements were also authorised with the South Wales, and joint committee appointed to be formed. New capital to the extent of 1,000*l.* to be raised in shares; and the Commissioners of Woods and Forests were authorised to grant an extension of time for repayment by the company of sums advanced by them, five years, instead of one twelvemonth, being now allowed.

By 24 and 25 Vic., cap. 184 (22nd July, 1861), the company was authorised to construct some new works for coal traffic, and to increase the capital of the undertaking by 15,000*l.*, in shares at 6 per cent., and 5,000*l.* in loans.

No. of Directors—7; minimum, 3; quorum, 4 ; if at minimum, 2. *Qualification*, 500*l.*

DIRECTORS :

Chairman—ARTHUR T. PRATT BARLOW, Esq., Taplow, Maidenhead, Berks.

Deputy-Chairman—OSMAN BARRETT, Esq., Mitcheldean, Gloucestershire.

Chas. I. B. Williams, Esq., M.D., F.R.S., 49, Upper Brook Street, Grosvenor Square, W.	Alfred Nash, Esq., Denmark Hill, S.
	Edmund Kendall, Esq., Thornton Heath, Surrey, S.
Francis Venn, Esq., 12, Clifton Gardens, Maida Hill West, W.	Chas. Greenwood, Esq., 61, Nelson Square, Blackfriars Road, S.

OFFICERS.—Sec., W. H. Wilson, 6, Victoria Street, Westminster, S.W. ; Eng., J. T. Williams, 49, Upper Brook Street, Grosvenor Square, W.; Solicitors, Baxter, Rose, and Norton, 6, Victoria Street, Westminster, S.W., and J. K. Smith, Newnham, Gloucestershire; Bankers, Ransom, Bouverie, and Co., 1, Pall Mall East, S.W.

Offices—6, Victoria Street, Westminster, S.W.

156.—FORTH AND CLYDE JUNCTION.

Incorporated by 17 Vic., cap. 125 (4th August, 1853), for a railway from Stirling (junction with the Scottish Central) to Alexandria (junction with the Caledonian and Dumbartonshire), near Balloch, foot of Loch Lomond. The line connects the east and west of Scotland, and the rivers Forth and Clyde, by the shortest possible route. Length, 30 miles. Opened, 20th May, 1856.

By 30 and 31 Vic., cap. 24 (13th July, 1857), the company was authorised to cancel certain forfeited shares, of the nominal value of 43,000*l.*, and to issue the same amount and also 21,000*l.* additional, at 6 per cent. preference. The Act also contains clauses for converting the share capital and mortgage debt, and the money to be borrowed, under the Act into stock, and to authorise the company to attach a preference to the shares for all or any of the additional money to be raised, and to fund the debt of the company, with various provisions in relation thereto,

By 24 and 25 Vic., cap. 230 (1st August, 1861), the company was authorised to raise new capital to the extent of 21,000*l.* in shares, and 7,000*l.* on loan. Also to construct a branch to Dalmonach print works. Length, 62 chains.

REVENUE.—It was reported in September, that the receipts exhibited a decrease of 228*l.* as compared with the corresponding period of last year. The ordinary working expenses were above those of the corresponding period, the excess being spent entirely in strengthening the permanent way and fencing the line. The balance, after deducting ordinary working expenses, and paying all public and parochial burdens, feu duties, interest on debenture loans and bank account, and providing for interest on deferred dividend warrants amounted to 2,215*l.* The directors, however, had again considered it necessary and prudent to expend a considerable sum as extraordinary outlay during the half-year, in further re-laying and renewing of the permanent way and bridges, particulars of which are given in the balance-sheet. The net revenue surplus, after deduction of ordinary working expenses, taxes, feu duties, interest on loans, &c., and extraordinary expenditure, amounted to 922*l.*, from which a dividend at the rate of 2½ per cent. per annum on the first preference stock in deferred dividend warrants, bearing interest at the rate of 4 per cent. was declared.

CAPITAL.—The expenditure on this account to 31st July amounted to 262,154*l.* showing a balance against receipts of 12,009*l.*, the latter being thus detailed:—

Consolidated stock	£106,373	
First 5 per cent. preference stock	58,772	
Second preference shares, bearing 5 per cent.	4,520	
Do. do. bearing 6 per cent.	16,480	
Loans on debentures	64,000	=£250,145
Balance		12,009=£262,154

Meetings half-yearly (at Stirling), in August or September, and February or March.

No. of Directors—9 ; quorum, 4 ; committee of directors, 3 to 5 ; quorum, the majority. *Qualification*, 50 shares.

DIRECTORS :

Chairman—6 His Grace the DUKE OF MONTROSE, K.T., Buchanan House, Drymen, Stirlingshire, and 45, Belgrave Square, S.W.

7 Henry Ritchie Cooper, Esq., of Ballin-dalloch.
1 James Morrison, Esq., of Livilands.
2 Alexander Wilson, Esq., Bannockburn.

3 John M. Douglas, Esq., Cupar-Fife.
4 Henry Kerr, Esq., Glasgow.
5 John Mc.Gaven, Esq., Glasgow.

The figures show the order of retirement.

OFFICERS.—Man. and Sec., Robert Young, Forth Place, Stirling; Engs., R. Young and Sons; Locomotive and Permanent Way Superintendent, Thomas Wood; Accountant, Thomas Ronald ; Auditors, James Thomas Wingate, Writer, Stirling, and Patrick Graham Morison, Writer, Stirling; Solicitors, J. and J. Mathie, Writers, Stirling, and T. L. Galbraith, Writer, Stirling.

157.—FULHAM.

Incorporated by 28 and 29 Vic., cap. 192 (29th June, 1865), to construct a line from the Hammersmith and City. through Fulham, to the north shore of the Thames. Length, 4¾ miles. Capital, 165,000*l.* in 16,500 10*l.* shares, and 55,000*l.* on loan. Mixed gauge. Arrangements with Great Western.

By 30 and 31 Vic., cap. 202 (15th August, 1867), the company obtained an extension of time till 15th August, 1869, wherein to complete its works, and also power to raise new capital to the extent of 35,000*l.* in shares, and 11,600*l.* on loan.

No. of Directors—6; minimum, 4; quorum, 3. *Qualification*, 500*l.*

DIRECTORS:

Thomas Eyre Foakes, Esq., 4, New Square, Lincoln's Inn, W.C.

Lieut.-Colonel Francis Beckford Ward, Welwyn, Herts.

James Hendrey, Esq., 78, Warwick Square, Pimlico, S.W.

Thomas Williams, Esq., Grove End Road, St. John's Wood, N.W.

OFFICERS.—Sec., George W. Harris, 6, Westminster Chambers, S.W.; Eng., H. H. Fulton, 22, Great George Street, Westminster, S.W.; Solicitors, Wilkins, Blyth, and Marsland, 10, St. Swithin's Lane, E.C.; Auditors, J. Waddell and Co., Accountants, New Poultry Chambers, 7, Poultry, E.C.

Offices—6, Westminster Chambers, S.W.

158.—FURNESS.

Incorporated by 8 Vic., cap. 22, for a line commencing at Barrow and Piel Piers, Morecambe Bay, mainly for the conveyance of minerals from Dalton and Kirkby Mines, opened for traffic in 1846. The line was subsequently extended to Broughton, and opened for traffic in 1848. Power was also obtained for an extension eastward from Dalton to Ulverston. This extension was opened to Lindal in 1851, to Halfway Bridge in 1852, and to Ulverston in 1864, where a junction was afterwards (1857) formed by the Ulverston and Lancaster.

CONISTON.—Incorporated by 20 and 21 Vic., cap. 110 (10th August, 1867), for making a railway from Broughton (junction with the Furness line) to Coniston Lake. Length, 9 miles. Capital, 45,000l.; loans, 15,000l. Opened 18th June, 1859. This undertaking was amalgamated with the Furness, under an Act passed on the 7th July, 1862, 25 and 26 Vic., cap. 133, under the following arrangements:—"That the Coniston shareholders receive a dividend in accordance with the terms of the present working agreement between the two companies for the period for which that agreement has been entered into. The agreement bore date the 17th June, 1859, and was for a period of five years. The terms of it are, that the Coniston shareholders should receive no dividend for the first year; for the second and third years a dividend equal to one-third of the dividend paid upon the ordinary shares of the Furness; and for the fourth and fifth years, a dividend equal to half of the dividend on the Furness ordinary shares. After the expiration of the term of the working agreement, the Coniston shareholders are, under the arrangement for amalgamation, to receive for the then ensuing five years, a dividend equal to two-thirds of the dividend on the Furness ordinary shares; and after the expiration of that period of five years, they are to receive the same dividend as the ordinary shareholders of the Furness."

ULVERSTON AND LANCASTER.—Incorporated by 14 and 15 Vic., cap. 102 (24th July, 1851), for a line from the Furness at Ulverston to a junction with the Lancaster and Carlisle, at Carnforth, 7 miles north of Lancaster. Length, 19 miles. Opened, August, 1857. Original capital, 220,000l. Additional capital, 150,000l. Debentures, 123,333l., under the powers of the Ulverston and Lancaster Act, 1858; the whole of this undertaking has been transferred to the Furness under the following arrangement, adopted on 21st January, 1862:—"The Furness to allot to the shareholders in the Ulverston, in exchange for their shares, preferential shares or stock of the Furness, bearing interest at 5 per cent. per annum, for the half-year ending 31st December, 1861, and at 6 per cent. per annum thenceforth in perpetuity, clear of all outgoings. The preferential shares or stock to be so created, and the existing preference shares of the Furness to rank equally in point of priority as a first charge on the divisible profits of the two undertakings, after satisfying a dividend of 2½ per cent. on 10,000l. to Lady le Fleming and her lessees. Neither the new nor the old preferential shares entitled to vote, and the Furness to be allowed two years from 1st January, 1862, to make the necessary arrangements with their present preference shareholders (who are redeemable) for effectuating these purposes." In connection with the purchase of the Ulverston and Lancaster railway, it was necessary for the Directors to arrange for the purchase of the Ulverston Canal, and an agreement was accordingly entered into for the sale of the canal to the Furness, for the sum of 22,000l.

By 25 and 26 Vic., cap. 89 (30th June, 1862), the Furness was authorised to construct a branch 2¼ miles, to Hawcoat Quarry, to purchase the Ulverston Canal, and to raise additional capital to the extent of 160,000l. (of which 30,000l. are 5 per cent. preference snares), and 40,000l. on loan.

By 26 and 27 Vic., cap. 82 (22nd June, 1863), the Furness jointly with the Midland was authorised to construct a line from a junction with the Furness line at Carnforth to a junction with the Midland line at Wennington.　Capital, 150,000*l.* in shares, and 50,000*l.* on loan; each company to subscribe in equal proportions.

By 26 and 27 Vic., cap. 89 (22nd June, 1863), the Harbour of Barrow was vested in the company, which was also authorised to construct docks and other works.　New capital, 137,000*l.* in shares, and 40,000*l.* on loan.

By 28 and 29 Vic., cap. 179 (29th June, 1865), the company was authorised to construct a loop line from Park Mines to Barrow, with a branch to Scarf Point on the Duddon.　Length, 9½ miles.　Capital, 200,000*l.* in shares, and 66,000*l.* on loan.

By 29 and 30 Vic., cap. 176 (16th July, 1866), the company was authorised to construct a branch from Ulverston to Newby Bridge, Windermere.　Length, 9½ miles, with short branches to the Ulverston Canal Basin, and from Dalton to Stainton. New capital, 300,000*l.* in shares, and 100,000*l.* on loan.

WHITEHAVEN AND FURNESS JUNCTION.—Incorporated 21st July, 1845, by 8 and 9 Vic., cap. 100, for a railway from Whitehaven to a junction with the Furness, near Dalton; subsequently extended to a junction at Whitehaven with the Whitehaven Junction, and fixing the junction with Furness at Foxfield, near Broughton.　Opened for traffic between Whitehaven and Ravenglass, July, 1849, and to Foxfield in November, 1850.　Total length, 35 miles.

By Act of 1853 the company was authorised to raise 25,000*l.* (authorised by Act of 1846), by preference shares; maximum, 6 per cent.; also 30,000*l.* additional, by the re-issue of a portion of the 6,125 forfeited shares, with the privileges, preferences, &c., meetings may determine.　Meeting of 26th August, 1853, sanctioned preference shares of 10*l.* each; of 5,500 shares then issued, 2,997 had been taken up, and 29,814*l.* paid thereon.　Arrangements authorised with Whitehaven Junction, and Whitehaven Cleator and Egremont.

By 20 and 21 Vic., cap. 122 (10th August, 1857), the company obtained authority to raise 70,000*l.* of additional capital by the issue of new preference shares.　Of this amount 46,787*l.* was raised to pay off liabilities, and the rest to be expended in providing increased facilities for an anticipated increase in the traffic.

By 28 and 29 Vic., cap. 143 (29th June, 1865), the company was authorised to construct a line across the Duddon estuary, and a branch to the Hodbarrow mines. Length, 4¼ miles.　Capital, 130,000*l.* in shares, and 29,900*l.* on loan.

By 29 and 30 Vic., cap. 132 (28th June, 1866), the Whitehaven and Furness jointly with the Whitehaven Cleator and Egremont, were authorised to construct a line from Egremont to Sellafield.　Length, 4¾ miles.　Capital, in equal proportions, 66,000*l.* in shares, and 22,000*l.* on loan.

By 29 and 30 Vic., cap. 236 (16th July, 1866), the Whitehaven and Furness was amalgamated with the Furness, at 8 per cent. on the ordinary stock.

By 30 and 31 Vic., cap. 104, the Furness was authorised to construct a line (5¼ miles) from a junction in the parish of Beetham, to a junction at Hincaster, on the Lancaster and Carlisle.　Also to effect a diversion of road and other works.　New capital, 200,000*l.* in shares, and 66,300*l.* on loan.　Running powers over this line were conceded to the London and North Western.　By the same Act the Furness and Lancaster and Carlisle was authorised to be abandoned, and the deposit of that company permitted to be released.

REVENUE.—The receipts for the half-year ending 31st December, including a balance of 2,656*l.* from previous account, were 148,276*l.*　The expenditure amounted to 73,371*l.*, while the preference dividends absorbed 25,717*l.*, and the interest on debentures 12,085*l.* The balance of 36,997*l.* permitted a dividend of 4*l.* for the half-year on the ordinary stocks, and left a balance of 1,291*l.*　The revenue account for the same half-year showed that 139,818*l.* had been received, and 62,107*l.* expended, leaving a balance of 77,711*l.*; to which was added 1,296*l.*, the balance from last half-year, making 79,007*l.*, out of which the usual dividend at the rate of 8 per cent. per annum was declared, and a balance of 832*l.* carried forward.　It was also reported that the Stainton branch was opened in February, and a large mineral traffic had been conveyed over the line.　The works of the Newby Bridge branch were progressing satisfactorily, and the line would be ready for opening by 1st May, 1869.　The Cleator and Furness branch would also be ready for opening early next year.　The directors had allotted to the ordinary shareholders the 363,000*l.* of new capital authorised to be issued and the larger proportion of which had been accepted.

CAPITAL. — The balance sheet to 30th June, detailed an expenditure of 2,737,472*l.*, which, with 25,244*l.* for stores, and 58,439*l.* for accounts due to the company made receipts appear as follow:—

Authorised.		Received.
£532,000	Ordinary stock	£532,000
137,000	Furness and Barrow Harbour Act, 1863 .... }	145,440
10,000	Furness Gas and Water Act, 1864 .... }	
25,000	Coniston shares (2-3rds ordinary dividend)	25,000
75,000	Furness and Midland Act, 1863 .... }	174,302
200,000	Furness Act, 1865 .... }	
300,000	Furness Act, 1866	297,627
£1,279,000	Total ordinary capital	£1,174,369
298,000	6 per cent. stock	298,000
170,000	5 per cent. do., redeemable at par......................................	170,000
30,000	5 per cent. do., irredeemable	30,000
10,000	2½ per cent. guaranteed	10,000
227,500	8 per cent. preference, W. and F. Junction............................	227,500
50,000	5 per cent. do. do.	50,000
52,000	5 per cent. do. do.	52,000
5,000	4½ per cent. do. do.	5,000
33,000	Cleator and Furness Act...	......
130,000	Whitehaven and Furness Junction Act, 1865	......
200,000	Furness Railway Act, 1867	......
£2,484,500		£2,016,869
782,066	Loans on debentures	603,406
£3,266,566		£2,620,275
	Revenue...	38,155
	Tradesmen's accounts...	9,874
	Sundry accounts due by the company..................................	34,953
	Reserve fund, 31st December, 1867....................£9,319	
	Less amount expended on renewal of Piel Pier................. 3,500 =	5,819
	Advances in anticipation of calls......................................	30,000
	Bills payable...	20,840
	Bankers' account..	61,238
		£2,821,157

The accounts are made up to 30th June and 31st December, and the statutory meetings are held in February and August every year.

Scale of Voting.—One for every 3 up to 24 shares; one for 7 above 24.

Fee charged for transfer, 2s. 6d. Stock coupons are required to accompany transfer deed. Several classes of shares may go on one stamp.

No. of Directors.—Maximum, 9; minimum, 4. *Qualification*, 500*l.* capital. Rotate, one every February.

DIRECTORS:

Chairman—His Grace The DUKE OF DEVONSHIRE, K.G., Devonshire House, Piccadilly, W.

His Grace The Duke of Buccleuch and Queensbury, K.G., Montague House, Whitehall, S.W.

Lord Frederick C. Cavendish, M.P., 21, Carlton House Terrace, S.W.

Frederick John Howard, Esq., Eastbourne.

Frederick I. Nicholl, Esq., 8, Howard Street, Strand, W.C.

Harry S. Thompson, Esq., Kirby Hall, York.

James Ramsden, Esq., Managing Director, Barrow-in-Furness, Lancashire.

OFFICERS.—Sec. and Traffic Man., Henry Cook; Engs., M'Clean and Stileman; Solicitors, Currey and Holland.

Head Offices—Barrow-in-Furness, Lancashire,

159.—FURNESS AND MIDLAND,

Incorporated by 26 and 27 Vic., cap. 82 (22nd June, 1863), by which the Furness and the Midland are authorised to construct a line from Carnforth to Wennington, connecting the Ulverston and Lancaster and the Little North Western. Length, 9½ miles.

Capital, 150,000*l.* in shares, to be provided in equal proportions by the two companies ; borrowing powers, 50,000*l.* Opened June, 1867, and worked by Midland.

OFFICERS.—Sec., William Currey, 14, Great George Street, Westminster, S.W.; Engs., M'Clean and Stileman, and J. S. Crossley ; Solicitors, Currey and Holland, and S. Carter.

Head Offices—Barrow-in-Furness, Lancashire.

160.—GARSTANG AND KNOTEND.

Incorporated by 27 and 28 Vic., cap. 149 (30th June, 1864), to construct a line from the Lancaster and Preston Junction to Knotend. Length, 11¾ miles. Capital, 60,000*l.* in 10*l.* shares, and 20,000*l.* on loan.

By 30 Vic., cap. 16 (3rd May, 1867), the time for completion of these works was extended till 1st July, 1869.

No. of Directors—6 ; quorum, 3. *Qualification*, 500*l.*

DIRECTORS :

Captain Mounsey, Inglewhite Lodge, Preston.
William Forrester, Esq., Leyland, Preston.

Henry Gardiner, Esq.
John Taylor, Esq., Garstang.

OFFICERS.—Sec., John Noble, Church Street, Garstang ; Engs., Galbraith and Tolmé, 1, Victoria Street, Westminster, S.W.; Solicitors, Hargrove, Fowler, and Blunt, 3, Victoria Street, Westminster, S.W., and Paul Catterai, Camden Place, Preston ; Auditors, Robinson and Rooking, Garstang.

Offices—Garstang.

161.—GIRVAN AND PORTPATRICK JUNCTION.

Incorporated by 28 and 29 Vic., cap. 358 (5th July, 1865), to construct a line from Girvan on the Maybole, to a junction with the Portpatrick at East Challock. Length, 30¾ miles. Capital, 250,000*l.* in shares, and 83,300*l.* on loan. Arrangements with Glasgow and South Western, which subscribes 50,000*l.* Works not commenced.

No. of Directors—6 ; minimum, 4 ; quorum, 3. *Qualification*, 500*l.*

DIRECTORS :

Chairman—DAVID GUTHRIE, Esq., Stranraer.

Colonel Macdowall, of Logan.
Sir J. C. D. Hay, Bart., M.P., of Park Place, and 108, St. George's Square, S.W.

J. P. Willison, Esq., of Dalpedder.
David Frederick, Esq., Dumbreddan, by Stranraer.

OFFICERS.—Auditors, J. Graham and W. Murray ; Solicitors, H. and R. Lamond, Glasgow, and Millar, Allardice, and Robson, Edinburgh.

Offices—Stranraer, and 64, West Regent Street, Glasgow.

162.—GLASGOW AND MILNGAVIE JUNCTION.

Incorporated by 24 and 25 Vic., cap. 198 (1st August, 1861), to construct a line from the Glasgow Dumbarton and Helensburgh, to Milngavie. Length, 3 miles 16 chains. Capital, 30,000*l.* in 10*l.* shares ; loans, 10,000*l.* Opened, 21st April, 1863. Worked by North British.

In consequence of the failure of the North British to meet its engagements, a new arrangement was entered upon in May, 1867, and which is reported as being fairly carried out. It was reported in September that the receipts had increased, and after clearing off the whole interest and other charges for the half-year there remained at the credit of revenue the sum of 90*l.*, which would be nearly sufficient to pay a dividend at the rate of 1 per cent.; the directors, however, considered it proper to carry over this sum to the credit of next half-year's account.

CAPITAL.—The expenditure to 31st July, 1868, extended to 36,080*l.*, which was provided for as follows :—

Share capital	£18,720
Mortgages	2,025
Surplus land and houses	14
Transfer fees	1
Balance	15,318=£36,080

Meetings in February or March, and August or September.

No. of Directors—5 ; minimum, 3 ; quorum, 2. *Qualification*, 200*l.*

DIRECTORS:

Chairman—ALEXANDER RONALDSON, Esq., Merchant, Glasgow.

John Campbell Colquhoun, Esq., Killer-mont.

Frederick M'Call, Esq.,Merchant,Glasgow.

Hugh Kirkwood, Esq., Factor and Banker, Killermont.

James Young,Esq.,Broadholm,Duntocher.

OFFICERS.—Sec., James Keyden; Engineers, Forman and M'Call, C.E., Glasgow; Auditors, John E. Watson and Theodore E. Keyden, Accountants, Glasgow ; Solicitors, Keyden, Strang, and Keyden, Glasgow.

Office—186, West George Street, Glasgow.

163.—GLASGOW AND SOUTH WESTERN.

An amalgamation of the GLASGOW PAISLEY KILMARNOCK AND AYR, and GLASGOW DUMFRIES AND CARLISLE, by 11 Vic., cap. 183, taking effect from the opening throughout from Cumnock to Gretna, 28th October, 1850. The terms were a reduction of the G. D. and C. shares from 25*l*. to 8*l*. 10*s*. each, and distribution of the remaining capital required to complete the line *pro rata* amongst the Shareholders of both companies. The main line, Glasgow to Ayr, 40 miles, was opened 12th August, 1843; the remainder, ending with completion of Dumfries line, on 28th October, 1850. The Ayr and Dalmellington was opened in August, 1856. In operation 249¼ miles.

The Consolidation Act, 18 and 19 Vic., cap. 97 (26th June, 1855), entirely reconstitutes the company. By the same Act a short extension of the Mayfield branch into the Grouger coal-field, and a small branch for connecting the main line with the Ardrossan, near the Eglington iron works, were approved of. The length of the first line is 5 furlongs 8 chains and 9 yards, and of the second 2 furlongs 7 chains and 18 yards.

By 21 and 22 Vic., cap. 73 (28th June, 1858), the company was authorised to create 60,000*l*. of additional capital in the Ayr and Dalmellington branch, for the purpose of paying off existing obligations, and to erect stations and otherwise complete works.

By 26 Vic., cap. 14 (4th May, 1863), the company was authorised to raise further capital, 286,000*l*. in shares, at 5 per cent., and 96,000*l*. on loan.

By 26 and 27 Vic., cap, 157 (13th July, 1863), the Glasgow and South Western was authorised to make a junction line to connect the Glasgow and Paisley with the Paisley and Renfrew. Length, 59 chains. Capital, 45,000*l*., at 5 per cent., and 15,000*l*. on loan.

By 26 and 27 Vic., cap. 148 (13th July, 1863), the Glasgow and South Western was authorised to make use of the Ayr and Maybole Junction, and to work, maintain, and renew the same, from 1st August, 1863, on the following terms:—When the gross receipts are under 1,575*l*. for the half-year, at 47 per cent. ; when above that amount, but under 2,000*l*., at 45 per cent. ; under 2,500*l*., 43 per cent.; when under 3,000*l*., 41 per cent. ; and when exceeding 3,000*l*., 39 per cent.

By 27 and 28 Vic., cap. 132 (30th June, 1864), the Glasgow and South Western and the Caledonian were authorised to construct branches and other works in connection with their joint line between Glasgow and Paisley. Length, 2 miles. Capital, 70,000*l*. in shares, and 22,000*l*. on loan, in equal proportions.

CITY OF GLASGOW UNION.—By 28 Vic., cap. 48 (26th May, 1865), the Glasgow and South Western subscribe 300,000*l*. to this undertaking which connects all the railways having termini in Glasgow. By 30 and 31 Vic., cap. 166 (25th July, 1867), the Glasgow and South Western was authorised to subscribe an additional amount of 140,000*l*. in aid of the City of Glasgow Union, which see.

KILMARNOCK DIRECT.—By 28 Vic., cap. 74 (2nd June, 1865), the Glasgow and South Western is authorised to construct new lines between Kilmarnock and Glasgow. Length, 22 miles. Capital, 500,000*l*. in shares, and 166,600*l*. on loan.

AYRSHIRE LINES.—By 28 and 29 Vic., cap. 246 (5th July, 1865), the Glasgow and South Western was authorised to construct six different branches of an aggregate length of 24 miles. New capital, 300,000*l* in shares, and 100,000*l*. on loan. Through booking in favour of the Caledonian. By 29 and 30 Vic., cap. 146 (28th June, 1866), the Glasgow and South Western was authorised to construct other lines in Ayrshire of about 14 miles in length, with a further capital of 100,000*l*. in shares, and 33,000*l*. on loan. Also to create debenture stock.

ADDITIONAL POWERS.—By 28 and 29 Vic., cap. 245 (5th July, 1865), the company was authorised to construct a line from Dalry to Kilbride, with other branches (8 miles), and to raise new capital for general purposes, to the extent of 120,000*l*. in shares, and 40,000*l.* on loan By 29 and 30 Vic., cap. 202 (16th July, 1866), the company was authorised to construct new lines and works. Length, 1½ mile. New capital, 26,000*l.* in shares, and 8,600*l.* on loan.

AMALGAMATIONS.—By 28 and 29 Vic., cap. 298 (5th July, 1865), the following companies were amalgamated with the Glasgow and South Western, as from 1st August, 1865 :—

CASTLE DOUGLAS AND DUMFRIES.—Incorporated by 19 and 20 Vic, cap. 114 (21st July, 1856), for making a railway from Castle Douglas, by Dalbeattie, to Dumfries, by a junction with the Glasgow and South Western, with which traffic arrangements are sanctioned. Capital, 120,000*l.*, in 10*l.* shares; loans, 40,000*l.* Length, 19¾ miles. By 22 and 23 Vic., cap. 29 (21st July, 1859), a deviation was sanctioned, to be completed in two years. The company was also authorised to raise 72,000*l.*, at a preference of not exceeding 6 per cent., and 24,000*l.* on mortgage, in addition to capital authorised by original Act. Opened in November, 1859.

MAYBOLE AND GIRVAN.—Incorporated by 19 and 20 Vic., cap. 99 (14th July, 1856), to make a railway from the town of Maybole to the town and harbour of Girvan. Capital, 68,000*l.*, in 10*l.* shares; loans, 22,600*l.* Length, 12½ miles. Opened, 21st May. 1860. By 22 and 23 Vic,, cap. 34 (21st July, 1859), certain deviations were authorised, but to be completed within one year, the estimate for which amounted to 2,960*l.* New capital to the extent of 45,000*l.*, in 5 per cent. preference shares, and 15,000*l.* on loan.

KIRKCUDBRIGHT.—Incorporated by 24 and 25 Vic., cap. 205 (1st August, 1861), to construct a line from Castle Douglas to Kirkcudbright. Length, 10¼ miles. Capital, 60,000*l.*, in 10*l.* shares, and 20,000*l.* on loan. Opened throughout 16th August, 1864.

BRIDGE OF WEIR.—Incorporated by 25 and 26 Vic., cap. 121 (7th July, 1862), to construct a line from Johnstone, on the Glasgow and South Western, to the village of Bridge of Weir. Length, 3¾ miles. Capital, 25,000*l.*, in 10*l.* shares, and 8,300*l.* on loan.

By 31 and 32 Vic., cap. 39 (25th June, 1868), the company obtained an extension of time for completion of the Kilmarnock Direct till 8th June, 1871, and for the West Kilbride till 5th July, 1871.

POSTPONEMENTS.—At the commencement of the year, the directors stated to the shareholders, that they had resolved to postpone for a period of two years the call of 2*l.* 10*s.* per share, with 5*s.* per share premium, payable on the 10th of February, 1868, on the 10*l.* ordinary shares, in consequence of having arranged with the directors of the Caledonian for the line between Glasgow and Kilmarnock, *viâ* Barrhead, becoming joint property, thus involving abandonment of the Kilmarnock Direct, and for which a bill is to be applied for in the session of 1869 to carry out this arrangement. The directors also took the opportunity of assuring the shareholders that the rolling stock and permanent way were in excellent condition, that no charge had been made against the capital for repairs or renewals. and that for several years past great improvements in the rolling stock, with regard to materials, construction, and value, had been made entirely at the cost of revenue.

REVENUE.—The receipts for the half-year ending 31st January, 1868, amounted to 295,226*l.*, the expenses to 138,132*l.*, the net receipts to 157,094*l.*, the interest on loans and calls in advance to 39,234*l.*, leaving a net balance of 122,860*l.*, to which was added 3,000*l.* from the contingent account (premiums), making 125,860*l.* available for dividend, on the ordinary stock and shares at the rate of 5 per cent. per annum, carrying forward 117*l.*

The receipts for the half-year ending 31st July, 1868, were 3,482*l.* in excess of those of the corresponding period. The net increase in the coaching traffic was 2,498*l.*; in merchandise, 1,961*l.*; live stock, 250*l.*; and the decrease in the mineral traffic, 1,227*l.* The amount expended on maintenance and renewal of way and works for the half-year ending 31st July, 1867, was 37,309*l.*, of which only 32,222*l.* was charged against revenue. During the half-year now ended, the amount expended for similar purposes had been 37,879*l.*, which had been wholly charged against revenue, being 570*l.* in excess of the amount expended, and 5,657*l.* in excess of the amount charged against revenue in the corresponding half-year. The line, works, and rolling stock had been thoroughly maintained. The total receipts amounted to 231,348*l.*, against 277,688*l.* for the corresponding period last year; and the expenses to 130,015*l.*, against 128,911*l.* The net receipts amounted to 151,333*l.*, against 148,777*l.* The balance available for dividend amounted to 117,701*l.*, against 134,275*l.* in 1867, showing a decrease of 16,574*l.* The unproductive capital on which dividend was paid out of revenue amounted to 750,000*l.* The dividend on the preference and guaranteed stocks and shares amounted to 32,449*l.*, leaving a balance of 85,252*l.*, out of which a dividend on the ordinary stock, at the rate of 4½ per cent. per annum, left a balance of 1,288*l.*

CAPITAL.—The expenditure on this account amounted on 31st July to 5,874,772*l.* with 663,500*l.* in subscriptions to other railways (see below). A balance on hand of 130,776*l.* accounts for the subjoined receipts:—

Consolidated stock	£3,131,740
Guaranteed consolidated stock	156,250
Preference consolidated stock	250,000
Perpetual guaranteed stock	342,110
Do. Do. No. 2	321,000
Castle-Douglas preference stock	36,000
Maybole and Girvan do.	25,000
Ordinary 10*l.* shares—calls received	624,697
20*l.* five per cent. preference shares—calls received	275,092
	£5,161,889
Loans on mortgage	1,453,351
Funded debt	51,893
	£6,667,133
Ayr and Dalmellington	1,914= £6,669,048

The Capital authorised for subscriptions to other undertakings was detailed as under:—

	Authorised	Sanctioned	Paid.
Portpatrick Act, 1857	£60,000	£60,000	£60,000
Glasgow and South Western (Glasgow Union Subscription) Act, 1865	300,000	300,000	300,000
Greenock and Ayrshire Act, 1865	300,000	300,000	300,000
Girvan and Portpatrick Junction Act, 1865	50,000	......	......
Ayr Harbour Act, 1866	10,000	10,000	......
Solway Junction (Capital) Act, 1866	100,000	......	......
Brampton and Longtown Act, 1866	30,000	......	......
City of Glasgow Union Act, 1867	140,000	140,000	......
Total	£990,000	£810,000	£660,000

NEW CAPITAL.—At a special meeting, held on 20th August, 1868, it was resolved:—
1. That the agreements now submitted to the meeting, viz.: an agreement between the City of Glasgow Union and the Glasgow and South Western; and an agreement between the City of Glasgow Union, the Glasgow and South Western, the North British, and Messrs. Thomas Brassey, John Kelk, and Charles Waring, of the City of London, Contractors, be, and the same are hereby approved and confirmed; and that the Directors be empowered to concur and assist in the promotion of a bill to be introduced in the next session of Parliament by the City of Glasgow Union, for the purposes of carrying out the provisions contained therein.
2. That under the provisions of the "City of Glasgow Union Act, 1867," the company be empowered to subscribe towards the undertaking, and to take and hold preference shares or stock in the capital of the City of Glasgow Union to the extent of 140,000*l.*, to be created in terms of the "City of Glasgow Union Act, 1867."
3. That in pursuance of and under the powers of the "City of Glasgow Union Act, 1867," the capital stock of the company be, and the same is hereby increased by the additional sum of 140,000*l.*, and that the same be raised by the creation and issue of 140,000*l.* of consolidated stock, which shall be entitled to a preferential dividend, without further participation of profits, and subject to all existing preferences, at the rate of 5*l.* per cent. per annum in perpetuity, payable half-yearly with the dividend on the ordinary stock, with the option to the holder to convert any portion of such stock into the ordinary general stock, on giving notice in writing, addressed to the secretary of the company, at any time on or before 31st July, 1873, and such conversion shall be considered as effected on and from 1st February or 1st August immediately preceding the date of such notice, and that the Directors be empowered to issue the said stock in such a manner and at such times as they may deem most to the advantage of the company.

The whole of this stock has since been issued.

The accounts are made up to 31st January and 31st July, and the meetings held in Glasgow in February or March, and August or September in every year.

Certificates must accompany transfer deeds. Registration fee, 2*s* 6*d.* each transfer, for each description of stock. Transfer books close 21 days before meetings. Proxies 48 hours before meeting. Several classes of stock may go on one stamp.

No. of Directors—10. *Qualification,* 1,000*l.* stock.

DIRECTORS:

1 Chairman—Sir ANDREW ORR, of Harviestoun and Castle Campbell.

9 Deputy-Chairman—ALEXANDER RONALDSON, Esq., 7, Park Terrace, Glasgow.

6 Robert Barclay, Esq., 21, Park Terrace, Glasgow.

10 Peter Clouston, Esq., 1, Park Terrace, Glasgow.

5 Andrew Galbraith, Esq., 163, St. George's Road, Glasgow.

3 James Rodger, Esq., 1, Claremont Gardens, Glasgow.

4 Wellwood H. Maxwell, Esq., M.P., of Munches, Dalbeattie.

8 James M'Clelland, Esq., 140, St. Vincent Street, Glasgow; and Reform Club, London, S. W.

2 William Stevenson, Esq., The Lea, Bridge of Allan.

7 Thomas Richardson, Esq., of Ralston, Paisley.

Retiring Directors are eligible without waiting.

OFFICERS.—Sec., W. J. Wainwright; Gen. Man., William Johnstone; Engs., William Johnstone and Andrew Galloway; Solicitor, James Kerr; Assist Man., W. Gilmour; Man. of Goods Traffic, David Dickie; Supt. of Loco. Dep., James Stirling; Accountant and Cashier, James Thomson, Registrar of Transfers, John Morton; Audit Inspector, William Brown; Auditors, William MacLean and Walter Mackenzie.

Head Offices—14, Bridge Street, Glasgow.

164.—GLOUCESTER AND DEAN FOREST.

Incorporated by 9 and 10 Vic., cap. 240 (27th July, 1846), for a line in connection with the Great Western at Gloucester, to the Hereford Ross and Gloucester, at Westbury, and also to the South Wales at Aure. Broad gauge. Length, 16 miles. The total capital subscribed for was 354,000*l.* The South Wales held 4,000 shares (100,000*l.*); subsequently in lieu thereof, the company took upon itself the construction of seven miles of the line, from Aure to Grange Court, and the capital became reduced, and the 4,000 shares treated as cancelled. The Great Western subscribed 50,000*l.* In 1847, the Gloucester and Dean Forest was empowered to construct a dock at Gloucester (canal). Powers were given by these Acts to either sell or lease the line to the Great Western; and in accordance with these powers, a lease of 999 years was entered into, under which the line is now being worked by the Great Western— terms, 4½ per cent. per annum upon the share capital of 254,000*l.* (any extra capital required found by the Great Western); that rate to be increased to 5 per cent. at the end of five years from the opening; and either of these rates increased to 5½ per cent. on the line being completed to Hereford, which was done in 1855.

Dividends for the half-years ending 31st December and 30th June were at the rate of 12*s.* 9*d.* per 25*l.* share, free of income tax.

CAPITAL.—The general statement of receipts and payments on this account to 30th June, 1868, presented the subjoined details:—

Received.	Expended.
Share capital £254,000	Construction, land, law, engineering, and general expenses £253,700
Cash received on debentures 24,900	Subscription to share capital of Hereford, Ross, and Gloucester 25,000
£278,900	£278,900

The accounts are made up to the 30th June and 31st December, and the statutory meetings held in Gloucester, in February and August every year.

Scale of Voting—C.C.C. Act, sec. 75.

Transfer fee, 2*s.* 6*d.* each deed. Certificates need not accompany transfer deed.

No. of Directors—9. *Qualification*, 1,000*l.*

DIRECTORS:

1 Chairman—WILLIAM PHILIP PRICE, Esq., M.P., Tibberton Court, Gloucester

2 Deputy-Chairman—D. MOWBRAY WALKER, Esq., Gloucester.

1 Thomas Charles Avery, Esq., Gloucester.

2 William Charles King, Esq., Warfield Hall, Bracknell, Berkshire.

3 W. H. K. Gibbons, Esq., Harley, Salop.

3 Charles Barton, Esq., Holbrook House, Wincanton.

The figures opposite the names indicate the number of years each party has to serve.

OFFICERS.—Sec., John Nash, Ross; Auditors, John Calton and Thomas Henry Pike, Gloucester.

Secretary's Offices—Ross.

165.—GREAT EASTERN.

Incorporated by 25 and 26 Vic., cap. 223 (7th August, 1862), and comprising the EASTERN COUNTIES, NORFOLK, EASTERN UNION, EAST ANGLIAN, EAST SUFFOLK, and other subsidiary undertakings in connection therewith. For special details in regard to this amalgamation, see APPENDIX to Vol. XV.

I. EASTERN COUNTIES, which is mainly formed of two arteries—the one to Colchester, and the other to Cambridge; the first was incorporated by 6 and 7 Wm. IV., cap. 106 (1836), for a railway from London to Norwich and Yarmouth, by Romford, Chelmsford, Colchester, and Ipswich. Owing, however, to difficulties in raising the requisite funds, the original scheme was not carried beyond Colchester, 51 miles from London.

NORTHERN AND EASTERN.—Incorporated by 6 and 7 Wm. IV., cap. 103 (4th July, 1856), for a line from Stratford to Newport, with a branch to Hertford (44 miles). By an Act of 1844 (7 and 8 Vic., cap. 20), this company was leased for 999 years to the Eastern Counties, in perpetuity, at 5 per cent. per annum, with surplus profits. These terms have been secured by the Amalgamated Act, and the capital is constituted and confirmed by an Act passed in 1847 (11 Vic., cap. 157), a first claim on the net revenue of the Great Eastern, before any other classes of shares. This company also receives 1,000l. per annum to cover the expenses of management.

NEWMARKET.—By resolutions 17th April, 1851. worked at the rate of 40 per cent on gross receipts, under an agreement dated 28th May, 1851 (confirmed by an Act obtained 28th May, 1852), which took effect from the opening of the branch to Cambridge (viz., from 9th October, 1851); whereby the Newmarket proprietors received such a sum, as with their own net earnings, were sufficient to make up a dividend of 3 per cent. per annum on their share capital (350,000l.)

NEWMARKET.—BURY EXTENSION.—Incorporated by 10 Vic., cap. 172 (16th July, 1846), as the NEWMARKET AND CHESTERFORD, for a line from Chesterford Junction (Eastern Counties) to Newmarket, with a branch to Cambridge, 23 miles. In 1847 the company obtained power to extend the line to Thetford, junction with Norfolk and its title was altered; also to make branches to Ely on the one hand, and Bury St. Edmunds on the other. The Eastern Counties purchased the original line at 15l. per share, payable in debentures at three years' date, bearing 4 per cent. interest in the meantime, and to work the extension at 5 per cent. upon the outlay, not exceeding 145,000l. The extension from Newmarket and Bury was opened on 1st April, 1854, when the Eastern Counties took possession, and the 5 per cent. dividend commenced.

II. NORFOLK.—An amalgamation of the YARMOUTH AND NORWICH and NORWICH AND BRANDON, under the powers of 8 and 9 Vic., cap. 41. The former was incorporated 18th June, 1842, by Act 5 and 6 Vic., cap. 82, for a line from Norwich to the port of Yarmouth. The latter was incorporated 1844, by Act 7 and 8 Vic., cap. 15, for a line in continuation from Norwich to Brandon (where a junction was formed with the Eastern Counties), and was opened simultaneously with that company's extension from Newport to Brandon (30th July, 1845), with a branch to East Dereham, which has since been continued to Fakenham.

WELLS AND FAKENHAM.—Incorporated by 17 and 18 Vic., cap. 180 (24th July, 1854). The line (10 miles) was promoted by residents in the districts, who determined to obtain possession of the land at reasonable prices before commencing the works. Capital, 70,000l., in 20l. shares; power to borrow extends to 23,000l. Opened December 1st, 1857. By 22 and 23 Vic., cap. 139 (13th August, 1859), the company was authorised to extend the line along the quay, at Wells, to raise additional capital to the extent of 3,800l. at 6 per cent. preference, with loan of 1,200l., and to convert the debenture debt into stock. By the same Act the Norfolk may guarantee interest or dividend on the new capital of 3,800l., provided the annual net revenue will so permit.

EPPING.—Incorporated by 22 and 23 Vic., cap. 117 (13th August, 1859), for establishing railway communication between Loughton, Epping, and Chipping Ongar Capital, 100,000l., in 10l. shares; loans, 33,000l. The first line commences by two junctions of the Woodford and Loughton Branch of the Great Eastern and terminates near Epping; the second by a junction with the first near Coopersale, and terminates near Chipping Ongar. By 25 and 26 Vic., cap. 187 (29th July, 1862), the Epping was transferred to the Eastern Counties, and thence became a portion of the Great Eastern.

III. EASTERN UNION.—An amalgamation (under powers obtained in 1847, by Act 11 Vic., cap. 174) of the original EASTERN UNION and the IPSWICH AND BURY. The Eastern Union was incorporated by 8 Vic., cap. 85, 1844, for a line (18 miles) from Colchester to Ipswich, which was opened for traffic 15th June, 1846. The Ipswich and Bury was incorporated by 9 Vic., cap. 97, for a line from Ipswich to Bury St. Edmunds,

with an extension from Haughley to Norwich. From Ipswich to Bury St. Edmunds
(27 miles) was opened 23rd December, 1846, the remainder of the 31 miles from
Haugley to Burston, 2nd July, and thence to Norwich, 12th December, 1819, and the
Trowse branch (2 miles), connecting the railway with the Eastern Counties system at
Norwich, in 1852. The extension to Woodbridge was opened 1st June, 1859. The
Eastern Union leases the Colchester and Stour Valley, which see.

WAVENEY VALLEY.—Incorporated by 14 and 15 Vic., cap. 66 (3rd July, 1851), for a
line from the Tivetshall Station of the Eastern Union, and terminating at Bungay,
Suffolk. Length, 13 miles. By the 26th and 28 in clauses of Act, this company and the
Eastern Union are to afford each to the other the necessary facilities for an interchange
of traffic, and they are also authorised to enter into mutual contracts for working and
joint use. An Act of the 4th of August, 1853 (17 Vic., cap. 144), authorised extension
of Waveney Junction with the " Halesworth " to Beccles. Length, 6 miles. Further
capital authorised 40,000l., and 9,000l. on loans. Compulsory powers, two and five
years. By 18 and 19 Vic., cap. 157 (July 22nd, 1855), the time for compulsory purchase
of land for this extension was extended to 4th August, 1856 ; and by 19 and 20 Vic.,
cap. 129 (29th July, 1856). the period of completion for whole line was postponed to 31st
August, 1858. By 22 and 23 Vic., cap. 115 (13th August, 1859), the company was
authorised to extend the line from Harlestone to Bungay and Ditchingham. No new
capital. By 23 and 24 Vic., cap. 157 (23rd July, 1860), the company was authorised to
extend its line from Bungay to Beccles on the East Suffolk. Length, 51 miles. Compulsory purchase, three years ; completion of works, four years. No new capital. By
24 and 25 Vic., cap. 171 (22nd July, 1861), the company obtained powers to increase its
capital by further loans, to the extent of 4,334l.; to issue cancelled shares at a preference of 5 per cent.; and to convert debentures into stock. Open from Tivetshall to
Harleston in October, 1860, 6½ miles ; further extension from Harleston to Bungay,
opened November 2nd, 1860, 6 miles ; Bungay to Beccles (6 miles), 2nd March, 1863.

By 25 and 26 Vic., cap. 195 (29th July, 1862), the Eastern Union was authorised to
make certain arrangements in regard to its capital account, to issue new 5 per cent.
preference shares to the extent of 250,000l.; of which 200,000l. was to discharge
existing liabilities, and 50,000l. as its contribution on the Waveney Valley.

IV. EAST ANGLIAN.—Incorporated by 11 Vic., cap. 275, being an amalgamation of
three distinct companies, viz., the LYNN AND ELY, incorporated by 9 Vic., cap. 55, for
a line from a junction with the Eastern Counties, at Ely, to the port of Lynn, with a
branch to Wisbeach, 36½ miles, all open; the LYNN AND DEREHAM, incorporated by 9
Vic., cap. 126, for a Line from a junction with a branch of the Norfolk and Dereham, to
join the Lynn and Ely, at Lynn, 26½ miles, all open; and ELY AND HUNTINGDON,
incorporated by 8 and 9 Vic., cap. 48, for a line from a junction with the Lynn and Ely,
at Ely, to Huntington, 22½ miles.—At a special meeting on 22nd September, 1863, it
was resolved to divide the East Anglian stock into two classes, one to be called No. 1
stock, amounting to 1,06,721l., to be entitled to fixed dividends at the rate of 5l. per cent.,
and the other to be called East Anglian No. 2 Stock, amounting to 826,885l., to be
entitled to a dividend thereon equal to one-half of the amount of dividend exceeding 3l.
per cent., which shall in any half-year be declared upon the ordinary stock. The practical effect of the arrangement is that every proprietor of 100l. stock became entitled
to 20l. of a new 5l. per cent. stock, and 80l. of a stock bearing a dividend equal to one-
half of the excess over 3l. per cent. paid at any time on Great Eastern ordinary stock,
one-half of such excess on 80l. being the same as two-fifths on 100l.

V. EAST SUFFOLK.—Incorporated as HALESWORTH BECCLES AND HADDISCOE
by 14 Vic., cap. 26 (June 5th, 1851), for a line from Halesworth to Beccles, and to join
the Lowestoft at Haddiscoe, in Norfolk, with a branch. By Act of 1854 (17 and 18
Vic., cap. 119) the name of the company was changed to "East Suffolk" and the
capital fixed at 450,000l. The borrowing powers extend to 150,000l., which, with the
share capital "shall be applied only in carrying into execution the object and purposes of the Act." Length of new main line, 24 miles 3 chains and 30 links, and that
of the branches respectively, as follow, viz.: Leiston branch 3 miles 4 furlongs 8
chains and 50 links ; Snap Bridge branch, 1 mile 4 furlongs 4 chains and 50 links;
Framlingham branch, 5 miles 5 furlongs 8 chains and 20 links. Total, 53 miles.
Opened 1st June, 1859. By 21 and 22 Vic., cap. 47 (28th June, 1858), the company
was authorised to construct a branch near Lowestoft, and to raise 360,000l. in shares,
and 120,000 on mortgage. Of this additional capital, 350,000l. was required for making
the East Suffolk a double line, and 10,000l. for the new branch. By 21 and 22 Vic.,
cap. 3 (23rd July, 1858), the two following undertakings are incorporated with the
East Suffolk;—Lowestoft and Beccles, incorporated by 19 and 20 Vic., cap. 53 (23rd
June, 1856), to make a railway from Lowestoft to join the East Suffolk at Beccles. Capital, 80,000l. in 10l. shares; loans, 23,000l.. Yarmouth and Haddiscoe, incorporated by

19 and 20 Vic., cap. 79 (7th July, 1856), for making line from Yarmouth to the East Suffolk, at Haddiscoe. Length, 8¼ miles. Capital 90,000*l.* in 10*l.* shares; loans, 25,000*l.* By 22 Vic., cap. 28 (19th April, 1859), the company was authorised to raise new capital in shares, 40,000*l.*, and on loans, 13,333*l.* Also to construct a branch to Aldborough. Length, 4½ miles. Estimate, 40,000*l.* Opened, 1860. By an Act 22nd July, 1861, the company was authorised to determine the lease to Sir Morton Peto. The Great Eastern issued to the East Suffolk 340,000*l.* debenture stock, bearing a guaranteed dividend of 4 per cent., and a further sum of 335,000*l.* 4½ per cent. preference stock. Out of this stock the East Suffolk indemnify the Great Eastern against the fixed liabilities of 340,000*l.* debenture stock, 86,488*l.* simple contract debts and 177,860*l.* East Suffolk stock convertible into preference stock, or redeemable at par. The Great Eastern is also bound to issue to the East Suffolk such an amount of ordinary stock, fully paid up, as Captain Galton shall determine to be the amount of that ordinary stock, which taking into consideration the probable natural future development of the traffic of the East Suffolk undertaking, ought to be so issued.

NEW WORKS, &c.—By 26 and 27 Vic., cap. 190 (21st July, 1863), additional powers were conferred on the Great Eastern, in respect of the East Anglian capital, and to divide that stock into two classes, &c. Also to dissolve the Waveney Valley, and to amalgamate that company with the Great Eastern; to authorise the Great Eastern to guarantee 4½ per cent. on the shares of the Lynn and Hunstanton and the Bishop Stortford. Also to raise new capital to the extent of 5,000*l.*

By 27 and 28 Vic., cap. 95 (23rd June, 1864), the company was authorised to construct a line from Leyton to Highbeech. Length, 6¼ miles. Capital, 120,000*l.* in shares, and 40,000*l.* on loan.

By 27 and 28 Vic., cap. 282 (25th July, 1864), the company was authorised to construct several short junctions, to shorten certain routes, and to facilitate traffic generally. Length 3¾ miles. New capital, 24,000*l.* in shares, and 8,000*l.* on loan.

By 28 Vic., cap. 62 (2nd June, 1865), the company was authorised to construct a branch from Somersham to Ramsey. Length, 8 miles. New capital, 52,000*l.* in shares, and 17,300*l.* on mortgage.

By 28 and 29 Vic., cap. 184 (29th June, 1865), the company obtained power to consolidate certain preference stocks, and to raise new capital to the extent of 1,500,000*l.* in shares, and 500,000*l.*, on mortgage.

METROPOLITAN STATION.—By 27 and 28 Vic., cap. 313 (29th July, 1864), the company was authorised to construct several short lines in and near the Metropolis, and to purchase lands for a station in the city of London. Length. 15½ miles. Capital, 1,363,000*l.* in shares, and 454,330*l.* on loan. By 30 Vic., cap. 52 (31st May, 1867), the company was authorised to carry on steamboat traffic between Harwich and Harlingen and Geestemunde.

By 28 Vic., cap. 118 (19th June, 1865), the company was authorised to make several short lines in connection with the metropolis, to purchase lands for stations., &c. Length, 7 miles. Capital, 196,000*l.* in shares, and 65,330*l.* on mortgage.

By 29 and 30 Vic., cap. 255 (23rd July, 1866), the company was authorised to purchase lands and buildings for station purposes, to alter the levels of the Ramsey branch, and also of part of the Metropolitan Extension. Also to construct two short branches in conjunction with the Hertford and Enfield branches. Length, ¾ mile. New capital, 76,000*l.* in shares, and 25,300*l.* on mortgage. The company also obtained power to raise a portion of their debentures, although one-half of their stock in relation thereto had not been paid up.

By 29 and 30 Vic., cap. 287 (30th July, 1866), the Great Eastern was authorised to construct an extension to connect the system with the Alexandra Park. Length, 3¼ miles. Capital, 112,000*l.* in shares and 70,000*l.* on loan.

STEAMBOATS.—By 26 and 27 Vic., cap. 225 (28th July, 1863), the company was authorised to employ steamboats between Harwich and Flushing, Rotterdam and Antwerp. New capital, 120,000*l.* By 30 and 31 Vic., cap. 119 (15th July, 1867), the Great Eastern was authorised to constitute their Metropolitan Extensions into a separate company, having obtained an extension of time for completion of works for three years.

MARCH AND SPALDING.—By 26 and 27 Vic., cap. 191, the Great Eastern obtained working powers over the Great Northern line from March to Spalding, but not to interfere with intermediate traffic.

TOTTENHAM AND HAMPSTEAD JUNCTION.—An agreement for working this line received the approval of the proprietors on the of June, 1862.

WARE, HADHAN, AND BUNTINGFORD.—The Great Eastern subscribed 22,000*l.* to this line, and works the traffic.

BLACKWALL.—By 28. Vic., cap. 100 (12th June, 1865), the Blackwall was leased to the Great Eastern from 1st January, 1866, at a fixed guarantee of 4½ per cent. on its ordinary stock, the London and North Western, the Great Northern, and the Midland obtaining various running powers.

BISHOP'S STORTFORD, DUNMOW, AND BRAINTREE.—Incorporated by 24 and 25 Vic., cap. 182 (22nd July, 1861), to construct a line from Bishop's Stortford, on the Great Eastern, through Dunmow to Braintree, on the line of the same company, with a branch to join the Epping at Dunmow. Length, 19 miles 14 chains. Capital, 120,000*l.*, in 10*l.* shares, loans, 40,000*l.* By 28 and 29 Vic., cap. 150 (29th June, 1865), this line is to be vested in the Great Eastern on opening of the line for traffic. By 31 and 32 Vic., cap. 170 (31st July, 1868), it is provided that the Great Eastern may pay in debentures and stock, an ascertained balance due to the contractors, on which the Bishop's Stortford shall become part of the Great Eastern system.

FINANCE ACT, 1867.—By 30 and 31 Vic., cap. 208 (20th August, 1867), special powers were conferred upon the company to raise 3,000,000*l.* in preference stock, in payment of its debts and other liabilities. The enacting clauses of this measure are given in the APPENDIX to the volume for 1868.

By 31 and 32 Vic., cap. 164 (31st July, 1868), the company obtained two years for purchase of lands in respect to its Acts of 1865 and 1866; and also three years for completion of works between Edmonton Station and the Tottenham and Hampstead Junction. Also a declaration as to the priority of the 4½ preference stock of 1861, and validification of agreement between the Great Eastern and the East Anglian, by which the latter might waive its privilege of appointing directors.

REVENUE.—The receipts for the half-year ending 31st December, amounted to 1,031,227*l.*, against a gross revenue of 996,293*l.* in the corresponding half-year of 1866 The increase was 34,934*l.*, or at the rate of 3½ per cent. The working expenses were 511,194*l.*, or about 49½ per cent. upon the gross revenue. In the corresponding half-year of 1866 the working expenses were 508,740*l.*, or about 51½ per cent. The net revenue was 509,198*l.*, against 483,677*l.* in December, 1866, showing an increase of 25,521*l.*, or 5½ per cent. The leased lines and the interest upon debentures absorbed 238,635*l.*, while a further sum of 12,076*l.* was required for payment of interest upon the floating debt. The remainder was sufficient to pay the half-year's dividends of all the preference shareholders falling due on the 31st of December, and also all the arrears due for the previous half-year to those preference shareholders whose dividends were not covered by the revenue of that half-year. The anticipation, therefore, expressed by the late chairman, that the revenue of the year 1867 would be sufficient to meet the preference dividends for that year, proved to be correct, a balance of 7,737*l.* remaining to next account.

For the June half-year there had been a gross revenue of 925,070*l.*, against 872,213*l.*, in the corresponding half-year of 1867. The increase had consequently been 52,857*l.*, or at the rate of 6 per cent. The working expenses were 473,600*l.*, or about 51 per cent. In the corresponding half-year of 1867 the working expenses were 479,279*l.*, or about 55 per cent. Notwithstanding the increased receipt of 52,857*l.*, there had been a saving on the working expenses of 5,679*l.* Adding the increase upon traffic and the saving in expenditure, the net revenue amounted to 451,470*l.*, against 392,934*l.* in June, 1867, showing an increase of 58,536*l.*, or 14¾ per cent. of net profit. The interest upon debentures and other obligations absorbed 266,899*l.* The remaining sum of 184,571*l.* was sufficient to cover the preference dividends for the half-year, amounting to 184,132*l.*, leaving a balance of 439*l.*, in addition to the balance from the previous half-year.

The directors were convinced that the expenditure on revenue account upon the permanent way and the rolling stock had been amply sufficient to repair the wear and tear of the half-year; and that the company's property in that respect was now in a better condition than at the beginning of the half-year. It had, in fact, been necessary for the last two years to spend more upon those two accounts than the legitimate repairs of the half-year would require, in consequence of the neglect into which they had been previously allowed to fall.

FINANCE.—It was reported in August that the agreement recently made with the Great Northern, and in the increase in goods traffic to which the present improved relations between the two companies might be expected to lead, rendered it a matter of urgent necessity that the deficiency in rolling stock under which the company laboured should not be allowed to continue. The directors were precluded under the Finance Act of last year from making any such capital outlay without the assent of the preference shareholders. The sum required would not fall far short of 150,000*l.* Heavy repairs were found to be required upon the steamboats in consequence of the state of neglect into which they had fallen, and the traffic in consequence still appeared upon the company's books as a cause of loss. But the directors hoped that a more satisfactory result would be obtained by next half-year. The debts to bankers had been paid. The preference shareholders had received debenture stock in satisfaction of their claims for dividend up to December last, so far as application had been made for it. The number who had applied represented three-fourths of the whole preference stock. The ordinary debts were being paid as fast as the amounts could be settled between the parties and the authority of the Court of Chancery for payment obtained. The unrenewed debentures had been paid off, or payment had been tendered for them, and provision had been made for the debentures about to fall in for several months to come. The coal depôt was being constructed as rapidly as possible. There was no other cause of embarrassment in the general financial condition of the company, except that the question of the metropolitan extensions had not yet been brought to a settlement.

RECEIVERS.—These functionaries were discharged by the Court of Chancery in November, and the entire management committed to the descretion and responsibility of the board.

CAPITAL —The subjoined tabular statement furnishes in full detail the stock and share capital of the company : —

	Authorized.		Received
Great Eastern ordinary	£8,376,981	....	£8,374,136
East Anglian ,,	826,885	....	826,885
Great Eastern 7 per cent.	80,654	....	80,654
,, 6 per cent.	761,817	....	761,817
,, 5½ per cent.	135,000	....	105,000
,, 5 per cent.	3,042,012	....	2,943,262
,, 4½ per cent.	975,129	....	898,454
,, 4 per cent.	672,360	....	669,375
,, 3½ per cent.	23,750	....	23,750
,, 5 per cent., 1862	1,122,600	....	1,122,600
,, 5 per cent., 1863	1,204,000	....	1,181,946
,, 5 per cent., 1864	1,716,930	....	308,185
,, 5 per cent., 1865	1,860,000	....	....
,, 5 per cent., 1866	188,000	....	....
	£20,986,118	....	£17,296,064

Deduct—
Amount repealed by Finance Act of 1867, viz :
Capital Act, 1865 ....£1,500,000
Metropolitan Act, 1864 ...£1,363,000
Highbeech Branch Act,
1864 120,000
Additional Powers Act,
1865 196,000
Additional Powers Act,
1866 76,000
Alexandra Park Act,
1866 112,000
—————
£1,867,000
Less—
Aggregate amount for
which powers to raise
capital are retained ... 867,000
—————— £1,000,000 = £2,500,000

	£18,486,118	....	£17,296,064
Raised in respect of the 6½ per cent. stock, 1866	....	....	55,084

	£18,486,118	....	£17,351,148
Debentures and debenture stock			6,271,144

Total capital £23,622,29

Scale of Voting.—One vote for each 100*l.* held.

No. of Directors—15, of which 3 are nominated by Northern and Eastern, and 2 elected by East Anglian proprietors; quorum, 5.   *Qualification*, 2,600*l.*

DIRECTORS:

Chairman—The MARQUIS OF SALISBURY, 1, Mansfield Street, Cavendish Square, W.

Deputy-Chairman—CHARLES HENRY TURNER, Esq., Litchurch, Derby.

James Chadwick, Esq., Miller Street, Manchester.
George Wodehouse Currie, Esq., 10, Hyde Park Street, W.
Robert William Kennard, Esq., 37, Porchester Terrace, Bayswater, W.
William Thomas Makins, Esq., 34, Holland Park, Bayswater, W.
Lightly Simpson, Esq., 50, Gower Street, Bedford Square, W.C.

Henry Lewis Smale, Esq., Doctor's Commons, E.C.
Robert Stuart, Esq , Ardwick Hall, Manchester.
Sir Edward William Watkin, Knt., Rose Hill, Northenden, near Manchester, and 18, Westbourne Terrace, Hyde Park, W.
Richard Young, Esq., Osborne House, Wisbeach.

OFFICERS.—Sec , J. B. Owen; Gen. Man., S. Swarbrick; Supt. J. Robertson; Goods Man., W. Birt; Loco. Supt., S. W. Johnson; Eng., H. W. Davis; Storekeeper, R. Scott; Land Agent, C. Dobbin; Law Clerk, W. H. Shaw; Solicitors, Baxter, Rose, Norton, and Co.; Cashier, W. Ellis.

Head Offices—Bishopsgate Terminus, E.C.

166.—GREAT MARLOW.

Incorporated by 31 and 32 Vic., cap. 100 (13th July, 1868), to construct a railway from the Wycombe branch of the Great Western to Great Marlow. Length, 2¾ miles. Capital 18,000*l.* in 10*l.* shares, and 6,000*l.* on loan.   Arrangements with Great Western.

Meetings in February or March, and in August or September.

No. of Directors—7; minimum, 5; quorum, 3.   *Qualification*, 100*l.*

DIRECTORS:

James Carson, Esq.
Peter Borgnio, Esq.
Thomas Owen Wethered, Esq., M.P.
Owen Peel Wethered, Esq.

James Rolls, Esq.
Thomas Rolls, Esq., M.P.
Robert Fottit, Esq.

167.—GREAT NORTH OF SCOTLAND.

Incorporated by 9 and 10 Vic., cap. 103, for a line from Aberdeen to Inverness, with branches to Banff, Portsoy, Garmouth and Burghead. Length, 138¼ miles. This and the Aberdeen were to have formed one undertaking, when half of the capital of each had been paid up; but an Act of 1850, 14 Vic., cap. 78, repealed the Amalgamation Act, 11 Vic., cap. 195.

The new lines and extensions authorised by Act of 1854, were Leithhall deviation, 3 miles 1 furlong 75 chains; canal branch, 1 mile 6 furlongs 22¾ chains; total 5 miles. Estimate, 43,000*l.*

By 18 Vic., cap. 28 (May 25th, 1855), the company was empowered to extend from Huntly to Keith, 12½ miles, at an estimated cost of 80,000*l.*

By 22 and 23 Vic., cap. 8 (31st July, 1859), the Acts of the company were consolidated and the tolls and charges revised.   The Act also fixed the capital at 1,050,000*l.*; original shares, 276,860*l.*; preference, 291,090*l.*; new preference, 482,050*l.* at 4½ per cent.; loans, 350,000*l.* Mortgage debt to be converted into stock at 4 per cent.

By 24 and 25 Vic., cap. 153 (11th July, 1861), the company was authorised to enlarge their stations at Kittybrewster and Aberdeen, and to alter the line and levels of the canal branch. No new capital.

By 25 and 26 Vic., cap. 62 (30th June, 1862), the company obtained power to guarantee, for ten years, the mortgage debt of the Alford Valley, the Keith and Dufftown, and the Aberdeen and Turriff; to subscribe additional capital, 48,000*l.*, to the Alford Valley, and 100,000*l.* to the Formantine and Buchan, and to raise additional capital to the extent of 360,000*l.*, at 4½ per cent., in shares, and 70,666*l.* on loan for these purposes. In addition to the above sums, the company are authorised to raise the following new share capital :—Stock and shares, authorised by "Strathspey Railway Act, 1861,"

100,000*l*.; by "Great North of Scotland Railway Act, 1863," as amended by "Denburn Valley Railway Act, 1864," 125,000*l*.; by "Banffshire Railway Act, 1863," 70,000*l*.; by "Banff Macduff and Turriff Extension Railway Act, 1863," 45,000*l*., by "Great North of Scotland Railway Act, 1864," 75,000*l*.; "Strathspey Railway Act, 1865," 40,000*l*. Debenture and debenture stock : By "The Great North of Scotland Railway Act, 1863," as amended by "Denburn Valley Railway Act, 1864," 41,600*l*. The total capital authorised up to 31st July, 1865, 237,266*l*.

MORAYSHIRE.—By agreement, the Great North of Scotland works the Morayshire at 45 per cent., and contributes 20,000*l*. to the new line through the glen of Rothes, with a view to a junction at Dufftown.

DENBURN VALLEY.—By 27 and 28 Vic., cap. 111 (23rd June, 1864), the Scottish North Eastern was authorised to construct a line through the city of Aberdeen to connect with the Great North of Scotland. Length, 1¾ miles. The capital of 190,000*l*. in shares is provided by subscription from the Great North of Scotland of 125,000*l*., and 70,000*l*. by the Scottish North Eastern, the obligation incurred by the former company in 1863, to construct the "Aberdeen Junction," being repealed. Through booking and mutual facilities. Borrowing powers, 41,600*l*.

By 27 Vic., cap. 26 (13th May, 1864), the Great North of Scotland was authorised to contribute additional sums to the following companies, as undermentioned, viz.,—Keith and Dufftown, 10,000*l*.; Strathspey, 50,000*l*.; and Morayshire, 15,000*l*.

By the following Acts the company obtained powers to contribute sums to the companies undermentioned, viz. :—Aberdeen and Turriff (Act 1859), 33,981*l*.; Keith and Dufftown (Acts 1857 and 1866), 26,000*l*.; Banff Extension (Acts 1857 and 1863), 50,000*l*.; Formartine and Buchan (Act 1863), 25,000*l*.; Strathspey (Acts 1861 and 1865), 140,000*l*.; Banffshire (Act 1863), 80,000*l*.

AMALGAMATION.—The whole system, however, was consolidated by 29 and 30 Vic., cap. 288 (30 July, 1866), which took effect on 1st August, 1866. The Act provided as regards the Alford Valley, Aberdeen and Turriff, Banff Macduff and Turriff Extension, Keith and Dufftown, and Strathspey, that the original share capital of these branches be cancelled, and a like amount of new ordinary shares in the amalgamated company created in lieu thereof, to be given off to the original shareholders in the branch lines, for like nominal amounts of their branch shares so cancelled; the shares created in lieu of those subscribed by the Great |North to be divided rateably among the original shareholders of that company. The contributions by the Great North and the public to the above lines amount as follow, viz.:—

	Great North.	Public.
Alford Valley	£59,920	£18,140
Aberdeen and Turriff	40,029	42,780
Banff Macduff and Turriff Extension	30,456	28,220
Keith and Dufftown	40,135	31,542
Strathspey	192,700	*12,360
	£363,231	£133,042

* Including 11,000*l*. from the Keith and Dufftown.

As regards the FORMARTINE AND BUCHAN, it is proposed to guarantee the original shares held by the public on 60 per cent. of the gross receipts of the Formartine and Buchan line proper, after the payment of the dividend on the 5 per cent. Formartine and Buchan preference shares, as follow, viz.:—

For year ending 31st August, 1867 .... 1½ per cent.
Do.　　　 do.　　1868 .... 2　 ,,
Do.　　　 do.　　1869 .... 2½ ,,
Do.　　　 do.　　1870 .... 3　 ,,

And in perpetuity thereafter, with the right of participating with the original shares of the company in any dividend beyond 3 per cent.

OLDMELDRUM JUNCTION.—This line, formerly leased to the Great North, is amalgamated with it, the rent (650*l*.) secured as a fixed charge against the Great North, and converted into a dividend of like amount on a preferential stock of 13,810*l*.—to be called "Great North of Scotland (Oldmeldrum) Preference Stock."

BANFFSHIRE.—Incorporated by 20 and 21 Vic., cap. 53 (27th July, 1857), to construct a line from the Grange Station of the Great North of Scotland, to the harbour of Banff, with a branch to the harbour of Portsoy. Capital, 90,000*l*. in 10*l*. shares; loans, 30,000*l*. Main line, 16¼ miles; length of branch to Portsoy, 3¼ miles. Opened, August, 1859. Arrangements, under usual restrictions with the Great North of Scotland. By 26 and

27 Vic., cap. 170 (21st July, 1863), the company was authorised to construct an extension to Port Gordon. Length, 14¾ miles. New capital, 160,000*l.* in shares of 5 per
cent., and 33,000*l.* on loan; but by 30 and 31 Vic., cap. 190 (12th August, 1867), the
extension was authorised to be abandoned, and the capital cancelled. By the same
Act the Banffshire line is amalgamated with the Great North.

FURTHER POWERS, 1867.—By 30 and 31 Vic., cap. 190 (12th August, 1867), the
Great North of Scotland was authorised to exercise its borrowing powers in respect
to the Denburn Valley, although the requisite amount of share capital had not been
paid thereon. By the same Act the entire capital of the Great North of Scotland,
including the Banffshire, was declared to consist of 2,554,443*l.* in stock, and 864,919*l*
on loan.

REVENUE.—It was reported in March, that, pending decision in the lawsuit in respect
to the proper division of revenue between certain sections of the preference stocks no
dividend could be declared. It was reported in September, however, that the first
preferences must be fully paid off before others participated in revenue. The receipts
during the half-year amounted to 90,658*l.*, and the expenditure to 58,426*l.*; the interest
on debentures and debenture stock to 18,318*l.*, leaving 13,915*l.*, to which was added
4,546*l.* from the preceding half-year, making 18,461*l.* The interest on bank accounts,
discount on bills, &c., amounted to 5,944*l.*; on the Old Meldrum 4½ per cent. stock, to
311*l.*; on the 5 per cent. Aberdeen and Turriff preference stock, to 635*l.*; on the
Formartine and Buchan 5 per cent. preference stock, to 3,195*l.*; on the Formartine and
Buchan ordinary stock at 2 per cent., to 1,064*l.*; on the 5 per cent. preference stock at
1*l.* per cent. for the year ending July 31st, to 2,911*l.*; and on the 4½ per cent. (A)
preference stock, at 18s. per cent. for the year ending July 31st, to 4,338*l.*, leaving a
balance of 63*l.* The gross traffic for the half-year was 89,290*l.*, and for the same period
of 1867, 87,452*l.*, showing an increase of 1,838*l.*; but there was a decrease on
miscellaneous receipts and dividends and interests from other companies of 1,036*l.*,
leaving the net increase on the half-year's revenue of 802*l.* Under locomotive power
there was an increase in repairs and renewals, but a decrease in the running expenses.
The total expenditure for the half-year on the maintenance and renewal of the plant
amounted to 8,986*l.*, being at the rate of 5d. per train mile. About 147,820*l.* of the
Formartine and Buchan and Aberdeen and Turriff 5 per cent. preference stocks had
been realised at par, and the proceeds applied in discharge of the floating debt. Of the
(B) 4½ per cent. preference stock held in security 136,010*l.* had been returned to the
company and cancelled.

CAPITAL.—The receipts and expenditure on this account to 31st July, furnished the
subjoined information:—

G. N. of S. 5 per cent. preference			£291,090
Do.	4½ per cent. (A) preference		482,050
Do.	4½ per cent. (B) preference (including 4,370*l.* in security)		222,400
Do.	(Oldmeldrum) 4½ per cent. preference		13,810
Do.	(Aberdeen and Turriff) 5 per cent. preference (including 7,500 in security)		32,900
Do.	(Formartine and Buchan) 5 per cent. preference	£127,786	
Do.	do. do. do. (in security)	70,740=	198,526
Do.	(Formartine and Buchan) ordinary	79,532	
Do.	do. (in security)	18,500	
Do.	do. (held for guarantors' obligations)	26,860=	124,892
Ordinary stock (including 7,170*l.* held for guarantors' obligations)			862,205
			£2,227,873
Debentures and debenture stock			833,859
			£3,061,732
Balance			182,695
Expenditure			£3,244,428

Accounts made up half-yearly to 31st January and 31st July. Meetings held at
Aberdeen, in March or April, September or October.

Scale of Voting.—One vote for each share held.

Certificates must accompany transfer deed, the free for registration of which is 2*s. 6d.*
each seller.

No. of Directors.—Maximum, 13; minimum, 7. *Qualification*, 20 shares.

DIRECTORS:

Chairman—JOHN DUNCAN, Esq., Advocate, Aberdeen.

Deputy-Chairman—GEORGE MILNE, Esq., of Kinaldie.

Thomas Adam, Esq., Banker, Aberdeen.

Newell Burnett, Esq., of Kyllachie, Aberdeen.

James Crombie, Esq., Manufacturer, Grandholm Works, by Aberdeen.

William Ferguson, Esq., of Kinmundy.

Robert Kaye, Esq., Fountain Bank, Partick Hill, near Glasgow.

William Leslie, Esq., Architect, Aberdeen.

John Ligertwood, Esq., Advocate, Aberdeen.

William Longmore, Esq., Distiller, Keith.

James Moir, Esq., Banker, Portsoy.

James Badenoch Nicolson, Esq., of Glenbervie,

Major John Ramsay, of Barra.

OFFICERS.—Gen. Man., Robert Milne; Manager's Assistant, John S. Stuart; Secretary, W. B. Ferguson; Secretary's Assistant, George Neilson; Passenger Supt., F. Morrison; Goods Man., William Walker; Loco. Supt., William Cowan; Eng., Patrick M. Barnett; Accountant, Samuel Paterson; Audit Clerk, James Rutherford; Traffic Cashier, Thomas Hector; Auditors, Robt. Fletcher and James Augustus Sinclair, Aberdeen; Solicitors, Adam, Thomson, and Ross, 75, Union Street, Aberdeen; Parliamentary Agents, Dyson and Company, London: Bankers, Union Bank, London: Commercial Bank, Liverpool; National Bank of Scotland, and Branches; North of Scotland Bank, Aberdeen.

Head Offices—Waterloo Station, Aberdeen.

168.—GREAT NORTHERN.

An amalgamation of the LONDON AND YORK and DIRECT NORTHERN. Incorporated 9 and 10 Vic., cap. 71 (26th June, 1846), for construction of a line from London to York, via Peterborough, Newark, and Retford, with a loop line from Peterborough, through Boston and Lincoln, rejoining the main line at Retford. Length, 275 miles. This company subsequently obtained power to construct branches to Spalding, Hertford, Hatfield, St. Albans, and Sutton, and the Isle of Axholme. Total parliamentary powers, 335½ miles. This company has leased the East Lincolnshire (Boston to Great Grimsby, 48 miles), and the Royston and Hitchin (19 miles). The following have been abandoned:—Main line, Askerne to York (1846), 26 miles, definitely determined 29th August, 1850; Loop, Gainsborough to Bawtry, 11 miles; Isle of Axholme Extension (12 Vic., cap. 114), 29 miles, and Snaith to Thorne Branch, 7 miles. Main Line, East Retford to Helpstone, via Newark and Grantham, 55 miles; Thorney, 5 miles; Sutton Bridge Line (10 Vic., cap. 286), 3 miles; branch to Bedford, from Boston, Stamford, and Birmingham Line to Wisbeach, 23 miles, and branch to Thorney, 5 miles; Bedford and Sandy branch, 8 miles; branches to Hertford and St. Albans (10 Vic., cap. 272), 14 miles; total, 181 miles abandoned. Productive mileage 233 miles.

An agreement with the York and North Midland permits the use of 20 miles from Knottingly into the station at York. The use of the intervening link from Askerne to Knottingley (belonging to the Lancashire and Yorkshire) is also permanently secured, and the agreement legalised by Act 14 and 15 Vic., cap. 45.

By 18 and 19 Vic., cap. 124 (July 2nd, 1855), the company became entitled to raise additional capital to the extent of 1,000,000l. in shares, and 333,000l. by loan. By the same Acts the agreements with the Lancashire and Yorkshire, and Leeds and Thirsk, as to purchase of part of lines, were legalised and confirmed.

By 22 Vic., cap. 35 (19th April, 1859), the company is authorised to form a junction with the North London, of 2 furlongs and 5 chains. By the same Act the company is authorised to convert its mortgage debt into 4 per cent. debenture stock, to redeem its present preference stock, and to re-issue the same under the following proviso:—"The new shares created under the powers of this Act shall be entitled to the preferential dividend, if any, which may be attached to them by the company as aforesaid, in priority to the ordinary shares and stock in the company; but if in any year ending the 31st day of December there shall not be profits arising to the company, available for the payment of the full amount of such preferential dividend for that year, no part of the deficiency shall be made good out of the profits of any subsequent year, or out of any other funds of the company.

METROPOLITAN JUNCTION.—By 23 and 24 Vic., cap. 168 (23rd July, 1860), the Great Northern was authorised to construct a communication from near King's Cross to the Metropolitan, to be completed within five years. New capital, 30,000l. at 4¼ per cent. in shares, and 10,000l. on loan. Opened June, 1863.

NOTTINGHAM AND GRANTHAM.—An arrangement was entered into as follows, in 1855:—"The Nottingham to complete line into the station at Nottingham. The Great Northern to work the line, exclusive of the Grantham and Nottingham Canals, at 30 per cent. of gross earnings, if the traffic be less than 37,000*l.* a year, or at 35 per cent. if it exceed that sum. The agreement for 10 years with power to the Great Northern to take the whole undertaking at a fixed annual rental of 4 per cent. within four years, or 4½ per cent. within nine years: or to amalgamate the two companies at par." A new arrangement has since been effected as follows :—To lease the line for 999 years on and from the 1st of August, 1861, on the terms of paying a dividend at the rate of 4*l.* 2*s.* 6*d.* per cent. per annum, on the capital of 1,014,000*l.*, with right to purchase the whole property on repayment of the capital at par value.

HERTFORD, LUTON, AND DUNSTABLE.—An amalgamation by 21 and 22 Vic., cap. 74 (28th June, 1858), of the Hertford and Welwyn Junction, and of the Luton Dunstable and Welwyn Junction. These companies were incorporated as follows:—

Hertford and Welwyn Junction.—By Act of 3rd July, 1854 (17th and 18th Vic., cap. 127). The line joins these two towns, and forms a connection between the Great Northern and Great Eestern, with both of which it may come in alliance. It has also running powers over the Great Eastern from Hertford to Ware. Capital, 65,000*l.*, in 20*l.* shares; power to borrow 21,600*l.* Opened, 7½ miles, 1st March, 1858.

Luton, Dunstable, and Welwyn Junction.—Incorporated by 18 and 19 Vic., cap. 146 (16th July, 1855), for constructing a railway from the London and North Wes'ern at Dunstable, to the Great Northern at Welwyn. Length, 17 miles. Estimate, 108,000*l.* Opened from Dunstable to Luton, 5½ miles, 13th May, 1858. The line was opened throughout on 1st September, 1860, and direct communication from Dunstable and Luton, *via* Hatfield, to Hertford and London (King's Cross station) established. Productive, 24½ miles.

MANCHESTEE, SHEFFIELD, AND LINCOLNSHIRE.—By 21 and 22 Vic., cap. 113 (23rd July, 1858), the Great Northern is authorised to enter into financial and traffic arrangements with this company, in accordance with which the former is entitled to receive, out of the earnings arising from through traffic, such a sum as would, with other receipts, make up the gross sum of 10,000*l.* per week, subject to being repaid when their gross receipts exceed 11,000*l.* per week.

CHESHIRE LINES.—By 26 and 27 Vic., cap. 147 (13th July, 1863), the Great Northern obtained power to subscribe to and pay interest on the capital of the Stockport and Woodley Junction, the Cheshire Midland, the Stockport Timperley and Altrincham, the West Cheshire, and the Manchester and South Junction, on completion of agreement with the Manchester Sheffield and Lincolnshire. New capital, 720,000*l.*, at 5 per cent., and 166,000*l.* on loan.

By 30 and 31 Vic., cap. 207 (15th August, 1867), the "Cheshire Lines Committee" was incorporated as one body corporate, with perpetual succession and a common seal.

EDGWARE, HIGHGATE, AND LONDON.—Incorporated by 25 Vic., cap. 46 (3rd June, 1862), to construct a line from the Great Northern through Highgate, Finchley, and Hendon to Edgware. Length, 9¼ miles. Capital, 220,000*l.* in 10*l.* shares; loans, 73,300*l.* Arrangements with Great Northern, which subscribes 78,300*l.* Opened 22nd August, 1867. By 27 Vic., cap. 29 (13th May, 1864), the company was authorised to form a branch to Alexandra Park. Length, 1¾ mile. New capital, 96,000*l.* in shares at 5 per cent., and 32,000*l.* on loan. Also to attach a preference not exceeding 5 per cent. to unissued original shares. The Great Northern subscribes 32,000*l.* of this new capital. By 28 and 29 Vic., cap. 191 (29th June, 1865), the company was authorised to construct a short line to connect with the Tottenham and Hampstead Junction. Length, 1¾ mile. New capital, 72,000*l.* in shares, and 24,000*l.* on loan. Great Northern may subscribe 50,000*l.* of this amount, and also lease or purchase the undertaking. By 29 and 30 Vic., cap. 206 (16th July, 1866), an extension to Barnet was authorised. Length, 3¾ miles. New capital, 75,000*l.* in shares, and 25,000*l.* on loan. By 30 and 31 Vic., cap. 131 (15th July, 1867), the Edgware was transferred to the Great Northern, under the subjoined arrangements:—From opening of the main line, the shareholders of the Edgware participate in the Great Northern dividend in the following proportions, viz.:—for the first year after the opening of the line, 4/14ths of the Great Northern dividend ; for the second year, 6/14ths; for the third year, 8/14ths; for the fourth year, 10/14ths; and for the fifth and all subsequent years, 11/14ths. At the end of the fourth year the Edgware stock will merge into and become the Great Northern stock ; each shareholder in the Edgware line receiving for every 100*l.* of Edgware stock 11/14ths of 100*l.* in Great Northern stock.

WATFORD AND EDGWARE JUNCTION.—Incorporated by 27 and 28 Vic., cap. 205 (14th July, 1864), to construct a line from the Watford and Rickmansworth at Watford, to the Edgware Highgate and London, at Edgware. Length, 6¾ miles. Capital, 150,000*l*., in 10*l*. shares, and 49,000*l*. on loan. By 30 and 31 Vic., cap. 131 (15th July, 1867), the Watford and Edgware was transferred to the Great Northern.

BOURN AND ESSENDINE.—Incorporated by 20 and 21 Vic., cap. 112 (12th August, 1857), to construct a line from the Great Northern station at Essendine, to the town of Bourn. Capital, 48,000*l*. in 10*l*. shares; loans, 16,000*l*. Length, 6¼ miles. Opened 16th May, 1860, and amalgamated with Great Northern by 27 and 28 Vic., 25th July, 1864.

BOSTON, SLEAFORD, AND MIDLAND COUNTIES.—Incorporated by 17 Vic., cap. 223 (20th August, 1853), for a line from the Great Northern. at Boston, Lincolnshire, to the G.N. at Barkstone (North of Grantham Junction). The line runs across the country (east to west) from the G.N. loop to the G.N. main or Towns line, and so connects with the Ambergate. Length, 28 miles. Opened from Grantam to Sleaford 11 miles, 16th June, 1856; from Sleafoid to Boston, 17 miles, 12th April, 1859. An agreement has been made with the Great Northern for working the line till 1886, at 50 per cent. A dividend equal to 4¼ per cent. was declared in February. The August report acknowledged an increase in traffic to the extent of 1,770*l*. The directors also reported that the bill promoted by the Great Northern authorising amalgamation on the terms that this company shall receive in respect of their share capital of 200,000*l*. preferential stock to that amount of the Great Northern, bearing dividend at the rate of 4*l*. 5*s*. per cent., in perpetuity, such dividend to commence from the 1st July, 1864, passed into law. The forfeited and unissued shares had been sold, and from the proceeds the directors were arranging for the discharge of their liabilities. After deducting debenture interest, and other expenses, the sum of 3,763*l*. permitted a dividend at the rate of 4 per cent. per annum, being 1 per cent. in excess of the dividend of 1863.

LEEDS, BRADFORD, AND HALIFAX JUNCTION.—Incorporated by 15 and 16 Vic., cap. 118 (30th June, 1852), for a line from the Bowling Junction (Lancashire and Yorkshire), Bradford to Leeds junction. In 1853 this company obtained power to make an independent branch into Bradford, one mile to colleries at Drighlington and Gildersome Street, 6 miles. The main line was opened for passengers 1st August, 1855, and for goods on the 7th. By working arrangements with the Lancashire and Yorkshire, the whole of the traffic belonging to that company, and from Leeds westward, is conveyed over this line. In 1854 the company obtained their Ardsley Extension, which was opened with the Bradford Wakefield and Leeds, on the 10th October, 1857. By 22 and 23 Vic., cap. 111 (13th August, 1859), the company was authorised to covert its mortgage debt into debenture stock at 5 per cent. By 24 Vic., cap. 40 (7th June, 1861), the company were authorised to construct a branch from the line at Drighlington to Batley on the Birstal Branch of the London and North Western. Length, 2¾ miles. Capital, 45,000*l*. in shares, and 15,000*l*. on loan. By 25 and 26 Vic., cap. 92 (30th June, 1862), some deviations and an extension (seven chains) of the Batley Branch were authorised, so as to communicate with the London and North Western. New capital, 15 000*l*. in shares and 5,000*l*. on loan. Opened, 2¼ miles, 19th August, 1863. By 27 and 28 Vic., cap. 145 (14th July, 1864), the company was authorised to acquire additional land, and to construct new works, including a branch from Bradford to connect with the Lancashire and Yorkshire. Length, ¾ mile. Capital, 80,000*l*. in shares, and 16,000*l*. on loan. By 28 and 29 Vic., cap. 330 (5th July, 1865), the Leeds Bradford and Halifax was amalgamated on equal terms with the Great Northern, as from 5th September, 1865.

WEST YORKSHIRE.—Incorporated by 17 and 18 Vic., cap. 140 (July, 1854). Capital, 180,000*l*., in 20*l*. shares, with power to borrow 60,000*l*. Length, 10 miles. Opened 5th October, 1857. By 22 and 23 Vic., cap. 71 (1st August, 1859), the company was authorised to raise additional capital to the extent of 40,000*l*. Mortgage debt converted into 5*l*. per cent. guaranteed stock. By 23 and 24 Vic., cap. 147 (23rd July, 1860), the company was authorised to construct a line to Ossett. Length, 2½ miles. New capital, 33,000*l*., at 4½ per cent. preference, borrowing powers extended to one-third of the entire share capital. Opened, April 6th, 1862. By 24 Vic., cap. 28 (17th May, 1861), the company was authorised to construct a branch from Ossett, to join the London and North Western at Batley. Length, 3 miles 69 chains. Capital. 40,000*l*. in shares, and 13,333*l*. on loan. By 25 and 26 Vic., cap. 63 (30th June, 1862), the Act of 1860 was amended, and provisions made in respect of completion of works on the Ossett branch. By 26 and 27 Vic., cap. 167 (21st July, 1863), the company were to construct a branch to Methley. Length, 3¼ miles. New capital, 75,000*l*. and 25,000*l*. on loan. By 27 Vic., cap. 55 (23rd June, 1864), the Lancashire and Yorkshire and North Eastern were each authorised to subscribe 25,000*l*. towards the Methley branch, so that the capital of 75,000*l*. should be provided in equal proportions by the three companies. By 28 and 29 Vic., cap. 275 (5th July, 1865), the West Yorkshire was authorised to raise new capital to the extent of 20,000*l*. in shares, for the purpose of assisting the Wakefield station of the West Riding and Grimsby. By 28 and 29 Vic., cap. 331 (5th July, 1865), the West Yorkshire was amalgamated with the Great Northern.

VESTED LINES.—By 28 and 29 Vic., cap. 327 (5th July, 1865), the following lines were vested jointly in the Great Northern, the Midland, and the Manchester and Sheffield :—

CHESHIRE MIDLAND.—Incorporated by 23 Vic., cap. 90 (14th June, 1860), to con‑struct a line from the South Junction, at Altrincham, to Northwich. Length, 12¼ miles. Capital, 100,000*l*. in 20*l*. shares. Loans, 33,000*l*. Under this Act the Manchester Sheffield and Lincolnshire was authorised to subscribe 30,000*l*. By 24 and 25 Vic., cap. 113 (11th July, 1861), a deviation near Knutsford was authorised. Powers are obtained in the same Act for the Manchester Sheffield and Lincolnshire to subscribe a further sum of 20,000*l*., and to guarantee a dividend of 4¼ per cent. to the Cheshire Midland. Running powers and facilities are granted to the London and North Western and Great Western. By the Great Northern (Cheshire Lines) Act, 1863, the Sheffield and Great Northern Companies contribute and guarantee equally the capital necessary for completing the undertaking, each company having equal rights and privileges in all respects. By this Act the Great Northern have powers to subscribe to this undertaking in the whole 65,000*l*., and by a further Act passed in 1864, the Manchester Sheffield and Lincolnshire obtained powers to increase their subscriptions to the same amount. Opened from Altrincham to Knutsford (7 miles) on the 18th May, 1862, and to Northwich (6 miles), on 1st January, 1863, since which date the shareholders became entitled to 4½ per cent., from the Sheffield and Great Northern.

GARSTON AND LIVERPOOL.—By 24 Vic., cap. 35 (17th May, 1861), the Great Northern and the Manchester Sheffield and Lincolnshire were authorised to construct a line between Garston and Liverpool. Length, 4¼ miles. Capital, 250,000*l*. to be furnished in equal proportions by the two companies. Loans, 75,000*l*. Opened 1st June, 1864. By this Act the two companies are authorised to use portions of the Warrington and Stockport, the St. Helens, and of the Edge Hill line of the London and North Western, the latter obtaining in lieu thereof, use of the Sheffield line up to that town, and of the Great Northern between Peterborough and Grimsby and New Holland, with access to other towns in Yorkshire.

LIVERPOOL CENTRAL STATION.—Incorporated by 27 and 28 Vic., cap. 290 (29th July, 1864), to construct a railway and general station in Liverpool. Length, 1¾ mile. Capital, 500,000*l*. in 10*l*. shares, and 166,000*l*. on loan. By 29 and 30 Vic., cap. 259 (30th July, 1866), the Liverpool Central Station was vested jointly in the Manchester and Sheffield, the Great Northern, and the Midland, and its management placed in the Cheshire lines committee, nominated by the three companies.

LIVERPOOL EXTENSION.—By 29 and 30 Vic., cap. 191 (10th July, 1866), the Great Northern was constituted with the Midland and the Sheffield joint owners of the Liverpool Extension, the Great Northern subscribing thereto 250,000*l*. Also by 29 and 30 Vic., cap. 192 (16th July, 1866), the Great Northern was authorised, in con‑junction with the Midland and Sheffield, to construct new lines in connection with the Liverpool Extension (length, 5½ miles), and a new canal in substitution of that to be stopped up under the Act. New capital, 120,000*l*. by each of the three companies, with one-third additional, by borrowing.

STOCKPORT, TIMPERLEY, AND ALTRINCHAM JUNCTION.—Incorporated by 24 and 25 Vic., cap. 175 (22nd July, 1861), to construct a line from the Stockport and Woodley to the Warrington and Stockport, and two branches connecting with the Manchester South Junction and Altrincham. Length, 9½ miles. Capital, 150,000*l*. in 10*l*. shares, and 50,000*l*. on loan. Opened about February, 1866.

STOCKPORT AND WOODLEY JUNCTION.—Incorporated by 23 Vic., cap. 16 (15th May, 1860), to construct a line from Stockport to Woodley, on the Newton and Compstall branch of the Manchester Sheffield and Lincolnshire line, and to the extensive coal fields in the neighbourhood of Hyde and Dukinfield. Length, 2½ miles. Capital, 60,000*l*. in 10*l*. shares ; loans, 20,000*l*. Opened 12th January, 1863.

WEST CHESHIRE.—Incorporated by 24 and 25 Vic., cap. 143 (18th July, 1861), to con‑struct a line from Northwich, on the Cheshire Midland, to Helsby, on the Birkenhead. Length, 6 miles. Capital, 200,000*l*. in 10*l*. shares ; loans, 66,000*l*. Running powers and facilities conceded to London and North Western and Great Western. The line to be efficiently worked by the Sheffield, with which, and Great Northern, traffic arrange‑ments may be made, and who may subscribe 65,000*l*. each. By 25 and 26 Vic., cap. 190 (29th July, 1862), the company was authorised to construct branches to Winsford and Winnington, and a deviation to Oakmere. Length, 7¾ miles. Capital, 63,000*l*. in shares, and 21,000*l*. on loan.

WEST RIDING AND GRIMSBY.—On the 1st February, 1866, the Great Northern and Manchester Sheffield and Lincolnshire took possession of this line, and since that date the traffic of the company to the West Riding of Yorkshire has passed over that line, and a saving in time of about twenty minutes between Leeds and London has been effected by adoption of this route.

ROYSTON AND HITCHIN.—This line which had been leased to the Great Eastern for fourteen years, reverted to the Great Northern on 1st April, 1866, since which date it has been worked by them. In anticipation of this event the Great Northern applied for powers in 1864 to extend their branch from its termination at Shepreth, to Cambridge. The Bill for the construction of the extension was, however, withdrawn by agreement with the Great Eastern, which undertook to double their single line from Shepreth and Shelford, to give the Great Northern running powers to Cambridge, and to provide proper accommodation for them at the latter place.

NEW WORKS, &c.—By 19 and 20 Vic., cap. 69 (7th July, 1856), a deviation from the Junction with the London and North Western at Dunstable, but no extension of time was permitted.

By 22 and 23 Vic., cap. 33 (21st July, 1859), the company was authorised to make certain arrangements with regard to the capital, and to postpone the completion of the Luton section for two years. By the same Act unissued shares to the extent of 10,540l. on the Hertford section were cancelled, and new shares in lieu thereof allowed to be issued, as well as additional capital, to the extent of 10,000l. The total amount of the Hertford capital is limited to 75,000l., part of which may be preference at 6 per cent.

By 24 Vic., cap. 70 (12th June, 1861), the line is amalgamated with the Great Northern, which pays for the Dunstable and Welwyn section a fixed dividend on the original capital, amounting to 70,000l., commencing at 3 per cent. for the first year, 4 per cent. for the second and third years, and 4½ per cent. per annum subsequently; for the Welwyn and Hertford section 1 per cent per annum until April, 1866, upon 55,000l., and 3½ per cent. per annum thereafter. The Great Northern also pays interest on mortgage and preference capital amounting to 152,500l.

By 25 Vic., cap. 1 (11th April, 1862), the company obtained power to acquire additional lands near Doncaster, as well as extension of time for ten years, for disposing of superfluous lands.

By 26 and 27 Vic., cap. 191 (21st July, 1863), the company was authorised to construct a line from Spalding to March. Length, 19½ miles. New capital, 225,000l. in shares, and 75,000l. on loan. Running powers to Great Eastern from March to Spalding, but not to interfere with intermediate traffic.

By 27 and 28 Vic., cap. 202 (14th July, 1864), the company was authorised to construct an extension to Barnet, and to improve the station at King's Cross. Length, 1½ mile. Capital, 200,000l. in shares, and 66,000l. on loan. By the some Act the arrangement with the Metropolitan (26th December, 1860), was confirmed, and arrangements authorised with the Chatham and Dover. By 29 and 30 Vic., cap. 166 (16th July, 1866), the extension to Barnet was authorised to be abandoned.

By 27 and 28 Vic., cap. 242 (25th July, 1864), the Great Northern was authorised to extend the line from Lincoln to Sleaford. Length, 17½ miles. Capital, 310,000l. in shares, and 103,000 on loan; also to amalgamate the Boston Sleaford and Midland Counties, and the Bourne and Essendine. Mutual facilities were likewise conceded to the Great Eastern in regard to traffic to and from Peterborough and Spalding.

By 27 and 28 Vic., cap. 243 (25th July, 1864), the Great Northern was authorised to complete the loop line between Doncaster and Gainsborough, and to improve the gradients south of that place. Length, 21 miles. Capital, 408,000l. in shares, and 136,000l. on loan.

By 28 Vic., cap. 105 (19th June, 1865), the company was authorised to construct a line from Hornsey to Hertford. Length, 16 miles. New capital, 650,000l. in shares, and 216,000l. on mortgage.

By 28 and 29 Vic., cap. 182 (29th June, 1865), the company was authorised to construct a line from Sleaford to Bourne. Length, 17¾ miles. Capital, 190,000l. in shares, and 63,000l. on loan.

By 28 and 29 Vic., cap. 216 (5th July, 1865), the company was authorised to construct certain short lines and junctions at Newark, Spalding, Essendine, and Barkstone. Length, 7¾ mile. Capital, 150,000l. in shares, and 50,000l. on loan. By the same Act the Great Northern obtained power to subscribe one-third of the capital of the Liverpool Central Station, and to guarantee 5 per cent. on all or any part of the capital required for that undertaking.

By 29 and 30 Vic., cap. 127 (28th June, 1866), the company obtained powers to double the line in the parish of St. Pancras, to acquire additional lands in several places, and to abandon the crossing of the river Trent in the constuction of the Doncaster and Gainsborough. New capital, 810,000l. in shares, and 270,000l. on loan.

By 29 and 30 Vic., cap. 351 (10th August, 1866), the Great Northern obtained running powers over a portion of the Newton and Compstall branch of the Sheffield; also in conjunction with that company and the Midland, to execute certain works, and to become joint owners of the Godley and Woodley branch. The Chester and West Cheshire was also, by the same Act, vested in the three companies, each of which were to raise 90,000l. in shares, and 30,000l. on loan, instead of the Chester and West Cheshire.

By 30 and 31 Vic., cap. 131 (15th July, 1867), the company was authorised to raise additional capital to the extent of 75,000l. in shares, and 25,000l. on loan.

By 31 and 32 Vic., cap. 53 (25th June, 1868), the company obtained power to make a new road in the town of Leeds.

REVENUE.—Subjoined is a comparative summary of the revenue accounts of the half-years ending respectively 31st December, 1866 and 67, which explains the appropriation of the receipts of those periods. The whole of the new ordinary deferred stock, amounting to 980,000l., and 735,367l. of the permanent preference stock, become entitled to dividend in addition to the capital at the corresponding period:—

	1867.	1866.
Receipts	£1,155,260	£1,089,490
Expenditure	566,751	552,808
Excess of receipts over expenditure	£588,509	£536,682
Sundry receipts, including balance	7,427	22,129
Net revenue	£595,936	£558,811
Fixed and preference charges	296,812	277,540
Balance for ordinary dividend	£299,124	£281,271

This balance enabled the proprietors to declare a dividend at the rate of 7l. 10s. per cent. per annum on the original stock, giving for the half-year 3l. 15s. to the original; 4l. 10s. to the A ; 3l. to the B stock.

The revenue accounts for the June half-year showed an increase in the receipts of 12,851l., and a decrease in the expenditure of 11,617l. During the half-year the toll from Midland amounted to 31,308l., while in the past half-year 16,546l only was derived therefrom. The expenditure amounted to 532,576l., against 544,193l., showing an increase of 11,617l. The excess of receipts over expenditure amounted to 472,647l., against 448,180l. After deducting fixed charges and interest on loans the balance applicable to dividend amounted to 317,301l. against 283,848l. The preference dividend amounted to 136,716l., against 119,894l., leaving for ordinary dividend 180,585l., against 163,954l. Notwithstanding the decrease in the coal traffic, the diminution of 14,762l. in the Midland toll, and the additional dividend of 30,281l. payable in respect of new stock, the net available balance enabled the proprietors to declare a dividend at the rate of 4l. 5s. per cent. per annum on the original stock, giving for the half-year 2l. 2s. 6d. to the original, 3l. to the B. and 1l. 5s. to the A, leaving a balance of 3,237l. against 64l.

GREAT EASTERN.—A traffic arrangement had been made with this company, by which they were enabled to collect and deliver goods and merchandise by their own agents, in all the chief towns and places on the Great Northern and Manchester Sheffield and Lincolnshire. The traffic was carried over the recently constructed March and Spalding, and Doncaster and Gainsborough lines, and there was reason to hope that the arrangements would prove satisfactory, and be profitable to both parties.

Subjoined is a comparative statement of the capital and revenue of the Great Northern during fifteen half years to 30th June, 1868.

Half-Year ending.	Capital.		Revenue.				Working Expenses.		Dividend.		
	Shares and Loans.	Fixed Charges.	Miles in work.	Gross Receipts.	Amount.	Per cent. on Earnings.			On Preference Capital.	On Ordinary Capital.	Per Cent. per Annum
June, 1861.	£ 11,990,711	£ 1,625,134	308	£ 650,798	£ 363,776	55·89			£ 196,929	£ 90,093	£ s. d. 3 15 0
Dec. 1861..	11,994,128	2,630,980	330	768,684	367,811	47·84			214,576	186,297	7 15 0
June, 1862.	12,579,660	2,348,740	330	672,458	345,697	51·40			217,371	109,390	4 10 0
Dec. 1862..	12,545,879	2,345,900	330	828,547	410,684	49·57			213,876	203,987	8 10 0
June, 1863.	12,757,244	2,345,900	330	706,993	386,840	54·72			217,554	102,599	4 5 0
Dec. 1863..	12,729,323	3,100,070	330	872,316	416,351	47·72			245,895	210,070	8 15 0
June, 1864.	13,144,236	3,144,800	330	833,814	441,453	52·94			257,640	134,721	5 10 0
Dec. 1864..	13,971,805	3,111,814	364	970,578	478,345	49·28			266,909	225,324	8 15 0
June, 1865.	14,362,607	3,574,900	364	910,335	479,403	52·66			279,374	151,558	5 10 0
Dec. 1865..	16,041,900	2,352,900	404	1,045,370	513,854	49·15			233,826	297,690	8 15 0
June, 1866.	16,808,614	2,580,910	422	960,784	526,345	54·78			258,885	175,553	5 0 0
Dec. 1866..	17,474,785	2,484,210	422	1,089,490	552,808	50·74			255,411	281,271	8 0 0
June, 1867.	18,035,350	2,484,210	441	992,373	544,193	54·84			284,226	163,953	4 10 0
Dec. 1867..	18,201,199	2,479,210	487	1,155,260	566,751	49·06			289,385	299,124	7 10 0
June, 1868.	18,339,713	2,479,210	487	1,005,223	532,576	52·98			292,061	180,585	

CAPITAL.—The following is a statement of the parliamentary powers of the company exercised up to 30th June, 1868.

			Shares.	Debentures	Total.
	GREAT NORTHERN AND BRANCHES.				
1846.	Great Northern		£5,600,000	£1,868,000	£7,468,000
1846-7.	London and York Extension		503,000	166,800	669,800
1846.	Witham Navigation Mortgages		....	24,692	24,692
,,	East Lincolnshire Borrowing Powers........		....	200,000	200,000
1851.	Great Northern		750,000	250,000	1,000,000
,,	Ditto		60,000	20,000	80,000
1853.	Ditto		750,000	250,000	1,000,000
1855.	Ditto		1,000,000	333,000	1,333,000
1860.	Great Northern and Metropolitan Junction		30,000	10,000	40,000
1861.	Great Northern		20,000	6,000	26,000
1862-3.	Ditto		500,000	166,000	666,000
1863.	Ditto	(Spalding and March)......	225,000	75,000	300,000
1864.	Ditto	(Doncaster and Gainsboro')	408,000	136,000	544,000
,,	Ditto	(Lincoln and Honington)..	310,000	103,000	413,000
,,	Ditto		200,000	66,000	266,000
1865.	Witham Drainage		10,000	....	10,000
,,	Great Northern (Sleaford and Bourn) ...		....	....	....
,,	Ditto	(Works and Junctions) ...	150,000	....	150,000
,,	Ditto	(Hornsey to Hertford)	....	....	....
1866.	Ditto	(Additional Powers) ..·.....	400,000	....	400,000
1867.	Ditto	(ditto)	....	....	....
,,	Ditto	(Westgate Station).........	....	....	....
,,	Ditto	(Midland and Eastern) ...	....	....	....
	AMALGAMATED LINES.		£10,916,000	£3,674,492	£14,590,492
1861.	Hertford Luton and Dunstable		218,400	61,600	280,000
1864.	Boston and Sleaford		200,000	66,600	266,600
,,	Bourn and Essendine		24,000	16,000	40,000
1864-5.	Leeds Bradford and Halifax................		80,000	....	80,000
1865.	Ditto		575,000	180,000	755,000
,,	West Yorkshire		494,568	115,500	610,068
1866.	West Riding and Grimsby Purchase........		210,000	....	210,000
1862.	Edgware Highgate and London		73,300	....	73,300
1864.	Ditto		32,000	....	32,000
,,	Watford and Edgware Junction		....	....	....
1865.	Tottenham and Hampstead Junction		....	....	....
1866.	Edgware Highgate and London—(Barnet Branch)................................		....	....	....
	SUBSCRIPTIONS.		£1,907,268	£439,700	£2,346,968
1861,	Garston and Liverpool		225,000	75,000	300,000
,,	Stockport Timperley and Altrincham Junction......................................		50,000	....	50,000
,,	West Cheshire		65,000	....	65,000
1862-3.	Cheshire Lines		228,000	....	228,000
,,	Hatfield and St. Alban's		20,000	....	20,000
1864.	London Chatham & Dover (City undertaking)		300,000	....	300,000
,,	Halifax and Ovenden		30,000	....	30,000
1865.	Cheshire Lines Transfer		125,000	....	125,000
1866.	Manchester Sheffield and Lincolnshire— Liverpool Extension		250,000	....	250,000
,,	Cheshire Lines..............:		40,000	....	40,000
,,	Manchester Sheffield and Lincolnshire— New Lines		....	....	....
,,	Bradford Eccleshill and Idle...............		....	....	....
,,	Keadby and Lincoln.....................		....	....	....
			£1,333,000	£75,000	£1,408,000

Powers Abandoned—

Shares.	Loans.				
£72,000	£24,000	Tottenham & Hampstead Jnc.	....	....	....
200,000	66,600	Keadby and Lincoln	....	....	....

		Shares.	Debentures	Total.
	Powers exercised	£14,156,268	£4,189,192	£18,345,460
	Do. not exercised	1,939,108	959,533	2,898,641
	Total Parliamentary Powers	£16,095,376	£5,148,725	£21,244,101

The receipts and expenditure to 30th June, 1868, were given as under :—

Received.		Expended.	
Shares and stock	£14,153,526	To 31st December, 1867	£18,053,312
Mortgage loans	1,332,458	Six months ended 30th June,	
Debenture stock	2,853,729	1868	191,183
		Total	18,244,496
		Balance	95,217
	£18,339,713		£18,339,713

The accounts are made up to 30th June and 31st December in every year ; and the statutory meetings held in February and August.

Scale of Voting.—C.C.C. Act, sec. 75. Holders of preference shares under Act of 1853 have same votes as if original shares. Holders of debenture stock to have no vote, unless three-fifths of a meeting specially notified shall so resolve.

Registration fee, 2s. 6d. each deed transferring stock. Fee, on transfer of bonds, 2s. 6d. each bond.

No. of Directors.—Maximum, 36 ; minimum, 10. *Qualification*, 50 shares.

DIRECTORS :

Chairman—COLONEL PACKE, Caythorpe, Grantham, and
41 Charles Street, Berkeley Square, W.

Deputy-Chairman—COLONEL THE HON. OCTAVIUS DUNCOMBE, M.P.,
Waresley Park, St. Neots, and 84, Eaton Square, S.W.

John Harvey Astell, Esq., Woodbury Hall, St. Neots.

The Right Hon. Lord Colville, 42, Eaton Place, S.W.

Edward Christopher Egerton, Esq., M.P., 45, Eaton Place, S.W., and Mountfield Court, Hurst Green, Sussex.

Charles Wilson Faber, Esq., Northaw, Barnet.

Major Wm. Amsinck, Richmond, Surrey, S.W.

Christopher B. Denison, Esq., M.P., Doncaster.

William Firth, Esq., Burley Wood, near Leeds.

Robert Tennant, Esq., Scarcroft Lodge, Shadwell, Leeds.

Chas. Turner, Esq., M.P., Dingle Head, near Liverpool.

George Walker, Esq., Osgathorpe, Sheffield

Samuel Waterhouse, Esq., M.P., Hope Hall, Halifax.

One-fourth of the Directors retire annually.

OFFICERS.—Gen. Man., Seymour Clarke ; Sec., Henry Oakley ; Assistant Sec., Alexr. Forbes ; Supt. of the Line, F. P. Cockshott : Assistant Supt. of the Line, Henry Conder ; Goods Man., John Ashley ; Assistant Goods Man., Richard H. Twelvetrees ; Mineral Man., William Newton ; Con. Eng., Joseph Cubitt, C.E., 6, Great George Street, S.W. ; Eng., Richard Johnson ; Loco. Eng., P. Stirling ; Storekeeper, William Nicholls ; Accountant, William Grinling ; Auditors, John Morgan and Captain Fitzmaurice ; Parliamentary Agents, Dyson and Co., Parliament Street, S.W. ; Solicitors, Johnston, Farquhar, and Leech, 65, Moorgate Street, E.C.

Head Offices—King's Cross, N.

169.—GREAT NORTHERN AND WESTERN.

Incorporated by 20 and 21 Vic., cap. 84 (27th July, 1857), for making railways from Athlone to Roscommon and Castlerea. Line to Roscommon, 18 miles ; that to Castlerea, 16½ miles. Agreements under the usual regulations made with the Midland Great Western. Capital, 240,000l., in 10l. shares ; loans, 80,00Cl. Opened from Athlone to Roscommon, 13th February ; to Castlerea, on the 15th November, 1860 ; to Ballyhaunis, 11½ miles, 9th September, 1861 ; to Claremorris, 11 miles, 19th May, 1862 ; to Castlebar, 14½ miles, 17th December, 1862. In operation, 71½ miles.

By 21 and 22 Vic., cap. 96 (12th July, 1858), the company was authorised to make certain deviations, and the Midland Great Western permitted to subscribe to the undertaking to the amount of 80,000l.

By 22 and 23 Vic., cap. 48 (1st August, 1859), an extension from Castlerea to Castlebar was authorised. New capital, 100,000l. in shares, and 33,000l. on loan. The Midland Great Western may hold to the extent of 73,333l., in addition to the above stated amount of 80,000l.

By 23 Vic., cap. 45 (15th May, 1860), the company was authorised to make certain deviations between Roscommon and Castlerea (5¼ miles).

By 24 Vic., cap. 67 (12th June, 1861), the company was authorised to make an extension from Castlebar to Westport. Length, 12 miles. New capital, 64,000l. in shares, and 21,000l. on loan. Opened.

By 25 and 26 Vic., cap 201 (29th July, 1862), the company was authorised to construct a line from Manulla to Ballina. Length, 20⅝ miles. Capital, 90,000l. in ordinary shares, and 30,000l on loan.

By 27 and 28 Vic., cap. 252 (25th July, 1864), the company was authorised to raise new capital to the extent of 30,000*l*. in shares, and 10,000*l*. on loan, and to convert mortgage debt into debenture stock.

By 27 and 28 Vic., cap. 299 (29th July, 1864), the company was authorised to use a portion of the Midland Great Western, near Athlone, and to cancel any unissued shares authorised to be created by the Acts of 1861 and 1862, or either of such Acts, to any extent not exceeding 51,000*l*., and in lieu thereof to issue new shares representing in nominal value the value of the shares cancelled, but not exceeding in the whole the sum of 51,000*l*, ; and the company may attach to such new shares, to the extent aforesaid, privileges of priority in payment of dividend to such extent not exceeding 5 per cent. per annum as the company may determine.

By 29 and 30 Vic., cap. 237 (16th July, 1866), the company obtained till 16th July, 1868, to complete the lines to Westport, and till 1869 to Ballina, and also to raise new capital to the extent of 30,000*l*. at 6 per cent.

REVENUE.—There has been a continued increase in the receipts ; those from the 30th June to the 31st of December, 1867, amounted to 12,570*l*., being in excess of the corresponding half-year of 2,161*l*. After providing 2,785*l*. for interest on debentures, 1,369*l*. for dividend on preference stock, and 1,573*l*. interest on unpaid land purchases and upon temporary loans, a balance of 6,843*l*. remained for dividend on the ordinary stock at the rate of 3*l*. 10*s*. per cent. per annum. The directors, however, could not recommend a dividend on the ordinary stock, as the whole of the revenue had been applied in the discharge of pressing liabilities. The revenue account for the half-year ending the 30th of June showed that 18,912*l*. had been received, and 7,741*l*. expended, leaving a balance of 10,871*l*. After paying 2,785*l*. for interest on debentures, 1,490*l*. for dividend on preference stocks, and 1,623*l*. interest on temporary loans and unpaid land purchases, a balance of 4,973*l*. remained. The outstanding liabilities made it still impracticable for the directors to recommend the payment of a dividend upon the ordinary stock. The extension to Foxford was opened for traffic on the 1st of May. From the impossibility of placing the preference stock the construction of this branch had exhausted the pecuniary resources of the company. The necessity for abandoning all further extension was, if possible, more than ever imperative.

No. of Directors.—Maximum, 12 ; minimum, 3 ; quorum, 3 and 2. *Qualification*, 1,000*l*. Qualification of Auditor, 100*l*.

DIRECTORS ;

Chairman—Lieut.-General the Right Hon. the EARL OF LUCAN, K.C.B., Castlebar, County Mayo, and 36, South Street, W.

The Right Hon. the Lord Crofton, Mote Park, Roscommon.

The Right Hon. the Lord Bingham, M.P., 7, Portland Place, W.

Alexander Lambert, Esq., Brook Hill, Claremorris, County Mayo.

Neal Davis, Esq., Castlebar, Ireland.

John Parson, Esq., Ham Common, Surrey.

George Clive, Esq., M.P., 31, Great Cumberland Place, W.

* John Ennis, Esq., Merrion Square, Dublin.

* Sir Percy Nugent, Bart., Donore, Multyfarnham.

* The Right Hon. the Earl of Clancarty, Garbally, Ballinasloe.

* Directors of the Midland Great Western Railway of Ireland.

The Midland Company have not named a fresh Director.

OFFICERS.—Sec., Benjamin Room ; Eng., Frederick Barry, 34, Great George Street, Westminster, S.W. ; Auditors, James Gildea and George Leeming.

Offices—3, Victoria Street, Westminster, S.W.

170.—GREAT SOUTHERN AND WESTERN.

Incorporated by Act 7 and 8 Vic., cap. 100 (6th August, 1844), and 8 and 9 Vic., cap. 24 (21st July, 1845), for a line from Dublin to Cork, passing by or near Portarlington, Thurles, Tipperary, and Mallow, with a branch to Carlow. Powers were subsequently obtained for making an extension to the river Lee, a branch from Portarlington to Tullamore, and incorporating the Clonmel and Thurles ; also authorising subscriptions to other companies to the following extent, viz.:—Killarney Junction, 100,000*l*.; Mallow and Fermoy, 100,000*l*.; Irish South Eastern, 90,000*l*. Total in operation, 330 miles.

The company obtained an Act, 15 Vic., cap. 80 (24th July, 1851), which removed any previous doubt as to the validity of the creation of the 6¼*l*. preference shares, owing to that capital having been raised under Acts for subscriptions to other lines, &c., and not strictly applied to those purposes ; as the capital raised thereby is now legally applicable to all or any of the purposes for which the company is legally authorised to apply the same. The company is also, by the same Act, enabled to construct a dock and warehouses at the river Lee, Cork, and to create 250,000*l*. additional capital for that and other purposes, on which, as well as on the preference shares already created, and any shares which may be hereafter raised for the capitalisation of the company's bonded debt, a preferential dividend, not exceeding 6 per cent. per annum, can be conferred by three-fifths of any special general meeting, the first created preference shares having reserved to them "a priority in the payment of the interest or dividend secured, or intended to be secured thereon, under the resolutions of the company, by virtue whereof the said new or preference shares were created over any other shares or stock which may be created *under the provisions of this Act, or subsequent to the passing thereof.*" All the 6 per cent. preference stock issued, has, however, merged into the original stock, in conformity with the terms of its creation.

By Act of 1851, this company's subscription to the Killarney Junction was reduced from 100,000*l.* to 60,000*l.* In order to hasten its completion, certain of the directors became personally responsible for payment of the interest and repayment of the principal in 20 years, of the loan of 100,000*l.* from government, in addition to the liabilities attaching to the counties of Cork and Kerry with respect to that loan.

By Act 28th May, 1852 (15 Vic., cap. 24), the compulsory powers as to the Tullamore branch (16 miles) were extended to 28th May, 1855 and 1857 respectively. The shareholders, on 28th August, 1852, authorised the directors to enter into such arrangements for construction of that branch as they might think fit. Length, 16 miles.

By 20 and 21 Vic., cap. 1 (26th June, 1857), the company is authorised to raise additional capital to the extent of 250,100*l.*, at 5 per cent. per annum.

By 24 and 25 Vic., cap. 148 (11th July, 1861), the company was authorised to raise, for general purposes, the sum of 280,000*l.* in shares at 5 per cent., and 50,000*l.* on loan. Power was also given to the Midland Great Western to transfer its shares in the Limerick and Castle Connell to the Great Southern and Western (10,000*l.*)

By 28 Vic., cap. 43 (26th May, 1865), the company was authorised to create and issue debenture stock in lieu of bonds.

ROSCREA AND PARSONSTOWN.—Incorporated by 17 Vic., cap. 113 (August 4th, 1853), for a line from the Great Southern and Western to Parsonstown. Length, 22½ miles. Capital, 100,000*l.* Scheme vested in Great Southern and Western on 17th November, 1855, when half capital was paid up. The line was opened to Roscrea (10 miles) on 19th October, 1857 ; thence to Parsonstown (12 miles), 8th March, 1858.

By 24 and 25 Vic., cap. 147 (11th July, 1861), the company was authorised to construct an extension from Roscrea to Nenagh and Birdhill. Length, 32 miles. New capital, 210,000*l.* in shares at 5 per cent., and 70,000*l.* on loan. Open to Nenagh (19 miles) on 5th October, 1863, and to Birdhill on the 1st June, 1864.

TRALEE AND KILLARNEY.—Incorporated by 17 and 18 Vic. cap. 142 (10th July, 1854), in lieu of the Act of 1853, for a line from Killarney Junction to Tralee. Length, 22 miles. Projected in connection with Killarney Junction, which subscribes 50,000*l.* Capital authorised :—Shares, 11,000 of 10*l.*, 110,000*l.* Loans, 55,000*l.* By 20 and 21 Vic., cap. 17 (20th June, 1857), power is given to borrow the whole of the loan capital, in certain proportions, before the shares have been fully subscribed. The board also succeeded in obtaining from the government a loan of 10,000*l.* By 22 Vic., cap. 10 (19th April, 1859), the time for completion of works was extended to 15th August, 1860, under penalty of 20*l.* for each day's delay. The line, however, was opened for passengers on the 18th July, and for goods on the 25th August, 1859, and has since been incorporated with the Great Southern and Western.

KILLARNEY JUNCTION.—Incorporated by 9 and 10 Vic. cap. 200 (1846), for a line from a Junction of the Great Southern and Western, near Mallow, to Killarney, 41 miles. The G. S. and W. had power, under the Act of incorporation, to amalgamate with, to lease or purchase this undertaking ; also to subscribe 60.000*l.*, and nominate three directors. The line was completed in May, 1854, and is now incorporated in the Great Southern and Western.

IRISH SOUTH EASTERN.—Carlow to Kilkenny, 25 miles (12 and 13 Vic., cap. 62). Opened to Bagnalstown, 10 miles, 24th July, 1848, and to Kilkenny, 15 miles 14th November, 1850. Incorporated with the Great Southern and Western, on 1st July, 1863, each share in the former being exchanged for 5*l.* stock in the latter company.

MALLOW AND FERMOY.—Incorporated by 17 and 18 Vic., cap. 132 (3rd July, 1854), for making a line from Great Southern and Western, near Mallow, to Fermoy. Length, 17 miles. Capital, 100,000*l.*, in 10*l.* shares ; calls, 2*l.*; intervals, three months. Borrowing powers, 30,000*l.* By 20 and 21 Vic., cap. 62 (27th July 1856), this company is dissolved, and its powers transferred to Great Southern and Western. The latter may raise 100,000*l.* (all of which must be applied to the purposes of the Mallow and Fermoy) at 5 per cent. preference. Opened, May 17th, 1860.

ATHLONE.—By 20 and 21 Vic., cap. 85 (27th July, 1857), the company is authorised to make a line from Tullamore to Athlone, at a cost of 160,000*l.*, which may be raised by 5 per cent. preference. 24 miles. Opened, October 21st, 1856.

LIMERICK AND CASTLE CONNELL.—Under the award of the arbitrators, the company had to pay the Midland Great Western 10,000*l.*, being the amount invested in the Castle Connel.

PARSONSTOWN AND PORTUMNA.—By 29 Vic., cap. 57 (11th June, 1866), the Great Southern and Western was authorised to purchase, lease, and subscribe to this undertaking.

CORK AND YOUGHAL.—By 29 and 30 Vic., cap. 144 (28th June, 1866), the company was authorised to form a junction with the Cork and Youghal, and to purchase that railway for the sum of 310,000*l.*

REVENUE.—The net surplus for the half-year ending 31st December, was 104,976*l.*, out of which a dividend at the rate of 4½ per cent. per annum was declared.

It was reported in August that the increase in receipts for the half-year ending 30th June, amounted to only 4,382*l.*, notwithstanding the large outlay that had been incurred in providing additional rolling stock. The dividend was at the rate of 5 per cent. per annum, with balance of 2,720*l.*

CAPITAL.—The expenditure on this account to 30th June, including subscription of 2,000*l.* to the Parsonstown and Portumna, amounted to 6,181,422*l.* The receipts were given as follow:—

Capital stock	£4,109,889	
Do. Parsonstown and Portumna Bridge.......................	2,000	
4 per cent. stock	1,329,100	=£5,440,989
Do. debenture stock	164,914	
Loan on debentures..	501,846	
Loan Commissioners, 4 per cent.	66,988	= 568,834
		£6,009,824
Balance...		171,598
		£6,181,422

The accounts are made up to 30th June and 31st December, and the statutory meetings held in Dublin in February and August.

Scale of Voting.—One vote for every 250*l.* original stock up to 2,500*l.*, and one additional vote for every 500*l.* original stock afterwards.

Certificates must accompany transfer deed. Registration fee, 2*s.* 6*d.* each deed.

No. of Directors.—Maximum, 27; minimum, 16. *Qualification,* 2,000*l.* stock; allowance, 3,000*l.*

DIRECTORS;

Chairman—WILLIAM HAUGHTON, Esq., 28, City Quay, Dublin.

Deputy-Chairman—JAMES W. MURLAND, Esq., Fitzwilliam Square, Dublin.

James B. Ball, Esq., 12, Merrion Square East, Dublin.
Edward Cane, Esq., 60, Dawson Street, Dublin.
Lord Cloncurry, Lyons, Hazlehatch Station, and White's Club, W.
Samuel H. Close, Esq., Henry Street, Dublin.
Lieut.-Col. George Thomson, C.B., Cork.
Henry Hutton, Esq., 5, Bachelor's Walk, Dublin.

The Hon. Judge Longfield, LL.D., Fitzwilliam Square, Dublin.
Michael B. Mullins, Esq., Fitzwilliam Square, Dublin.
Valentine O. B. O'Connor, Esq., 3, Beresford Place, Dublin.
George Pim, Esq., Brenanstown House, Cabinteely.
Nicholas Philpot Leader, Esq., Dromagh Castle, Kanturk, County Cork, and Carlton Club, S.W.
Joseph Shaw, Esq., Celbridge.

OFFICERS.—Sec., William Taylor; Traffic Supt., George Edward Ilbery; Loco. Eng., Alexander M'Donnell; Permanent Way Engs., Valentine Browne, Dublin, and Charles G. Napier, Cork; Auditors, James Haughton, and Luke J. McDonnell; Solicitors, Barrington and Jeffers, Ely Place, Dublin and Limerick; Bankers, Glyn, Mills, Currie, and Co., Lombard Street, E.C., and Bank of Ireland, Dublin.

Head Offices—Kingsbridge Terminus, Dublin.

171.—GREAT WESTERN.

This undertaking was remodelled by the Amalgamation Act of 1863 (given in the APPENDIX to Vol. XVI.), by which the WEST MIDLAND and the SOUTH WALES were embodied with the GREAT WESTERN. These various sections which are to be kept distinct for purposes of revenue may be designated as follows:—

I. GREAT WESTERN PROPER.—Originally incorporated by 5 and 6 Wm. IV., cap. 107 (31st August, 1835), for a line from London to Bristol (118¼ miles), but since extended by Acts of Incorporation, lease, or purchase to a system embracing 542¾ miles of railway and canal, all of which are in operation. This undertaking comprises the following sections and engagements:—

GREAT WESTERN PROPER.—London to Bristol (118¼ miles), with the following branches diverging therefrom, viz., West Drayton to Uxbridge, 2½; Slough to Windsor, 3; Twyford to Henley, 4¾; Didcot to Oxford, 10. Total, 138¼.

BERKS AND HANTS.—Reading to Basingtoke, and Fork to Hungerford, 38¼ miles.

CHELTENHAM UNION.—From Swindon to Gloucester (37) with a short branch to Cirencester (4), Gloucester to Cheltenham (7½ miles). Total, 48.

WILTS, SOMERSET, AND WEYMOUTH.—Chippenham to Melksham, Devizes, Bradford, Bathampton, Trowbridge, Warminster, Salisbury, Frome, Yeovil, and Weymouth,
123 miles. The total payments on this branch of the undertaking up to 30th June
amounted to 1,676,054*l.*

GLOUCESTER AND DEAN FOREST.—From Gloucester to Grange Court, 7½ miles.
Great Western investment, 103,434*l.* This line is leased on the following terms:—A rent
of 4½ per cent. on the share capital of 254,000*l.*, for five years, and five per cent. afterwards:—a *possible* further outlay of 12,600*l.* to be raised on the mortgage of Dean
Forest, interest to be borne by Great Western. A covenant, however, provides for a
rent of 5½ per cent. on the 254,000*l.*, as soon as a line shall be finished from the terminus
at Grange Court to Hereford; and towards which the Dean Forest have subscribed
25,000*l.* to the "Hereford Ross and Gloucester," defrayed under general borrowing
powers. South Wales had power to subscribe 100,000*l.*, but in lieu undertook construction of seven miles. This amount is therefore deducted from capital.

HEREFORD, ROSS, AND GLOUCESTER.—Incorporated by 15 Vic., cap. 40 (1851), for a
line at Grange Court, 7 miles from Gloucester, *via* Ross, to Hereford, junction with
the Shrewsbury and Hereford. Broad gauge. The Gloucester and Dean Forest subscribed 25,000*l.* Opened on 1st June, 1855. This line, by 25 and 26 Vic., cap. 196 (29th
July, 1862), is finally transferred to Great Western, which guarantees 5 per cent. on the
preference and 3 per cent. on the ordinary share capital.

YEOVIL.—By 23 Vic., cap. 69 (26th May, 1860), the company was authorised to construct a short branch line and station near Yeovil, where the South Western (Exeter)
crosses Great Western (Weymouth) line. Completion of works, three years.

WEST LONDON.—A moiety of the lease (30,300*l.*) to the London and North Western
is borne by and belongs to the Great Western. For further arrangements with this
company, see "West London." By 22 and 23 Vic., cap. 1 (31st July, 1859), the company
obtained powers to deviate the West London by bridge over the Great Western at
Wormwood Scrubbs, instead of by a level crossing.

BIRMINGHAM AND OXFORD (65¾ miles).—Purchased at 30 per cent. premium and
constructed thereafter on the mixed gauge, which now extends from Wolverhampton
to Basingstoke. The narrow gauge from the latter place to Oxford has cost 136,709*l.*;
and the Didcot deviation (1 mile), by which the through traffic is worked, 45,598*l.*; on
the western fork at Reading, also attached to the same system, there has been expended 33,788*l.*; and it is calculated that the extension of the narrow gauge from this
fork to Reading, there to meet the Staines and Wokingham Junction from the Reading
Guildford and Reigate, will incur a further liability of about 10,400*l.*

BIRMINGHAM AND WOLVERHAMPTON (12¼ miles).—Purchased on the same terms
as above, and worked on both gauges, in conjunction with the Liverpool, Manchester,
and Birkenhead traffic.

NANTWICH AND MARKET DRAYTON. -Incorporated by 24 Vic., cap. 44 (7th June,
1861), to construct a line from the London and North Western, at Nantwich, to Market
Drayton. Length, 10¾ miles, single line. Capital, 60,000*l.* in 20*l.* shares, 20,000*l.*
Opened 19th October, 1863. By 27 and 28 Vic., cap. 152 (30th June, 1864), the company
obtained an increase of capital to the extent of 60,000*l.*, in shares, and 20,000*l.* on loan.
These shares were created and issued on 31st August, 1865, the whole being guaranteed
4½ per cent. by the Great Western.

SHREWSBURY AND BIRMINGHAM (29½ miles), with branch to Madeley, and shares
in Stour Valley. Amalgamated at 3½ per cent. on ordinary stock, and half surplus
profits. The Great Western holds preference and other stocks to the amount of 35,124*l.*

SHREWSBURY AND CHESTER (46 miles), with branch to Oswestry. Amalgamated on
the same terms as above, with exercise of running powers over the latter branches of the
Birkenhead, viz., to the Mersey, and to the junction on the Warrington and Stockport;
the Great Western investments on Shrewsbury and Chester stock reach 74,031*l.*

HAMMERSMITH AND CITY.—Incorporated by 24 and 25 Vic., cap. 164 (22nd July, 1861),
to construct a line from the Great Western, at Green Lane Bridge, to Hammersmith, with branch to Kensington. Mixed gauge. Capital, 180,000*l.*, in 10*l.* shares;
loans, 60,000*l.* Arrangements with Great Western and Metropolitan. Open from
Hammersmith to the Great Western Junction, 2 miles 50 chains, on 13th June, and
Kensington branch, 55 chains, 1st July, 1864. Total, 3 miles 25 chains. By 26 and 27
Vic., cap. 172 (21st July, 1863), the company was authorised to make a second junction
with the Great Western, in the parish of Paddington. Length, 45 chains. New
capital, 60,000*l.*, preference, 5*l.* per cent., issued 14th April, 1864, not cumulative; and
20,000*l.* on loan. By 28 Vic., cap. 101 (19th June, 1865), the company was authorised
to alter some of the works on the line, to purchase additional land, and to lease the
undertaking to the Great Western and Metropolitan. New capital, 100,000*l.* in shares,
and 33,000*l.* on loan; also to create and issue debenture stock. By the Great Western
Additional Powers Act, 1867, the line is leased jointly to the Great Western and the
Metropolitan.

METROPOLITAN.—The Great Western runs a portion of the trains on this line,
carrying the local passengers of the Metropolitan, along with those from Hammersmith, Ealing, &c.

SOUTH DEVON.—The Great Western subscription to this line amounts to 225,000*l*.

CORNWALL.—The Great Western, in addition to subscribing 60,000*l*. to this line, guarantees, in conjunction with the Bristol and Exeter and South Devon, its proportionate share of the debenture debt of that company.

STRATFORD-ON-AVON.—Arrangements made for working this line at cost price, under sanction of three-fifths of shareholders and Board of Trade.

PLYMOUTH DOCKS.—The Great Western subscription to this undertaking is 17,500*l*.

GREAT WESTERN AND BRENTFORD.—This line, although constructed without contribution from the Great Western, is of the greatest importance to that company. It provides cheap and prompt means of conveyance for all heavy traffic passing to the river, or destined for the docks in the port of London.

BRIDPORT.—By 22 and 23 Vic. (August 13th, 1859), arrangements are authorised with this company, for which see "Bridport."

ABINGDON.—This short line (3 miles single line), is worked by Great Western at cost price, under a provisional arrangement, until it be ascertained what changes can be made.

EAST SOMERSET.—An agreement is in operation for working this railway between the junction at Witham and Wells at an agreed per centage on the receipts.

LLANGOLLEN.—An agreement is made for working this railway (5¼ miles in length) on terms of a per centage upon receipts as in the case of the East Somerset ; together with a fixed annual sum of 400*l*., in consideration of a saving of expense to the Great Western, by dispensing with the Llangollen Road station.

NEW LEASES.—The Great Western also leases the Wellington and Severn Junction. Working agreements have also been made with the East Somerset, the Wycombe extension to Thame, and the Berks and Hants extension from Hungerford to Devizes.

LONDON, CHATHAM, AND DOVER.—This company having obtained an Act for bringing a railway through populous districts, south of the river Thames, into connection with the Metropolitan, in the neighbourhood of Farringdon Market and Victoria Street, powers have been conferred upon the Great Western and the London Chatham and Dover to agree with the Victoria Station, for joint lease and occupation of a portion of passenger station in Pimlico.

LONDON AND NORTH WESTERN.—By arrangements with this company, Great Western traffic to Manchester is now conveyed by the London and North Western from Chester, *via* Warrington.

BIRKENHEAD.—This agreement, jointly with the London and North Western, was not sealed till July, 1860, but took effect from 1st January previous, under the following provisions :—The two companies to assume debenture stock, mortgage debt and liabilities on capital account, not exceeding in the whole 512,000*l*., to pay half-yearly dividends upon ordinary share capital, not exceeding 2,000,000*l*., after the rates following, viz. :—For the years 1860 and 1861, 2½ per cent. per annum ; 1862, 1863, 1864, 1865, 3½ per cent. per annum ; 1866 and thereafter, 4 per cent. per annum.

SHREWSBURY AND HEREFORD.—This line is leased one-half by the London and North Western, and the other moiety by the Great Western and West Midland.

VARIOUS POWERS.—By 22 and 23 Vic., cap. 40 (21st August, 1859), the company, in conjunction with Midland, is authorised to abandon Gloucester and Chelthenham tram-roads.

By 24 Vic., cap. 36 (17th May, 1861), the company is authorised to raise new capital, to the extent of 1,000,000*l*., in shares ; 333,000*l*. on loan, for general purposes, including narrow gauge from Reading and Brentford to Paddington.

By 24 and 25 Vic., cap. 204 (1st August, 1861), the company obtained power to construct a short branch to Lightmore. length 2 miles, to be constructed out of existing capital. By the same Act, the Great Western and the West Midland were authorised to lease the Wellington and Severn Junction, and to enter into arrangements with the Wenlock, the Vale of Llangollen, and the Llangollen and Corwen.

By 25 and 26 Vic., cap. 196 (29th July, 1862), the Great Western leased the Ely Valley and purchased the Hereford Ross and Gloucester.

By 25 and 26 Vic., cap. 127 (7th July, 1862), the company was authorised to construct a connection between its Birmingham line and the Stourbridge extension of the West Midland. Also to acquire additional lands in Stafford and Warwick. New capital, 70,000*l*., in shares, and 23,000*l*. in loans.

By 26 and 27 Vic., cap. 151 (21st July, 1863), the company obtained power to construct a line from the Wolverhampton and Dudley, at½West Bromwich, to Great Bridge, on the London and North Western. Length, 49 chains. New capital, 54,000*l*., in shares, at 5 per cent., and 18,000*l*. on loan.

By 27 and 28 Vic., cap. 306 (29th July, 1864), the company obtained power to acquire lands and to construct several new works. Length, half a mile. Also to enter into arrangements with the Cambrian, with regulations for certain stations on the Birkenhead. New capital, 1,000,000*l.*, in shares, and 250,000*l.* on loan. The same Act conferred on the company a power to establish a superannuation fund for such of its officers as should contribute to the same.

II.—WEST MIDLAND.—Incorporated by 23 Vic., cap. 81 (16th June, 1860), being an amalgamation of the three following undertakings, with their respective leases and financial obligations:—

1. OXFORD, WORCESTER, AND WOLVERHAMPTON.—Incorporated by 8 and 9 Vic., cap. 184 (4th August, 1845), for a line from Wolvercott, near Oxford, junction with the Great Western, through Worcester to Wolverhampton, with branches. Capital, 1,500,000*l.*, and loans 500,000*l.*

By an Act of 1856, new capital to the extent of 35,000*l.*, was created as a 4½ per cent. pre-preference or debenture stock, the first preference being made second, with a fixed guarantee of 6 per cent. The first dividend on the second guarantee (5*s.* per cent.) was declared on 30th July, 1858, the arrears on which then amounted to 14*l.* 11*s.* 7*d.*

By 21 and 22 Vic., cap. 123 (23rd July, 1858), the company was authorised to abandon the Diglis branch and prospective substitution of a short branch from the Worcester and Hereford to the Severn, called the Butts branch, to replace the Stourbridge branch of 1855 by a shorter and cheaper line; to abandon part of Kingswinford branch; to extend the time for formation of Stratford branch; to arrange with holders of second guaranteed shares for adjustment of their arrears, and to make certain alterations in the constitution of Stratford canal rent-charges.

By 22 and 23 Vic., cap. 76 (8th August, 1859), the company was enabled to carry out the following objects:—1st. Abandonment of the broad gauge as provided for in the agreement with the Great Western. 2nd. To use capital allotted to completion of the broad gauge by Parliament, for the following purposes, viz.:—completion of Stratford, Kingswinford, and Stourbridge branches, for which no means were provided in the Act of 1856; to pay a certain sum to the Great Western under the terms of the agreement. Doubling of the line between Charlbury and Campden, and substitution of solid embankment or masonry for wooden viaducts between Worcester and Dudley. 3rd. To issue debenture stock in lieu of rent-charges and annuities payable on account of purchase of Stratford canal. 4th. To purchase the Chipping Norton branch on the following terms, viz.:—First year, 3¼ per cent.; second year, 3½ per cent; third year, 3¾ per cent.; fourth year, and in perpetuity, 4 per cent. 5th. To make arrangements with the holders of second guaranteed shares, based upon the principle of substituting an *irredeemable* for a *redeemable stock*, contingent upon a fair arrangement being made for a partial liquidation af the arrears.

Chipping Norton.—Incorporated 17 and 18 Vic., cap. 209 (31st July, 1854). The West Midland works the line for 50 per cent. of gross receipts, and pays one-third of gross receipts of any increase of traffic that may arise to main line from construction of this branch. The entire cost of the line, including stations, did not exceed 32,000*l.* The dividends are 4 per cent.

Severn Valley.—Incorporated by 17 Vic., cap. 227 (20th August, 1853), for a line from near Hartlebury station on Oxford Worcester and Wolverhampton line to Shrewsbury, joining the Shrewsbury lines; also for a railway or tramway, Benthall to Madeley, supplying Stourport, Bewdley, Coalbrookdale, &c., main line, 40½; branch, ¼ mile; total, 40½ miles. By 18 and 19 Vic., cap. 183 (July 30th, 1855), the company was empowered to reduce its capital to 480,000*l.*, in 20*l.* shares, with power to borrow 160,000*l.* Power to use part of the Shrewsbury and Hereford, also the Shrewsbury station; and the Wellington and Severn Junction is to afford facilities for the transmission of traffic. By 19 and 20 Vic., cap. 111 (21st July, 1856), certain deviations were permitted, and the period for compulsory purchase of land in relation thereto extended for two years; completion of works, three years. By same Act an option is given to convert shares into halves, the first of which to guarantee dividend to second. By 21 and 22 Vic., cap. 135 (23rd July, 1858), an extension of time for three years was obtained. By 23 Vic., cap. 76 (14th June, 1860), the Severn Valley was leased to the West Midland per agreement (ratified 1st November, 1860), for 999 years. The West Midland has since made the following arrangement with the Severn Valley, consequent on amalgamation with the Great Western. That for two years from the opening the Severn Valley be guaranteed 3 per cent. per annum; that for the third year from the opening, 3½ per cent.; for the fourth, fifth, and sixth years from the opening 4 per cent.; and thenceforward, in perpetuity, 4½ per cent.

2. NEWPORT, ABERGAVENNY, AND HEREFORD.—Incorporated by Act 10 Vic., cap. 303 (3rd August, 1846), for a line with various branches commencing at the Pontypool junction of the Monmouthshire, thence to Abergavenny and Hereford, by a junction with the Shrewsbury and Hereford, 33 miles. In 1847, power was also obtained by 11 Vic., cap. 86 and cap. 177, to make a line to connect this line with the Taff Vale. In 1853 the company obtained power (17 Vic., cap. 178), to make deviations and short branches to the Taff Vale Extension; also cap. 179 to form a cheaper junction with the Shrewsbury and Hereford branch to Hereford Ross and Gloucester. By 20 and 21 Vic., cap. 119 (10th August, 1857), extensions into the Aberdare and Barford Valley were authorised. The length of the former, 4¾ miles; of the latter, 5 miles. The estimate is 122,000*l.*, which may be raised at 6 per cent. The works must be completed within 5 years. By

21 and 22 Vic., cap. 126 (23rd July, 1848), the company is authorised to make a deviation in the line at Aberdare, and also to convert borrowed capital into debenture stock.

3. WORCESTER AND HEREFORD.—Incorporated 17 Vic., cap. 184 (August 15th, 1853), for a narrow gauge line connecting the North with the Welsh districts, from Worcester to Hereford, 29¾ miles, with branches to the Oxford Worcester and Wolverhampton, at Worcester, ¼ mile, and two to the Shrewsbury and Hereford, at Shelwick Court and Barr's Court, ¼ mile. By 21 and 22 Vic., cap. 142 (2nd August, 1858), the period for completion of works extended to 15th August, 1861. The Midland, the Oxford Worcester and Wolverhampton, and the Newport Abergavenny and Hereford, severally acquired powers to subscribe towards the Worcester and Hereford to any extent not exceeding 37,500l. Opened 16th August, 1861. By 22 and 23 Vic., cap. 16 (21st July, 1859), the company is authorised to construct a branch from Worcester to the river Severn, and to enlarge the station at Hereford.

By 25 and 26 Vic., cap. 168 (17th July, 1862), the West Midland was authorised to construct several additional works, to provide facilities for its traffic to Newport and to make several junctions or short lines. Length, 6¼ miles. New capital, 120,000l., in shares of 5 per cent., and 40,000l. on loan. The company also obtained power to use the Monmouthshire line, to exercise the borrowing powers of the Severn Valley, and the Coleford Monmouth Usk and Pontypool; also to create debenture stock in lieu of borrowing powers.

By 26 and 27 Vic., cap. 136 (13th July, 1863), the West Midland was authorised to construct a branch to Bargoed. Length, 6¾ miles. New capital, 150,000l., at 5 per cent. and 49,800l. by loan. Also to convert mortgage debt of Coleford Monmouth and Usk, and of Severn Valley into debenture stock.

III. SOUTH WALES.—Incorporated by 8 and 9 Vic., cap. 190 (4th August, 1845), for a line from Fishguard Bay, Pembroke, and running thence along the northern shore of the Bristol Channel, through Carmarthen, Llanelly, Swansea, Neath, Cardiff, and Newport, to the west bank of the river Wye, at Chepstow, with a branch from Newport to Monmouth. By subsequent Acts, an extension from Chepstow to Grange Court was authorised, the railway to Fishguard was abandoned, and an extension of the railway from Haverfordwest to Neyland (Milford Haven) was also sanctioned. The company obtained an Act, 17 Vic., cap. 210 (August 20th, 1853), for an extension of Pembroke line to Pennarmouth, 6 miles; Pembroke deviation, 8 miles; ¾ mile to Swansea Harbour, junction with the Newport and Pontypool of ¼ mile; cost, 170,000l., for which new capital was authorised, with power to borrow 56,000l.

IV.—VALE OF NEATH.—Incorporated by 9 and 10 Vic., cap. 341 (3rd August 1846), for a line from the South Wales, at Neath, to Merthyr Tydfil, with branches to the Aberdare and to certain collieries. In 1847, other small branches were obtained, and in 1848 the South Wales was also authorised to subscribe 127,780l. towards the under-taking. In 1852 the company obtained powers to substitute new branches. Broad and narrow gauge. Productive mileage, 43¾ miles.

By 18 Vic., cap. 25 (May 25th, 1855), the company became entitled to raise additional capital to the amount of 120,000l., for station accommodation. Of this amount 79,190l. was raised by ordinary shares, and now forms part of the consolidated stock of the company. The remainder (40,810l.) was raised by preferential shares currently with the 10,000l. which the Vale of Neath were authorised to raise by the Swansea and Neath Act, 1861.

By 22 and 23 Vic., cap. 22 (21st July, 1859), the company is authorised to enter into arrangements with other companies, and to regulate its capital and borrowing powers. The South Wales may dispose of part of the Neath station to the Vale of Neath; the company may guarantee 6 per cent. on the Briton Ferry Dock shares, to the extent of 40,000l., or lease the docks. New capital may be raised to the extent of 150,000l. for general purposes; 16,000l. for acquisition of Aberdare Valley. Forfeited shares may be cancelled, and new shares issued instead. Debenture debt may be converted into debenture stock at not exceeding 5 per cent. The entire capital, either in shares, by borrowing, or in debenture stock, not to exceed 333,333l.

By 26 and 27 Vic., cap. 120 (13th July, 1863), in addition to amalgamating the Swansea and Neath, the company was authorised to construct several new works and Junctions. Also to create new capital, to the extent of 15,000l. in shares, and 5,000l. on loan. Arrangements with Taff Vale and Brecon and Merthyr Junction.

By 28 and 29 Vic., cap. 316 (5th July, 1865), the company was authorised to complete its arrangements with the Aberdare Valley, to enter into agreements with the London and North Western, and to raise new capital to the extent of 275,000l. in shares, and 91,600l. on mortgage. By 29 and 30 Vic., cap. 126 (10th August, 1866), the Vale of Neath was amalgamated with the Great Western as from 31st February, 1865, at 4½ per cent.

SOUTH WALES.—An agreement secures for Neath traffic, to and from Briton Ferry, those facilities necessary for the proper conduct of the large amount of tonnage which will at once, or may ultimately, pass between that line and the docks. The fixed rental is upon a comparatively small tonnage, and will not commence until a specified amount of shipping accommodation at the docks is available for traffic.

BRITON FERRY DOCKS.—This undertaking, to which this company subscribes 20,000l. will afford shipping accommodation to the produce of the Aberdare and Merthyr districts within a less distance than the port of Cardiff. At a special meeting on 19th June, 1860, the directors were authorised to guarantee and secure payment of dividend or interest on all or so much as they shall approve (but not to exceed 40,000l.) of the unissued share capital of the Briton Ferry Dock authorised by that company's Acts, such dividend or interest being at such rate and payable at such times, and for such period, or perpetually, and being secured or guaranteed by this company on such terms and conditions as the directors may deem necessary or expedient, and best calculated to secure the subscription and due appropriation of the capital to be so created by the Briton Ferry. The directors were further authorised to make and enter into all such contracts and arrangements with the Briton Ferry Dock, and any other companies or persons as they shall from time to time deem expedient for these purposes. By 25 and 26 Vic., cap. 178 (29th July, 1862), these arrangements were sanctioned and the Briton Ferry Dock company were authorised to raise new capital to the extent of 30,000l. in shares.

SWANSEA AND NEATH.—By 25 and 26 Vic., cap. 132 (29th July, 1862), the Vale of Neath was authorised to hold the whole of the capital in the Swansea and Neath (7¾ miles), as well as to furnish the loans on debenture, namely, 120,000l. and 40,000l.; also to lay down the narrow gauge on the whole of the company's lines, and to raise new capital to the extent of 160,000l. in shares of 5 per cent., and 33,300l. on loan. By Act 1863, the line was incorporated with the Vale of Neath, and was opened for coal traffic on 15th July, and for passengers on 1st August, 1863.

SWANSEA HARBOUR.—By 25 and 26 Vic., cap. 132 (29th July, 1862), this company is leased to the Vale of Neath, but with power to the South Wales to use the same.

BRECON AND MERTHYR TYDFIL.—The Act obtained by this company for a line to join the Taff Vale at Merthyr contains clauses to the following effect :—That if the Vale of Neath shall lay down narrow gauge rails into the Merthyr station, and shall obtain the authority of Parliament for the Brecon to form a junction with the Vale of Neath, the Brecon shall make such junction, and shall run a minimum number of five trains per day into and out of Neath station at Merthyr, and shall use that station for the purposes of their traffic. The importance of this junction will be apparent from the fact that it will place the system of the Vale of Neath in connection with the narrow gauge lines converging upon Merthyr from the north and north-east.

ABERDARE VALLEY.—Incorporated by 18 and 19 Vic., cap. 120 (2nd July, 1855), for making a line through Aberdare Valley, from Middle Duffryn coal pits, to join the Vale of Neath. Length, 1½ mile. Capital, 12,000l. in 600 shares of 20l. each ; loan, 4,000l. Transferred to Vale of Neath, as from 1st January, 1864. The interest received by the holders of the Aberdare Valley shares at the rate of 7l. 10s. per cent, is secured by annuities in the Vale of Neath, one annuity of 30s. per annum being given in exchange for each 20l. share in the Aberdare Valley.

CONSOLIDATION ACT.—By this measure all the Acts relating to the Company were consolidated, and power obtained for construction of a branch to New Docks at Cardiff, 1½ mile in length. An alteration was authorised in construction of the main line near Llansamlet, and additional powers and facilities as to capital granted. The company was also empowered to borrow a further sum of 114,941l.

BRITON FERRY.—By 25 and 26 Vic., cap. 178 (29th July, 1862), the South Wales is authorised to lease part of these docks, &c., to subscribe 15,000l. to the undertaking, and to appoint a director thereto.

SWANSEA HARBOUR.—By 25 and 26 Vic., cap. 167 (17th July, 1862), the South Wales is authorised to make use of this harbour, under arrangement with the Vale of Neath.

BRISTOL JOINT STATION.—By 28 Vic., cap. 98 (19th June, 1865), the company is authorised to contribute its proportion in conjunction with the Bristol and Exeter and the Midland, towards erection of a joint station at Bristol.

HAMMERSMITH AND CITY.—By 28 Vic., cap. 101 (19th June, 1865), the Great Western and the Metropolitan were authorised to lease the Hammersmith and City, and which has since been carried into effect at 5½ per cent.

ADDITIONAL POWERS.—By 28 and 29 Vic., cap. 299 (5th July, 1865), the company obtained power to construct a variety of new works, to acquire land, and to raise new capital to the extent of 300,000l. in shares, and 100,000l. on mortgage. New mileage in Hereford, Acton, and Ruabon, 7½ miles. Arrangements with Midland for joint stations at Worcester and Gloucester ; arrangements as to Chester and Birmingham guaranteed shares; agreements with Wenlock and Much Wenlock, for vesting Shrewsbury and Welshpool, jointly, in Great Western and London and North Western ; and confirming agreement with Metropolitan in regard to lease to Hammersmith and City. Also authorising lease of the Great Western and Wycombe to the Great Western.

LLANGOLLEN AND CORWEN.—An agreement with this company provides for the maintenance, working, and use of that railway by the Great Western at 60 per cent. of the gross receipts, after payment of the interest on their debentures, with an allowance in lieu of the rebate on traffic passing over the Great Western.

WYCOMBE.—In accordance with the terms of an agreement with the Wycombe, and under the powers of the Great Western (Wycombe Transfer) Act, 1866, a resolution was adopted at the meeting in August for creation of rent-charged stock to the amount of 420,000l., bearing interest at the rate of 5 per cent. per annum. The Wycombe was dissolved on 31st January, 1867, and the undertaking is now transferred to and vested in the Great Western.

FURTHER POWERS.—By 29 and 30 Vic., cap. 307 (30th July, 1866), the Great Western obtained further powers in relation to its own undertakings as well as in respect to others, viz. ; to construct 4 short lines in Glamorganshire, 3 miles in length; to effect several deviations in authorised lines; to acquire additional lands; to consolidate various separate stocks or shares into one stock, embracing the whole of the sections of which the undertaking is composed ; to cancel Berks and Hants Extension shares and to issue preference stock in lieu thereof ; to convert the Henley subscription into stock ; to convert the Wilts and Somerset redeemable into irredeemable stock; and also to create a new stock in lieu of the unissued 4½ per cent. redeemable preference. The company likewise obtained power to create and issue new capital to the extent of 1,220,953l. in shares, at 6 per cent., and 400,000l. on loan. Agreements and arrangements were also authorised with the Forest of Dean Central, the Stratford-on-Avon, as well as transfer of the Wellington and Drayton, the Nantwich and Market Drayton, the Stourbridge, the Henley-in-Arden, the Berks and Hants Extension, and the Stratford-on-Avon. The Tenby was also authorised to be leased to the Great Western, and the London and North Western jointly. Agreements were also authorised with the South Western in regard to the Weymouth and Portland, by which the latter has become the joint property of the two companies.

ADDITIONAL POWERS.—By 30 and 31 Vic., cap. 150 (15th July, 1867), the company obtained various powers in relation to its own undertaking as well as of other companies, among the more prominent of which may be stated the widening and improving of bridges ; arrangements with Rhymney for joint construction of five miles of railway ; similar arrangements with the Taff Vale to construct about half a mile of railway ; also with the London and North Western to make a new road at Hereford; acquisition of additional lands and completion of works within five years ; suspension of sale of superfluous lands for ten years; use of portion of Cambrian between Buttington and Welshpool without toll, and to use other portions on payments to be agreed upon facilities being offered by the Cambrian, and the Great Western to employ its own officers and servants if necessary; arrangements with London and North Western in respect to joint ownership and occupation of certain parts of the Great Western system, and also in respect to joint station at Manchester. Running powers to Brecon and Merthyr, between Newport and Cardiff, to Taff Vale over parts of the Newport Abergavenny and Hereford, and the Vale of Neath, with reciprocal powers to the Great Western over the Taff Vale. The Act also provided for dissolution of the Hammersmith and City, and for transfer of the Llangollen and Corwen, the Vale of Llangollen, the Corwen and Bala, the Bala, and the Wenlock on such terms as may be agreed upon. The Great Western was also authorised to create new capital to the extent of 150,000l. for works under the Act, and 459,000l. to carry out the transfer of the five companies before-mentioned, at a preference not exceeding 6 per cent. Also to borrow 50,000l. on mortgage, and to create debenture stock in lieu of borrowing at a rate not exceeding 5 per cent. interest. Conversion of various affiliated stocks was also authorised by the Act, so as to combine the whole within the more direct action of the company, and to facilitate its financial management, with rent-charges in lieu of Chester and Birmingham preferences, and consolidation of the mortgage debts of the West Midland and South Wales into Great Western debentures or debenture stock.

DIVIDENDS ON STOCK.—By 31 and 32 Vic., cap. 54 (25th June, 1868), the previous payments of dividends on stocks of the company was fully legalized, the several shares and stocks so paid being confirmed and declared to be good and valid, and entitled to dividend *pari passu* with the other shares and stocks of the same class and description

FURTHER POWERS.—By 31 and 32 Vic., cap. 145 (31st July, 1868), the company obtained a series of further powers in relation to its own undertaking as well as that of other companies, viz. :—To construct a line, 1 mile in length, from the main line of the West Midland, near Stourbridge station to the Stourbridge station of the latter company ; to revive a line from Kidderminster, on the Severn Valley, to the West Midland at the Kidderminster station ; to stop up or alter certain roads in the parish of Aylesbury ; to acquire additional lands in Aberdare, Glamorgan, Monmouthshire, Gloucester ; an extension of time for ten years, for sale of certain superfluous lands; extension of time for three years for purchase of lands for the Ruabon and Wrexham lines and for three years for completion of the works ; for abandonment of the line to Hatton, authorised by the Act of 1862, as well as that to Church Honeybourne, authorised by the Act of 1832. Also to abandon portions of the South Wales Union. The same Act provides that a rent charge stock of the company might be substituted for shares and stock in the Stratford ; to enter upon agreements with the Llanelly ; to validify the agreement with the South Wales Union, the text of which is given in the APPENDIX to the present volume, and to create and issue Great Western (South Wales Union) preference stock and ordinary stock, and their consolidation with the other stocks of the Great Western. By the same Act the company obtained powers to dispose of unappropriated shares and stock, to create new shares and stock, and to assign preferential dividends thereto ; to cancel unissued shares and stocks, and to regulate payment and disposal of the same. Also to borrow on mortgage the sum of 13,330l. in addition to other sums authorised, and to create debenture stocks to the full amount of exercised borrowing powers.

REVENUE.—The receipts for the half-year ending the 31st of January, 1868, when compared with the accounts for the half-year ending the 31st January, 1867, presents the following results :—

RECEIPTS.	1867		1868		Increase.		Decrease.
Passengers, parcels, mails, &c.	£966.466	..	£982,918	..	£16,452	..	..
Merchandise, coal, &c.............	973,827	..	1,004,000	..	30,173	..	..
	£1,940,293	..	£1,936,918	..	£46,625	..	

EXPENDITURE.							
Maintenance of way..............	£201,044	..	£200,862	..	...	..	£182
Locomotive and carriage stock....	329,458	..	336,211	..	£6,753	..	...
Traffic expenditure	322,328	..	309,220	..	..	..	13,108
Government duty and rates and taxes...........................	65,629	..	67,143	..	1,514	..	..
Other expenditure................	51,177	..	52,530	..	1,353	..	..
Total......................	£969,636		£965,966		£9,623	..	£13,290

There was thus an increase in the receipts of 46,625l. while the expenses were reduced. The Shrewsbury and Chester and Birkenhead sections benefited from the exceptionally large shipments of coal in the Mersey. After making provision for fixed and preference charges, the balance of 143,673l. authorised declaration of the following dividends :— On Great Western (Vale of Neath) consolidated stock at the rate of 5l. per cent. per annum, as against 5l. for the corresponding half-year ; on South Wales at the rate of 3l. 5s. per cent , as against 3l. 5s.; on Great Western at the rate of 1l. 10s., as against 1l.; on West Midland (Newport) at the rate of 15s., as against 7s. 6d.: on West Midland (Oxford) at the rate of 12s. 6d., as against 5s., leaving to be carried forward a balance of 17,575l. The following table exhibits the revenue and expenses of the half-year ending the 31st of July last, in comparison with those of the corresponding period of 1867 :—

RECEIPTS.	1868.		1867.		Increase.		Decrease.
Passengers, parcels, mails, &c.....	£979,845	..	£955,422	..	£24,423	..	..
Merchandise, coal, &c.............	971,246	..	967,787	..	3,459	..	..
	£1,951,091	..	£1,923,209	..	£27,882	..	..

EXPENDITURE.							
Maintenance of way..............	£179,554	..	188,245	..	...	..	£8,691
Locomotive and carriage stock....	325,809	..	328,480	..	2,329	..	...
Traffic expenditure	302,309	..	311,868	..	..	..	9,559
Government duty, and rates and taxes...........................	65,556	..	66,407	..	...	..	851
Other expenditure................	55,271	..	54,054	..	1,217	..	..
	£928,499	..	£944,054	..	£3,546	..	£19,101

After payment of the dividends on all the preference and guaranteed stocks, the available balance admitted of payment of the following dividends :—On Great Western stock, at the rate of 1l. 5s per cent. per annum ; on West Midland (Oxford) stock, at the rate of 5s. per cent.; on West Midland (Newport) stock, at the rate of 10s. per cent.; on South Wales, at the rate of 3l. 10s. per cent. Balance carried forward, 17,852l., against 17,575l. 5s. 4d. in the last half-year.

VALE OF NEATH.—It was reported in September that in accordance with the provisions of " The Great Western (Vale of Neath Amalgamation) Act, 1866," and in pursuance of the resolution passed at the last general meeting, the arrangement then sanctioned for the exchange of the Vale of Neath stocks for a like amount of joint rent charge stock has been carried out, and the accounts of the Vale of Neath have become merged in the joint accounts. By this arrangement the adjustment of the disputed accounts between the Vale of Neath and the other sections of the company, in reference to matters prior to the amalgamation was rendered necessary, and the unsettled balances were accordingly dealt with on a principle which seemed equitable to the directors. The directors also thought it desirable to deal at the same time with the accounts in difference between the South Wales and Great Western sections prior to their amalgamation. Although the questions between these sections were not finally settled, the directors apportioned by estimate, in the accounts submitted, the total charges involved. This apportionment will be adjusted so soon as an equitable settlement of the points in difference has been effected, it being understood that the rights of the sections will, in the meantime, be in no way prejudiced.

DIVIDENDS ON STOCK.—It was also reported in September that the bill to confirm the issue of stocks and shares in payment of dividends had become law. Having regard to the opinion expressed by the proprietors when this bill was under their consideration, and to the improved financial position of the company, that portion of it which contained powers for the future issue of stock in lieu of dividends was withdrawn, and the provisions of the Act to the confirmation of the stocks and shares issued.

METROPOLITAN.—An agreement, mutually beneficial to the two companies, has been come to with the Metropolitan, for an alteration in the terms of the arrangement of the 14th January, 1865. On the one hand, the new agreement relieves the company from the obligation to take over the spare lands at Farringdon Street, and will diminish the other obligations imposed by the agreement of 1865. On the other hand, this company have agreed, as from the 1st of March, 1869, to abandon the use of the broad gauge over the Metropolitan, and to reduce the number of trains which they were entitled to run over that line. Many disputed points have also been settled which, but for this arrangement, might have involved the two companies in serious and protracted litigation.

NARROW GAUGE.——In reference to the important subject of an alteration in the gauge the directors anounce that they were prepared to take further steps towards giving effect to the policy which has more than once received the approval of the proprietors, and with this view they propose to discontinue the broad gauge over about 96 miles, on which the mixed gauge already exists. It is intended to take up the third rail between Oxford and Wolverhampton (81 miles), and between Basingstoke and the Junction near Reading (15 miles), and to conduct the service of those districts for the future by means of narrow gauge trains only. It is also proposed to convert the present broad gauge between Hereford and Grange Court into narrow gauge, and to lay a third rail within the broad gauge between the latter point and Gloucester, and from Gloucester to Standish Junction, so as to form, in connection with the Midland a complete through narrow gauge route between Bristol and the narrow gauge lines north and south of Hereford. The value of the materials released between Oxford and Wolverhampton, and on the Basingstoke Branch, will go far to meet the outlay to be incurred in the Hereford and Gloucester districts; an additional vote of 15,640l. being required to complete the work. The directors are satisfied that the expenditure, thus incurred will have the effect of improving the working of the line, increasing the traffic thereon, while at the same time the permanent way expenses will be diminished. It will be necessary to expend a sum of 71,700l., for which a vote is also asked, in additional narrow gauge rolling stock, to provide for the services on these lines as well as on the Metropolitan. By the Pembroke and Tenby Act, 1866, an obligation was imposed upon the Great Western to provide a narrow-gauge communication between Carmarthen and Whitland—the point of junction of the Pembroke and Tenby with the South Wales—a length of about 15 miles. Under the provisions of the same Act, the Pembroke and Tenby contributed 20,000l. towards the cost of the work. Desirous of avoiding as much as possible the construction of additional mixed gauge lines, a new narrow gauge line has been substituted for the broad gauge on the up side, that line being appropriated exclusively to narrow gauge traffic, the down line being continued on the broad gauge only and reserved for broad gauge traffic.

CAPITAL.—This account to 31st July showed that 21,121,136l. had been received on account of the Great Western ; 4,316,946l. on account of West Midland ; 3,461,494l. on account of South Wales, and 17,445,276l. on Great Western joint account ; total, 46,344,852l. The expenditure on the Great Western (Original) undertaking, including 1,843,720l. subscriptions to other undertakings, amounted to 28,232,609l.; on the West Midland, to 5,856,674l.; on the South Wales, including 125,580l. subscriptions to other undertakings, to 4,646,903l.; and on Great Western joint account, including 152,200l. subscriptions to other undertakings, to 6,861,266l., making the total expenditure 45,597,452l., and leaving a balance of 747,400l. The following details give a complete summary of the various capital accounts :—

GREAT WESTERN (ORIGINAL).

Stock and shares	£17,383,936	
Loans on debentures	3,737,200	= £21,121 136

WEST MIDLAND.

	Oxford.	Newport.	Joint.	
Stock and shares (Abstract A)	£2,760,410	£1,120,516	£352,720	
Stratford canal annuities	83,300	....	....	
Total West Midland	£2,843,710	£1,120,516	£352,720=	4,316,946

SOUTH WALES.

Stock and shares	3,461,494

GREAT WESTERN (JOINT).

Stock and shares	£4,656,659	
Loans on debenture	8,938,390	
Rent-charges	29,763	
Debenture stocks	3,727,344	
Kennet and Avon canal loans	53,600	
Temporary loans	39,520=	17,445,276
		£46,344,852

The subjoined elaborate compilation exhibits the whole of the multifarious stocks of the company in their priorities :—

GREAT WESTERN (ORIGINAL).

	Received.	Balance.	Authorised.
5 per cent. rent charge guaranteed	£28,130 ..	....	..
Ditto (represented by Hereford Ross and Gloucester shares)	157,788 ..	....	⎫
Canal	147,462 ..	£1,878,282	⎪ £2,666,600
6 per cent. Birmingham preference......	129,128 ..	....	⎪
8 per cent. Chester preference	171,000 ..	....	⎬
5 per cent. Chester preference	154,810 ..	....	⎭
5 per cent. Berks and Hants Extension guaranteed	59,062 ..	.... ..	59,062
5 per cent. Henley guaranteed..........	6,010 ..	50 ..	6,060
4 per cent. Wilts Somerset and Weymouth annuity	825,100 ..	.... ..	825,100
4 per cent. irredeemable preference, 1850	1,471,000 ⎱ ..	.... ..	3,499,000
4½ per cent. irredeemable preference, 1850	2,028,000 ⎰		
5 per cent. redeemable preference, 1855.	1,325,000 ..	.... ..	1,325,000
4½ per cent. redeemable preference, 1860.	224,356 ..	.... ..	224,356
4½ per cent. irredeemable preference, 1863	810,402 ..	17,160 ⎱ ..	1,278,206
5 per cent. irredeemable preference	.... ..	450,644 ⎰	
5 per cent. perpetual guaranteed, 1866..	.... ..	2,571,250 ⎱	
Birmingham guaranteed	973,676 ..	26,024 ⎬ ..	4,368,550
Chester guaranteed......................	692,391 ..	105,209 ⎰	
Ordinary	8,180,621 ..	100,638 ..	8,281,259
	£17,383,936	£5,149,259	£22,533,193

OXFORD.

	Received.	Balance.	Authorised.
6 per cent. first guaranteed..............	850,000 ..	.... ..	850,000
6 per cent. second guaranteed	485,910 ..	.... ..	485,910
4 per cent. Chipping Norton	24,000 ..	.... ..	24,000
Ordinary stock	1,400,500 ..	.... ..	1,400,500
	£2,760,410	....	£2,760,410

NEWPORT.

	Received.	Balance.	Authorised.
5 per cent. first guaranteed..............	444,572 ..	.... ..	444,572
6 per cent. second preference...........	135,000 ..	.... ..	135.000
Ordinary stock	540,944 ..	£906 ..	541,850
	£1,120,516	£906	£1,121,422

WEST MIDLAND.

	Received.	Balance.	Authorised.
5½ per cent. guaranteed, 1863............	£220,000 ..	.... ..	£220,000
5 per cent. preference, 1863............	132,720 ..	£7,280 ..	140,000
	£352,720	£7,280	£360,000

SOUTH WALES.

	Received.	Balance.	Authorised.
4 per cent. irredeemable guaranteed ..	£165,558 ..	.... ..⎱	£522,178
4½ per cent. irredeemable guaranteed ..	356,620 ..	.... ..⎰	
5 per cent. redeemable guaranteed....	318,900 ..	1,080 ..	319,980
4½ per cent. irredeemable guaranteed, 1859	194,000 ..	....	194,000
Ordinary	2,426,416 ..	526 ..	2,426,942
	£3,461,494	£1,606	£3,463,100

GREAT WESTERN (JOINT).

	Received.	Balance.	Authorised.
5 per cent. rent charge guaranteed....	£1,298,816	£107,933	£1,406,749
5 per cent. Vale of Neath perpetual preference......................	68,420 ..	.... ..	68,420
5 per cent. Vale of Neath perpetual guaranteed	53,240 ..	.... ..	53,240
4½ per cent. Vale of Neath preference shares, 1862	18,360 ..	.... ..	18,360
5 per cent. Vale of Neath perpetual preference, 1865	28,510 ..	.... ..	28,510
5 per cent. Hereford perpetual........	579,903 ..	97 ..	580,000
5 per cent. perpetual preference, 1865..	985,294 ..	14,706 ..	1,000,000
6 per cent irredeemable preference and 20l. shares, 1866	1,624,116 ..	1,035,524 ..	2,659,640
Authorised by Acts of 1865, 1867, and 1868, but not created	.... ..	849,000 ..	849,000
	£4,656,659	£2,007,260	£6,663,919

SUMMARY.

Great Western (original)	£17,383,936	..	£5,149,257	..	£22,553,193
Oxford................................	2,760,410	..	....	..	2,760,410
Newport	1,120,516	..	906	..	1,121,422
West Midland	352,720	..	7,280	..	360,000
South Wales	3,461,494	..	1,606	..	3,463,100
Joint................................	4,656,659	..	2,007,260	..	6,663,919

Stocks and shares..............	£29,735,735	£7,166,309	£36,902,044

The accounts are made up to the 31st January and 31st July, and the statutory meetings held in February and August.

Scale of Voting.—One vote per every 100*l.* stock, up to 2,000*l.*, and one additional vote every 500*l.* beyond 3,000*l.*

Certificates must accompany transfer deeds. Registration, 2*s.* 6*d.*

No. of Directors—16. *Qualification*, 1,000*l.* ordinary stock.

DIRECTORS :

Chairman—Sir DANIEL GOOCH, Bart., M.P., London.

Deputy-Chairman—CHARLES ALEXANDER WOOD, Esq., London.

Richard Bassett, Esq , Cardiff.
F. L. Bodenham, Esq., Hereford.
Captain Bulkeley, Windsor.
Lewis L. Dillwyn, Esq., M.P., Swansea, and 10, Prince's Terrace, S.W
W. C. King, Esq., Bracknell, Berks.
Edward Leeming, Esq., Richmond.
Richard Michell, Esq., London.
F, N. Micklethwait, Esq., London.

John William Miles, Esq., Bristol.
C. G. Mott, Esq., Birkenhead.
The Hon. Fredk. G. B. Ponsonby, London.
Christopher R. M. Talbot, Esq., M.P., Margam Park, South Wales, and 3, Cavendish Square, S. W.
Edward Wanklyn, Esq., Slough.
Sir Watkin W. Wynn, Bart., M.P., Wynn-stay, and 18, St. James's Square, S. W.

OFFICERS.—Sec., Frederick G. Saunders ; Gen. Man., James Grierson ; Registrar, T. M. Ward ; Loco. Supt., Joseph Armstrong, Swindon ; Chief Eng., W. G. Owen, Paddington, W.; Chief Accountant, Frederick Cleetsom, Paddington, W.; Supt. of Line, G. N. Tyrrel, Paddington, W.; Goods Man., John Grant, Paddington, W.; Storekeeper. H. Dunn, Swindon ; Auditors, Edward Harper, J. G. T. Child, and James William Bowen ; Solicitors, Young, Maples, Teesdale, and Young, Paddington Station, W.

Chief Offices—Paddington Terminus, W.

172.—GREAT WESTERN AND BRENTFORD.

Incorporated by 18 and 19 Vic., cap, 191 (14th August, 1855), to make a railway from the Great Western at Southall to Brentford, with docks, &c. Broad gauge. Length, 4½ miles. Estimate, 90,000*l.* There is a dock in connection with the railway, at the terminus at Brentford. Extra land, ten acres.

By 20 and 21 Vic., cap. 13 (26th June, 1857), the company was authorised to raise additional capital to the extent of 45,000*l.*, at 5 per cent. preference; also to borrow 15,000*l.* on mortgage. Opened for goods, 18th July, 1859; for passengers, 1st May, 1860.

By 28 and 29 Vic., cap. 299 (5th July, 1865), the Great Western and Brentford was authorised to be transferred to the Great Western on such terms as might be agreed upon.

GREAT WESTERN.—An agreement sanctioned by 22 Vic., cap. 15 (19th April, 1859), authorises a lease of the railway and dock to the Great Western for a term of 99 years from completion and opening for traffic. The Great Western to pay in each year to the Brentford a tollage of 1*s.* 2*d.* per ton on the first 100,000 tons of goods and minerals (other than coal, coke, and stone), conveyed over the railway to and from the dock ; for all goods and minerals (other than coal, coke, and stone), exceeding 100,000, but not exceeding 150,000 tons, 1*s.* per ton ; for 150,000 tons (other than coal, coke, and stone), and not exceeding 180,000 tons, 9*d.* per ton ; for all exceeding 180,000 tons 6*d.* per ton, subject to a reduction on the contingency referred to below ; for all coal, coke, and stone, 6*d.* per ton, but subject to a reduction on the same contingency ; for goods, minerals, and all other articles not conveyed over the railway, but imported into or exported from the dock, 4*d.* per ton for dock and wharfage dues. For passengers, cattle, horses, and carriages, the following fixed annual sums by way of rent, viz., for the first year nothing ; for the second year, 200*l.* ; for the third year, 300*l.* ; for the fourth year, 400*l.* ; and for the fifth and all subsequent years, 500*l.* each year. The Great Western undertake to send not less than 100,000 tons of goods, exclusive of coal, coke, and stone in every year, or to pay for the same by way of rent, at the prescribed tollage of 1*s.* 2*d.* per ton for that quantity. If found necessary to supply the wants of increasing traffic (after the rent shall amount to 10,500*l.* per annum), the two companies are to find additional capital in equal moieties. If the Great Western shall provide any such additional capital, the rate on the excess tonnage, whether of goods or minerals, or of coal, coke, and stone, is to be reduced from 6d. to 4d. per ton over and above the quantity representing the said rent of 10,500l. per year, and the Brentford are guaranteed at least 5 per cent. per annum on any additional capital provided by them.

REVENUE.—The net income for the half-year ending 31st December, 1867, admitted of a dividend for the half-year of 1l. 2s. 6d. per cent., and for the June half-year to the same extent.

CAPITAL.—The construction account to 30th June showed that 219,717l. had been expended, the receipts having been as under :—

9,000 shares at 10l. each, Act 18 and 19 Vic.	£90,000
592 shares at 10l. each, Act 20 and 21 Vic.	5,920
3,908 shares at 10l. each, bearing a preferential dividend of 5 per cent. per annum, Act 20 and 21 Vic.	39,080
3,000 shares at 10l. each, bearing a preferential dividend of 5 per cent. per annum, Act 22 Vic.	30,000
	£165,000
Debentures	55,048=£220,048

The accounts are made up to 30th June and 31st December.

Meetings in February and August. Dividends paid 15th March and 15th September in each year.

No. of Directors—6 ; quorum, 3. *Qualification*, 25 shares.

DIRECTORS:

Chairman—PETER DAVEY, Esq., Horton, Colnbrook, Bucks.

Deputy-Chairman—HENRY DONKIN, Esq., Grange Road, Bermondsey, S.E.

Arthur S. Davey, Esq., Old Barge House, Blackfriars, S. | Captain Bulkeley, Clewer Lodge, Windsor. Henry Browse, Esq., Upper Tooting, Surrey.

OFFICERS.—Sec., Charles Eley, 5, Westminster Chambers, Victoria Street, Westminster, S.W.; Solicitor, R. H. Wyatt, 28, Paliament Street, Westminster, S.W.; Auditors, George Wyatt, 7, St. George's Villas, St. Paul's Road, Highbury, and William Moates, Public Accountant, 28, Moorgate Street, E.C.

Offices—5, Westminster Chambers, Victoria Street, Westminster, S.W.

173.—GREENOCK AND AYRSHIRE.

Incorporated by 28 and 29 Vic., cap. 301 (July 5th, 1865), for making a railway from Greenock, by Bridge of Weir, to Howood, with a junction with Glasgow and South Western company's line at both those places. The capital of the company is 350,000l., in 10l. shares, and 116,600l. in loans. Length, 15 miles. The Glasgow and South Western contribute 300,000l., and have entered into an agreement to work the line in perpetuity, which is confirmed by the Act. Works in progress.

By 31 and 32 Vic., cap. 136 (13th July, 1868), the company obtained power to construct three short and local lines, about 1 mile in length in all, and also a new street in Greenock. New capital, 150,000l. in shares, and 50,000l. on mortgage, as well as to create and issue debenture stock.

CAPITAL.—The expenditure to 31st January, 1868, amounted to 364,723l., leaving a balance due to bankers of 6,535l.

No. of Directors—10 ; quorum, 3. *Qaulification*, 500l.

DIRECTORS:

Chairman—PETER CLOUSTON, Esq., 1, Park Terrace, Glasgow.

Deputy-Chairman—Sir ANDREW ORR, of Harviestoun and Castle Campbell.

Robert Barclay, Esq., 21, Park Terrace, Glasgow. | James Morton, Esq., Iron Merchant, Greenock.
Archibald Finnie, Esq., of Springhill, Kilmarnock. | Neil Robson, Esq., C.E., 127, St. Vincent Street, Glasgow.
David Johnstone, Esq., Belleaire, Greenock. | James Rodger, Esq., 1, Claremont Gardens, Glasgow.
John Kerr, Esq., Greenock. | Alexander Ronaldson, Esq., 7, Park Terrace, Glasgow.

OFFICERS.—Sec., W. J. Wainwright ; Engs., Forman and Mc.Call, Glasgow ; Auditors, William Stevenson, Crosslee House, Johnstone, and — Welsh, Greenock ; Solicitors, Mathew Anderson, Glasgow, and Thomas King, Greenock ; Bankers, Union Bank of Scotland.

Offices—14, Bridge Street, Glasgow.

174.—GREENOCK AND WEMYSS BAY.

Incorporated by 25 and 26 Vic., cap. 160 (17th July, 1862). to construct a line from the Greenock branch of the Caledonian at Port Glasgow to Wemyss Bay. Length 9½ miles. Capital, 120,000l. in 10l. shares; loans, 40,000l. Arrangements with Caledonian which subscribes 30,000l. Opened 15th May, 1865.

By 26 Vic., cap. 47 (8th June. 1863), the company was authorised to construct an extension (16 chains), and a pier in connection therewith. New capital, 30,000l. in shares, at 5 per cent. preference, and 10,000l. on loan.

REVENUE.—The receipts for the half-year ending 31st January were 5,869l., in comparison with 4,510l. for the corresponding period of 1867. For the half-year ending 31st July the receipts were 6,234l.. in comparison with 5,768l. It was reported in September that the liability to the contractors had been reduced from 15,619l. to 10,619l.; and that, although the revenue would not admit of dividend, the affairs of the company were upon a sound basis.

CAPITAL.—The expenditure to 31st July, 1868, was reported at 194,245l. The receipts having been as follow :—

Share capital—ordinary...	£90,061
Do. —preference, 5 per cent.................................	29,936
Mortgages	35,396
Upper Greenock new goods station	3,167
Balance..	35,685=£194,245

Meetings in February or March, and in August or September. Accounts to 31st July and 31st January.

No. of Directors- 5; minimum, 3; quorum, 2. *Qualification*, 500l.

DIRECTORS :

Chairman –ALEXANDER STRUTHERS FINLAY, Esq., of Castle-Toward.

Deputy-Chairman—ALEXANDER RONALDSON, Esq., Merchant, Glasgow.

James Lamont, Esq., of Knockdow. | Col. David Carrick Robert Carrick Bu-
James Stewart, Esq., Merchant, Greenock. | chanan, of Drumpellier, Coatbridge.

OFFICERS.—Sec., James Keyden; Engs., Forman and M'Call, C.E., Glasgow; Solicitors, Keyden, Strang, and Keyden, Glasgow; Auditors, Walter Mackenzie and William Anderson, Accountants, Glasgow.

Offices—186, West George Street, Glasgow.

175.—GWENDRAETH.

Incorporated by 29 and 30 Vic., cap. 297 (30th June, 1866), out of an extension of the Carmarthen and Cardigan to Kidwelly. Length, 7½ miles. Capital, 170,000l. in shares, and 56,600l. on loan. No shares have as yet been taken up.

Meetings in February or March and in August or September.

No. of Directors—6; minimum, 4; quorum, 3. *Qualification*, 500l.

DIRECTORS :

William Parsons, Esq., Nottingham. | Joseph Ivimey, Esq., 8, Staple Inn, W.C.

176.—HALESOWEN AND BROMSGROVE.

Incorporated by 28 and 29 Vic., cap. 333 (5th July, 1865), to construct several short lines in the county of Worcester, connecting the Midland and the West Midland section of the Great Western. Length, 7¼ miles. Capital, 120,000l., in 12,000 10l. shares, and 40,000l. on mortgage. Arrangements with Midland and Great Western.

By 29 and 30 Vic., cap. 317 (6th August, 1866), the company was authorised to construct two small branches in the county of Worcester. Length, 3¾ miles. New capital, 48,000l. in shares and 16,000l. on loan.

No. of Directors—6; minimum, 3; quorum, 3. *Qualification*, 500l.

DIRECTORS :

The Right Hon. Lord Lyttelton, Hagley Park, Worcestershire, and 21, Carlton House Terrace. S.W.
Thomas Eyre Foakes, Esq., 4, New Square, Lincoln's Inn, W.C.
Frederick Blyth, Esq.. 120, Adelaide Road, Hampstead, N.W.

John Corbett. Esq., Stoke Salt Works, near Bromsgrove.
Edward Gem, Esq., Messrs. Edward Gem and Co., Birmingham.
Captain Charles Miller Layton, Glasbury House, Glasbury, Brecon.

OFFICERS.—Sec., George W. Harris; Auditors, J. Waddell and Co., Accountants, New Poultry Chambers, 7, Poultry, E.C.; Solicitors, Wilkins, Blyth, and Marsland, 10, St. Swithin's Lane, E.C., and Scott and Horton, Bromsgrove; Surveyors, Jeremiah Matthews and Sons, Birmingham. and W. Rogers Penn, Bromsgrove.

Offices—6, Westminster Chambers, S.W.

177.—HALIFAX AND OVENDEN.

Incorporated by 27 and 28 Vic., cap. 143 (30th June, 1864), to construct a line from Lancashire and Yorkshire, near Halifax, to Ovenden. Length, 2¾ miles. Capital, 90,000*l.* in 10*l.* shares, and 30,000*l.* on loan. Arrangements with Great Northern and Lancashire and Yorkshire, which each subscribe 30,000*l.* Works in progress.

By 30 and 31 Vic., cap. 178 (12th August, 1867), the company was authorised to make several variations in the line, and to increase the capital by 90,000*l.*, in shares, and 30,000*l.* on loan. The Great Northern and the Lancashire and Yorkshire may each subscribe 30,000*l.* to this new capital.

CAPITAL.—The receipts and expenditure on this account to 30th June, 1868, were stated as follow :—

Received.		Expended.	
Calls	£69,395	Per last report	£58,529
		During half-year :—	
		Parliamentary expenses	300
		General expenses	70
		Land purchases expenses	358
		Works	142
			£59,401
		Balance	9,993
	£69,395		£69,395

No. of Directors—15 ; 5 by the shareholders, and 5 by each of the Great Northern and Lancashire and Yorkshire ; minimum, 9 ; quorum, 3. *Qualification*, 1,000*l.*

DIRECTORS :

Chairman—EDWARD AKROYD, Esq., M.P., Bankfield, Halifax, and 40, Lowndes Street, S.W.

Sir Francis Crossley, Bart., M.P., Belle Vue, Halifax.
William Foster, Esq., Queensbury, Bradford.
*Joshua Radcliffe, Esq., Rochdale.
*George Anderton, Esq., Cleckheaton.
*Samuel Fielden, Esq.. Todmorden.
*George Wilson. Esq., Manchester.
*Joshua Appleyard, Esq., Clare Hall, Halifax.

†William Firth, Esq., Burley Wood, near Leeds.
†Colonel Packe, Caythorpe, Grantham.
†Robert Tennant, Esq., Scarcroft Lodge, Shadwell, near Leeds.
†Samuel Waterhouse, Esq., M.P., Hope Hall, Halifax, and 66, Pall Mall, S.W.
†George Walker, Esq., Osgathorpe, Sheffield.

* Represent Lancashire and Yorkshire.   † Represent Great Northern.

OFFICERS.—Sec., C. N. Wilkinson, Halifax ; Eng., John Fraser, Leeds ; Auditor, Robert Midgley, Salterlee, Halifax ; Solicitors, Wavell, Philbrick, Foster, and Wavell. Offices—Halifax.

178.—HARBORNE.

Incorporated by 29 and 30 Vic., cap. 101 (28th June, 1866), for constructing a line from the Birmingham Wolverhampton and Stour Valley section of the London and North Western, in Birmingham, to the town of Harborne, in Staffordshire. Length, 3 miles. Capital, 100,000*l.*, in 10*l.* shares, and 33,000*l.* on loan, with power to create and issue debenture stock. Arrangements with London and North Western.

No. of Directors—5 ; minimum, 3 ; quorum, 2. *Qualification*, 30 shares.

DIRECTORS :

Sir William Smith, Bart., 10, Greville Place, Kilburn, N.W.
Thomas Eyre Foakes, Esq., 4, New Square, Lincoln's Inn, W.C.
Charles William Earle, Esq., Little Elms, Watford.

Frederick Blyth, Esq., 120, Adelaide Road, Hampstead, N.W.
Francis Housman, Esq., 5, New Square, Lincoln's Inn, W.C.

OFFICERS.—Sec., George W. Harris, 6, Westminster Chambers, S.W.; Eng., J. H. Tolmé, 1, Victoria Street, Westminster, S.W. ; Solicitors, Wilkins, Blyth, and Marsland, 10, St. Swithin's Lane, E.C.; Surveyors, J. Mathews and Sons, Birmingham. Offices—6, Westminster Chambers, S.W.

179.—HATFIELD CHASE.

Incorporated by 17 and 18 Vic., cap. 9 (1854), for the purpose of draining, working, and otherwise improving part of the level of Hatfield Chase. Authorised by 29 and 30 Vic., cap. 163 (16th July, 1866), to construct a railway from Haxey, on the Doncaster and Gainsborough branch of the Great Northern, to Owston, on the river Trent. Length, 3¼ miles. New capital, 44,000*l.* in shares and 14,600*l.* on loan. Arrangements with Great Northern and Manchester and Sheffield.

180.—HATFIELD AND ST. ALBANS.

Incorporated by 25 and 26 Vic., cap. 86 (30th June, 1862), to construct a line from the Great Northern, at Hatfield, to the London and North Western, at St. Albans. Length, 6 miles. Capital, 70,000*l.*, in 10*l.* shares; loans, 23,000*l.* Arrangements with the Great Northern, which subscribed 20,000*l.*, and works the line. Opened 1st November, 1865. Powers for raising additional capital, to the amount of 15,000*l.* in shares and 5,000*l.* in mortgages, have been granted by a Board of Trade certificate, in accordance with the Companies Powers Act of 1864.

Meetings in February and August.

No. of Directors—7; minimum, 3; quorum, 3. *Qualification, 300l.*

DIRECTORS:

Chairman—LORD EBURY, Moor Park, Rickmansworth, and 107, Park Street, Grosvenor Square, W.

Deputy-Chairman—JOSEPH CARY, Esq., 49, Pall Mall, S.W.

The Hon. Reginald Algernon Capel, Little Cashiobury, Watford, and 21, Chesham Place, S. W.	John Henry Dillon, Esq., K 5, The Albany, Piccadilly, W.
* Colonel the Hon. Octavius Duncombe, M. P., Waresley Park, St. Neots, and 84, Eaton Square, S.W.	*John Harvey Astell, Esq., Woodbury Hall, St. Neots.

* Represent the Great Northern.

OFFICERS.—Sec., Alexander Forbes; Eng., J. Pierce, 5, Westminster Chambers, Westminster, S. W.; Solicitor, F. F. Jeyes, 28, Parliament Street, Westminster, S.W.; Bankers, Smith, Payne, and Smith, 1, Lombard Street, E. C.

Offices—King's Cross Station, N.

181.—HAWES AND MELMERBY.

Incorporated by 28 and 29 Vic.. cap. 244 (5th July. 1865), to construct a line between these places. Length, 41 miles. Capital, 350,000*l.* in shares, and 116,000*l.* on loan.

No. of Directors—8; minimum, 5; quorum, 5 and 3. *Qualification, 500l.*

DIRECTORS:

Colonel Henry Van Straubenzee, Spennithorne.	*Henry Pease, Esq., Pierremont, Darlington.
George Lightfoot. Esq., Masham.	*Isaac Wilson, Esq., Nunthorpe Hall, Middlesbro'.
* George Hicks Seymour, Esq., Clifton, near York.	* William Rutherford Hunter, Esq., Lovaine Crescent, Newcastle
*George Leeman, Esq., York.	* North Eastern representatives.

Secretary, J. Cleghorn, York.

182.—HAYLING.

Incorporated by 23 and 24 Vic., cap. 166 (23rd July, 1860), to construct a line from near Havant, on the Brighton, to Hayling, with branch to the Portsmouth. Capital, 50,000*l.*, in 10*l.* shares; call, 2*l.*, with intervals of two months. Loans, 16,000*l.* Arrangements may be made with South Western. which may make use of the line for its own traffic, and exercise running powers thereon.

By 27 and 28 Vic., cap.177 (14th July, 1864), the company was authorised to construct two extensions (1¼ miles), to make and maintain docks, and to raise further capital, to the extent of 10,000*l.* for general purposes, 60,000*l.* for the docks, and 6,000*l.* for the extensions, with borrowing powers equal to 25,300*l.*

By 30 and 31 Vic., cap. 189 (12th August, 1867), the company was authorised to abandon some portions of the line, and to substitute others in place thereof; also to apply a preference to unissued shares not exceeding 6,000*l.* Completion of works, 12th August, 1869.

Meetings in February and August.

No. of Directors—4; quorum, 3. *Qualification, 100l.*

DIRECTORS:

Chairman—FRANCIS FULLER, Esq., 3, Whitehall Gardens, S.W.

Admiral Sir Henry J. Leeke, K.C.B., K. H., Thoydon Place, Epping.	Robert Hume, Esq., 65, Berners Street, W. Richard Crowley, Esq.

OFFICERS.—Sec., W. H. Wilson; Consulting Eng., James Abernethy, M.I.C.E.; Acting Eng., Thomas J. Hay, C. E.; Solicitors, George T. Potter, 4, Victoria Street, Westminster, S.W., and George F. Smith, 65, Golden Square, W.; Bankers, Glyn, Mills, and Co., Lombard Street, E.C.

Offices—6, Victoria Street, Westminster, S.W.

183.—HELSTON AND PENRYN.

Incorporated by 27 and 28 Vic., cap. 197 (14th July, 1864), to construct a line from Helston to the Cornwall at Penryn. Length, 9¾ miles. Capital, 120,000l., in 20l. shares, and 40,000l. on loan. Broad gauge. Arrangements with Cornwall.

No. of Directors—5; quorum, 3. *Qualification*, 500l.

DIRECTORS:

Chairman—JOHN JOPE ROGERS, Esq.

T. J. Agar Robartes, Esq., Lanhydrock, near Bodmin.
J. F. Basset, Esq., Tehidy Park.

John St. Aubyn, Esq., M.P., 42, Upper Grosvenor Street, S.W.
Major Grylls, R. A., Helston.

OFFICERS.—Sec., P. Grenfell Hill; Eng., W. Humber: Solicitors, Grylls, Hill, and Hill, Helston; Bankers, Union Bank of London (Temple Bar Branch), E.C., and Vivian, Grylls, Kendall, and Co., Helston.
Offices—Helston.

184.—HEMEL HEMPSTEAD.

Incorporated by 26 and 27 Vic., cap. 152 (12th July, 1865), to construct a line from the London and North Western, at Boxmoor, to Hemel Hempstead. Length, 1¾ mile. Capital, 20,000l. in 10l. shares, and 6,600l. on loans. Arrangements with London and North Western.

By 29 and 30 Vic., cap. 215 (16th July, 1866),. the company obtained power to construct a line from Hemel Hempstead to Harpenden on the Hertford Luton and Dunstable branch of the Great Northern. Also a short branch to the Midland. Length, 9¼ miles. Capital, 170,000l. in shares, and 56,600l. on loan.

No. of Directors—5; quorum, 3. *Qualification*, 100l.

DIRECTORS:

John Barrow, Esq., 35, Westbourne Terrace, Hyde Park, W.
Henry Balderson, Esq.
James Stuart Tulk, Esq.

John Rennie Fulton, Esq.
Charles Lempriere, Esq., Delahay Street, Westminster, S.W.

Secretary, Joseph Butler.

Office—6, Raymond Buildings, Gray's Inn, W.C.

185.—HENLEY-IN-ARDEN.

Incorported by 24 and 25 Vic., cap. 76 (28th June, 1861), to construct a line from the Birmingham and Oxford, at Rowington, to Henley-in-Arden. Length, 3 miles 15 chains. Capital, 18,000l. in 10l. shares; loans, 6,000l. Mixed gauge. Arrangements with Great Western.

By 27 and 28 Vic., cap. 134 (30th June, 1864), an extension of time for one year was conceded, with power to raise additional capital to the extent of 12,000l. in shares, and 4,000l. on loan.

No. of Directors—5; minimum, 3; quorum, 3 and 2. *Qualification*, 200l.

DIRECTORS:

Robert Dolphin, Esq.
T. H. Goodwin Newton, Esq.
Edward Cooper, Esq.

S. H. Agar, Esq.
G. R. Dartnell, Esq.

186.—HEREFORD, HAY, AND BRECON.

Incorporated by 22 and 23 Vic., cap. 84 (8th August, 1859), to construct a line from Brecon, through Hay, to the Shrewsbury and Hereford, at the latter town. Capital, 280,000l. in 20l. shares; loans, 23,000l.; calls, 2l. 10s. Length, 34 miles. By 23 and 24 Vic., cap. 127 (3rd July, 1860), the company was authorised to relinquish the junction of the line with the Shrewsbury and Hereford, and in lieu thereof to form a communication with the Newport Abergavenny and Hereford Section of the West Midland, at Barton Station. By 23 and 24 Vic., cap. 179 (6th August, 1860), the Hay railway is vested in the Hereford Hay and Brecon, but parts of the line transferred to the Mid-Wales Brecon and Merthyr Tydfil Junction, and a portion disused. The Hereford and Brecon allots to every Hay share of 100l. two Herefords of 20l. each, and 2l. 8s. as interest due, or 20l. in cash, according to option of Hay shareholders. By 25 and 26 Vic., cap. 95 (30th June, 1862), various alterations of levels and deviations of the line were authorised; all to be completed by 6th August, 1864. In operation, 27 miles. By 26 Vic., cap. 9 (4th May, 1863), the company was authorised to raise new capital to the extent of 75,000l. in shares at 5 per cent., and 25,000l. on loan. By 28 and 29 Vic., cap. 324 (5th July, 1865), the Hereford Hay and Brecon was amalgamated with the Brecon and Merthyr, on a share capital not exceeding 355,000l.

By 30 'and 31 Vic., cap. 142, the Hereford Hay and Brecon was remitted to its former position as a separate company.

Application is being made to Parliament for renewal of debentures; conversion of debenture and other debts into debenture stock ; variation of priorities of debenture-holders ; running powers over a portion of the Mid-Wales, over the Neath and Brecon, and over the railways of the Brecon and Merthyr Tydvil Junction ; working and traffic agreements with the London and North Western, the Great Western, and the Midland.

DIRECTORS:
Chairman—S. E. BOLDEN, Esq., Lancaster.

F. A. Fynney, Esq., Queen's Chambers, Manchester.
William Laurence Banks, Esq., F.S.A., Pontywell Hall, Brecon.

G. Heginbottom, Esq., Southport.
G. A. Addison, Esq., 29, Lombard Street, London.
Samuel Turnbull, Esq., Manchester.

OFFICERS.—Sec., James Fraser, 7, Bank Buildings, Lothbury, E.C. ; Solicitors, Tilleard, Son, Godden. and Holme, 34, Old Jewry, E. C.

Offices—7, Bank Buildings, Lothbury, E.C.

187.—HEXHAM AND ALLENDALE.

Incorporated by 28 Vic., cap. 87 (19th June, 1865). to construct lines : No. 1 from the Newcastle and Carlisle, near Hexham. to Allendale Town, length, 13 miles ; and No. 2, from Allendale Town to Allenheads ; length, 7 miles. Capital in 10l. shares, for No. 1, 75,000l. and 25,000l. on loan. No. 2, 45,000l. and 15,000l. on loan. Total 120,000l. and 40,000l. on loan. The North Eastern subscribe 10,000l., and by 29 Vic., cap. 78 (11th June, 1866) they subscribe a further sum of 10,000l., and the Comptroller of the Greenwich Hospital Estate is registered as a shareholder for 10,000l. Opened to Langley, about 8 miles, for goods and cattle traffic on 19th August, 1867. From Langley to Catton Road, 4½ miles, opened for goods and cattle traffic 13th January, 1868.

An extension of time for construction of works is being sought for from the Board of Trade.

REVENUE.—By this account from August 19th to December 31st, 1867, it appeared that the working expenses had been 315l.: income-tax. 5l., making 321l.; balance carried to profit and loss, 356l.; total. 677l. By goods traffic, 496l.; minerals, 170l.; live stock, 9l.; total, 677l. The revenue account for the half-year ending June 30th, showed :—working expenses, 456l.; income-tax, 3l.; balance carried to profit and loss, 573l.; total, 1.033l. By goods traffic, 697l.; minerals, 331l.; live stock, 2l.; parcels, 2l.; total, 1,033l. The general balance showed the balance of capital to be 122l.; balance of profit and loss, 930l.; total, 1,052l. By traffic accounts unpaid, 11l.; by bankers' balances, 1,041l.; total, 1,052l.

CAPITAL.--The receipts on this account have been 72,661l.; and the expenditure, 72,539l.

Scale of Voting.—One vote for every 10l. share.

No. of Directors—7 ; minimum, 2: quorum, 3. *Qualification*, 250l.

DIRECTORS:

2 Chairman—WENTWORTH BLACKETT BEAUMONT, Esq., M.P., Allenheads, Haydon Bridge; Bretton Park Wakefield ; and 144, Piccadilly, W.
Deputy-Chairman—*WILLIAM RUTHERFORD HUNTER, Esq. (North Eastern), Lovaine Crescent, Newcastle-upon-Tyne.

3 Joseph Dinning, Esq., Langley Lead Works, Haydon Bridge.
1 Wm. Campbell Arnison. Esq., Allendale Town.

3 Wm. James Johnson, Esq., Pods Bank, Allendale.
* Charles Grey Grey, Esq., (Greenwich Hospital), Dilston, Corbridge-on-Tyne.

* Do not rotate ; the others do.
1. Retire in 1871; 2, in 1869 ; 3, in 1870. All eligible for re-election.

OFFICERS.—Sec. and Eng., Thomas J. Bewick, C.E., Haydon Bridge, and Neville Chambers, Newcastle-upon-Tyne ; Auditors. James Dewar. Newcastle-upon-Tyne, and James May Fothergill, Newcastle-upon-Tyne ; Solicitor. R. R. Dees, Newcastle-upon-Tyne ; Bankers, Lambton and Co., Newcastle-upon-Tyne and Hexham.

Offices—Haydon Bridge.

188.—HIGHLAND.

An incorporation of the INVERNESS AND ABERDEEN and the INVERNESS AND PERTH JUNCTION, sanctioned by 28 and 29 Vic., cap. 168 (29th June, 1865). In operation, 246 miles.

INVERNESS AND ABERDEEN JUNCTION.—Incorporated by 19 and 20 Vic., cap. 110 (21st July, 1856), to make a railway from Nairn to Keith. Capital, 325,000l. in 10l. shares ; loans, 108,300l. Length, single line, 40 miles. Opened throughout 18th August, 1858.

By 23 Vic., cap. 9 (3rd April, 1860), the company was authorised to raise new capital to the extent of 150,000l. in shares, and 50,000l. on loans. At the meeting on 27th April, 1860, it was resolved that 150,000l. be raised by creation of 15,000 shares of 10l. each,, bearing a dividend at the rate of 4½ per cent. in perpetuity.

By 24 Vic., cap. 18 (17th May, 1861), the company was authorised to construct a branch from Alves station to Burghead. Length, 5½ miles. New capital, 20,000l. in shares at 5 per cent., and 6,650l. on loan. By the same Act provision was made for additional station at Inverness. Opened 23rd December, 1862.

By 24 Vic., cap. 8 (17th May, 1861), the INVERNESS AND NAIRN was consolidated with the Inverness and Aberdeen Junction. The former company was incorporated by 17 and 18 Vic., cap. 176 (1854). Capital, 80,000l., in 8,000 shares of 10l. each. Length, single line, 15 miles ; a branch to Harbour at Inverness, 4 furlongs. Opened 5th November, 1855. By 20 and 21 Vic., cap. 5 (26th June, 1857), the company was authorised to issue 25,000l. in preference stock, which amply sufficed to meet all liabilities. Power was also taken to dispose of unissued stock. with preferential dividend of 5 per cent.

By 25 and 26 Vic., cap. 113 (30th June, 1862), the INVERNESS AND ROSS-SHIRE was incorporated with the Inverness and Aberdeen Junction. The former included a line from Inverness and Invergordon. Length, 31¼ miles. Capital, 215,000l. in 10l. shares ; loans, 71,600l., which may be converted into debenture stock. Opened to Dingwall, 18 miles, on 11th June, 1862 ; to Invergordon on 23rd May, 1863. The Act of Amalgamation provides that a preferential dividend of 3 per cent. be paid to the Ross-shire share-holders the first year after the opening of the line throughout to Invergordon, and ½ per cent. additional each year thereafter until it reaches that paid on the Inverness and Aberdeen Junction ordinary stock at the time, after which both stocks go on together, and carry the same dividend ever after.

By 26 Vic., cap. 32 (11th May, 1863), the company was authorised to construct an extension from Invergordon to Tain and Bonar Bridge. Length, 26½ miles. New capital, 160,000l. in shares at 3 per cent., to be increased 10s. per annum until dividend reaches that on ordinary stock, when it will take rank with the same. Loans, 53,000l. Opened to Meikle Ferry on 1st June, and completed to Bonar Bridge on 1st October, 1864.

INVERNESS AND PERTH JUNCTION.—Incorporated by 24 and 25 Vic., cap. 186 (22nd July, 1861), to construct a line from Forres, on the Inverness and Aberdeen, to Birnam, on the Perth and Dunkeld, with a branch to Aberfeldy. Length, 112 miles. Branch to Aberfeldy, 9 miles. Opened on 3rd July, 1864. Capital, 654,000l., in 10l. shares ; loans, 218,000l. Preference shares, 4½ per cent. Traffic agreements with Scottish North Eastern, Scottish Central, and North British. The line was opened from Dunkeld to Pitlochry on the 1st of June, from Forres to Aviemore on 3rd August, and throughout on the 9th September, 1863. By 26 Vic., cap. 61 (8th June, 1863), the company was authorised to make certain deviations, to cancel certain shares, and to re-issue the same at 5 per cent. preference.

PERTH AND DUNKELD.—Incorporated by 17 and 18 Vic., cap. 148 (July 10th, 1854), for a line (8¾ miles) commencing by junction with Scottish Midland, near Stanley, and terminating in Dunkeld. Opened 7th April, 1856. Capital, 80,000l. in 25l. shares ; loans, 20,000l. Amalgamated under Act of 1863, with the Inverness and Perth, at a preferential dividend of 6 per cent. on 28th February, 1864. The new capital authorised by the Amalgamation Act extended to 400,000l. in shares, and 133,000l. on loan. Traffic arrangements with Scottish North Eastern and Great North of Scotland.

SCOTTISH NORTH EASTERN.—The tolls between Stanley Junction and Perth general station were reduced to 5,000l. a year in perpetuity, irrespective of the quantity of traffic going over the line. This had been secured by Act of Parliament, as well as clauses protecting this company against an undue diversion of traffic via the Aberdeen route. The tolls during the last year amounted to very nearly 10,000l., and the amount was yearly increasing.

REVENUE.—The receipts for the half year ending 29th February amounted to 98,454l., and the expenditure to 46,448l., or 46·82 per cent., leaving a balance of 52,006l., to which was added 1,716l., balance from preceding half-year, making 53,722l. From this was deducted 28,591l. for interest on debentures, temporary loans, &c,, and 25,012l. for dividends on the preference stocks, including 3,650l. for the proposed dividend on the ordinary stock at the rate of 1 per cent. per annum, leaving a balance of 118l. The increase in the traffic during the half-year over the corresponding half-year was 5,446l., and if it had not been for the extraordinary expenses incurred in repairing the damage to the line at various points by the severe floods of 31st January, coupled with the loss of traffic during the temporary stoppage, a higher dividend would have been paid. The revenue for the half-year ending August 31st last amounted to 107,165l., and the expenditure to 42,745l., leaving a balance of 64,420l. From this was deducted 29,942l. for interest on debentures and loans ; and 32,329l. for dividends on the 4½ per cent., 5 per cent., and 6 per cent. preference shares, including 10,949l. for the proposed dividend at the rate of 3 per cent. per annum on the ordinary stock, leaving a balance of 2,149l. The dividend for the corresponding period of last year was at the rate of 2 per cent., while the working expenses amounted to 38½, as compared with 35 per cent. The directors had just completed arrangements by which 375,000l. of the temporary loans, at 5 and 4½ per cent., would be renewed for two years at 4¼ ; the saving of interest by this transaction would be about 2,000l. per annum. The debentures falling due at Martinmas, amounting to 299,000l., had almost all been renewed or replaced on favourable terms. The liabilities of the company were reduced to about 29,000l.

SUTHERLAND.—The company commenced to work this line on the 13th April last in terms of the agreement between the companies, and the directors are glad to say the result of the working is satisfactory. The expenses have not amounted to 75 per cent., which is the limit in the agreement, while the unity of management, and the utilising of a portion of the Highland company's rolling stock, have contributed considerably to the decrease in this company's working expenses.

FOCHABERS AND GARMOUTH.—This was the only line ever promoted by the directors for defensive purposes ; six miles in length, with a capital of 30,000*l*., and borrowing powers to the extent of 10.000*l*. Fortunately, the only expense incurred in connection with the scheme was that of procuring the Act, and during the last half-year the directors obtained from the Board of Trade the necessary warrant for abandoning it.

DINGWALL AND SKYE.—This railway was undertaken by the landowners and others in the district, who found necessary capital. In these circumstances, and seeing that it will be a valuable feeder to the Highland the directors entered into negotiations with the Skye board with the view of maturing a working agreement, which was sanctioned at the meeting on 30th October, 1868. The leading principle of the agreement is that the Highland work and maintain the Skye for a period of ten years—the line to be then handed over in good order, ordinary tear and wear excepted—receiving for two trains each way daily the rate of 2s. per train mile, and for all trains beyond two daily 1s. 10d. per train mile ; the Skye paying the Highland a rent for the Dingwall station and the passenger duty on their own line. These rates are higher than those at which the Highland is worked, with its numerous stations and a considerable amount of night duty. The Highland have already sufficient engines and carriages to work the line, and the directors satisfied themselves that it is to be substantially made, the rails being double-headed and weighing 70 lb. per yard and fish-jointed, with sleepers of natural Strathspey pine. The traffic to and from the Skye will be in a great measure through traffic, and it will pass over 162 miles of the Highland from Dingwall to Perth.

CAPITAL.—The receipts on this account to 31st August, 1868, including 565,000*l*. of temporary loans, were 2,850,864*l*. The expenditure, including 30,000*l*. of subscription to the Sutherlandshire, amounted to 2,839,912*l*., and left a balance in hand of 10,952*l*. The general statement gave the parliamentary powers of the company, and its receipts thereon, as follows :—

Stock and Shares.			Authorised.	Raised.	Still to raise.	In arrear.
Dunkeld....6 per cent. preference			£76,000 ..	£76,000 ..	— ..	
Nairn 5	„	„	45,000 ..	44,960 ..	— ..	£40
Nairn 6	„	„	59,080 ..	59,080 ..	— ..	
Class A 4½	„	„	513,650 ..	395,245 .. £118,350 ..		55
Class B 5	„	„	400,000 ..	293,130 .. 106,280 ..		590
Ordinary			1,115,350 ..	716,815 .. 385,390 ..		13,144
			£2,209,080 ..	£1,585,230 .. £610,020 ..		£13,829
Loan capital and debenture stock			£700,880 ..	£700,634 ..	£245 ..	—
Total share and loan capital			£2,909,960 ..	£2,285,864 .. £610,265 ..		£13,829

Meetings in March or April, and September or October, in Inverness. Quorum, 15 shareholders, in person or by proxy, and holding 30,000*l*.

Scale of Voting—2 to 10 shares, one vote ; for each 10 additional shares to 100, one vote ; and for every 20 shares above 100, one vote.

No. of Directors—18 ; minimum. 9 ; quorum, 3. *Qualification*, 2,000*l*.

DIRECTORS :

Chairman—ALEX. MATHESON, Esq., of Ardross, M.P., Ardross Castle, Ross-shire, and 38, South Street, W.
Deputy-Chairman—Hon. THOS. CHARLES BRUCE, 13, Hertford Street, Mayfair, W.

The Right Hon. the Earl of Seafield, Castle Grant, Grantown, Inverness-shire, and 169, New Broad Street, W.
George Loch, Esq., M.P., 2, Albemarle Street, W.
Eneas W. Mackintosh, Esq., M.P., of Raigmore, Inverness.
William James Tayler, Esq.,of Rothiemay, Huntly.
Alexander Inglis Robertson, Esq., of Ault-naskiah, Inverness.
Major Cumming Bruce, of Dunphail, Forres.
Ewen Macpherson, Esq., of Cluny Mac-pherson, Cluny Castle, Kingussie.
His Grace the Duke of Sutherland, Dun-robin Castle, Sutherlandshire, and Staf-ford House, St. James's, S.W.

Colonel William Fraser-Tytler, of Aldourie, Inverness.
Lieut. R. W. Duff, of Fetteresso, M.P., R.N., Stonehaven, and 40, Mount Street, W.
Colonel Hugh Inglis, of Kingsmills, Inver-ness.
The Hon. Simon Fraser, Master of Lovat, Beaufort Castle, Beauly, Inverness-shire.
R. B. Æ. Macleod, Esq., of Cadboll, Inver-gordon Castle, Invergordon.
James Merry, Esq., of Belladrum, M.P., Beauly, and 68, Eaton Square, S.W.
Charles Waterston, Esq., Banker, Inver-ness.
James Falshaw, Esq., 26, Castle Street, Edinburgh.

The directors who retire annually have their places supplied by the election of the shareholders in terms of the Companies Clauses Consolidation (Scotland) Act, 1845.

OFFICERS.—Sec. and Gen. Man., Andrew Dougall; Goods Mans., Thomas Mackay and Thomas C. Lowson; Supt. of Line, William Roberts; Supt. of Permanent Way, John W. Buttle; Loco. Supt., William Stroudley; Accountant, William Fenwick; Assistant Secretary, William Gowenlock; Chief Audit Clerk, C. S. M'Hardy; Auditors, Robert Smith and William R. Grant, Inverness; Solicitors, H. and A. Inglis, W.S., Edinburgh, and Stewart and Rule, Inverness; Parliamentary Solicitors, Martin and Leslie, London; Bankers, Barclay, Bevan, Tritton, and Co., 54, Lombard Street, E.C., Commercial Bank of Scotland, British Linen Company Bank, and Caledonian Bank.

Head Offices—Inverness.

189.—HOLYWELL.

Incorporated by 27 and 28 Vic., cap. 328 (29th July, 1864), to construct railways or tramways from Holywell to Greenfield, and to the Holywell station of the Chester and Holyhead. Length. 2 miles. Capital, 30,000l. in 10l. shares, and 10,000l. on loan. Arrangements with London and North Western.

By 31 and 32 Vic., cap. 122 (13th July, 1868), the company was authorised to divert and relinquish the line authorised as above, and to substitute other railways. New capital, 10,000l. in shares, and 3,300l. on loan. Works to be completed by July, 1871. Arrangements with London and North Western.

Meetings in February and August.

No. of Directors—6; minimum, 4; quorum, 3 and 2. *Qualification, 500l.*

DIRECTORS:

Thomas Linklater Lockington, Esq. | James Langhorne, Esq.
H. Laurence Bunn, Esq.

190.—HORNCASTLE.

Incorporated by 17 and 18 Vic., cap. 143 (1854), and estimated to cost 45,000l. Length, 8 miles. Capital, 48,000l. in 10l. shares. Loans, 73,000l. Single line. Opened 11th August, 1855. The line forms a junction with the Great Northern at Kirkstead, about 123 miles from London. Worked by the Great Northern for 50 per cent. of gross receipts.

The Board of Trade, upon the application of this company, and with the concurrence of the Great Northern, made an order for the continuance of the existing arrangements between the two companies as prescribed by the Horncastle Act, 1854, for a further period of 10 years from 1865, and the agreement of 11th February, 1855, has likewise been renewed for the same period.

REVENUE.—The sum received from the Great Northern permitted declaration of a dividend equal to 6l. 15s. per cent. per annum for the half-year ending 31st December, and of 5l. 5s. for the six months ending 30th June.

No. of Directors—8; minimum, 4. *Qualification, 20 shares.*

DIRECTORS:

Chairman—JAMAS BANKS STANHOPE, Esq., Revesby Abbey.

William Martin, Esq., Scamblesby. | John Elsey, Esq., Horncastle.
The Rev. Thomas Livesey, Stourton Hall, | William Robinson, Esq., Asgarly.
  near Horncastle. | Charles Hill, Esq., Winceby.
Timothy Collinson, Esq., Horncastle. | John Hindley Wright Scott, Esq., Horncastle.

The directors retire in rotation, one-third yearly, but are eligible for re-election.
OFFICERS.—Sec. and Solicitor, Fred. W. Tweed, Horncastle; Auditors, Robert Clifton Armstrong and Henry Nicholson, Horncastle.

191.—HORSHAM, DORKING, AND LEATHERHEAD.

Incorporated by 25 and 26 Vic., cap. 151 (17th July, 1862), to construct a line from Horsham and Dorking. Length, 13¼ miles. Capital, 120,000l., in 10l. shares, and 40,000l. on loan. Opened 1st May, 1867. Arrangements with the Brighton, which contributed 75,000l., and guaranteed 4 per cent. on capital, under Amalgamation Act, of 1864. To be embodied in the Brighton.

CAPITAL.—The expenditure to 31st December, 1866, which appears to have been the latest published, amounted to 139,362l., the receipts for which have been as follows:—

Deposit of 1l. 10s. per share on 12,000 shares	£18,000
First call of 2l. per share on 11,500 shares, payable to 31st December..	23,000
Payments in anticipation of calls	75,400
Temporary loans	20,000
	£136,400
	2,962=£139,362

Meetings in February and August.
Scale of Voting.—For 1 to 5 shares, one vote, and an additional vote for every 5 shares.
No. of Directors—4; minimum, 3; quorum, 3. *Qualification, 500l.*

DIRECTORS:

*Leo Schuster, Esq., Roehampton, S.W. | *Edward Kerrich, Esq., Arnolds, Capel,
*Charles Smith Mortimer, Esq., Morden | Dorking, Surrey.
  Park, Surrey.

* Nominated by the London, Brighton, and South Coast.

OFFICERS.—Sec., George William Brown; Eng., R. Jacomb Hood, M.I.C.E., C ,
Little George Street, Westminster, S.W.; Solicitor, William Gascoigne Roy, 28, Grea :
George Street, Westminster, S.W.; Surveyor, Francis Fuller, 3, Whitehall Gardens,
S.W.; Bankers, Williams, Deacon, and Co., Birchin Lane, E.C.; Auditor, Edward
Bellamy, 7, Victoria Chambers, Westminster, S.W.
  Offices—28, Great George Street, Westminster, S.W.

192.—HOUNSLOW AND METROPOLITAN.

Incorporated by 29 and 30 Vic., cap. 336 (5th August, 1866), to construct a line from
the Acton and Brentford, at Hanwell, to Hounslow, with a junction with the Great
Western and Brentford. Length, 4 miles. Capital, 120,000l., in 10l. shares, and 40,000l.
on loan. Mutual facilities with Great Western.

No. of Directors—5 ; minimum, 3 ; quorum. 3 and 2. *Qualification*, 200l.

DIRECTORS :

Chairman—Sir JAMES CARMICHAEL, Bart., Oakdene, Edenbridge.

Charles Neve Cresswell, Esq., Spring | Thomas Eyre Foakes, Esq., 4, New Square,
  Greve, Isleworth. | Lincoln's Inn, W.C.
George Wyatt, Esq., Highbury.

193.—HOYLAKE.

Incorporated by 26 and 27 Vic., cap. 207 (28th July, 1863), to construct a line from a
point immediately contiguous to Seacombe Ferry, proceeding near the Northern side of
the Birkenhead docks, through Poolton village to Bidston, and thence by way of More-
ton, Saughall-Massey, Great Meols, and Hoose, to the Hoylake terminus, adjoining the
racecourse. From Bidston a branch will run into Birkenhead, terminating at Wallasey
Bridge Road, near the dock cottages. Length, 8 miles. Capital, 100,000l. in 10l. shares,
and 33,300l. on loan. Opened, 5½ miles, on 2nd July, 1866.

By 28 and 29 Vic., cap. 236 (5th July, 1865). the company was authorised to make an
extension to New Brighton. Length, 4¾ miles. New capital, 90,000l., in shares, and
30,000l. on loan. Also to attach a preference to unissued on cancelled shares, and to
create debenture stock.

By 29 and 30 Vic., cap. 186 (16th July, 1866), the company was authorised to extend
the line to Parkgate. Length, 8¼ miles. New capital, 200,000l. in divided shares and
66,000l. on loan.

Agreements have been entered upon with the Manchester and Sheffield and the
Great Northern for a full and free interchange of traffic on completion of line.

REVENUE.—The receipts are extremely small, and little prospect exists of the undertaking being able to pay its working expenses.

No. of Directors—7 ; minimum, 5 ; quorum, 3. *Qualification*, 500l.

DIRECTORS :

Chairman—JOHN EVERITT, Esq., Banker, London.

Richard Kyrke Penson, Esq., Ludlow. | Frederick Adolphus Fynney, Esq., Queen's
  | Chambers, Manchester.

OFFICERS.—Sec., Braithwaite Poole, Liverpool ; Traffic Man., James Goulding ;
Eng., Benjamin Piercy, C.E., 19, Duke Street, Westminster, S.W.; Solicitors, John-
ston. Farquhar, and Leech, Moorgate Street, E.C.; Bankers, North and South Wales
Bank, Liverpool and Birkenhead.
  Offices—5, Jackson Chambers, South Castle Street, Liverpool.

194.—HULL AND SELBY.
(LEASED TO NORTH EASTERN.)

Incorporated by 6 and 7 Wm. IV., cap. 80 (1836), for a line connecting those towns
subsequently extended (Act 1843 and 1845) by a branch from Hull to Bridlington.
Length, 61 miles ; main line opened 1st July, 1840, the branch in October, 1846.

The lease to the York and North Midland provides for 10 per cent. in perpetuity on
700,000l. The lessees had the option, any time after the expiration of five years from
date of the lease (30th June, 1845), to pay off the whole of the capital at the rate of
112½l. per 50l., of 56¼l. per 25l., 28⅛l. per 12½l. share, on giving six months' notice of such
intention. By resolution of the next general meeting (25th February, 1846), the Lancashire and Yorkshire were allowed to participate equally in this lease, and any agreements which the two companies might enter into with that view were sanctioned by

Act 9 and 10 Vic., cap. 241, which gives this company the power to lease or sell to the York and North Midland, or the Lancashire and Yorkshire; and all agreements made prior to the passing of the Act (27th July, 1846), were made binding on the companies. The various lawsuits that arose out of these arrangements terminated by the North Eastern accepting the whole of the engagements.

Dividends of 2l. 9s. 6d. per 50l. share, and pro rata for half and quarter shares, are declared each half year.

DIRECTORS:

Chairman—JOHN LOFT, Esq., Beverley Road, Hull.

Deputy-Chairman—WILLIAM ALTOFT SUMMERS, Esq., Leicester Place, Beverley Road, Hull.

Isaac Whitaker, Esq., Hessle, near Hull.
Thomas Barton Holmes, Esq., Anlaby Road, Hull.
Henry Garbutt, Esq., Regent's Terrace, Anlaby Road, Hull.

Benjamin Whitaker, Esq., Hessle, near Hull.
William Tudor, Esq., Cottingham, near Hull.

OFFICERS.—Sec., John P. Tomlinson; Auditors, George Bucton, Hull, and Elijah Meggitt, Hull; Law Clerk, Charles H. Phillips, Solicitor, Hull.
Head Office—Hull.

195.—IDLE AND SHIPLEY.

Incorporated by 30 and 31 Vic., cap. 179 (12th August, 1867), to construct a line from the Bradford Eccleshill and Idle to Shipley. Length, 2½ miles. Capital, 55,000l. in 10l. shares, and 18,300l. on loan. Facilities over Bradford Eccleshill and Idle, and part of Great Northern. Meetings in February or March and in August or September.

No. of Directors—5; quorum, 3. Qualification, 1,000l.

DIRECTORS:

Samuel Waterhouse, Esq., M.P., 66, Pall Mall, S.W., and Hope Hall, Halifax.
William Firth, Esq.

George Vint, Esq.
William Bower, Esq.
Thomas Booth, Esq.

196.—IPSWICH AND FELIXTOW.

Incorporated by 28 and 29 Vic., cap. 303 (5th July, 1865), to construct a line from the Westerfield station of the Great Eastern to Felixtow. Length, 11 miles. Capital, 65,000l. in shares, and 21,800l. on loan. Arrangements with Great Eastern.

No. of Directors—7; minimum, 5; quorum, 5. Qualification. 200l.

DIRECTORS:

George Tomline, Esq., M.P., 1, Carlton House Terrace, S.W.
Thomas Brassey, Jun., Esq., M.P.

Charles A. Schreober, Esq.
James Scott, Esq.
George Charles Stackpole, Esq.

197.—IRISH NORTH WESTERN.

Incorporated by 8 and 9 Vic., cap. 96 (July, 1845), for a railway communication between Dundalk and Enniskillen, with two branches therefrom. Original capital, 750,000l. in shares, and 250,000l. on loan; total, 1,000,000l.

On the 14th August, 1855, the line was open to Newbliss, being an extension of 10 miles; 16 miles to Lisnaskea, on 26th June; 6 miles to Lisbellaw, on the 16th August, 1858. The remaining 4 miles to Enniskillen were opened in January, 1859. On the extension from Ballybay to Cavan, 8 miles to Cootehill were opened on the 18th October, 1860.

By 20 and 21 Vic., cap. 104 (27th July, 1857), several deviations were sanctioned, and an extension of time on old line obtained. By the same Act the Dublin and Drogheda and the Dublin and Belfast Junction are each authorised to contribute 30,000l. towards completion of Dundalk and Enniskillen, each appointing two Directors to sit at the board of the latter.

By 21 Vic., cap. 16 (21st May, 1858), the company is authorised to raise 75,000l. in shares at 6 per cent., out of profits of each year only. The company may also borrow, in addition to previous powers, 24,900l. on mortgage.

By 22 and 23 Vic., cap. 51 (1st August, 1859), the company was authorised to construct a line between Clones and Cavan, to which the Ulster, Dublin and Drogheda, and the Dublin and Belfast Junction are contributors. Length, 15 miles. Compulsory purchase of land, three years; completion of works, five years. The extension of the Ulster from Monaghan to Clones completes the communication from the north-east to the west of Ireland. New capital, 130,000l. at 6 per cent. Opened 1st March, 1864.

By 25 and 26 Vic., cap. 139 (7th July, 1862), the company was authorised to issue new shares to the extent of 198,200*l.* in shares, and 109,500*l.* on loan for the purpose of completing the Belturbet and other unfinished works. In consideration of the amalgamation of the Londonderry and Enniskillen with the Dundalk and Enniskillen the name of the company was changed to the "Irish North Western."

By 26 and 27 Vic. cap. 236 (28th July. 1863), the company was authorised to extend its line along the quays at Dundalk, but no new capital was authorised.

By 27 and 28 Vic., cap. 253 (25th July, 1864), various financial and other arrangements were authorised, by which existing debts were extinguished, and compensation stock given in exchange. The capital of the company was thus made to consist of 900,000*l.* in shares and 300,000*l.* on loan. Working or leasing arrangements were also authorised with the Dublin and Belfast, the Dublin and Drogheda, and the Ulster. Productive, 145 miles.

ARRANGEMENTS.—Working and traffic arrangements have been entered upon with the Bundoran and Sligo. the Dundalk and Greenore, and the Finn Valley. Also with the London and North Western for through traffic.

REVENUE.—The receipts for the half-year ending 31st December, 1867, were 51,366*l.*, in comparison with 50,828*l.*, showing an increase of 538*l.* The working expenses were 24,688*l.* ; compensation, taxes, interest. and rent of Londonderry amounted to 23,316*l.*, making a total gross expenditure of 48,005*l.* The net profit of the half-year (3,361*l.*) with the balance from the preceding half-year, were carried to the credit of next account.

The revenue of the Clones and Cavan Extension exhibited a surplus of 940*l.*, and a dividend on the separate capital of that line was declared at the rate of 1*l.* 10*s.* per cent. per annum. This, when brought to the credit of the revenue account of the main line, will benefit the receipts by 643*l.*

Should the traffic receipts of the main line in any year exceed 95,000*l.*, the Londonderry, under agreement, were entitled to receive, in addition to their rent of 26,000*l.*, 20*l.* per cent. of such excess. The receipts of the year 1867 having been 98,162*l.*, the Londonderry consequently became entitled to an additional rent of 632*l.*

The receipts on the main line for the six months ending 30th June amounted to 48,345*l.*, in comparison with 47,906*l.*, exhibiting an increase of 438*l.* The working expenses were 23,892*l.*, and disbursements under the heads of rents, interests, claims, &c., amounted to 23,359*l.*, making a total expenditure of 47,251*l.* The balance, when added to the sum of 7,913*l.* remaining at the credit of the revenue account of 31st December, amounted to 9,006*l.* The cash representing that balance had been applied to the retirement of debentures to the amount of 6,122*l.*, and to other exigencies of capital. The directors, therefore, consider it expedient to recommend declaration of a dividend until the debenture securities became canvertible into money.

FINANCE.—The scheme of arrangement with the company's mortgage creditors, having been confirmed by the Master of the Rolls and subsequently enrolled, has now the effect of an Act of Parliament. Under its terms the several mortgages held against the company (except those in the hands of the Loan Commissioners) have been cancelled, and the holders have, in lieu of their mortgages, been registered as proprietors of an equal amount of 5 per cent. irredeemable debenture stock. The directors are of opinion that this arrangement, which carries out a previous resolution of the shareholders, will, in its ultimate results, be most beneficial, by preventing the absorption of the revenue into the capital account, and thus enabling the company to resume the payment of dividends.

AMALGAMATION.—The three companies between Dublin and Belfast having it in contemplation to amalgamate, have expressed their willingness to admit this company to a joint purse agreement when they are so amalgamated.

CAPITAL.—The expenditure to 30th June, 1868, including 48,680*l.* to the Clones and Cavan Extension, and 17,685*l.* for works and improvements on the Londonderry, amounted to 992,479*l.* The receipts were detailed as under :—

5,714 Ordinary shares at 30*l.*	£171,420
23,538 Preference shares, Class A, at 10*l.* each	235,380
9,000 Preference shares, Class A, in respect of which has been received	89,811
A. Preference stock issued in pursuance of Act of 1864, viz. :—	
Debt compensation stock	104,280
Dividends compensation stock	15,463
2,534 Preference shares, Class B (under Act of 1857)	25,340
Government loan account	58,361
Debenture stock, 1st Class	169,516
Debenture stock issued under Act of 1864	61,311
Forfeited and merged shares	35,631
Sundries, including interest from shareholders	8,645
	£975,160
Balance	17,319
	£992,479

CLONES AND CAVAN.—The expenditure on this extension has amounted to 113,984*l.*, the contributions having been as follows —

Dublin and Belfast Junction	£18,546
Dublin and Drogheda	18,546
Ulster	27,887
Irish North Western	48,680
	£113,659
Balance	324=£113,984

The accounts are made up to the 30th June and 30th December, and the statutory meetings held in February and August in each year, at Dublin.

Scale of Voting—One vote for every share up to 10 ; one vote for every five beyond 10 up to 100 ; and one for every 10 beyond the first 100.

Transfer books closed 14 days previous to the close of the meetings. Certificates must accompany transfer deed. Fee for registration, 2*s.* 6*d.*

No. of Directors—12. *Qualification*, 20 shares.

DIRECTORS :

Chairman—Hon. HENRY CAVENDISH BUTLER, D.L., Innis Rath, Lisnaskea.

Deputy-Chairman—RICHARD A. MINNITT, Esq., J.P., Derrygooney Lodge, Cortubber, Ballybay.

Major F. Ellis, J.P., Fecarry House, Omagh.
Richard Mayne, Esq., J.P., Glynch House, Newbliss.
Patrick James Byrne, Esq., Lisnawilly, Dundalk.
A. J. Macrory, Esq., Duncairn, Belfast, and 48, Rutland Square, Dublin.
Philip Callan, Esq., M.P., Cookstown, Ardee.

John Jameson, Esq., Bow Street, Dublin.
R. G. Collis, Esq., Leeson Park House, Dublin.
Captain Johnston, Roselawn, Celbridge.
W. Mc.Carter, Esq., J.P., Londonderry.
Alexander Parker, Esq., J.P., 59, William Street, Dublin.

OFFICERS.—Sec., W. Eykelbosch ; Eng., John Stokes, Enniskillen ; Loco. Supt., F. Pemberton, Dundalk ; Traffic Man., Henry Plews, Enniskillen ; Bookkeeper, Thos. Medcalf ; Auditors, H. Guinness and R. Jackson ; Solicitor, Alexander Boyd ; Bankers, Bank of Ireland, Dublin ; Belfast Banking Co., Enniskillen ; Glyn, Mills, and Co., Lombard Street, E.C.

Head Offices—43, Lower Gardiner Street, Dublin.

198.—ISLE OF WIGHT.

Incorporated by 23 and 24 Vic., cap. 162 (23rd July, 1860), to construct a line from Ryde to Ventnor. Length, 12 miles. Capital, 125,000*l.* in 10*l.* shares ; calls, 2*l.*, with intervals of two months ; loans, 41,600*l.* Opened from Ryde to Shanklin (8 miles) on 23rd August, 1864, and from Shanklin to Ventnor, October, 1866.

By 26 and 27 Vic., cap. 232 (28th July, 1863), an extension from Newport to Wrexhall (15¾ miles) was obtained, thus forming a connection with the line from Ryde to Ventnor. New capital, 105,000*l.* in shares, and 68,000*l.* on loan.

By 28 and 29 Vic., cap. 157 (29th June, 1865), the company was authorised to provide and work steam vessels, and to raise new capital for that purpose to the extent of 20,000*l.* in shares, and 5,000*l.* on loan, to be kept distinct from the other capital and revenue of the company.

By 28 and 29 Vic., cap. 224 (5th July, 1865), the company obtained power to construct several extensions. Length, 13½ miles ; and also to raise new capital to the extent of 39,000*l.* for the eastern lines ; 20,000*l.* for the central lines ; and 160,000*l.* for the new or western lines ; in all, 219,000*l.* in shares, and 72,300*l.* by borrowing. Each capital to be kept distinct.

By 30 and 31 Vic., cap. 174 (12th August, 1867), the company was authorised to raise additional capital for the eastern lines, to the extent of 50,000*l.* in shares, and 16,600*l.* on loan, one-half of which may be raised when one-half of the new capital of 50,000*l.* is subscribed for, issued, and accepted, and one-half thereof paid up. The company may also create debenture stock at a rate not exceeding 5 per cent.

REVENUE.—The receipts for the half-year ending 31st December, 1867, were 11,309*l.*, in comparison with 8,259*l.* for the corresponding period of 1866. The receipts for 1867 amounted to 18,261*l.*, and the working expenses, including passenger duty, rates, taxes, rents, &c., to 9,443*l.*, leaving a balance of 8,818*l.*, which, after payment of interest on debentures, left 5,942*l.* applicable to dividend on the preference capital.

The receipts for the June half-year were 8,035*l.*, which exhibited an increase of 1,082*l.* over the corresponding period of 1867. The working expenses were 4,360*l.*, being 690*l.* more than in the half-year for 1867. It was reported in August that after providing for the actual working of the line, and the payment of government duty, rates, taxes, &c.,

the attention of the directors had been given to meet the payments for interest on the debenture debt regularly as they became due. This they had effected by a system of setting apart the necessary amount out of the weekly receipts, and paying the same to a trust account, to be strictly applied to that purpose. By this means the debenture interest for the half-year was punctually met, and the directors believed that in this way the credit of the company, as to the debenture bonds and stock, had been put on a firm basis. After charging the interest on the debentures, loans, and advances on preference shares held by the company's bankers, amounting to 2,499l., there remained a balance of 361l., which would have been applicable as dividend on the remainder of the preference shares, but the necessity for cash payments on account of rolling stock, together with provision for other pressing claims on capital account, absorbed the whole of the revenue balance for the time being, and consequently prevented its division among the shareholders.

CAPITAL.—The balance sheet to 30th June gave a total expenditure of 290,953l., which had been provided for as follows:—

Ordinary share capital authorised, £125,000—
Received...£109,274
(1,539 shares are in the hands of the bankers, to be returned to the company.)
First preference share capital, authorised £25,000—
Received on shares issued £16,992
   Do.   deposited at bankers .... 4,500= 21,492
Second preference share capital, authorised £39,000—
Received on shares issued 14,790
   Do.   deposited at bankers .... 24,210= 39,000
Third preference share capital, authorised £50,000—
Received on shares issued 36,619
Debentures, authorised £62,900—
Issued 60,760
Debenture stock, authorised £16,600—
Issued (on account of first moiety) 7,776
Transfer fees.. 2
Overdrawal of banking accounts 4,011
Revenue account... 12,019= £290,953
Meetings in February and August.

No. of Directors—6; minimum, 5; quorum, 3. *Qualification*, 250l.

DIRECTORS:

Chairman—ALEXANDER BEATTIE, Esq., Summerhill, Chislehurst, Kent.

Joseph Bravo, Esq., 20, Lancaster Gate, W.
A. D. De Pass, Esq., Langbourne Chambers, Fenchurch Street, E.C.
Thomas Norton, Esq., 13, Bolton Row, May Fair.

James Simpson, Esq., 29. Great George Street, Westminster, S.W.
George Young, Esq., Apley Towers, Ryde, Isle of Wight.

Retire as provided by C.C.C. Act; all eligible for re-election.

OFFICERS.—Sec., R. Hicks; Eng., J. Fowler, 2, Queen Square Place, Westminster, S.W.; Solicitor, George T. Porter, 4, Victoria Street, Westminster, S.W.; Bankers, The City Bank, and the National and Provincial Bank of England, Ryde Branch; Auditors, William Phillips, Coal Exchange, E.C., and C. L. Christian, Great George Street, E.C.

General Offices—4, Victoria Street, Westminster, S.W.

199.—ISLE OF WIGHT—NEWPORT JUNCTION.

Incorporated by 31 and 32 Vic., cap. 181 (31st July, 1868), to construct railways to connect Newport and Cowes with Sandown, Ryde, and Ventnor. Length, 9½ miles. Capital, 84,000l. in 10l. shares, and 28,000l. on loan. Joint stations at Newport and Sandown, with running powers over parts of the Isle of Wight and Cowes and Newport.

No. of Directors—5; minimum, 3; quorum, 3 and 2. *Qualification*, 500l.

DIRECTORS:

George Frederick Anderson, Esq.
Jonathan Joliffe, Esq.
Edwin Lankester, Esq.

Alfred Pearson, Esq.
Thomas Webster, Esq.

200.—KEIGHLEY AND WORTH VALLEY.

Incorporated by 25 and 26 Vic., cap. 90 (30th June, 1862), to construct a line from the Leeds and Bradford Extension of the Midland at Keighley to Haworth and Lowertown. Length, 4¾ miles. Capital, 36,000l. in 10l. shares; loans, 12,000l. Arrangements with Midland, which is to work the line at 50 per cent. of receipts.

No. of Directors—9; minimum, 7; quorum, 4. *Qualification*, 500l.

DIRECTORS:

Chairman—ISAAC HOLDEN, Esq., Oakworth House.

Deputy-Chairman—JONATHAN NOWELL CRAVEN, Esq., High Thorn House, York.

John Craven, Esq., High Thorn House, York.

Robert Newsholme Sugden, Esq., Dockroyd.

John Speake, Esq., Lowertown.

Michael Merrall, Esq., Law House, near Haworth.

Edwin Greaves Hattersley, Esq., Mytholme House, near Haworth.

Seven in number. Three rotate at the end of each year, but are eligible for re-election.

OFFICERS.—Sec., Robert Fawcett, Keighley; Engs., J. S. Crossley, C.E., Derby and J. Mc.Landsborough, C.E., Bradford; Solicitor, William Haggerty, 32, Great George Street, Westminster, S.W.

Offices—Keighley.

201.—KENT COAST.

Incorporated by 20 and 21 Vic., cap. 152 (17th August, 1857), to construct a line between Herne Bay and Faversham. Capital, 80,000*l.* in 20*l.* shares; loans. 26,000*l* Length, 10¾ miles. Opened to Whitstable on 1st August, 1860; to Herne Bay on 13th July, 1861; to Ramsgate, on 2nd October, 1861.

By 22 and 23 Vic., cap. 116 (15th August, 1859), the company are authorised to extend their line to Margate. Length, 11½ miles. Estimate, 105,000*l.* New share capital to that extent is created in shares or half shares, at 5 per cent., and an additional 35,000*l.* in loans authorised.

By 24 and 25 Vic., cap. 241 (6th August, 1861), the company was authorised to extend their line to Ramsgate. Length, 5¼ miles. Capital, 96,000*l.* in shares, at 6 per cent., and 32,000*l.* on loan. Opened 5th October, 1863.

By 25 and 26 Vic., cap. 197 (29th July, 1862), the company was authorised to make some deviation, to construct tramways at Ramsgate, and to increase the capital of the undertaking by 264,000*l.* in shares, and 88,000*l.* on loan.

By 27 and 28 Vic., cap. 93 (23rd June, 1864), the Kent Coast was authorised to acquire additional lands, to raise more money, and to make further provision for lease to the Chatham and Dover. New capital, 120,000*l.* in shares, and 40,000*l.* on loan.

LONDON, CHATHAM, AND DOVER.—This company was represented as having leased the Kent Coast in perpetuity, on the following terms:—"1. The Chatham and Dover to work the line between Faversham and Ramsgate, when completed to the satisfaction of the engineer of the London Chatham and Dover, maintaining the line, and paying all expenses of working, including rates, taxes, and government duty. 2. The receipts for all traffic passing between stations on the Kent Coast and stations on the Chatham and Dover, and between stations on the Kent Coast, to be set apart, 50 per cent. of the same to be paid to the Chatham and Dover, for their expense of working and maintaining the line, the remainder up to 45,420*l.* a year to be paid to the Kent Coast, anything above that amount to be divided in the proportion of three-fourths to the Chatham and Dover, and one-fourth to the Kent Coast. 3. The line from Faversham to Ramsgate to be completed and opened for traffic as a double line by 1st September, 1863. The extra line between Faversham and Herne Bay, and the lines from Herne Bay to Ramsgate to be maintained for twelve months after opening at the expense of the contractors." This agreement, however, was set aside, by the Court of Chancery, and the Kent Coast is now worked by the Chatham provisionally, under an award by Captain O'Brien, until a definitive arrangement can be obtained.

It was reported in August, that when the question of the provisional working of the line by the Chatham and Dover was referred to Captain O'Brien, he was directed to make his award without reference to the agreement of April, 1862. That agreement provided that the Kent Coast should take 50 per cent. of the gross receipts arising from traffic to, from, and on the line up to 45,500*l.* per annum, and 25 per cent. of any further receipts. The award made by Captain O'Brien on the limited reference yields only about 20,000*l.* per annum to the company. This sum, although more than sufficient to pay the debenture interest, is obviously a very inadequate return for the great advantages resulting to the Chatham and Dover from the construction of the Kent Coast, and the directors are satisfied that more equitable terms will be obtained by arbitration or otherwise. The directors are satisfied that the best interests of the company require the speedy release of their affairs from the control of the Court, but this can only be effected by the creation of debenture stock, and by either applying it in exchange for debentures or offering it to the public.

CAPITAL.—This account to 30th June showed that 968,322*l.* had been expended, the receipts being detailed as follows:—

B stock £302,500
Ordinary stock .... 422,500= £725,000
Debentures 238,212
Balance .... 5,110= £968,322

DIRECTORS:

Chairman—Sir R. B. HARVEY, Esq., Langley Park, Bucks.

E. J. Coleman, Esq., Stoke Park, Bucks. | Captain Slarke, Herne Bay.
W. Rigden, Esq., Faversham. |

OFFICERS.—Sec., W. E. Johnson; Eng., F. T. Turner; Solicitors, Maynard and Co ; Bankers, Glynn, Mills, and Co.

202.—KETTERING, THRAPSTON, AND HUNTINGDON.

Incorporated by 25 and 26 Vic., cap. 173, and 26 and 27 Vic., cap. 203, and the Midland, under agreement, work it for 40 per cent. of the gross receipts for seven years, and afterwards for 50 per cent. in perpetuity. Opened 1st March, 1866.

This railway branches from the Midland at Kettering, passes under the London and North Western at Thrapston. under the Great Northern, with which it communicates, near Huntingdon, and effects a junction with the Great Eastern at Huntingdon. Length, 26 miles. By agreement with the Great Eastern, the Midland had powers of running through trains, passing over the Kettering and Thrapston from Leeds, Bradford, Sheffield, Nottingham, Derby, Leicester, &c., to Cambridge, thus establishing direct communication between the whole of the Great Eastern systems, and the northern and midland manufacturing and mineral districts.

It was reported in September that the accounts rendered by the Midland for the half year ending 30th June, exhibited an increase of 1,184l., as compared with the corresponding period of last year. The increase was chiefly derivable from goods and cattle, the passenger traffic remaining nearly stationary, while the minerals show even a decrease. Deducting 40 per cent. for working expenses, the net receipts due to this company under each head to 30th June were 3,792l. From this amount was deducted the following charges :—interest on debenture debt, 1,617l.; rent, rates, taxes, and miscellaneous expenses, 358l.; total, 2,005l., leaving a balance of 1,786l. Add 237l. from previous half-year's account, there was a total available balance of 2,023l., which admitted of a dividend at the rate of 2½ per cent. on the Consolidated A Stock, and left a balance of 408l. to next account. The dividend sanctioned and declared by the shareholders at the half yearly meeting held in February has not yet been paid, owing to the retention by the Midland of the balance due to this company at that time, pending the settlement of an alleged agreement for the execution of certain works on the line.

CAPITAL.—The expenditure to 30th June, 1868, amounted to 305,600l., the receipts being reported as under :—

Consolidated A Stock	£130.000
Do. B Stock	100,000= £230,000
Debentures	75,510
Surplus land sold	2
Balance	98= £305,600

No. of Directors—5; quorum, 3. Qualification, 300l.

DIRECTORS :

Chairman—GENERAL ARBUTHNOT, Woodford House, Thrapston.

Herbert Murray, Esq., 16, Chester Square, S.W. | A. C. Sherriff, Esq., M.P., Perdiswell Hall, Worcester, and 6, Westminster Chambers, Victoria Street, S.W.
James Macdonald, Esq., 7, Lothbury, London, E.C. | Charles Waring, Esq., 6B, Albany, W.

OFFICERS.—Sec., Arthur Lankester, 2. Westminster Chambers, Victoria Street, S.W.: Eng., George B. Bruce, 2, Westminster Chambers, Victoria Street, S.W.; Auditors, Henry W. Notman. 2, Leadenhall Street, E.C., and John Seath, 3, Prince's Street, Westminster, S.W.; Solicitors, Hodding, Townsend, and Co., 3, Prince's Street, Westminster, S.W.

Offices—2, Westminster Chambers, Victoria Street, S.W.

203.—KILKENNY JUNCTION.

Incorporated by 23 and 24 Vic., cap. 153 (23rd July, 1860), to construct a line from the Waterford and Kilkenny, at the latter town, to Mountrath. Length, 25¼ miles. Capital, 140,000l., in 10l. shares. Loans, 46,000l. Opened from Kilkenny to Abbeyleix, 19 miles, on 1st March, 1865.

The Waterford and Kilkenny subscribe 20,000l., and create new shares for that purpose. Traffic arrangements under usual conditions.

By 24 and 25 Vic. cap. 232 (6th August, 1861), the company was authorised to abandon a portion of the line between Abbeyleix and Mountrath station, and construct in lieu thereof a main line from Abbeyleix to Maryborough, with a view of ultimately proceeding through Mountmellick, Geashill, and Philipstown, to Mullingar, and a branch from Attanagh, through Durrow and Rathdawney to the Roscrea and Parsonstown Junction.

By 27 and 28 Vic., cap 300 (29th July, 1864), the company obtained an extension of time for three years for completion of the Kilpurcell branch, and also powers to use stations at Kilkenny.   New capital, 74,000*l.* in shares and 24,600*l.* on loan.

By 29 and 30 Vic., cap. 257 (23rd July, 1866), the Kilkenny Junction was authorised, in conjunction with the Waterford and Kilkenny, to construct the "Central of Ireland," which see.

By 30 and 31 Vic., cap. 159 (25th July, 1867), the company was authorised to abandon construction of the Kilpurcell branch, and the capital reduced by the sum of 60,000*l.* in shares and 20,000*l.* on mortgage.

No. of Directors—9 ; minimum, 6.   *Qualification,* 500*l.*

DIRECTORS :

Michael Cahill, Esq., Ballyconra House, County Kilkenny.
James Delahunty, Esq., M.P., Waterford.
James B. Dunn, Esq., Threadneedle Street, E.C.
Arthur Kavanagh, Esq., M.P., Borris House, County Carlow.

Sir Benjamin Morris, Mall, Waterford.
Edmond Power, Esq. Eastlands, Tramore, County Waterford.
Edmond Smithwick, Esq., Kilcreene House, Kilkenny.
James M. Tidmarsh, Esq., Kilkenny.

OFFICERS.—Sec., Henry Sargent ; Eng., George Willoughby Hemans, 1, Westminster Chambers, Victoria Street, S.W.; Solicitors, Radcliffe and Davis, 20, Craven Street, Strand, W.C.

Offices—2, Bank Place, Waterford.

204.—KILRUSH AND KILKEE.

Incorporated by 23 and 24 Vic., cap. 155 (23rd July, 1860), to construct a line from Kilrush to Kilkee ; length, 8¼ miles ; and for embanking and reclaiming certain waste lands, in the estuary of Poulnasherry, County Clare.   Capital, 37,000*l.* for railway ; 7,200*l.* for reclamation, in 10*l.* shares.   Loans, 1,500*l.*

By 24 Vic., cap. 29 (17th May, 1861), the company were authorised to make some deviations in the line, as well as to deepen the harbour of Kilrush. New capital, 15,000*l.* in shares, and 5,000*l.* on loan.

By 28 Vic., cap. 133 (19th June, 1865), an extension of time for completion of works for two years was obtained. Various alterations in the line were sanctioned, and powers granted to issue 20,000*l.* in preference shares.   In abeyance.

205.—KINGSBRIDGE.

Incorporated by 27 and 28 Vic., cap. 287 (29th July, 1864), to construct a line from South Brent, on the South Devon, to Kingsbridge. Length, 12¼ miles. Capital, 130,000*l.* in 10*l.* shares, and 43,000*l.* on loan.   Arrangements with South Devon.

By 29 and 30 Vic., cap. 264 (23rd July, 1866), the company was authorised to make several deviations, and to raise new capital to the extent of 60,000*l.* in shares, and 17,000*l.* on loan. Works commenced on 24th June, 1867.

CAPITAL.—The borrowing powers were resorted to at the end of September to the extent of 43,000*l.* at 5 per cent. The income and expenditure to 30th June, was described as follows :—

Received.		*Expended.*	
Share capital—		To December 31st, 1867	£7,962
On Deposit and calls	£13,934	Land purchases, compensation, and costs	1,390
On shares fully paid up	20	Engineering	300
	£13,954	Works	3,016
Interest—general account (balance)	85	Salaries and office expenses, including rent of offices, clerks, auditors, postage, &c.	147
		Travelling expenses	31
		Law expenses	34
			£12,882
		Cash at Bankers and in hand	1,156
	£14,038		£14,038

No. of Directors—5 ; minimum, 3 ; quorum, 3.   *Qualification,* 100*l.*

DIRECTORS:

Chairman—WILLIAM B. FORTESCUE, Esq., Octon, Torquay.

The Right Hon. Earl of Devon, Powderham Castle. Exeter, and 23, Brook Street, W.
John Elliot, Esq., Kingsbridge.

William Roope Ilbert, Esq., Bowringsleigh, Kingsbridge.
Willoughby Shortland, Esq., Kingsbridge.

OFFICERS.—Sec., E. Bellamy, 7, Westminster Chambers, S.W.; Eng., W. Mc.N. Harkness. Parliament Street, S.W.; Auditors, P. O. Hingston and A. Brown ; Surveyor, J. Drew, Jun., Powderham Castle, Exeter ; Solicitors, Hargrove, Fowler, and Blunt, 3, Victoria Street, S.W., and G. B. Lidstone, Kingsbridge.

Offices,—7, Westminster Chambers, Victoria Street, S.W.

206.—KING'S LYNN.

Incorporated by 28 and 29 Vic., cap. 88 (19th June, 1865), to construct a short line from Purfleet, on the Great Eastern; also to construct docks and other works at King's Lynn. Length, ½ mile. Capital, 66,000*l*. in shares, and 22,000*l*. on loan. Powers to corporation of King's Lynn, and to the Lynn and Sutton Bridge, and the Peterborough Wisbeach and Sutton to subscribe.

No. of Directors.—Maximum, 8; minimum, 3; quorum, 3. *Qualification*, 200*l*.

DIRECTORS:

Lewis Whincope Jarvis, Esq., Lynn.
William Burkitt, Esq.
W. Moyse, Esq., Lynn.

William Bunce Greenfield, Esq., 59, Porchester Terrace, Hyde Park, W.

207.—KINGTON AND EARDISLEY.

Incorporated by 25 and 26 Vic., cap. 67 (30th June, 1862), to construct a line from the Leominster and Kington to the Hereford Hay and Brecon, at Eardisley. Length, 7¾ miles. Capital, 100,000*l*., in 10*l*. shares, and 33,000*l*. on loans. Arrangements with Leominster and Kington, and Hereford Hay and Brecon. In abeyance.

By 27 and 28 Vic., cap. 199 (14th July, 1864), the company was authorised to extend the line to Presteign, and to use a portion of the Leominster and Kington; also to enter into agreements with that company and the Great Western. Length of new line, 7¼ miles. Capital, 90,000*l*., in shares, and 30,000*l*. on loan.

By 28 Vic., cap. 44 (26th May, 1865), the company was empowered to divide the capital into half-shares preferred and deferred.

By 31 and 32 Vic., cap. 107 (13th July, 1868), the company was authorised to make certain deviations, to abandon portions of lines, to revise and extend its powers for compulsory purchase of lands, and to use a portion of the Leominster and Kington. Works to be completed within three years.

DIRECTORS:

Chairman—WILLIAM LAURENCE BANKS, Esq., F.S.A., Brecon.

Deputy-Chairman—R. GREEN-PRICE, Esq., M.P., Norton Manor, Presteign, and 3, Suffolk Place, S.W.

The Rev James Davies, Moor Court, Kington, Herefordshire.
Captain Layton, Glasbury House, Glasbury, Brecon.

Stephen Robinson, Esq., The Moor, Kington, Herefordshire.
Captain Corbett, Greenfields, Presteign.

OFFICERS.—Sec., W. Roberts; Eng., Thomas David Roberts, M.I.C.E.; Auditors, Thomas Price, Bank, Kington, and Thomas Stanton, Bank, Presteign; Solicitors, Tilleard, Son, Godden, and Holme, 34, Old Jewry, E.C., and Crawley, Arnold, and Green Price, 20, Whitehall, S.W.; Bankers, Robarts, Lubbock, and Co., Lombard Street, E.C., and Davies, Banks, and Davies, Kington.
Offices—Brecon.

208.—LANCASHIRE UNION.

Incorporated by 27 and 28 Vic., cap. 273 (25th July, 1864), to construct several lines between Blackburn, Chorley, Wigan, and Hindley. Length, 21 miles. Capital, 250,000*l*., in 100*l*. shares, and 83,000*l*. on loan. Arrangements with London and North Western, which may subscribe 100,000*l*.

By 28 Vic., cap. 21 (26th May, 1865), certain portions of the line near Blackburn were vested jointly in the Lancashire and Yorkshire and Lancashire Union, and a joint committee appointed.

By 28 and 29 Vic., cap. 193 (29th June, 1865), the company was authorised to construct an extension to St. Helens, with other branches. Length, 12¾ miles. Capital, 200,000*l*., in shares, and 66,000*l*. on mortgage. Lancashire and Yorkshire to obtain access to St. Helens.

By 29 and 30 Vic., cap. 233 (16th July, 1866), the company obtained powers to construct new lines in the townships of Parr, Haydock, and Ashton-in-Makerfield. Length, 4 miles. New capital, 80,000*l*. in shares, and 26,000*l*. on loan.

By 31 and 32 Vic., cap. 14 (13th July, 1868), the Lancashire and Yorkshire and the Lancashire Union obtained extensions of time till 25th January, 1870, for completion of the works authorised by the Act of 1864. The Act of 1868 also vested a further portion of the Lancashire Union in the two companies, agreements with the London and North Western, however, not to be interfered with.

By 31 and 32 Vic., cap. 115 (13th July, 1868), the company was authorised to abandon a portion of the line, and also to extend the time for completion of works till 1869.

No. of Directors—9: minimum, 6; quorum, 3. *Qualification*, 1,500*l*.

209.—LANCASHIRE AND YORKSHIRE.

This company is an amalgamation of the MANCHESTER AND LEEDS, the MANCHESTER BOLTON AND BURY, the LIVERPOOL AND BURY, the HUDDERSFIELD AND SHEFFIELD, the WAKEFIELD PONTEFRACT AND GOOLE, the WEST RIDING UNION, and the EAST LANCASHIRE. The present title was conferred by 10 and 11 Vic., cap. 163 (1847). Productive, 411½ miles.

I. MANCHESTER AND LEEDS.—This company, incorporated by 6 and 7 Wm. IV., cap. 111 (4th July, 1836), for a line from Manchester to Normanton Junction, and subsequently extended to and connected with the London and North Western and Sheffield lines at Ardwick station. Opened throughout to Normanton, 1st, October, 1844. In 1844 the Ashton and Stalybridge was transferred to this undertaking.

MANCHESTER, BOLTON, AND BURY.—This company was incorporated for a canal by the 31 Geo. III. (1791), and for railway in 1831 (2 Wm. IV., cap. 69), 11 miles. Amalgamated with the Manchester and Leeds by 9 and 10 Vic., cap. 378, the agreement taking effect as from 1st July, 1845 : the proprietors received 7*l*. dividend per share (93*l*. paid) in 1845 ; 8*l*. per share in 1846 ; and afterwards a *pro rata* dividend with M. and L. old shares.

LIVERPOOL AND BURY.—This scheme was incorporated in 1845, 9 Vic., cap. 166, 31⅝ miles. Amalgamated with M. and L. by 10 Vic., cap. 282 (July, 1846), terms being—a dividend 1 per cent. less than M. and L. 50*l*. shares for two years from the opening of this railway (20th November, 1848) ; the L and B. 50*l*. and M. and L. 50*l*. shares, in respect to calls being placed on an equal footing, and also with respect to dividends, after the two years. No interest on calls was allowed during construction. This agreement was modified at general meeting, 7th March, 1849 ; viz.—In consideration of the delay of half-a-year, the opening of the line beyond the time promised, a rebate of 17*s*. per share was allowed on the call due 15th October, 1849 ; and the difference in the dividends of 1 per cent., for two years, less than the general dividend, deducted at once from that of the half-year due 30th June, 1849, the amount as thus reduced being fixed at 7*s*. 6*d*. per share. From 1st July, 1849, these shares were converted into stock, and have taken equal dividend with the rest of this company's ordinary stock.

HUDDERSFIELD AND SHEFFIELD.—A company incorporated June, 1845 (9 Vic., cap. 39), to Huddersfield—14¾ miles. Amalgamated with the M. and L. by 10 Vic., cap. 277, taking effect one month after the close of the session (1846), terms being on equal dividend, *pro rata*, from opening, with that payable on the M. and L. 50*l*. shares. Interest was paid on calls at 4 per cent. during construction. Opened 1st July, 1850.

WAKEFIELD, PONTEFRACT, AND GOOLE.—Incorporated by 8 and 9 Vic., cap. 172 (1845), 28¾ miles. Further branches 15½ miles, and a jetty at Goole. Under the Acts previous agreements for amalgamation at par were sanctioned. Interest at 4 per cent. was paid during construction. First dividend in March, 1849. for half-year, 30th December, 1848. Shares are now converted into Lancashire and Yorkshire stock.

WEST RIDING UNION.—Incorporated 18th August, 1846 (10 Vic., cap. 390), for a series of lines--in all 45½ miles. By the same Act the whole scheme was incorporated with the Manchester and Leeds three months after the passing of the Act, the capital to form part of the Manchester and Leeds company. The Lancashire and Yorkshire Company's Act (1852), authorises the abandonment of those portions between Bowling and Leeds ; Salter Hebble and Huddersfield ; Birstal and the Brighouse station, Halifax, Birstal to Dewsbury.

SHEFFIELD, ROTHERHAM, BARNSLEY, WAKEFIELD, HUDDERSFIELD, AND GOOLE.—Incorporated by Act 9 and 10 Vic , cap. 354 (7th August, 1846), for a line from Wakefield to Barnsley ; formerly leased to Lancashire and Yorkshire for 13,500*l*. per annum, equal to 5 per cent. ; but by 21 and 22 Vic., cap. 143 (2nd August, 1858), the line is finally vested in the latter company, and the former dissolved. The Lancashire and Yorkshire created stock to the amount of 260,000*l*., bearing dividend at 5*l*. 3*s*. 10*d*. per cent. per annum, to be designated "The Lancashire and Yorkshire (Barnsley) Stock."

LEASES, &c.—The following other engagements have also been entered into by the Lancashire and Yorkshire, viz. :—
North Union.—This company is vested by 10 Vic., cap. 231, in the Lancashire and Yorkshire and London and North Western, at an annual perpetual rent of 66,053*l*. 18*s*.,

from 1st January, 1864, and the interest of mortgage debt. The proportion borne by the Lancashire and Yorkshire is 34-94ths of the profit or loss. Line worked in divisions.

Preston and Wyre.—This company, incorporated 1835, capital 130,000*l.*, and loans 40,000*l.*; further 307,000*l.* and 126,000*l.*; total, 666,000*l.*, leased to L. & Y. under Acts of 1846, 10 Vic., cap. 306. The L. and N. W. participate in this lease under 13 Vic., cap, 74, 18l9; the larger proportion, viz., two-thirds, is borne by the L. and Y. The terms of this lease are a rent of 7*l.* 1*s.* 6*d.* per cent.. 35*s.* 4½*d.* per share, till the end of 1854, when it advanced to 7*l.* 17*s.* 2*d.* per cent.. 39*s.* 3½*d.* in perpetuity, per share, on a total capital of 668,000*l.* By 28 Vic., cap. 22 (26th May, 18 5), the Lancashire and Yorkshire was authorised to raise new capital to the extent of 16,000*l.* in shares and 4,000*l.* on loan; and the London and North Western 8,000*l.* in shares and 2,000*l.* on loan, for widening and otherwise improving the Preston and Wyre.

Liverpool, Crosby, and Southport.—Incorporated by 11 Vic., cap. 105 (2nd July, 1847), for a line joining the Lancashire and Yorkshire Bury line, at 1¾ mile from Tithebarn Street, Liverpool, over the L. & Y. and East Lancashire to Crosby and the bathing village of Southport, 18½ miles, of which 1¾ mile to the Kirkdale Junction belongs to the L. & Y. and E. L. At a special meeting of the Liverpool Crosby and Southport, on June 14th, 1855, an agreement was entered into with the Lancashire and Yorkshire on these terms :—"That the Lancashire and Yorkshire become purchasers of the Liverpool Crosby and Southport ; shall assume its entire engagements and liabilities ; and pay to the proprietors upon the share capital a dividend of 2½ per cent for the year 1855, 3½ per cent. for the years 1856 and 1857 respectively, and from and after 31st December, 1857, affix the common seal of the company thereto, at the same dividend as that payable to holders of Lancashire and Yorkshire ordinary stock."

Blackburn.—Under the provisions of the Act authorising a purchase of this line (1858) the joint owners are authorised to redeem the preference and ordinary stock of the Blackburn, upon terms which make it the interest of the two companies that such redemption should take place.

Leeds and Liverpool Canal.—In 1851, the East Lancashire, Midland, London and North Western, and Lancashire and Yorkshire companies undertook a joint lease of the tolls of the Leeds and Liverpool canal, for 21 years, determinable at the end of 15 years, at the option of the railway companies, at the rate of 40,000*l.* per annum, divisible in proportion to the traffic in the district.

Rochdale Canal.—The sanction of the proprietors was obtained to a lease, for not exceeding 21 years, of the tolls and duties authorised to be taken by the proprietors of this canal. The lease is tak n jointly with the North Eastern, the Manchester Sheffield and Lincolnshire, and the London and North Western. An arrangement had been in operation for some time with the canal company, by which Lancashire and Yorkshire traffic was protected, and its interests secured within certain limits : the lease, with but a slight increase of liability, affords protection over a much wider field.

II. EAST LANCASHIRE.—This undertaking is an amalgamation of the EAST LANCASHIRE (originally incorporated as the Manchester Bury and Rossendale) and the BLACKBURN and PRESTON, under an Act passed 3rd August, 1846 (10 h Vic., cap. 302), by which the united capital was fixed at 1,010,000*l.* in shares, and 296,000*l.* in loans.

Manchester, Bury, and Rossendale.—This line was incorporated by 8 Vic., cap. 60 (4th July, 1844), for a line to connect Manchester with Bury, which was subsequently extended to Rawtenstall. Length, 14 miles. Commencing with a capital of 300,000*l.* in shares, and loan powers 100,000*l.* By the Extension Act, 9 Vic., cap. 35, the capital was increased by 530,000*l.* in shares, and 176,000*l.* in loans ; 24 miles were authorised. The Act 9 Vic., cap. 101, gave further powers. The Act 10 Vic., cap. 267 for branches, and allow six miles and additional capital, 300,000*l.*; loans, 100,000*l.*

Blackburn and Preston.—This company was incorporated by 7 Vic., cap. 34 (1844), for a line from Blackburn to Farrington (junction with North Union), near Preston. Length, 9¾ miles. Capital authorised—shares, 120,000*l.*, and loans, 40,000*l.* By 9 Vic., cap. 103, the line was altered, and further capital authorised of 30,000*l*, and 10,000*l.* By 10 Vic., cap. 26ₒ, branches were authorised, with further capital of 30,000*l.*, and 10,000*l.* Length, 6 miles.

Extensions.—On the 30th June, 1845, an Act (9 Vic., cap. 35) was obtained by the "Blackburn Burnley Accrington and Colne Extension," extending the original scheme from Rawtenstall to Blackburn, via Accrington, with a branch eastward through Burnley to Colne. where a junction is effected with the Midland (Leeds and Bradford). This Act provided for its immediate transfer to the Rossendale, the united undertakings assuming thenceforward the name of the "East Lancashire."

In 1846 the amalgamated line was extended by the incorporation of the "Liverpool Ormskirk and Preston," from Farrington junction (through Ormskirk) to Liverpool Exchange (capital, 750,000*l.* and 250,000*l.*: length, 36⅝ miles), where a station has been erected at the joint expense of this company and the Lancashire and Yorkshire, as owners of the Liverpool and Bury.

On the 22nd July, 1847, an Act was obtained (10 and 11 Vic., cap. 289), authorising an extension to Preston, and an independent station at that place. Capital authorised, 217,000*l.* in shares, and 72,300*l.* in loans.

By Act 12 and 13 Vic., cap. 71 (July 28th, 1849), the company was authorised to raise an additional capital of 304,000*l.* in shares, and 101,000*l.* in loans. By Act 14 and 15 Vic., cap. 56 (July 3rd, 1851), the company was authorised to raise 304,000*l.* in shares, for the purpose of redeeming the preference fifth shares, and also 425,533*l.* in loans. The redemption of the fifth shares was not, however, effected, nor the share capital authorised by this Act raised.

On 4th August, 1853, an Act was obtained (16 and 17 Vic., cap. 163) for an extension to Rainford, to join the St. Helens, and also for empowering the company to convert their mortgage debt into annuities. Additional capital authorised, 80,000*l.* in shares, and 20,000*l.* in loans.

By East Lancashire and Lancashire and Yorkshire Act, 1854, 17 and 18 Vic., cap. 117 (July 3rd, 1854), the companies became joint owners of the lines between Clifton and Manchester and Burscough and Southport, and were authorised to erect an independent station at Southport. Capital under this Act, 200,000*l.* in shares, and 66,000*l.* in loans.

III.—AMALGAMATION.—By 22 and 23 Vic., cap. 110 (13th August, 1859), the line is amalgamated with Lancashire and Yorkshire, and from that date ceased to exist as an independent company. By the same Act the board of directors may be reduced to 12; the power to create perpetual annuities is repealed; power given to convert mortgage debt into debenture stock; and the through traffic from Penistone and Huddersfield facilitated and regulated; provision is also made for the enlargement of stations; the North Union and Preston and Wyre engagements continued; and the tolls on the united railways revised. These tolls, however, may again be revised and reduced, when the dividend on the paid-up capital stock of the company, upon the average of three years, last preceding, shall equal or exceed 8 per cent. per annum. Power is also given to convert the borrowed capital into debenture stock at a fixed dividend, not exceeding 4 per cent. The directors will take advantage of this provision whenever the state of the money market offers the opportunity of doing so with advantage.

By 22 and 23 Vic., cap. 129 (13th August, 1859), the company was authorised to construct lines from Oldham to Rochdale and Royton. New capital, 200,000*l.* in shares, and 66,000*l.* in loans. Opened in November, 1863.

By 24 Vic., cap. 34 (17th May, 1861), the company was authorised to construct a line from Aintree to Bootle, with other small branches. Length, 5¼ miles. Capital, 210,000*l.*, in shares, and 70,000*l.* on loan.

By 24 and 25 Vic., cap. 101 (28th June, 1861), the company was authorised to construct a line from Salford to the Victoria Station at Manchester. Length, 53 chains. Capital, 150,000*l.* in shares, and 50,000*l.* on loan. Opened August, 1865.

By 24 Vic., cap. 50 (7th June, 1861), the company was authorised to construct branches to Dewsbury, Heckmondwike, and Meltham (length, 7 miles): also to purchase additional land at Rochdale and Miles Platting. New capital, 173,000*l.* in shares, and 57,600*l.* on loan.

By 24 Vic., cap. 37 (17th May, 1861), the company was authorised to raise new capital for general purposes, to the extent of 500,000*l.*, at a preference not exceeding 4½ per cent. The period for sale of superfluous lands was also extended for ten years from date of Act.

By 25 and 26 Vic., cap. 97 (30th June, 1862), the company was authorised to construct a branch to Shawforth (5½ miles), and to raise new capital to the extent of 187,750*l.* in shares, and 62,500*l.* on loan.

By 26 Vic., cap. 5 (4th of May, 1863), the company was authorised to raise new capital to the extent of 50,000*l.*, at 5 per cent., with one-fourth on loan, for the purpose of the North Union and Preston and Wyre.

By 27 Vic., cap. 32 (13th May, 1864), the company was authorised to acquire additional land, and to execute several new works, including the Beswick branch. Length, ¼ mile. Capital, 315,000*l.* in shares, and 105,000*l.* on loan.

By 27 Vic., cap. 55 (23rd June, 1864), the Lancashire and Yorkshire and the North Eastern were each authorised to subscribe 25,000*l.* towards the Methley branch of the West Yorkshire, so that the share capital of 75,000*l.* required for that branch shall be provided in equal proportions by the three companies.

By 27 and 28 Vic., cap. 270 (25th July, 1864), the company was authorised to construct lines between Blackburn, Chorley, Horwich, and Wigan. Length, 11¾ miles. Capital, 210,000*l.* in shares, and 70,000*l.* on loan.

By 28 Vic., cap. 21 (26th May, 1865), certain portions of the line near Blackburn were vested jointly in the Lancashire and Yorkshire and the Lancashire Union, and a joint committee appointed.

Br 28 and 29 Vic., cap. 332 (5th July, 1865), the company was authorised to construct branches to Ripponden and Stainland, establish new works, and to acquire additional lands. Length, 4½ miles. Capital, 140,000*l.* in shares, and 46,000*l.* on mortgage.

By 29 Vic., cap. 43 (18th May, 1866), the company obtained an extension of time for construction of lines authorised in 1861 and 1862, and also to acquire additional lands and raise new capital to the extent of 6,000*l.*, and 200,000*l.* on loan.

By 29 Vic., cap. 44 (18th May, 1866), the company was authorised to construct a line between Blackburn and Padiham. Length, 6¾ miles. Capital, 128,000*l.* in shares, and 42,600*l.* on loan. Extension of time to 11th August, 1871.

By 29 Vic., cap. 71 (11th June, 1866), the company was authorised to construct three short branches in the West Riding, and also to lay down additional rails on the Halifax branch. Length, 6½ miles. Capital, 205,000*l.* in shares, and 68,000*l.* on loan.

By 30 and 31 Vic., cap. 136 (15th July, 1867), the Lancashire and Yorkshire were authorised to complete the North Lancashire Loop Line between Blackburn and Burnley (2¼ miles). New capital, for this and other purposes, 700,000*l.*, in shares, and 233,000*l.* on loan. Also to issue debenture stock at a rate not exceeding 4½ per cent.

By 31 and 32 Vic., cap. 64 (25th June, 1868), the company obtained an extension of time to complete the Ripponden and Stainland branches till 5th July, 1872, and also authority to subscribe 50,000*l.* to the Hull Docks.

By 31 and 32 Vic., cap. 114 (13th July, 1868), the Lancashire and Yorkshire and the Lancashire and Yorkshire Union obtained extensions of time till 25th January, 1870, for completion of the lines authorised by Act of 1864. The Act of 1868 also vested a further portion of the Lancashire Union in the two companies, agreements with the London and North Western, however, not to be interfered with.

FLEETWOOD, PRESTON, AND WEST RIDING.—By 30 Vic., cap. 95 (17th June, 1867), the London and North Western and the Lancashire and Yorkshire were jointly authorised to lease the Fleetwood Preston and West Riding, which see.

MILEAGE.—There are now 411½ miles open for traffic. During the year the Bootle and Aintree and Hindley and Horwich lines have been opened, and in the course of the coming year it is probable that the Lockwood and Meltham, the Shawforth, and the Heckmondwike and Thornhill branches will also be opened.

REVENUE.—This account for the half-year ending 31st December, 1867, stated that 1,289,911*l.* had been received, against 1,230,866*l.* in the same period of 1866, showing an increase of 59,045*l.* The expenses amounted to 546,791*l.*, against 506,408*l.*, showing an increase of 40,383*l.* The balance of revenue applicable to the payment of dividend on the ordinary stock was 424,777*l.*; and out of this amount, a dividend at the rate of 6½ per cent. per annum, left a balance of 12,235*l.* to next account.

The receipts during the June half-year amounted to 1,251,756*l.* against 1,201,538*l.* for the corresponding period of 1867, showing an increase of 50,218*l.* The disbursements amounted to 555,022*l.*, against 541,894*l.*, showing an increase of 13,128*l.* The balance of revenue applicable to dividend was 440,093*l.*; and out of this amount a dividend at the rate of 6¾ per cent. per annum, left a balance of 11,684*l.*, to next account. The gross increase of traffic for the half-year was 50,218*l.*, earned at an additional cost, in working expenses of 13,128*l.*

NEW CAPITAL.—At a special meeting held on 19th February, 1868, it was resolved :—
"That for the purposes, under the authority and subject to the provisions of the following Acts of Parliament and the Acts of Parliament incorporated therewith, the company doth determine to raise, by the creation of new shares, additional capital in the undertaking, amounting in the aggregate to the sum of 641,000*l.*, that is to say, under 'The Lancashire and Yorkshire (Blackburn, Chorley, Horwich, and Wigan lines) Act, 1864,' the sum of 210,000*l.* ; under 'The Preston and Wyre, 1865,' the sum of 16,000*l.*; under 'The London and North Western and Lancashire and Yorkshire companies' (Fleetwood Preston and West Riding Junction vesting) Act, 1867,' the sum of 65,000*l.*; and under 'The Lancashire and Yorkshire (North-Lancashire Loop Line and Capital) Act, 1867,' the sum of 350,000*l.*, for general purposes; and the company doth determine that the said sum of 641,000*l.* shall be raised in new shares of the amount, class, and description, and bear the dividend, and shall be appropriated and disposed of in the manner and on the terms and conditions hereinafter appearing, that is to say,—

"1. That the said additional capital shall be raised in shares of a nominal value of 5*l.* each, entitled in preference to the ordinary stock of the company from the 15th day of April, 1868, to the 1st day of July, 1871, out of the profits available for dividend in each year, to a dividend at the rate of 4½ per cent. per annum and no more on the amount paid up in calls thereon ; and such new shares shall, as and from the said 1st day of July, 1871, become part of the ordinary shares or stock of the company, and be entitled to dividends accordingly ; and until such new shares shall fall into the ordinary shares or stock of the company, they shall be called 'The Lancashire and Yorkshire Railway New 5*l.* Shares, 1868 ;' and until such new shares shall become part of the ordinary shares or stock of the company they shall not entitle the holders thereof to participate in any future issue of shares or stock.

"2. That the directors of the company be authorised to offer such new shares to the holders of ordinary stock in the company as registered this day, in the proportion of one 5*l.* share for every 100*l.* stock held by them (omitting fractions), or to the nominees of such holders duly appointed in writing, every such offer being conditional upon payment of a deposit or call of 1*l.* per share on or before the 15th day of April next ; and in case any allottee or his or her nominee shall fail to accept the same, and to pay the said sum of 1*l.* per share on that day, then the allotmet so made to him or her of new shares shall be cancelled, and the right of such allottee or his or her nominee to the new shares comprised therein shall be forfeited.

"3. That the remaining 4*l.* per share shall be called up in such manner and at such times as the directors shall think proper, provided that the whole amount shall be called up on or before the 1st day of July, 1871, and that 1*l.* per share shall be the greatest amount of each future call, and that there shall be an interval of two months at the least between successive calls.

"4. That in case any of the holders of the said new shares shall neglect to pay the calls due thereon on the respective days or times appointed for payment thereof, interest at such rate as the directors may from time to time determine upon shall be paid upon any call or calls in arrear.

"5. That the directors of the company may receive from the allottees or holders of the said new shares payments in anticipation of all or any part of the deposit or calls thereon, in such manner, and at such times, and at such rate of interest, whether by way of rebate or otherwise, as they may from time to time determine upon.

"6. That the directors be authorised to take such steps and to make such regulations, in conformity with this resolution and the provisions of the said several Acts of Parliament and the Acts incorporated therewith as they may deem necessary or expedient in reference to the said new shares and the issuing thereof."

CAPITAL.—The following is a statement of the capital authorised, and on which dividends were paid as from 30th June, 1868. according to their priorities:—

Per cent.	Created.	Received.	In Arrear	Uncalled.	Unissued.
Guaranteed 6	£794 040	£794,040	....	....	....
Preference 6	283,375	2·7,793	....	....	£582
,, 5	304,000	297,490	....	....	6,510
,, 5	65,700	53,230	....	....	12,740
,, 4½	100,000	90,780	....	....	9,220
Barnsley branch £5 3s. 10d. ..	260 050	260,050	....	....	....
Blackburn purchase 4½	538,048	538,035	£13	....	....
Preference 4½	1,233,000	1,232,808	192	....	....
,, 4½	607,750	607,551	199	....	....
New 5*l.* shares 4½, till July, 1871, then ordinary	641,000	189,745	29,737	329,223	92,295
Consolidated stock	12,769,995	12,683,936	3,607	....	76,401
	£17,601,958	£17,041,503	£33.748	£329,223	£197.478

	Dec. 31, 1867.	June 30, 1868.	Total.
Shares and stock..................... ..	£16,851,403	£190,105	£17,041,508
		Less	
Loans	5,108,514	60,078	5,048,436
		£130,027	
Debenture stock	492,321	11,700	504,021
Advance of calls	......	130,686	130,686
Forfeited and merged shares...............	75,525	......	75,525
	£22,527,763	£272,413	£22,800,176
Balance	......	......	133,220
Expenditure			£22,933,396

The account are made up to 30th June and 31st December, in every year, and the meetings held in Manchester, February and August.

Scale of Voting.—One Vote for every 100*l.* stock, nomiral amount.

Certificates must accompany transfer deed. Registration fee, 5s. each deed or bond. Parts of 1*l.* may not be transferred. Several classes of shares or stock may go on one deed. Transfer books close usually 22 days before meetings.

No. of Directors.—Maximum, 26; minimum, 12. *Qualification,* 2,500*l.* stock, nominal value. Allowance, 5,000*l.* Present board, 16.

DIRECTORS:

Chairman—GEORGE WILSON, Esq., Manchester.
Deputy-Chairman—THOMAS DUGDALE, Esq., Blackburn.

George Anderton, Esq., Cleckheaton, near Leeds.
Joshua Appleyard, Esq., Clare Hall, Halifax.
Thomas Barnes, Esq., Farnworth, near Bolton.
William T. Blacklock, Esq., Hopefield, near Manchester.
George S. Beecroft, Esq., Abbey House, Kirkstall, near Leeds.
Samuel Fielden, Esq., Todmorden.

James Hatton, Esq., Manchester.
John Hargreaves, Esq., Silwood Park, Berks.
James Holme, Esq., Liverpool.
William Henry Hornby, Esq., M.P., Blackburn, and 24, Pall Mall, S.W.
Theodore J. Hare, Esq., 4, Promenade, Southport.
John R. Kay, Esq., Bury.
James Pilkington, Esq., Blackburn.
Joshua Radcliffe, Esq., Rochdale.

OFFICERS.—Sec., William S. Lawn; Traff. Man., William Thorley, Manchester; Treas., Samuel William Bulteel; Res Eng., Sturges Meek, Manchester; Audit Accountant, W. J. Benbow; Loco. Supts., William Hurst and William Yates, Manchester, John Jaques and R. Mason, Bury; Supts. Passenger Traffic, Henry Blackmore (Western Division), Victoria Station, Manchester; C. H. Binstead (Eastern Division), Wakefield: Goods Man., T. Collin; Supt. of Merchandise Traffic, E. M. Grundy; Bankers, Cunliffes, Brooks and Co., Manchester; Solicitors, T. A. and J. Grundy and Co., King Street, Manchester.

Head Offices—Hunt's Bank, Manchester.

210.—LANCASTER AND CARLISLE.

(LEASED TO LONDON AND NORTH WESTERN).

Incorporated by 7 and 8 Vic., cap. 37 (1844), for a single line in the first instance until the Act authorising the Caledonian was passed, when it was made a double line, continuing the Lancaster and Preston to Carlisle, and there forming a junction with the Caledonian. Length, 70 miles.

An Act 13 Vic., cap. 87 (1st August, 1849), sanctioned an agreement between this company and the Lancaster and Preston, as follows:—That the Lancaster and Preston receives 7-22nds and the Lancaster and Carlisle the remaining 15-22nds of net profits derived from working of both lines. Out of their proportion the Lancaster and Preston paid interest on mortgage debt, 113,000*l*.

By 20 and 21 Vic., cap. 161 (25th August, 1857), the Lancaster and Carlisle was authorised to construct the connecting link between Tebay and Ingleton. Additional capital, 300,000*l*.; loan, 100,000*l*. Length of main line is 19 miles; that of the branch, 1 mile 2 furlongs 1 chain. By 21 and 22 Vic., cap. 14 (23rd July, 1858), the company obtained power to abandon part of Lowgill Junction, the connection between Little North Western and Lancaster and Carlisle being in no way impaired. Opened October 1st, 1861.

By 22 and 23 Vic., cap. 124 (August 13th, 1859), the Acts of the company were consolidated, and lease and amalgamation with the Kendal and Windermere and Lancaster and Preston authorised.

LANCASTER AND PRESTON JUNCTION.—Incorporated by 7 Wm. IV., cap. 22 (1837), for a line between those towns. Length, 20¼ miles. Opened throughout, 30th June, 1840. Leased to the Lancaster Canal for 21 years, from 1st September, 1842, per agreement, dated 14th July, 1852, at an annual rental of 13,000*l*. By Act 13 Vic, cap. 87 (1st August, 1849), the Lancaster and Carlisle assumed the management of the two undertakings, under agreement of 13th November, 1848. This company's relations with the Canal company are as follows, viz.: On 1st August, 1849, the canal relinquished their lease, paying their portion of the stipulated rent up to that date; receiving from the Preston company 4,875*l*. a year. The option of purchasing this annuity was reserved to this company; at the meeting of 12th April, 1850, it was agreed to be exercised—the "*twelfth*" shares were created, and the canal was paid 48,155*l*. 3*s*. 6*d*., principal and expenses, less proceeds of certain sales in 1849 (2,976*l*. 13*s*. 5*d*.); balance, 44,137*l*. 10*s*. The Lancaster and Preston agreed to the terms of lease with the Lancaster and Carlisle, which took effect on 10th September, 1859, the Preston proprietors receiving 101*l*. 18*s*. 1½*d*. for every 100*l*. stock.

KENDAL AND WINDERMERE.—Incorporated by 8 and 9 Vic., cap. 32 (1845), for a line from the Lancaster and Carlisle, at Oxenholme, to Birthwaite, near Windermere Lake, 10¼ miles. Opened 21st April, 1847. Leased in perpetuity to the London and North Western, at 3 per cent.

PORTPATRICK.—The Lancaster and Carlisle subscribed 100,000*l*. to this undertaking, and the London and North Western exercises the power of nominating two directors.

LONDON AND NORTH WESTERN.—This company leased the Lancaster and Carlisle and the Lancaster and Preston, for 900 years, from 1st August, 1859, on the following terms:—On the London and North Western paying a dividend at the rate of 4 per cent. or under, the Lancaster and Carlisle to receive a dividend of 8 per cent.; on paying 4¼, to receive 8½; on paying 4½, to receive 9; on paying 4¾, to receive 9¼; on paying 5, to receive 9½; on paying 5¼, to receive 9¾; on paying 5½, to receive 10; on paying 5¾, to receive 10¼; and on the London and North Western paying 6 per cent., Lancaster and Carlisle to receive 10½, and so on for any greater or less fraction than ¼ per cent., increasing in the same ratio as London and North Western. The dividends paid to the Lancaster and Carlisle, under this arrangement, have been as follow:—

Half-year.	£	s.	d.	£	s.	d.	Half-year.	£	s.	d.	£	s.	d.
31st January, 1860 ……	4	17	6	9	12	6	31st January, 1865 ……	5	15	0	11	0	0
31st July, 1860 ……….	4	15	0				31st July, 1865 ……….	5	5	0			
31st January, 1861 ……	4	17	6	8	17	6	31st January, 1866 ……	5	17	6	11	2	6
31st July, 1861 ……….	4	0	0				31st July, 1866 ……….	5	5	0			
31st January, 1862 ……	4	12	6	8	12	6	31st January, 1867 ……	5	12	6	10	10	0
31st July, 1862 ……….	4	0	0				31st July, 1867 ……….	4	17	6			
31st January, 1863 ……	5	0	0	9	5	0	31st January, 1868 ……						
31st July, 1863 ……….	4	5	0				31st July, 1868 ……….						
31st January, 1864 ……	5	5	0	10	7	6							
31st July, 1864 ……….	5	2	6										

By 28 and 29 Vic., cap. 333 (5th July, 1865), it is provided that shareholders in the Lancaster and Carlisle shall participate *pro rata* in future allotments of London and North Western stock.

The accounts made up to the 31st January and 31st July ; and the statutory meetings held about February and August every year, at Lancaster.

Scale of Voting—One vote per share up to 20 ; and one for every additional four shares. Certificates must accompany transfer deed. Registration fee, 2s. 6d. each deed, except when both ordinary and preference stock are inserted in the same deed, then the fee is 2s. 6d. for each class of stock

No. of Directors—17 ; five of whom are nominated by the London and North Western

DIRECTORS:

Chairman—E. W. HASELL, Esq., Dalemain, Penrith.

Deputy-Chairman—WILLIAM JACKSON, Esq., Lancaster.

Samuel Edward Bolden, Esq., Lancaster.
Edward Hughes Satterthwaite, Esq., Lancaster.
George H. Head, Esq., Rickerby House, Carlisle.
William Birley Esq., The Larches, Preston.
*John T. Hibbert, Esq., M.P., Urmston Grange, Stretford, near Manchester, and 29, Grosvenor Street West, S.W.
*Henry Cotton Tunnicliffe, Esq., Brunswick Street, Liverpool.
*James Cropper, Esq., Ellergreen, Kendal.
*James Bancroft, Esq., 5, Police Street, Manchester.

*Alex. Brogden, Esq., M.P., Ulverston.
William Nicholson Hodgson, Esq., M.P., Newby Grange, Carlisle, and Carlton Club, S.W.
Henry Garnett, Esq., Wyreside, near Lancaster.
W. A. F. Saunders, Esq., Wennington Hall, Lancaster.
John Barker, Esq., of Broughton Lodge, Grange, Lancashire.
John Stamp Burrell, Esq., Parkfield House, near Lancaster.
†Henry Lowther, Esq., M.P., Barley Thorpe, Oakham, Rutlandshire.

* Nominated by the L. and N. W.   † Nominated by the Earl of Lonsdale.

OFFICERS.—Sec., William King ; Auditors, Joseph Salkeld and Henry Crosfield ; Solicitor, J. B. Batten, 32, Great George Street, S.W. ; Bankers, The Lancaster Banking Company, Lancaster.
Head Offices—Lancaster.

211.—LANDPORT AND SOUTHSEA TRAMWAY.

Incorporated by 26 Vic., cap. 43 (8th June, 1863), to construct a tramway from the Portsea line of the Brighton and South Western to the Southsea Pier, in Southsea. Length, 1 mile 8 chains. Capital, 10,000l. in 10l. shares, and 2,500l. on loan. Arrangements with Brighton and South Western.

No. of Directors—6 ; minimum, 4 ; quorum, 3. *Qualification*, 200l.

DIRECTORS:

William Grant Chambers, Esq., J.P., Portsmouth.

Alderman Nance, J.P., Baffin's Farm.
Edward Kent Parson, Esq., Southsea.

OFFICERS.—Sec., Henry Hollingsworth, Southsea ; Eng., R. Jacomb Hood, C.E., 6, Little George Street, Westminster, S.W.; Bankers, The National Provincial Bank, Portsea, Landport, and Southsea Branches.

212.—LAUGHARNE.

Incorporated by 29 and 30 Vic., cap. 279 (30th July, 1866), to construct a line from the South Wales at St. Clears, to Laugharne. Length, 5½ miles. Capital, 50,000l. in shares, and 16,600l. on loan. Arrangements with Great Western.

No. of Directors—5 ; minimum, 3 ; quorum 3 and 2. *Qualification*, 200l.

DIRECTORS:

Chairman—FRANK HOWARD, Esq.

John Carter, Esq.
W. T. Lyon, Esq.

John Muddelle, Esq.

OFFICERS.—Sec. and Man., *pro tem.*, Matthew Shield ; Engs., Sir Charles Fox, Knt., and Son, New Street, Spring Gardens, S.W.
Offices—49, Victoria Street, Westminster, S.W.

213.—LAUNCESTON AND SOUTH DEVON.

Incorporated by 25 and 26 Vic., cap. 111 (30th June, 1862), to construct a line from Tavistock, on the South Devon and Tavistock, to Launceston. Length, 19 miles. Capital, 180,000l., in 10l., shares, and 60,000l. on loan. Broad gauge. Arrangements with South Devon, which works the line, and guarantees interest on debenture stock. Rebates on traffic from Great Western, Bristol and Exeter, South Devon and Cornwall.

By 26 and 27 Vic., cap. 105 (28th June, 1863). some deviations were authorised to be completed by 30th June, 1867. Opened 1st July, 1865.

By 29 and 30 Vic., cap. 147 (28th June, 1866), the company obtained power to cancel certain shares, and to raise new capital to the extent of 36,000*l.* in shares, and 12,000*l.* on loan. The narrow gauge to be laid down on application from the Devon and Cornwall.

This company is in future to be embodied in the South Devon.

REVENUE.—The net earnings for the half-year ending 31st December were 2,841*l.*, against 2,639*l.* in corresponding six months, while for the whole year they were 5,472*l.*, against 4,949*l.* There was a balance on the revenue occount of 1,347*l.*, about equal to 1 per cent. on the original share capital, but the directors deemed it expedient to defer declaration of a dividend.

Scale of Voting.—One vote for every 10*l.* share.

No. of Directors—7; minimum, 5; quorum, 3. *Qualification,* 250*l.*

DIRECTORS:

Chairman—EDWARD ARCHER, Esq., Trelaske, near Launceston.

Deputy-Chairman—WILLIAM RICHARD DERRY, Esq., Launceston.

Thomas Hender, Esq., Launceston.	Daniel Shilson, Esq., Launceston.
Edmund Pearse Nicolls, Esq., Launceston.	Thomas Woollcombe, Esq., Devonport.
Edward Pethybridge, Esq., Launceston.	

OFFICERS.—Sec., John Dingley; Auditors, J. B. Geake and Geo. Mitchell Gifford, Launceston.

Offices—Launceston.

214.—LEOMINSTER AND KINGTON.

Incorporated by 17 and 18 Vic., cap. 144 (1854). Length, 13¼ miles, single line. Capital, 80,000*l.*, in 10*l.* shares, with power to borrow 26,000*l.* Opened, 2nd August, 1857.

By 22 Vic., cap. 34 (19th April, 1859), power was given to the company to issue the shares not taken up at not exceeding 5 per cent. preference. These shares were issued at 4½ per cent. preference.

By 26 and 27 Vic., cap. 127 (13th July, 1863), the company was authorised to enter into working arrangements with the West Midland, and to devise a lease of the line to that company. By provisions of a lease to the Great Western, in accordance with this Act, the shareholders receive a minimum of 4 per cent., with a future increase in proportion to increase of traffic. The directors have stipulated for the purchase of the line at 5 per cent., whenever the traffic is sufficient to warrant the purchase. Dividends at the rate of 4 per cent. are declared on the ordinary shares, and at the rate of 4½ per cent. on the preference.

At the meeting in August the chairman congratulated the shareholders on the success of the undertaking. The traffic had steadily increased, and a mutual arrangement for running powers, &c., had been made with the Kington and Eardisley, with the view of avoiding parliamentary expenses. He also alluded to the desirability of an extension of the line, so as to bring it into connection with the Welsh and other railways.

CAPITAL.—This account now stands as under in regard to income and expenditure:—

Received.		Expended.	
Ordinary shares	£59,010	Parliamentary and preliminary	£5,384
Preference shares	19,280	Land and compensation	20,849
		Works—contractor	71,600
	£78,290	„ engineer	2,735
Loans on mortgage	26,000	Advertising	91
		Printing, lithographing, &c.	192
	£104,290	Office expenses, &c.	438
Balance due to revenue	899	Rates and taxes	81
		Interest, commission, &c.	2,243
		Travelling expenses	20
		Salary to secretary	497
		Direction and audit	1,055
	£105,189		£105,189

DIRECTORS:

Chairman—The Right Hon. LORD BATEMAN, Shobdon Court, Shobdon, Herefordshire.

Deputy-Chairman—Admiral Sir THOMAS HASTINGS, K.C.B., 61, Upper Seymour Street, W.

James King King, Esq., Staunton Park, Staunton-on-Arrow, Herefordshire, and 97, Eaton Place, S.W.
John Samuel Bannister, Esq., Weston Court, Pembridge, Herefordshire.

James Bedford, Esq., Leominster.
John Percy Severn, Esq., The Hall, Pen-y-bont.
Thomas Bristow Stallard, Esq., Leominster.

OFFICERS.—Sec., William Daggs; Auditors, V. W. Holmes and E. A. Williams.; Solicitors, Baxter, Rose, and Norton, 6, Victoria Street, Westminster, S.W.

Offices—Leominster.

215.—LESLIE.

Incorporated by 20 and 21 Vic., cap. 86 (7th July, 1857), to construct a line from Markinch to Leslie, with three small branches. Length, 6¼ miles. Capital, 35,000l. in 10l. shares, and 11,500l. on loan. Opened 11th February, 1861. Arrangements with North British, which works the line.

DIRECTORS:

Chairman—WILLIAM TULLIS, Esq., Rothes, by Markinch.

Deputy-Chairman—ANDREW WYLIE, Esq., Prinlaws, by Leslie.

James Thrift Smith, Esq., Auchmuty, by Markinch.

OFFICERS.—Solicitor and Sec., Adam Morrison, S.S.C.; Eng., Thomas Bouch, A.I.C.E.; Auditors, William Elder and Arthur Russell; Bankers, Union and Royal Banks of Scotland.

Offices—45, York Place, Edinburgh.

216.—LETTERKENNY.

Incorporated by 23 and 24 Vic., cap, 99 (3rd July, 1860), for making a railway from Cuttymanhill, to the town of Letterkenny. Length, 15¼ miles. Capital, 100,000l. in 10l. shares. Calls, 2l., with intervals of three months. Loans, 33,300l.

By 26 and 27 Vic., cap. 116 (13th July, 1863), the company was authorised to alter and reduce their line 10 miles in county Donegal; to extend and enlarge their powers, and to enter into arrangements with the Londonderry and Lough Swilly which may subscribe 25,000l.

By 29 Vic., cap. 60 (11th June, 1866), the Letterkenny obtained an extension of time for completion of works, and was authorised to enter into arrangements with Londonderry and Lough Swilly. New capital to purchase the latter line. The Letterkenny was also authorised to be leased to Peter Roe. New capital, 50,000l. in shares, and 16,500l. on loan. The works have been suspended since February, 1865. The contractors then became insolvent, and the directors have since been unable to proceed with the works, so that, after much labour and serious expenditure, the undertaking has completely failed.

Meetings in April and October.

No. of Directors—9; minimum, 5; quorum, 3. *Qualification*, 300l.

DIRECTORS:

Chairman—ALEXANDER JOHN ROBERT STEWART, Ards, County Donegal, and Belgrave Square, London, S.W.

Deputy-Chairman—JAMES GROVE WOOD, Esq., Castle Grove, Letterkenny.

John Vandeleur Stewart, Esq., Rockhill, Letterkenny.
Captain Patterson, Gortlea, Letterkenny.
James T. Macky, Esq., Belmont, Londonderry.
Joseph Cooke, Esq., Londonderry.

Wybrants Olphert, Esq., Ballyconnel House, Dunfanaghy.
Bartholomew Mc. Corkell, Esq., Londonderry.
John Munn, Esq., Londonderry.

The second three directors retire by rotation in October. All eligible for re-election.

OFFICERS.—Sec., John Storey, Letterkenny; Eng., John Bower, V.P., Institution of Civil Engineers of Ireland, 10, South Frederick Street, Dublin; Solicitors, Newtons and Armstrong, Dungannon and Dublin; Bankers, the Belfast Banking Company.

217.—LEVEN AND EAST OF FIFE.

Incorporated by 15 Vic., cap. 95 (17th June, 1852), for a line from Thornton Junction, Markinch, Fife (Edinburgh Perth and Dundee), to Burnmill, in Scoonie ; branches to Kirkland Works and Leven Harbour. Length, 6 miles. Opened 3rd July, 1864.

By 24 and 25 Vic.. cap. 158 (22nd July, 1861), the EAST OF FIFE was amalgamated with the Leven. New capital, 17,000*l.* The former company was incorporated by 18 and 19 Vic., cap. 165 (23rd July, 1855), to make a railway from the Leven at the town of that name to Kilconquhar, in the County of Fife. Length, 7 miles 5 chains. Capital, 32,000*l.* in 10*l.* shares ; borrowing powers, 10,606*l.* By 19 Vic., cap. 24 (5th June, 1856), the terminus at Kilconquhar was changed to the North of Muircambus Mill. Opened 18th August, 1867.

REVENUE.—It was reported for the half-year ending 31st January, that the free revenue available for division was 2,318*l.* The proportion falling to the holders of the Leven capital stock was 1,545*l.*, with 33*l.* from last half-year, together 1,578*l.*, out of which a dividend at the rate of 7½ per cent., leaving a balance of 92*l.* to next half-year. The proportion falling to the holders of East of Fife capital stock was 772*l.*, with 11*l.* from last half-year, together 784*l.*, out of which a dividend at the rate of 3 per cent., left a balance of 20*l.* to next half-year. For the half-year ending 31st July, the free revenue, after setting aside 100*l.* to meet contingencies, was 2,286*l.* The proportion of which accruing to the holders of the Leven capital stock, was 1,524*l.*, with 92*l.* from last half-year's account, together 1,616*l.*, out of which a dividend at the rate of 7½ per cent. per annum, left a balance of 110*l.* to next account. The proportion accruing to the holders of East of Fife capital stock was 762*l.*, with 20*l.* from last half-year, together 782*l.*, out of which a dividend at the rate of 3 per cent. per annum, left a balance of 28*l.*

CAPITAL.—The receipts on the Leven line have been 36,460*l.* in shares, and 5,000*l.* on debenture ; debts due (599*l.*) make the total amount 42,059*l.* The East of Fife receipts have been 34,940*l.* in shares and 10,600*l.* on debentures. Debts due (60*l.*) make the amount 45,600*l.* The receipts on Extension capital account have been 40,330*l.* in preference stock, 20,250*l.* in debentures, and 3,631*l.* in debts due, making a total of 64,211*l.*

The accounts are made up to 31st January and 31st July, and the statutory meetings are held in March or April, and September or October.

Scale of Voting.—From 2 to 10 shares, one vote ; one vote for every 10 shares above 10 to 100 ; one vote for every 20 above 100 shares.

No. of Directors—Maximum, 7 ; minimum, 3. *Qualification*, 15 shares Leven capital, and 30 shares East of Fife capital.

DIRECTORS :

Chairman—JOHN HAIG, Esq., Distiller, Cameron Bridge.

John Wood, Esq., Banker, Collingsburgh. | John Luke, Esq., of Brownhills.
James Anderson, Esq., Durie Foundry. |

Secretary and Solicitor, Andrew Wilkie, Writer and Banker, Leven.

218.—LIMERICK, CASTLE CONNELL, AND KILLALOE.

Incorporated by 18 and 19 Vic., cap. 76 (June 26th, 1865), to construct a railway from the Waterford and Limerick, at Killonan, to Castle Connell. Length, 9¾ miles. Completed at the original estimate of 5,000*l.* per mile. Opened 28th August, 1858.

By 21 and 22 Vic., cap 144 (2nd August, 1858), the company was authorised to extend the line from Castle Connell to Killaloe, at an outlay of 37,000*l.* in 10*l.* shares, and 12.333*l.* on loan. Length, 7½ miles. Opened to Birdhill on 10th July, 1860 ; from Birdhill to Killaloe (2¾ miles) on 12th April, 1862. In operation, 13 miles.

By 29 and 30 Vic., cap. 339 (6th August, 1866), the company was authorised to extend the line from Castle Connell to the river Shannon. Length, 1 mile. Capital, 7,500*l.* in shares, and 2,500*l.* on loan. Total mileage open, 17¼ miles.

REVENUE.—The receipts for the half-year ending 31st December, were 1,392*l.*; showing a decrease of 161*l.* For the June half-year they were 1,384*l.*, representing a decrease of 157*l.*

CAPITAL.—The receipts to June 30th were on the Castle Connell 32,615*l.*, while the expenditure amounted to 27,082*l.*, leaving a balance in favour of receipts of 5,532*l.* On the Killaloe extension the receipts have been 49,211*l.*, and the expenditure, including interest and discount, 51,352*l.*

Meetings in February and August ; quorum, 5 shareholders, representing 2,500*l.*

Scale of Voting.—5 shares, one vote ; 10 shares, two votes : one additional for each 10 shares excess ; but no shareholder to have more than 10 votes.

No. of Directors—5 ; minimum, 3 ; quorum, 3. *Qualification,* 50 shares ; Auditors, same qualification.

DIRECTORS :

Chairman—WILLIAM MALCOMSON, Esq., Portlaw, County Waterford.

Deputy-Chairman—ABRAHAM STEPHENS, Esq., Duncannon, County Wexford.

Joseph Robinson, Esq., Corbally House, Limerick.	Samuel B. Pim, Esq., Portlaw.
	James Martin, Esq., M.D., Portlaw.

OFFICERS.—Traffic Man., Thomas Ainsworth ; Sec., Thomas Naan, Limerick ; Eng., James Tighe ; Solicitors, Murdock, Green, and Co., 52, Lower Sackville Street, Dublin.

Offices—Limerick;

219.—LIMERICK AND ENNIS.

By 17 Vic., cap. 114 (4th August, 1853), the company was incorporated by this new title ; empowered to abandon the branches to Killaloe, the Great Southern and Western. and near Limerick. Reduced length, 24¾ miles, single line. Worked by Waterford and Limerick, under Act of 1862, at 45 per cent.

LIMERICK, ENNIS, AND KILLALOE.—Incorporated by 10 Vic., cap. 195 (1846), for a line from Limerick Junction to Ennis (Clare), and branches to Killaloe Junction with the Great Southern and Western, and a branch to Clare.

The first portion of the line, between the Shannon and Clare, was opened on 17th January, 1859 ; the bridge across that river, with the section to Limerick, on 26th March ; the remainder, from Clare to Ennis, 1⅛ mile, 2nd July ; total, 24¾ miles.

By 23 Vic., cap. 56 (25th May, 1860), the company was authorised to maintain the line over certain roads on a level, to purchase lands, and to make alterations in respect to meetings, &c.

REVENUE.—The receipts for the half-year ending 31st December, were 4,952*l.,* showing a decrease of 479*l.,* but an improvement in the net revenue balance of 317*l.* It was reported in September that the gross receipts for the half-year had been 5,597*l.,* being an increase of 283*l.* over those of the corresponding half of last year ; and was the largest amount received during any half-year since the opening of the line. After paying working expenses there remained a balance of 2,829*l.,* out of which was deducted 2,422*l.* for interest on loans and floating debt, leaving a net profit of 398*l.,* which was applied to the reduction of the debt on revenue account. The directors stated that if they could succeed in placing the company's debts at a reasonable rate of interest, the present receipts of the line would pay a fair dividend to the shareholders.

CAPITAL.—The expenditure on this account to 30th June, 1868, amounted to 198,354*l.,* being 19,327*l.* in excess of receipts, which were as follows :—

Ordinary shares—Calls paid	£84,563
Forfeited	7,415
5*l.* per cent. preference shares	12,325
Total received on account of shares	£104,303
Loans—From Public Works Loan Commissioners	21,723
On ordinary debentures	53,000
Total received on capital account	£179,026
Balance—Excess of expenditure over receipts	19,327
	£198,354

The meetings are held half-yearly, in March and September, at Limerick. The accounts are made up to June and December.

Scale of Voting.—1 and not exceeding 5 shares, one vote ; 6 and not exceeding 10, two votes ; and for more than 10, a vote for every 10.

Transfer books close 14 days before meetings. Certificates must accompany deeds—fee, 2*s.* 6*d.* on transfers ; 5*s.* on deaths and marriages.

No of Directors.—Maximum, 15 ; minimum, 8. Elections in March.

DIRECTORS:

Chairman—WILLIAM MALCOMSON, Esq., Portlaw.

Deputy-Chairman—MARCUS KEANE, Esq., Beech Park, Ennis.

Richard Russell, Esq., Limerick.
Abraham Stephens, Esq., Duncannon, County Wexford.
James Martin, Esq., M.D., Portlaw.
William Spaight, Esq., Limerick.
Richard Stacpoole, Esq., Edenvale, Ennis.
Joseph Robinson, Esq., Limerick.

Samuel B. Pim, Esq., Portlaw.
Major Henry William Massy, Rosanna, Tipperary.
Joseph S. Richardson, Esq., Waterford.
Augustine Butler, Esq., D.L., Ballyline, Crusheen.

Four directors go out by rotation every year, but are eligible for re-election.

OFFICERS.—Sec., Thomas Naan; Traffic Man., Thomas Ainsworth; Res. Eng., John Long; Auditors, Hon. Robert O'Brien, Old Church, Limerick, and William Phayer, Limerick; Solicitors, Barrington, Son, and Jeffers, 10, Ely Place, Dublin; Bankers, Bank of Ireland.

Offices—Limerick.

220.—LIMERICK AND FOYNES.

Incorporated by 17 Vic., cap. 168 (4th August, 1853), for a line from Limerick to Foynes, Island Quay, Limerick, and the Lower Shannon. Length, 26½ miles. Opened, October, 1859.

By 18 and 19 Vic., cap. 78 (26th June, 1855), the company was permitted to borrow one-third of its share capital, when one-half thereof should have been paid up, but whether or not the whole of such capital had been subscribed.

By 21 and 22 Vic., cap. 93 (12th July, 1858), the company was afforded new powers to raise the funds requisite to complete the undertaking. Unissued shares may be converted into preference, at 5 per cent., to the extent of 31,975l. Cancelled shares also to be issued as preference, if within the above amount.

By 24 and 25 Vic., cap. 99 (28th June, 1861), the company was authorised to raise new capital to the extent of 40,000l. at 5l. per cent.

Meetings half-yearly, March and September. Quorum, 10 shareholders, holding 10,000l. Shareholders' requisitions, quorum, 10, holding 20,000l. Books balanced 31st December and 30th June; inspection 14 days before, and 14 days after, each ordinary meeting.

Scale of Voting—Above 5 to 20 shares, one vote; every 10 above 50, one vote.

No. of Directors—15 to 10. *Qualification*, 40 shares own right; quorum, 3. Committee of directors, minimum, 3—chairman's casting vote; quorum 3 or 2. Auditors' qualification same as directors.

DIRECTORS:

Chairman—WILLIAM MALCOMSON, Esq., Portlaw.

The Earl of Dunraven, Adare, and 4, Buckingham Gate, S.W.
Thompson Russell, Esq., Limerick.
John White, Esq., Nantinan, Rathkeale.
Joseph Robinson, Esq., Limerick.
Thomas S. Harvey, Esq., Waterford.
Henry White, Esq., Waterford.

J. Lapham, Esq., Waterford.
Abraham Stephens, Esq., Duncannon.
J. W. Murland, Esq., Dublin.
Lieut.-Col. Thompson, C.B., Cork.
Valentine O'B. O'Connor, Esq., Dublin.
John George Fennell, Esq., Cahir.
Samuel Bewley Pim, Esq., Portlaw.

OFFICERS.—Sec., William Carroll, Limerick; Res. Eng., James Tighe, Waterford; Traffic Man., Thomas Ainsworth, Limerick; Solicitors, Barrington, Son, and Jeffers, Limerick and Dublin.

Offices—Limerick.

221.—LIMERICK AND NORTH KERRY.

Incorporated by 28 and 29 Vic., cap. 369 (5th July, 1865), to construct a line from the Rathkeale and Newcastle, at the latter place, to Listowel. Length, 22¾ miles. Capital, 130,000l. in shares, 43,000l. on loan. Arrangements with Rathkeale and Newcastle, and other companies.

No. of Directors—6; quorum, 3. *Qualification*, 200l.

DIRECTORS:

Right Hon. Earl of Devon, Powderham Castle, Exeter, and Brook Street, W.
Frederick William Sedgwick, Esq.
H. B. Harenc, Esq., William Street, Lowndes Square, W.

Lieut.-Colonel Samuel Auchmuty Dickson, Croom Castle, County Limerick, and Chapel Street, Belgrave Square, S.W.
Hamilton Geale, Esq., J.P., Tem E.C., and Darragh, Kilfinane, Co Limerick.

OFFICERS.—Sec., H. Williams Wood; Engs., Sir John Benson and William Barington; Solicitors, P. Burrowes Sharkey, London, and Michael Leahy, Newcastle.

222.—LISKEARD AND CARADON.

Incorporated by 7 Vic., cap. 42 (27th June, 1843), to construct a mineral line between these places in Cornwall. Length, 8¾ miles. Opened in March, 1846.

By 23 Vic., cap. 20 (15th May, 1860), the company was authorised to regulate its capital as follows :—The sum of 18,825*l*. in shares of 1,000*l*. due on mortgage or bond, with power to raise further sums of 12,000*l*. by new shares, and 9,000*l*. by borrowing ; to empower the company to make alterations in two portions, length 6 miles, of their existing railways, and also a new railway, length 2 miles, from a junction with the main line near Trecarne Farm to Gonomena, on Cheesewring branch, and a new branch, length 1 mile, from Crow's Nest to Tokenbury Corner.

This Act also authorises the company to take on lease or purchase or arrange for working of the Kilmar railway, belonging to the Cheesewring Granite Company (Limited) ; and to arrange with the commissioners of Looe Harbour with respect to laying down rails at, and the use of, the works of the commissioners. The dividends are at the rate of 5 per cent.

Meetings on the 2nd Tuesday in February in each year.

No. of Directors—8 ; minimum, 6 : quorum, 3.   *Qualification*, 100*l*.
Offices—Liskeard.

223.—LISKEARD AND LOOE.

Incorporated by 21 Vic., cap. 11 (11th May, 1865), to construct a line from Liskeard, 7 miles in length, to join the Liskeard and Caradon. Both are intended for conveyance of minerals in Cornwall, and may be used as feeders to the trunk line in that county. The steepest gradient is 1 in 63. Capital, 13,000*l*., in 25*l*. shares, to be provided by the Liskeard and Looe Canal, and loan, 4,000*l*. Estimate, 12,000*l*. Land for extra purposes, ten acres ; compulsory purchase, 3 years ; completion of works, five years.

Working arrangements with Liskeard and Caradon, which has been open since 1846,
Offices—Liskeard.

224.—LLANELLY.

Incorporated (dock portion) by 9 Geo. IV., cap. 91 (1828), and (railway) by Wm. IV., cap. 96 (1835), for a line from Llanelly, to Llandilo, with branches to Cwmamman Spitty, Mynyddmawr, Brynamman, &c.

By 17 Vic., cap. 169 (6th August, 1853), branches were granted to Cylyrchan (2 furlongs) and Pistillishaff (3 furlongs) from its new line to Llandilo. Extension from Cross Inn Junction to Llandilo, 7⅛ miles. The line forms a junction with the South Wales at Llanelly, and extends 28¼ miles, with the Vale of Towy, 11¼ miles. Productive 65¼ miles.

By 23 and 24 Vic., cap. 161 (23rd July, 1860), the company was empowered to take a lease in perpetuity of the Vale of Towy. The company were also authorised to issue share and debenture bonds to a further amount for various purposes, to the extent of 155,000*l*.

By 24 and 25 Vic., cap. 217 (1st August, 1861). the company was authorised to construct a line to Swansea, with branches to Llanrhidian, and to the Carmarthen and Cardigan. Length, 30 miles. Capital, 270,000*l*. in shares, and 89,900*l*. on loan. Opened to Carmarthen, 13¼ miles, on the 1st June, 1865 ; to Swansea, 12½ miles, on 14th December, 1867.

By 25 and 26 Vic., cap. 161 (17th July, 1862), the company was authorised to make certain deviations in the Swansea and Carmarthen lines, to lay down narrow gauge rails on the Carmarthen and Cardigan, and to raise new capital of 25,000*l*., in shares. and 8,320*l*. on loan. Also to enter into agreements with the Vale of Neath and South Wales.

By 26 and 27 Vic., cap. 103 (29th June, 1863), the company was authorised to raise additional capital, namely 114,000*l*. for the Swansea lines, and 8,000*l*. for the Carmarthen line, with 40,000*l*. on mortgage. Among the new works sanctioned the principal was a branch to the south side of the south docks at Swansea. Length, 5 miles. An agreement has been made with the Duke of Beaufort for a lease of wharf lands and frontage on that side of the dock, with regard to which arrangements have been made with the Swansea Harbour trustees and the Vale of Neath, whereby those parties as well as the company make use of them.

By 27 Vic., cap. 1 (28th April, 1864), the company was authorised to re-arrange its capital, and to affix preferences to certain parts thereof, as well as to divide portions into half shares.

By 27 and 28 Vic., cap. 218 (25th July, 1864), the powers of the company were extended in regard to deviations and crossings, and also to construct a line, called the Gower Road Junction, to connect with the Great Western at Gower Road. Length, ½ mile. Capital, 18,000*l*. in shares, and 6,000*l*. on loan.

By 28 and 29 Vic., cap. 158 (29th June. 1865), the company was authorised to raise additional capital to the extent of 120,000*l*. in shares, and 40,000*l*. on loan.

By 28 and 29 Vic.. cap. 349 (5th July, 1865), the company was authorised to extend the line to Mumblesj Swansea Bay. Length, 2¾ miles. Capital, 36,000l. in shares and 12,000l. on loan.

By 29 and 30 Vic., cap. 289 (30th July, 1866), the Llanelly was authorised to construct a pier at the Mumbles. Capital, 40,000l. in shares, and 13,300l. on loan.

By 30 Vic., cap. 93 (17th June, 1867), the Llanelly obtained further powers in extension of time for completion of works, and for amalgamation of the capital of the separate undertakings, &c. The Central Wales, the Central Wales Extension, and the Knighton were also authorised to subscribe 50,000l. each to the Llanelly.

VALE OF TOWY.—This line, which is a virtual continuation of the communication to Llandovery, was opened on 1st April, 1858. By an Act of 1858 the two lines might be worked under one management. The terms were : Capital of the Vale of Towy not to exceed 50,000l. in shares, and 18,000l. in debentures—together, 68,000l. The Llanelly to pay interest not exceeding 5 per cent. on the debenture capital, and on the share capital 2 per cent. for five years ; 3 per cent. for next five years ; with power to the Llanelly to determine the lease at the end of the fifth year, and giving a year's notice, and paying a penalty of 1,000l. to the Vale of Towy. This line has since been jointly leased by the London and North Western and the Llanelly, so as the more efficiently to develop the traffic on the Central Wales, &c.

REVENUE.—The earnings during the half-year ending 31st December were, on the original undertaking, 24,012l., the working expenses, 11,177l. Out of the net income of 12,834l.. the sum of 2,549l. was paid for hire and purchase of wagons and engines. From the balance there were written off 626l. for bad and doubtful debts. From 9,665l. remaining the rent of the Vale of Towy and debenture interest had to be deducted. After payment of the preference stock, there were 3,926l. left for dividend on the ordi-nary stock, which would have permitted payment at the rate of 5 per cent., but the directors recommended only 3½, which left 478l. to next account. The income of the original undertaking for the year 1867, amounted to 45,377l., showing an increase of 7,061l. over the receipts of the previous year. The net receipts on the Carmarthen line was 1,163l. The dividend on the ordinary stock of the original undertaking. for the half-year ending 30th June, was reduced to the rate of 3 per cent. per annum. The net earnings of the Carmarthen were 488l., which was applied in part payment of the interest on debentures. The amount due by the Swansea lines to the original under-taking is 16,425l.

CAPITAL.—The receipts on the original undertaking to 30th June were 389,708l., of which 13,287l. remained on hand.

Scale of Voting.—For evrey 25l. up to 250l. nominal value of shares, 1 vote ; for every sum of 125l. beyond 250l. and up to 2,500l., 1 additional vote ; and for every sum of 250l. beyond 2,500l., 1 additional vote.

Certificates must accompany transfer deeds. Registration fee, 2s. 6d.

No. of Directors.—Maximum, 12 ; quorum, 3. *Qualification,* 1,000l., nominal. Com-mittees, 3 and 5 ; quorum, 2.

DIRECTORS :

2 Chairman—JOHN BIDDULPH, Esq., Swansea.

1 Deputy-Chairman—JOHN TOWNSEND KIRKWOOD, Esq., Yeo Vale, Bideford.

2 David Lewis, Esq., Stradey, Llanelly.
2 Henry Lewis Smale, Esq., 2, Dean's Court, Doctors' Commons, E.C.
3 Charles William Christie, Esq., 10, Hyde Park Square, W.
3 James Kitson, Esq., Elmete Hall, Leeds.
3 Major Rice Watkins, Llwynybrain.

1 William Blount, Esq., Orchhill House, Gerard's Cross.
1 Samuel Hawksley Burbury, Esq., New Square, Lincoln's Inn, W.C.
1 Charles Townsend Murdoch, Esq., 1, Pall Mall East, S.W.
1 John Worrall Walker, Esq., Highfield House, Hawkhurst, Kent.

1, Retire in January, 1869 ; 2, January, 1870 ; 3, January, 1871.

OFFICERS—Supt. and Sec., Richard Glascodine, Llanelly ; Eng. E. H. Lloyd, Llan-dilo, Carmarthenshire ; Solicitors, Maynard, Son, and Co., 57, Coleman Street, E.C.; Bankers, Cocks, Biddulph, and Co., 43, Charing Cross, S.W.

Head Offices—Llanelly, Carmarthenshire.

225.—LLANGOLLEN AND CORWEN.

Incorporated by 23 and 24 Vic., cap, 188 (6th August, 1860), to construct a single line from the Vale of Llangollen to Corwen, to join the Denbigh Ruthin and Corwen, and thus complete communication from Shrewsbury to the Chester and Holyhead. Length, 10 miles. Capital, 90,000l., in 10l. shares. Loans, 30,000l. Arrangements with Great Western and Vale of Llangollen. Opened, 1st May, 1865.

The line continues to be satisfactorily worked by the Great Western. The dividends on the ordinary stock for the year have been at the rate of 2½ per cent. per annum.

CAPITAL.—The statement of this account to 30th June, gave the receipts and disbursements as follows:—

Received.		Expended.	
Calls	£88,900	Parliamentary and law	£3,975
Eorfeited shares, calls received, prior to forfeitures	40	Engineering	1,000
Mortgages	30,000	Land and compensation	14,262
		Works and permanent way	94,541
		Electric telegraph	372
		Directors, secretary, auditors, stationery, &c.	971
		Commission and interest, including interest on debenture loans.	3,127
		Balance	620
	£118,940		£118,940

No. of Directors—9; minimum, 5; quorum, 3.   Qualification, 500l.

DIRECTORS:

Chairman—CHARLES JOHN TOTTENHAM, Esq., Plâs Berwyn, Llangollen.

Sir W. W. Wynn. Bart., M.P., Wynnstay, Ruabon, and 18, St. James's Square, S.W.
William Henry Darby, Esq., Brymbo, Wrexham.
William Wagstaff, Esq., Corwen.

J. R. Ormsby Gore, Esq., M.P., The Mount, Oswestry, and 11, Park Place, St. James's S.W.
John Robertson, Esq., Siamberwen, Llangollen.
John Taylor, Esq., Hatherton Hall, Stafford.

All eligible for re-election.

OFFICERS.—Sec., Charles Richards; Eng., Henry Robertson; Solicitors, Longueville, Williams, Jones, and Williams, Oswestry, and C. Richards, Llangollen; Auditors, William Patchet and George Haswell.
Offices—Llangollen.

226.—LLANTRISSANT AND TAFF VALE.

Incorporated by 24 Vic., cap. 51 (17th June, 1861), to construct a line from the Taff Vale, at Llantwit Vairdre, to Llantrissant, with a branch to the Ely Valley and another to Llantrissant Common.   Length, 5½ miles.   Capital. 40,000l., in 10l. shares.   Loans, 13,000l.   Power was taken to purchase the Llantwit railway, and to authorise the Taff Vale to subscribe 13,000l., also to lay down the narrow gauge on the Ely Valley.

The Taff Vale undertake maintenance of railway and works and entire management of the traffic, and collection of tolls and charges incidental thereto, and pay the Llantrissant 5 per cent. upon share capital of 40,000l., interest upon debenture debt for the time being, with an additional annual payment of 250l. for management.   In operation, 5½ miles.

By 29 and 30 Vic., cap. 248 (23rd July, 1866), the Llantrissant and Taff Vale was authorised to construct extensions to the Penarth and the Ely Valley.   Length, 10 miles. Capital, 120,000l. in share, and 47,000l. on loan.   Works in progress.

CAPITAL.—The statement of this account, to 30th June, set forth an expenditure of 76,274l., the receipts having been as under :—

Capital, 4,000 in 10l. shares	£40,000
Ditto 2,100 ditto on account	17,152
Mortgage debentures	13,000
Balance	6,122=£76,274

No. of Directors—6; minimum, 4; quorum, 3.   Qualification, 300l.

DIRECTORS:

1 Chairman—JAMES POOLE, Esq., Wick House, Durdham Down, Bristol.

2 William Done Bushell, Esq., Cambrian Place, Cardiff.
2 Henry Jones Evans, Esq., Brecon Old Bank, Cardiff.

3 John Whitlock Nicholl Carne, Esq., D.C.L., Dimland Castle, Glamorganshire.

The rotation is indicated by the figures, 1, 2, 3.   All eligible for re-election.
Directors elected at the half-yearly meeting in February.

OFFICERS.—Sec., Fredk. Marwood; Eng., George Fisher; Auditors, Wilberforce Tribe and Fulke L.W. Barnard, Bristol; Bankers, Wilkins and Co., Cardiff.
Offices—Taff Vale railway station, Cardiff.

227.—LLYNVI AND OGMORE.

An amalgamation of the Llynvi Valley and Ogmore Valley systems, the capital being kept distinct.

LLYNVI VALLEY.—Originally incorporated by 9 and 10 Vic., cap. 353, and various other Acts, all of which are of a purely local character, and refer to creation of capital by which to convert the original tramway into a broad gauge line in connection with the South Wales. By 18 Vic., cap. 50 (June 15th, 1855), Parliament conferred the long-sought power to make a locomotive line on the broad gauge, from the end of the valley to Bridgend. The Act authorised new capital to the extent of 130,920l., borrowing powers, 17,425l. The length of the main line from Tywith Bridge to the South Wales is 9¼ miles, of the branch from Foce Toll-house to Ynis-awdre, is 2¼ miles. Opened August, 1861.

By 25 and 26 Vic., cap. 115 (30th June, 1862), the company was authorised to raise new capital to the extent or 40,000l. in shares at 5 per cent., and 3,300l. on loan.

By 27 and 28 Vic., cap. 48 (23rd June, 1864), arrangements were authorised between the Llynvi Valley and the Ogmore in respect to improvements in the harbour of Porth-cawl and other works. Also to construct a short line of half a mile in length. Capital to each 30,000l. in shares, and 10,000l. on loan.

By 29 and 30 Vic., cap. 117 (28th June, 1866), the Llynvi Valley was authorised to con-struct two short extensions and to acquire additional lands. Length, 2¾ miles. Capital, 100,000l. in shares, and 33,000l. on loan.

OGMORE VALLEY.—Incorporated by 26 and 27 Vic., cap. 139 (13th July, 1863), to con-struct railways in Glamorganshire, from the Llanvi Valley to Nant-y-Moel, and a branch. Length, 9 miles. Capital, 90,000l., in 20l. shares; loans, 30,000l. Arrangements with Llynvi Valley. Opened, 1st August, 1865.

By 27 and 28 Vic., cap. 48 (23rd June, 1864), arrangements were authorised between the Ogmore and the Llynvi Valley, in respect to improvements in the harbour of Porth-cawl and other works. Also to construct a short line (length, ½ mile). Capital, to each 30,000l. in shares, and 10,000l. on loan.

By 29 and 30 Vic., cap. 252 (23rd July, 1866), the Ogmore was authorised to construct five short extensions in Glamorganshire. Length, 11½ miles. Capital, 123,000l. in shares, and 41,000l. on loan. Amalgamated with Llynvi Valley under the name of "Llynvi and Ogmore" by 29 and 30 Vic., cap. 120 (28th June, 1866).

By 30 and 31 Vic., cap. 95 (15th July, 1867), the Llynvi and Ogmore was authorised to increase its capital by the sum of 100,000l in shares, and 33,300l. on loan. Also to enter into arrangements with the South Wales Mineral.

ELY VALLEY EXTENSION.—Incorporated by 26 and 27 Vic , cap. 199 (28th July, 1863), to construct a line from the western terminus of the Gellyrhaidd branch of the Ely Valley to Pelfachgoch ; broad gauge. Length, 1½ mile. Capital, 12,000l., in 10l. shares; loans, 4,000l. Arrangements with Ely Valley and Great Western. Amalgamated with Ogmore Valley by 28 and 29 Vic., cap. 205 (5th July, 1865).

REVENUE.- This account for the half-year ending 30th June showed that 20,579l. had been received, and 10,034l. expended on working, and 627l. for interest on loans and on wagon purchases, leaving a balance of 4,275l., which, with balance on hand, admitted of dividends being declared at the rate of 5 per cent. per annum on the first and second preference shares, at the rate of 5 per cent. on the preference redeemable shares, and at the rate of 1¼ per cent. per annum on the Llynvi ordinary stock, leaving a balance of 40l. The amount outstanding for dividends declared in September, 1867, had been reduced from 9,112l. to 4,279l. by proprietors accepting preference redeemable shares for the difference. The dividend declared in March, 1868, had been in like manner reduced from 3,790l. to 3,378l., which, with the dividends proposed to be now declared, would make a total amount of 12,413l. due on this account. The directors had used every endeavour also to raise money by the issue of preference redeemable shares, but they had not succeeded in placing 1,076 altogether, for which they had received 11,016l. This amount had been appropriated partly in payment of urgent claims and partly for works which were now almost completed. The certainty that the additional traffic and harbour rates would bring a considerable increase of net revenue afforded a better assurance that preference redeemable shares would now be taken up by the public, and the company relieved from financial difficulty.

CAPITAL.—The receipts and expenditure to the 30th June, 1868, were detailed as follows:—

Received.		*Expended.*	
Llynvi ordinary stock and shares	£112,180	Works, to date of amalgamation	£452,510
Ogmore ordinary stock	153,020	Parliamentary and law	9,254
1st preference stock (1855)	130,920	Engineering, surveying, and land	
2nd do. (1862)	20 730	valuers	5,966
Preference redeemable shares	19,294	Direction	150
(Ogmore Valley Railways Act, 1866)		Office expenses, printing, &c.	370
Loans on security :—	436,144	Land and compensation	3,333
Preference redeemable shares..	16,500	Stations, workshops, &c.	7,850
2nd preference stock	14,227	Permanent way and sidings	12,751
Debentures	143,216	Rolling stock	59,402
Bond for land compensation.	1,200	Harbour works	114,925
		Interest account	4,579
	£611,288	Discount on preference redeem-	
Balance	62,840	able shares	3,033
	£674,129		£674,129

*No. of Directors—*12; maximum, 14; minimum, 6; quorum, 3. *Qualification,* 500l.

DIRECTORS:

Chairman—ALEXANDER MACGREGOR, Esq., 7, Sussex Place, Hyde Park Gardens, W.

Deputy-Chairman—ALEXANDER BROGDEN, Esq., M.P., Ulverston.

Henry Brogden, Esq., Mersey Lea, Brooklands, Sale, Manchester.
James Brogden, Esq., Tondû, Bridgend.
John Halcomb, Esq., Chieveley, near Newbury, Berks.

Piers F. Legh, Esq.,Grange, near Ulverston.
Archibald F. Paull, Esq., 33, Devonshire Place, Portland Place, W.
Philip Rose, Esq., 6, Victoria Street, Westminster, S.W.

OFFICERS.—Sec., George F. Saunders; Eng., R. P. Brereton; Traff. Man., George Howell; Loco. Supt., John Routledge; Auditors, Wm. W. Deloitte and Robert Fletcher; Solicitors, Baxter, Rose, Norton, and Co., and C. and H. Tahourdin; Bankers, National Provincial Bank of England, 112, Bishopsgate Street, E.C., and National Provincial Bank of England, Bridgend.

Offices—Bridgend, Glamorganshire.

228.—LONDON AND BLACKWALL.

Incorporated by 6 and 7 Wm. IV., cap. 123, for a line from Minories to Blackwall. Cost, 266,000l. per mile.

By 18 and 19 Vic., cap. 90 (June 26th, 1855), the company were authorised to create 100,000l. additional capital for widening the line. The amount to be raised on loan is 33,000l. The length of line to be widened, but which is partly on land already acquired by the company, is 2 miles 3 chains and 70 links. Estimate, 100,000l.; period of completion, five years. Arrangements with Great Eastern, and London Tilbury and Southend, which see.

By 23 and 24 Vic., cap. 123 (3rd July, 1860), the company was authorised to raise 300,000l., to effect various improvements, and to construct a branch to the London Docks, at a cost limited to 73,555l., upon which the Dock Company guarantee interest at 5 per cent.

By 25 Vic., cap 7 (16th May, 1862), the company was authorised to construct new works, and to take additional lands, and also to attach a preference of not exceeding 5 per cent. to the capital created under the Act of 1860.

By 27 and 28 Vic., cap. 219 (25th July, 1864), the company was authorised to enlarge several stations, and to improve other works as well as widen part of the line. Capital, 75,000l. in shares, and 24,000l. on loan.

LONDON, BLACKWALL, AND MILLWALL EXTENSION.—By 28 Vic., cap. 116 (19th June, 1865), the Blackwall was authorised to construct lines in the parishes of Stepney, Poplar, and Limehouse. Length, 5¼ miles. Capital, 250,000l. in shares, and 83,000l. on loan. Arrangements with Great Eastern, which is to work the line.

By 31 and 32 Vic., cap. 120 (13th July, 1868), an extension of time for completion of works till 1871 was obtained.

GREAT EASTERN.—By 28 Vic., cap. 100 (19th June, 1865), the Blackwall was leased to the Great Eastern under a guarantee of 4½ per cent. on its ordinary stock; the London and North Western, the Great Northern, and the Midland, obtaining running powers over certain portions of the line.

CAPITAL.—The following is a statement of the capital account to 30th June, 1868:—

	Received.	Due.	Total.
Consolidated stock (1,459,050l.), being 145,905 shares converted into stock, at 10l. per share	£1,452,870	....	£1,452,870
Preference stock, (250,055l.). 4½ per cent., being 17,051 new shares, 1860, and 21,419 preference shares, 1862, converted into stock at 6l. 10s. each	250,055	....	250,055
Extension shares	....	£23,075	23,075
	£1,702,925	£23,075	£1,726,000
Debentures			552,230

The expenditure to 30th June amounted to 2,252,713l., leaving a balance on hand of 2,441l.

The accounts are made up to 30th June and 31st December in every year; and the statutory meetings held in February and August.

Certificates are required with transfer deeds. Registration fee, 2s. 6d. each seller.

DIRECTORS:

Chairman—FRANCIS MACNAGHTEN, Esq., Chester Square, S.W.

Deputy-Chairman—CHARLES WHETHAM, Esq., Gordon Square, W.C.

F. W. Haigh, Esq., Bickley, Bromley, Kent. | John Venables, Esq., 34, Aldgate, E.

OFFICERS.—Sec., John F. Kennell; Registrar, Samuel Le Cren; Surveyor, William Tite, M.P.; Auditors, George Smith and Thomas Wrake Ratcliff; Solicitors, Pearce and Co., Gresham House, Broad Street, E.C., and Hollingsworth, Tyerman, and Green, 4, East India Avenue, Leadenhall Street, E.C.

Offices—Fenchurch Street, E.C.

229.—LONDON, BRIGHTON, AND SOUTH COAST.

An†amalgamation of the Croydon and Brighton, under the powers of 9 and 10 Vic., cap. 283 (27th July, 1846). By the Act of amalgamation, each holder of a Brighton 50l. share received 50l. of stock; and each holder of a Croydon 20l. share, 18l. 10s. of stock in new company. Before amalgamation, the Brighton had created 25,694 quarter or 12½l. shares, in substitution of a like number of loan notes of 10l. each, in accordance with the terms on which those loan notes were originally issued : that involved a loss of 2½l. per quarter (or 10l. per whole) share, loss, 66,735l.; in like manner the Croydon had previously issued 4,280 shares (part of the above 55,340 shares, nominally 20l., but on which only 15l. had been received, thereby losing 3½l. per share. The additions to capital taking dividend (being balance of loss on these conversions and on the amalgamation) amounted to 429,753l.

By 21 and 22 Vic., cap. 57 (28th June, 1858), the company is authorised to create additional capital to the extent of 200,000l. By the same Act authority is given to purchase on lease the East Grinstead and Wimbledon and Croydon.

By 20 and 21 Vic., cap. 143, and 21 and 22 Vic., cap. 104 (10th August, 1857), the company was authorised to purchase on lease the West End and Crystal Palace.

By 21 and 22 Vic., cap. 84 (12th July, 1858), the company was authorised to construct a line between Shoreham and Henfield. Capital, 155,000l. in shares, and 50,000l. by loan. Length, 17¼ miles. Opened September, 1861.

By 22 and 23 Vic., cap. 69 (1st August, 1859), the company was authorised to make (1) a deviation (West Grinstead deviation) from the authorised line of the Shoreham and Henfield ; (2) a short line (Norwood Junction) in the parish of Croydon, to connect the main line with Farnborough extension of the West End of London and Crystal Palace ; (3) a widening of the bridge carrying the main line over the Montpelier Road, near Brighton ; (4) an embankment in substitution for the viaduct on the Horsham branch ; (5) for the improvement of their stations, to purchase additional lands, and to stop up a footpath ; (6) to take on lease or purchase the undertakings of the Mid Sussex and the Lewes and Uckfield. Additional capital for new works, additional land, &c., 100,000l.; loan, 33,000l.

By 23 and 24 Vic., cap. 171 (23rd July, 1860), the company was authorised to make certain alterations in its coast lines, and in the West End and Crystal Palace. The company was also authorised to subscribe 30,000l. to the Midhurst, and also to raise new capital to the extent of 355,500l. in shares, and 116,833l. on mortgage.

By 23 and 24 Vic., cap. 109 (3rd July, 1860), the company was authorised to construct a line from Croydon to Balham Hill, on the West End and Crystal Palace. Length, 5 miles 14 chains. New capital, 103,000l., and 33,000l. by mortgage. Opened 1st December, 1862.

By 25 and 26 Vic., cap. 68 (30th June, 1862), the company was authorised to enlarge the stations at |London Bridge and Bricklayers' Arms, and to own and work steam vessels. New capital, 355,500l. in preference shares, and 116,500l. on loan.

By 25 and 26 Vic., cap. 78 (30th June, 1862), the company were authorised to construct new lines in Surrey and Sussex, including a junction at Brixton with the Chatham and Dover, and a line from Newhaven to Seaford. Length, 5½ miles. New capital, 340,000l. in preference shares, and 113,000l. on loan.

By 26 and 27 Vic., cap. 137 (13th July, 1863), the company was authorised to construct a line from Dorking to Leatherhead. Length, 5 miles. New capital, 90,000l., and 30,000l. on loan. Opened 11th March, 1867.

By 26 and 27 Vic., cap. 142 (13th July, 1863), the company was authorised to construct certain new lines and extensions in Camberwell and Lambeth. Length, 4½ miles. New capital, 300,000l., and 100,000l. on loans.

By 26 and 27 Vic., cap. 192 (21st July, 1864), the company was authorised to construct a new line at Croydon, 2½ miles, and a tramway at Newhaven. New capital, 100,000l. in shares, and 33,300l. on loan.

By 26 and 27 Vic., cap. 218 (28th July, 1863), the company was authorised to construct new lines in connection with South London, Tooting, &c. Length, 14¼ miles. New capital, 360,000l. in shares, and 120,000l. on loan.

By 26 and 27 Vic., cap. 227 (28th July, 1863), the company obtained power to widen and improve the line to Pimlico, so as to obtain independent access to Victoria Station. New capital, 450,000*l.* in shares, and 150,000*l.* on loan.

By 27 Vic., cap. 35 (13th May, 1864), the company was authorised to provide station accommodation at Kemptown, and to construct a new line in connection therewith. Length, 1¾ miles. Capital, 75,000*l.* in shares, and 25,000*l.* on loan.

By 27 and 28 Vic., cap. 123 (23rd June, 1864), the company was authorised to construct lines from the Ouse Viaduct to Uckfield and Hailsham. Length, 20 miles. Capital, 330,000*l.* in shares, and 126,000*l.* by loan.

By 27 and 28 Vic., cap. 154 (13th June, 1864), the company was authorised to run steam vessels between Littlehampton and certain places on the coast of France, as well as to and from the Channel Islands. Capital, 100,000*l.* in shares, and 25,000*l.* on loan.

By 27 and 28 Vic., cap. 172 (14th July, 1864), the company was authorised to construct lines between Tunbridge Wells and Eastbourne. Length, 15¾ miles. Capital, 250,000*l.* in shares, and 83,000*l.* on loan. Interchange of facilities with South Eastern.

By 27 and 28 Vic., cap. 274 (25th July, 1864), the company was authorised to construct certain lines and works in and near Battersea. Length, 4¾ miles. Capital, 430,000*l.* in shares, and 143,000*l.* on loan.

By 27 and 28 Vic., cap. 314 (29th July, 1864), the company was authorised to construct several short lines in Surrey and Sussex. Length, 7¾ miles. New capital, 390,000*l.* in shares, and 130,000*l.* on loan. Also to amalgamate the Horsham, the Guildford, the Bognor, the Uckfield, the Banstead, and the Groombridge undertakings.

BANSTEAD AND EPSOM DOWNS.—Incorporated by 25 and 26 Vic., cap. 158 (17th July, 1862), to construct a line from the Sutton Station of the Croydon and Epsom branch of the Brighton, to Banstead and Epsom Downs. Length, 4¼ miles. Capital, 85,000*l.* in 10*l.* shares, and 28,300*l.* on loan. Amalgamated with Brighton by Act of 1864. Opened 22nd May, 1865.

BOGNOR.—Incorporated by 24 and 25 Vic., cap. 120 (11th July, 1861), for making a line from Eastergate to Bognor. Length, 3½ miles. Capital, 30,000*l.* in shares, and 10,000*l.* by loan. Amalgamated with the Brighton by Act of 1864, but amalgamation not yet completed.

UCKFIELD AND TUNBRIDGE WELLS.—Incorporated by 24 and 25 Vic., cap. 174 (22nd July, 1861), to construct a line at Uckfield to Tunbridge Wells. Length, 15 miles 18 chains. Capital, 200,000*l.*, in 20*l.* shares. Loans, 65,000*l.* Amalgamated with the Brighton by the Act of 1864.

HORSHAM AND GUILDFORD DIRECT.—Incorporated by 23 and 24 Vic., cap. 180 (6th August, 1860), to construct a line from the Mid-Sussex (Brighton) to Godalming branch of the South Western, at Guildford. Length, 14 miles. Capital, 160,000*l.* Loans, 50,000*l.* Amalgamated with the Brighton by Act of 1864.

MID-SUSSEX AND MIDHURST JUNCTION.—Incorporated by 22 and 23 Vic., cap. 125 (13th August, 1859), for making a railway from the Coultershaw branch of Mid-Sussex to Midhurst. Capital, 70,000*l.*, in 10*l.* shares ; loans, 20,000*l.* Length, 5½ miles. By 25 and 26 Vic., cap. 210 (7th August, 1862), the company obtained till 1863 to complete its works, and also power to sell or lease the undertaking to the Brighton. Opened 15th December, 1866.

WEST LONDON EXTENSION.—The Brighton joins the London and North Western, the Great Western, and South Western, in providing capital for the extension of this line to Pimlico. The estimated outlay is 555,000*l.*, and the proportion contributed by the Brighton is 92,500*l.*, and took effect from 1st July, 1859.

VICTORIA STATION.—Opened 1st October, 1860. The Brighton owns half of this station, and the London Chatham and Dover and Great Western are accommodated in the other portion.

WEST END OF LONDON AND CRYSTAL PALACE.—Incorporated by 17 Vic., cap. 180 (4th August, 1853), for a line from the London and South Western (Windsor and Richmond) to the Crystal Palace Park (5¾ miles) ; branch to the London and Brighton, at Norwood, 1¾ mile ; branch to Chelsea Suspension Bridge, with wharf and pier on Thames, south side, 2½ miles. The following arrangement with the Brighton was sanctioned on the 16th May, 1859 :—That the Brighton pays the company's fixed charges, viz., the interest on the existing mortgage bonds ; 7 per cent. per annum on the 220,000*l.* B. shares ; 6*l.* per cent. per annum on the amount of the 6*l.* per cent. shares now paid up, commencing on the 1st July, 1859, and to pay a perpetual dividend of 4 per cent. per annum on the 220,000*l.* A shares, commencing from 1st January, 1865. The purchase-money of the line between Norwood and Bromley was paid January, 1864.

MID-SUSSEX.—Incorporated by 20 and 21 Vic., cap. 133 (10th August, 1857), to construct a line from the Brighton, at Horsham, to Pulborough, with a branch to Petworth. Length, 17 miles. Opened 10th October, 1859. Purchased by the Brighton, on 31st May, 1860, for 100,000*l.* 4 per cent. preference stock, the Brighton taking the mortgage debt, 50,000*l.*

LEWES AND UCKFIELD.—Incorporated by 20 and 21 Vic., cap. 60 (27th July, 1857). to make a railway from Lewes to Uckfield. Capital, 59,000*l.* in 50*l.* shares ; loans, 16,500*l.* Length, 7¼ miles. Its termini are at the end, a junction with the Keymer branch of the Brighton, in the parish of Hamsey, and at the other end the town of Uckfield. Opened 18th October, 1858. Purchased by the Brighton on 31st May, 1860, for 33,900*l.* 4 per cent. preference stock, and takes the mortgage debt. The resolution of 31st May, was as follows :—" That for the purpose of the transfer to this company of the Lewes and Uckfield, the company, under the powers conferred upon them by the company's Act, 1859, do create and issue to the Lewes and Uckfield, or their nominees, 33,900*l.* of stock in the undertaking of the company, and for the purpose of the transfer to this company of the Mid-Sussex the company do create and issue to that company, or their nominees, 100,000*l.* of stock in the undertaking of the company, the whole of such stock, instead of entitling the holders thereof to participate in the profits of the company, to have attached thereto a preferential fixed dividend of 4 per cent. per annum, payable half-yearly, at the same time and with the other dividends of the company ; but such stock not to confer upon the holders thereof any right of voting at meetings of the company, or any qualification, or any right or privilege, except the right to receive the fixed specified dividend thereon. And also for the purpose of such transfers respectively, that the company borrow on mortgages or bonds on the security of the undertaking of the company, and upon such terms and conditions as the directors may deem expedient, such sums of money as may be necessary for paying off any mortgages or bonds exclusively charged on the Lewes and Uckfield and the Mid-Sussex respectively."

EAST GRINSTEAD.—Incorporated by 17 Vic., cap. 88 (8th July, 1853), for a line from the Brighton, at Three Bridges, to East Grinstead. Length, 6⅝ miles. Opened 9th July, 1855. Capital, 50,000*l.* This line was purchased in January, 1865, for 50,000*l.*, 4 per cent. stock, the Brighton taking upon itself the mortgage debt.

ST. LEONARDS.—By 28 Vic., cap. 50 (26th May, 1865), the company was authorised to construct new lines from St. Leonards to the Ouse Valley and the Tunbridge Wells and Eastbourne   Length, 18 miles.   New capital, 300,000*l.* in shares, and 100,000*l.* by mortgage. By 29 and 30 Vic., cap. 234 (16th July, 1866), the company was authorised to construct several new lines in substitution of those sanctioned as above ; also to raise new capital to the extent of 100,000*l.* in shares, and 33,000*l.* on loan.

ADDITIONAL POWERS.—By 28 and 29 Vic.. cap. 66 (19th June, 1865), the company obtained power to construct several short junctions in the county of Surrey. Length, 1½ mile. Capital, 90,000*l.*, in shares, and 30,000*l.* on loan.

TOOTING, MERTON, AND WIMBLEDON.—Incorporated by Act 27 and 28 Vic., cap. 325 (29th July, 1864), for lines from Wimbledon, *via* Tooting and Merton, to join the Brighton line at Streatham. Length, 5¼ miles. Capital, 95,000*l.* Loans, 31,600*l.* By 28 and 29 Vic., cap. 273 (5th July, 1865), this undertaking was vested jointly in the Brighton and South Western, and a further junction of half a mile, authorised. New capital, 52,500*l.* in shares, and 17,500*l.* on loans.

CAPITAL AND POWERS.—By 29 and 30 Vic., cap. 281 (30th July, 1866), the company obtained power to construct several new junctions, extending to 1¼ mile ; to purchase additional lands: and also to vest the Crystal Palace line, the Victoria Station, the Uckfield, the Guildford, the Dorking, the Groombridge, the Banstead, the Uckfield and Tunbridge Wells, the East Grinstead, and the Tooting in the Brighton. By the same Act the company's powers in regard to raising money on these several undertakings were consolidated, and new capital authorised to the extent of 500,000*l.* in shares, and 166,600*l.* on loan. Power was also given to create 5 per cent. consols in lieu of the different preference shares issued at various times. The Brighton was also authorised to acquire the Mid-Sussex, and to subscribe to the Surrey and Sussex and the Chichester and Midhurst.

By 30 and 31 Vic., cap. 163 (25th July, 1867), the company was authorised to execute new works as well as to effect alterations in those already authorised ; to acquire additional lands in Surrey, Sussex, and Kent ; to extend the time for completion of the Ouse Valley, the Tunbridge Wells and Eastbourne, and the St. Leonards for three years. Also to abandon construction of the first junction authorised by Act of 1865. Also to issue ordinary stock not taken up, at such discount as a special meeting might determine.

By 31 and 32 Vic., cap. 134 (13th July, 1868), the company was authorised to abandon the Ouse Valley, the St. Leonards, and the Eastbourne, the lands acquired for which to be sold within two years. An extension of time for sale of other superfluous lands was obtained for ten years. Authority was also obtained to raise new capital to the extent of 1,000,000*l.* in shares, at a discount, one-third additional of the sum realised to be borrowed on mortgage. The fares on the company's system were also raised to 2¾*d.* first class express, and 2*d.* per mile second class. In ordinary trains the fares were raised to 2¼*d.* per mile first class ; 1¾*d.* second class ; and 1*d.* third class.

MILEAGE.—In operation 365 miles.

REVENUE.—The gross revenue of the half-year ending 31st December was 709,654*l.*, to which, for the purpose of comparison with the corresponding half-year of 1866, must be added the tolls from other companies, amounting to 4,885*l.*, showing an increase of

53,896*l.* over the corresponding period of 18^{.6}. The gross revenue of the year 1867 therefore, amounted to 1,262,650*l.*, as compared with 1,189,944*l.* in 1866, showing an increase of 72,706*l.*

The subjoined statement furnishes a comparison of receipts and expenses for three half-years :—

Half-years ending	Dec. 31, 1866.	June 30, 1867.	Dec. 31. 1867.
Miles open	314¾	335	335¾
Total traffic receipts	£643,541	£534,559	£700,793
Maintenance of way, &c.	41,184	69,710	70,126
Locomotive power	89,339	102,033	104,329
Carriage and wagon department	31,904	42,665	30,829
Coaching traffic charges	118,681	94,290	83,749
Goods traffic charges	39,857	37,958	38,942
General charges	8,247	9,277	11.412
Law and parliamentary charges	2,180	44,803	13,359
Rates and taxes	23,005	27,006	32.217
Government duty	16,147	12,611	17,782
Tolls to other companies,rents of leased lines, &c.	26,913	6,479	4,188
Total working expenses and renewals	£397,457	£446,832	£406,933

The interest payable on the various preference stocks prior to 1865 amounted to 207,054*l.* for the year 1867, and the balance available sufficed to pay this interest, carrying forward the sum of 1,008*l.*

A similar table for the following half-year, with its comparisons, produced the following results :—

Half-years ending	June 30, 1867.	Dec. 31, 1867.	June 30, 1868.
Miles open	335	335¾	336¼
Total traffic receipts	£534,559	£700,793	£575,358
Maintenance of way, &c.	69,710	70,126	£53,188
Locomotive Power	102,033	104,329	92,877
Carriage and wagon department	42,665	30,829	25,137
Coaching traffic charges	94,290	83,749	72,067
Goods traffic charges	37,958	38,942	38,248
General charges	9,277	11.412	9,560
Law and parliamentary charges	44,803	13,359	9,958
Rates and taxes	27,006	32,217	24,001
Government duty	12,611	17,782	13,945
Tolls to other companies, rents of leased lines, &c.	2,184	4,188	2,255
Total working expenses and renewals	£442,537	£406,933	£341,236

The receipts were thus increased by 40,799*l.* over the corresponding half-year, while the expenses diminished by no less than 101,301*l.*, so that the increase of net profit amounted to 142,100*l.* The accounts indicated a balance of revenue over expenditure of 243,578*l.*, to which must be added the balance from last half-year, 1,003*l.*; making a total of 244,587*l.* Of this the payment of debenture and other interest required 94,908*l.*, leaving available towards payment of the preference interest, 149,679*l.*, which sufficed to pay the full half-year's interest on all the preference stocks up to the issue of 1,661,335*l.* 5 per cent. stock No. 6, 1866, on which half the half-year's interest was paid, amounting in all to 146,064*l.* As the gross revenue of the second half-year always exceeds that of the first by about 150,000*l.*, while the expenses are not above 30,000*l.* or 40,000*l.* in excess, it is morally certain that there will be enough net income at the end of next half-year to pay the full year's interest on the entire preference stock for the year 1868, with a small surplus.

AMALGAMATION.—The directors reported in August that the principle of the working union was unanimously sanctioned, after full inquiry, by committees of both Houses ; but a clause was introduced by the committee of the House of Lords limiting the tolls over the whole system to the *maximum* tariff sanctioned for the Brighton. The South Eastern were of opinion that this would involve a serious sacrifice of their present receipts, and accordingly the bill was withdrawn with the concurrence of the three companies interested. The directors regret the loss of a measure which would have been attended with so much advantage both to the shareholders and the public, but they will endeavour to mitigate it as far as possible by taking advantage of the amicable relations which now so happily prevail with neighbouring companies to make equitable arrangements respecting the traffic at all competing points.

CAPITAL.—The receipts on this account to 30th June, 1868, have been detailed in the manner and to the extent subjoined:—

Ordinary stock and shares	£6,839,882
7 per cent. stock	220,000
6 per cent. stock	411,177
5 per cent. stock and shares	3,703,840
4½ per cent. stock and shares	2,441,616
4 per cent. stock	449.400
	£14,065,916
Deduct discount and commission	885,195
	£13,180,721

MORTGAGE AND DEBENTURE DEBT.

Mortgage debt	2,787,072	
Debenture stock	1,305,744=	£17,273,537
Total authorised capital		£18,671,000
Expended to 30th June, 1868	17,192,205	
Add discount and commission on shares issued	885,195=	£18,077,400
Unexpended capital		£593,599

NEW CAPITAL.—The following resolutions were adopted at a special meeting on the 4th February, 1868:—

That under the powers conferred upon the company by the several Acts hereinafter mentioned, and "The (Capital and Powers) Act, 1866," and "The Act, 1867," or some one or more of the said Acts, or otherwise, the following sums be raised by the creation of new ordinary shares or stock, and as part of the capital of the company (that is to say):

1. 15,000*l.*, being the unissued balance of the sum of 60,500*l.* authorised to be raised by "The (Various Powers) Act, 1863," or otherwise, with respect to the Wimbledon and Croydon.

2. 20,000*l.*, part of the capital authorised to be raised by "The (Additional Powers) Act, 1864," or otherwise, with respect to the Horsham Dorking and Leatherhead.

3. 30,000*l.*, being the capital authorised to be raised by "The (Additional Powers) Act, 1864," or otherwise, with respect to the Bognor.

4. 30,000*l.*, being the capital authorised to be raised by "The Epsom and Leatherhead (South Western and Brighton) Act, 1860," and "The (Additional.Powers) Act, 1863," or one of such Acts, or otherwise with respect to the Epsom and Leatherhead.

5. 100.000*l.*, being the capital authorised to be raised by "The (St. Leonard's Deviations) Act, 1866."

And further, that the directors be, and they are hereby authorised to issue the whole or any part of the new ordinary shares or stock created as aforesaid, and also to issue as new ordinary shares or stock the whole or any part of the remaining balance of the shares or stock created under the powers of "The (Capital and Powers) Act, 1866." but not actually issued.

And further, that the directors be, and they are hereby authorised to dispose of the whole, or any part of the several new shares or stock respectively authorised to be issued as aforesaid, at such rate or rates, and upon such terms and conditions, and at such times, and to such persons, and in such manner as the directors may from time to time think advantageous to the company, and notwithstanding that less than the full nominal amount of any share or portion of stock may be payable or paid in respect thereof.

At another special meeting, held on 30th July, 1868, the subjoined resolutions were also adopted:—

That for the purpose of exercising the power of borrowing conferred on this company by the 18th section of the London Brighton and South Coast Act. 1868, debenture stock to an amount which, together with the existing mortgage debt and debenture stock, shall be equal to one-third of the sum of 14,066,273*l.* be, and the same is hereby created, and that such debenture stock may be issued and disposed of at such a rate of interest, at such discount, if any, at such times, to such persons, in such manner, and on such terms and conditions, as the directors may from time to time think advantageous to the company, provided that any part which may be issued at a discount be offered in the first instance, to the ordinary shareholders *pro ratâ.*

That the board of directors be, and they are hereby authorised, to raise all, or any part, of the money which for the time being the company has raised or are authorised to raise, on mortgage or bond, by the creation and issue at such times, in such amounts and manner, on such terms, subject to such conditions, and with such rights and privileges as the board may think fit, of debenture stock, instead of and to the same amount as the whole or any part of the money which may at the time being be owing by the company on mortgage or bond, or which they may from time to time have power to raise on mortgage or bond, and to attach to such debenture stock such fixed and perpetual preferential interests. and at such rate and payable half-yearly or otherwise, and commencing at once or at any future time or times, when and as the debenture stock is issued or otherwise, as the board of directors shall from time to time think fit.

That in pursuance of the powers conferred on the company by "The Additional Powers Act, 1864," and the other acts relating to the company, preference stock to the amount of 100,000l., the balance of the sum of 120,000l. authorised to be raised by the said Act of 1864, in respect of the Horsham Dorking and Leatherhead, be and the same is hereby created, and that such preference stock be entitled to a preferential dividend of 4 per cent. per annum, to rank immediately after the dividends payable on the existing preference stocks and preference shares of the company, and that the same be from time to time issued by the directors as they may determine."

The following is a synopsis of the new stock and shares issued during the year:—

Ordinary Stock, authorised at general meeting of 4th February, 1868.
215,405l. at 45 per cent.

On which has been received....................	£96,910
To be received.................................	22
Discount on same, 55 per cent,.................	118,473
	£215,405

Debenture Stock, 4½ per cent. authorised at general meeting of 30th July, 1868.
416,100l. issued at 95 per cent.

On which there has been received..............	£304,002
To be received.................................	91,293
Discount on same, 5 per cent.	20,805
	£416,100
Balance to be issued...........................	133,900
Total authorised	£550,000

The accounts are made up t ` 30th June and 31st December, and the statutory meetings are held in London within one month of 31st January and 31st July.

Scale of Voting.—50l. shares, three votes for every share up to 10; then three for every five beyond 10.

Certificates must accompany transfer deeds of stock. Registration fee, 2s. 6d. each deed. Fractions of 1l. stock allowed. Transfer books close usually 14 days before each meeting. Regulated by special acts as well as C.C.C. Act.

Qualification for Directors, 1,000l. stock.

DIRECTORS:

Chairman—SAMUEL LAING, Esq., 6, Kensington Gardens Terrace, Bayswater, W.

Deputy-Chairman—JONAS LEVY, Esq., Kingsgate Castle. Isle of Thanet, Kent.

Christopher Baldock Cardew, Esq., East Hill, Lyss, near Petersfield.

Thomas Francis Fremautle, Esq., 22, Chesham Place, S.W.

Lord George Gordon Lennox, M.P., 50, Portland Place.

Ralph Ludlow Lopes, Esq., Sandridge Park, Melksham, Wiltshire.

Arthur John Otway, Esq., M.P., 9, Harley Street, Cavendish Square, W.

George Edward Wythes. Esq., 22, Westbourne Terrace, Hyde Park, W.

OFFICERS.—Sec., Allen Sarle; Res. Eng., Fred. D. Banister; Loc. and Car. Supt., John Chester Craven; Traffic Man., George Hawkins; Auditors, William Cash and J. C. Fitzmaurice; Solicitors, Baxter, Rose, Norton, and Co., 6, Victoria Street, Westminster Abbey, S.W.

Head Offices—Terminus. London Bridge, S.E.

230.—LONDON, CHATHAM, AND DOVER.

Incorporated by 17 Vic., cap. 132 (4th August, 1853), for a line from Strood to Canterbury, continuing the South Eastern (North Kent); length, 29 1-10th miles, with branches to Faversham Quays. ¾ mile, and Chilham 1⅜ mile. Total length, 31½ miles. Opened between Strood and Faversham, 19¼ miles, on 25th February, 1858; to Canterbury, 10 miles, on 18th July, 1860.

By 18 and 19 Vic., cap. 94 (June 26th, 1855), the company obtained release of its deposit, on condition of expending the same on the construction of the Medway Bridge.

By 18 and 19 Vic., cap. 187 (July 16th, 1855), the company obtained power to extend the line from Canterbury to Dover, and to increase the share capital by 500,000l., and the borrowing powers by 166,000l. The length of Dover extension is 16¾ miles; branch to Admiralty Pier, 3 furlongs and 2 chains; branch to Dover Harbour, 1 furlong 5½ chains.

By 20 and 21 Vic., cap. 76 (27th July, 1857), the period for compulsory purchase of land was extended one year. The capital for the Dover extension was raised (under resolution, 31st August, 1856), by a preference guarantee of 5 per cent.

By 21 and 22 Vic., cap. 51 (28th June, 1858), the company obtained an extension of time for completing the works on the line to Dover till 29th December, 1860.

By 22 and 23 Vic., cap. 54 (1st August, 1859), the company was authorised to change its name from "East Kent" to "London Chatham and Dover;" to unite its original and Dover extension capitals, and to raise a further sum not exceeding 80,000l. in shares, and 26,000l, on mortgage, and half-shares may be allotted.

WESTERN EXTENSION.—By 21 and 23 Vic., cap. 107 (23rd July, 1858), the company was authorised to construct a line from Strood to St. Mary's Cray. New capital, shares, 300,000l.; loans, 100,000l. Length, 20½ miles. Traffic arrangements authorised with West End and Crystal Palace, so that the Chatham may obtain access to Victoria station. Opened, 12th October, 1861.

METROPOLITAN EXTENSIONS.—By 23 and 24 Vic., cap. 177 (6th August, 1860), the company was authorised to construct the following works :—

1. A railway (4 miles 21 chains) from a junction at Beckenham with the Farnborough extension of the West End of London and Crystal Palace to Herne Hill; two junctions (length 29 chains and 39 chains respectively) to connect No. 1 with the Brighton at Penge.

2. A railway (4 miles 32 chains) in extension of No. 1 from Herne Hill across the river Thames at Blackfriars, to the eastward side of Farringdon street; and two junctions (length 27 chains and 11 chains respectively) to connect No. 2 with the Metropolitan near Victoria Street, and West Smithfield.

3. A railway (2 miles 65 chains) in extension of No. 1 from Herne Hill to a junction with the authorised line of the Victoria Station and Pimlico, at Battersea; two junctions (29 chains) to connect No. 3 with the main line of the South Western at Battersea and a junction (60 chains) to connect Nos. 2 and 3 in the parish of St. Mary, Lambeth. Extra land, eight acres ; compulsory purchase, three years ; completion of works, five years. The company authorised to run over the Mid-Kent, the West End of London and Crystal Palace, the Metropolitan, the Pimlico, and the West London Extension, and to enter into arrangements with respect to construction and working of their undertaking, and interchange of traffic with the Great Northern, Great Western, Metropolitan, and Victoria Station and Pimlico. The company is empowered to raise further sums of 1,650,000l. by new shares, and 550,000l. by borrowing.

ARRANGEMENTS ACT, 1860.—By 23 and 24 Vic., cap. 187 (6th August, 1860), the share and debenture stock of the company were regulated and constituted as under :—

Original Capital.—Ordinary		....	£700,000
	Preference, 1855	....	500,000
	Ditto 1859	....	80,000
	Ditto 1860	....	300,000=£1,580,000
Western Extension	1858	....	300,000
Ditto	1860	....	90,000= 390,000

Un issued shares may be cancelled and re-issued at 6 per cent. preference. Half-shares may be created as preferred or deferred. Calls not to exceed one-fifth per share, with intervals of two months. New loans, 100,000l. for original undertaking, and 30,000l. for Western Extension. Debenture stock may be created at interest not exceeding 5 per cent., and issued in lieu of bonds on mortgage.

KENT COAST.—By 24 and 25 Vic., cap. 239 (August 6th, 1861), the Margate, with its extension to Ramsgate, was leased to the London Chatham and Dover, under resolution of 2nd April, 1842, upon the following terms :—1. The London Chatham and Dover to work the line of the Kent Coast, between Faversham and Ramsgate, when completed to the satisfaction of the engineer of the London Chatham and Dover line, maintaining the line, and paying all expenses of working, including rates, taxes, and government duty. 2. The receipts for all traffic passing between stations on the Kent Coast line to be set apart, 50 per cent. of the same to be paid to the London Chatham and Dover, for their expenses of working and maintaining the line, the remainder, up to 45,420l. a year, to be paid to the Kent Coast, anything above that amount to be divided in the proportion of three-fourths to the London Chatham and Dover and one-fourth to the Kent Coast. 3. The line from Faversham to Ramsgate to be completed, and opened for traffic as a double line, by 1st September, 1863. The extra line between Faversham and Herne Bay, and the lines from Herne Bay to Ramsgate, to be maintained for twelve months, after opening, at the expense of the contractors. This agreement has since been set aside by the Court of Chancery, and the Kent Coast is worked provisionally until a definitive arrangement is agreed upon.

VARIOUS POWERS.—By 25 and 26 Vic., cap. 240 (August 6th, 1861), the company is authorised to make certain deviations in the Metropolitan Extensions, as well as to construct a line of 4 miles parallel with the Bromley to St. Mary's Cray, in the event of the latter remaining under lease to the South Eastern. The new capital authorised by this Act amounts to 129,000l. in new shares, and 43,000l. on loans.

By 25 and 26 Vic., cap. 163, the London Chatham and Dover was authorised to extend the line to Walmer and Deal. Length, 9½ miles. Capital, 150,000*l*. in shares, and 50,000*l*. on loan. Dividend restricted to 6 per cent., remainder of earnings, when any, to go to Chatham and Dover.

By 25 and 26 Vic., cap. 192 (29th July, 1862), the company was authorised to construct a junction at Battersea, &c. Length, 1¼ mile. Also to acquire additional land in Kent and Surrey. New capital, 1,700,000*l*. in shares, at 6 per cent., and 566,600*l*. on loan.

By 25 and 26 Vic., cap. 224 (7th August, 1862), the company was authorised to lease the Mid-Kent (Bromley to St. Mary's Cray), as from 1st September, 1863, at a rental equal to 4 per cent. on the outlay.

By 26 and 27 Vic., cap. 204 (28th July, 1863), the company obtained power to extend its line from Peckham to Greenwich, as well as several other extensions and junctions. Also to complete arrangements with the Brighton and the Great Western, in respect to occupation of the Victoria Station. New line, 4 miles. New capital, 1,220,000*l*. in shares, and 406,000*l*. on loan.

By 27 and 28 Vic., cap. 96 (23rd June, 1864), the company was authorised to run steam vessels from Ramsgate to certain foreign ports. No new capital.

WEST END AND CRYSTAL PALACE.—An agreement has been entered into with this company. The following article occurs in this agreement:—" The said West End shall provide, or cause to be provided, for the East Kent, such accommodation for engines, carriages, and stores, as well as for goods, minerals, and passenger traffic at the Battersea station of the West End Company, as the said East Kent may require ; the extent and nature of such accommodation, and the terms of payment in respect thereof, to be agreed upon between the companies. or in the event of difference to be settled by arbitration." By 23 and 24 Vic., cap. 174 (23rd July, 1860), the Farnborough branch of the Crystal Palace line is transferred to the London Chatham and Dover, and an extension of time to the 8th August, 1862, conceded. The Bromley section is also sold to the Chatham, which may raise a further capital of 190,000*l*. for these purposes.

VICTORIA STATION.—An agreement has been made between the Victoria Station and Pimlico, and the London Chatham and Dover, and Great Western. for joint use of a certain portion of the Victoria Station, and of the Pimlico railway, from the 1st October, 1860, temporary station accommodation being provided at a reduced rate till 1862, when more permanent station buildings were provided. The cost of the accommodation works is limited to 105,000*l*. The rent for the station accommodation and use of the railway on the mixed gauge is to be 13,250*l*. for the first year, 18,000*l*. for the second year, and so on, increasing for about seven years, until the rent amounts to 32,000*l*. a-year.

CITY UNDERTAKING.—By 27 and 28 Vic., cap. 212 (25th July, 1864), the company was authorised to form into a separate undertaking so much of the Metropolitan Extensions as lies between the north side of East Street, Blackfriars and the Junction with the Metropolitan. To these works the Great Northern was authorised to subscribe 300,000*l*., at 3½ per cent. New capital to general undertaking 1,500,000*l*., and to Metropolitan Extensions, 1,600,000*l*.; and City Lines, 1,000,000*l*. Borrowing powers : City lines, 333,300*l*.; general undertaking, 500,000*l*.; and on Metropolitan Extensions, 533,000*l*. Total capital authorised by Act : shares, 4,100,000*l*.; loans, 1,366,300*l*.

NEW LINES.—By 27 and 28 Vic., cap. 195 (14th July, 1864), the company obtained power to acquire additional lands, to deviate lines. and to alter works, as well as to amend the Acts of the company. New capital for Battersea works, 150,000*l*. in shares, and 50,000*l*. on loan ; for Kent works, 220,000*l*. in shares, and 73,300*l*. on loan.

By 28 and 29 Vic., cap. 268 (5th July, 1865), the South Western was authorised to contribute 400,000*l*. in shares, and 133,300*l*. on loan, towards construction of a part of the Metropolitan Extensions, and to obtain use of the same. By 28 and 29 Vic., cap. 269 (5th July, 1865), the Chatham was authorised to make several connecting links, and to abandon part of the Crystal Palace and South London Junction. Also to consolidate existing capital, and to provide for dividend on preference shares.

By 28 and 29 Vic., cap. 347 (5th July, 1865), the company was authorised to make a short connecting link at Beckenham, to abandon some other junctions, and enter into traffic arrangements with the South Eastern.

By 29 and 30 Vic., cap. 282 (30th July, 1866), the company obtained power to construct a branch to Chatham Dockyard. Length, 1¼ mile. New capital, 100,000*l*. in shares, and 33,300*l*. on loan.

By 29 and 30 Vic., cap. 283 (30th July, 1866), the company was authorised to execute a variety of new works in Kent and Surrey ; to acquire additional lands in London, Middlesex, Surrey, and Kent ; and also to acquire the Sittingbourne and Sheerness, at a yearly sum of 7,000*l*. An extension of time for three years was also obtained for construction of Greenwich and other lines.

By 29 and 30 Vic., cap. 303 (10th August, 1866), the company was authorised to enlarge the Ludgate Station, by making two new streets and altering another street, and to take part of the property of Apothecaries' Hall, in which the society have carried on business for two centuries. The new streets are to be in Union Street, Earl Street, and Church Entry, Blackfriars, and to join the new street. The city commissioners to act with the company as to the land taken, and among the improvements contemplated is the widening of Ludgate Hill. The corporation may contribute towards the expenses and agree with the railway company as to the alteration. The Act also authorises a new road to be made at Ramsgate by the Kent Coast from East Cliff to the Royal Harbour.

ARRANGEMENTS ACT, 1867.—By 30 and 31 Vic., cap. 209 (20th August, 1867), the company obtained extraordinary powers to raise additional capital, as well as to effect arrangements with its creditors on the one hand, and the various classes of its debenture holders on the other. The leading provisions of the Act are given *in extenso* in the APPENDIX to Volume XX., but the subjoined synopsis may not be unacceptable to the general reader. All existing legal proceedings and claims against the company are placed in abeyance for ten years, and during that time which is called the "suspense period," the management is vested in a board o eight directors, of whom four represent the shareholders and four the debenture holders. The board are authorised to dispose of superfluous lands, and to apply the proceeds to certain special purposes, and they are given power to create and issue debenture stocks of three classes, called respectively A, B, and C debenture stocks, all of which are to be charged upon the entire undertaking, and not, as heretofore, on separate sections of the company. "A" debenture stock may be issued to the extent of 600,000*l.*, and bear interest not exceeding 6*l.* per cent. per annum; but with priority only over those existing mortgages the holders of which consent in writing to be postponed; but not over mortgagees who do not consent to such postponement. It is provided that any increase in the net revenues beyond the amount for the year ending 30th June, 1867, shall go in the first place towards payment of interest to the holders of "A" debenture stock. For present arrears of interest due to mortgagees, and for accruing interest which the income of the company may be insufficient to satisfy, deferred dividend warrants, bearing 5*l.* per cent. interest, and conferring the same rights as regards the payment thereof, and the interest thereon, as the mortgages in respect of which they are issued, are to be given to all mortgagees, whether consenting to the creation of "A" stock or not; at their option, they may take, instead, "B" debenture stock, the "B" and "C" debenture stock ranking *after* existing mortgages. The existing rights and priorities of debenture holders, except so far as they are affected or disturbed by the Act, are preserved by a special clause. The Act further provides a form of circular, and of consent to the creation of "A" stock, to be sent by the board, with copies of the clauses relating to that stock, to all mortgagees. No part of this capital has yet been raised, although in the opinion of the directors it was thought desirable that the company should be in a position to issue the A debenture stock as it might be found necessary, and as the increase of net revenue for the year just ended exceeded 70,000*l.*, the security for the A stock might be considered ample and satisfactory.

NEW CAPITAL.—The following resolution was adopted by the Board of Directors, on 8th August, 1867 :—" That there be now created and issued 155,556*l.* Sheerness rent-charge 4½ per cent. stock, as provided by the London Chatham and Dover (Various Powers) Act, 1866, and that such stock be dealt with on the terms of the said Act and the heads of arrangement set forth in the schedule thereto."

The subjoined resolution was also adopted at a board meeting. held on 14th August, 1867 :—" That there be now created and issued ordinary stock of an amount not exceeding 25,000*l.*, as provided by the London Chatham and Dover (Various Powers) Act, 1866, and that such stock be dealt with on the terms of the said Act and the heads of arrangement set forth in the schedule thereto."

MILEAGE.—Main line and branches, 136 miles.

REVENUE.—The directors reported in February that the gross receipts upon the railways worked by the company, including steamboats, for the half-year ending 31st December, amounted to 368,355*l.*, against 320,740*l.* in the same period of 1866, showing an increase of 47,615*l.* The gross expenses, including 14,804*l.* expended on renewal of the permanent way and 5,000*l.* charged towards legal and parliamentary expenses, had been 213,714*l.*, against 226,356*l.* in 1866. showing a decrease of 12,647*l.* The net result of the traffic for the half year was a balance of 154,641*l.*, earned at a per centage of 58·01 for working expenses as compared with 94,384*l.* for the corresponding half of 1866, earned at 70·57 per cent. The result of the half-year's working was considered satisfactory—first, as regarded the absolute reduction of working expenses; and next, when it was borne in mind that during the whole period all direct communication with the Great Northern had been wholly closed for passenger traffic, and partially for goods. A considerable part of the increase in the receipts was no doubt attributable to the Paris Exhibition, though the traffic from this source had not realised expectations.

The directors made a similar report in August, stating that the result of the half-year's working was again satisfactory. The gross receipts upon all systems worked by the company amounted to 290,489*l.*, which, compared with 265,747*l.* for the corresponding period of 1867, showed an increase of 9·31 per cent. The gross expenses, including 23,795*l.* for renewal of permanent way, were 207,636*l.*, as compared with 200,546*l.* in 1867, or an increase of 3·53 per cent. The net result for the half-year was a balance of 82,853*l.*, earned at a per centage of 71·47, as compared with a net balance of 65,202*l.* for the corresponding period of 1867, earned at 75'46 per cent. of the receipts. The sum of 23,795*l.* expended during the half-year on renewal of permanent way was included in the working expenses and charged to revenue. This item was in addition to 19,756*l.* for ordinary maintenance. For the half-year ending the 30th June, 1866, the net result of the traffic amounted to 62,301*l.*, earned at 75'39 per cent., in 1867 to 65,202*l.* earned at a cost of 75'46 per cent.; and for 1868 to 82,853*l.* earned at 71'47 per cent. The goods traffic had improved, although but little had resulted from the opening of the through communication with the Great Northern.

Deferred dividend warrants and B debenture stock have been issued in exchange for over-due debenture coupons to the extent of—

To the 30th June, 1868, deferred dividend warrants £147,044
Ditto   B debenture stock...... 17,855

AMALGAMATION.—The directors regretted the non-success of the bill for establishing a working union between the three southern companies. The result had not disturbed the friendly relations of the three companies.

MESSRS. PETO AND CO.—The directors also reported in August that the claim of the company in Messrs. Peto and Co.'s bankruptcy had been admitted so far as any practical benefit could be obtained. The bankrupts in the first balance-sheet claimed to be creditors of the company to the extent of upwards of 210,000*l.*, but after an examination the bankrupts withdrew all claim against the company, and admitted the company creditors against the joint estate of the three bankrupts for 365,030*l.*, and against the estate of Peto and Betts for 119,848*l.*, thus altering the position of the accounts in favour of the company to the extent of 694,878*l.* A dividend of 1*s.* 10*d.* in the pound on the 119,848*l.* had lately been received. With the exception of the two suits instituted by the finance companies and the cross bill found indispensable in defence of those suits, the directors were happy to congratulate the mortgagees and shareholders on the company being comparatively free from litigation.

CAPITAL.—The subjoined compilation is made as carefully as possible from the disjointed statements issued by the company :—

GENERAL UNDERTAKING.

First preference stock (5 per cent.)		£500,000
First preference arrears of interest (5 per cent.)		170,000
Second preference (6 per cent.)		800,000
Ordinary stock...................................	£3,000,000	
Do. (issued to extinguish Sittingbourne and Sheerness Ordinary Stock)	18,435=3,018,435	
		£4,488,435
Western extension stock		622,726
		£5,111,161
Debentures	£1,427,131	
Ditto Western extension........................	190,242=1,617,373	
Joint capital account, B debenture stock issued		1,657
		£6,730,191
Balance, excess of expenditure over receipts		163,176= £6,893,367

METROPOLITAN EXTENSIONS.

First preference B stock (6 per cent.)		£825,000
Second preference C stock (6 per cent.)		1,050,000
A or ordinary stock:—		
Created under the powers of the Act of 1860, at special general meeting, 12th October, 1860........	825,000	
Created under the powers of the Act of 1864, at special general meeting, 26th August, 1864	1,600,000=2,425,000	
		£4,300,000
Debentures—Act, 1860	550,000	
Act, 1862	350,000	
Act, 1864	533,000	
	£1,433,000	
Excess	8,645=1,441,645	
		£5,741,645
Joint capital account, B debenture stock issued		1,772
		£5,743,417
Balance, excess of expenditure over receipts		67,877= £5,811,295

COMMON FUND.

Created under the powers of the Act of 1862, at an extraordinary
   general meeting, 19th June, 1863.. £750,000
Debentures now outstanding .... 248,883 = £993,883
Parliamentary limit..£250,000

CITY LINES.

Created under the powers of the Act of 1864 :—

   Deferred A shares, 50,000 at 10l. each £500,000
   Preferred B shares, 50,000 at 10l. each 500,000

                                  £1,000,000

Received thereon :—
   Contribution A and B shares Great Northern £300,000
   Subscribed for by and issued—as paid up—to Peto and Co.
     and since transferred to other parties £700,000
   On which the company has received, partly in cash from
    Peto and Co., and partly by credit in account with them.. 150,000

                                £450,000
Debentures—Parliamentary limit £333,300
Excess .... 127,378= £460,678
Joint capital account—B Debenture stock issued............ 169

                                £910,848
Balance, excess of expenditure over receipts .... 677,360=£1,588,208

VICTORIA STATION IMPROVEMENTS.

Share capital £520,000
Created under the powers of Acts of 1863 and 1864, at special general
   meeting, 4th August, 1865, subscribed for by, and issued—as paid
   up—to Peto and Co., and since transferred to other parties. The
   company has had credit in account with Peto and Co. thereon for £366,000
Debentures (parliamentary limit, 173,000l.)......................... 172,813
Joint capital of B debenture stock issued 73

                                £538,886
Balance, excess of expenditure over receipts....................... 263,955 = £802,842

EASTERN SECTION.

   Deferred shares A, 53,500 of 10l. each £535,000
   Preferred shares B, 53,500 of 10l. each 535,000

                              £1,070,000
Created under the powers of Acts of 1863 and 1864 at special general
   meetings, 26th February and 12th of August, 1864, subscribed for
   by Peto and Co., and now registerred in the name of Sir S. M.
   Peto, but no money has been received in respect thereof.
Debentures £356,300
Joint capital account, B debenture stock issued 14,182

                              £370,482
Balance, excess of expenditure over receipts .... 7,859 = £378,341

                              £16,472,936

No of Directors −8. Qualification, 1,000l.

DIRECTORS :

Chairman—GROSVENOR HODGKINSON, Esq., M.P., Newark, Notts.

Deputy-Chairman-MAJOR JELF SHARP, The Meadowside, Twickenham
   Meadows, S.W., and Junior United Service Club.

Joshua Dixon, Esq., Winslade, Exeter.
W. E. Hilliard, Esq., Cowley House, Uxbridge.
Richard Hodgson, Esq., F.R.A.S., Hawkwood, Chingford, Essex.

J. H. Powell, Esq., Mayfield, Streatham.
G. C. Taylor, Esq., 42, Elvaston Place, South Kensington, W.
H. D. Warter, Esq., Longden Manor, Shrewsbury.

OFFICERS—Sec., G. W. Brooke ; Gen. Man., J. S. Forbes ; Goods Man., C. H. Chapman ; Res. Eng., W. Mills ; Loco. Supt., W. Martley ; Accountant, J. Morgan ; Auditors, S. B. Bristowe and G. Hogarth ; Solicitor, W. Cleather ; Bankers, The London and County Bank.

General Offices—Victoria Station, Pimlico, S.W.

231.—LONDON AND GREENWICH.

This line (3½ miles) is leased to the South Eastern for 45,000l. per annum, on a rent-charge on the whole of the lines for 999 years. The guaranteed 5 per cent. interest is on 222,720l. capital, payable 31st March and 30th September. The ordinary capital of the company, 861,540l., pays a half-yearly dividend in the middle of January and July of 5s. 5d. per share, or 1l. 7s. 1d. per cent. clear of income tax. The debenture debt of 233,300l. at 4 per cent. pays interest half-yearly on 1st January and 1st July.

Qualification of Directors—50 unprivileged shares.

Scale of Voting.—10 shares, one vote; 20 shares, two votes; 35 shares, three votes; 50 shares and upwards, four votes.

Transfer fee, 2s. 6d. each seller. Several shares may go on one transfer. Certificates must accompany transfer deed. Books close about ten days before each half-yearly meeting.

DIRECTORS:

Chairman—ROGER KYNASTON, Esq.

Deputy-Chairman—THOMAS BARKER, Esq.

Capt. Wm. Scott Murray. | James Holbert Wilson, Esq.
Alfred Rhodes Bristow, Esq. |

OFFICERS.—Sec., H. Adron; Transfer Clerk, Harry Forster.

Offices—173, Gresham House, Old Broad Street, E.C.

232.—LONDON AND NORTH WESTERN.

The company was formed out of the LONDON and BIRMINGHAM, GRAND JUNCTION, and MANCHESTER and BIRMINGHAM (9 and 10 Vic., cap. 204, 16th July, 1846).

I.—GRAND JUNCTION.—An amalgamation of the Liverpool and Manchester, the Grand Junction proper, the Bolton and Leigh (Kenyon and Leigh), Warrington and Newton, and Chester and Crewe railways, under powers granted by 8 and 9 Vic., cap. 198 (1846) viz.:—

Liverpool and Manchester, incorporated in 1826 by 7 Geo. IV., cap. 49 for a line between those towns. Opened throughout 14th September, 1830. Capital at amalgamation was taken at 1,692,600l.

Bolton and Leigh, capital 82,025l., but reduced on amalgamation to 32,810l.

Warrington and Newton, 1830, was merged into the Grand Junction.

Grand Junction (proper) was projected in 1824, but was defeated several times: in 1832 it was revived, but did not obtain the Act of incorporation until 1833, 3 Wm. IV., cap. 34, for a line from Birmingham to Warrington Junction of L. and M., and in the following year for a junction in Birmingham and a Branch to Wolverhampton. Opened throughout on 6th July, 1837. In 1840, the CHESTER and CREWE was amalgamated with the Grand Junction; its capital at the amalgamation was 3,098,387½l. Conflicting interests with L. & B. were finally set at rest by a complete amalgamation, and with the M. & B. as from 1st July, 1845. The G. J. was allowed, as a consideration for such amalgamation, an allotment of 20l. per 100l. of stock; this increased the amalgamated stock of the three by 20 per cent., amounting to 964,759½l., thus making a total amount of amalgamated stock 1,788,500l.

II. LONDON AND BIRMINGHAM.—Incorporated 1833, by Act 3 Wm. IV., cap. 36. Opened throughout, 20th September, 1838. This company subsequently obtained power to purchase the Warwick and Leamington, in 1843; to construct the Peterborough branch; to subscribe 100,000l. to the Lan. and C., 1,000,000l. to the C. and H., and 277,780l. to the Trent Valley. By the Act of amalgamation the capital of this company, which was then 8,250,000l., was fixed at 8,653,750l.

III. MANCHESTER AND BIRMINGHAM.—Incorporated 1837, by 1 Vic., cap. 69, for a line from Manchester to Crewe; opened throughout in August, 1842. Loan powers, 700,000l. Capital fixed at 2,800,000l. Further power was obtained to the extent of 175,000l., as subscription to the South Junction and Altrincham, and 277,780l. for the Trent Valley subscription, which have been included in the authorised power of the amalgamated companies.

HUDDERSFIELD and MANCHESTER.—Incorporated by 9 Vic., cap. 105. Share capital, 1,041,570l. The Oldham branch of this section (4 miles) was opened in July, 1855.

NORTHAMPTON and MARKET HARBRO'.—By Act 17 Vic., cap. 160 (4th August, 1853).

power was given to make a branch to **Market Harbro'** junction of Rugby and Stamford branch, from Hardingston junction, and a short branch from Hardingston, 18¾ miles.

ST. ALBANS.—By Act 17 Vic., cap. 161 (4th August, 1853), the L. and N. W. was empowered to make a branch to St. Albans. Reduced length, 7½ miles. Opened 5th May, 1858.

SHREWSBURY and CREWE.—By Act 17 Vic., cap. 216 (20th August, 1853), power was given to make a railway from Crewe to Shrewsbury, 33 miles. Opened 2nd Sept., 1858.

LEEDS, DEWSBURY, and MANCHESTER.—Incorporated 1845, 9 Vic., cap. 36. Total capital authorised previous to amalgamation, 600,000l. This amount is reduced by 3-10ths as the portion of share capital, entered as part of the L. and N. W. parliamentary capital.

IV. SUBSIDIARY LINES.—The London and North Western is likewise interested, by subscription or lease, in the following undertakings:—

BIRMINGHAM, WOLVERHAMPTON, and STOUR VALLEY.—Incorporated in 1846. Capital, 1,110.000l., leased under 11 Vic., cap. 120 (1847), in perpetuity, at a rental on a fixed capital of 760,350l. at 2-3rds of the dividend of the L. and N. W. to participate in all new creation of stock; and L. and N. W. to find any further capital.

BUCKINGHAMSHIRE.—Incorporated 1846. Length, 41½ miles. Capital, 795,000l. Consolidated by 11 Vic., cap. 236 (1847). Under the Acts of 1846-7, this company subscribed for 422,375l. Leased to L. and N. W. at 4 per cent. per annum, and half surplus profits on the authorised capital; but as a considerable portion of that capital, say 25,714 shares of 17½l. each=449,995l. and all the extra cost of construction will fall upon this company, the actual liability is limited to the above rate on 794,990l.

BEDFORD.—The company was incorporated 1845—15¾ miles. Opened November, 1846. Capital, 2,500 shares of 50l., all paid, 125,000l. Loan powers, 41,650l. Leased by L. and N. W. at 4 per cent., half surplus profits on one-half of the capital; the public hold 978 shares, the remainder, 1,522, subscribed by this company. This branch treated as an integral portion of the main line, cost 264,265l.

HAMPSTEAD JUNCTION.—Incorporated by 17 Vic., cap. 222 (August 20th, 1853), for a line from Willesden to the North London, with a branch to the North and South Western Junction. Length, main line, 6½ miles; branch, ½ mile. L. and N. W. subscribed 150,000l. Capital, 250,000l., in 10l. shares; loans on mortgage or bond, 83,333l. By Act 19 and 20 Vic., cap. 52 (23rd June, 1856), an extension of one year for completion of works was obtained. By 22 and 23 Vic., cap. 13 (21st July, 1859), another extension of time for one year was concluded, and certain deviations authorised. New capital to the extent of 150,000l. was also authorised, but without any preference being attached. Traffic included in receipts of London and North Western.

BIRMINGHAM CANAL, leased (through the Stour Valley), under Act 10 Vic., cap. 244 (1846), at rent sufficient, with the net amount of the tolls and other income arising from the canal and other property, after deducting all proper expenses and interest on the unallocated debt, to produce a dividend of 4l. per share, clear of deduction (except property and income tax), upon each of the present shares, 17,600l. (in 1849 were 19,360¾ shares of 39l. 17s. 6d. at 4 per cent.); and also upon each share upon which the unallocated debt shall be converted. Clause 16 extends the guarantee to 2,066 shares of the Dudley Canal Navigation; clause 20 provides for a previous arrangement made by the canal company, whereby a deduction is made of 35s. 6d. from certain unallocated shares on which the proportion of debt attaching thereto had not been paid; and of 19s. 6d. from certain unallocated Wyrley shares. If the canal profits exceed the above *minimum* guarantee, no more shall be payable out of such profits than will be sufficient to pay 5l. per share, the remainder to be set apart for a reserve fund, not to exceed 500,000l., and out of any accumulation thereon (if any) a dividend of 5l. is to be maintained. The primary liability of the L. and N. W. to make up such dividend to 4l. per share remains undisturbed. No charge has fallen upon the L. and N. W. revenue.

NORTH UNION.—Leased conjointly with the Lancashire and Yorkshire, for joint workings, and fixed divisions of proceeds.

PRESTON and WYRE.—Leased conjointly with the Lancashire and Yorkshire. This company takes one-third only of the loss or profit. By 28 Vic., cap. 22 (26th May, 1865), the L. and N. W. was authorised to raise 8,000l. in shares, and 2,000l. on loan; and the Lancashire and Yorkshire 16,000l. in shares, and 4,000l. on loan, for the purpose of widening and otherwise improving the Preston and Wyre.

WEST LONDON.—Leased jointly with the Great Western.—See West London, and also West London Extension.

MANCHESTER, BUXTON, MATLOCK, and MIDLANDS (incorporated 1846).—Reduced to 11½ miles opened: purchased the Cromford Canal for 101,200l. Act of 1851 gave powers to raise capital, and to mortgage to canal proprietors. Purchase completed 30th

August, 1852. The L. and N. W. held 7,500 shares. By Act 1851 capital reduced to 82,500 5½*l.* shares=153,750*l.*, and loans, 151,250*l.* (15 Vic., cap. 126). By Act (1852) is leased to this company and the Midland conjointly, on an agreement confirmed by the lessors, 2nd September, 1852; Act 15 Vic., cap. 98 (17th June, 1852), for 19 years from 1st July, 1852, at an annual sum equal to 2½ per cent. upon the share capital, then 421,300*l.*

North and South Western Junction.—Incorporated in 1851, for a line of about 4 miles, connecting this line with the S.W., and south of the Thames and Southampton, under an agreement to allow toll of 6 miles for minerals and 4 miles for passengers, and to secure to it a *minimum* of traffic sufficient to yield the shareholders at least 3 per cent. net on their paid-up share capital. All profits beyond, and interest on debts, and 6 per cent. to be divided, one-half to the shareholders, and the remainder to the two contracting companies.

Shropshire Union.—Incorporating the Newtown and Crewe, 1846; share capital, 1,500,000*l.*; the Chester and Wolverhampton, 1846; share capital, 1,000,000*l.*; Shrewsbury and Stafford, 1846; share capital, 800,000*l.*=total, 3,300,000*l.*, and 1,099,999*l.* on loans. 154 miles, besides Ellesmere and Chester and Shrewsbury and Montgomery canals, purchased for 482,920*l.*, as stated under S.U., and loans about 814,207*l.* L. and N.W. subscribed 101,732*l.*; and 11 Vic., cap. 121 (1847), L. and N.W. agreed to lease and guarantee dividend on 600,000*l.* (cost of line), and canal capital (now called up 1,552,564*l.*), equal to one-half of the dividend on L. and N. W. ordinary consolidated stock. A considerable portion of the original scheme is abandoned; and the remainder, with the canal leased by the L. and N. W., by 20 and 21 Vic., cap. 108 (27th July, 1857), and ratified by proprietors on 9th October, 1857.

Chester and Holyhead.—Incorporated by 7 and 8 Vic., cap. 65 (4th July, 1844), for a line from Chester to Holyhead harbour, 85 miles. The Mold (12¼) is incorporated under 11 Vic., cap. 162 (1847). The Bangor and Canarvon (7¼ miles) is also included in the Chester and Holyhead. Total mileage 105. Sea passage, passenger route, 66 miles to Kingstown; merchandise, 70 miles to Dublin. By 21 and 22 Vic., cap. 130 (23rd July, 1858), the Chester and Holyhead was authorised to be leased to or amalgamated with the London and North Western, at a price not exceeding 50*l.* per 100*l.* stock. This arrangement was adopted by both parties in March, 1859, and has been acted upon, the Chester and Holyhead as a separate company being now dissolved. By 22 and 23 Vic., cap. 113 (13th August, 1859), the company is authorised to use locomotive power on the tramways at Holyhead harbour, under regulation of the Board of Trade. By 25 and 26 Vic., cap. 104, the powers of the two companies for raising money were more clearly defined, which were explained as follows to a meeting on the 21st August, 1862:—"The chairman moved that under the powers guaranteed by the London and North Western Act, 1862, authorising the Chester and Holyhead to create and issue one uniform stock, in substitution for several descriptions of stock now existing, 2,468,000*l.* new capital be created, bearing a preference dividend at the rate of 5 per cent. per annum, to be guaranteed by the London and North Western, and to be called 'Chester and Holyhead (London and North Western) guaranteed 5 per cent. stock,' such stock to be, with the consent of the London and North Western, applied exclusively in substitution for the surrendered stock or shares of the Chester and Holyhead in the following proportions—namely, for and in lieu of every 100*l.* stock of the Chester and Holyhead entitled to a dividend at the rate of 5 per cent. per annum, there shall be issued the said guaranteed stock to the amount of 101*l.* for and in lieu of every 100*l.* of stock, the Chester and Holyhead to be entitled to a dividend at the rate of 5½ per cent. per annum in respect of guaranteed stock of 110*l.*; and for and in lieu of every 100*l.* of ordinary stock of Chester and Holyhead there shall be issued, after the 1st of March, 1863, guaranteed stock to the amount of 50*l.* This arrangement will not interfere with the interest of the original proprietors, but is simply for the purpose of consolidating into one the varieties of stock now existing.

Lancaster and Carlisle.—The London and North Western lease this undertaking for a period of 900 years, the share capital not to exceed 1,600,000*l.*, including 350,000*l.* held by London and North Western, the loan capital not to exceed 430,000*l.*, making together 2,030,000*l.* Neither the share nor loan capital to be increased without the consent of London and North Western. In no case is the Lancaster and Carlisle to receive less than 8 per cent. per annum (less income tax), and to increase according to the following scale, viz., on the London and North Western paying a dividend at the rate of 4½ per cent. per annum, the Lancaster and Carlisle are to receive at the rate of 8½ per cent.; on the London and North Western paying 4½ per cent., the Lancaster and Carlisle to receive 9 per cent.; on paying 4¾ per cent. the Lancaster and Carlisle to receive 9¼ per cent.; on paying 5 per cent. the Lancaster and Carlisle to receive 9½ per cent.; and on the London and North Western paying 6 per cent. the Lancaster and Carlisle to receive 10½, and so on for any greater or less fraction than ¼ per cent. The Lancaster and Preston and Kendal and Windermere receive their due proportion of dividend according to the Act of 1849, and the agreement for amalgamation. The London and North Western to provide needful office accommodation, and pay direction, audit, secretary, and transfer expenses, but they are not to exceed 1,525*l.*

WARRINGTON AND STOCKPORT.—By 22 and 23 Vic., cap. 138 (13th August, 1859), this line is leased to the London and North Western at 5 per cent. on its preference capital, and 4 per cent. on its ordinary stock.

BLACKWALL.—Under an Act passed 1852, the London and Blackwall have constructed a short branch to connect their line with the warehouses in Haydon Square, which this company purchased for goods traffic. This company have agreed to pay the interest of the cost of that branch, and a certain fixed annual amount as toll.

WHITEHAVEN JUNCTION.—Incorporated 30th June, 1844, for a railway from the Maryport junction (Maryport to Carlisle) to Workington junction (Cockermouth and Workington), and Whitehaven (Whitehaven and Furness). Branch to Maryport Dock for traffic, 1 mile, opened, September, 1859. Length, 13 miles. By Act 11 and 12 Vic., cap. 91 (22nd July, 1848), the company were authorised to raise the sum of 33,000l. in preference shares, and 11,000l. on mortgage, and by Act 17 Vic., cap. 24 (2nd June, 1854), the sum of 12,000l. in preference shares, and 4,000l. on mortgage, the whole of which powers were exercised by the issue of 25,000l. in 5l. shares at 6 per cent., 7,000l. in 7l. shares at 4½ per cent., 10,000l. in 10l. shares at 5 per cent., and 3,000l. in 6l. shares at 5 per cent.; total, 45,000l. in shares and 15,000l. on mortgage. By 21 and 22 Vic. (23rd July, 1858), the company was authorised to raise new capital to the extent of 65,000l., at 5 per cent. per annum, which power was exercised on 25th August, 1858, by an issue of 20l. preference shares. By 28 Vic., cap. 68 (2nd June, 1864), the company was authorised to enlarge the station accommodation at Whitehaven, and to raise new capital to the extent of 50,000l. by mortgage. By 29 and 30 Vic., cap. 190 (16th July, 1866) the Whitehaven Junction was vested at a fixed dividend of 10 per cent., in the London and North Western, which thereby obtained running powers over a portion of the Whitehaven and Furness.

COCKERMOUTH AND WORKINGTON.—Incorporated by 8 and 9 Vic., cap. 120 (July 1845). A line from Cockermouth to Workington Harbour; it is three-fourths coal traffic line; joins the Whitehaven there. Length, 8½ miles. Opened throughout, 28th April, 1847. An Act was passed 13 Vic., cap. 48 (1849), for a branch from Marron Foot to Bridge Foot, ½ mile. By 26 Vic., cap. 43 (8th June, 1863), the company was authorised to construct a small branch and several works. Length, ¼ mile. New capital, 20,000l. in shares, to participate in dividend same as original shares, and 4,000l., at a guarantee of 4½ as preference A shares. By 29 and 30 Vic., cap. 189 (16th July, 1866), the Cockermouth and Workington was vested in the London and North Western on the terms following:—For 18 months ending 31st December, 1866, 7 per cent.; for the next year, 8 per cent.; for the year 1868, at the rate of 9 per cent.; and 10 in perpetuity thereafter.

STOCKPORT, DISLEY, AND WHALEYBRIDGE.—Incorporated by 17 and 18 Vic,, cap. 200 (July 31st, 1854), for making a railway from the London and North Western, near Stockport, to Disley and Whaley Bridge. The line branches off from the London and North Western, near Stockport, runs along between that railway and Hazlegrove, passes through the Norbury coal-field, not far from Poynton, under the Macclesfield canal, skirts the eminence of Lyme Park, and the pond at Disley, crosses under the turnpike road by a short turn, and then runs for the greater part of its course between the canal and the road to Whaley Bridge. Capital, 150,000l., in shares of 20l. each. Power to borrow 50,000l. Length of line 10 miles 6½ chains. By 18 and 19 Vic., cap. 130 (July 16th, 1855), the London and North Western may hold shares to an amount not exceeding 85,000l. The sum was voted, and an agreement to work the line entered into. Opened to Whaley Bridge on 9th June, and the junction with the Cromford and High Peak on the 17th August, 1867. By 20 and 21 Vic., cap. 98 (27th July, 1857), an extension to Buxton (9 miles) was sanctioned. New capital, 200,000l. in shares, and 66,000l. in loans. Estimate, 200,000l. Compulsory purchase of land, three years; completion of works, four years. The London and North Western subscribe 105,000l. to this extension. Opened 15th June, 1864. By 23 and 24 Vic., cap. 136 (3rd July, 1860), the company was authorised to raise additional capital, in shares, to the extent of 35,000l., and on loan to 10,000l. By Act of 1866, the Stockport Disley and Whaley Bridge, including the Buxton Extension, was transferred to the London and North Western, the following resolutions being adopted on the 16th November, 1866:—"That additional new capital, not exceeding 385,000l., be created for the conversion of the shares of the Stockport Disley and Whaley Bridge into an equivalent amount of stock of the London and North Western Company, bearing a preferential dividend, without further participation of profits, at 4½ per cent, per annum, payable half-yearly."

GREAT NORTHERN.—The negotiations between the directors of London and North Western, the Great Northern, and Manchester Sheffield and Lincolnshire resulted in the admission and adoption of the important principle of equality of charge between all points of competition, at rates to be fixed by arbitration in case of difference; the heads of an agreement were exchanged on the 26th November, 1858, providing for the interchange of traffic at through rates; for co-operation between the several parties, for the conduct of competitive traffic at equal rates, to be settled by arbitration; and for the adjustment, on satisfactory terms, of all questions connected with the London Road station, Manchester. On 23d December, 1858, a further agreement was signed, providing for a division of competitive traffic, and for arrangements generally, which will tend to the advantage of the companies, and promote also the public convenience.

GREAT WESTERN.—By an agreement with this company it is provided that they are to use the lines and stations of the London and North Western for their Manchester traffic, for a period of years, upon mutually advantageous conditions. Arrangements for division of traffic at all competitive places have also been effected.

BIRKENHEAD.—The terms of arrangement with this company in conjunction with the Great Western, are as follows:—The two companies, as from 1st January, 1860, assume the Birkenhead debenture stock, mortgage debt, and liabilities on capital account, not exceeding in the whole 512,000*l*. The two companies to pay half-yearly, as from 1st January, 1866, dividends upon Birkenhead ordinary capital of 1,941,505*l*. after the rates following, viz.:—For the years 1860 and 1861, 2½ per cent. per annum; for the years 1862, 1863, 1864, and 1865, 3½ per cent. per annum: and for the year 1866 and thereafter, 4 per cent. per annum. If during the year 1852 the earnings of the Birkenhead, after deduction of interest on debt, and an estimated per centage for working expenses, shall exceed the rate of 2½ per cent. per annum, then the next higher rate of 3½ per cent. per annum shall commence, and be paid in respect of the year 1861, the certificate of the auditors of the two companies on that point being final and conclusive. The two companies to keep the Birkenhead register of stock, and to distribute the dividend, &c. This arrangement was finally completed in August, and the leasing companies took possession on 18th November, 1860.

OLDHAM, ASHTON, AND GUIDE BRIDGE.—By 22 and 23 Vic. (13th August, 1859), the London and North Western was authorised to contribute 50,000*l*. towards completion of this undertaking; and by 25 and 26 Vic , cap. 98 (30th June, 1862), that line is vested mutually in the London and North Western and Manchester Sheffield and Lincolnshire.

NORTH STAFFORDSHIRE.—At a meeting in August, 1860, the following resolution was adopted:—"That the articles of agreement, with a scheme for a traffi agreement between this company and North Staffordshire, submitted to this meeting, are hereby approved, but subject to the due approval thereof by an extraordinary general meeting of the shareholders of the North Staffordshire. And this meeting hereby authorises the directors of this company, after such approval on the part of the North Staffordshire, to affix the common seal of this company to the engrossments thereof in duplicate, one part to be held by this company, and the other part thereof to be held by the North Staffordshire; and this meeting hereby authorises the directors of this company, from time to time, to make, do, execute, and assent to all such lawful acts, deeds, and things whatsoever as shall, from time to time, be proper and sufficient for giving full effect to those articles of agreement, or as they shall, from time to time, think expedient, for attaining all or any of the objects of those articles of agreement and of the scheme respectively."

LEEDS NEW CENTRAL STATION.—By 28 and 29 Vic., cap. 267 (5th July, 1865), the London and North Western and the North Eastern obtained power to erect a new Central Station, in Leeds. New capital to each company, 100,000*l*. in shares, and 33,000*l*. on mortgage.

V. NEW WORKS, &c.—By 20 and 21 Vic., cap. 108 (27th July, 1857), in addition to amalgamation with the Shropshire Union, the following new works are authorised :—

1. Construction of a line, occupying in its course portions of the site of the Shropshire canal, and the discontinuance for public navigation of parts of that canal. The length of the line is 7 miles 7 furlongs and 7 chains ; and the amount of the estimate is 80,000*l*. 2. Acquisition by the London and North Western of additional lands at Watford. 3. Power for London and North Western and Great Western to enter into agreements with respect to the acquisition or user by the former company of the lands at Shrewsbury belonging to the latter company. 4. Further provision as to the station at Chester, in which the London and North Western, the Great Western, and other companies are interested.

By 21 and 22 Vic., cap. 131, the company was further authorised to construct the following additional works :—1. A branch and other works, and the acquisition of additional lands at Shrewsbury in connection with Crewe and Shrewsbury. 2. Diversion or alteration of certain roads, and the execution of certain miscellaneous works in connection with the undertaking, and acquisition of additional lands at Willesden, Linsdale, Crewe, Stafford, Northampton, Pitsford, and North Kilworth, and the alteration of the terminus at St. Albans. 3. Substitution of a viaduct and embankment for a viaduct on the Coventry and Nuneaton. 4. Power for the London and North Western, the Chester and Holyhead railways and the City of Dublin Steam Packet Companies to enter into agreements with reference to the objects and purposes of the "Improved Postal and Passenger Communications between England and Ireland Act, 1855," 5. Acquisition of additional lands, and widening of bridge over the Irwell.

By 22 and 23 Vic., cap. 2 (21st July, 1859), the London and North Western is authorised to construct a line from its station at Edge Hill, near Liverpool, to the St. Helens, at Garston. Length, 4½ miles. Opened 15th February, 1863. Arrangements for traffic over this junction, made with Great Northern and Manchester Sheffield and Lincolnshire.

By 22 and 23 Vic., cap. 88 (8th August, 1859), the London and North Western is authorised to construct a line from Aston Station to Sutton Coldfield. No new capital. Opened, 2nd June, 1862.

By 22 and 23 Vic., cap. 113 (13th August, 1859), the company was authorised to construct new works, and to acquire additional land in the counties of Lancaster and Northampton ; also to subscribe 50,000*l*. to the Oldham Ashton and Guide Bridge, and enter into working arrangements therewith. No new capital.

By 23 Vic., cap. 77 (14th June, 1860), certain arrangements were sanctioned with reference to the use by the London and North Western of the station at Normanton, and the railway between the same and Goosehill.

By 24 and 25 Vic., cap. 110 (28th June, 1861), the company was authorised to construct new lines from near Stockport to Cheadle, and from Chelford to Knutsford. Length, 13 miles. New capital, 133,500*l*. in shares, and 44,500*l*. on loan.

By 24 and 25 Vic., cap. 123 (11th July, 1861), the company acquired additional lands in connection with the Chester and Holyhead, and a renewal of the steamboat contract for a further period of nine years from end of 1862.

By 24 and 25 Vic., cap. 128 (11th July, 1861), the company was authorised to construct lines from Edge Hill to Bootle, from Winwick to Golborne, and from Aston to Ditton, with a branch to Runcorn, and bridge across the Mersey, with other powers to enlarge the stations at Lime Street and Wapping, in Liverpool. Length, 15 miles 33 chains. New capital, 1,000,000*l*. in shares, and 333,000*l*. on loan. Partially opened, 1st August, 1863.

By 24 and 25 Vic., cap. 130 (11th July, 1861), the company was authorised to construct a line from Eccles through Tyldesley and Wigan, with branches to Bedford and Leigh. Length, 13 miles. New capital, 350,000*l*. in shares, and 115,000*l*. on loan. Opened 24th August, 1864.

By 24 and 25 Vic., cap. 208 (1st August, 1861), additional powers were conferred on the company, including new lines at Burton-on-Trent, new provisions respecting the West London, relating to abandonment of part of Sutton Coldfield, &c. Length, 1 mile 16 chains. New capital, 100,000*l*., and 33,000*l*. on loan.

By 24 Vic., cap. 66 (12th June, 1861), further powers were conferred on the London and North Western and Manchester Sheffield and Lincolnshire, with respect to the division and regulation of the Manchester London Road station. No new capital.

By 24 and 25 Vic., cap. 166 (22nd July, 1861), further arrangements were authorised with the Lancaster and Carlisle and the Caledonian, respecting the Citadel Station in Carlisle. New capital, 45,000*l*. in shares, and 50,000*l*. on loan ; the Caledonian proportion of which being 33,000*l*.

By 24 and 25 Vic., cap. 219 (1st August, 1861), the company was authorised to take on lease or to purchase the St. George's Harbour.

By 25 and 26 Vic., cap. 208 (7th August, 1862), various additional powers were conferred upon the company, including branches, extending to 2⅓ miles. New capital, 180,000*l*. in ordinary shares, and 60,000*l*. by loan.

By 26 Vic., cap. 5 (4th May, 1863), the company was authorised to raise 50,000*l*. at 5 per cent., for purposes of North Union and Preston and Wyre.

By 26 and 27 Vic., cap. 177 (21st July, 1863), the company was authorised to construct several small branches to the West Cheshire, and to abandon part of the Chelford and Knutsford line. New lines, 10½ miles. Capital, 60,000*l*. in shares, and 20,000*l*. on loan.

By 26 and 27 Vic., cap. 217 (28th July, 1863), several additional powers were conferred on the company, including new lines in Yorkshire ; new arrangements respecting Chester joint station, and confirming agreements with Llanrwst, South Leicestershire, and Hampstead Junction, &c. New lines, 4½ miles. New capital, 150,000*l*. in shares, and 50,000*l*. by borrowing. Arrangements authorised with the Monmouthshire and Cheshire Midland, also to absorb the Cannock Mineral, and to convert Stour Valley stock into that of London and North Western.

By 27 and 28 Vic., cap. 226 (25th July, 1864), additional powers were conferred on the company in regard to alteration in works, abandonment of certain small lines, and agreements with other companies. New lines, 8½ miles. Capital, 265,000*l*. in shares, and 88,300*l*. on loan.

By an Act passed in 1855, the London and North Western, in conjunction with the Chester and Holyhead Railway, and the City of Dublin Steam Packet Companies, was authorised to contract with government for a better postal and passenger service between London and Kingstown. This contract is now extended to 1871. By 27 and 28 Vic., cap. 194 (14th July, 1864), the company was authorised to enter into traffic arrangements with the Irish North Western, the Dublin and Belfast, and the Dublin and Drogheda, with a view to still further improve the communication between the two countries.

By 28 and 29 Vic., cap. 333 (5th July, 1865), the company acquired further additional powers, including construction of several short lines and junctions. Length, 12⅞ miles. Capital, 800,000*l*. in shares, and 266,000*l*. on mortgage. Also, to dissolve the Bedford and Cambridge, and to incorporate that company with the London and North Western.

By 28 and 29 Vic., cap. 334 (5th July, 1865), the company obtained power to construct several short lines in Wales, 23½ miles in extent, and to raise new capital, 100,000*l.* in shares, and 33,000*l.* on loan.

By 29 and 30 Vic., cap. 168 (16th July, 1866), the company was authorised to construct several new lines in the West Riding, in Shropshire, Cheshire, and Flint. Length, 27 miles. Capital, 640,000*l.* in shares, and 213,000*l.* on loan.

By 29 and 30 Vic., cap. 249 (23rd July, 1866), the company obtained several additional powers in relation to their own undertaking, in purchasing land, constructing works, &c. New capital, 4,327,000*l.* in shares, and 375,300*l.* on loan. Also power to subscribe to the North Western and Charing Cross to the extent of 200,000*l.*, and to guarantee 5 per cent. on all or any part of the undertaking.

By 30 and 31 Vic., cap. 113 (15th July, 1867), the company was authorised to construct new branches to the extent of 9½ miles, to make certain deviations and other works, and to raise new capital, 200,000*l.* in shares, and 66,600*l.* on loan. Also to make arrangements with the Rhymney and the Brecon and Merthyr.

By 31 and 32 Vic., cap. 118 (13th July, 1868), the company acquired additional powers to construct new works in relation to its own as well as the undertakings of other companies. These included alterations in various roads, purchase of additional lands for its own uses, and also in conjunction with the Great Western at Kensington and the Midland at Huddersfield. An extension of time till 11th July, 1869, was obtained for completion of the Bridge over the Mersey at Runcorn; and also for two years with respect to the branches authorised by Act of 1863. Also to abandon part of the station works at Whitehaven. Compulsory sale of superfluous lands postponed for ten years, which may be sold either by way of rent-charge or for a sum in gross. Power to grant building leases on certain superfluous lands was also conceded, with a power likewise for the company to obtain the appointment of special constables to act in protection of its property. Debenture stock to be issued in lieu of debentures on any or all of the affiliated undertakings; agreements with Sheffield and the Midland (for which see APPENDIX to present Volume); and power, in conjunction with the Great Western, to purchase or hire steamboats for railway traffic between Birkenhead and Liverpool. The London and North Western was also authorised to subscribe to the Brynmawr to the extent of 15,000*l.*, and to appoint directors.

ASHBY AND NUNEATON.—By 20 Vic., cap. 94 (17th June, 1867), the London and North Western was authorised, jointly with the Midland, to construct and maintain these lines, which had been conceded to the Midland in the previous session.

By 31 and 32 Vic., cap. 49 (25th June, 1868), the Midland and the London and North Western obtained power to make certain deviations on these lines, and to construct others in substitution of parts abandoned. New capital 35,000*l.* in shares, and 11,200*l.* by borrowing, by each of the companies. New works to be completed by 6th August, 1871.

NEW WORKS AND ADDITIONAL POWERS.—By 30 and 31 Vic., cap. 144 (15th July, 1867), the company was authorised to construct a dock and embankments on the Mersey, and also to execute a variety of minor works relating to roads, bridges, &c.; also to acquire additional lands in or near Manchester, and a great number of other places. New capital, 1,500,000*l.* in shares, and 403,300*l.* on loan. Debenture stock to be re-sold at a rate of interest not exceeding 5 per cent. Mutual running powers over and for the North Staffordshire; arrangements with the Sirhowy, and power to subscribe 70,000*l.* to the Lancashire Union, 20,000*l.* to the Harborne, 50,000*l.* to the Central Wales, and 150,000*l.* to the Central Wales Extension. The London and North Western also to grant and issue its own mortgages for those of the Bangor and Carnarvon, the Warrington and Stockport, the Hampstead Junction, the Conway and Llanrwst, the Vale of Clwyd, the Stour Valley, South Staffordshire, and the South Leicestershire. The shares of the undermentioned companies were also to be converted into stocks of the London and North Western, viz., the Vale of Clwyd at 5 per cent., the Birmingham, Wolverhampton, and Stour Valley at two-thirds of the London and North Western dividend; the South Staffordshire at 4½ per cent. in perpetuity on its preference stock, and 4½ on its ordinary stock till 31st July, 1871, and 5 per cent. on the B shares till that date, and 4 per cent. thereafter; and the South Leicestershire and the Bangor and Carnarvon at 5 per cent., the whole of these undertakings being then vested in perpetuity in the London and North Western.

FLEETWOOD, PRESTON, AND WEST RIDING JUNCTION.—By 30 Vic., cap. 95 (17th June, 1867), this undertaking was vested jointly in the London and North Western and the Lancashire and Yorkshire.

SOUTH STAFFORDSHIRE.—The agreement has been completed by a settlement with the lessee, under which all questions, the subject of arbitration, were withdrawn, on payment of the sum of 110,099*l.*, including the lessee's interest in the unexpired term of the eleven years in the agreement known as the "Four Town's Agreement."

MERTHYR, TREDEGAR, AND ABERGAVENNY.—Incorporated by 22 and 23 Vic., cap. 59 (1st August, 1859), to supply railway communication to the district between Merthyr and Abergavenny. Capital 150,000*l.* in 20*l.* shares. Loans, 49,900*l.* The length of the first railway is 9½ miles; the second, 4⅜ miles. By 25 and 26 Vic., cap. 209 (7th August,

1862), the line was leased for a thousand years to the London and North Western, at 5 per cent., with special facilities to the Great Western. By 26 and 27 Vic., cap. 126 (13th July, 1863), the company was authorised to execute some deviation and new works, and to raise additional capital to the extent of 70,000*l.* in shares, and 23,000*l.* on loan, for the purpose of doubling the line. By the London and North Western (Additional Powers in Wales) Act of 1865, the time for doubling this line was extended to 1st August, 1868. The company was dissolved, as from 30th June, 1866, the line now forming part of the London and North Western system, the shares being converted into 5 per cent. preference stock, the London and North Western undertaking the debenture debt and every other liability.

BEDFORD AND CAMBRIDGE.—Incorporated by 23 and 24 Vic., cap. 183 (6th August, 1860), to construct a line commencing by a junction with the Bletchley and Bedford Branch of London and North Western, and terminating at Cambridge, by a junction with Great Eastern. Length, 29¾ miles. Capital, 240,000*l.*, in 10*l.* shares. Opened 1st August, 1862. Worked by London and North Western, which subscribed 70,000*l.* By 27 and 28 Vic., cap. 62 (23rd June, 1864), further arrangements were authorised with the London and North Western. New capital was also authorised to the extent of 50,000*l.* in shares. The line is leased to the London and North Western at 4 per cent. in perpetuity, and has ceased to exist as an independent company.

CONWAY AND LLANRWST.—Incorporated by 23 and 24 Vic., cap. 149 (23rd July, 1860), to construct a line from Chester and Holyhead, near Conway, to Llanrwst. Length, 11½ miles. Capital, 50,000*l.* in 10*l.* shares; loans, 16,666*l.* By 24 and 25 Vic., cap. 179 (22nd July, 1861), the company was authorised to make a deviation and alteration in the line, to be completed within three years. Also to raise additional capital, 10,000*l.* in shares, and 3,300*l.* on loan. Opened 17th June, 1863 : by 26 and 27 Vic., cap. 217 (28th July, 1833), transferred to London and North Western, at a rent equal to 5 per cent. on the share capital. The London and North Western Act of 1865, conveys power to that company to convert Conway and Llanrwst stock into London and North Western capital.

ST. GEORGE'S HARBOUR.—Incorporated by 16 and 17 Vic., cap. 213 (1853), to construct a harbour, with pier and other works, at Llandudno, with a railway to the Chester and Holyhead. Capital, 150,000*l.*, in 20*l.* shares, and 50,000*l.* on loan. By Act of 1853, new capital was authorised, but power to construct the harbour became extinct. By 24 and 25 Vic., cap. 219 (1st August, 1861), a lease or sale of the railway to the London and North Western was permitted, but power to construct the undertaking restricted to 70,000*l.* in shares. Loans, 20,000*l.* Rent not to exceed 2,500*l.*, which may be redeemed by London and North Western allotting stock bearing fixed dividend equal to that amount.

SHREWSBURY AND HEREFORD—This line is leased at 6 per cent., one-half by the London and North Western, and the other moiety by the Great Western.

SHREWSBURY AND WELSHPOOL.—Incorporated by 19 and 20 Vic., cap. 132 (July 1856), to construct a line from general station at Shrewsbury to junction with Oswestry and Newtown at Welshpool, with branch to Minsterley. Capital, 150,000*l.*, in 10*l.* shares. Loans, 50,000*l.* Length of main line, 16¼ miles, and of branch. 5 miles. Company may use part of Shrewsbury and Hereford. Board of Trade to decide in case of disagreement. By 21 and 22 Vic., cap. 110 (23rd July, 1858), an extension of time for two years was conceded. The directors entered into a contract with Mr. Alexander Thomas Gordon, by which he engaged to purchase land, construct the railway, and pay all incidental expenses up to opening of line, and to keep it in repair for one year after opening, for a sum equal to that upon which the interest and dividends are secured by undermentioned arrangements with London and North Western. By 23 Vic., cap. 25 (18th May, 1860), the company was authorised to make certain deviations and alterations in levels, to raise further capital to the extent of 30,000*l.*, which has been issued at 4½ per cent. preference. Extension of time till 15th May, 1862. By 24 Vic., cap. 13 (17th May, 1861), the company was authorised to widen the Minsterley branch, and to raise further capital, 12,000*l.* in shares, and 4,000*l.* on loan. By 26 and 27 Vic., cap. 97 (29th June, 1863), the company was authorised to raise new capital to the extent of 54,000*l.*, in shares at 5 per cent., and 18,000*l.* on loan, for the purpose of doubling the line to Llanwood. Also to authorise sale or lease to London and North Western and Great Western jointly. By 27 and 28 Vic., cap. 196 (14th July, 1864), the Shrewsbury and Welshpool was leased to the London and North Western, or jointly to that company and the Great Western, for 300,000*l.* in perpetual 4 per cent. preference stock.

SOUTH LEICESTERSHIRE.—Incorporated by 22 and 23 Vic., cap. 104 (18th August, 1859), to construct a line from the Trent Valley, at Nuneaton, to Hinckley, in Leicestershire. Capital. 45,000*l.*, in 10*l.* shares; loans, 14,000*l.* Single line. Length, 4½ miles. Estimate, 42,000*l.* Extra land, two acres; compulsory purchase, two years; completion of works, three years. Traffic and working arrangements with London and North Western under usual restrictions calculated to realise 4½ per cent. Company or London and North Western to use Midland between Rugby and Leicester, and Midland, in return, to use the line between the Wigston Magna and Nuneaton, and London and North Western, as far as Coventry. Mutual accommodation in respect to stations, and regulations in regard to tolls. By 23 Vic., cap. 91 (14th June, 1860), the company was authorised to change its name as above, and to extend its line from Hinckley to Wigston Magna, on the Midland. Length, 10½ miles. New capital, 150,000*l.* in shares, and 50,000*l.* on loan. The Midland also entered into an agreement with the directors and those of the London and North Western for mutual accommodation of the traffic of the district. including terminal station arrangements. Opened from Nuneaton to Hinckley, 4½ miles, on 1st January, 1862; from Hinckley to Wigston Junction, 1st January, 1864. Dividends at the rate of 4½ per cent. have been regularly declared.

ST. HELENS.—An amalgamation of the SANKEY BROOK NAVIGATION and ST. HELENS and RUNCORN GAP RAILWAY, under the powers of an Act passed in 1845 (8 and 9 Vic., cap. 117). In 1846 powers were acquired to construct a branch from the original line at Widnes to Garston, four miles south of Liverpool, and to make docks at Garston : and in 1847 to improve the main line, and to construct branches to Warrington and to Blackbrook. In 1853, to make branches to Rainford and to Eccleston. Productive mileage, 36 railway (including 14 in lease to London and North Western) and 16 canal. By 20 and 21 Vic., cap. 16 (26th June, 1857), new capital was authorised to the extent of 100,000l. of 6 per cent., for the general purposes of the undertaking. By Acts of 1859, the London and North Western were authorised to construct a line from Edgehill to the St. Helens, near Garston, making a new route to Manchester of 36 miles in length ; also to lease the Warrington and Stockport. By 23 and 24 Vic. (14th June, 1860), a portion of the St. Helens (from Warrington to Garston, 14 miles, was leased to the London and North Western, at a rent of 12,000l. per annum. The St. Helens was also authorised, by the same Act, to create new capital, to the extent of 100,000l., at 5 per cent. preference, and 33,000l. on loan. By 27 and 28 Vic., cap. 296 (29th July, 1864), the remainder of the St. Helens became vested in the London and North Western, the latter company guaranteed the ordinary stock at 4 per cent. for 1865, 4½ for 1866, and 5 in perpetuity thereafter. Power to Lancashire and Yorkshire to use part of St. Helens.

CENTRAL WALES.—Incorporated by 22 and 23 Vic., cap. 121 (13th August, 1859). to construct a line from Knighton to Llandrindod, in Radnorshire. Length, 20 miles. Capital, 160,000l. in 10l. shares ; loans, 53,300l. Opened in September, 1865, and worked by London and North Western. By 26 and 27 Vic., cap. 79 (22nd June, 1863), amalgamation with the Knighton (12 miles) was authorised. The two lines extend from Craven Arms, on the Shrewsbury and Hereford, to the Central Wales Extension, at Llandrindod. United existing capital, 326,000l. in shares, with one-third additional on loan. New shares may be issued by the Knighton, to the extent of 40,000l.. and by the Central Wales, 60,000l. each at 5 per cent., with 33,000l. on loan, vested in the London and North Western at 4 per cent.

CENTRAL WALES EXTENSION. –Incorporated by 23 and 24 Vic., cap. 141 (3rd July, 1860). The company is authorised to construct an extension from Llandrindod to Llandovery. Length, 26¼ miles. Capital, 208,000l. in 10l. shares. Loans, 69,338l. Traffic with Mid-Wales to be facilitated. Working agreements with the Llanelly, Knighton, Central Wales, and Shrewsbury and Hereford, during which whole system to be considered one continuous line. Joint committee to be appointed. By 26 and 27 Vic.. cap. 77 (1863), the company was authorised to raise further capital to the extent of 120,000l. in shares at 5 per cent., and 40,000l. on loan. Also to enter into arrangements with London and North Western. These shares were created at the meeting on 29th August, 1864. Opened. By 29 Vic., cap. 3 (30th April, 1866), the company obtained an extension of time for completion of works until 3rd July, 1867, and also to create new capital to the extent of 150,000l. in shares, and 50,000l. on loan. At a special meeting held in Westminster Chambers, London, on 10th July, 1866. it was resolved to authorise the creation and issue of additional capital to the amount of 150,000l. in shares of 10l. each ; 130,000l. being in 5 per cent. preference shares, and 20,000l. in ordinary shares. Vested in the London and North Western at 2½ per cent.

KNIGHTON.—Incorporated by 21 Vic., cap. 19 (21st May, 1858), to construct a line from Craven Arms, on the Shrewsbury and Hereford, to Knighton. Length, 12 miles. Capital, 66,000l. in 10l. shares : loans, 22,000l. Opened to Bucknell, 9 miles, on 1st October, 1860 : to Knighton, 3 miles, on 6th March, 1861. By 26 and 27 Vic., cap. 79 (22nd June, 1863), the Knighton passed into the hands of the London and North Western on 30th June, 1862, and is in receipt therefrom of dividend at the rate of 4 per cent.

VALE OF TOWY.—By 31 and 32 Vic., cap. 37 (25th June, 1868), these three companies were authorised to take a joint lease of the Llanelly of the Vale of Towy, which is thus brought into co-operation with the London and North Western.

VALE OF CLWYD.—Incorporated by 19 and 20 Vic., cap. 45 (23rd June, 1856), to construct a railway from the Chester and Holyhead, near Rhyl, to the town of Denbigh, 10 miles. Capital, 60,000l. in 10l. shares with 20,000l. on loan. The line is single, but the bridges and other works are formed for a double line. By 24 and 25 Vic., cap. 192 (22nd July, 1861), the company was authorised to create new shares to the extent of 50,000l., to redeem personal advances made by the directors, and to complete certain works, including a double line of rails when required. By 25 and 26 Vic., cap. 93 (30th June, 1862), the company was authorised to divert a portion of the existing line. and to extend it to the north-west shore of the river Clwyd, at Foryd. Length, 1 mile. Capital, 10,000l. at 5 per cent. preference. and 3,300l. on loan. Opened in October, 1865. Embodied in London and North Western at 5 per cent., by Act of 1868.

MILEAGE —In operation, 1,372 miles, '.½ having been added during the year, consisting of branches and junctions by lease or otherwise.

REVENUE.—As compared with the corresponding period of 1866, the amount received for passengers, &c., goods, minerals, and cattle, for the half-year ending 31st December, were as follows:—

	1867.	1866.	Increase.
Passenger, &c., receipts	£1,544,913	£1,529,408	£15,505
Goods, mineral, and cattle receipts	1,875,584	1,788,886	86,698
Total	£3,420,497	£3,318,294	£102,203

After discharging the debenture and preference interest, rents of leased lines, &c., the net proceeds of the half-year's working were 1,143,811*l.*, which, with balance from last account of 28,676*l.*, made a disposable balance of 1,172,487*l.*, out of which a dividend at the rate of 6¾ per cent. per annum left a balance of 34,658*l.*

The receipts for the half-year ending 30th June were 3,053,481*l.*, and the expenditure 1,531,162*l.*, including 66,661*l.* compensation for accidents and losses in respect of passengers, goods, &c., 25,003*l.* for parliamentary and legal proceedings, 57,931*l.* for parish rates and taxes, and 37,414*l.* for duty on passenger traffic, leaving a balance of 1,522,319*l.* To this was added 34,658*l.*, from the preceding half-year, 22,737*l.* for interest account, 35,651*l.*, ror rents of lands and buildings, 6,195*l.* for Manchester, Buxton, and Matlock lease one year, 3,000*l.* for Great Western moiety of Shrewsbury and Welshpool dividend, and 74,947*l.* for dividends on investments in nine other railway companies, making the total receipts on general revenue account 1,699,507*l.* From this was deducted 324,400*l.*, for interest on loans and debenture stock, 19,255*l.* chief rents and interest on land purchases, 24,900*l.* Buckinghamshire lease, 2,750*l.* Cannock mineral lease, 28,172*l.* for North Union guaranteed dividend, &c., and 307,747*l.* for the rents of 14 railway and canal undertakings, leaving a disposable balance of 992,283*l.* available for dividends, out of which 179,570*l.* was deducted for guaranteed dividends, varying from 10 to 3½ per cent. on 15 separate undertakings belonging to the company, and 784,327*l.* for ordinary dividend at the rate of 5¼ per cent. per annum, leaving a balance of 28,386*l.* for next account.

NEW CAPITAL.—At a special meeting held on 21st February, 1867, it was resolved :—

That in pursuance of the powers of "The London and North Western (New Works and Additional Powers) Act, 1867," an additional capital of 20,510*l.* be created, for the conversion of the preference shares of the Warrington and Stockport into stock of the company, bearing a dividend at the rate of 5*l.* per cent. per annum, payable half-yearly, at the same periods as the dividends on the ordinary stock of the company are payable.

That in pursuance of the powers of "The London and North Western (New Works and Additional Powers) Act, 1867," an additional capital of 506,770*l.* 14*s.* be created, for the conversion of the shares or stock of the Birmingham, Wolverhampton, and Stour Valley into stock of the company, bearing a dividend equal to two-thirds of the dividend paid from time to time by the company on their ordinary stock, and payable half-yearly, at the same perods as the dividends on the ordinary stock of the company are payable.

That in pursuance of the powers of "The London and North Western (New Works and Additional Powers) Act, 1867," an additional capital of 1,302,000*l.* be created, for the conversion of the shares or stock of the South Staffordshire into stock of the company, bearing a dividend as follows:—On the existing preference shares or stock of the South Staffordshire at the rate of 4*l.* 10*s.* per cent. per annum in perpetuity. On the ordinary shares or stock of the South Staffordshire at the rate of 4*l.* 10*s.* per cent. per annum until the 31st July, 1871, and thereafter at the rate of 4*l.* per cent. per annum in perpetuity. On the B shares of the South Staffordshire at the rate of 5*l.* per cent. per annum until 31st July, 1871, and thereafter at the rate of 4*l.* per cent. per annum in perpetuity ; and the said dividends, respectively, to be payable half-yearly at the same periods as the dividends on the ordinary stock of the company are payable.

That in pursuance of the powers of "The London and North Western (New Works and Additional Powers) Act, 1867," an additional capital of 195,000*l.* be created, for the conversion of the shares or stock of the South Leicestershire into stock of the company, b aring a dividend at the rate of 5*l.* per cent. per annum, payable half-yearly, at the same periods as the dividends on the ordinary stock of the company are payable.

That in pursuance of the powers of "The Carnarvon and Llanberis Act, 1867," this meeting authorises the directors to subscribe towards the undertaking of the Carnarvon and Llanberis to an extent not exceeding 80,000*l.*

That in pursuance of the powers of "The London and North Western (New Works and Additional Powers) Act, 1867," an additional capital of 150,000*l.* be created, for the conversion of the shares or stock of the Bangor and Carnarvon into stock of the company, bearing a dividend at the rate of 5*l.* per cent. per annum, payable half-yearly at the same periods as the dividends on the ordinary stock of the company are payable.

That in pursuance of the powers of "The London and North Western (New Works and Additional Powers) Act, 1867," an additional capital of 120,000*l.* be created, for the conversion of the shares or stock of the Vale of Clwyd in stock of the company, bearing a dividend at the rate of 5*l.* per cent. per annum, payable half-yearly, at the same periods as the dividends on the ordinary stock of the company are payable.

CAPITAL.—This account to 30th June showed that 43,581,901*l.* had been authorised to be raised on shares and stocks, including conversion of the capitals of subsidiary companies, and 16,522,182*l.* on loans, making a total of 60,104,083*l.*, of which 53,685,720*l.* had been created or sanctioned. The amount raised on debentures and by debenture stocks was 15,105,814*l.* The receipts amounted to 36,712,895*l.* on stocks and shares, to 12,770,291*l.* on debentures, and to 2,335,523*l.* on debenture stocks ; total, 51,818,709*l.* The amount expended. including subscriptions to other companies, has been 50,243,787*l.*, leaving a balance of 1,574,922*l.* The general statement is as follows :—

DESCRIPTION.	Amount.	Received.	In arrear.	Unissued
	£	£	£	£
Consolidated	29,817,152	29,501,619	5,393	310,138
Capital created 24th February, 1865, for conversion of Shropshire Union and Stour Valley stocks	1,283,182	372,124	....	911,057
Ordinary consolidated	31,100,334	29,873,744	5,393	1,221,195
Coventry and Nuneaton	270,000	270,000	....	....
Perpetual 5 per cent. preference	2,425,576	2,425,576	....	....
St. Helens	911,480	911,480	....	....
Bedford and Cambridge	240,000	239,436	563	....
Shrewsbury and Welshpool	300,000	300,000	....	....
St. George's Harbour	62,500	62,500	....	....
Merthyr, Tredegar, and Abergavenny	220,000	220,000	....	....
Whitehaven Junction	230,000	230,000	....	....
Cockermouth and Workington	129,000	129,000	....	....
Stockport, Disley, and Whaley Bridge	385,000	385,000	....	....
Warrington and Stockport	20,510	20,510	....	....
South Leicestershire	195,000	179,226	64	15,710
Birmingham, Wolverhampton, & Stour Valley	506,770	467,131	....	39,639
South Staffordshire	1,302,300	1,300,485	146	1,369
Vale of Clwyd	120,000	100,000	....	20,000
Bangor and Carnarvon	150,000	150,000	....	....
Total Joint Stock Capital	38,568,170	37,264,089	6,167	1,297,914

Addition to capital, per 9 and 10 Vic., cap. 204 .... £964,759				
Exchanged for Shropshire Union stock, 353,290*l.* 14*s.* 6*d.*, at 50*l.* per cent. 176,645				
	£1,141,404			
Less—Reduction of capital of Huddersfield and Manchester, Leeds and Dewsbury, and Birmingham, Wolverhampton, and Stour Valley 590,210		....	551,194	
		36,712,894		

The receipts and disbursements on revenue account for the half-year ending 30th June, were detailed in the statements subjoined :—

Receipts.—Disposable balance 31st December £1,172,487
Less dividend ordered 21st February .... 1,137,829 = £34,658
Balance of traffic account, this date   1,522,318
Interest account..   22,737
Rents of land and buildings........................... 44,835
Less repairs and Sundries .... 9,184 = £35,650
Manchester Buxton and Matlock lease .... 1 year   6,195
Great Western moiety of Shrewsbury and Welshpool dividend   3,000
Dividends received from Lancaster and Carlisle........ 19,125
     South Staffordshire 4,185
     Manchester and South Junction 8,864
     North London 36,220
     Scottish North Eastern 150
     Manchester, Buxton, and Matlock 633
     Shropshire Union.................................. 5,572
     Stockport Disley and Whaley Bridge 801
     Cockermouth and Penrith 281
                                £75,833
Estimated December half-year 73,062
                                 £2,771
Estimated June half-year.... .... 72,175 = £74,946 = £1,699,506

Expenditure.—Interest on loans...................... £278,466
Ditto on debenture stock .... 45,933=£324,400
Chief rents and interest on land purchases 19,254
Buckinghamshire lease 24,900
Cannock Mineral do. 2,750
North Union guaranteed dividend 21,084
     Interest—Chief rents, &c. .... 7,087 = 28,171
Preston and Wyre ....lease 4,188
Chester and Holyhead .... „ 86,108
Lancaster and Carlisle .... „ 127,217
Kendal and Windermere..................................... „ 4,337
Shropshire Union.. „ 29,673
West London .... „ 450
Leeds and Liverpool and Rochdale .... „ 2,454
Birkenhead.. „ 28,108
Oldham Ashton and Guide Bridge .... „ 1,265
Shrewsbury and Hereford................................... „ 12,031
Cromford and High Peak................................... „ 2,000
Central Wales ....agreement 2,845
Fleetwood Preston and West Riding .... „ 732
Disposable Balance .... 992,282=£1,699,506

The accounts are made up to 30th June and 31st December, and the statutory meetings held in London in February and August.

Scale of Voting.—One vote for every 100*l.* stock up to 1,000*l.*; then one for every 500*l.* up to 10,000*l.*; above that one vote additional for every 1,000*l.*

Certificates of shares not required to accompany transfer deed. Registration fee, 2*s.* 6*d.* each deed. Certificates of stock must accompany transfers; 1*l.* lowest sum transferable; several classes of shares may go on one transfer.

No. of Directors (consolidated by Act 1846)—30; of whom one is appointed by the Duke of Sutherland. *Qualification,* 1,000*l.* stock.

DIRECTORS:
Chairman—RICHARD MOON, Esq., Wigginton Lodge, Tamworth.
Deputy-Chairman—J. P. BROWN-WESTHEAD, Esq., M.P., 13, Eaton Square, S.W., and Lea Castle, near Kidderminster.

James Bancroft, Esq., 5, Police Street, Manchester.
Robert Benson, Esq., 16, Craven Hill Gardens, Hyde Park, W.
John Pares Bickersteth, Esq., Southcot, Leighton Buzzard.
Richard Birley, Esq., Seedley, Pendleton, Manchester.
Lieut.-Col. James Bourne, M.P., 16, Suffolk Street, S.W., and Heathfield House, Wavertree, near Liverpool.
Thomas Brassey, Junr., Esq., M. P., Beauport, Battle, Sussex.
The Hon. T. C. Bruce, 13, Hertford Street, May Fair, W.
James Timmins Chance, Esq., Handsworth, near Birmingham.
Richard Ryder Dean, Esq., 97, Gloucester Place, Portman Square, W.
Hardman Earle, Esq., Allerton Tower, near Liverpool.
George Carr Glyn, Esq , 67, Lombard Street, E.C.
Samuel Robert Graves, Esq.. M.P., 5, Cleveland Row, S.W., and The Grange, Liverpool.
William Edwards Hirst, Esq., Lascelles Hall, Huddersfield.

Wm. Nicholson Hodgson, Esq., M.P., Newby Grange, Carlisle, and 33, Duke Street, St. James's, S.W.
The Hon. C. W. G. Howard, M.P., 122, Park Street, W.;. and Naworth Castle, near Brampton. Cumberland.
George Hall Lawrence, Esq., Mossley Hill, Liverpool.
Matthew Lyon, Esq., Leamington.
Michael Linning Melville, Esq., Tunbridge Wells.
Sam Mendel, Esq., Manchester.
Arthur Mills, Esq., 34, Hyde Park Gardens, W.
Lord Alfred Paget, 56, Queen Anne Street, London, W.
George Sheward, Esq., 17, Leinster Square, Bayswater, W.
Oscar Leslie Stephen, Esq., Bardon Hall, Leicester.
The Duke of Sutherland, K.G., Stafford House, St. James's, S.W.
William Tipping, Esq., M.P., Brasted Park, Sevenoaks, Kent.
Edward Tootal, Esq., The Weaste, Manchester.
Henry Cotton Tunnicliffe, Esq., Brunswick Street, Liverpool.

OFFICERS.—Sec., Stephen Reay. Gen. Man., William Cawkwell. Assistant Man., C. Mason. Man. of Goods Traff., George Findlay. Out-Door Supt., G. P. Neele. Supts. of Traff., H. P. Bruyeres, London; J. Shaw, Liverpool; W. Sutton. Manchester; J. O. Binger, Chester.; J. H. Roberts, Birmingham. District Goods Mans., D. Stevenson, Rugby; G. Greenish, Camden Station, London; D. Taylor, Liverpool; T. Kay, Manchester; J. Fitzsimons, Lancaster; E. Huntley, Wolverhampton; E. Wood, Shrewsbury; J. Bishop, Abergavenny; E. Farr, Chester; J. Mason, Birmingham; J. Thurstan, Warrington; J. Myson, Whitehaven. Civil Eng., W. Baker. Supts. of Permanent Way, H. Woodhouse, Stafford; H. Lee, Bangor; S. B. Worthington, Manchester; W. Smith, Crewe. Mechanical Eng., J. Ramsbottom, Crewe. Marine Supt., Captain Dent, R.N., Holyhead. Auditors, H. Crosfield and R. W. Hand. Solicitor, James Blenkinsop.

Offices—Euston Station, Euston Square, N.W.

233.—LONDON AND SOUTH WESTERN.

Incorporated in 1834, by 4 and 5 Wm. IV., cap. 88, under the title of the LONDON and SOUTHAMPTON, which is retained until 1839, when it was altered by 2 Vic., cap. 28. This line commences at London, near Waterloo Bridge, proceeding thence south-west of Basingstoke ; then southerly to Southampton, the original terminus ; thence by the incorporation of the SOUTHAMPTON and DORCHESTER, extended along the South Coast to Dorchester. Also has branches to Hampton Court, Chertsey, and Guildford, Farnham, Alton, and by Andover to Salisbury and Exeter and Exmouth, also from Bishopstoke to Romsey and Salisbury, and to Gosport ; a short branch from Fareham connects this line with the London Brighton and South Coast ; a joint interest in the portion from the junction of the two lines at Cosham into Portsmouth (4½ miles) has been purchased from the Brighton for 60,000*l*.   By the complete incorporation of the WINDSOR STAINES and SOUTH WESTERN, this company also possesses an important branch through Richmond to Windsor, with a loop at Barnes, crossing the Thames to Kew, Brentford, and the main line branch beyond Hounslow.

By 18 and 19 Vic., cap. 188 (August 14th, 1855), the whole of the company's Acts were consolidated, and other powers conferred.   It removed certain irregularities which had in the course of years grown up in the creation of portion of the ordinary share capital, and settles its amount at 7,354,650*l*.   It in like manner defines the borrowing power at 2,400,416*l*.   It consolidates into stock the amount paid up on the 7 per cent. preference shares (171,276*l*. 13*s*. 4*d*.), and repeals the power of issuing any more of those shares, and of calling any more upon those already issued (total repeal power, 1,933,723*l*. 6*s*. 8*d*.), and it confines the right of voting to the amount actually paid up.   It authorises raising of additional sums of 9,000*l*. in shares, and 3,000*l*. in loans, for the new works.   It also authorises an alteration in the mode of constructing the Basingstoke and Salisbury, as well as an improvement of the company's wharf premises at Nine Elms, and a new connection by railway between the parts of the company's goods yards, lying on the opposite sides of the Nine Elms line.   It likewise enables the company to complete four lines of rails between Vauxhall and Falcon Bridge.

By 20 and 21 Vic., cap. 136 (10th August, 1857), the company obtained several deviations and improvements of its line at Salisbury.   By 21 and 22 Vic., cap. 89 (12th July, 1858), the company is authorised to lease the Salisbury and Yeovil, to extend their works, and further to regulate the capital.

By 19 and 20 Vic., cap. 120 (21st July, 1856), the company was empowered to construct a line from Yeovil to Exeter, 50 miles.   Contracts with the Salisbury and Yeovil declared valid ; the South Western may hold shares to the extent of 100,000*l*. in the Salisbury and Yeovil, on a preference dividend of 5 per cent. ; and may lend to that company 100,000*l*., as well as nominate two directors to that board.

By 22 and 23 Vic., cap. 44 (1st August, 1852), various amendments and extension of power were authorised.   Besides authorising arrangements with the Brighton respecting the through traffic between London and Portsmouth, and enabling the South Western to execute a branch in the Kingston district, the Act authorised an enlargement of the West Station at Southampton, and also to enable the proprietors to reduce, if they see fit, the number of directors to nine.   Additional capital, in shares, 100,000*l*.; on loan, 33,000*l*.   Opened 1st June, 1863.

By 23 and 24 Vic., cap. 185 (6th August, 1860, Kingston Extension), the company received additional powers, and was authorised to abandon a portion, near Kingston Bridge, and in lieu thereof to make a railway (length, 72 chains), to extend the remainder across the Thames; also to abandon railways at Havant and station at Portsea.   To authorise leases or transfers of the Stokes Bay, Isle of Wight Ferry, Lymington, and Exeter and Exmouth, and lease of the Dorset Central from the Southampton and Dorchester to Blandford.   To authorise arrangements for making and working of the works of the Stokes Bay and Isle of Wight Ferry, and also for working the Epsom and Leatherhead.   To make perpetual the powers given to the South Western for fourteen years by their Acts of 1848, of working steam vessels between English and French Ports and the Channel Islands.   To enable the company to raise additional sums of 50,000*l*. by new shares, and 16,666*l*. by borrowing, and 300,000*l*. by new shares, and 100,000*l*. by borrowing for general purposes.

By 23 and 24 Vic., cap. 103 (3rd July, 1860), the company was authorised to extend the Exeter line, and to connect it with the Bristol and Exeter ; also to make alterations in the St. David's station of that line, and to lay down and work over narrow gauge rails from Exeter to Bideford.   Completion of works, three years.   The Exeter and Crediton, North Devon, and Bideford may be leased to the South Western, and when so to be deemed one continuous line.   New capital : South Western, 120,000*l*.; Exeter and Crediton, 15,000*l*.; Bideford, 7,500*l*.; all at 5 per cent. preference.   Borrowing powers : South Western, 40,000*l*. ; Exeter and Crediton, 5,000*l*.; Bideford, 2,500*l*.

By 25 Vic., cap. 42 (3rd June, 1862), the company obtained several additional powers, includng new works, transfer of the Wimbledon and Dorking, and various arrangements respecting increase of capital by creation of new shares, to the extent of 500,000*l*., and 166,666*l*. on loan.

By 27 and 28 Vic., cap. 87 (23rd June, 1864), the company was authorised to construct a line from Chertsey to the Staines and Wokingham and Egham. Length, 2¾ miles. Capital, 45,000*l.* in shares, and 15,000*l.* on loans.

By 27 and 28 Vic., cap. 166 (14th July, 1864), the company was authorised to construct a line from the Hammersmith and City and the North and South Western Junction at Kensington to Richmond. Length, 6¾ miles. Capital, 330,000*l.* in shares, and 110,000*l.* on loan.

By 27 and 28 Vic., cap. 227 (25th July, 1864), various powers of amalgamation (see below) were given to the company. New capital, 27,000*l.* in shares, and 9,000*l.* on loan.

By 28 Vic., cap. 89 (19th June, 1865), the company was authorised to abandon the lines at Kensington and Hammersmith, and to construct others instead. Also to work over and interchange traffic with the Hammersmith.

By 28 Vic., cap. 102 (19th June, 1865), the company was authorised to construct certain new lines in Surrey. Length, 6½ miles. Capital, 120,000*l.* in shares, and 40,000*l.* on mortgage.

By 28 Vic., cap. 103 (19th June, 1865), the company obtained power to construct a line from Pirbright, by Aldershot, to Farnham. Length, 9 miles. Capital, 160,000*l.* in shares, and 53,330*l.* on mortgage.

By 28 Vic., cap. 104, the company was authorised to construct a line from Bideford to Great Torrington. Length, 5¼ miles. Capital, 80,000*l.* in shares, and 26,600*l.* on loan.

By 28 and 29 Vic., cap. 304 (5th July, 1865), the South Western obtained power to construct several new works, to amalgamate the Salisbury and Yeovil, and the Exeter and Exmouth, and to regulate and increase the capital and borrowing powers of the company. New capital, 517,500*l.* in shares, and 172,500*l.* by mortgage. Transfer of part of the Chatham line is also regulated by this Act.

By 28 and 29 Vic., cap. 268 (5th July, 1865), the South Western was authorised to contribute towards construction of a part of the Chatham Metropolitan Extensions, and to obtain uses of the same. New capital, 400,000*l.* in shares, and 133,300*l.* on mortgage. By the same Act power is taken to amalgamate the Salisbury and Yeovil, and the Thames Valley, when these companies shall so agree.

By 29 and 30 Vic., cap. 216 (16th July, 1866), the South Western obtained power to construct curves at Kew Bridge and Brentford; to enter into arrangements with the Great Western in respect of the Weymouth and Portland; and to lease the Devon and Cornwall. Also to lay down additional lines of rails on several parts of the system. New capital to the extent of 200,000*l.* in shares, and 66,600*l.* on loan. Completion of the Kensington and Richmond lines was likewise postponed till 31st December, 1867.

By 29 and 30 Vic., cap. 217 (16th July, 1866), the South Western were authorised to construct lines from the Southampton and Dorchester to the Poole and Bournemouth. Length, 4½ miles. New capital, 54,000*l.* in shares, and 18,500*l.* on loan.

By 30 and 31 Vic., cap. 156 (25th July, 1867), the South Western was authorised to construct certain deviations and new works, as well as to enter upon arrangements with the Great Western, the Chatham, the Metropolitan, and the Hammersmith, and to lease the Salisbury and Dorset Junction, and the Salisbury and Yeovil. The South Western was authorised to complete the connection with the Chatham and Dover at its own expense, any excess over 92,500*l.* to be repaid by the latter. By this Act the South Western capital was declared to consist of 12,807,558*l.*, which amount is liable to increase by the creation of stock already authorised but not issued, by subscription to the Waterloo and Whitehall, and to the Salisbury and Dorset. An amalgamated stock at 5 per cent. was also authorised, to take the place of the various existing preference liabilities, and also to create and issue debenture stock in lieu of mortgages.

By 31 and 32 Vic., cap. 69 (25th June, 1868), the company obtained an extension of time for its Kensington and Richmond till 31st December, 1868, and for its Aldershot works till 31st July, 1870. A public carriage road, toll free, to be constructed near Brookwood station ; other roads to be stopped up or diverted; and building leases to be granted on superfluous lands.

STOKES BAY.—An arrangement has been concluded with the Stokes Bay, by which the South Western leases and works that undertaking, in perpetuity, at a yearly rent of 1,800*l.*; but such arrangement is to cease if the sea service between Stokes Bay and the Isle of Wight should at any time not be sufficiently worked or provided for by the Stokes Bay or Ferry Company.

WIMBLEDON AND CROYDON.—The Brighton and South Western are authorised to accept a lease of this line, about 8¼ miles in length. The rent is 1,820*l.* per annum, being a rate of interest of 4 per cent. on cost of line.

WIMBLEDON AND EPSOM.—The line was opened on the 4th April, 1859, and has since been purchased by the South Western.

SALISBURY.—These works are to be constructed and maintained at the cost of the promoters ; and, by largely increasing the market accommodation at Salisbury, they cannot fail to contribute to the traffic of this company. It has been arranged that the market branch line shall be worked by the South Western, and that they shall have the control of the persons employed thereon.

STAINES AND WOKINGHAM.—This line was opened for traffic on 4th June, 1856, as far as Ascot, and on the 9th July, to Reading. The line is leased by the South Western at 50 per cent. on the receipts, for 42 years, from 25th March, 1858. The rent is to be half of the gross receipts between Staines and Wokingham, but not less in any year than 7,000l., the South Western paying toll for the use of the portion of the South Eastern, and retaining the whole of the fares and rates received for the traffic.

EXETER AND CREDITON.—The South Western has also leased, as from 1st January, 1862, the Exeter and Crediton at 55 per cent. of gross receipts.

LYMINGTON.—Worked by South Western at 50 per cent. of gross receipts.

EPSOM AND LEATHERHEAD.—Incorporated by 19 and 20 Vic., cap. 92 (14th July, 1856), to construct a line from Epsom, on the Brighton, to Leatherhead. Capital, 30,000l., in 10l. shares, and 10,000l. in loans. Length, 3¾ miles. Opened 1st February, 1859. By 22 Vic., cap. 3 (8th April, 1859), the company is authorised, in conjunction with the Wimbledon and Dorking, to provide a joint station at Epsom. Compulsory purchase of land, two years. The line was taken over and opened by the South Western on the 1st February, 1859. By 23 and 24 Vic., cap. 158 (23rd July, 1860), the undertaking was transferred solely to the South Western, on terms agreed to at a special meeting on the 30th September, 1861, when it was agreed that the consideration to be given for purchase of the railway should be 44,444l. of the South Western 4½ per cent. guaranteed stock, giving an income equal to the present rent of 2,000l. per annum. From this amount of stock the South Western was to deduct 10,000l., and take upon itself the debenture debt of the company, amounting to 10,000l. Of the residue of the stock, 33,000l., bearing interest from 1st July, 1861, was allotted to the shareholders at the rate of 11l. per share, the balance of 1,444l. being retained until the few unsettled matters of the company had been adjusted, when the sum in hand was divided pro rata among the shareholders, and the company became extinct.

WIMBLEDON AND DORKING.—Incorporated by 20 and 21 Vic., cap. 72 (27th July, 1857), to construct a line from the South Western, at Wimbledon, to the town of Epsom. Length, 5¾ miles. Opened 4th April, 1859. Line to be laid with double rails whenever required by the Board of Trade. By 22 Vic., cap. 3 (8th April, 1859), the company, in conjunction with the Epsom and Leatherhead, was authorised to construct a joint station at Epsom. By 23 and 24 Vic., cap. 152 (23rd July, 1860), the company was authorised to raise further capital to the extent of 24,500l., in 5 per cent. preference shares, and 8,000l. on loan. By 25 Vic., cap. 42, the undertaking is transferred to the South Western. The South Western has allotted 4½ per cent. stock to yield 4 per cent. in perpetuity on this company's shares, upon receiving in cash the difference between 3½ and 4 per cent. for four years upon the company's capital.

PORTSMOUTH.—Incorporated by 17 Vic., cap. 99 (July 8th, 1853), for a line from Godalming station of South Western to Havant junction with the London and Brighton line, and the Fareham Extension of the London and South Western, and direct to Portsmouth. Length, 32¼ miles. Opened January, 1859. By 18 and 19 Vic., cap. 177 (July 23rd, 1855), the company were permitted to make deviations, and also to borrow 33,000l., in addition to former power to borrow to the extent of 100,000l.; the capital of the company thus consists of—shares, 400,000l.; loans, 133,000l.; total, 533,000l. By 20 and 21 Vic., cap. 18 (3rd July, 1857), the company obtained various deviations, power to create preference shares, and permitting arrangements with neighbouring companies. By 21 and 22 Vic., cap. 101 (12th July, 1858), the company was authorised to make some further deviations, to acquire additional lands, to use a portion of the Brighton and South Western. By 22 and 23 Vic., cap. 31 (21st July, 1859), the line and works were authorised to be leased to or amalgamated with the South Western, which has been completed under the following arrangement:—"Debenture debt, 92,000l., interest at 4½ per cent. thereon will annually absorb 3,910l. of the 18,000l., and leave 14,090l. to be paid to the Portsmouth. The whole 18,000l. a year is divided into 144,000 annuities of 2s. 6d. per annum each. Of these, 31,280, amounting to 3,910l. per annum, is retained to cover debenture interest at the agreed rate; 87,500, amounting to 10,937l. 10s. per annum, have been issued to Portsmouth proprietors; that is to say, five (or 12s. 6d.) per annum in respect of each of these 17,500 shares of 20l. each, and the rest of the annuities (25,220), amounting to 3,152l. 10s. per annum (or at 25 years' purchase equal to 78,812l. in money) are retained by the South Western until all the remaining liabilities of the Portsmouth shall have been satisfied. The final balance, after every unadopted claim on the Portsmouth shall have been discharged, will be distributed among the proprietors of that company." A meeting of the Portsmouth was held on the 12th August, 1861, when the arrangements with South Western were finally concluded, and the company declared to be at an end.

ANDOVER AND REDBRIDGE.—Incorporated by 21 and 22 Vic., cap. 82 (12th July, 1858), to construct a railway between Andover and Redbridge, and to convert the Andover canal into a railway. Capital, 130,000l., in 10l. shares; loans, 43,000l.; calls 2l. 10s. per share, with intervals of three months. Length, 22½ miles; broad gauge; estimate, 13,000l. Land for extra purposes, five acres; completion of works, two years. Purchase of canal, 12,500l. in money, and 1,250 shares in railway. First sod cut by Lord

Palmerston, on 20th September, 1859. By 23 Vic., cap. 53 (15th May, 1860), certain deviations were authorised, and the period of completion of works fixed for 12th July, 1863. By 25 and 26 Vic., cap. 177 (29th July, 1862), the company was authorised to cancel forfeited shares, and to raise new capital to the extent of 15,000*l*., at 6 per cent. preference, and 5,000*l*. on mortgage. Extension of time till 1st January, 1864. By 26 and 27 Vic., cap. 109 (29th June, 1863), the Andover was amalgamated with the South Western, the latter taking up the debenture debt and certain liability of the Andover, and securing to the shareholders an annuity equal to 3 per cent. on the payment they had made. Opened 23½ miles, on 6th March, 1865.

TOOTING, MERTON, AND WIMBLEDON.—Incorporated by Act 27 and 28 Vic., cap. 325 (29th July, 1864), for lines from Wimbledon, *via* Tooting and Merton, to join the Brighton line at Streatham. Length, 6 miles. By 28 and 29 Vic., cap. 273 (5th July, 1865), this undertaking was vested jointly in the Brighton and South Western, and a further junction of half a mile authorised. New capital, 52,500*l*. in shares, and 17,500*l*. on loan, to absorb amounts named in the first act.

AMALGAMATIONS.—By 26 and 27 Vic., cap. 90 (22nd June, 1863), the Chard and Petersfield were amalgamated with the company; provisions were enacted for authorising further arrangements with the Ringwood and Christchurch and the Bishop's Waltham; and with the Brighton as to the joint ownership of the Epsom and Leatherhead.

PETERSFIELD.—Incorporated by 23 and 24 Vic., cap. 173 (23rd July, 1860), to construct a line from the Mid-Sussex and Midhurst Junction, in Midhurst, to Petersfield, on the Direct Portsmouth. Length, 10¼ miles: capital, 100,000*l*., in 10*l*. shares; loans, 30,000*l*. Amalgamated with London and South Western, by 26 and 27 Vic., cap. 90 (22nd June, 1863).

CHARD.—Incorporated by 23 Vic., cap 64 (25th May, 1860), to construct a line from the London and South Western Extension to the town of Chard, with tramroad to canal. Length, 3 miles. Capital, 25,000*l*. in 10*l*. shares; calls, 2*l*. 10s. with intervals of three months. Loans, 8,300*l*. Amalgamated with London and South Western, by 26 and 27 Vic., cap. 90 (22nd June, 1863). Opened 8th May, 1863.

SOUTHAMPTON AND NETLEY.—Incorporated by 24 and 25 Vic., cap. 220 (1st August, 1861), to construct a line from the South Western, near Southampton, to Netley. Length, 4¾ miles. Capital, 48,000*l*., in 10*l*. shares; loans, 16,000*l*. Extra land, one acre; compulsory purchase, two years; completion of works, three years. South Western contributed 5,000*l*. By 26 and 27 Vic., cap. 70 (22nd June, 1863), several deviations were permitted, the whole of which were to have been completed by 22nd June, 1866. Amalgamated with South Western as from 1st January, 1865, by 27 and 28 Vic., cap. 174 (14th July, 1864).

NORTH DEVON.—Incorporated as TAW VALE, by Act 1 and 2 Vic., cap. 27 (11th June 1838), revived 21st July, 1845, by 9 Vic., cap. 107, for a line from Crediton (Exeter and Crediton, to Barnstaple, with a branch to the docks at Fremington Pill, also included in this company's undertaking, and effecting a junction across from the Bristol to the English Channel. By 10 Vic., cap. 355, the value of the works and land at the docks was estimated at 15,000*l*., and the amount divided into 750 shares of 20*l*. each, considered as paid up. By an Act obtained 1847 (10 and 11 Vic., cap. 273), this company obtained power to construct branches to Bideford and South Molton, and for enlargement of the docks; the powers of compulsory purchase, &c., granted by this Act, expired in 1851, but the line from Fremington to Bideford (6 miles) was promoted in 1853 by the "BIDEFORD EXTENSION." An Act was obtained 24th July, 1851, 15 Vic., cap. 83, which altered the title of the company, extended the limit of compulsory purchase and completion to three and four years respectively, authorised deviations, and reduced the original capital from 970,666*l*. to 441,003*l*., and loans involving a reduction of the shares from 20*l*. to 16*l*. each, with the option of subdividing them still further. Also sanctioned the contract with Mr. Brassey for leasing to him the line for seven years from opening, paying a fixed rent of 12,000*l*. a year, a sum sufficient to enable the company to pay about 2½ per cent. At a special meeting on 30th July, 1862, the following terms of lease to the South Western, for 1,000 years, from 1st January, 1863, was unanimously agreed to:—The South Western to pay the interest on the North Devon debenture debt, and on the 6 per cent. redeemable preference stock and dividends on the original share capital, as follows:—

For seven years, ordinary stock,	2 per cent.	(and afterwards)	2½ per cent.
,, ,, A stock	1 per cent.	in	1 per cent.
,, ,, B stock	4 per cent.	perpetuity	5 per cent.

The sanction of the South Western proprietors was given at the same time to an agreement (subject to parliamentary approval) to be obtained at the option and expense of the South Western for amalgamating the two companies on the following terms:—The debenture debt of the North Devon to become debenture debt of the South Western. The 6 per cent. preference stock to become preferential redeemable stock of the South Western. Ordinary stock of the South Western to be given in exchange for the North Devon stock in the following proportions, viz:—

50*l*. South Western stock for every 100*l*. North Devon ordinary stock.
20*l*.	ditto	ditto	100*l*.	ditto	A	stock.
100*l*.	ditto	ditto	100*l*.	ditto	B	stock.

This Act was obtained in the session of 1864, to take effect from 1st January, 1865.

BIDEFORD EXTENSION.—Incorporated by 17 Vic., cap. 140 (4th August, 1853), for a line from North Devon terminus at Fremington Pill to Bideford. Length, 6 miles, 4 chains. Broad and narrow gauge. Opened for traffic on 2nd November, 1865. The South Western obtained power in 1861 to add the narrow gauge and to lease the line, which it effected on the following terms :—From and after 1st August, 1862, to 31st December, 1862, rent at the rate of 2,250l. per annum, and from 1st January, 1863, to 31st December, 1869, an annual rent of 1,925l., being at the rate of 3½ per cent. on 55,000l., together with the interest on the debenture of 10,000l. (the authorised capital), and from 1st January, 1870, an increase of rent equal to 4 per cent. net dividend on the ordinary stock, in addition to the debenture debt before referred to. By Act of 1864, this undertaking was amalgamated with the South Western as from 1st January, 1865.

MID-HANTS.—This line is to be leased to the South Western, but the terms do not appear to be finally arranged.

EXETER AND EXMOUTH.—Incorporated by 18 and 19 Vic., cap. 122 (July 22nd, 1855), to construct a railway from the South Devon to Exmouth, with a branch to the Exeter Canal. By 20 and 21 Vic., cap. 24 (28th June, 1858), the capital was reduced to 50,000l. in shares, and 16,000l. on loan. By the same Act a new line to the South Western at Topsham, was authorised, 1½ mile in length, the connection with the broad gauge having been abandoned. By 24 Vic., cap. 15 (17th May, 1861), the company obtained power to raise additional capital to the extent of 30,000l. in shares at 5 per cent., to cancel forfeited shares, and to re-issue others in lieu thereof. By 28 and 29 Vic., cap. 304 (5th July, 1865), the Exeter and Exmouth was amalgamated, as from 1st January, 1866, with the South Western on the following terms :—The preference shareholders to accept and receive 4½ per cent. preference South Western stock to the amount of 27,000l. at par. The ordinary shareholders to accept and receive 4½ per cent. preference, or at their option, ordinary South Western stock at par, in the proportion of 50l. for every 100l., that is, 18,400l. for 36,800l.

SALISBURY AND DORSET JUNCTION.—For agreement with this company, see APPENDIX to volume for 1868.

MILEAGE.—Total mileage of railways constructed and owned by the company, 487 miles 49 chains ; lines not owned by the company, but worked at a per centage on the traffic, or under running powers, 124 miles 22 chains ; lines partly owned, 31 miles 30 chains, making a gross total of 643 miles 21 chains. The Tooting Merton and Wimbledon, the small piece of line constructed between Knight's Hill and Herne Hill, the Kensington and Richmond, and the Kingston and Wimbledon Extension were opened for traffic 1st January, 1869.

REVENUE.—The receipts in the half-year ending the 31st December amounted, on 506½ miles, to 853,129l., against 807,499l. in the same of 1866, showing an increase of 45,630l. The working expenses, including taxation, amounted to 420,883l., against 416,721l., showing an increase of 4,162l. The net revenue amounted to 432,246l., and for the corresponding period of 1866 to 390,778l., showing an increase of 41,468l. ; earned at an additional cost of 4,162l., or about 10 per cent. The balance available for dividend was 214,342l., from which a dividend at the rate of 5¼ per cent. per annum left a balance of 10,303l.

The revenue for the June half-year, after deducting interest on loans and all other preferential charges, was 156,263l.: adding surplus at December, 1867, 10,303l., the balance available for dividend amounted to 166,566l. Dividend at the rate of 4 per cent. per annum, amounting on 7,772,886l. of paid-up capital to 155,457l., left a balance of 11,108l. The gross revenue showed an increase, as compared with the amount for the corresponding period of 1867, of 38,403l., which had been earned on a similar length of line, and showing a progressive development of the resources of the country served by the railway and its branches.

WORKS IN PROGRESS.—It was reported in August, that the contractor for the Aldershot was making good progress between Aldershot and Pirbright, most of the bridges and one of the tunnels being completed.

SOUTH EASTERN.—At the special meeting held on the 28th May, the directors reported the result of the negotiations with the South Eastern in reference to a new transfer station at Waterloo, and the consequent withdrawal of the clauses in the bill deposited by the company in reference to the construction of this station. They had the pleasure of informing the proprietors that the South Eastern had commenced the works, which were being carried on with expedition, and it was hoped that in the course of a few months the Charing-cross and Cannon-street stations would be accessible to passengers arriving at Waterloo from all parts of this company's system.

BRIGHTON.—Pending the progress of the Working Union Bill of the South Eastern, Brighton, and Chatham, an agreement of the date of the 30th April, 1868, was entered into with the Brighton, and submitted to the special meeting of the proprietors in May. Notwithstanding the subsequent withdrawal of the Working Union Bill by its promoters, important parts of the agreement remain unaffected, and the most friendly spirit continues to exist between the Brighton and this board in the various relations subsisting between the two companies.

POOLE AND BOURNEMOUTH.—In the spring of 1866, the directors informed the proprietors that, looking at the rapidly increasing importance of Bournemouth, and the necessity for a more convenient access to Poole, they had decided that it was expedient for the South Western to adopt the Poole and Bournemouth, and to form the needful connections between it and the existing railways of the district. Looking to the agreement entered into with the Poole and Bournemouth, and with contractors, who are bound to construct the line between Poole and Bournemouth on favourable terms to this company, the directors determined to submit that agreement to the proprietors, in connection with the making of the Junction authorised in 1866 to be executed by this company. The aggregate estimated cost of the works, including those comprised in the above-mentioned contract, is 106,000l. The rapid increase of Bournemouth and its neighbourhood, which induced the directors in 1866 to enter into these engagements, still continues. The extension of the Ringwood and Christchurch from its present terminus at Christchurch to the Eastern side of Bournemouth is to be forthwith completed by the Ringwood Christchurch and Bournemouth. Notwithstanding this appeal, the proprietors, almost unanimously, rejected the proposal, and left the Poole and Bournemouth to arrange with its contractors as it could.

CAPITAL.—A summary of the capital of the company, in stocks, shares, and mortgage bonds, to 30th June, presented the subjoined particulars :—

Ordinary stock—registered	£7,772,886	
,, uncalled	619,525=	£8,392,412
Preference 7 per cent.	171,276	
Gosport 5 per cent.	14,400	
4 per cent. stock	4,400	
4¼ ,, preference stock	1,450,000	
4½ ,, new ,,	500,000	
4¾ ,, preference stock 1865	929,976	
5 ,, preference stock 1866	1,332,013	
5 ,, North Devon preference	8,074	
Andover and Redbridge annuities	5,006=	£4,415,146
Mortgage bonds	3,296,734	
Perpetual 4 per cent. mortgage stock	873,560	
,, 4½ ,,	679,562	
Remaining to be borrowed ,,	184,973=	£5,014,830=£17,822,388

The receipts on this account have been 16,637,521l., of which 190,525l. remained unexpended on 30th June. The financial statement to same date furnished the following details :—

Total receipts as above	£16,637,521
Less—Profit on shares, interest, surplus land and rails sold, &c.	50,446
	£16,587,074
Discount on shares, 1837	400,000
,, ordinary stock	1,405
,, new 4½ per cent. preference stock	1,684
,, ,, ,, 1865	25,470
,, perpetual 4 per cent. mortgage stock	2,228
Uncalled	619,525
Preference scrip purchased	25
Mortgage bonds unissued	184,973
Total capital	£17,822,388
Capital entitled to dividend	£7,380,480
Discount on shares, 1837	400,000
,, ordinary stock	1,405
4 per cent. stock exchanged for ordinary	5,400
	£7,787,286
Less—5 per cent. Gosport stock	14,400
Entitled to dividend to 30th June, 1868	£7,772,886

The accounts made up to 30th June and 31st December, and the statutory meetings held in August and February in every year.

Scale of Voting.—One vote for every 50l. of stock up to 500l.; one additional vote for every 250l. of stock above 500l. up to 5,000l.; and one additional vote for every additional sum of 500l. above 5,000l.

Certificates must accompany transfer deed. Registration fee, 2s. 6d. each seller.

No. of Directors—12. *Qualification,* 3,000l.

DIRECTORS :

Chairman—Capt. CHARLES E. MANGLES, Poyle Park, Farnham, Surrey.

Deputy-Chairman—CHARLES CASTLEMAN, Esq., Glasshayes, Lyndhurst, Hants.

The Rt. Hon. Viscount Bury, M.P., 65, Prince's Gate, Hyde Park, S.W.	The Count Eyre, 7, Hinde Street, Manchester Square, W.
Hon. R. H. Dutton, Timsbury Manor, Romsey, Hants.	Captain Johnston, 8, York Terrace, Regent's Park, N.W.
Mr. Sergeant Gaselee, 2, Cambridge Square, Hyde Park, W.	H. C. Lacy, Esq., Withdeane Hall, near Brighton.
Lieut.-Col. Luard, Farnham, Surrey.	C. S. Mortimer, Esq., Wigmore House, Capel, Surrey, S.
Edward J. Hutchins, Esq., Beenham House, Reading, and 10, Portland Place, London.	William P. Snell, Esq., Belmont, near Havant, Hants.

OFFICERS.—Sec., F. Clarke ; Traffic Man., A. Scott; Supt. of the Line, W. M. Williams; Res. Eng., J. Strapp; Loc. and Car. Supt., J. Beattie; Goods Man., J. T. Haddow; Treas., A. Morgan; Auditors, A. Hoyes, Bitterne Grove, Southampton, and J. Ashmore, 27, Westbourne Terrace, Hyde Park, W.; Solicitor, F. T. Bircham, Parliament Street. S. W.; Law Clerk, L. Crombie.

Head Offices—Waterloo Bridge Station, S.

234.—LONDON, TILBURY, AND SOUTHEND.

This company was originally an incorporation of acquiescing shareholders in the Eastern Counties and Blackwall, who by 15 Vic., cap., 84 (17th June, 1852), are authorised to make a railway from Ilford to Tilbury Fort (opposite Gravesend) and Southend. A contract was entered into with Messrs. Peto, Brassey, and Betts, for construction on lease for 25 years, guaranteeing a net return of 6 per cent. from 1st January, 1853, upon a share capital of 600,000l. and half surplus profits. The line branches off the Blackwall at Stepney, and is carried on to the Great Eastern, at Bow station, where it takes the main line nearly as far as Ilford. It then proceeds to the east of Purfleet, and, passing through Grays, directs its course to West Tilbury and Tilbury Fort, where the North Gravesend station is erected. The Town Pier, Gravesend, is leased to the company, and steamers convey passengers across the river to and from the trains.

By 19 Vic., cap. 15 (5th June, 1856), the company was authorised to raise new capital to the amount of 60,000l. and obtain additional borrowing powers to the extent of 40,000l. By the same Act the company was authorised to sell water at Southend station, but not to expend capital on such purpose.

By 19 and 20 Vic., cap. 76 (7th July, 1856), the following extensions and branches were authorised ; a junction between the Blackwall and North London, and two branches to the North Woolwich branch of Eastern Counties. New capital, 150,000l., in shares, and 50,000l. on loan. The lessees to pay 6 per cent. on all new capital called up.

By 25 Vic., cap. 8 (16th May, 1862), the proprietors were incorporated into a distinct company, the Great Eastern and Blackwall still nominating each one-third of the board.

By 26 and 27 Vic., cap. 69 (22nd June, 1863), the company was authorised to enter into arrangements with the Great Eastern and the Blackwall with reference to a modification of the lease by Messrs. Peto and Betts, but the shareholders have refused to entertain the subject.

REVENUE.—The accounts, as furnished by the lessees, showed that the receipts amounted to 38,169l., and the expenses to 21,838l., leaving a balance of 16,331l. The receipts show an increase of 3,210l., and the expenses of 2,137l., as compared with the same period of 1866, leaving a net increase of 1,073l. Adding to the above receipts the passenger tolls and proportions of goods receipts derived by the Great Eastern and North London from the traffic of the line during the half-year, amounting to 15,983l., the gross receipts for Tilbury traffic amounted to 54,152l.

The revenue account for the half-year ending the 30th June, as furnished by the lessees, showed that the receipts amounted to 26,503l. and the expenses to 19,424l., leaving a balance of 7,079l., being an increase of 1,166l. as compared with the corresponding period last year. The returns of passenger tolls and proportions of goods receipts derived by the Great Eastern and North London from the traffic of this line during the half-year had been supplied by those companies, and were as follows:—Great Eastern, 8,875l.; North London, 636l.; and, adding the above 26,503l. receipts, made the gross receipts for Tilbury traffic during the half-year, 36,014l.

CAPITAL.—The expenditure on this account to 30th June, amounted to 798,677l. The receipts, which left a balance of 1,973l., were as under :—

Capital stock £650,650
Debentures .... 150,000=£800,650

DIRECTORS:

Chairman—CHARLES JOHN ELEY, Esq., Elm Cottage, Old Brompton, S.W.

Deputy-Chairman—THOMAS MOXON, Esq., 29, Throgmorton Street, E.C.

Francis Macnaghten, Esq., Chester Square, S.W.
F. W. Haigh, Esq., Bickley, Bromley, Kent.
John Venables, Esq., 34, Aldgate, High Street, E.
Lincoln Phené, Esq., 10, Lansdowne Circus, Leamington.

Lightly Simpson, Esq., 50, Gower Street, Bedford Square, W.C.
G. W. Currie, Esq., 10, Hyde Park Street, W.
Charles Henry Turner, Esq., Litchurch, Derby.

OFFICERS.—Sec., John F. Kennell; Man., Joseph Louth; Engs., G. P. Bidder and John Fowler, Westminster, S.W.; Auditors, Thomas Adams and John Jackson Gosset; Solicitors, Maynard, Son, and Co., Coleman Street, E.C., and Hollingsworth and Co., 4, East India Avenue, Leadenhall Street, E.C.

Offices—Blackwall Railway Terminus, Fenchurch Street, E.C.

235. LONDON, WORCESTER, AND SOUTH WALES.

Incorporated by 28 and 29 Vic., cap. 270 (5th July, 1865), to construct a line from Worcester, on the Great Western, to the East and West Junction at Old Stratford. Length, 23¼ miles.   Capital, 320,000l. in shares, and 106,000l. on loan.   Facilities with East and West Junction.

By 29 and 30 Vic., cap. 144 (16th July, 1866), the company was authorised to make several deviations and other alterations in the line of route, and also to enter into arrangements with the Great Western.

It was reported in October that the provisional arrangement made with a contractor for the completion of the railway had been broken off, and, owing to the state of the money market, they had not entered into any new arrangement.

No. of Directors—7; minimum, 3; quorum, 3 and 2.   *Qualification*, 500l.

DIRECTORS :

Sir Charles Henry Rouse Boughton, Bart., Downton Hall, Ludlow.
The Hon. Richard Howe Browne, The Crouch Oak, Addlestone, Surrey.
W. Bickerton Evans, Esq., Worcester.

Josiah Stallard, Esq., Worcester.
Clarence Holcombe Judd, Esq., Brompton.
Stevenson Forbes, Esq., Kensington.
William Blackmore, Esq., Lothbury.

OFFICERS.—Sec., C. Banks; Eng., J. B. Burke, Westminster, S.W.; Solicitors, John Stallard, Worcester, and Jones and Son, Alcester ; Bankers, Smith, Payne, and Smiths, London, Worcester City and County Bank, and The Old Bank, Worcester.

Offices—3, Westminster Chambers, Victoria Street, S.W.

236.—LONDONDERRY AND COLERAINE.

Incorporated by 8 and 9 Vic., cap. 187 (4th August, 1845), but dissolved and re-incorporated under the same title by an Act obtained 23rd May, 1852 (15 Vic., cap. 43), wherein this undertaking is defined to consist of—1st, a main line from the Foyle Bridge at Londonderry, to the Bridge over the Bann, near Coleraine; 2nd, a branch near the river Broharris, on lands reclaimed from Lough Foyle, and known as "*Robertson's reclamation,*" or the *Myroe Level*, to Newtownlimavady ; 3rd, the estate and interest of the company in the waste lands, mud banks, and slopes of Lough Foyle, which have been acquired, from the undertakers of the reclamation, authorised by an Act, entitled an *Act for draining and embanking certain land in Lough Swilly and Lough Foyle*, and the various subsequent Acts relating thereto.   Length, 36 miles.

The company in 1856 obtained an Act (18 and 19 Vic., cap. 167), authorising them to lease the railway, the object being a lease to W. M'Cormick, who was then working the line under agreement, but difficulties having arisen in arranging the terms, the Public Works Loan Commissioners, under the powers vested in them, executed a lease to W. M'Cormick for a term of seven years from the 10th April, 1858, at a net rental of 8,500l. for each of the two first years, and 10,000l. for each of the remaining five years.

By 22 and 23 Vic., cap. 131 (13th August, 1859), the company was authorised to raise additional capital to the extent of 75,000l., in preference or A debentures, at 4½ per cent.; 95,763l. in B debentures at 4 per cent.; 25,900l. in B B debentures 2½ per cent., 60,000l. in C debentures at 3 per cent.   These powers must be exercised within twelve months after passing of the Act, but not until the mortgage, judgment, and other creditors of the company (except the Public Works Loan Commissioners) have consented to accept the new clauses in lieu of the present securities.   The whole of this money to be applied to the payment of existing debts.   Arrears on A debentures to be made good before any payment to B, and so on in rotation.   This Act could not be put in force in the 12 months, and became a dead letter.

By 25 and 26 Vic., cap. 170 (17th July. 1862). the company obtained power to facilitate arrangements with its creditors, the whole undertaking to be sold if debentures were not taken in lieu of debts.

The line is now worked under special arrangement by the Belfast and Northern Counties.

The statutory meetings held in London in February or March, and September or October.

Certificates must accompany transfer deed. Registration fee, 2s. 6d. each' seller. Transfer books close 14 days before meetings.

No. of Directors—8. *Qualification*, 20 shares.

DIRECTORS:

Chairman—JOHN ROBERT HALL, Esq., The Grange, Sutton, S.

Deputy-Chairman—HENRY LAVER, Esq., Pembridge Gardens, W.

Joseph Henry, Esq., Westbourne Terrace, | Arthur Sinclair, Esq., St. Helens.
W.

OFFICERS.—Hon. Sec., Henry Laver ; Auditors, Hugh P. Fuller, Abbey Road, Regent's Park, N.W., and Charles Whetham, Gordon Square, W.C.; Solicitors, Payne and Layton, London, and John Burgess, Londonderry.

Head Offices—4, Coleman Street Buildings, E.C.

237.—LONDONDERRY AND ENNISKILLEN.

Incorporated by Act 8 and 9 Vic., cap. 98 (1845), but dissolved and re-incorporated under the same title by Act obtained 28th May, 1852 (15 Vic., cap. 44) wherein the objects of this undertaking are defined to be those already sanctioned, and as subsequently restricted to a line from the bridge over the river Foyle, at Londonderry, to Omagh ; by the new Act thence to Enniskillen. Productive, 60 miles.

For the purpose of extending the line to Enniskillen, the company by Act of 1852 was authorised to create new shares to the extent of 25,000l.; and for the new bridge across the Foyle, and the Quay of Londonderry, to subscribe 15,000l. to guarantee on the shares which may be created for those purposes, dividend *maximum* 6 per cent. per annum. The 32nd section provides that the revenue shall be applied, 1st, in payment of 1st preference dividend on the shares created under 12 Vic., cap. 79 ; 2nd, of preferential dividend as on new capital under Consolidation Act 1852 ; 3rd, to dividend on any other shares. It has been found, however, during the progress of the works, that additional capital would be required, and, accordingly, an Act was obtained in 1854, 17 and 18 Vic., cap. 135 (July 3rd), to raise funds to pay for 10 miles of double line from Newtown Stewart to Omagh, as well as for the construction of the Fintona branch (1 mile, 2½ chains), and for lengthening the line at Derrybridge, enlarging station ground, and providing the necessary plant. The Act authorised new capital to the extent of 75,000l., to be raised by preference interest at 5 per cent. Power to borrow 25,000l., in addition was also obtained.

At a special meeting on the 3rd November, 1854, it was resolved :—"That the new capital of 75,000l. be raised by the issue of shares at 12l. 10s. each, to be called guaranteed preference shares. That such shares take claim immediately after the existing preference shares, and subject to them to be entitled to a preference dividend of 5 per cent. Should the profits in any half-year be insufficient to pay such a dividend, the difference to be carried to credit of such shares, and paid from future profits."

By 19 and 20 Vic., cap. 124 (21st July, 1856), the company is authorised to issue the unissued stock, in amount 32,025l., as a first preference, excluding only from the operations of such first preference the sum of 3,062l. 10s. held by two preference'shareholders, who formally dissented from the Bill. It also permits the issue of 20,000l. out of the 25,000l. debentures sanctioned by the Act of 1854, the remaining 5,000l. to be issued when the shares are fully subscribed for, and empowers the company to convert the mortgage debt into permanent debenture stock. It was accordingly decided in August, 1856, to raise 32,000l. on preference 10l. shares, entitled to dividend not exceeding 6½ per cent. for ten years, and 5 per cent. afterwards. This stock bears interest at 6 per cent. until 1st October, 1866, and afterwards 5 per cent. in perpetuity.

IRISH NORTH WESTERN.—By Act of 1859 the Dundalk was authorised to lease the Londonderry for 999 years, which was carried into effect on 1st January, 1860, on the following terms :—Rent of 26,000l. per annum, with a gradual increase after three years from date of lease, of 20 per cent. on all gross receipts from the two railways above 95,000l. per annum, until the rent reached 33,000l. per annum, at which it is then fixed in perpetuity. This would pay preference and guaranteed dividends, and also a dividend of 5 per cent. on the ordinary shares, with something over for contingencies.

The dividends remaining due at the date of the August report were to

Stock B ....£26,879, equal to £10 17 per cent.

Stock C 27,529,   „   63 16   „

Total arrears......................£54,409

CAPITAL.—The expenditure on this account to 30th June was stated at 709,604l., the receipts having been as follow : –

Capital receipts to June 30th, 1868...................................£529,569
Amount received on debentures, debenture stock, and government loan 144,303
Amount transferred from revenue, as per account, to 31st Dec., 1867.. 28,558=£702,430
Balance   7,173

£709,604

The accounts are made up to 30th June and 31st December, and the statutory meetings held in London, in February or March, and August or September, in every year.

Certificates must accompany transfer deed ; fee for registration, 2s. 6d. each seller.

No. of Directors—8 ; Qualification, 20 shares ; allowance, 500l.; of this the directors take but 300l.

DIRECTORS :

Chairman—JAMES CLAY, Esq., M.P., 25, Montagu Square, W.

Deputy-Chairman—HENRY LAVER, Esq., Pembridge Gardens, Bayswater, W.

Peter W. Barlow, Esq., F.R.S., Great George Street, Westminster, S.W.
Philip Hanbury, Esq.; Lombard Street, E.C.

Captain Daniel Warren, 68, Porchester Terrace, Hyde Park, W.

OFFICERS.—Hon. Sec., Henry Laver ; Eng.-in-Chief. Peter W. Barlow, F.R.S.; Solicitors, Francis Kearsey, London, and Archibald Collum. Enniskillen ; Auditors, Hugh P. Fuller, Abbey Road, Regent's Park, N.W.; and Charles Whetham, Gordon Square, W.C.

Head Offices—4, Coleman Street Buildings, E.C.

238.—LONDONDERRY AND LOUGH SWILLY.

Incorporated by Act of 1843. Revised by 22 and 23 Vic., cap. 50 (1st August, 1859), to construct a line from the Western shore of Lough Foyle to Carrowan, in the county Donegal. Length, 12 miles. Capital, 40,000l. in 10l. shares, and 13,300l. on loan.

By 24 and 25 Vic., cap. 161 (22nd July, 1861), the company was authorised to extend the line to Buncrana. Length, 6½ miles. Capital, 20,000l. in shares, and 6,600l. on loan. Arrangements with the Letterkenny and the Finn Valley.

By 27 and 28 Vic., cap. 228 (25th July, 1864), the company was authorised to extend the line towards Londonderry. Length, 5 chains. New capital, 20,000l. in shares, and 6,600l. on loan. In operation, 12 miles.

By 29 Vic., cap. 60 (11th June, 1866), the Lough Swilly may be purchased by the Letterkenny at a price to be mutually agreed upon by the parties.

REVENUE.—The following is a statement of the traffic for six months, compared with the corresponding period of last year :—

31st July.	1868.	1867.	Increase.	Decrease.
Passengers	£1,665	£1,422	£242	....
Parcels, horses, carriages, and dogs	69	47	22	....
Goods..	558	438	119	....
Live stock...................................	29	35	....	£5
	£2,322	£1,944	£383	£5
Increase £383				
Less decrease................... 5		378		
	£2,322	£2,322		

CAPITAL.—The expenditure to 31st July amounted to 102,562l., the receipts from which have been as under :—

Shares and stock £34,489
Loans .... 19,600= £54.089
Balance .... 48,472= £102,562

DIRECTORS :

Chairman—JAMES THOMPSON MACKY, Esq., J. P., Belmont, Londonderry.

Joseph Cooke, Esq., Boomhall, Londonderry.
John Munn, Esq., J.P., Crawford's Square, Londonderry.
Samuel Gilliland, Esq., J.P., Brookhall, Londonderry.
Isaac Colquhoun, Esq., Rockfort, Buncrana.

T. M. M'Clintock, Esq., J.P., Hampstead Hall, Londonderry.
B. M'Corkell, Esq., J.P., Glenburnie, Moville.
James Corscaden, Esq., Ballyarnet, Londonderry.

OFFICERS.—Sec., A. H. Stewart : Man., Joseph Mc Donald : Auditors, G. H. Mitchell, St. Helens, Buncrana ; and Richard Waller, Troy, Londonderry ; Solicitor, Robt. Knox, Londonderry.

Offices—Londonderry.

239.—LONGTON. ADDERLEY GREEN. AND BUCKNALL.

Incorporated by 29 and 30 Vic., cap. 174 (16th July, 1866), to construct a line from Longton through Adderley Green to Bucknall, in Staffordshire.   Length, 4¾ miles. Capital, 50,000*l.* in 10*l.* shares, and 16,000*l.* on loan, with power to create debenture stock. Arrangements with North Staffordshire.   In abeyance.

No. of Directors—5 ; minimum, 3   quorum, 3 and 2.   *Qualification,* 500*l.*

DIRECTORS :

James Stott, Esq., Manchester.
Joseph Hulse, Esq., Longton.
Frederic Bishop, Esq., Stoke-on-Trent.

John Hackett Goddard, Esq., Longton.
William Rigby, Esq., Church Lawton, Cheshire.

240.—LOSTWITHIEL AND FOWEY.

Incorporated by 25 and 26 Vic., cap. 69 (30th June, 1862), to construct a line from the Cornwall, near Lostwithiel, to Fowey.   Length, 5¼ miles.   Capital, 30,000*l.* in 20*l.* shares ;   loans, 10,000*l.*   Arrangements with Cornwall, which is to work the line at 50 per cent.   Opened to Carne Point on 1st December, 1868.

By 28 Vic., cap. 30 (29th May, 1865), the company's capital was remodelled in accordance with the provisions of the general Act 26 and 27 Vic., cap. 118, in regard to the cancellation and surrender of shares, and their re-issue as preference.

CAPITAL.—The abstract of receipts and payments, to 30th June, 1868, furnished the following details :—

Received.		*Expended.*	
Calls, &c., to 31st December, 1867 ..	£31,137	Payments to 31st December, 1867 ..	£30,898
June 30th, 1868.....................	76	To 30th June, 1868	249
		Balance due from bankers	48
		Balance in secretary's hands	17
	£31,214		£31,214

No. of Directors—6 ; minimum, 3.   *Qualification,* 200*l.*

DIRECTORS :

Chairman—ROBERT THOMAS HEAD, Esq., The Briars, Alphington, Exeter.

Deputy-Chairman—EDWARD LAMBERT, Esq., 8, John Street, Bedford Row, W.C.

William West, Esq., Tredenham House, St. Blazey, Cornwall.

William Lowry, Esq., Fowey, Cornwall.
Wm. Thos. Sobey, Esq., Fowey, Cornwall.

Two Directors retire annually, but are eligible for re-election.

OFFICERS.—Sec., William Polkinghorne, Par Office, Cornwall ; Engs., Jenkin, Trathan, and Triscott ; Auditor, Edmund Carlyon, St. Austell ; Solicitors, Joseph Burgin, 8, John Street, Bedford Row, W.C., and Gidley and Head, 15, Bedford Circus, Exeter ; Bankers, The East Cornwall Bank, St. Austell, Cornwall.

241.—LOUTH AND LINCOLN.

Incorporated by 29 and 30 Vic., cap. 344 (6th August, 1866), to construct a railway from Louth to the Great Northern Loop line at Lincoln.   Length, 21 miles.   Capital, 250,000*l.* in 10*l.* shares, and 83,000*l.* on loan.   Arrangements with Great Northern.

No. of Directors—5 ; minimum, 3 ; quorum, 3 and 2.   *Qualification,* 25*l.*

DIRECTORS :

Edward Heneage, Esq., 5, Grosvenor Crescent, S.W.
Henry Chaplin, Esq., M.P., Blankney, Lincolnshire.

William Thomas Kime, Esq.
Robert Norfolk, Esq.
Charles Edward Lucas, Esq.

242.—LUDDENDEN VALLEY.

Incorporated by 28 Vic., cap. 23 (26th May, 1865), to construct a line from the Lancashire and Yorkshire at Luddenden Foot to Little Holme House.   Length, 2 miles. Capital, 22,000*l.* in shares, and 7,300*l.* on loan.   Arrangements with Lancashire and Yorkshire, which subscribes one-half of the share capital.

No. of Directors—6 ; quorum, 4.   *Qualification,* 200*l.*

One-half of the board to be appointed by the Lancashire and Yorkshire ; and the quorum in all cases to consist of two of each section of the directors.

DIRECTORS :

Chairman—WILLIAM AMBLER, Esq., Royd's House, Luddenden, near Halifax.

James Eastwood, Esq., Mill House, Luddenden.
Wm. Murgatroyd, Esq., Oates Royd, Luddenden.

George Anderton, Esq., Cleckheaton.
Samuel Fielden, Esq., Todmorden.
Joshua Radcliffe, Esq., Rochdale.

OFFICERS.—Sec., J. E. Norris, Halifax ; Eng., Sturges Meek, Manchester ; Auditors, Edward Harper and James Wrigley ; Solicitors, Grundy and Co., Manchester, and Norris and Foster, Halifax.
Offices—Halifax.

243.—LUDLOW AND CLEE HILL.

Incorporated by 24 and 25 Vic., cap. 187 (22nd July, 1861), to construct a line from Ludlow, on the Shrewsbury and Hereford, to Clee Hill. Length, 6 miles. Capital, 30,000*l*. in 10*l*. shares ; loans, 10,000*l*. Powers for Shrewsbury and Hereford to subscribe 5,000*l*. Opened August 24, 1864. The line is now worked by the Great Western and London and North Western. as from the 1st June, 1867, for the first two years 90 per cent., for the second 2 years 80 per cent., for the remaining two years 70 per cent., of the gross receipts from traffic, with option of purchase, on terms to be fixed, in case of difference, by arbitration.

CAPITAL.—The receipts on this account, including 9,700*l*. on debentures, have been 39,700*l*. The expenditure amounted to 52,302*l*.

Meetings in February or March, and in August or September.

No. of Directors—6 ; minimum, 3 ; quorum, 3. *Qualification*, 300*l*.

DIRECTORS :

Chairman—Sir CHARLES H. ROUSE BOUGHTON, Bart., Downton Hall, Ludlow.

Andrew Johnes Rouse Boughton Knight, Esq., Downton Castle, Ludlow. | William Thomas Carlisle, Esq., 8, New Square, Lincoln's Inn, W.C.

OFFICERS.—Sec., Cecil Peele ; Auditor, Mr. Bell, Shrewsbury ; Solicitors, Loxdale, Peele, and Sons ; Bankers, Rocke, Eyton, and Co., Shrewsbury and Ludlow.
Offices—Shrewsbury.

244.—LUGG VALLEY.

Incorporated by 28 and 29 Vic., cap. 185 (29th July, 1865), to construct a line from Presteign to Llangunllo, on the Central Wales. Length, 10¾ miles. Capital, 90,000*l*. in shares, and 30,000*l*. on loan. Arrangements with Great Western, Central Wales, Kington and Eardisley, and Leominster and Kington.

No. of Directors—5 ; minimum, 5 ; quorum, 3 and 2. *Qualification*, 200*l*.

DIRECTORS :

Richard Green Price, Esq., M.P., Norton Manor, Radnorshire, and 3, Suffolk Place, S.W. | Sir H. J. J. Brydges, Bart. Henry Wagner, Esq. George Thomas Edwards, Esq.

245.—LYMINGTON.

Incorporated by 19 and 20 Vic., cap. 71 (7th July, 1865), to make a railway from Lymington to the South Western, at Brockenhurst, with a landing place at Lymington. Capital, 21,000*l*., in 10*l*. shares ; loans, 7,000*l*. Length, 4 miles. Opened 1st July, 1858. Contracts or working agreements authorised with the South Western, by which the traffic is worked at 50 per cent.

By 22 and 23 Vic., cap. 15 (21st July, 1859), the company is authorised to acquire the ferry across the Lymington river, and to raise 11,860*l*. for the purpose of the undertaking. The entire share capital is limited to 34,000*l*.; and loans to 7,000*l*. Unissued shares may be cancelled, and 5 per cent. preference shares created in lieu thereof.

The dividend declared on the ordinary stock for the half-year ending 31st December was at the rate of 2½ per cent. per annum, but the total net receipts for the six months ending 30th June being only 479*l*., this amount was carried to current account. The working agreement with the South Western was renewed for 10 years from 1867.

CAPITAL.—The receipts on this account to 30th June were 42,556*l*., all of which had been expended, except 44*l*.

Meetings in January or February, and July or August.

No. of Directors—6 ; minimum, 3 ; quorum, 3. *Qualification*, 350*l*.

DIRECTORS :

Chairman—GEORGE FOSTER ST. BARBE, Esq., Lymington.

Deputy-Chairman—WILLIAM PEERE WILLIAMS-FREEMAN, Esq., Pylewell Park, near Lymington.

Henry Daniell, Esq., Lymington. George Inman, Esq., Lymington. | Warren Peacocke, Esq., Efford House, near Lymington.

OFFICERS.—Sec. and Solicitor, E. H. Moore ; Auditors, Richard Sharp and James Furner, Lymington : Bankers, St. Barbe and Co., Lymington.

246.—LYNN AND HUNSTANTON.

Incorporated by 24 and 25 Vic., cap. 199 (1st August, 1861), to construct a line from Lynn, on the East Anglian, to Hunstanton. Length, 15 miles. Capital, 60,000*l*. in 10*l*. shares ; loans, 20,000*l*. Arrangements with Great Eastern, Opened 3rd October, 1862.

REVENUE.—It was reported in February that there was a balance of 2,554*l*. available, out of which dividend at the rate of 8*l*. 5*s*. per cent. per annum for the half-year ending December 31st, 1867, left 79*l*. to be carried forward. This dividend, with that paid up to June 30th, made 6*l*. 10*s*. per cent. for the whole of 1867. The August report stated that the balance of net revenue for the half-year ending June 30th was 1,709*l*., out of which a dividend at the rate of 5½ per cent. per annum, left a balance of 59*l*. This balance would, however, be absorbed by the expenses attending the conversion of the company's debenture debt into 4½ per cent. debenture stock, an operation which was proceeding satisfactorily as debentures fell due.

Meetings in February or March, and August or September.

No. of Directors—7 ; minimum, 3 ; quorum, 2. *Qualification*, 200*l*.

DIRECTORS:

Chairman—LIGHTLY SIMPSON, Esq., 50, Gower Street, Bedford Square, W.C.

Edward Elmer Durrant, Esq., Lynn.	Edward Self, Esq,, Lynn, Norfolk.
Humphery John Hare, Esq., Docking, Lynn.	Charles Henry Turner, Esq., Litchurch, Derby.

OFFICERS.—Sec., Thomas Paul Bond, 5, Great Queen Street, Westminster, S.W. ; Eng., John Sutherland Valentine, 11, Park Street, Westminster, S.W. ; Solicitor, Henry Edwards, Lynn ; Auditors, John Thorley and William Plews, Lynn.

247.—MACCLESFIELD, BOLLINGTON, AND MARPLE.

Incorporated by 27 and 28 Vic., cap. 204 (14th July, 1864), to construct a line from Macclesfield, through Bollington, to Marple. Length, 10½ miles. Capital, 200,000*l*. in 10*l*. shares, and 66,600*l*. on loan. Arrangements with North Staffordshire and Manchester and Sheffield, which each subscribe 80,000*l*. Works in progress.

CAPITAL.—The receipts on this account to 30th June were 118,100*l*., and the expenditure, 147,993*l*.

No. of Directors—9 ; minimum, 7 ; quorum, 5 and 3. *Qualification*, 250*l*.

DIRECTORS:

William Worthington, Esq., Brockhurst Hall, Northwich, Cheshire.	Sir Edward William Watkin, Knt., Northenden, near Manchester, and 18, Westbourne Terrace, Hyde Park, W.
Lieut-Col. Charles Pearson, Cheltenham.	William Fenton, Esq., Beaumonds, near Rochdale.
Lieut-Col. Frederick Wright Tomlinson, Leamington.	Richard Withers, Esq., Royal Bank Buildings, Liverpool.
William Brownfield, Esq., Hanley, Staffordshire.	
John Chapman, Esq., Hill End, Mottram.	

OFFICERS.—Sec., Edward Ross ; Joint Engineers, J. C. Forsyth and Charles Sacré ; Joint Solicitors, J. R. Lingard and William Burchell ; Auditors, R. G. Underdown, Manchester, and Jonathan Samuda, Stoke-upon-Trent.

248.—MACCLESFIELD, KNUTSFORD, AND WARRINGTON.

Incorporated by 29 and 30 Vic., cap. 159 (28th June, 1866), to construct a line from Macclesfield, on the North Staffordshire, to Warrington, &c. Length, 25¾ miles. Capital, 400,000*l*. in 10*l*, shares, and 133,300*l*. on loan. Running powers over portions of the Warrington and Stockport and Cheshire Midland. Arrangements with the London and North Western, the Manchester and Sheffield, the North Staffordshire, and the Great Northern. The construction of the line is not yet commenced, and the issue of shares has been stayed for the present.

No. of Directors—6 ; quorum, 3. *Qualification*, 500*l*.

DIRECTORS:

Chairman—JOHN SMITH, Esq., Langley, Macclesfield.

Vice-chairman—THOMAS OLIVER, Esq., Water House, Bollington, Macclesfield.

David Chadwick, Esq., M.P., 21, Finch Lane, E.C.	Charles Edward Proctor, Esq., Ashfield House, Macclesfield.
William Coare Brocklehurst, Esq., M.P., 33, Milk Street, E.C., and Butley Hall, Macclesfield.	John Rylands, Esq., Oxford Lodge, Warrington.

OFFICERS. — Sec., George William Clarke ; Eng., John Isaac Mawson, Bank Chambers, Essex Street, Manchester ; Solicitors, Parrott, Colville, and May, Church Side, Macclesfield.

Offices—Bank Buildings, Chestergate, Macclesfield.

249.—MAIDSTONE AND ASHFORD.

Incorporated by 29 and 30 Vic., cap. 353 (10th August, 1866), to construct a line, No. 1, from Maidstone to Ashford, with junction at Ashford with South Eastern, and at Maidstone with Seven Oaks Maidstone and Tunbridge; and a line, No. 2, from the terminus of No. 1 at Maidstone to join the South Eastern Company's line at Maidstone. Length of line No. 1, 19¾ miles.   Length of line No. 2, ¾ of a mile.   Capital, 350,000*l.* in 20*l.* shares, and 116,000*l.* on loan.   Arrangements with South Eastern and London Chatham and Dover.

No. of Directors—5; minimum, 3; quorum, 3 and 2.

DIRECTORS :

The Right Hon. Earl of Romney, the Mote, Maidstone, and 48, Green Street, Park Lane, W.
William Laurence, Esq., Maidstone.
Alexander Randall, Esq., Maidstone.

Charles Wykeham Martin, Esq., M.P., Leeds Castle, Kent, and 25, Cumberland Street, W.
James Whatman, Esq., M.P., Vinters, Maidstone, and 6, Carlton Gardens, S.W.

OFFICERS.—Sec., *pro tem.*, Henry Hughes ; Engs., John Wright, Rochester, and Park Street, S.W., and Joseph Kincaid, 20, Spring Gardens, S.W. ; Solicitors, King, Hughes, and King, Maidstone.
Offices—Mill Street, Maidstone.

250.—MANCHESTER, BUXTON, MATLOCK, AND MIDLANDS JUNCTION.

Incorporated by 9 and 10 Vic., cap. 192 (16th July, 1846), for a line from the Midland at Ambergate, through Derbyshire, to Cheadle Station (London and North Western). Length, 45 miles, as projected.   In 1848, the original plan was altered, and the capital reduced.   The scheme is limited to the portion constructed, viz., 11½ miles between Ambergate and Rowsley, near Chatsworth. Opened, 4th June, 1848, and worked by Midland.

This company, by powers under Act of Incorporation, and the Cromford Canal Sale Act (9 and 10 Vic., cap. 290), has acquired the Cromford Canal for 101,200*l.* : but as no authority was given to appropriate ordinary capital to such purpose, and further capital for railway would be required, the company's borrowing powers could not be made available, an Act was obtained, 1st August, 1851 (15 Vic., cap. 126), which, whilst limiting the share capital to the amount already called, viz., 453,750*l.* (equal to 5*l.* per share) on the original 82,500 shares, has given the company power to borrow one-third of that capital, viz., 151,250*l.*, and to apply the same in payment of the canal purchase ; the canal proprietors are enabled to accept debentures in lieu of purchase money. This company entered into possession of the canal, 30th August, 1852.

Under provisions of an Act, 7th June, 1852 (15th Vic., cap. 98), which authorised this company, the London and North Western, and the Midland, to lease this line to the two companies, the shareholders, on 2nd September, 1852, sanctioned a lease of the railway and canal to the London and North Western and Midland, jointly, for 19 years, from 1st July, 1852, upon terms of agreement dated 3rd September, 1851, under which the two companies pay an annual sum equal to 2*s.* 9*d.* per share=2*l.* 10*s.* per cent. per annum upon the paid-up share capital, and also pay interest on capital of the canal, not exceeding 110,000*l.*   The directors receive the rent from the lessees, and pay a dividend of 1*s.* 4*d.* per share half-yearly ; one half-penny per share each six months being deducted for current expenses.

The lease, originally for 19 years, expires on 1st July, 1871.
CAPITAL.—The receipts have been 436,789*l.* on shares, and 109,128*l.* on loan. The expenditure is set down at 545,109*l.*, leaving a balance in hand of 808*l.*

Accounts are made up to 30th June and 31st December in every year, and the statutory meetings held in Derby, in February and August.

Certificates are not required to accompany transfer deed.   Registration fee, 2*s.* 6*d.* each deed.

No of Directors.—Maximum, 12 ; minimum, 3.   *Qualification*, C. C. C. Act, sec. 75.

DIRECTORS :

Chairman—

Deputy-Chairman—J. G. COTTINGHAM, Esq., Chesterfield.

Joseph Whitworth, Esq., Darley Dale, Derbyshire, and Manchester.
W. S. Roden, Esq., M.P., Etruria Hall, near Stoke-on-Trent.
* Samuel Beale, Esq., Warfield Grove, Bracknell, Berks.

* W. E. Hutchinson, Esq., Oadby Hill, Leicester.
† James Bancroft, Esq., 5, Police Street, Manchester.
† Richard Birley, Esq., Seedley, Pendleton, Manchester.

* Represent the Midland Railway.   † Represent the London and North Western.

OFFICERS.—Sec., Frederick Wragge ;, Auditors, P. Hubbersty and Wm. Richardson.
Offices—Derby.

251.—MANCHESTER AND MILFORD.

Incorporated by 23 and 24 Vic., cap. 175 (23rd July, 1860), to construct a line from Llanidloes to Pencader. Length, 51½ miles. Capital, 555,000l., in 10l. shares ; loans, 185,000l.

By 24 and 25 Vic., cap. 150 (11th July, 1861), the company was authorised to construct a branch from Devil's Bridge to Aberystwyth. Length, 11½ miles. Capital, 111,000l., in 10l. shares, and 37,000l. on loan. Arrangements with London and North Western, Great Western, and Cambrian.

By 28 and 29 Vic., cap. 305 (5th July, 1865), the company obtained power to construct certain lines in substitution of others, and also an extension of time for two years for completion of previous works. Length, 21¼ miles. Capital, 15,300l. in shares, and 5,100l. on loan. The company is also to complete the harbour line of the Aberystwyth and Welsh Coast, to lay down the mixed gauge on the Carmarthen and Cardigan, and also to enter into traffic and working arrangements with the Cambrian. Opened 12th August, 1867, thus completing a narrow gauge line from Carmarthen to Aberystwyth, where it joins the Cambrian, and affords a free and direct communication with the northern and midland districts.

DIRECTORS :

Chairman—WILLIAM CHAMBERS, Esq., University Club, and Hafod, Cardiganshire.

John Barrow, Esq., 35, Westbourne Terrace, Hyde Park, W.
Hon. Robert F. Greville, Milford.
Frederick Harrison, Esq., 15, Carlton Villas, Maida Hill, W.

Lieut.-Col. W. T. R. Powell, 83, Gloucester Street, Pimlico, S.W.
Charles Locock Webb, Esq., 1, Hanover Terrace, Notting Hill, W.

OFFICERS.—Sec., Joseph Butler ; Traf. Man., E. Hamer, Lampeter ; Eng., Hamilton H. Fulton, 4, Victoria Street, Westminster, S.W.; Solicitors, Marriott and Jordan.

Offices—6, Raymond Buildings, Grays Inn, W.C.

252.—MANCHESTER, SHEFFIELD, AND LINCOLNSHIRE.

An Amalgamation of the SHEFFIELD, ASHTON-UNDER-LYNE, and MANCHESTER, the GREAT GRIMSBY and SHEFFIELD JUNCTION, the SHEFFIELD and LINCOLN-SHIRE, the SHEFFIELD and LINCOLNSHIRE EXTENSION, and the GREAT GRIMSBY DOCK companies, by virtue of powers conferred by Act 9 and 10 Vic., cap. 268 (1846). The Act 10 and 11 Vic., cap. 190 (1847), authorised amalgamation with the MANCHESTER and LINCOLN UNION : the whole were dissolved and re-incorporated as one company, under this title, by the "Consolidation Act," of 1849 (13 Vic., cap. 81). Mileage in operation, including South Yorkshire, 249 miles.

The Grimsby New Dock possesses 47¾ acres of dock accommodation, and 7,200 feet of quays available for the wharfage of goods. The company's own first-class steam ships sail regularly between Grimsby, Hamburg, Rotterdam, and Antwerp, carrying passengers and goods. Communication by steam is also made with Dieppe, Ghent, and Rouen ; and, during the season, with St. Petersburg, and other ports in the Baltic.

The *Chesterfield and Gainsborough Canal* (46 miles) was obtained by the purchase of the then existing 986 shares of 100l. at par, and the discharge of a debt of 52,672l. These amounts were paid out of the Manchester and Lincoln Union 4l. 2s. shares.

This company has engagements under perpetual leases, with respect to three canals, constructed by previously independent companies, viz.: (under Act 9 and 10 Vic., cap. 267), the *Peak Forest* (21¼ miles) purchased for an annuity of 9,324l. 18s., or 3l. 18s. per share of 78l., subject also to an interest on a debt of 41,800l.; the *Macclesfield Canal* (26¼ miles), for an annuity of 6,605l., or 2l. 10s. per share of 59l., subject also to interest on a debt of 60,000l., also by virtue of Act 11 and 12 Vic., cap. 86, the *Ashton and Oldham Canal* (17¾), for an annuity of 12,363l. 15s., or 7l. per 100l. share, subject also to interest on a debt of 12,000l. Total liability under these three leases, 28,293l. 13s. per annum, besides interest on loans of 113,800l.

In August, 1847, were created 87,200 shares of 10l. each, guaranteed a dividend of 6 per cent., with a view of relieving shareholders from too great pressure for calls and to expedite the works. This creation was paid in full, not a single share in arrear. In 1849 very stringent clauses confirmed the privileged dividend guaranteed at their creation.

By 13 and 14 Vic., cap. 94 (August 30th, 1850), the company was authorised to raise 1,035,000l. in 6l. shares, bearing interest at 6 per cent. for 20 years. The company has then the option of redemption at par ; but if this option is not exercised within five years, these shares are to bear 6 per cent. in perpetuity. These shares are entitled to priority in dividend over all others in the company at present created, with the exception of the debenture stock.

By 17 Vic., cap. 145 (4th August, 1853), power is given to deviate and construct a branch to Barnsley station, on the Lancashire and Yorkshire (3 miles), cost 45,000l. out of existing capital powers, in substitution of line authorised by Act 1847. Opened throughout in August, 1857.

By Act 1853, June 30th (17 Vic., cap. 52), the company is entitled to borrow 2,370,000*l.*, and the Act states that the company has borrowed 2,370,000*l.* That the Act of 1847 authorised 43,210 shares of 8*l.* 2*s.* (the "M. and L. Union") and that 4*l.* 2*s.* has been paid; and gives power to create "*Debenture Stock*" for *not* above 2,370,000*l. maximum* guaranteed interest at 4 per cent. preference over other shares (as three-fifths of a special meeting may determine), but not to prejudice rights of holders of annuities, debentures, or other charges or securities, made payable or granted before the creation of such "Debenture Stock." A receiver may be appointed, if arrears, on application of holders of 20,000*l.* Powers with consent of holders, to convert the "M. and L. Union" shares and the amount paid into stock. To create new shares or stock for uncalled portion, as a meeting under 11 Vic., cap. 102, may determine. The new stock and shares confer same rights as existing shares. By 21 and 22 Vic., cap. 75, power was given to increase the maximum dividend to 6 per cent.

In August, 1858, were created 62,830 new shares of 10*l.* each, guaranteed dividend 6 per cent. per annum, to rank next after the existing preference stocks and shares of the company, but to take precedence of, and priority over, all dividends on consolidated stock; guaranteed to continue ten years certain from 8th September, 1858; company then to have the option of redemption at 10 per cent. premium.

By 18 and 19 Vic., cap. 129 (16th July, 1855), the whole Acts of the company were consolidated, for ample abstract of which see APPENDIX to Volume for 1856.

By 21 and 22 Vic., cap. 75 (28th June, 1858), the company was authorised to construct a line from Newton station to Compstall. Length, 5½ miles.

By 24 and 25 Vic., cap. 86 (28th June, 1861), the company was authorised to enter upon various additional works and branches, extending to 4 miles 56 chains. New capital, 218,500*l.* in shares, and 72,000*l.* on loan.

By 25 and 26 Vic., cap. 112 (30th June, 1862), several additional powers were conferred upon the company, including construction of a branch from Godley to Woodley. Length, 2¼ miles. New capital, 56,000*l.*, in shares at 5 per cent.; and 18,600*l.* on loan.

By 27 and 28 Vic., cap. 78 (23rd June, 1864), the subscriptions of the Sheffield to the Stockport and Woodley, the Cheshire Midland, the Stockport and Timperley, and the West Cheshire, were regulated as stated below, and new capital authorised to the extent of 250,000*l.* in shares, and 83,000*l.* on loan.

By 27 and 28 Vic., cap. 320 (29th July, 1864), the company was empowered to run steam and other vessels between Great Grimsby and foreign ports. Capital, 250,000*l.* in shares, and 83,300*l.* on loan.

By 29 and 30 Vic., cap. 158 (28th June, 1866), the Sheffield company obtained power to widen part of the line from Gorton to Hyde, and to enlarge the station in Sheffield. New capital, 195,000*l.* in shares, and 230,000*l.* on loan.

GREAT NORTHERN.—By 21 and 22 Vic., cap. 113 (23rd July, 1858), the company was authorised to enter into arrangements with the Great Northern. The Act enables the division and apportionment of traffic, the working of the line of one company by the other, the purchase of stock, the provision of capital for common purposes, and the appointment of a joint committee with full powers. An agreement is made with the Great Northern, by which the latter subscribe, in equal proportions with the Sheffield, to the following undertakings in Lancashire and Cheshire, viz.:—The Stockport and Woodley Junction, Stockport Timperley and Altrincham, Cheshire Midland, West Cheshire, and Garston and Liverpool.

SOUTH JUNCTION.—The Sheffield and London and North Western companies are joint owners of this line.

OLDHAM, ASHTON, AND GUIDE BRIDGE.—By 25 and 26 Vic., cap. 98 (30th June, 1862), this line is vested in the London and North Western and the Sheffield, the latter being thereby authorised to raise additional capital to complete its share of the purchase of the Oldham.

SOUTH YORKSHIRE.—By 27 and 28 Vic., cap. 77 (23rd June, 1864), the South Yorkshire was leased to the Sheffield company for 999 years, at 5 per cent. on the ordinary stock, with certain contingent advantages.

LIVERPOOL CENTRAL STATION.—By 28 and 29 Vic., cap. 248 (5th July, 1865), the Sheffield was authorised to contribute 250,000*l.* to this undertaking, as well as to raise 5,000*l.* for purchase of additional lands.

MARPLE, NEW MILLS, AND HAYFIELD JUNCTION.—Incorporated by 23 Vic., cap. 15 (15th May, 1860), to construct a line from the Newton and Compstall branch of the Manchester Sheffield and Lincolnshire, at Marple, to New Mills and Hayfield. Junction with Disley and Hayfield. Length, 6 miles. Capital, 150,000*l.* in 10*l.* shares; loans, 50,000*l.* By 27 Vic., cap. 7 (28th April, 1864), some alterations were authorised, and an extension of time for two years conceded. New capital, 10,000*l.* in shares, and 3,300*l.* on loan. By 28 and 29 Vic., cap. 248 (5th July, 1865), this company was amalgamated with the Manchester and Sheffield. Shares to be surrendered to latter company upon such terms as may be mutually agreed upon, not exceeding 90,000*l.*

ADDITIONAL POWERS.—By 30 Vic., cap. 4 (5th April, 1867), the company obtained additional powers in respect to the construction and abandonment of certain works, and also to divide the stock into preferred and deferred. In conjunction with the South Yorkshire, the Sheffield was also authorised to construct a line and colliery tramway, less than a mile in length. Also to subscribe to the Trent Ancholme and Grimsby, any sum not exceeding 30,000l., as well as 35,000l. in new capital, at not more than 6 per cent. preference, with 21,500l. on mortgage. By the same Act the South Yorkshire is also authorised to borrow 10,000l. Sec. 27 of this Act declares the capital of the company to be in shares or stock 11,769,998l., and in loans, 2,700,000l.

By the Act 30 Vic., cap. 49 (31st May, 1857), the company is authorised to raise and subscribe for the purposes of the station at Wakefield in shares, 20,000l., and 6,600l. in loans.

VESTED LINES.—By 28 and 29 Vic., cap. 327 (5th July, 1865), the following lines were vested jointly in the Great Northern, the Midland, and the Manchester and Sheffield :—

CHESHIRE MIDLAND.—Incorporated by 23 Vic., cap. 90 (14th June, 1860), to construct a line from the South Junction at Altrincham, to Northwich. Length, 12¼ miles. Capital, 100,000l., in 20l. shares. Loans, 33,000l. Under this Act the Manchester Sheffield and Lincolnshire were authorised to subscribe 30,000l. By 24 and 25 Vic., cap. 113 (11th July, 1861), a deviation near Knutsford was authorised. Powers were obtained in the same Act for the Manchester Sheffield and Lincolnshire to subscribe a further sum of 20,000l., and to guarantee a dividend of 4½ per cent. to the Cheshire Midland. Running powers and facilities are granted to the London and North Western and the Great Western. By the Great Northern (Cheshire Lines Act), 1863, the Sheffield and Great Northern companies are to contribute and guarantee equally the capital necessary for completing the undertaking, each company having equal rights and privileges in all respects. By this Act the Great Northern have powers to subscribe to this undertaking in the whole 65,000l., and by a further Act passed in 1864, the Manchester Sheffield and Lincolnshire company obtained powers to increase their subscriptions to the same amount. Opened from Altrincham to Knutsford (7 miles), on the 18th May, 1862, and to Northwich (6 miles), on 1st January, 1863, since which date the shareholders became entitled to 4½ per cent. from the Sheffield and Great Northern.

GARSTON AND LIVERPOOL.—By 24 Vic., cap. 35 (17th May, 1861), the Great Northern and the Manchester Sheffield and Lincolnshire were authorised to construct a line between Garston and Liverpool. Length, 4½ miles. Capital, 250,000l., to be furnished in equal proportion by the two companies. Loans, 75,000l. Opened 1st June, 1864. By this Act the two companies are authorised to use portions of the Warrington and Stockport, the St. Helens, and of the Edge Hill line of the London and North Western, the latter obtaining in lieu thereof use of the Sheffield line up to that town, and of the Great Northern between Peterborough and Grimsby and New Holland, with access to other towns in Yorkshire.

EXTENSION TO LIVERPOOL.—By 28 and 29 Vic., cap. 378 (6th July, 1856), the Sheffield was authorised to construct a line from the South Junction, in Manchester, to the Garston, in Liverpool. Length, 32⅔ miles. Capital, 750,000l. in shares, and 250,000l. on loan. By 29 and 30 Vic., cap. 191 (11th July, 1866), the Great Northern and the Midland were constituted in conjunction with the Sheffield, joint owners of the Liverpool Extension, these two companies each subscribing 250,000l. Also by 29 and 30 Vic., cap. 192 (16th July, 1866), the Great Northern and the Midland were authorised, in conjunction with the Sheffield, to construct new lines in connection with the Liverpool Extension. Length, 5½ miles ; and a new canal in substitution of that stopped up by the Act. New capital, 120,000l. by each of the three companies, with one-third additional by borrowing.

LIVERPOOL CENTRAL STATION.—Incorporated by 27 and 28 Vic., cap. 290 (29th July, 1864), to construct a railway and general station in Liverpool. Length, 1¾ miles. Capital, 500,000l. in 10l. shares, and 166,000l. on loan. By 29 and 30 Vic., cap. 294 (30th July, 1866), the Liverpool Central Station was vested jointly in the Manchester and Sheffield, the Great Northern, and the Midland, and its management placed in the Cheshire lines committee, nominated by the three companies.

STOCKPORT, TIMPERLEY, AND ALTRINCHAM JUNCTION.—Incorporated by 24 and 25 Vic., cap. 175 (July 22nd, 1861), to construct a line from the Stockport and Woodley to the Warrington and Stockport, and two branches connecting with the Manchester South Junction and Altrincham. Length, 9½ miles. Capital, 150,000l. in 10l. shares, and 50,000l. on loan.

STOCKPORT AND WOODLEY JUNCTION.—Incorporated by 23 Vic., cap. 16 (15th May, 1860), to construct a line from Stockport to Woodley, on the Newton and Compstall branch of the Manchester Sheffield and Lincolnshire line, and to the extensive coal fields in the neighbourhood of Hyde and Dukinfield. Length, 2½ miles. Capital, 60,000l. in 10l. shares. Loan, 20,000l. Opened 12th January, 1863.

WEST CHESHIRE.—Incorporated by 24 and 25 Vic., cap. 143 (18th July, 1861), to construct a line from Northwich, on the Cheshire Midland, to Helsby, on the Birkenhead. Length, 16 miles. Capital, 200,000l. in 10l. shares : loans, 66,600l. Running powers and facilities conceded to London and North Western and Great Western. The line to be efficiently worked by the Sheffield, with which, and Great Northern, traffic arrangements may be made, and who may subscribe 65,000l. each. By 25 and 26 Vic., cap. 190 (29th July, 1862), the company was authorised to construct branches to Winsford and Winnington, and a deviation at Oakmere. Length, 7¾ miles. Capital, 63,000l. in shares, and 21,000l. on loan. By 29 and 30 Vic., cap. 351 (10th August, 1866), the Great Northern obtained running powers over a portion of the Newton and Compstall branch of the Sheffield ; also, in conjunction with that company and the Midland, to execute certain works and to become joint owners of the Godley and Woodley branch. The Chester and West Cheshire was also by the same Act vested in the three companies, each of which were to raise 90,000*l*. in shares, and 30,000*l*. on loan, instead of the Chester and West Cheshire.

REVENUE.—The receipts for the half-year ending 31st December, were 591,158*l*., the expenditure 267,697*l*., and the net profit 323,460*l*., which, with the balance from the previous half-year, amounted to 323,958*l*. The debenture and other interest chargeable against revenue amounted to 79,370*l*., the canal annuities to 14,148*l*., the dividends on the various classes of preference stock and shares to 114,794*l*., and the South Yorkshire interest and dividends to 70,581*l*., making a total charge of 278,892*l*., and leaving a balance of 45,065*l*., out of which a dividend at the rate of 2*l*. per cent. per annum left a balance of 1,139*l*. to next account. The receipts for the half-year ending 30th June, amounted to 533,891*l*., the expenses to 245,878*l*., and the net profit, 288,013*l*., which, with balance from the previous half-year, made a total of 289,153*l*. The debenture and other interest chargeable amounted to 83,169*l*., the canal annuities to 14,143*l*., the dividends on the various classes of preference stocks and shares to 115,357*l*., and the South Yorkshire interest and dividends to 74,992*l*., making a total charge of 287,662*l*., leaving a balance of only 1,491*l*. There was consequently no dividend on the ordinary stock.

GREAT NORTHERN.—The directors reported in February that they thought it right to explain that they had an unsettled claim against the Great Northern, under the agreement of 1857, for interest upon capital expended for the accommodation of the through traffic exchanged between the two companies. The directors trusted that the Great Northern Board would meet the claim in a fair spirit.

CAPITAL.—The expenditure on this account to 30th June, 1868, amounted to 12,489,726*l*. The balance of 52,258*l*. accounting for a receipt of 12,541,984*l*., the details of which were stated as under :—

6*l*. preference shares	£1,034,555
3¼ per cent. stock	366,698
6*l*. per cent. preference	872,000
Redeemable 10*l*. preference shares (5*l*. called up)	263,101
5 per cent. guaranteed (conversion)	106,904
Garston and Liverpool extension	225,000
5 per cent. perpetual preference	182,967
5 per cent. redeemable preference 10*l*. shares	472,685
Consolidated stock	4,392,553
Shares forfeited	170,678
Loans on debenture	3,447,095
Debenture stock at 4 per cent.	79,576
Debenture stock at 5 per cent.	156,670
Loans on security of preference shares	160,790
Calls in advance on Lincoln Union shares	6,712
Advance by Great Northern on account of improvement to Fishing Craft Dock at Grimsby	4,000
	£12,541,984

The accounts are made up to the 30th June and 31st December, and the statutory meetings are held in January and July every year.

Scale of Voting.—One vote for each 100*l*. of nominal capital up to 1,000*l*. ; beyond that amount one vote additional for every 300*l*.

Certificates of shares are not required to accompany transfer deed, but coupons of stock must be sent in. Registration fee, 2*s*. 6*d*. each seller of shares. Several classes may go on one transfer stamp. Parts of a pound may be transferred. Registers of shares close three weeks before meetings. Fee for registration of bonds, 2*s*. 6*d*. each bond.

No. of Directors.—Maximum, 18 ; minimum, 9. *Qualification*, 1,000*l*. of stock.

DIRECTORS :

Chairman—Sir EDWARD WILLIAM WATKIN, Knt., Rose Hill, Northenden, Cheshire, and 18, Westbourne Terrace, Hyde Park, W.

Deputy-Chairman—WILLIAM FENTON, Esq., Beaumonds, near Rochdale.

Thomas Rawson Barker, Esq., The Edge, near Sheffield.
Sir John Brown, Sheffield.
John Chapman, Esq., Hill End, Mottram, Cheshire.
The Hon. William George Eden, Cantley, Doncaster.
Lieut.-Colonel George Morland Hutton, Gate Burton, near Gainsborough.

John William Maclure, Esq., Manchester.
Alexander Shand, Esq., Maryton Grange, near Liverpool.
Charles Turner, Esq., M.P., Dingle Head, Liverpool, and 5, Cleveland Row, S.W.
Richard Withers, Esq., Liverpool.
The Rt. Hon. Lord Wharncliffe, Wortley Hall, near Sheffield, and 15, Curzon Street, W.

OFFICERS.—Gen. Man., R. G. Underdown ; Sec., Edward Ross ; Eng. and Supt. of Loco. and Stores Dept., Charles Sacré ; Goods Man., Alfred Ormerod ; Solicitor, J. R. Lingard ; Accountant, Robert Williams : Supt. of Line, W. Bradley ; Auditors, Smith P. Robinson, Manchester, and J. G. T. Child, Manchester ; Bankers, Smith, Payne, and Smiths, and Williams, Deacon, and Co., London ; Liverpool Commercial Bank ; Yorkshire Banking Co., Leeds ; Manchester and Salford Bank ; Sheffield Banking Company ; and Smith, Ellison, and Co., Lincoln.

Head Offices—London Road Station, Manchester.

253.—MANCHESTER, SOUTH JUNCTION, AND ALTRINCHAM.

Incorporated by act 9 Vic., cap. 111 (1845). This line is in two divisions—1st, the South Junction line (1½ mile), connecting the lines at London Road, Manchester, with the London and North Western, at Ordsal Lane, Salford. 2nd, the Altrincham branch, 7¾ miles from Manchester, South Junction, to Altrincham and Bowdon.

By 21 and 22 Vic., cap. 136 (23rd July, 1858), the management was so far improved as to authorise the appointment of a standing arbitrator, who shall attend at the meetings of the joint board and affirm, modify, or negative such resolution as could only be carried by casting vote of chairman, which is abolished.

Capital authorised—1st Act, 40,000l., Act 1848, 250,000l. ; loans, 216,666l. The London and North Western, and the Manchester Sheffield and Lincolnshire, each subscribed half the authorised capital, which is included in their capitals. No reports are published. Returns of traffic are rendered conjointly to the partner companies, the dividend on which appears in their respective accounts.

DIRECTORS:

Matthew Lyon, Esq., Leamington.
Edward Tootal, Esq., The Weaste, near Eccles.
Sir Edward Wm. Watkin, Knt., Rose Hill, Northenden, and 18, Westbourne Terrace, Hyde Park, W.

Charles Turner, Esq., M.P., Dingle Head, Liverpool, and 5, Cleveland Row, S.W.
James Bancroft, Esq., 5, Police Street, Manchester.
Richard Withers, Esq., Royal Bank Buildings, Liverpool.

OFFICERS.—Sec. and Man., James Kirkman ; Res. Eng., Henry Woodhouse.

Offices—Station, Oxford Road, Manchester.

254.—MANCHESTER AND STOCKPORT.

Incorporated by 29 and 30 Vic., cap. 207 (16th July, 1866), to construct a line from Manchester, on the Sheffield and Lincolnshire, to the Stockport and Woodley Junction, with a branch to the Newton and Compstall branch of the Sheffield. Length, 7½ miles. Capital, 200,000l. in 10l. shares, and 66,600l. on loan. Arrangements with the Sheffield, which may guarantee interest on capital. Works not commenced.

It is proposed to hand over this concern to the Manchester and Sheffield.

No. of Directors—7 ; minimum, 5 ; quorum, 3. *Qualification*, 300l.

DIRECTORS:

Sir Edward William Watkin, Knt., Rose Hill, Northenden, and 18, Westbourne Terrace, Hyde Park, London, W.
James Marshall, Esq., Stockport.
George Wilkinson, Esq., Stockport.
Robert Maclure, Esq., Stockport.

William Fenton, Esq., Beaumonds, near Rochdale.
John Chapman, Esq., Hill End, Mottram, Cheshire.
Charles Turner, Esq., M.P., Dingle Head, Liverpool, and 5, Cleveland Row, S.W.

---

255. MARLBOROUGH.

Incorporated by 24 and 25 Vic., cap. 167 (22nd July, 1861), to construct a line from the Berks and Hants Extension to Marlborough. Length, 5¾ miles. Capital, 45,000l. in 10l. shares ; loans, 15,000l. Arrangements with Great Western, which may subscribe 20,000l. Opened 30th March, 1864.

Meetings in February or March, and August or September.

No. of Directors—5 ; maximum, 8 ; minimum, 3 ; quorum, 3. *Qualification*, 300l.

DIRECTORS:

Chairman—The Right Hon. LORD ERNEST BRUCE, M.P., 6, St. George's Place, Hyde Park Corner, S.W.
Deputy-Chairman, R. E. PRICE, Marlborough.

H. B. Baring, Esq., 36, Wilton Place, Belgravia, S.W.
F. A. Mc. Geachy, Esq., Shenley Hill, Barnet, Herts, N.

H. R. Tomkinson, Esq., 7, Lower Seymour Street, W.

OFFICERS.—Sec., W. H. Wilson, 6, Victoria Street, Westminster, S.W.; Eng.. R. J. Ward, C.E., 6, Victoria Street, Westminster, S.W.; Solicitors, Cope, Rose, and Pearson, 26, Great George Street, Westminster, S.W.; and Merriman and Gwillim, Marlborough; Bankers, Ward, Merriman, and Co., Marlborough, and Robarts, Lubbock, and Co., Lombard Street, E.C.

Offices—6, Victoria Street, Westminster, S.W.

256.—MARYPORT AND CARLISLE.

Incorporated by Act 1 Vic., cap. 101 (1837). The Act of June 26th, 1855 (18 and 19 Vic., cap. 79), provided for new capital for doubling the rails and other improvements, to the extent of 77,712*l*. 10*s*. in 12*l*. 10*s*. shares, making a total of 420,000*l*., with borrowing powers to the extent of 135,000*l*. Productive, 38 miles.

By 25 and 26 Vic., cap. 80 (30th June, 1862), the company were empowered to construct branches to Bolton and Wigton (7½ miles), to purchase additional land, and to raise new capital to the extent of 75,000*l*. in 12*l*. 10*s*. shares, and 20,000*l*. on loan. These shares were created at a meeting on 20th August, 1862, and issued to the proprietors as ordinary stock. although the Act authorised a preference not exceeding 5 per cent. Opened 26th December, 1866.

By 28th Vic., cap. 84 (19th June, 1865), the company was authorised to construct the Derwent branch (6 miles), to enlarge the Bull Gill station, to purchase additional lands, and to raise further capital to the extent of 60,000*l*. in shares, and 20,000*l*. by mortgage. Opened, 1st December, 1867.

By completion of the Derwent Branch between the Bull Gill station and the junction with the Cockermouth and Workington at Brigham, a short and direct communication has been opened out between Scotland and Newcastle and the extensive iron ore mines and iron furnaces of West Cumberland. This branch also gives direct connection with the Cockermouth and Workington (now part of the London and North Western system), the Whitehaven Cleator and Egremont, and the Cockermouth Keswick and Penrith.

REVENUE.—The receipts for the half-year ending 31st December amounted to 43,751*l*. and the expenditure, including rates and taxes, to 19,151*l*. The balance, after carrying 1,662*l*. to the credit of the contingency account, was 18,851*l*., which authorised a dividend on the ordinary shares at the rate of 7½ per cent. per annum.

By the half-yearly statement to the 30th June, the receipts amounted to 41,748*l*. and the expenditure, including rates and taxes, to 18,410*l*. The balance for the half-year, after carrying 137*l*. to the credit of the contingency account, was 19,106*l*., which enabled declaration of a dividend on the ordinary shares at the rate of 7½ per cent. per annum.

CAPITAL.—This account on the original line is closed at 555,000*l*., with a balance of 845*l*. on hand. The receipts on the Bolton and Wigton branches have been 94,982*l*., 305*l*. being on hand on 30th June. On the Derwent Branch the expenditure had been 82,348*l*., and the receipts 70,400*l*., showing a balance against the account of 11,948*l*.

On the 1st October, 1867, a call of 2*l*. per share was made on the new 12*l*. 10*s*. shares (1865), on the 1st June, 1868, the remaining call of 2*l*. per share was made upon the new 12*l*. 10*s*. shares (1862), and on the 1st October, 1868, the remaining call of 2*l*. per share was made upon the new 12*l*. 10*s*. shares (1865).

DIRECTORS:

3 Chairman—GILFRED WILLIAM HARTLEY, Esq., Rosehill, Whitehaven.

2 Deputy-Chairman—JOSEPH POCKLINGTON SENHOUSE, Esq., Netherhall, Maryport.

1 Robert Ritson, Esq., Ellen Bank, Maryport.
3 Sir Wilfrid Lawson, Bart., M.P., Brayton Hall.

2 George Gill Mounsey, Esq., Carlisle.
2 William Ostle, Esq., Birkby, Maryport.
1 Caleb Hodgson, Esq., Carlisle.

1, retire in the autumn of 1869; 2, in 1870; 3, in 1871, but eligible for re-election.

OFFICERS.—Sec. and Gen. Man., John Addison, C.E.; Loco. Supt., George Tosh; Accountant, Hugh Carr; Auditors, William Cowan, LL.D. and James Lainton, Public Accountant; Solicitors, Tyson and Hobson.

Head Offices—Maryport.

257.—MELLIS AND EYE.

Incorporated by 28 and 29 Vic., cap. 249 (5th July, 1865), to construct a line from the Great Eastern, at Mellis, to Eye. Length, 3 miles. Capital, 15,000*l*. in shares, and 5,000*l*. on loan. Opened in April, 1867. Arrangements with Great Eastern, which works the line.

CAPITAL.—It was reported in August that the receipts had been 13,847*l*., and the expenditure 15,844*l*., leaving a balance of 1,997*l*. against the company.

The traffic had averaged for the past 16 months 85*l.* per month, but the chairman thought, however, that the traffic had suffered of late from the Great Eastern having "put on the screw" too tight in various directions.

No. of Directors—6 ; quorum, 3. *Qualification*, 100*l.*

DIRECTORS :

Chairman—SIR EDWARD KERRISON, Bart., Brome Hall and Oakley Park, Suffolk.

Edgar Chenery, Esq., Eye.
Benjamin Cotton Etheridge, Esq., Eye.
Robert Chase, Esq., Eye.

The Hon. John Major Henniker-Major, M.P., Woodlands, Ipswich.
Samuel Pech, Esq., Eye.

OFFICERS.—See Great Eastern.

258.—MERRYBENT AND DARLINGTON.

Incorporated by 29 Vic., cap. 75 (11th June, 1866), to construct a line and branch from the Darlington and Barnard Castle to Melsonby, in the North Riding of Yorkshire. Length, 6¾ miles. Capital, 60,000*l.* in 10*l.* shares, and 20,000*l.* on loan. Arrangements with North Eastern.

No. of Directors—7; minimum, 5 ; quorum, 3. *Qualification*, 500*l.*

DIRECTORS:

Henry King Spark, Esq.
Joseph Boyer, Esq.
Robert Wardell, Esq.

Henry Currer Briggs, Esq.
Joseph Johnson, Esq.

Secretary, Samuel Richardson, Land Agent, Darlington.

259.—MERSEY.

Incorporated by 29 and 30 Vic., cap. 139 (28th June, 1866), to construct a line to connect Birkenhead with Liverpool by a passage beneath the river Mersey. Length, 1½ mile. Capital, 350,000*l.* in 20*l.* shares, divided, and 116,600*l.* on loan. Power to create debenture stock.

By 31 and 32 Vic., cap. 161 (31st July, 1868), an extension of time for purchase of lands and completion of works was obtained, the latter till 31st July, 1873.

No. of Directors—7 ; minimum, 3 ; quorum, 4 and 2. *Qualification*, 500*l.*

DIRECTORS:

Robertson Gladstone, Esq., Liverpool.
Edward Lawrence, Esq., Liverpool.
Edward Stewart Jones, Esq.

Harold Littledale, Esq., Liverpool, and Liscard Hall, Cheshire.
Augustus De Metz, Esq.

260.—METROPOLITAN.

Re-incorporated by 17 and 18 Vic., cap. 221 (7th August, 1854), being an extension of the North Metropolitan Act of the previous session.

By 18 and 19 Vic., cap. 102 (July 2nd, 1855), some economic deviations were authorised. By 19 and 20 Vic., cap. 109 (21st July, 1856), the company obtained an extension of time for one year for completion of works. By 20 and 21 Vic., cap. 125 (10th August, 1857), some further deviations were authorised, and another extension of time for one year conceded. By 22 and 23 Vic., cap. 97 (8th August, 1859), the company obtained a third extension of time for one year, and was authorised to carry the line clear of Clerkenwell Prison, and to get rid of the Post-Office terminus. By 23 Vic., cap. 58 (25th May, 1860), the company was authorised to acquire additional land, and to provide enlarged station accommodation. The period for completion of railway was further extended for another year.

By 24 and 25 Vic., cap. 133 (11th July, 1861), the company was authorised to make certain improvements in communication with the Great Northern, and with the new market in Smithfield, also to enter into arrangements with the corporation of London, which subscribes 200,000*l.* to the undertaking. New capital, 200,000*l.* in shares, and 100,000*l.* on loan.

By 24 and 25 Vic., cap. 283 (6th August, 1861), the company was authorised to extend the line from Smithfield to Finsbury Circus. Length, 53 chains. New capital, 500,000*l.* in shares, and 166,000*l.* on loan ; completion of works, five years.

By 25 and 26 Vic., cap. 58 (30th June, 1862), the company was empowered to purchase additional lands, and to attach a preference of 5 per cent. to the 300,000*l.* authorised by the Act of 11th July, 1861.

By 26 and 27 Vic., cap. 165 (21st July, 1863), the company was authorised to acquire certain additional lands, and three year's additional time given for completion of the line, in Praed Street, to the front of the Great Western Hotel, under a penalty of 50*l.* per day, if not opened by 21st July, 1866.

By 27 and 28 Vic., cap. 200 (25th July, 1864), several new works were authorised, and new capital obtained, to the extent of 450,000*l.* in shares, and 150,000*l.* on loan.

By 27 and 28 Vic., cap. 291 (29th July, 1864), the company was authorised to extend the line to Notting Hill, Kensington, and Brompton. Length, 2¾ miles. Capital, 1,200,000*l.* in shares, and 400,000*l.* on loan. Opened 1st October, 1868.

By 27 and 28 Vic., cap. 315 (29th July, 1864), the company was authorised to construct an extension from Finsbury Circus to Tower Hill. Length, 1 mile. Capital, 700,000*l.* in shares, and 233,000*l.* on loan.

By 28 Vic., cap. 117 (19th June, 1865), the company obtained various powers in respect to holding land and works, and to create separate mortgages thereon ; also to lease the Hammersmith and City in conjunction with the Great Western.

By 29 and 30 Vic., cap. 160 (28th June, 1866), the company acquired powers to improve existing works, to obtain additional lands, to authorise agreements with the Great Western, Great Northern, and Midland, and to extend the time for two years for completion of works. New capital, 1,000,000*l.* in shares, and 333,000*l.* on loan.

By 30 Vic., cap. 85 (17th June, 1867), the company obtained further powers and also authority to subscribe to the Metropolitan and St. John's Wood, and also to form a junction with that line at Baker Street Station.

By 31 and 32 Vic., cap. 109 (13th July, 1868), the company was authorised to construct a junction line to unite the Meat Market with the London, Chatham, and Dover, and also to enter into arrangements with the latter company and the Midland. Also to regulate the extension capital until it shall become united with the general undertaking on 1st January, 1870. Also to set aside 5,000*l.* per annum out of revenue for discharge of the mortgage debt. The company were likewise authorised to sell the shares for which it had subscribed in the Metropolitan and St. John's Wood.

REVENUE.—The receipts for the half-year ending the 31st of December amounted to 118,738*l.*, as compared with 107,295*l.* for the corresponding period of 1866, showing an increase of 11,443*l.*, which had been earned without a corresponding increase in the expenses. A net available balance (exclusive of the dividend of 6 per cent. paid on the extension stock) of 91,633*l.*, permitted the payment of dividends on the preference stock at the rate of 5 per cent. per annum, and upon the consolidated stock at the rate of 7 per cent. per annum, carrying forward a balance of 6,999*l.* to the credit of the current half-year.

From the report of Mr. Myles Fenton, general manager, it appeared that 23,405,282 passengers had been conveyed over the railway in the year 1867, that the gross receipts amounted to 233,180*l.*, and the net receipts, after deducting expenses, to 143,109*l.* The aggregate number of passengers conveyed during five years was 81,619,357, the gross receipts were 803,131*l.*, and the net receipts, 482,113*l.* During the half-year ending 31st December, the number of passengers was 11,916,924, and the amount of gross receipts 118,731*l.*, showing an increase of 947,215 passengers, and 11,443*l.* in the receipts over the corresponding period of 1866. This return has been secured with an increase of only 422*l.* in the working expenses. The traffic to and from the Hammersmith railway continued steadily to increase. In 1867 it amounted to 40,866*l.*, against 32,520*l.* in 1866, and 19,165*l.* in 1865.

The number of passengers conveyed, and the amount of traffic receipts in each year since the opening of the line, has been as follow :—

Year.	Passengers.	Receipts.	Net Receipts.
1863	9,455,175	£101,707	£56,537
1864	11,721,889	116,489	70,776
1865	15,763,907	141,513	86,008
1866	21,273,104	210,242	125,683
1867	23,405,282	233,180	143,109
	81,619,357	£803,131	£482,113

During the June half-year of 1868 the number of passengers was 11,916,924, and the amount of gross receipts 118,738*l.*, showing an increase of 947,215 passengers and 11,443*l.* in receipts over the corresponding period of 1866. This had been secured with an increase of only 422*l.* in the working expenses.

It was reported in August that the amount applicable for payment of interest and dividends was 156,582*l.*, and dividends were declared at the following rates, viz. : on the preference stock at the rate of 5*l.* per cent. per annum, on the Extension stock at the rate of 6*l.* per cent., on the ordinary stock at the rate of 7*l.* per cent., and the balance of 1,673*l.* was carried forward. The revenue from the surplus property, subject to the new redeemable share trust, was steadily increasing, and the directors had every reason to believe that their expectations as to its ultimate value would be fully realized. On the opening of the Western Extension the entire undertaking would, with the exception of the Eastern Extension, be substantially completed.

The details of revenue income and expenditure for the half-year ending 30th June, gave the following particulars :—

Receipts, &c.

Undivided dividend	£13,500	
Balance from last half-year	6,998	
Traffic account	128,474	
Messrs. Kelk and Co. (Extension revenue)	57,000	
Surplus land account to meet interest on new redeemable shares to 30th June	9,375	
Rents	1,259	
Interest on revenue balances	1,084	
Transfer fees	270	= £217,962

Expenditure.

Locomotive and carriage charges	£14,852		
Maintenance of way and works	5,511		
Salaries and wages	8,942		
Water, gas, and general charges	3,219		
Rates, taxes, and passenger duty	10,629	= £43,155	
Compensations		1,578	
Office expenses		1,620	
Directors and Auditors		1,400	
Half-year's annuity to Mrs. Pearson		125	= £47,880
Undivided dividend			13,500
Available balance—			
Interest on 699,330*l.* debenture capital		15,734	
Interest on new redeemable shares at 5 per cent.		9,375	
Dividend on 300,000*l.* 5 per cent. preference stock		7,500	
* Ditto on 2,259,761*l.* consolidated stock at 7 per cent.		79,000	
Dividend on 1,440,239*l.* extension stock at 6 per cent.		43,207	
Balance carried to next account		1,673	= 156,582

* This includes 459,761*l.* converted extension stock.   £217,962

PARLIAMENTARY.—The Act of 1868 was thus described by the directors in their report for August :—" By the new Act, which received the Royal assent on the 13th July, the arrangement made when the Extension capitals were created, that they were not to become chargeable upon revenue until the extensions were opened for traffic, was recognised and confirmed, and until the period of the amalgamation of the capitals, viz. : the 1st of January, 1870—the general revenue was to be charged only with the dividends and interest upon so much of the Extension capital as would represent from time to time the portions of the extensions earning revenue, the 6 per cent. dividend upon the balance of the Extension capital being paid under the arrangement with the contractors as heretofore. The Act sanctioned the vesting of the surplus lands in trustees, and contained a provision that 5,000*l.* should be annually set aside with a view to the creation of a fund for the gradual redemption of the debenture debt."

CAPITAL.—The general statement of receipts and disbursements to 30th June, 1868, furnished the subjoined particulars :—

Receipts.—Consolidated capital of 1,800,000*l.*	£1,799,992	
5*l.* per cent. preference capital 300,000*l.*	300,000	
Extension share capital of 1,900,000*l.*	1,899,720	
New redeemable share capital of 600,000*l.*	515,387	
Debenture capital of 1,533,333*l.*	1,532,944	
Temporary loans	147,140	=£6,195,183

Expenditure.—To 30th June, 1868		£5,653,363	
Purchase of lands	£220,536		
Works	140,367		
New rolling stock	20,936		
Interest on loans and debentures (Extension capital)	24,486	= 406,327	=£6,059,690
Subscription to Metropolitan and St. John's Wood			100,000
Cash balance			35,492

                                                                                                         £6,195,183

NEW REDEEMABLE CAPITAL SURPLUS LAND ACCOUNT.—The particulars of this account to 30th June, were detailed as under :—

Receipts.—From last account	£4,975	
Amount received on mortgage of land	33,448	
Amount received for rents	7,000	
Interest on deposits	16	= £45,441
Expended.—Paid to revenue to meet interest to 30th June	£9,375	
Interest on land mortgages	195	
Purchase of 3,379 new redeemable shares paid in full	34,222	
Balance in hands of trustees	1,647	= £45,441

DIVISION OF STOCK.—It was resolved, at a special meeting on 19th August, to divide the ordinary stock into preferred and deferred, in accordance with the regulation of Railways Act, 1868.

DIRECTORS:

Chairman—JOHN PARSON, Esq., Bitton House, Teignmouth, Devon.

Deputy-Chairman—CHARLES GILPIN, Esq., M.P., 10, Bedford Square, W.C.

William Lee, Esq., M.P., Holborough, Rochester, and 16, Upper Ground Street, Blackfriars, S.

Alex. Clunes Sherriff, Esq., M.P., Perdiswell Hall, Worcester, and 10, Dean's Yard, Westminster, S.W.

William Austin, Esq., Farningham, Kent.

Mr. Alderman Hale, 71, Queen Street, Cheapside, E.C.

Mr. Alderman Dakin, Creechurch Lane, E.C.

Russell Scott, Esq., 10, Cornwall Terrace, Regent's Park, N.W.

James Nasmyth, Esq., Penshurst, Kent.

OFFICERS.—Sec., John Henchman ; Man., Myles Fenton ; Eng., John Fowler ; Res. Eng. and Loco. Supt., Robert Harvey Burnett ; Auditors, B. J. Armstrong, Upper Wimpole Street, W., and Sampson Copestake, Bow Church Yard, E.C.; Solicitors, Messrs. Burchell, 5, Broad Sanctuary, S.W.; Bankers, London and County Bank, 21, Lombard Street, E.C.

Offices—3, Old Palace Yard, S.W.

261.—METROPOLITAN DISTRICT.

Incorporated by 27 and 28 Vic., cap. 322 (29th July, 1864), to construct a series of lines to complete an inner circle of railway north of the Thames, extending from Kensington by Westminster Bridge and the north bank of the Thames to Tower Hill. Length, 8 miles. Capital, 3,600,000l., in shares of 20l. each, and 1,200,000l. on loan. Arrangements with Metropolitan, and facilities to London and North Western. Opened between Kensington and Westminster Bridge on 24th December, 1868.

By 28 and 29 Vic., cap. 151 (29th June, 1865), certain deviations were authorised, as well as new capital to the extent of 150,000l. in shares, and 50,000l. on loan. Traffic arrangements with the Metropolitan. Works in progress.

By 29 and 30 Vic., cap. 178 (16th July, 1866), the company was authorised to acquire additional lands, and obtained renewed facilities in regard to the mode of construction of several works. Also to exercise its borrowing powers on subscription to the first section of its capital, on one part thereof having been paid up.

By 31 and 32 Vic., cap. 108 (13th July, 1868), the company obtained power to purchase additional lands, and to extend the time for completion of works in connection with the Thames embankment till 1st August, 1871, and for other works till 1873.

METROPOLITAN.—This company is efficiently to work and maintain the portions of the District as they are successively opened for traffic ; to extend the running of all their Notting Hill and Brompton trains over the District, and run additional trains if deemed necessary by a joint committee to be appointed by the two boards, and hand over monthly to the Metropolitan District 55 per cent. on the gross receipts, whether from local traffic or their proportion of through traffic. This agreement is terminable at any time by either company at eighteen months' notice, after the end of twelve months from the opening of the line between Brompton and Westminster Bridge.

CAPITAL.—The expenditure on this account to 30th June, 1868, was 2,784,450l., leaving a balance at the bankers of 16,842l. The receipts to the same period were detailed as follow :—

Share capital, as per statement to 31st December, 1867	£1,846,271	
Additional to 30th June, 1868	170,618=	£2,016,889
Loans and debentures to 31st December, 1867	325,486	
Less loans repaid	59,466=	266,020
Debenture stock to 31st December, 1867	53,014	
Additional to 30th June, 1868	465,368=	518,382
		£2,801,292

At a special meeting held on 19th December, 1868, it was resolved to issue the remainder of the ordinary share capital (1,500,000l.) at 80l. for every 100l., with a right to take a preference dividend of 4 per cent. When the company could pay more than 5 per cent. on the ordinary capital, the 4 per cent. preference should participate in any surplus dividend above 5 per cent. with the ordinary shareholders. If the ordinary shareholders got 6 per cent., the 4 per cent. holders would have 5 per cent. on the 100l. stock ; and if the ordinary shareholders got 7 per cent., the 4 per cent. preference holders were to receive 6 per cent. ; but before the remaining share capital could be issued as a preference stock, the authority of Parliament would be required.

DIRECTORS:

Chairman—The EARL OF DEVON, Powderham Castle, Exeter.

Deputy-Chairman—ALEXANDER CLUNES SHERRIFF, Esq., M.P., Perdiswell Hall, near Worcester, and 10, Dean's Yard, Westminster, S.W.

William Austin, Esq., The Mount, Farningham, Kent.

Thomas Dakin, Esq., Alderman, 2 and 3, Creechurch Lane, E.C.

Ralph Anstruther Earle, Esq., 27, Park Street, Grosvenor Square, W.

Charles Gilpin, Esq., M.P., 10, Bedford Square, W.C.

Viscount Gort, 10, Warwick Square, Pimlico, S.W.

Colonel the Hon. W. P. Talbot, 2, Cromwell Road, W.

Sir Henry Drummond Wolff, K.C.M.G., 15, Rutland Gate, S.W.

George Worms, Esq., 17, Park Crescent, Portland Place, N.W.

OFFICERS.—Sec., George Hopwood ; Eng.-in-Chief, John Fowler ; Eng., T. Marr Johnson ; Solicitors, Baxter, Rose, Norton, and Co., 6, Victoria Street, Westminster, S.W., and Messrs. Burchell. 5, Broad Sanctuary, Westminster, S.W.; Valuers, Henry Arthur Hunt and Robert Ritchie ; Bankers, Glyn, Mills, Currie, and Co., 67, Lombard Street, E.C., Robarts, Lubbock, and Co., 15, Lombard Street, E.C., and Herries, Farquhar, and Co., 16, St. James's Street, S.W.

Offices—6, Westminster Chambers, Victoria Street, S.W.

262.—METROPOLITAN AND ST. JOHN'S WOOD.

Incorporated by 27 and 28 Vic., cap. 303 (29th July, 1864), to construct a line from the Baker Street Station of the Metropolitan, through St. John's Wood, to the Hampstead Junction, near Finchley Road Station. Length, 2½ miles. Capital, 300,000l., in 10l. shares, and 100,000l. on loan. Arrangements with Metropolitan. Opened 13th April, 1868.

By 28 Vic., cap. 31 (26th May, 1865), the company was authorised to construct an extension to Hampstead. Length, 1 mile. New capital, 200,000l. in shares, and 66,000l. on loan.

By 29 and 30 Vic., cap. 107 (28th June, 1866), the company was authorised to raise additional capital to the extent of 250,000l. in shares, and 83,000l. on loan.

By 31 and 32 Vic., cap. 149 (16th July, 1868), the company obtained a renewal of its powers to purchase lands in Hampstead (Act of 1864) until 1st November, 1868, and for other lands in Hampstead (under Act of 1865) till 1st October, 1869, completion of the Hampstead Extension being postponed till 26th July, 1871. Certain additional arrangements with the Metropolitan were also authorised, as well as contracts with the Midland in respect to joint construction of the Finchley Road station.

REVENUE.—The statement of this account from 13th April to 30th June furnished the subjoined particulars :—

Received.		Expended.	
50 per cent. of gross traffic, less passenger duty	£1,623	Proportion of directors' fees and office expenses	£350
Rebate on Metropolitan proportion of traffic	391	Proportion of interest on debentures due 15th July, 1868	1,116
	£2,014	Balance	663
Proportion of rents to 30th June	115		
	£2,129		£2,129

CAPITAL.—The receipts and expenditure on this account to 30th June, 1868, were as under :—

Received.		Expended.	
Ordinary share capital fully paid up	£300,000	To 31st December, 1867	£495,291
£5 per cent. preference ditto, deposit and calls	178,170	Purchase of land	59,213
Mortgage debt	96,910	Works	42,363
Temporary loans	30,000	Direction, salaries, &c.	447
		Interest, commission, &c.	2,493
			£599,809
		Land and compensation deposit account	1,766
		Balance	3,504
	£605,080		£605,080

Meetings in February and August.

No. of Directors—5 ; maximum, 5 ; quorum, 3. Qualification, 500l.

DIRECTORS:

Chairman—WILLIAM AUSTIN, Esq., Farningham, Kent.

William Lee, Esq., M.P., Holborough, Rochester, and 16, Upper Ground Street, Blackfriars, S.

Robert Mc.Kim, Esq., Belsize Park, Hampstead, N.W.

Donald Nicoll, Esq., Oaklands Hall, West End Park, Kilburn, N.W.

Alexander Clunes Sherriff, Esq., M.P., Perdiswell Hall, Worcester, and 10, Dean's Yard, Westminster, S.W.

OFFICERS.—Sec., John Henchman; Eng.-in-Chief, John Fowler; Eng., T. Marr Johnson; Solicitors, Hargrove, Fowler, and Blunt, 3, Victoria Street, Westminster, S.W.; Bankers, Herries, Farquhar, and Co., 16, St. James's Street, S.W.

Offices—3, Old Palace Yard, Westminster, S.W.

263.—MID-HANTS.

Incorporated by 24 and 25 Vic., cap. 111 (28th June, 1861), to construct a line at Alton, on the South Western, to Alresford, and thence to Winchester on the same railway. Length, 18½ miles. Capital, 150,000*l.* in 10*l.* shares; loans, 50,000*l.* Opened 2nd October, 1865.

At a special meeting on the 2nd December, 1861, an agreement to lease to the South Western was adopted. The terms include, in addition to maintenance, the provision by the South Western, at their own cost, of the engines, carriages, and wagons which will be required, and the payment of an annual rent equal to 57½ per cent. of the gross receipts.

By 27 and 28 Vic., cap 298 (29th July, 1864), the company was authorised to construct extensions to the Petersfield and Bishop's Waltham. Length, 9 miles. Also to change its name to that of "Mid-Hants," and to raise new capital to the extent of 180,000*l.* in shares, and 59,900*l.* on loan.

A scheme is now before the Court of Chancery for arrangements between the company and its creditors.

Meetings in February and August.

No. of Directors—6; minimum, 4; quorum, 3. *Qualification*, 200*l.*

DIRECTORS:

Chairman—EDWARD KNIGHT, Esq., Chawton House.

Deputy-Chairman—ROBERT COLE, Esq., Holybourne Lodge, Alton.

Henry Hall, Esq., Alton. | John Taylor, Esq., Gracechurch St., E. C.

OFFICERS.—Eng., J. H. Tolmé, 19, Duke Street, Westminster, S.W.; Solicitor, G. T. Porter, 4, Victoria Street, Westminster, S.W.; Auditors. J. F. Adams, Alresford, and C. Collins, Bishop's Sutton; Bankers, Bulpett and Hall, Alton, Alresford, and Winchester.

264.—MID-KENT (BROMLEY TO ST. MARY'S CRAY).

Incorporated by 19 and 20 Vic., cap. 125 (21st July 1865), to construct a line from Bromley, at the West End of London and Crystal Palace line, to St. Mary's Cray. Capital, 70,000*l.* in 10*l.* shares. Loans, 23,000*l.* Opened from Bromley to Southborough Road, 2½ miles, on 5th July, 1858.

By 25 and 26 Vic., cap. 224 (7th August, 1862), the line was leased to the London Chatham and Dover, from 1st September, 1863, at a rent equal to 4 per cent. on the share capital.

CAPITAL.—The expenditure to 30th June, 1868, amounted to 84,967*l.*, the receipts being as follow:—

Share capital £61,550
Debenture capital .... 23,000 = £34,550
Transfer from general revenue account, August, 1864, being the excess of expenditure over 84,550*l.* capital received .... 417 = £34,967

DIRECTORS:

Chairman—WILLIAM DENT, Esq., 110, Cannon Street, E.C.

John Allan, Esq., Heathfield Lodge, Chislehurst, Kent. S.E.

Coles Child, Esq., The Palace, Bromley, Kent.

Charles Hill, Esq., 29, Threadneedle Street, E.C.

N. W. J. Strode, Esq., Camden Place, Chislehurst, S.E.

John Tredwell, Esq., Leigham Court, Streatham, S.

OFFICERS.—Sec., William Aggas; Auditors, W. Dallison Starling and Robinson Latter.

Offices—1, King's Arms Yard, E.C.

265.—MID-WALES.

Incorporated by 22 and 23 Vic., cap. 63 (1st August, 1859), to construct a line from Llanidloes to Newbridge. Several deviations have since been authorised by various Acts of Parliament, as well as additional capital. Length, 52 miles. Opened 1st September, 1864.

By 27 and 28 Vic., cap. 142 (30th June, 1864), the Mid-Wales was authorised to construct a line to join the Central Wales. Length, 17 chains. Also to lease the line to Messrs. Watson and Overend. New capital, 90,000l. in shares, and 30,000l on loan.

By 28 and 29 Vic., cap. 159 (29th June, 1865), the company was authorised to construct a line to communicate with the Central Wales. Length, 9½ miles. New capital, 120,000l. in shares, and 40,000l. on loan.

By 28 and 29 Vic., cap. 371 (5th July, 1865), the company was authorised to construct extensions to the Manchester and Milford. Length, 26⅔ miles. Capital, 380,000l. in shares, and 126,500l. on loan.

By 29 and 30 Vic., cap. 210 (16th July, 1866), the company acquired powers to raise new capital to the extent of 200,000l. in shares, and 66,000l. on loan.

It was reported in August that the directors had been enabled to carry through a scheme of arrangement under the Companies' Act of 1867. They, however, regretted that, in consequence of the late period at which the order to stay all proceedings in the suit in Chancery was made, the fund in court could not be obtained until after the vacation, and the company was therefore unable to pay more than one year's interest up to 1st January last to the debenture-holders ; but the money would be obtained as soon as the Chancery offices were re-opened, and the half-yearly interest up to July discharged. Provisions were made for the continuance of the debentures, or for exchange into a perpetual debenture stock. The increasing favour with which debenture stocks were now regarded would probably induce many of the debenture-holders to avail themselves of this opportunity of securing a perpetual debenture stock carrying 5 per cent. after the first five years. The directors had put in operation the company's powers to run over the Hereford Hay and Brecon, and were so satisfied that the public interests were well served by the arrangement that it was intended immediately to commence carrying the goods traffic exchanged between the Mid-Wales and that railway. The London and North Western having obtained powers to purchase the Central Wales, this company were successful in securing facility clauses, binding them to book Mid-Wales traffic through all parts of their system.

The half-year's dividend, to 1st July, has since been paid.

No. of Directors—8 ; minimum, 5 ; quorum, 3.   *Qualification,* 500l.

DIRECTORS;

Francis Philips, Esq., Lee Priory, Wingham, Sandwich, Kent.
Abel Chapman, Esq., 79, Old Broad Street, E.C.
John Borradaile, Esq., 4, St. Helen's Place, E.C.
Jasper Wilson Johns, Esq., Wolverton Park, Newbury, Hants.

A. S. Wildy, Esq., South Sea House, E.C.
Wm. Lefeaux, Esq., Glandwr, Llanidloes.
Edward Parker, Esq., Barnsley, Yorkshire.
John Overend, Esq., Morecambe, Lancaster.
Samuel Gurney Sheppard, Esq., 28, Threadneedle Street, E.C.

OFFICERS.—Gen. Man., F. Broughton, Brecon : Sec., John Wade, 75, Ethelburga House, Bishopsgate St., E.C.; Solicitor, S. F. Noyes, 1, Broad Sanctuary, Westminster, S.W.; Auditors, Mr. Chandler, Shrewsbury, and Mr. Wilding, Montgomery.

Offices—75, Ethelburga House, Bishopsgate Street, E.C.

266.—MIDLAND.

An amalgamation of the NORTH MIDLAND, MIDLAND COUNTIES, and BIRMINGHAM AND DERBY, since 10th May, 1844, under the powers of the Act of Amalgamation (7 and 8 Vic., cap. 18).

The NORTH MIDLAND was incorporated 4th July, 1836, by Act 7 Wm. IV., cap. 107, for a line from Leeds to Derby (74½ miles) ; the MIDLAND COUNTIES for a continuation line from Derby to Rugby (49¼ miles), was incorporated 21st June, 1836, by 7 Wm. IV., cap. 78. The BIRMINGHAM AND DERBY, for a line from Derby to Birmingham, with a fork branch to the London and North Western at Hampton (48½ miles), was incorporated 19th May, 1836, by Act 6 and 7 Wm. IV., cap. 35. Total, 181½ miles.

With the company thus amalgamated there have been incorporated, by an issue of Midland Guaranteed shares, the following railways, viz.: Bristol and Gloucester, and Birmingham and Gloucester (95½ miles), Sheffield and Rotherham (9¼ miles), Leicester and Swannington (16 miles), and Leeds and Bradford (43 miles). In addition to which the following extensions have been authorised and constructed since the amalgamation, viz.:—Syston and Peterborough (48¼ miles), Nottingham and Lincoln and Southwell branch (36 miles). Leicester and Swannington extensions (21¼ miles), the Erewash Valley (21½ miles), the Nottingham and Mansfield (12¾ miles), and the Mansfield and Pinxton (7½ miles).

LEICESTER AND HITCHIN.—The Midland had power by Act of 1847-48 to make this line, but abandoned it on arrangements with Great Northern. In 1853 it obtained an Act (17 Vic., cap. 108), 4th August, to make a line from Wigston Station, Leicester, to Hitchin station, and branch to Wellingboro' station of London and North Western, 62 miles, branch 1 mile ; also to lay down additional rails on Rugby and Stamford. Opened 8th May, 1858.

An Act passed 3rd July, 1851 (14 and 15 Vic., cap. 57), recites that at a special meeting, 28th October, 1846, it had been determined to create 66,500 shares, at 50l., representing capital of 3,175,000l., but instead thereof, 77,245 shares of 50l. were in fact issued, representing a capital of 3,862,250l., being an excess over the amount authorised of 687,250l.; that over issue has been confirmed, and the capital increased to that extent; but, before the payment of any dividend, the Midland shall set apart half-yearly, 500l., to be employed exclusively in paying off an equivalent amount of mortgage debt, until a sum equal to 687,250l. be discharged. This Act also legalises the resolutions passed at a special meeting on the 19th July, 1850, which sanctioned the arrangement whereby the 50l. shares have been divided into two shares, one of 33½l.—which has been converted into stock—and the other of 16¾l., on which the payment of 4½ per cent. per annum is guaranteed, until the same shall be redeemed at par.

By 17 Vic., cap. 33 (14th June, 1853), three-fifths of a special meeting may resolve to convert existing mortgages or bonds into shares, *with a fixed and irredeemable dividend,* or in perpetual irredeemable annuities, at *maximum* of 4 per cent. per annum, may pay off and create in lieu of reborrowing.

By 19 and 20 Vic., cap. 54 (23rd June, 1856), the company was authorised to raise additional capital, to the extent of 400,000l., at 5 per cent. preference, and also to borrow 153,000l. The necessity for this measure was thus explained :—"The shares forfeited and unissued, and which constitute the present margin of capital, cannot be made available so long as the stock remains under par, there being no power to issue them at a discount, or to make them preference shares ; and as it is impossible to look forward even for a few years without seeing that the requirements of traffic will necessitate an increase in the capital expenditure, it is proposed to take power to raise a somewhat larger sum than the forfeited and unissued shares would give." Accordingly in August, 1856, power was given to the directors to borrow 200,000l.

By 22 and 23 Vic., cap. 130 (13th August, 1859), the company was empowered to construct an extension of the Erewash Valley to Clay Cross on the main line. New capital, 190,000l. in shares at 4½ per cent. preference.

By 22 and 23 Vic., cap. 136 (13th August, 1859), the company is authorised to construct certain branches in and near Burton, as well as to build and remove bridges over the Trent. New capital, 60,000l., at 4½ per cent. preference.

By 23 Vic., cap. 66 (25th May, 1860), the company was authorised to construct a line between Rowsley and Buxton, length 15 miles, from a junction with the Manchester Buxton Matlock and Midland, near its northern terminus, at Rowsley to Buxton, with a branch, length 25 chains, at Buxton, and a branch, length 25 chains, to extend from the first railway to a junction with the authorised extension of the Stockport Disley and Whaley Bridge at Buxton ; also a railway, length 40 chains, to connect the main line to Derby with the main line to Nottingham, at Long Eaton ; to be completed in five years ; and for those purposes the company were empowered to raise additional sums of 450,000l. by new shares, and 150,000l. by borrowing. The Act also contains powers for creation of 4 per cent. preference stock, for conversion of money borrowed, or for raising money which might be borrowed.

By 23 Vic., cap. 65 (25th May, 1860), further powers were conferred on the company relating to the new lines in or near Burton-on-Trent. New capital, 30,000l. in shares, and 10,000l. on loan.

By 23 Vic., cap. 67 (25th May, 1860), the company was authorised to construct a station in the parish of St. Pancras, London, and to effect arrangements with the Great Northern and North London, and with the Regent's Canal. New capital, 200,000l. in shares, and 66,000l. on loan.

By 23 Vic., cap. 91 (14th June, 1860), the Midland obtained power to run over South Leicestershire, from Leicester to Coventry.

By 23 Vic., cap. 91 (14th June, 1860), the Midland was authorised to enter into contracts with the North London, the Great Eastern, the Blackwall, and the Tilbury and Southend for the use of any of these undertakings.

By 24 Vic., cap. 57 (7th June, 1861), the company was authorised to construct eight new lines or branches, including one from Shustoke, on the Tame Valley, to Nuneaton, by a junction with the South Leicestershire ; another from Ashchurch to Evesham, on the West Midland ; and a third connecting the Midland main line, near Worcester, with the Tewkesbury branch. Also from Erewash Valley, at Blackwell, to Feversham, and from Beighton. on the Midland, to Aston, on the Manchester and Sheffield. Length, 28 miles 13 chains. Capital 390,000l. in shares, and 127,000l. on loan.

By 24 and 25 Vic., cap. 106 (28th June, 1861), the company was authorised to construct new works, and to acquire additional land in Derby, Lancaster, Nottingham, Warwick, Gloucester, and Yorkshire. Also to acquire certain hotels, and to accept the Dursley and Midland Junction, for which see below. New capital, 100,000*l.* in shares, and 33,300*l.* on loan.

By 24 and 25 Vic., cap. 139 (11th July, 1861), the company was authorised to construct a line in extension of the Leeds and Bradford section to Otley and Ilkley. Length, 12 miles 50 chains. New capital, 185,000*l.* in shares, and 61,600*l.* on loan.

By 25 and 26 Vic., cap. 81 (30th June, 1862), the company obtained power to construct new works and some small branches, and to create new capital, 120,000*l.* in shares, and 40,000*l.* on loan.

By 25 and 26 Vic., cap. 91 (30th June, 1862), the company was authorised to extend the Rowsley and Buxton to a connection with the Marple and New Mills (14 miles), and to raise 380,000*l.* in shares, and 126,000*l.* on loan. It is by this line and its connection with the Sheffield that the Midland obtains access to Manchester.

By 26 and 27 Vic., cap. 74 (22nd June, 1863), the company obtained power to construct a line from Bedford to London. Length, 51 miles. Capital, 1,750,000*l.* in shares, and 583,330*l.* on loan.

By 26 and 27 Vic., cap. 182 (21st July, 1863), the Midland was authorised to construct a connecting link with the Bristol and Exeter. New capital, 15,000*l.* in shares, and 5,000*l.* on loan.

By 26 and 27 Vic., cap. 183 (21st July, 1863), the company was also authorised to construct several small new lines and other works in Yorkshire; in the counties of Warwick, Leicester, and Gloucester; in the towns of Worcester, Nottingham, and Northampton. New lines, 21½ miles. New capital, 225,000*l.* in shares, and 75,000*l.* on loan.

By 27 and 28 Vic., cap. 164 (14th July, 1864), the company obtained power to construct a line from Mangotsfield to Bath and Thornbury. Length, 17½ miles. Capital, 236,000*l.* in shares, and 78,600*l.* on loan.

By 27 and 28 Vic., cap. 230 (25th July, 1864), the company was authorised to construct a line from Chesterfield to Sheffield. Length, 13¾ miles. Capital, 455,000*l.* in shares, and 150,000*l.* on loan. Facilities to Manchester and Sheffield.

By 27 and 28 Vic., cap. 231 (25th July, 1864), the company were enabled to enter upon arrangements with the Metropolitan, and to construct a branch in the parish of St. Pancras. Length, 1 mile. Capital, 150,000*l.* in shares, 50,000*l.* on loan.

By 27 and 28 Vic., cap. 245 (25th July, 1864), the company acquired additional powers in regard to works, as well as to construct several short branches. Length, 11¾ miles. Capital, 166,000*l.* in shares, and 55,000*l.* on loan.

By 28 and 29 Vic., cap. 335 (5th July, 1865), the Midland was authorised to construct 15 short lines in connection with its existing system. Length, 31¾ miles. Capital, 1,000,000*l.* in shares, and 333,000*l.* on mortgage.

By 28 and 29 Vic., cap. 359 (5th July, 1865), the Midland was authorised to construct a line from Mansfield to Southwell and Worksop. Length, 33¾ miles. Capital, 500,000*l.* in shares, and 166,000*l.* on loan.

By 29 Vic., cap. 90 (11th June, 1866), the Midland obtained power to acquire additional lands, and to give effect to arrangements authorised with the Great Western in respect to lines and stations at Malvern. New capital, 130,000*l.* in shares.

By 29 and 30 Vic., cap. 223 (16th July, 1866), the Midland was authorised to construct a line from Settle to Hawes, Appleby, and Carlisle. Length, 78 miles. Capital, 1,650,000*l.* in shares, 550,000*l.* on loan. Midland to use Citadel station at Carlisle, and North Eastern at Hawes and Melmerby to make use of portions of Midland.

By 29 and 30 Vic., cap. 298 (30th July, 1866), the Midland was authorised to construct seven branches on various parts of its system. Length, 18¼ miles. Capital, 350,000*l.* in shares, and 116,000*l.* on loan. Also to make a deviation on the Hertford Luton and Dunstable branch, to acquire land at Shirland, to make roads and execute other works. The Midland also obtained power to use parts of the Lancashire and Yorkshire, and the Manchester and Sheffield, between Beighton, Penistone, and Huddersfield. The North Staffordshire also acquired the right to use part of the Midland, and *vice versa.*

By 29 and 30 Vic., cap. 315 (6th August, 1866), the Midland was authorised to construct four lines between Ashby-de-la-Zouch and Nuneaton, and other places. Length, 25 miles. Capital, 330,000*l.* in shares, and 110,000*l.* on loan.

ADDITIONAL POWERS.—By 30 and 31 Vic., cap. 170 (12th August, 1867), the company obtained power to construct two small branches, 2 miles in length, and to raise new capital to the extent of 75,000*l.* in shares, and 25,000*l.* on loan. Also to acquire additional lands in a great number of places for stations and other purposes. The Midland also obtained power to use part of the South Staffordshire, and to run over the London and North Western between Bescot and Wolverhampton, so as to make use of the Wolverhampton and Walsall. By the same Act the Midland and South Western Junction was authorised, on its completion, to be vested in the Midland.

DERBY GAS WORKS.—By 30 Vic., cap. 27 (31st May, 1867), the Midland was authorised to acquire the land and property of these works, as also to sell other land to the gas company wherever gas works might be erected. New capital, 30,000*l.* in shares.

By 31 and 32 Vic., cap. 43 (25th June, 1868), the company acquired several additional powers, including power to raise 3,750,000*l.* in shares, and 1,250,000*l.* on loan; to construct the Darfield Junction (1 furlong 6 chains), and a line at the St. Pancras station

(209 yards), and also a deviation and curve at Codnor Park ; power to stop up or deviate roads in several parts of the company's system, and to acquire additional lands ; an extension of time for two years for completion of Barnsley Branch ; for three years for Bristol Junction. The agreement with the Metropolitan (as given in the volume for 1868) was also confirmed.

By 31 and 32 Vic., cap. 49 (25th June, 1868), the Midland and the London and North Western obtained power to make certain deviations in their lines, and to construct others in substitution of parts abandoned. New capital, 35,000*l.* in shares, and 11,200*l.* on loan, by each of the companies. New works to be completed by 6th August, 1871.

VESTED LINES.—By 28 and 29 Vic., cap. 327 (5th July, 1865), the following lines were vested jointly in the Great Northern, the Midland, and the Manchester and Sheffield :—

CHESHIRE MIDLAND.—Incorporated by 23 Vic., cap. 90 (14th June, 1860), to construct a line from the South Junction, at Altrincham, to Northwich. Length, 12¼ miles. Capital, 100,000*l.*, in 20*l.* shares. Loans, 33,000*l.* Under this Act the Manchester Sheffield and Lincolnshire were authorised to subscribe 30,000*l.* By 24 and 25 Vic., cap. 113 (11th July, 1861), a deviation near Knutsford was authorised. Powers were obtained in the same Act for the Manchester Sheffield and Lincolnshire to subscribe a further sum of 20,000*l.*, and to guarantee a dividend of 4½ per cent. to the Cheshire Midland. Running powers and facilities are granted to the London and North Western and the Great Western. By the Great Northern (Cheshire Lines) Act, 1863, the Sheffield and Great Northern companies are to contribute and guarantee equally the capital necessary for completing the undertaking, each company having equal rights and privileges in all respects. By this Act the Great Northern have powers to subscribe to this undertaking in the whole 65,000*l.*, and by a further Act passed in 1864 the Manchester Sheffield and Lincolnshire company obtained powers to increase their subscriptions to the same amount. Opened from Altrincham to Knutsford (7 miles), on 18th May, 1862, and to Northwich (6 miles), on 1st January, 1863, since which date the shareholders became entitled to 4½ per cent. from the Sheffield and Great Northern.

GARSTON AND LIVERPOOL.—By 24 Vic., cap. 35 (17th, May, 1861), the Great Northern and the Manchester Sheffield and Lincolnshire were authorised to construct a line between Garston and Liverpool. Length, 4½ miles. Capital, 150,000*l.*, to be furnished in equal proportion by the two companies. Loans, 75,000*l.* Opened 1st June, 1864. By this Act the two companies are authorised to use portions of the Warrington and Stockport, the St. Helens, and of the Edge Hill line of the London and North Western, the latter obtaining in lieu thereof use of the Sheffield line up to that town, and of the Great Northern between Peterborough and Grimsby and New Holland, with access to other towns in Yorkshire.

LIVERPOOL CENTRAL STATION.—Incorporated by 27 and 28 Vic., cap. 290 (29th July, 1864), to construct a railway and general station in Liverpool. Length, 1¾ miles. Capital, 500,000*l.* in 10*l.* shares, and 166,000*l.* on loan. By 29 and 30 Vic., cap. 294 (30th July, 1866), the Liverpool Central Station was vested jointly in the Manchester Sheffield and Lincolnshire, Great Northern, and the Midland, and its management placed in the Cheshire Lines committee, nominated by the three companies.

LIVERPOOL EXTENSION.—By 29 and 30 Vic., cap. 191 (16th July, 1866), the Midland was constituted with the Great Northern and the Sheffield a joint owner of this line, the Midland subscribing thereto 250,000*l.* Also by 29 and 30 Vic., cap. 192 (16th July, 1866), the Midland was authorised, in conjunction with the Great Northern and the Sheffield, to construct new lines in connection with the Liverpool Extension. Length, 5½ miles, and a new canal in substitution of that to be stopped up under the Act. New capital, 120,000*l.*, by each of the three companies, with one-third additional by borrowing.

STOCKPORT, TIMPERLEY, AND ALTRINCHAM JUNCTION.—Incorporated by 24 and 25 Vic., cap. 175 (July 22nd, 1861), to construct a line from the Stockport and Woodley to the Warrington and Stockport, and two branches connecting with the Manchester South Junction and Altrincham. Length, 9½ miles. Capital, 150,000*l.* in 10*l.* shares, and 50,000*l.* on loan.

STOCKPORT AND WOODLEY JUNCTION.—Incorporated by 23 Vic., cap. 16 (15th May, 1860), to construct a line from Stockport to Woodley, on the Newton and Compstall branch of the Manchester Sheffield and Lincolnshire line, and to the extensive coal fields in the neighbourhood of Hyde and Dukinfield. Length, 2¼ miles. Capital, 60,000*l.* in 10*l.* shares. Loans, 20,000*l.* Opened 12th January, 1863.

WEST CHESHIRE.—Incorporated by 24 and 25 Vic., cap. 143 (18th July, 1861), to construct a line from Northwich, on the Cheshire Midland, to Helsby, on the Birkenhead. Length, 16 miles. Capital, 200,000*l.* in 10*l.* shares ; loans, 66,000*l.* Running powers and facilities conceded to London and North Western and Great Western. The line to be efficiently worked by the Sheffield, with which, and Great Northern, traffic arrangements may be made, and who may subscribe 65,000*l.* each. By 25 and 26 Vic., cap. 190 (29th July, 1862), the company was authorised to construct branches to Winsford and Winnington, and a deviation at Oakmere. Length, 7¾ miles. Capital, 63,000*l.* in shares, and 21,000*l.* on loan.

By 29 and 30 Vic., cap. 351 (10th August, 1866), the Great Northern obtained running powers over a portion of the Newton and Compstall branch of the Sheffield; also, in conjunction with that company and the Midland, to execute certain works, and to become joint proprietors of the Godley and Woodley branch. The Chester and West Cheshire was also, by the same Act, vested in the three companies, each of which were to raise 90,000l. in shares, and 30,000l. on loan, instead of the Chester and West Cheshire.

DURSLEY AND MIDLAND JUNCTION.—Incorporated by 18 Vic., cap. 17 (May 25th, 1855), for making a railway from the Parish of Cam, in Gloucestershire, by a junction with the Bristol and Birmingham (Midland), to the town of Dursley. Length, 2¼ miles. Capital, 12,000l. in 20l. shares; loans, 4,000l. Opened 22nd September, 1856, and vested in Midland by 24 and 25 Vic., cap. 106. The purchase money amounted to 10,750l., on which the Midland allows 4 per cent.

WORCESTER AND HEREFORD.—By Act of 1858 the Midland subscribed 37,500l. to this undertaking.

NORTH WESTERN.—The Midland leases this line on the following terms:—That the Midland pay every expense connected with the North Western, including debenture interest and dividends on debenture stock, and a half-yearly sum equal to a net dividend, without deduction, except for income tax, upon ordinary shares, after the following scale:—Half-year ending June 30th, 1859, 1l. 10s. per cent. per annum; ditto December 31st, 1859, 1l. 10s. ditto; ditto, June 30th, 1860, 2l. ditto; ditto December 31st, 1860, 2l. ditto; ditto, June 30th, 1861, 2l. 10s. ditto; ditto December 31st, 1861, 2l. 10s. ditto; ditto June 30th, 1862, 3l. ditto; ditto December 31st, 1862, 3l. ditto; ditto June 30th, 1863, 3l. ditto; ditto December 31st, 1863, 3l. ditto; ditto June 30th, 1864, 3l. 10s. ditto; ditto December 31st, 1864, 3l. 10s. ditto; and so on for a term of 999 years, from 1st January, 1859, with such additional dividends, if any, as one half of the excess net earnings of the North Western undertaking will pay beyond the rates aforesaid; working expenses, to be deducted from gross traffic, being taken at the same per centage as on whole of Midland. Ordinary stock on which guarantee takes effect, 800,000l.; preference stock at 5 per cent., 126,285l.; debenture debt, about 260,000l. No further shares or debentures to be issued, or debentures renewed, without consent of Midland.

TEWKESBURY AND MALVERN.—The Act of this company provides that the Midland may become shareholders to the extent of 40,000l. and appoint two directors by virtue of holding this amount. A resolution authorising that subscription was agreed to at the meeting in August, 1862, but no further steps appear to have been taken in the matter.

BRISTOL JOINT STATION.—By 28 Vic., cap. 98 (19th June, 1865), the Midland was authorised, in conjunction with the Great Western and Bristol and Exeter to furnish its proportion of new capital (150,000l. in shares, and 50,000l. by mortgage) for erection of a Joint Station at Bristol.

REVENUE.—The receipts for the half-year ending December 31, 1867, as compared with the corresponding half-year of 1866, showed the following results:—An increase from coaching of 38,543l.; from cattle, 5,609l.; from merchandise of 37,654l.; from minerals of 40,452l.; total increase, 122,258l. This increase, however, was to be ascribed to the traffic brought by the new lines which had been opened since 31st December, 1866. The balance available for dividend was 525,633l., and the following dividends were declared:—2l. 15s. upon each 100l. consolidated Midland Stock, 2l. 1s. 3d. upon each 100l. consolidated Birmingham and Derby stock, 3l. upon each 100l. consolidated preferential stock, and the usual dividends on the other preference stocks and shares, leaving a balance of 12,069l. The revenue account for the half-year ending June 30 showed that 1,488,809l. had been received, and 700,072l. expended in working, including 39,671l. for rates and taxes and government duty, leaving a balance of 788,737l. From this was deducted 263,689l. for interest on debentures, debenture stock, and dividends on guaranteed stocks of four other companies, 23,681l. for the North-Western rental, 1,254l. for the Redditch rental, 3,750l. for the Midland and Eastern rental, and 500l. for redemption of mortgage debentures, leaving, with a balance of 12,070l. brought from the preceding half-year, a disposable sum of 507,933l. Out of this was deducted 283,890l. for the proposed dividend on the Midland Consolidated Stock, at the rate of 5 per cent. per annum, 17,736l. for the proposed dividend on the Birmingham and Derby stock, at the rate of 3l. 12s. 6d. per cent. per annum, and 202,867l. on 11 preference stocks, having dividends of 6 per cent., of 5 per cent., of 4½ per cent., and of 4 per cent. per annum, leaving a balance of 3,440l. These dividends were less by 5s. per cent. upon the open stock than those declared for the corresponding period of 1867, the reduction having been occasioned by the bad state of trade, and the continued large outlay upon lines and works, some of which at present produced but little, while others were entirely unproductive.

MILEAGE.—Messrs. Barlow and Liddell reported that the Bedford and London was in good working order, and nearly finished; that a sufficient portion of the station might be ready to receive the through passenger traffic in the month of September next; and that the canal basin and the remainder of the coal drops would be ready for traffic about the same time. The line between Bedford and Moorgate Street was opened for suburban and local passenger traffic on the 13th of July. In operation, 774½ miles.

LONDON AND NORTH WESTERN.—With respect to the Settle and Carlisle, the directors reported in August that they had had several interviews with the directors of the London and North Western ; negotiations were still pending, though not so far advanced as to enable them to lay any definite result before the meeting, but no effort would be spared on the part of the Midland directors to bring the negotiations to a successful termination. An agreement has since been entered upon, for which see APPENDIX to present volume.

CAPITAL.—This account to 30th of June showed that 26,856,453*l*. was received on stocks and shares, 5,737,895*l*. on debentures, and 137,030*l*. premiums on shares sold ; together 32,731,378*l*., including 1,328,007*l*. received during the half-year. The expenditure amounted to 32,971,118*l*., including 961,335*l*., during the half-year, leaving a balance of 239,740*l*. against the account. The expenditure on rolling stock was 3,587,635*l*. The parliamentary powers and assets amounted to 40,326,111*l*., of which 32,971,118*l*. were expended to the 30th of June, leaving 7,354,993*l*. to complete an estimated outlay of 7,238,808*l*. The lines authorised, but not commenced, were, in the aggregate, 172 miles in length, and the capital amounted to 3,788,558*l*. The general statement of stocks and shares, with the rate of dividend on each, according to their priorities, furnished the subjoined information :—

DESCRIPTION.	Recd. June 30th, 1868.	Calls to make.	Total.	Rate of Dividend per annum.
Consolidated stock, on which dividend is payable	£11,355,617	....	£11,355,617	Uncertain.
80 9*l*. shares, created February 15th, 1865	286	434	720	
Birmingham and Derby.......	978,533	....	978,533	1*l*. 7*s*. 6*d*. less than consolidated stock.
Midland preferential	25,000	....	25,000	6 per cent. minimum.
Consolidated Erewash Valley ..	145,000	....	145,000	6 per cent. minimum.
Sheffield and Rotherham preferential	150,000	....	150,000	6 per cent. in perpetuity.
Leicester and Swannington	140,000	....	140,000	8 per cent. in perpetuity.
Bristol and Birmingham 6 per cent.	1,799,902	....	1,799,902	6 per cent. guaranteed, redeemable with 150*l*. for each 100*l*.
Consolidated 4½ per cent. preferential	1,239,466	....	1,239,466	4½ per cent., subject to redemption at par.
Consolidated Midland Bradford preferential	1,800,000	....	1,800,000	4 per cent. in perpetuity.
Consolidated Leicester and Hitchin preferential	675,000	....	675,000	4 per cent. in perpetuity.
Consolidated irredeemable 4½ per cent. preferential	613,620	....	613,620	4½ per cent. in perpetuity.
A 5 per cent. preference	640,000	....	640,000	5 per cent. in perpetuity.
B 5 per cent. preference	500,000	....	500,600	
114,722 18*l*. 5 per cent. preference shares	2,015,098	49,898	2,064,996	[See * Note.]
128,609 18*l*. inconvertible 5 per cent. preference shares ·.....	1,996,565	318,397	2,314,362	5 per cent. in perpetuity.
125,227 22*l*. 5 per cent. preference shares	1,650,141	1,104,853	2,754,994	[See † Note.]
	£25,724,229	£1,473,582	£27,197,811	
Mortgage preference stock issued.....................	1,041,373	....	1,041,373	4 per cent. in perpetuity.
Mortgage preference stock.. issued.....................	81,273	....	81,273	4½ per cent. in perpetuity.
Cancelled shares..............	9,576	....	9,576	
	£26,856,453	£1,473,582	£28,330,035	

* NOTE.—5*l*. per cent. in perpetuity, with an option to convert the shares into ordinary general stock on giving notice to the company not later than 1st September, 1869, such conversion to be considered as effected on that date, and the shares entitled to the ordinary dividend of the company, accruing from and after the 30th June, 1869.

† NOTE.—5*l*. per cent. in perpetuity, with an option to convert any of such shares into the ordinary general stock, on giving notice not later than 31st August, 1872, to the company of the intention to exercise such option. And such conversion shall be considered as effected on the said 31st August, 1872, and the shares as entitled to the ordinary dividend of the company, accruing from and after 30th June, 1872.

The accounts are made up to 30th June and 31st December, and the statutory meeting held in Derby in February and August every year.

Scale] of Voting.—One vote for every 100*l*., as far as 2,000*l*., and one vote additiona for every 500*l*. above 2,000*l*.

Certificates of shares need not accompany transfer deed. Fee for registering the transfer of a bond, 2*s*. 6*d*. ; for registering stock or shares, 2*s*. 6*d*. each deed.

No. of Directors.—Maximum, 20 ; present board, 15. *Qualification*, 2,000*l*. stock.

DIRECTORS:

Chairman—WILLIAM EVANS HUTCHINSON, Esq., Oadby Hill, Leicester.

Deputy-Chairman—WILLIAM PHILIP PRICE, Esq., M.P., Tibberton Court, Gloucester, and 105, Pall Mall, S.W.

Edward Shipley Ellis, Esq., Leicester.
Francis Carbutt, Esq., Leeds.
Richard Birkin, Esq., Aspley Hall, Nottingham.
George Hounsfield, Esq., The Hazles, Sheffield.
Sir Isaac Morley, Beech Field, Doncaster.
George Braithwaite Lloyd, Esq., Birmingham.
Charles Henry Jones, Esq., Huddersfield.

Matthew William Thompson, Esq., Park Gate, Guiseley, near Bradford.
Samuel Beale, Esq., 10, Park Street, Westminster, S.W.
Timothy Kenrick, Esq., Edgbaston, Birmingham.
William Unwin Heygate, Esq., Roecliffe, Loughborough.
Josiah Lewis, Esq., Edge Hill, Derby.
John Mercer, Esq., Clifton, Bristol.

OFFICERS.—Gen. Man., James Allport; Assis. Gen. Manager, John Noble; Sec., James Williams; Assistant Sec., John Moore; Consulting Eng., William Henry Barlow, Great George Street, Westminster, S.W.; Eng., J. S. Crossley, Derby; Supt. of Loc. Dept., Matthew Kirtley, Derby; Supt. of Passenger Traffic, E. M. Needham, Derby; Man. of Goods Dept. W. L. Newcombe, Derby; Accountant, William H. Hodges; Auditors, Robt. Heane, Gloucester, and Alfred Allott, Sheffield.

Head Offices—Derby.

267.—MIDLAND COUNTIES AND SHANNON JUNCTION.

Incorporated by 24 and 25 Vic., cap. 246 (6th August, 1861), to construct a line from Clara, on the Great Southern and Western, to Meelick, on the Shannon. Length, 21¼ miles. Capital, 115,000l. in 10l. shares, and 38,300l. on loan.

Powers are given in the Act to make arrangements with the Great Southern and Western "for the use, working, and management of so much of the undertaking as lies to the east of the Shannon."

By Act 29 and 30 Vic., cap. 182 (16th July, 1866), the company was authorised to purchase additional lands, and also to extend the time for purchasing lands to the 16th of July, 1868, and for completion of works to 16th July, 1869. Powers are conferred by the same Act to cancel 50,000l. of original shares, and to issue in lieu thereof an equal amount of preference capital, bearing interest at the rate of 5 per cent.

This undertaking has been in abeyance for the past three years, and of the 18 miles which constitute it, from the junction with the Great Southern and Western, at Clare, to Banagher on the Shannon, the whole of the earthworks and bridges are completed, and about half of the distance is laid with rails, at an outlay of 80,000l., but with a debt incurred to various creditors, amounting at present to about 20,000l., the arrangement of which has retarded, for the time named, the progress of the works.

Arrangements are now, however, under the proposals made by Mr. Nicoll, the secretary, progressing satisfactorily, by which the creditors undertake to withdraw their recorded judgments against the company, and by so doing, permit the borrowing powers of the company, which are at present untouched to the extent of 38,000l., to take priority. This arrangement will be completed by the middle of December, and immediately thereon application will be made to the Public Works Commissioners to increase their promised grant of 17,000l. to 35,000l., which last sum, with the unissued preference capital of 50,000l., will prove amply sufficient to complete the works and stations, and pay off all incumbrances.

Accounts balanced to 30th June and 31st December. Meetings to be held in April or October, in Banagher or Dublin.

No. of Directors—6; minimum, 3; quorum, 3, with reduced number, 2. Qualification, 1,000l.

Directors retire and are elected in accordance with the Companies' Clauses Act.

DIRECTORS:

Chairman—JOSEPH BOYCE, Esq., D.L., 52, Upper Mount Street, Dublin.

Deputy-Chairman—HENRY R. PERRY, Esq., Dublin.

The Rev. J. A. Bell, Cuba House, Banagher.
John Eyre, Esq., Eyrecourt Castle, Eyrecourt.

John D. Lauder, Esq., J.P., Moyclare, Ferbane.

OFFICERS.—Sec., John Fowler Nicoll; Engs., John Hill, Ennis, and Henry Brett, Dublin; Solicitors, F. Edwards, Westminster, S.W., and James Dillon Meldon, Dublin; Auditors, Thomas Perry and Thomas Hynes.

Head Offices—53, Lower Dominick Street, Dublin.

268.—MIDLAND COUNTIES AND SOUTH WALES.

Incorporated by 26 and 27 Vic., cap. 220 (28th July, 1863), to construct a line from Blisworth to Farthinghoe. Capital, 140,000l. in 10l. shares; loans, 46,000l. Works in progress

By 28 and 29 Vic., cap. 361, Northampton and Banbury Railway (Branch) Act, 1865, the company were empowered to make a branch line to connect their railway with the Northampton and Peterborough line of the London and North Western, and to raise additional capital to the extent of 193.300*l*.; viz., by shares, 145,000*l*.; on loan, 48,300*l*. Compulsory powers under this Act, three years; completion of works, five years. Power to enter into traffic arrangements with Great Western. An agreement is scheduled to this Act by which the company obtains running powers over the Buckinghamshire line of the London and North Western from Cockley Brake to Banbury, with use of the London and North Western and Great Western Stations.

By 28 and 29 Vic., cap. 362, Northampton and Banbury Railway (Extensions) Act, 1865, the company were empowered to extend their railway to Chipping Norton and Blockley, and to raise additional capital to the extent of 666,600*l*., viz., by shares 500,000*l*.; on loan, 166,600*l*. Compulsory powers under this Act, three years. Completion of works, five years. Works in progress.

By 29 and 30 Vic., cap. 310, Northampton and Banbury Junction Railway Act, 1866, the company were empowered to extend their railway from Blockley to Ross, and to raise additional capital to the extent of 733,000*l*.; viz., by shares 550,000*l*;. on loan, 183,000*l*. Compulsory powers under this Act, three years; completion of works, five years. By this Act the company obtain running powers over the Midland Company's lines between Bickford and Tewkesbury, over the Ross and Monmouth, and over the Worcester Dean Forest and Monmouth, between Newport and Monmouth, and the name of the company has been changed from the Northampton and Banbury Junction to the Midland Counties and South Wales. Total length of line now authorised, 96½ miles. In April, 1866, the portion of the railway from Blisworth to Towcester was opened for traffic.

Meetings in February and August.

No. of Directors.—Maximum, 8 : minimum, 5 ; quorum, when more than five directors, 4 ; when five directors, 3. *Qualification,* 300*l*.

DIRECTORS :

Chairman—The Right Hon. Lord ERNEST BRUCE, M.P., 6, St. George's Place, S.W.

Deputy-Chairman—ALEXANDER BEATTIE, Esq., M.D., 45, Porchester Terrace, Hyde Park, W.

Jasper Wilson Johns, Esq., J.P., Wolverton Park, near Newbury, Hants.	Charles Kelson, Esq., Gresham House, Old Broad Street, E.C.
Wm. Laurence Banks, Esq.,Watton House, Brecon.	L. M. Rate, Esq., King's Arms Yard, E.C.
H. J. Sheldon, Esq., Brailes House, Shipston-on-Stour, Worcestershire.	W. R. Drake, Esq., Parliament Street, Westminster, S.W.

OFFICERS.—Sec. and Gen. Man., J. Wilson Theobald, 6, Victoria Street, Westminster, S.W.; Engs., John Collister, C.E., 28, Great George Street, Westminster, S.W., and Charles Liddell, C.E., 24, Abingdon Street, Westminster, S.W.; Solicitors, Gregory, Champion, and Eady, 18, Park Street, Westminster, S.W., and 12, Clements Inn, W.C.; Bankers, The Union Bank of London (Temple Bar Branch), Chancery Lane, W.C., and The Northamptonshire Banking Company, Northampton.

Offices—6, Victoria Street, Westminster, S.W.

269.—MIDLAND AND EASTERN.

Incorporated by 29 and 30 Vic., cap. 265 (23rd July, 1866), and being a union of the Lynn and Sutton Bridge and Spalding and Bourne.

The united capital of the new company to consist of 213,000*l*. in 20*l*. shares, and 71,000*l*. on loan. Arrangements with Midland and Great Northern. By the same Act the Midland and Eastern was authorised to take a lease of the Norwich and Spalding, and also to amalgamate that company at a future period.

LYNN AND SUTTON BRIDGE.—Incorporated by 24 and 25 Vic., cap. 245 (6th August, 1861), to construct a line from Lynn, on the East Anglian, to Sutton Bridge, on the Norwich and Spalding. Length, 9 miles and 43 chains. Capital. 100,000*l*. in 20*l*. shares; loans, 37,000*l*. Opened, 1st March, 1865, and worked by Great Northern. By 26 and 27 Vic., cap. 193 (21st July, 1862), the company were relieved from certain onerous obligations in respect to building a new bridge at Sutton. By 27 and 28 Vic., cap. 229 (25th July, 1864), the use by the company of the Cross Keys Bridge, over the river Neve, was regulated. By 28 and 29 Vic., cap. 194 (29th June, 1865), the company were permitted to execute certain works at Sutton, and to raise additional capital to the extent of 15,000*l*. in shares, and 5,000*l*. on mortgage. Also to attach a preference to unissued and cancelled shares.

SPALDING AND BOURNE.—Incorporated by 25 and 26 Vic., cap. 199 (29th July, 1862), to construct a line from Spalding, on the Great Northern, to Bourne. Length, 9½ miles. Capital, 100,000*l*. in 20*l*. shares ; loan, 32,500*l*.

By 30 and 31 Vic., cap. 185 (12th August, 1867), certain agreements with the Midland and Great Northern were confirmed, by which these two companies agree to work the lines jointly, and to aid completion of the same by subscriptions towards the capital. The Midland may apply any amount it can spare from capital already authorised to be raised, while the Great Northern is permitted to create and issue new capital for the purposes of this Act to the extent of 24,000*l*. in shares, and 8,000*l*. on loan.

Meetings in February or March, and in August or September.
No. of Directors—7 ; minimum, 5 ; quorum, 3. *Qualification,* 400*l.*

DIRECTORS :

Lewis Whincop Jarvis, Esq., Kings Lynn. | C. Waring, Esq., 10, Victoria Chambers,
W. Waring, Esq., 10, Victoria Chambers, | S.W.
S.W. | W. Eckersley, Esq., 5, Victoria Street, S.W.

OFFICERS.—Sec., T. P. Bond, 5, Great Queen Street, S.W. ; Eng., J. Brunlees, 5,
Victoria Street, S.W. ; Solicitor, James Wheeler, 4, Victoria Street, S.W.

270.—MIDLAND GREAT WESTERN.

Incorporated by 9 Vic., cap. 119 (21st July, 1845), for a line from Dublin to Mullingar,
with a branch to Longford. In 1846 the scheme was extended to Athlone. In 1847 the
company obtained power to continue the line to the port of Galway. By 16 Vic., cap.
137 (1852), further power was obtained to deviate the extension to Longford, and for a
branch to Cavan (24 miles), opened 8th February, 1856. The extension line from Mullingar to Longford was opened for public traffic on 8th November, 1855 ; the branch to the
river Liffey on the 1st of April, 1864, length, 26 miles ; from Castlebar to Westport, 11½
miles, on the 29th January, 1866 ; and from Manulla to Foxford, 11¼ miles, on 1st May,
1868. Total in operation, including Athenry and Tuam, 222 miles of railway and 92 of
canal.

With this undertaking is also incorporated the " Royal Canal," running parallel with
the railway from Dublin as far as Mullingar, whence it diverges to Longford. The
Royal Canal (said to have cost the original proprietors 1,500,000*l.*) was purchased under
the Act of incorporation by this company for 298,059*l.*

By 20 and 21 Vic., cap. 77 (27th July, 1857), the company was authorised to make an
extension to Sligo, with branches therefrom. New capital, 510,000*l.*, in 25*l.* shares
(calls, 10 per cent.), and loans, 193,000*l.* The length of the extension, commencing at
the terminus of the existing railway at Longford, and terminating at the town of Sligo,
is 57 miles ; the length of the branch, commencing from the extension in Ballysadare,
is 2 furlongs ; and the length of the branch, commencing from the extension, in Rathed-
mond and terminating near Sligo, is 4 furlongs. Opened from Longford to Sligo,
December 3rd, 1862.

By 20 and 21 Vic., cap. 113 (10th August, 1857), the company was authorised to construct a line from Streamstown to Clara. New capital, 80,000*l.*, in 25*l.* shares, and loans,
26,000*l.* Length, 7 miles. Opened, 1st April, 1863.

By 22 and 23 Vic., cap. 53 (1st August, 1859), the company was authorised to construct
a branch from Glasnevin to the river Liffey. Length, 3 miles. New capital, 50,000*l.*, in
20*l.* shares, and 16,000*l.* on loan. Opened 1st April, 1864. By the same Act power was
given to raise 135,860*l.* to discharge debt due in respect of Royal Canal.

By 22 and 23 Vic., cap. 62 (1st August, 1859), the company was authorised to abandon
a portion of its line between Longford and Boyle, and to construct a new line in substitution thereof.

By 28 Vic., cap. 40 (26th May, 1865), the capital of the company was defined at 2,750,000*l.*
in shares, 702,200*l.* by mortgage, and 500,000*l.* on loan from the public works, and subject
to increase in event of the purchase of the Royal Canal being completed by 135,800*l.*

By 28 and 29 Vic., cap. 210 (5th July, 1865), an arrangement was legalised with the
baronies, in Roscommon and Galway, by which their contributions to the company in
respect to deficiencies in revenue were to cease as from 28th October, 1870.

By 29 Vic., cap. 34 (18th May, 1866), the company was authorised to acquire additional
lands, and also to reduce the number of directors to nine, with ultimate power to still
further reduce the number to six.

GRAND CANAL.—The lease of the tolls of the canal expired on 1st July, 1860, when
the undertaking was handed back to the directors of that company. It is now worked
in unison with the Great Southern and Midland Great Western, the lease by these companies having been withdrawn from parliament last session only in consequence of an
inadequate scale of tolls having been insisted on by a committee of the Lords.

DUBLIN AND MEATH.—An amicable arrangement has been effected with this company,
and a new and separate entrance into Dublin avoided.

GREAT NORTHERN AND WESTERN.—The Midland Great Western works this line,
83¼ miles.

REVENUE.—The receipts for the half-year ending 31st December amounted to
131,064*l.*, and the working expenses to 66,365*l.*, for suspense account to 3,761*l.*, interest
on debentures, &c., 25,000*l.*, leaving a balance of 35,937*l.*, to which was added 1,888*l.*
from the preceding half-year, making the total, 37,825*l.*, out of which a dividend at the
rate of 5 per cent. per annum on the preference stock, and at the rate of 2¾ per cent.
on the consolidated stock, left a balance of 3,079*l.* The receipts during the June half-
year amounted to 112,170*l.*, against 110,185*l.* in the corresponding period, showing an
increase of 1,985*l.* The total receipts from all sources were 124,939*l.*, the working expenses 68,371*l.*, and the interest on debentures and taxes 23,313*l.*, making 91,684*l.*,

leaving a balance of 33,255l., to which was added 3,079l. from the preceding half-year, making 36,334l., out of which a dividend at the rate of 5 per cent. per annum on the preference stock, and at the rate of 2½ per cent. per annum on the consolidated stock, left a balance of 3,262l. The traffic receipts during the half-year ended 30th June last on the Athlone to Galway amounted to 13,881l., and the working expenditure to 12,754l., to which was added the interest at the rate of 3½ per cent. per annum (on 470,000l.), amounting to 8,225l., making 20,979l., and consequently leaving a balance of 7,098l. against the Baronies.

GALWAY LOAN.—It was reported in September that the directors had pressed on the government the justice of affording the company some relief regarding the repayment of the Galway Loan. The Chancellor of the Exchequer expressed his readiness to meet the wishes of the deputation, but the law officers gave it as their opinion "that under the existing law the Lords of the Treasury have not power to grant the relief sought for." Under these circumstances the directors considered it desirable that a bill should be promoted enabling the government to relieve the company by making the terms less oppressive. The repayments had increased from 2,290l. in June, 1861, to 9,401l. in June, 1868, making the total repayments 61.385l.

ATHENRY AND ENNIS.—This line having been reported as nearly completed, the directors of the Midland Great Western stated that they would have been prepared to carry out the wishes of the shareholders for the working of that line on equitable terms, but they were informed that the Waterford and Limerick declined to abandon an agreement entered into in the year 1863 with that company.

CAPITAL.—This account to 30th June showed that 3,733,078l. had been expended, leaving a balance against the account of 36,564l. The receipts have been as under :—

Consolidated stock...£2,157,175
Preferential 5 per cent. stock .... 264,412=£2,421,587
Royal Canal, mortgage due thereon 135,860
Debenture stock 29,440
Debenture bonds.. 671,011
Athlone to Galway—Loan, under 12 and 13 Vic., cap. 62.......... £500,000
                    Less paid off .... 61,385= 438,614

                                                            £3,696,514
        Balance 36,564

                                                            £3,733,078

The accounts are made up to 30th June and 31st December, and the statutory meetings held in Dublin in March and September in every year.

Scale of Voting.—One vote for every 200l. stock : an additional vote for every 200l. beyond, up to 2,000l.; and an additional vote for every 500l. after first 2,000l. M.G.W.R. Act, 1866.

Certificates must accompany transfer deeds. Registration fee, 2s. 6d. each deed ; 2s. 6d. for replacement of lost certificate.

No. of Directors—8. Qualification, 2,000l. consolidated stock.

DIRECTORS :

*Chairman—RALPH SMITH CUSACK, Esq., 24, Rutland Square, Dublin.

1 Robert Preston Bayley, Esq., Rookwood, Athleague.
1 Right Hon. Earl of Clancarty, Garbally, Ballinasloe, and Palace Hotel, Buckingham Gate, S.W.
* James Digges La Touche, Esq., Woodlawn, Dundrum, County Dublin.

2 George Woods Maunsell, Esq., 10, Merrion Square South, Dublin.
2 Thomas James Smyth, Esq., Ballynegall, Mullingar.
2 Laurence Waldron, Esq., 38, Rutland Square, Dublin.
1 Robert Warren, Jun., Esq., 40, Rutland Square, Dublin.

* Re-elected, September, 1868.

The figures opposite the names indicate the number of years each party has to serve.

OFFICERS.—Sec., Henry Beausire ; Res. Eng., James Price ; Loco. Eng., Robert Ramage ; Traffic Supt., William G. Skipworth ; Accountant, Thomas Bennett ; Auditors, Alexander Parker and Robert G. Collis ; Solicitor, Walter P. Kirwan, Dublin.
Head Offices—Broadstone Terminus, Dublin.

271.—MIDLAND AND SOUTH WESTERN JUNCTION.

Incorporated by 27 and 28 Vic., cap. 190 (14th July, 1864), to construct a line from the North and South Western Junction. at Acton, to the London Extension of the Midland at Hendon. Length, 4 miles. Capital, 90,000l. in 10l. shares, 53,000l. of which have already (September, 1867), been paid up, and 30,000l. on loan. To be vested in the Midland on completion of works, and opening for traffic at an annual rental, equal to 5 per cent. on the share and debenture capital, amounting to 120,000l. Opened 1st October, 1868.

CAPITAL.—The expenditure on this account to 31st July, 1868, amounted to 89,139*l.*, which left a balance at bankers of 1,415*l.* The receipts have been as under :—

Share capital—Received £61,900		£61,900
Due to respect of calls 2,980		
To call 25,120		
Authorised £90,000		
Debentures—Borrowed.. 26,000		26,000
Of unexercised power............................ 4,000		
Authorised £30,000		
Interest		636
Sundry creditors, viz.:—On bills payable £1,500		
Interest on debentures .... 518 =		2,018
		£90,554

Meetings in February or March, and in August or September.
No. of Directors—3; maximum, 5; quorum, 2. *Qualification*, 100*l.*

DIRECTORS :

Chairman—W. LANSDOWNE BEALE, Esq., Waltham, St. Lawrence, Berks.

John Charles Morice, Esq., Throgmorton Street, City, E.C. | George Charles Ring, Esq., Great Knight-rider Street, E.C.

OFFICERS.—Sec., Benjamin Humphries Tromp, 4, Old Palace Yard, Westminster, S.W.; Solicitors. Johnston, Farquhar, and Leech, 65, Moorgate Street, E.C.; Bankers, The Union Bank of London. Prince's Street, E.C.; Auditors, John Ball and William Quilter, Moorgate Street, E.C.
Offices—24, Abingdon Street, Westminster, S.W.

272.—MILFORD.

Incorporated by 19 Vic., cap. 14 (5th June, 1856), for making a line from Johnston station of Neyland Extension of the South Wales to the town of Milford. Broad gauge. Capital, 60,000*l.* in 10*l.* shares ; loans, 20,000*l.* Calls, 2*l.* 10s. per share, with intervals of two months. Length, 3½ miles.
By 26 and 27 Vic., cap. 200 (28th July, 1863), an extension of time to 28th July, 1864, was conceded. New capital, 10,000*l.* in shares, and 3,000*l.* on loan.
The line was opened for traffic in September, 1863, and is worked by the Great Western, under agreement.

DIRECTORS :

Chairman—RICHARD BASSETT, Esq., Bonvilstone, Cardiff.

Admiral Stokes, Scotchwell House, Haverfordwest.
Frederick George Saunders, Esq., Westbourne Lodge, Paddington, W.
Charles Whetham, Esq., 52, Gordon Square, W.C. | F. N. Micklethwait, Esq., 43A, South Street, Park Lane, W.
J. W. Williamson, Esq., 4, Gloucester Villas, Warwick Road, W.

OFFICERS.—Sec., J. W. Mellis ; Eng., W. G. Owen ; Auditors, W. R. Barwis and R. G. Marwood ; Solicitors, Marriott, Jordan, and Cooper, 52, Parliament Street, Westminster, S.W.
Offices—Paddington Station, W.

273.—MILFORD HAVEN.

Incorporated by 23 and 24 Vic., cap. 156 (23rd July, 1860), to construct a railway, docks, and other works on the north side of Milford Haven. Length, 1¼ mile. Capital, 140,000*l.* in 10*l.* shares ; calls, 2*l.* 10s., with intervals of three months. Loans, 46,000*l.* Traffic arrangements with Great Western.
By 26 and 27 Vic., cap. 163 (21st July, 1863), an extension of time for completion of works was obtained till 21st July, 1866.
By 30 Vic., cap. 6 (12th April, 1867), the company obtained an extension of time till 1870 for completion of the works authorised in 1860 and 1863.
The railway and pier are in a forward state, and will be completed early in this year.
No. of Directors—6 ; minimum, 4 ; quorum, 3. *Qualification*, 200*l.*

DIRECTORS :

Chairman—CHARLES REED, Esq., M.P.
Deputy-Chairman—JOSEPH FREEMAN, Esq.

Henry Constable. Esq.
Alfred Beeston, Esq. | G. A. Hillier, Esq.
J. W. Williamson, Esq.

OFFICERS.—Sec., Saml. Jeffryes ; Traff. Man., John Milnes ; Eng., J. M. Toler.
Offices—7, Westminster Chambers, Westminster, S.W., and Milford, South Wales.

274.—MINEHEAD.

Incorporated by 28 and 29 Vic., cap. 317, to construct a line from Watchet, on the West Somerset, to Minehead. Length, 8¾ miles. Capital, 70,000l. in 10l. shares, and 23,300l. on loan. Arrangements with Bristol and Exeter and West Somerset.

Meetings in February or March, and August or September.

No. of Directors.—Maximum, 5: minimum, 3; quorum, 3. *Qualification*, 300l.

DIRECTORS:

Chairman—GEORGE FOWNES LUTTRELL, Esq., Woodlands, Bridgewater.

Lawrence Walker, Esq., 12, Bryanstone | John Halliday, Esq., Chapel Cleve,
Square, W. | Somerset.
Thos. Abraham, Esq., Dunster, Somerset. |

OFFICERS.—Sec., William Henry Wilson, 6, Victoria Street, Westminster, S.W.; Eng., R. P. Brereton, 18, Duke Street, Westminster, S.W.; Solicitors, Radcliffe and Davies, 20, Craven Street, Strand, W.C., and Charles E. Rowcliffe, Stogumber, Somerset; Bankers, Stuckey's Banking Company, Taunton.

Offices—6, Victoria Street, Westminster, S.W.

275.—MISTLEY, THORPE, AND WALTON.

Incorporated by 26 and 27 Vic., cap. 178 (21st July, 1863), to construct a line from Mistley, on the Great Eastern, to Walton-on-the-Naze. Length, 12 miles. Capital, 60,000l. in 10l. shares, and 20,000l. on loan. Arrangements with Great Eastern, which subscribes 20,000l., appoints two directors, and is to work the line at 48 per cent.

By 27 and 28 Vic., cap. 144 (30th June, 1864), the company was authorised to construct an extension to join the Tendring Hundred. Length, 2½ miles. Capital, 15,000l. in shares, and 5,000l. on loan.

By 28 Vic., cap. 4 (9th May, 1865), the capital of the company was reduced to 36,000l. in shares, and 12,000l. by loan, in consequence of the Tendring Hundred being authorised to construct a portion of the line previously conceded to the Mistley, from Thorpe to Walton.

No. of Directors—6; minimum, 3; quorum, 3. *Qualification*, 500l.

DIRECTORS:

Chairman—The Right Hon. The MARQUIS OF SALISBURY, 1, Mansfield Street, W.

Richard Young, Esq., Wisbeach. | William H. Wilson, Esq., 6, Victoria St.,
| Westminster, S.W.

OFFICERS.—Sec., John Sizer, Manningtree; Eng., James S. Cooke, 12, Abingdon Street, Westminster, S.W.; Solicitors, Patteson and Cobbold, 17, New Bridge Street, Blackfriars, E.C., and Charles Spencer Owen, Manningtree.

Offices—Manningtree, and 12, Abingdon Street, Westminster, S.W.

276.—MOLD AND DENBIGH JUNCTION.

Incorporated by 24 and 25 Vic., cap. 247 (6th August, 1861), to construct a line from the Mold branch of the Chester and Holyhead to Denbigh, on the Vale of Clwyd. Length, 18 miles. Capital, 125,000l. in 20l. shares; loans, 41,000l. Arrangements with London and North Western. In abeyance.

By 28 and 29 Vic., cap. 172 (29th June, 1865), the company was authorised to make several deviations, and to raise further capital to the extent of 100,000l. in shares, and 33,000l. on loan.

By 28 and 29 Vic., cap. 271 (5th July, 1865), the company was authorised to make certain new lines and to abandon a portion of the authorised railway. Length, 17½ miles. Capital, 100,000l. in shares, and 33,000l. on loan.

By 29 and 30 Vic., cap. 250 (23rd July, 1866), the company was authorised to construct four short branches, and to make a deviation in another part of the line. Length, 8 miles. Capital, 134,000l. in shares, and 44,000l. on loans.

By 30 and 31 Vic., cap. 164 (25th July, 1867), the company was authorised to exercise running powers over parts of the Vale of Clwyd and of the Wrexham Mold and Connah's Quay; to divide the shares into deferred and preferred; to create debenture stock; and to pay 6 per cent. to the Vale of Clwyd for outlay on extension of station at Denbigh.

A scheme of redemption was filed in the Court of Chancery in March, which recited the various powers conferred upon the company by Parliament in 1861-5-6-7, for the construction of a main line between Mold and Denbigh and sundry branches; and also power to raise capital. The capital raised under the said powers is stated to be mortgages 107,000l., preference shares 100,000l., ordinary shares 225,000l., total 432,000l. It is further stated the company are indebted in various sums to landowners for land taken and required for the purposes of the main line of railway, and to other creditors for work and labour done, materials provided, and money paid on behalf of the company: and in respect of a portion of these debts they have issued acknowledgments in the form of "Lloyd's Bonds," to the extent of 50,000l. The company are unable to pay landowners and other creditors, and also unable to pay the interest on the mortgages and Lloyd's Bonds, the arrears of which on the 30th of June were 18,835l.

Article 1 bars the further issue of capital under the powers given the company by their several Acts of Parliament (the whole of the capital authorised had not been issued).

Article 2 empowers the company to offer rent charges in lieu of money to such unpaid landowners as may be willing to accept the same at 5 per cent. per annum.

Article 3. The company may create and issue a 5 per cent. debenture stock to an amount not exceeding 40,000l., to complete the main line, and to pay such landowners as do not accept rent charges ; and also to pay the cost of preparing and obtaining the scheme from the Court of Chancery.   This debenture stock to be called "debenture stock A," and such debenture stock and annual rent charges to be a first charge on the company's undertaking, and to rank *pari passu* the one with the other of such charges.

Article 4. The existing mortgage debt and mortgages, 107,000l. (excluding interest), may be converted into debenture stock of the company, bearing interest at the rate of 4 per cent. per annum for the first five years, and after five years 5 per cent. per annum.   It is to be called "debenture stock B," and is to be a second charge upon the undertaking.

Article 5. The company may raise by debenture stock, at 4 per cent. per annum for the first five years, and 5 per cent. afterwards, a sum not exceeding 30,000l., to pay existing debts of the company not provided for in articles 2, 3, and 6 of the scheme. This also to be called debenture stock B, and to be, together with the amount to be raised under article 4, a second charge on the company's undertaking.

Article 6. The company may raise, at the same rates of interest as above, a sum not exceeding 70,000l. to satisfy the principal sum of Lloyd's Bonds and the arrears of interest, and also the interest on the existing mortgage debts of the company.   Such stock to be called "debenture stock C," and to be a third charge on the undertaking.

Article 7 declares that no dividend exceeding 4 per cent. per annum shall be paid on preference or preferred shares for the first five years after the passing of the scheme.

No. of Directors—5 ; minimum, 3 ; quorum, 3.   *Qualification*, 200l.

DIRECTORS:

Henry Keate, Esq., Shrewsbury.
Philip Pennant Pennant, Esq., Brynbella, St. Asaph.
George Moore Dixon, Esq., Bucknowle House, Wareham, Dorset.

A. T. Roberts, Esq., The Tower, Mold.
F. A. Hamilton, Esq., Founder's Court, E.C.

OFFICERS.—Sec., John Broughall, Shrewsbury ; Engs., John Ashdown, 7, Westminster Chambers, Victoria Street, S.W., and George Bellis, Mold ; Solicitors, S. F. Noyes, 1, Broad Sanctuary, Westminster, S.W., and Kelly, Keene, and Roper, Mold.
Offices—Shrewsbury.

277.—MONMOUTHSHIRE.

Incorporated by 8 and 9 Vic., cap. 169 (31st July, 1845), for a line from Newport to Pontypool, 12 miles (with several branches and canal).   This railway was authorised to be made by the Monmouthshire Canal Navigation (which, as a canal company, has previously been in existence more than 50 years), by raising additional capital. Productive, 44 miles.

By 18 Vic., cap. 10 (May, 6th, 1855), the company obtained power to raise further capital to the extent of 202,510l., at a preference not exceeding 6 per cent. Power to borrow 67,500l. by mortgage was also given by the same Act.

At a special meeting on the 30th May, 1855, the company resolved to raise the sum of 202,500l. by creation of 6,750 shares of 30l. each, bearing a preferential interest, in perpetuity, at the rate of 5 per cent. The company subscribes 20,000l. to Newport Docks.

By 24 and 25 Vic., cap. 218 (1st August, 1861), the company was authorised to construct some short connecting lines.   Length, 5 miles 8 chains.   Completion of works, three years. New capital, 100,000l. in 5 per cent. preference shares, and 25,000l. on loan. Unissued and forfeited shares to be cancelled, and reissued at 5 per cent. preference. These shares were issued as ordinary stock, on 18th September, 1862.

The West Midland obtained powers to use compulsorily the Eastern Valley between Coed-y-gric and Newport.   The London and North Western have obtained power to enter into agreements with the Monmouthshire for working and transmission of traffic. By 28 and 29 Vic., cap. 281 (5th July, 1865), the company was authorised to raise further capital to the extent of 200,000l. in shares, and 50,000l. on loan ; also to purchase the Brecon and Abergavenny canal and to construct two short branches in the mineral district, and to purchase new rolling stock.   By the Alexandra Dock Act, the Monmouthshire may subscribe 20,000l. to that undertaking.

REVENUE.—The receipts and disbursements for three years have been as follow :—

	Dec., 1865.	June, 1866.	Dec., 1866.	June, 1867.	Dec. 1867.	June, 1868.
Receipts	£74,965	£74,851	£72,109	£71,227	£77,514	£66,360
Expenses	38,621	34,248	34,153	34,330	34,141	35,695
Net	£36,344	£40,603	£37,956	£36,897	£43,373	£30,665
Per cent.	51	46	47½	48¼	44	53¾
Dividend	£3 5 0	£3 0 0	£2 15 0	£2 10 0	£2 10 0	£2 6 0

CAPITAL.—The receipts on this account to 30th June were 1,466,159*l.*, which left a balance in hand of 70,280*l.*

Election and Scale of Voting—In accordance with "The Companies' Clauses Act, 1845. *No. of Directors*—Limited to 13.   *Qualification*—5 shares of 100*l.* each.

DIRECTORS :

Chairman—The Right Hon. LORD TREDEGAR, Tredegar Park, Newport, and 39, Portman Square, W.

Charles Octavius Swinnerton Morgan, Esq., M.P., The Friars, Newport, and 9, Pall Mall, S.W.

Crawshay Bailey, Esq., Nantyglo.

Thomas Brown, Esq., Hardwick, Chepstow.

Thomas Gratrex, Esq., King's Hill, Newport.

O. A. Wyatt, Esq., Troy House, near Monmouth.

George Cave, Esq., Burfield House, Westbury-on-Trim, near Bristol.

Charles Walter Savage, Esq., Westbury, near Bristol.

Edward J. Phillips, Esq., Maindee, near Newport.

Thomas Powell, Esq., Coldra, near Newport.

Francis Tothill, Esq., Ebbw Vale, near Newport.

John Lawrence, Esq., Crick House, near Chepstow.

William Evans, Esq., The Fields, Newport.

OFFICERS.—Sec. and Gen. Man., George Harrison ; Traffic Supt., William Lane ; Eng., Robert B. Sayer ; Loco. Supt., H. Appleby ; Auditor, W. Tribe, Bristol ; Solicitors, Waddington and Gustard, Newport ; Treasurers, National Provincial Bank of England, Newport.

Offices—Dock Street, Newport, Monmouthshire.

278.—MONTROSE AND BERVIE.

Incorporated by 23 and 24 Vic., cap. 142 (3rd July, 1860), to construct a line from Inverbervie to the Montrose branch of the Scottish North Eastern. Length, 13 miles. Capital, 70,000*l.* in shares. Loans, 23,000*l.* Agreements and arrangements with the Scottish North Eastern, which subscribes 15,000*l.* Opened 1st November, 1865.

REVENUE.—The receipts for the half-year ending 31st January were 1,712*l.* as compared with 1,691*l.* for the corresponding period in the previous year. There was a decrease in the working expenses, exclusive of interest and feu-duties, to the extent of upwards of 123*l.* But in consequence of the interest account embracing some adjustments applicable to former periods, the balance against revenue was increased by the sum of 86*l.* The receipts for the half-year ending the 31st July amounted to 1,721*l.*, and the expenditure to 1,212*l.*, leaving a balance of 509*l.*

CAPITAL.—This account showed that 82,000*l.* had been received, and 86,494*l.* expended, leaving a balance against the company of 4,494*l.*

CAPITAL.—The total capital authorised consists of 70,000*l.* in shares, and 23,333*l.* on loan. The sum of 11,000*l.* still remains to be raised on debentures. The expenditure has been 85,999*l.*, leaving a balance of 3,999*l.* against receipts.

No of Directors—6 ; minimum, 3.   *Qualification,* 200*l.*

DIRECTORS :

Chairman—HERCULES SCOTT, Esq., of Brotherton.

James Farquhar, Esq., of Hallgreen, | Captain Forsyth Grant, of Ecclesgreig.
Alexander Porteous, Esq., of Lauriston. | David Mitchell, Esq.

OFFICERS.—Secretary, James Crockatt ; Auditors, James Marquis and James Meston, Accountants, Aberdeen.

Offices—Stonehaven.

279.—MORAYSHIRE.

Incorporated by Act 9 and 10 Vic., cap. 178 (16th July, 1846), for a line from Stottfield and Lossiemouth Harbour to Elgin (6 miles). Capital, 29,700*l.* in 10*l.* shares, and 9,900*l.* in loans. Opened 10th August, 1852.

By 19 and 20 Vic., cap. 86 (14th July, 1856), the company was again authorised to construct a railway from Orton to Craigellachie. Length, 5½ miles. Capital, 25,000*l.* in 10*l.* shares ; loans, 8,333*l.* Power to enter into agreements with Inverness and Aberdeen, as to use of station at Elgin, and traffic arrangements with that company and Inverness and Nairn, under usual stipulations. Opened to Rothes on 23rd August, 1858, and throughout on 23rd December, 1858.

By 23 and 24 Vic., cap. 116 (3rd July, 1860), the company was authorised to construct a direct line from Elgin to Rothes, and so avoid use of the Inverness and Aberdeen, to obtain access to its Craigellachie extension. Length, 9½ miles. Additional capital, 40,000*l.* in 10*l.* shares ; loans, 13,300*l.* Opened on 1st January, 1862.

By 24 Vic., cap. 30 (17th May, 1861), the company was authorised to extend its line over the river Spey, forming a junction with the Strathspey at Craigellachie. Length, 51 chains. New capital, 20,000l. in 10l. shares, and 6,600l. on loan. Opened 1st July, 1863. Arrangements with Great North of Scotland, Keith and Dufftown, and Strathspey. Productive, 21 miles 53 chains.

By 26 and 27 Vic., cap. 210 (28th July, 1863), the company was authorised to create new capital to the extent of 25,000l. in 10l. shares, at 5 per cent. and 8,300l. on loan. Also to contribute to communication by sea from Lossiemouth (otherwise than by steam vessels) to Caithness, to the extent of 600l. per annum.

By 29 Vic., cap. 30 (18th May, 1866), the company was authorised to create and issue new shares (in lieu of others cancelled) at a preference of 5 per cent. Also to create debenture stock at the same rate of interest.

By 29 and 30 Vic., cap. 288 (30th July, 1866), the Morayshire obtained power to amalgamate with the Great North of Scotland on terms to be agreed upon.

REVENUE.—It was reported to the annual meeting in November, that the receipts amounted to 8,085l., and the expenditure to 4,380l., leaving a balance of 3,705l. to pay interest on debentures, guaranteed shares, and floating debt, and after paying those charges there remained a balance of 215l. The passenger traffic during the year amounted to 3,891l., and the ordinary working expenses to 3,507l. There was no dividend either for the preference or ordinary shareholders. The passenger traffic showed a considerable increase, as compared with that of the preceding year, while the goods traffic indicated a slight falling off. The Chairman, however, stated the affairs of the company were improving, and he had reason to believe in future that the returns would be more encouraging. They had transferred 4,993l. from the general balance account to capital. That sum included a profit and loss account of 3,002l. incurred during nearly three years when the company could not meet all the claims upon them, a suspense account of 1,448l., and also 542l. for bad debts. The circumstances of the company would not admit of those sums being paid out of revenue, and they were therefore transferred to capital, but the net revenue would be sufficient to meet the interest on those items, as well as on the debentures and other sums.

CAPITAL.—The expenditure to 30th Sepetmber, 1868, including 4,993l. of ledger balances transferred from general balance account, extended to 174,060l., the receipts for which were given as under:—

Ordinary share capital received		£52,887
Preference share capital received		34,820
Preference shares held by Great North Company (convertible)		12,620
	(Guaranteed)	£100,327
Ordinary and preference share capital "redeemable"	£12,900	12,900
		£113,227
Capital floating debt account (A.)	16,274	16,274
Total Guaranteed	£29,174	
Capital floating debt account (B.)		6,428
Loans on mortgage		38,130
Authorised Capital　£186,133		
		£174,060

The accounts are closed annually on the 30th September, and meetings held in Elgin annually.

Scale of Voting.—C.C.C. Act (Scotland).

No. of Directors.—Maximum, 12; minimum, 5. *Qualification,* 20 shares.

DIRECTORS:

Chairman—JAMES GRANT, Esq., Writer, Elgin.

Deputy-Chairman—ALEX. URQUHART, Esq., Agnes Villa, Elgin.

George Smith, Esq., Minmore, Glenlivat.
W. J. Wainwright, Esq., Glasgow.
The Right Hon. The Earl of Caithness, 17, Hill Street, Berkeley Square, W.

Alex. Russell, Esq., Lord Provost of Elgin.
W. H. Mills, Esq., C.E., London.
George Hay, Esq., Bon-accord Villa, Elgin.

OFFICERS.—Sec., Alexander Watt; Consulting Engineers, James Samuel, F.R.A.S., and W. H. Mills, C.E., London; Auditors, John Milne, Accountant, Elgin, and Alexander Morrison, Writer, Elgin; Solicitors, Grant and Jameson, Elgin; Parliamentary Agent, R. M. Muggeridge, 26, Duke Street, Westminster, S.W.

Head Office—Elgin.

280.—MORETONHAMPSTEAD AND SOUTH DEVON.

Incorporated by 25 and 26 Vic., cap. 128 (7th July, 1862), to construct a line from the South Devon, at Wolborough, to Moretonhampstead. Length, 12¼ miles. Capital, 105,000*l.* in 10*l.* shares, and 35,000*l.* on loan. Arrangements with South Devon, which grants a rebate on 25,000*l.*, equal to 5 per cent. per annum. Opened 4th July, 1866.

REVENUE.—The receipts for the half-year ending 31st December were 2,167*l.*, while the June report stated that there had been an increase of 113*l.* over the corresponding period of 1867.

CAPITAL.— The expenditure on this account to 30th June amounted to 135,830*l.*, which left a balance in hand of 864*l.* The receipts were as under :—

To 31st December, 1867	£133,625
In Half-year ended 30th June, 1868—	
Ordinary shares	£1,110
Special shares	1,290
Temporary loans	669=£3,069= £136,694

Scale of Voting—One vote for every share held.

No. of Directors—6 ; minimum, 3 ; quorum, 3 and 2. *Qualification*, 300*l.*

DIRECTORS:

Chairman—*The EARL OF DEVON, Powderham Castle, Exeter, and 68, Brook Street, W.

W. R. Hole, Esq., Park, Bovey Tracey.	*John Divett, Esq., Bovey Tracey.
Elias Cuming, Esq., Linscott, Moreton-	Thomas Wills, Esq., East Wrey, Lustleigh.
hampstead, Devon.	Thomas Woollcombe, Esq., Devonport.

OFFICERS.—Sec., Alexander E. Lhoyd, Newton Abbot ; Engs., John Fowler, 2, Queen's Square Place, Westminster, S.W., and P. J. Margary, Plymouth ; Auditors, Symon N. Neck, and *Edward Bowring ; Solicitors, Whiteford and Bennett, Plymouth ; Bankers, The Devon and Cornwall Banking Co. (London Correspondents, Barclay, Bevan, and Co., 54, Lombard Street, E.C.), and Sanders and Co., Exeter.

* Retire in 1868, but are eligible for re-election.

Offices—Newton Abbot.

281.—MOUNTSORREL.

Incorporated by 22 and 23 Vic., cap. 55 (1st August, 1859), from a point 20½ miles from Derby, to Mountsorrel, in Leicestershire. The line is the sole property of Lord Lanesborough, and is intended to facilitate the working of certain valuable granite quarries in the immediate vicinity of the town. Length, 1 mile 2 furlongs and 3-70 chains. Estimate, 8,300*l.*

282.—MOWDDWY.

Incorporated by 28 and 29 Vic., cap. 306 (5th July, 1865), to construct a line from the Cemmes station of the Cambrian, to the town of Dinas Mowddwy. Length, 6¾ miles. Capital, 21,000*l.* in shares, and 7,000*l.* on loan. Arrangements with Cambrian.

The line was opened for traffic in September, 1867.

No. of Directors—6 ; minimum, 3 ; quorum, 3 and 2. *Qualification*, 300*l.*

DIRECTORS:

Sir Edmund Buckley, Bart., M.P., of Plas	Edmund Shaw, Esq., Dinas Mowddwy.
Dinas Mowddwy, Merionethshire, and	William Rees, Esq., Llandovery.
33, Hyde Park Square, W.	

OFFICERS.—Sec., David Howell, Machynlleth ; Eng., George Owen, Oswestry ; Solicitors, Howell and Morgan, Machynlleth.

283.—MUCH WENLOCK AND SEVERN JUNCTION.

Incorporated by 22 and 23 Vic., cap. 26 (21st July, 1859), to construct a line from Much Wenlock, in Shropshire, to the Severn Valley, and the river Severn. Capital, 24,000*l.* in 10*l.* shares ; loans, 8,000*l.* Length, 4½ miles, including communication with the river Severn. Extra land, one acre ; compulsory purchase, two years ; completion of works, four years. Running powers over part of the Severn Valley. Opened, 1st February, 1862.

By 25 Vic. cap. 14 (16th May, 1862), the company was authorised to raise additional capital to the extent of 24,000*l.* in shares, and 8,000*l.* on loan ; also to subscribe a further sum of 10,000*l.* to the Wenlock, &c.

By 27 and 28 Vic., cap. 302 (29th July, 1864), arrangements were authorised with the Wenlock line that both be worked by the Great Western for ten years, ending July, 1872.

No. of Directors—7 ; minimum, 4 ; quorum, 3. *Qualification*, 250*l.*

DIRECTORS:

Chairman—ANDREW GOOD BROOKES, Esq., Shrewsbury.

Joseph Amphlett, Esq., Much Wenlock.
George Adney, Esq., Much Wenlock.
Ralph Augustus Benson, Esq., Wenlock, Salop.

William Penny Brookes, Esq., Much Wenlock.
John Horton, Esq., Much Wenlock.

OFFICERS.—Solicitor and Secretary, R. C. Blakeway, Wenlock; Engineer, John Fowler, 2, Queen's Square Place, S.W.; Auditors, Richard Palin, Shrewsbury, and C. J. Cooper, Bridgnorth.

284.—MUSWELL HILL.

A company established under limited liability, but incorporated by Act 29 and 30 Vic., cap. 290 (30th July, 1866), to construct certain railways over the estate, and to establish access to the Great Eastern, the Great Northern, and the Edgware Highgate and London. Length, 1¾ mile. New capital, 70,000l. in shares. No borrowing powers. Works not commenced.

Arrangements may be made with the three railway companies mentioned, or either of them. In abeyance.

285.—NANTWICH AND MARKET DRAYTON.

Incorporated by 24 Vic., cap. 44 (7th June, 1861), to construct a line from the London and North Western. at Nantwich, to Market Drayton. Length, 10¾ miles, single line. Capital, 60.000l. in 20l. shares; loans, 20,000l. Opened, 19th October, 1863. By 27 and 28 Vic., cap. 152 (30th June, 1864), the company obtained an increase of capital to the extent of 60,000l. in shares, and 20,000l. on loan. These shares were created and issued on 31st August, 1865, the whole being guaranteed 4½ per cent. by the Great Western. This undertaking, in conjunction with the Wellington and Drayton, is embodied in the Great Western system.

No of Directors—7; minimum, 4; quorum, 4 and 3. *Qualification, 500l.*

DIRECTORS :

Chairman—HENRY REGINALD CORBET, Esq., Adderley, Market Drayton.

William Tayleur, Esq., Buntingsdale, Market Drayton.
Thomas Twemlow, Esq., Peatswood. Market Drayton.
H. B. Clive, Esq., Styche, Market Drayton.

E. W. Harding, Esq., Old Springs, Market Drayton.
Mr. William Rodenhurst, Market Drayton.
Rev. Athelstan Corbet, Adderley, Market Drayton.

OFFICERS. — Sec., W. M. Wilkinson, Market Drayton; Eng., John Gardner, 9, Victoria Chambers, Westminster, S.W. ; Solicitors, Cobb and Southey, 4, Westminster Chambers, S.W., and Warren and Onions, Market Drayton ; Bankers, The Manchester and Liverpool District Bank. Market Drayton and Nantwich ; Auditors, H. B. Hoy, Euston Station, N.W., and William Welch Deloitte, 5, Lothbury, E.C.

Offices—Market Drayton.

286.—NAVAN AND KINGSCOURT.

Incorporated by 28 and 29 Vic., cap. 350 (5th July, 1865), to construct a railway from Navan, on the Dublin and Meath, to Kingscourt. Length, 11 miles. Capital, 120,000l. in shares, and 40,000l. on loan. Arrangements with Dublin and Meath, which may subscribe 40,000l.

By 30 and 31 Vic., cap. 146 (15th July, 1867), the company obtained power to make certain deviations, as well as an extension of time for completion of works till 15th July, 1871. The number of directors was also increased from five to seven.

A bill is now before parliament for an extension to Carrickmacross, as well as for an extension of time for completion of authorised works, for additional capital, and for powers to Dublin and Meath.

DUBLIN AND MEATH.—A special meeting was held in October. 1867, for the purpose of considering the terms on which a subscription of 40,000l. on the part of the Dublin and Meath should be accepted. It was explained that the project had remained dormant since 1865, in consequence of the commercial panic. Since then deviations had been authorised by parliament, which would effect a saving in the outlay. The Meath were prepared to lend 40,000l. at 5½ per cent. upon preferential shares, and proposed to work the line for 40 per cent. on gross receipts. A resolution was passed acceding to those terms.

No. of Directors—7; quorum, 3. *Qualification, 500l*

287.—NEATH AND BRECON.

Incorporated by 25 and 26 Vic., cap. 193 (29th July, 1862), to construct a line from the Vale of Neath to certain collieries in Breconshire. Length, 9¼ miles. Capital, 60,000l. in 10l. shares; loans, 20,000l. Mixed gauge. Arrangements with Vale of Neath. Opened for goods and minerals to Onllwyn iron works, 10¼ miles, on 2nd September, 1864. Opened throughout for passengers, 1867.

By 26 and 27 Vic., cap. 130 (13th July, 1863), certain deviations were authorised, as well as an extension to Brecon. Length, 8 miles. The name of the undertaking was also changed to that of the "Neath and Brecon." Arrangements with the Vale of Neath, Brecon and Merthyr Tydfil, and Hereford Hay and Brecon. New capital, 405,000l. in shares, and 135,000l. on loan.

By 27 and 28 Vic., cap. 316 (29th July, 1864), the company was authorised to extend the line to the Central Wales, and to construct two branches to collieries. Length, 15¼ miles. Capital, 210,000l. in shares, and 70,000l. on loan. Arrangements with Central Wales.

By 29 Vic., cap. 15 (18th May, 1866), the company was authorised to raise additional capital to the extent of 150,000l. in shares (preferred and deferred), and 50,000l. on loan.

SWANSEA VALE AND NEATH AND BRECON JUNCTION.—Incorporated by 27 and 28 Vic., cap. 293 (29th July, 1864), to construct a line from the Swansea to the Neath and Brecon. Length, 8 miles. Capital, 120,000l. in 10l. shares, and 40,000l. on loan. By 28 and 29 Vic., cap. 239 (5th July, 1865), the company obtained power to construct a branch from Ystradgynlais to Alecrane. Length, 1½ miles. Capital, 15,000l. in shares, and 5,000l. on loan. By 29 and 30 Vic., cap. 212 (16th July, 1866), this undertaking was vested in the Neath and Brecon for 999 years, from the 1st January, 1867, at 5 per cent.

By 30 and 31 Vic., cap. 122 (15th July, 1867), the company was authorised to acquire certain lands at and near Swansea, to acquire the Oystermouth tramway and part of the Brecon Forest tramway; also to create new shares to the extent of 75,000l., and to borrow 35,000l.

No details of revenue or capital have been forthcoming.

No. of Directors—8; minimum, 5; quorum, 3. *Qualification*, 300l.

DIRECTORS:

3 Chairman—THOMAS CAVE, Esq., M.P., 66, Lancaster Gate, Hyde Park, W.

2 Vice-Chairman—J. W. WILLIAMSON, Esq., 4, Stone Buildings, Lincoln's Inn, W.C.

1 W. Laurence Banks, Esq., F.S.A., Ponty-
Wal Hall, Bronllys, Hereford.
2 John Whittington, Esq., Clifton, Bristol.

3 W. M'Andrew, Esq., 57, King William
Street, City, E.C.

1, Retire in 1869; 2, in 1870; 3, in 1871.

OFFICERS.—Sec., D. Howell Morgan, Westminster Chambers, Victoria street, Westminster, S. W., and Neath; Con. Eng., John Gordon M'Kenzie, C.E.; Res. Eng., Hans St. George Caulfeild, B.A., C.E.: Auditor, W. Whittington, Neath; Solicitors, Dean and Taylor, and James Kempthorne, Neath; Bankers, The Union Bank of London, Temple Bar Branch, E.C., The Glamorganshire Banking Company, Neath, and the National Provincial Bank of England, Brecon.

Offices—1, Westminster Chambers, Victoria Street, Westminster, S.W.

288.—NEWCASLE (COUNTY DOWN).

Incorporated by 25 and 26 Vic., cap. 219 (7th August, 1862), to construct a railway from the Downpatrick and Newry, at Wateresk, to Newcastle. Length, 3 miles. Capital, 20,000l. in 5l. shares; loans, 6,600l. Arrangements with Downpatrick and Newry, and Belfast and County Down.

Meetings in February or March, or in August or September.

No. of Directors—4; minimum, 3; quorum, 3 and 2. *Qualification*, 50

DIRECTORS:

Major - General Chesney, R.A., D.C.L.,
F.R.S., F.R.G.S.
Captain Edward Hare Croker.

William M'Cormick, Esq., 41, Parliament.
Street, S.W.

289.—NEW MILFORD DOCKS.

Incorporated by 26 and 27 Vic., cap. 219 (July 28th, 1863), to construct a railway, docks, and other works at Milford Haven, near the estuary, called Neyland Pill, at its junction with Milford Haven.

Traffic arrangements with the Gt. Western. Capital, 220,000l. in 10l. shares; loans, 73,300l.

By 29 Vic. (1866), the company obtained an extension of powers. Additional capital, 50,000l. in 10l. shares; loans, 16,600l.

No. of Directors—5; minimum, 3; maximum, 6; quorum, 3. Qualification, 250l.

OFFICERS.—Eng., R. P. Brereton, Duke Street, Westminster, S.W.; Solicitors, Gregory, Champion, and Eady, 18, Park Street, Westminster, S.W.

Offices—18, Park Street, Westminster, S.W.

290.—NEWPORT.

Incorporated by 29 and 30 Vic., cap. 329 (6th August, 1866), to construct a railway from the North British, at Ferry-port-on-Craig, to Newport, in the County of Fife. Length, 6 miles. Capital, 96,000l. in 10l. shares, and 32,000l. on loan. Arrangements with North British.

By 30 and 31 Vic., cap. 157 (25th July, 1867), the company was authorised to make a deviation as well as to relinquish several sections of the original line. Capital reduced from 96,000l. to 46,000l. in shares, and the borrowing powers from 33,000l. to 15,000l.

No. of Directors—5; minimum, 4; quorum, 3. Qualification, 200l.

DIRECTORS:

John Berry, Esq.
William Heriot, Esq.
Maitland Dougal, Esq.

Harry Walker, Esq.
Peter Christie, Esq.
James Hendry Thoms, Esq.

291.—NEWPORT PAGNELL.

Incorporated by 26 and 27 Vic., cap. 110 (29th June, 1863), to construct a line from the London and North Western, at Wolverton, to Newport Pagnell, and to purchase the Newport Pagnell canal. Length, 4 miles. Capital, 45,000l. in 10l. shares, and 15,000l. on loan. Arrangements with London and North Western. Opened, 2nd September, 1867.

By 28 Vic., cap. 56 (2nd June, 1865), the company was authorised to construct an extension to Onley. Length, 5¼ miles. New capital, 80,000l. in shares, and 26,000l. on loan, which sums were authorised to be raised at the meeting in August; the shares a 5 per cent. preference.

By 29 and 30 Vic., cap. 354 (10th August, 1866), the company was authorised to extend the line to the Northampton and Peterborough branch of the London and North Western, and also to the Bedford and Northampton. Length, 11 miles. Capital, 225,000l. in shares, and 75,000l. on loan. Arrangements with Midland and Bedford and Northampton.

Meetings in February or March and August or September.

No. of Directors—5; maximum, 5; quorum, 3. Qualification, 200l.

DIRECTORS:

Chairman—WILLIAM FOWLER, Esq., Whittington Hall, Chesterfield.

Charles Magnay, Esq., The Terrace, Richmond Hill.
James B. Dunn, Esq., South Sea House, Threadneedle Street.

C. M. Tatham, Esq., 14, Cleveland Gardens, Hyde Park, W.
John Livesey, Esq., Reform Club, Pall Mall.

OFFICERS.—Sec., Edward Bellamy; Man., J. Talbot; Eng., J. H. Tolmé; Solicitors, Hargrove, Fowler, and Blunt; Surveyor, Robert Ritchie.

Offices—7, Westminster Chambers, S.W.

292.—NEWPORT AND USK.

Incorporated by 28 and 29 Vic., cap. 360 (5th July, 1865), to construct a line from the Eastern Valleys of Monmouthshire to a junction with the Coleford Monmouth Usk and Pontypool at Gwetrelog. Length, 11½ miles. Capital, 138,000l. in shares; loan, 46,000l. Arrangements with Great Western and Monmouthshire.

No. of Directors—7; minimum, 4; quorum, 3. Qualification, 200l.

DIRECTORS:

Chairman—WILLIAM GRAHAM, Esq., Newport, Monmouthshire.

Deputy-Chairman—WILLIAM LAURENCE BANKS, Esq., Watton House, Brecon.

Francis M'Donnel, Esq., Usk, Monmouthshire.
James Murphy, Esq., Newport, Monmouthshire.
J. J. William Fredericks, Esq., Abermellte, Glyn-Neath, Glamorganshire.

Thomas William Eady, Esq., Gothic House, Richmond, W.
John Logan, Esq., Maindee, near Newport, Monmouthshire.

OFFICERS.—Eng., Charles Liddell, C.E., 24, Abingdon Street, Westminster, S.W.; Auditors, — Craig and T. W. Theobald; Solicitors, Gregory, Champion, and Eady, 18, Park Street, Westminster, S.W.

Offices—18, Park Street, Westminster, S.W.

293.—NEWQUAY AND CORNWALL JUNCTION.

Incorporated by 27 and 28 Vic., cap. 163 (4th July, 1864), to construct a line from the Cornwall, near Burngullow, to the St. Dennis branch of the Newquay. Length, 5¼ miles. Capital, 27,000l. in 20l. shares, and 9,000l. on loan. Arrangements with Cornwall.

By 30 Vic., cap. 6 (29th May, 1868), the company was authorised to make a deviation in the line, and to extend the time for completion of works till 1871. Also, to cancel unissued shares, to assign a preferential dividend not exceeding 6 per cent. on 7,000l., and to raise additional capital to the extent of 3,000l., and to borrow thereon by instalments.

It was reported in August that the great difficulties which had so long stood in the way were now removed. The works were rapidly being pushed forward, and the opening of the line to Drinnick Mill might be expected at no remote period. A resolution, cancelling 7,000l. of unissued shares, and authorising the directors to issue preferential shares to that amount, at a dividend not exceeding 6 per cent., and a discount not exceeding 10 per cent., was agreed to. It was also stated that at that moment the company were not liable for a single preference share, and they had not a single debenture nor a single Lloyd's bond.

CAPITAL.—The expenditure to 30th June, 1868, amounted to 16,158l., which left a balance due to bankers of 3,778l. A special meeting was held on 6th October, at which it was resolved to raise 3,000l. on mortgage, which sum has since been obtained.

No. of Directors—6; minimum, 3; quorum, 3. *Qualification*, 200l.

DIRECTORS:

Chairman—E. BRYDGES WILLYAMS, Esq., M.P., Nanskeval, St. Columb.

Deputy-Chairman—WILLIAM LANGDON MARTIN, Esq., St. Austell.

Robert Thomas Head, Esq., The Briars, Alphington, Exeter.
Edward Lambert, Esq., 28, York Terrace, Regent's Park, N.W.

Edward Stocker, Esq., Glenview, Saint Austell.

Two directors retire annually, but are eligible for re-election.

OFFICERS.—Sec., William Polkinghorne, Woodlands, near Par Station, Cornwall; Engs., Jenkin, Trathan, and Triscott, Liskeard; Auditor, George Petterick, St. Austell; Solicitors, Joseph Burgin, 8, John Street, Bedford Row, and Gidley and Head, 15, Bedford Circus, Exeter; Bankers, Willyams, Treffoy, West, and Co., South Cornwall Bank, St. Austell.

294.—NEW ROMNEY.

Incorporated by 29 and 30 Vic., cap. 305 (30th July, 1866), to construct a line from the South Eastern, at Appledore, to New Romney, with a branch to Denge Beach. Length, 13¾ miles. Capital, 85,000l., in 10l. shares, and 28,300l. on loan. Arrangements with South Eastern.

Meetings in March and September.

No. of Directors—7; minimum, 5; quorum, 4 and 3. *Qualification*, 200l.

DIRECTORS:

Chairman—Colonel SIR CHARLES JOHN JAMES HAMILTON, Bart., C.B.

James Oliver Mason, Esq., The Crescent, Birmingham.
Robert Alured Denne, Esq., Lydd, Kent.
William Dering Walker, Esq., Honeychud Manor, New Romney, Kent.

John William Whitelock, Esq., Fyning House, Petersfield, Hants.
Thomas William Eady, Esq., Gothic House, Richmond, S.W.
William Henry Wilson, Esq., Chapel House, Battersea Park, S.W.

OFFICERS.—Sec., John Wilson Theobald; Engs., Shelford and Robinson, 7, Westminster Chambers, S.W.; Solicitors, Gregory, Champion, and Eady, 18, Park Street, Westminster, S.W. and 12, Clement's Inn, W.C.; Local Solicitor, Henry Stringer, New Romney; Surveyor, William Adams, 1, Lancaster Place, Strand, W.C.; Bankers, London Joint Stock Bank, Prince's Street, E.C., and Jemmet and Co. Ashford.

Offices—6, Victoria Street, Westminster, S.W.

295.—NEWRY AND ARMAGH.

Incorporated 31st July, 1845, for a line from Newry, by way of Armagh, to Enniskillen. Productive, 21 miles.

By 20 and 21 Vic., cap. 156 (17th August, 1857), the portion from Armagh to Enniskillen was abandoned, and the capital was consolidated to 55,660*l.* and "deferred." On the "deferred" shares, 9*l.* per share is considered as paid up, and no further call will be made until 9*l.* per share has been paid up on the new capital created by that Act, which amounts to 192,000*l.* in shares, and 78,000*l.* in loans. In addition, by 22 and 23 Vic. (1860), the company was authorised to issue debentures for 12,000*l.* for its moiety of the cost of junction with Warrenpoint ; but at the end of two years these debentures must be extinguished, and their places supplied with shares.

By 22 and 23 Vic., cap. 38 (1st August, 1859), the company was authorised to make certain alterations in the line, and to construct a short branch at Newry to an important depôt on the Ship Canal. Opened 1st September, 1861. Compulsory purchase of land, two years. By same enactment the company may use, by arrangement, the Ulster station, at Armagh.

By 25 and 26 Vic., cap. 75 (30th June, 1862), further powers were conferred, and debenture stock authorised instead of terminable loans. "By section 10 of this Act it is enacted that the holders of shares in series A of the dissolved Newry and Enniskillen, shall, within eight months, send in certificates of such shares to the secretary of the company, to be dealt with in accordance with the provisions of sec. 36 of Act 1857," otherwise all such shares become liable to forfeiture.

By 27 and 28 Vic., cap. 185 (14th July, 1864), the company obtained power to issue new shares to the extent of 250,000*l.*; also, to cancel forfeited and unissued shares, still keeping the total capital at 408,120*l.* Those new shares to rank for dividend *before* the shares created by 20 and 21 Vic. (17th August, 1857).

ULSTER.—The Newry and Armagh still complains of ill treatment at the hands of the Ulster, notwithstanding the judicial decision to the effect that the latter company had to pay damages for obstruction to the extent of 3,300*l.*

DUBLIN AND BELFAST JUNCTION.— An amicable arrangement has been effected with this company, under which through facilities are extended to all the traffic passing between the lines of the two companies.

REVENUE.—The receipts for the half-year ending 31st December, 1867, were 7,602*l.*, in comparison with 7,439*l.* for the corresponding period of 1866, and 6,459*l.* for 1865. The receipts for the June half-year were 5,323*l.*, in comparison with 6,412*l.* in 1867, and 5,331*l.* for 1866.

CAPITAL.—The old account shows a receipt of 136,425*l.*, being 4,304*l.* less than an expenditure of 140,730*l.* The expenditure of new extension capital to 30th June amounted to 432,158*l.*, which left a balance against receipts of 249,814*l.*

The accounts are made up to 30th June and 31st December ; and the statutory meetings held in February and August in every year, the books being closed 14 clear days previously.

Scale of Voting.—Voting according to C.C.C. Act.

Certificates must accompany transfer deed. Registration fee, 2*s.* 6*d.* each seller.

No. of Directors—12 ; minimum, 6 ; quorum, 3. *Qualification*, 60 new or 60 deferred 10*l.* shares. Meetings alternately in London or Newry or Armagh.

DIRECTORS:

ENGLISH BOARD.

Chairman—CHARLES HIGBY LATTIMORE, Esq., Wheathampstead, near St. Albans.

W. B. Heaton, Esq., Gainsborough, Lincolnshire.

J. R. Burbidge, Esq., 27, Clifton Hill, Brighton.

E. Jeggins, Esq., Park Road, East Moulsey, Surrey.

Joseph Roscoe Allen, Esq., Lentworth, Lancaster.

IRISH BOARD.

Chairman—WILLIAM KIRK, Esq., M.P., Annvale, Keady.

John Overend, Esq., Morecambe.

William Henry, Esq., Newry.

Samuel Gardner, Esq., J.P. Armagh.

Jacob Orr, Esq., Loughgall.

All eligible for re-election.

OFFICERS.—Sec. and Man., Benjamin L. Fearnley ; Eng.-in-Chief, G. W. Hemans, C.E. ; Auditor for England, Samuel Jeggins, Park Lodge, St. John's Park, N.W. Auditor for Ireland, John Moore, Newry ; Solicitor, Edward Greer, Trevor Hill, Newry. Head Offices—Edward Street, Newry.

296.—NEWRY AND GREENORE.

Incorporated by 26 and 27 Vic., cap. 229 (28th July, 1863), to construct a line from Newry to Carlingford Lough. Length, 15 miles. Capital, 102,000*l.* in 10*l.* shares, and 34,000*l.* on loan. Arrangements with Newry and Armagh. Works in progress.

By 27 Vic., cap. 3 (28th April, 1864), the company was permitted to raise additional capital to the extent of 50,000*l.* in shares, and 16,600*l.* on loan.

By 28 and 29 Vic., cap. 307 (5th July, 1865), the company was authorised to make certain deviations and raise new capital to the extent of 50,000*l.* in shares, and 16,600*l.* on loan.

By 30 Vic., cap. 96 (17th June, 1867), the company obtained an extension of time for completion of works, till 17th June, 1870.

Meetings in February or March and August or September.

No. of Directors—10 ; minimum, 5 ; quorum, 3. *Qualification,* 2,000*l.*

DIRECTORS:

Chairman—JOHN OBINS WOODHOUSE, Esq., J.P., Omeath Park, Newry.

Samuel Gardner, Esq., J.P., Armagh.	John Moore, Esq., J.P., Newry.
Daniel F. Brady, Esq., LL.D., Gardners Row, Dublin.	William McCulla, Esq., Newry.
James Overend, Esq., London.	George McCracken, Esq., Newry.

OFFICERS.—Sec., Benjamin L. Fearnley, Newry ; Eng., G. W. Hemans, 1, Westminster Chambers, Victoria Street, Westminster, S.W.; Solicitor, Edward Greer, Newry.

297.—NEWRY, WARRENPOINT, AND ROSTREVOR.

Incorporated by 10 Vic., cap. 245 (27th July, 1846), for a line from Newry to Rostrevor, with a branch to Warrenpoint (8½ miles). Six miles from Newry to Warrenpoint have been opened since 28th May, 1849.

By 20 and 21 Vic., cap. 61 (27th July, 1857), the company is authorised to extend its line at Newry and at Warrenpoint (length, ¾ mile), and to enter into arrangements with the Newry and Armagh. New capital, 20,000*l.* by shares, and 6,000*l.* by loan. Opened 2nd September, 1861.

By 23 Vic., cap. 87 (14th June, 1860), the company was authorised to regulate its 6 per cent. preference capital, and to create new shares at 5½ per cent.; to define its borrowing powers as extending to 39,900*l.* The Newry and Armagh was authorised to subscribe 12,500*l.*, and agreements between the companies legalised. New works were also permitted, principally connected with water conveyance.

REVENUE.—The receipts for the half-years ending 31st December compare with each other as follows :—

	Passengers.	Goods, &c.	Mileage.	Total.
1864	£2,165	£854	£317	£3,337
1865	2,358	831	192	3,382
1866	2,527	1,165	52	3,745
1867	2,596	966	292	3,855

The following comparative statement for the June half-years shows the progress made during four years :—

1865	£1,576	£742	£158	£2,416
1866	1,475	1,218	28	2,722
1867	1,590	1,143	180	2,915
1868	1,538	1,187	109	2,836

The directors, in August, expressed their regret at the non-development of the coal traffic, consequent upon the still unsatisfactory interruptions of proper arrangements between the Ulster and the Newry and Armagh. It was, however, to be hoped that the recent trial, in which the latter company gained substantial damages, might prove the means of bringing about a more satisfactory feeling between the two companies, through which the Newry and Warrenpoint must materially benefit.

CAPITAL.—The balance sheet to 30th June set forth an expenditure of 171,720*l.*, the receipts for which were given as follows :—

Deposit of 2*l.* per share on 5,000 shares	£10,000
1st call of 3*l.* per share on 4,500 shares	13,500
2nd call of 5*l.* per share on 4,450 shares	22,250
3rd call of 2*l.* 10*s.* per share on 3,850 shares	9,625
4th call of 2*l.* 10*s.* per share, on 3,850 shares	9,625
5th call of 5*l.* per share on 3,725 shares	18,625
Sale of forfeited shares	7,713
6 per cent. preference shares, 2*l.* per share on 6,450 ....£12,900	
5½ ,, ,, ,, 3,550 .... 7,100=	20,000
Loans on mortgage ,,	39,500
Bankers	2,455
Newry and Armagh, account of	12,984
Open accounts, sundry creditors	976
Balance of general revenue account	4,118
Balance due secretary	346=£1,171,720

Scale of Voting.—One vote for every five shares ; no proprietor can have more than 20 votes.

No. of Directors.—Maximum, 13 ; minimum, 5 ; under Act, 1853. *Qualification,* 20 shares ; allowance, nil.

DIRECTORS:

Deputy-Chairman—CHARLES HOLLAND, Esq., Liverpool.

Joseph Lupton, Esq., Newry.   James Kennedy, Esq., Liverpool.
Peter Quinn, Esq., Newry.   J. T. Fitzadam, Esq., Wigan.
*John Reilly, Esq., Dublin.

* Retires by rotation in February, 1869, but is eligible for re-election.

OFFICERS.—Secretary, Robert Cochran, Liverpool; Superintendent, Peter Roe;
Auditors, Joseph Wren and James Bryn.

Secretary's Office, 71, Tower Buildings, Liverpool.

298.—NORTH BRITISH.

An incorporation (by 25 and 26 Vic., cap. 189, 29th July, 1862), of the original North
British, the Edinburgh Perth and Dundee, the West of Fife, and their several subsidiary connections; and by 28 and 29 Vic., cap. 217 (5th July, 1865), the Monkland was
amalgamated with the Edinburgh and Glasgow, which was by an Act of the same session,
28 and 29 Vic., cap. 308 (1865), amalgamated with the North British as from 31st July,
1865. The following particulars refer to the undertakings now forming component
parts of the united company.

I. NORTH BRITISH.—Incorporated 19th July, 1844, for a line from Edinburgh to
Berwick junction with North Eastern (York Newcastle and Berwick), with a branch
to Haddington (62 miles). In 1845 powers were given to purchase the Edinburgh and
Dalkeith (14 miles), and to construct a small branch (two miles) to connect it. The
powers of the Edinburgh and Hawick (43½ miles), were transferred to this company in
the same year. In 1846 the company obtained power to construct branches to Selkirk,
Jedburgh, Kelso, Tranent, Cockenzie, North Berwick, and Dunse (42 miles). The first
two of these schemes have since been made by local parties. A deviation and short
extension were authorised in 1847.

19 and 20 Vic., cap. 63, cancelled forfeited shares to the extent of 72,272l.; gave power
to raise 152,000l. new capital, and to convert mortgage debt into debenture stock.

By 21 and 22 Vic., cap. 109 (23rd July, 1858), the Acts of the company were consolidated,
and an alteration sanctioned on Leith branch, so as to permit use of locomotives.

By 23 and 24 Vic., cap. 159 (23rd July, 1860), the company obtained power to enlarge
its station at Edinburgh, and also to use the Citadel station in Carlisle. Authority was
also given to the company to raise new capital to the extent of 30,000l. in shares, at 5
per cent. preference, and 10,000l. on mortgage; and by 28 and 29 Vic., cap. 152 (29th
June, 1865), an agreement with the corporation of the city of Edinburgh was sanctioned
and confirmed, in virtue of which and of another agreement since concluded, the whole
of the vegetable markets are to be conveyed to the company for the enlargement and
improvement of the Edinburgh station.

CARLISLE AND SILLOTH BAY.—Incorporated by 18 and 19 Vic., cap. 153 (16th July,
1855), to make a railway from Port Carlisle, at Drumburgh, to the boat lighthouse in Silloth
Bay, and a dock and jetty at the latter place (12¾ miles). Opened 4th September, 1856.
The dock at Silloth was opened on 3rd August, 1859. It measures 600 feet in length
and 300 in width, giving an area of water surface of upwards of four acres, with a width
at the entrance gate of 60 feet. Share capital, 165,000l.; loans, 55,000l. Leased to North
British by 25 and 26 Vic., cap. 47 (3rd June, 1862), for 999 years, at an annual fixed rent
of 2,000l., and a further contingent rent to commence from 1st February, 1863, equal to
the same rate per cent. on 165,000l. as the dividend for the time being on the North
British ordinary stock.

PORT CARLISLE.—Incorporated by 17 Vic., cap. 119 (4th August, 1853), for converting
a canal into a railway. By 59 Geo. III., cap. 13, the canal was authorised from Carlisle
to Solway Firth (Fisher's Cross), Bowness, Cumberland ("Port Carlisle"), and "The
Carlisle Canal Company" was incorporated with a capital of 80,000l. and 40,000l. By 7
Wm. IV., cap. 50 (Dock Act), power was given to make docks at Port Carlisle, and raise
40,000l. Length, 11½ miles. Opened 22nd May, 1854, for goods, and on 22nd June for
passengers. Ordinary share capital 70,600l. Preference capital, 35,000l. at 5 per cent.,
and 40,000l. at 5½ per cent., mortgage debts, 73,537l. 10s., now converted into debenture
stock, to bear 3 per cent. per annum. Leased to North British by 25 and 26 Vic., cap.
48 (3rd June, 1862), for 999 years, at a fixed annual rent of 3,100l., and an additional
contingent rent when the dividend on the North British stock exceeds 4 per cent. per
annum, equal to such an amount per cent. on 70,600l. as shall be the difference between
4 per cent. per annum and the rate of dividend on such ordinary stock.

By 25 and 26 Vic., cap. 49 (3rd June, 1862), the North British was authorised to construct branches from their railway in the parish of Inveresk, and to create new capital
to the extent of 220,000l., and 73,000l. on loan. By 25 and 26 Vic. (17th July, 1862), the
North British were authorised to contribute 50,000l. towards the Berwickshire, which
connects the company's Berwick and Hawick lines.

PEEBLES.—Incorporated by 17 Vic., cap. 78 (8th July, 1853), for a line from the Hawick branch of the North British (Eskbank station), to Peebles (single line). Length, 18¾ miles. Sidings, &c., 2¼ miles. Total, 21. Opened 4th July, 1855. By 20 and 21 Vic., cap. 14 (26th June, 1857), the Peebles was authorised to create additional capital to the extent of 27,000l. in shares, at 5 per cent. preference, and 9,000l. on loan. Power also given to convert mortgage debt into debenture stock, not exceeding 4 per cent. Leased to North British by 24 and 25 Vic., cap. 114 (July 11th, 1861), on a guarantee of 5 per cent. minimum dividend. After 6 per cent. shall be earned, further surplus profits go equally between the two companies.

JEDBURGH.—Incorporated by 18 Vic., cap. 30 (May 25th, 1855), to construct a line (7 miles 1 furlong 8 chains) from Jedburgh to the Roxburgh station of North British. Capital, 35,000l. in 10l. shares, with power to borrow 11,500l. Opened 17th July, 1856. By 23 and 24 Vic., cap. 140 (3rd July, 1860), the line is leased to the North British at 4 per cent., with increase above that rate equal to difference between that rate and any higher rate of dividend paid on North British ordinary stock.

SELKIRK AND GALASHIELS.—Incorporated by 17 and 18 Vic., cap. 199 (July 31st, 1854), for a line between these towns. Capital, 24,000l., in 10l. shares; loans, 8,000l. The line (6¼ miles) commences on "town haugh," near Selkirk, and terminates by a junction with the Hawick branch of North British, near Galashiels station. Opened 5th April, 1856. By 21 Vic., cap. 29 (4th June, 1858), the company was authorised to raise additional capital—6,000l. in shares at 5 per cent., and 2,000l. on mortgage. By 22nd and 23rd Vic., cap. 14 (21st July, 1859), the company is amalgamated with North British, at par, the ordinary stock of the latter being exchanged for that of the former. At a meeting on 18th October, 1859, the company was formally wound up, the balance in hand being divided, and the undertaking handed over to the North British.

BORDER UNION.—By 22 and 23 Vic., cap. 24 (21st July, 1859), the company was authorised to construct a line from Hawick to Carlisle, with branches as under :—Main line, 44 miles; Langholm, 7 miles; Canobie coal field, ¼ mile; Gretna, 3 miles; total, 54¼ miles. The main line is double and the branches are single. Capital, 495,000l. ; loans, 165,000l. It was resolved at the half-yearly meeting in September, 1859, to raise so much of the capital as had not been raised by ordinray shares in shares of 10l., not exceeding 400,000l. in the whole, to which a perpetual dividend of 5½ per cent., in perpetuity, commencing from and after 31st December, 1861, shall attach, without participation in surplus profits (over 5½ per cent.) out of Border Union revenue. Opened throughout from Carlisle (Citadel station), for passengers, and Canal station for goods, to Edinburgh, July, 1862.

BORDER COUNTIES.—Incorporated by 17 and 18 Vic., cap. 212 (July, 1854), for a line from Hexham, on the North Eastern (Newcastle and Carlisle), by the Valley of North Tyne, to Wark, Reedsmouth, Hareshaw Iron Works, Bellingham, Falstone, and Kielder. Length, 26 miles. Capital, 250,000l. in 20l. shares; loans, 83,333l. By 22 and 23 Vic., cap. 43 (1st August, 1859), the company was authorised to construct the Liddesdale section, to deviate some parts of the North Tyne section, and to raise further capital to the extent of 100,000l. in shares, and 33,333l. on loan. The Liddesdale section (15 miles) commences by a junction with the Border Counties, and terminates on the Border Union (Hawick to Carlisle), near Riccarton. By 23 and 24 Vic., cap. 195 (13th August, 1860), amalgamated with North British. Running powers obtained over the portion of the Newcastle and Carlisle between the junction of the Border Counties therewith and Newcastle, and the use of stations on such portion, and security for the free passage of traffic between the two railways. Opened throughout, 1st July, 1862.

WANSBECK.—Incorporated by 22 and 23 Vic., cap. 85 (8th August, 1859), to construct lines from Morpeth to the Border Counties, the Blyth and Tyne, and the North Eastern. Capital, 120,000l. in 10l. shares; loans, 40,000l. Length of main line, 28 miles, to commence at Morpeth, and terminate at Chollerton, by junction with North Tyne section of Border Counties ; branch to Blyth and Tyne, 6½ furlongs ; branch to North Eastern, 2¼ furlongs. Opened from Morpeth to Reedsmouth, 1st May, 1865. By 26 and 27 Vic., cap. 194 (21st July, 1863), the company was authorised to create new capital to the extent of 10,000l. in shares and 3,300l. on loan, and also to amalgamate with the North British, which was effected on 20th July, 1862.

GALASHIELS AND PEEBLES.—By 24 and 25 Vic., cap. 102 (28th June, 1861), the North British is authorised to construct a line from Galashiels, on the Hawick section, to Peebles, there joining the Peebles as well as Symington Biggar and Broughton. Length, 18 miles 12 chains. Capital, 95,000l. in shares, and 31,600l. on loan. Completion of works, five years. Opened throughout, 17½ miles.

II. EDINBURGH, PERTH, AND DUNDEE.—This company, under an Act of 1847 (11 Vic., cap. 239), is an amalgamation of the EDINBURGH, LEITH, and GRANTON, incorporated 1836 by Act 6 and 7 Wm. IV., cap. 131, and the EDINBURGH and NORTHERN, incorporated by 8 and 9 Vic., cap. 158. These two lines are connected by a steam ferry across the Firth of Forth.

The above companies were dissolved and re-incorporated under this title, by Act 13 Vic., cap. 79 (1849), and again dissolved and re-incorporated by Act 14 and 15 Vic., cap. 55 (1851), the undertaking being defined to be a line from Edinburgh, in conjunction with the North British and Edinburgh and Glasgow, to Leith Harbour, Granton

Pier, Burntisland (on the opposite shore), and Ladybank : a junction with the Scottish Central, near Perth, to Cupar and Ferry-Port-on-Craig, opposite Dundee and Broughty Ferry to join the Dundee and Arbroath to Dundee and the North : a branch from Thornton to Dunfermline, to join the Stirling and Dunfermline, and to Kirkaldy Harbour. Length of railways and ferries, 78 miles.

KINROSS-SHIRE.—Incorporated by 20 and 21 Vic., cap. 124 (10th August, 1857), for making a railway from the Dunfermline branch of the Edinburgh Perth and Dundee to Kinross, with a branch to Kingseat. Capital, 53,000*l.* in 10*l.* shares ; loans, 17,666*l.* Length, 7 miles ; branch, 3½ miles. Opened 20th June, 1866. By 24 and 25 Vic., cap. 177 (22nd July, 1861), the company was authorised to substitute for the Kingseat branch, formerly authorised for effecting a junction with the West of Fife Mineral, another but shorter and less expensive branch for the same purpose ; as also to construct a branch (length, 1 mile 79 chains), to join the Devon Valley, near Kinross. The former is nearly completed, and the latter has been abandoned, in virtue of power to that effect in 25 and 26 Vic., cap. 181 (29th July, 1862), the connection being attained by a junction with the Fife and Kinross, at Kinross. By 24 and 25 Vic., cap. 214 (1st August, 1861), the line is amalgamated with the Edinburgh Perth and Dundee, and a dividend of 5 per cent. per annum on the Kinross-shire share capital is to be paid out of the gross revenue earned upon the Kinross-shire, after payment of public burdens and interest on loan debt ; the working charges being defrayed by the Edinburgh Perth and Dundee, from its own revenue, after payment of preferential interest and dividend.

FIFE AND KINROSS.— Incorporated by 18 and 19 Vic., cap. 127 (16th July, 1855), to make a railway from Ladybank, on the Edinburgh Perth and Dundee, by Auchtermuchty and Strathmiglo, to Milnathort and Kinross. Capital, 70,000*l.* in 10*l.* shares. Borrowing powers, 23,000*l.* Length, 14 miles. By 20 and 21 Vic., cap. 129 (10th August, 1857), certain deviations were sanctioned, and the company allowed to extend the line from Milnathort to Kinross. Additional capital, 12,000*l.* by 5 per cent. preference, and 4,000*l.* on loan. By 21 and 22 Vic., cap. 65 (28th June, 1858), a junction was authorised with the Kinross-shire, with joint station at Kinross. Estimate, 13,500*l.* By 24 and 25 Vic., cap. 131 (11th July, 1861), the company was authorised to raise additional capital to the extent of 53,850*l.* in new shares, to which a preferential dividend of 4½ per cent. has now been attached, cancelling 25,850*l.* of unissued share capital, authorised by previous Acts, the share capital of the undertaking is fixed at 110,000*l.* Borrowing powers, 36,600*l.* Length, 15 miles 62 chains. By 25 and 26 Vic., cap. 181 (29th July, 1862), the Fife and Kinross was amalgamated with the Edinburgh Perth and Dundee.

III. WEST OF FIFE.—Incorporated by 19 and 20 Vic., cap. 98 (14th July, 1856), for making a line from Dunfermline to Killairnie, 6¾ miles, with a branch to Kingseat, 1 furlong. Capital, 45,000*l.* in 10*l.* shares, with power to borrow 15,000*l.* By 20 and 21 Vic., cap. 91 (27th July, 1857), the company is authorised to construct a branch to Roscobie, 2½ miles. New capital, 7,000*l.* in 10*l.* shares ; loans, 2,300*l.* By 23 and 24 Vic., cap. 145 (23rd July, 1860), the company was authorised to extend the Kingseat branch, to Beath, where it unites with the Kinross-shire. Length, 3¼ miles. Additional capital, 12,000*l.* in 10*l.* shares.

CHARLESTOWN. — Incorporated by 22 and 23 Vic., cap. 96 (8th August, 1859), to enable the company to purchase the coast line (constructed by private parties) and to improve the harbour of Charlestown. Capital, 72,000*l.* in 10*l.* shares ; loans, 24,000*l.* Length of main line, 5 miles ; it commences at the harbour of Charlestown, and terminates by a junction with the West of Fife Mineral, near Dunfermline. This line transferred to the West of Fife Mineral, and various improvements effected in the gradients so as to make the railways more available for passengers as well as mineral traffic. By 24 and 25 Vic., cap. 226 (1st August, 1861), the Charlestown and the West of Fife were amalgamated. Total share capital, 136,000*l.,* to which a preference dividend of 5 per cent. is now attached. Loans, 45,000*l.*

By 26 and 27 Vic., cap. 213 (28th July, 1863), the company obtained power to construct a line from Queensferry to Dunfermline, and by several extensions and continuations to join the Edinburgh Perth and Dundee, so as to form a new and shorter route between Edinburgh and Perth. Also, to construct extensions and other improvements in regard to the Leith branch. Length, 22 miles. Capital, 460,000*l.* in shares, and 153,300*l.* on loan.

By 26 and 27 Vic., cap. 194 (21st July, 1863), the company was authorised to raise new capital to the extent of 500,000*l.* in shares, and 166,600*l.* on loan.

By 26 and 27 Vic., cap. 226 (28th July, 1863), the North British was authorised to purchase and employ steam boats between Silloth and Belfast. New capital, 30,000*l.* in shares, and 10,000*l.* on loan.

By 27 and 28 Vic., cap. 100 (23rd June, 1864), an agreement is sanctioned with the Scottish Central, by which the North British, on payment of an annual sum of 5,000*l.,* may use the line of the Scottish Central into Perth. New capital for additional station accommodation at Perth, 21,000*l.* in shares, and 7,000*l.* on loan.

IV. MONKLAND.—An amalgamation of the MONKLAND and KIRKINTILLOCH, the BALLOCHNEY and the SLAMANNAN, under Act 12 Vic., cap. 134 (14th August, 1848). These lines were constructed chiefly as m neral from Kirkintilloch, Coatbridge, Airdrie Bathgate, and Bo'ness on the Forth.

In 1853, July 8th (17 Vic., cap. 90), the Monkland was empowered to form five connecting lines, &c., with the Edinburgh and Glasgow, Bathgate Mineral Fields, &c.

Estimated cost, 73,085l. Subscription contract signed for 71,250l.; deposits, 7,125l.

Power to raise 75,000l. additional capital, with preferences, maximum, 6 per cent. not to affect prior guarantees, and loans, 25,000l.

By 20 and 21 Vic., cap. 78 (27th July, 1857), the Monkland is authorised to construct certain extensions in the counties of Lanark and Linlithgow. From Cowdenhead to Boghead ; from Clarkston to Cowdenhead ; to near Planes ; to Craig Mill ; from Kipps to Browneside. New capital : shares, 137,000l.; loans, 45,000l.

By 23 and 24 Vic., cap. 178 (6th August, 1860), the Monkland obtained power to form a branch of about 5 miles in length, through the mineral fields extending from the new line in course of formation towards the Shotts iron works. New capital, 50,000l. in shares, with or without preference, and 16,000l. on loan. Opened February, 1862.

V. EDINBURGH AND GLASGOW.—Incorporated originally by 1 and 2 Vic., cap. 58, for a railway from Edinburgh to Glasgow, with a branch to Falkirk. Capital, 900,000l. in shares, and 300,000l. on loan. By Act 15 Vic., cap. 109 (17th June, 1852), this company was re-incorporated under the same title, and every Act previously obtained repealed, except special Acts as to other companies specified. The Union Canal became embodied in the company of 1848. The company was re-incorporated and consolidated by 15 Vic., 1852.

By 18 and 19 Vic., cap. 158 (July 23rd, 1855), the Edinburgh and Glasgow undertook to subscribe 50,000l. to the Dumbartonshire and Helensburgh. Power was also taken to subscribe 150,000l. by shares, to enlarge the Queen Street station, and for other purposes, and also to raise a further sum of 30,000l. By 24 and 25 Vic., cap. 84 (28th June, 1861), the Edinburgh and Glasgow was authorised to raise additional capital to the extent of 160,000l. in shares at 5 per cent. By 26 and 27 Vic., cap. 237 (28th July, 1863), the Edinburgh and Glasgow was authorised to construct a line from Ratho to South Queensferry, with subsidiary branches. Length, 6½ miles. New capital, 270,000l. in shares, and 90,000l. on loan. By 27 and 28 Vic., cap. 279 (25th July, 1864), the Edinburgh and Glasgow was authorised to construct railways at Cowlairs, and between Maryhill and the River Clyde, as also to construct a tramway at the h rbour of Glasgow. Length, 9½ miles. Capital, 270,000l. in shares, and 90,000l. on loan. Running powers and separate stations to Caledonian harbour line, with a joint station in Glasgow.

STIRLING AND DUNFERMLINE.—By 21 and 22 Vic., cap. 64 (28th June, 1858), this undertaking was vested in the Edinburgh and Glasgow at 4 per cent. on 450,000l., and interest on debentures to the extent of 130,000l.

EDINBURGH AND BATHGATE.—This line was leased to the Edinburgh and Glasgow for 999 years.

CALEDONIAN AND DUMBARTONSHIRE JUNCTION.—Incorporated by 9 and 10 Vic., cap. 81 (June, 1846), for a line from Bowling to Loch Lomond, 8½ miles. The agreement entered into between the directors and the Edinburgh and Glasgow for amalgamation was unanimously approved at a general meeting, and the fusion has since taken place, in accordance with the provisions of 25 and 26 Vic., cap. 135 (7th July, 1862).

GLASGOW, DUMBARTON, AND HELENSBURGH.—Incorporated by 18 and 19 Vic., cap. 190 (15th August, 1855), to make a line from the Edinburgh and Glasgow, at Cowlairs, to the Caledonian and Dumbartonshire, at Bowling, with a branch to Helensburgh. Capital, 240,000l. in 10l. shares. Power to borrow, 60,000l. The Edinburgh and Glasgow subscribed 80,000l. Opened 31st May, 1858. It commences by a junction near Cowlairs, and proceeds westward to Maryhill, 4 miles ; to Dalmuir, 9½ miles ; to Kilpatrick, 11 miles ; to Bowling, 12¼ miles ; it then runs for 3¾ miles along the Leven to Dumbarton, 15¾ miles ; and to Dalreoch Junction, 16 miles. Up to this point the new line is double, but beyond it to Cardross and Helensburgh, 23¾ miles from Glasgow, the line is single.

ALVA.—Incorporated by 24 and 25 Vic., cap. 195 (22nd July, 1861), to construct a line from the Cambus station of the Stirling and Dunfermline, to Alva. Length, 3¼ miles. Capital, 15,000l. in 10l. shares ; loans, 5,000l. Opened 11th June, 1863. Amalgamated with Edinburgh and Glasgow by 27 and 28 Vic., cap. 81 (23rd June, 1864), at a cost of 12,500l. Edinburgh and Glasgow stock, and assuming a debenture debt of 5,000l.

LEADBURN, LINTON, AND DOLPHINTON.—Incorporated by 25 Vic., cap. 51 (3rd June, 1862), to construct a line from the Peebles, at its Leadburn Station, to Linton. Length, 10 miles. Capital, 40,000l., in 10l. shares ; loans, 13,300l. Opened 1st July, 1864. By 29 and 30 Vic., cap. 172 (16th July, 1866), the Leadburn Linton and Dolphinton was amalgamated with the North British, the dividend of the latter in one half-year becoming a preference charge for the next ensuing for the Leadburn.

NEW WORKS, &c.—The company have power to construct new lines and works as follows :—

By 28 and 29 Vic., cap. 309 (5th July, 1865), the company was authorised to construct a pier at Burntisland, enlarge the Bonnington and North Leith stations: and same Act confirmed the purchase of land for the enlargement of the company's station at Newcastle-on-Tyne. New capital, 49,500l. in shares, and 16,500l. on loan.

By 28 and 29 Vic., cap. 206 (5th July, 1865), the company was authorised to extend their railway at Carlisle to the goods line on the southern side of the Carlisle Citadel station, and to acquire land for additional station accommodation at Carlisle. New capital, 66,000*l.* in shares, and 22,000*l.* on loan.

By 28 and 29 Vic., cap. 125 (19th June, 1865), the company was authorised to make railways to Liberton, Lasswade, and other places in the suburbs of Edinburgh. New capital, 195,000*l.* in shares, and 65,000*l.* on loan.

By 28 and 29 Vic., cap. 328 (5th July, 1865), the company (as coming in place of the Edinburgh and Glasgow) was authorised to make a railway from Glasgow to Coatbridge, and a junction with the Glasgow City Union. New capital, 280,000*l.* in shares, and 93,000*l.* on loan.

By 28 and 29 Vic., cap. 200 (20th June, 1865), the company (as coming in place of the Edinburgh and Glasgow) was authorised to purchase land, and form a station at the College of Glasgow, and to subscribe 300,000*l.* towards the undertaking of the Glasgow City Union. New capital authorised, 350,000*l.* in shares.

By 28 and 29 Vic., cap. 356 (5th July, 1865), the company was authorised to subscribe, in addition to their former subscription of 17,000*l.*, the further sum of 30,000*l.* towards an extension of the Blane Valley, and were empowered to raise the latter amount by shares.

By 28 and 29 Vic., cap. 201 (29th June, 1865), the company (as coming in place of the Monkland) was authorised to construct railways in the county of Lanark, and to raise new capital to the amount of 30,000*l.* in shares, and 10,000*l.* on loan.

COATBRIDGE BRANCHES.—By 29 and 30 Vic., cap. 219 (16th July, 1866), the company was authorised to construct certain lines in connection with its system in the counties of Lanark, Linlithgow, and Stirling, as well as a deviation on the Forth and Clyde Canal. Length, 7 miles. New capital, 72,000*l.* in shares, and 24,000*l.* on loan. Also to create and issue debenture stock.

STIRLING BRANCHES.—By 29 and 30 Vic., cap. 173 (16th July, 1866), the company was authorised to construct new lines in the counties of Lanark, Dumbarton, and Stirling, in connection with the system of the Monkland. Length, 5¾ miles. New capital, 81,000*l.* in shares, and 27,000*l.* on loan.

NEW WORKS, &c.—By 29 and 30 Vic., cap. 266 (23rd July, 1866), the company obtained power to construct several small lines of about 1½ miles, and also an extension of time for completion of various works, especially in regard to the system crossing the Firth of Forth. Also, to enter into arrangements with the corporation of Edinburgh in regard to the site of the fruit and vegetable markets, and with the Midland as to a goods station at Carlisle. Finally, by this Act the Fife and Kinross was vested in the North British. New capital, 181,380*l.* in shares, and 51,700*l.* on loan.

GLASGOW BRANCHES.—By 29 and 30 Vic., cap. 285 (30th July, 1866), the company was authorised to construct two small branches near Glasgow. Length, 3¾ miles. Capital, 60,000*l.* in shares, and 20,000*l.* on loan.

CAMPS, &c.—By 29 and 30 Vic., cap. 291 (30th July, 1866), the North British was authorised to construct three short branches in connection with its system in Linlithgow, Stirling, and Edinburgh. Length, 5¾ miles. Capital, 40,000*l.* in shares, and 13,000*l.* on loan.

DEVON VALLEY.—By 29 and 30 Vic., cap. 326 (6th August, 1866), the North British was authorised to lease or amalgamate the Devon Valley, as well as to subscribe 60,000*l.* thereto.

ESK VALLEY.—By 29 and 30 Vic., cap. 200, the company are authorised to lease the Esk Valley, when opened, for 999 years.

DEVON VALLEY AND NORTH BRITISH BRANCHES.—By 29 and 30 Vic., cap. 277, the company was authorised to construct branches to connect their system with the Devon Valley, and with the mineral districts of Fife and Clackmannan. Length, 14¼ miles. New capital, 95,000*l.* in shares, and 31,600*l.* on loan.

GENERAL POWERS.—By 30 and 31 Vic., cap. 145 (15th July, 1867), the North British was authorised to make certain deviations in the Glasgow Branches and on the Forth and Clyde Canal. Also, to deviate a portion of the railway authorised under the Edinburgh and Glasgow Extension Act of 1864, and to extend the time for the completion of the works.

FINANCE ACT, 1867.—The financial powers obtained by this Act (30 and 31 Vic., cap. 198, 12th August, 1867), are given in extenso in the APPENDIX to the Volume for 1868. At a special meeting held on 20th September, 1867, it was resolved—That the directors be, and they are hereby, empowered to borrow on mortgage to the extent of 843,850*l.*, under the provisions of sections 29 and 30 of "The North British Financial Arrangements Act, 1867."

ABANDONMENTS.—By 31 and 32 Vic., cap. 63 (25th June, 1868), the company was authorised to abandon certain portions of the railways by the Bridge of Forth Act 1845, and obtained an extension of time for completion of the works on the remainder till 1872.

By 31 and 32 Vic., cap. 139 (13th July, 1868), the company was authorised to construct new works and railways, and to abandon others, including conveyance of Baird's railway to the company and construction of a line (2 furlongs) in connection with the Monkland and Kirkintilloch; another (1 furlong) from that railway to the Langloan ironworks; several deviations and other alterations; and a railway (2 furlongs) from Carlisle to a junction with the Port Carlisle branch of the Caledonian, the whole to be completed within five years. Also, to abandon Railway No. 1 of the Act of 1865; the railways and works authorised by the Dundee branch Act of 1866; St. Margaret's diversion of 1866; the Camps branches of 1866; and Nos. 1 and 3 of the Devon Valley branches of 1866. Also, Railway No. 2 of the General Powers Act of 1867, and No. 2 of the Financial Arrangements' Act of 1867. By the same Act the capital of the company was reduced by the several amounts of 125,000*l.* and 74,000*l.*, or 199,000*l.* in all. Extensions of time for purchase of lands and completion of works were also obtained, the latter for three years. The North British, by the provisions of this Act, are to pay the Caledonian 600*l.* a-year for running over the Port Carlisle branch of the latter company, and also for running over the main line between Port Carlisle and the Citadel station 1,200*l.* for the first year; 1,300*l.* for the second; 100*l.* a-year, extra, for each year till the seventh, when the annual payment in perpetuity is to be 1,800*l.*, the payments in respect to which are to be made monthly through the Clearing House. The same Act also prescribed that the railway from Inverkeithing to Dunfermline, and from Lasswade to Penicuik might be converted into separate undertakings, and also confirmed an agreement between the company and the subscribers to the Coatbridge.

The North British works the Berwickshire, St. Andrews, Leslie, Devon Valley, Blane Valley and Milngavie railways.

MILEAGE.—N. B. Proper, 739 miles 1 chain. Peebles (leased by N. B., but receipts not included in their accounts), 18 miles 60 chains. Lines worked by N. B., 51 miles 5 chains.—Total, 808 miles 66 chains. Opened on 2nd March, 1868, Edinbro', Leith, and Granton new branches, 3 miles 49 chains. On June 1st, 1868, Dalmeny to South Queensferry, 1 mile 49 chains. No further openings of importance in prospect for some time.

REVENUE.—It was reported in March that the balance of revenue applicable to dividend was 135,818*l.*, as against 101,801*l.* in the corresponding period of 1867, or an increase of 34,016*l.*, equal to 33·41 per cent. It was recommended that the said sum of 135,818*l.*, with the balance of 56*l.* brought from the previous half-year, be credited by way of dividend on the several stocks enumerated, which absorbed 135,867*l.* The circumstances of the company did not admit of these dividends being now paid in cash, and they were, therefore, deferred, except on those stocks to which a lien is attached for the payment of the dividends secured to them.

The revenue account for the half-year to 31st July, 1868, as compared with that for the half-year to 31st July, 1867, shows the following results:—

Receipts.	July, 1868.	July, 1867.	Increase.	Decrease.
Passengers, parcels, mails, &c.......	£278,147 ..	£269,553 ..	£8,594 ..	....
Merchandise, minerals, & live stock	396,636 ..	378,535 ..	18,100 ..	....
Miscellaneous	6,948 ..	10,247 ..	.... ..	3,299
Total receipts................	£681,731 ..	£658,335 ..	£23,395 ..	....
Expenditure.....................	392,105 ..	383,646 ..	26,750 ..	£18,291
Less remuneration for working other lines.............................	7,978 ..	7,616 ..	361 ..	....
	£384,127 ..	£376,030 ..	£8,098 ..	....

The interest on debentures, temporary loans, prepaid calls, the expenses of loans, &c., and the interest on debenture stocks, amounted to 156,946*l.* The balance of revenue applicable to dividend was 131,406*l.*, and it was recommended that, in terms of the arrangement as to the interim division of gross receipts hereafter explained, the said sum, with the balance of 7*l.* from previous half-year, be credited by way of dividend on the several stocks enumerated in the net revenue statement. This absorbed 131,372*l.*; the balance of 41*l.* being carried forward. The circumstances of the company did not admit of these dividends being paid in cash, and they were, therefore, deferred, except on these stocks to which a lien is attached for the payment of the dividends secured to them.

The resolution declaring these several dividends was framed on the following terms: —"That in respect of the application of revenue receipts in payment of obligations on capital account, the dividends, less income-tax for the half-year ending 31st July last, on the following guaranteed and preference stocks be deferred—viz., on Granton preference stock, at the rate of 4*l.* per cent. per annum; on Monkland 6*l.* per cent. guaranteed stock, at the rate of 6*l.* per cent. per annum; on Monkland 5*l.* per cent. guaranteed stock, at the rate of 5*l.* per cent. per annum; on Monkland 4½ per cent. guaranteed stock, at the rate of 4*l.* 10*s.* per cent. per annum; on North British No. 1 guaranteed stock, at the rate of 5*l.* per cent. per annum; on Edinburgh Perth and Dundee second preference stock, at the rate of 4*l.* per cent. per annum; on Edinburgh and Glasgow No. 1 preference stock, at the rate of 5*l.* per cent. per annum; on North British No. 2 guaranteed stock, at the rate of 5*l.* per cent. per annum; on Border Union guaranteed stock, at the rate of 5*l*. 10*s*. per cent. per annum ; on North British guaranteed stock (1861) at the rate of 5*l*. per cent. per annum ; on Fife and Kinross preference stock, at the rate of 4*l*. 10*s*. per cent. per annum; on Edinburgh and Glasgow No. 2 preference stock, at the rate of 5*l*. per cent. per annum : on North British preference stock (1862), at the rate of 5*l*. per cent. per annum ; on North British 5 per cent. preference stock (1863), at the rate of 5*l*. per cent. per annum ; on Edinburgh and Glasgow 5 per cent. No. 3 preference stock, at the rate of 2*l*. 8*s*. per cent. per annum ; and that warrants, payable on advice from the company's office, be issued therefor, bearing interest at the rate of 4*l*. per cent. per annum, from the 30th day of September, 1868, until paid.

FINANCE.—In the Session of 1868, the company were authorised to abandon the lines and works aftermentioned, estimated to cost the sums stated opposite to each, viz.:— Forth Bridge (except a subsidiary connection, which will now be abandoned), 819,990*l*.; St. Margaret's diversion, 40,000*l*.; Dundee branches, 80,000*l*.; Lasswade branches, to the extent of 12,000*l*.; Devon Valley branches, to the extent of 74,000*l*.; Railway No. 4 of Camps Branch Act, 5,000*l*.; Railway No. 2 of General Powers Act of 1867, 28,988*l*.= 1,059,978*l*.; and the Glasgow and Coatbridge (authorised share capital, 280,000*l*.) is now being carried out in a modified form and on a principle which does not impose any additional burden on the revenues of the company. There are also other lines and works which the company are empowered to construct, but as the directors see no prospect of any of them being carried out within a reasonable time, they have resolved, unless the requisite capital shall, in the interim, be provided by local interests, to apply to Parliament in next Session to abandon the following, which were estimated to cost the respective amounts specified—Devon Valley branches, so far as not abandoned, 21,000*l*.; Lasswade branches, so far as not abandoned, 183,000*l*.; Glasgow branches and Stobcross branch, 301,012*l*.; Coatbridge branches, 1866, so far as not executed or contracted for, 40,000*l*.; Edinburgh Dunfermline and Perth, so far as not constructed, 250,000*l*.; Stirling branches, 81,000*l*.; new works, 1866, to the extent of 81,380*l*.; Langdale branch, 30,000*l*.=987,392*l*. The company are also authorised to improve and enlarge the Waverley station, Edinburgh ; to erect a station at the College, Glasgow ; to construct, at the joint expense of the Midland and North British, a goods station and access thereto, at Carlisle; and to execute other minor works. These works would involve an expenditure of from 250,000*l*. to 300,000*l*.; and, although the requirements of the traffic and other considerations justify the outlay, the circumstances of the company do not admit of the same being in every case carried out as originally intended.

DEFERRED WARRANTS.—In accordance with the pledge given in their report of last half-year the directors anxiously considered how the deferred dividend warrants can be liquidated, and the company placed in a position to admit of the future net earnings of the line being distributed among the shareholders with regularity. In pointing out how, in their opinion, this can best be effected, the directors would recal to the recollection of the shareholders the position in which the company was placed when they came into office two years ago. At that time, the committee of investigation reported that the financial affairs of the company were in confusion—that there were debts and current obligations to the amount of 1,875,625*l*. requiring to be immediately provided for, and that the company were under statutory obligation to construct new lines and works, involving an estimated outlay of a further sum of 2,600,000*l*. The directors have already explained the steps they have taken to obtain relief from the latter, and it therefore remains for them to point out how the amount constituting the debts and current obligations can be liquidated. In the last six months, the debts to the public have been reduced from 1,119,743*l*. to 566,348*l*., but until this sum can be cleared away, it would be inexpedient to resume cash dividends. The only course that appears open, therefore, is to apply the surplus revenue of the year to 31st July, 1869, estimated to amount to 260,000*l*., and which, with 110,294*l*. of unissued debentures, or together 370,294*l*., will place the debt at 31st July next, at the comparatively moderate amount of 196,053*l*. But while the company will thus be all but freed from debt to the public, they will stand indebted at 31st July, 1869, to the shareholders in about 800,000*l*.; and as the company have no resources from which this large amount can then be paid in cash, there is no other alternative but to convert the warrants into preference stock. This operation, although accompanied with inconvenience to many, the directors are convinced will ultimately prove beneficial to the shareholders generally. The only preference stock created which the directors can offer for the acceptance of the shareholders is the 1865 preference stock, of which 1,180,000*l*. is available. The present net earnings of the line, however, being insufficient to admit of a dividend on that stock, the directors propose, in place of issuing it in the first instance, to apply in next session for authority to cancel the uncreated share capital specially granted by Parliament in 1867, in substitution for other capital then applied for to liquidate the company's debts, and to issue in lieu of it a like amount of stock, to be designated "dividend stock," ranking (for seven years) immediately after the debenture stocks of the company, bearing 4 per cent. dividend until 31st July, 1876, when it shall be converted into the 5 per cent. 1865 preference stock at par, but with the option to the holders of effecting the conversion at an earlier date. The operation of the scheme on the revenue account will be as follows :—I. As under the present arrangement—interest at 4 per cent. (the rate fixed by the shareholders) on say 850,000*l*. of deferred dividends, and accrued interest as at 31st July, 1869—yearly from that date, 34,000*l*. II. As proposed—dividend on

350,000*l.* of dividend stock at 4 per cent.—yearly 34,000*l.*: or precisely the same charge on the revenue, and with no difference whatever in priority. It is impossible to overrate the advantages to the company which would result from the adoption of the scheme now submitted, and the directors therefore feel that they cannot too strongly urge the necessity that exists for the unanimous assent of the shareholders to it. The resumption of cash dividends will, in addition to improving the credit of the company, at once raise the value of all the preference stocks, and therefore a shareholder, in accepting dividend stock in payment of his deferred warrants, will receive not only a valuable and easily negotiable security, yielding a fair return, but he will have the further satisfaction of knowing that, in doing so, the market value of his holding is enhanced. With the view of carrying the scheme into effect, the directors are applying for Parliamentary sanction, the bill for which having been submitted to a meeting on 23rd December, and carried by a large majority.

JOINT-PURSE WITH CALEDONIAN.—The details of this arrangement were given in the ADDENDA to the Volume for 1868. On this subject the directors reported as follows, in September :—" Proportion of the joint traffic receipts of the Caledonian and North British to be drawn by each company, under the joint-purse agreement of 16th January last, has not yet been finally ascertained, but it is in course of adjustment. In the meantime, by arrangement between the two boards, the actual receipts earned on each line for the half-year to 31st July last are given in the respective revenue accounts ; but it is understood that neither company shall be in the slightest degree prejudiced by this interim arrangement when the provisions of the agreement come to be applied. Under the direction of the joint-committee, and by the united action and good mutual understanding of the companies' officers, the traffic is being satisfactorily conducted. Unless the shareholders of either company desire otherwise, it is proposed to postpone to a future session application to Parliament for sanction of the joint-working agreement. The directors of both companies concur in recommending the postponement."

DEBENTURE STOCK.—At a special meeting held on 30th September, 1868, it was resolved :—

That, in pursuance of the Acts relating to the company, First-Class Debenture Stock to the amount of 1,000,000*l.* be now created, and that the same be issued and applied in discharge and liquidation of an equivalent amount of outstanding debentures ranking prior to those authorised by the North British (Financial Arrangements) Act, 1867, and which debenture stock shall be entitled, in perpetuity, to a fixed rate of interest of 4*l.* 10*s.* per cent. per annum, payable half-yearly.

That the said debenture stock be allotted to the shareholders at par, and that the same be payable in instalments, as follows :—

10*l.* per cent. on 11th November, 1868,
30*l.* per cent. on 15th May, 1869,
30*l.* per cent. on 11th November, 1869,
30*l.* per cent. on 15th May, 1870,

with the option to the allottees at any time to anticipate instalments.

That in the event of any portion of such stock not being taken up, the directors be authorised to dispose of the same at such times, on such terms, and in such manner as they may think best for the benefit of the company.

CITY OF GLASGOW UNION.—At a special meeting on 20th August, 1868, it was resolved :—

That a Proposed Minute of Agreement between the City of Glasgow Union Railway Company, of the first part, and the North British Railway Company, of the second part, varying the authorised arrangements for constructing the lines of the City of Glasgow Union and Glasgow and Coatbridge Railways, eastward of the College at Glasgow, having been submitted to the meeting, the same be, and is hereby approved, under the express stipulation that the North British are to become joint owners with the City of Glasgow Union of the lines of railway above referred to, situate between certain points in the City of Glasgow, near to Hunter Street and Sword Street, and that it be remitted to the directors to carry the same into effect.

That a Proposed Minute of Agreement between the City of Glasgow Union, of the first part ; the Glasgow and South Western, of the second part ; the North British, of the third part ; and Messrs. Thomas Brassey, John Kelk, and Charles Waring, of the City of London, Contractors, of the fourth part—providing for the completion of the City of Glasgow Union—having been submitted to the meeting, the same be, and is hereby approved, subject to such further conditions and stipulations as the directors may consider proper, and that it be remitted to them, in conjunction with the other parties to the agreement, to execute the same. [For these agreements see APPENDIX to the present volume.]

COATBRIDGE.—At the same meeting it was also resolved :—

1. That the Articles of Arrangement adjusted between the North British, of the first part, and the committee referred to in the subscription lists of the subscribers to shares in the Coatbridge undertaking of the North British, of the second part, dated the 27th day of March and 20th and 21st days of April, 1868, having been submitted to the meeting, be, and the same are hereby approved, subject to the modifications thereon

with respect to the restriction of the capital, and the extension of time for constructing the works, as explained in the directors' report, dated 6th August current ; and to the end of carrying into effect such Articles of Arrangement, the meeting further resolve that, in pursuance of the North British (Financial Arrangements) Act, 1867, and the North British (General Powers) Act, 1868, the Railways and Works authorised by the Edinburgh and Glasgow (Coatbridge Branch) Act, 1855, subject to the variations authorised by the City of Glasgow Union Act, 1867, or agreed to with the City of Glasgow Union, and subject also to the abandonment, under the said Act second above recited, of a portion of the Railway, No. 1, in the said Act third above recited, shall, within the meaning, and for the purposes of the said Acts first and second above recited, be, and the same are hereby, constituted a separate undertaking, under the name of "The Coatbridge Undertaking."

2. That, whereas the estimated amount of the capital required for the said undertaking is 200,000*l.*, this meeting, in further pursuance of the said Articles of Arrangement, and of the North British (Financial Arrangements) Act, 1867, and the North British (General Powers) Act, 1868, do hereby cancel 200,000*l.*, unissued, of the 1,614,810*l.* of preference stock created by the company on 12th October, 1865, and authorise the directors to re-issue the same in shares of 10*l.* each, as capital for the Coatbridge undertaking, in terms of the said Acts, or either of them.

3. That a proposed agreement between the subscribers to the Coatbridge undertaking, of the first part, and the North British, of the second part, following upon the said Articles of Arrangement, and providing for the subscription of the capital for the said undertaking, having been submitted to the meeting, the same be, and is hereby, approved, and that it be remitted to the directors to carry the same into effect, subject to such additions or alterations as they may approve of, and that the directors be empowered to affix the Corporate Seal of the company to the agreement then concluded.

CAPITAL.—The receipts and expenditure on this account to 31st July, 1868, have been detailed as follows :—

Receipts.—North British ordinary	£2,758,931
Border Union ordinary	98,222
Edinburgh Perth and Dundee, ordinary, including Fife and Kinross ordinary	1,327,266
Stirlingshire Midland preference 5½ per cent.	150,000
Granton preference, 4 per cent.	95,925
Monkland 6 per cent. guaranteed	55,000
Monkland 5 per cent. guaranteed	90,000
Monkland 4½ per cent. guaranteed	2,950
North British guaranteed, No. 1, 5 per cent., including Selkirk preference	783,080
Edinburgh Perth and Dundee second preference, 4 per cent.	549,641
Stirling and Dunfermline, 4 per cent.	450,000
Edinburgh and Glasgow No. 1 preference, 5 per cent.	275,000
North British guaranteed, No. 2, 5 per cent.	223,128
Border Union guaranteed 5½ per cent.	391,591
Jedburgh preference, 4 per cent.	30,580
Kinross-shire preference, 5 per cent.	39,470
North British 10*l.* guaranteed (1861) 5 per cent	295,415
Fife and Kinross preference	46,660
Edinburgh and Glasgow No. 2 preference, 5 per cent.	404,092
West of Fife ordinary, converted into 5 per cent. preference, in terms of Amalgamation Act (1862)	115,940
North British 5*l.* preference (1862), 5 per cent.	325,160
North British 12*l.* 10*s.* preference (1863), 5 per cent.	782,659
Wansbeck preference, 3¾ and 4 per cent.	59,695
Edinburgh and Glasgow No. 3 preference, 5 per cent.	555,083
Monkland ordinary, converted into 6 per cent. preference, in terms of Amalgamation Act, 1865	563,379
Edinburgh and Glasgow ordinary, converted into preference in terms of Amalgamation Act, 1865	2,419,572
North British preference shares (1865), 5*l.* per cent. £114,740	
Do. do. do. second issue.......... 55,055=	169,795
Leadburn preference	20,291
	£13,078,528
Debenture stock, 3½ per cent £45,000	
Debenture stock, 4 per cent. 122,146	
Debenture stock, B, 5 per cent 400,679	
	£567,825
Loans on mortgage ....4,590,015=	5,157,811
(Balance to issue, 26,615*l.*)	
Loans on Mortgage, Financial Act, 1867	760,170
(Balance to issue, 83,679*l.*)	
Balance	609,924
	£19,606,464

Expenditure.—Preliminary and parliamentary	£837,377
Interest to shareholders, and interest on loans during construction of works,&c.	562,244
Land and compensation, including cost of ferries and Union canal	3,074,478
Construction of line and stations, including engineering and general expenses	10,150,847
Rolling stock	2,482,656
Ferry stock	161,691
Loss on Tyne Valley, Border Counties, and Edinburgh Perth and Dundee stocks, including purchase of stock on other lines, and unallocated expenditure	986,622
Port Carlisle and Silloth	53,309
Galashiels and Peebles	179,505
Monktonhall and Ormiston Branches	175,505
Edinburgh Dunfermline and Perth	244,420
Queensferry branch	166,497
Stobcross branch	88,580
Bridge of Forth and Railways	40,999
Leadburn Linton and Dolphinton	47,815
	£19,252,553

Lines in which the company have an interest :—	
Berwickshire	78,627
Blane Valley	47,892
Glasgow City Union	201,764
Devon Valley	25,626
	£19,606,464

The accounts are made up to 31st January and 31st July ; and the statutory meetings held in Edinburgh, London, or elsewhere, in February or March, and August or September in each year.

Scale of Voting.—One vote for 50*l.* up to 500*l.* ; then one vote additional for every 200*l.* up to 10,000*l.* ; then one vote additional thereafter for every 500*l.* No voting in respect of debenture stock.

Certificates must accompany transfer deed. Registration fee, 2*s.* 6*d.* each deed, and each seller on the deed.

No. of Directors.—Maximum, 15 ; minimum, 6. *Qualification,* 1,000*l.* stock. Allowance, 4,100*l.*

DIRECTORS :

Chairman—JOHN STIRLING, Esq., Kippendavie, Dunblane, Perthshire.

Deputy-Chairman—JOHN BEAUMONT, Esq., Ravensknowle, Huddersfield.

William P. Adam, Esq., M.P., Blairadam, and 2, Ennismere Place, W.
Robert Orr Campbell, Esq., of Crosslet, Dumbartonshire.
Peter Garnett, Esq.,Thornton Hall, Bedale, Yorkshire.
George Harrison, Esq., Merchant, Edinburgh.
Alexander Harvie, Esq., Glasgow.
Alexander Crombie Matthew, Esq., M.D., Aberdeen.
William Muir, Esq., Leith.

Francis Maxwell, Esq., St. Vincent Place, Glasgow.
William Miller, Esq., of Manderston, Berwickshire.
George Robertson, Esq., W.S., 17, Royal Circus, Edinburgh.
John Ronald, Esq., S.S.C., 20, Hill Street, Edinburgh.
John. J. Stitt, Esq., Merchant, Liverpool.
Robert Young, Esq., 107, Buchanan Street, Glasgow.

OFFICERS.—Gen. Man., S. L. Mason. Sec., John Walker. Cashier, J. Macdonald. Accountant, George Simpson. Audit Accountant, David Anderson. Registrar, A. B. Scott. Eng., James Bell, Edinburgh. District Res. Engs.,William Barrie, Burntisland; Robert Bell, Portobello; Charles Boyd, Carlisle ; and James Deas, Glasgow. Gen. Goods Man., P. Mac Pherson, George Square, Glasgow. District Goods Mans., William Hardie, Edinburgh, and William Peat, Dundee. Gen. Pass. Supt., James M'Laren, Edinburgh. Loco. Supt., Thomas Wheatley, Cowlairs, Glasgow. Auditors, Walter Mackenzie and J. Wyllie Guild, Accountants, Glasgow. Solicitor, Adam Johnstone, Edinburgh.
Head Offices—Canal Street, Edinburgh.

299.—NORTH EASTERN.

The company originally comprised the York Newcastle and Berwick, the York and North Midland, Leeds Northern, and Malton and Driffield companies amalgamated in 1854, but other companies have been amalgamated with it at different times since that date, more particularly the Newcastle and Carlisle, in 1862, the Stockton and Darlington, 1863, and the West Hartlepool and Cleveland companies in 1865. Productive miles, 1,254.

The following particulars refer to the undertakings which have been amalgamated since 1854 :—

HARTLEPOOL DOCK AND RAILWAY.—Incorporated by 2 and 3 Wm. IV., cap. 67, for docks at Hartlepool, a line thereto, with branches to collieries ; length, 16 miles. Opened 1st July, 1835, and dock and tide harbour, 40 acres. Under provisions of an Act of 1848 (11 and 12 Vic., cap. 81), this undertaking was leased to the York Newcastle and Berwick for 31 years, from 1st July, 1848, with a provision that after the expiration of the lease, or sooner, if thought proper, the companies shall amalgamate. This amalgamation was effected in 1857. The rent payable up to 1879 is 8 per cent. on the share capital of 440,570l., together with interest on the company's mortgage debt, and after 1879 the Hartlepool shareholders will receive the same dividend as the Berwick.

NORTH YORKSHIRE AND CLEVELAND.—Incorporated by 17 and 18 Vic., cap. 151 (10th July, 1854). The line originally authorised was to commence at the Grosmont station of the Whitby and Pickering, and proceed westward along the vale of Esk, Fryupdale, Danby Dale, Westerdale, Stokesley, and through the Whorlton hills, all abounding in ironstone, to Picton, near Yarm, and thus secure communication with the North Eastern main line. The portion between Picton and Castleton was first constructed, and the continuation from Castleton to Grosmont was opened in October, 1865 (see below). By 18 and 19 Vic., cap. 116 (July 2nd, 1855), the company obtained authority to construct a branch to Guisboro' of about five miles, to unite the main line with Middlesbro' and the iron works there, also a branch of two miles to bring the ironstone from Whorlton to the main line. By 21 and 22 Vic., cap. 134 (23rd July, 1865), the company was authorised to purchase the Ingleby branch ; to construct the Rosedale branch ; and to enter into traffic arrangements with, or to sell the line to, the North Eastern. Under the powers of the last mentioned Act, the North Eastern purchased the North Yorkshire and Cleveland, and took possession of it on 1st January, 1859. By 22 and 23 Vic., cap. 91, the North Eastern had the power to construct the Rosedale Branch transferred to them. That branch was opened in April, 1861.

BEDALE AND LEYBURN.—Incorporated by 17 Vic., cap. 137 (4th August, 1853), for a line from Bedale branch of York Newcastle and Berwick to Leyburn. Opened November 2nd, 1856. By 22 and 23 Vic., cap. 91, the Bedale and Leyburn was amalgamated with the North Eastern, and the Bedale capital has been merged into the North Eastern 4 per cent. stock.

DEARNESS VALLEY.—Incorporated by 18 and 19 Vic., cap. 180 (July 30th, 1855), for making a line from the Bishop Auckland Branch of the North Eastern to the Stanley branch of the Stockton and Darlington. The North Eastern purchased the line, which was opened on 1st January, 1858.

HULL AND HOLDERNESS.—Incorporated by 17 Vic., cap. 93 (8th July, 1852), for a line from Hull to Withernsea. Opened 27th June, 1854. Dissolved by 25 and 26 Vic., cap. 120 (7th July, 1862), and vested in the North Eastern at 4 per cent.

NEWCASTLE AND CARLISLE.—Incorporated by 10 Geo. IV., cap. 72 (22nd May, 1829), for a line between these towns, crossing from the east to the west coast of England ; also, a branch of 12 miles to Alston and a short branch to Redheugh. By 25 and 26 Vic., cap. 145 (17th July, 1862), the Newcastle and Carlisle was amalgamated with the North Eastern on the same principle as the amalgamation of 1854. The Carlisle section of shareholders now receives 8·58 per cent. of the joint net revenue of the whole North Eastern.

STOCKTON AND DARLINGTON.—By 26 and 27 Vic., cap. 122 (13th July, 1863), the Stockton and Darlington was amalgamated with the North Eastern, the Darlington section of shareholders receiving 13·90 of the joint net revenue. Provision is made for certain matters more particularly affecting that section, and for the traffic of the Darlington district being managed for a period of years by a committee consisting of ten members appointed by the Darlington section, and two by North Eastern ; three of the Darlington directors having, also, seats at the North Eastern board.

WEST HARTLEPOOL.—An incorporation by Act 16 Vic., cap. 142 (30th June, 1852), of the Stockton and Hartlepool, Clarence and Hartlepool, and the Hartlepool West Harbour and Docks. By 20 and 21 Vic., cap. 43 (13th July, 1857), the company was authorised to convert loans into debentures or preference stock, and to exchange or substitute by consent any existing shares or stocks for other shares or stocks, and to provide additional capital for securing increased traffic and benefiting the undertaking. By 24 and 25 Vic., cap. 249, the authorised capital was altered to 2,100,000l. in shares, and 700,000l. on loan. By 26 and 27 Vic., cap. 154 (13th July, 1863), the whole financial constitution of the company was remodelled ; and by Act of 1865 the West Hartlepool was amalgamated with the North Eastern, as from 30th June, 1865, on the following terms :—That the North Eastern shall substitute for the West Hartlepool classes A and B stocks a corresponding amount of North Eastern preferential stock, carrying a perpetual guaranteed dividend at the rate of 4l. per cent. per annum, from 1st July, 1868, with intermediate guaranteed dividends for the year commencing 1st July, 1865, at 3l. 5s., for the year commencing 1st July, 1866, at 3l. 10s., and for the year commencing 1st July, 1867, at 3l. 15s. per cent. per annum.

CLEVELAND.—Incorporated by 21 and 22 Vic., cap. 114 (23rd July, 1858), to construct railways from Guisbrough to Skinningrove, and other places in the North Riding. Capital, 120,000*l.* in 50*l.* shares; loans, 40,000*l.* By Act of 1865, the Cleveland was amalgamated with the North Eastern, at 5½ per cent., with option to either shareholders or company to redeem the shares at 122*l.* 5*s.* per cent.

HULL AND HORNSEA.—Incorporated by 25 and 26 Vic., cap. 100 (30th June, 1862), to construct a line from the North Eastern, near Hull, to Hornsea. Length, 13 miles. Capital, 70,000*l.* in 10*l.* shares. Opened 28th March, 1864. By 29 and 30 Vic., cap. 187 (16th July, 1866), the Hull and Hornsea was amalgamated with the North Eastern. A separate account is kept of the receipts, &c., of this section in terms of the arrangement.

METHLEY.—By 27 and 28 Vic., cap. 55 (23rd June, 1864), the North Eastern and the Lancashire and Yorkshire were each auhorised to subscribe 25,000*l.* towards the Methley branch of the West Yorkshire, so that the share capital of 75,000*l.* required for that branch shall be provided in equal proportions by the three companies. This line is opened for traffic.

NEW WORKS.—The company have obtained powers to construct the following new lines and works since 1854 :—

TYNE DOCK.—This Dock (at Jarrow, near South Shields), was opened on March 3rd, 1859, having been completed in little more than three years. The water area covers 48 acres, and it possesses capabilities for the shipment of coal unequalled in any other dock in the United Kingdom, and accommodation has also been provided for general merchandise traffic.

LANCHESTER VALLEY.—By 20 and 21 Vic., cap. 46 (13th July, 1857), the company obtained powers to construct this line (12 miles) at an estimated cost of 120,000*l.* New capital, 120,000*l.* Opened 1st September, 1862.

NIDD VALLEY.—By 22 and 23 Vic., cap. 10 (21st July, 1859), the North Eastern was authorised to construct this branch at a cost of 90,000*l.* Opened 1st May, 1862.

HARROGATE BRANCHES.—By 22 and 23 Vic., cap. 100 (8th August, 1859), the North Eastern was empowered to construct branches to connect the Leeds and Thirsk, and the Church Fenton and Harrogate. New capital, 100,000*l.* Opened 1st August, 1862.

CASTLETON AND GROSMONT, &c.—By 24 and 25 Vic., cap. 135 (11th July, 1861), the company was authorised to extend, and thereby to complete, the Cleveland line from Castleton to Grosmont, on the Pickering and Whitby line ; and also to deviate part of the Whitby line, in order to avoid the incline at Goathland, and convert the Whitby branch into a locomotive line throughout. Capital, 180,000*l.* in shares, and 60,000*l.* on loan. Opened on 1st August, 1865.

OTLEY AND ILKLEY.—By 24 and 25 Vic., cap. 141 (11th July, 1861), the company was authorised to construct a line between Arthington and Otley, and also in conjunction with the Midland, to construct a joint line from Otley to Ilkley. Capital, 135,000*l.* in shares, and 45,000*l.* on loan. Opened on 1st August, 1864.

MARKET WEIGHTON AND BEVERLEY.—By 25 and 26 Vic., cap. 85 (30th June, 1862), the company was empowered to construct a branch from Market Weighton to Beverley, and a short curve line at Hull ; new capital, 88,000*l.* in shares, and 29,300*l.* on loan. Opened 1st May, 1864.

BLAYDON AND CONSIDE.—By 25 and 26 Vic., cap. 146 (17th July, 1862), the North Eastern was authorised to construct a branch between Blaydon and Conside. Capital, 165,000*l.* in shares, and 55,000*l.* on loan. Opened 2nd December, 1867.

TEAM VALLEY.—By 25 and 26 Vic., cap. 154 (17th July, 1862), the company was authorised to construct the Team Valley and a short branch at Bishop Wearmouth. New line, capital, 200,000*l.* in shares, and 96,000*l.* on loan. The Bishop Wearmouth branch was opened 1st October, 1865. The Team Valley was opened December 1st, 1868.

NEWCASTLE QUAY BRANCH.—By 26 and 27 Vic., cap. 221 (28th July, 1863), the North Eastern was authorised to construct a branch to the Quay at Newcastle. Length, 1 mile, with other works in connection therewith. New capital, 56,000*l.* in shares, and 18,000*l.* on loan. Works nearly completed.

HULL AND DONCASTER.—By 26 and 27 Vic., cap. 238 (28th July, 1863), the North Eastern was authorised to construct a line from Staddlethorpe, on the Hull and Selby, to Thorne, on the South Yorkshire. Running powers to Lancashire and Yorkshire and South Yorkshire. Length, 14½ miles. New capital, 310,000*l*. in shares, and 103,000*l*. on loan. Works nearly finished.

CHURCH FENTON, &c.—By 27 Vic., cap. 20 (13th May, 1864), a branch was sanctioned between Church Fenton and Micklefield. Length, 4 miles. Capital, 80,000*l* in shares, and 26,000*l*. on loan. The object of this line is to improve the connection between York and Leeds. Works completed, and line will shortly be opened.

YORK AND DONCASTER.—By 27 and 28 Vic., cap. 49 (24th June, 1864), the company obtained power to construct a line from York to near Doncaster. Length, 27 miles. Capital, 330,000*l*. in shares, and 110,000*l*. on loan. Running powers conceded to Great Northern. This line will shorten and improve the East Coast line of communication. Works in progress.

CLEVELAND BRANCHES.—By 28 and 29 Vic., cap, 363 (5th July, 1865), the company was authorised to construct six short branches, about 7¼ miles in length. Capital, 129,000*l*. in shares, and 43,000*l*. in loan. Not commenced.

LEEDS EXTENSION.—By 28 and 29 Vic., cap. 251 (5th July, 1865), the company was authorised to construct a short extension through the town of Leeds. Length, 1¼ mile. Capital, 150,000*l*. in shares, and 50,000*l*. on loan. Works nearly completed.

LEEDS NEW CENTRAL STATION.—By 28 and 29 Vic., cap. 267 (5th July, 1865), the North Eastern and the London and North Western were authorised to construct a central station at Leeds. New capital to each company, 100,000*l*. in shares, and 33,000*l*. on mortgage. This station will shortly be opened.

PELAW BRANCH, &c.—By 28 and 29 Vic., cap. 368 (5th July, 1865), the company was authorised to construct a line from Pelaw to South Shields, and to extend the Team Valley line to a point on the present main line near Ferryhill. Length, 17¾ miles. New capital, 320,000*l*. in shares, and 106,000*l*. on mortgage. The Pelaw branch not yet commenced, but the Team Valley Extension is in progress.

GILLING AND PICKERING.—By 22 Vic., cap, 10 (18th May, 1866), the company was authorised to construct a line from Gilling to Helmsley and Pickering, Length, 16¾ miles. Capital, 280,000*l*. in shares, and 93,000*l*. on loan.

DURHAM.—By 29 Vic., cap. 11 (18th May, 1866), the company was authorised to acquire additional lands; to establish a timber pond at Hartlepool Slake, and to construct five small branches in the county of Durham. Length, 3½ miles. Capital, for these works and for general purposes, 1,133,000*l*. in shares, and 377,000*l*. on loan.

YORKSHIRE.—By 29 and 30 Vic., cap. 251 (23rd July, 1866), the company was authorised to construct a new station, &c., at York; also a line from Knaresboro' to Boroughbridge, and certain short lines in various parts of Yorkshire, all in connection with its existing system, as well as purchase additional lands. Length, 11½ miles. New capital for these works and for general purposes, 1,370,000*l*. in shares, and 456,000*l*. on loan. None of these works are commenced.

LEEDS AND WETHERBY.—By 29 and 30 Vic,, cap. 295 (30th July, 1866), the company obtained power to construct a line from the Leeds and Selby, at Austhorpe, to the Church Fenton and Harrogate branch at Wetherby. Length, 10¾ miles. Capital, 210,000*l*. in shares, and 70,000*l*. on loan. Not commenced.

AMALGAMATION PROPORTIONS.—The amalgamation with the Carlisle and Darlington having added their revenues to those of the North Eastern, a re-adjustment of the proportions of joint net receipts due to the several sections of the united company became necessary. These proportions, which will in future regulate the division of the joint receipts, represent in their results precisely those previously agreed upon, and have been fixed by the Stockton and Darlington Amalgamation Act, as follows:— Berwick section, 44·10; York, 25·41; Leeds, 7·72; Malton, ·29; Carlisle, 8·58; Darlington, 13·90.

By 20 and 21 Vic., cap. 19 (3rd July, 1857), the company was authorised to cancel unissued and forfeited shares, and to create new shares in lieu thereof. This arrangement was considered a natural and proper sequence to the Amalgamation Act, giving the united company the unexercised powers previously possessed by the Berwick, York, Leeds, and Malton respectively. These powers were exercised in August, 1862.

REVENUE —The receipts for the half-year ending the 31st of December amounted to 2,036,165*l*., against 1,964,442*l*. in the corresponding six months of 1866, showing an increase of 71,723*l*. The working expenses, including rates and taxes, amounted to 1,001,366*l*. against 961,047*l*., showing an increase of 40,319*l*. The net receipts for the half-year were 1,034,799*l*., against 1,003,395*l*., showing an increase of 31,404*l* After providing for interest on the debenture debt, rents of leased lines, and dividends on all classes of preference stocks and shares, the following balances remained to the credit of the different sections :—Out of 242,725*l*. on the Berwick account, a dividend at the rate of 6 per cent. per annum left a balance of 1,016*l*. ; out of 95,061*l*. on York account, 5½ per cent., left a balance of 3,335*l*. ; out of 25,418*l*. on Leeds account, 3½ per cent. per annum, left a balance of 1,016*l*.; out of 50,172*l*. on Carlisle account, 8 per cent., left a balance of 972*l*.; out of 82,717*l*. on Darlington account, 8¼ per cent. per annum, left 322*l*.; and out of 1,106*l*. on Thirsk and Malton account, 4 per cent., left a balance of 106*l*.

The receipts for the half-year ending the 30th of June, were 1,821,025*l*. on 1,246 miles, against 1,800,437*l*. on 1,228 miles, showing an increase of 20,588*l*. The working expenses, taxes, &c., amounted to 903,489*l*., against 872,923*l*., showing an increase of 30,566*l*. After providing for interest on borrowed capital, for rents of leased lines, and dividends on all classes of preference stocks and shares, the following balances remained to the credit of the different sections—viz., on Berwick account a balance of 183,749*l*, and a dividend at the rate of 4½ per cent. per annum, left 1,775*l*. ; on York account a balance of 61,377*l*., 3¾ per cent., leaving 999*l*. ; on the Leeds account, 15,410*l*., 2½ per cent. per annum, 595*l*. ; on Carlisle account, 38,182*l*., a dividend at the rate of 6¼ per cent., leaving 400*l*. ; on Darlington account, 65,291*l*., a dividend of 6½ per cent., leaving 360*l*. ; and on Thirsk and Malton account, 1,048*l*., a dividend at the rate of 4 per cent., leaving 48*l*.

LIABILITIES.—The directors reported in February last that the amount of capital to be expended during the years 1868 and 1869 would not, in all probability, exceed 1,500,000*l*., and that if the directors succeeded in their applications for extension of time, or for power to abandon the schemes specified, the expenditure after 1869, to which the company was pledged, would be comparatively light. That although the new capital (1,500,000*l*.) to be expended during 1868 and 1869 would, it raised at 5 per cent., throw an additional charge of 75,000*l*. on the revenue of subsequent years, and require an increase of gross traffic of 150,000*l*. to meet it, the increase of revenue for five years had been on the average 198,000*l*. per annum, and should the traffic on the existing lines increase at half that rate during 1868 and 1869 the receipts (even if the new lines and works should contribute nothing to the available revenue) would more than suffice to pay the above charge of 75,000*l*., without diminishing the net balance available for ordinary dividends, so that the shareholders might be satisfied that the further liabilities on capital account were not such as to cause anxiety or alarm.

NEW STOCK.—The directors also reported in February that since the previous half-yearly meeting they had further exercised the powers given them on the 19th of February, 1867, and had created 633,000*l*. additional 5 per cent. preference stock, which, with the 500,000*l*. previously created, completed the share capital (1,133,000*l*.) authorised by the " County of Durham Lines Act, 1866." Of this amount, 941,865*l*. had been issued to the present time, and the remainder would be allotted to those shareholders who might apply for it. The directors further reported in August, that since the February meeting the directors had created 510,000*l*. five per cent. preference stock, being part of the capital authorised by the "Yorkshire Lines Act, 1866." Of this new capital, 420,890*l*. had been issued, and the remainder would be allotted as occasion required.

POSTPONEMENT, &c.—At a special meeting, held on the 16th October, 1868, it was resolved;—" That no money be expended in respect of the construction of the York station and railway, the doubling of the railway from Pilmoor to Gilling, or the Hawes and Melmerby, without an express vote of the shareholders."

" That the directors endeavour to make arrangements with the landowners and others interested in the Gilling and Pickering, Knaresborough and Boroughbridge, and Leeds and Wetherby branches, with the view to diminishing the cost of their construction, and do apply to Parliament for an extension of the time within which those branches are required to be made, and for its sanction to any alteration that may be found desirable, the construction of these branches and of the Pilmoor branch being proceeded with at such times as the directors think proper."

" That the directors be authorised to proceed with the improvements in the dock at Middlesborough, as recommended in the last half-yearly report, involving an outlay of 90,000*l*.

CAPITAL.—This account to 30th June showed that 39,917,820*l.* had been expended, leaving a balance of 138,809*l.* The receipts were given as follows:—

Berwick capital stock	£9,271,044
York	3,887,675
Leeds	1,736,746
Carlisle	1,460,000
Malton	159,801
Thirsk and Malton	50,000
Darlington	4,032,891
Ditto 4½ per cent. debenture stock	133,220
Hornsea	62,483
North Eastern preferential stocks—	
4 per cent.	482,821
4½ per cent.	2,665,441
5 per cent.	2,418,875
West Hartlepool	2,788,818
Cleveland	10,900
West Hartlepool primary charges—shares	251,480
Ditto ditto —loans	59,164
Debentures	10,194,281
North Eastern 4 per cent. debenture stock	201,027
Ditto 4½ per cent. ditto	219,962
	£40,056,629

DEBENTURE STOCK.—At a special meeting, held on 20th February, 1868, it was resolved:—" That under the powers of 'The York and North Midland (Victoria Dock) Act, 1852,' 'The North Eastern Act, 1854,' and 'The Company's Act, 1867,' this meeting sanctions and authorizes an increase in the rate of dividend or interest on such amounts of the unissued North Eastern debenture stock, authorised to be created at the special meeting of the company held on the 22nd day of February, 1856, as the directors may from time to time determine, and hereby guarantees and attaches thereto, in lieu of the dividend or interest of 4*l.* per cent. per annum attached to the said debenture stock by the company at that meeting, a fixed preference dividend or interest not exceeding the rate of 4*l.* 10*s.* per cent. per annum, to be payable and paid at the same time and in the same manner as the dividend or interest on the North Eastern debenture stock already issued; and this meeting authorises the issue of such amounts of the said unissued stock as the directors may from time to time determine, on the terms last aforesaid, and declares that the debenture stock already issued under the resolution passed at the special meeting of the company, held on the 19th day of November last, shall be treated and considered as if the same had been issued by the directors under the authority of this resolution, with a fixed preference dividend of 4*l.* 10*s.* per cent. per annum."

No. of Directors.—Maximum, 21; minimum, 15, during continuance of Darlington committee, and afterwards not less than 12. *Qualification*, 1,000*l.* in stock or shares.

DIRECTORS:

Chairman—HARRY STEPHEN THOMPSON, Esq., Kirby Hall, York.

Deputy-Chairman—GEORGE LEEMAN, Esq., York, and 7, Dean's Yard, Westminster, S.W.

Isaac Lowthian Bell, Esq., The Hall, Washington.

William Charles Copperthwaite, Esq,, The Lodge, Malton.

George Dodsworth, Esq., Clifton, York.

John Fogg Elliot, Esq., Elvet Hill, Durham.

George Fenwick, Esq., Bywell Hall, Stocksfield-on Tyne.

James Hartley, Esq., Ashbrook, Sunderland.

William Rutherford Hunter, Esq., Lovaine Crescent, Newcastle.

James Kitson, Esq., Elmete Hall, Leeds.

Harcourt Johnstone, Esq., Hackness Grange, near Scarborough.

Alfred Kitching, Esq., Elm Field, Darlington.

Henry Oxley, Esq., Weetwood, Leeds.

Samuel Priestman, Esq., East Mount, Hull.

Henry Pease, Esq., Pierremont, Darlington.

Joseph Whitwell Pease, Esq., M.P., Hutton Hall, Guisbro', and 18, Prince's Gardens, W.

George Hicks Seymour, Esq., Clifton, York.

Isaac Wilson, Esq., Nunthorpe Hall, Middlesborough.

OFFICERS.—Gen. Man., William O'Brien, York. Sec., John Cleghorn, York. Eng.-in-Chief, Thomas E. Harrison, Newcastle-on-Tyne. Engs., Southern Division, Thomas Cabry, York; Northern Division, John Bourne, Newcastle-on-Tyne. Goods Man., James Wilson, York. Gen. Passenger Supt., Alexander Christison, York. Mineral Traffic Managers, Southern Division, R. W. Bailey, York; Northern Division, J. G. Quelch, Newcastle-on-Tyne. Supt. of Newcastle and Carlisle Section, H. Smiles, Newcastle-on-Tyne. Supt. of West Hartlepool Section, W. S. Leng, West Hartlepool. Accountant, Henry Tennant, Newcastle-on-Tyne. Solicitors, Richardson, Gutch, and Co., York, and Newton, Robinson, and Brown, York. Auditors, A. H. Wylie, Edinburgh, and J. R. Bywater, Leeds.

Head Offices—York; Accountant's Office, Newcastle-on-Tyne.

300.—NORTH KENT EXTENSION.

Incorporated by 28 and 29 Vic., cap. 375 (6th July, 1865), to construct a line from the North Kent branch of the South Eastern, at Denton, to a point in the Isle of Grain, on the banks of the Medway, opposite Sheerness, with a pier there. Length, 15¾ miles. Capital, 120,000*l.* in shares, and 40,000*l.* on loan.

No. of Directors—4; quorum, 3.   *Qualification*, 250*l.*

DIRECTORS:

Colonel Charles Robert Wynne, Jermyn | Octavius Ommaney, Esq., Great George
Street, W. | Street, Westminster, S.W.

Brinsley De C. Nixon, Esq., St. James's Terrace, Harrow Road, N.W.

OFFICERS.—Solicitors, Edwards and Co., 8, Delahay Street, Westminster, S.W.; Engs., John Wright, Park Street, Westminster, S.W., and Joseph Kincaid, 20, Spring Gardens, S.W.

301.—NORTH LONDON.

Incorporated by 9 and 10 Vic., cap. 396 (26th August, 1846), for making a railway from London and North Western goods station, at Camden Town, to West India Docks, at Blackwall; and authorised by Act of 1850 to make a branch to Blackwall Extension, near Bow. Traverses the northern and eastern suburbs of London, and by junctions with the Great Northern, Eastern Counties, and the Blackwall, at Stepney, passes into the heart of the city, and to the steam packet wharf at Blackwall.

Act 17 Vic., cap. 97 (8th July, 1853), authorised 250,000*l.* further capital, in 10*l.* shares, to be offered to old shareholders ; and loans, 83,000*l.* after half paid up. Debentures may be converted into stock, *maximum*, 4 per cent.

By Acts 17 and 18 Vic., cap. 80 (3rd July, 1854), the company was enabled to construct a station, or depôt, and sidings, near to the new metropolitan cattle market.

By 23 Vic., cap. 14 (15th May, 1860), the company was authorised to purchase additional land for widening and otherwise improving a portion of their railway, length, 50 chains, in the parish of St. Pancras ; and for that purpose, and for general purposes, to raise 150,000*l.* by new shares, and 50,000*l.* by mortgage.

By 24 and 25 Vic., cap. 132 (11th July, 1861), the company was authorised to widen various portions of the railway. New capital, 100,000*l.* in shares, and 33,300*l.* on loan.

By 24 and 25 Vic., cap. 196 (22nd July, 1861), the company was authorised to construct a line from Kingsland station to Liverpool Street, in the city of London. Length, 2 miles. New capital, 1,000,000*l.* in shares, and 233,000*l.* by loan. London and North Western take 300,000*l.*, and arrangements authorised by which that company are to erect a station in the city, or to lease the same from the North London. Opened 1st November, 1865.

By 27 and 28 Vic., cap. 246 (25th July, 1864), the company obtained power to construct additional works at Poplar, &c. Capital, 50,000*l.* in shares, and 16,600*l.* on loan.

By 28 Vic., cap. 72 (2nd June, 1865), the company obtained power to widen several portions of the line, and to effect other improvements. New capital, 100,000*l.* in shares ; 33,300*l.* by mortgage.

By 30 Vic., cap. 78 (17th June, 1867), the company was authorised to widen several portions of the line, to purchase additional lands and to raise new capital to the extent of 300,000*l.* in shares, and 100,000*l.* on loan, power being given to the London and North Western to take its moiety of these amounts.

By 30 Vic., cap. 4 (29th May, 1868), the company obtained power to construct a variety of works for the improvement of the line and facilitation of the traffic. Also to purchase additional lands within three years. In operation, 11 miles.

REVENUE.—The dividends for the half-years ending 31st December and 30th June were at the rate of 6 per cent. per annum. The condition of the traffic is shown by the subjoined synopsis of the latter six months:—

30th June.	1868.		1867.		Increase.		Decrease.
Passengers	£112,178	...	£95,887	...	£16,291	...	—
Merchandise	31,227	...	28,152	...	3,075	...	—
Minerals	19,298	...	23,757	...	—	...	£4,459
Live Stock	1,683	...	1,230	...	453	...	—
Total	£164,386	...	£149,026		£15,360		

CAPITAL.—There have been issued, during the year, 30,000 new 10*l.* shares, realising 300,000*l.* The receipts and disbursements to 31st June were detailed as under:—

Received.		*Expended.*	
Ordinary stock	£1,525,000	Land and compensation	£655,722
„ 10*l.* shares (1866)	150,000	Construction, fixed plant and	
„ „ (1868)	7,080	machinery	668,840
Preference stock	700,000	Rolling stock	287,561
Debenture stock, 4 per cent.	7,075	City Extension, Widening, and	
„ 4½ „ ...	25	Additional Powers Acts... ...	1,567,723
Debenture loans	729,441		
Temporary loan in anticipation of issue of debenture stock	50,000		
Balance	11,227		
Total	£3,179,848	Total	£3,179,848

The accounts are made up to 30th June and 31st December, and the statutory meetings are held in London in February and August of each year.

Certificates must accompany transfer deeds. Registration fee, 2*s.* 6*d.* each deed.

DIRECTORS:

Chairman—JAMES BANCROFT, Esq., Noah's Ark, Broughton, near Manchester.

George Allender, Esq., 35, Kensington Park Gardens, Bayswater, W.
Thomas Brassey, Jun., Esq., M.P., Beauport, Battle, Sussex.
Harry Chubb, Esq., 18, Endsleigh Street, Tavistock Square.
Henry Davidson, Esq., 3, Corbet Court, Gracechurch Street, E.C.
Richard Ryder Dean, Esq., 97, Gloucester Place, Portman Square, W.
M. L. Melville, Esq., Tunbridge Wells.

Henry Morris Kemshead, Esq., 46, Lime Street, E.C.
George Grenfell Glyn, Esq., M.P., 67, Lombard Street, E.C.
James R. Robertson, Esq., 12, Leadenhall Street, E.C.
Alexander Stewart, Esq., 2, Talbot Road, Westbourne Park, W.
Matthew Lyon, Esq., Leamington.
William Tipping, Esq., M.P. Aqûes, near Dieppe.

OFFICERS.— Sec. and Man., Robert S. Mansel; Asst. Sec., G. Bolland Newton, Euston Station, N.W.; Auditors, Henry Crosfield and F. E. Greenaway; Solicitors, Paine and Layton, 47, Gresham House, E.C.; Bankers, Glyn and Co.

Head Offices—Euston Station, N.W.

302.—NORTH METROPOLITAN.

Incorporated by 29 and 30 Vic., cap. 299 (30th July, 1866), to construct railways from the Great Western at Southall to the Victoria Docks on the river Thames, with links to the Great Western, the London and North Western, the Midland and South Western Junction, the Great Eastern, and the Tilbury and Southend. Length, 26½ miles. Capital, 1,600,000*l.* in 20*l.* shares, and 533,000*l.* on loan. Arrangements with the various companies mentioned. In abeyance.

By 30 Vic , cap. 86 (17th June, 1867), the company was authorised to make a deviation and construct a branch in substitution of other works, and to establish better communication with the Midland and South Western Junction.

No. of Directors—8; minimum, 6; quorum, 4 and 3. *Qualification,* 500*l.*

DIRECTORS:

Chairman—WILLIAM HAWES, Esq., 17, Montague Place, Russell Square, W.C.

Deputy-Chairman—Major General BROWNRIGG, C.B., 91, Victoria Street, Westminster, S.W.

James Childs, Esq., Summerfield, Putney, Park Lane, Roehampton, S.W.

Peter Graham, Esq., Queen's Road, Regent's Park, N.W.

Alfred Smee, Esq., F.R.S., Finsbury Circus, London Wall, E.C.

John Sale Barker, Esq., 11, Palace Gardens Terrace, Kensington, W.

Edwin Fox, Esq.

H. M. Brownrigg, Esq.

303.—NORTH AND SOUTH WESTERN JUNCTION.

Incorporated by Act 14 and 15 Vic., cap. 100 (24th July, 1851), for a line from the L. and N. W. Willesden station to Windsor branch of L. and S. W., near Kew. Length, 4 miles 65 chains.

The line is worked jointly by the L. and N. Western and S. Western, under an agreement sanctioned by Parliament. By its terms the two companies undertake—1st, to provide rolling stock, and to work the Junction for 33 per cent. of the gross receipts; 2nd, to allow this company a mileage toll of 6 miles on goods and 4 miles on passengers; and in any case to guarantee a *minimum* net revenue from toll on mileage alone of 2,250*l.* per annum; 3rd, that company shall be entitled to divide 6 per cent. as dividend after payment of interest on debentures, &c., before the companies participate in the profits. Surplus above 6 per cent. to be apportioned between the three companies as follows, viz.:—one half to this company, and remainder to working companies. Commencing from 27th November, 1852, date of certificate of government inspection.

By 16 and 17 Vic., cap. 69 (28th June, 1853), this company was authorised to make a branch to Hammersmith—1¼ mile. Guarantee not extended thereto. Opened 1st May, 1857. By agreement with the London and North Western and South Western, it will be necessary to keep the accounts of the branch distinct from those of the main line, in order that the rights of those companies to participate in the profits exceeding 6 per cent. may not be interfered with; but as respects the shareholders in the branch, their shares will rank equally with those of the main line from the time of opening.

By 27 and 28 Vic., cap. 113 (23rd June, 1864), the company was authorised to purchase additional land and to raise new capital to the extent of 10,000*l.* in shares, and 3,000*l.* on loan.

By 30 and 31 Vic., cap. 50 (25th June, 1868), the company was authorised to make a deviation in the main line, and to raise further capital to the extent of 15,000*l.* in shares, and 5,000*l.* on mortgage.

REVENUE.—The dividend for the half-year ending 31st December was at the rate of 5½ per cent. per annum, and for June 5 per cent. The details of revenue for the latter six months were as follow:—

	1868.	1867.	Increase.	Decrease.
Passengers	£2,883	£2,418	£465	......
Merchandise	909	832	76	......
Live stock	84	52	32	......
Minerals	2,284	2,786	......	£502
Total	£6,162	£6,089	£72	

CAPITAL.—The various details connected with this account to 30th June have been given as under:—

	Authorised.	Received.
Capital stock	£90,000	£90,000
Share capital (1867)	} 28,600	18,386
Debenture loans		12,400
Authorised but not yet raised, viz.:—Act of 1868	26,000	......
	£138,600	£120,786

Expended.

Land and compensation	£49,543
Construction	65,908
Balance	5,334
	£120,786

No. of Directors.—Maximum, 9; minimum, 7; quorum, 4. *Qualification*, 50 shares. Committees, 5 to 3; quorum, 2.

DIRECTORS:

Henry Charles Lacy, Esq., Withdean Hall, near Brighton.
Harry Chubb, Esq., 18, Endsleigh Street, W.C.
Thomas Hill, Esq., Tower House, Winchester.

George Cooper, Esq., Brentford, W.
Charles Jack, Esq., Beech Hill Park, Barnet.
George Allender, Esq., 35, Kensington Park Gardens, W.

OFFICERS.—Sec. and Man., Robert S. Mansel; Asst. Sec., G. Bolland Newton; Res. Eng., William Butterton, 17, Great George Street, S.W.; Auditors, T. R. Cobb and Henry Browne; Solicitor, H. Toogood, 16, Parliament Street, S.W.; Bankers, Glyn, Mills, Currie, and Co., Lombard Street, E.C.

Offices—Euston Station, N.W.

304.—NORTH AND SOUTH WILTSHIRE JUNCTION.

Incorporated by 28 and 29 Vic., cap. 338 (5th July, 1865), to construct a line from the Wilts and Gloucestershire, at Christian Malford, to Beechingstoke, on the Berks and Hants. Length, 17½ miles. Capital, 270,000l. in shares, and 90,000l. on loan. Arrangements with Great Western. An extension of time is being sought for in the present session.

No. of Directors—8; minimum, 5; quorum, 3. *Qualification*, 1,000l.

DIRECTORS:

Joseph Cary, Esq., 49, Pall Mall, S.W.
Henry Hawes Fox, Esq., 27, Leadenhall Street, E.C.
George Ford, Esq.

Captain Robert O'Brien Jameson, The Albany, Piccadilly, W.
— Bayley, Esq.

Offices—41, Parliament Street, S.W.

305.—NORTH STAFFORDSHIRE.

Incorporated by three separate Acts in 1846, but now acting under consolidation Act of 1847 (10 and 11 Vic., cap. 108). In operation, 144 miles of railway and 116 of canal.

By 22 and 23 Vic., cap. 126 (13th August, 1859), the company was authorised to make an extension from Earl Granville's branch in Stoke-upon-Trent to Miles Bank. Compulsory purchase of land, 18 months; completion of works, two years. By same Act an extension of time for completion of works authorised in 1854, conceded for one year. Power also given to contract with London and North Western for use of North Staffordshire for division and apportionment of traffic thereon. Contract to be public, and to be under usual restrictions. Debenture stock to be created in lieu of mortgage debt at 5 per cent.

By 23 Vic., cap. 114, the company was permitted to relinquish a portion of the works authorised by Act of 1854; to convert the capital into 17l. 10s. shares, or into stock; to enter into agreements with the Silverdale and Newcastle, and Newcastle-under-Lyme canal, with respect to working and traffic of the two latter undertakings; and to take tolls on the Canal Extension, constructed by the Newcastle-under-Lyme canal without authority from parliament.

By 26 and 27 Vic., cap. 158 (13th July, 1863), the company was authorised to construct a line (6¾ miles), to lessen the distance between Leek and the Potteries, and a short branch to secure a convenient access for goods to the important town of Burton-upon-Trent, and also to legalise the conversion of the ordinary shares into stock, at the nominal value of 20l. per share. New capital, 100,000l. in shares, at not exceeding 5 per cent., and 33,300l. on loan. Opened on 1st July for goods, and on 1st November for passengers.

POTTERIES, BIDDULPH, AND CONGLETON.—Incorporated by 17 and 18 Vic., cap. 194 (24th July, 1854). The line is in six sections. The first commences on the main line, at Stoke-upon-Trent, and terminates at Congleton (opened August 3rd, 1859); the second diverges from the new branch near the junction with the main line, and terminates in a field in the parish of Stoke; the third leaves the branch at Ashbury, and proceeds until it again meets the main line; the fourth also leaves the branch at Ashbury, and joins the main line at Congleton station; the fifth likewise diverges from the first branch, running between the parishes of Bucknall and Caverswall; the next leaves the first at Burslem, and terminates in the same parish at Stoneybank.

NEWCASTLE-UNDER-LYME CANAL.—This canal, and the canal extensions belonging thereto, were vested in the North Staffordshire by 27 and 28 Vic., cap. 118 (23rd June, 1864), on payment by the latter of a rent of 520l. per annum, and liquidation of mortgage debt.

TUNSTALL.—By 27 and 28 Vic., cap. 232 (25th July, 1864), the North Staffordshire was authorised to construct a line from the Potteries to Tunstall. Length, 2¼ miles. Capital, 66,000*l.* in shares, and 22,000*l.* on loan.

By 27 and 28 Vic., cap. 308 (29th July, 1864), the company was authorised to construct several small branches. Length, 15 miles. Capital, 250,000*l.* in shares, and 83,300*l.* on loan.

By 27 and 28 Vic., cap. 309 (29th July, 1864), the company was authorised to construct lines from the Silverdale and Newcastle to Madeley, and thence to the Nantwich and Market Drayton and the London and North Western. Length, 12¾ miles. Capital, 175,000*l.* in shares, and 58,000*l.* on loan. Expected to be opened during the year.

By 28 and 29 Vic., cap. 339 (5th July, 1865), the company was authorised to construct a loop line in the Potteries district. Length, 7¾ miles. Capital, 300,000*l.* in shares, and 100,000*l.* on loan.

By 30 and 31 Vic., cap. 142 (15th July, 1867), the company acquired various powers, including widening of certain sections of its system, and an extension of time for completion of works till 15th July, 1872. Running powers in exchange for mutual facilities were conceded to the London and North Western.

REVENUE.—The receipts for the half-year ending 31st December were 192,835*l.*, including 12,926*l.* under the agreement with the London and North Western, and for the same period of 1866 184,020*l.*, showing an increase of 8,815*l.* The working expenses amounted to 81,165*l.* against 81,085*l.*, showing an increase of 80*l.* The canal revenue amounted to 50,581*l.* against 50,601*l.*; and the expenditure to 19,527*l.*, against 18,317*l.*, leaving a balance of 31,054*l.*, against 32,284*l.* The net revenue amounted to 142,725*l.*, against 135,219*l.*, showing an increase of 7,506*l.* The balance available for dividend, after payment of interest on debentures and preference charges, with the sum brought forward from June last, amounted to 59,767*l.* Dividend at the rate of 3½ per cent. per annum, amounted to 56,527*l.*, and left a balance of 3,239*l.* Although the increase in the net general revenue, as compared with the corresponding period of 1866, amounted to 7,505*l.*, the charges for additional interest, Parliamentary expenses, and reconstruction of rolling stock, &c., exceeded by 10,530*l.* the corresponding charges in 1866, which, with 3,143*l.* less brought forward, explained the reduction of ½ per cent. in the dividend.

The receipts on the railway and canal for the half-year ending 30th June, compared as under with previous periods:—

RAILWAY.	1866.	1867.	1868.
Goods (Local	£10,782	£5,935	£6,300
and ⟨ Local through	49,136	42,300	46,052
Cattle (Direct through	4,940	3,621	4,059
Minerals	52,036	61,795	59,442
Total	£116,894	£113,651	£115,853
Passengers	£45,243	£43,729	£45,370
Horses, parcels, mails, &c.	3,362	3,903	4,204
	£48,605	£47,632	£49,574
CANAL	£42,311	£38,770	£36,172

The net balance, together with the sum brought forward from 31st December, after providing for interest on debentures and preference charges, amounted to 43,202*l.*, out of which a dividend at the rate of 2½ per cent. per annum on the ordinary stock, left the balance of 2,825*l.*

The exceptionally heavy payment for parliamentary expenses, for interest on unproductive capital amounting to 3,802*l.*, and for the renewal of permanent way, all charged to revenue, more than account for a reduced dividend.

CAPITAL.—The expenditure on this account to 30th June, amounted to 5,171,008*l.*, the receipts being detailed as under :—

Railway Capital, created 1847 (representing 3,230,140 stock) ...	£3,200,000
New Preference 5 per cent. Stock..	355,000
Ditto part 250,000*l.*, last issue..................................	67,630
Debentures	1,541,286
	£5,163,916
Balance	7,091=£5,171,008

NEW PREFERENCE STOCK.—It was resolved in August to give the shareholders the option of taking the remainder of the unissued New Preference (5 per cent.) Stock, amounting to 150,000*l.* The price fixed by the directors was 97*l.* per hundred, payment to be made in full on the 1st October—dividend to accrue from that date.

The accounts are made up to 30th June and 31st December; and the statutory meetings held in February and August in each year.

Scale of Voting.—C. C. C. Act, sec. 75.

Certificates must accompany transfer deed, registration fees charged since 1st January, 1861.

No. of Directors—Reduced to 12 by meeting of 11th August, 1868, of whom 3 must be elected from amongst the canal preference shareholders. *Qualification*, 2,000*l.* ordinary stock (the ordinary stock having been converted into stock); the directors representing the canal proprietors, 100 preference shares.

DIRECTORS:

Chairman—Lieut.-Colonel CHARLES PEARSON, Cheltenham.

*Sir Smith Child, Bart., M.P., Stallington Hall, near Stone.

William Brownfield, Esq., Hanley, Staffordshire.

John Bramley-Moore, Esq., Gerrard's Cross, Bucks.

Lord Alfred Paget, 56, Queen Anne Street, Cavendish Square, W.

John Adamthwaite, Esq., Oak Hill, Tean, Staffordshire.

Francis Stanier Broade, Esq., Silverdale, near Stoke-upon-Trent.

Frederick Wright Tomlinson, Esq., Leamington.

William Worthington, Esq., Brockhurst Hall, Northwich.

*Viscount Sandon, M.P., Sandon Hall, Staffordshire.

Colin Minton Campbell, Esq., Woodseat, Staffordshire.

Thos. Salt, junr., Esq., Stafford, Banker.

* Represent the Canal preference shareholders.

Go out in rotation annually, in July. Eligible for re-election.

OFFICERS—Gen. Man., Percy Morris; Sec., Jonathan Samuda; Goods Man., James Cordon; Canal Supt., Edward Pamphilon; Coaching Supt., Charles Lockhart; Eng., John Curphey Forsyth; Res. Eng., James Johnson; Eng. Canal Dept., Joseph S. Forbes; Accountant, Robert Steele; Auditors, William Hopes and George Smith; Solicitor, William Burchell, 5, Broad Sanctuary, Westminster, S.W.; Bankers, Glyn, Mills, Currie, and Co., London, and Lloyd's Banking Company (Limited), Longton.

Head Offices—Stoke-upon-Trent, Staffordshire Potteries.

306.—NORTH UNION.

An amalgamation of the Wigan and Preston and Wigan branch, under the name of the North Union, by virtue of 4 Wm. IV, cap. 25, with which was afterwards incorporated the Bolton and Preston, by 7 and 8 Vic., cap. 2, established for lines from Parkside junction with the L. and N. W. to Preston; and from Preston to Bolton. Productive mileage, 39 miles 60 chains.

The undertaking is vested for ever, jointly in the L. and N. W., and the L. and Y. under powers of Act 9 and 10 Vic., cap. 231 (27th July, 1846), for a fixed annuity of 66,063*l.* 18*s.* from 1st January, 1846, payable in net moneys, free of deductions, except income tax, half-yearly, 15th February and 15th August, whereof 60-94ths are to be paid by the L. and N. W., and 34-94ths by L. and Y. This annuity is divided, 47,732*l.* 13*s.* 4½*d.* amongst holders of A stock, and 18,331*l.* 14*s.* 8½*d.* to B stock, equal to 10 per cent. and 7 per cent. respectively.

The books are generally closed about a fortnight previous to the date when the dividend warrants are payable, viz., 15th February and 15th August. Certificates must accompany transfer deeds. Registration fee, 2*s.* 6*d.* each seller, and for each new certificate or coupon. Both classes may go on one deed.

DIRECTORS:

Chairman—1 WILLIAM BIRLEY, Esq., Preston.

2 Samuel Henry Thompson, Esq., Thingwall Hall, Knotty Ash, near Liverpool.

3 James Glover, Esq. Southport.

4 Dr. Reynolds, Coed-du, near Mold.

5 John Bairstow, Esq., Preston.

6 H. Earle, Esq., Liverpool.

8 John Stevenson, Esq., Iron Founder, Preston.

Numbered according to seniority—all at present re-eligible.

OFFICERS.—Sec., Thomas H. Carr; Eng.-in-Chief, same as London and North Western and Lancashire and Yorkshire Companies; Eng., Charles Axon; Goods Agent, J. Nichols, Preston.

Joint Lessees' Office, Preston.

307.—NORTH WESTERN.
(LEASED TO MIDLAND.)

Originally incorporated by 10 Vic., cap. 92 (30th June, 1846), for a railway from the Leeds and Bradford, at Skipton, to the Lancaster and Carlisle, at Low Park, Kendal, with a diverging line to Lancaster. Various acts of parliament have reduced the undertaking to a line from Skipton to Ingleton and Poulton, a connection with Lancaster and Carlisle. Length, 47 miles.

By 27 and 28 Vic., cap. 71 (23rd June, 1864), the company was authorised to divide its 20l. shares into one of 12l., and another of 8l., the former bearing a perpetual fixed dividend of five per cent., and the latter taking the residue of the rent with any contingent advantage that may arise out of the lease to the Midland. This alteration was duly effected at a meeting of the company, on 11th July, 1864.

MIDLAND.—The following arrangement was effected in December, 1858, with this company—"That the Midland pay every expense connected with the North Western, including debenture interest and dividends on preference shares, and a half-yearly sum equal to a net dividend, without deduction, except income tax, upon the ordinary stock, after the following scale:—Half-year ending June 30th, 1859, 1l. 10s. per cent. per annum; ditto, December 31st, 1859, 1l. 10s. ditto; ditto, June 30th, 1860, 2l. ditto; ditto. December 31st, 1860, 2l ditto; ditto, June 30th, 1861, 2l. 10s. ditto; ditto, December 31st, 1861, 2l. 10s. ditto; ditto, June 30th, 1862, 3l. ditto; ditto, December 31st, 1862, 3l. ditto; ditto, June 30th, 1863, 3l. ditto; ditto, December 31st, 1863, 3l. ditto; ditto, June 30th, 1864, 3l. 10s. ditto; ditto, December 31st, 1864, 3l. 10s. ditto; and so on for a term of 999 years, from 1st January, 1859, with such additional dividends, if any, as one half excess net earnings of North Western will pay beyond the rates aforesaid; the working expenses to be deducted from the gross traffic being taken at the same per centage as on the whole Midland. The ordinary stock on which the guarantee takes effect is 800,000l. preference stock at 5 per cent., 126,285l.; debenture debt, 260,000l. No further shares or debentures to be issued, or debentures renewed without consent of Midland.

For the half-year ending 31st December, dividends were declared in February, as follows:—On 471,336l. A consolidated stock, at the rate of 5 per cent. per annum, as guaranteed by the Midland, and on 314,224l. B consolidated stock at the rate of 1¼ per cent. per annum. Both dividends are guaranteed by the Midland, but the A stock is preferential. The dividend on the B stock has never exceeded 1¼ per cent. per annum.

CAPITAL.—The receipts on this account have been 1,257,579l. An expenditure of 1,257,465l., leaves a balance on hand of 114l.

Registration fee, 5s. for each deed.

No. of Directors.—Maximum, 7 ; minimum, 5. *Qualification.*, 50 shares.

DIRECTORS:

Chairman—HUMPHREY JOHN HARE, Esq., Docking Hall, King's Lynn.

Deputy- Chairman—ISAAC BURKILL, Esq., Westwood Park, Scarbro'.

Henry Alcock, Esq., Aireville, Skipton.	Abraham Clapham, Esq., Ramsdale Bank,
William Douglas, Esq., Ilkley.	Scarbro'.
Joseph Holt, Esq., Leeds.	

Two directors retire annually in February, and are eligible for re-election.

OFFICERS.—Sec., William F. Dean, Leeds ; Auditors, Robert Frost, Leeds, and Benjamin Bailey, Leeds.

Head Offices— 22, Commercial Street, Leeds.

308.—NORTH WESTERN AND CHARING CROSS.

Incorporated by 27 and 28 Vic., cap. 115, to construct lines from the Hampstead Road to the Charing Cross, with a branch to the London and North Western. Length, 4½ miles. Also to construct several new streets from Tottenham Court Road to the Strand, &c. Capital, 990,000l. in 10l. shares, and 330,000l. on loan. Arrangements with the South Eastern. Application has been made to the Board of Trade for authority to abandon the undertaking.

No. of Directors—12 ; quorum, 4. *Qualification*, 500l.

DIRECTORS:

309.—NORTHERN AND EASTERN.

Incorporated by 6 and 7 Wm. IV., cap. 103 (July, 1863), for the construction of a line commencing from a junction with the Great Eastern at Stratford, 4 miles from London, and terminating at Newport, with a branch to Hertford. Total, 44 miles.

The line is leased to the Great Eastern for 900 years under parliamentary powers obtained in 1844, at 5, and a portion at 6 per cent., with half profits when Great Eastern reaches the former amount. Dividends on shares, 50*l.* guaranteed 5 per cent. per annum, 1*l.* 5*s.* each; on shares of 50*l.* guaranteed 6 per cent. per annum, 1*l.* 10*s.* each.

CAPITAL.—The general statement of receipts and expenditure to 30th June furnished the subjoined details:—

Received.		*Expended.*	
Calls on 19,200 shares of 50*l.* each.....................................	£959,810	Cost of the railway, as per account to 31st December.........	£963,166
Cash received of the Great Eastern (being excess of capital expenditure over 960,000*l.*)	3,166		
Balance carried down	120		
	£963,166		£963,166

The accounts are made up to 30th June and 31st December, and the half-yearly meetings (for the declaration of the dividend) are held in London on or before the 21st February and 21st August in every year; the transfer books close one week previously.

Scale of Voting—One vote for each share up to 20; then one for every 5.

Certificates of shares need not accompany transfer deeds. Registration fee, 2*s.* 6*d.* each deed.

No. of Directors.—Maximum, 12; minimum, 3. *Qualification*, 1,000*l.*

DIRECTORS:

2 Chairman—ROBERT W. KENNARD, Esq., 37, Porchester Terrace.

One-sixth of the directors retire annually, and are eligible for re-election. August meeting fills up vacancies.

OFFICERS.—Sec., William Bourne; Solicitors, Maynard, Son, and Co., 57, Coleman Street, E.C.

Offices—Bishopsgate Station (Great Eastern), E.C.

310.—NORTHUMBERLAND CENTRAL.

Incorporated by 26 and 27 Vic., cap. 335 (28th July, 1863), to construct a line from the Wansbeck, at Hartburn, to Ford, and thence to the Kelso and Berwick branch of the North Eastern. Length, 49¾ miles. Capital, 270,000l. in 10l. shares, and 90,000l. on loan. Arrangements with North Eastern and North British.

By 30 Vic., cap. 9 (12th April, 1867), the company was authorised to abandon the southern part of the line to the extent of 13 miles, the capital being reduced from 270,000l. to 75,000l. in shares, and from 90,000l. to 25,000l. on loan.

It was reported in August, 1868, that the directors were in a position to re-commence the works, and that the difficulties in obtaining the requisite funds to complete the line to Rothbury had been overcome. The negotiations which were some time since opened with the Duke of Northumberland had resulted in an agreement with his Grace, which, they felt called upon to admit, while liberal, was at the same time fair to both parties. The conditions of this agreement were as follow:—The capital required to complete the line was 44,250l., and from the fact that this was the sum arrived at, after a most careful investigation by the engineer of the company, and revised by Mr. Bruce, an eminent engineer, there could be no doubt that it would be amply sufficient to complete the line. Of this amount the Duke of Northumberland subscribed 13,860l.; the debentures taken up represented 20,000l.; and the stock issued at a discount and also taken up, 9,640l., made up 43,500l.

It was accordingly resolved that on the execution of the agreements between the Duke of Northumberland and the company the debentures to the extent of 20,000l., agreed to be taken be issued, and the shares subscribed for at 50 per cent. discount be also issued.

CAPITAL.—The expenditure to 31st December, 1867, had been 42,779l., which showed a balance overdrawn of 1,982l.

No of Directors—9; minimum, 6; quorum, 3. *Qualification*, 500l.

DIRECTORS.

Chairman—Sir WALTER CALVERLEY TREVELYAN, Bart., Wallington, Northumberland.

Sir Horace St. Paul, Bart., Ewart Park, Northumberland.

Sir John Swinburne, Bart., Capheaton, Northumberland.

George Annett Grey, Esq., of Milfield, Northumberland.

William Forster, Junr., Esq., Burradon, Rothbury.

John Ord, Esq., of Nizbet, Kelso, Northumberland.

OFFICERS.—Sec., Benjamin Woodman, Solicitor, Morpeth; Eng., John Furnes Tone, Newcastle-on-Tyne; Auditors, Wm. Wightman, Wooler, Northumberland, and Thos. Arkle, Shafto, Northumberland; Bankers, W. H. Lambton and Co., Newcastle-on-Tyne, and Alnwick and County Bank, Wooler, Northumberland.

Offices—Morpeth, Northumberland.

311.—NORWICH AND SPALDING.

Incorporated by 17 Vic., cap. 124 (4th August, 1853), for a line from the Great Northern, at Spalding, to Holbeach. Length, 16 miles.

By 22 and 23 Vic., cap. 118 (13th August, 1859), the company was authorised to extend the line from Holbeach to Sutton Bridge. Opened to Sutton Bridge, 3rd July, 1862.

By an Act passed in 1865, this company, or any company working the line, has running powers over the Peterboro' Wisbeach and Sutton from Sutton Bridge to Wisbeach.

Under an agreement by which the Great Northern and Midland work the line the company is secured a minimum net rent of 7,000l. a year, with half surplus profits beyond this sum.

No. of Directors.—Maximum, 10; minimum, 10; quorum, 3. *Qualification*, 25 shares

DIRECTORS:

Chairman—WILLIAM ECKERSLEY, Esq., 7, Victoria Street, S.W.

Adderley Howard, Esq., Long Sutton, Lincolnshire.

Thomas Edward Savage, Esq., Holbeach, Lincolnshire.

William Skelton, Esq., Sutton Bridge, Lincolnshire.

Peter Sers, Esq., Acton, W.

Charles Waring, Esq., 10, Victoria Chambers, Westminster, S.W.

William Waring, Esq., 10, Victoria Chambers, Westminster, S.W.

OFFICERS.—Sec., W. H. Dawson, 9, Victoria Chambers, Westminster, S.W.; Solicitor, James Wheeler, 4, Victoria Street, Westminster, S.W.; Auditors, A. G. Lovell, 20, Chalcot Terrace, Regent's Park, N.W.; Bankers, the Imperial Bank, Westminster, S.W.

Offices—9, Victoria Chambers, Westminster, S.W.

312.—NOTTINGHAM AND GRANTHAM.
(LEASED TO GREAT NORTHERN.)

Incorporated by 9 and 10 Vic., cap. 155, for construction of a line commencing as projected, in conjunction with the Midland, and in continuation thence of the Manchester Buxton Matlock and Midlands Junction, at Ambergate, and terminating in conjunction with the Great Northern, at Spalding, with Branches to Sleaford and Boston (90 miles); but, by resolution of general meetings it was determined to confine all operations to a line from Grantham (where a junction is formed to the Great Northern). The portion in operation is 23 miles, viz., from Grantham to Nottingham. Under Act of incorporation, this company had agreed to purchase the Nottingham Canal for 225l. in cash, or nine railway shares of 25l. each, paid up; and the Grantham Canal for 100l. in cash, or five railway paid-up 25l. shares for each canal share.

By 23 Vic., cap. 36 (15th May, 1860), the name of the undertaking was changed to "Nottingham and Grantham," the capital reduced to 1,014,000l. in lieu of 1,056,250l., and of the borrowing powers from 358,333l. to 265,000l.; various provisions for consolidation of shares into stock, and for regulating the transfer thereof, were also made.

The line has since been leased to the Great Northern for 999 years, at a rental of 4l. 2s. 6d. on a capital of 1,014,000l., with a right to the Great Northern to purchase the undertaking at par. The rent is regularly paid, and the dividends declared half-yearly. The borrowing powers are exercised by the Great Northern.

The revenue accounts are made up to 31st January and 31st July in every year; and the half-yearly meetings held in Grantham, generally, in February and August.

Coupons are required at the office before a transfer can be registered. Fee for registration, 2s. 6d. each seller. Transfer books close 14 days before each meeting.

No. of Directors.—Maximum, 9; minimum, 5. *Qualification*, 1,000l. Present board, 6; receiving 300l. a year.

DIRECTORS:
Chairman—RICHARD SEPTIMUS WILKINSON, Esq., 3, St. Mildred's Court, Poultry, E.C.

Deputy-Chairman—JOHN FOWLER BURBIDGE, Esq., St. Peter's Hill, Grantham.

W. Durham, Esq., Wilton Lodge, Addison Road, Notting Hill, W.

Col. George Hussey Packe, Caythorpe, Grantham, and 41, Charles Street, Berkeley Square, W.

Samuel Newham, Esq., The Park, Nottingham.

John Alexander Thompson Smyth, Esq., 4, Cumberland Terrace, Regent's Park, N.W.

OFFICERS.—Sec., John Gough, Nottingham; Registrar, Henry Lasalle, Nottingham; Auditors, William Vernon Stephens and Hugh Oxenham; Solicitor, John Thompson Brewster, Nottingham; Bankers, Hardy, Johnstone, and Hardy, Grantham.

Head Offices—London Road Station, Nottingham.

313.—OLDHAM, ASHTON-UNDER-LYNE, AND GUIDE BRIDGE JUNCTION.

Incorporated by 20 and 21 Vic., cap. 137 (10th August, 1857), for the construction of railways to supply direct communication between these places. Capital, 140,000l. in 10l. shares; loans, 46,600l. The length of first railway is 4 miles and 7 yards, commencing by a junction of the Oldham branch of the London and North Western, at or near the Oldham station, and terminating by a junction with the Ashton and Stalybridge branch of Lancashire and Yorkshire; length of the second is 1 mile 3 furlongs and 17 yards, commencing by a junction with the Ashton and Stalybridge branch of Lancashire and Yorkshire, at Peccatties, and terminating by a junction with Manchester Sheffield and Lincolnshire, at Guide Bridge; the length of the third is 2 furlongs 6 chains and 17 yards, commencing by a junction with the first railway, in the parish of Ashton, and terminating near the service reservoir of the Ashton waterworks; the length of the fourth is 5 furlongs 8 chains and 11 yards, commencing by a junction with the first railway near Wood Lane, and terminating at or near Moss coal pit; and the length of the fifth is 2 furlongs 6 chains and 8 yards, commencing by a junction with the first railway near Lower Allhil, terminating in Rochervale. The Manchester Sheffield and Lincolnshire and London and North Western subscribe 50,000l. each, and each appoint one-third of the directors. Opened 26th August, 1861.

By 25 and 26 Vic., cap. 98 (30th June, 1862), the line is vested mutually in the London and North Western and Manchester and Sheffield at 4¾ per cent.

No. of Directors—9 ; minimum, 6 ; quorum, 3.   *Qualification*, 100 shares.

DIRECTORS:

Chairman—NATHANIEL BUCKLEY, Esq., Ashton-under-Lyne.

Thomas Rawson Barker, Esq., The Edge, Sheffield.
James Bancroft, Esq., 5, Police Street, Manchester.
John Chapman, Esq., Hill End, Mottram, Cheshire.
William Fenton, Esq., Beaumonds, near Rochdale.

John Tomlinson Hibbert, Esq., M.P., Urmston Grange, near Manchester, and 29, Grosvenor Street West, S.W.
Jonathan Mellor, Esq., Pole Field, Prestwich, near Manchester.
Sam Mendel, Esq., Manley Hall, Whalley Range, Manchester.
Edward Tootal, Esq., The Weaste, near Manchester.

OFFICERS.—Man., James Kirkman; Sec., Edward Ross, Manchester; Eng., Charles Sacré, Manchester; Auditors, Sir Edward Wm. Watkin, Manchester, and Frederick Hughes, Oldham; Solicitor, John Stevenson, Manchester; Bankers, Fenton and Sons, Rochdale.

Offices—London Road Station, Manchester.

314.—PARSONSTOWN AND PORTUMNA BRIDGE.

Incorporated by 24 and 25 Vic., cap. 142 (11th July, 1861), to construct a line from the Great Southern and Western, at Parsonstown, to Portumna Bridge, on the Shannon. Length, 12½ miles. Capital, 65,000l. in 10l. shares; loans, 21,600l. The company may provide and use steam vessels. Opened November 5th, 1868.

The Great Southern and Western have entered into an agreement to work and maintain the line for 10 years for 40 per cent. of the gross receipts.

By 29 Vic., cap. 57 (11th June, 1866), the company obtained an extension of time till 11th June, 1868, for completion of the works; also to issue preference shares, and to sell or lease the undertaking to the Great Southern and Western.

No. of Directors—8 ; minimum, 6 ; quorum, 3.   *Qualification*, 300l.

DIRECTORS:

Chairman—The MARQUIS OF CLANRICARDE, K.P., P.C., Portumna Castle, and 17, Stratton Street, W.

Sir Thomas John Burke, Bart., Marble Hill, Loughrea.
Thomas Butler Stoney, Esq., J.P., Portland, Roscrea, Co. Tipperary.
William Meara, Esq., Merchant, Parsonstown, King's Co.

*Edward Cane, Esq., 60, Dawson Street, Dublin.
*Michael Bernard Mullins, Esq., 18, Fitzwilliam Square, Dublin.
*Valentine O'Brien O'Connor, Esq., Merchant, 3, Beresford Place, Dublin.

* Directors of Great Southern and Western.

OFFICERS.—Sec., Daniel Molloy; Engs., Nixon and Denis, 3, Victoria Street, Westminster, S.W. ; Solicitors, Barrington and Jeffers, 10, Ely Place, Dublin.
Offices—Kingsbridge, Dublin.

315.—PARSONSTOWN & PORTUMNA BRIDGE EXTENSION.

Incorporated by 27 and 28 Vic., cap. 301 (29th July, 1864), to construct an extension from the Portumna Bridge line across the river Shannon to the town of Portumna. Length, 1½ mile. Capital, 24,000l. in 10l. shares, and 8,000l. on loan. In abeyance.

316.—PEEBLES.

Incorporated by 17 Vic., cap. 78 (8th July, 1853), for a line from the Hawick branch of the North British (Eskbank station) to Peebles (single line). Length, 18¾ miles. Sidings, &c., 2¼ miles. Total, 21 miles. Opened 4th July, 1855.

By 20 and 21 Vic., cap. 14 (26th June, 1857), the company was authorised to create additional capital to the extent of 27,000*l.* in shares, at 5 per cent. preference, and 9,000*l.* on loan. Power also given to convert mortgage debts into debenture stock not exceeding 4 per cent. Leased to North British by 24 and 25 Vic., cap. 102 (11th July, 1861), on a guarantee of 5 per cent. minimum. North British to pay interest on 20,000*l.* of Peebles loans, leaving only interest of 12,100*l.* to be paid by Peebles.

The dividend paid for the half-year ending 31st January was at the rate of 6½ per cent., and for the six months ending 31st July, 6¾ per cent. per annum, and this out of the 50 per cent. of gross traffic payable by lessors to lessees, besides considerable surplus paid to lessors.

It was remarked by the Chairman, at the meeting in September, that the Peebles was about the most prosperous railway in the kingdom. For the past half-year they proposed to pay a dividend at the rate of 6¾ per cent. per annum on the ordinary shares, and 5 per cent. on the preference; but, besides dividing this profit on the stock, they gave under agreement a share of the surplus to the North British, on account of working the line, amounting for the half-year to 283*l.* The reason it paid so well was because it was constructed cheaply, had not had its revenues eaten up by bad-paying lines, and was administered at small expense. The line had kept itself to itself; not meddled with what it had nothing to do with. In consequence of that it was solvent in the midst of universal disaster. They remembered how the North British offered to absorb them at 4½ per cent. for a permanence, and how that generous offer was rejected, though not without a pang to some timorous shareholders. Had they accepted that offer, would it have been realised? Ask the shareholders of the Edinburgh and Glasgow what had been the consequences of their absorption. Had that grand offer been accepted, the shares of the Peebles would not at present have been worth much, whereas by minding their own small business they were getting 6¾ per cent., every shilling of which was honestly earned. His anticipations were that they would some day pay 10 per cent., and they might almost have done so but for the branch line pushed down the Tweed to Peebles by the Caledonian, which took away part of the goods traffic that would naturally have come to them, without apparently yielding any benefit to the parent company. They had before them the melancholy spectacle of two gigantic companies unable to pay any dividends on the ordinary shares or stocks. There was a universal apprehension of dishonesty in railway management, but he hoped, through the patient and orderly management of companies, that things would mend, and that public confidence would be restored.

CAPITAL.—The expenditure on this account is closed. The ordinary capital is 70,000*l.*, preference (at 5 per cent.), 27,000*l.*; loans, 32,000*l.* (but see above). After making provision for the dividends, and all rates and charges, there was paid to the working company, in terms of the lease, the sum of 293*l.*, being one-half of the surplus income beyond a 6 per cent. dividend on the ordinary shares; and a balance was carried forward of 82*l.*

Scale of Voting—2 shares to 10, one vote; every 10 to 100, one vote, afterwards one for every 20,

No. of Directors.—Maximum, 9; minimum, 5; quorum, 3.   *Qualification*, 30 shares.

DIRECTORS:

2 Chairman—The Right Hon. WILLIAM CHAMBERS, of Glenormiston,
Lord Provost of Edinburgh.

3 The Right Hon. Lord Elibank.	1 Robert Balfour Wardlaw Ramsay, Esq..
3 George W. Muir, Esq., Caberston.	of Whitehill.
2 Alexander Tod, Esq., St. Mary's Mount.	1 William Duncan, Esq., S.S.C., Edinburgh.
2 Archd. Ainslie, Esq., Dodridge, by Ford.	
3 William Anderson, Esq., of Hallyards.	1 Andrew Buchan, Esq., Peebles.

1, retire in 1869; 2, in 1870; 3, in 1871.

OFFICERS.—Sec., J. D. Bathgate, Peebles; Eng., Thomas Bouch, A.I.C.E., Edinburgh; Auditors, William Stuart, Writer to the Signet, and Robert Thorburn, Bank Agent, Peebles; Bankers, the Union Bank of Scotland.

Offices—Peebles.

317.—PEMBROKE AND TENBY.

Incorporated by 22 and 23 Vic., cap. 6 (21st July, 1859), to make railways from Pembroke Dock to Tenby, and from the former place to Hobb's Point. Capital, 80,000*l.* in 10*l.* shares; loans, 26,600*l.* Length of first line, to commence at or near Pembroke Docks and to terminate at Tenby, 11¾ miles; and length of second, to commence at or near Pembroke Docks and to terminate at Hobb's Point, two furlongs and 7¼ chains. Estimate, 80,000*l.* Opened, 27½ miles.

By 27 and 28 Vic., cap. 183 (14th July, 1864), the company was authorised to construct several short lines, including an extension to Whitland. Length, 18 miles. Capital, 200,000*l.* in shares, and 66,000*l,* on loan.

By 29 and 30 Vic., cap. 330 (6th August, 1866), the company was authorised to extend the line to Carmarthen and to Milford Haven. Length, 15¾ miles. Capital, 200,000*l.* in shares, and 65,600*l.* on loan. Arrangements with Great Western, Cambrian, Central Wales, Llanelly, and Manchester and Milford. Opened for goods traffic only.

REVENUE.—The receipts for the half-year ending 31st December, 1867, amounted to, 10,142*l.,* being 3,117*l.* in excess of the previous six months.

The report for the June half-year stated that the revenue continued most satisfactory, showing an increase of 1,351*l.* over that of the corresponding six months of the previous year. The directors congratulated the shareholders on the extension of the line from Whitland to Carmarthen, and the consequent connection of the district by the narrow-gauge system with the Northern and Midland Counties. The line had been worked by Messrs. Davies and Roberts in a satisfactory manner. The dividends for the year have been at the rate of 5 per cent. upon the ordinary and preference shares.

CAPITAL.—The receipts and expenditure on this account to 30th June, 1868, have been as follows:—

Received.		Expended.	
Ordinary shares	£75,748	On account of contractors	£9,336
5 per cent. preference shares	150,680	To contractors, under contracts 1 and 2	299,875
Loans on debentures at 5 per cent.:—		To contractors, under contract No. 3	28,100
Under Act of 1859	£26,400		
Under Act of 1864	63,320		£337,311
Under Act of 1866	20,000		
Sundries	1,220	Balance at bankers	£7
	£337,369		£337,369

Meetings in February and August.

No. of Directors—7; minimum, 5; quorum, 3. *Qualification,* 300*l.*

DIRECTORS:

Chairman—WILLIAM OWEN, Esq., Whithy Bush, Haverfordwest.

Deputy-Chairman—GEORGE MATHIAS, Esq., Tenby.

Charles Allen, Esq., Tenby.
Stephen Robinson, Esq., The Moor, Kingston, Herefordshire.

F. L. Clark, Esq., Pembroke.
John Barrow, Esq., Ringwood, Chesterfield.

OFFICERS.—Sec., Thomas Stokes, Pembroke Dock; Traffic Man., Isaac Smedley, Pembroke Dock; Auditors, R. Greenish, Haverfordwest, and J. Phelps, Tenby; Solicitor, Wm. Davies, Haverfordwest.

Offices—Pembroke Dock.

318.—PENARTH.

(LEASED TO TAFF VALE.)

Incorporated as the ELY TIDAL by 19 and 20 Vic., cap. 122 (21st July, 1856), to construct a line from the Taff Vale, 5¾ miles from Cardiff, to river Ely, County of Glamorgan, and for converting part of that river into a tidal harbour. Capital, 130,000*l.* in 100*l.* shares; loans, 43,000*l.* Length, 6½ miles; narrow gauge. Board of Trade may appoint auditor to examine accounts.

By 20 and 21 Vic., cap. 69 (27th July, 1857), the name of the company was changed to the "PENARTH HARBOUR DOCK AND RAILWAY." Various deviations and improvements were sanctioned, and the period of completion extended to five years from date of Act, and of others to ten years. New capital authorised to the extent of 192,000*l.*, in 100*l.* shares, 10*l.* calls, with intervals of two months. Power to borrow extended to sum of 107,000*l.* Opened July, 1859.

By 24 and 25 Vic., cap. 124 (11th July, 1851), the company was authorised to raise further capital to the extent of 300,000*l.* in shares, and 100,000*l.* on loan, for the purpose of completing the works, the purchase of steamers, &c.

At a special meeting of the Taff Vale, and of the Penarth, on 12th August, 1862, a lease of the Penarth for 10 years was agreed to, in the following terms:—At a rent, till the dock works are open for traffic, that will pay the Penarth interest upon 73,000*l.* of existing debentures, and 4½ per cent. upon 157,000*l.* share capital, with one-half divisible profits. After the dock is open for traffic, the rent will be the interest upon all the debentures, and 4½ per cent. upon all the share capital expended, with one-half divisible profits. Parliament, by 26 and 27 Vic., cap. 75 (22nd June, 1863), sanctioned a lease for 999 years upon the above terms.

REVENUE.—The directors, in their report for the half-year ending 31st December, regretted that they could not recommend a dividend. The capital account showed an apparent balance in hand, arising from the extra cost of the dock works above the contract prices, together with a considerable sum for interest, being held to the debit of the contractors, and not yet charged to the capital account.

The report presented to the shareholders in August contained the following announcement:—" The revenue account has been modified as the result of an arrangement by which the company's disputes and litigation with the Taff Vale have been terminated. This arrangement involves the abatement of rent as shown in the revenue account with the complete settlement of the accounts as rendered by the Taff Vale, amounting to 31,880*l.*, by the payment on the part of this company of 22,000*l.*, with a further payment of 1,000*l.* for any claim the Taff Vale may have for all other matters relating to your undertaking. This settlement with the Taff Vale ensures from the 1st January, 1868, and in perpetuity, the receipt by this company of rent at 4½ per cent., with half profits, on the total share capital, interest half-yearly on all the debenture capital, and a further sum of 4½ per cent. on 3,245*l.*, half the cost of the entrance to the Graving Dock."

A balance of 28,635*l.* stood to the credit of revenue account, which the directors have retained to meet, if required, the above allowance of 23,000*l.*

CAPITAL.—The receipts on this account to 30th June amounted to 795,234*l.*, and the expenditure to 720,428*l.*, leaving a balance in hand of 74,805*l.*

No. of Directors—9; minimum, 7; quorum, 5. *Qualification*, 2,500*l.*

DIRECTORS:

Chairman—CRAWSHAY BAILEY, Esq., Llanfoist, Abergavenny.

William S. Cartwright, Esq., Newport, Monmouthshire.
James H. Insole, Esq., Cardiff.
Henry Jones Evans, Esq., Banker, Cardiff.
Thomas Powell, Esq., Newport, Monmouthshire.

John Batchelor, Esq., Cardiff.
Lewis Davis, Esq., Preswylfa, Cardiff.
John Nixon, Esq., Cardiff.
Lieut.-Col. The Hon. G. H. W. Windsor Clive, M.P., 53, Grosvenor Street, W.

OFFICERS.—Sec., Booth Bacon; Auditors, James S. Batchelor and William P. Stephenson; Engs., John Hawkshaw, London, and Samuel Dobson, Cardiff; Solicitors, Elsdale and Byrne, Whitehall, S. W., and B. Matthews, Cardiff; Bankers, Wilkins and Co., Cardiff.

Offices—Cardiff.

319.—PETERBOROUGH, WISBEACH, AND SUTTON.

Incorporated by 26 and 27 Vic., cap. 222 (28th July, 1863), to construct a line from Peterborough to Thorney, Wisbeach, and Sutton, on the Norwich and Spalding. Length, 26¾ miles. Capital, 180,000*l.* in 20*l.* shares; and 60,000*l.* on loan. Arrangements with Great Northern and Midland. Works in progress.

By 27 and 28 Vic., cap. 240 (25th July, 1864), the company was authorised to extend the line to the Great Eastern. Length, 2¼ miles. Capital, 105,000*l.* in shares, and 35,000*l.* on loan.

By 28 and 29 Vic., cap. 340 (5th July, 1865), the company was authorised to construct an extension to Crowland, and to make certain deviations. Length, 11 miles. Capital 39,500*l.* in shares, and 13,000*l.* on loan.

By 29 and 30 Vic., cap. 267 (23rd July, 1866), the company obtained power to regulate its early capital, class B shares being converted into preferred original shares, at 5 per cent., and the class A shares into deferred original shares, to rank after the other.

REVENUE.—The receipts for the half-year ending 31st December were 6,055l., showing an increase of 970l. The increase for the June half-year was 839l. The Midland still continued to work and maintain the line, but the directors were of opinion that its capabilities were not properly developed.

NEW CAPITAL.—At the half-yearly meeting in March the directors were authorised to raise additional capital, not exceeding 25,000l., by the issue of new shares. The expenditure to 30th June amounted to 352,173l., the receipts having been as under:—

	Authorised.	Received.
6,750 deferred shares, 20l. each	£135,000	£110,000
7,500 preferred shares, 20l. each	150,000	150,000
Loans	95,000	93,472
		£353,472

No. of Directors—10; minimum, 6; quorum, 5 and 4. *Qualification*, 1,000l.

DIRECTORS:
Chairman—JOSEPH CARY, Esq., 49, Pall Mall, S.W.

Alexander Clunes Sherriff, Esq., M.P., Perdiswell Hall, Worcester, and 10, Dean's Yard, Westminster, S.W.

Augustus Samuel Wildy, Esq., 116, Regent's Park Road, N.W.

Captain Robert O'Brien Jameson, The Albany, Piccadilly, W.

Richard Young, Esq., Osborne House, Wisbeach, and 8, Austin Friars, E.C.

OFFICERS.—Sec., W. H. Dawson ; Solicitors, Messrs. Burchells, Broad Sanctuary, Westminster, S.W.

Offices—9, Victoria Chambers, Westminster, S.W.

320.—PETERSFIELD AND BISHOP'S WALTHAM.

Incorporated by 27 and 28 Vic., cap. 310 (29th July, 1864), to construct a line from Petersfield to Bishop's Waltham. Length, 12¾ miles. Capital, 150,000l. in 10l. shares, and 50,000l. on loan. Arrangements with South Western.

Meetings in February and August.

No. of Directors—6; minimum, 3; quorum, 3 and 2. *Qualification*, 500l.

DIRECTORS:
Henry Lacy, Esq.

Admiral Sir Henry J. Leeke, K.C.B., K.H., United Service Club, S.W.

Sir Sibbald David Scott, Bart.

Bettsworth Pitt Shearer, Esq.

321.—PLYMOUTH AND DARTMOOR.

Incorporated by 59 Geo. III., cap. 115, to make a tramroad from Crabtree to the prison in the Forest of Dartmoor. Capital, 35,000l. Remodelled by 28 Vic., cap. 131 (19th June, 1865). New capital, 75,000l. in shares, and 25,000l. on loan. Arrangements with South Devon.

No. of Directors—5; minimum, 3; quorum, 3 and 2. *Qualification*, 300l.

DIRECTORS:
William Bowles, Esq., 31, Upper Hamilton Terrace, St. John's Wood, N.W.

Charles John Johnson, Esq.

Charles Harrison, Esq.

James Brend Batten, Esq., 32, Great George Street, Westminster, S.W.

322.—PONTYPOOL, CAERLEON, AND NEWPORT.

Incorporated by 28 and 29 Vic., cap. 364 (5th July, 1865), to construct a line from the Newport Abergavenny and Hereford, at Pontypool, to Newport, on the Great Western. Length, 12 miles. Capital, 100,000l. in shares, and 33,300l. on loan. Arrangements with Great Western.

By 31 and 32 Vic., cap. 137 (13th July, 1868), the time limited for completion of works was extended to 5th July, 1871.

No. of Directors—8; minimum, 5; quorum, 3. *Qualification*, 500l.

DIRECTORS:
Francis Moggridge, Esq.

Richard Padmore, Esq.

Martin Abell, Esq.

Charles Conway, Esq.

Richard Steven Roper, Esq.

323.—POOLE AND BOURNEMOUTH.

Incorporated by 28 Vic., cap. 19 (26th May, 1865), to construct a line between these places. Length, 8¾ miles. Capital, 90,000*l.* in shares, and 30,000*l.* on loan.

No progress has been made with this company, although the South Western obtained an Act in 1866 to connect it with their system. An agreement was entered into between this company and the South Western, whereby the Messrs. Waring were to construct the line, but the shareholders of the South Western, at their meeting in August, refused to ratify the agreement.

No. of Directors—6; minimum, 4; quorum, 3. *Qualification*, 250*l.*

DIRECTORS:

Frederick Styring, Esq.
George Bellen, Junr., Esq.
William Pearce, Esq.
Charles Augustus Lewin, Esq.

The Right Hon. Viscount Gort, 10, Warwick Square, Pimlico, S.W.
Charles Waring, Esq.

324.—PORT CARLISLE.

(LEASED TO NORTH BRITISH.)

Incorporated by Act 17 Vic., cap. 119 (August 4th, 1853), for converting a canal into a railway. By 29 Geo. III., cap. 13 the canal was authorised from Carlisle to Solway Firth (Fisher's Cross), Bowness, Cumberland ("Port Carlisle"), and "Carlisle Canal Company," was incorporated, with a capital of 80,000*l.* and 40,000*l.* By 7 Wm. IV., cap. 50 (Dock Act), power was given to make docks at Port Carlisle, and raise 40,000*l.* Length, 11½ miles. Opened 22nd May, 1854, for goods, and on 22nd June for passengers.

By 23 and 24 Vic., cap. 134 (3rd July, 1860), the Port Carlisle was authorised to raise an additional sum of 40,000*l.* by shares, to which a 5 per cent. preferential dividend may be assigned, payable next after the dividends on existing preference stock of 35,000*l.*, and before principal or interest of any of the existing mortgages or charges on the undertaking. The same Act gives to the Port Carlisle and the Carlisle and Silloth running powers over the portion called the canal branch in Carlisle (1½ mile), and rights to traffic facilities over the Newcastle and Carlisle, upon terms to be settled in default of agreement by arbitration; and to commute tolls payable to the corporation of Newcastle in respect of the traffic of the two former companies into or out of that town, for a payment to be ascertained, in default of agreement, by arbitration.

By 25 Vic., cap. 47 (3rd June, 1862), the Port Carlisle is leased to the North British for 999 years, at a rent of 3,100*l.* Under provisions of this Act the capitals raised for the purpose of converting the Carlisle canal into a railway, and increasing the station accommodation at Carlisle, namely, 35,000*l.* 5 per cent. first preference stock, and 7,380*l.* 5½ second preference stock, have been transferred to, and have become preference stocks of, the North British; and all the debts and liabilities (except mortgage debt) of the Port Carlisle remaining undischarged on the 1st August, 1862, become debts and liabilities of the North British, thus leaving to the Port Carlisle only the original mortgage debt. This mortgage debt is by the Act converted into an irredeemable debenture stock, receiving from 1st August, 1862, a perpetual fixed dividend of 3 per cent. out of the annual rent of 3,100*l.*, payable by the North British, and leaving sufficient to pay a dividend of 1 per cent. at least on original stock. The dividends have been at the rate of 1*l.* 4*s.* per cent. on the ordinary stock.

It was reported in August that, after paying a dividend at the rate of 3 per cent. per annum upon the debenture stock for past half-year, there remained a balance of 433*l.*, out of which the directors recommended the payment of a dividend at the rate of 1*l.* 4*s.* per cent. upon the ordinary stock, leaving 20*l.* to be carried forward.

DIRECTORS:

Chairman—WILLIAM MARSHALL, Esq., Patterdale Hall, Westmorland.

The Rev. John Heysham, Lazonby, Cumberland.
William Bousfield Page, Esq., Carlisle.

William Forster, Esq., Carlisle.
William Edward James, Esq., Barrock Park, Carlisle.

OFFICERS.—Sec., John Nanson, Town Clerk, Carlisle; Auditors, John Laver and Silas Saul; Solicitor, John Nanson, Carlisle.

Offices—Carlisle.

325.—PORTADOWN, DUNGANNON, AND OMAGH.

Incorporated by 11 Vic., cap. 153 (1857), for a line from Portadown to Dungannon, north of Ireland. Length, 13½ miles. Capital, 154,775*l*., and loans, 51,585*l*. On 28th June, 1853, a further Act was obtained (16 and 17 Vic., cap. 57), for reviving the powers to take lands and completion of works for four years. Opened 5th April, 1858

By 20 and 21 Vic., cap. 120 (10th August, 1857), an Act to amend and enlarge the powers of the company, and to extend the line to the town of Omagh, was obtained. Arrangements were authorised with the Ulster, and new capital to the extent of 100,000*l*. in 10*l*. shares, and 33,000*l*. in loans created. Length of extension is 27 miles.

By 23 and 24 Vic., cap. 121 (3rd July, 1860), the company was authorised to alter the extension line, and to make a short branch at Omagh, to be completed in four years; and to enter into arrangements with Ulster and Londonderry and Enniskillen.

By 24 Vic., cap. 69 (12th June, 1861), the company was authorised to construct a branch from Dungannon to Auchnacloy. Length, 12 miles. Capital, 75,000*l*. in shares, and 24,000*l*. on loan. Completion of works, five years.

By 26 and 27 Vic., cap. 153 (13th July, 1863), the company obtained power to raise new capital to the extent of 75,000*l*. in shares, at 5 per cent., and 24,800*l*. on loan.

The Ulster contributes 40,000*l*. to the undertaking, and works the line till 1868, at 55 per cent. In operation, 41 miles.

REVENUE.—The following is a comparative statement of traffic for five years, ending 30th June, 1867 :—

	Half-Yearly.	Yearly.	Increase.
June 30, 1863	£8,813		
December 31, 1863	9,094	£17,908	£1,061
June 30, 1864	9,458		
December 31, 1864	9,786	19,244	1,336
June 30, 1865	9,934		
December 31, 1865	11,242	21,177	1,932
June 30, 1866	10,507		
December 31, 1866	11,579	22,087	909
June 30, 1867	11,997		
December 31, 1867	13,094	25,091	3,004
June 30, 1868	11,769		

CAPITAL.—The receipts to 30th June, 1868, have been 490,212*l*., the expenditure from which leaves a balance in hand of 4,570*l*. The balance sheet to same date sets forth the subjoined particulars:—

Dr.		Cr.	
Capital account	£4,570	Ulster railway	£4,971
Revenue account	444	Provincial Bank of Ireland	677
Messrs. Newtons and Armstrong	638	Cash in secretary's hands	5
	£5,654		£5,654

The directors have been authorised to borrow 3,500*l*. on mortgage.

DIRECTORS:

2 Chairman—Colonel the Hon. WILLIAM STUART KNOX, M.P., Dungannon Park, Dungannon, and 13, St. James's Place, S.W.

1 Deputy-Chairman—JOHN DOUGLAS COOPER, Esq., J.P., Killymoon Castle, Cookstown.

3 Jacob Orr, Esq., Laurel Hill, Loughgall. | 2 Colonel Caulfield, J.P., Drumcairn,
4 John W. Greer, Esq., J.P., Lurgan. | Stewartstown.

1, Retires in 1869; 2, in 1870; 3, in 1871; 4, representative of the Ulster company.

OFFICERS.—Sec., William Mackay; Solicitors, Longfield, Davidson, and Kelly, 62, Upper Sackville Street, Dublin, and Dungannon; Bankers, Provincial Bank of Ireland.

326.—PORTPATRICK.

Incorporated by 20 and 21 Vic., cap. 149 (10th August, 1857), to construct a line from Castle Douglas to Portpatrick. Capital, 460,000*l*. in 10*l*. shares; loans, 150,000*l*. Length of main line, 61 miles; Stranraer branch, 7 furlongs and 37 yards; branch to Portpatrick Harbour, 4 furlongs and 32 yards; total, 62½ miles. Main line commences by a junction with the Castle Douglas and Dumfries, at Castle Douglas, and terminates near Portpatrick; the Stranraer branch diverges from the main line in the parish of Inch, and terminates near Stranraer harbour; and the other branch diverges from the main line at Portpatrick, and terminates at the north pier of that harbour. Worked by Caledonian.

By 27 and 28 Vic., cap. 317 (29th July, 1864), the company obtained power to alter certain works, to increase the capital, and to arrange with the London and North Western and the Caledonian as to working the line. New capital, 20,000l. in shares, and 10,000l. on loan. Facilities to Glasgow and South Western.

By 27 and 28 Vic., cap. 318 (29th July, 1864), the company was authorised to establish steam communication between Portpatrick and Donaghadee, and between Stranraer and Belfast and Larne. New capital, 72,000l. in shares, and 24,000l. on loan. London and North Western, Glasgow and South Western, and Belfast and County Down subscribe.

REVENUE.—The statement of accounts for the half-year ending 31st January, 1868, showed a balance at the credit of revenue, after payment of working expenses and other charges, of 3,623l., which allowed a dividend on the ordinary shares at the rate of 1½ per cent. per annum, being the same as for the corresponding period of last year. There had been a small increase on the receipts for the half-year, but the addition to the taxes, arising from an increase on the valuation of the line, absorbed the whole additional revenue.

It was reported for the half-year ending 31st July that the balance at credit of revenue, after paying working expenses and other charges, amounted to 3,003l., which was sufficient for a dividend on the ordinary shares of 1¼ per cent. per annum, free of income tax. It was also reported that, after vainly exhausting every means to obtain from government the fulfilment of their engagement to adopt the Portpatrick route for the mail service to the North of Ireland, the directors deemed it necessary to settle on the most favourable terms that could be obtained. After a long negotiation, the treasury eventually agreed to pay a sum of 20,000l., and to grant a loan of the whole debenture debt for a period of 35 years, at 3½ per cent., in satisfaction of the company's claims, and an Act of Parliament was passed in last session sanctioning these terms of settlement.

CAPITAL.—The receipts on this account to 31st July were 557,772l.; the expenditure from which left a balance of 4,474l. The share capital is 436,151l., and the amount borrowed 121,621l.

Meetings may be held in Stranraer, Carlisle, or such other places as the directors may appoint.

No. of Directors.—In addition to those to be appointed by the Lancaster and Carlisle, Glasgow and South Western, and the Belfast and County Down, 10; quorum, 4. *Qualification,* 500l.

DIRECTORS:

Chairman—8 The EARL OF STAIR, Loch Inch Castle, Stranraer, and 32, Albemarle Street, W.

Deputy-Chairman—9 Sir WILLIAM DUNBAR, Bart., Mertonhall.

10 Sir Andrew Agnew, Bart., of Locknaw, Wigtownshire.
1 Captain Viscount Garlies, M.P., Galloway House, Wigtownshire.
2 John C. Moore, Esq., of Corsewall, Wigtownshire.
3 Horatio G. M. Stewart, Esq., of Cally, Gatehouse.
4 Colonel James M'Douall, of Logan, Wigtownshire.
5 Lieut.-Col. Salkeld, Holmhill, Carlisle.
† Sir James Lumsden, Lord Provost of Glasgow

6 Sir John C. D. Hay, Bart., M.P., of Park Place, and 108, St. George's Square, S.W.
7 George Guthrie, Esq., of Appleby, Stranraer.
* James Mackie, Esq., of Bargally, and 99, Piccadilly, W.
* William Nicholson Hodgson, Esq., M.P., Newby Grange, Carlisle, and 33, Duke Street, St. James's, S.W.
† Andrew Galbraith, Esq., Glasgow.
‡ William Nevin Wallace, Esq., Downpatrick.

* Appointed by the Lancaster and Carlisle.   † Appointed by the Glasgow and South Western.   ‡ Appointed by the Belfast and County Down.

The numbers prefixed to the names indicate the order in which they retire.

OFFICERS.—Sec., Alexander Ingram, Writer, Stranraer; Auditors, George Agnew Main, Banker, Whithorn, and Alexander Guthrie, Writer, Stranraer.

Head Office—Stranraer.

327.—POTTERIES, SHREWSBURY, AND NORTH WALES.

An amalgamation by 29 and 30 Vic., cap. 201 (16th July, 1866), of the undermentioned undertakings:—

1. Shrewsbury and North Wales.—Incorporated by 25 and 26 Vic., cap. 185 (29th July, 1862), to construct a line from Westbury, on the Shrewsbury and Welshpool, to Llanymynech, on the Oswestry and Newtown. Length, 13¾ miles. Capital, 90,000l. in 10l. shares; loans, 30,000l. By 26 and 27 Vic., cap. 145 (13th July, 1863), the company was authorised to make certain deviations in branches, and to enter into arrangements with the London and North Western, Great Western, Shrewsbury and Welshpool, and the Oswestry and Newtown. Length, 8¼ miles. Capital, 60,000l. and 20,000l. on loan. By 27 and 28 Vic., cap. 126 (30th June, 1864), the company was authorised to construct seven new lines, and to use a portion of the Oswestry and Newtown. Length, 20 miles. Capital, 200,000l. in shares, and 66,000l. on loan. By 27 and 28 Vic., cap. 156 (30th June, 1864), the company obtained power to change its name to that of the "Shrewsbury and North Wales," to construct several smaller branches (18¾ miles), to raise new capital to the extent of 100,000l. in shares, and 33,000l. on loan. London and North Western and Cambrian to use the railway. By 28 Vic., cap. 29, the company was authorised to make certain deviations, and to raise certain capital to the extent of 100,000l. in shares or half shares, and 33,000l. on loan. By 29 and 30 Vic., cap. 220 (10th July, 1866), the Shrewsbury and North Wales obtained power to make certain deviations, and also to construct a line to Bryn Tanat. Length, ¼ mile. New capital, 80,000l. in shares, and 26,000l. on loan. Arrangements with Cambrian and Drayton Junction.

2. Shrewsbury and Potteries Junction.—Incorporated by 28 and 29 Vic., cap. 341 (5th July, 1865), to construct various lines from Market Drayton on the Wellington and Drayton, and connecting with the Shrewsbury and Crewe, the Welshpool, the Severn Valley, and the Shrewsbury and Hereford. Length, 23½ miles. Capital, 400,000l. in shares, and 133,300l. on loan. By 29 and 30 Vic., cap. 211 (16th July, 1866), the Shrewsbury and Potteries obtained power to make certain deviations, and also to participate in the ownership of the Wellington and Drayton. New capital, 80,000l. in shares, and 26,600l. on loan.

By 31 and 32 Vic., cap. 73 (25th June, 1868), the company was authorised to make a "substituted" line, and also to abandon portions of the railway. Works to be completed in two years.

The sections of the Shrewsbury and North Wales line from Llanymynech to Red Hill, and the Shrewsbury and Potteries from Red Hill to Shrewsbury, were opened on 13th of August, 1866.

No. of Directors—8; minimum, 5; quorum, 3. *Qualification, 500l.*

DIRECTORS:

Chairman—ELIAS MOCATTA, Esq., 5, Scarisbrick Street, Southport, Lancashire.

Major-General Henry Pelham Burn, 94, Inverness Terrace, Bayswater, W.
Joseph Bravo, Esq., 20, Lancaster Gate, Hyde Park, W.

John Alldin Moore, Esq., Red Hill, Surrey.
Augustus Samuel Wildy, Esq., 34, Great Winchester Street, E.C.

OFFICERS.—Gen. Man., J. B. Cooper, Shrewsbury; Sec., Charles Chandler, Shrewsbury; Assistant Sec., John Wade, 75, Ethelburga House, Bishopsgate Street, E.C.; Eng., John Ashdown, 7, Westminster Chambers, S.W.; Auditors, Henry Billson and W. F. Cattlow; Solicitor, S. F. Noyes, 1, Broad Sanctuary, Westminster, S.W.

Offices—75, Ethelburga House, Bishopsgate Street, E.C., and Talbot Chambers, Shrewsbury.

328.—PRESTEIGN, CLUN, AND BISHOP'S CASTLE.

Incorporated by 29 and 30 Vic., cap. 243 (23rd July, 1866), to construct lines from the Kington and Eardisley between Presteign and Clun, and Craven Arms on the Central Wales and Knighton. Length, 19¾ miles. Capital, 220,000l. in 10l. shares, and 73,000l. on loan.

No. of Directors—5; quorum, 3. *Qualification, 300l.*

OFFICERS. — Sec., W. Roberts; Solicitors, Stephens and Bellamy, Presteign, Thomas Griffiths, Bishop's Castle, and Wm. Wilding, Montgomery; Bankers, Barnett, Hoare, & Co., Lombard Street, E.C., Parsons and Co., Presteign, and North and South Wales Bank, Bishop's Castle.

Office—Brecon.

329.—RAMSEY.

Incorporated by 24 and 25 Vic., cap. 194 (22nd July, 1861), to construct a line from Holme, on the Great Northern, to Ramsey, Huntingdonshire. Length, 5 miles 51 chains. Capital, 30,000*l.* in 10*l.* shares, and 10,000*l.* on loan. Opened in July, 1863. Worked by the Great Northern for seven years from that date.

Meetings in February or March, and in August or September, in Ramsey or in London.

No. of Directors—3; quorum, 2. *Qualification*, 500*l.*

DIRECTORS:

Chairman—EDWARD FELLOWES, Esq., M.P., 3, Belgrave Square, S.W.

W. Staffurth, Esq.

OFFICERS.—Sec., Thomas James, Solicitor, Ramsey, Huntingdonshire; Solicitor, F. W. Thorp, St. Ives, Hunts.

Offices—Ramsey, Huntingdonshire.

330.—RATHKEALE AND NEWCASTLE JUNCTION.

Incorporated by 24 and 25 Vic., cap. 168 (22nd July, 1861), to construct a line from the Limerick and Foynes, near Rathkeale, to Newcastle, county Limerick. Length, 10 miles 11 chains. Capital, 50,000*l.* in 10*l.* shares; loans, 16,600*l.* Arrangements with Limerick and Foynes, and Waterford and Limerick, which subscribed 5,000*l.* each, the Waterford and Limerick having also agreed to work the line. Opened, 1st January, 1867.

By 30 and 31 Vic., cap. 191 (12th August, 1867), the company was authorised to issue preference shares at 5 per cent., to the extent of 13,000*l.*, in lieu of unissued ordinary capital, and also to raise new capital to the extent of 25,000*l.*, also at 5 per cent. preference, and 15,000*l.* on mortgage. Also to create debenture stock.

The company obtained a loan of 16,600*l.* from the Public Works Loan Commissioners at 5 per cent. to replace debenture debt.

An Act of parliament was obtained in 1865 by an independent company for extending this line to Abbeyfeale and Listowel, which, when completed, will only leave a short length of 20 miles of railway to be constructed between Listowel and Tralee to connect the Limerick, Newcastle, and Listowel districts by rail with the Tralee, Killarney, Mallow, and Cork systems of railway communications.

By 31 and 32 Vic., cap. 172 (31st July, 1868), the Public Works Loan Commissioners have power to lend to this company should they think fit, all or any part of the money it is entitled to borrow on mortgage, viz., 31,600*l.*

Scale of Voting.—One vote for each share held.

No. of Directors—5; minimum, 3; quorum, 3.

DIRECTORS:

Chairman—The Right Hon. The EARL OF DEVON, Powderham Castle, Exeter, and 68, Brook Street, W.

William Malcomson, Esq., Portlaw, Waterford.	Joseph William Holland, Esq., Birley House, Forest Hill, S.
Edward Curling, Esq., J.P., Newcastle West, County Limerick.	Lord Courtenay, M.P., 68, Brook Street, W.

OFFICERS.—Sec., H. Williams Wood, 6, Westminster Chambers, Victoria Street, Westminster, S.W.; Eng., William Barrington; Traffic Man., Thomas Ainsworth; Solicitors, Tracy and Nagle, Cork, Michael Leahy, Newcastle, and P. Burrowes Sharkey, 42, Blessington Street, Dublin, and Carlton Chambers, 12, Regent Street, W.; Bankers, Provincial Bank of Ireland, and National Bank.

Offices—6, Westminster Chambers, Victoria Street, Westminster, S.W.

331.—REDDITCH.

Incorporated by 21 and 22 Vic., cap. 137 (23rd July, 1858), to construct a line from Redditch to the Midland at Barnt Green. Capital, 35,000*l.* in 10*l.* shares; loans, 11,500*l.* Length, 4¾ miles. Opened 19th September, 1859. Leased to and worked by Midland.

By 25 and 26 Vic., cap. 214 (7th August, 1862), the company was authorised to raise new capital to the extent of 15,000*l.*, on shares at not exceeding 6 per cent.; and 5,000*l.* on loan. Also to create debenture stock in lieu of loans. Dividend, 4 per cent.

Meetings in February or March and August or September.

No. of Directors—4; minimum, 3; quorum, 3. *Qualification*, 300*l.*

DIRECTORS:

1 Chairman—HENRY MILWARD, Esq., Redditch.

2 Samuel Thomas, Esq., Redditch.   4 John Osborne, Esq., Redditch.
3 J. E. Clift, Esq., Redditch.

The figures denote the order of retirement—all eligible for re-election.

OFFICERS.—Sec., Charles Swann; Auditors, W. T. Heming and Richard Harrison, Redditch; Solicitors, Browning and Son, Redditch, and Bolton and Sanders, Dudley. Offices—Redditch.

332.—REDRUTH AND FALMOUTH JUNCTION.

Incorporated by 27 and 28 Vic., cap. 269 (25th July, 1864), to construct a line from the Cornwall, at Perran-Arworthal, to Redruth, and form a junction with the West Cornwall. Mixed gauge. Length, 5¼ miles. Capital, 80,000*l.* in 20*l.* shares, and 26,600*l.* on loan. Arrangements with Cornwall.

No. of Directors—6; quorum, 3. *Qualification*, 500*l.*

DIRECTORS:

John Solomon Bickford, Esq.   William Teague, Esq.
Francis Pryor, Esq.

333.—RHONDDA VALLEY AND HIRWAIN JUNCTION.

Incorporated by 30 and 31 Vic., cap. 188 (12th August, 1867), to construct four short lines in the county of Glamorgan, connecting the Taff Vale and the Vale of Neath. Length, 7 miles. Capital, 135,000*l.* in 10*l.* shares, and 45,000*l.* on loan.

No. of Directors—6; quorum, 3. *Qualification*, 300*l.*

DIRECTORS:

Handel Cossham, Esq.   David Joseph, Esq.
Thomas Joseph, Esq.   James Marychurch, Esq.
John Daniel Thomas, Esq.   Evan Davies, Esq.

334.—RHYMNEY.

Incorporated by 17 and 18 Vic., cap. 193 (July 24th, 1854). Capital, 100,000*l.* in 10*l.* shares. Borrowing powers, 30,000*l.* The main line extends from Rhymney to a junction with the Great Western Company's Newport Abergavenny and Hereford line at the Hengoed (called by the G. W. Co. the Rhymney) Junction, the distance being over 9 miles. By the Act 18 and 19 Vic., cap. 110 (July 2nd, 1855), the company was authorised to raise 100,000*l.* additional capital in shares, and 30,000*l.* on loan, and to extend their main line from the Hengoed Junction to a Junction with the Taff Vale at Walnut Tree Bridge (about 18 miles from Rhymney), to run over 6 miles of the Taff Vale on to Cardiff, and to make the Bargoed branch, also branches to the Bute East Dock and Tidal Harbour at Cardiff, leading from and out of the Taff Vale, which terminates at the Bute West Dock. Thus, by the main line, a through communication is opened between Rhymney and Cardiff, the distance being from Rhymney to Cardiff Station, 24½, and to the docks, 26 miles. Also by the junction with the Great Western system at Hengoed, through routes are established from Cardiff and Rhymney to all parts of the west and north of England, through Pontypool Road and Hereford, and to Merthyr, Aberdare, and the Vale of Neath in South Wales. Through the Bargoed branch, now completed, access is also given to Dowlais, and to the Brecon and Merthyr, Mid-Wales, and other Welsh railway systems.

By 20 and 21 Vic., cap. 140 (10th August, 1857), the company is authorised to raise 100,000*l.* additional capital in shares, and 100,000*l.* on loan, inclusive of the debenture debt of 60,000*l.*

By 24 and 25 Vic., cap. 144 (11th July, 1861), the powers of the company to construct the Bargoed branch were revived, and authority given to raise new capital by 141,000*l.* and 47,000*l.* on loan.

By 27 and 28 Vic., cap. 275 (25th July, 1864), the company was authorised to construct extensions to join the Brecon and Merthyr and the Merthyr Tredegar and Abergavenny. Length, 3 miles. Capital, 45,000*l.* in shares, and 15,000*l.* on loan.

By 27 and 28 Vic., cap. 264 (25th July, 1864), the company was authorised to construct a line from Cardiff to Caerphilly. Length, 12½ miles. Capital, 210,000*l.* in shares, and 70,000*l.* on loan. By this Act, access to Cardiff, independent of the Taff Vale, was secured.

By 29 and 30 Vic., cap. 259 (23rd July, 1866), the Rhymney was authorised to construct two small branches. Length, 127 chains. Capital 66,000*l.* in deferred and preferred shares, and 22,000*l.* on loan.

By 30 and 31 Vic., cap. 171 (12th August, 1867), the Rhymney was authorised to construct a line (1½ mile) from Llanfabon to a junction with the Vale of Neath Extension, and to raise additional capital to the extent of 100,000*l.* in shares, and 33,300*l.* on loan; to divide the shares into deferred and preferred, and to grant 6 per cent. on the capital raised under the Acts of 1864. Also to exercise running powers over part of the Great Western system.

LONDON AND NORTH WESTERN.—It was reported in 1867 that the London and North Western had obtained an Act whereby about a mile and a half of the company's extension line north of Rhymney would be made and worked by the two companies jointly. The construction of a short line about 3 miles in length, would, with running powers over a portion of the London and North Western, enable the company to convey to Cardiff the produce of some of the principal works in Monmouthshire. It would also enable the two companies to interchange north of Rhymney a considerable traffic which was at present exchanged at Hengoed. The result of this alteration in the point of interchange would be that this traffic would pass over 27 miles of the company's railway, instead of over about ten miles, as at present.

CARDIFF AND CAERPHILLY.—In order to construct the Cardiff and Caerphilly and other works the Rhymney directors proposed cancelling 213,000*l.* of existing 5 per cent. preference shares, and the re-creation of those shares with a preferential dividend of 6 per cent.

REVENUE.—The receipts for the half-year ending the 30th of June amounted to 32,961*l.*, and for the corresponding period in 1867 to 33,799*l.*, showing a decrease of 838*l.* A strike of the colliers in a considerable portion of the district occupied by the railway occurred in the early part of the past half-year and continued for some months. The result was a greatly diminished supply of coal and a consequent diminution of receipts from coal and coke traffic. The balance at credit of revenue was 1,777*l.*, out of which a dividend at the rate of 1¾ per cent. left a balance of 111*l.*

CAPITAL.—This account to 30th June showed that 668,255*l.* had been expended, leaving a balance of 83,045*l.* against the company.

DIRECTORS:

Chairman—2 JOHN BOYLE, Esq., 6, Barnard's Inn, Holborn, E.C.

3 William Austin, Esq., The Mount, Farningham, Kent.
5 C. T. Simpson, Esq., 7, Old Buildings, Lincoln's Inn, W.C.
6 Thomas Dakin, Esq., Alderman, 2 and 3, Creechurch Lane, E.C.

1 John S. Gilliat, Esq., 4, Crosby Square, E.C.
4 Lieut.-Colonel George H. Tyler, Cottrel, Cardiff.

The numbers prefixed to the names of the directors show the order in which they go out of office. They are all eligible for re-election.

OFFICERS.—Sec., John B. Shand; Traffic Man. and Eng., Cornelius, Lundie*;* Auditors, Geo. Wm. Horn and Wm. P. Stephenson; Solicitor, W. Gascoigne Roy.

Offices—Cardiff.

335.—RIBBLESDALE.

Incorporated by 27 and 28 Vic., cap. 80 (23rd June, 1864), to construct a line from Chatburn, on the Lancashire and Yorkshire, to Settle. Length, 14½ miles. Capital, 180,000*l.* in 10*l.* shares, and 60,000*l.* on loan. Arrangements with Midland and Lancashire and Yorkshire.

No. of Directors—8; minimum, 5; quorum, 4. *Qualification*, 1,000*l.*

DIRECTORS:

Right Hon. Lord Ribblesdale, Gisburn Park, Yorkshire.
Hector Christie, Esq.
Captain H. Gandy, Eden Grove, Kirkby Thore.

James Garnett, Esq.
Richard Hardacre, Esq.
R. C. Mercer, Esq.
J. B. S. Sturdy, Esq.
Robert Watson, Esq.

336.—RICKMANSWORTH, AMERSHAM, AND CHESHAM.

Incorporated by 25 and 26 Vic., cap. 171 (17th July, 1862), to construct a line from Rickmansworth, on the Watford and Rickmansworth, to Chesham, and a junction with the Uxbridge and Rickmansworth. Length, 8½ miles. Capital, 90,000l. in 10l. shares; loans, 30,000l. Works in progress.

By 27 and 28 Vic., cap. 276 (25th July, 1864), the company was authorised to make a level crossing at Rickmansworth. London and North Western may contribute 30,000l. and enter into working agreements.

By 28 and 29 Vic., cap. 147 (29th June, 1865), the company obtained an extension of time for completion of works till 1st August, 1867.

No. of Directors—6; minimum, 3; quorum, 3 and 2. *Qualification*, 300l.

DIRECTORS:

Chairman—LORD EBURY, Moor Park, Rickmansworth, and 107, Park Street, Grosvenor Square, S.W.

Deputy-Chairman—JOSEPH CARY, Esq., 49, Pall Mall, S.W.

The Hon. Reginald Capel, Little Cashio-bury, Watford, and 21, Chesham Place, S.W. | John Henry Dillon, Esq., 5K, Albany Piccadilly, W.

OFFICERS.—Sec., Alexander Forbes; Eng., John Sampson Peirce, 6, Victoria Street, Westminster, S.W.; Solicitors, Hargrove, Fowler, and Co., 3, Victoria Street Westminster, S.W.; Bankers, The National Bank, Old Broad Street, E.C.

Offices—3, Victoria Street, S.W.

337.—RINGWOOD, CHRISTCHURCH, AND BOURNEMOUTH.

Incorporated by 22 and 23 Vic., cap. 95 (8th August, 1859), to construct a line from the South Western, at Ringwood, to Christchurch. Capital, 45,000l. in 10l. shares, and 15,000l. on loans. Length, 7¾ miles. Opened 13th November, 1862. Worked by South Western, under usual restrictions.

By 26 and 27 Vic., cap. 134 (13th July, 1863), the company was authorised to extend the line to Bournemouth. Length, 3½ miles. New capital, 30,000l. in shares, and 10,000l. on loan.

Meetings in September or October. Accounts to be balanced yearly to 30th June.

No. of Directors—5; quorum, 3. *Qualification*, 500l.

DIRECTORS:

Chairman—Sir HENRY DRUMMOND WOLFF, K.C.M.G., 15, Rutland Gate, S.W.

Sir William Rose, K.C.B., New Bond Street, W. | James Grant Fraser, Esq., Surbiton.
James Druitt, Esq., Christchurch. | Henry Harrison, Esq., 4, Great George Street, S.W.

OFFICERS.—Eng., John Strapp, London and South Western Railway; Solicitors, Townsend, and Co., 3, Prince's Street, Westminster, S.W.; Auditors, Samuel Price and John Scath.

338.—ROSS AND MONMOUTH.

Incorporated by 28 and 29 Vic., cap. 312 (5th July, 1865), to construct a line from Ross, on the Hereford Ross and Gloucester, to Monmouth, on the Coleford Monmouth Usk and Pontypool. Length, 11 miles. Capital, 160,000l. in shares, of 20l. each. Arrangements with Great Western.

The report for August stated that the subscriptions, with few exceptions, had been satisfactorily paid up, and the works would shortly be commenced, the contract having been let to Mr. Firbank.

No. of Directors—6; quorum, 3. *Qualification*, 500l.

DIRECTORS:

Chairman—Colonel JOHN FRANCIS VAUGHAN.

Colonel H. Morgan Clifford, Llantilio House, near Abergavenny. | John Partridge, Esq., Bishop's Wood, near Ross.
Henry Richards Lückes, Esq., Ross. | William Partridge, Esq., Wyelands, near Ross, and 49, Gloucester Place, Hyde Park, London.
Colonel A. W. H. Meyrick, Goodrich Court, near Ross. |

OFFICERS.—Sec., John Edward Stower Hewett, Ross; Engs., Charles Liddell and Edward Richards; Solicitors, Henry Minett, Ross, Powles and Evans, Monmouth; Auditors, Thomas Blake, Ross, and Robert James Skynner, Monmouth.

Offices—Ross.

339.—ROYSTON AND HITCHIN.

Incorporated by 9 and 10 Vic., cap. 170 (16th July, 1846), for a line commencing from a junction with the Great Northern, at Hitchin, and terminating at Royston. The capital in that Act was fixed at 800,000*l*. In 1848 by Act 11 and 12 Vic., cap. 119, powers were given to extend the line from Royston to a point of junction with the Great Eastern branch to Bedford, near Shepreth, with the view of giving the company access to Cambridge. In 1851, another Act was obtained, reducing the nominal value of the original shares to 6¼*l*. at which rate they are now converted into stock. Length of main line, 12½ miles, which was opened 21st October, 1850; and of the extension, 5 miles, opened 1st August, 1851; cost of works, 3,500*l*. per mile.

By 27 and 28 Vic., cap. 124 (23rd June, 1864), the Great Northern and the Great Eastern were authorised to enter upon arrangements with regard to the future occupation of the Royston and Hitchin, which has again reverted to the former company.

The stock having long been converted into "Royston Hitchin and Shepreth Stock," the accounts are made up in February and August, and meetings held in these months. Registration fee, 2*s*. 6*d*. Stock certificates must accompany transfer deed, and a part of a pound allowed. Transfer books close 14 days before half-yearly meetings.

DIRECTORS:

Chairman—JOHN CHEVALLIER COBBOLD, Esq., Ipswich.

John George Fordham, Esq., Royston.	Major Wm. Amsinck, Richmond, S.W.
John Phillips, Esq., Royston.	Charles Wilson Faber, Esq., Northaw,
Joseph Sharples, Esq., Hitchin.	near Barnet.
Sir Robert Walter Carden, 2, Royal Ex-	Henry Fordham, Esq., Royston.
change Buildings, E.C.	Fred. Seebohm, Esq., Hitchin.

OFFICERS.—Sec., John C. Janson; Solicitors, Bircham, Dalrymple, and Drake, Parliament Street, S.W.; Bankers, City Bank.

Head Offices—61, Gracechurch Street, E.C.

340.—RYDE (ISLE OF WIGHT).

Incorporated by 29 and 30 Vic., cap. 303 (30th July, 1866), to construct a railway and central station, and also to erect slaughter-houses at Ryde, in the Isle of Wight. Length, 1 mile. Capital, 65,000*l*. in 10*l*. shares, and 21,600*l*. on loan. Arrangements with Isle of Wight.

By 30 Vic., cap. 59 (31st May, 1867), the company was authorised to construct a railway instead of tramways, and to enter into agreements with the Isle of Wight.

No. of Directors—5; minimum, 3; quorum, 3 and 2. *Qualification*, 500*l*.

DIRECTORS:

Edward Henry Bramah, Esq.	Binney Douglas, Esq.
Francis Cobb, Esq.	

341.—SAFFRON WALDEN.

Incorporated by 24 and 25 Vic., cap. 178 (22nd July, 1861), to construct a line from Wendon, on the Great Eastern, to Saffron Walden. Length, 2 miles. Capital, 25,000*l*. in 10*l*. shares, and 8,000*l*. on loan. Opened 21st November, 1865.

By 26 and 27 Vic., cap. 83 (22nd June, 1863), the company was authorised to construct an extension to Bartlow, on the Great Eastern. Length, 6¼ miles. New capital, 70,000*l*. in 10*l*. shares, and 23,000*l*. on loan. Arrangements with Great Eastern, which subscribed 23,000*l*. Opened October 26th, 1866.

It was reported in September that a settlement of certain matters in dispute with the Great Eastern has not yet been arrived at. The receipts for the half-year ending 30th June, amounted to 1,254*l*., as compared with 1,193*l*. in the corresponding six months of 1867, showing an increase of 61*l*. It is hoped that negotiations now in progress will bring the line into a more satisfactory state.

Meetings in February or March, and in August or September.

No. of Directors—5; minimum, 3; quorum, 3. *Qualification*, 100*l*.

DIRECTORS:

Chairman—WYATT GEORGE GIBSON, Esq.

George Stacy Gibson, Esq.	Joshua Clarke, Esq.
John Stephenson Robson, Esq.	James Starling, Esq.

342.—ST. ANDREWS.

Incorporated by 14 and 15 Vic., cap. 54 (3rd July, 1851), for a line from Milton Junction, on Edinburgh Perth and Dundee, to St. Andrews. Length, 4¾ miles. Opened 1st July, 1852. Worked by North British.

REVENUE.—The receipts for the half-year ending 31st January amounted to 2,206*l*., and the expenditure to 1,342*l*. The sum of 106*l*. was applied to paying interest on loans, 461*l*. for a dividend of 4½ per cent. on 21,000*l* share capital, and 606*l*. for working the railway, leaving a surplus of 169*l*., which, according to agreement, was equally divided between the St. Andrew's and the North British. The directors of the St. Andrew's were thus enabled to pay a dividend at the rate of 5 per cent. per annum. The increase in the revenue was 112*l*. over the corresponding period. The balance at the credit of the dividend reserve fund was 251*l*., and at the credit of the sinking fund, 500*l*.

The receipts to 31st July were 2,050*l*., and the expenditure 726*l*. The balance of 1,324*l*. was applied as follows:—Interest on 5,300*l*. of debenture loans, at 4 per cent. per annum, less tax, 101*l*.; dividend on 21,000*l*. of share capital, at 4½ per cent., less tax, 460*l*.; mileage of carriage power and plant to North British, 11,900 miles, at 1*s*. per mile, 595*l*. Surplus, 167*l*., which was equally divided between the two companies.

CAPITAL.—The statement of this account to 31st July furnished the subjoined particulars of income and expenditure:—

Original stock	£21,000	
On debentures	5,300	= £26,300
Expended		26,211

Balance in Bank of Scotland £88

The accounts are made up to 31st January and 31st July, and the statutory meetings are held at St. Andrews, in March or April, and September or October.

Transfer fee, 2*s*. 6*d*. Certificates must accompany.

DIRECTORS:

Chairman—WILLIAM SMITH, Esq., St. Andrews.

*John Orphat, Esq., Guard Bridge, near St. Andrews.
Andrew Aikman, Esq., St. Andrews.

Walter Thomas Milton, Esq., St. Andrews.
*John Purvis, Esq., Kinaldie.
John Adamson, Esq., M.D., St. Andrews.

* Retire in March, but are eligible for re-election.

OFFICERS.—Secretary and Solicitor, William Murray, St. Andrews; Eng., Wm. Barrie; Auditors, A. K. Lindesay and John Jamieson.

Head Offices—Albert Buildings, St. Andrews.

343.—ST. IVES AND WEST CORNWALL JUNCTION.

Incorporated by 26 and 27 Vic., cap. 230 (28th July, 1863), to construct a line from St. Erth, on the West Cornwall, to St. Ives. Length, 3¼ miles. Capital, 42,000*l*. in shares, and 14,000*l*. on loan. Arrangements with West Cornwall.

By 31 and 32 Vic., cap. 121 (13th July, 1868), the company obtained an extension of time for completion of works until 28th July, 1870.

No. of Directors—5; quorum, 3. *Qualification*, 250*l*.

DIRECTORS:

Edwin Bray, Esq.
Henry William Carr, Esq.

John Roseley, Esq.
John Child, Esq.

344.—SALISBURY.

Incorporated by 19 and 20 Vic., cap. 93 (14th July, 1856), to make a market-house and railway at Salisbury, to join the South Western. Length, 2 furlongs 20 yards. Capital, 12,000*l*. in 25*l*. shares; loans, 3,600*l*. Agreements made with the South Western and Salisbury and Yeovil.

By 27 Vic., cap. 21 (13th May, 1864), the company obtained power to increase its capital by 5,000*l* in shares, and 1,000*l*. on loan.

No. of Directors—9; minimum, 3; quorum, 5, and 3 when reduced. *Qualification*, 100*l*.

DIRECTORS:

Chairman—EDWARD HINXMAN, Esq., Durnford House, Salisbury.

F. R. Fisher, Esq., Salisbury.
Stephen Eldridge, Esq., Salisbury.
William Osmond, Jun., Esq., Salisbury.
F. Stephen Long, Esq., Bulford, Wilts.
Robert Stokes, Esq., Salisbury.

C. H. M. Finch, Esq., Bemerton Lodge, Salisbury.
John Waters, Esq., Salisbury.
Francis Attwood, Esq., The Close Salisbury.

Secretary, C. R. Norton.

Offices—Salisbury.

345.—SALISBURY AND DORSET JUNCTION.

Incorporated by 24 and 25 Vic., cap. 190, to construct a line from Salisbury to West Parley, near Wimborne. Length, 18½ miles. Capital, 160,000l. in 10l. shares; loans, 53,300l. Worked by South Western for 45 per cent. of the gross receipts. Opened 20th December, 1866.

By the Board of Trade (additional capital) certificate, 1867, the company was authorised to increase its capital by 15,000l. in shares, and 5,000l. on loan.

The undertaking is now in Chancery, under a receiver, the debenture interest not having been duly paid.

CAPITAL.—The receipts and expenditure on this account have been published as under :—

Received.		Expended.	
Share capital	£149,772	Land and compensation	£17,259
Debentures	45,384	Works of construction	185,899
Balance carried down	11,856	Expenses of administration, stationery, and general charges	608
		Commission and interest	1,478
		Debenture interest	1,767
	£207,012		£207,012

No. of Directors—7 ; quorum, 3. *Qualification*, 500l.

DIRECTORS :

Chairman—MATTHEW HENRY MARSH, Esq., Ramridge House, near Andover.
Deputy-Chairman—THOMAS PAIN, Esq., Ugford, Wilts.

S. Cook Frankish, Esq., Parliament Street, Westminster, S.W.
William Blackmore, Esq., Founder's Court, Lothbury, E.C.

Octavius Ommanney, Esq., Parliament Street, S.W.

OFFICERS.—Sec., G. W. Horn; Eng., Hamilton H. Fulton, 4, Victoria Street, Westminster, S.W.; Solicitors, Hoddings, Townsend, and Lee, 3, Prince's Street, Westminster, S.W.

Offices—2, Westminster Chambers, Victoria Street, Westminster, S.W.

346.—SALISBURY AND YEOVIL.

By this scheme (17 and 18 Vic., cap. 215, 1854), it is intended to construct a single line from the South Western at Salisbury, to the junction at Yeovil of the Great Western and Bristol and Exeter. The length of the main line is 40 miles, and of a branch to join the Wilts Somerset and Weymouth, 3 furlongs. Capital, 400,000l., in shares of 20l. each. Borrowing powers, 133,333l., and the line has now been doubled throughout its length.

By 18 Vic., cap. 62 (June 15th, 1855), a deviation of 6½ miles was authorised between Semley in Wilts, and Gillingham in Dorset. Powers to purchase this land expire in two years, and deviation to be completed within three years.

By 20 and 21 Vic., cap. 121 (10th August, 1857), the company is authorised to make certain deviations, which are to be completed within two years. The arrangement with the South Western is also legalised by this Act, as also authority to the latter to guarantee the Salisbury and Yeovil debentures to the extent of 133,000l.

By 21 and 22 Vic., cap. 67 (28th June, 1858), an extension of two years for completion of work was conceded. Under same Act the South Western took a lease of the undertaking, to work and maintain it for 42½ per cent. of traffic receipts. Opened to Gillingham (22 miles) on 1st May, 1859; to Sherborne (12 miles) on the 7th May, 1860; and to Yeovil (6 miles), 1st June, 1860.

By 23 and 24 Vic., cap. 124 (3rd July, 1860), certain deviations were authorised, and the Bristol and Exeter permitted to lay down the mixed gauge at Yeovil. Forfeited shares were also allowed to be cancelled and the company authorised to create and issue others instead, at a preference not exceeding 5 per cent. Additional capital in shares was likewise sanctioned to a preference to the extent of 150,000l., which may be raised at 5 per cent. preference, and further loans, amounting to 49,500l. South Western may guarantee interest on Salisbury and Yeovil mortgages, and also 4 per cent. on the capital raised by Act of 1854.

By 27 and 28 Vic., cap. 88 (23rd June, 1864), the company was authorised to acquire additional lands, and raise new capital to the extent of 150,000l. in shares, and 49,900l. on loan. Power was also given in the Act for the South Western to provide the whole of this amount.

By 29 and 30 Vic., cap. 204 (16th July, 1866), the company was authorised to form a connection with the Somerset and Dorset, and also to acquire additional lands at

Templecombe. Length, ¾ mile. These works are now in progress. Arrangements with South Western and Somerset and Dorset.

REVENUE.—The gross earnings for the half-year ending 31st December amounted to 41,899*l*.,or 40*l*. 5*s*. 8*d*. per mile per week, against 41,433*l*. for the same period of 1866, showing an increase of 466*l*. The traffic for the year 1867 amounted to 74,680*l*., against 76,271*l*. in 1866, showing a decrease of 1,591*l*. After deducting working expenses, interest, and other preference charges, a balance of 11,487*l*. allowed a dividend on the ordinary share capital at the rate of 7 per cent. per annum, leaving 52*l*., which, added to balance of 3,793*l*. from the previous half-year, made the balance carried forward, 3,845*l*.

The earnings for the June half-year compared with those for the corresponding period of 1867 as follows:—

30th June.	Coaching.	Goods.	Total.	Per mile per week.
				£ s. d.
1868	£19,082	£15,124	£34,206	32 17 10
1867	18,296	14,484	32,781	31 10 5
Increase	£785	£639	£1,425	£1 7 5

The receipts for the year ending 30th June, 1868, amounted to 36*l*. 11*s*. 9*d*. per mile per week, or 76,105*l*.; the traffic for the previous twelve months averaged 35*l*. 13*s*. 7*d*. per mile per week, or 74,214*l*., showing an increase of 1,891*l*. After deducting working expenses, passenger duty, interest, and other charges, the accounts for the half-year showed a balance of 13,610*l*., to which, adding the balance brought from last account, viz., 3,844*l*., there were available for dividend 17,455*l*. The dividend on the 150,000*l*. 5 per cent. preference shares of 1860 amounted to 3,750*l*., and on the 5 per cent. preference capital raised under the Act of 1864 to 2,437*l*., which left 11,267*l*. for dividend on the ordinary capital, at the rate of 5½ per cent. per annum, absorbing 8,984*l*., and leaving a balance to be carried forward to next account of 2,283*l*.

CAPITAL.—The receipts and expenditure on this account to 30th June, 1868, were detailed as under:—

Receipts.—Capital account	£594,076
Loans on debentures	133,250
Loans on mortgage bonds	49,500
Loans on debenture stock, at 4¼ per cent. per annum	200
Transfer fees	5
Interest on overdue calls	9
	£777,041
Balance	10,919 = £787,960

Expenditure.—Preliminary and parliamentary expenses, lands, works of construction, and all other expenditure from formation of company to 31st December, 1867 ... £782,829
Works of construction ... 400
Sidings, stations, and fittings ... 873
Cottages at Temple-Combe ... 898
Engineering and plans ... 550
Land and compensation ... 167
Law and Conveyancing ... 153
Temple-Combe Junction ... 2,661

£788,534

Deduct sum previously overcharged on account of doubling the line as ascertained on final settlement with the contractor ...... 574 = £787,960

No. of Directors.—Maximum, 9; minimum, 6; quorum, 3. *Qualification*, 50 shares.

DIRECTORS:
Chairman—JOHN CHAPMAN, Esq., 2, Leadenhall Street.

Sir William Coles Medlycott, Bart., Milborne Port, Sherborne.
Captain Charles E. Mangles, Poyle Park, Farnham.
H. Danby Seymour, Esq., Knoyle, Wilts.

Mr. Sergt. Gaselee, 2, Cambridge Square, Hyde Park, W.
Thomas Pain, Esq., Ugford, Wilts.
William Wagstaff, Esq., 4, Great George Street, Westminster, S.W.

OFFICERS.—Sec., Henry W. Notman; Eng., James G. Fraser, 9, Great Queen Street, Westminster, S.W.; Auditors, Isaiah Butt, Haverstock Hill, N.W., and John Williams Bell. Middle Temple; Solicitors, Hoddings, Townsend, and Co., 3, Prince's Street, Westminster, S.W.

Offices—2, Leadenhall Street, E.C.

347.—SALTASH AND CALLINGTON.

Incorporated by 28 and 29 Vic., cap. 373 (6th July, 1865), to construct a line from the Cornwall, at Saltash, to Callington on the Tamar and Kit Hill. Broad gauge. Length, 10 miles. Capital, 100,000*l.* in shares, and 33,300*l.* on loan. Arrangements with the Great Western.—No progress has yet been made with this undertaking.

No. of Directors—7 ; minimum, 3 ; quorum, 3 and 2.   *Qualification*, 200*l.*

DIRECTORS:

William Symons, Esq. | William Gilbert, Esq.
John Kempthorne, Esq.

348.—SCARBOROUGH AND WHITBY.

Incorporated by 28 and 29 Vic., cap. 272 (5th July, 1865), to construct a line from Scarborough to Whitby, on the North Eastern. Length, 21½ miles. Capital, 275,000*l.* in shares, and 91,600*l.* on loan. Arrangements with North Eastern.

No. of Directors—5 ; minimum, 3 ; quorum, 3 and 2.   *Qualification*, 500*l.*

DIRECTORS:

William Henry Hammond, Esq. | Charles Bell, Esq., M.P.

OFFICERS.—Sec., J. Mc.Millan, 7, Westminster Chambers, S.W. ; Eng., E. Birch, M.I.C.E., 7, Westminster Chambers, S.W.

349.—SEATON AND BEER.

Incorporated by 26 and 27 Vic., cap. 118 (13th July, 1863), to construct a line from the Colyton station of the South Western to Seaton. Length, 4¼ miles. Capital, 36,000*l.* in 10*l.* ordinary shares, 12,000*l.* on loan. Opened 16th March, 1868. Arrangements with South Western, which works the line at 45 per cent.

CAPITAL.—Additional capital to that authorised by parliament has been raised under certificate from Board of Trade, to the extent of 12,000*l.* in 5 per cent. preference, and 4,000*l.* on loan.

No. of Directors—5 ; minimum, 3 ; quorum, 3.   *Qualification*, 200*l.*

DIRECTORS:

Sir WALTER CALVERLEY TREVELYAN, Bart., Nettlecomb, Somerset, and Wallington, Northumberland.

Deputy-Chairman—GEORGE EVANS, Esq., Seaton, Axminster.

William Dommett, Esq., Chard. | John Latoysonere Scarbrough, Esq., Coly
John Babbage, Esq., Nettlecomb, Taunton. | House, Colyton, Devon.

OFFICERS.—Sec., C. E. Rowcliffe, Stogumber, Taunton ; Eng., W. R. Galbraith, Victoria Street, Westminster, S.W. ; Solicitors, Radcliffe and Davies, 20, Craven Street, Strand, W.C.

350.—SEVENOAKS, MAIDSTONE, AND TUNBRIDGE.

Incorporated by 22 and 23 Vic., cap. 45 (1st August, 1859), from Sutton at Hove, on the London Chatham and Dover, to Sevenoaks. Length, 8 miles. Capital, 120,000*l.* in 20*l.* shares ; loans, 40,000*l.* Five miles opened 2nd June, 1862.

By 25 and 26 Vic., cap. 166 (17th July, 1862), the company obtained power to double the line to Sevenoaks, and to construct a line to Maidstone. Length, 24 miles. Capital, 825,000*l.* in 10*l.* shares at 6 per cent. preference, and 271,000*l.* on loan. The name of the company was thereupon changed from Sevenoaks as above.

By 28 and 29 Vic., cap. 199 (29th June, 1865), an extension of time for 15 months was conceded for the purchase of certain lands.

By 30 and 31 Vic., cap. 184 (12th August, 1867), the company obtained an extension of time for the completion of works till 12th August, 1870.

The London Chatham and Dover works the line for 50 per cent. of gross receipts, the Sevenoaks paying for management, rates, taxes, &c.

SOUTH EASTERN.—By arrangement the Sevenoaks is to make the extension to Maidstone, and the South Eastern to Tunbridge, but the former is to form a junction at Sevenoaks with the latter line, and the South Eastern to book passengers and goods over the Sevenoaks between Hastings, Tunbridge Wells, and Tunbridge, and the stations of the London Chatham and Dover at the City and West End.

CHATHAM AND DOVER.—By 27 and 28 Vic., cap. 129 (30th June, 1864), the several capitals of the Sevenoaks were consolidated, and a sale or lease to the Chatham authorised. New capital, 100,000*l.* in shares, and 33,000*l.* on loan.

DIRECTORS:

Lord Sondes, 32, Grosvenor Square, W.
Sir P. H. Dyke, Bart., Lullingstone Castle, Farningham.

Lieut.-Colonel Evelyn, Onslow Crescent, Brompton, S.W.
G. F. Holroyd, Esq., 8, Sussex Square, Hyde Park, W.

OFFICERS.—Sec., W. E. Johnson; Eng., F. T. Turner; Solicitors, Freshfields and Newman; Bankers, Union Bank of London.
Offices—Victoria Station, S.W.

351.—SEVERN JUNCTION.

Incorporated by 28 and 29 Vic., cap. 366 (5th July, 1865), to construct several lines in Gloucestershire, to connect with railways on the east and west of the Severn, with a bridge over that river. Length, 15¾ miles. Capital, 420,000l. in shares, and 140,(00l. on loan. Arrangements with Midland.

By 29 and 30 Vic., cap. 155 (16th July, 1866), the company was authorised to construct two short branches to the South Wales and to the Forest of Dean Central. Length, 2 miles. No new capital, and no progress in works.

No. of Directors.—Maximum, 9; minimum, 3; quorum, 3.   *Qualification*, 300l.

DIRECTORS:

Chairman—
William Evans, Esq.
William Bunce Greenfield, Esq., 59, Porchester Terrace, W.

Samuel Stephens Marling, Esq., M.P.
Samuel Ford, Esq.

352.—SEVERN VALLEY.

Incorporated by Act 17 Vic., cap. 227 (20th August, 1853), for a line from near Hartlebury station, on Oxford Worcester and Wolverhampton line, to Shrewsbury, joining the Shrewsbury lines; also for a railway or tramway, Benthall to Madeley, supplying Stourport, Bewdley, Coalbrookdale, &c. Main line, 40⅛; branch, ¼ mile; total, 40½ miles. By 18 and 19 Vic., cap. 183 (July 30th, 1855), the company was empowered to reduce its capital to 480,000l., in 20l. shares, with power to borrow 160,000l. Power to use part of the Shrewsbury and Hereford, also the Shrewsbury station, and the Wellington and Severn Junction is to afford facilities for transmission of traffic. By 19 and 20 Vic., cap. 111 (21st July, 1856), certain deviations were permitted, and the period for compulsory purchase of land in relation thereto extended for two years; completion of works, three years. By same Act an option is given to convert shares into halves, the first of which to guarantee dividend to the second. By 21 and 22 Vic., cap. 135 (23rd July, 1858), an extension of time for three years was obtained. By 23 Vic., cap. 128 (14th June, 1860), the Severn Valley is leased to the West Midland, per agreement (ratified 1st November, 1860), for 999 years. By 24 and 25 Vic., cap. 212 (1st August, 1861), the Severn Valley and its lessees are authorised to construct a short line in the parish of Kidderminster, by which to form a junction with the West Midland. New capital, 60,000l., in shares at 5 per cent., and 20,000l. on loan. Opened 1st February, 1862.

By 25 and 26 Vic., cap. 182 (29th July, 1862), it is provided that the rent shall be as under:—the preference shareholders to receive their dividend at the rate of 4½ per cent. from 30th June, constantly, the ordinary shareholders until 31st December, 1863, at the rate of 3l. per cent., for the following year, 3l. 10s, and for the years 1865, 1866, and 1867 at 4 per cent., and thenceforth at the rate of 4l. 10s. for the remainder of the term. On 31st December, 1871 (or earlier if required), the Great Western to purchase the. Severn Valley, paying to the holders the amount they shall have paid for their shares.

By 27 and 28 Vic., cap. 151 (30th June, 1864), the company was authorised to execute several new works, and to raise additional capital to the extent of 120,000l. in shares, and 40,000l. on loan; arrangements in respect thereof with Great Western.

No. of Directors—7; minimum, 5; quorum, 3.   *Qualification*, 50 shares.

DIRECTORS:

Chairman—Major-General the Right Hon. G. C. W. FORESTER, M.P., 3, Carlton Gardens, Pall Mall, W.
Deputy-Chairman—JOHN PARSON, Esq., Bitton, Teignmouth, Devon.

John Alfred Chowne, Esq., 153, Westbourne Terrace, Hyde Park, W.
J. Slaney Pakington, Esq., Kent's Green, Powick, Worcester.

William Wagstaff, Esq., 45, Westbourne Terrace, Hyde Park, W.

OFFICERS.—Sec., Robert Hicks, 4, Victoria Street, Westminster, S.W.; Auditors, C. L. Christian and W. Phillips; Law Clerk, George T. Porter, 4, Victoria Street, Westminster, S.W.; Eng., John Fowler, 2, Queen's Square Place, Westminster, S.W.; Surveyors, Fuller and Withall, 21, Parliament Street, Westminster, S.W.; Bankers, Imperial Bank, Westminster, and Pritchards and Co., Bridgnorth.

Offices—Victoria Street, Westminster, S.W.

353.—SEVERN AND WYE.

By 49 Geo. III., cap. 159 (1809), the Lydney and Lydbrook Railway Company were incorporated and empowered to make a "railway" from Lydbrook (Wye) to Lower Forge, Newerne, Lydney, and "other railways" in the Forest of Dean, Gloucestershire. Extended by 50 Geo. III., cap. 215 (1810), and name changed to the above; and further powers by 51 and 54 Geo. III. and 3 Geo. IV. (1822).   An Act of 1853 recites, that the company are also possessed of various tramways, a harbour and canal, and are desirous to improve the same, supply motive power and become carriers. Additional tramway authorised, 3¾ miles. Gauge of 3½ feet.

This is a mineral railway, worked partly by horse power, and partly by steam power, but the former is being gradually superseded by the latter. The main line, leading from the Severn to the Wye, and branches to the mines, collieries, and stone quarries, &c., lying on either side thereof, chiefly in the Forest of Dean, are, together, about 30 miles in length; for the most part open for traffic ever since the year 1813. Great improvements have been effected therein under the provisions of the Act of 1853—embracing ample facilities for the transfer and transmission of traffic by the South Wales railway, at Lydney junction. The company have recently completed the laying of about 8 miles of broad gauge, by the side of their tramway, in order to enable the freighters to convey their coal and other merchandise direct from their works on to the Great Western railway at the said junction, without shifting, which has hitherto been unavoidable by tramway. Powers for effecting a further extension of the broad gauge for the accommodation of more distant collieries, the gradual removal of the tramway, alteration of tolls, and other purposes, will be applied for in the present session of parliament, of which due notice has been given. The canal and harbour of the company, one mile in length, lie between the said junction and the river Severn. Nearly 200 vessels are employed in conveying, seaward and inland, the coals and merchandise shipped at this port, and the quantity so conveyed at present exceeds 200,000 tons annually.

CAPITAL.—The original capital consists of 3,762 shares of 50*l.* each, authorised and created under the powers granted by the several Acts, viz.:—49 Geo. III., cap. 159, and subsequent Acts. The new capital authorised by the Act of 1853, consists of 1,500 shares of 20*l.* each. To these shares a guaranteed rate of interest at 4 per cent. per annum was attached, also a participation in surplus profits. Under the provisions of the Railway Companies' Powers Act, 1864, a certificate was granted by the Board of Trade in April, 1868, enabling the company to raise, for the purposes of their undertaking, a further sum of 38,000*l.* in shares, and one-third of that sum cn mortgage. Also enabling them to commute the 1853 shares for shares of equal nominal amount at the fixed rate of 4½ per cent. per annum, the shares so commuted retaining their priority of dividend. This commutation has been generally accepted by the holders of the 1853 shares.

At a special general assembly of proprietors, held at Lydney on the 12th November, 1868, a resolution was unanimously passed to create 20,000*l.* (part of the aforesaid sum of 38,000*l.*), and to issue the same in preference shares of 10*l.* each, which will be entitled to a preferential dividend at the rate of 5½ per cent. per annum.

Under the powers of the Act of 1853, the company have issued debenture bonds to the amount of 20,000*l.* bearing interest partly at 4½ per cent. and the remainder at 5 per cent per annum.

DIRECTORS:

Chairman—JOHN GRAHAM CLARKE, Esq., J.P., The Manor House, Frocester, near Stonehouse.

Deputy-Chairman—RICHARD WILLIAM GILES, Esq., Clifton.

Timothy Sampson Powell, Esq., Charlton, Filton, near Bristol.
John Jenner Mogg, Esq., West Park, Bristol.
Thomas Allaway, Esq., J.P., Lydney.
Capt. C. B. Jarrett, Bathampton House, Wilts.

George Thomas, Esq., Bristol.
John Longman, Esq., Melcombe Villas, Bristol.
Alfred William Hooper, Esq., Clevedon, Somerset.
John Hewitt, Esq., Kingsdown Parade, Bristol.

OFFICERS.—Sec., George Baker Keeling, Lydney, Gloucestershire; Eng., George William Keeling, Lydney, Gloucestershire; Treasurer, Timothy Sampson Powell, Charlton, Filton, near Bristol; Solicitors, Wintle and Maule, Newnham; Bankers, Gloucestershire Banking Company, Lydney, Gloucestershire.
Offices—Lydney, Gloucestershire.

354.—SHREWSBURY AND HEREFORD.
(LEASED TO LONDON AND NORTH WESTERN AND GREAT WESTERN.)

Incorporated by 9 and 10 Vic., cap. 325 (3rd August, 1846), for a line commencing at Hereford (in conjunction with the Newport Abergavenny and Hereford), and terminating at the joint station at Shrewsbury. Productive, 51 miles, all of which are now double line.

An Act was obtained in 1854 (13 and 14 Vic., cap. 26), reconstructing the share capital. It is provided therein that the original 40,000 shares of 20l. each, reduced by forfeiture to 29,710, shall be hereinafter considered as 29,710 shares of 10l. each, on which the 5l. then called, if paid, should be credited. In addition to the above 29,710 original shares, the forfeited (4,943), the unissued (5,201), and the unclaimed (146) shares under 1st Act—10,292 shares were re-created, and a further creation of 5,000 shares was sanctioned; thus 15,209 new shares were authorised to be issued and distributed, in the first instance, among the original holders, at 1l. discount, or 9l. per share, and entitled to the same privileges as the original shares.

By 19 and 20 Vic., cap. 47 (23rd June, 1856), the company is enabled to raise a further additional capital beyond that sanctioned in 1850, of 300,000l., namely, 225,000l. by the creation of shares at 5 per cent. preference, and 75,000l. by borrowing on mortgage of bonds. The Act also contains a power to convert any borrowed money into a fixed and irredeemable stock, at any rate not exceeding 4½ per cent.

By 25 and 26 Vic., cap. 198 (29th July, 1862), the Shrewsbury and Hereford is leased to the London and North Western and Great Western. These lessees on 1st February and 1st August annually pay the guaranteed dividend of 6l. per cent. on the consolidated stock, and on so much of the ordinary share capital as shall from time to time be called up. They are also to pay dividend on the preferential stock, and all interest on moneys borrowed, and interest at 4½ per cent. on moneys paid in advance of and until absorbed in calls. Neither the company nor the lessees to raise or apply further capital for any purposes connected with the undertaking until the money remaining unpaid upon the new shares shall have been called up. The Act provides that the undertaking shall be placed under the control of a joint committee of eight members, four being nominated by the London and North Western and four by the Great Western, and of an independent chairman to be appointed in case of difference by the Board of Trade. The same Act authorised the Shrewsbury and Hereford or the London and North Western to subscribe 30,000l. to the Knighton or Central Wales.

TENBURY.—By the Act of this company power was given to the Shrewsbury and Hereford to subscribe 5,000l. towards that undertaking, and also to enter into working and traffic arrangements, &c. The Tenbury (6 miles) was opened on 1st August, 1861, and is worked by the Shrewsbury and Hereford lessees for seven years from that date.

No. of Directors.—Maximum, 12; minimum, 6. Qualification, 600l. stock, or 60 shares of 10l. each, paid up.

DIRECTORS:

Great Western.	London and North Western.
Sir D. Gooch, Bart., M.P., 3, Warwick Road, Maida Hill, W.	R. Moon, Esq., Wigginton Lodge, Tamworth.
C. A. Wood, Esq., 25, Chesham Place, S.W.	J. P. Brown-Westhead, Esq., M.P., 13, Eaton Square, S.W., and Lea Castle, near Kidderminster.
Hon. F. G. B Ponsonby, 3, Mount Street, Grosvenor Square, W.	
Capt. Bulkeley, Clewer Lodge, Windsor.	J. Bancroft, Esq., 5, Police Street, Manchester.
C. G. Mott, Esq., Sunnyside, Birkenhead Park, Birkenhead.	O. L. Stephen, Esq., Bardon Hall, Leicester.
	J. P. Bickersteth, Esq , Southcot, Leighton, Beds.

JOINT OFFICERS.—Sec., J. Wait, Birkenhead; Eng., R. E. Johnston; Supt., W. Patchett, Shrewsbury.

355.—SHROPSHIRE UNION.
(LEASED TO THE LONDON AND NORTH WESTERN.)

This company is an amalgamation of railways and canals, with a view originally of converting the latter into the former. This object it was found impracticable to carry out, especially after an arrangement had been entered into with L. and N. W., which was itself invalid until sanctioned by parliament. The supervening difficulties were got rid of by 17 and 18 Vic., cap. 179 (July 24th, 1854), which may be regarded as the incorporating of the company. Length of railway, 29¼ miles. Opened June, 1849.

By lease to the London and North Western, under the powers of the Shropshire Union Leasing Act, 10 and 11 Vic., cap. 121 (1847), the proprietors of Shropshire Union stock are secured half London and North Western dividend in perpetuity, with all profits above that rate up to 6 per cent.

A supplemental agreement between the two companies of even date with the lease (25th March, 1847), as confirmed by parliament, authorising the two companies to agree upon a composition in lieu of the surplus profits to which the Shropshire Union is entitled, over and above the half London and North Western dividend, and also empowering individual Shropshire Union shareholders to exchange their Shropshire Union stock into stock of the London and North Western, at the rate of 50l. London and North Western for 100l. Shropshire Union Stock. Under this agreement a "lease capital account" has been raised, in which both companies are interested, and to which the proceeds of all carrying stock, &c., sold, are to be carried—and the unappropriated balance to the credit of this account to the 30th June, 1866, amounted to 61,032l. 7s. 6d.

The dividend declared for the half-year ending 31st December was 1l. 13s. 9d., and for the June half-year 1l. 6s. 3d., being 3l. for the year.

The accounts are made up to 30th June and 31st December, and the statutory meetings are held in March and September in each year.

Stock coupons are required to accompany transfer deeds. Registration fee, 2s. 6d. each deed.

Transfer books close 14 clear days before the meeting.

DIRECTORS:

Chairman—The Right Hon. the EARL OF POWIS, Powis Castle, Welshpool, and 45, Berkeley Square, W.

Richard Moon, Esq., Wigginton Lodge, Tamworth.

The Hon. Rowland Clegg Hill, Hawkstone, Salop.

J. P. Brown-Westhead, Esq., M.P., Lea Castle, near Kidderminster, and 13, Eaton Square, S.W.

George Holyoak, Esq., Neachley, near Shifnal, Salop.

Henry Newbery, Esq., Docklands, Ingatestone, Essex.

George Stanton, Esq., Coton Hill, Shrewsbury.

Lightly Simpson, Esq., 50, Gower Street, Bedford Square, W.C.

T. C. Eyton, Esq., Eyton, Wellington, Salop.

OFFICERS.—Sec. and Man., Alfred Wragge; Eng., John Beech, Ellesmere, Salop; Auditors, Charles Townshend and Richard George Jebb; Public Accountants, S. E. Cottam and Son, Manchester; Solicitors, Potts and Roberts, Chester; Bankers, Dixons and Co., Chester, and Glyn and Co., London.

Principal Office—Tower Wharf, Chester.

356.—SIDMOUTH.

Incorporated by 25 and 26 Vic., cap. 227 (7th August, 1862), to construct a line from Ottery Road station, on the South Western, to Sidmouth, with harbour thereat. Length, 8 miles. Capital, 120,000l. in 10l. shares, and 40,000l. on loan. Capital applicable to railway only, 90,000l. The South Western to lease the line in perpetuity on the clear annual payment of 5,000l. per annum.

By 28 and 29 Vic., cap. 237 (5th July, 1865), the company was authorised to construct a short branch in the parish of Sidmouth. Length, ½ mile. No new capital.

By 30 and 31 Vic., cap. 105 (20th June, 1867), the company was authorised to make certain deviations with extension of time till 20th June, 1872. Also to divide the capital into deferred and preferred shares.

No. of Directors—8; maximum, 9; quorum, 3. Qualification, 150l.

DIRECTORS:

Chairman—WILLIAM LAURENCE BANKS, Esq., Whitehall Gardens, S.W.

Deputy-Chairman—GEORGE ALFRED HILLIER, Esq., Gresham House, Old Broad Street, E.C.

Major Robert Wilberforce Bird, Stoke, Suffolk.

Edmund Burke, Esq (Messrs. J. Russell and Co.), Upper Thames Street, E.C.

Richard Henegan Lawrie, Esq., Inner Temple, E.C.

John Foster Vesey Fitzgerald, Esq., 11, Chester Square, Belgravia, S.W.

M. G. Nasmyth, Esq., 1, Victoria Street, Westminster, S.W.

C. J. Tahourdin, Esq., 29, Cleveland Gardens, Hyde Park, W.

OFFICERS.—Sec., Raymond Yates; Engs., Galbraith and Tolmé; Solicitors, C. and H. Tahourdin, 1, Victoria Street, Westminster, S.W., and Radford and Williams, Sidmouth; Bankers, Milford, Snow, and Co., Exeter.
Offices—1, Victoria Street, Westminster, S.W.

357.—SIDMOUTH AND BUDLEIGH-SALTERTON.

Incorporated by 26 and 27 Vic., cap. 234 (28th July, 1863), to construct a line from Tipton on the Sidmouth Railway, to Budleigh-Salterton. Length, 6¼ miles. Capital, 80,000l. in 10l. shares, and 26,600l. on loan. Arrangements with Sidmouth and London and South Western, which latter is to work the line. By 28 and 29 Vic., cap. 282 (5th July, 1863), deviation was authorised.

DIRECTORS:
Chairman—RICHARD HENEGAN LAWRIE, Esq., The Temple, E.C.

John Foster Vesey Fitzgerald, Esq., 11, Chester Square, Belgravia, S.W.
John James Williams, Esq., Mount Place, Brecon.

William Torrens McCullagh Torrens, Esq., M.P., 49, St. George's Road, Westminster, S.W.

OFFICERS.—Sec., Thomas Edward Watkins; Engs., William Robert Galbraith and Julian Horne Tolmé, 1, Victoria Street, Westminster, S.W.; Auditors, Samuel Patch, County House, Dorchester, and D. Glyn Watkins, Christ's College, Cambridge; Solicitor, Kedgwin Hoskins Gough, 19, Parliament Street, Westminster, S.W.
Offices—19, Parliament Street, Westminster, S.W.

358.—SIRHOWY.

Incorporated by 42 Geo. III., cap. 115, and remodelled by 23 and 24 Vic., cap. 71, and 28 and 29 Vic., cap. 342. Extent of railway from Nine Mile Point, on the Monmouthshire, past Tredegar, to Sirhowy, 15 miles. Share capital, 145,000l., and loan, 48,300l.

The dividends declared for the half-year ending 31st December were at the rate of 5 per cent. on the preference shares, and of 9 on the ordinary stock (free of income tax). The dividend on the latter for the June half-year was at the rate of 10 per cent., also free of income tax, with a balance of 543l., out of a total net receipt of 6,793l.

CAPITAL.—The expenditure to 30th June amounted to 194,133l., the receipts having been as follows:—

300 original shares, Act of 1802	.... £30,000	
750 do. do. 1860	.... 75,000=	£105,000
400 preference shares, Act of 1865	....	40,000
Debentures, Acts 1802, 1860, and 1865	....	48,300
		£193,300
Balance	....	833=£194,133

The company has been authorised by the Board of Trade to raise additional capital, partly in ordinary or preference shares and partly on loan.

DIRECTORS:

* Rowland Fothergill, Esq., Hensol Castle, Cowbridge, Glamorganshire.
* William Henry Forman, Esq., 28, Queen Street, Cheapside, E.C.

George Hardy, Esq., 28, Queen Street, Cheapside, E.C.
James Reed, Esq., Tredegar Ironworks, Monmouthshire.

* Retire in February, 1869; eligible for re-election.

OFFICERS.—Sec. and Accountant, Theophilus Bevan; Gen. and Traff. Man., Robert Bond; Loco. Supt., Benjamin Samuel Fisher; Auditors, Charles Widdowson and Evans Jones Davies; Bankers, West of England and South Wales District Bank, Tredegar.
Offices—Tredegar, Monmouthshire.

359.—SITTINGBOURNE AND SHEERNESS.

Incorporated by 19 and 20 Vic., cap. 75 (7th July, 1856), to make a railway from Sittingbourne to Sheerness. Capital, 80,000l. in 10l. shares; loans, 26,600l. Length, 7½ miles. Opened June 19th, 1860.

By 20 and 21 Vic., cap. 151 (17th August, 1857), the company was authorised to alter the line and levels, to abandon a portion of the line, and to construct new branches.

By 22 and 23 Vic., cap. 90 (8th August, 1859), the company was authorised to lease the line to the London Chatham and Dover, and to raise additional capital to the extent of 40,000l. at 5½ per cent. preference, and 13,000l. on loan. The line is worked under agreement with that company, and under the superintendence of a joint committee, the London Chatham and Dover taking 55 per cent. of gross receipts until July, 1865, after which it will pass into the hands of the London Chatham and Dover, by whom the undertaking (exclusive of road-bridge and pier) is to be leased in perpetuity, at a rent to be determined by arbitrators. The rent to be not less than 5,000l., nor more than 11,000l. a year.

By 24 and 25 Vic., cap. 127 (11th July, 1861), the company was authorised to raise additional capital to the extent of 30,000l. in shares at 5½ per cent., and 10,000l. by loan.

By the London Chatham and Dover Arrangements Act of 1867, the Sittingbourne and Sheerness is fully secured in priority to the debenture holders of the Chatham.

It was stated in August that the debenture debt was in liquidation in the Court of Chancery, in consequence of the debenture holders having refused to acccept the 4½ per cent. rent-charge stock at par. Could this arrangement be effected, the affairs of the company would speedily be brought to a settlement.

CAPITAL.—The balance sheet to 30th June gives the capital and other financial resources of the undertaking as follows:—

Share capital, viz.:—4,805 ordinary shares, 10l. each £48,050		
4,802 first preference „ 40,820	=	£88.870
Sundry creditors secured by deposit of 1,500 first preference shares		11,999
Sundry creditors for land and interest		19,333
„ „ debentures and interest, January 1st, 1868 ... £51,148		
Interest accrued since £1,039		
Less income tax .... 21 = 1,017	=	52,166
Unsecured creditors, January 1st, 1868 44,978		
Interest accrued since 12		
Auditors' fees and balance due G. B. Roach 16	=	45,007
Gross revenue to January 1st, 1868 ...—.................................. 34,513		
Revenue, six months to June 30th, 1868 3,522	=	38,035
Forfeited shares..		3,734
Total		£259,146

No. of Directors—6; maximum, 8; quorum, 3. *Qualification*, 200l.

DIRECTORS:

Chairman—LIGHTLY SIMPSON, Esq., 50, Gower Street, Bedford Square, W.C.

Deputy-Chairman—WILLIAM HARTRIDGE, Esq., 80, Old Broad Street, E.C.

Richard Comyn, Esq., Queenborough, and 31, Lincoln's Inn Fields, W.C.
Frederick Leese, Esq., Bredgar, Sittingbourne, Kent.

Captain Dumergue, Esher, Surrey.
Sidney Beisley, Esq., Laurie Park, Sydenham, S.E.

OFFICERS.—Sec., W. H. Burton; Accountant, L. H. Evans; Auditors, W. G. Head and Wm. West; Solicitor, A. Scott Lawson, 31, Lincoln's Inn Fields, W.C.

Offices—31, Lincoln's Inn Fields, W.C.

360.—SKIPTON AND WHARFDALE.

Incorporated by 28 and 29 Vic., cap. 203 (5th July, 1865), to construct a line from Skipton, on the Little North Western, to Wharfdale. Length, 8 miles. Capital, 80,000l. in shares, and 26,000l. on loan. Arrangements with Midland. No progress in raising capital, or in commencing works.

No. of Directors—5; quorum, 3. *Qualification*, 500l.

DIRECTORS:

Chairman—MATHEW WILSON, Esq., Eshton Hall.

John Robert Tennant, Esq., Kildwick Hall.
William Montagu Baillie, Esq., Old Bank, Bristol.

Thomas Vaughan, Esq., Middlesborough.
William Wilkinson, Esq.

OFFICERS.—Sec., George Kendall; Engs., G. B. Bruce and A. L. Light, Westminster Chambers, S.W.; Solicitors, Edwards, Webb, and Co., 8, Delahay Street, Westminster, S.W., and George Robinson, Skipton.

Office—Town Hall, Skipton.

361.—SLIGO AND BALLAGHADERREEN.

Incorporated by 26 and 27 Vic., cap. 160 (13th July, 1863), to construct a line from the Midland Great Western, at Kilpee, to the town of Ballaghaderreen. Length, 9½ miles. Capital, 40,000l. in 10l. shares, and 13,300l. on loan. Arrangements with Midland Great Western.

By 29 and 30 Vic., cap. 360 (10th August, 1866), the company obtained renewal and extension of its powers, the line to be completed by 10th August, 1869. No progress towards this consummation appears, however, to have been made.

No. of Directors—7 ; minimum, 5 ; quorum, 3. *Qualification*, 200l.

DIRECTORS:

Right Hon. John Wynne.
Viscount Dillon.
Thomas H. Williams, Esq.
Charles Strickland, Esq.

Thomas Strickland, Esq.
James O'Connor, Esq.
Henry Lyons, Esq.

362.—SOLWAY JUNCTION.

Incorporated by 27 and 28 Vic., cap. 158 (30th June, 1864), to construct a line from the Caledonian, near Kirtlebridge, to the Brayton station of the Maryport and Carlisle, and branches in connection therewith. Length, 25¼ miles. Capital, 320,000l. in 10l. shares, and 106,600l. on loan. Works in progress, and the line expected to be opened in February.

By 28 and 29 Vic., cap. 186 (29th June, 1865), certain deviations were authorised, power given to use part of the Glasgow and South Western, to make use of the Maryport and Carlisle station, and an agreement with the North British confirmed.

By 29 and 30 Vic., cap. 243 (23rd July, 1866), the company was authorised to raise additional capital to the extent of 60,000l. in shares, and 20,000l. on loan. Power was also given to the North British and the Glasgow and South Western to subscribe 100,000l. each to the Solway Junction.

By 30 and 31 Vic., cap. 116 (15th July, 1867), the company was authorised to construct a junction with the Carlisle and Silloth Bay. Length, 13 chains, and to divide the capital into deferred and preferred shares. The Caledonian was also authorised to guarantee the debenture debt of the Solway Junction, as well as to subscribe a sum not exceeding 100,000l. towards the share capital of the undertaking. An extension of time for three years for completion of works was also obtained, while traffic facilities were given to the Furness and London and North Western.

It was reported in August that the completion of the viaduct over the Solway was a subject of congratulation, while the remaining works on this important estuary were being prosecuted as rapidly as possible. The bad weather at the beginning of the year retarded the works, but the continued dryness of the later months had been of great advantage to the contractors. The opening of the line throughout might be looked forward to with tolerable certainty, the contractors having agreed to complete it by 1st February, 1869.

CAPITAL.—The expenditure on this account to 30th June amounted to 303,673l., the receipts, which left a balance on hand of 16,876l., having been as follows :—

Capital account...................................... £197,752
Do.   (5 per cent. preference...... 20,000
Loans on debentures 91,715
Sundry creditors .... 1,083=320,550

Meetings in February and August.

No. of Directors—6 ; quorum, 3. *Qualification*, 300l.

DIRECTORS:

Chairman—ALEX. BROGDEN, Esq., M.P., Ulverstone.

Deputy-Chairman—JAMES DEES, Esq., Whitehaven and Bellingham, Northumberland.

Joseph Fletcher, Esq., Kelton House, Dumfries and Whitehaven.
Hugh Ker, Esq., Annan.

Lieut.-Col. Salkeld, Holm Hill, Carlisle.
*Andrew Buchanan, Esq., Auchentorlie, Dumbartonshire.

* Directors of the Caledonian Railway Company.

Directors go out of office 1st meeting after opening of the line ; eligible for re-election.

OFFICERS.—Sec., H. F. Tahourdin, 1, Victoria Street, Westminster, S.W.; Chief-Eng., James Brunlees, C.E., 5, Victoria Street, Westminster, S.W. ; Solicitors, Messrs. Tahourdin, 1, Victoria Street, Westminster, S.W., and Alexander Downie, Town Clerk, Annan.

363.—SOMERSET AND DORSET.

An incorporation by 25 and 26 Vic., cap. 225 (7th August, 1852), of the Somerset Central and Dorset Central, the combination of interests taking place from 1st September, 1862.

SOMERSET CENTRAL.—Incorporated by 15 Vic., cap. 63 (17th June, 1852), for the following purposes, viz:—1st—Construction of a railway, commencing at the harbour of Highbridge, north side of the river Brue, and thence crossing the Bristol and Exeter, and forming a junction therewith, near Highbridge station, and terminating at Glastonbury. 2nd—Appropriation of the Glastonbury navigation and canal for the railway and works. 3rd—Making a new cut from the Highbridge station, from one point on the canal to another point thereon. 4th—The appropriation of that much of the existing canal. Length, 13½ miles. Broad gauge. Opened 28th August, 1854. The Bristol and Exeter, former owners of the Glastonbury canal, sold that property to this company for 8,000l., and became shareholders to the extent of 10,000l., of which sum 8,000l. is deemed the purchase money of the canal. By 18 and 19 Vic., cap. 182 (July 30th, 1855), extensions to Wells and Burnham (and pier at latter place) were authorised. Length of new lines, Glastonbury to Wells, 5½ miles; Highbridge to Burnham, 1½ mile; branch to pier, 1 furlong; total, 7 miles. The Burnham was opened 3rd May, 1858. The line from Glastonbury to Wells was opened on 15th March, 1859. By 19 and 20 Vic., cap. 102 (24th July, 1856), the company was authorised to construct a line from Glastonbury to Bruton. Additional capital, 100,000l., and 33,000l. on loan. Length, 12 miles (broad gauge). Opened February, 1862. By 22 and 23 Vic., cap. 56 (1st August, 1859), the company was empowered to lay down narrow gauge rails to work in connection with the South Western system, and to raise additional capital, by shares and borrowing, for that purpose. New capital, 75,000l. in shares at 6 per cent.; loans, 24,000l. Debentures converted into stock at 5 per cent.

BURNHAM TIDAL HARBOUR.—By 23 and 24 Vic., cap. 130 (6th August, 1860), the Somerset Central was authorised to subscribe 12,000l. to this undertaking, and to issue new shares to that amount at 6 per cent. preference. The Somerset Central to work the line, and to enter into traffic and other arrangements under the usual restrictions.

GLASTONBURY TO BRUTON.—By 24 and 25 Vic., cap. 209 (1st August, 1861), an extension of time, till August, 1862, was obtained, in which to construct the line from Glastonbury to Bruton, to be provided with rails for both gauges. The company was also authorised to raise new capital to the extent of 85,000l. in shares, and 29,800l. on loan.

DORSET CENTRAL.—Incorporated by 19 and 20 Vic., cap. 135 (29th July, 1856), to construct a line from Wimborne, on the Southampton and Dorchester branch of the South Western, to Blandford, in the county of Dorset. Capital, 100,000l. in 20l. shares; loans, 33,000l. Length, 10¼ miles. Opened from Wimborne to Blandford, 10 miles, 1st November, 1860.

By 20 and 21 Vic., cap. 139 (10th August, 1857), the line is extended from Blandford along the Vale of Blackmore, a distance of 24 miles, to the Somerset Central, at Bruton. Opened to Temple Coombe, 9 miles, in November, 1861. Capital, 300,000l. in 20l. shares; loans, 100,000l.; of which there may be borrowed 60,000l., when 200,000l. of the capital shall have been subscribed for, and one-half thereof paid-up, and 40,000l. when the balance of the capital is subscribed for and one-half paid-up. Length, No. 1, 16½ miles; No. 2, 3 furlongs 1 chain; No. 3, 8¾ miles; No. 4, 2 furlongs 2·25 chains; No. 5, 3 furlongs 2·80 chains. By 23 and 24 Vic., cap. 130 (3rd July, 1860), an extension of time for completion of works was obtained for three years. The line was completed and opened on 31st August, 1863.

AMALGAMATION.—The capitals of the two companies are amalgamated on equal terms. The Somerset and Dorset will thus be 66 miles in length, commencing at Burnham, on the Bristol Chanel, and extending to Wimborne, on the London and South Western, and by virtue of an arrangement with the London and South Western Company, the trains of the Somerset and Dorset Company run into Poole, thus forming a through connection between the English and Bristol Channels.

By 27 and 28 Vic., cap. 223 (25th July, 1864), the company was authorised to acquire additional lands, and to raise new capital to the extent of 100,000l. in shares, and 33,000l. on loan.

By 29 and 30 Vic., cap. 268 (23rd July, 1866), the company obtained power to acquire additional lands, and to raise new capital to the extent of 300,000l. in shares, and 100,000l. on loan. Also to enter into further arrangements with South Western.

A scheme is now before the Court of Chancery, by which it is proposed to effect certain arrangements with the creditors of the company.

No. of Directors.—Maximum, 10; minimum, 7. *Qualification*, 500*l*. Bristol and Exeter directors, two, whilst subscribing 13,000*l*.; if the subscription is reduced below 13,000*l*., one director only; if the subscription is below 7,000*l*., then power to appoint any director will cease.

DIRECTORS:

Chairman—CHARLES WARING, Esq., 10, Victoria Chambers, Westminster, S.W.

Henry Danby Seymour, Esq., East Knoyle, Hindon, Wilts.
Sir Edward Baker Baker, Bart., Ranston, near Blandford.
Sir Ivor Bertie Guest, Bart., Canford Manor, Wimborne.
James Clark, Esq., Street, Somerset.
George Reed, Esq., Burnham, Somerset.

William Waring, Esq., 10, Victoria Chambers, Westminster, S.W.
George Warry, Esq., Shapwick House, Somerset.
John Clavell Mansel, Esq., Longthorns, Blandford.
* Richard King Meade King, Esq., Walford, near Taunton.

* Representative of Bristol and Exeter.

OFFICERS.—Sec. and Gen. Man., Robert Arthur Read; Eng. and Loco. and Carriage Supt., Frederick George Slessor; Chief Accountant, Richard J. Rees; Bankers, Stuckey's Banking Co., Glastonbury.

Chief Offices—Glastonbury, Somerset.

364.—SOUTHAM.

Incorporated by 27 and 28 Vic., cap. 200 (14th July, 1864), to construct a line from the Great Western, at Harbury, to the London and North Western, near Birdingbury. Length, 7¼ miles. Capital, 70,000*l*. in 10*l*. shares, and 23,000*l*. on loan. Mixed gauge. Arrangements with Great Western.

Meetings in April and October.

No. of Directors—3; maximum, 5; quorum, 2 and 3. *Qualification*, 300*l*.

DIRECTORS:

Chairman—DOUGLAS YEOMAN BLAKISTON, Esq., St. Leonard's-on-Sea.

Robert Poole, Esq., Welford.

The Rev. John Copeland Poole, Clay Coton Rectory, Rugby.

Solicitor—Edward Poole, Southam, near Rugby.

365.—SOUTH DEVON.

Incorporated by 7 and 8 Vic., cap. 68 (4th July, 1844), for a broad gauge line from the Bristol and Exeter, at Exeter, to Plymouth, whence, the Cornwall having been completed the broad gauge system is extended to Falmouth. In 1846 branches to Torquay and other places were authorised. In 1847 additional powers were obtained to extend the line to Torquay and to Brixham. Productive, 110½ miles.

By Act of incorporation, and subsequent Acts, this company may be leased to the Great Western, or Bristol and Exeter. The Devonport branch was transferred to the Cornwall, the South Devon having received 11,100*l*. on account of purchase money, which sum has been deducted from general expenditure.

In 1854 the company obtained an Act for improving the Sutton Harbour branch, and adapting it for the working of locomotive engines. This Act also empowers the company to acquire additional land for station purposes, and extends the period for disposal of surplus lands.

By 20 and 21 Vic., cap. 8 (26th June, 1857), the company's stocks are consolidated, and additional shares created.

By 21 and 22 Vic., cap. 102 (12th June, 1858), the South Devon is authorised to lease the South Devon and Tavistock.

By 23 Vic., cap. 10 (15th May, 1860), the company was authorised to improve its Plymouth and other stations, to widen certain parts of the line, and to apply existing capital for these purposes.

By 28 and 29 Vic., cap. 255 (5th July, 1865), the company was authorised to construct a short branch at Exeter; to enter into an arrangement with the Tavistock, and to establish a superannuation fund. New capital, 360,000*l*. in shares, and 120,000*l*. on loan.

By 29 and 30 Vic., cap. 153 (28th June, 1866), the company was authorised to acquire additional lands, to construct new works, and to raise new capital to the extent of 150,000*l*. in shares, and 80,000*l*. on loan. Also to acquire shares in the Launceston, and to guarantee interest on part of the capital of that company as well as of the Dartmouth and Torbay.

LAUNCESTON AND MORETONHAMPSTEAD.—The South Devon subscribe 500*l*. to each of these undertakings, in order to give it a place at the respective boards of these companies.

SOUTH DEVON AND TAVISTOCK.—Incorporated by 17 and 18 Vic., cap. 189 (July 4th, 1854). Length, 13 miles. Opened 22nd June, 1859. By 28 and 29 Vic., cap. 255 (5th July, 1865), the Tavistock was amalgamated with the South Devon, at a perpetual d ividend of 3½ per cent. on its ordinary stock.

REVENUE.—The receipts for the half-year ended 31st December, were 123,252l., and the working expenses 53,627l., leaving an available balance of 123,252l. After payment of charges arising out of the Dartmouth, Launceston, and Moretonhampstead, a surplus of 40,355l. met the whole of the preference charges, and afforded a dividend on the ordinary stock at the rate of 3 per cent. per annum.

The receipts for the half-year ending 30th June showed that 114,226l. had been received, against 109,129l. for the corresponding period of 1867, showing an increase of 5,097l. The working expenses amounted to 54,004l., or 47·28 per cent., as compared with 51,791l. or 47·46 per cent. for the corresponding period. An outlay of 1,400l. had been incurred in substituting wrought-iron girders and masonry for wood in the renewal of bridges, and in cutting back cliffs between Dawlish and Teignmouth, to protect the line from slips. The auditors recommended that those and similar expenses be charged to revenue, but spread over six half-years, and the board concurred and acted upon the recommendation. The revenue account was now debited with this company's proportion of the ascertained deficits on the working of the Cornwall and West Cornwall to the 31st December, as well as with the estimated deficits to the 30th June. The interest account was also debited with an exceptional item of 2,517l., being the amount accruing to the 30th June, but payable during the half-year, on debentures, debenture stock, and rent-charges. This item and the additional debit in respect of the Cornwall together represented 6,407l. A credit of 5,333l. was derived by charging the half-year with the proportion of preferential dividends accruing to the 30th June, and the balance to debit on the altered and improved statement was thus reduced to 1,074l. The disposable revenue balance was 23,759l.; and, after making provision for preference charges, left a dividend on the ordinary stock at the rate of 1l. 10s. per cent. per annum, left a balance of 288l.

CAPITAL.—The expenditure during the June half-year had been 5,130l., chiefly for land and works. The debenture debt amounted to 668,966l., of which 130,860l. had been converted into debenture stock. The whole of the latter sum, on and after 1st March, 1869, would bear interest in perpetuity at 4 per cent. per annum. This account also showed that 2,926,726l. had been expended, leaving a balance against receipts of 144,444l. These receipts have been derived as follows:—

Consolidated Ordinary Stock.

20 and 21 Vic., cap. 8 .... £1,469,425		
28 and 29 Vic., cap. 255—Tavistock	28,875=	£1,498,300
* Annuities—		
20 and 21 Vic., cap. 8, per annum	10,141	......
† Tavistock Preference Shares—		
28 and 29 Vic., cap. 225—1,347 @ 25l.	......	33,675
‡ Tavistock Annuities—		
28 and 29 Vic., cap. 255	......	115,875
Issuable	7,450	......
§ New Shares of 10l.—		
11 and 12 Vic., cap. 98, Plymouth Great Western Dock Act ...	15,000	......
14 and 15 Vic., cap. 53, South Devon Act, 1851	85,000=	£100,000
‖ Additional Shares of 10l.—		
20 and 21 Vic., cap. 8, 27,012 shares	......	270,120
¶ 28 and 29 Vic., cap. 255, 36,000 shares	360,000	56,340
29 and 30 Vic., cap. 153, 15,000 shares	150,000	......
Total received to 30th June, 1868		2,074,310
** Debenture Stock—		
14 and 15 Vic., cap. 53, to 30th June, 1868		130,860
		£2,205,170

* The annuities have preference of all shares and stock, excepting debenture stock.
† The Tavistock preference shares bear 4½ per cent. in perpetuity.
‡ The Tavistock annuities bear 3½ per cent. in perpetuity.
§ The new shares bear 4½ per cent. in perpetuity, in preference to all shares or stock, excepting debenture stock and annuities.
‖ The additional shares bear 4½ per cent. in perpetuity.
¶ The additional shares (1865) bear 5 per cent. in perpetuity. They are subject to the above-named preferences, and rank in preference to the consolidated ordinary shares.
** The debenture stock, in substitution of mortgage debentures, has preference of all other shares or stock. The debenture stock, 1852, bears 4 per cent. in perpetuity; that of 1859 bears 4½ per cent. to 1st March, 1869, and thereafter 4 per cent. in perpetuity.

The accounts are made up to 30th June and 31st December; and the statutory meetings held at Exeter and Plymouth, in February and August every year.

Scale of Voting.—1 vote for every share of 50*l.* up to 20 ; and after that 1 vote for every 5 shares. The associated companies have one vote for every 2 shares.

Certificates of stock required to accompany transfer deed. Registration fee, 2*s.* 6*d.*

No of Directors—11, of which two represent the Great Western, three the Bristol and Exeter, and one the Midland Company, in right of the subscription of those companies. *Qualification,* 1,000*l.* stock.

DIRECTORS:

Chairman—THOMAS WOOLLCOMBE, Esq., Devonport.

Deputy-Chairman—Sir MASSEY LOPES, Bart., M.P., Maristow, near Plymouth, and 4, Buckingham Gate, S.W.

Henry Brown, Esq., Plymouth.

C. Seale Hayne, Esq., Dartmouth, and 3, Eaton Square, S.W.

*Richard Bassett, Esq., Bonvilstone, near Cardiff.

*Richard Michell, 3, Kensington Park Gardens, W.

George Pridham, Esq., Plymouth.

†Francis Fry, Esq., Cottiam, Bristol.

†Michael Castle, Esq., Clifton, Bristol.

†William Adair Bruce, Ashley, Chippenham.

‡W. P. Price, Esq., M. P., Tibberton Court, Gloucester, and 105, Pall Mall, S.W.

Eligible for re-election.

* Representatives of Great Western.   † Representatives of Bristol and Exeter.
‡ Representative of Midland.

OFFICERS.— Sec. and Gen. Man., L. J. Seargeant; Goods Man., W. H. Avery; Supt., C. E. Compton; Eng., P. J. Margary; Loco. Supt., John Wright; Accountant, A. P. Prowse; Auditors, George Henderson, Plymouth, and C. G. Millman, Dawlish; Solicitors, Whiteford and Bennett, Plymouth.

Offices—Plymouth.

366.—SOUTHSEA.

Incorporated by 30 and 31 Vic., cap. 194 (12th August, 1867), to construct a line through Southsea to the joint line of the Brighton and South Western at Union Bridge, with a branch from Fratton Bridge. Length, 2 miles. Capital, 30,000*l.* in 10*l.* shares and 10,000*l.* on loan. Running powers to Brighton and South Western.

A bill is now before parliament for the abandonment of this undertaking.

No. of Directors.—5; minimum, 3; quorum, 3. *Qualification,* 100*l.*

DIRECTORS:

George Absalom, Esq.
Thomas Bailey, Esq.
Edwin Galt, Esq.

Henry Lawrence, Esq.
Daniel West, Esq.

367.—SOUTH EASTERN.

Incorporated by 6 Wm. IV., cap. 75 (21st June, 1836), as the SOUTH EASTERN AND DOVER. 334 miles are now in operation; but 12¾ miles to Reigate have been constructed by the Brighton, 6¾ miles between Reading and Reigate by the London and South Western, for which a toll is paid; and 4½ miles are leased lines; leaving 310 miles as constructed out of South Eastern capital. The original scheme commenced at Reigate, and terminated near Dover. In 1839 the company obtained power to run over the Croydon to Croydon, on payment of tolls: from Croydon to Reigate (12 miles) was constructed, in the first instance, by the Brighton; this company afterwards purchased for 340,000*l.* (with interest on the cost up to the date of purchase), one-half of that length, from the Brighton, and to contribute a share of the expense of erecting a joint station at London Bridge. In 1843 the company obtained power to extend the main line into Dover (88 miles), to make a branch to Maidstone, to purchase the station at Bricklayers' Arms, and to make a branch thereto. In 1844 extensions were obtained to Canterbury, Ramsgate, and Margate, the Folkestone branch and harbour. In 1845 the Tunbridge Wells branch was authorised; also the widening of the Greenwich; and of the Gravesend and Rochester (previously leased); to make the Minster and Deal, the Ashford and Tunbridge Wells, and Hastings branches. In 1846 power was also obtained to construct branches from Rye to Rye harbour; Tunbridge Wells to Hastings; to enlarge the Ashford station, and to construct the "North Kent," being a line from a junction with the Greenwich, and terminating at Gravesend; also to extend that line to Rochester, by purchase of the Gravesend and Rochester canal, which was in the same year authorised. The North Kent is now extended to Maidstone. In 1852 this company obtained possession of the Reading Guildford and Reigate, which merged into the South Eastern system. Also the Whitstable, London and Greenwich, with a coal branch at Charlton to the Thames (Angerstein's). The company are proprietors of the Pavilion Hotel, at Folkestone, and of the Lord Warden Hotel, at Dover; also of the Folkestone Harbour, &c., under Act of 27th June, 1843; the dues arising therefrom being entered to credit of revenue.

By 18 Vic., cap. 16 (25th May, 1855), this company became entitled to raise additional capital to the extent of 500,000*l.*, to borrow to the extent of one-third of the entire capital, and to convert debentures into stock.

By 20 and 21 Vic., cap. 155 (17th August, 1857), the company is enabled to form a better junction at Tunbridge, and the qualification of a director raised from 600*l.* to 2,000*l.*

By 24 and 25 Vic., cap. 191 (22nd July, 1861), the company obtained further powers with respect to steam vessels, &c.

CHARING CROSS.—By 22 and 23 Vic., cap. 81 (8th August, 1859), the South Eastern was authorised to subscribe 300,000*l.* to this undertaking, to participate in its management, and to work the line when opened. The amount was voted by meeting of 1st September, 1859, to be raised in 4½ per cent. preference shares. An extension to Cannon Street, with a bridge over the Thames, was authorised by 24 and 25 Vic., cap. 93 (28th June, 1861), to which the South Eastern subscribed the further sum of 250,000*l.* By 24 Vic., cap. 12 (17th May, 1861), the company was authorised to add to its contributions to the original Charing Cross scheme the sum of 350,000*l.*, making in all 900,000*l.*, to the lines from Charing Cross to Cannon Street, and to London Bridge. By Act of 1863, the South Eastern was authorised to amalgamate with the Charing Cross Railway Company on terms to be agreed upon, which arrangement was carried into effect by resolutions adopted on 25th August, 1864.

By 27 and 28 Vic., cap. 192 (4th July, 1864), the Charing Cross was authorised to raise new capital to the extent of 90,000*l.* in shares, and 30,000*l.* on loan. Opened from London Bridge to Charing Cross, in August, 1864; to Cannon Street, on 1st September, 1866.

CATERHAM.—Incorporated by 17 and 18 Vic., cap. 68 (1853). The lines run from the town of Caterham to the Brighton line. Length, 4 miles 5 furlongs 1½ chain. Opened on 5th August, 1856. By 22 and 23 Vic., cap. 35 (21st July, 1859), this line is sold to the South Eastern for 15,200*l.*, having cost 40,000*l.*

TUNBRIDGE AND DARTFORD.—By 25 and 26 Vic., cap. 96 (30th June, 1862), the South Eastern was authorised to construct lines to Tunbridge and Dartford, and to widen a portion of the North Kent. Length, 34⅔ miles. Capital, 1,200,000*l.* in shares, and 400,000*l.* on loan. Opened to Dartford on 1st September, 1866. From Chislehurst to Sevenoaks in March, 1868, and from Sevenoaks to Tunbridge in May, 1868.

WESTERHAM.—By 27 and 28 Vic., cap. 98 (23rd July, 1864), the South Eastern was authorised to construct an extension to Westerham. Length, 4¾ miles. Capital, 70,000*l.* in shares, and 23,000*l.* on loan.

CRANBROOK, HYTHE, &c.—By 27 and 28 Vic., cap. 99 (23rd June, 1864), the South Eastern was authorised to construct extensions to Cranbrook, Hythe, and Sandgate. Length, 13 miles. Capital, 280,000*l.* in shares, and 93,000*l.* on loan.

LONDON AND GREENWICH.—The company leases this line for 45,000*l.* per annum, on a rent-charge on the whole of the lines for 999 years. The guaranteed 5 per cent. interest is on 222,720*l.* capital, payable 31st March and 30th September. The ordinary capital of the company, 861,540*l.*, pays a half-yearly dividend in the middle of January and July of 5*s.* 5*d.* per share, or 1*l.* 7*s.* 1*d.* per cent. clear of income tax. The debenture debt of 333,300*l.* at 4 per cent pays interest half-yearly on 1st January and 1st July.

MID-KENT.—By 27 and 28 Vic., cap. 311 (29th July, 1864), this company was amalgamated with South Eastern, by purchase, at a premium of 60,000*l.* The Mid-Kent was incorporated by 18 and 19 Vic., cap. 169 (28th July, 1855), to construct a railway from near Beckenham, on the Farnborough extension of the West London and Crystal Palace, to the North Kent branch of the South Eastern at Lewisham. Length, 4½ miles. By 25 and 26 Vic., cap. 153 (17th July, 1862), the company was authorised to make an extension to Addiscombe. Length, 3¾ miles. Capital, 40,000*l.* in shares, and 15,000*l.* on loan. By 26 and 27 Vic., cap. 138 (13th July, 1863), the company was authorised to raise additional capital to the extent of 15,000*l.* at 5 per cent., and 5,000*l.* on loan. The following resolution was adopted at a meeting of the South Eastern, on 25th August, 1864:—"That under the powers and provisions of 'The South Eastern (Mid-Kent) Act, 1864,' there be created for the purpose of the amalgamation with the Mid-Kent new stock to the aggregate nominal amount of 60,000*l.*, and that there be attached to such stock a right to a preferential dividend at the rate of 5*l.* per cent. per annum, such new stock to be issued in exchange for the shares representing the first and second preferential capitals of the Mid-Kent, and the rights, priorities and privileges, attached thereto to be such as are defined by the said Act." The report presented to the concluding meeting of this proprietary. in August, 1866, stated that the many and serious questions which had arisen with the South Eastern had at length been settled. The negotiations led to an agreement for a final reference of all matters in difference to Mr. John Buller, whose award had just been received. Under its provisions the South Eastern were to hand to the shareholders in the Mid-Kent, and the shareholders were to accept in discharge of the purchase-money of the line, 116,800*l.* of South Eastern 5 per cent. preference stock of 1865, being at the rate of 36*l.* 10*s.* of that stock for every 25*l.* share in the Mid-Kent, and giving the shareholders in perpetuity 7*l.* 6*s.* per cent. upon their original investment. The award provided for the transfer of all the rights, powers, obligations, and liabilities of the Mid-Kent to the South Eastern; aud was rendered valid and legally binding by an Act passed in the Session of 1866. As the dividends upon the South Eastern stock were not due until the 1st of August and 1st of February in each year (being payable within 15 days from those dates), the South Eastern had paid the interest on the purchase-money of the line, at the usual rate, to the 31st July; and the final accounts of the company made up and audited to the 14th August, 1866, would be forwarded to the shareholders. The directors had only to add that they considered the settlement to be, under all circumstances, an advantageous one for both companies; and, in taking leave of the shareholders, congratulated them upon the satisfactory issue to which their undertaking had been brought. The capital account showed that 179,869*l.* had been expended, leaving a balance of 131*l.* The revenue account for the seven months ending July 31st authorised a final distribution of 1*l.* per share on 3,200 shares, leaving 74*l.* in the hands of the secretary to meet contingencies.

LONDON, CHATHAM, AND DOVER.—With a view to the avoidance of injurious competition and the economising of working expenses in the conduct of the continental traffic, *via* Dover and Folkestone, an arrangement was concluded with this company, in 1863 under parliamentary sanction.

EXTENSIONS.—By 28 and 29 Vic., cap. 343 (5th July, 1865), the company was authorised to construct several short extensions of its lines at Greenwich, Woolwich, and Cranbrook. Length, 4½ miles. Capital, for these lines, the completion of the Charing Cross line and other purposes, 905,000*l.* in shares, and 301,600*l.* on loan.

By 29 and 30 Vic., cap. 227 (16th July, 1866), the company was authorised to construct some short branches or extensions in Greenwich, and to the Weald of Kent, &c. Length, 8¼ miles. Capital, 204,000*l.* in shares, and 68,000*l.* on loan. Running powers to Chatham and Dover over Greenwich lines.

By 30 Vic., cap. 8 (12th April, 1867), the South Eastern obtained various powers for regulating its capital and debt, and dividing its stock into deferred and preferred moieties. Also to consolidate the various preference shares of the company into one consolidated 5 per cent. stock, and the debenture loans into debenture stock.

By 31 and 32 Vic., cap 172 (31st July, 1868), the company obtained powers to divide its ordinary stock into deferred and preferred, to alter the levels and approaches at Woodside Bridge, and to establish savings banks for its servants, &c.

REVENUE.—The receipts for the half-year ending 31st January showed that 784,267*l.* had been received, against 704,212*l.* in the corresponding period of 1867, showing an increase of 80,055*l.* The working expenses and other deductions amounted to 357,914*l.*, against 365,728*l.*, showing a decrease of 7,814*l.*, leaving the net receipts for the half-year 429,353*l.*, against 338,484*l.*, showing a net increase of 87,869*l.* After making provision for all fixed charges, rents, and interest on the whole of the capital expenditure on lines and stations productive and open for traffic, the sum remaining applicable to the dividend on the consolidated stock was 176,635*l.*, being equal to a dividend at the rate of 4*l.* 12*s.* 6*d.* per cent. per annum ; but the directors recommended that the whole of the interest on capital invested on unproductive works, including the Direct Tunbridge, be charged to revenue ; deducting this sum there would remain 153,820*l.*, which was equal to a dividend at the rate of 4 per cent., as against 3 in the corresponding period, leaving a balance of 1,092*l.*

The receipts for the half-year ending 31st July amounted to 727,488*l.*, and for the corresponding period of 1867 to 714,718*l.*, showing an increase of 12,769*l.* The working expenses and other charges amounted to 354,188*l.*, against 366,795*l.*, showing an increase of 12,607*l.* The net receipts amounted to 373,300*l.*, against 347,923*l.*, showing an increase of 25,377*l.* After providing for all outgoings, as well as dividend and interest on all loan and preferential capital, there remained 99,097*l.*, but from this was deducted the cost of damage by fire at the Charing-cross station, and of the Fusion Bill in the past Session—leaving 90,414*l.* available, out of which a dividend at the rate of 2*l.* 5*s.* per cent. left a balance of 4,504*l.*

DEBENTURE STOCK.—The directors reported in September, that they had created 4,359,263*l.* of debenture stock to be used in the extinction of the old bond debt as such fell due, and they had allotted to the holders of original stock debenture stock at par amounting to 3,818,440*l.*, of which 3,294,350*l.* had been taken up. 255,000*l.* had been issued to capitalists, who joined in guaranteeing the issue, and also 28,500*l.* to others (not being directors), entitled to an allotment; thus 3,577,850*l.* out of 4,359,263*l.* created had been issued. The directors had offered the remaining amount to the debenture and preference stockholders, as well as to the holders of consolidated stock, at a premium of 10 per cent. The directors proprosed to appropriate the premiums on this stock as it was disposed of by them to the reduction of the capital account.

AMALGAMATION.—Referring to the Bill for the working union of the South Eastern and Brighton and of the London Chatham and Dover, and the rejection of the proposal by the Lords' committee to assimilate the *maximum* tolls on their very costly railways to those proposed for the Brighton section, the directors stated that this would have entailed a loss of net revenue at the rate of 60,000*l*. a year, or, in other words, such a reduction of the dividend upon the ordinary capital as would have been equivalent to the giving away or extinction of about 1,200,000*l*. of that capital. There remained no alternative but to withdraw those portions of the Bill effecting the fusion of net revenue. The committee, however, afterwards gave to the Brighton the moderate increase of tolls demanded by that company. It had been contended in high quarters that the scale of tolls granted to railway companies in the Acts authorising the construction of their works constituted a sort of treaty with parliament and the public, and should not be raised by future legislation. The directors thought that the same argument would apply with more force where shareholders had laid out millions of money on the faith of certain powers of charge. As much misrepresentation had appeared to exist, the directors finally repeated—1. That no toll clauses whatever were inserted in the Fusion Bill as presented to the committee of the Commons. 2. That this company never proposed any increase whatever in the *maximum* rates of charge, on the faith of which the shareholders subscribed capital and constructed the South Eastern system. 3. That the toll clauses proposed in the Bill while in committee were so proposed at the instance of the committee, and not of the promoters. And 4. That if passed they would have largely reduced the *maximum* power of charge, except in a very few cases, and have led, of necessity, to a reduction in existing fares on portions of the company's system, such reduction being counterbalanced by that saving in needless working expense which the directors believed it was the interest, both of the public and of the proprietors, to secure. The Brighton having stated their intention of putting in operation the increased toll powers specially given to them as above (and which, it would be observed, were lower in amount than their actual charges to the public in 1862), the question of a revision of fares was referred to the general managers of the three companies, and on their recommendation various changes have been made. The moderate advance of rates on the South Eastern did not affect the "residental" or periodical and season tickets, or the Charing-cross service, or, in fact, the bulk of the passenger traffic of the company, while the time of all the return tickets had been extended and a new and special service had been established for the working classes. Valuable portions of the Fusion Bill were retained, and the important clause, sanctioning the division of the original stock of the company into equal parts of preferred and deferred stock, after encountering opposition in the House of Lords, was, nevertheless, eventually carried through both Houses of Parliament and received the Royal assent on the 31st of July.

DIVIDED STOCK.—At a special meeting, held on 27th August, 1868, it was resolved—"That the directors are hereby authorised to carry into effect the powers of the South Eastern Act, 1868, in respect of the division of the paid-up ordinary stock of the company into two classes, and to issue the same as in the said Act provided."

CAPITAL.—The consolidated stock and share account to 31st July, 1868, is constituted as follows:—

	Received.	Not Received.	Total.
"Consolidated South Eastern Stock"	£7,637,049	£ 831	£7,637,880
"Consolidated South Eastern Stock. guaranteed 4½ per cent. in perpetuity"	481,300	....	481,300
Fixed 4½ per cent.	503.000	....	503,000
South Eastern 4½ per cent., No. 2	300,000	....	300,000
South Eastern 5 per cent, preference consolidated (1861)	591,500	....	591,500
South Eastern 4½ per cent. preference shares (1862)— Deposit ....£113,282 Instalments, Nos. 2 to 4 ....1,017,828 = 1,131,110		68,890	1,200,000
5 per cent. preference shares (Charing Cross, 1863)— Deposit...............£70,000 Instalments, Nos. 2 to 5 ....629,775 = 699,775		225	700,000
South Eastern 5 per cent. perpetual preference (1864)	685,820	....	685,820
South Eastern 5 per cent. preference shares (1865) ..	759,337	495,663	1,255,000
South Eastern Annuities—Capital represented	800,000	....	800,000
	£13,588,891	£565,609	£14,154,500

The receipts and expenditure for the half-year ending 31st July, were detailed in the following form :—

Received.		Expended.	
5 per cent. preference shares (1865)	£3,560	To 31st January, 1868 ....£18,247,350	
4½ per cent. debenture stock	1,500	Received to 31st January, 1868..	18,092,409
5 per cent. debenture stock (1867)..	21,500		
5 per cent. debenture stock certifi-			£154,940
cates (1868).....................	141,302	Main line and branches, North	
		Kent, and Greenwich, less re-	
	£167,862	ceived for sale of surplus lands	10
Balance....................	194,338	Carriages and wagons—Reten-	
		tions on stock purchased in	
		previous year	1,116
		Purchase of land on Addiscombe	
		branch	2,656
		Tunbridge and Dartford lines..	28,205
		Charing Cross lines	7,323
		Loans........................	167,948
	£362,201		£362,201

The accounts are made up to 31st January and 31st July, and the meetings are held in London half-yearly.

Scale of Voting.—One vote for 30*l.* stock up to 600*l.*; and one vote additional for every 150*l.* beyond the first 600*l.*

Registration fee, 2*s.* 6*d.* each seller.   In transfers, Reading annuities may be described as so many "Perpetual annuities of 20*s.* 6*d.*, 15 Vic., cap. 103, of and in the undertaking called the S. E. R. Co.," &c.

No. of Directors—12.   *Qualification,* 2,000*l.* of stock, held three months previous to their nomination.

DIRECTORS:

Chairman—Sir EDWARD WILLIAM WATKIN, Knt., Rose Hill, Northenden, near Manchester, and 18, Westbourne Terrace, Hyde Park, W.

Deputy-Chairman—The Hon. JAMES BYNG, Great Culverden, Tunbridge Wells.

John Barlow, Esq., 99, Piccadilly, London, W.

Alexander Beattie, Esq., Summerhill, Chislehurst, Kent, S. E.

Nathaniel Buckley, Esq., Ryecroft, Ashton-under-Lyne.

Charles Gilpin, Esq., M.P., 10, Bedford Square, W.C.

Jonathan Mellor, Esq., Polefield, Prestwich, near Manchester.

Captain Daniel Warren, 68, Porchester Terrace, Bayswater, W.

John Bibby, Esq., Hart Hill, Liverpool.

Thomas Norton, Esq., 13, Bolton Row, May Fair, W.

John Stuart, Esq., 41, Corporation Street, Manchester.

James Whatman, Esq., M.P., Vinters, near Maidstone, and 6, Carlton Gardens, S.W.

OFFICERS.—Gen. Man., C. W. Eborall; Sec., John Shaw; Treas., Thos. A. Chubb; Goods Man., E. B. Noden, Bricklayers' Arms Station; Traffic Supt., J. P. Knight; Chief Res. Eng., Peter Ashcroft; Loco. Supt., James I'Anson Cudworth, Ashford; Carriage Supt., R. C. Mansell, Ashford; Auditors, Charles Whetham, 52, Gordon Square, W.C., and J. G. T. Child, Parker Street, Manchester.

Head Offices—London Bridge Station, S.E.

368.—SOUTH ESSEX.

Incorporated by 28 and 29 Vic., cap. 344, to construct a line from Brentwood, on the Great Eastern, to Southminster, with a Branch to Maldon.   Total length, 31¼ miles. Capital, 250,000*l.* in 10*l.* shares, and 83,000*l.* on loan.   Compulsory purchase, three years.   Completion of works, 5 years.

By 29 and 30 Vic., cap. 340 (6th August, 1866), the company obtained power to construct a line from Rettendon to Pitsea, on the London Tilbury and Southend.   Length, 5½ miles.   Capital, 60,000*l.* in shares, and 20,000*l.* on loan.

Meetings in February or March, and August or September.

No. of Directors.—Maximum, 7; minimum, 5; quorum, 3.   *Qualification,* 300*l.*

DIRECTORS:

Chairman—The Hon. HENRY WILLIAM PETRE, Chelmsford.

William Lawrence Banks, Esq., Watton House, Brecon.

Alfred Champion, Esq., Epsom, Surrey.

Captain Owen Henry Strong, Iffley, near Oxford.

OFFICERS.—Sec., J. Wilson Theobald, 6, Victoria Street, Westminster, S.W.; Engs., G. W. Hemans, C. E., and Travers H. Falconer, 1, Westminster Chambers, Victoria Street, S.W.; Solicitors, Gregory, Champion, and Eady, 18, Park Street, Westminster, S.W., and 12, Clement's Inn, Strand, W.C.

Offices—6, Victoria Street, S.W.

369.—SOUTHERN OF IRELAND.

Incorporated by 28 and 29 Vic., cap. 353 (5th July, 1865), to construct a line from the Great Southern, and Western at Thurles, to Clonmel, on the Waterford and Limerick. Length, 22¼ miles. Capital, 171,000l. in shares, and 57,000l. on loan. Arrangements with Great Southern and Western and Waterford and Limerick. Works in progress.

By 29 and 30 Vic., cap. 271 (23rd July, 1866), the company obtained power to make several deviations, and also to construct three branches. Length, 9½ miles. Capital, 60,000l. in shares, and 20,000l. on loan.

No. of Directors—7 ; quorum, 3. *Qualification*, 250l.

DIRECTORS:

Chairman—PETER GRAHAM, Esq., Queen's Road, Regent's Park, N.W.

William Forbes, Esq.
J. Lyster O'Beirne, Esq., M.P., 36, Sackville Street, W.

Edward Nathan Burgess, Esq.
Major-General Brownrigg, C.B., 91, Victoria Street, Westminster, S.W.

Secretary, R. F. Mulvany.

Offices—70, Bishopsgate Street, E.C.

370.—SOUTH NORTHUMBERLAND.

Incorporated by 28 and 29 Vic., cap. 256 (5th July, 1865), to construct a line from the Wallbottle branch of the Blyth and Tyne to Dyke House. Length, 11 miles. Capital, 60,000l. in shares, and 20,000l. on loan. Arrangements with Blyth and Tyne. In abeyance.

No. of Directors—7 ; minimum, 3 ; quorum, 3 and 2. *Qualification*, 500l.

DIRECTORS:

Sir Edward Blackett, Bart.
Richard Hodgson, Esq., of Carham Hall, Coldstream.

John Frederick Bigge, Esq.
Thomas James, Esq.
John Hodgson Hinde, Esq.

371.—SOUTH WALES AND GREAT WESTERN DIRECT.

Incorporated by 28 and 29 Vic., cap. 367 (5th July, 1865), to construct a line from Chepstow, on the South Wales, to Wootton Bassett, on the Great Western, with a bridge over the Severn. Length, 40¾ miles. Capital, 1,800,000l. in shares, and 600,000l. on loan. Arrangements with Great Western. In abeyance.

No attempt has yet been made to raise the capital required for this undertaking.

No. of Directors—9 ; minimum, 5 ; quorum, 3. *Qualification*, 1,000l.

DIRECTORS:

Chairman—THE EARL OF DEVON, Powderham Castle, Exeter, and 68, Brook Street, W.

The Hon. Howe Browne, The Crouch Oak, Addlestone.
Henry Hussey Vivian, Esq., M.P., Swansea, and 7, Belgrave Square, S.W.
Francis Tothil, Esq., Clifton.

Chris. Rice Mansel Talbot, Esq., M.P., Margam Park, Glamorganshire, and 3, Cavendish Square, W.
Thomas Brown, Esq., Hardwick House, Chepstow.

OFFICERS.—Sec., B. C. Stephenson ; Eng., John Fowler; Solicitors, Hargrove, Fowler, and Blunt, Victoria Street, Westminster, S.W.

Offices—6, Westminster Chambers, Victoria Street, Westminster, S.W.

372.—SOUTH WALES MINERAL.

Incorporated by 17 Vic., cap. 197 (15th August, 1853), for a line from Briton Ferry station of South Wales to Glyncorrwg, Glamorganshire, and a branch, from Baglan to Mitchelstone-super-Avon and Forcedwn Colliery. Length (main line, 11⅚, branch ⅘) 12¼ miles.

By 18 Vic., cap. 23 (May 25th, 1855), the line is leased to the Glyncorrwg Coal Company, at 5 per cent. for two years; 5½ per cent. for the next 14 years; and 6 per cent. for remaining 14 years of lease.

By 24 and 25 Vic., cap. 210 (1st August, 1861), the company was authorised to construct an extension to Briton Ferry Docks. Length, 1½ mile. Capital, 30,000l. in shares, and 10,000l. on loan.

By 27 and 28 Vic., cap. 297 (29th July, 1864), the company obtained power to extend the undertaking from Glyncorrwg to Blaen Afon and other places. Length, 4½ miles. Capital, 30,000l. in shares, and 10,000l. on loan.

Meetings in February or March, and August or September, in London or Neath.

No. of Directors.—Maximum, 9; minimum, 6; quorum, 3. *Qualification,* 50 shares.

DIRECTORS:

Chairman—ROBERT DUDLEY BAXTER, Esq., The Oaks, Frognals, Hampstead, N.W.

Deputy-Chairman—ARTHUR T. PRATT BARLOW, Esq., Taplow, Maidenhead, Berks.

Edward Nugent Ayrton, Esq., 19, Old Square, Lincoln's Inn, W.C.
James Pratt Barlow, Esq., Hyde Park Gate, W.

John Nathaniel Foster, Esq., Biggleswade, Beds.

OFFICERS.—Sec., Thomas John Woods, 6, Victoria Street, Westminster, S.W.; Registrar and Accountant, Robert Smith, 6, Victoria Street, Westminster, S.W.; Solicitors, Baxter, Rose, Norton, and Co., 6, Victoria Street, Westminster, S.W.; Bankers, Glyn, Mills, and Co., 67, Lombard Street, E.C., and the Glamorganshire Banking Company, Neath.

Offices—6, Victoria Street, Westminster, S.W.

373.—SOUTH YORKSHIRE.

Incorporated by 11 Vic., cap. 291 (22nd July, 1847), for a line from Doncaster to Midland at Swinton, intersecting which the line is continued to a junction with the Sheffield R. B. W. H. and Goole at Barnsley. In 1850 power was also given to effect certain deviations, to construct branches to Elsecar and Worsbro', and to change the name of the company to the "South Yorkshire Railway and River Dun Company." In 1851 further deviations were authorised. Opened in September, 1859.

The Act of incorporation also provided for the purchase of the DUN NAVIGATION, subject to that company's existing liabilities, which are secured a preference over all mortgages and bonds authorised by the Railway Act. The capital of the canal consisted of 150 shares, on which a profit of 150l. per annum had been *made*, and 120l. *divided* for some time previous. These shares, by that Act, were secured in lieu of profits from the canal, until the opening of the railway, the sum of 120l. per share per annum, one canal share to have 150 railway shares of 20l. each, paid up in full, and entitled to dividend *pro rata* with ordinary railway shares. Power to redeem these "paid up" shares within ten years from the opening of the railway, at par, being 3,000l. for each Old Dun Navigation share. By an Act passed in 1850 this company was authorised to guarantee a fixed dividend on any of these shares, instead of fluctuating dividends. By resolution of 28th February, 1851, a 4 per cent. guarantee stock was created for that purpose.

Under the same Act it was also provided that the company should purchase the DEARNE AND DOVE NAVIGATION, and create new shares to the extent required. The capital of canal consisted of 600 shares, on which a profit of 17l. per annum had been made, and 16l. per annum actually divided for some time previous; it was paid off at the rate of 350l. per share, 2nd January, 1856.

By 22 and 23 Vic., cap. 101 (8th August, 1859), the company is enabled to convert its debt into debenture stock, and authorised to charge on the new line from Doncaster through Thorne to Keadby (10 miles) the same rates and tolls as are taken on the main line.

By 24 and 25 Vic., cap. 169 (22nd July, 1861), the company was authorised to extend the line across the Trent from Keadby, to join the Trent Ancholme and Grimsby. Capital, 100,000l. in shares, and 33,000l. on loan. Arrangements with Trent Ancholme and Grimsby, and the Manchester Sheffield and Lincolnshire.

By 25 and 26 Vic., cap. 129 (7th July, 1862), the South Yorkshire was authorised, in conjunction with the Manchester and Sheffield, to contribute towards and to acquire the Trent Ancholme and Grimsby, which see.

By 25 and 26 Vic., cap. 141 (17th July, 1862), the South Yorkshire was authorised to construct a line from Doncaster to Thorne, and a railway to join the Manchester Sheffield and Lincolnshire, at Sheffield. Length, 12¼ miles. Capital, 100,000l. in shares, and 33,000l. on loan. Completion of works, three years.

By 26 and 27 Vic., cap. 146 (13th July, 1863), several deviations were authorised, as well as new capital to the extent of 20,000l. in shares at 5 per cent., and 6,000l. on loan. Agreements with Great Northern and North Eastern.

By 29 Vic,, cap. 86 (11th June, 1866), the company was authorised to widen and improve a portion of the railway, and to abandon other portions, which extensions or deviations had rendered necessary. New capital, 150,000l. in shares, and 50,000l. on loan.

TRENT, ANCHOLME, AND GRIMSBY.—The following resolution was adopted at a meeting of South Yorkshire proprietors, on 6th September:—"That the directors are hereby authorised to subscribe and hold shares in the Trent Ancholme and Grimsby to the extent of 40,000l., as authorised by the Trent Ancholme and Grimsby Act of 1862, and to apply in payment of such subscriptions any sums of money which the company is authorised to receive, or which they may have raised by any Act or Acts relating to the undertaking."

BARNSLEY COAL.—Incorporated by 24 and 25 Vic., cap. 165 (22nd July, 1861), to construct a line from the South Yorkshire, at Darfield, to Notton. Length, 4 miles. Capital, 40,000l. in 10l. shares; loans, 13,000l. By 26 and 27 Vic., cap. 146 (13th July, 1863), this line was authorised to be purchased by the South Yorkshire, which had subscribed 10,000l. to the undertaking.

By 27 Vic., cap. 19 (13th May, 1864), the South Yorkshire was authorised to extend this line to the Midland at Barnsley. Length, 1¼ mile. No new capital.

There are now in operation 70 miles of railway and 60 of canal, and the Trent Ancholme and Grimsby, 15 miles, is also completed.

TRANSFER.—By 27 and 28 Vic., cap. 77 (23rd June, 1864), the South Yorkshire was leased to the Manchester and Sheffield, at a *minimum* dividend of 5 per cent. on the ordinary stock, and a half of the clear profits remaining thereafter.

REVENUE.—The statement for the year 1867 showed the gross traffic to be for the
half-years ending 30th June...£111,208
      and 31st December... 125,715
    Making the gross traffic for 1867 ....————£236,923
    which, after deducting 38 per cent. 90,030

left the sum hypothecated as rent to this company £146,893

The amounts receivable as rent from the Manchester and Sheffield, to
meet the interest and dividends, were for the half-years ending 30th
 June £71,043
    and 31st December.. 70,580
making a total amount for 1867 of ....————141,623

So that the guarantee fund was £5,270
above the amount required. After deduction, however, of the working expenses at the agreed on rate of 42 per cent. (99,508l.), there remained a net profit for 1867 of 137,415l., so that the net profits were less by 4,208l. than the amount required for the interest and dividends, and consequently there were no additional profits divisible.

For the June half-year of 1868 the receipts from traffic and rents from the railway and navigations for the same period were 109,102l. The sum payable by the Manchester Sheffield and Lincolnshire to cover rents, interests, and charges and guaranteed dividends, amounted to 71,992l. The extension line from Tinsley to Rotherham had been opened for traffic on the 1st August. After deducting 30,665l. for interest on loans, there remained a balance available for dividend of 47,029l., out of which, after the dividends on the 4 per cent. and 5 per cent. preference stocks and shares had been deducted, there was left 17,619l. for dividend on the ordinary stock at the rate of 5 per cent. per annum.

CAPITAL.—The expenditure on this account to 30th of June was stated at 3,334,079*l.*, which left a balance against the company of 96,224*l.* The receipts were detailed as follow:—

Consolidated ordinary stock and shares	£657,036	
Unconveyed River Dun shares (entitled to ordinary dividend)...	47,000 =	£704,036
Guaranteed 4 per cent. stock	403,220	
Unconveyed River Dun shares (entitled to guaranteed dividend)	45,760 =	448,980
Redeemable guaranteed 5 per cent. stock, 1860		500,000
Redeemable 5 per cent. preference stock, 1863		260,000
Irredeemable preference 5 per cent. 10*l.* shares, created August 25th, 1866		57,200
Canals, Capital Account:—		
Dearne and Dove Canal	£58,450	
Keadby Canal	150 =	58,600
Mortgage debt—railway and navigations		1,134,665
Forfeited shares		49,373
Temporary loans		25,000
Total receipts to 30th June, 1868		£3,237,855
Balance due by company		96,224
		£3,334,079

The statutory meetings are held half-yearly (for the purpose of declaring the dividend) in February and August. Certificates must accompany transfer deed. Registration fee, 2*s.* 6*d.* each seller.

DIRECTORS:

Chairman—The Hon. WILLIAM EDEN, Elmfield, Doncaster.

Deputy-Chairman—G. S. LISTER, Esq., Tattingston Park, Ipswich.

Thomas Rawson Barker, Esq., The Edge, Sheffield.
R. J. Bentley, Esq., Rotherham.
Wm. Fenton, Esq., Beaumonds, Rochdale.
Wm. Hutton, Esq , Gate Burton, Lincoln.
William Newman, Esq., Darley Hall, Barnsley.
Col. George Hussey Packe, Caythorpe, near Grantham, and 41, Charles Street, Berkeley Square, W.

Richard Withers, Esq., Royal Bank Buildings, Liverpool. .
The Right Hon. J. Parker, Darrington, Pomfret.
Samuel Roberts, Esq., Queen's Tower, Sheffield.
S. H. Staniforth, Esq., Sheffield.
C. Bartholomew, Esq., Broxholme, Doncaster.

OFFICERS.—Sec., J. B. Renton; Eng., Charles Sacré; Auditors, J. Rhodes and J. G. T. Child, 104, King Street, Manchester.
Head Offices—Doncaster.

374.—SPILSBY AND FIRSBY.

Incorporated by 28 and 29 Vic., cap. 238 (5th July, 1865), to construct a line from Spilsby to a junction with the East Lincolnshire at Firsby. Length, 4 miles. Capital, 25,000*l.*, in shares; and 8,333*l.* on loan. Arrangements with Great Northern, which is to work the line.
No. of Directors—5; quorum, 3. *Qualification*, 200*l.*

DIRECTORS:

Henry Valentine Bantham, Esq.
Harwood Mackinder, Esq.
John Wilby Preston, Esq.

Rev. Edward Rawnsley.
George Walker, Esq., Osgathorpe, near Sheffield.

375.—STAFFORD AND UTTOXETER.

Incorporated by 25 and 26 Vic., cap. 175 (29th July, 1862), to construct a line from Stafford, on the London and North Western, to Uttoxeter, on the North Staffordshire, with a branch to the Colwich station of the latter company. Length, 13¼ miles. Capital, 130,000*l.* in shares, and 43,300*l.* on loan. Reciprocal facilities, through booking, &c., with London and North Western and North Staffordshire. Opened December, 1867.

By 28 Vic., cap. 45 (26th May, 1865), further powers were granted to the company, including power to divide the shares, and to raise new capital to the extent of 50,000*l.* in shares, and 16,600*l.* on loan.
Meetings in March and September.

No. of Directors—6; minimum, 3; quorum, 2 and 3. *Qualification*, 250*l.*

DIRECTORS :

Chairman—THOMAS CAMPBELL EYTON, Esq., Eyton, Wellington, Salop.

William Buxton, Esq., Stafford. | John Taylor, Esq., 27, Warwick Crescent,
Thomas Wynne, Esq., Stone, Staffordshire. | Kensington, W.

OFFICERS.—Sec., R. D. Newill, Wellington, Salop; Eng., T. C. Townsend, C.E.,
Shrewsbury; Solicitors, R. D. Newill, Wellington, and J. Brend Batten, Great George
Street, Westminster, S.W.

Offices—Wellington, Salop.

376.—STAINES, WOKINGHAM, AND READING.

Incorporated by 17 Vic., cap. 85 (July 8th, 1853), for a line from Staines Junction,
S.W., Windsor line, to Wokingham, junction with Reading Guildford and Reigate, and
branch over Chobham, to the London and South Western line at Woking. Length,
22¾ miles. By 18 and 19 Vic., cap. 139 (July 16th, 1855), the company was authorised
to make certain deviations, with power to run over the extended Reading Guildford
and Reigate, and to use part of Great Western land.

Opened from Staines to Ascot, 10 miles, 4th June, 1856; from Ascot to Wokingham,
8 miles, 9th July. The trains are run into Reading, the company having running
powers over that portion of the South Eastern.

By 21 and 22 Vic., cap. 58 (28th June, 1858), the company is authorised to lease the
line to the South Western; to cancel and re-issue forfeited shares. In respect to the
latter, the following resolution was adopted on 30th August:—" That 2,245 new shares
be created and issued in lieu of the 2,245 shares to be surrendered; and that there shall
be attached to the 2,245 new shares, and also 255 of the 500 shares which were created
under the 'Reading Railways Junction Act, 1857,' making together 2,500 shares at 20l.
each, a dividend at the rate of 5l. per cent. per annum on the amount from time to
time paid up on the said shares, such dividend to be paid in perpetual and absolute
preference and priority to any dividend or dividends upon any other shares in the
company."

SOUTH WESTERN.—A lease of the line, including portion of Reading junction was
granted to this company for 42 years from 25th March, 1858. The lessees to work and
maintain line, and to pay duty, parish rates, and all outgoings appertaining to proper
working and maintaining of line, and to pay by way of rent to the company, 50 per
cent. of the gross receipts, guaranteeing that the amount shall never be less than
sufficient to pay the interest (at a rate not exceeding 5 per cent.) on 140,000l., the
amount of debentures and preferential share capital.

REVENUE.—The increase of the passenger traffic during the December half-year had
been 355l., and on the goods traffic 419l., total, 774l.; being an increase of about 5 per
cent. on the passengers, and nearly 13 per cent. on goods.

The following dividends were declared at the rate of 5 per cent. per annum on the
preference shares, amounting, less income tax, to 1,218l.; and 4s. per share, or 2 per
cent. per annum, on the ordinary shares, against 3s. 3d. per share, or 1⅝ per cent. per
annum, for the corresponding half-year of 1866, amounting, less income tax, to 2,487l.,
and leaving a balance of 33l.

It was reported in August that on comparing the receipts of the half-year ending
30th June with the corresponding period of 1867 there was an increase in the passenger
traffic of 379l., and in the goods traffic of 190l., together, 569l. The increase in passenger receipts was greater than in the preceding statement, as the proportion of the
traffic carried by the South Eastern and Brighton to Ascot during the races was not
included in that half-year's return, although it formed part of that for 1867. The
result, therefore, showed that the resources of the railway would ultimately be developed. The following dividends were declared, viz:—At 5 per cent. per annum on
the preference shares, less income tax; and 6s. per share, or 3l. per cent. per annum, on
the ordinary share, less income tax, leaving a balance of 74l. The dividend for the
same half-year of 1867 was 5s. 6d. per share, or 2¾ per cent. per annum.

No. of Directors.—Maximum, 6; minimum, 3; quorum, 3.   *Qualification,* 25 shares.

DIRECTORS :

Chairman—JAMES GARRARD, Esq., Pinner Place, near Watford.

3 Richard Blanshard, Esq., Fairfield, | 1 Robert William Kennard, Esq., 37, Por-
  Lymington, Hampshire. | chester Terrace, W.
2 Richard Davis, Esq., 9, St. Helen's | 2 Charles Wilkin, Esq., 10, Tokenhouse
  Place, Bishopsgate Street, E.C. | Yard, E.C.

Two directors go out annually, but are eligible for re-election.

OFFICERS.—Sec., Theodore Morris Walford, 1, Broad Sanctuary, Westminster, S.W.; Auditors, Joseph George, Goldsmith's Hall, E.C., and Walter Prideaux, Goldsmith's Hall, E.C.; Solicitor, S. F. Noyes, 1, Broad Sanctuary, Westminster, S.W.; Bankers, National Bank, Old Broad Street, E.C.

Offices –1, Broad Sanctuary, Westminster, S.W.

377.—STAMFORD AND ESSENDINE.

Incorporated by 17 Vic., cap. 199 (August 5th, 1853), for a line from Stamford to Essendine. Length, 3¾ miles. Company may use the Great Northern line, and *vice versa.* Capital authorised in 1,000 shares of 50*l.* each, 50,000*l.*; loans, 16,000*l.*; powers to three-fifths of general meeting to attach preference to 10,000*l.* of capital; which was exercised in August, 1857; total, 66,000*l.* Maximum interest, 5 per cent. Opened 1st November, 1857, and worked under arrangements with Great Northern.

By 20 and 21 Vic., cap. 82 (27th July, 1857), the company was authorised to create new capital, 20,000*l.* in shares at 5 per cent. preference, and 15,000*l.* by loan. At a special meeting on 19th of March, resolutions were adopted authorising the directors to raise 20,000*l.* by creation of new preference shares, to bear interest at 5 per cent. for 10 years—the company to have option, at the expiration of that period, of either purchasing the shares at par, or reducing interest to 4 per cent.

By 27 and 28 Vic., cap. 220 (25th July, 1864), the company was authorised to construct a line to join the Northampton and Peterborough branch of the London and North Western. Length, 6 miles. Capital, 75,000*l.* in shares, and 25,000*l.* on loan. Opened.

No. of Directors—4; quorum, 3. *Qualification*, 6 shares.

DIRECTORS:

Chairman—The MARQUIS OF EXETER, Burghley House, Stamford.

Charles Ormiston Eaton, Esq., Tolethorpe | W. Brydone, Esq., Whitehall, S.W.
Hall, Rutland. |

OFFICERS.—Sec., John Ford, Stamford; Traffic Manager, Henry Edwards, Stamford; Eng., William Hurst, 46, Bedford Row, W.C.; Auditor, William Higgs, Stamford; Solicitors, Messrs. Walford, Bolton Street, Piccadilly, W., and Thompsons, Phillips, and Evans, Stamford.

378.—STIRLING AND DUNFERMLINE.
(EMBODIED IN NORTH BRITISH.)

Incorporated by 9 and 10 Vic., cap. 202 (16th July, 1846), for a line from Stirling to Dunfermline, with branches to Tillicoultry and Alloa Harbour. In 1848 deviations and new works were authorised. In 1849 other deviations were authorised in the Alloa branch, private railways diverted, and an extension of time obtained for the construction of the line between Alloa and Stirling. Length authorised, 24 miles.

The disputes with the Edinburgh and Glasgow were finally arranged and settled by 21 and 22 Vic, cap. 64 (28th June, 1858), the Stirling and Dunfermline being vested in that company from that date. By this Act the Edinburgh and Glasgow is burdened with the whole debenture debt of this company, as well as to hand over 450,000*l.* of now guaranteed stock, entitled "Edinburgh and Glasgow (Stirling and Dunfermline) 4 per cent. guaranteed stock," to be distributed among the shareholders, or otherwise applied in lieu of original share capital of 390,000*l.* This new stock is in every respect most amply secured, having not only a preferable lien on the Stirling and Dunfermline, but also (as regards the Edinburgh and Glasgow) having precedence of the ordinary and preference stocks of that company. The dividends, as guaranteed, continue to be regularly paid by the North British.

379.—STOCKTON AND DARLINGTON.

Incorporated by Act 1 and 2 Geo. IV., cap. 44 (1821), for a tram-road from the river Tees at Stockton to Witton Park Colliery, with several branches therefrom, and was first opened for traffic (coals) on 27th September, 1825. Productive, 201¼ miles.

MIDDLESBOROUGH AND REDCAR.—On 29th September, 1847, Act 8 and 9 Vic., cap. 127, this company was leased for 999 years, from 1st October, 1847, at an annual rental of 2,880*l.*, equal to 6 per cent. on share capital then created, with an additional annual rent equal to interest payable on amount then held, and thereafter taken upon loan.

WEAR VALLEY.—This company was also leased under powers of Act 8 and 9 Vic, cap. 152, which subsequently became incorporated with the Bishop Auckland and Weardale, the Wear and Derwent, the Weardale Extension, and the Shildon Tunnel, all for the yearly rental of 47,037l., equal to 6 per cent. upon the share capital, commencing 1st October, 1847. Under authority of an Act of 1851 (14th Vic., cap. 23), the lessees became responsible for a further loan debt of 40,000l. Productive mileage, about 44 miles. Sealed 16th February, 1848.

MIDDLESBOROUGH AND GUISBROUGH.—Incorporated by 15 Vic., cap. 73 (17th June, 1852), for a line from a junction with the Middlesborough and Redcar at Middlesborough to Guisbrough, with two branches to the Cleveland hills. Length, main line, 9 miles; branches, 3 miles. Opened 25th February, 1854.

DARLINGTON AND BARNARD CASTLE.—Incorporated by 17 and 18 Vic., cap. 115 (1854). Capital, 100,000l. in 20l. shares; 30,300l. on loan. Length, 15¼ miles. Opened 8th July, 1856. By the terms of amalgamation, 21 and 22 Vic. (3rd July, 1858), the Stockton and Darlington, from 3rd September, pays all debts and liabilities, issuing in lieu of existing shares a preferential stock, bearing dividend at 6 per cent. per annum, from 1st January, 1859.

These four companies were amalgamated with the Stockton and Darlington by 21 and 22 Vic., cap. 116 (23rd July, 1858).

The Act 17 and 18 Vic., cap. 128 (July 3rd, 1854), had for its objects:—1. Construction of branch to Shildon Tunnel. 2. Acquisition of additional lands for general purposes. 3. Purchasing or taking on lease part of Wear Valley, formerly held only on way leaves. 4. Raising of additional capital to the extent of 200,000l., of which 45,170l. were required for construction of proposed branch, and acquisition of additional lands, and residue of general purposes. Length of branch, 2½ miles.

By 18 and 19 Vic., cap. 149 (July 16th, 1855), a sum of 110,000l. was authorised to be raised for construction of new lines, diversion of roads, and purchase of additional lands for station purposes, and also 90,000l. for the general purposes of the undertaking. The length of the several lines are as follow:—Junction to connect Stockton and Darlington with Darlington and Barnard Castle, 407 furlongs; branch from Wear Valley, near Waskerley, to Whitehall, 3 miles; branch from Wear Valley, near Scot's Isle, to High Stoop, 3 miles; branch in Parish of Brancepeth, 2¾ miles.

By 21 and 22 Vic., cap. 117 (23rd July, 1858), the company obtained power to construct new lines in the North Riding, as follow:—Redcar to Saltburn, 6½ miles. 6¼ miles opened 12th August, 1861. New capital, 45,000l.

By 21 and 22 Vic., cap. 115 (23rd July, 1858), the company was authorised to construct a line in the county of Durham, in connection with the Wear Valley and the main line. New capital, 30,000l. Length, 1½ mile, with portion of existing line to be altered, widened and improved, 2½ miles.

By 22 and 23 Vic., cap. 127 (13th August, 1859), the company was authorised to construct a junction from its main line at Stockton to the North Eastern in the same place. By the same Act the tolls to be taken by the North Eastern for certain traffic are regulated, and facilities afforded for the traffic of the Cleveland. No new capital.

By 23 Vic., cap. 44 (15th May, 1860), the company was authorised to raise 333,000l. in shares, and 83,000l. on loans, which have since been issued in 25l. shares. Calls, 2l. per share, with intervals of one year.

By 24 Vic., cap. 63 (12th June, 1861), the company was authorised to abandon the branch to Skelton, authorised by the North Riding Act of 1858, and to substitute a branch from Marske to Skelton instead.

By 24 and 25 Vic., cap. 157 (22nd July, 1861), the company was authorised to raise additional capital to the extent of 220,000l. in 25l. shares, and 67,000l. on loan.

By 25 Vic., cap. 54 (3rd June, 1862), the company was authorised to construct branches from Tow Law to Crook, and from Crook to the West Durham. Length, 4¼ miles. Debenture stock to be created to the extent of 500,000l. in lieu of loans; a portion at 4½ per cent. has been issued at a premium of 5½ per cent.

By 25 and 26 Vic., cap. 106 (30th June, 1862), the Eden Valley and South Durham and Lancashire were amalgamated with Stockton and Darlington.

EDEN VALLEY.—Incorporated by 21 Vic., cap. 14 (21st May, 1858), to construct a line from the Lancaster and Carlisle, near Penrith, to the South Durham and Lancashire, near Kirkby Stephen. Capital—shares, 135,000l., of 25l. each, loans, 45,000l. Length, 22 miles. Opened 9th June, 1862. By 25 and 26 Vic., cap. 118 (7th July, 1862), the Eden Valley was authorised to construct branches 5½ miles in length, and to raise new capital to the extent of 65,000*l.* in shares, and 21,666*l.* on loan. By 25 and 26 Vic., cap. 106 (30th June, 1862), the Eden Valley was amalgamated with the Stockton and Darlington, as from 1st January, 1863, at 4 per cent. preference on its outlay for three years, for next two years, 5, and in perpetuity thereafter, 5½ per cent.

SOUTH DURHAM AND LANCASHIRE UNION.—Incorporated by 20 and 21 Vic., cap. 40 (13th July, 1857), to construct a line from the Haggerleases branch of Stockton and Darlington to Tebay on Lancaster and Carlisle. Capital, 400,000*l.* in 25*l.* shares; loans, 133,000*l*, Length, 44 miles. Opened from Barnard Castle to Tebay, 8th August, 1861, from Barnard Castle to Bishop Auckland, on 1st February, 1863. By 25 and 26 Vic., cap. 106 (30th June, 1862), the South Durham and Lancashire was amalgamated with the Stockton and Darlington as from 1st January, 1863, at the rate of 4½ per cent. for 18 months from the date of amalgamation; 5 per cent. for the next two years; and 5¼ in perpetuity thereafter.

FROSTERLEY AND STANHOPE.—Incorporated by 24 and 25 Vic., cap. 72 (28th June, 1861), to construct a line from the Stockton and Darlington, at Frosterley, to Newland-side, near Stanhope, County Durham. Length, 2 miles 16 chains. Capital, 10,000*l.* in 20*l.* shares; loans, 3,300*l.* Opened 22nd October, 1862. By 25 Vic., cap. 40 (3rd June, 1862), the company was authorised to make certain deviations, to construct a branch (21 chains), and to make other improvements in the works; also to raise additional capital to the extent of 5,000*l.* in shares, and 1,000*l.* on loan. By 25 and 26 Vic., cap. 106 (30th June, 1862), the Frosterley and Stanhope is dissolved, and merged into the Stockton and Darlington, the latter repaying the capital to the subscribers of the former with 5 per cent. interest to 1st July, 1863.

NORTH EASTERN.—By 26 and 27 Vic., cap. 122 (13th July, 1863), the Stockton and Darlington was amalgamated with the North Eastern, the former company, however, maintaining the distinct management of its own system by a committee, consisting chiefly of its own directors, and to hold separate meetings till 1873. Three Stockton and Darlington directors have also seats at the North Eastern board.

The dividends declared on behalf of the Stockton and Darlington ordinary stock, since the amalgamation, have been as follow :—

	£	s	d			£	s	d
1863, December	4	0	0		1866, June,	4	2	6
1864, June	4	0	0		1866, December	4	5	0
1864, December	4	10	0		1867, June	3	12	6
1865, June	4	2	6		1867, December	4	2	6
1865, December	4	12	6		1868, June	3	5	0

Scale of Voting.—One vote for each share up to 20, and one vote for every 5 shares beyond the first 20 shares.

No. of Directors.—Maximum, 12: minimum, 8. *Qualification,* 500*l.*

DIRECTORS:

Chairman—1 HENRY PEASE, Esq., Pierremont, Darlington, and Stanhope Castle.

Deputy-Chairman—2 ALFRED KITCHING, Esq., Elm Field, Darlington.

2 John Castell Hopkins, Esq., The Firs, Kingston-on-Thames.
3 Isaac Wilson, Esq., Nunthorpe Hall, near Middlesborough-on-Tees.
2 Joseph Whitwell Pease, Esq., M.P., Hutton Hall, near Guisbro', and 18, Prince's Gardens, W.
1 William Randolph Innes Hopkins, Esq., Grey Towers, near Middlesborough-on-Tees.

1 William Thompson, Esq., Darlington.
2 W. C. Stobart, Esq., Etherley Lodge, near Bishop Auckland.
* W. C. Copperthwaite, Esq., Malton.
* William Rutherford Hunter, Esq., Lovaine Crescent, Newcastle-on-Tyne.
3 Henry Fell Pease, Esq., Brinkburn, Darlington.

1, Retire in 1869 ; 2, 1870; and 3, in 1871. * Nominated by North Eastern Company;

OFFICERS.—Sec. and Gen. Man., Thomas MacNay; Managers—Goods and Pass. Traffic, George Stephenson; Minerals, Richard Pickering and William Smith; Eng., William Cudworth; Loco. Supts., William Bouch and David Dale; Treas., Joseph Pease, Darlington; Accountant, E. Towns, Jun.; Auditors, Robert Wilson and Charles Robson; Solicitors, Hutchinson and Lucas; London Bankers, Dimsdale, Fowler, and Barnard, 50, Cornhill, E.C.

Head Office—Northgate, Darlington.

380.—STOKES BAY.

Incorporated by 18 and 19 Vic., cap. 192 (August 14th, 1855), to make a railway from Gosport (South Western) to Stokes Bay, and a Pier thereat. Length of railway 1mile 4 furlongs and 5 chains. The Act also authorises construction of a pier in connection with the railway, which will enable passengers to land at all times of tides.

By 21 and 22 Vic., cap. 50 (28th June, 1858), an extension of time for three years is conceded.

By 22 and 23 Vic., cap. 65 (1st August, 1859), the company was authorised to raise additional capital to the extent of 16,000l. in shares at 6 per cent. preference, and 5,000l. on loans; total, 40,000l. in shares, and 13,000l. by loan.

SOUTH WESTERN.—The agreement with this company is to the following effect:— 1. The South Western to work the line, pay all necessary outgoings for repairs, provision of rolling stock, and collection of tolls—paying to the Stokes Bay for the same the sum of 1,800l. per annum, as a commuted toll for the use of the line and pier for their through traffic to and from the island. 2. The Stokes Bay to have the advantage of any other than railway traffic using pier. The Isle of Wight Ferry have been made parties to the arrangement.

No. of Directors—6; minimum, 3; quorum, 3. *Qualification*, 25 shares.

DIRECTORS:

Chairman—THOMAS WILLIS FLEMING, Esq., Southampton.

T. Webster, Esq., Beachfield, Sandown Bay, Isle of Wight.
Edw. Woods, Esq., Gloucester Crescent, Hyde Park, W.
William Wagstaff, Esq., 4, Great George Street, Westminster, S.W.

OFFICERS.—Sec., W. P. Sutherland; Eng., H. H. Fulton; Parliamentary Agents, Wyatt and Hoskins, 28, Parliament Street, Westminster, S.W.; Solicitor, J. Brend Batten, 32, Great George Street, Westminster, S.W.

Offices—4, Great George Street, Westminster, S.W.

381 —STONEHOUSE AND NAILSWORTH.

Incorporated by 26 and 27 Vic., cap. 132 (13th July, 1863), to construct a line from Stonehouse, on the Bristol and Birmingham line of the Midland, to Nailsworth. Length, 5¾ miles. Capital, 66,000l. in 20l. shares; loans, 22,000l. Extra land, one acre; compulsory purchase, two years; completion of works, four years. Arrangements with Midland, which is to work the line. Opened January, 1867.

By 28 and 29 Vic., cap. 177 (29th June, 1865), the company was authorised to extend the line from Dudbridge to the Great Western, at Stroud. Length, 1¼ mile. Capital, 35,000l. in shares, and 11,600l. on loan. Midland to subscribe 35,000l. Great Western may call for broad gauge to be laid down, and employ its clerks on the stations.

No. of Directors—6; minimum, 3; quorum, 2. *Qualification*, 1,000l.

DIRECTORS:

Chairman—WILLIAM PLAYNE, Esq., Longfords, Minchinhampton, Gloucestershire.

Charles Playne, Esq., Nailsworth, Gloucestershire.
Alfred Selfe Leonard, Esq., Ebley, near Stonehouse, Gloucestershire.
George Ford, Esq., Ryeford, near Stonehouse, Gloucestershire.

OFFICERS.—Sec., G. B. Smith, Nailsworth, Gloucestershire; Auditors, E. Kimber and J. Dowrick; Solicitor, Henry Carnsew, 41, Parliament Street, S.W.

382.—STOURBRIDGE.

Incorporated by 23 Vic., cap. 94 (14th June, 1860), to make a railway from Stourbridge to Old Hill, with branches to Cradley Park and Coingreaves Iron Works. Length, 3¼ miles. Capital, 80,000l. in 10l. shares; loans, 26,600l.

By 24 and 25 Vic., cap, 221 (1st August, 1861), the company was authorised to extend its line to Smethwick, on Stour Valley branch of the London and North Western. Length, 5 miles. New capital, 120,000l. in 10l. shares, and 40,000l. on loan. Through booking facilities provided over and for the London and North Western. Opened 1st April, 1867.

By 26 and 27 Vic., cap. 95 (29th June, 1863), the company was authorised to raise new capital to the extent of 45,000l. in shares, at 5 per cent., and 15,000l. on loan.

By 28 and 29 Vic., cap. 226 (5th July, 1865), the company was authorised to construct a short branch into Stourbridge. Length, ¾ mile. Capital, 107,000*l*. in shares, and 35,000*l*. on loan.

By 29 and 30 Vic., cap. 221 (16th July, 1866), the company was authorised to construct a deviation at Stourbridge. New capital, 33,000*l*. in shares, and 9,900*l*. on loan. By this Act also the Stourbridge was transferred to the Great Western.

By 31 and 32 Vic., cap. 91 (13th July, 1868), the company obtained an extension of time for completion of the branch to Stourbridge till 31st December, 1869.

The minimum dividend secured by the working agreement with the Great Western is at the rate of 4 per cent. per annum.

CAPITAL.—The receipts on shares have been 105,905*l*., and on loans, 31,600*l*. Total, 137,505*l*. The Extension receipts have been 193,428*l*. on shares, and 70,000*l*. on loan. Meetings in February or March, and August or September.

No. of Directors—6; minimum, 3; quorum, 3. *Qualification*, 200*l*.

DIRECTORS:

Chairman—WILLIAM AKROYD, Esq., Parkfield, near Stourbridge.

G. K. Harrison, Esq., Hagley, near Stourbridge.

C. E. Swindell, Esq., The Quarry, Stourbridge.

Alexander Clunes Sherriff, Esq., **M.P.**, Perdiswell Hall, Worcester, and **10,** Dean's Yard, Westminster, S.W.

OFFICERS.—Sec., W. T. Adcock, Worcester; Eng., Edward Wilson, Worcester, and 9, Dean's Yard, Westminster, S.W.; Solicitor, John Harward, Stourbridge; Auditor, James B. Fisher, Greenfield, Stourbridge.

Offices—Worcester.

383—STRATFORD-ON-AVON.

Incorporated by 20 and 21 Vic., cap. 116 (10th August, 1857), to construct a line from Stratford-on-Avon to Hatton (Birmingham and Oxford section of Great Western). Mixed gauge. Capital, 65,000*l*. in 20*l*. shares; loans, 21,000*l*. Length, 9¼ miles. Opened 10th October, 1860.

By 24 Vic., cap. 31 (17th May, 1861), the company formed a junction with the West Midland. Length, 29 chains, which is completed, and in operation. New capital, 17,500*l*, in 10*l*. shares at 5 per cent., and 6,000*l*. on loan. These shares were created and issued in August, 1861.

GREAT WESTERN.—The following arrangement is made with this company:—Great Western to work the line, finding plant and staff, and maintain railway after first year and pay to Stratford the following per centage of gross earnings, viz.:—

If traffic receipts do not exceed 15*l*. per mile per week, 45 per cent.
If they exceed 15*l*. and do not exceed 20*l*. ,, 50 ,,
If they exceed 20*l*. ,, 55 ,,

Working arrangements to be for 10 years, renewal for 10 years, and all facilities to be given for through as well as for local traffic. A joint committee to manage all matters not directly affecting Great Western expenditure.

The dividend for the half-year ending 31st December was equal to 5 per cent. per annum, and that for the six months ending 30th June to 4*l*. 5*s*., equal to 4*l*. 12*s*. 6*d*. for the year.

CAPITAL.—The expenditure on this account is stated at 107,997*l*., leaving a balance against the company of 209*l*.

No. of Directors—7; minimum, 3. *Qualification*, 20 shares.

DIRECTORS:

Chairman—2 RICHARD GREAVES, Esq., The Cliff, Warwick.

Deputy-Chairman—1 EDWARD FORDHAM FLOWER, Esq., Stratford-on-Avon.

3 John Branston Freer, Esq., Stratford-on-Avon.
3 John Caleb Adkins, Esq., Milcote, near Stratford-on-Avon.
2 George Branson, Esq., Birmingham.

3 William Baldwin, Esq., Payton Street, Stratford-on-Avon.
1 William Bevington Lowe, Esq., Eatington, near Stratford-on-Avon.

1, Retire in February, 1869; 2, in February, 1870; 3, in February, 1871.

OFFICERS.—Sec., John C. Bull; Eng., T. Macdougal Smith; Auditors, William Gibbs and James Cox, Junr.; Bankers, Greenway, Smith, and Co., Warwick.

Offices—Warwick.

384.—SUNNINGDALE AND CAMBRIDGE TOWN.

Incorporated by 27 and 28 Vic., cap. 207 (14th July, 1864), to construct a line from the Staines Wokingham and Woking, near Sunningdale, to Cambridge Town. Length, 6¾ miles. Capital, 70,000*l.* in 10*l.* shares, and 23,000*l.* on loan. Arrangements with South Western. Works in progress.

By 28 and 29 Vic., cap. 197 (29th June, 1865), to construct a line from Frimley to the Blackwater station of the Reading Guildford and Reigate branch of the South Eastern. Length, 12¾ miles. Capital, 20,000*l.* in shares, and 6,600*l.* on loan.

By 29 and 30 Vic., cap. 141 (28th June, 1866), the company obtained power to alter the levels of the line, and to effect other improvements in its construction. New capital, 200,000*l.* in shares, and 6,600*l.* on loan.

No. of Directors—4; maximum, 6; quorum, 3. *Qualification*, 500*l.*

DIRECTORS:

John Fairhurst, 7, Markham Square, Chelsea, S.W.
M. F. Blakiston, Stoke-upon-Trent.

Charles Raleigh Knight, Esq.
Robert Spring, Esq.

Solicitor, J. Brend Batten, 32, Great George Street, Westminster, S.W.

385.—SURREY AND SUSSEX JUNCTION.

Incorporated by 28 and 29 Vic., cap. 379 (6th July, 1865), to construct a line from the Brighton, at Croydon, to junctions with the East Grinstead and Uckfield and Tunbridge branches of the same system. Length, 24¼ miles. Capital, 705,000*l.* in shares, and 235,000*l.* on loan.

By 30 and 31 Vic., cap. 140 (25th July, 1867), the company was authorised to make certain alterations in the mode of constructing the line, to acquire additional land, and the spare capital reduced from 705,000*l.* to 655,000*l.* In abeyance.

For intelligence respecting arbitration case with the Brighton before the Duke of Richmond, see ADDENDA.

No. of Directors—7; quorum, 3. *Qualification*, 1,000*l.*

DIRECTORS:

Chairman—LEO SCHUSTER, Esq., Roehampton, S.W.

James Scott, Esq., Lincoln's Inn Fields, W.C.
Colonel W. B. Barttelot, M.P., Helier's, Petworth, Sussex, and 10, St. James's Place, S W.
W. Coningham, Esq., Brighton.

P. Northall Laurie, Esq., Park Crescent, Regent's Park, N.W.
John Nix, Esq., The Hall, Worth, Sussex.
James Whishaw, Esq., York Terrace, Regent's Park, N.W.

Auditor, Mr. Burnett.

386.—SUTHERLAND.

Incorporated by 28 and 29 Vic., cap. 169 (29th June, 1865), to construct a line from Bonar Bridge, on the Highland, to Brora, in the county of Sutherland. Length, 32¼ miles. Capital, 180,000*l.* in shares, and 60,000*l.* on loan. Arrangements with Highland, which subscribes 15,000*l.*

By 29 and 30 Vic., cap. 181 (16th July, 1866), the diversion in one part of the line was authorised, and another relinquished. New capital, 30,000*l.* in shares, and 10,000*l.* on loan. Opened from Bonar Bridge to Golspie (26½ miles) on 13th April, 1868.

REVENUE.—The traffic to 31st August, averaged 99*l.* per mile, and from the 31st August 152*l.* per mile.

The working charges paid to the Highland, under the agreement, amount to 64 per cent. of the receipts.

CAPITAL.—The sum of 150,491*l.* has been received to 31st August, and 160,191*l.* expended. The revenue account to the same date showed a balance against the company of 557*l.* The balance sheet exhibited the subjoined particulars:—

Debtor.		*Creditor.*	
Debenture interest due to date ...	£806	Balance on capital account	£9,699
Amount due Caledonian Bank ...	9,697	„ revenue account	557
Income tax	43	„ due by Highland Co. ...	270
		Cash on hand	20
	£10,547		£10,547

No. of Directors—5; quorum, 2. *Qualification*, 500*l.*

DIRECTORS:

Chairman—His Grace the DUKE OF SUTHERLAND, Dunrobin Castle, Golspie, and Stafford House, St. James's, S.W.

Deputy-Chairman—ALEXANDER MATHESON, Esq., M.P., of Ardross, and 38, South Street, W.

George Loch, Esq., M.P., Uppat, Golspie, and 12, Albemarle Street, W.	The Right Hon. The Earl of Caithness, Barrogill Castle, Wick, and 17, Hill Street, Berkeley Square, W.
The Hon. Thomas C. Bruce, 13, Hertford Street, Mayfair, W.	

OFFICERS.—Sec., Andrew Dougall; Accountant, Wm. Gowenlock; Eng., Wm. Baxter; Solicitors, Stewart and Rule, Inverness, and Loch and Maclaurin, London; Auditors, A. Penrose Hay, Inverness, and G. Peacock, Golspie.

Head Offices—Inverness.

387.—SWANSEA AND ABERYSTWYTH JUNCTION.

Incorporated by 27 and 28 Vic., cap. 175 (14th July, 1864), for making a railway from the Llanelly, at Llandilo, to the Manchester and Milford, near Tregaron, with branch to Lampeter. Capital, 375,000l. in 10l. shares; loans, 125,000l.; calls, 2l. per share. Length: Main line, 25½ miles; branch, 4¼; total, 29⅜ miles. Facilities over Vale of Towy, and traffic arrangements with Llanelly.

By 28 and 29 Vic., cap. 211 (5th July, 1865), the company obtained power to construct three short branches, to divide the capital into half shares, and to raise new capital to the extent of 9,000l. in shares, and 3,000l. on loan.

388.—SWANSEA VALE.

Incorporated by 18 Vic., cap. 60 (June 15th, 1855), to convert the company from a registered undertaking into one acting under authority of parliament; to maintain and extend the line, and render it fit for passenger traffic and other purposes. The original line extends from the port of Swansea to the parish of Cadoxton-juxta-Neath.

Length of extension to Fabin's Bay, 6 chains, and of branch to Swansea Harbour Float, 13¾ chains; with provisions for laying down additional rails so as to adapt to broad gauge, between Swansea and the point where South Wales crosses the line. Capital, 147,000l. in 25l. shares, and 49,000l. by loan.

By 19 and 20 Vic., cap. 95 (14th July, 1856), the company was authorised to make an extension and branches. Length, 6 miles; of Ystalyfera branch, 8 chains; of Twrch branch, 1 furlong 7 chains; and of Yniscedwyn branch, 2 furlongs 3 chains, narrow gauge.

By 22 Vic., cap. 2 (8th April, 1859), the company was authorised to raise additional capital, 33,000l. on shares at 6 per cent., and 11,000l. on mortgage. At a meeting on 2nd May, 1859, these shares were issued at 15l. each, with a preference interest of 6 per cent.

By 24 and 25 Vic., cap. 162 (22nd July, 1861), the company was authorised to construct some new works, and an extension and branch, forming a junction with the Llanelly. Length, 6 miles. New capital, 33,000l. in shares, and 11,000l. on loan. Opened 1st January, 1864. Productive, 20 miles.

By 27 Vic., cap. 18 (28th April, 1864), the company was authorised to raise new capital to the extent of 36,000l. in shares, and 12,000l. on loan.

By 29 and 30 Vic., cap. 274 (23rd July, 1866), the Swansea Vale obtained facilities over part of the South Wales to Swansea, and to lay down the narrow gauge to effect that purpose. Also to raise new capital to the extent of 21,000l. in shares, and 7,000l. on loan. Arrangements with Great Western, Vale of Neath, and Llanelly.

By 30 Vic., cap. 98 (17th June, 1867), the company was authorised to construct two branches. Length, 5 miles. New capital, 65,000l. in shares, and 21,600l. on loan.

REVENUE.—The receipts for the half-year ending 31st December amounted to 12,795l., being an increase over the corresponding half-year of 1,166l. The working expenses were 5,868l., against 4,774l., showing an increase of 1,094l. The available balance after payment of interest on mortgages was 3,675l., out of which the usual dividends were recommended on the preference shares, and a dividend of 1 per cent. per annum on the ordinary shares left a balance of 319l.

The report for the June half-year stated that the net profit, including balance from the previous half-year, amounted to 5,338*l*., from which 2,279*l*. had to be deducted for interest on debentures and loans, leaving a divisible balance of 3,059*l*., for payment of dividend on the preference shares, the balance to next account being 341*l*. The Brynaman section had been opened for passenger traffic, and a through communication had been established with the whole of the London and North Western system.

CAPITAL.—The receipts and payments on this account to 30th June, 1868, have been detailed as under :—

Received.		Expended.	
Original shares £130,212		Parliamentary and law expenses..	£16,285
6*l*. per cent. preference................	71,380	Engineering expenses	11,132
5*l*. per cent. preference...............	11,000	Debenture stamps, commission,	
4*l*. per cent. preference...............	17,800	&c...	1,111
		Works, stations, &c.	266,936
	£230,392	Rolling stock, tools, and machinery	28,270
Loans on debentures...................	313,392	Furniture and fittings	273
Other loans..............................	14,648		
Sundry accounts due by company	1,056		£324,010
Available balance	3,059	Sundry accounts due to company	8,145
	£332,156		£332,156

No. of Directors—6, may be increased to 8; quorum, 3.   *Qualification*, 1,000*l*.

DIRECTORS :

Chairman—S. BENSON, Esq., Fairy Hill, Swansea.

Pascoe St.Leger Grenfell, Esq., Maesteg House, Swansea.
C. H. Smith, Esq., Gwernllwynwith, Glamorganshire.
George Burden Strick, Esq., West Cross, Swansea.

A. M. S. Maskelyne, Esq., Basset Down House, Swindon, Wiltshire, and Senny, Breconshire.
Henry James Bath, Esq., Swansea and Altyferrin, Carmarthenshire.

OFFICERS.—Sec., J. E. Morrice; Man., F. W. Mortimer; Eng., D. H. Jones, C.E.; Auditors, William Harries Francis and George Young, Swansea; Solicitors, Coke and Jones, Neath ; Bankers, Glamorganshire Banking Company, Swansea.

Head Offices—Railway Terminus, New Cut, Swansea.

389.—SWANSEA VALE AND NEATH AND BRECON JUNCTION.

Incorporated by 27 and 28 Vic., cap. 293 (29th July, 1864), to construct a line from the Swansea to the Neath and Brecon. Length, 8 miles. Capital, 120,000*l*. in 10*l*. shares, and 40,000*l*. on loan.

By 28 and 29 Vic., cap. 239 (5th July, 1865), the company obtained power to construct a branch from Ystradgynlais to Alecrane. Length, 1½ mile. Capital, 15,000*l*. in shares, and 5,000*l*. on loan.

By 29 and 30 Vic., cap. 212 (16th July, 1866), this undertaking was vested in the Neath and Brecon for 999 years, from 1st January, 1867, at 5 per cent.

DIRECTORS:

3 Chairman—THOMAS CAVE, Esq., M.P., 66, Lancaster Gate, Hyde Park, W.

2 Vice-Chairman—J. W. WILLIAMSON, Esq., 4, Stone Buildings, Lincoln's Inn, W.C.

1 W. Laurence Banks, Esq., F.S.A., Pont-y-wal Hall, Bronllys, Hereford.
1 Capt. C. Miller Layton, 57A, Wimpole Street, Cavendish Square, W.

2 W. M'Andrew, Esq., 57, King William Street, City, E.C.

1, Retire in 1869; 2, in 1870; 3, in 1871.

OFFICERS.—Sec., D. Howell Morgan, Westminster Chambers, Victoria Street, Westminster, S.W., and Neath ; Consulting Eng., John Gordon M'Kenzie, C.E.; Res. Eng., Hans St. George Caulfeild, B.A.,C E.; Auditors, W. Whittington, Neath; Solicitors, Dean and Taylor, and James Kempthorne, Neath ; Bankers, The Union Bank of London, Temple Bar Branch, E.C., The Glamorganshire Banking Company, Neath, and the National Provincial Bank of England, Brecon.

Offices—1, Westminster Chambers, Victoria Street, S.W.

390.—TAFF VALE.

Incorporated by 6 and 7 William IV., cap. 82 (21st June, 1836), for a line commencing at Merthyr Tydfil, in Glamorganshire, to the docks at Cardiff, with two short branches. Length, 54 miles. Includes Aberdare, leased in perpetuity at 10 per cent. In operation, 63 miles.

By an Act obtained in 1852 this company was empowered to make agreements with South Wales for junction of lines at Cardiff, ¼ mile.

By 20 and 21 Vic., cap. 152 (17th August, 1857), the company obtained power to raise 550,000*l.*, of which the sum of 350,000*l.* was for new works, and 200,000*l.* for rolling stock, and for alterations in the existing line, to accommodate the traffic. Borrowed capital to the extent of 267,000*l.* was also converted into debenture stock.

ABERDARE.—Incorporated by Acts 8 and 9 Vic., cap. 159 (31st July, 1845), for construction of a line at Aberdare, and terminating by a junction with Taff Vale, near Ynis Meyric, with branch to Cwmbach Colliery. Length, 8¾ miles. Leased by Taff Vale.

LLANTRISSANT AND TAFF VALE.—The Taff Vale subscribes 13,000*l.* to this undertaking, with the privilege of working the line. It was reported in February that the directors had arranged with the Llantrissant and Taff Vale Junction to extend the working agreement existing between the two companies from 10 years to 35 years from the 29th September, 1863, and this arrangement had since received the approval of the Board of Trade.

COWBRIDGE.—The directors have consented to work this line at cost price for 12 months, in connection with the Llantrissant and Taff Vale Junction, as a guide to more permanent arrangements, should such be considered desirable.

PENARTH.—The Taff Vale directors have been authorised to lease this undertaking at 4½ per cent. and half surplus profits. It was reported in August that the disputes hitherto existing between the Penarth and Taff Vale had been amicably adjusted. The leases would be forthwith completed in accordance with the terms now arranged.

The Taff Vale is also in possession of permissive powers to subscribe 60,000*l.* to the Brecon and Merthyr Tydfil Junction, and 3,000*l.* to the Cowbridge.

REVENUE.—The directors reported in February that the pressure on revenue by the working charges and rent of the Penarth harbour, dock, and railway, had been relieved by an increased revenue. The revenue account for the half-year ending 31st December stated that 171,020*l.* had been received and 86,522*l.* or 50·59 per cent. expended, leaving a balance of 84,498*l.* After placing 750*l.* to the credit of depreciation fund, the directors were enabled to recommend a dividend at the rate of 9 per cent. per annum upon the ordinary stock and C shares, leaving a balance of 2,331*l.* The revenue for the June half-year showed that 157,072*l.* was received and 77,071*l.* expended, leaving a balance of 80,001*l.* against 78,198*l.* in the same period of 1867. The directors recommended that a dividend at the rate of 8½ per cent. be declared upon the ordinary stock and C shares, and on the preference stock No. 1 ; also, that the usual sum of 750*l.* be placed at credit of the depreciation fund, leaving a balance of 850*l.*

CAPITAL.—This account to the 30th of June showed that 1,781,762*l.* had been expended, leaving a balance of 8,646*l.* The receipts were detailed as follow :—

Capital stock	£877,300	
23,270 " C " 10*l.* shares, Act, 1857	139,620	
Preference stock, No. 1	165,000	
4½ per cent. perpetual preference stock	53,225	
5 per cent. perpetual preference stock	66,775	
Mortgage debentures	398,183	
Irredeemable stock	38,817	
Premiums received on shares, &c., sold	34,196=	£1,773,116
Balance		8,646
		£1,781,762

The accounts are made up to 30th June and 31st December, and the statutory meetings are held in February and August in every year.

Scale of Voting—20 votes for first 20 shares, and then one vote for every five shares. Certificates are required to accompany transfer deeds; transfer fee, 2*s.* 6*d.* each deed.

No. of Directors—11. *Qualification*, 10 original shares, or their equivalent.

DIRECTORS:

Chairman—4 JAMES POOLE, Esq., Wick House, Durdham Down, Bristol.

Deputy-Chairman—4 WILLIAM DONE BUSHELL, Esq., Cardiff.

1 John Whitlock Nicholl Carne, Esq., D.C.L., Dimland Castle, Glamorganshire.
4 Hubert Churchill Gould, Esq., Thornford, Sherborne.
2 John Perry, Esq., Claremont Place, Clifton.
1 Robert Henry Webb, Esq., Kingsdown, Bristol.

3 Henry Jones Evans, Esq., Cardiff.
3 Thomas William Hill, Esq., Stoneleigh House, Clifton Park, Clifton.
1 John Jenner Mogg, Esq., West Park, Bristol.
2 John Richards Homfray, Pwll-y-wrach, Glamorganshire.
2 James Ford, Esq., Clifton Park, Clifton.

The rotation is indicated by the figures 1, 2, 3, 4; all eligible for re-election. Nos. 4 re-elected 25th August last.

OFFICERS.—Sec., Frederick Marwood; Eng., George Fisher, C. E.; Traffic-Manager, Edwin E. Page; Supt. of Loco. Dept., J. Tomlinson, Junr.; Accountant, George Robertson; Solicitor, Benjamin Matthews; Auditors, George Thomas and Wilberforce Tribe, Accountants, Bristol; Bankers, National Provincial Bank of England.

Head Offices—Crockherbtown, Cardiff.

391.—TALACRE.

Incorporated by 29 Vic., cap. 35 (18th May, 1866), to construct a pier, harbour, and railway in the parish of Llanasa, county of Flint. Length, quarter of a mile. Capital, 150,000l. in 10l. shares, and 50,000l. on loan.

No. of Directors—5; minimum, 3; quorum, 2. *Qualification*, 1,000l.

DIRECTORS:

George Elliot, Esq., M.P.
Ralph Elliot, Esq.
William Hunter, Esq.

Moses John Jonasshon, Esq.
William Henry Ashwin, Esq.
Adam Eyton, Esq.

392.—TALYLLYN.

Incorporated by 28 and 29 Vic., cap. 315 (5th July, 1865), to construct a line from the Aberystwyth and Welsh Coast, at Towyn, towards Talyllyn. Length, 6¾ miles. Capital, 15,000l. in shares, and 5,000l. on loan. Arrangements with Cambrian.

No. of Directors—6; minimum, 3; quorum, 3 and 2. *Qualification*, 300l.

DIRECTORS:

Thomas Houldsworth McConnell, Esq., 30, Pall Mall, Manchester.
James Murray, Esq., Ancoats Hall, Manchester, and Bryanston Square, W.
James McConnell, Esq., Manchester

Thomas Swannick, Esq., 56, Fountain Street, Manchester.
Murray Gladstone, Esq., 24 Cross Street, Manchester.
Samuel Holker Norris, Esq., Altrincham.

OFFICERS.—Sec. and Manager, J. P. Williams; Solicitors, Howell and Morgan, Machynlleth.

Office—Towyn, Machynlleth.

393.—TAMAR, KIT HILL, AND CALLINGTON.

Incorporated by 27 and 28 Vic., cap. 297 (29th July, 1864), to construct a line from the river Tamar, at Calstock, to Callington. Length, 7¼ miles. Capital, 70,000l. in 10l. shares, and 23,000l. on loan.

By 29 and 30 Vic., cap. 312 (30th July, 1866), the company was authorised to lay down the mixed gauge or the broad gauge only, and also to enter into arrangements with the Saltash and Callington, the Cornwall, the South Devon, the Bristol and Exeter, and the Great Western.

Meetings in March or September.

No. of Directors—6; minimum 3; quorum, 3 and 2. *Qualification*, 250l.

394.—TEES VALLEY.

Incorporated by 28 Vic., cap. 91 (19th June, 1865), to construct a line from the South Durham, at Lartington, to Middleton-in-Teesdale. Length, 7 miles. Capital, 50,000l. in 25l. shares, and 16,000l. on loan. Working arrangements with North Eastern, which subscribes 25,000l. Opened.

No. of Directors—9; quorum, 3. *Qualification*, 500l.

DIRECTORS:

Chairman—The Rev. THOMAS WITHAM, Lartington Hall.

Henry Pease, Esq., Pierremont, Darlington.
W. T. Scarth, Esq., Keverston Hall.
Thomas MacNay, Esq., Darlington.
Thompson Richardson, Esq., Barnard Castle.

Robert Thompson, Esq., Darlington.
Henry Fell Pease, Esq., Brinkburn, Darlington.

OFFICERS.—Sec., Lancelot Railton, Barnard Castle; Treasurers, J. and J. W. Pease, Darlington; Engs.. Nimmo and MacNay, C.E., 21, Abingdon Street, Westminster, S.W.; Solicitor, R. T. Richardson, Barnard Castle; London Bankers, Dimsdale, Fowler, and Barnard, 50, Cornhill, E,C.
Offices—Witham Testimonial Buildings, Barnard Castle.

395.—TEIGN VALLEY.

Incorporated by 26 and 27 Vic., cap. 159 (13th July, 1863), to construct a line from the Moretonhampstead and South Devon, at Bovey Tracey, to Chudleigh and Doddiscombsleigh. Length, 7¾ miles. Capital, 45,000l. in 20l. shares, and 15,000l. on loan. Broad gauge.

By 28 and 29 Vic., cap. 154 (29th June, 1865), the company was authorised to divide the shares and to raise new capital to the extent of 30,000l. in shares, and 10,000l. on loan. Also to create debenture stock. Working arrangements with South Devon.

By 31 and 32 Vic., cap. 99 (13th July, 1868), the company were authorised to make a deviation in the line, and to postpone completion of the works till 13th July, 1870.

At a meeting of the Company, it was resolved to authorise the directors to raise by the creation and issue of debenture stock, any sum or sums of money not exceeding in the whole, 79,000l., in accordance with the scheme of arrangement between the company and their creditors, confirmed by and enrolled in the Court of Chancery, in pursuance of the Companies' Act, 1867; and also to exercise the powers of borrowing and other powers conferred on the company by the said scheme as they might deem expedient.

No. of Directors—6; maximum, 7; quorum, 3. *Qualification,* 500l.

DIRECTORS:

Chairman—Sir LAWRENCE PALK, Bart., M.P.. Haldon House, Exeter,
and Grosvenor Gardens, S.W.

Edward Gulson, Esq , Teignmouth.
William Kitson, Esq., Torquay.
John Fleming, Esq., Bigadon, Devon.

Thomas Eales Rogers, 'Esq., Waye, Ashburton.
Charles Langley, Esq., Chudleigh.

OFFICERS.—Eng., J. F. Tone, Newcastle-upon-Tyne; Solicitor, W. Toogood, 16, Parliament Street, Westminster, S.W.; Auditors, C. Wescomb, Exeter, and J. Rendall, Coffinswell, Devon.

396.—TEME VALLEY.

Incorporated by 29 and 30 Vic., cap. 345 (6th August, 1866), to construct a railway from Worcester to Tenbury. Length, 21¼ miles. Capital, 350,000l. in 10l. shares, and 116,000l. on loan. Arrangements with London Worcester and South Wales.
No. of Directors—6; minimum, 3, quorum, 3 and 2. *Qualification,* 500l.

DIRECTORS:

Chairman—SEPTIMUS HOLMES GODSON, Esq., of Tenbury, and 14, Rutland Gate,
Hyde Park, W.

Sir Thomas Edward Winnington, Bart., Stanford Court, near Worcester.
The Hon. Richard Howe Browne, Brighton.
Sir Charles Rouse-Boughton, Bart., Downton Hall, Salop.

William Hyde Cooke, Esq., The Green, Stanford, near Worcester.
Thomas Henry Davis, Esq., Orleton, near Worcester.

OFFICERS.—Sec., C. Banks; Eng., S. G. Purchas, Worcester; Solicitor, Henry Moore, Leominster; Surveyor, Henry Webb, Worcester; Bankers, The Worcester City and County Banking Company (Limited), Worcester and Tenbury, and the London Joint Stock Bank, Princes Street, London.
Offices— 3, Westminster Chambers, Victoria Street, S.W.

397.—TENBURY.

Incorporated by 22 and 23 Vic., cap. 16 (21st July, 1859), to construct a railway from the Wooferton station of the Shrewsbury and Hereford to Tenbury.　Length, 5¼ miles. Capital, 30,000l. in 10l. shares; loans, 10,000l.　Opened 1st August, 1861.

The Shrewsbury and Hereford disposed of part of the Leominster canal to the company, and agreed to work the Tenbury for seven years, paying out of the first receipts 500l. per annum, and 40l. per cent. of the balance of such receipts, retaining the residue to cover working expenses and maintenance.　The Shrewsbury and Hereford having passed into the hands of the London and North Western and the Great Western, the lease of this line has become vested in those companies.

The dividends for the year ending 30th June have been at the rate of 3 per cent.

CAPITAL.—The expenditure on this account, to 30th June, amounted to 40,112l.

The receipts having been from calls £24,608
Loans on debenture 10,000
Loans 5,008
Cash, Great Western and London and North Western .... 500 = £40,110

Meetings in February or March, and August or September.

No. of Directors—7; minimum, 5; quorum, 3.　*Qualification*, 200l.

DIRECTORS:

1 Chairman—The Right Hon. LORD NORTHWICK, Burford House, Tenbury,
　　　　and 22, Park Street, Grosvenor Square, W.
2 Deputy-Chairman—EDWARD VINCENT WHEELER, Esq., Kyrewood House,
　　　　Tenbury.

2 George Pardoe, Esq., Nash Court, near Tenbury.
3 Thomas Bangham, Esq., Tenbury.
The figures show the order of retirement.

5 William Davis, Esq., Dean Park, near Tenbury,
6 Ambrose Grounds, Esq., Ludford Villa, Ludlow.

OFFICERS.—Sec., William Norris; Auditors, John Cranstoun and Benjamin Home.

Offices—Tenbury.

398.—TENBURY AND BEWDLEY.

Incorporated by 23 and 24 Vic., cap. 128 (3rd July, 1860), to construct a line from the Severn Valley, near Bewdley, to the town of Tenbury. Length, 14 miles. Capital, 120,000l. in 10l. shares; loans, 40,000l.　Opened 13th August, 1864.　Worked by Great Western, the dividend for the half-year ending 30th June having been at the rate of 2¾ per cent. per annum.

CAPITAL.—The expenditure on this account to 30th June amounted to 165,185l., which left a balance due to bankers of 336l.

Meetings in February or March, and August or September, in Tenbury.

No. of Directors—6; quorum, 3.　*Qualification*, 200l.

DIRECTORS:

6 Chairman—The Right Hon. LORD NORTHWICK, Burford House, Tenbury,
　　　　and 22, Park Street, Grosvenor Square, W.
1 Deputy-Chairman—Sir E. BLOUNT, Bart., Mawley Hall, near Cleobury.

2 Edward Vincent Wheeler, Esq., Kyrewood House, Tenbury.
4 William Davis, Esq., Dean Park, near Tenbury.

3 Samuel Clarke Good, Esq., Aston Court, near Tenbury.
5 Thomas Bangham, Esq., Tenbury.
The figures show the order of retirement.

OFFICERS.—Sec., William Norris; Auditors, John Cranstoun and Benjamin Home.

Offices—Tenbury.

399.—TENDRING HUNDRED.

Incorporated by 22 and 23 Vic., cap. 119 (13th August, 1860), to construct a new line from Hythe, on the Colchester and Stour Valley, to Wivenhoe.　Length, 2½ miles. Capital, 15,000l. in 10l. shares; loans, 5,000l.　Opened 8th May, 1863.

By 25 Vic., cap. 34 (3rd June, 1862), the company was authorised to extend the line into Colchester.　Length, 1 mile.　New capital, 25,000l. in shares, and 8,300l. on loan. Opened 1866.

By 26 and 27 Vic., cap. 143 (13th July, 1863), the company was authorised to construct extensions to Weeley and Walton. Length, 14 miles. New capital, 85,000*l.* in 10*l.* shares, and 28,000*l.* by loan. Arrangements with Great Eastern, which subscribes 28,000*l.*, and appoints two directors. Opened 11½ miles in February, 1866. The remainder was opened to the terminus at Walton, in May, 1867. This line and its capital is to be kept separate.

By 27 and 28 Vic., cap. 79 (23rd June, 1864), the company was authorised to make an alteration in the line to Walton.

By 30 Vic., cap. 43 (31st May, 1867), the company obtained power to raise new capital to the extent of 30,000*l.* in shares, at a preference not exceeding 7 per cent., and also 10,000*l.* by borrowing.

Meetings in February or March, and August or September.

No. of Directors—7; quorum, 3.

DIRECTORS:

Chairman—JOHN CHEVALLIER COBBOLD, Esq., Holywells, Ipswich.

The Right Hon. William Beresford, The Palace, Hampton Court.	John Stuck Barnes, Esq., Colchester.

Elected by the shareholders of the Extension Lines of 1863.

Col. Septimus M. Hawkins, Alresford, Colchester.	James Shum, Esq., Kirby, Essex.

Nominated by the Great Eastern Company.

The Marquis of Salisbury.	C. H. Turner, Esq., Litchurch, Derby.

OFFICERS.—Sec., Arthur L. Laing, Colchester; Eng., Peter Bruff, Handford Lodge, Ipswich; Auditors, The Rev. William Yorick Smythies, Hill Side, Weeley, Essex, and ; Solicitors, Messrs. Philbrick and Son, Colchester. Offices—Trinity Street, Colchester.

400.—TEWKESBURY AND MALVERN.

Incorporated by 23 Vic., cap. 72 (25th May, 1860), to construct a line from the Ashchurch branch of the Midland to Great Malvern. Length, 14¼ miles. Capital, 145,000*l.* in 10*l.* shares; loans, 48,000*l.* Agreements with Midland. Opened from the Malvern junction with the West Midland to Malvern Hill station on 1st July, 1862, and throughout on 1st May, 1864.

By 25 and 26 Vic., cap. 56 (30th June, 1862), the company was empowered to raise additional capital to the extent of 120,000*l.* in shares, and 40,000*l.* on loan.

This undertaking continues in abeyance, no arrangement having yet been effected with the Midland.

No. of Directors—8; quorum, 3. *Qualification*, 500*l.*

DIRECTORS:

Chairman—DAVID JOSEPH HENRY, Esq., 55, Kensington Garden Square, W.

Bassett Smith, Esq.	Robert F. Gordon, Esq., Belfast.
Alfred Beeston, Esq., 4, Regent's Park Terrace, N.W.	Timothy Kenrick, Esq., Edgbaston, Birmingham
Edward Harrison Barwell, Esq., Northampton.	William P. Price, Esq., M.P., Tibberton Court, Gloucester, and 105, Pall Mall, S.W.
John Edward Campbell Koch, Esq., 1, Threadneedle Street, E.C.	

OFFICERS.—Sec., Richard Stephens; Eng., George Willoughby Hemans, 1, Westminster Chambers, Victoria Street, S.W.; Auditor, E. Bellamy, 7, Victoria Chambers, Westminster, S.W.; Solicitors, S. F. Noyes, 1, Broad Sanctuary, Westminster, S.W., and Thomas Holland, Malvern. Offices—

401.—THETFORD AND WATTON.

Incorporated by 29 and 30 Vic., cap. 198 (16th July, 1866), from Thetford on the Great Eastern to Watton. Length, 9 miles. Capital, 45,000*l.* in 10*l.* shares; 15,000*l.* on loan. Arrangements with Great Eastern.

No. of Directors—5; minimum, 3; quorum, 3 and 2. *Qualification*, 200*l.*

DIRECTORS:

Wyrley Birch, Esq.	George Perkins, Esq.
Thomas Barton, Esq.	J. Cronshey, Esq., Thetford, Norfolk.

402.—THORPE AND CLACTON.

Incorporated by 29 and 30 Vic., cap. 194 (16th July, 1866), to construct a line from the Tendring Hundred, at Thorpe, to Clacton. Length, 4¾ miles. Capital, 40,000l. in 10l. shares, and 13,300l. on loan. Arrangements with Tendring Hundred.

No. of Directors—5; minimum, 4; quorum, 3. *Qualification*, 200l.

DIRECTORS:

William Martin Hazard, Esq.
William F. G. Bruff, Esq.

Charles Lemprière, Esq.

403.—TORBAY AND BRIXHAM.

Incorporated by Act 27 and 28 Vic., cap. 247 (26th July, 1864), for making a railway from the Dartmouth and Torbay, at Brixham Road station, to Brixham, in the county of Devon, and a tramway in connection therewith, and for other purposes.

Capital, 18,000l. in shares of 10l. each; and 6,000l. on loan. Length of the railway, 2 miles. The gradients and curves are generally favourable, the steepest gradient being 1 in 82½. Opened on the 28th of February, 1868, for passenger traffic, and on the 1st May following, for goods traffic, and worked under arrangement with the South Devon.

There are only four shareholders. Mr. R. W. Wolston, who constructed the line under a share contract (assigned to him by the first contractor, who failed to carry out his contract), is the holder of 1,770 shares, and may be considered to have a local interest in the line. The rest of the shares are held by the present directors.

The result of the working of the line to the present time (31st December, 1868) is highly satisfactory. The earnings for the last six months, having averaged over 100l. per month, fully justify the conviction that the expectations under which the construction of the line was undertaken will be fully realised.

The following were the grounds of such expectations:—The population of Brixham is between 7 and 8,000. It is one of the largest fisheries in England, and nearly 20,000 tons of shipping, owned by residents, hail from the port, trading to all parts. A considerable mineral traffic is opening up, or rather reviving, especially in the article of lime and building stone, Brixham, before railways were in vogue, being the chief locality whence Exeter and the large surrounding agricultural district drew its supplies of limestone.

It was the landing place of King William III., the spot being indicated by a neat obelisk, with a part of the stone on which he first set foot, inserted in front. This, and the bold scenery of Berry Head attract large numbers of visitors from Torquay and elsewhere.

The tramway has merged into the railway with the sanction of the Board of Trade.

No. of Directors—5; quorum, 3. *Qualification*, 10 shares.

DIRECTORS:

A. H. Wolston, Esq.
Mr. W. P. Spark.

W. T. P. Wolston, Esq., M.D.

General Man., Sec., and Registered Officer, R. W. Wolston, Esq.
Offices—New Road, Brixham.

404.—TOTTENHAM AND HAMPSTEAD JUNCTION.

Incorporated by 25 and 26 Vic., cap. 200 (29th July, 1862), to construct a railway from the main line of the Hampstead Junction to Tottenham, thence to the Northern and Eastern; and a line from the Hampstead Junction to the Great Northern at Hornsey. Length, 5¾ miles. Capital, 160,000l. in 10l. shares, and 53,300l. on loan. Opened between Highgate Road and Fenchurch Street on 1st July, 1868. Worked by Great Eastern at cost price until such time as the junction with the Midland at Kentish Town can be carried out.

By 26 and 27 Vic., cap. 205 (28th July, 1863), the company was authorised to construct a short extension. Length, ¾ mile. New capital, 50,000l. in shares, at 5 per cent. preference, and 16,600l. on loan. Arrangements with Great Eastern, which subscribes 50,000l., and appoints two directors.

By 27 and 28 Vic., cap. 221 (25th July, 1864), the company was authorised to construct a line in the parish of Islington to join the Midland Extension into London. Length, 1½ mile. Capital, 100,000l., in shares, and 333,000l. on loan. Arrangements with Midland and Great Eastern, which may each subscribe one-third of the new capital.

By 28 and 29 Vic., cap. 178 (29th June, 1865), the company was authorised to make a number of deviations, as well as to enter into enlarged arrangements with the Great Eastern and Midland, which may each subscribe one-third of the capital.

By 29 and 30 Vic., cap. 175 (16th July, 1866), the company was authorised to raise new capital to the extent of 100,000*l.* in shares (deferred and preferred), and 33,333*l.* on loan. The Midland and the Great Eastern were also authorised to subscribe any sum not exceeding 33,333*l.* each. These companies were likewise authorised to accept a transfer of the Tottenham and Hampstead on terms to be ageeed upon.

By 31 and 32 Vic., cap. 101 (13th July, 1868), the company was authorised to raise further capital to the extent of 100,000*l.* in perpetual 6 per cent. shares, and 33,333*l.* on loan. Also, to attach a preference of 6 per cent. to the unissued ordinary capital.

It was reported in September that the "traffic was very inconsiderable, and there was little hope of any substantial increase of it so long as the line was disconnected with that of the Midland. The difficulties arising out of land purchases and other liabilities were still pressing heavily on the company, so that it was difficult to see how it could be retrieved from the unfortunate pecuniary position in which it was placed, without the assistance and co-operation of all the parties interested in it, whether as creditors, debenture holders, or shareholders."

CAPITAL.—The expenditure on this account to 30th June amounted to 472,130*l.* The receipts were as follow:—

Share capital under Act of 1862	£160,000
Share capital under Act of 1863 and 1864	113,170=£273,170
Debentures	53,300
Transfer fees	51
Sale of surplus property	1,453
Rents	158
Interest on Great Eastern stock	1,832
Balance to general account	142,163=£472,130

No. of Directors—9; minimum, 5; quorum, 5. *Qualification*, 500*l.*

DIRECTORS:

Chairman—Captain Sir FREDERICK ARROW, Pilgrim's Hall, Brentwood.

James Joseph Allport, Esq., Littleover, Derby.
Francis Carbutt, Esq., Leeds.
Samuel Swarbrick, Esq., Oaklands, Upper Clapton, N.
Lightly Simpson, Esq., 50, Gower Street, Bedford Square, W.C.

*Wm. Philip Price, Esq., M.P., Tibberton Court, Gloucester, and 105, Pall Mall, S.W.
†Charles Henry Turner, Esq., Litchurch, Derby.

* Director of the Midland.　† Director of the Great Eastern.

OFFICERS —Sec., George William Horn; Engs., Mc.Clean and Stileman, 23, Great George Street, Westminster, S.W.; Solicitors, G. B. Townsend, 3, Prince's Street, Westminster, S.W., and Henry Toogood, 16, Parliament Street, Westminster, S.W.

Offices—2, Westminster Chambers, Victoria Street, S.W.

405.—TRENT, ANCHOLME, AND GRIMSBY.

Incorporated by 24 and 25 Vic., cap. 156 (22nd July, 1861), to construct a line from Keadby, on the river Trent, to the Barnetby Station of the Manchester Sheffield and Lincolnshire. Length, 16 miles. Capital, 120,000*l.* in 10*l.* shares; loans, 40,000*l.* Opened, 11th October, 1866.

By 25 and 26 Vic., cap. 129 (7th July, 1862), the South Yorkshire and the Manchester and Sheffield are authorised to contribute towards, as well as to acquire, the Trent Ancholme and Grimsby. Each company may subscribe 40,000*l.*, appoint directors, and vote at general meetings. It is also provided by clause 6, that the proprietors in the Trent Ancholme and Grimsby may sell or transfer their undertaking to the two companies, or either of them.

By 27 and 28 Vic., cap. 65 (23rd June, 1864), the company was authorised to raise new capital to the extent of 60,000*l.* in shares, and 20,000*l.* by borrowing.

REVENUE.—This account for the half year ending 31st December, 1867, showed a balance after the payment of working expenses, interest of mortgages, and interest on advances made by the South Yorkshire and Sheffield companies, of 299*l.* The revenue accounts for the June half year showed a balance of profit of 375*l.*, after paying the interest on mortgages, and all other interest on preference charges.

Meetings in February or March, and in August or September.

No. of Directors—6; minimum, 4; quorum, 3. *Qualification*, 500*l.*

DIRECTORS:

Chairman—† The Hon. WILLIAM GEORGE EDEN, Elmfield, near Doncaster.

Rowland Winn, Esq., M.P., Appleby Hall, Brigg.

George Dawes, Esq., Milton and Elsecar Ironworks, near Barnsley.

*William Fenton, Esq., Beaumonds, Rochdale.

*William Hutton, Esq., Gate Burton, near Gainsborough.

†George S. Lister, Esq., Hirst Priory, Bawtry.

* Sheffield representatives.   † South Yorkshire representatives.

OFFICERS.—Sec., Edward Ross; Eng., Charles Sacré; Solicitors, Baxter, Rose, and Co., 6, Victoria Street, Westminster, S.W.

Offices—London Road Station, Manchester.

406.—ULSTER.

Incorporated by 6 and 7 Wm. IV., cap. 33 (19th May, 1836), for a line from Belfast to Armagh (36 miles), partly opened August, 1839, and to Portadown in 1842. Powers for purchase of land under original Act having expired, an Act was obtained in 1845 to extend line to Armagh (11 miles) without additional capital, which was completed and opened 1st March, 1848.

By 18 Vic., cap. 53 (15th June, 1855), the company was authorised to construct an extension to Monaghan (16¾ miles), opened 25th May, 1858.

By 19 and 20 Vic., cap. 18 (15th June, 1856), the Ulster was empowered to subscribe 28,000l., as well as to work the Portadown and Dungannon.

By 22 and 23 Vic., cap. 41 (1st August, 1856), the company obtained power to extend the line from Monaghan to Clones, 12 miles. Capital, 225,000l. in ordinary shares, of which 40,000l. may be subscribed to Portadown Dungannon and Omagh. Loans, 50,000l. Opened 2nd March, 1863.

By 22 and 23 Vic., cap. 51 (1st August, 1859), the Ulster was authorised to subscribe 30,000l. to the joint undertaking of the Clones and Cavan Extension, the Dublin and Drogheda and Dublin and Belfast each subscribing 20,000l., and the Dundalk and Enniskillen the remainder. Opened April, 1862.

BANBRIDGE, LISBURN, AND BELFAST (15 miles).—The Ulster subscribed 25,000l. at the guaranteed rate of 4 per cent. interest, on an undertaking to lease the line for 21 years, which was carried out under the provisions of 25 and 26 Vic., cap. 108 (30th June, 1862). The lease is to be for 21 years, and may be renewed for another 10 years, for whatever rent or other consideration may be agreed upon between the parties.

BANBRIDGE EXTENSION.—At a meeting on 14th May, 1862, the Ulster resolved to subscribe 9,000l. to this undertaking, and to raise the money by issue of debenture stock, at 4 per cent.

PORTADOWN, DUNGANNON, AND OMAGH.—This line is worked by the Ulster (42 miles) under lease for 999 years, at the following rent, viz., 10,500l. per annum, until on the average of a period of years the receipts shall have been 23,000l. per annum. When the receipts shall reach 23,000l., and not exceed 25,000l. per annum, the Ulster shall pay to the Dungannon 10,500l. per annum, and one-half the surplus receipts beyond 23,000l. Between 25,000l. and 30,000l. per annum, the Ulster shall pay to the Dungannon company 47½ per cent. on the gross receipts. Beyond 30,000l. and not exceeding 35,000l. per annum, the Dungannon company to receive 50 per cent. of the gross receipts. The Ulster subscribed 10,000l. to the undertaking, 2,500l. being preference shares, and the remainder ordinary stock in the Dungannon.

MILEAGE.—The present productive mileage of the Ulster is 64¼ miles; of the Portadown Dungannon and Omagh, 41¼ miles; and of the Banbridge and Lisburn, 15 miles; making a total of 120 miles.

REVENUE.—The receipts for the half year ending 31st December, 1867, amounted to 80,105l., being an increase of 2,234l. over the income of the corresponding half year in 1866. The working expenses, after deduction of 2,740l. for working the Banbridge, were 35,968l., and the dividend equal to 4 per cent. per annum. The receipts for the six months ending 30th June amounted to 74,788l. in comparison with 76,615l., the working expenses, after deduction of 2,654l. for the Banbridge, were 34,014l., being

2,751*l*. less than for the corresponding period of 1867. After paying interest at the rate of 4½ per cent. on preference and ordinary stocks, 1,000*l*. were applied in liquidation of the renewal account, and 1,908*l*. carried forward.

NEWRY AND ARMAGH.—The differences with this company were reported upon in August as follows :—" Since the last meeting the Newry and Armagh applied to the Court of Queen's Bench for an injunction to compel this company to book through with, and afford other advantages to, the Newry and Armagh. The court ruled in favour of this company on the point of through booking, and left the other questions over to be hereafter dealt with. In the course of its judgment the court expressed an opinion that the terms of through booking which the Ulster had offered to the Newry and Armagh were fair and reasonable, and such as ought to have been accepted. An action, at suit of the same company, against this company, was tried at the recent assizes at Armagh. Damages, laid at the sum of 10,000*l*., were claimed for alleged neglect and want of impartiality in this company's performance of that company's business at Armagh station. The jury found a verdict in favour of the plaintiff for 3,300*l*. This subject engages the earnest attention of your directors."

BANBRIDGE, LISBURN, AND BELFAST.—This company having sought to give priority over this company's preference shares in that company to a sum of 15,000*l*., which had been advanced by certain directors of that company for completion of its undertaking, the directors, acting under the advice of eminent counsel, felt themselves constrained to oppose that proceeding, and accordingly applied to the Court of Chancery for an injunction to prevent it. The court, however, decided in favour of the Banbridge Lisburn and Belfast, thus making this company's investment rank after the 15,000*l*. referred to. The question of the payment to be made by the Banbridge to this company for station services at Lisburn, and dispensing with a station at Knockmore Junction, having been referred to arbitration, 250*l*. per annum has been awarded as the amount to be paid.

CAPITAL.—Of the 200,000*l*. of 4½ per cent. preference stock authorised by the Board of Trade certificate, 1865, there had been issued, up to 30th June, 1868, the sum of 107,770*l*. The expenditure on capital account to that date amounted to 1,450,418*l*. the receipts having been detailed as follow :—

	Authorised.	Unissued.	Raised.
Shares	£1,000,000	......	£1,000,000
Bonds	309,000	£5,090	303,910
4 per cent. debenture stock			
4½ per cent. preference stock	200,000	92,230	107,770
	£1,509,000	£97,320	£1,411,680
Balance			38,738
			£1,450,418

The accounts are made up to 30th June and 31st December, and the statutory meetings are held in Belfast in August and February.

Scale of Voting.—One vote for every five original shares, ten half-shares, or twenty quarter-shares.

Certificates are required to accompany transfer deed. Fee for registration, 2*s*. 6*d*.

No. of Directors—12. *Qualification*, twenty original shares, forty half-shares, or eighty quarter-shares.

DIRECTORS:

Chairman—WILLIAM COATES, Esq., Belfast.

Deputy-Chairman—JAMES GRAY, Esq., Belfast.

William Thompson, Esq., M.D., Lisburn.
Lieut.-Col. Mc.Clintock, Tynan.
Samuel Murland, Esq., Castlewellan.
Francis Watson, Esq., Lurgan.
George Pim, Esq., Dublin.

John W. Greer, Esq., Lurgan.
E. H. Thompson, Esq., Belfast.
C. A. W. Stewart, Esq., Carrickfergus.
Thomas Walkington, Esq., Ballinderry.
John Brady, Esq., Clones.

OFFICERS.—Sec., Foster Coates; Man., Thomas Shaw; Accountant, James Dawson; Treas., Bank of Ireland; Eng., Charles R. Atkinson, M.I.C.E.; Loco. Supt., John Eaton; Auditors, James G. Bell and John Raphael; Solicitors, Crawford and Lockhart.

Head Offices—Belfast.

407.—UXBRIDGE AND RICKMANSWORTH.

Incorporated by 24 and 25 Vic., cap. 73 (28th June, 1861), to construct a line from the Great Western, at Uxbridge, to join the Watford and Rickmansworth at the latter place, with a branch to Scot's Bridge Mills. Length, 8 miles 13 chains. Capital, 70,000l. in 10l. shares; loans, 23,000l. Arrangements with Great Western. Works in progress.

By 25 Vic., cap. 36 (3rd June, 1862), a deviation was authorised, but the whole works to be completed by 28th June, 1864.

By 26 and 27 Vic., cap. 173 (21st July, 1863), an extension of time for completion of works was conceded till 1st January, 1866.

By 29 and 30 Vic., cap. 141 (28th June, 1866), the company obtained an extension of time for completion of works till 28th June, 1868. Also to raise new capital to the extent of 43,000l. in shares, and 14,000l. on loan.

By 31 and 32 Vic., cap. 51 (25th June, 1868), the company obtained another extension of time, viz., till 1870, for completion of works.

The directors expressed a hope in August that they would be in a position to report that some active measures had been taken for the construction of the railway.

CAPITAL.—This account showed that in the four calls 17,810l. had been raised, which, with 23l. received for rents, made the total receipts 17,833l. The expenditure amounted to 17,208l., leaving a balance of 625l.

No. of Directors—7; minimum, 3; quorum, 3 and 2. *Qualification,* 300l.

DIRECTORS:

Chairman—Capt. the Hon. R. W. GROSVENOR, M.P., 48, Grosvenor Place, S.

Hon. Reginald Capel, Little Cashiobury, Watford.
Colonel William Elsey, West Lodge, Ealing, W.

Joseph Cary, Esq., 49, Pall Mall, S.W.
Capt. J. Bulkeley, Windsor.
D. Ogilvie, Esq., Sydenham, S.E.

OFFICERS.—Sec., Alexander Forbes; Eng., J. S. Peirce, 6, Victoria Street, Westminster, S.W.; Solicitors, Hargrove, Fowler, and Co., 3; Victoria Street, Westminster, S.W.

Offices—3, Victoria Street, S.W.

408.—VALE OF CRICKHOWELL.

Incorporated by 27 and 28 Vic., cap. 188 (14th July, 1864), to construct a line from the Merthyr Tredegar and Abergavenny, at Llanfoist, to Crickhowell Bridge. Length, 5¼ miles. Capital, 48,000l. in 10l. shares; and 11,000l. on loan. Arrangements with London and North Western and Great Western.

By 29 and 30 Vic., cap. 313 (30th July, 1866), the company was authorised to extend the line from Crickhowell to Brecon, so as to form a junction with the Neath and Brecon. Length, 14¾ miles. Capital, 186,000l. in shares, and 62,000l. on loan. Running powers over Brecon and Merthyr Tydfil, and arrangements with Neath and Brecon.

It was reported in February that the board had been unable to enter into a contract for construction of the line, the subscription list being too small. It had been arranged that deferred shares to the amount of 24,000l. should be issued for the preliminary expenses, the same not to receive any dividend until 4 per cent. was paid on the ordinary capital. The cost of constructing the line would depend materially on the landowners, who, if they accepted rent-charges, would greatly assist the company.

No. of Directors—6; minimum, 3; quorum, 3 and 2. *Qualification,* 300l.

DIRECTORS:

Chairman—THOMAS DAVIES, Esq., Neuadd, Crickhowell.

William Lewis, Esq., Crickhowell.
Henry Jeffreys, Esq., Crickhowell.
William Christopher, Jun., Esq., Crickhowell.

George Augustus Spreece Davies, Esq., Crickhowell.
John Jayne, Esq., Panty Bailey, Crickhowell.

OFFICERS.—Sec., E. J. C. Davies, Crickhowell; Eng., Isaac Davies, Brecon; Auditors, John Thomas Stephen and Thomas Price, Crickhowell; Solicitors, David Thomas, Brecon, and E. J. C. Davies, Crickhowell.

409.—VALE OF LLANGOLLEN.

Incorporated by 22 and 23 Vic., cap. 64 (1st August, 1859), to construct a line from Ruabon, on the Shrewsbury and Chester, to the town of Llangollen. Capital, 45,000*l.* in 10*l.* shares; loans, 15,000*l.* Length, 6 miles. Opened for minerals December 1st, 1861; for passengers, June 2nd, 1862.

By 26 Vic., cap. 20 (11th May, 1863), the company was authorised to raise new capital to the extent of 24,000*l.* at 5 per cent., and 8,000*l.* by loan. Also to agree with Llangollen and Corwen as to the joint station at Llangollen.

Traffic arrangements, under usual restrictions, with Great Western, by which that company work the line, and practically adopt it as part of their railway.

The directors reported in September that the gross receipts for the half-year ending 30th June exhibited an increase of upwards of 10 per cent. over those of the corresponding half-year of 1867, whereas the receipts in the corresponding periods of 1866 and 1867 were exactly the same.

The dividends on the ordinary stock were 2*s.* per 10*l.* share for December half-year, and 2*s.* 6*d.* for June.

CAPITAL.—This account to the 30th June, 1868, furnished the subjoined detail of income and expenditure:—

Received.		Expended.	
Ordinary 10*l.* shares	£44,619	Parliamentary and law	£4,411
Preference 10*l.* shares	24,000	Engineering	3,000
Mortgages	23,000	Land and compensation	25,526
		Works and permanent way	46,988
		Stations	8,510
		Electric telegraph	239
		General expenses	848
		Commission, interest, &c., prior to opening of the line	1,456
			£90,982
		Balance	637
	£91,619		£91,619

Meetings in February or March, and in August or September, at Llangollen.

No. of Directors—7; minimum, 5; quorum, 3. *Qualification, 500l.*

DIRECTORS:

Chairman—COLONEL TOTTENHAM, Plas Berwyn, Denbighshire.

William Henry Darby, Esq., Brymbo.	William Wagstaff, Esq., Rhug, Corwen.
J. R. O. Gore, Esq., M.P., The Mount, Oswestry, and 3A, King Street, St. James's, S.W.	J. Robertson, Esq., Llangollen. Three go out of office each year, eligible for re-election.

OFFICERS.—Sec., Charles Richards, Llangollen; Eng., Henry Robertson; Auditors, W. Patchett and George Haswell; Solicitors, Longueville, Williams, Jones, and Williams, Oswestry, and C. Richards, Llangollen.

410.—VALE OF TOWY.

Incorporated by 17 and 18 Vic., cap. 150 (July 10th, 1854), for a line from Llandovery, Carmarthen, to join the Llanelly at Llandilofaur. Length, 11¼ miles. Capital, 60,000*l.* in shares; loans, 18,000*l.* Mixed gauge, if company think fit, or if required by South Wales, in which case the latter bears portion of expense.

By 21 and 22 Vic., cap. 147 (2nd August, 1858), the line was leased for a term of ten years to the Llanelly.

By 23 and 24 Vic., cap. 161 (23rd July, 1860), the line was authorised to be leased to the Llanelly in perpetuity, but by Act of 1868, one moiety of the lease is transferred to the London and North Western. Dividends at the rate of 3¼ per cent. per annum.

CAPITAL.—The receipts have been 69,055*l.*, and the expenditure 68,884*l.*, leaving a balance in hand of 171*l.*

No of Directors—6; quorum, 3. *Qualification, 100l. shares.*

DIRECTORS:

Chairman—WM. FULLER MAITLAND, Esq., Stanstead Park, Bishop's Stortford.

Deputy-Chairman—W. D. H. CAMPBELL-DAVYS, Esq., Neuaddfawr, Carmarthenshire.

Richard Moon, Esq., Bevere, Worcester. | Thomas Brassey, Junr., Esq., M.P., 4, Great
Oscar Leslie Stephen, Esq., Bardon Hall, | George Street, Westminster, S.W.
Leicester. | J. P. Bickersteth, Esq., London.

All are eligible for re-election.

OFFICERS.—Sec., C. Bishop, Jun., Llandovery; Auditors, William Rees, Tonn, Llandovery, and David Jeremy, Bank, Llandovery; Solicitor, Charles Bishop, Llandovery.

Offices—Llandovery and Euston Square Station.

411.—VICTORIA STATION AND PIMLICO.

Incorporated by 21 and 22 Vic., cap. 118 (23rd July, 1858), to construct a general station, near Victoria Street, Pimlico, and a line to be connected with the West End and Crystal Palace at Battersea. Capital, 675,000l. in 10l. shares, and 225,000l. on loan. Including 450,000l. on the part of the Brighton. Length, 1¼ mile, including bridge over the Thames. Opened 2nd October, 1860.

By 22 and 23 Vic., cap. 112 (13th August, 1859), the company was empowered to raise additional capital to the extent of 75,000l. in 10l. shares, and 25,000l. on loan, the whole of which sums are to be devoted exclusively to the purposes of the undertaking. By the same Act authority is given to arrange with Great Western, so as to provide broad gauge rails to accommodate that company to or from the station.

By 24 and 25 Vic., cap. 81 (28th June, 1861), a lease was sanctioned to the Great Western and Chatham and Dover, for use of one-half of the station for 999 years, at an increasing rental in lieu of tolls; further powers were also conceded to the company in reference to division and apportionment of its capital; also to raise a portion thereof by preference at 5 per cent.

The dividends are now securely placed at 9 per cent. per annum.

CAPITAL.—The expenditure on this account extends to 481,426l., the receipts leaving a balance of 39,545l.

Ordinary stock	£225,000
4½ per cent. preference stock	130,000
4½ per cent. debenture stock	98,972
Loans on debentures—4¼ per cent. ... £14,550	
Do. —4½ per cent. ... 52,450=	67,000
	£520,972

Meetings in January and July, or such other months as the company may determine. *No. of Directors.*—Maximum, 7; minimum, 3. *Qualification*, 500l.

DIRECTORS:

Chairman—WILLIAM LEE, Esq., M.P., Holborough, Rochester, Kent, and 16, Upper Ground Street, Blackfriars, S.

Philip Patten Blyth, Esq., Wimpole Street, | Colonel C. Fladgate, 6, Queen Square,
Cavendish Square, W. | Westminster, S.W.
John Elger, Esq., 1, Lewes Crescent, | George Witt, Esq., 22, Princes Terrace,
Brighton. | Knightsbridge, S.W.

OFFICERS.—Sec., Edward Bellamy; Engs., John Fowler and William Wilson, Westminster, S.W.; Solicitors, Fladgate, Clark, and Finch, Craven Street, Strand, W.C.; Auditors, J. Ball and E. Brooks; Surveyors, Hunt and Stevenson, Parliament Street, S.W.

Offices—7, Westminster Chambers, Victoria Street, Westminster, S.W.

412.—WALLINGFORD AND WATLINGTON.

Incorporated by 27 and 28 Vic., cap. 266 (25th July, 1864), to construct a line from the Great Western, at Cholsey, to Wallingford and to Watlington. Length, 9 miles. Capital, 80,000l. in 10l. shares, and 26,000l. on loan. Narrow gauge. Opened to Wallingford 2nd July, 1866.

No. of Directors—4; minimum, 6; quorum, 3. *Qualification*, 300l.

DIRECTORS:

Chairman—GEORGE W. HASTINGS, Esq., Temple, E.C., and Barnards Green, Malvern.

William Hawes, Esq., London. | Andrew Edgar, Esq., Kensington, W.
James Childs, Esq., Roehampton, S.W. | Edward Poole, Esq., Southam, Warwickshire.

OFFICERS.—Sec., C. S. Collard; Eng., James B. Burke, 4, Queen Square, Westminster, S.W.; Solicitors, Wilson, Bristows, and Carpmael, 1, Copthall Buildings, E.C.; Bankers, London and Westminster Bank, St. James's Square, S.W.

Offices -4, Skinner's Place, Sise Lane, Bucklersbury, E.C.

413.—WANTAGE AND GREAT WESTERN.

Incorporated by 29 and 30 Vic., cap. 231 (16th July, 1866), to construct a line from the Great Western, at Wantage Road station, to Wantage. Length, 2½ miles. Capital, 25,000*l.* in 10*l.* shares, and 8,300*l.* on loan. Arrangements with Great Western.

No. of Directors – 5; minimum, 3; quorum, 3 and 2. *Qualification*, 50*l.*

DIRECTORS:

J. J. William Fredericks, Esq., Abermellté, Glyn Neath, Glamorganshire. | Edward Roberts, Esq., 25, Parliament Street, Westminster, S.W.
George Newington, Esq., Goudhurst, Staplehurst, Kent. | J. Roberts, Esq., Parliament Street, Westminster, S.W.
Owen Henry Strong, Esq., Iffley, near Oxford. |

OFFICERS.—Eng., James Wilkinson, Duke Street, Westminster, S.W.; Solicitors, Gregory, Champion, and Eady, 18, Park Street, Westminster, S.W.

Offices—18, Park Street, Westminster, S.W.

414.—WARRINGTON AND STOCKPORT.

Incorporated by Act 14 and 15 Vic., cap. 71 (3rd July, 1851), for a line commencing from the St. Helens, at Warrington, to the South Junction and Altrincham, at Timperley, with a branch to join the Birkenhead Lancashire and Cheshire Junction, at Lower Walton. Productive mileage, 11 miles.

By Act 17 Vic., cap. 122 (4th August, 1853), the company obtained a branch to Stockport, from canal at Altrincham, crossing the South Junction at Timperley, 7¾ miles. Further capital authorised, 110,000*l.* in shares, and 36,600*l.* on loan. This branch was not made.

By 21 and 22 Vic., cap. 150 (2nd August, 1858), the capital was further regulated.

By 22 and 23 Vic., cap. 2 (13th August, 1859), the line is leased to the London and North Western and St. Helens, for 999 years, from 1858 at a dividend on the capital of 4¼ per cent., with 100*l.* per annum to the directors for transacting routine business. By the same Act the London and North Western (with consent of St. Helens) may purchase Warrington and Stockport, the price to be 9*l.* 5s. of London and North Western stock for every 10*l.* of Warrington ordinary stock; preference shareholders guaranteed by London and North Western. This option has been exercised.

OFFICERS. — Goods Man., Thomas Kay, London Road Station, Manchester; Resident Engineer, Henry Woodhouse.

Offices—Arpley, Warrington, and London Road Station, Manchester.

415.—WATERFORD AND CENTRAL IRELAND.

Incorporated by Act 8 and 9 Vic., cap. 87 (21st July, 1845), for a line from Waterford to Kilkenny, with a branch to Kells (6 miles). In 1848 an Act was obtained authorising the creation of further capital to the extent of 120,000*l.*, should the railway commissioners require the company to alter the construction of the permanent way, and repealing that clause in the Act of incorporation which required the company to make and open the Kells branch within one year after the opening of the main line. In 1850 another Act was obtained, giving the company power to raise fresh capital for the completion of the line into Waterford. In operation, 31 miles.

By 14 and 15 Vic., cap. 110, the company obtained power to purchase the Waterford and Limerick, and by another Act (14 and 15 Vic., cap. 141), power to sell the junction to the Waterford and Limerick, and purchase bridge over the river Suir; it also further provides that a separate account be kept of cost of the line from junction between this railway and the Limerick into Waterford, and station there. The Limerick to pay rent equal to 5 per cent. on half of outlay for its use thereof. The Great Southern and Western also pay a rent of 1,025*l.* for use of junction and station at Kilkenny.

By 21 and 22 Vic., cap. 48 (28th June, 1858), the company was authorised to raise money by perpetual mortgage, or by conversion of such mortgage into stock, which privilege was exercised at a meeting on 19th July of that year.

By 29 and 30 Vic., cap. 257 (23rd July, 1866), the Waterford and Kilkenny, in conjunction with the Kilkenny Junction, was authorised to construct the "Central of Ireland," which see.

By 31 and 32 Vic., cap. 141 (13th July, 1868), the company obtained power to acquire additional lands for stations, &c., in the county of Waterford; also to borrow on mortgage 10,000*l.* for substituting stone or iron viaducts for those now made of wood; also to establish a sinking fund for redemption of mortgages. and to sell or mortgage the rent-charge of the company to the Great Southern and Western, and to change the name of the undertaking from the Waterford and Kilkenny to the "Waterford and Central Ireland."

REVENUE.—The receipts for the half-year ending 25th March were 12,164*l.*; the working expenses 5,783*l.*; and the balance of 6,381*l.* permitted a dividend at the rate of 2 per cent. per annum on the preference shares. The receipts for the six months ending 29th September were 13,180*l.*; the working expenses 6,173*l.*; the balance of 7,007*l.* authorising a dividend equal to 2 per cent. on the preference shares, with a surplus of 201*l.*

WATERFORD AND LIMERICK —The proceedings of this company towards the Waterford and Central were reported as follows in May:—"The illegal and forcible eviction of your traffic from the joint station at Waterford by the Waterford and Limerick, and which station cost this company over 40,000*l.* has been put an end to by the award of the arbitrator of the Board of Trade, and this company is now declared legally entitled to equal rights with said company to that station.

GREAT SOUTHERN AND WESTERN.—The differences existing with this company, with respect to the interchange of traffic at the Maryborough junction station, were settled and arranged on the 2nd of May, and measures adopted to give effect to such settlement. The board have no doubt that the facilities will develop and increase a traffic heretofore shut out from the system.

ROLLING STOCK.—In addition to the 7,610*l.* worth of rolling stock handed back by the Waterford and Limerick, on the termination of the line working, over 20,000*l.* worth of new stock has been purchased to work the two lines; and, as in order to secure the safe working of the railway, it is necessary to relay a portion of the line with new rails, to fish the rest, and to replace the timber viaducts with those of iron, the board promoted the bill, to provide funds to pay off these liabilities, and effect those renewals, so as not to interfere with the payment of the usual dividend on the preference stock, the amount of which must increase from the certain development of the traffic. It was further reported in November that the rolling stock had been well maintained; a portion of the old stock had been rebuilt, but that increased traffic would require more stock from time to time. The directors, however, were of opinion that in a year or two, when the permanent way, stations, and rolling stock expenses were settled, there would be a steady increase of dividend.

CAPITAL.—The receipts and expenses on this account to 29th September, 1868, were reported as follow:—

Received.		*Expended.*	
Original stock	£250,000	To March, 1868	£573,474
Preference stock	196,885	Works executed for Irish South	
Debenture stock	61,364	Eastern, now Great Southern	
Government mortgage loan	42,477	and Western	20,560
Government loan, 1866	12,776	Waterford and Limerick on account of rolling stock	
Debentures	29,898	count of rolling stock	1,118
Balance	2,301	New goods shed, carriage shop, iron store, and locomotive office at Waterford	608
	£595,702		£595,702

The accounts are made up to 25th March and 29th September in every year, and the statutory meetings held in London in May and November.

Scale of Voting.—One vote for every share up to 10; then one vote for every 5 up to 100; then one vote for every 10 shares beyond.

Certificates required to accompany transfer deed. Fee for registration, 2s. 6d. each seller.

No. of Directors.—Maximum, 12; minimum, 8. *Qualification*, 20 shares.

DIRECTORS:

Chairman—JAMES DELAHUNTY, Esq., M.P., Waterford.

Deputy-Chairman—EDMOND POWER, Esq., J.P., Eastlands, Tramore.

Michael Cahill, Esq., Ballyconra House, Co. Kilkenny.
John O'Brien, Esq., Waterford.
Walter Charles Venning, Esq., 9, Token-house Yard, E.C.

Edmond Smithwick, Esq., Kilkenny.
James M. Tidmarsh, Esq., Kilkenny.
Charles Whetham, Esq., 52, Gordon Square, W.C.

OFFICERS.—Sec., William Williams; Auditors, John Makesey, Waterford, and Charles H. Robinson, London; Solicitors, Radcliffe and Davies, 20, Craven Street, Strand, W.C., and Dobbyn and Tandy, Waterford; Bankers, The National Bank, Waterford, and 13, Old Broad Street, E.C.

Head Offices—Waterford Terminus.

416.—WATERFORD AND LIMERICK.

Incorporated by 8 and 9 Vic., cap. 131 (21st July, 1845), for a line from Waterford to Limerick. Length, 22 miles, double line, 55 single. Opened in 1854.

The company obtained power in 1850, with regard to the purchase of land, whereby immense cost and litigation are spared. Power was also obtained to re-issue the 4,725 shares forfeited and merged into the company, as well as any other shares to be forfeited, and to grant a preference dividend on such re issue, and in 1851, by Act 14 and 15 Vic., cap. 110, the hitherto dubious course of the line has been decided by the authority therein given to carry it from Fiddown to the North of the river Suir; and to form a junction with the Kilkenny, near Waterford. Either of these companies may sell or lease their undertakings to the other, with the consent of three-fifths of special meetings respectively, and may raise the capital necessary to effect such purpose, &c.

The completion between Tipperary and Waterford was undertaken under the influence of a loan from government of 120,000l.

By 18 and 19 Vic., cap. 73 (26th June, 1855), the company raised 94,000l., at 6 per cent., which has since been redeemed, and a consolidated 4½ per cent. stock issued instead. By the same Act working arrangements authorised with Limerick and Foynes, and Limerick and Ennis.

By 23 and 24 Vic., cap. 160 (23rd July, 1860), the company was authorised to construct a tramway to the Market Place, at Limerick, and a half-a-mile of line with pier or wharf at Waterford; both of which works have been completed. Preferential shares to be consolidated into 5 per.cent. stock, and additional capital not exceeding 50,000l. in 5 per cent. preference shares, and 16,000l. on loan. Mortgage debt to be converted into debenture stock at 4½ per cent.

By 25 and 26 Vic., cap. 191 (1862), authority has been obtained to divert the tramway at Limerick, and to work or lease the Limerick and Ennis, existing working agreement with that company being also confirmed. Power is also given to raise 23,000l. by shares, and to attach thereto preference dividend up to 5 per cent.; also to borrow 7,000l.

By 29 and 30 Vic., cap. 272 (23rd July, 1866), the Waterford and Limerick was authorised to enter into traffic arrangements with the Great Southern and Western and the Great Western, or either of them.

By 31 and 32 Vic., cap. 88 (13th July, 1868), the company was authorised to raise additional capital to the extent of 50,000l. in shares, and 16,600l. on loan.

LIMERICK AND ENNIS.—This line has been worked by the Waterford and Limerick, since April 22nd, 1861, on a 20 years' lease, at 45 per cent. on the receipts. The management is vested in a joint committee, under 25 and 26 Vic., cap. 191 (29th July, 1862), by which the Waterford and Limerick was authorised to raise 23,000l. new preference capital, for the purpose of taking up the plant of the Ennis.

LIMERICK AND CASTLE CONNELL.—This line, of which 13 miles are open, commencing 4½ miles from Limerick, and ending at Killaloe, on the Shannon, is traffic worked under a mileage agreement.

ATHENRY AND ENNIS.—By 26 and 27 Vic., cap. 133 (1863), working arrangements are sanctioned with the Waterford and Limerick, and the latter authorised to subscribe thereto.

LIMERICK AND FOYNES.—This line, 26¼ miles, is likewise worked for a fixed annual sum terminable by either party. The Waterford and Limerick originally subscribed 17,500l. to this undertaking, and has since added 5,850l. in preference shares.

RATHKEALE AND NEWCASTLE JUNCTION.—By 27 and 28 Vic., cap. 236 (25th July, 1864), the Waterford and Limerick was authorised to work the Rathkeale and Newcastle (10 miles), to contribute 5,00ℓ. to that undertaking, as well as to raise 35,000ℓ., with 7,000ℓ. on loan, to provide rolling stock for the same, and for their own general purposes.

MILEAGE.—The total length of miles worked by the company extends to 155¼.

REVENUE.—The receipts for the half-year ending 31st December amounted to 42,372ℓ., and for the same period of 1866 to 42,346ℓ., showing an increase of 26ℓ. ; but the receipts of 1866 were the largest the company ever had, and were swelled by a traffic in Indian corn and other breadstuffs, which they had not had to the same extent in the first half-year. Having regard to the large unexpected plant depreciation which had become needful to write off, the Board had felt it right to transfer to reserve the surplus balance of 2,316ℓ., in reduction of that debit. They much regretted that this absorbed for the present the dividend on the ordinary stock otherwise available. but as such a charge was not likely to again occur, they trusted that the shareholders would approve the course taken.

The receipts for the June half-year were 37,084ℓ.; and for the half-year ending 30th June, 1867, 36,180ℓ.: increase, 975ℓ. The profit was, after defraying working expenses, 20,137ℓ., out of which had to be deducted interest on bonds and temporary advances, &c. amounting to 9,167ℓ. From the balance the usual dividend at the rate of 5 per cent. per annum were paid on the old and new preference shares, and also at the rate of 4½ per cent. on the perpetual stocks. This absorbed 10,545ℓ., and the sum of 424ℓ. remaining being applied in reduction of the reserve fund debt.

WATERFORD AND KILKENNY.—It was reported in August that an award, dated 18th March, had been made by Mr. Seymour Clarke, with reference to the old premises, between Dunkitt and Waterford, and the works constructed thereon. The differences between the two companies relative thereto were of rather a serious character ; we claimed that the sum of 16,779ℓ. was due to us by the Kilkenny ; they did not admit that their liability exceeded 8,840ℓ.—the amount declared to be due by a former award of Mr. Le Fanu's, made some years since. The award now made and being acted on is, that the amount due to us is 14,462ℓ., on which sum the Waterford and Kilkenny are bound to pay us for ever 5 per cent. interest. "We regret, however, that there still remain unsettled differences with the Waterford and Kilkenny. We have offered to have all differences between us referred to the Board of Trade, or to the late Arbitrator ; but they have not assented to this amicable mode of settlement."

CAPITAL.—The expenditure on this account to 30th June, 1868, was stated at 1,339,017ℓ., being 25,215ℓ. in excess of the undermentioned receipts :—

Original shares existing, 50ℓ. each	£499,650	
Quarter shares at 12ℓ. 10s. each	1,850=£501,500	
5 per cent. 50ℓ. preference shares redeemable	246,700	
New 5 per cent. 50ℓ. ditto	102,000	
4½ per cent. 100ℓ. consolidated preference (perpetual)	91,200	
Forfeited shares gain, less discount allowed on issuing shares	25,632	
Public works loan—Balance	71,501	
Mortgages—General	23⁸,310	
Debentures—Perpetual	16,000	
Loans on deposit (temporary)	20,958	
	£1,313,802	

The accounts are made up to 30th June and 31st December in every year, and the statutory meetings held in Waterford in February and August.

Scale of Voting.—5 shares of 50ℓ. each, one vote ; 10 shares, two votes ; 15 shares, three votes ; 20 shares, four votes ; 40 shares, five votes : then one vote for every 10 shares to 90 ; ten votes maximum.

Certificates must accompany transfer deed. Registration fee 2s. 6d. each deed. Registration of death or marriage, 5s.

No. of Directors.—Maximum, 18 ; minimum, 6. Qualification, 1,000ℓ. capital.

DIRECTORS :

Chairman—WILLIAM MALCOMSON, Esq., Milford House, Portlaw, County Waterford.

Deputy-Chairman—ABRAHAM STEPHENS, Esq., Duncannon, County Wexford.

Walter Breen, Esq., Slade, Feathard, County Wexford.
Thomas White Jacob, Esq., Tramore, County Waterford.
Sir Benjamin Morris, J.P., D.L., The Mall, Waterford.
Joseph Strangman Richardson, Esq., Merchant, Waterford.
Joseph Robinson, Esq., Corbally House, Limerick.
John George Fennel, Esq., Cahir Cottage, Cahir.
Frederick Malcomson, Esq., Woodlock, Portlaw.

OFFICERS.—Sec. and Traffic Man., Thomas Ainsworth, Waterford ; Loco. Supt., Martin Atock, Limerick ; Eng., James Tighe. Waterford ; Auditors, T. S. Harvey and Robt. Ardagh, ; Solicitor, Joseph Ambrose, Waterford ; Bankers, the Bank of Ireland.
Head Offices—The Terminus, Waterford.

417.—WATERFORD, LISMORE, AND FERMOY.

Incorporated by 28 and 29 Vic., cap. 351 (5th July, 1865), to construct lines from Waterford to Dungarvan, and from Lismore to Fermoy. Length, 59½ miles. Capital, 400,000*l.* in shares, and 133,000*l.* on loan. Arrangements with Great Southern and Western.

Application will be made to the Board of Trade for liberty to abandon.

Solicitors—Edwards and Co., 8, Delahay Street, Westminster, S.W., and Edmund Power, Clonmel.

418.—WATERFORD, NEW ROSS, AND WEXFORD.

Incorporated by 29 and 30 Vic., cap. 348 (10th August, 1866), to construct lines between Waterford, Kilkenny, and Wexford. Length, 34 miles. Also to purchase the Bagenalstown and Wexford for the sum of 25,000*l.* Capital, 330,000*l.* in 10*l.* shares, and 90,000*l.* on loan. Arrangements with Great Southern and Western and Dublin Wicklow and Wexford.

By 30 and 31 Vic., cap. 129 (15th July, 1867), the company was authorised to make certain deviations, to construct lines or extensions (5½ miles), and also to purchase the Bagenalstown and Wexford.

No. of Directors—4; minimum, 3; quorum, 3 and 2.   *Qualification,* 200*l.*

DIRECTORS:

William Henry Forman, Esq., 28, Queen Street, Cheapside, E.C.
Standish Motte, Esq.
Edward Staunton, Esq.

Arthur Kavanagh, Esq., M.P., Borris House, Borris, Co. Carlow, and 13, Chapel Street, Belgrave Square, S.W.

419.—WATERFORD AND PASSAGE.

Incorporated by 25 and 26 Vic., cap. 217 (7th August, 1862), to construct a line from the Waterford and Tramore to Passage. Length, 9 miles. Capital, 60,000*l.* in 10*l.* shares, and 20*l.* on loan. Extra land, two acres; compulsory purchase, two years; completion of works, three years. Arrangements with Waterford and Tramore.

The Act gives power to construct a line branching off from the Waterford and Tramore, at about three-quarters of a mile from the Waterford Terminus, and, passing near Woodstown, terminates at the deep water harbour, and town of Passage, where it is proposed to build a jetty, where there is 11 fathoms depth of water, at lowest tide. for the steamers to land and embark passengers and mails for England, saving the tortuous and tedious river navigation up to Waterford. and saving one hour and a quarter at least in the passage between Waterford and Milford. It is also proposed to place a steam ferry between Passage and Arthurstown (in connection with the railway) on the Wexford side, and thus bring the traffic from the whole southern portion of the County of Wexford over the Passage railway to Waterford, which is at present the market town. The line will be cheaply constructed, and can be completed in 12 months. It is also proposed to connect this railway with the Waterford and Wexford Railway, thus completing through railway communication between Waterford and Dublin, and by means of a new harbour at Wexford, giving a new and short route to England, *via* Fishguard and South Wales.

By 26 and 27 Vic., cap. 224 (28th July, 1863), the company was authorised to extend the line to the south-west shore of the Suir, at Passage, and to establish ferries across the estuary. Length, ½ mile. New capital, 20,000*l.* in shares, and 6,600*l.* on loan.

By 28 and 29 Vic.. cap. 381 (6th July, 1865), an extension of time for purchase of lands, for six months, and completion of works, for two years, was obtained.

By 30 and 31 Vic., cap. 161 (25th July, 1867), the company obtained an extension of time for completion of works till 25th July, 1869.

No. of Directors—6; minimum, 3; quorum, 3.   *Qualification,* 200*l.*

PATRONS:

The Most Noble the Marquis of Waterford, Curraghmore, Waterford, and 30, Charles Street, St. James's, S.W.
The Right Hon. Lord Templemore, Arthurstown, near Passage, and 32, Bruton Street, W.

DIRECTORS:

Edward Roberts, Esq., Agent to the Marquis of Waterford, Waterford.
Frederick William Sedgwick, Esq., Stone Cottage, Doddington Grove, S.

Hamilton Geale, Esq., J.P., Monkstown, Dublin.
Robert Ford, Esq., Merchant, 38, Cannon Street, E.C., and Sydenham, S.E.

OFFICERS.—Sec., H. Williams Wood; Eng., Peter Robert Roddy, 35, South Mall, Cork; Solicitors, P. Burrowes Sharkey, 42, Blessington Street, Dublin, and Carlton Chambers, 12, Regent Street, W., and Thomas Babington, Cork.
Offices—6, Westminster Chambers, Victoria Street, S.W.

420.—WATERFORD AND TRAMORE.

Incorporated by 14 and 15 Vic., cap. 112 (24th July, 1851), for a railway commencing in the city of Waterford, and terminating at Tramore, on the coast. Length, 7½ miles.

By 20 and 21 Vic., cap. 27 (3rd July, 1857), the company is authorised to raise additional capital of 10,000l. in shares at 5 per cent. preference, and 3,350l. in loans, in aid of "new works," station accommodation, &c.; but an extension was refused. This new capital was created on 29th September, 1857, at 5 per cent.

REVENUE.—The accounts showed an increase of 318l. for the half-year ending 31st December, 1867. The available balance for dividend, after paying interest, &c., was 1,016l., of which the original 10l. shareholders obtained 4s. on each share.

DIRECTORS:

Chairman—SIR JAMES DOMBRAIN, Woodstock, Sandford, Dublin.

Abraham Denny, Esq.. J. P., Tramore.
John Blood, Esq., Mountjoy Square, Dublin.

Edmond Power, Esq., Eastlands, Tramore, Waterford.
John Malcomson, Esq., Waterford.

OFFICERS.—Sec. and Traffic Man., George N. Baker, Waterford; Eng., Charles Tarrant, C.S., Waterford; Auditor, Dr. Macessy, Waterford.

Offices—Terminus, Waterford.

421—WATERFORD AND WEXFORD.

Incorporated by 27 and 28 Vic., cap. 216 (25th July, 1864), to construct a railway from the river Suir, at Arthurstown, in connection with the Waterford and Passage railway and ferry to the town of Wexford, on the Dublin Wicklow and Wexford, with a harbour in Greenore Bay, opposite to Fishguard Coast, establishing a short sea route from Wexford, via Fishguard, to South Wales, London, &c., and completing railway communication between the city of Waterford and Dublin. Length. 35 miles. Capital, 330,000l. in 10l. shares, and 110,000l. on loan. Arrangements with Dublin Wicklow and Wexford.

By 30 and 31 Vic., cap. 190 (15th July, 1867), the company obtained an extension of time for completion of works till 15th July, 1870, and also to exercise the borrowing powers, as certain fixed proportions of the general capital were paid up.

No. of Directors.—Maximum, 7; minimum, 5; quorum, 5. Qualification, 300l.

DIRECTORS:

Chairman—GEORGE LE HUNTE, Esq., Wexford.

Joseph William Holland, Esq., Birley House, Forest Hill, S.
Edward Corry, Esq., Merchant, 8, New Broad Street, E.C.

Fred. William Sedgwick, Esq., Stone Cottage, Doddington Grove. London, S.
John Greene, Esq., J.P., Wexford.

OFFICERS.—Sec., H. Williams Wood: Eng., Peter Robert Roddy, Cork; Solicitor, P. Burrowes Sharkey, 42. Blessington Street, Dublin, and Carlton Chambers, 12, Regent Street, W.; Bankers, National Bank, 13, Old Broad Street, E.C.

Offices—6, Westminster Chambers, Victoria Street, Westminster, S.W.

422.—WATERLOO AND WHITEHALL.

Incorporated by 28 and 29 Vic., cap. 258 (5th July, 1865), to construct a line on the pneumatic principle from Waterloo Station to Charing Cross. Length, ¾ of a mile. Capital, 100,000l. in shares, and 33,000l. on loan.

By 30 and 31 Vic., cap. 197 (12th August, 1867), the company was authorised to raise additional capital to the extent of 75,000l., at a preference not exceeding 8 per cent., and to borrow 24,000l. on mortgage. Extension of time for completion of works, one year. Arrangements may be made with London and South Western.

By 31 and 32 Vic., cap. 169 (31st July, 1868), an extension of time for completion of works was obtained till 5th July, 1871.

CAPITAL.—The expenditure on this account to 30th June, 1868, amounted to 67,140l., which left a balance at interest of 4,266l., the receipts having been as under:—

Deposit and calls	....	£66,331
Payments in advance	....	4,424 = £70,755
Interest on calls in arrear, moneys on deposit, &c.	....	651
		£71,406

No. of Directors—6; maximum, 10; minimum, 3; quorum, 3 and 2. Qualification, 300l.

DIRECTORS:

Chairman—JOHN PARSON, Esq., Bitton, Teignmouth, Devon.

J. St. George Burke, Esq., Q.C., The Auberies, Sudbury, Suffolk.
The Hon. R. H. Dutton, Timsbury Manor. Romsey, Hants.
Samuel Lucas, Esq., 6, Cork Street, Burlington Gardens, W.

Charles Mortimer, Esq., Wigmore House, Capel, Surrey.
Arthur John Otway, Esq., M.P., 9, Harley Street, W.

OFFICERS.—Sec., Edward Bellamy; Engs., T. W. Rammell, Westminster Chambers, S.W., and Sir Charles Fox and Son, Spring Gardens, S.W.; Surveyor, R. Ritchie, 4, Parliament Street, Westminster, S.W.; Solicitors, Messrs. Burchell, 5, Broad Sanctuary, Westminster, S.W.; Bankers, Union Bank of London, Pall Mall East, S.W. Offices—7, Westminster Chambers, Victoria Street, S.W,

423.—WATFORD AND RICKMANSWORTH.

Incorporated by 23 and 24 Vic., cap. 111 (July 3rd, 1860), to construct a line from Watford, on the London and North Western, to Rickmansworth. Length, 4½ miles. Capital, 40,000l. in 10l. shares, and 13,000l. on loan. Opened 1st October, 1862.

By 26 and 27 Vic., cap. 131 (14th July, 1863), the company obtained power to create additional capital to the extent of 30,000l., at 5 per cent., and 10,000l. on loan.

The London and North Western works the line, having subscribed 10,000l. of the new capital, at 5 per cent. preference.

Meetings in January and February, and June or July.

No. of Directors—8; minimum, 4; quorum, 3.   *Qualification,* 300l.

DIRECTORS:

Chairman—LORD EBURY, Moor Park, Rickmansworth, and 35, Park Street, Grosvenor Square, S.W.
Deputy-Chairman—JOSEPH CARY, Esq., 49, Pall Mall, S.W.

Hon. Reginald Capel, Little Cashiobury, Watford.
John Henry Dillon, Esq., 5k, Albany, Piccadilly, W.

Hon. R. W. Grosvenor, M.P., Moor Park, Rickmansworth, and 48, Grosvenor Place, S.W.

OFFICERS.—Sec., Alexander Forbes; Eng., J. S. Peirce, 6, Victoria Street, S.W.; Solicitors, Hargrove, Fowler, and Co., 3, Victoria Street, Westminster, S.W.
Offices—3, Victoria Street, S.W.

424.—WEALD OF KENT.

Incorporated by 27 and 28 Vic., cap. 233 (25th July, 1864), to construct a line from Hartley and Cranbrook to Tenderden. Length, 20 miles. Capital, 200,000l. in 20l. shares, and 66,000l. on loan.

By 28 Vic., cap. 82 (19th June, 1865), the company was authorised to make various deviations.

Meetings in February and August.

No. of Directors—7; minimum, 5; quorum, 3.   *Qualification,* 500l.

DIRECTORS:

William Francis Lawrence, Esq.
Walter Freeth, Esq.
Walter Joseph Fry, Esq.
Joseph Cary, Esq., 49, Pall Mall, S.W.

Capt. Robert O'Brien Jameson, 60, St. James's Street, Piccadilly, S.W.
Hugh Ward Saunders, Esq.

425.—WEEDON AND DAVENTRY.

Incorporated by 31 and 32 Vic., cap. 171 (31st July, 1868), to construct a line from Daventry to Weedon, on the London and North Western. Length, 3¾ miles. Capital, 30,000l. in 10l. shares, and 10,000l. on mortgage. Arrangements with London and North Western.

It was stated in October that all the anticipations formed of the company would be fully realised. Up to the present time the progress of the line had not been so rapid as the directors could wish, but no doubt was entertained that all difficulties would soon be removed, and that the works would be carried forward to a satisfactory conclusion.

No. of Directors—3; quorum, 2.   *Qaulification,* 150l.

DIRECTORS:

Chairman—JOHN JOHNSTONE, Esq.
Francis Anderson, Esq. | Harry Lennard Wright, Esq.

Offices—Victoria Street, Westminster, S.W.

426.—WELLINGTON AND DRAYTON.

Incorporated by 25 and 26 Vic., cap. 226 (7th August, 1862), for a railway from Wellington, on the Great Western, to Drayton, in connection with the Nantwich and Market Drayton. Length, 15½ miles. Capital, 200,000l. in 10l. shares; loans, 66,600l. The company and the Nantwich and Market Drayton may reciprocally work over each other's lines, and both may enter into traffic arrangements with Great Western. Opened 16th October, 1867.

By 27 and 28 Vic., cap. 176 (14th July, 1864), the company was authorised to make several deviations, and to transfer the undertaking to the Great Western.

By 29 and 30 Vic., cap. 211 (16th July, 1866), the Shrewsbury and Potteries was authorised to participate in the ownership of the Wellington and Drayton, but is not likely to avail itself of the option.

Meetings in February or March, and in August or September.

No. of Directors—5 ; maximum, 10 ; quorum, 3. *Qualification*, 500*l*.

DIRECTORS :

Chairman—WILLIAM FENTON, Esq., Beaumonds, near Rochdale.

A. C. Sherriff, Esq., M.P., 10, Dean's Yard, Westminster, S.W.
Sir Watkin W. Wynn, Bart., M.P., Wynnstay, Ruabon, and 18, St. James's Square, S.W.
Richard Potter, Esq., Standish House, Stonehouse, Gloucestershire.

Captain Bulkeley, Clewer Lodge, Windsor.
W. C. King, Esq., Warfield Hall, Bracknell, Berks.
John Williams, Esq., Chester.
Joseph Loxdale Warren, Esq., Market Drayton.

OFFICERS.—Sec., Gordon Graham ; Auditors, Mr. Wood and Mr. Williams.
Offices—Great Malvern.

427.—WELLINGTON AND SEVERN JUNCTION.

Incorporated by Act 17 Vic., cap. 214 (August 28th, 1853), for a line by junction with Shrewsbury and Birmingham, at Wellington, and extension to Coalbrookdale. Length, 5½ miles. Capital, 6,000 shares, of 10*l*.; loans, 10,000*l*.

By 24 and 25 Vic., cap. 212 (1st August, 1861), the line is leased to the Great Western for a term of 999 years. The dividend for the first three years was at the rate of 4*l*. 10*s*. per cent., and is to be 5 per cent. for the remainder of the term.

Meetings in January or February, and in August or September.

No. of Directors.—Maximum, 8 ; minimum, 6 ; quorum, 3 ; committees, 3.

DIRECTORS :

Chairman—HENRY DICKINSON, Esq., Coalbrookdale.

John Slaney, Esq., Wellington.
Joseph Robinson, Esq., Berkhampstead.

William Henry Darby, Esq., Brymbo Hall, near Ruabon.

Eligible for re-election.

OFFICERS.—Solicitor and Sec., R. D. Newill, Wellington, Salop ; Eng., Henry Robertson, Shrewsbury ; Auditors, John Hiatt Slaney and John Barber, Wellington ; Bankers, The Shropshire Banking Company, Wellington.
Offices—Wellington, Salop.

428.—WENLOCK.

Incorporated by 24 and 25 Vic. (22nd July, 1861), to construct a railway, No. 2, from the Buildwas station, of the Much Wenlock and Severn Junction and Severn Valley companies, across the River Severn to the Coalbrookdale iron works ; also to construct a railway, No. 1, commencing by a junction with the Much Wenlock and Severn Junction at the town of Much Wenlock, and terminating by a junction with the Shrewsbury and Hereford, in the parish of Winstanstow, near the Craven Arms. Length of railway No. 2, 1 mile. Length of railway, No. 1, 14 miles. Capital, 125,000*l*. in 10*l*. shares ; loans, 41,500*l*. Running powers over Great Western to Ketley ironworks ; over Shrewsbury and Hereford to Craven Arms station ; over the Much Wenlock and Severn Junction line ; and a part of Severn Valley.

By agreement dated March, 1864, the Great Western subscribes 20,000*l*. and the Much Wenlock 20,000*l*. towards the construction of railway No. 2 (the Coalbrookdale), and pay the latter 1,000*l*. a year rent for their share of profit.

Meetings in March or September.

No. of Directors—7 ; minimum, 5 ; quorum, 3. *Qualification*, 250*l*.

DIRECTORS :

Chairman—WILLIAM PENNY BROOKES, Esq., Much Wenlock.

Moses George Benson, Esq.
Richard Butcher, Esq.
William Wagstaff, Esq., 4, Great George Street, Westminster, S.W.

Thomas Brassey, Jun., Esq., M.P., 4, Great George Street, Westminster, S.W.
Ralph Augustus Benson, Esq., Much Wenlock.

Secretary, R. C. Blakeway.

Offices—Much Wenlock.

429.—WEST CORK.

Incorporated by 23 and 24 Vic., cap. 203 (28th August, 1860), to construct the following railways, viz.:—1 (10 miles 3 chains) from a junction with the Cork and Bandon, near Bandon, to Ballineen ; 2 (7 miles 34 chains), from Ballineen to Dunmanway ; 3 (7 miles 55 chains), from Dunmanway to Dromoleague ; 4 (8 miles 13 chains), from Dromoleague to Skibbereen. Capital, 200,000*l*. in 10*l*. shares. Agreements with Cork and Bandon. Separate accounts to be kept of money borrowed on baronial guarantees. The Cork and Bandon empowered to subscribe 20,000l. towards the West Cork, agreed to subscribe 10,000l. when the first section of 10 miles to Ballineen is finished, and the remaining 10,000l. on completion of the line to Dunmanway.

By 28 and 29 Vic., cap. 232 (5th July, 1865), the company obtained an extension of time for completion of works, and was also authorised to raise new capital to the extent of 120,000l. in shares and 40,000l. on loan, and to divide the capital in half-shares.

By 30 and 31 Vic., cap. 192 (12th August, 1867), the company was authorised under written consent of three-fourths of the preference shareholders to attach an absolute priority of dividend not exceeding 6 per cent. to any shares unissued or which may be forfeited and reissued, with power to redeem the same. Also to borrow on mortgage 15,000l. to discharge the existing liabilities. Extension of time for completion of works till 12th August, 1869.

It was reported in September, that, since the report of the committee of investigation (for which see APPENDIX to present volume) was adopted, the objects recommended in that report have been carried into effect and the management of the line completely changed, but no further details appear to have been forthcoming.

Meetings in February and August.

No. of Directors—5 ; minimum, 5 ; quorum, 5. *Qualification,* 500l.

DIRECTORS :

Chairman—Sir JOHN ARNOTT, Kt., Woodlands, Cork.

J. P. Ronayne, Esq., Queenstown, Cork.	* William Gray, Esq., 5, Tokenhouse Yard, London.
William H. Massey, Esq., Massey Town, Macroom.	* Fras. T. Mackreth, Esq., Hercules Passage, Threadneedle Street, London.
Timothy Mahoney, Esq., Ardsulla, County Cork.	* F. W. Sedgwick, Esq., Doddington Grove, Kennington.
* John Everitt, Esq., 49, Lombard Street, London.	

* The four last named directors constitute the Finance Committee in London.

OFFICERS.—Sec., G. Purcell, 91, South Mall, Cork ; Sec. of Finance Committee in London, W. J. Mitson, 6, Westminster Chambers, Victoria Street, S.W. ; Solicitors, Thomas Babington, Cork, T. Mc. Carthy Downing, Skibbereen, and P. Burrowes Sharkey, 42, Blessington Street, Dublin, and Carlton Chambers, 12, Regent Street, W. ; Bankers, The Munster Bank, Cork, and National Bank, London.

Offices—91, South Mall, Cork.

430.—WEST CORNWALL.

Incorporated by 9 and 10 Vic., cap. 336 (3rd August, 1846), for a line from Carredas to Penzance, with a branch to the Cornwall. Under provisions of the Act the company purchased the Hayle (which had been incorporated since 1834), the consideration paid being the issue of 4,000 shares of 20l., and the assumption of its then existing mortgage debt. It was sought to carry on the line from Hayle to Penzance, by the Act of 1850, authorising the issue of No. 9 forfeited shares in hand, at 6l. discount : the dividends from the traffic of the whole line to be shared *pro rata* on all shares up to 5 per cent.; any surplus to be additional dividends on the 4,000 paid up (Hayle company), up to 5 per cent. on the whole capital paid up ; then further dividends to be rateably divided.

By an Act of 1850, modifications of the original agreement were sanctioned : and by an Act of 1853 (17 Vic., cap. 187), the clauses of Act 1850 are repealed, as main line open, but without prejudice to that half-year's dividend. The Act of 1850 also sanctions the construction of the extension to Penzance, on the narrow instead of the broad gauge ; therefore obviating the necessity of widening the existing Hayle railway, and altering the rolling stock, &c. When, however, any railway shall be made in Cornwall on the broad gauge, this railway must be altered to the broad, or an additional line of rails be laid down.

The Act 17 Vic., cap. 187 (5th August, 1853), authorised extensions and alterations : to widen main line 5½ miles ; to make extension line to Kenwyn, Garas Wharf and Truro river side (2½ miles) ; a junction line from Kenwyn (2 furlongs) to West Cornwall line ; to maintain the Hayle branch (6 furlongs). Productive mileage, 27½ miles.

By 24 Vic., cap. 54 (7th June, 1861), the company was authorised to attach a preference of 5 per cent. to the shares (35,000l.) created under the Act of 1853 ; and to create debenture stock in lieu of loans extinguished.

By 28 and 29 Vic., cap. 219 (5th of July, 1865), the company was authorised to enter into working arrangements with the Great Western, Bristol and Exeter, and South Devon, and its ultimate dissolution provided for on terms of agreement,

The line is now worked by the associated companies at a fixed rental equal to 5 per cent. on the preference stock and 2¼ on the ordinary.

REVENUE.—The receipts for the half-year ending 31st December furnished a disposable balance of 5,184l., which admitted of 4,234l. being divided among the proprietors of original stock, at the rate of 2¼ per cent. per annum, leaving 332l. to be carried forward.

The report for 30th June stated that 109,415l. of debentures, of which 24,235l. bore 5 per cent. interest, had become payable, and had been renewed at 4½ per cent. On the revenue account the six months' rent, 9,000l., had been received from the associated companies, and, after paying debenture interest, the disposable balance was 5,292l., out of which a dividend of 5 per cent. per annum on the preference stock and of 2½ per cent. on the ordinary stock left 415l. to credit of the current half-year.

CAPITAL.—The expenditure to 30th June, 1868, left a balance of 1,060l. on account of the subjoined receipts :—

Original stock	£346,900
Preference stock	30,000
Debentures at 5 per cent.............	£55,525
„ 4½ per cent............	108,920
„ 4 per cent...	5,000 = 164,945=£550,845

The accounts are made up to 30th June and 31st December, and the statutory meetings held in Bristol or Penzance, in February and August in every year.

Registration fee, 2s. 6d. each seller.

No. of Directors.—Maximum, 18; minimum, 8. *Qualification*, 50 shares.

DIRECTORS :

Chairman—LOUIS VIGURS, Esq., Rosehill, Penzance.

John Ching, Esq., Launceston.
J. Claude Daubuz, Esq,, Killiow, Truro.
Charles Evan Thomas, Esq., Cranmers, Mitcham, Surrey.

O. B. C. Harrison, Esq., 4, Paper Buildings, Temple, E.C.
Thomas Porter Jose, Esq., Bristol.
William Bolitho, Junr., Esq., Penzance.
Thomas Robins Bolitho, Esq,, Penzance.

OFFICERS.—Sec., Henry Roach; Auditors, Robert Hart Pike and George Thomas; Solicitors, Radcliffe and Davies, 20, Craven Street, Strand, W.C., and Rodd and Cornish, Penzance.

Head Offices—Penzance.

431.—WEST DURHAM.

A local line, 7 miles in length, connecting the West Hartlepool and the Stockton and Darlington, chiefly employed in the carriage of minerals.

The North Eastern has obtained power to absorb the West Durham with its own system.

DIRECTORS :

Chairman—JAMES PULLEINE, Esq., Clifton Castle, Bedale.

George Leeman, Esq., York.
George Allison, Esq., Darlington.

William Rutherford Hunter, Esq., Newcastle-on-Tyne.
John Buckton, Esq., Darlington.

OFFICERS.—Sec., John Close, York; Eng., Edward Willis; Auditor, Michael Middleton, Darlington.

432.—WEST GRINSTEAD, CUCKFIELD, AND HAYWARD'S HEATH JUNCTION.

Incorporated by 27 and 28 Vic., cap. 251 (25th July, 1864), to construct a line between the West Grinstead and Hayward's Heath stations of the Brighton. Length, 10 miles. Capital, 110,000l. in 10l. shares, and 36,000l. on loan. Arrangements with Brighton. In abeyance.

No. of Directors—5; quorum, 3. *Qualification*, 500l.

DIRECTORS :

Walter Wyndham Burrell, Esq.
Frederick Weekes, Esq.
William Marshall, Esq.

Frederick Waller, Esq.
William Warren Smith, Esq.

433.—WEST LONDON.

Incorporated by Act 6 Wm. IV., cap. 79 (21st June, 1836), under the title of "THE BIRMINGHAM BRISTOL AND THAMES JUNCTION," the object being to unite the London and North Western and Great Western with the western districts of the metropolis, and communicate with the river Thames, through the medium of the Kensington canal. The canal was purchased for 36,000l. The title of the railway was altered by 3 and 4 Vic., cap. 105. Total mileage authorised, 9½ ; of which 3 miles 75 yards, forming a junction with L. and N. W., near Kensall Green Cemetery, to the Kensington canal, have been opened since 27th May, 1844.

By 8 Vic., cap. 156, the railway was leased to the L. and N. W. and G. W. conjointly, for 999 years, commencing 11th March, 1845, at a rent of 1,800l. per annum.

By 22 and 23 Vic., cap. 134 (13th August, 1859), the Kensington canal and all other properties of the West London were absolutely transferred to the "West London Extension" which is composed of the London and North Western, the Great Western, the South Western, and the Brighton. These companies secure the following guarantees to the different classes of properties in West London : viz., 14s. per 20l. share, first class, preference, which were issued at 10l. per cent. discount, 24s. per 20l. share, second class preference, all paid up. 4s. per share to original shareholders after opening of new line, which took place on 2nd March, 1863 ; 6s. per share three years after opening of line ; 8s. per share six years after opening of line. The company is to dissolve under provisions of the Act 26 and 27 Vic., cap. 208 (28th July, 1863), so soon as an agreement with the West London Extension is finally resolved upon.

The accounts are made up to 30th June and 31st December, and the statutory meetings held in the third week of the months of February and August, or within 20 days therefrom, in every year.

Scale of Voting.—One vote for 5 shares, and one additional vote for every 5 additional shares, but no proprietor can have more than 20 votes.

Certificates must accompany transfer deed. Registration fee, 2s. 6d. each seller.

DIRECTORS:

Great Western.
Sir D. Gooch, Bart., M.P., Fulthorpe House, London.
C. A. Wood, Esq., 25, Chesham Place, S.W.
Hon. F. G. B. Ponsonby, 3, Mount Street, Grosvenor Square, London.
Captain Bulkeley, Clewer Lodge, Windsor.
C. G. Mott, Esq., Sunnyside, Birkenhead Park, Birkenhead.

London and North Western.
R. Moon, Esq., Bevere, Worcester.
J. P. Brown-Westhead, Esq., M.P., 13, Eaton Square, S.W., and Lea Castle, Kidderminster.
James Bancroft, Esq., 5, Police Street, Manchester.
O. L. Stephen, Esq., Bardon Hall, Leicester.
J. P. Bickersteth, Esq., Southcot, Leighton. Beds.

JOINT OFFICERS.—Sec., J. Wait, Birkenhead ; Supt., W. Patchett, Shrewsbury ; Eng., R. E. Johnston, Birkenhead.

434.—WEST LONDON EXTENSION.

Incorporated by 22 and 23 Vic., cap. 134 (13th August, 1859), to construct the undermentioned lines and works, viz. :—

1. A railway, length 4 miles 6 chains, from a junction with the West London at Kensington, crossing the Thames by a bridge to a junction with the authorised line of the Victoria Station and Pimlico at Battersea. This bridge will be 340 yards in length, with six arches of 120 feet span each, seven arches of 25 feet span each, and with a headway under each arch of 20 feet above Trinity high water mark.

2 and 3. Branches of the respective lengths of 63 chains and 35 chains, to connect (1) with the West End of London and Crystal Palace near its Clapham Station, and with the South Western, near the junction of its Richmond branch with the main line.

4. A branch from Battersea to the South Western.

5. A branch, length 27 chains, from the main line near the basin of the Imperial Gas Company to the Thames near the mouth of the Kensington canal.

6. A dock in the parish of Fulham.

7. A diversion of a part of the Kensington canal, belonging to the West London, who are to be authorised to discontinue the use of the part of the canal north of King's Road, Chelsea.

By 24 and 25 Vic., cap. 234 (6th August, 1861), the company obtained an increase of capital to the extent of 105,000l., to which the London and North Western and Great Western each contribute 35,000l., and the South Western and Brighton, 17,500l. each. Further borrowing powers, amounting to 35,000l., were also conceded. Opened 2nd March, 1863. West Brompton station on 1st October, 1866.

By 26 and 27 Vic., cap. 208 (28th July, 1863), the four subscribing companies were authorised to furnish new capital in the following proportions :—

London and North Western .. £50,000
Great Western 50,000
South Western £25,000
Brighton 25,000

The new borrowing powers extend to 50,000l. These lines and branches (except the junction with the South Western) are constructed on the mixed gauge.

WEST LONDON.—The purchase of this line, with its absorption by the new company is regulated by the following scheme of compensation :—Holders of first-class preferred 20l. shares to receive per annum 14s. per share ; holders of second-class preferred 20l. shares to receive per annum 1l. 4s. per share ; holders of original 20l. shares, from and after the completion and opening for public traffic of any part of the new railways, per annum 4s. per share ; from and after the expiration of three years from such completion and opening per annum, 6s. per share ; and from and after the expiration of six years from such completion and opening, per annum 8s. per share. The West London capital consists of 185,960l. in the following shares, there being no mortgage or bond debt :— 5,338 ordinary shares of 20l. each, 106,760l. ; 3,200 first-class preference shares, 64,000l. ; 760 second class preference shares of 15,200l. The yearly rent of 1,800l.,formerly payable to the West London by the London and North Western and the Great Western, is now paid to the company constituted by this Act, which may also, by agreement, disburse the dividends due half-yearly to the original and preference shareholders in the West London.

No. of Directors—12 ; quorum, 5.   Appointed as under by the four contributing companies.

SPECIAL CHAIRMAN.—The directors, when they think fit, may select a special chairman, not being one of themselves, to act for any period ; but no such appointment to be made except by unanimous resolution of a meeting of which at least one director from each of the four companies is present.   In event of the assembled directors failing to agree in the appointment of a special chairman, then the Board of Trade, on the application of any two or more of the companies, may appoint any person not being one of the directors, to act as a special chairman for as long a period as it may think fit.

DIRECTORS.
London and North Western.

Richard Ryder Dean, Esq., 2, New Square, Lincoln's Inn, W.C., and 97, Gloucester Place, Portman Square, W.
Robert Benson, Esq., 16, Craven Hill Gardens, Hyde Park, W.

J. P. Brown-Westhead, Esq., M.P., 13, Eaton Square, S.W., and Lea Castle, Kidderminster.
George Sheward, Esq., 17, Leinster Square, Bayswater.

Great Western.

Edward Leeming, Esq., Spring Grove, Richmond, S.W.
Richard Michell, Esq., Kensington Park Gardens, W.

Edward Wanklyn, Esq., Fulmer Place, Slough.
Captain Thomas Bulkeley, Clewer Lodge, Windsor.

London and South Western.

William P. Snell, Esq., Belmont Park, near Havant, Hants.

Captain J. G. Johnston, 8, York Terrace, Regent's Park, N.W.

London, Brighton, and South Coast.

Thos. F. Fremantle, Esq., Hamilton Place, Piccadilly.

Ralph L. Lopes, Esq., Sandridge Hall, Melksham.

OFFICERS.—Sec., Edward Bellamy ; Supt., S. Grew, Kensington Station : Eng., W. Baker, of London and North Western Company ; Surveyor, F. Fuller. 3, Whitehall Gardens, S.W. ; Auditor, W. W. Deloitte, 4, Lothbury, E.C. ; Solicitor, S. Carter, 32, Great George Street, Westminster, S.W.

Offices—7, Westminster Chambers, Victoria Street, S.W.

435.—WEST NORFOLK JUNCTION.

Incorporated by 27 and 28 Vic., cap. 90 (23rd June, 1864), to construct a line from the Lynn and Hunstanton, at Heacham, to the Great Eastern, at Wells. Length, 18½ miles. Capital, 75,000*l.* in 10*l.* shares, and 25,000*l.* on loan. Arrangements with Great Eastern, which subscribes 30,000*l.*, and works the line at 50 per cent. Opened August 17th, 1866.

REVENUE.—It was reported in March that after paying interest on the debenture debt and temporary loan there was a balance of 398*l.*, which might be applied to the reduction of the debt owing by the company on capital account. The traffic had increased to the extent of about 50 per cent. in the past half-year, as compared with the corresponding half-year of 1866.

The report for the June half-year stated that the receipts amounted to 1,998*l.*, as compared with 1,515*l.* for the corresponding six months of 1867. The result of the working to June 30th, 1868, after payment of debenture interest, was a balance of 663*l.* of net revenue, which the directors recommended should be applied in the reduction of the cost of certain extra works.

CAPITAL.—This account to 30th June showed that 99,898*l.* had been received and expended.

Meetings in February and March, and in August or September.

No. of Directors—8 ; minimum, 3 ; quorum, 3 and 2. *Qualification*, 200*l.*

DIRECTORS :

Chairman—HUMPHREY JOHN HARE, Esq., Docking Hall, Norfolk.

Henry Etheridge Blyth, Esq.
Edward Self, Esq., Lynn, Norfolk,

Edward Elmer Durrant, Esq.
J. S. Valentine, Esq., 11, Park Street, S.W.

OFFICERS.—Sec., T. P. Bond, 5, Great Queen Street, Westminster, S.W. ; Eng., J. S. Valentine, 11, Park Street, Westminster, S.W. ; Solicitors, Partridge and Edwards, Lynn ; Bankers, Jarvis and Jarvis, Lynn, and Prescott and Company, 62, Threadneedle Street, E.C.

436.—WEST RIDING AND GRIMSBY.

Incorporated by 25 and 26 Vic., cap. 211 (6th August, 1862). to construct a line from the Bradford Wakefield and Leeds, at Wakefield, to the South Yorkshire, at Barnby-upon-Don, with a branch to Doncaster, and several minor branches. Length, 28½ miles. Capital, 360,000l. in 10l. shares, and 120,000l. on loan. Extra land, six acres; compulsory purchase, three years; completion of works, five years. South Yorkshire and Sheffield appoint four directors, and guarantee interest on debentures, and a minimum dividend of 4½ per cent. on share capital. Opened 1st January, 1866.

By 27 and 28 Vic., cap. 91 (23rd June, 1864), the company was authorised to construct a station at Wakefield. Length of new line, ½ mile. Capital (to be kept separate), 80,000l. in shares, and 26,600l. on loan. West Yorkshire may contribute 15,000l. of this amount. Arrangements for the use of stations by Midland, West Yorkshire, and Manchester and Sheffield.

By 28 and 29 Vic., cap. 321 (5th July, 1865), the company was authorised to construct a line from Keadby, on the South Yorkshire, to Lincoln, on the Great Northern. Length, 29¼ miles. Capital, 400,000l. in shares, and 133,000l. on loan. This Act was repealed by 31 and 32 Vic., cap. 55 (25th June, 1868).

By 28 and 29 Vic., cap. 259, the West Riding and Grimsby was authorised to raise additional capital to the extent of 60,000l. in shares, and 20,000l. on loan. An extension of time was also conceded in respect to construction of one of the branches.

By 29 and 30 Vic., cap. 162 (28th June, 1866), the West Riding and Grimsby was transferred jointly to the Great Northern and the Manchester Sheffield and Lincoln-shire, the company to become extinct within one year from the passing of the Act.

By 30 Vic., cap. 49 (31st May, 1867), power was given to the Great Northern and the Sheffield, each to raise additional capital, for the purposes of the Wakefield station, to the extent of 20,000l., with 6,600l. on mortgage. Arrangements with Midland for use of Wakefield station.

By 30 Vic., cap. 162, the line was vested in the Great Northern and the Sheffield, ceasing to exist as an independent undertaking on 28th June, 1867. The West Riding and Grimsby is now worked jointly, and is managed by a committee of three directors from each of the two leasing companies.

DIRECTORS :

Great Northern.	*Manchester, Sheffield, and Lincolnshire.*
Samuel Waterhouse, Esq., M.P., Hope Hall, Halifax, and 66, Pall Mall, S.W.	T. R. Barker, The Edge, Sheffield.
William Firth, Esq., Birley Wood, Leeds.	Hon. William Eden, Doncaster.
Christopher B. Denison, Esq., M.P., Doncaster.	Richard Withers, Esq., Royal Bank Buildings, Liverpool.

Secretary to the committee and Manager of line, William West.

Offices—Wakefield.

437.—WEST SOMERSET.

Incorporated by 20 and 21 Vic., cap. 145 (17th August, 1857), to construct a railway from the Bristol and Exeter, at Taunton, to the harbour at Watchet. Capital, 120,000l. in 10l. shares; loans, 40,000l. Length, 14½ miles. Broad gauge. Opened 31st March, 1862.

By 23 Vic., cap. 51 (15th May, 1860), certain new works were authorised. Forfeited shares to be cancelled, and re-issued at 5 per cent. preference.

The Bristol and Exeter lease the undertaking, find all necessary plant, and work the line, paying to West Somerset 55 per cent. of gross receipts, with guarantee that such proportion of receipts shall not be less than 4,500l. a year. The dividends are at the rate of 2½ per cent.

Revenue.—The receipts were for the six months ending the 30th June, 3,397l., as compared with 7,077l. in the corresponding half of 1867, showing an increase of 320l. In the twelve weeks between the 28th June and 20th September the receipts were 2,666l., while in the corresponding twelve weeks of 1867 they had been 2,128l., showing an increase of 138l. The minimum rental for the six months, after payment of the interest on the debenture bonds, left a balance of 1,247l. applicable to the payment of a dividend on the first issue of 5,220 preference shares and of the current expenses. A dividend at the rate of 4½ per cent. per annum on the 5 per cent. dividend shares was declared.

Meetings in February or March, and in August or September.

No. of Directors—8 ; minimum, 3 ; quorum, 3 and 2. *Qualification*, 300l.

DIRECTORS :

Chairman—Sir P. P. F. P. ACLAND, Bart., Fairfield, Somerset.

Deputy-Chairman—Sir A. A. HOOD, Bart., Bridgewater, Somerset.

Lawrence Walker, Esq., 12, Bryanston Square, W.	John Halliday, Esq., Old Cleeve, Somerset.
George Furness, Esq., 36, Great George Street, Westminster, S.W.	R. Herniman, Esq., Taunton, Somerset.
	Henry Turle, Esq., Taunton, Somerset.
	William Stoate, Esq., Watchet, Somerset.

OFFICERS.—Sec., William Henry Wilson, 6, Victoria Street, Westminster, S.W.; Eng., R. P. Brereton, 18, Duke Street, Westminster, S.W.; Solicitors, Radcliffe and Davies, 20, Craven Street, Strand, W.C., and Beadons and Sweet, Taunton, Somerset; Bankers, Stuckey's Banking Company, and H. and R. Badcock, Taunton, Somerset.

Offices—6, Victoria Street, Westminster, S.W., and 11, Hammet Street, Taunton, Somerset.

438.—WEST SOMERSET MINERAL.

Incorporated by 20 and 21 Vic., cap. 66 (July 27th, 1857), for making a railway from the Quay, at Watchet, to the parish of Exton, with a branch therefrom. Length of main line, 13 miles; length of branch, 1 furlong. Share capital under this Act, 65,000l., divided equally into A and B shares. Loan capital, 21,500l. By the Watchet Harbour Act, 1860, the company were authorised to create, and they have created 10,000l. of additional class B shares.

The line is worked by the Ebbw Vale Company (Limited), for 55½ years, from 24th June, 1864. That company guarantees interest on the mortgage capital, as well as 6 per cent. on the 32,500l. A shares, and 5 per cent. on the 42,500l. B shares. These are regularly paid.

CAPITAL.—This account is constituted as follows, the expenditure to 30th June, 1867, having been 109,950l. :—

3,250 Class A shares at 10l. each		£32,500
3,250 ,, B ,,		32,500
1,000 Additional Class B 10l. each (Watchet Harbour Act)		10,000
Mortgages, in substitution for which debenture stock was created on 21st November, 1867	£21,500	
Less paid off to 30th June, 1868	3,500=	18,000
Debenture stock issued to 19th September, 1868	3,396	3,500
Balance to be issued	104=	
Bonds		8,500
Total capital, the income of which is guaranteed by the Ebbw Vale Company Limited		105,000
The company hold Watchet Harbour Mortgages (subject to a loan thereon of 4,950l. 14s. 10d.) for		10,000
		£115,000

No. of Directors—5; minimum, 3; quorum, 3.   *Qualification,* 500l.

DIRECTORS:

Chairman—ABRAHAM DARBY, Esq., Ebbw Vale Park, Monmouthshire.

Deputy-Chairman—JOSEPH ROBINSON, Esq., 7, Laurence Pountney Hill, E.C.

Charles Rowcliffe, Esq., Milverton, Somerset. | Charles King Anderson, Esq., 7, Laurence
Francis Tothill, Esq., 77, Laurence Pount- | Pountney Hill, E.C.
ney Hill, E.C.

Solicitor and Secretary, Charles E. Rowcliffe.

Offices—Stogumber, Taunton, Somerset.

439.—WEST SUSSEX JUNCTION.

Incorporated by 27 and 28 Vic., cap. 278 (25th July, 1864), to construct a line from Hardham to Steyning. Length, 11¾ miles. Capital, 125,000l. in 10l. shares, and 41,600l. on loan. Arrangements with Brighton.

By 28 Vic., cap. 127 (19th June, 1865), the company was authorised to make several deviations in the original route.

By 30 and 31 Vic., cap. 154 (25th July, 1867), an extension of time for completion of works was obtained till 25th July, 1870. In abeyance.

No. of Directors—4; quorum, 3.   *Qualification,* 300l.

DIRECTORS:

Col. Walter Barttelot Barttelot, M.P., | John Kemp Jacomb Hood, Esq.
Heliers, Petworth, Sussex, and 10, | Solomon Atkinson, Esq.
St. James's Place, S.W.

440.—WEYMOUTH AND PORTLAND.

Incorporated by 25 and 26 Vic., cap. 71 (30th June, 1862), to construct a line from Weymouth to the Isle of Portland, and an extension of the Wilts Somerset and Weymouth, to the Harbour. Mixed gauge. Length, 5½ miles. Capital, 75,000l. in 10l. shares, and 25,000l. on loan. Opened 9th October, 1865. Leased to Great Western and South Western, which conjointly work the line, and pay 4,500l. a year rent, being equivalent to 4½ per cent. on the share and debenture capital, and this sum, after payment of the interest on debentures (25,000l. at 4½ per cent.) and expenses of management, is divided among the shareholders, ¼ per cent. is calculated to cover these expenses, so that a dividend of 4l. 7s. 6d. per cent. per annum has been, and will, in future, be paid, depending on renewing the debentures at 4½ per cent.

CAPITAL.—The receipts and payments on this account to 30th June, 1868, have been as under :—

Received.		Expended.	
Shares, 7,500 at 10l. each .... (Full authorised amount.)	£75,000	Parliamentary....................	£3,280
Debentures .... (Full parliamentary limit.)	25,000	Land and compensation, works, engineering, and law	96,120
		Direction, secretary, and office expenses........................	600
	£100,000		£100,000

Meetings in February or March, and August or September.

No. of Directors.—Maximum, 5; minimum, 4; quorum, 3. *Qualification,* 250l.

DIRECTORS:

Chairman—JOHN REMINGTON MILLS, Esq., Kingswood Lodge, Tunbridge Wells.
Deputy-Chairman—A. T. P. BARLOW, Esq., Taplow, Maidenhead, Berks.

Capt. J. W. B. Browne, Weymouth. | John Stewart, Esq., 4, Bank Buildings, Lothbury, E.C.

OFFICERS.—Sec., William Fraser, 26, Great George Street, Westminster, S.W.; Engs., John Fowler, 2, Queen's Place, Westminster, and R. J. Ward, 11, Great Queen Street, Westminster, S.W.; Auditors, J. W. Weldon, 1, St. James's Square, S.W., and Robert Fletcher, 2, Moorgate Street, E.C.; Solicitors, Cope, Rose, and Pearson, 26, Great George Street, Westminster, S.W.

Offices—26, Great George Street, Westminster, S.W.

441.—WHITBY, REDCAR, AND MIDDLESBOROUGH UNION.

Incorporated by 29 and 30 Vic., cap. 195 (16th July, 1866), to construct a line in the North Riding of York, from the Whitby branch of the North Eastern to the Cleveland. Length, 16 miles. Capital, 250,000l. in 10l. shares, and 83,300l. on loan. Arrangements with North Eastern.

No. of Directors—7; minimum, 4, quorum, 3. *Qualification,* 300l.

DIRECTORS:

Marquis of Normanby, Palace Hotel, S.W. | John Henry Dillon, Esq., 5K, Albany,
Charles Mark Palmer, Esq. | Piccadilly, W.

442.—WHITEHAVEN, CLEATOR, AND EGREMONT.

Incorporated by 17 and 18 Vic., cap. 64 (June 16th, 1854). Length of main line, 4½ miles, and of branch, 2 miles. Opened for goods on 11th January; for passengers on the 1st July, 1867, 6½ miles.

By 20 Vic., cap. 3 (21st March, 1857), the company was authorised to raise new capital to the extent of 25,000l.

By 24 Vic., cap. 62 (7th June, 1861), the company was authorised to widen and enlarge the railway and works, and to construct an extension from Frizington to Lamplugh. Length, 3½ miles. New capital, 45,000l. in 6l. ordinary shares, and 15,400l. on loan. Opened for minerals in November, 1862, and for passengers, 12th February, 1864.

By 26 Vic., cap. 64 (8th June, 1863), the company was authorised to construct an extension from Lamplugh to join the Cockermouth and Workington, and make some deviation on the Frizington branch. New capital, 75,000l., at 5l. per cent., and 20,000l. on loan.

By 28 Vic., cap. 86 (19th June, 1865), the company was authorised to construct a line from Cleator to Briggrigg Moor, and other small branches. Length, 1¼ mile. New capital, 15,000l. in shares, and 4,600l. on loan. Productive, 20 miles.

By 29 and 30 Vic., cap. 132 (28th June, 1866), the Whitehaven Cleator and Egremont, jointly with the Whitehaven and Furness, were authorised to construct a line from Egremont to Sellafield. Length, 4¾ miles. Capital, in equal proportions, 66,000l. in shares, and 22,000l. on loan. Works in progress.

REVENUE.—The receipts for the half-year ending 31st December were 22,246l., and the expenditure, 8,420l., leaving a balance of 14,826l. This amount, with 143l. from previous half-year, after payment of interest on unsettled land claims, interest on mortgages, and other preferential charges, left 12,389l. for division amongst the proprietors, at the rate of 10 per cent. per annum (less income-tax) on the consolidated stock, and on the amount paid up to the 31st December, 1867, and on the 10l. (C) shares. Out of the balance remaining (727l.), the directors placed 500l. to credit of reserve fund, and carried forward 227l. to next half-year's account.

The receipts for the June half-year were 24,426*l.*, as against 21,236*l.*, and the expenditure, 9,722*l.*, as compared with 8,625*l.* The increased expenditure had been caused principally by relaying portions of the old line. After deductions for preference charges, 12,191*l.* was available for dividend, of 10 per cent.

CAPITAL.—The statement of this account to 30th June, 1868, furnished the subjoined particulars :—

Consolidaded stock £195,000	
New 10*l.* shares (C)	41,595
Preference shares...	14,611
Ditto (1867) ....;.	3,291
Loans on mortgage	84,600=£339,098
Balance	5,503

Expenditure..£344,601	

No. of Directors—12 ; minimum, 6 ; quorum, 4. *Qualification,* 500*l.* stock.

DIRECTORS :

Chairman—*ANTHONY BENN STEWARD, Esq., Newton Manor, Gosforth, near Whitehaven.

8 The Earl of Lonsdale, Whitehaven Castle, and 14, Carlton House Terrace, S.W.
9 George Head Head, Esq., Rickerby House, Carlisle.
10 Wm. Barwick Clarke, Esq., Barwickstead, Beckermet, near Whitehaven.
11 James Lumb, Esq., Homewood, near Whitehaven.
1 Henry Jefferson, Esq., Springfield, near Whitehaven.

2 Samuel Lindow, Esq., Ingwell, near Whitehaven.
3 Sir Robert Brisco, Bart., Low Mill House, Egremont, and Crofton Hall, Wigton.
5*James Dees, Esq., Floraville, Whitehaven.
6*John Stirling, Esq., Bridekirk, near Cockermouth.
7*John Lindow, Esq., Eden Hall, Cleator.
12 Charles Fisher, Esq., Distington Hall, Whitehaven.

* Re-elected 30th August, 1866. Rotate according to C.C.C. Act.

OFFICERS.—Sec. and Gen. Man., Thomas S. Dodgson ; Traffic Man., John Russell ; Auditors, Edward Jobling and James Lainton ; Solicitor, John Musgrave.

Offices—Lowther Street, Whitehaven.

443.—WILTS AND GLOUCESTERSHIRE.

Incorporated by 27 and 28 Vic., cap. 222 (25th July, 1864), to construct a line from Christian Malford to Nailsworth. Length, 23 miles. Mixed gauge. Capital, 243,000*l.* in 10*l.* shares, and 81,000*l.* on loan. Traffic arrangements with Midland. Works in abeyance.

By 30 Vic., cap. 57 (31st May, 1867), an extension of time for completion of works (till 25th July, 1872), was obtained. Shares to be divided into deferred and preferred.

It was reported in 1866 that Captain Galton, as arbitrator, had decided that the Midland, under its agreement with the Great Western, could not be permitted to work the Wilts and Gloucestershire.

An application, however, is to be made during the present session, for an Act which shall contain such a declaration of the meaning and effect of a clause in the Act of 1864, as may enable the Great Western or the Midland to work the line or any portion of it when made, if they shall be so disposed.

CAPITAL.—The receipts on calls have been 13,674*l.*, while the expenditure has left a balance at bankers of 2,244*l.*

Meetings in February and August.

No. of Directors—9 ; minimum, 5 ; quorum, 3. *Qualification,* 500*l.*

DIRECTORS :

Chairman—SAMUEL S. MARLING, Esq., M.P., Stanley Park, Stroud.

Deputy-Chairman—The Right Hon. T. H. S. SOTHERON ESTCOURT, Estcourt House, Tetbury.

Samuel B. Brooke, Esq., Cowbridge House, Malmesbury.
Robert Stayner Holford, Esq., M.P., Weston-birt, Tetbury, and Dorchester House, Park Lane, W.

William Capel, Esq., The Grove, Stroud.
Edwin Cook, Esq., Tetbury.
W. J. Stanton, Esq., The Thrupp, Stroud.
George Thomas, Esq., Lasborough, Wootton-under-Edge.

OFFICERS.—Sec., Charles F. Hart ; Eng., R. J. Ward, 11, Great Queen Street, Westminster, S.W. ; Solicitors, Helps and Son, 37, Great George Street, Westminster, S.W., and Pauls and Rogers, Tetbury.

Offices—Devizes, Wilts.

444.—WILTSHIRE.

Incorporated by 28 and 29 Vic., cap. 318 (5th July, 1865), to construct a line from the South Western, at Idmiston, in Wiltshire, to Pewsey, on the Berks and Hants. Length, 47¾ miles. Capital, 240,000l. in shares, and 80,000l. on loan. Arrangements with South Western and Midland.

No. of Directors—9; minimum, 7; quorum, 3. *Qualification,* 500l.

DIRECTORS:

Sir Edmund Antrobus, Bart.
Edmund Antrobus, Esq., M.P., 11, Grosvenor Crescent, Belgrave Square, S.W.
Henry Danby Seymour, Esq., Knoyle, Wilts.

Sir M. E. H. Beach, Bart., M.P., 33, Eaton Place, S.W.
William W. B. Beach, Esq., M.P., 33, Mansfield Street, W.
Thomas Pain, Esq., 22, Great George Street, Westminster, S.W.

445.—WINCHCOMB AND MIDLAND.

Incorporated by 29 and 30 Vic., cap. 196 (16th July, 1866), to construct a line from near Beckford, on the Ashchurch and Evesham, to Winchcomb. Length, 5¾ miles. Capital, 42,000l. in 10l. shares, and 14,000l. on loan. Arrangements with Midland, which may subscribe 10,000l.

The first meeting of shareholders was held on 16th January, 1866, the report of the directors stated that more than one-third of the gross estimated cost of the undertaking had already been subscribed in the locality, and that several tenders were under consideration, but none would be accepted, pending the conclusion of working arrangements with the Midland.

No. of Directors—5; minimun, 3; quorum, 3 and 2. *Qualification,* 500l.

DIRECTORS:

Chairman—JOHN COUCHER DENT, Esq., Sudeley Castle.
William Smith, Esq., Winchcomb.
John James Sexty, Esq., Winchcomb.

William Gates Adlard, Esq., Postlip.
William Montague Baillie, Esq., Bristol.

OFFICERS.—Eng., Kinnaird B. Edwards, Westminster, S.W.; Solicitors, Edwards, Webb, and Co., 8, Delahay Street, Westminster, S.W., and Henry Plumbe, Winchcomb.

446.—WITNEY.

Incorporated by 22 and 23 Vic., cap. 46 (1st August, 1859), to construct a line from the Oxford Worcester and Wolverhampton, at Yarnton, to the town of Witney. Capital, 50,000l. in 10l. shares; loans, 16,000l. Opened November 20th, 1861.

By 24 Vic., cap. 22 (17th May, 1861), the company was authorised to cancel shares and to re-issue others at 5 per cent.; and, at a special meeting on 8th June, 1861, 1,200 preference shares at 5 per cent. in perpetuity, were created, representing 12,000l. of capital, in lieu of unissued ordinary shares. Agreement in respect to working, maintenance, management, &c., with Great Western.

By 27 Vic., cap. 101 (23rd June, 1864) the company was authorised to raise additional capital, to the extent of 30,000l. in shares, and 10,000l. on loan.

No. of Directors—6; minimum, 6; quorum, 3. *Qualification,* 200l. or 20 shares.

DIRECTORS:

Chairman—WALTER STRICKLAND, Esq., Cokethorpe Park, Witney.

Deputy-Chairman—CHARLES LOCOCK WEBB, Esq., Barrister-at-Law,
5, New Square, Lincoln's Inn, W.C.

Henry Akers, Esq., Black Bourton, near Faringdon.
Joseph Druce, Esq., Eynsham, Oxon.

Charles Early, Esq., Witney.
Joseph Thompson, Esq., 5, St. Stephen's Square, Westbourne Park, W.

OFFICERS.—Sec., George Broom, Jun., 80, Coleman Street, E.C.; Eng., Charles Douglas Fox, 8, New Street, Spring Gardens, S.W.; Solicitors, Marriott, Jordan, and Cooper, 52, Parliament Street, S.W.; Bankers, The Union Bank of London (Temple Bar Branch) E.C., and Clinch and Sons, Witney; Auditors, James Clinch, Banker, Witney, and Charles Titian Hawkins, Accountant, Oxford.
Offices—80, Coleman Street, E C.

447.—WIVENHOE AND BRIGHTLINGSEA.

Incorporated by 24 and 25 Vic., cap. 119 (11th July, 1861), to construct a line from Wivenhoe, on the Tendring Hundred, to Brightlingsea, in the county of Essex. Length, 5 miles. Capital, 25,000l. in 10l. shares; loans, 8,000l. Great Eastern subscribes 8,500l., and works the line.

By 29 and 30 Vic., cap. 213 (16th July, 1866), the company obtained power to raise additional capital to the extent of 15,000l. in shares (deferred and preferred), and 5,000l. on loan. Also to transfer the undertaking to the Great Eastern.

It was reported in February and August that no account had been delivered by the Tendring Hundred of the amount of toll owing by them, and consequently the balance could not be included in the statement of accounts. The revenue account for the half-year ending December 31st showed that the Great Eastern had paid 182*l.* for traffic, the receipts being 251*l.* After paying 177*l.* to debenture-holders, there remained 9*l.* The August report stated that the improvement in traffic was equal to about 15 per cent. After payment of interest on debentures and sundry expenses, the balance in hand amounted to 110*l.*

CAPITAL.—The receipts to 30th June, 1868, were 48,467*l.*, all of which had been expended except 7*l.*

No. of Directors—6; minimum, 3; quorum, 3. *Qualification*, 500*l.*

DIRECTORS:

* Chairman—RICHARD MOXON, Esq., J.P., Pontefract.

C. H. Turner, Esq., J.P., Litchurch, Derby.
James Edward Robinson, Esq., Pontefract.

Richard Young, Esq., Wisbeach.
*Edward Westwood, Esq., Old Swinford, Stourbridge.

* Retire in 1869; eligible for re-election.

OFFICERS.—Sec., H. Rowbotham, Pontefract; Auditors, William Sherlcliff and R. W. Nicholson, Pontefract; Solicitor, G. Bradley, Castleford.

448.—WOLVERHAMPTON AND WALSALL.

Incorporated by 28 and 29 Vic., cap. 181 (29th June, 1865), to construct a line between these places. Length, 6 miles. Capital, 120,000*l.* in shares, and 40,000*l.* on loan.

By 29 and 30 Vic., cap. 276 (23rd July, 1866), the company was authorised to make a deviation from the original line, and to construct a branch in Wolverhampton. Length, ¾ of a mile. Capital, 25,000*l.* in shares, and 8,300*l.* on loan. Arrangements with London and North Western and Great Western.

By 30 and 31 Vic., cap. 180 (12th August, 1867), the company was authorised to make a deviation, and an extension of time till 12th August, 1870, was obtained.

By 31 and 32 Vic., cap. 196 (13th July, 1868), to construct new roads, so as to avoid level crossings, and to raise new capital to the extent of 50,000*l.* in shares, and 16,600*l.* on loan. The London and North Western to subscribe 2,000*l.*, to aid in construction of the new road at Walsall.

No. of Directors—14; minimum, 7; quorum, 3. *Qualification*, 500*l.*

DIRECTORS:

Chairman—The Right Hon. The EARL OF LICHFIELD, Shugborough, Stafford.

Deputy-Chairman—EDWIN DIXON, Esq., Wolverhampton.

Thomas Barker, Esq., The Birches, near Codsall.
Moses Ironmonger, Esq., Graiseley, Wolverhampton.
Samuel Loveridge, Esq., Chapel Ash, Wolverhampton.
Frederick Charles Perry, Esq., Dunston, near Stafford.
James Tyldesley, Esq., Willenhall.

George Lees Underhill, Esq., New Bridge, Wolverhampton.
Benjamin Urwick, Esq., Willenhall.
Sampson Lloyd Foster, Esq., Old Park Hall, near Walsall.
Charles Frederick Clark, Esq., Perton Grove, near Wolverhampton.
Matthew Lyon, Esq., Leamington.
O. L. Stephen, Esq., Bardon Hall, Leicester.

OFFICERS.—Joint Secs., H. Underhill and H. H. Fowler; Eng., John Addison; Solicitors, Baxter, Rose, Norton, and Co., 6, Victoria Street, S.W., H. and J. E. Underhill, and Corser and Fowler, Wolverhampton.

Offices—57, Darlington Street, Wolverhampton.

449.—WORCESTER, BROMYARD, AND LEOMINSTER.

Incorporated by 24 and 25 Vic., cap. 213 (11th August, 1861), to construct a line from the West Midland, at Bransford Bridge, to the Shrewsbury and Hereford, at Leominster. Length, 24½ miles. Capital, 200,000*l.* in 10*l.* shares; loans, 66,500*l.* Works in abeyance.

By 27 and 28 Vic., cap. 171 (14th July, 1864), the company obtained power to purchase additional land, with an extension of time for two years for completion of works.

By 29 and 30 Vic., cap. 138 (28th June, 1866), the company obtained an extension of time for completion of works till 28th June, 1869. Also to issue 50,000*l.* in preference shares.

The Great Western is to work the line for 52½ per cent.: and the West Midland section, which subscribed 50,000*l.* to the undertaking, is to allow a rebate sufficient to pay interest and other fixed charges, in event of 47½ per cent. not being sufficient for that purpose.

It was reported in September that the Great Western board had given permission to issue 40,000*l.* debenture bonds or stock to pay off the company's liabilities, and to complete the line to Suckley Road, provided some slight modifications were made in the working agreement. The directors were therefore in hopes that the several creditors who had obtained judgments, or who were sueing the company, would have come to terms of arrangement proposed by the directors and partially accepted by them, but, unfortunately, executions were issued, and the property of the company seized and sold. Writs of *eligit* were also issued, and the sheriffs of Worcestershire and Hereford-shire had delivered over the lands purchased by the company for the purpose of their railway to one of their creditors. The effect of those proceedings has been to delay, if not entirely to prevent, the resuscitation of the undertaking, and the only chance now left would be for the creditors to come to an arrangement among themselves and join the board in raising funds to complete the line to Suckley Road. If this were done it is believed that all the creditors might eventually be paid in full, with interest.

CAPITAL.—The expenditure on this account to 30th June amounted to 125,492*l*., including 74*l*. in hands of secretary. The receipts were stated as follow :—

On shares	£107,116
Bonds—acknowledgment of debt....................................	10,966
Loan account, balance of	13
Registration fees..	4
Interest	1,746
Sundry accounts owing...	179
Bankers...	5,466 =£125,492

Meetings in March and September.

No. of Directors—12 ; minimum, 5 ; quorum, 3. *Qualification,* 500*l.*

DIRECTORS;

Chairman—JOHN WHEELEY LEA, Esq., Worcester.

Deputy-Chairman—EDWARD BICKERTON EVANS, Esq., Whitbourne Hall, near Worcester.

Thomas Rowley Hill, Esq., Worcester.
Josiah Stallard, Esq., Worcester.
William Fenton, Esq., Beaumonds, near Rochdale.
Alexander Clunes Sherriff, Esq., M.P., Perdiswell Hall, Worcester, and 10, Dean's Yard, Westminster, S.W.

F. L. Bodenham, Esq., Hereford.
John Freeman, Esq., Gaines, Worcester-shire.
Richard Green Price, Esq., M.P., Norton Manor, Presteign, and 3, Suffolk Place, S.W.

OFFICERS.—Sec., W. T. Adcock, Worcester ; Engs., W. B. Lewis, Westminster, S.W., and E. Wilson, Worcester, and 9, Dean's Yard, Westminster, S.W.; Solicitors, Charles Pidcock and Son, Worcester ; Auditors, Joseph Hall and Richard West, Worcester.

Offices—Worcester.

450.—WORCESTER, DEAN FOREST, AND MONMOUTH.

Incorporated by 26 and 27 Vic., cap. 185 (21st July, 1863), to construct a line from Great Malvern, on the Great West-rn, through the Forest of Dean to the Coleford Monmouth Usk and Pontypool, at Monmouth. Length, 37 miles. Capital, 450,000*l.* in 10*l.* shares ; loans, 150,000*l.*

By 27 and 28 Vic., cap. 295 (29th July, 1864), the company was authorised to construct an extension from Newent to Gloucester. Length, 8¼ miles. Capital, 150,000*l.* in shares, and 50,000*l.* loan. Arrangements with Great Western.

By 28 and 29 Vic., cap. 319 (5th July, 1865), the company was authorised to make several deviations on the Gloucester Extension, and to raise new capital to the extent of 120,000*l.* in shares, and 40,000*l.* on loan.

No. of Directors—12 ; minimum, 5 ; quorum, 3. *Qualification,* 500*l.*

DIRECTORS :

Chairman—ABRAHAM DARBY, Esq., Ebbw Vale, Monmouth.

Deputy-Chairman—JOSEPH ROBINSON, Esq., Berkhampstead, and 7, Laurence Pountney Hill, E.C.

William Thompson Adcock, Esq., Wor-cester.
Thomas Brown, Esq., Hardwick House, Chepstow.
Frederick Levick, Esq., Newport, Mon-mouthshire.
Peter Hardy, Esq., Worcester.
William Lewis, Esq., The Mount, Rain-bow Hill, Worcester.

J. D. Perrins, Esq., Lansdown Crescent, Worcester.
G. R. G. Relph, Esq., Usk.
Richard Wood, Esq., Rainbow Hill, Wor-cester.
O. A. Wyatt, Esq., TroyHouse, Monmouth.
Alexander Clunes Sherriff, Esq., M.P., Perdiswell Hall, Worcester, and 10, Dean's Yard, Westminster, S.W.

OFFICERS.—Sec., F. Higgins ; Eng., E. Wilson, Worcester, and 9, Dean's Yard, Westminster, S.W.; Solicitors, T. Holland, Fern Lodge, Malvern Link, and Messrs. Burchell, 5, Broad Sanctuary, Westminster, S.W.

Offices—Worcester.

451.—WORKINGTON.

Authorised by 24 and 25 Vic., cap. 83 (28th June. 1861). Promoter, the Earl of Lons-dale. The works comprise a dock or tidal basin at Workington, with a railway, 61 chains in length, to join the Whitehaven Junction, with which, and Cockermouth and Work-ington, arrangements may be made. Capital for dock, 21,000*l.*; for railway, 3,000*l.*, borrowing powers, 8,000*l.*

452.—WREXHAM AND MINERA.

Incorporated by 24 Vic., cap. 32 (17th May, 1861), to construct a line from the Wrexham to the Minera Station of the Shrewsbury and Chester. Length, 3 miles 7 chains. Capital, 36,000*l.*, in 10*l.* shares; loans, 12,000*l.* Opened for minerals, 22nd May, 1862. Arrangements with Great Western.

By 28 and 29 Vic., cap. 260 (5th July, 1865), the company was authorised to construct two short lines connected with the Mold and Denbigh. Length, 4 miles. Capital, 60,000*l.* in shares, and 20,000*l.* on loan.

By 29 Vic., cap. 87 (11th June, 1866), the line is leased jointly to the London and North Western and the Great Western.

No. of Directors—5; minimum, 3; quorum, 3 and 2.   *Qualification,* 500*l.*

DIRECTORS:

Chairman—WILLIAM HENRY DARBY, Esq., Brymbo Works, Wrexham.

William Low, Esq., Fron, Wrexham.
John Williams, Esq., Chester.

John Robertson, Esq., Llangollen.
Capt. Bulkeley, Clewer Lodge, Windsor.

OFFICERS.—Sec., John Jones, Oswestry; Eng., Henry Robertson, Shrewsbury; Auditors, Edward Tench, Wrexham, and John Evans, Oswestry; Solicitors, Longueville, Williams, Jones, and Williams, Oswestry.

Offices—Upper Brook Street, Oswestry.

453.—WREXHAM, MOLD, AND CONNAH'S QUAY JUNCTION.

Incorporated by 25 and 26 Vic., cap. 221 (7th August, 1862), to construct a line from Wrexham to Buckley, with certain branches. Length, 12½ miles. Capital, 150,000*l.* in 10*l.* shares, and 50,000*l.* on loan. Mutual facilities with London and North Western, Great Western, Buckley, and Wrexham and Minera. Open from Wrexham to Buckley.

By 27 and 28 Vic., cap. 234 (25th July, 1864), the company obtained power to construct an extension to Whitchurch and Brymbo. Length, 20 miles. Capital, 200,000*l.* in shares, and 66,600*l.* on loan.

By 28 and 29 Vic., cap. 176 (29th June, 1865), the company was authorised to construct an extension to Farndon, in the Dee Valley. Length, 8 miles. Capital, 90,000*l.* in shares, and 30,000*l.* on loan.

By 28 and 29 Vic., cap. 261 (5th July, 1865). the company was authorised to construct an extension to Connah's Quay. Length, 18 miles. Capital, 100,000*l.* in shares, and 30,000*l.* on loan.

By 29 Vic., cap. 38 (18th May, 1866), the company was authorised to raise additional capital to the extent of 180,000*l.* in shares, deferred and preferred, with 60,000*l.* on loan.

By 29 and 30 Vic., cap. 358 (10th August, 1866). the company was authorised to extend the line from Hawarden to Buckley. Length, 3¼ miles. Capital, 45,000*l.* in shares, and 15,000*l.* on loan.

By 29 and 30 Vic., cap. 359 (10th August, 1866), the company was authorised to construct an extension to Connah's Quay. Length, 7¼ miles. And also to make a deviation in the authorised route. Capital, 100,000*l.* in shares, and 33,300*l.* on loan.

By 30 and 31 Vic.. cap. 200 (15th August, 1867), the company obtained an extension of time for purchase of land, and for completion of the line to Whitchurch till 1870.

No. of Directors—9; minimum, 5; quorum, 3.   *Qualification,* 500*l.*

DIRECTORS :

Chairman—THOMAS BARNES, Esq., The Quinta, Chirk, Denbighshire.

Deputy-Chairman—CHARLES HUGHES, Esq., Brynhyfryd, Wrexham.

Richard Kyrke Penson, Esq., Dinham House, Ludlow.
James Richardson Barnes, Esq., Brookside, Chirk, Denbighshire.
F. A. Fynney, Esq., 14, Queen's Chambers, Manchester.

John Everitt, Esq., 49, Lombard Street, E.C.
George Lewis, Esq., The Grange, Frankton, near Oswestry.

OFFICERS.—Sec. and Gen. Man., John Broughton, Railway Station, Wrexham; Consulting Eng., Geo. Owen, Oswestry; Auditors, William Overton and John Allmand; Bankers, The North and South Wales Bank, Wrexham and Mold, and the London and South Western Bank, 27, Regent Street, S.W.

Offices—Railway Station, Wrexham.

454.—WYCOMBE.

Incorporated by Act 9 and 10 Vic., cap. 236 (26th July, 1847), for a line from Great Western, at Maidenhead, to High Wycombe. Revised by 15 and 16 Vic., cap. 147 (30th June, 1852). Capital, 102,600*l.*; loans, 33,600*l.* Leased to Great Western at an annual rent of 3,600*l.* Length, 10 miles, broad gauge.

By 20 and 21 Vic., cap. 158 (17th August, 1857), the company was authorised to extend the line to Prince's Risborough and to Thane, 15 miles. Opened 1st August, 1862. New capital, 60,000*l.* in shares ; and 20,000*l.* on loan. The receipts of extension to be applied in the first instance in payment of interest on 40,000*l.* of debentures, and the remainder to be divided in the following proportions, namely, 60 per cent. to Great Western for working expenses, and 40 per cent. to Wycombe. The gross receipts of present Wycombe, in excess of 7,200*l.* per annum, to be appropriated to make up 4 per cent. on whole share capital (both original and extension) of Wycombe. The dividends at present are equal to 3½ per cent.

By 24 and 25 Vic., cap. 87 (28th June, 1861), the company was authorised to construct extension to Aylesbury and to Oxford. Length, 20 miles. Capital, 260,000*l.* in shares at 5 per cent., and 86,000*l.* on loan. Arrangements with Great Western, which subscribes 100,000*l.* Opened to Oxford, 15 miles, October 25th, 1864.

By 25 Vic., cap. 5 (16th May, 1862), the capital was further arranged by re-issue of cancelled shares, and provision made that no dividend should be declared on either of the extensions until each had been opened six months.

By 28 and 29 Vic., cap. 299 (5th July, 1865), the Wycombe was authorised to be transferred to the Great Western on such terms as might be agreed upon.

By 29 and 30 Vic., cap. 254 (23rd July, 1866), the line was absorbed in the Great Western system, and will in future be dealt with as one of its branches.

DIRECTORS:

Chairman—F. R. WARD, Esq., 1, Gray's Inn Square, W.C.

Deputy-Chairman—A. T. PRATT BARLOW, Esq., Taplow, Maidenhead, Berks.

Captain Bulkeley, Clewer Lodge, Windsor. | Randolph Crewe, Esq., High Wycombe,
Charles Venables, Esq., Bath. | Bucks.
William Rose, Esq., High Wycombe, Bucks. |

OFFICERS.—Sec., William Henry Wilson, 6, Victoria Street, Westminster, S.W.; Eng., R. J. Ward, 6, Victoria Street, Westminster, S.W.; Solicitors, Pinniger, Rose, and Wilkinson, 26, Great George Street, Westminster, S.W.; Bankers, Glyn, Mills, and Co., 67, Lombard Street, E.C.; The Union Bank of London (Temple Bar Branch), 13, Fleet Street, E.C.; R. and T. Wheeler, High Wycombe, Bucks ; Bucks and Oxon Union Bank, Thame, Oxon ; London and County Bank, Thame, Oxon.

Offices—6, Victoria Street, Westminster, S.W.

455.—WYE VALLEY.

Incorporated by 29 and 30 Vic., cap. 357 (10th August, 1866), to construct railways from the South Wales to the Coleford Monmouth Usk and Pontypool, and to the South Wales and Great Western Direct. Length, 15 miles. Capital, 230,000*l.* in 20*l.* shares, and 76,600*l.* on loan. Arrangements with Great Western and South Wales and Great Western Direct.

No. of Directors—5 ; minimum, 3 ; quorum, 3 and 2. *Qualification*, 500*l.*

DIRECTORS:

Jasper Wilson Johns, Esq., Wolverton | James Murphy, Esq.
Park, Newbury, Hants. | Joseph Cary, Esq., 49, Pall Mall, S.W.
Osmond A. Wyatt, Esq., Troy House, | Capt. Robert O'Brien Jameson, 60, St.
Monmouth. | James's Street, Piccadilly, S.W.

II.—CONTINENTAL, &c.

In order to render this division of the Work more perfect, it is necessary that Officers should forward to the publishers in England (or to the care of Mr. Middleton, 94, Montagne de la Cour, Brussels, their agent for "Guides," &c.), copies of official documents, reports, &c.

Latest information as to miles opened, &c., will be found in each current number of "BRADSHAW'S CONTINENTAL GUIDE."

456.—ANTWERP AND ROTTERDAM.

Société Anonyme, with limited liability.   Capital, 500,000*l.* in 10*l.* shares ; bonds, 80,000*l.* Instituted under convention with Holland and Belgium, 4th August, 1852. Trunk line, 37¼ miles ; branch to Breda, 14¼ miles ; and including the space traversed by steam boats the length of working about 73¾ miles English.

LIERRE AND TURNHOUT.—The Antwerp and Rotterdam lease the Lierre and Turnhout, on the terms of receiving from the Government, and handing over to the Lierre and Turnhout shareholders, the 4 per cent. guaranteed to the latter, in case of deficiency in the traffic, and of working the Turnhout line for a per centage of 65 per cent. for the first two years, 60 per cent. for the second two years, and 50 per cent. for the remainder of the concession, of the gross receipts of the Turnhout, the Antwerp and Rotterdam allowing, in addition, an annual sum of 20,000*fr.*, equal to 5 per cent. on the cost of rolling stock provided by the Turnhout.

The Antwerp and Rotterdam, in conjunction with the East Belgian and the Sambre and Meuse, is now worked under the title of the Great Central Belgian   The network thus constituted comprises 310 miles, but the three companies thus united still retain independent financial existencies.   The terms under which the traffic is being worked in common are substantially as follow : The Antwerp and Rotterdam is to deduct from the receipts annually the sum of 41,480*l.* the amount of profits in 1863, including certain guarantees accorded by the Belgian Government.   On the expiration of these guarantees this preliminary deduction is to be reduced to 35,480*l.*   The remainder of the receipts to be divided to the extent of 177,120*l.* in the following proportions :—

> 1866 : East Belgian, 0·478 ; Antwerp and Rotterdam, 0·522.
> 1867 : East Belgian, 0·473 ; Antwerp and Rotterdam, 0·527.
> 1868 : East Belgian, 0·468 ; Antwerp and Rotterdam, 0·532.
> 1869 : East Belgian, 0·464 ; Antwerp and Rotterdam, 0·536.
> 1870 : East Belgian, 0·460 ; Antwerp and Rotterdam, 0·540.
> 1871 : East Belgian, 0·456 ; Antwerp and Rotterdam, 0·544.
> 1872 : East Belgian, 0·452 ; Antwerp and Rotterdam, 0·548.
> 1873 : East Belgian, 0·448 ; Antwerp and Rotterdam, 0·552.

In 1874 the share of the Antwerp and Rotterdam is to rise to 0·565, and will continue at that point until the concessions expire.   The surplus profits remaining after these arrangements have been carried out, are to be divided between the three companies, thus : Antwerp and Rotterdam, 0·467 ; East Belgian, 0·372 ; Sambre and Meuse, 0·161.

The net profit of the Antwerp for the year 1867 amounted to 37,645*l.*, and for the year 1866 to 32,107*l.*, showing an increase of 5,538*l.*   A dividend of 5*l.* 12*s.* per cent. left 3,120*l.* to the extraordinary redemption of bonds, 5,817*l.* to credit of reserve fund for renewal of rails and sleepers, and to create a reserve to meet advances which are to be made to the Aix-la-Chapelle to Masselt carrying to it 5,141*l.*

457.—BELGIAN EASTERN JUNCTION.

A line from Manage, a station on the Belgian State Railway from Bruxelles to Namur, to Wavre, on the Charleroi Louvain Railway.   Runs through the valley of the Dyle.   Length, 26½ miles.

The amended statutes approved the convention with the Government, confirmed by a royal decree, dated 16th August, 1862, constituting it a *Société Anonyme*.   The Govern-

ment guarantees to the company, during a period of fifty years, a minimum annua
interest according to the following basis :—

A.   So long as the annual gross receipts from the working do not exceed 375,000fr.
(15,000l.) the minimum is to be fixed at 187,500fr. (7,500l.) say 4 per cent. of a capital of
4,687,500fr. (187,500l.)

B.   When any annual increase of receipts above 375,000fr. (15,000l.) there shall be
a proportional reduction of the minimum, namely : of ¹0 per cent. of the amount of
increase if this be less than 1,000fr. (40l.) ; of $10\frac{125}{1000}$ per cent. if the amount be 1,000fr.
and does not exceed 2,000fr. (80l.) ; of $10\frac{250}{1000}$ per cent. if the amount be 2,000fr. (80l.)
and does not exceed 3,000fr. (120l.) ; of $10\frac{375}{1000}$ per cent. if the same be 3,000fr. (120l.)
and does not exceed 4,000fr. (160l.) ; and so on, the rate of the reduction of minimum
being increased by $\frac{125}{1000}$ for every 1,000fr. (40l.) of augmentation of the receipts.

The guarantee of minimum interest shall cease when the annual receipts exceed
725,000fr. (29,000l.)

This guarantee is specially hypothecated to the payment of the interest on the
debenture capital, and to provide a sinking fund to extinguish the debt in fifty years.

MANAGE PIETON.—The company have entered into an agreement with the Conces-
sionare for working this railway and its extensions, which are important feeders to the
Belgian Eastern Junction, during a period of ten years, but with the right to terminate
the agreement at the end of five years.

CAPITAL.—42,500 shares at 5l. each, 212,500l.; debentures 1852, 110,480l. ; debentures
1858, 78,720l. ; debentures, 1862, 39,780l.

The line is worked by the Société Générale d'Exploitation, for a fixed rent, which
resulted in the declaration of a dividend of 1s. per share for the year ending 31st.
December, 1867.

DIRECTORS :

Chairman—CHARLES WARING, Esq. (of the firm of Waring Brothers),
10, Victoria Chambers, Victoria Street, Westminster. S.W.

Deputy-Chairman—Mons. EDOUARD PERROT, Paris.

James Wheeler, Esq., 4, Victoria Street, Westminster, S.W.
Mons. Henri Davignon, Rue Royale, ex-térieure, Brussels.
Mons. Charles Gréban, Brussels.

William Waring, Esq. (of the firm of Waring Brothers), 10, Victoria Chambers, Victoria Street, Westminster, S.W.
Mons. Dumonceau de Bergendael, Baulers, near Nivelles.

OFFICERS.—Sec., L. L. Barnes, 10, Victoria Chambers, Victoria Street, Westminster, S.W. ; Directeur-Gérant, Mons. S. Gheude, Nivelles.

458.—BELGIAN GENERAL RAILWAYS WORKING.

This reorganised company is now working 337½ miles of line, divided, however, into
six groups, completely isolated from each other, viz., the West Flanders, the Gand,
Lokeren, and Selzaete, the Hainaut and Flanders, the Flénu and St. Ghislain, the Centre, and the Tamines, Landen, and Tirlemont. The isolation of the lines worked has
had the effect of reducing the receipts ; but in a few months this disadvantage will be
overcome by the opening of the following sections :—Ostend to Thouront, Nieuport to
Dixmude, Roulers to Ypres, Courtrai to Audenarde, St. Ghislain to the Flénu, Frameries
and Monns to Bonne Esperance, and Piéton to Laval, or altogether 71⅞ miles. The
company will also undertake as from 1st January, 1868, the working of the Manage
and Wavre and the Manage and Piéton, 31⅝ miles more, so that 441¼ miles of Belgian
line will be brought under one general administration, each of the companies whose
undertakings are worked retaining, however, an independent financial existence.

459.—BELGIUM.

The miles in operation amount to 1,073, of which 346 have been constructed
and worked by the Government, 117½ constructed by companies but worked by
Government, 601¾ miles constructed and worked by companies, and 6¼ miles constructed
by the Government, but worked by company. The lines, constructed by companies, are
as under :—

Lierre and Turnhout.
Antwerp and Rotterdam.
Antwerp and Gand.
Brussels and Gand by Alost.
Audenaerde and Lupinte.
West Flanders.
Tournay and Jurbise.
Lichtervelde and Furnes.
L'Ath and Lokeren.
Mons and Hautmont.
Mons and Manage.

Erquelines and Ecaussines.
Erquelines and Charleroi.
Sambre and Meuse.
Mariembourge and Momignies.
East Belgian.
Belgian Eastern Junction.
St. Frond-von-Maestricht.
Pepinster and Spa.
Namur and Liége.
Great Luxembourg.

Of these lines the State now works the Gand and Brussels, L'Ath and Lokeren, the Mons and Manage, and the Tournay and Jurbise. The lines constructed by the State comprise the following:—

Brussels and Malines.	Gand and Ostend.
Malines and Antwerp.	Gand and Courtrai.
Contich and Lierre.	Courtrai and Tournay with line from
Malines and Louvain.	Mouscron to French Frontier.
Louvain and Tirlemont.	Dendre and Waes.
Tirlemont and Waremme.	Brussels and Tubize.
Waremme and Ans.	Tubize and Soignies.
Ans and Meuse.	Soignies and Monf.
Liége and Frontier.	Mons and Quiévrain.
Malines and Gand.	Braine-le-Comte and Namur.

In 1861 the average return realised upon the capital expended was 5·51 per cent, while in 1866 the corresponding rate of profit had sunk to 5·05 per cent., showing a decline of 0·46 per cent. In 1861 the length of line worked in Belgium was 1,093½ miles ; in 1866, 1,703¾ miles. In 1861 the capital expended was 19,601,314l. : in 1866 it had increased to 29,755,399l., so that in the five years ending 1866 inclusive, Belgium appears to have expended no less than 10,154,085l. in the work of additional construction. The working expenses rose in 1867 to 60·73 per cent. of the receipts, as compared with 57·29 in 1866, and 51·09 in 1865. The share of the net receipts paid over to the miscellaneous companies whose lines are worked in connection with the system has also been increasing of late. The result is that the net profit derived by the Belgian Treasury from the lines declined in 1867 to 500,847l., while in 1866 it was 534,009l., and in 1865, 655,251l. The return realised on the capital employed by the Government declined in consequence to 4·80 per cent. in 1867, as compared with 5·33 in 1866, and 6·88 in 1865.

GREAT CENTRAL.—The receipts from 1st January to the end of November, 1868, amounted to 422,467l., and for the corresponding period of 1867, to 355,647l., showing an increase of 66,820l., or 18·8 per cent.

460.—BRANCH RAILWAYS OF FRANCE.

Société Anonyme.—Capital, 1,000,000l. sterling: dividend in shares "to bearer" 4l. each. Interest at 5l. per cent. during construction.

The company has obtained the concession of the line Auteuil and St. Cloud, through the Champs Élysées : the line from Rennes to the sea (37 miles), passing through Benon, Aubin, Sene, Tremblay, Antrain, Pontorson, and Moïdry.

DIRECTORS:

C. Bart, ex-Préfet, Paris.	Marquis de St. Paul, Paris.
Count d'Avigdor, Director of the Sardinian Railways, Paris.	Count Luillier d'Orcières, Paris.
	— Collignon, Banker, Paris.
Marquis de Lefressange, Paris.	— Collasson, Iron Manufacturer, Paris.
Viscount Mazenod, Paris.	Sir Thomas H. Roberts, Bart., London.
J. Boncaruc, Paris.	Major Gregory Way, London.
De Moncuit, Mayor of Rennes.	

Managing Director—A. LAURENT de BLOIS.
Bankers—In Paris, the Bank of France.

461.—CHARENTES.

The concessions acccorded by a new convention, coupled with those previously granted, may be said to constitute a seventh great French network, which, although less considerably than others, does not the less possess a real importance. The first concession of the Charentes comprised a line from Napoleon-Vendée to Rochefort and from Rochefort to Angoulême, with a branch from St. Jean d'Angely to Coutras. The system was thus purely and simply confined to the two Charentes ; but the new convention extends the line from Rochefort and La Rochelle as far as Limoges and adds a branch from St. Jean d'Angely to Niort, with two ramifications to Marennes and Blaye, and another branch to Nontron. The domain of the Charentes has thus been extended over the departments of the Vendée, the Deux-Sèvres, the Vienne, and the Gironde. These lines will not be without value, those from Limoges to La Rochelle uniting the centre of France to the western parts, while that from Coutras to Napoleon-Vendée constitutes the greatest part of a direct route from Bordeaux to Nantes, the line from Coutras and Libourne to Niort being also the first section of a direct route from Bordeaux to Angers and Rouen. Further from the subventions accorded, the lines will be carried out at a comparatively moderate cost to it.

The Charantes, although it has been the subject of a convention with the State in 1868, is not placed under the *régime* created by the convention of 1858 and 1863, and confirmed by the conventions of 1868, as regards the six great companies. The position of these latter companies may be summed up in two striking points—a guarantee of an interest of 4·65 per cent. per annum on the capital employed for the new network, and a fixation of a reserved net revenue for the old network. The revenue of the shares is thus for a rather long period limited to the totals prescribed by the conventions, and can only increase when the new networks cover their annual charges, and when the State shall have been repaid the sums it may have advanced in fulfilment of its engagements as regards the guarantee of interest. The arrangements with the Charentes are completely different. The engagement of the State are confined to the payment of a subvention; and on the other hand, the company does not divide its lines into two networks, but has only one annual account, leaving to the shares all the net profit which may remain after the loan service has been provided for.

The subvention given by the State is adjusted so that the outlay to be made by the company upon its lines will not exceed 6,400*l.* per mile; and with an annual rough receipt of 960*l.* per mile per annum, it is calculated that the capital, shares and obligations alike, will be assured a return at the rate of 6 per cent. per annum. By this combination the guarantee is indirect but none the less real. During 1868, with 73¾ miles in operation, the company has been acquiring receipts at the rate of 1,100*l.* per mile per annum; and, even assuming working expenses at the rate of 65 per cent., the requisite net profit to assure the shares a return of 6 per cent. would appear to be secured. At present the company is only paying interest at the rate of 5 per cent. per annum upon its shares, but it is pushing forward its works with activity, and it is expected that it will have all its lines completed by 1871. The new lines are being carried out by obligations which are being placed at 12*l.* 12*s.* each; on these conditions, the company's loan capital only costs it 5½ per cent. per annum for interest and redemption.

462.—COPENHAGEN TRAMROAD.

This company purchased, as of 1st January, 1866, the undertaking of the Copenhagen Railway Company Limited (an English company), being a line from Fredericksberg, through the city of Copenhagen, to Vibenshuiss, a distance of about 5 miles, the whole of which has been completed and in operation.

The capital of the company is divided into 4,250 shares of 10*l.* fully paid up, the shares being issued either in name or to bearer. Of the shares 2,090 are A shares, bearing a preferential dividend of 5 per cent., and 2,160 B shares. When both classes of shares have received 5 per cent., the surplus, if any, is to be equally divided between the A and B shares, and after both classes shall have received a dividend of 5 per cent. for two consecutive years, all distinction between A and B shares shall thenceforward cease.

The directors are all resident in Copenhagen, viz.: Councillors of State, M. J. A. Bech and F. Eskildsen, Colonel C. Just, M. J. P. Nörgaard, and M. C. F. Tietjen.

Agents in England, Ashurst, Morris, and Co., 6, Old Jewry, E.C.

463.—DANUBE AND BLACK SEA.

Incorporated under the Limited Liability Act. A concession from the Imperial Ottoman Government, for 99 years from date of opening, in terms of which the company has deposited in the Turkish embassy, 6,000*l.* in Turkish bonds, which cost 5,415*l.* Capital, 400,000*l.* in shares, and 100,000*l.* in debentures. Length from Tchernavodo to Kustendjie, 40 miles. All public land given by the Turkish Government. Line opened 4th October, 1860.

REVENUE.—It was reported in February that the traffic, after a period of great depression, had begun to improve. The gross receipts for the half-year ending 31st May were 29,444*l.*, against 10,865*l.* last year, and 20,631*l.* in the best corresponding half year that the company had had—viz., that of 1866. Up to the end of June they were 34,843*l.*, against 11,616*l.* last year. and there was every prospect of a steady trade during the remainder of the year. Under those circumstances the Board hoped to be in a position to pay the 2 per cent. dividend which had been declared on the ordinary stock.

CAPITAL.—The first mortgage, which had been reduced from 35,000*l.*, at which it stood in 1865, to 19,500*l.*, fell due on 22nd November. It was desirable that it should be paid off, and for this purpose the remaining 8 per cent. mortgage bonds to a like amount should be taken up. The issue of 100,000*l.* 8 per cent. bonds would then be completed, and would be a first charge on the undertaking.

Meetings in February and August.

DIRECTORS:

Deputy-Chairman—W. P. PRICE, Esq., M.P., Tibberton Court, Gloucester, and 105, Pall Mall, S.W.

William Johnstone Newall, Esq., 3, Crown Court, Philpot Lane, E.C.
Thomas Moxon, Esq., 3, Copthall Court, Throgmorton Street, E.C.
Charles Liddell, Esq., 24, Abingdon Street, Westminster, S.W.
Wm. Tipping, Esq., M.P., Brasted Park, Sevenoaks.

Josiah Lewis, Esq., Edge Hill, Derby.
Wm. Lansdowne Beale, Esq., 10, Park Street, Westminster, S.W.
J. Trevor Barkley, Esq., Kustendjie, Turkey.
Charles Paget, Esq., Ruddington Grange, Nottingham.

Three retire at the meeting held in February in each year, but are eligible for re-election.

OFFICERS.—Sec., C. W. Eddy; Gen. Man., Edward Harris; Auditors, Richard Potter and Timothy Kenrick; Solicitors, Johnston, Farquhar, and Leech, 65, Moorgate Street, E C.; Bankers, Barnett, Hoare, and Co., Lombard Street, E.C., and Hanson and Co., Constantinople.
Offices—24, Abingdon Street, Westminster, S.W.

464.—DENMARK.

The Danish Parliament during the year 1833 passed several Bills, whereby the net of State railways may be regarded as settled. The net spreads over North Jutland and Fuen, and consists of a trunk line from Aalborg, in the north of Jutland, over Aarhuus and Fredericia, to Vamdrup, on the Slesvig border, and a branch from Aarhuus over Viborg to the west of the Linfiord. On Fyen the line will run from Niborg over Odense to Strib, opposite Fredericia in Jutland. The connection between the Zealand and the Fyen, and between this and the Jutland, will be by means of a steam ferry for goods and passenger wagons. As soon as a similar communication is established between Helsingborg, in Sweden, and Elsinore, in Zealand, the whole Scandinavian North will have a satisfactory iron route to the European continent.

The execution of this railway net has been intrusted to Sir Morton Peto. Its whole length is about 300 English miles, and its total expense about 16 millions of Danish dollars. In order to complete the system, Sir Morton is bound to connect the Jutland with the long since finished South Slesvig; while the Zealand, whose line runs from Copenhagen to Korsör and the Great Belt, is now throwing out a line from the capital, over Fredericksburgh, the king's former residence, to Elsinore.

The first section from Aarhuus to Randers (40 miles) was opened in September, 1862, in July, 1863, the second section from Langaa to Viborg (24 miles) was opened. The existing state of affairs has of course caused some delay in the prosecution of the works in general, but upon many sections they are in an advanced stage, and vigorous progress continues to be made. A section of about 25 miles from the Flensburg Junction northward to Rodekro' was opened on the 15th of April, 1865, upon the North Slesvig, but little actual progress appears to have been made during the past year.

465.—DUNABURG AND WITEPSK.

Incorporated with Limited Liability under the Joint Stock Companies' Act, 1862. The line constructed under a concession granted by the Emperor of Russia, dated 19th of March (O.S.), 1863.

Nominal capital (fixed by the concession), 2,600,000l., on which the Russian Government guarantees an annual interest of 5l. per cent., amounting to 130,000l. in sterling money for 85 years, and an additional 1-12 per cent., to redeem the capital at par in 85 years, by annual drawings, commencing the first year after the completion of the line.

The capital is issued in 26,000 shares, at 100l. each, bearing a minimum interest of 5l. per share, which, on an outlay of 83l. per share, amounts to a fraction above 6 per cent. Interest on calls at the rate of 6 per cent. per annum paid during construction.

This railway, 161 English miles, connects Dunaburg, the terminus of the Riga and Dunaburg, with Witepsk. Among the distinguished features of the concession are the following:

1. The company is constituted according to English Law, with the board of directors in London, and an agency of three directors in Riga.
2. The Government guarantees the interest in sterling money, not as in previous cases, in roubles.
3. The Government also guarantees an additional sum payable half-yearly on the capital of 2,600,000l., sufficient to redeem the whole capital at par in 85 years.
4. Both the interest and the sinking fund are payable half-yearly at fixed rates.
5. The net receipts of the line are applicable in relief of the Government guarantee; but the company is authorised, in priority, to set apart 10 per cent. of such net receipts, to the extent of 100,000l., to form a reserve fund against contingencies.
6. The shareholders are entitled to all net profits of the line, up to 6 per cent., on the nominal capital of 2,600,000l. They are further entitled to one-half of all further profits, over and above the 6 per cent., until the Government is reimbursed the moneys which it may have paid in respect of the guaranteed interest beyond the net earnings of the line; after which reimbursement the shareholders are entitled to the whole of the net profits, whatever they may be.

The receipts, including Government guarantee, will be distributed rateably over the shares, according to the amount paid on each.

Opened 100 miles from Dunaburg to Polotzk, on 5th June, and 61 miles from Polotzk to Witepsk, on 17th October, 1866. In operation, 161 miles.

It was reported in April that the whole undertaking had been completed for a sum rather less than 80l. per share, instead of 83l. as originally estimated. The dividends for the year ending 30th June, 1868, were at the rate of 5 per cent. per annum. From the return of receipts, the shareholders were informed of the steady improvement of the undertaking, the working of which in every department continued to prove highly satisfactory. The receipts for the first six months of 1868 amounted to 521,182 roubles, against 328,036 roubles for the same period of 1867, showing an increase of 193,146 roubles, or nearly 59 per cent. During the last few months several new lines had been opened for traffic in Russia, some of which were so situated as to justify the expectation of their bringing considerable traffic to the company's railway and of increasing the receipts of the line.

It was reported in November that the directors had received the sanction of the Emperor to the reduction of capital, and other changes in the constitution of the company sanctioned at the meeting in July.

CAPITAL.—The capital of the undertaking is now reduced to 2,076,160l. in 129,760 shares, of 80l. each, but this reduction is not to affect any provision for its future increase.

DIRECTORS :

Chairman—T. A. MITCHELL, Esq., M.P. (Messrs. Mitchell, Yeames, and Co.), 50, Charles Street, Berkeley Square, W.

H. L. Bischoffsheim, Esq. (Messrs. Bischoffsheim and Goldschmidt).

Ch. H. Göschen, Esq. (Messrs. Frühling and Göschen).

William Miller, Esq., (Messrs. William Miller and Co., St. Petersburgh), 135, Piccadilly, W.

Jervoise Smith, Esq. (Messrs. Smith, Payne, and Smiths), 1, Lombard Street, E.C.

Loftus Fitz-Wygram, Esq., 58, Curzon Street, Mayfair, W.

OFFICERS.—Sec , S. H. Godefroi ; Con. Eng., John Hawkshaw ; Auditors, James E. Coleman and Alexander Sim ; Solicitors, Messrs. Freshfields, 5, Bank Buildings, E.C.; Bankers, Smith, Payne, and Smiths, 1, Lombard Street, E.C.

Offices—15, Angel Court, Throgmorton Street, E.C.

466.—DUTCH RHENISH.

Projected by the late King of Holland, who partly completed the portion from Amsterdam towards Prussia ; in order to raise funds for the purpose, he issued by royal decree, dated 30th April, 1838, and May 12th, 1838, 9,000 bonds of 1,000fl. (1s. 8d. each)=750,000l., bearing interest at the rate of 4½ per cent. per annum ; guaranteed—first by the railway, and second by the king himself. Open in 1853, 57½ miles, on 21st May, 1855, from Utrecht to Goude, 20 miles ; to Rotterdam, 12½ miles, on 1st August ; from Arnheim to Emmerich in October, 1856, thus completing the whole length of the Dutch Rhenish, which is 109 miles.

REVENUE.—The traffic for the book-year ending 30th April, 1857, amounted to 126,174l., and for the following years respectively to 156,823l., 160,737l., 166,621l., 186,467l., 205,412l., 218,607l., 242,096l., 288,786l., 317,417l., 295,569l., and ending 30th April, 1868, to 323,955l. The working expenses amounted for each year during the preceding 12 years to 75,568l., 86,522l., 67,600l., 66,676l., 71,632l., 78,949l., 85,444l., 92,387l., 100,563l., 117,051l., 115,772l., and to 126,301l. respectively, the expenses having been gradually reduced from 60 in 1857 to 39 per cent. The earnings were increased from 5s. 5d. per train mile in 1857 to 7s. 9½d. in 1865, and to 7s. 4½d. in 1868. The per centage of dividend on capital was increased from 2·2 per cent. for 1857, to 2·8 in 1858, to 3 66 in 1859, to 4·1 in 1860, to 4·89 in 1861, to 5·37 in 1862, to 5·60 in 1863, to 6·48 in 1864, to 8·25 in 1865, to 8·88 in 1866, to 7·40 in 1867, and to 7·90 per cent. in 1868. The revenue for the year amounted to 323,955l., showing an increase over the previous year of 28,387l. The working expenses amounted to 176,304l., showing an increase of 10,531l. After making the deductions prescribed by the statutes the whole dividend for the year ending 30th April, 1868, was at the rate of 7l. 18s. 4d. per cent.

The receipts since the commencement of the book year, on the 1st of May last, including the above, amounted to 221,685l., showing an increase, as compared with the corresponding period of the preceding year, of 9,205l. The working expenses for the fortnight amounted to 4,834l., or 37·69 per cent. of the receipts, and for the corresponding period of last year to 5,249l., or 42·14 per cent., showing a decrease of 415l. The working expenses from the 1st of May, 1868, to 31st December, 1868, amounted to 89,923l., or 40·56 per cent., and for the corresponding period of the preceding year to 41·07 per cent.

It was announced in December that the direction had been empowered to pay a provisional dividend as follows, viz. : 17s. 9d. on the shares paid up before 1st of May last ; 17s. 2d. on the shares paid up 1st of July last ; and 4s. 9d. on the new shares on which the third call was paid on 1st July last, making (6l.) 72fl. paid.

CAPITAL.—The total expenditure on this account to 30th April, 1868, amounted to 2,384,043l.

467.—EASTERN OF FRANCE.

Established by concession for 44 years, but by decree, March, 1852, the term was extended to 99 years from 27th November, 1853. The line occupies a rich and populous district, and connects Paris and Meux, Chateau-Thierry, Epernay, Chalons, Vitry, Bar-le-duc, Toul, Nancy, Luneville, Saverne, Rheims, Mentz, and Strasburg. Thus it connects France with Germany and Central Europe. A branch to Starbruck connects the line with the Prussian and Bavarian systems. The Government retains its right to redeem the line, but upon condition that such purchase can only be exercised in reference to the whole (and not a part) of the undertaking : and, moreover, only after the expiration of the first 15 years from 27th November, 1855.

By convention of September, 1853, Government conceded new lines from Paris to Mulhausen, with branch to Coulommierres ; from Nancy to Gray ; from Paris to Vincennes and St. Maux. There have also been annexed the lines from Montereau to Troyes, from St. Dizier to Gray, and the Strasburg to Basle and Wesserling.

ARDENNES.—In accordance with the conventions with the Eastern of France, approved by an Imperial decree, dated 11th June, 1863, 84,000 shares of the Ardennes were exchanged for a like number of Eastern of France. The actual exchange took place on 1st July, 1864; as from 1st January, regarding the two companies as amalgamated, the number of Eastern of France shares is increased to 584,000. These shares took dividends in common as from 1st January, 1864.

The dividends declared by this company for ten years, including its fusion with the Ardennes in 1863, have been as follow:—

Year.	Dividend.	Year.	Dividend.
1857	£1 12 6	1863	£1 6 5
1858	1 12 6	1864	1 6 5
1859	1 10 11	1865	1 6 5
1860	1 12 0	1866	1 6 5
1861	1 12 0	1867	1 6 5
1862	1 8 0		

Average for ten years, $7\frac{1}{4}$ per cent.

The length of line in working at the close of 1867 was 1,660 miles, as compared with 1,601$\frac{1}{4}$ at the close of 1866, the average for the year being 1,625$\frac{5}{8}$ miles.

The total earnings of the old network, included the Vincennes, the lines of the Luxembourg, and 2$\frac{1}{2}$ miles of the Bâle, amounted to 2,591,453*l.*, while the new network acquired 1,636,912*l.*, of which 45,896*l.* accrued on lines only partially worked, making the total revenue 4,228,365*l.* After deducting the tax of 10 per cent. levied on the quick train receipts and the receipts of the Luxembourg division, the revenue still amounted to 4,198,220*l.*, as compared with 3,923,361*l.* in 1866, showing an increase of 274,859*l.*

468.—EUPHRATES VALLEY.

A project to extend from the Mediterranean to the Persian Gulf. Registered under the Limited Liability Act, but to be incorporated by parliament. The Ottoman Government grant a lease of the land necessary for the railway and works for 99 years, free of charge. At the expiration of 99 years, the land with the railway and works pertaining thereto, became the property of the Ottoman Government, who will at the same time purchase the rolling stock at a valuation, to be settled by arbitration. The Ottoman Government guarantee the company against all competition from works of a similar character, and grant the right of land, woods, forests, and quarries, the property of the State, at a certain distance at each side of the line. It is proposed first, to execute the Section, about 88 miles of railroad, from the ancient part of Seleucia on the Mediterranean, to Aleppo.

The scheme has been for several years in abeyance, but hopes are still entertained by its projectors of some active measures being taken on its behalf.

DIRECTORS:

Chairman—WILLIAM PATRICK ANDREW, Esq., (Chairman of the Scinde), 26, Montague Square, W.

J. Edmund Anderdon, Esq., Henlade House, Taunton.
Sir Frederick Arthur, Bart., 24, Queen's Gate, Kensington, W.
Harry Borradaile, Esq. (late Bombay Civil Service).
Thomas Williams, Esq., Grove End Road, Regent's Park, N.W.
Sir T. Herbert Maddock (late Deputy-Governor of Bengal).

OFFICERS.—Consulting Eng., Major-General Chesney, R.A., D.C.L., F.R.S., and F.R.G.S.; Bankers, Glyn, Mills, and Co., 67, Lombard Street, E.C., and the Ottoman Bank; Solicitors, Baxter, Rose, and Norton.

Office—Gresham House, Old Broad Street, E.C.

Agents in Syria and Mesopotamia, Stephen Lynch and Co.

469.—FRANCE.

The extent of the concessions of the six great French companies at the close of 1866 was as follows:—

System.		Old network.	New network.	Total.
Northern	Miles.	687$\frac{1}{2}$	321$\frac{1}{4}$	1,008$\frac{3}{4}$
Eastern		609$\frac{3}{8}$	1,320$\frac{5}{8}$	1,930
Western		562$\frac{1}{2}$	1,023$\frac{1}{8}$	1,585$\frac{5}{8}$
Orleans		1,260$\frac{5}{8}$	1,368$\frac{3}{4}$	2,629$\frac{3}{8}$
Lyons-Mediterranean		1,638$\frac{3}{4}$	2,020	3,658$\frac{3}{4}$
Southern		498$\frac{3}{4}$	908$\frac{1}{8}$	1,406$\frac{7}{8}$

The total extent of the lines conceded to the six companies at the close of last year was thus 12,219$\frac{3}{8}$ miles. There was also conceded to small miscellaneous companies at the same date an aggregate of 936$\frac{7}{8}$ miles, making the general total distance conceded at the close of 1866, 13,156$\frac{1}{4}$ miles.

The extent of line opened for traffic in 1866 was 590 miles, of which $533\frac{3}{4}$ referred to the six great networks. To this new mileage the contribution made by each of the six companies was as annexed :—

Northern—Soissons to Laon, $21\frac{1}{4}$ miles.

Eastern—Châtillon-sur-Seine to Chaumont, $26\frac{7}{8}$ miles.

Western—Mayenne to Laval, $12\frac{1}{2}$; Dreux to Laigle, $37\frac{1}{2}$; Argentan to Flers, $26\frac{7}{8}$; Laigle to Conches, $20\frac{5}{8}$; total, $97\frac{1}{2}$ miles.

Orleans—Chalonnes to Cholet, $25\frac{5}{8}$ miles; Nantes to Napoléon-Vendée, $46\frac{7}{8}$; Massiat to Murat, $21\frac{7}{8}$; Aurilac to Figeac, $40\frac{5}{8}$; Decazeville Branch, $1\frac{1}{4}$; total, $136\frac{1}{4}$ miles.

Lyons-Mediterranean—Le Coteau to Amplepins, $16\frac{1}{4}$; Tarare to St. Germain au Mont-d'Or, $20\frac{5}{8}$; Gray to Ougne, $16\frac{7}{8}$; Cercy-la-Tour to Nevers, $33\frac{1}{8}$; Brioude to Langeac, 20; Montbrison to Andrézieux, $11\frac{1}{4}$; the Puy to the Pont-du-Lignon, $28\frac{1}{8}$; and Aix to Annecy, $30\frac{5}{8}$; total, $176\frac{7}{8}$ miles.

Southern—Langan to Bazas, $6\frac{1}{4}$; Tarbes to Lourdes, $18\frac{1}{8}$; Pau (Billeres) to Pau (Axe), $1\frac{1}{4}$; Bayonne (Mousserolles) to Bayonne, $1\frac{1}{4}$; Boussens to St. Girons, $19\frac{3}{8}$; Castres to Mazamet, $11\frac{7}{8}$; Perpignan to Collioure, $16\frac{7}{8}$; total, 75 miles.

The total length of line in operation in France at the close of 1866 being $9,066\frac{1}{4}$ miles, it follows that the distance remaining to be completed amounted at the same date to 4,090 miles.

Of this considerable extent of line the Northern had still to complete $239\frac{3}{8}$; the Eastern, $333\frac{1}{8}$; the Western, $327\frac{1}{2}$; the Orleans, $576\frac{1}{4}$; the Lyons-Mediterranean, $1,463\frac{1}{8}$; and the Southern, $396\frac{7}{8}$; total, $3,336\frac{1}{4}$ miles. The balance of $753\frac{3}{4}$ miles remained to be executed by the small miscellaneous companies, whose undertakings will, no doubt, be eventually fused with the six great networks.

The outlay made on capital account by the six great companies, and the first establishment expenditure still remaining to be made by them, stood as follows at the close of 1866 :—

Company.	Outlay made.	To make.	Total.
Northern	£23,983,200	£3,407,880	£27,391,080
Eastern	40,732,000	6,868,000	47,600,000
Western	34,536,000	9,984,000	44,520,000
Orleans	44,206,000	9,514,000	53,720,000
Lyons-Mediterranean	76,633,600	28,338,400	104,972,000
Southern	21,377,640	6,108,360	27,486,000
Total	£241,468 440	£64,220,640	£305,689,080

The outlay made by other minor companies to the same date was 5,459,360*l*., and the total remaining to be made by them was 8,051,480*l*. These further totals increase the outlay made on all the railways of France to the close of 1866 to 246,927,800*l*., and the amount remaining to be expended to 72,272,120*l*.—making an expenditure on French railways, actual and contemplated, of 319,199,120*l*.

The length of the lines conceded in France extends to 13,156 miles. Of this considerable network, $9,062\frac{1}{2}$ miles are now opened for traffic, so that there is about three-fourths as much railway communication in France as in the United Kingdom.

TRAFFIC.—Combining the earnings of the old and new concessions, the annexed totals show the receipts of each company for ten years :—

Year.	Eastern.	Southern.	Northern.	Orleans.	Western.	Lyons-Med.
1858	£2,181,316	£646,696	£2,239,862	£2,575,722	£1,750,750	£4,006,773
1859	2,389,706	849,916	2,320,134	2,926,490	2,000,899	4,728,381
1860	2,575,872	992,745	2,475,178	3,058,788	2,063,683	4,869,957
1861	2,810,972	1,246,463	2,627,187	3.262,058	2,303,500	5,864,532
1862	2,710,351	1,378,143	2,829,437	3,306,693	2,192,912	6,607,683
1863	2,751,408	1,397,988	2,859,823	3,536,807	2,377,758	6,909,536
1864	3,365,536	1,468,780	3,002,839	3,795,406	2,652,530	7,160,462
1865	3,716,023	1,573,545	3,247,894	3,980,558	2,878,909	7,420,481
1866	3,981,283	1,734,183	3,465,160	4,303,284	3,135,048	7,955,489
1867	4,187,233	1,783,516	3,787,055	4,570,645	3,579,656	8,576,782

The traffic of the six systems has enormously increased during the last six years and with scarcely any check. Of course great additions have been made to mileage, but the receipts per mile worked were in every case larger in 1867 than in 1858.

The receipts on the whole of the French Railways for the year 1867 amounted, on 9,738 miles, to 26,259,763*l*., and for the year 1866, on 9,030 miles, to 24,227,218*l*., showing an increase of 708 miles, or 7·27 per cent. in the mileage, and of 2,032,545*l*., or 8.39 pe cent. in the receipts.

The receipts on the seven old lines of the principal companies, 4,676 miles in the aggregate, amounted in 1867 to 19,987,480*l*., and for the year 1866, on the same mileage, to 18,795,762*l*., showing an increase of 1,191,718*l*., or 6·34 per cent. The receipts on the new railways belonging to those companies, on 4,853 miles, amounted in 1867 to

6,085,672*l*., and for the year 1866, on 4,230 miles, to 5,298,095*l*., showing an increase in the length of 623 miles, or 14·73 per cent, and of 787,577*l*., or 14·87 per cent. in the receipts.

The receipts on ten short "independent" railways, 209 miles in the aggregate, amounted for the year 1867 to 186,612*l*.. and for the year 1866, on 124 miles, to 133,360*l*., showing an increase of 85 miles, or 68·55 per cent. in length, and of 53,252*l*., or 40 per cent. in the revenue.

The receipts on the old lines in 1867 amounted to 4,274*l*. per mile, on the new lines belonging to them to 1,254*l*., and on the short "independent" lines to 833*l*.

For later intelligence see ADDENDA.

470.—FRANCO-AUSTRIAN.

Deducting a section on the Orawitza and Steyerdorf, 20⅜ miles in length, opened in November. 1863, and which up to the close of that year was used only for the transport business of the company—the length of the lines worked remained at 827½ miles, in which total the Northern figured for 293¾ miles, the South Eastern 415 miles, and the Vienna and Neu-Szony for 118¾ miles.

The dividend was fixed at 14*s*. per 20*l*. share, in addition to interest paid, in accordance with the statutes, at the rate of 5 per cent., total dividend for 1867 was thus at the rate of 8½ per cent. per annum. The receipts derived from working were 3,347,843*l*., and the working expenses 1,116,360*l*., showing a net balance of 2,231,483*l*. After deducting 491,450*l*. for interest on shares and 550,829*l*. for interest on the obligations, and after making various payments, a balance remained of 947,331*l*. After deducting again from this sum the 5 per cent. applied to the statutory reserve, the 10 per cent. appertaining to the directors and the loss sustained on the exchange account, there still remained a balance of 576,849*l*., out of which the council declared the dividend of 14*s*. per share, leaving a balance of 296,849*l*. to the credit of 1868.

The revenue has been pretty well maintained of late, although in 1867, the concern was doing a large business (supposed to be exceptional) in the conveyance of Hungarian wheat. In the forty weeks ending October 6th, 1868, the revenue showed an increase of 480,795*l*. as compared with the corresponding period of 1867. The grain-producing resources of Hungary are large, and appear likely to be turned to greater account in future years.

The Hungarian Government is negotiating with a Belgian company with reference to the concession of a line commencing at Esseg and running on one side to Semlin, and, on the other side, to Sissek Carlstadt, Fiume, and Zengg, with a branch from Brod to Gradisca.

A subscription has been opened at Vienna for 50,000 shares of the North-West Austrian. The share capital is to be divided into 170,000 shares, and the present issue is being made at a rate ranging from 80 to 85 per cent.

CAPITAL.—The aggregate amount raised to the close of 1867 for the old lines was 18,396,360*l*., of which 9,280,356*l*. was derived from shares, and 9,116,004*l*. from obligations. The expenditure to the close of 1867 was 17,537,229*l*., leaving a disposable balance of 859,131*l*. Of the 17,537,229*l*. expended, 14,566,761*l*. related to the railways, and 2,970,468*l*. to estates, mines, ironworks, &c. Taking account of sums derived from the sale of stores, lands, &c., the add'tions made to capital in 1867 were not considerable, putting the supplementary network out of the calculation. The total sum raised to the close of 1867 by obligations issued for the supplementary network was 1,525,066*l*., of which 196,689*l*. had been expended, leaving a disposable balance of 1,328,177*l*.

471.—GELLIVARA.

A coal and mining company, in Sweden, which purposes to construct a railway, which starting from the Kaptens Grufvan, a mine or quarry on the Gellivara mountain, proceeds for a distance of 14 miles to the eastward, ard then taking nearly a southern direction, terminates on the river Lulea, at Norvick, which river will be navigable after the formation of the canals from this point to the sea, Gauge, 3 ft. 6 in.

Little or no progress in construction of works appears to have been made during the past four years, owing to want of capital, the calls on the shares not being responded to

472.—GERMANY.

In 1866 the average return realised upon the 80,283,295*l*. embarked in private German railways—that is, railways independent of the State—was 7·57 per cent. per annum. The Prussian lines produced an average return of 9 04 per cent.; the Austrian, 7·66 per cent.; the South German, 6·05 per cent.; and the North German, 6·52 per cent. The dividends paid upon two German lines in 1866—viz., the Leipzic and Dresden, and the Magdeburg and Leipzic—were upwards of 20 per cent. per annum. At the close of 1867 there were 13,161 miles in working order in the German States, of which 5,831 miles were in Prussia, and 4,191 miles in Austria.

473.—GRAND DUCAL WILLIAM LUXEMBOURG.

The company was constituted in 1857, under the patronage of the King of Holland, who is Grand Duke of Luxembourg.

The line forms almost a perfect cross in the middle of the Grand Duchy, the town of Luxembourg being the centre. The west branch of the cross is formed by the line from Luxembourg to Arlonn, where it joins the Belgian (Great Luxembourg). The southern arm is formed by the line from Luxembourg to Thionville, where it joins the Eastern of France. The eastern branch is formed by the line from Luxembourg to the Prusian frontier town of Treves. The northern branch runs to the northern frontier of the Duchy and will ultimately join the Belgian system at Spa, or the Prussian lines at or near Cologne, total 88 miles.

There are also two short branches leaving the French arm at Bettenburg, and running up to the iron-stone quarries of Esch sur-l'Alzette and Rummetange. These iron-stone quarries are most remarkable. There are hundreds of acres of iron-stone, completely upon the surface of the ground. and averaging five or six yards thick. This iron-stone, now largely employed in the Zollverein, will be put into the railway trucks at a price varying from 8d. to 1s. per ton. The dividend for 1867 was at the rate of 1 per cent. per annum.

In consequence of the remainder of the network having been brought into operation in 1867, the profits of the year were higher than those for 1866, being estimated at 83,400l., a sum which, after providing interest on obligations and sundry expenses for management and maintenance, as well as the dividend accruing on the preference shares, would still admit of a dividend of 8s. per share on the old shares, with a balance of 3,654l. to be carried forward.

DIRECTORS:

President—MARQUIS D'ALBON.
Vice-President—MONS. J. R. BISCHOFFSHEIM.
Director-General—J. VANDEWYNCKELE.

OFFICERS.—Secretary, Mons. H. De Groux ; Consulting-Engineer, Mons. Vuigner ; Engineer-in-Chief, Mons. Grenier.

474.—GREAT RUSSIAN.

The Goverment conceded, in 1857, to a mixed French and English association, represented chiefly by the Credit Mobilier of France, the following lines :—

St. Petersburgh to Warsaw ....English Miles	670
Kowno Branch	60
Moscow to Nijni-Novgorod	280
Moscow to Sebastopol....................................	933
Little Archangel to Lihan	750=2,693

To be constructed at an outlay of about 45,000,000l. sterling. The interest is regularly paid by the Russian Government.

The share capital is composed of 600,000 shares of 20l. each, and the company has besides issued 70,000 obligations of 80l. each, and 18,877 of 20l. each. The works of establishment have involved an outlay of nearly of 24,000,000l. In 1864 the net profits realised on the Warsaw and St. Petersburgh were 202,717l. as compared with 257,473l. in 1863. On the other hand the net profits of the line from Moscow to Nijni-Novgorod rose in 1864 to 286,189l. as compared with 232,899l. in 1863. The total profits realised on the two combined were thus 488,906l. as compared with 490,372l. in 1863. After making various deductions and additions, the net profits of 1864 were finally returned at 459,225l. The Russian Government guarantees 5 per cent. upon all the capital engaged in the enterprise. This guarantee involves a charge of at least 900,000l. for 1864, so that upon all the interest paid, the Russian Treasury contributed 50 per cent.

The receipts show a sensible progress. The Warsaw, with its Prussian branches, acquired in May 686,031 roubles, and the Moscow and Nijni-Novgorod 418,763 roubles, making a total receipt for May of 1,104,793 roubles. In the four preceding months of the year the amount acquired was 4,027,070 roubles, making the total receipts of the system to May 31st, 5,131,863 roubles as compared with 4,153,096 in the corresponding period of 1867. The advance for the first five months was thus 978,767 roubles, an equally steady progress in receipts being manifested.

The Russian Government has transferred the St. Petersburgh and Moscow to the Great Russian.

475.—GREAT LUXEMBOURG.

Commences in Brussels (Quartier Leopold), and proceeds in a direct line to Namur, 34 miles. A junction with the Namur and Liége, and extends to Arlon, near Luxembourg The Government agreed to guarantee a *minimum* dividend at 4 per cent. on 900,000l., from opening of any integral section.

The original concession was for 90 years from the date of completion. and embraced an extension of the lines from Luxembourg to Thionville and Metz, where it would join the Paris and Strasburg. The whole history of the past, however. may be considered valueless. A new era commenced from date of new charter (September 6th, 1855), granted by the Belgian Government.

WILLIAM LUXEMBOURG. — "Negotiations were arranged with the Government, having for objects the substitution for the canalisation of the river Ourthe beyond the point to which the works are already executed, of a railway which would connect the city of Liége with the main line of the Great Luxembourg railway ; owing, however, to certain objections on the part of the William Luxembourg, it became necessary, in consequence, to enter upon new negotiations, 'and on the 5th January, a new agreement with that company was entered into, which has been finally ratified by all the parties concerned. Under this new agreement the working of the William Luxembourg will be divided between the East of France and the Great Luxembourg, the latter obtaining from the date of the opening of the Spa line, the portion which connects its own lines with those of central Germany.'"

LONGWY BRANCH.—"The extension of this branch from Longwy to Longuyon (point of junction with the main line of the Ardennes), constructed by the Ardennes, has been opened for traffic."

OURTHE.—This branch, 38 miles, was opened in August, 1866, it being stated that the cost would not exceed the estimate. In operation, 172 miles.

REVENUE.—The receipts for the half-year ending 31st December, 1867, amounted to 151,208l., against 147,218l. in 1866, and 155,282l. in 1865 ; the net earnings being respectively 74,770l., 67,987l., and 80,202l. The expenditure during the half-year, amounted to 76,438l., or 50½ per cent., against 79,231l., or 53¾ per cent. in 1866, showing a reduction in the expenditure of 2,793l., although the quantity of merchandise conveyed was larger than in the same period of 1866. The falling off in the traffic had arisen from a considerable reduction of tariffs, and from the industrial and commercial crisis which had prevailed with more or less intensity in the whole of Europe during the last two years, and which had especially affected the trade of Belgium and France. On the first of February last, the Government had introduced certain modifications in its tariffs, and these were applied to the Great Luxembourg, but more remained to be done to yield satisfactory results. The receipts of the Ourthe from the 1st of August, 1866, to 1st January, 1867, five months, amounted to 13,023l., being at the rate of 2,605l. per month ; equal to 15,627l. for an entire half-year. The receipts for the half-year ending 31st December, 1867, amounted to 15,372l., showing a decrease of 275l. After deducting 58,707l. for interest and reimbursement of obligations, and 5,500l. for dividend on the preference shares, there remained a balance of 21,033l., from which a dividend of 3s. 6d. per share left 1,049l. towards repayment of the sum advanced by Government as guarantee of interest on the Namur and Arlon, and a balance of 2,484l. to next half-year. On 134 miles, for the six months ending 30th June, the gross net earnings were as follow :—

	Gross receipts.	Net earnings.
1866	£147,882	£66,435
1867	132,737	58,300
1868	151,472	77,268

The gross receipts for the half-year thus exhibit an excess over the corresponding period of 1866 by 3,588l., and over 1867 of 18,735l. The working expenses for the six months ending 30th June, 1867, were 74,437l., or 56 per cent., while those of 1868 were 74,203l., or 49 per cent. This reduction is ascribed to diminution in the cost of fuel, to the exercise of general economy, "and to the facilities arising from the laying down, along a portion of the railway, of the second line of rails." This additional line is being proceeded with, and it was expected that by the close of the year a continuous length of double way of twenty miles would have been brought into operation. The Ourthe fails to answer expectation, the receipts (14,660l.) being only 647l. in advance of the receipts for the corresponding period of 1867. The working of the part of the William Luxembourg between the Belgian and Prussian frontiers yielded a profit of 1,179l., while the net earnings of the canal amounted to 145l. After deducting 62,110l. for interest and reimbursement of obligations, and 5,500l. for dividend on the preference shares, there remained a balance of 20,128l., out of which a dividend of 3s. 6d. per share, and 1,048l. towards repayment of the sum advanced by the Belgian Government as guarantee of interest on the Namur to Arlon, left 1,580l.

CAPITAL.—The balance sheet, to 30th June, 1868, furnished the subjoined particulars of income and expenditure to that date :—

Received.		Expended.	
Shares	£2,000,000	Main line and extensions	£2,920,980
Preference shares	220,000	Bastogne branch	36,083
Obligations of 4l.	437,516	Ourthe line	808,472
Obligations of 20l.	2,369,300	Rolling stock, tools, and furniture	549,365
		Canal construction account	403,506
	£5,026,816	Real estate	11,823
Amortization of obligations of 4l.	16,052	Stores, coal, &c., on hand	47,770
Ditto ditto of 20l.	25,080	Unissued obligations of 20l. on hand	190,880
	£5,067,948	Discount on issue of obligations	
Reserve fund	6,600	of 20l. (4th issue)	98,720
Balance of revenue	19,080	Due to company, &c.	90,957
Owing by company, &c.	134,551	Cash in hand	69,619
	£5,228,180		£5,228,180

DIRECTORS:

Chairman—WILLIAM FENTON, Esq., Beaumonds, near Rochdale.

James Aikin, Esq., Liverpool.
Mons. J. Brasseur, Ostend.
Thomas Close, Esq., Nottingham.
James Hutchinson, Esq., London.

Mons. Edouard de Moor, Brussels.
B. B. Reed, Esq., Red Hill, Surrey.
Mons. Victor Tesch, Brussels.

OFFICERS.—Sec. in London, Frederick Horncastle, 156, Gresham House, Old Broad Street, E.C. ; London Bankers, London and County Bank, 21, Lombard Street, E.C.; Agent in Liverpool, Henry Christie Beloe, 22, Lord Street.

476.—HOLLAND.

The works of the State system are advancing rapidly, as of the whole system projected, less than 90 miles remain to be opened for traffic. Three lines—from Utrecht to Waardenburg, 20 miles ; from Winschooten to the frontier of Prussia, 7½ miles ; and from Herzogenbusch to Bught, 1⅞ miles—were to be completed before the close of the year. There will then remain to open for traffic lines from Meppel to Groningen, from Maerdrick to Rotterdam, from Herzogenbusch to Waardenburg, and from Floe to Fliessingen, presenting altogether a development of 85⅜ miles.

The report of the company for working the State lines for 1867 confessed to a loss of 16,944l. The company also works two private lines—the Almelo and Salzbergen, and the Liége and Limbourg—with what result does not appear.

477.—INTERNATIONAL.

A line from Terneuzen, a Dutch port on the Scheldt, to Malines, the central station of Belgium. Length, 43 miles. Société Anonyme authorised by the Governments of Belgium and Holland. Capital, 640,000l., divided into 16,000 shares of 20l. each, bearing 5 per cent. interest during construction ; and 32,000 bonds issued at 10l. bearing 6 per cent. interest on the price of issue, reimbursable at 20l. per bond, by annual drawings.

DIRECTORS :

President—Monsieur AUGUSTE DE COCK, Senator, Echevin of the town of Ghent, President of the Société Linière of Ghent, &c.

Vice-President—Mons. W. VANS TETS VAN GOODRIAAN, late Finance Minister, Holland, the Hague.

Mons. Theodore Janssens, Member of the Chamber of Representatives, Brussels.
Mons. Auguste Wauters, Member of the Chamber of Commerce of St. Nicolas.

Mons. Francois Lancelot, Advocate of the Court of Appeal in Brussels.

Offices in Brussels, 33, Boulevard d'Observatoire.

478.—LEGHORN.

This is a combination of three separate companies, consolidated by the parliament of Italy.

I. LUCCA AND PISTOJA.—Established under a concession from the Tuscan Government for 10 years as a Société Anonyme. From Lucca it traverses the left bank of the Arno, through Peschia to Pistoja, junction with Leopolda and Maria Antonia, which run to Florence, with branches to Leghorn. Capital authorised 280,000l. Government guarantee 4 per cent. per annum interest, from opening of first section from Lucca to Peschia. Government may redeem the concession after open 15 or 20 years, at average of five preceding years, the purchase money converted into a permanent annuity, under guarantee of the Government. 150,000l. in 30,000 preference shares, was created in November, 1852, for second section of line, bearing preferential interest at 5 per cent. per annum. secured on the whole Government grant, which is made a real charge upon the property and revenue ; after 2½ per cent. have been paid on ordinary capital (also secured on the guarantee), net revenue to be provided pro ratá amongst the two classes of shareholders. The line from Bologno to Vergato, 23¾ miles, was opened for traffic in November, 1863, and the line as far as Pistoja in 1864.

II. MARIA ANTONIA.—Formed for the construction of a railway from Florence to Pistoja, junction with the Lucca line from Pisa. Length, 21 miles ; opened on 12th July, 1851. The concession of Government from 60 to 100 years.

III. LEOPOLDA.—The directors of this company entered into an agreement with the Maria Antonia for the purchase of the shares of the latter upon terms nearly identical with those offered by the Lombardo-Venetian. The Leopolda, on the 17th November, 1858, approved the agreement.

479.—LEMBERG-CZERNOWITZ.

Capital, 1,250,000l., in 62,500 shares, of 20l. each. Established under a guarantee from the Austrian Government, producing a net minimum dividend of 7 per cent. per annum, payable in silver.

Provision is made for payment by the contractor (Mr. Brassey) of interest at 6 per cent. per annum during construction, which is not to exceed 2,450,000*l*.

The concession, the duration of which is 90 years, stipulated for the commencement of the works previous to the 11th January, 1865, and for their completion within three years; but provision is made for extension of these periods in case of political or financial crises. The Government guarantee a fixed sum of 150,000*l*. in silver money as a net annual revenue of the line. The line is still under construction by Mr. Thomas Brassey, the contractor.—Dividend at the rate of 7 per cent.

The traffic returns from January 1st to December 31st, 1868, amounted to 1,720,848*fl*., and for the year 1867 to 1,450,527*fl*., showing an increase of 270,321*fl*., or 18·64 per cent.

At a special meeting, held at Vienna on 15th October, a report was submitted in respect to a concession for a line from Czernowitz to Jassy and branches to Roman and Botuschani. The extension of the Lemberg and Czernowitz to the Black Sea, had always been the ultimate desire and ambition of the direction since the establishment of the company. The guarantees of a prosperous future lie in this extension, be it either to Odessa or to Galatz. A committee consisting of members of the direction, and the well-known contractor, Mr. Thomas Brassey, and with the co-operation of several great banking establishments, were successful, in the beginning of the year, in obtaining from the Roumanian Government a promise that the whole of the Moldo-Wallachian network should be under one supervision. The Roumanian Government by making it a condition that the whole network should be expeditiously carried out, divided the network as follows:—To the Austrian committee the line to Jassy and the branch lines to Roman and Botuschani; to the Prussian the construction of a line to Galatz. The committee accepted the concession, and had already commenced the construction of the line, upon the understanding that, should the Lemberg and Czernowitz refuse to ratify the concession, no loss should accrue to the original concessionnaires. The directors recommended the acquisition of this concession for the following advantageous reasons:—The proposed line will form a middle branch of the South Russian as also of the Moldo-Wallachian, and gives the long-sought-for connection with the Black Sea on the one side to Odessa, and on the other to Varna, irrespective of the connection which will lead from Roman to Galatz, the port of the Danube. The construction of this new line, particularly with the use of the projected, Lemberg-Warsaw, will be the means of diverting the traffic from the North and Baltic Seas on the one side, and from the Black Sea on the other, on the Lemberg and Czernowitz, and will release the company from the danger, hemmed in between two companies, of being obliged to submit to any pressure put upon it. The concession itself stipulates that, for every kilometre of the 217 kilometres, the Roumanian Government shall furnish a sum of 40,000 *fl*., and that, if the concession is acquired by any company already established, the Government further guarantees a net profit of 7½ per cent.—*i. e.*, 1,497,300 *fl*. in silver currency for the whole line ; also grants an immunity of taxes and of the interest for the guaranteed advance, and stipulates only for a sixth of the surplus of the guaranteed amount after the guaranteed advance has ceased, and this only to cover the cost of its subvention. The next point to be considered is the financial part of the project for the construction of the lines, which will be carried out as follows:— 1. The subvention of the Roumanian Government, amounting to 8,680,000*fr*. 2. By the issue of debentures to the nominal amount of 15,600,000 *fl*., and of shares to the nominal amount of 10,000,000 *fl*. These debentures, like the other debentures of the company, to receive interest at the rate of 5 per cent., and to be redeemed in 75 years. The interest and redemption to be provided in the first instance out of the revenue of the new line. The shares to be issued as shares of the second emission in the like nominal amount, and to bear the same interest as the shares of the first emission, and receive 7 per cent. during construction. By these issues the company would have to provide

For interest, debentures, 1st June			*Fl*.600,000
Do.	do.	2nd June	600,000
Do.	do.	3rd June (at present proposed)	780,000
		Total	*Fl*.1,980,000

Against this amount the guaranteed profits are—

Guarantee Lemberg and Czernowitz Railway		*Fl*.1,500,000
Do.	Lemberg and Sczawa	700,000
Do.	Roumanian, &c.	1,497,300
		Fl.3,697,300
After deducting interest as above		1,980,000
	Leaves	*Fl*.1,717,300
To provide the 7 per cent. interest, which is		1,575,300
		Fl.142,000
From which must be deducted the redemption fund, amounting to		65,800
	Leaving a surplus of	*Fl*.76,200

The construction of the line is undertaken by Mr. Thomas Brassey for a fixed sum. This gentleman has also taken upon himself the responsibility of the Roumanian subvention, of the issue of the new shares and debentures, of furnishing the whole of the necessary materials for construction, of refunding to the concessionaires all expenses appertaining to their obtaining the concession, and to hand over to the company a reserve fund of 2,500,000f. on the completion of the line. Mr. Brassey, on his part, has made a contract with the Anglo-Austrian Bank, by which the latter agrees to take over the debentures and shares at a fixed rate, with the sole condition that the shareholders of the Lemberg-Czernowitz be entitled to receive for every original share four new shares at a rate of 70 per cent.

The resolutions adopted at the meeting were as follow :—1. To acquire the concession for the prolongation of the line from Suczawa to Jassy, with the branch lines to Roman and Botuschani. 2. To increase the capital of the company by the issue of shares of the value of 1,000,000l. sterling, and bonds of the value of 1,560,000l. sterling. 3. To alter the statutes in consequence of the company's acquiring the said concession.

NEW CAPITAL.—These obligations comprised creation of new capital to the extent of 1,000,000l. in 20l. shares, which have been subscribed, and of 1,500,000l. in bonds. In the first instance, the amount of bonds offered was reduced to one-half, or 780,000l., in 26,000 bonds of 30l. each, which were offered at 20l. 6s. The rate of interest is 5 per cent., but the issue price showed 7½ per cent. interest to the subscriber. The deposit is fixed at 10 per cent., and the balance will be due on allotment, though there is an option of deferring the payment. The total amount of annual interest on the entire bonded debt of the company will be 198,000l., and as security for this, there is the guarantee of the Austrain Government, amounting in the aggregate to 220,000l., and that of the Roumanian Government, amounting to 149,73)l., in addition to revenue itself. The bonds, including those issued ard those now offered, form, of course, a first charge on the whole of these revenues. Interest accrues from 1st instant, and will be payable half-yearly at the Anglo-Austrian Bank in London. The bonds are to be redeemed in 70 years, by annual drawings, the first of which is to take place in 1871.

The first and present members of the Council of administration are—Prince Leo Sapieha, Prince Carl Jablonowski, Chevalier Wladimir de Borkowski, Carl Klein, Dy. Carl Griskra, Baron Alexander Petrino, Chevalier Constantine de Tchorznicki, Chevalier Octav de Pietruski. In England, W. R. Drake, Esq. ; L. M. Rate, Esq. ; Somerset Beaumont, Esq., M.P.; and H. G. Edlmann, Esq. Secretary, Miximilian Zingler.

480—LERIDA, REUS, AND TARRAGONA.

It was reported in August 1867, that, of the concessions of 64¾ miles, only 33¼ miles are at present worked; but of the remaining 30 miles, 15 have been constructed. The receipts for 1866 were 21,914l., and the working expenses 20,292l., leaving a net profit of 1,622l. This amount being inadequate to meet interest on the capital expended (1,835,124l.) the council of administration proposed to cut the Gordian knot of the difficulties with which it has to deal by reducing the share capital to one-fourth, and transforming the obligation capital into shares. The company would thus be reconstituted with 40,000 new shares, of which 31,024 would be given in exchange for 62,048 existing obligations, and 8,956 in exchange for 35,820 present shares. It is urged that the company being thus relieved of its existing obligations may be able to borrow the sum required to pay its present debts and complete the line in its entirety. The receipts to 9th December, 1867, were 947,317l., as compared with 881,365l. at the corresponding date of 1866.

481.—LIERRE AND TURNHOUT.

Capital, 172,000l., in 8,600 shares of 20l. each (guaranteed by the Belgian Government. Length, 24½ miles. Opened for traffic on 23rd April, 1855, but the guarantee of the minimum interest did not commence until the 22nd of May following.

The working of the line is leased to the Antwerp and Rotterdam under an agreement ratified by general meetings, by which that company took the rolling stock of the Turnhout, paying a fixed sum equal to an additional ½ per cent. per annum for its use, and as a rent for the line, paying 35 per cent. of the gross receipts for the first two years, 40 per cent. for the next two years, and thereafter to the end of the concession (which is 90 years), 50 per cent.

DIRECTORS :

H. T. Matthyssens, President of the Chamber of Commerce, Antwerp.	A. Stoclet, Director of the Antwerp and Rotterdam, Brussels.
Samuel Laing, Esq., 6, Kensington Gardens Terrace, Bayswater, W.	

482.—MADRID, SARAGOSSA, AND ALICANTE.

The original network (from Madrid to Alicante, and from Madrid to Saragossa) has been some time in operation, the Alicante having been worked since 1858, and the Saragossa since June, 1863. But to these lines the company has successively added others to Ciudad-Real, Cordova, and Carthagena, which carry the total undertaking to 892½ miles. The line from Alcazar to Ciudad-Real has been worked since 1861, and when a line from that point to Badajoz is completed, the company will be in communication with the Portuguese lines and with the Atlantic Ocean.

The shareholders received no dividend for 1866, a year which proved equally as profitless to them as 1865.

As regards the traffic of 1867 the 892½ miles forming the entire network of the company were in operation all through 1867, while in 1866 the average length of line worked was 810. The rough receipts were 1,016,835*l*., and the net 532,737*l*. In 1866 the rough earnings were 949,941*l*., and the net 497,840*l*.

483.—MONT CENIS.

Established with Limited Liability, with a capital of 250,000*l*. in shares, and 125,000*l*. on loan, since increased to 202,600*l*., the latter bearing interest at 7 per cent.

This railway crosses the Alps from St. Michael, in Savoy, to Susa, in Piedmont, a distance of forty-eight miles, connecting the railways of France with those of Italy, thus completing the last link of a direct line of 1,400 miles from Calais to the Port of Brindisi on the Adriatic, whereby an improved route is created from England and France to Italy, Egypt, and the East, and a saving of two days may be effected in the transit of the Indian Mail.

The railway is constructed on the existing Imperial road, the grant of a sufficient width of which, free of charge, has been made by the two Governments, and this grant may be considered equal to a subvention of 200,000*l*. For working this line the centre rail system of locomotives is adopted, the practicability of which had been previously proved by trials made on the Cromford and High Peak in England, and afterwards on the Mont Cenis, where the system was submitted to every variety of test before commissioners of engineers appointed by the French, Italian, English, Russian, and Austrian Governments.

The line has now been worked since the 15th June, 1868, and, although at first opposed by the Diligences, is now able to take all the traffic which presents itself and is worked with the utmost regularity. The total amount of traffic receipts to the 31st December, 1868, is 533,589*fr*.

It was resolved, at a special meeting in November, 1867, to authorise the directors to borrow an additional sum of 77,600*l*., making the total bond capital 202,600*l*. as above stated.

The profits of the company in each year are to be applied—1st. In payment of interest on bonds. 2nd. In payment of a dividend of 7 per cent. per annum upon the shares. 3rd. For the purpose of creating a "Bond Redemption Fund." 4th. After the Bond Redemption Fund is completed, for the purpose of creating a "Bonus Fund," to be applied in payment of a bonus of 20*l*. per share. After which payment the preferential dividend of 7 per cent. per annum will cease in respect of such share. 5th. One-half of the residue or surplus profits in each year will be divided among the shareholders, and the other moiety will be paid to the concessionaires.

DIRECTORS :

Lord Abinger, 48, Chester Square, S.W.
Duke of Vallombrosa, Cannes, France.
Sir R. C. Dallas, Bart., 52, Rutland Gate, S.W.
Thos. Brassey, Esq., 4, Gt. George Street, S.W.
Edward Blount, Esq., 3, Rue de la Paix, Paris.

Alex. Brogden, Esq., M.P., Ulverstone.
William Barber Buddicom, Esq., Penbedw, Flintshire.
John B. Fell, Esq., Spark Bridge, Ulverstone.
J. A. Longridge, Esq., Clapham Park, S.W.
James Brunlees, Esq., 5, Victoria Street, S.W.

Secretary, Walter J. Cutbill, 13, Gresham Street, E.C.

Offices—13, Gresham Street, E.C.

484.—NAMUR AND LIEGE—MONS AND MANAGE.

1.—NAMUR AND LIEGE, 45 miles.—The principal line leaving Namur from the State station, follows the left bank of the Meuse to the Val St. Lambert, and passes that point on the right bank of the terminus at the Longdoz station at Liége. The branch detaches itself from the main line at the station at Flemalle, a little before the crossing of the Meuse, and unites with the State line near Liége, in order to be unloaded at the station of the Guellemins belonging to the State. Leased to the Northern of France, and the annual rental is applied to the payment of interest and redemption of the debentures. The coupons are payable half-yearly.

2.—MONS AND MANAGE, 21 miles.—Leased to the Belgian Government, and the annual rental is applied to the payment of the 6 per cent. interest on the 10,000*l.* preference shares, and the payment of dividends (about 2¾ per cent.) on the 26,595 original shares.

DIRECTORS:

Fred. John Sidney Parry, Esq., Onslow Square, S.W.
Robert Bridgman Barrow, Esq., Sydnope Hall, Matlock.

George Blagden, Esq., Tollington Park Hornsey, N.
Richard Lamarche, Esq., Liége.
Alexander Poppe, Esq., Managing Director, Brussels.

OFFICERS.—Solicitor, H. Wellington Vallance Moorgate House, Moorgate Street, E.C.; Bankers, London and Westminster Bank, Lothbury, E.C., Banque de Belgique, Brussels, and Banque Liegeoise, Liége.

485.—NORTHERN OF FRANCE.

From Paris to Amiens, Lille to the Frontiers of Belgium, with branches to St. Quentin, Calais, and Dunkirk, Valenciennes, Roubais, and Tourcoing, the whole (445 English miles) are open.

The original concession was for 38 years; but in consideration of new lines agreed to be made, by a decree of 19th February, 1852, the concession has been extended to 99 years, and will expire on both sections 10th September, 1947. Government cannot take possession of the line until after February, 1876. The sum to be placed aside each year for the reduction of the social capital is reduced from 2,236,384*fr.* to 168,200*fr.*

This company constructed branches:—1st, Quentin to Érquelinnes, *via* Maubeuge (53 miles); 2nd, from the Boulogne to Nouyelle to St. Vallery (3½ miles); 3rd, to unite that of Maubeuge with that of Valenciennes, *via* Somain and Le Cateau, with a deviation to take in Cambray (22 miles), and 4th, to join the St. Quentin with Paris and Strasburg, *via* La Fere and Rheims (50 miles).

LILLE TO STRASBURG.—By this line the Northern, Ardennes, and Strasburg, are, united together. The Northern construct from Busigny to Hirson; the Ardennes, from Hirson to Thionville: and the Strasburg, thence to Strasburg.

The dividends on each of the 16*l.* shares of this company, for eleven years, have been as follow:—

Year.	Dividend.	Year.	Dividend.
1857	£2 8 0	1863	£2 9 7
1858	2 8 10	1864	2 13 7
1859	2 12 5	1865	2 17 2
1860	2 1ʒ 5	1866	2 16 0
1861	2 12 10	1867	3 0 0
1862	2 9 7		

The average dividend was at the rate of 16¼ per cent. per annum. This result was all the more satisfactory when it was considered that 125,000 new shares of 16*l.* each were admitted to dividend as from January, 1863. The receipts of 1867 on the old network amounted to 3,511,045*l.*, while the working expenses were 1,465,227*l.*, leaving a net profit of 2,045,818*l.*, which was applied as follows:—Interest and redemption of shares, 339,733*l.*; interest and redemption of loans, 460,214*l.*: dotation to the pension fund, 18,573*l.*; stamps, 7,522*l.*; deficiency on the new network, 37,415*l.*; dividend at the rate of 2*l.* 4*s.* 9*d.* per share, 1,176,000*l.*; leaving a balance of 6,368*l.* to be carried forward to the credit of 1868. The total dividend and interest paid on the shares for 1867 was at the rate of 18 per cent. per annum on the paid-up share capital, and even what are termed the *actions de jouissance*, although not entitled to interest, received a dividend of 2*l.* 4*s.* 9*d.* per share, or 14 per cent. on their redeemed capital.

If a convention prepared in 1864 had been carried out, this company would have been relieved of the necessity of rendering any account of its position to the State All its concessions would have been united into one single network, and the State would not have been entitled to a division of profits in excess of the amount prescribed by the conventions of 1858 and 1862, which would thus have been almost rendered mere waste paper. The company would have gladly seen the convention of 1864 approved by the legislative body of France; but, notwithstanding that a favourable report was presented upon the subject by a committee, the Minister of public works deemed it prudent not to expose it to a public discussion and withdrew it, thus preserving to the State, apparently in spite of himself, the participations of profits reserved by the conventions of 1858 and 1862,

CAPITAL.—The company has adjourned until 1872 the closing of its first establishment account, and has been competing of late with the Belgian General Railways Working Company for the concession of several new lines. Assuming that the establishment account is definitely closed in 1872, the old network, on which a line from Dulnoye to Hirson alone remains to be brought into working, will have cost only 20,840,000*l.*, and the new network 7,120,000*l.*, making an aggregate of 27,960,000*l.* At the commencement of the current year 19,480,000*l.* had been expended on the old network, and 6,040,000*l.* on the new network, making a total of 25,520,001*l.* The quantity of additional capital which will have to be provided during 1868, 1869, 1870, and 1871 will thus be 2,420,000*l.*

486.—NORTHERN OF SPAIN.

This company's network is finished, the section from Alar del Rey to Santander
having become available for traffic July 6th, 1866. The rough receipts in 1866, amounted
to 745,016*l*., as compared with 757,480*l*. in 1865, showing a decrease last year of 12,464*l*.
The net profits realised, after provision had been made for working expenses, amounted
to 419,314*l*., as compared with 381,299*l*. in 1865, showing an increase of 38,015*l*. This
result was attributable to a rigorous economy introduced into every department of
management; but notwithstanding these efforts the year's accounts resulted in a deficit
of 48,483*l*., the whole available profit having been more than absorbed by the charges of
the obligation service. A reserve of 119,548*l*. brought forward from 1865 appears to
have been also consumed. The only hope of the company appears to be that Government may be induced to extend some assistance to the concern in the matter.

REVENUE.—For the last three years the revenue may be said to have remained
stationary, having amounted to 727,120*l*. in 1867, as compared with 726,672*l*. in 1866, and
720,978*l*. in 1865. Unfortunately 1868, which opened favourably, exhibited in its turn a
depression of traffic in a part of the districts accommodated by the system. In the
first ten months of the year the average increase in the receipts as compared with the
corresponding period of 1867 was 5·62 per cent.; but then the precarious state of the
crops, and fears as to their insufficiency in some of the important centres of production
in Old Castile, checked the movement of cereals. Notwithstanding this adverse influence, the company's revenue only declined to 1st June to the extent of 1·95 per cent.,
as compared with the corresponding five months of 1867.

CAPITAL.—The receipts on this account to the close of 1867 were shares, 4,000,000*l*.;
obligations, 6,253,681*l*.; subventions paid by Government, 2,264,136*l*.; total, 12,517,817*l*.
The expenditure was 14,260,517*l*., leaving a deficit of 1,742,700*l*., represented by an
unmanageable floating debt, also swollen by the outlay made for stores and interest in
arrear on obligations and liabilities contracted *extra vires*.

487.—NORWAY.

The railway system of this country is being constructed with a gauge of 3 feet 6
inches, under the direction of M. Carl Pihl, State engineer. Two lines have been
completed; the one from Grundsett to Hamar, a distance of 24 English miles, at a cost
of 3,000*l*. per mile, including rolling stock and stations; and the other, from Trondhjem
to Storen, a distance of 30 English miles, at a cost 6,000*l*. per mile, including also
rolling stock and stations; but in the latter case the country was more difficult, the
works generally heavy, so that steep gradients and short curves were unavoidable.

488.—NORWEGIAN TRUNK.

Concession for 100 years from 1852. Line to connect Norway with the two great
lakes of Ogeron and Miosen into communication with Christiania; facilities to transport
timber, &c. Capital, 450,000*l*. Land conveyed by Government at annual rent of 4 per
cent. on its value not exceeding 1,200*l*. a year.

Net profits to be applied to pay, 1st, 5 per cent. on the shareholders' 225,000*l*.; 2nd, 4
per cent. on Government advance surplus to be divided equally. At the end of 100
years Government has option of taking possession of railway, on the payment of shareholders' portion of capital.

The first section extending from Christiania and Strommen, a length of about 11 miles, was opened for timber traffic in July, 1853; the second section to Dahl, making a total length of 36 miles, was opened in November, and the line throughout to the termination of Eidsvold, in September, 1854. Total, 42 miles.

DIRECTORS IN ENGLAND:

Thamas Brassey, Esq., 56, Lowndes Square, S.W., and 8, Adam Street, Adelphi, W.C.

Sir S. M. Peto, Bart., Palace Gardens, W., and 9, Great George Street, Westminster, S.W.

DIECTORS IN NORWAY:

(Named under the contract by the Norwegian Government):

Dr. Broch. | A. Stabell. | M. Heftye.

OFFICERS.—Representative at Christiania of the English Directors, J. R. Crowe, British Consul-General; Eng., G. P. Bidder: Agents for the payment of dividends, A. and W. Ricardo, 11, Angel Court, Throgmorton Street, E.C., to whom all inquiries are to be addressed.

489.—NOVARA AND LAKE ORTA.

This undertaking (limited) is intended to form the first section of the "European Junction," uniting Italy with Germany and France. Capital, 200 000l. in 20,000 shares, at 10l. each, with power to raise 75,000l. in debentures, retaining shares to that amount, 12,500 shares only being issued. The concession for this line (27 English miles) was granted for 100 years by the Sardinian Government in July, 1860, and time fixed for its being opened, February, 1862, the rate of charges being the same as on the Government lines. The line was opened from Novara to Gozzano on 10th of March, 1864, and is worked by the Italian Government, on terms which the directors consider satisfactory.

DIRECTORS:

The Hon. Thomas C. Bruce, 13, Hartford Street, May Fair, W.
Alan Lambert, Esq., Heath House, Putney, S.W.
Nicholas Philpot Leader, Esq., Dromah Castle, Kanturk, County Cork.

Charles Liddell, Esq., Abingdon Street, Westminster, S.W.
R. S. Newall, Esq., Gateshead, Durham.
Thomas Collett Sandars, Esq., Michenden House, Southgate, N.

OFFICERS.—Sec., Edward Bellamy; Eng., G. Barkley; Solicitors, Hughes, Masterman, and Co.

Offices—7, Westminster Chambers Victoria Street, Westminster S.W.

490.—OTTOMAN—SMYRNA TO AIDIN.

Established by concession from the Turkish Government, who guarantee the company 112,000l. per annum. The following is an outline of the principal clauses of the concession :—

1. It is perpetual, subject to the right of purchase by the Ottoman Government upon agreed and equitable terms, at the end of 50, 75, 95, and every subsequent 20 years. 2. A guarantee as above-mentioned for 42 years. The line to be opened in sections, and the guarantee to come into operation as each section is opened. Profits over 8 per cent. to be divided with Government. 3. Government lands and materials to be taken and made use of by the company gratuitously. 4. Materials for constructing, working, and renewing the railway, to be imported duty free. 5. Power of working all coal mines within 30 miles of any part of the lines on payment of a fixed royalty. 6. The privileges of erecting warehouse, with a custom house attached, on company's premises at Smyrna. 7. Government not to grant a concession to any competing line. 8. Unrestricted power of management.

The railway, 80¾ miles in length, connects Smyrna, the most important seaport in the Levant, with Guzel Hissar or Aidin, the grand entrepot of the internal trade of Asia Minor. The works were commenced on 24th September, 1858, and 27 miles were opened on 24th December, 1860; 10 on 9th September, 1861: and 3 (completing the first section) on 14th November, 1861. The extension to Ephesus (7½ miles), was opened on 15th September, 1862; the line being opened to Aidin on 1st July, 1866, when the guarantee of 112,000l. a year, by the Turkish Government, should have come into operation.

The company has been sadly disturbed during the year by differences of opinion among the shareholders, and by the withholding of the guarantee by the Turkish Government in consequence of assertions to the effect that the line and stations have not been completed according to the contract. The council regret that, notwithstanding their unceasing exertions have been directed to obtain a settlement with the Ottoman Government, they are unable to report the receipt of funds on account of the arrears. The amount due to the company, to the 1st January, 1868, is 190,632l.

The entire income for the half-year ending 30th June amounted to 22,217*l.*, being an increase of 4,921*l.* over the corresponding half of last year. The ordinary working expenses amounted to 20,432*l.*, to which had to be added 1,661*l.*, the expenses in London and Constantinople, including the cost of being specially represented at the latter place, making a total of 22,093*l.*, leaving a balance of 123*l.* ; while for the corresponding period of 1867 the loss on the working, after deducting 2,950*l.* brought forward from the preceding half-year, amounted to 2,061*l.* The rolling stock was in an improved condition, and was fully equal not only to the present requirements of the line, but for all anticipated increase for some time to come. The expenditure under this head had been 4,174*l.*, of which 1,763*l.* had been expended in additional rolling stock, and 2,408*l.* on works required to be borne by capital. The remainder of the works, specified in the report of the special commissioner of the Ottoman Government, would be executed gradually within the dates fixed by the Government.

CAPITAL.—This account to 30th June last showed that 1,818,612*l.* had been expended, leaving a balance against the account of 76,255*l.*

DIRECTORS :

Chairman—Sir R. MACDONALD STEPHENSON, 72, Lancaster Gate, W.

Deputy-Chairman—ALEXANDER DEVAUX, Esq., 62, King William Street, E.C.

William John Lysley, Esq., 23, Prince's Gardens, W.

Eric Carrington Smith, Esq., 1, Lombard Street, E.C.

Major-General Tremenheere, Spring Grove, Isleworth, W.

Seymour Toulon, Esq., Tenchleys Park, Limpsfield, Surrey.

Joseph Henry Trewby, Esq., Chancellor, Turkish Embassy, 1, Bryanston Sq., W.

Edward Warner, Esq., Quorn Hall, near Loughborough.

OFFICERS.—Sec., S. J. Cooke ; Traffic and Loco. Supt., Edward Purser, C.E., Smyrna ; Agent, Henry James Hanson, Constantinople : Auditors, George Smith and Henry Lloyd Morgan ; Solicitor, George Rooper, 26, Lincoln's-Inn-Fields, W.C. ; Accountant, S. J. Smithers ; Bankers in London, Smith, Payne, and Smiths, 1, Lombard Street, E.C.; Bankers in Turkey, C. S. Hanson and Co., Constantinople ; the Ottoman Bank, Smyrna.

Offices—47A, Moorgate Street, E.C.

491.—PARIS CIRCULAR.

This line *de ceinture*, which goes great part of the way round Paris, to unite the different lines, was completed in October, 1854. It was executed by the administration des Pontes-et-Chaussees, and has cost 540,000*l.* Of this sum, the Rouen, Northern, Strasburg, Lyons, and Orleans, each contributed 1,000,000*fr.*, and the State gave the remainder, viz., 7,000,000*fr.* The entire length of the line is nearly 11 miles, including the junctions.

The concession of an extension of the Girdle of Paris (left bank) has been granted to the Western. By this arrangement the termini of five of the great systems—the Northern, the Orleans, the Lyons-Mediterranean, the Eastern, and the Western—will be united to each other.

492.—PARIS, LYONS, AND MEDITERRANEAN.

This is a confederation of the PARIS and LYONS, LYONS and MEDITERRANEAN, LYONS and GENEVA, and all the subsidiaries of these companies.

DAUPHINE.—In conformity with the resolution of 18th July, 1863, the 35,000 shares were exchanged for 58,333 three per cent. obligations of the Paris, Lyons, and Mediterranean, at the rate of 1⅔ obligation for each share. These obligations bear interest from 1st January, 1864.

The network in Algeria conceded to the company by a decree dated June 11th, 1863, comprises two lines, viz., that from Algiers to Oran, about 286¼ miles ; and from Phillippeville to Oran, 54⅘ miles.

As this undertaking dates in its present form only from July 3rd, 1857, we cannot extend our retrospect of the dividends on each 20*l.* share over a longer period than ten years :—

Year.	Dividend.	Year.	Dividend.
1858	£2 2 6	1863	£3 0 0
1859	1 19 7	1864	2 12 0
1860	2 10 10	1865	2 8 0
1861	2 10 10	1866	2 8 0
1862	3 0 0	1867	2 8 0

It is expected that the dividend of 2*l.* 8*s.* per 20*l.* share will be maintained until 1872 or 1873.

The amount derived from the working of the old network in 1867 amounted to 6,961,609*l.* After deducting the tax of 10 per cent. imposed on the quick train traffic and the subventions to external services, the amount was still 6,641,097*l.* The working expenses were 2,237,543*l*., leaving the net profits at 4,403,554*l*., increased to about 4,514,840*l*. by temporary investments and miscellaneous receipts, and reduced again to 4,311,280*l*. by an expenditure of 203,560*l*. for renewal of way. The 4,311,280*l*. forming the definite net profit of the old network was applied thus :—Fixed charges of the old network, 1,293,487*l*. ; insufficiencies of the new network, 966,144*l*. ; special reserve, 120,000*l*.; dividend of 2*l*. 8*s*. per share (or 12 per cent. for the year on the share capital), 1,920,000*l*.; balance carried forward to 1868, about 11,000*l*.

A new division has been made of the lines conceded. Thus lines to the aggregate length of 977½ miles, representing a total capital of 33,024,000*l*., are transferred from the new to the old network, the length of which is increased to 2,594⅜ miles. This modification has more particularly the effect of comprising in one and the same network the two lines from Paris to Lyons, *via* Burgundy and the Bourbonnais, so that the company has no interest in diverting traffic in passengers and goods to either of these routes—that is, through traffic to Lyons. The new arrangement also forms groups of lines united to each other by their geographical position like those from Nevers and Moulins to Chagny and from Santenay to Étang which attach themselves to the Bourbonnais group just at the Dauphiné and Savoy lines are the complement of the lines from Mâcon and Lyons to Geneva. The majority of the lines added to the old network are open for traffic, and their earnings, when contrasted with the present accruing on their estimated cost, lead to the conclusion that their profits are by no means sufficient to cover the charges resulting from the outlay made on first establishment account. Interest guaranteed at the rate of 4·65 per cent. per annum on a total capital of 33,024,000*l*. is a considerable annual charge, and by the new arrangements made the responsibilities of the state will be diminished to this extent. Earnings of the old network will be sufficient to provide for this new state of affairs ; but if by a combination of unfortunate circumstances the case should prove otherwise, the insufficiency must be provided for out of the balance available for dividend on the company's share capital, and will not fall on the French Treasury. Further, by the new arrangements the length of the new network is reduced to 1,026⅞ miles, and the amount of the new network capital on which a guarantee of interest is given is reduced to 22,720,000*l*. By the convention of 1863 the new network capital was fixed at 50,200,000*l*. Various supplementary charges will probably increase it even now to 25,200,000*l*.

London Agency—Devaux and Co., 62, King William Street, E.C.

493.—PARIS AND ORLEANS.

With its extension to Nevers, Roanne, Clermont, Limoges, Bordeaux, Rochfort, La Rochelle, and Nantes, comprises an aggregate length of 981 English miles ; an amalgamation of PARIS AND ORLEANS, ORLEANS AND BORDEAUX, CENTRAL OF FRANCE, and TOURS AND NANTES, fused 27th March, 1852. Concession, 99 years, from 1st January, 1852, to 31st December, 1950. The Grand Central has been leased by the Paris and Orleans also.

The dividends for 11 years on this line have been, on each 20*l*. share, as under :—

Year.	Dividend.	Year.	Dividend.
1857	£3 12 0	1863	£4 0 0
1858	3 9 7	1864	4 0 0
1859	3 17 6	1865	2 4 10
1860	4 0 0	1866	2 4 10
1861	4 0 0	1867	2 4 10
1862	4 0 0		

The company in 1868 obtained a concession from Government of two lines from Chateaubriant to Nantes, and from Romorantin to the line from Tours to Vierzon—lines which must be executed in eight years from January 1, 1870. The state grants a subvention of 348,000*l*. for the first, and 44,000*l*. for the second ; these subventions are to be paid in sixteen equal half-yearly instalments in proportion to the progress made with the works. The state reserves to itself at the same time the right to convert this subvention into eighty-seven annuities or to deliver in payment lands, earthworks, and works of art, this faculty being extended to all the subventions allowed by the convention of 1863.

The net revenue reserved to the old network by the convention of June 11, 1863, was 1,684*l*. per mile, on 1,103⅜ miles. The first establishment capital of the old network was fixed at 21,480,000*l*., of which 12,000,000*l*. was represented by shares, and 9,480,000*l*. by obligations ; but this amount will now be reduced by 880,000*l*. representing the cession of the Bourbonnais. Further, the length of the old concessions has been increased to 1,262½ miles, by the transference to the old network of a line from Brétigny to Tours, and 1,664*l*. per mile on 1,262½ miles comes to about 2,100,800*l*., while 1,684*l*. on 1,103⅜ miles makes 1,860,000*l*. The old network will have to sustain a charge of 1·10 per cent. per annum on the additional new network obligation capital which is proposed to be created ; but even after providing for this, it is calculated that the net revenue account will not be affected, as regards the balance for dividend.

The traffic for 1867 showed receipts of 3,344,640*l*. on the old network, and 1,062,400*l*. on the new. The receipts per mile on the old network were nearly three times the corresponding amount per mile realised on the new. The net profit of the old, calculated on the *déversoir* system, amounted, for 1867, to 1,907,963*l*., which was applied as follows :—Loan charges, 308,363*l*.; difference of 1'10 per cent. between the guarantee of the State and the effective charges of the loans of the new net work, 209,044*l*.; redemption of shares, 25,576*l*.; pension to M. Lecomte, 410*l*.: leaving a balance of 1,364,564*l*. available for distribution on the shares. The amount paid to the shareholders October 1, 1867 (16*s*. per share) as a provisional distribution was 480,000*l*.; and the balance (1*l*. 8*s*. 9*d*. per share) absorbed 864,000*l*.; making a total of 1,344,000*l*.; a sum of 20,564*l*. thus remained to be carried forward. The amount which had to be paid in 1867 by the State, in respect to its guarantee, was 389.280*l*., as compared with 422,202*l*. in 1866.

There seem to be still 435 miles to complete on the new work, as regards the concessions granted up to and in 1863. The convention of 1868 increases the new network by five new lines, having an aggregate length of 114⅜ miles. Two only of these five new lines—that from Nantes to Châteaubriant (39⅜ miles), and a branch to Romorantin (5 miles)—are conceded definitively. A subvention of 348,000*l*. is granted for the first line out of 960,000*l*., forming the estimated expense ; and a subvention of 44,000*l*. is granted for the second, the estimated cost of establishment being 80,000*l*. The three lines conceded eventually extend from Libourne to Bergerac (39⅜ miles) ; from Bergerac to the Buisson de Cabans (23¾ miles) ; and from St. Eloi to the line from Commentry to Gannat (6⅞ miles).

The whole of the concessions of the Orleans extend over a distance of 2,751⅞ miles, of which 1.262½ miles are comprised in the old network, and the balance in the new network. Before the conclusion of the convention of 1868, the cost of establishing this vast mileage was estimated at 52,120,000*l*. ; and this sum has now been increased to 55,640,000*l*., as well in consequence of the new lines conceded as in consequence of additions to the estimated cost of the old lines. The augmentation relates entirely to the capital of the guaranteed network, which has been increased from 30,640,000*l*. to 34,160,000*l*. The 758¾ miles worked on the new network in 1867 produced a net profit of 437,256*l*., while the service—that is, the charge for interest and redemption—of the capital of 20,120,000*l*. engaged absorbed 1,146,550*l*. There is thus a heavy deficit to be made good either by carrying a portion of the obligation interest charges to first establishment account as regards certain lines of the new network, or by putting in force on others the guarantee of interest given by the State on the new network capital,—this guarantee being 4 per cent. per annum for interest, and 0'65 per cent. per annum for redemption. As the charge of the obligations for interest and redemption averages 5'75 per cent , the difference of 1'10 per cent. per annum has in any case to be made good out of the profits realised by the company on its old network over and above the reserved revenue of that portion of the system.

CAPITAL.—At the close of 1867 the amount raised for construction and equipment of the old net work was 19,633,001*l*., of which 19,483,251*l*. had been expended, leaving a balance of 149,750*l*. A sum of 654,442*l*. had also been raised on capital account for the Aubin mines and ironworks. The receipts on the new net work were 26,892,447*l*., of which 25,904,978*l*. had been expended, leaving a balance of 987,469*l*. The total amount raised at the close of 1867 was thus no less than 47,179,890*l*. The amount expended on the old net work in 1867 was 696,000*l*.; and on the new net work, 1,744,000*l*.

Offices—Bouleval de l'Hospital, Paris ; for transfers, &c., 4, Rue Drouet.

494.—RIGA AND DUNABURG.

Provisionally registered 7th and 8th Vic., cap. 110. Established by special decree of His Imperial Majesty the Emperor of Russia, dated 18th May, 1853, granting a guarantee of a minimum interest of 4 per cent. on the sum of 12,000,000s. *rs*. of capital, which is equal to a guarantee of 5 per cent. on the sum required for the construction of the railway, with other valuable privileges. An additional half per cent. is also guaranteed on the above sum, to form a sinking fund to redeem the shares at par within 56 years. Length, 140 miles.

Capital (authorised by the Imperial Government), 2,000,000*l*. in 20,000 shares of 100*l*. each, bearing a guaranteed minimum interest of 4 per cent. to be issued at 80*l*. Deposit, 1*l*. per share. 3,000 shares reserved for shareholders in Russia.

Several modifications in the concession were announced in March, 1857. The more prominent were as follows :—"The term of the concession has been extended from 56 to 75 years, dated from the opening of the whole line. during which period the company will enjoy the profits. The Imperial Government has not reserved to itself the right to purchase the line during the term of concession. The terms as now arranged enable the directors to substantiate the original representation of a *minimum interest of 5 per cent*. upon the required capital ; and the terms of the contract for the construction of the line, as approved by the Engineer-in-Chief, leave such a margin as to justify the directors in anticipating an increase on that per centage. The company is not required to account to the Imperial Government for its expenditure, but the guarantee applies to the fixed capital for 75 years ; hence, any saving in the cost of the works enhances the value of the guarantee." Opened September, 1861.

DIRECTORS :

Chairman—The Councillor of State, G. VON CUBE, Riga.
Deputy-Chairman—Coll. Ass. A FALTIN, Riga.

A. Hollander. Esq., Riga.	Henry Robinson, Esq., Riga.
Councillor Dolmatow.	

The number of Directors is limited to 5.

495,—ROMAN.

Described as the first section of a grand line from Rome to Naples, is founded on a concession for 99 years,—*Société Anonyme*, authorised by decree of Pontifical Government, dated November, 8th, 1854. Capital, 320,000*l.* divided into 32,000 shares of 10*l.* each. In operation, 762½ miles.

Advances are made by the Italian Government, to be made good afterwards out of the mileage subventions promised, and which are, in fact, to be discounted. The first advance is 440,000*l.*, required for the payment of the interest due for 186 , on the ordinary obligations issued by the company. The second advance is 320,000*l.* to meet the most urgent debts of the company, including the arrears due for works on the section from San Severino to Solofra. The third advance is a sum of 184,000*l.*, the definitive application of which has not been yet determined on, and which will probably be absorbed in great part in the payment of amounts due from the company to the Government. The fourth advance is 256,000*l.*, which is to be applied to the execution of urgent works on the line from Torricelle to Foligno, to works remaining to be completed on two lines from Orvieto to Orte, and from Nuziatella to Chiarone (in order that those lines may be opened for traffic as soon as possible), and to the improvement of the plant upon the network. The company deposit with the Government 100,000 obligations authorised but not yet placed ; these obligations serve as security for the advances to be made by the Government, and the latter may, by the arrangement entered into, dispose of them in whole or part, on the condition that the selling price is 6*l.* per obligation at the least.

By statements submitted to the annual meeting in October, the expenditure had been 18,573,335*l.*, represented by 1,047½ miles of line, of which, however, 88¾ miles have been ceded to the Italian Government, leaving 958¾ miles still to be worked by the company. The Italian and Pontifical Governments have given mileage guarantees : and in representation of the sale of part of its network to the South Italian, the Roman is also to receive a rent from that company to the amount of 142,400*l.* per annum. The charges for the year were 1,696,000*l.* ; and deducting these charges from the various receipts, subventions, &c., there remained a surplus of 97,600*l.* for division among the shareholders. The difference of 97,600*l.* enabled the directors to declare a dividend of 4*s.* per share for 1869. The subvention of the Pontifical Government for the next five years is to be 100,000*l.* per annum. Great efforts have been made to come to some arrangement with the Italian Government to secure the extinction of the floating debt. A scheme for the purchase of the system by the State proved abortive, but the State consented to postpone until 1872 the repayment of its debt. At June 30th, 1868, the floating debt was 3,406,725*l.* of which 1,408,560*l.* were due to the State ; this is the debt, the repayment of which is to be postponed. The company also succeeded in inducing the Pontifical Government to come to some arrangement with reference to the arrears of its guarantees, which amounted for the five years ending 1867, inclusive, to 209,994*l.*; of this sum the Pontifical Government undertook to pay 125,797*l.* in November and December 1868, and January 1869. In exchange for this partial satisfaction, the company undertakes to construct in the course of the next ten years a central station at Rome.

With regard to the Italian Government, the Ligurian is retroceded to the State : and the line from Florence to Massa, *via* Pistoja and Lucca, is sold to the Government for a sum of 1,400,000*l.*, which will be applied in reduction of the floating debt. The Roman undertakes to work a line from Florence to La Spezzia in consideration of a rent of 52 per cent. on the rough receipts, and an annual indemnity of 4,000*l.* for shelter for the plant employed. Not only does the Italian Government agree to pay 1,400,000*l.* for the Florence and Massa, but it also promises to make an advance of 400,000*l.* to the company.

The affairs of the company are in future to be administered by a council of sixteen members, four of whom will be nominated by the Italian Government, and must be Italians. Of the other twelve members of the council, who are to be chosen by the shareholders, six are to be Frenchmen, and six Italians. Of the twelve gentlemen elected, eight were old directors and four were new candidates. Altogether, the management of the company appears to have been greatly modified. Signor Perruzzi is named as probable future director-general of the company.

496.—ROYAL PORTUGUESE.

A *Company Anonyme.* Share capital, 1,400,000*l.*, in 70,000 shares of 20*l.* each. Bonds are authorised in addition, to complete the undertaking. Concession granted to M. José de Salamanca by Act of 14th September, 1859, and ratified by the Cortes, on the following conditions :—

1. The concession is granted for 99 years.
2. Tariffs similar to those of the French railways.
3. Subvention granted by the Portuguese Government, amounting on an average to 7,258*l.* per English mile.

The concession is for a line from Lisbon to Badajoz on the Spanish frontier, to join the line from Badajoz to Madrid ; also from Lisbon to Oporto ; length, 310 English miles. The capital is represented by 70,000 shares of 20*l.*, now fully paid up, and by debentures. Guaranteed interest of 8 per cent. during construction. The obligations of the company are for 20*l.* each, being the nominal amount ; but according to the continental system they are issued at 10*l*., the other half being the bonus payable when the obligations are drawn. The interest is 3 per cent. on the nominal amount, being 6 per cent. on the cash. Drawings take place every year, and each drawing increases annually from the accumulations of interest on the amortisated bonds. The subvention of the Government was from 4,500*l*. to 5,400*l*. per kilometre, according to the nature of the ground. The first section of 47 miles was opened 1st July, 1861.

The difficulties of the company continue, no arrangement having yet been effected with the Portuguese Government, but the floating debt has been reduced to 64,000*l*., while it stood a year since at 160,000*l*. This appears the one hopeful feature in the position of the company, which in other respects is about as bad as it well can be. The Portuguese Government requires help almost as much as the company, and has not rendered it at present any tangible assistance. Even auxiliary common roads to the stations remain uncompleted. The directors appear still to possess the confidence of the shareholders. Thus the report and accounts for 1868 were adopted at the annual meeting, held at Lisbon, in December, and the retiring directors—M. Daru, M. Delahante, Senor don José de Salamanca, and Senor Mendoza—were re-elected.

DIRECTORS:

MM. Marshal Duke of Saldanha (late President of Portuguese Council of Ministers).
Viscount Paiva, Minister of Portugal in Paris.
Fortunato Chamico, Banker in Lisbon.
Roldau, Banker in Lisbon.
José de Salamanca.
A. Llorente.
I. de Zaragoza.
De la Grandara.
José de la Fuente, Ex-Deputé.
Ch. Devaux, Banker, London.

William Barber Buddicom, Esq., Penbedw Hall, near Mold, Flintshire.
E. Blount, Banker in Paris.
Litchlin, Vice-President of Société Générale de Crédit Industriel et Commercial.
Joseph de la Bouillerie, Director of Société Générale de Crédit Industriel et Commercial.
Chatelus, Chief Engineer of Mines.
Gustave Delahante.
M. Daru.
Senor Mendoza.

Agents in London, G. E. Balleras and Co., 13, Austin Friars, E.C.

497.—ROYAL SARDINIAN.

Guaranteed by the Italian Government. A *Société Anonyme*: the liability of shareholders limited to the amount of their shares. Share capital, 1,000,000*l*. sterling, in 50,000 shares, of 20*l*. to bearer, with power to issue 2,000,000*l*. nominal capital, in obligations or debentures.

The shares to be redeemed by lot, at par, out of the proceeds of freehold landed estates granted to the company, to bear interest at 6 per cent. per annum during construction, and subsequently an estimated minimum annual dividend of 32*s*. (equal to 8 per cent.) per share, based upon the Government guarantee, and payable during the whole term of 99 years, on all shares whether redeemed or not.

Debentures or obligations 20*l*. each, to bear interest at 3 per cent. per annum, repayable by annual drawings within 41 years, at par; to be issued at 11*l*. each. Every subscriber for shares to have a preferential option of claiming two obligations or debentures for each share allotted to him.

The Government of Italy, by virtue of an Act bearing the royal confirmation under date of the 4th January, 1863, conferred the following concessions, which have been purchased by this company:—

1. The exclusive privilege of constructing railways in the Island of Sardinia.
2. A guarantee or subvention for the lines now proposed of 9,000 lire for each kilometre of railway, or 58*l*. sterling per English mile, per annum, net revenue, for the period of 99 years, payable as each section is opened for traffic; and
3. An immediate grant to the company, in perpetuity and absolutely, of freehold landed estates, belonging to the Crown, in the Island of Sardinia, containing 200,000 hectares, or 480,000 English acres, the present value of which is officially returned at 500,000*l*., but which it is manifest will be largely increased by the completion of the railways.

The works are for the present in abeyance in consequence of the Italian Government not having been able, from its political necessities, to fulfil its engagements,

Shareholders in England desiring information as to the company's affairs may obtain the same either by direct communication with the secretary at the offices, No. 28, Via della Scala, Florence, or at the offices of Messrs. Bircham and Co., 46, Parliament Street, Westminster.

COUNCIL OF ADMINISTRATION IN ITALY:

Honorary President—MARQUIS DE BOYL and VILLAFLOR.

Signor Guiseppe Sanna-Sanna, Deputy of the Italian Parliament.
The Baron Sabino Leonino (Leonino Brothers, Bankers), Genoa.

Secretary, *pro. tem.*, G. B. Gaja, Florence.

DIRECTORS IN ENGLAND:

Chairman—H. R. GRENFELL, Esq. (Pascoe Grenfell and Sons), 15, St. James's Place, S.W.

Deputy-Chairman—CHARLES BELL, Esq., M.P. (Thomson, Bonar, & Co., London.)

Thomas Barnes, Esq., Farnworth, near Bolton, Lancashire, and the Quinta, near Chirk.

The Chevalier Ippolito Leonino (I. Leonino and Co.), London.

John Pender, Esq. (John Pender and Co.), Manchester.

OFFICERS.—Secretary in London, C. de Tivoli, 1, Great Winchester Street Buildings; Eng., Benjamin Piercy, C.E., Duke Street, S.W.; Solicitors, Bircham and Co., Parliament Street, S.W.

498.—ROYAL SWEDISH.

Originally established under royal charter. Constructed from Arboga to Orebro. Opened in March, 1856, 10 miles; in August, 1857, 25 miles. The ascertained nominal capital of the company is as follows:—92,000 original shares of 5l. each ; 38,000 preference shares of 4l. each ; and 32,000 obligation shares of 4l. each, which are in gradual process of liquidation.

ARBOGA AND KOPING EXTENSION.—A line has lately been constructed by an independent company from Uttersburg to Koping, a distance of 15 English miles north of the latter town, for the accommodation of a mineral district, from whence is brought a considerable supply of rough ore, and also manufactured iron. The port of Koping, on the Malar lake, however, is closed by ice during several months of the year ; and a necessity has arisen for securing communication all the year round with the southern ports of Sweden (and especially Gothenberg) over the Government state railways. This has revived the question of completing this company's line between Arboga and Koping, by which means, and passing over the entire line, the Southern and other districts might be reached. So important is this deemed to be by those interested in the Uttersburg-Koping, that they have united to raise the necessary funds for finishing the Arboga-Koping Extension, one-half being granted by the Government, as is usual under such circumstances, to enterprises of this kind. This extension was opened in October, 1867.

REVENUE.—The receipts for the year 1867 were 17,083l.; the working expenses and other charges left a balance of 4,151l., which enabled the directors to make a further payment to the obligation-holders of 2s., the amount of one coupon, per obligation on account of the arrears of interest due to them.

CAPITAL.—The nominal capital now consists of 92,000 original shares of 5l. each ; 38,000 preference shares of 4l. each ; and 32,500 obligations of 4l. each. The assets of the company to 31st December, 1867, exclusive of the line, plant, rolling stock, and fixtures, consisted of—

Balance at Banker's, in England £12
Calls due on preference shares.................................... 50
Balance of capital account in Sweden £31
　　,,　　　revenue 4,151
　　,,　　　reserve fund 471
Value of stores and materials 5,785
530 shares in Arboga-Koping Company of 100 rix dols. each 2,944
900 shares of Netherlands Land Company of 10l. each.

DIRECTORS IN SWEDEN:

Count A. E. Von Rosen. | P. G. Hjelm.

Manager, Marcus Agrelius ; Engineer, J. J. Cronin.

DIRECTORS IN LONDON:

G. E. Seymour, Esq., 38, Throgmorton Street, E C.

F. L. Austen, Esq., 26, Hyde Park Square, W.

Ernest Chaplin, Esq., Brooksby Hall, Leicester.

William Hartridge, Esq., 80, Old Broad Street, E.C.

Secretary, G. A. Hillier.

Offices—208, Gresham House, Old Broad Street, E.C.

499.—RUSSIA.

The net work in this country now comprises—1. The lines of Poland. 2. Lines from Warsaw to St. Petersburg and from St. Petersburg to Moscow. 3. A line from Moscow to Odessa. 4. A line from Riga cutting that from Warsaw to St. Petersburg at the Dunaburg station and terminating at the line from Moscow to Odessa, at the Orel station. 5. A line leaving Moscow in order to direct itself to the north to Sergnievsk, another also leaving Moscow and directing itself to the east to Nijni-Novgorod, and finally a third directing itself to the south-east to Vorsnech. 6. Lines from Helsingfors to Tavastchus, in Finland ; from Poté to Tiflis, in Georgia ; and from Odessa to Kerbinety, in Bessarabia. This network will probably be completed by the adjunction of the following :—1. A line running from Koursk to the line from Moscow to Odessa and directing itself to Taganrog, a port on the Sea of Azof. 2. Another uniting Orel and Moscow with the Volga and the Don. 3. Another from Moscow to Warsaw. 4. Two lines uniting, one Siberia and the other Tartary to Russia. 5. A line from St. Petersburg to Helsingfors, in Finland. 6. One uniting the Volga to the Dwina. 7. One uniting Kiel to the line from Moscow to Warsaw. 8. A line from St. Petersburg to various ports of the Baltic. 9. Another from Liebau to the line from St. Petersburgh to Warsaw. 10. Finally another from Rybinsk on the Volga to Osnetschinsk on the line from Moscow to St. Petersburgh. When all these lines are executed, Russia, which is now behind other European nations as regards the development of railway communication, will perhaps find herself in advance of them. But it will take many years to fulfil the programme, although the cost does not exceed 9,000l. to 13,000l. per mile. On the other hand, some of them will run through very thinly populated districts,—it may almost be said through undeveloped wildernesses.

The concession has been approved of a line from Port Baltic to St. Petersburg. The length of the line is considerable (343 verstes) ; it will fall into the St. Petersburg and Warsaw. The capital has been fixed at 24,010,000 metallic roubles, represented by 192,080 shares of 125 roubles each. This capital is stated to have been subscribed in Russia.

500.—SAMBRE AND MEUSE.

This Anglo-Belgian company was formed in 1844, to construct a line from the coal basin at Charleroi, on the Sambre, to Vireux, on the Meuse. The length of the trunk line from Marchiennes to terminus on the Meuse is 38½ miles ; the branch to Morialmé, 8¼ miles ; and to Llaneffe, 3¾ miles. These two branches were opened on 1st December, 1848, at the same time as the first portion of the trunk line, 12 miles to Walcourt. The trunk to the terminus at Vireux on the Meuse was opened in August, 1854 ; the branch to Couvin, about 3¼ miles, on 16th June of same year. The branch from Walcourt to St. Lambert, on 20th December, 1853, and thence to Florennes on 12th July, 1854, together about 11¼ miles ; and the branch from Proidmont to Phillipeville, 3 miles, on 20th November, 1854. These three last named branches have a net income of 8,000l. per annum for 50 years, guaranteed by the Belgian Government, by whom any deficit is to be made up. The railway from Chimay to the French frontier, a continuation of that from Marienburg to the former place was opened for traffic on the 17th September, 1859. Trunk and branches, 68 miles.

The dividends for the half-years ending 31st December and 30th June were at the rate of 4s. per share.

CAPITAL.—This account to 30th June showed that the expenditure had amounted to 1,108,597l., which exhibited a balance against receipts of 21,107l.

Original capital	£620,000	
Less shares in hands of the company	32,460 =	£587,540
		199,910
Preference capital	200,000	
4 per cent. loan guaranteed by Belgian Government	40,000 =	160,000
Less discount on issue	155,600	
4½ per cent. debentures	15,560 =	140,040
Less discount on issue		21,107
Balance		
		£1,108,597

DIRECTORS :
Chairman—GEORGE SHEWARD, Esq., Leinster Square, Bayswater, W.

William Austin, Esq., The Mount, Farningham, Kent.
*Henry Harrison, Esq., Maple Lodge, Surbiton.
*Henry T. Taylor, Esq., Salisbury Place, Turnham Green, W.

Thomas Brassey, Esq., Lowndes Square, S.W., and 4, Great George Street, Westminster, S.W.
*Re-elected in September.
All eligible for re-election.

OFFICERS.—Sec., A. Snellgrove ; London Bankers, Consolidated Bank, Threadneedle Street, E.C.

Offices—61, Moorgate Street, E.C.

501.—SARAGOSSA, PAMPELUNA, AND BARCELONA.

At the close of April, 1867, this company had a floating debt of 210,526l., while the obligation service (suspended in October, 1866), was in arrear to the extent of 10,526l., making a total of 221,051l. From this amount, however, must be deducted 42,105l. for cash and securities held, leaving a balance of 178,936l. In order to pay this sum, the council of administration proposed that the obligation-holders should consent to receive, during a period of two years, only half their coupon interest, subject to the reception of the other at some future time. The receipts slightly declined last year, while the working expenses increased, so that the net profit realised in 1866 declined to 181,656*l.*, as compared with 201,258*l.* in 1865. The company received last year from the Government a supplementary subvention of 112,421*l.* in reparation of a loss experienced by the old Barcelona company in the negotiation of State securities representing the value of the subventions originally accorded.

The debt on running account has been brought down to 86,052*l.*, and it is being progressively reduced out of receipts. The net profits of last year fell short of the total amount due for obligation interest by about 20,000*l.*; they amounted, however, to 228,425*l.*, presenting an advance of about 25 per cent. as compared with 1866. The company is paying its obligation coupons as far as it can, but they are still about eighteen months in arrear.

502.—SAXONY.

The Government has undertaken the following sections at the cost of the State :— Leipzig and Chemnitz, estimated at 7,000,000 *thalers;* Raderberg and Kamenz, 2,500,000 *thalers;* Grosschonau and Warnsdorf, 150,000 *thalers;* Warnsdorf and Lobau, 1,850,000 *thalers;* and Aue and Jagersgrun, 2,500,000 *thalers;* total, 14,000,000 *thalers.* This sum is being obtained by means of a loan. The construction by the State of other lines is also decreed, but their execution is adjourned while other lines are abandoned to private enterprise. In order to provide for the works which it has on hand, the Saxon Government issued a loan of 20,000,000 *thalers*, at 4 per cent., of which 17,500,000 *thalers* were to be applied to railway works, and 2,500,000 *thalers* to the construction of barracks.

503.—SMYRNA AND CASSABA.

A Limited Liability Association, with a guarantee of 40,000*l.* a year from the Turkish Government. Capital, 800,000*l.* in shares, and 230,000*l.* in debentures. Length, 61 miles. Opened 15th March, 1866.

It was reported in May that from 7th October, 1866, to 14th April, 1867, the weekly receipts averaged 1,167*l.*, and the receipts per mile per week, 19*l.* 2*s.* 6*d.*, showing a weekly increase. The line had been taken by the company on 1st January, 1867, and was under the management of Mr. Price pending definitive arrangements with the company. The commissioner of the Turkish Government had signed the certificate for the payment of the balance due on account of the guaranteed interest for the first year ending 31st December, 1866. It was further stated that 30,000*l.* a year would pay the interest on debentures, &c., and leave 10,000*l.* for dividend on the ordinary capital. The amount of the Government certificate to the end of the year was 11,000*l.* If the traffic earned a net profit on the working of 25,000*l.* a-year the Government would have to pay the difference, only 15,000*l.*, under the guarantee of 40,000*l.* a year. The receipts for the three months ending 31st March amounted to 14,037*l.*, and the expenses to 8,315*l.*, leaving a net balance of 5,722*l.*, or an average of 22,800*l.* a year for the first three months, which were not the best for traffic. The total cost of the railway would be about 800,000*l.* for 61 miles. The guarantee would pay all preference charges, and leave something more than 2 per cent. for the ordinary capital.

REVENUE.—The receipts for the half-year ending 31st December amounted to 44,490*l.*, or 28*l.* per mile per week, against 28,961*l.*, or 19*l.* per mile per week for the corresponding period of 1866, showing an increase of 15,529*l.*, or about 53½ per cent. The expenditure amounted to 31,008*l.*, leaving a net revenue of 13,482*l.*, consequently 6,518*l.* only was required from the Ottoman Government to make up the guaranteed income. The Imperial Commissioner had examined the accounts and given the official certificate as to their correctness. The payment of the half-year's interest on the debenture debt had absorbed 8,050*l.*, leaving a balance of 23,900*l.*, which was appropriated to the amount of 5,766*l.* in payment of dividends for the first half of 1867 on the ordinary stock at the rate of 3 per cent. per annum, 10,500*l.* for one year's dividend at 7 per cent. on the preference shares, 5,625*l.* for the redemption of shares, and 1,922*l.* for dividend at the rate of 1 per cent. per annum on the ordinary stock, leaving 86*l.*

DIRECTORS :

John Wingfield Larking, Esq., Imperial Ottoman Bank, 4, Bank Buildings, E.C.
William Quilter, Esq., 3, Moorgate Street, E.C.

Charles Gilpin, Esq., M.P., 10, Bedford Square, W.C.
Henry Robertson, Esq., Shrewsbury.
Charles Joyce, Esq.

OFFICERS.—Sec., G. A. Cape; Eng., C. E. Austin, 7, Broad Sanctuary, Westminster, S.W.; Solicitors, Messrs. Burchell, 5, Broad Sanctuary, Westminster, S.W.; Brokers, Messrs. Scrimgeour, 18, Old Broad Street, E.C.; Auditors, John Ball, 3, Moorgate Street, E.C.; at Smyrna, Samuel Bayliss, C.E., Manager.

Offices—8, Old Jewry, E.C.

504.—SOUTH AUSTRIAN-LOMBARDO-VENETIAN.

The original capital was 6,000,000l. sterling, in 300,000 shares of 20l. each. The Austrian Government granted a guarantee for the whole period of the concession of 90 years of 5 2-10ths per cent. per annum, for interest and sinking fund on the whole of the present or any future capital expended. The further concession of the Vienna and Trieste and other lines were granted in September, 1858.

A convention of an important character has been concluded between this company and the Austrian Government. The convention refers to the construction of a port at Trieste, of a line from a point between Kottozi and Kanissa to Barcs, and a branch from Bruck to Leoben. The first of these new lines was to be completed by July 1st, 1868, and the second by July 1st, 1870. The port at Trieste is to be completed by December 31st, 1873, and for its construction the company is to receive a sum of 1,350,000l., payable in twelve annual instalments. The company is to be exempted until January 1st, 1880, from all taxes on its revenue, as well as from all other direct taxation. A certain amount of revenue is guaranteed on all the company's lines in operation on the Austrian territory, the guarantee dating from January 1st, 1866. The duration of the concession of all the lines conceded to the company is fixed for 99 years, dating from 1870. The separation of the company into two, independent of each other, which was provided for by a convention of November 20th, 1861, commenced January 1st, 1867, from which date the administration of the Austrian network has been entirely distinct from that of the Italian. To complete the financial separation a period of five years is allowed, dating from January 1st, 1867 ; during this period the share and obligation capital of each of the two networks is to be definitively established, and the exchange of the present shares against shares of the two new companies is to be effected.

The net profits of the South Austrian network in 1867 were 1,417,640l. ; of the Venetian, 177,720l. ; of the Lombard, 261,160l. ; of the Central Italy, 254,160l. ; and of the Piedmontese, 550,000l. ; making a total of 2,663,080l., increased to 2,673,880l. by a sum of 10,800l. derived from temporary investments. The obligation charges of last year, after deducting the portion relating to lines still in course of construction, amounted to 1,596,360l., leaving a balance of 1,077,480l. : reduced to 1,017,480l. by the deduction of 60,000l. for cost of renewal of way. From the balance of 1,017,480l., 750,000l. was paid as interest on the shares, at the rate of 5 per cent., while 26,720l. was carried to the reserve, leaving a sum of 271,480l. available for dividend purposes. Of this sum there was applied 240,000l. to payment of a dividend of 6s. 6d. per share, making the total dividend for 1867 1l. 6s. 6d. per share, of which 16s. was paid in November, leaving 10s. 6d. per share to be distributed on 1st May, 1868.

CAPITAL.—The expenditure on first establishment account at the close of 1866 stood at 41,700,060l., and a further sum of 3,828,000l. was expended in the course of 1867, making an aggregate of 45,588,000l. The amount received was 43,789,520l., viz. : 15,000,000l. from shares, 19,348,480l. from obligations, and 8,108,560l. from bonds, plus 1,520,000l. from a syndicate representing certain bonds and obligations. A discussion, it may be observed, has arisen on the interruption of the contract between the company and the syndicate, and arbitrators appointed to determine the matter have decided that certain advances made by the syndicate should be covered by bonds. It will be observed that the expenditure made on first establishment account at the close of 1867 exceeded the resources realised by 1,800,000l., covered in part by the profits derived by the company from its last year's working. These figures refer only to first establishment expenditures properly so called. Including certain other items, the entire outlay at the close of 1867 was 48,480,000l., an amount exceeding the resources realised by about 3,920,000l., so that it has become necessary to issue further bonds to the extent of 4,000,000l.

505.—SOUTH EASTERN OF PORTUGAL.

Incorporated with Limited Liability under the Joint Stock Company's Act of 1856 and 1857. Capital, 3,000,000l., of which 1,500,000l. is raised in 75,000 shares of 20l. each, and 1,500,000l. bonds bearing 7 per cent. interest.

The railway will be about 300 miles in length ; it commences at Barreiro (opposite Lisbon) and runs to Evora, Estremoz, and Crato, where it forms a junction with the Royal Portuguese line. On the east it runs to the Spanish frontier in the direction of Seville, and on the south, through Beja and the Algarves to the sea.

The Government made a free grant, in aid of the construction of the railway, of about 1,500,000l.

The shareholders authorised the directors to conclude a contract with the Portuguese Government for the purchase of the Barreiro and Vendas Novas, and for extensions of an undertaking to the Spanish frontier, on the east in the direction of Seville, and on the north in the direction of Badajoz, also through the Algarves to one of the ports on the southern coast of Portugal. This contract not having been carried out by the company, the whole of the undertaking has been confiscated by the Portuguese Government. The arrangement effected on behalf of the debenture and shareholders, subject to ratification by the Portuguese Chambers, is in effect, a guarantee of 7 per cent. interest, and of one half per cent. amortisation (sinking fund) upon the amount obtained by the company on debentures, as also on the amount actually expended in the construction of works and rolling stock, with a reduction of 20 per cent. on these last amounts.

At a meeting of bondholders, held on 7th November, 1867, it was resolved—"That this meeting approves of the settlement made by Mr. Laing, and declares that on its being ratified by law and carried into effect there will no longer be any reclamation to make against the Government of Portugal ; and the meeting desires to record its high sense of the conduct of the Portuguese Government in making a settlement of this affair, alike advantageous for Portugal and equitable towards the interests of British capitalists, who have invested their capital in the construction of railways in that kingdom."

Various attempts have since been made to effect an arrangement with the Portuguese Government, but hitherto without effect.

DIRECTORS :

Chairman—G. BARNARD TOWNSEND, Esq., 3, Prince's Street, St. James's Park, S.W.

William F. Fergusson, Esq., Langham Place, W.C.
Alfred Cowan, Esq., 4, Connaught Square, Hyde Park, W.

Philip Rose, Esq., 6, Victoria Street, S.W.
Robert Castle Jenkins, Esq., Beachley, Chepstow.
Julius Beer, Esq., 1, Angel Court, E.C.

OFFICERS.—Sec., Alfred Wilson ; Consulting Eng., J. R. Mc.Clean, M.P., 2, Park Street, Westminster, S.W.; Solicitors, Bircham, Dalrymple, and Drake, 46, Parliament Street, Westminster, S.W.; Bankers, The Union Bank of London, 2, Prince's Street, E.C.
Offices—9, Old Broad Street, E.C.

506.—SOUTHERN OF FRANCE.

Established by concession, dated August 24th, 1852, for 99 years from completion, uniting the two seas ; Bordeux to Cette, with branches to Bayonne and Perpignan. The State guarantees a minimum 4 per cent., and a sinking fund calculated at the same rate of interest on the loan capital for 50 years, and 4 per cent. on the share capital. The State has further ceded (gratis) to the company the lateral canal, à la Garonne, the tolls, &c., being fixed by Government.

GRAISSESSAC AND BEZIERS.—Conceded 27th March, 1852, for 99 years from completion, joins the Bordeux and Cette, and the Canal du Midi. Establishes a connection with the coal districts, Marseilles, Toulon, and Mediterranean ports. The colliery proprietors guarantee the transport of 100,000 tons of coal a year. Merged into the Southern of France.

The dividends paid by this company, on each of its 20l. shares, have been as follow, since 1857 :—

Year.	Dividend.	Year.	Dividend.
1857	£0 16 0	1863	£1 16 0
1858	0 16 0	1864	1 14 0
1859	1 1 8	1865	1 12 0
1860	1 8 0	1866	1 12 0
1861	2 0 0	1867	1 12 0
1862	2 1 8		

The average rate of dividend has been at the rate of 7½ per cent.

The company is concessionaire of 1,412½ miles. Of this system 498¾ miles belonging to the first network are concluded, with the exception of some improvements and extensions which have become necessary in the station-buildings ; the whole of the first network is now opened for traffic. Of the 913¾ miles belonging to the second network 582½ miles are completed and worked, the balance still remaining to be constructed, a part being in course of execution, either by the company or by the State. The length of line worked on the first and second networks had cost at the close of 1867, 24,071,414l., of which 13,494,759l. related to the first network and the balance to the second network. Working of these lines produced in 1867 a total receipt of 1,876,121l., of which 1,578,177l., was acquired on the first network, and the balance on the second.

The receipts of the old network amounted in 1867 to 1,408,640l., exclusive of the sums derived from "accounts of order ;" and the working expenses having been 490,840l. a net profit remained of 917,800l. The receipts presented an augmentation of 19,400l. as compared with 1866, while the working expenses showed a decrease of 22,680l. The balance of net profit as compared with 1866 was 42,080l. The ratio of the working expenses accordingly declined from 36·81 per cent. in 1866, to 34·59 in 1867. The sum to be paid by the State, in respect to its guarantee for the new network, declined to 680l. The net profit remaining from the working of the old network was 917,800l., but the various conventions concluded with the State reduced the disposable balance to 785,800l. This sum was applied as follows :—Paid on account on the shares in July, 1867, and January, 1868, 1l. 4s. per share, 300,000l. ; difference of 1·10 per cent. to be made good on the obligations of the new network, 29,004l.; balance of the dividend, 8s. per share, 100,000l.; leaving 72,680l. to be carried forward.

The net result, after payment of expenses and fixed charges, and after paying 148,375*l.* over to the state in reduction of its guarantee of interest, was to leave the company for application either to its reserve fund or its shareholders a sum of 412,753*l.*; the revenue of each share for 1867 was 1*l.* 12*s.* The expenditure made by the State on all the lines worked by the company has been 4,440,000*l.* As a set-off for this outlay, the State received, in stamps, taxes, &c., paid by the company, 159,417*l.*, while it realised besides, in connection with the postal service, military transports, &c., economies to the aggregate amount of 201,884*l.*, making a total direct or indirect gain to the public treasury of 361,331*l.* The return thus obtained by the State upon the amount of capital expended by it in aid of the construction of the network was at the rate of 8·14 per cent. per annum for 1867. When account is taken of the general benefits which railways confer upon a country, it must be owned that the French Government has made a good bargain in dealing with the Southern of France.

The convention of 1868 had the following principal objects in view:—1. The definitive or eventual concession of seven new lines of an aggregate length of 205 miles, and which will involve an estimated outlay of 4,560,000*l.*, of which 2,520,000*l.* will remain at the charge of the State, and 2,040,000*l.* at the charge of the company. 2. The mode of executing the works of these lines, either by the company alone, or by the State and the company combined. 3. Modifications in the old conventions by which the State undertakes to execute on certain previously conceded lines the works which should have been carried out by the company. 4. Arrangements for payment of the subventions given to the company, and for payment by the company to the State of advances involved by the works of which the State undertakes the execution. 5. The designation of the lines intended to form part of the old and new networks. 6. The fixation of the capital guaranteed for the new network and the period when the guarantee is to commence. 7. Certain arrangements for a division of net profits between the State and the company, and the rate per cent. above which these profits become divisible.

507.—SOUTH ITALIAN.

Messrs. Brassey and Co. have three contracts on this network—viz., from Monopoli to Brindisi, 43¾ miles; from Brindisi to Otranto, 53¾ miles, and from Bari to Tarento, 71⅞ miles, making a total of 169⅜ miles. The additional network of the South Italian will comprise altogether 853⅓ miles, and has been divided into fourteen sections, viz.:—

Ancona and Benedetto.	Foggia and Conza.
San Benedetto and Osento.	Conza and Salerno.
Osento and Foggia.	Salerno and Naples (with a branch
Foggia and Barletta.	to Castellamare).
Barletta and Monopoli.	Voghera and Pavia.
Monopoli and Brindisi.	Pavia, Cremona, and Brescia.
Brindisi and Otranto.	Pescara and Ceprano.
Bari and Tarento.	

A royal decree, dated December, 1867, approves a convention concluded between the Minister of Finance and this company. The principal clause is that which approves the advance by anticipation of the mileage subvention due to the company after January 1, 1867. This advance, amounting to 480,000*l.*, will be remitted by instalments in Treasury bonds bearing legal interest. The company is to charge itself with the construction of two sections of a line from Foggia to Naples, between Bovino and Caserta and between the Ariano and the Uffite.

There were 105 new miles opened for traffic in 1866, and the works are still being prosecuted with vigour. The receipts from traffic, however, continue very meagre, having regard to the extent of the system, which now comprises 798¾ miles in operation, a section from Gioja to Tarentum having been opened for traffic on September 15th, 1868. The aggregate receipts of the system from January 1st to September 15th were 274,795*l.*, as compared with 224,744*l.* in the corresponding period of 1867, showing an advance of 50,051*l.*

By a convention with the Minister of Public Works, the company is relieved from its obligation to construct lines from Termoli to Campobasso, and from Pescara to Aquila and Rieti. By way of compensation, the company abandons 80,000*l.* of the annual subvention accorded to it: this annual sum of 80,000*l.* is to be devoted to the construction of ordinary roads in the southern provinces. Finally, the Goverment anticipates to the benefit of the company three half-years' subventions, amounting altogether to 1,360,000*l.*

508.—SPAIN.

The Pampeluna, Barcelona, and Saragossa is endeavouring to obtain from the Spanish Government a grant of 160,000*l.* out of the 1,200,000*l.* promised to be doled out to meet the most pressing exigencies of the Spanish systems. If this company obtains the 160,000*l.*, it will be enabled to extinguish a floating debt of 80,000*l.*, with which it is now embarrassed, and to construct a bridge over the Ebro at an estimated cost of 60,000*l.*, by which the regular payment of the obligation coupons would be secured.

509.—TOURNAY TO JURBISE—LANDEN TO HASSELT.

Those railways unite the railways in Belgium on the west and south ; and the former, in accordance with a convention with the Northern of France, is to be placed on the same footing as the Belgian State lines. Length of Tournay and Jurbise portion, 30 miles, of which 9 miles (from Jurbise to Maffles) were opened 15th September, 1847, and the remainder delivered over to the Belgian Government on the 11th November, 1848, from which date the concession begins. Entire opened 1st July, 1849. The Landen and Hasselt, 17½ miles, was opened on 8th December, 1847. Total, 47½ miles, constructed at a cost of 10,638*l.* per mile, including 4 per cent. interest paid during construction. The terms of the concession are peculiar. Term, 99 years, redeemable by Government at the end of 45 years, upon payment of an annuity, for the remainder of the term, equal to the net average income of the preceding five years, with 25 per cent. added. On completion of the line Government took possession, finding working stock, and being at the charge of maintaining and working it, handing over monthly to proprietors 50 per cent. of gross receipts. This 50 per cent. is divided :—1st, 5 per cent. on amounts paid up to shareholders, and quarter per cent. in lieu of sinking fund ; 2nd, 3-20ths of surplus to Fondateurs ; and 17-20ths as addition to dividend. Capital, 500,000*l.*, in 25,000 shares of 20*l.* each. New shares have been issued (half in preference at 3 per cent., and half in ordinary stock), in lieu of the original shares.

The sinking fund of the preferential shares, which had been fixed, in 1862, at the sum of 43,000*fr.* per annum, has been raised to the sum of 45,000*fr.*, in order to make it coincident with the duration of the concession, which, starting from the year 1864, has but 75, instead of 77, years to run.

The net receipts for the half-year ending 30th June were 19,029*l.*, which, after deducting cost of management (1,209*l.*) left a balance of 17,820*l.*, which was appropriated as under :

1st. To be reserved for sinking funds of both kinds	£1,400
2nd. To be distributed 3 per cent. on preferential shares	7,500
3rd. To be distributed on dividend shares	8,920

Dividend, 1st October, 1868, preference shares, 6*s.* per share ; do., dividend shares, 7*s.* 1½*d.* per share ; total, 13*s.* 1½*d.* The dividend for the corresponding half-year of 1867 was 12*s.* 10¼*d.*

DIRECTORS :

President—R. W. KENNARD, Esq., 67, Upper Thames Street, E.C., and
37, Porchester Terrace, Hyde Park, W.

Managing Director—A. B. BRUNEAU, Esq., Brussels.

Thomas Brassey, Esq., Lowndes Square, S.W., and 4, Great George Street, Westminster, S.W.	W. Gladstone, Esq., 57½, Old Broad Street, E.C.
G. Bayley, Esq., 2, Half-Moon Street, Piccadilly, W., and Stock Exchange, E.C.	J. P. Kennard, Esq., Threadneedle Street, E.C.
	Herbert Dolez, Esq., Brussels.
	Thomas Westwood, Esq., Brussels.

OFFICERS.—Brussels Sec., Thomas Westwood ; London Sec., John Cross.
Head Offices—Brussels ; and Union Chambers, Old Broad Street, E.C.

510.—TURIN AND SAVONA.

The Italian Government has granted the definitive concession for 99 years of the railway from Turin to Savona, with a branch to Acqui, by means of which the most direct access will be secured to the Mediterranean from the whole system of the Italian railways, whilst the sea-coast line now being constructed from Nice to Genoa will complete the connection with all the railways of France. The leading features of the concession are :—

1. The use of the Government line from Turin to Carmagnola ; 16 miles subject only to a toll of 10 per cent. of the gross receipts.
2. A Government subvention, or free gift, of 400,000*l.*
3. A Government subvention of 80,000*l.*
4. A Government guarantee of a minimum receipt of 1,600*l.* per mile per annum on the branch to Acqui.

The distance from Turin to Savona is.......................	90
The length of the branch line to Acqui	30=120 miles.

The Italian Government has also voted 8,000*l.* to secure the continuation of the works of the Belbo tunnel.

During the last three years numerous memorials from the committee of English shareholders had been sent to the Italian Government without meeting with the favour of an answer ; and yet, without consultation with the shareholders, the Government were stated to have entered into a convention with the firm of Guestalla and Co., contractors. The matter excited the more notice in consequence of Mr. Guestalla having been a member of the board. The particulars given of the convention are evidently imperfect, but its object is to enable the Government to take the line on their own account.

At a meeting of English shareholders, held early in January, it was resolved to oppose this arrangement, and a committee appointed, with a view to "prosecute the just views of the English shareholders."

DIRECTORS:

COUNCIL OF ADMINISTRATION IN ITALY:

President—SIGNOR RATTAZZI.

Vice-President—SIGNOR PALEOCAPA, Senitor (late Minister of Public Works).

Signor Brombirni, Director of the National Bank, Turin.
Marqui de Cavour, Member of the Chamber of Deputies.
Count Cossilla, Syndic of Turin, Member of the Chamber of Deputies.
Count Corsi, Syndic of Savona, Member of the Chamber of Deputies.

Chevalier Genero, President of the Bank of Discount, Turin, Member of the Chamber of Deputies.
Colonel Pescetto, Royal Engineer Department, Mem. of the Chamber of Deputies.
General Solaroli, Aide-de-Camp to the King of Italy, Member of the Chamber of Deputies.

DIRECTORS IN LONDON :

Chairman—
Vice-Chairman—COLERIDGE J. KENNARD, Esq., 4, Lombard Street, E.C.

Wm. Dent, Jun., Esq. (late of the firm of Dent and Co., Hong Kong).
William Bunce Greenfield, Esq., Porchester Terrace, W.
Patrick D. Hadow, Esq. (Deputy-Chairman of the Peninsular and Oriental Steam Navigation Company).

Alexander Mackenzie, Esq. (late of the firm of Arbuthnot and Co., Madras).
Bonamy Price, Esq., 11, Prince's Terrace, Prince's Gate, S.W.
W. Gordon Thomson, Esq., 14, Clifton Gardens, Maida Hill, W.
Major-General Tremenheere (late Bengal Engineers).

OFFICERS.—Sec., John Wilson Pillans ; Solicitors, Wilkinson, Stevens, and Wilkinson, 4, Nicholas Lane, E.C.; Bankers in London, Consolidated Bank. 4, Lombard Street, E.C.; in Turin, the National Bank.

London Offices—61, Gresham House, Old Broad Street, E.C.

511.—VARNA.

Constituted in 1863 by statutes under the law of Turkey, with limited liability. Concessions, 99 years. Share capital, 900,000*l.*, in 45,000 shares to bearer of 20*l.* each, bearing a minimum interest of 5 per cent. per annum guaranteed by the Turkish Government. The shares to be redeemed at par by a sinking fund guaranteed by the Turkish Government by annual drawings, to commence the year after opening of the line, viz. :—12,500 shares during the first 33 years ; 20,000 during the second 33 years ; 12,500 during the third 33 years. Total, 45,000.

The holder of each share drawn and paid off at 20*l.* will receive a dividend warrant entitling him to participate in all profits earned by the railway in excess of the guaranteed interest during the remaining term of the concession.

This railway connects Rustchuck, on the banks of the Danube, with Varna, the principal port in the Black Sea, and will traverse for the entire distance of about 138 English miles, most populous districts in the province of Bulgaria. Opened October, 1866.

In the report of September, the shareholders were informed that the railway was accepted by the Government, and the guarantee acknowledged as from 1st March ; that the rolling stock had been found inadequate for the demands of the traffic ; and that an agent had been sent to Constantinople for the purpose of obtaining further assistance from the Government, either in the shape of a loan or as payment in anticipation of a guarantee. The request, although favourably received by the Government, had not been complied with. The directors had, therefore, been unable to liquidate the three unpaid coupons on the obligations, which led to the proposals on the part of the bondholders, to capitalise the said three coupons, and to accept in payment bonds, redeemable in ten years, bearing interest at 6 per cent. For the acceptance of these propositions the directors desired the sanction of the shareholders in February, when the following resolution was unanimously adopted :—"That the council of administration be empowered to accept on behalf of the company the said propositions, with such variations or modifications as in the interests of the company, they, the council of administration, may deem expedient, and to take, execute, and to do all such proceedings, instruments, and things, as in their judgment may be necessary or proper to giving effect thereto, and to such modifications as may be found expedient."

DIRECTORS:

Chairman—WILLIAM GLADSTONE, Esq., 57½, Old Broad Street, E.C.

H. Wollaston Blake, Esq., 11, London Street, E.C.
Charles Kelson, Esq., London.
Henry McChlery, Esq., London.

Maurice J. Posno, Esq., London.
Mons. L. Emerique, Brussels.
Mons. F. Pauwels, Brussels.
Mons. V. Tercelin-Monjot, Brussels.

OFFICERS.—Sec., J. F. Walsh; Consulting Eng., G. P. Bidder; Eng., William McCandlish; Contractors, Peto, Betts, and Crampton; Solicitors, Messrs. Freshfields, 5, Bank Buildings, E.C.; Bankers, Robarts, Lubbock, and Co., 15, Lombard Street, E.C. Offices—15, Angel Court, E.C.

512.—WEST FLANDERS.

This line from Comines to Ypres was opened for traffic on 23rd January, 1855, and thence to Poperinghe on the 20th March. The fixed liabilities of the company consist of 7,700*l*. per annum, interest on the 5½ per cent. preference shares; 6,000*l*. per annum, interest on the 3 per cent. bonds; 520*l*. per annum, as sinking fund on the 3 per cent. bonds; which sums are met by Government guarantee. 74 miles. Opened throughout on 1st January, 1856.

The dividend for the half-year ending 31st December was at the rate of 5*s*. 3*d*. per share, and for June, 5*s*. 6*d*. The increased rental of 1,000*l*. per annum, making 33,000*l*., commenced on the 1st January last. The rental for 1869 and 1870 will be 34,000*l*., and subsequently to the end of the concession, 36,000*l*. per annum. The Roulers and Ypres was opened in April, and the Société Générale d'Exploitation reported that the line from Poperinghe to Hazebrouck would be completed early in the year.

CAPITAL.—The expenditure amounted to 598,354*l*., leaving a balance of 1,180*l*. The bond redemption account on the two issues shows that 8,300 had been redeemed on the first, and 2,200 on the second.

DIRECTORS:

President—ROBERT TEMPLE FRERE, Esq.

Alexander Greig, Esq.
Edward Vaughan Richards, Esq.

Thomas Dyer Edwardes, Esq.
Thomas Robert Tufnell, Esq.

OFFICERS.—Sec., F. Smith; London Bankers, Glyn, Mills, and Co., 67, Lombard Street, E.C.

Offices—61, Moorgate Street, E.C., and Place de la Station, Bruges.

513.—WESTERN OF FRANCE.

This great confederation was constituted in January, 1855, under sanction of Government, and is composed of the Paris and Rouen; Paris Caen and Cherbourg; Rouen and Havre; St. Germain; Western of France; and other affiliations and concessions.

The new network comprises a contemplated aggregate length of 1,006⅞ miles, divided into two categories, completely distinct from each other. The first, comprising lines entirely opened for traffic on their whole extent before January 1st, 1865, and which must profit after that date from the guarantee of interest, presents a total length of 371⅞ miles. The second part, composed of lines still in course of execution on January 1st, 1865, and which will not profit from the guarantee of interest until more remote periods, presents a total length of 635 miles.

The dividends on the 20*l*. shares of this undertaking, for ten years, have been declared and paid as under:—

Year.	Dividend.	Year.	Dividend.
1857	£1 10 0	1862	£1 8 0
1858	1 6 6	1863	1 10 0
1859	1 10 0	1864	1 11 8
1860	1 10 0	1865	1 10 0
1861	1 14 0	1866	1 8 0

Average for ten years, 7½ per cent.

The rough receipts of the three networks—that is, the old network, the new network, and the new network worked on first establishment account—amounted in 1867, after deducting taxes, to 3,400,057*l*. The working expenditure was 1,615,011*l*., leaving a net profit of 1,785,046*l*. From this sum, however, deductions to the aggregate amount of 284,258*l*. had to be made for expenses relating to closed exercises, the partial renewal of way, the renewal of rolling stock, the rent of workshops and central buildings devoted to the new network, the rent of the stations of Redon, Angers, Amiens, and Longneau, various intersts at the debit of the new network, subventions for omnibus services, carting, &c., stamps on shares and obligations, statutory reserve of 2 per cent. on the net profits, &c. After making these deductions, and adding a sum of 43,747*l*. for miscellaneous receipts relating to the old and new network, a balance of 1,544,500*l*. was divided between the three networks, in the following manner:—Old network, 1,293,905*l*.; new network (first part), 154,924*l*.; and new network (second part), 95,671*l*. The receipts of the first part of the new network were applied in attenuation of the guarantee of interest, and those of the second part were carried in reduction of the cost of construction as prescribed by a convention concluded with the State on 1st May, 1863.

A new convention between this company and the Government makes the following additions to the network :—First, a line from St. Lo to Lamballe, forming the remainder of a line from Cherbourg to Brest, *via* Coutances, Avranches, Dol, and Dinan ; the length of this line is 109⅔ miles, and it is estimated to cost 2,800,000*l*. ; the State undertakes to furnish a subvention of 1,040,000*l*. Secondly, a line from Sablé to Châteaubriant, the first section of a line from Sablé to Nantes, 53⅛ miles in length, and estimated to cost 1,360,000*l*. ; the State proposes to grant a subvention of 480,000*l*. Thirdly, a line from Laval to Angers, *via* Segré, 53¾ miles in length, and estimated to cost 1,360,000*l*. ; the State proposes to grant a subvention of 480,000*l*. The total length of the new lines conceded is thus 215⅜ miles, the estimated cost being 5,520,000*l*., and the aggregate subventions proposed to be granted 2,000,000*l*. In accepting these new concessions, the company solicited from the Government a revision of the calculations on which the guarantee of interest is established. Besides the new capital of 3,520,000*l*., placed at its charge, the company called attention to augmentations indicated in the cost of lines conceded up to 1863, and for the Girdle of Paris (left bank). The new capital guaranteed has consequently been fixed as follows :—Guarantee of 1863, 22,800,000*l*. ; increase of expenses in reference to concessions granted previously to 1863, 1,920,000*l*. ; Girdle of Paris, 520,000*l*. ; new concessions, 3,520,000*l*. ; total, 28,760,000*l*. Authority has been taken to carry this sum to 33,800,000*l*., in consequence of the additional expenses which may be incurred during the next ten years. The net revenue per mile reserved to the old network is increased, the alteration being based on calculations intended to secure to the shares the same privileges as hitherto. A division of profits with the State is to commence when the new network capital attains a net revenue of 6 per cent.

CAPITAL.—This account was made up as follows at the close of 1867 :—Shares, 6,000,000*l*.; subventions to be received, 1,081,102*l*.; loans, 30,992,445*l*.; total, 38,073,547*l*. The amount expended on the two networks, to the close of 1867, deducting subventions received, was 36,581,711*l*., leaving a nominal surplus of 1,491,836*l*. in hand, of which, however, 1,081,102*l*. consisted of subventions still to be received. In the course of 1867, 170,583 obligations of the 11th and 12th series were issued and produced 2,084,669*l*., or rather more than 12*l*. 4*s*. per obligation.

514.—ZEALAND (Denmark).

Established 1833, and holds a concession from the Danish Government for 90 years from the date of opening. Line is to unite Copenhagen, crossing the island of Zealand, to Korsöer, a port on the West Coast ; in effect an extension of the Roskilde line, and thoroughfare to Germany and Southern Europe. Length, 49 English miles.

Government guarantee a *minimum* dividend at 4 per cent. per annum for 90 years ; after 25 years the State may purchase the share capital at par.

The railway was opened for public traffic, in its entire length, on 27th April, 1856. The guarantee of the Danish Government for payment of the stipulated interest commenced from that day, and continues to be regularly paid.

The directors are Messrs. V. Rothe, F. Dreyer, and F. Gotschalck. Eng. for the line, W. Bauditz ; Eng. for the locomotive department, F. Busse. All residing at Copenhagen.

III.—COLONIAL, AMERICAN, INDIAN, &c.

AFRICA.

515.—ALGERIA.

The length of this network is 339⅔ miles—viz., from Phillipville to Constantine, 53¼ miles ; and from Algiers to Oran, 286¼ miles. The expenditure made to the close of 1863 on the Algerian lines amounted to 596,188*l*., of which 530,017*l*. was disbursed by the original company, which became merged into the Paris Lyons and Mediterranean, July 29th, 1863. The outlay made by the company upon these lines, to the close of 1867, was 2,744,947*l*. A great deal of work still remains to be done, and they will not be fully completed before 1870. The French Government has granted a subvention to the amount of 3,200,000*l*., and a guarantee of 5 per cent. per annum on the capital expended in excess of that amount.

A section from Relizane to Oran was opened for traffic on 1st November, 1868. This section forms the western end of the Algiers and Oran, completed at the other extremity for several years, as between Algiers and Blidah. There are thirteen stations upon the new section, which is 78⅝ miles in length. One other section of the Algiers and Oran—viz., from Relizane to Blidah—still remain to be completed.

ENGLISH DIRECTORS :

H. T. Hope, Esq. | William Gladstone, Esq., 57½, Old Broad
                                   | Street, E.C.

OFFICERS.—Bankers, La Société Génerale du Credit Industriel, Paris; Brokers,
Laurence, Son, and Pearce, Auction Mart, London; Sec., Charles Pons.

Offices—38, Throgmorton Street, E.C.

516.—CAPE.

Incorporated by 18 and 19 Vic., cap. 140 (July 16th, 1855), for making railways and
docks within the colony of Cape Town. Length, 57½ miles. Capital, 600,000*l.* in 20*l.*
shares, of which 500,000*l.* have been issued. Debentures, 200,000*l.*

The first portion of the line, from the Parade in Cape Town to the Eerste river, 21
miles, was opened for traffic on 13th February, 1862, and an additional 10 miles, as far as
Stellenbosch, on the 4th May, 1863. The last portion was opened on 3rd November,
1863.

The Suburban line, from the Salt River station to Wynberg, is now open, making a
total of 63 miles in operation.

The guarantee from the Cape Government is at the rate of 6 per cent. per annum,
upon a sum not exceeding 500,000*l.*, and is paid as at a rate in aid towards making a
dividend at 6 per cent.

By 30 Vic., cap. 53 (31st May, 1867), the company was authorised to increase its
capital to the extent of 500,00u*l.* for construction of a line to Worcester, and 350,000*l.*
for another line to Malmesbury, of which separate accounts are to be kept, and with
one-third additional in debentures. By this Act also the name of the company was
changed from "Cape Town" to that of "Cape."

REVENUE.—The receipts for the half-year ending 31st December were 19,723*l.*, showing
an increase of 1,168*l.* The working expenses, including 500*l.* placed to the credit of
Wynberg rolling stock depreciation fund, had been 17,941*l.*, showing an increase of
1,668*l.* This increase arose mainly from the facts of 1 342*l.*, the cost of replacing decayed
sleepers, having in the corresponding period been transferred by the vote of the shareholders to capital account, and the cost of cartage and delivery of goods in Cape Town,
399*l.*, deducted from the receipts. The outlay on renewals, amounting to about 1,100*l.*,
including the purchase and placing of a portion of the experimental mile of iron sleepers,
had been charged against revenue, and the cost of cartage included in the working expenses. The result of the working, after all deductions, showed a profit of 1,782*l.* in
addition to the amount paid by the Colonial Government on account of guaranteed
interest, leaving a balance, after payment of dividend interest and home charges, of
9,604*l.* Deferred dividend warrants amounting to 7,412*l.*, together with 1,133*l.* in cash,
had been paid in purchase of preference stock. Up to the 1st March 12,844*l.* had been
paid of the floating debt, leaving about 15,000*l.* still to be provided for. With a view to
resume the cash payment of dividends at the earliest possible period, the directors had
settled the whole of the floating debts by the payment of 9,538*l.* in cash, and the issue
of 12,109*l.* original stock taken at 45 per cent. Dividend at the rate of 6 per cent. per
annum was declared on the preferential stock for the half-year ending the 31st of
December, payable in cash on 1st May, and at the rate of 3½ per cent. per annum,
free of income-tax, on the ordinary stock payable in deferred warrants. The board was
authorised to receive the deferred warrants for the present and past dividends at par, in
purchase of the 6 per cent. preferential stock on payment in cash of such small balances
as might be required to make up sums of not less than 1*l.*

A considerable increase in traffic was reported for the half-year ending June 30th,
both in comparison with the corresponding period in 1867 and that ending on 31st
December. The receipts were 25,406*l.*, against 22,495*l.* for the corresponding period of
1867, showing an increase of 2,911*l.* The working expenses in the colony for the like
periods were 19,616*l.*, against 19,090*l.*, showing an increase of only 526*l.*, and leaving a
profit of 5,790*l.* in addition to the amount paid by the Government on account of
guaranteed interest. The whole balance available on dividend account, after deducting
interest on debenture debt and other current home charges, amounted to 13,621*l.*
Arrangements had been completed by which the remainder of the outstanding deferred
dividend warrants were taken up and converted into preference stock, and the balance
of that stock subscribed. Dividend at the rate of 6 per cent. per annum was declared
on the preference stock, and at the rate of 4½ per cent. on the ordinary stock ; leaving
a balance of 1,100*l.* to next account. The floating debts had all been paid, and the
whole of the debentures falling due, amounting to 62,400*l.*, have either been paid off,
renewed, or re-subscribed.

Committees of both Houses of the Cape Legislature have taken into consideration
the question of extension in both provinces, but at present without any practical result,
and the board is still in communication with the Government as to the settlement of
the company's claim for an addition to the guaranteed capital.

CAPITAL.—The balance sheet, to 30th June, 1868, exhibited the subjoined details:—

Received.		*Expended.*	
Consolidated stock	£523,109	In England and Cape Town	£693,147
Debentures	199,600	Arbitration charges, including	
Preference stock	25,827	2,965*l.* for chancery suit........	14,331
		Law charges ditto (miscellaneous)	280
	£748,536	Loss on sale of consolidated stock	5,890
Wynberg Debentures	10,000		
			£713,649
	£758,536	Winberg rolling stock	18,660
Due on deferred warrants:—		Ditto fittings and plant	204
England..........................	1,540	Ditto advances on security of⎫	
Cape Town	362	their debentures, at rate of ⎬	10,000
		6 per cent. per annum ......⎭	
			£742,514
		Deduct outstanding liabilities....	1,793
			£740,720
		Stores in transit..................	931
		Branches – Bills receivable	4,042
		Cash at bankers and in hand	4,328
		Balance of amounts transferred⎫	
		to revenue ledger, less remit-⎬	10,416
		tances from Cape ....⎭	
	£760,439		£760,439

DIRECTORS:

Chairman—HARRISON WATSON, Esq. (of the firm of J. R. Thomson and Co.,
London ; and Thomson, Watson, and Co., Cape Town.)

Deputy-Chairman—JOHN BORRADAILE, Esq. (Chairman of Calcutta and South
Eastern Railway.)

Managing Director—G. LATHOM BROWNE, Esq.

Harry Borradaile, Esq. (Director of Scinde Railway.)
Thomas Dyer Edwardes, Esq. (Director of the London Chartered Bank of Australia)
William Durham, Esq., Wilton Lodge, Kensington, W.

W. Little, Esq., Park Square, Regent's Park, N.W.
Rothwell Pounsett, Esq. (of the firm of Grimble and Co., London.)

LOCAL COMMITTEE AT CAPE TOWN:

J. Bardwell Ebden, Esq. (Chairman of the Cape of Good Hope Bank.)
Hercules Crosse Jarvis, Esq.
C. J. Busk, Esq. (of the firm of McDonald, Busk and Co.)

J. T. Eustace, Esq. (of the firm of Borradaile, Thompson, Hall, and Co.)
Thomas Watson, Esq. (Director of the Cape of Good Hope Bank.)
John Barry, Esq., (Director of the London and South African Bank.)

OFFICERS.—Agent and Gen. Man. in the Colony, Thomas Watson, Esq.; Consulting Eng., Sir Charles Fox, Knt.: Auditors, Alderman Dakin, Creechurch Lane, E.C., and John Wyld Brown, Moorgate Street, E.C.; Solicitors, Merrick, Gedge, and Loaden, 4, Storey's Gate, Westminster, S.W., and J. and H. Reid and Nephew, Cape Town; Brokers, Philip Cazenove and Co., 52, Threadneedle Street, E.C.; Bankers, The London and County Bank ; Ransom, Bouverie, and Co.; Cape of Good Hope Bank.

Offices—261, Gresham House, Old Broad Street, E.C.; 40, Heerengracht, or Adderley Street.

517.—EGYPT.

This country possesses the following lines :—From Alexandria to Cairo, 131 miles ; to Mariouth, 17 ; to Meks, 6 ; to Rassateen, 3 : from Tanto to Samanud, 21 ; from Cairo to Suez, 91 ; to Barragd, 15 ; to Beni Sueff, 76—in all 360 miles. Besides these, there are smaller branches, from Cairo to the Citadel and Kasr Nin ; from Samanud to Mansoura and Damietta ; from Damanhour to Afte, which last extends to Rosetta.

518.—NATAL.

NATAL CENTRAL.—This project contemplates a line from Durban to Maritsburg, which will be about 69 miles.   Estimated capital, 600,000*l.*

NATAL MINERAL.—This scheme which is intended to pass through a district abounding in coal, limestone, and iron, suggests a line from Zugela to Durban. Length, 60 miles.

Several other projects have been before the Provincial Legislature, but no practical steps have yet been taken to carry them out.

AUSTRALASIA.

519.- QUEENSLAND.

There are a number of railways in course of construction in this colony, the chief object of which is to open up the interior of the country by providing easy access to the seaboard, and that at a cost which, while making the roads as efficient and durable as possible, will not saddle the colony with a heavy or unprofitable expenditure. The Government determined on constructing a 3ft. 5in. gauge single line, with the necessary passing places, so as to make it capable of accommodating the traffic which might be expected in future years. Only a couple of years have elapsed since the plan was decided upon, and already a railway has been opened from Ipswich to Helidon, a distance of 50 miles, while another extension of 130 miles in a western direction towards Toorroomba is now under construction. From this the line runs off to Dably in one direction and to Warwick in the other, and the greater portion of these several lines, forming a total length of about 180 miles, it was proposed to open about the autumn of 1867. While this has been going on in the South, the northern district has also been moving in the same direction. A line having its terminus at Rockhampton, running also towards the west as far as Westwood, is anticipated to be opened in May. The country traversed by the railway from Ipswich to Toorroomba presents many serious obstacles to cheap construction, as there are two ranges of hills to be surmounted, of 700ft. and 1,400ft., respectively, above the level of the country. The sides of these ranges are cut up by numerous deep ravines, and their slopes are likewise steep. This has involved the construction of a large number of viaducts, bridges, and culverts. The spurs between them, in some instances have been tunnelled through, there being as many as eleven tunnels, one of which is over three-quarters of a mile in length. The low-lying country at the basis of these two mountain ranges is intersected by streams and watercourses, which in the wet seasons become heavy torrents, overflowing their banks, and thus necessitating an amount of bridging and waterways greater, perhaps, than what appears on any 78 miles yet made in any country. Notwithstanding these exceedingly heavy and costly works, this part of the line has been constructed at an average cost of about 15,000l. per mile, while a mile of a section, presenting but ordinary difficulties, is being made at a cost of about 6,000l. The line is paying at the rate of 8 per cent. per annum.

520.—MELBOURNE AND HOBSON'S BAY UNITED.

This is a combination of the "Melbourne and Hobson's Bay," the "Melbourne," and the "St. Kilda and Brighton." The paid-up share capital of the united companies is 534,700l., on which dividends at the rate of 10 per cent. per annum have been declared as the result of the first year's working since the amalgamation. The total amount borrowed on debenture bonds, including 50,000l. now on offer by the Colonial Bank of Australasia, is 358,000l., and the company have power to issue a further sum of 80,300l., making a total share and debenture capital of 1,000,000l. The debentures are a first charge on the property of the company. Interest and principal—the latter due in July, 1880—are payable either in London or Melbourne.

521.—SOUTH AUSTRALIA.

Intended to have been established under powers of an Act of the legislature of South Australia, assented to in Her Majesty's name on October 21st, 1862, granting 128,000 acres of freehold land, for 100 miles of railway. Capital, 300,000l., in 60,000 shares of 5l. each. First issue, 30,000 shares. In abeyance.

DIRECTORS:

Henry Hills, Esq.
George Humby, Esq.
Henry Martin, Esq.
Joseph Turnley, Esq.
Thomas Hancock, Esq.

} Directors of the Yudanamutana Copper Mining Company of South Australia, Limited.

OFFICERS.—Sec., Mr. Dickeson; Solicitors, Pattison and Wigg, 10, Clement's Lane, Lombard Street, E.C.; Bankers, Bank of London, 52, Threadneedle Street, E.C.

Offices—1, Charlotte Row, Mansion House, E.C.

522.—VICTORIAN.

These railways consist of two main lines, one from Melbourne to Castlemain (Mount Alexander Goldfields) and Sandhurst (Bendigo Goldfields), 110 miles in length, and the other from Melbourne to Geelong and Ballarat, with a short branch to Williamstown (the port of Melbourne), 96 miles. The Geelong and Melbourne was purchased by the Government, in 1860, and an extension from Sandhurst to the river Murray, at Echuca (56 miles), is now in progress. The gauge is 5ft. 3in.

The following statement showing the debenture capital raised for the construction of Victorian Railways, also the debenture capital raised per mile open, together with the revenue per mile per annum, for the years ending December, 1863, to December, 1867 :—

	Year.	Miles open.	Raised.	Per Mile open.	Revenue per Mile.	Per centage
Murray	1863	97	£4,880,046	£50,309	£2,488	4·94
	1864	115	5,040,800	43,833	2,571	5·86
	1855	156	5,194,773	33,293	2,217	6·66
	1866	156	5,210,974	33,405	2,172	6·50
	1867	156	5,463,875	35,025	1,965	5·61
Williamstown.............	1863	5½	£387,305	£70,428	£5,105	7·21
	1864	5½	400,064	72,739	5,148	7·07
	1865	6	368,134	61,356	4,736	7·73
	1866	6	376,894	62,815	6,103	9·71
	1867	6	387,815	64,636	6,261	9·69
Ballarat..................	1863	90	£2,478,754	£27,541	£2,170	7·84
	1864	90	2,560,406	28,449	2,116	7·44
	1865	92	2,617,838	28,455	2,295	8·07
	1866	92	2,605,487	28,320	2,328	8·22
	1867	92	2,766,410	30,070	2,260	7·51
Totals	1863	192½	£7,746,105	£40,250	£2,414	5·99
	1864	210½	8,001,270	38,034	2,444	6·42
	1865	254	8,180,745	32,208	2,305	7·16
	1866	254	8,193,355	32,257	2,321	7·19
	1867	254	8,618,100	33,930	2,173	6·40

BRITISH NORTH AMERICA.

523.—BUFFALO AND LAKE HURON.

This line, formerly the BUFFALO, BRANTFORD, AND GODERICH, is leased by its present occupants on the following terms': For first seven years, 30,000l. a year; for eighth year, 32,500l.; for ninth year, 35,000l.; for tenth year, 37,500l.; for eleventh and every subsequent year, 40,000l.—such rental being in fact paid by the adoption of the following 6 per cent. bonds of the old company :—Active bonds, 500,000l. falling due in 1872, 1873, and 1874, requiring 30,000l. a year for interest. Deferred bonds, four equal series, each 41,666l. 13s. 4d., and each requiring 2,500l. a year for interest. Such interest commencing 7, 8, 9, and 10 years hence, simultaneously with and exactly absorbing the successive increase of rental.

HAMILTON AND PORT DOVER.—This proposed line, 17 miles in length, was finally made over to the Buffalo and Lake Huron in June, 1863, subject to the condition that it shall be completed and opened for traffic within two years; and arrangements have been made for the provisional purchase of bonds and other outstanding claims, including right of way, on moderate terms. The estimate of 80,000l. for the completion of this access to Lake Ontario, including purchase of bonds, claim of right of way, wharfs, elevators, and thirty acres of water frontage in the city of Hamilton, will not be exceeded.

GRAND TRUNK.—The arrangements made with this company provides for the Buffalo and Lake Huron being managed by a joint committee. "The capital, both share and bond, of the two companies, to be kept entirely distinct, but the gross receipts to be put together, and after payment of working expenses and renewals, to be apportioned as follows :—   Grand Trunk.   Buffalo and Lake Huron.

	Grand Trunk. per cent.	Buffalo and Lake Huron. per cent.
1st year	87	13
2nd year	86	14
3rd year	85	15
4th year	84½	15½
5th year	84	16
6th and subsequent years	83½	16½

Also that the Buffalo and Lake Huron shall, out of its own separate resources, raise 75,000l. towards the laying down of a third rail on its railway between Buffalo and Stratford, and the erection of the intended International Bridge at Buffalo, so as to aid in establishing that through route, via Buffalo, the development of which is a main object of the arrangement between the two companies; but that all further capital, if any, required hereafter for the still further development of the through traffic shall not fall on either company separately, but shall be a charge on their joint receipts, like working expenses."

It was reported in November that it would be seen from the Grand Trunk report that the gross revenue for the half-year ending 30th June was 646,797l.; the ordinary working expenses, 426,477l.; the renewals of permanent way, 36,020l.; and the loss by fires, 4,110*l.*—leaving a net available balance of 180,190*l.* From this was deducted 31,383*l.* transferred from suspense account, 10,807*l.* for Montreal and Champlain proportion, and 18,882*l.* loss on American Currency—leaving a balance of 119,118*l.* divisible between the two companies, in the proportion of 84½ per cent. to the Trunk, and 15½ per cent. to the Buffalo ; thus making the latter company's share 18,456*l.*, and not 22,045*l.*, as published in the Grand Trunk report. In partial explanation of this discrepancy the directors referred to their previous report, in which the proprietors would see that the amount due to the Buffalo for the half-year ending 31st December, 1867, was 18,429*l.*, although the Trunk only made the amount 12,284*l.* This was done by dealing with the 31,284*l.* then carried to the debit of suspense account. The amount really due for the half-year ending December, 1867, was 18,429*l.*, and for June, 1868, 18,456*l.*, making 36,885*l.* The Grand Trunk make the figures 34,329*l.* Of this amount the directors of the Buffalo regretted that they had not received any portion.

In the Grand Trunk report was the following paragraph :—"Every effort that the directors had made to bring about an amicable settlement of the differences of account with the Buffalo had hitherto failed. The Buffalo Board would neither agree upon nor allow an impartial officer of the Board of Trade to settle a deed of arbitration. Recent further negotiations through Messrs. Creak and Ritter had ended in nothing, as while the president of the company signed a memorandum of settlement of all matters, as Mr. Creak suggested, the representatives of the Buffalo had refused to do the same." On this statement the Buffalo Board remarked that their chairman did certainly refuse to sign a document put before him by Mr. Creak, having the signature of Sir E. Watkin, because it was drawn up in such a loose and inexact manner, leaving blank spaces for amounts to be afterwards settled, and still proposing to refer most points to arbitration. There was also introduced a fresh claim which, until that moment, had never been heard of. This also was to go to the arbitrators. To evince, however, the desire for peace, Mr. Heseltine, while refusing to sign Sir E. Watkin's paper, put into Mr. Creak's possession a carefully drawn up memorandum, based on the verbal recommendations of Messrs. Creak and Ritter, which paper left nothing open, no point unsettled, but disposed of all subjects in dispute without arbitration. The directors had heard nothing more of this paper. It stated that Sir E. Watkin had lost no opportunity of impressing upon his shareholders the small value to them of the Buffalo line, urging an alteration of the lease. The board uniformly replied that they would be surprised, indeed, if the line did pay, seeing the manner in which the traffic was conducted. Loud complaints were made all along the line of the want of accommodation. The directors were ready, however, as soon as the Grand Trunk would fairly carry out the present agreement, and pay, or make arrangements for paying, the balance due to this company, to discuss terms for an alteration in the lease. They did not intend, however, to be coerced into any fresh agreement by Sir E. Watkin withholding the balance due. Although prepared to discuss terms for an alteration of the lease, the board would prefer to entertain the question of cancelling it entirely. The directors had no hesitation in saying the value of the property was worth all and more than the Grand Trunk had given for it, and if the line were in other hands, and the power over its contributions of local traffic and "through" United States' traffic were cut off from the Grand Trunk system, their loss would be much more than this company's present share of joint revenue.

The following resolution, adopted by the Grand Trunk board on 21st October, was read to the meeting of that company by the chairman on the following day :—

"The board having considered the suggestion offered by the Buffalo and Lake Huron directors in their last report to their shareholders, to the effect that the existing agreement between them and this company should be entirely cancelled,

"Resolved—That it is desirable to accept that offer, and that (subject to the approval of to-morrow's Grand Trunk general meeting) the Buffalo and Lake Huron be requested to concur at once in the needful application to the Canadian Parliament for the cancelling of the agreement accordingly.

"And that, as part of this arrangement, the other offer of the Buffalo and Lake Huron to leave 'all subjects in dispute between the two companies to the arbitration of Mr. Geo. Grenfell Glyn, without any deed of submission, each side stating their own case in their own way,' be also accepted, proper provision being made, in the New Act of Parliament, for giving full effect to his award, irrespective of any informality in the business."

It was reported, however, to an adjourned meeting of Buffalo bondholders, held on 3rd December, that a partial arrangement had been effected with the Grand Trunk, and that other measures would be brought before the proprietors on a future occasion. The chairman, in his remarks, furnished the subjoined explanation :—"I wish you to understand that whatever our agreement binds us to, or did bind us to before the 5th of November, with regard to the 75,000*l.* for the Buffalo bridge, it still binds us to. Then there was another thing which had been a matter of dispute between the two companies, and that was the charge for the extra weight of rails. The Grand Trunk each half-year deducted a certain amount on account of extra weight of rails, and we always resisted it ; and now we have the principle admitted that in future, from 30th June last, any extra weight will form part of the separate working expenses, and will not form a charge against this company. Then we had another point in dispute, and that was relative to the administration expenses. A large sum was deducted out of working revenue on behalf of the administration expenses and other charges of the Grand

Trunk, and we thought ours should be allowed off, and we have got the principle of that admitted. That principle being admitted, a great deal is knocked off from our claim against the Grand Trunk, because each half-year from August, 1864, we have sent in a rather large claim, being a per-centage on their total administration expenses. We have now necessarily reduced our total claim by a considerable amount in consequence of that principle being conceded. Another point we had to deal with was the extra capital, which was a most difficult account. We have got that settled by agreeing for the present to a certain sum—2,000*l*. a-year from the 30th of June last. On that item of 2,000*l*., we gain about 700*l*. a year. Then we agreed to accept 30,000*l*. in discharge of all claims up to 30th June last. We have got 10,000*l*. paid to us, and two sums of 10,000*l*. will mature during the next six or seven months, and that will close up our money account with the Grand Trunk to the 30th June, 1868."

CAPITAL.—The statement of this account to 30th June showed the expenditure to have been 1,701,056*l*., leaving a balance of 74,017*l*. The bonded debt of the company extends to 666,666*l*., the receipts on shares having been as under :—

Ordinary shares	£1,230,000
Shares of preference capitalised arrears	84,000
Preference shares	150,000
Do. or redeemable shares	250,000
Capitalised coupon bonds	61,070=£1,775,070

DIRECTORS :

Chairman—EDWARD HESELTINE, Esq., London.

Philip Rawson, Esq., London.   Alfred Cox, Esq., London.
Charles Langton, Esq., Liverpool.

Secretary, Thomas Short, Great Winchester Street Buildings, E.C.

524.—CANADIAN LOCAL LINES.

The following list of other railways open to traffic in Canada may be interesting, although they are local lines, and the capital has been supplied in the Province :—

ERIE AND ONTARIO.—17 miles. From Chippewa, opposite to Niagara Falls, to Niagara City, on Lake Ontario. Worked during the summer months only.

GRENVILLE AND CARILLON.—13 miles. Opened October, 1854.

ST. LAWRENCE AND INDUSTRIE.—12 miles. Opened May, 1850. These two short lines are in Canada East, and are worked in the summer months only, in connection with the steamboats, as is also the Erie and Ontario.

STANSTEAD AND CHAMBLY.—28 miles.

MONTREAL AND CHAMPLAIN.—81 miles in Canada.—From Montreal to Rouse's Point, on Lake Champlain, 44 miles ; and from Montreal to Plattsburgh, in the State of New York, 62 miles, now incorporated with the Grand Trunk, which see.

COBURG AND PETERBOROUGH.—28 miles. Opened May, 1854 ; running into the Grand Trunk, but now closed.

PORT HOPE, LINDSAY, AND BEAVERTON.—56 miles. Opened December, 1857

PRESCOTT AND OTTAWA.—54 miles   Opened December, 1854.

BROCKVILLE AND OTTAWA.—To Perth and Landpoint, 86 miles.

PRESTON AND BERLIN.—11 miles.—Connecting the Great Western of Canada with the Grand Trunk, but now closed.

LONDON AND PORT STANLEY.—The length of the line is 24 miles, extending from London, C.W., to Port Stanley on Lake Erie. It was constructed in 1856 at a total cost, including rolling stock, of $1,025,000.

All the railways in the Province of Canada are constructed on the medium gauge of 5ft. 6in., except the following, which have the narrow gauge of 4ft. 8½in., viz.:—Montreal and Champlain, Prescott and Ottawa, St. Lawrence and Industrie, and Sanstead and Chambly.

525.—EUROPEAN AND NORTH AMERICAN.

Incorporated by Act of local legislature, to connect St. John, New Brunswick, with the railway system of the United States and Canada. It runs from Nova Scotia to Maine, U.S.; length, 108 miles. The line was completed from the St. Lawrence to the Bay of Fundy, on 1st August, 1860.

The Province subscribed 1,200*l*. sterling per mile, not exceeding 250,000*l*. in aggregate under the Money Facility Act of 1851, to be paid in provincial bonds redeemable in twenty years, with interest of 6 per cent., with bonds to the contractors as cash, at par. Also, loan to the company of 1,800*l*. sterling per mile, in provincial bonds, bearing 6 per cent. interest, to be a first charge on the loan. Interest at 6 per cent. secured on the line and earnings only, and subject to first mortgage.

It was reported in September that the Western Extension was rapidly progressing, and that there was a probability of its being opened for traffic to Fredericton on 1st January, and to Woodstock and the border of Maine in June following. The treasurer acknowledges receipt of cash from the province, the City St. John, and from shareholders amounting to about $430,000 of which $392,000 has been paid to the contractors, $10,000 for material and expenses, leaving some $28,000 at present in the treasury towards meeting a liability of some $60,000 now or shortly to become due. Sleepers for the whole road have been procured, and the most of them distributed along the line. Upwards of 2,000 tons of rails have been purchased in England, a portion of these being now on the ocean and the balance ready for shipment. Two locomotives and a quantity of rolling stock have been procured in the United States, the bonds of the company having been taken in exchange. The share lists show that the larger portion of the subscribers have responded to the several calls for payments, and that those who seem desirous of repudiating are few and their subscriptions small. The calls on the City Corporation for its stock have been promptly met.

A great part of this line having been adopted as an integral part of the Intercolonial, it is anticipated, when the latter is completed, that some reasonable return may be established for the projectors of the European and North American. The traffic, to this date, continues discouraging and unimportant.

526.—GRAND TRUNK OF CANADA.

The Act of incorporation of this vast undertaking, which passed the Canadian legislature in 1852, amalgamated seven incorporated lines, viz.:—The QUEBEC and RICHMOND, the ST. LAWRENCE and ATLANTIC, the OLD GRAND TRUNK, the GRAND JUNCTION, the TORONTO, GUELPH, and SARNIA, and the MAIN TRUNK.

The mileage of the different sections, all of which are in operation, may be stated as follows :—

Portland and Montreal	Miles 293	Miles brought forward	1,024
Quebec and Richmond	95	Detroit and Sarnia	66
Montreal and Toronto	333	Buffalo and Lake Huron	161
Toronto and Sarnia	169	Montreal and Champlian	84
London and St. Mary's	22	Three Rivers and Arthabaska	35
Quebec and Rivière du Loup	110	Berlin and Doon	7
Kingston Branch	2		
Miles carried forward	1,024	Total miles	1,377

ARRANGEMENTS ACT.—This important measure, given in extenso in the APPENDIX to the Volume of 1863, provides for a number of alterations in the legal and established rights of the shareholders, as well as postpones and reduces payment of the rate of interest on the bonds.

MONTREAL AND CHAMPLAIN.—The use by the Grand Trunk under agreement of the Bonaventure Street Station at, and of the lines near, Montreal, also of the New Junction, connecting the mixed gauge near the Tanneries with the lines of the Montreal and Champlain (whose railways of 83 miles connect at Rouse's Point with the Vermont Central for Boston, at Moer's Junction with the Plattsburg company for New York, and at St. John's with the Chambly line), has tended much to promote better access to the city of Montreal, and greater facility and convenience of working generally.

BUFFALO AND LAKE HURON.—For arrangement with this company, and the disagreements existing, see Buffalo and Lake Huron.

REVENUE.—The receipts for the half year ending 31st December compared as under with the corresponding period of 1866 :—

1866.		1867.
	Upon the whole undertaking, including the Buffalo and	
£719,370	Champlain	£704,379
	Deduct—Ordinary working expenses (being at the rate of	
413,608	63·50 per cent.)	£447,306
£305,762		
72,392	Renewals of permanent way and works debited to revenue	85,819
	Amounts paid on account for loss by fires at Sarnia and Toronto	6,164
	Debit balance from last half-year	17,677 = 556,966
£233,370	Leaving an available net balance of	£147,413

From this amount had to be deducted the loss on American currency, say 39,385l., leaving a cash balance of £108,028

From this again was deducted—for amount of postal and military revenue for half-year due to the postal and military bonds 19,253

Leaving the balance of £88,775

Applicable for the following payments, viz. :—

Interest, &c., paid on lands		£1,695	
Do.	on mortgage to Bank of Upper Canada	4,423	
Do.	on loans, banker's balances, promissory notes, European exchange, &c.	2,533	
Do.	on British American Land Company's debentures	616	
Do,	on Montreal Seminary debentures	616	
Do.	on Island Pond debentures	2,700	
Half-yearly instalment on Portland Sinking Fund		2,311 = £14,897	
Atlantic and St. Lawrence (in full)		32,786	
Detroit line lease (in full)		11,250	
Montreal and Champlain		6,777	
Buffalo and Lake Huron		12,284 = 63,098	
Equipment bond interest			10,779
			£88,775

The gross receipts upon the whole undertaking, including the Buffalo and Champlain, for the half year ending 30th of June amounted to 646,797*l*., against 609,121*l*. in the June half-year of 1867, showing an increase of 37,676*l*.: the ordinary working expenses being 426,477*l*., or 65·93 per cent., against 429,792*l*., or 70·53 per cent., showing a decrease of 3,315*l*. The renewals of permanent way amounted to 36,020*l*., against 54,973*l*., showing a decrease of 18,953*l*. The amount paid on account for loss by fires at Sarnia and Toronto was 4,110*l*., against 10,274*l*., leaving an available net balance of 180,190*l*., against 114,082*l*. The loss on American currency amounted to 18,882*l*., against 21,554*l*., which, being deducted, left the net amount 161,308*l*., against 92,528*l*., or an increase of 68,780*l*. From this balance of 161,308*l*. was deducted 31,383*l*., the renewal suspense debit from previous half-year, and 17,82·*l*. for the postal and military bondholders, leaving 112,096*l*. From this was again deducted 16,688*l*. for interest charges, 31,692*l*. for rent of Atlantic and St. Lawrence lease in full, 11,250*l*. for Detroit lease in full, 10,807*l*. for Montreal and Champlain, 22,045*l*. for the Buffalo and Lake Huron, and 10,779*l*. for the equipment bond interest, leaving 8,834*l*. for next account. Comparing the results of the half year with the corresponding period of 1867, there was an increase in the gross receipts of 37,679*l*., and a decrease in the ordinary working expenses of 3,215*l*., in renewals of 18,953*l*., and in the amount of damages paid on account of the Toronto and Sarnia fires 6,164*l*. The charges for renewals, adding 31,383*l*. placed to suspense account in December, now wiped off, amounted to 67,403*l*. The loss on American currency showed a decrease of 2,672*l*., being 18,882*l*. against 21,554*l*., so that the net revenue balance, after deducting this loss on the conversion of the American "greenbacks," amounted to 161,308*l*. sterling, against 92,528*l*. in the corresponding period of 1867. The total loss on American currency since 1862 amounted to 370,203*l*. From 1861 to 1868 the total profit on working was 1,823,569*l*., the loss on American currency 370,203*l*., and the total renewal to 781,037*l*. Out of the profit of 1,823,569*l*., averaging 213,14·*l*. per annum, there had been paid in cash on leased lines 874,000*l*., and for interest and other claims 624,500*l*., and since 1862 on the first, second, and third preference bonds and stocks 325,000*l*.

CITY OF PORTLAND BONDS.—The bonds issued by the City of Portland 20 years ago in aid of the construction of the Atlantic and St. Lawrence, amounting in the agregate to $1,500,000, began to fall due in December. The amount then maturing would be $200,000, of which about one-half would be provided by the sinking fund attached to the loan; the other half would have to be provided by the Grand Trunk. The balance of the above debt—viz., $1,300,000—would fall due at various periods between December and January, 1871. As the sinking funds would, in the aggregate, only be capable of providing about one-half of the whole amount, it followed that the remainder would have to be found by the Grand Trunk. To meet this payment of, say, $750,000*l*., it would be necessary to issue new bonds, either in American currency or in sterling. The latter mode would, of course, be preferable in consequence of the high rate of premium now paid for gold in the United States. The bonds, wherever they are issued, would be protected by a sinking fund—they formed part of the working expenses of the Grand Trunk—and the only mortgage that would take precedence of them was one for $1,500,000. The bonds would bear 6 per cent. interest per annum, payable half-yearly.

CAPITAL.—The expenditure on this account to 30th June, 1868, amounted to 17,717,786*l*., which left a nominal balance in hand of 450,536*l*., the receipts having been as under:—

Share stock:—Shares consolidated into stock	£2,810,144	
*Shares not yet consolidated	61,643	
Received on shares forfeited	1,801=	£2,873,589
Debentures:—Island Pond debentures	90,000	
British American land company's debentures	20,547	
Montreal seminary debentures	20,547=	131,095
Mortgage to bank of Upper Canada		221,190
Atlantic and St. Lawrence deferred interest certificates (1872), for arrears to 31st December, 1862		77,180
Preference bonds and stocks:—Equipment mortgage bonds		500,000
Postal and military service bonds		1,200,000
First preference bonds	2,513,975	
Do. do. stock	69,653=	2,583,629
Second preference bonds	1,469,877	
Do. do. stock	41,626=	1,511,504
Third preference stock		701,256
Fourth do.		5,258,806
Provincial debentures:—Issued on account of Grand Trunk railway		3,111,500
Amount received on unissued debentures and debenture certificates allotted with forfeited shares.—Company's	3,650	
Provincial	3,650=	7,300

Total £18,177,322

* Shares in the St. Lawrence and Atlantic Line, held by City of Montreal.

GENERAL BALANCES.—The assets and liabilities on this account were given as under:

Assets.		Balance of capital account........£459,536
To securities on hand, pledged, &c.:—		Balance of net revenue account for
On hand £271,091		half-year 8,834
Pledged 148,100		*Liabilities.*
Calls in arrear...... 8,328=£427,520		Agent, postal and military bond-
Cash at bankers 28,735		holders 8,556
Stores, fuel, &c., on hand 210,274		Loans on securities and otherwise 100,000
Sundry outstanding accounts .. 73,203		Bills payable...................... 19,319
Outstanding traffic accounts.... 53,379		Mortgages on real estate 25,028
		Interest on capital, &c., unpaid.. 21,554
		Sundry outstanding liabilities (cur-
		rent accounts) 122,636
		Wages unpaid at 30th June, 1868 27,646
£793,112		£793,112

DIRECTORS IN LONDON :

President—Sir EDWARD W. WATKIN, Knt., Northenden, near Manchester; and 18, Westbourne Terrace, W.

Thomas Baring, Esq., M.P., 6, Bishopsgate Street, E.C.

George Carr Glyn, Esq., 67, Lombard Street, E.C.

Richard Potter, Esq., Standish House, Stonehouse, Gloucester.

A. W. Young, Esq., Twyford, Berks,

John Swift, Esq., Portland Place, W., and Southfield Lodge, Eastbourne.

H. Wollaston Blake, Esq., 11, London Street, E.C.

Kirkman Daniel Hodgson, Esq., St. Helen's Place, E.C.

Captain Tyler, Board of Trade, Whitehall.

DIRECTORS IN CANADA:

Hon. James Ferrier, Montreal.

Charles John Brydges, Esq., Montreal.

Wm. Molson, Esq., Montreal.

OFFICERS.—Sec. in London, John M. Grant, 21, Old Broad Street, E.C.; Managing Director, C. J. Brydges, Montreal; Sec. and Treasurer in Canada, Joseph Hickson, Montreal; Solicitor in London, J. B. Batten, 32, Great George Street, S.W.; Solicitor in Canada, The Hon. G. E. Cartier, Montreal; Auditors, Thomas Morland and J. Baillie, Montreal, Canada, and William Newmarch, F.R.S., 67, Lombard Street, London.

Offices—21, Old Broad Street, E.C.

527.—GREAT WESTERN OF CANADA.

Empowered by various Acts of the Canadian legislature, between 1834 and 1858, for a line in the interior (or western) district of Canada, commencing at Niagara Falls and passing through Hamilton, at the west-end of the lake Ontario, and terminating at Windsor, Canada West (opposite Detroit, and on the straits connecting Lakes Erie and Huron), being the remaining link of communication from New York to the Far West of America, and joining at Detroit the Michigan Central, the Michigan Southern, and the Detroit and Milwaukee railways.

The main line from Suspension Bridge, Niagara Falls, to Windsor, opposite to Detroit, is 229 miles long. The productive mileage is 345 miles, viz., Main Line, 229 ; Hamilton and Toronto line, 38 ; Galt branch, 12 ; Sarnia branch, 51. The Galt and Guelph line, 15 (this last having now been taken by the Great Western for the amount of its debt).

The company has obtained legislative power to hold board meetings in London, and also giving a legal character to meetings of shareholders in England, which in future will form the rule of this company.

NARROW GAUGE TRACK.—This company laid down a third rail along their main line to suit the American gauge, and built an iron car ferry boat to carry the trains across the Detroit River, both of which have been of most material assistance to the traffic.

REVENUE.—The receipts for the half-year ending 31st January amounted to 400,813l., and the working expenses, including renewals, to 193,667l., leaving a balance of 207,146l. From this was deducted 50,911l. for interest on bonds, &c., 66,612l. loss on conversion of American claims, 4,110l. for Detroit fire claims, and 1,258l. for deficiency in working the Erie and Niagara, leaving a profit of 84,255l., to which was added 1,681l., surplus from previous half-year, making 85,936l. Dividend at the rate of 4½ per cent. per annum, free of income tax, left a surplus of 5,725l., of which was set apart 3,000l. for renewal of ferry steamers, making the renewal fund 5,000l., leaving 2,725l. The loss on the conversion of American funds for the half-year amounted to 66,612l., as compared with 48,229l. The working expenses, including renewals, were 48 31 per cent., against 50·26. The cost of maintenance and renewals was 43,589l., against 39,682l., an increase of 3,907l.

The receipts for the half-year ending 31st July amounted to 346,649l., and the working expenses, including renewals, to 208,462l., leaving a balance of 148,187l., out of which was deducted 52,270*l*. for interest on bonds, loan, &c., 54,749*l*. loss on conversion of American funds, 529*l*. loss on working Erie and Niagara, 476*l*. loss on working Galt and Guelph, 4,110*l*. Detroit fire claims, final charge, and 2,000*l*. set aside for renewal of ferry steamers, leaving 34,054*l*. as net profit. To this was added 2,725*l*. from the preceding half-year. Dividend at the rate of 2 per cent. per annum, free of income tax, left a surplus of 1,129*l*. to credit of next half-year. The renewal fund for the ferry steamers amounted to 7,125*l*. The average rate of conversions made during the half-year was 139⅞, the average price of gold for the same period having been 140½. The unconverted American funds in hand at 31st July amounted to $153,146. The total receipts showed a decrease of 8,887*l*., as compared with the corresponding period of 1867. There was a decrease of 20,214*l*. in local and foreign passenger traffic and local freight and mails; and an increase of 8,822*l*. in foreign freight, and of 2,505*l*. in emigrant traffic, leaving the total decrease 8,887*l*. This decrease was owing to the diminished rates adopted on the parallel routes for through passengers and freight, and to the total interruption of the traffic on three separate occasions during several days, by snow storms and floods, over their own and connecting lines, at the commencement of the half-year. If the tariff of through rates and fares in force at the corresponding period had been maintained during the past half-year the receipts for this traffic would have been augmented by upwards of $100,000, without incurring any increase in the working expense. The increase in the amount of working expenses was 25,693*l*., as compared with the corresponding period.

CAPITAL.—The receipts to 31st July amounted to 5,260,829*l*. The aggregate expenditure to the same date, 5,382,594*l*., leaving a balance to the debit of capital account of 121,765*l*. The outlay during the half-year had been 20,789*l*. This expenditure included a portion of the cost of rebuilding in stone the bridge over Twenty Mile creek at Jordan; sundry additions to stations: the cost of raising the level of track at Prairie siding, as a protection against floods; payment on account of building a new warehouse at Detroit for the better concentration of freight business; proportion of the cost of rebuilding in brickwork the passenger station at Paris, originally of wood: the cost of five new locomotive engines and ten new composite cars for the accommodation of emigrant traffic, and for mixed trains on the branch lines.

PROVINCIAL LOAN.—It was reported in March that the finance minister of the Government of Canada has lately brought to the notice of the directors the position of the provincial aid afforded by the late province of Canada to this company. In 1861, a petition, approved by the shareholders, was presented to the legislature of the province of Canada, praying for the relief to be granted to the Great Western that had been conceded to the other Canadian companies; and the directors feel they are justified in expecting that the Government will give the whole subject their favourable consideration, and with this conviction they are now in communication with the finance minister.

DIRECTORS:

Chairman—Mr. Alderman THOMAS DAKIN, Creechurch Lane, E.C.

Alexander Hoyes, Esq., Bitterne Grove, Southampton.
Francis S. Head, Esq., 24, Manchester Square, W.
Thomas Faulconer, Esq., 12, Copthall Court, E.C.
Paul Margetson, Esq., Clapham Common, S.

George Smith, Esq., 57, Conduit Street, London.
John Fildes, Esq., Manchester.
Hon. William McMaster, M.I.C., Canada.
Charles Hunt, Esq., Canada.
Donald Mac.Innes, Esq., Canada.
Hon. John Carling, M.P., Canada.

OFFICERS.—In LONDON.—Sec., Brackstone Baker; Registrar, Walter Lindley; Auditors, John Young, 16, Tokenhouse Yard, E.C., and Sidney Smith, 31, Bush Lane, E.C.; Bankers, London Joint Stock Bank, 5, Princes Street, E.C. In CANADA.— Gen. Man., Thomas Swinyard; Treasurer, Joseph Price; Eng., George Lowe Reid; Loco. and Car. Supt., W. A. Robinson; Bankers, Canadian Bank of Commerce.

Offices—126, Gresham House, Old Broad Street, E.C., and Hamilton, Canada.

528.—INTERCOLONIAL.

An Act conceding an imperial guarantee on 3,000,000*l*. passed the British parliament in the session of 1867, and the scheme is now under consideration in the Canadian legislature. A company to carry out the project has also been registered in London, under the Limited Liability Act. The route is not yet definitely fixed. The enacting clauses of the Act of 12th April, 1867, are as follows:—

Subject to the provisions of this Act, the Commissioners of her Majesty's Treasury may guarantee, in such manner and form as they think fit, payment of interest at a rate not exceeding 4 per cent. per annum, on any principal money not exceeding the sum of 3,000,000*l*. sterling, to be raised by way of loan by the Government of Canada for the purpose of the construction of the railway; and the Commissioners of her Majesty's Treasury may from time to time cause to be issued out of the consolidated fund of the United Kingdom, or the growing produce thereof, any money required for giving effect to such guarantee.

The Commissioners of her Majesty's Treasury shall not give any guarantee under this Act unless and until an Act of the parliament of Canada has been passed providing to the satisfaction of her Majesty's Treasury as follows :—

1. For the raising, appropriation, and expenditure, for the purpose of the construction of the railway, of a loan not exceeding 3,000,000l. sterling, bearing interest at a rate not exceeding 4 per cent. per annum.

2. For charging the Consolidated Revenue Fund of Canada with the principal and interest of the loan immediately after the charges specifically made thereon by sections 103, 104, and 105 of the British North America Act, 1867.

3. For the payment by the Government of Canada by way of sinking fund of an annual sum, at the rate of 1 per cent. per annum on the entire amount of principal money whereon interest is guaranteed, to be remitted the Commissioners of her Majesty's Treasury by equal half-yearly payments in such manner as they from time to time direct, and to be invested and accumulated under this direction in the name of four trustees, nominated from time to time, two by the Commissioners of her Majesty's Treasury and two by the Government of Canada, such sinking fund and its accumulations to be invested in securities of the provinces of Canada, Nova Scotia, and New Brunswick, issued before the Union of Canada, or, at the option of the Government of Canada, in such other securities as may be proposed by that government and approved by the Commissioners of her Majesty's Treasury, and to be applied under the direction of the Commissioners of her Majesty's Treasury in discharge of principal money whereon interest is guaranteed.

4. For charging the Consolidated Revenue Fund of Canada with the amount of the sinking fund, immediately after the principal and interest of the loan.

5. For charging the Consolidated Revenue Fund of Canada with any sum issued out of the consolidated fund of the United Kingdom under this Act, with the interest thereon, at the rate of 5 per cent. per annum, immediately after the sinking fund.

6. For continuance of the sinking fund until all principal and interest of the loan, and all sums issued out of the consolidated fund of the United Kingdom under this Act, and all interest thereon, are fully discharged, or until the sinking fund and its accumulations are adequate to discharge so much thereof as remains undischarged.

7. For the raising by the Government of Canada (without guarantee by the Commissioners of her Majesty's Treasury) of all such money (if any) beyond the sum of 3,000,000l., sterling, as, in the opinion of one of her Majesty's principal Secretaries of State, will be requisite for the construction of the railway, and for charging the Consolidated Revenue Fund of Canada with the money so raised and interest immediately after the charges made thereon, in pursuance of the foregoing provisions of this section.

There shall be laid before both houses of parliament, within fourteen days next after the beginning of every session, a statement and account showing what has been done from time to time in execution or pursuance of this Act by us under the direction of the Commissioners of her Majesty's Treasury and one of her Majesty's principal Secretaries of State and the parliament and Government of Canada.

A dispatch from the Colonial Secretary, dated July 22nd, 1868, settled the route of this railway. Three routes were proposed, called respectively the Frontier, the Central, and the Bey of Chaleur routes. The last named has been selected, its remoteness from the American frontier and the communication it affords with the Gulph of St. Lawrence, at various points, outweighing the commercial advantages urged in favour of the others. The Bay of Chaleur route is undoubtedly the longest and the most expensive of the three, but for military uses it is likely to prove the best. Three commissioners were appointed to superintend the construction of the railway, one of them being Mr. Bridges, the manager of the Grand Trunk. Tenders will be invited for the construction of certain portions of the Intercolonian between Rivière du Loup and Remouski, in Quebec; between Truro and Amherst, in Nova Scotia; and between Dalhousie and Bathurst, in New Brunswick. It is intended to let the work in sections, ranging from 15 to 35 miles, according to situation.

529.—NEW BRUNSWICK AND CANADA.

This was a revival of the St. Andrew's and Quebec intended to form part of the Intercolonial to the Canadas through the British territory, forming a junction at Trois Pistolles with the Grand Trunk and at Toronto with the Great Western of Canada. Incorporated by Act of parliament, 20 and 21 Vic., cap. 154 (August 17th, 1857). Capital, 800,000l., in 40,000 shares at 20l. each. The company is still in liquidation.

It was announced in October, 1867, by circular from the liquidators, that the railway has been seized for a debt of 7,200l., and was to be sold at Fredericton, New Brunswick, on 7th December. It appears that all the lands belonging to the company have been sold by the judgment creditors, while the interest of the shareholders is further reduced by accrued interest on debentures, with the outlay in sustaining the permanent way and in providing rolling stock. These items have increased the debenture debt to about 250,000l. The liquidators had not succeeded in obtaining an offer of even 200,000l. for purchase of the property, although several branches and connecting links are in course of construction which ought, naturally, to improve its prospects and enhance its value.

The only hope for the shareholders is that the projected Intercolonial may embrace the New Brunswick and Canada in its route.

Solicitors for the liquidators and for committee of bond-holders: Chilton, Burton, Yeates, and Hart, 25, Chancery Lane, W.C.

530.—NORTHERN OF CANADA.

The length of this line is 94 miles. It runs nearly in a direct route from Toronto, on Lake Ontario, to Collingwood, on the Georgian Bay of Lake Huron; Lake Simcoe spreads out its two arms to meet the line in the centre. The first opening (30 miles) took place on the 15th May, 1853; the second (12) on 13th June; another (21) on 11th October; and the next (31) on 2nd January, 1855. The branches owned by the company (included in the above) amount to 15 miles, and of the whole only 33 are "double track." In operation 97 miles.

REVENUE.—The receipts of the year 1867 amounted to 115,350*l.*, in comparison with 105,385*l.* in 1866, showing an increase in earnings of 9,964*l.*, or equivalent to 9½ per cent. The receipts for the half-year ending 30th June amounted to 56,521*l.*, as against 55,768*l.*, being an increase of 2·81 per cent. over the corresponding period of 1867. The net revenue amounted to 16,289*l.*, as against 15,479*l.* The interest dividends of both classes of the company's bonds having been paid, a balance was carried forward of $29,567 to credit of interest fund.

The traffic receipts from the 1st of July to the 26th of December amounted to 55,539*l.*, and for the corresponding period of 1867 to 58,945*l.*, showing a decrease of 3,406*l.*

During the last session of the Dominion Legislature an Act was passed empowering the company to create, under certain conditions, a new and additional class of securities, to a limited amount, and to rank next after the existing second preference bonds; the proceeds of such securities to be applied (with the sanction of the Governor in Council) to the construction of elevators, the extension of the rolling stock, and other similar provisions for meeting the growth of the traffic of the line.

CAPITAL.—The balance sheet gave the receipts and expenditure in dollars as follows:—

Received.		*Expended.*	
First preference bonds	$1,216,666	Capital account (old)	$4,595,120
Second do.	1,381,646	Works of restoration	862,668
Government lien	2,311,666	Cash on hand	2,195
Interest arrears debentures	534,708	Bank of Toronto	8,011
Debentures not entitled to priority	48,189	London and Westminster Bank.	36,940
Revenue account	26,690	Board of Directors, London	47,406
Interest on 1st preference bonds	38,187	Station masters, local	4,406
Interest on 2nd preference bonds	34,733	Do. through	55
Bills payable	31,500	Head office accounts, local	2,161
All other accounts	78,250	Bills receivable	500
		Stores on hand	54,743
		Fuel do.	6,833
		All other accounts	81,197
	$5,702,241		$5,702,241

DIRECTORS:

Chairman—Hon. JOHN BEVERLEY ROBINSON, Toronto.

Vice-Chairman—HENRY WHEELER, Esq., Wandsworth Common, S.W.
(Chairman of the London Board).

Managing Director—FRED. W. CUMBERLAND, Esq., M.P.P., Toronto.

Lewis Moffat, Esq., Toronto.
R. J. Reekie, Esq., Montreal.
John A. Chowne, Esq., Westbourne Terrace, Hyde Park, W.
H. M. Jackson, Esq., New Square, Lincoln's Inn, W.C.

John Kean, Esq., Ex-Officio Warden, County Simcoe.
Mr. Alderman J. B. Harman, Ex-Officio for Corporation of Toronto.

OFFICERS.—Gen. Man., Fred. W. Cumberland, M.P.P.; Sec. and Accountant, Thomas Hamilton; Auditors, W. Gamble and James Browne.

London Agency—Cutbill, Son, and De Lungo, 13, Gresham Street, E.C.

531.—NOVA SCOTIA.

This system comprises two lines, one between Halifax and Truro, and the other between Halifax and Windsor, the whole length of the main and branch being 92 miles.

The Nova Scotian Government secured the passage of an Act to authorise the extension of the trunk line from Truro to the New Brunswick frontier, and of the branch from Windsor to Annapolis. The former is provided for by a subsidy of 4 per cent. for twenty years on a capital of 10,600*l.* per mile, and the latter of 4 per cent. on a capital of 6,000*l.* per mile for the same period. The trunk line will, on the terms proposed, cost the province 30,000*l.* per annum for twenty years, and the 85 miles to Annapolis will cost 23,600*l.* a year for the same period.

532.—WELLAND.

The length is 25 miles, uniting Lakes Erie and Ontario, and running parallel with the Welland canal. Opened July 27th, 1859.

NEW BONDS.—An Act for raising 50,000*l.* received the assent of the Colonial Legislature in June, 1864. A resolution was adopted on the 12th October, authorising the directors to issue preference bonds or debentures to the amount of 50,000*l.* as a first charge on the railway and works, the rolling stock, vessels, elevators, and other property of the company, on such terms of years and rates of interest as the directors might determine, not exceeding 8 per cent. per annum.

The receipts for the year 1867 were 14,099*l.*, the working expenses 13,717*l.*, and the loss on American currency 1,018*l.*, showing a loss for the year of 636*l.*

CAPITAL.—The expenditure on this account amounts to 382,585*l.*, the receipts and liabilities having been as follows :—

Share capital	£164,118
First mortgage bonds	85,506
Second mortgage bonds	48,323
Preference bonds	31,300
Liabilities to creditors	53,338= £382,585

DIRECTORS IN LONDON :

Chairman—Major KITSON, 6, Riverdale Road, Twickenham Park.

Thomas Brassey, Esq., 4, Great George Street, Westminster, S.W.
Thomas Ogilvy, Esq., 62, Prince's Gate.
S. P. Bidder, Esq., Hillfield, Mitcham, Surrey.

J. W. Bosanquet, Esq., 73, Lombard Street, E.C.
R. B. Wade, Esq., 58, Upper Seymour Street, Portman Square, W.

DIRECTORS IN CANADA :

Thomas R. Merritt, Esq. | R. James Reekie, Esq.

OFFICERS.—Sec., H. D. Stead, 2, Queen Street Place, Southwark Bridge, E.C.; Auditor, Wm. Thomson Sinclair, 4, Addison Crescent, Kensington, W.; Gen. Man., J. G. M'Grath.

Head Office—2, Queen Street Place, Southwark Bridge, E.C.

533.—WINDSOR AND ANNAPOLIS (Nova Scotia.).

This undertaking has been incorporated under the Limited Liability Act of 1862, as well as by special Act of the legislature of Nova Scotia in 1867. The length of line is to be 85 miles. Capital, 500,000*l.* The first issue being represented by an issue of 15,000 shares of 20*l.* each. The Colonial Government is to contribute towards the construction, as a free gift or subvention—

In cash and 6 per cent. Government bonds	£220,600
All the land required for the line (including compensation) estimated at	60,000
Free use of timber, stone, and gravel, or other material on government land ; and a rebate of import duties on all machinery, plant, and materials, &c., imported for the construction and equipment of the line, estimated at	20,000= £300,600

It is calculated that the line may be constructed and fully equiped at a cost not exceeding 5,882*l.* per mile. The net annual income, assuming the receipts to be 18*l.* per mile per week, and allowing 50 per cent. for working expenses, are calculated to be equivalent to a dividend of 9 per cent. on the share capital, after providing interest on 200,000*l.* of debentures at 6 per cent.

DIRECTORS IN ENGLAND :

Chairman—GEORGE SHEWARD, Esq., Chairman of the Sambre and Meuse Railway Company.

Charles Capper, Esq., Chairman of the Southampton Dock Company, the East London Bank, &c.
Latimer Clark, Esq., 5, Westminster Chambers, Westminster, S.W.

James Hendrey, Esq., Director of the English and Foreign Credit Company.
Walter Stevenson, Esq., Bridge House, Paddington, W.

OFFICERS.—Sec., S. Jeffryes ; Solicitor, Charles Morgan, 15, Old Jewry Chambers, E.C.; Bankers, Robarts, Lubbock, and Co., Lombard Street, E.C.

Offices—6, Westminster Chambers, Victoria Street, S.W.

INDIA.

534.—ABSTRACT SUMMARY OF PROGRESS.

Mr. Juland Danvers, the Government director, reports that there have been 349 miles of new railway opened for traffic during the year ending 31st March, 1868, making the the whole extent of line then opened 3,943 miles.

Upwards of 9,000,000*l.* has been added to the capital accounts during the year, making the whole amount which has been raised for railways in India to the close of March, 1868, to be 76,579,016*l.* Of this sum 60,048,871*l.* consists of shares or stock, and 16,530,145*l.* of debentures.

The total expenditure on the railways opened, and on those in course of construction, amounted during the same period to 75,071,656*l.*

The expenditure during the year was about 7,000,000*l.*, and of this upwards of 4,000,000*l.* was expended in England for permanent way materials, locomotives, stores, &c., sent out from that country. This is the largest expenditure which has been incurred in any one year in England.

The estimated expenditure for the current year is 5,177,000*l.*, of which 1,791,000*l.* will be required in England, and 3,386,000*l.* in India.

The 75,000,000*l.* just mentioned as the amount already expended does not, however, represent the whole cost of the undertakings. It shows only what the railway companies have paid. In addition to that, Government has granted all the land, the value of which cannot be taken at less than 2,500,000*l.* Inasmuch, too, as the rate of exchange for converting the pound sterling, subscribed by the companies, into rupees is fixed by the contracts at 1*s.* 10*d.* the rupee, and the value of the rupee has, during the construction of the works, averaged about 2*s.*, the Government has contributed about 8 per cent. to the capital expended in India. This upon 45,000,000*l.* would amount to 3,600,000*l.* The actual cost of the railways is thus raised from 75 to 81 millions.

The revenue for the years 1866-'67 was only 32,337*l.* in excess of the previous year; but there was an increase of 962,984*l.* in that year's receipts over those of 1864-'65; so that in two years the revenue has increased upwards of 1,000,000*l.*

The gross receipts for the year ending 30th June, 1867, were 4,878,527*l.*, as compared with 4,537,235*l.* of the previous year. The working expenses were 2,537,812*l.* and 2,225,495*l.* respectively. The net receipts in 1867 were 2,337,300*l.* and 2,304,534*l.* in 1866. In 1867 the number of passengers was 13,746,354, of whom 13,074,980 were third class. In 1866 the number was 12,867,000. The sum paid by passengers last year for fares was 1,376,812*l.*, as against 1,278,580*l.* of the previous year; and the amount received for the conveyance of goods was 3,320,607*l.*, as against 3,091,723*l.* The train miles run were 10,980,319 and 10,120,920 respectively.

Some idea of the progress which has been going on may be formed by bringing the present in juxtaposition with ten years ago. Then about 300 miles of railway were open throughout all India, and about 2,000,000 people travelled on them; now there are nearly 4,000 miles, traversed by 13,746,300. The capital expended ten years ago amounted to about 26,000,000*l.*; now it amounts to upwards of 75,000,000*l.*

In 1857-'58 the net revenue derived from the railways was 111,446*l.*; last year it was 2,336,871*l.*; and, what is more remarkable, although the capital had increased from 20 to 75 millions, and the guaranteed interest in proportion, the net amount paid by the Government for guaranteed interest in the ten years 1857-'67 was about the same, viz.: 700,000*l.*

The amount for which the Government was last year responsible on account of guaranteed interest was 3,237,937*l.* Of this sum, however, about 2,500,000*l.* was paid by the companies themselves, so that the advances by Government really only amounted to little more than 700,000*l.* In the previous year the net amount so advanced was 800,000*l.*, and for the year before that 1,450,000*l.*

The whole sum which has been paid by Government for guaranteed interest since the commencement of the guarantee system now amounts to 22,215,505*l.*, of which about 9,500,000*l.* has been recovered from the railway companies, leaving about 12,000,000*l.* as their present debt, which is chargable against the half surplus profits over 5 per cent. This sum represents the amount which the Government has actually paid. Spread over eighteen years it gives an average annual charge upon the revenues of India of 666,666*l.*

Mr. Danvers observes that one great advantage of the guarantee system is that it provides effectual means for keeping the capital and revenue accounts perfectly distinct. Every sixpence which is advanced by the Government for interest on the capital, both before and after the lines are opened, is charged against revenue. An account is kept of the sums so advanced, and the Government is reimbursed, under the terms of the contracts, out of the half excess profits over 5 per cent. Rules have, moreover, been laid down for the guidance of those who have to make up and examine the half-yearly revenue accounts. True and real profits are carefully defined, and it is shown how they are to be ascertained. The confusion between capital and revenue accounts, which has prevailed so much among railways in England, and which has led to the undue increase of capital, and to the conferring upon the undertakings a deceptive value, is thus rendered impossible. Under these rules all the proper and legitimate outgoings and charges of a half year, whether applicable to the working or maintenance of the line, have to be determined and paid, or, if not actually paid, laid aside out of the receipts, before the amount applicable to dividend is arrived at. Some companies have gone even beyond this, and have, Mr. Danvers thinks, wisely established reserve funds for maintenance purposes, the expenses attending the repairs and revenues of a railway being thus more equally and therefore more justly distributed.

535.—BOMBAY, BARODA, AND CENTRAL INDIA.

Formed for a trunk line to connect Bombay with Agra and Central India by way of Surat, Baroda, and Neemuch, and the Valleys of the Mhye and the Chumbul, and thus to form a junction between the trunk line of the East Indian and the Presidency of Bombay ; also to construct a line from Surat, along the Valley of the Taptee, into the great cotton districts of Candeish and Berar, and the coal and mineral districts of the Nerbudda, with branches.

Incorporated by 18 and 19 Vic., cap. 113 (2nd July, 1855), by which the company is authorised to enter into contracts with the East India Company, to regulate and increase its capital, to issue debentures, and to register shares and transfers in India. A further concession, dated 2nd November, 1857, was made of an extension from Surat to Bombay, 163 miles. In operation, 306 miles. Six additional miles may be opened during the year.

By 22 and 23 Vic., cap. 102 (13th August, 1859), the company was authorised to convert shares into stock, and otherwise to regulate and define the capital, as follows :—

$$
\left.\begin{array}{r}
\text{£500,000 original} \ldots\ldots\ldots\ldots \\
250,000 \text{ A} \ldots\ldots\ldots\ldots\ldots \\
1,000,000 \text{ B} \ldots\ldots\ldots\ldots\ldots \\
700,000 \text{ C} \ldots\ldots\ldots\ldots\ldots \\
200,000 \text{ D} \ldots\ldots\ldots\ldots\ldots
\end{array}\right\}
\begin{array}{l}
\text{Converted into Stock.} \\
\text{£2,650,000.}
\end{array}
$$

REVENUE —The following is a comparative statement of gross receipts for the years ending 30th June, 1867, and 30th June, 1868, upon 306 miles open for traffic :—

Year ending	Receipts.	Per mile.
June 30th, 1868..................	£412,440	£1,347 16 10
„ „ 1867....................	433,725	1,417 8 0
Decrease	£21,285	£69 11 2

The gross revenue receipts for the half-year ending 30th June, 1868, amounted to 252,056l., as compared with 264,666l., and showed a decrease of 12,610l. The half-year's receipts, though actually less in amount, had increased per train mile from 10s. 3d. to 10s. 10d., in consequence of the reduction of 50,102 miles in the train mileage. The working expenses amounted to 153,217l., or 6s. 7d. per train mile, against 156,488l., or 6s. 1d. per train mile, in the same half of 1867, showing a decrease of 3,271l., and an increase of 6d. in the cost of working per train mile. The net revenue of the half-year amounted to 98,839l., as compared with 108,178l. in the corresponding period of 1867, showing a decrease of 9,339l. But from the 98,839l. was deducted 27,500l., as a special reserve for bringing the fencing on the line into good conditoin.

With regard to the extension lines, surveys were successfully made, during the last season, of the whole line from Wassud to Delhi and Agra, via Neemuch, including, also, the alternative line, via Pallee, which was surveyed at the request of the Bombay Government. The Board looked forward with satisfaction to the early completion of the line to Colaba, and the accommodation now proposed by Government, including a passenger station at the Marine lines, and a goods station at Carnac Bunder, on the Elphinstone Land Company's site on the harbour side of the island, in addition to that at Colaba. When those works and arrangements were carried out, convenient provision would be made for both passenger and goods traffic in Bombay, and a large expense in cartage would be saved.

CAPITAL.—The amount received on consolidated stock, shares, and debentures to the 30th June was 7,442,713l., of which 101,914l. was received on the half-year. The total expenditure to the same period in England and India amounted to 7,256,706l. The half-year's outlay of capital had been incurred principally for the strengthening of the larger bridges, the completion and furnishing of the permanent locomotive and carriage workshops, &c., at Parel, the construction of the additional line from Grant Road to

Churney Road, in Back Bay, including the temporary station there, additions to stations, and sidings for the traffic, and Suburmutee extension at Ahmedabad. The capital account is constituted as follows :—

Consolidated Stock, viz :—

Original, A, B, C, D, and E capitals consolidated, &c...........			£3,822,996
F capital consolidated £443,980			
G ditto	466,200		
H ditto	888,920=	£1,799,100	
Total share capital consolidated			£5,622,096
Debentures, 1st issue (converted)	242,800		
Ditto 2nd ,, ,, ...	167,100		
Ditto 1867 ,, ,, ...	29,500		
Ditto 1870 ,, ,, ...	11,200		
Ditto 1871 ,, ,, ...	7,600=	458,200	
Total consolidated stock			£6,080,296

Amount received on shares, viz :—

F capital	55,602	
G ,, ...	29,126	
H ,, ...	58,894=	143,622

Amount received on debentures, viz :—

Third issue, 1867	£299,995		
Less, converted as above £29,500			
,, repaid	32,900=	62,400=237,595	
4½ per cent.		100,000	
Fifth issue, 1870	400,000		
Less, converted as above	11,200=388,800		
Sixth issue, 1871	500,000		
Less, converted as above	7,600=492,400=	1,218,795	
		£7,442,713	

Total to 31st December, 1867..			£7,340,799
Received June half-year, viz:—F	£4,840		
Ditto ditto G	6,330		
Ditto ditto H..............................	90,744=	101,914	
		£7,442,713	

DIRECTORS:

3 Chairman—Lieut.-Col. P. T. FRENCH, 8, Duke Street, St. James's, S.W.

1 Deputy-Chairman—WILLIAM HARTRIDGE, Esq., 80, Old Broad Street, E.C.

Ex-officio Director—JULAND DANVERS, Esq., Government Director of the Indian Railway Companies, India Office, Whitehall, S.W.

3 The Right Hon. Viscount Gort, 10, Warwick Square, S.W.   2 James Mitchell, Esq., 8, Portugal Street, W.

2 Henry Haymen, Esq., 12, Clarendon Road, Kensington, W.   1 Samuel J. Wilde, Esq., Bromley, Kent, S.E.

1 Retire in 1869; 2, in 1870; 3, in 1871.

OFFICERS.—In LONDON.—Sec., John A. Baynes; Consulting Eng., Lieut.-Col. John Pitt Kennedy, 66, St. George's Square, S.W.; Auditors, Robert Fisher, 38, Threadneedle Street, E.C., and William Cooper, 13, George Street, Mansion House, E.C.; Solicitors, Howard, Dollman, and Lowther, 141, Fenchurch Street, E.C. In INDIA.—Agent, Charles Currey, Bombay; Chief Res. Eng., Francis Mathew, Bombay; Chief Auditor, T. W. Wood, Bombay.

Offices—45, Finsbury Circus, E.C.

536.—CALCUTTA AND SOUTH EASTERN.

Incorporated by 20 and 21 Vic., cap. 23 (3rd July, 1857). This Act authorises the company to enter into agreement with the East India Company, and to make provision for the establishment of offices, and the issue and registry of shares and transfers, and for the recovery of penalties in India. From Intally to the Mutla, 28 miles.

The East India authorities made a free gift of all the land required for the construction of the first section of the works, and also gave the use of the whole of the surveys of Colonel Baker, consulting engineer to the Government of India, which enabled the directors to commence the works without encountering any heavy expenses. The line was officially opened from Calcutta to Canning on 15th May, 1863. The capital is now constituted in stock at 325,200*l.*, and in debentures at 174,800*l.*, making a total of 500,000*l.* At a special meeting, 11th July, 1865, it was resolved: "That the directors may from time to time increase the capital by creation and issue of new stock or shares, and they may also issue and raise money on debentures, as the directors shall from time to time see fit, provided that no such increase of capital or issue of debentures shall be made unless with the consent of the Secretary of State for India, in Council."

The line is now worked for the Indian Government by the Eastern of Bengal, which see.

537.—EAST INDIAN.

Incorporated by 12 and 13 Vic., cap. 93, for a line from Calcutta to the Northern Provinces.

By 18 Vic., cap. 38 (25th May, 1855), the company was enabled to register shares, transfers, and securities in India.

By 19 and 20 Vic., cap. 121 (21st July, 1856) the company was authorised to convert its paid up capital into stock, as well as issue shares at various rates of interest.

By 27 and 28 Vic., cap. 157 (30th June, 1864), the Acts of the company were amended, and power given to raise further capital to the extent of 7,000,000*l.*

REVENUE.—The net earnings since the opening of the line are reported to have been as follow :—

15th August, 1854, to 31st December, 1862	£1,122,426
31st December, 1863	439,964
31st December, 1864	625,894
31st December, 1865	928,751
31st December, 1866	1,119,315
31st December, 1867	1,076,741

The gross earnings for the half-year ended 30th June amounted to 1,084,634*l.*, against 1,213,069*l.* in the same half of 1867, showing a decrease of 128,435*l.* The net earnings, however, amounted to 590,022*l.*, as compared with 679,596*l.* in the same half of 1867. The falling off in the gross receipts had been followed by a reduction of 38,860*l.* in the working expenses, and the net deficiency as compared with the corresponding half-year was therefore reduced to 89,575*l.* There appeared to be marked signs of improvement in the current half-year, the returns for the first 20 weeks, as compared with the corresponding period of last year, showing an increase nearly equal to the deficiency in the past six months. Should the weekly increase be maintained to the end of the half-year the net receipts for the year 1868, notwithstanding the depressed state of trade in the first half, would not fall far short, if at all, of the receipts for the year 1867.

The Jubbulpore line having been only opened on the 1st of August, 1867, the Board had no complete corresponding half-year with which to compare the present one. But, looking to the want of connection with the Bombay system, they could not regard the result as other than satisfactory. The gross receipts for the half-year ended the 30th of June last were 41,283*l.*, and the working expenses 28,645*l.* —leaving a net revenue of 12,638*l.* The gross receipts for the first 15 weeks after opening were 8,742*l.*, and for the corresponding weeks in the current half-year they amounted to 21,668*l.*—showing an increase of 12,926*l.*

The question relating to the proposed bridge over the Hooghly had been settled by the decision of the Secretary of State that a road bridge at Armenian ghât was likely to embrace all essential requirements, and by his having sanctioned the construction of such a bridge between Calcutta and Howrah, "leaving it to the Government to decide whether the work shall be undertaken by direct Government agency or committed to the municipality with Government assistance."

CAPITAL.—The sum of 450,000*l.* was raised early in the year in debentures at 4½ per cent. A resolution was adopted on 16th July authorising the directors to issue 1,000,000*l.*, to be raised in shares or paid-up stock, and to be offered rateably to the shareholders, at such price as may be agreed upon with the Secretary of State. Since the above date the Board had issued 1,000,000*l.* of 5 per cent. paid-up stock, bearing interest from the 1st of July, at 106*l.* 15s., the price agreed upon with the Secretary of State, which was in the first instance offered to the shareholders. The premium had been carried to the credit of capital. There remained still to be raised 2,868,000*l.* to complete the capital authorised by the shareholders, and of this sum the Board proposed to issue—either in stock or shares, or debentures, on such terms as might be agreed upon with the Secretary of State—1,000,000*l.* during the early part of next year.

DIRECTORS:

Chairman—ROBERT WIGRAM CRAWFORD, Esq., M.P., 71, Old Broad Street, E.C.

Ex-Officio Director—JULAND DANVERS, Esq., Government Director of the Indian
Railway Companies, India Office, Whitehall, S.W.

Joseph Baxendale, Esq.	John Clarke Marshman, Esq., 7, Kensing-
James Beaumont, Esq.	ton Palace Gardens, W.
James Denis de Vitré, Esq.	Sir Macdonald Stephenson, 72, Lancaster
Richard Ryder Dean, Esq., 2, New Square,	Gate, W.
Lincoln's Inn, W.C.	David Innes Noad, Esq.
George Lyall, Esq., 22, Rutland Gate, S.W.	

OFFICERS.—Managing Director, D. I. Noad ; Consulting Engineer, A. M. Rendel ;
Chief Eng., George Sibley ; Board of Agency, Edward Palmer, George Sibley, and Cecil
Stephenson ; Auditors, Thomas Palmer Chapman, Joseph Silvester Godfrey, and
Arthur Morgan ; Chief Auditor in Calcutta, Robert Roberts ; Solicitors, Messrs. Fresh-
fields, 5, Bank Buildings, E.C. ; Bankers, The Bank of England, and Glyn, Mills, Currie,
and Co., 67, Lombard Street, E.C.

Offices—East Indian Railway House, Nicholas Lane, E.C.

538.—EASTERN BENGAL.

Incorporated by Act 20 and 21 Vic., cap. 159 (25th August, 1857). To construct a
line from Calcutta to Dacca, *viâ* Pubna, with a branch to Jessore. Length, 112 miles.
Opened throughout on 15th November, 1862.

The company has resolved to construct an extension beyond the Ganges, as far as
Para Pukee, on the Jumoonara branch of the Bhurampooter, a distance of about 40 or
50 miles ; and to provide a ferry across the Ganges, on its own responsibility, rather than
accept a diminished guarantee from Government of 4¾ per cent.

By 29 and 30 Vic., cap. 136 (28th June, 1866), the company were authorised to execute
several new works, and to raise the necessary capital under sanction of the Secretary of
State for India.

REVENUE.—The following comparative tabular statement shows the progress made
in the traffic :—

	Receipts.	Expenses.	Net.
31st December, 1865	£62,551	£37,825	£24,716
30th June, 1866	72,477	39,752	32,725
31st December, 1866	68,548	38,099	30,449
30th June, 1867	87,516	42,812	44,704
31st December, 1867	81,949	47,365	34,584

The following comparative statement shows the progress made in the traffic during
the last three half-years, ending 30th June, 1868 :—

Railway and Steamer Traffic.

Half-year ending—	Receipts.	Expenses.	Net.
30th June, 1867	£87,516	£42,812	£44,704
31st December, 1867	81,949	47,365	34,584
30th June, 1868	94,631	48,136	46,495

Receipts per mile Open.

30th June, 1867, on 110 miles		£714 17 5
31st December, 1867 } on 112 miles		619 13 1
30th June, 1868 }		707 17 7

The general traffic returns for the last half-year show an increase of 7,115*l.* over the
receipts of the corresponding half-year of 1867.

The working expenses during the half-year amount to 45·86 per cent. of the gross
receipts, against 45·29 of the corresponding period of last year.

CALCUTTA AND SOUTH EASTERN.—On the 8th June, 1868, in pursuance of an
arrangement made with Government, this company undertook the working of the
Calcutta and South Eastern for a period of one year. No formal agreement had been
executed at the date of the last advices, but the arrangement contemplates that the
Government shall pay a certain sum of money to this company for superintendence,
and also specified terminal charges for the use of this company's passenger station at
Sealdah, between which and the South Eastern a junction had been previously made.
The receipts from that railway belong to Government, who will pay all expenses and
take upon themselves all liabilities in respect to it.

DIRECTORS :

Chairman—JOHN FARLEY LEITH, Esq., 79, Gloucester Terrace, Hyde Park, W.

Ex-Officio Director—JULAND DANVERS, Esq., Government Director of the Indian Railway Companies, India Office, Whitehall, S.W.

Henry Hulse Berens, Esq., Sidcup, Kent.	William Miller, Esq., 135, Piccadilly, W.
Sir Henry Byng Harington, K.S.I.	Colonel George Sim, R.E.
Joseph Spencer Judge, Esq., 1, Stanley Gardens, Kensington Park, W.	The Directors are eligible for re-election.

OFFICERS.—Sec., James T. Wood; Con. Eng. in England, John Hawkshaw; Chief Eng. in India, Bradford Leslie ; Agent in India, Franklin Prestage; Solicitors, Upton, Upton, and Johnson ; Bankers, Smith, Payne, and Smiths, 1, Lombard Street, E.C.; Auditors, J. A. Franklin and Edward Cheshire.

Offices—13, Gresham Street, E.C.

539.—GREAT INDIAN PENINSULA.

Incorporated by Acts in 1849 and 1854, and acting under contracts and agreements with the East India Government.

REVENUE.—The traffic statistics for the half-year ending 31st December exhibited an increase in gross receipts upon 852 miles as compared with 777, while they also set forth the extra expenditure to which the operations of the period have been subjected. The receipts upon 852 miles were 509,755l., or 598l. 8s. per mile, in comparison with 440,203l., or 566l. 11s. per mile. The expenditure, on the other hand, was enlarged by 43,890l., in consequence of increased outlay on all the items excepting carriage and wagon repairs, in which there was a diminution to the extent of 10,347l. The increase in locomotive charges was 18,109l.; in merchandise, 7,486l.; in maintenance, 5,631l.; in coaching, 4,782l.; and in general charges, 4,672l. There remained to be added to these extra expenses a sum of 13,555l. incurred in working the traffic over the high road as well as at the break, in consequence of the fall of the Mhow-Lee-Mallow viaduct. The net revenue amounted to 128,138l., in comparison with 102,478l. for the half-year ending 31st December, 1866.

The average length of line worked over during the June half-year was 869·11 miles, as compared with 843·98 miles, being an increase of 25·13 miles. The following tables exhibited the traffic receipts and expenditure, compared with those of the corresponding half-year of 1867 :—

30th June.	Receipts.	Expenditure.
1868	£869,943	£489,174
1867	976,956	446,388
Increase 1868		£42,786
Decrease 1867	£107,012	....

The net revenue amounted to 380,769l., against 530,570l., showing a decrease of 149,801l. The falling off in the gross receipts occurred almost entirely in the item of public merchandise ; the quantity carried was 248,869 tons, being 29,550 tons more than in the corresponding half of 1867. The receipts from that source only amounted to 599,173l., being 131,710l. less than was received on account of similar traffic in the same half of 1867. This result was occasioned by a reduction in the rates of charge for pressed and half-pressed cotton, which were made at the commencement of the working season of 1867-68, with a view to meet the condition of the cotton trade at that time.

CONDITION OF WORKS.—Mr. Berkeley, consulting engineer, had visited India, under instructions from the Board, "to inquire and report fully as to the causes which led to the failure of works, and as to the measures necessary for placing the whole railway upon a footing of permanent durability." On his return home he prepared schedules of the defective works, from which it appeared that the failure of the masonry works was in a great measure owing to defects in the provisions of the specification, a desire on the part of the engineers to economise to the utmost extent the cost of the works, and insufficient supervision, during construction, out of which arose the introduction of imperfect materials, principally in the forms and sizes of stone and quality of mortar used in "rubble work." The directors had given full effect to their consulting engineer's recommendations, and had accordingly reorganised and strengthened the company's engineering department, and they had reason to believe that the railway and works would be shortly placed in a thoroughly satisfactory condition.

CAPITAL.—The expenditure on this account to 30th June, 1868, amounted to 16,077,200l., leaving a balance of 2,545,750l. The receipts to the same date had been as follow :—

Shares	£14,399,310
Debentures at 5 per cent.	3,016,050
Debentures at 4½ per cent.	883,900
4 per cent. debenture stock	293,690 = £18,622,950

NEW CAPITAL. — At a special meeting held on 27th November, 1868, it was resolved—

"That the present share capital of the company be increased by the amount of 2,000,000l. sterling ; and that such amount be created and issued at such time or times, in such manner, and upon such terms in all respects as shall be agreed on and sanctioned by her Majesty's Secretary of State in Council of India ; and that the Board of Directors be, and are hereby, authorised to create and issue such capital stock accordingly."

This stock was "sold" by tender to the highest bidders—the average being 103½ per cent. The other conditions were that the stock should be paid for as under :—

29th December, 1868—25l. per cent. and the premium at which the stock is tendered for, the deposit being credited to such payment.

29th April, 1869—25l. per cent. | 28th August, 1869—25l. per cent.
28th December, 1869—25l. per cent.

Interest is allowed upon the stock paid up by instalments as follows, viz. :—

On 25l. per cent. from 1st January, 1869.
On 50l.   ,,   from 1st May, 1869.
On 75l.   ,.   from 1st September, 1869, and
On 100l.   ,,   from 1st January, 1870.

The interest paid half-yearly, on the 10th January and 10th July, by means of warrants.

DIRECTORS :

Chairman—WILLIAM NICOL, Esq., 41, Victoria Street, Westminster, S.W.

Ex-officio Director—JULAND DANVERS, Esq , Government Director of the Indian Railway Companies, Indian Office, Whitehall, S.W.

Acton Smee Ayrton, Esq., M.P., 33, Upper Brook Street, W.
Henry Wollaston Blake, Esq., 8, Devonshire Place, W.
Thomas Stock Cowie, Esq., 15, Hyde Park Square, W.

Lostock R. Reid, Esq., 122, Westbourne Terrace, W.
Col. James Holland, Hampden Villa, Talavera Road, Upper Norwood, S.
Thomas Rossiter Watt, Esq., Managing Director.

OFFICERS.—Agent in India, Walter Knox ; Con. Eng., George Berkeley, C.E., 24, Great George Street, Westminster, S.W. ; Auditors, George Smith, 17 and 18, Park Row, Greenwich, S.E., and Charles Packer, Kilravock House, Streatham, S. ; Solicitors, White, Borrett, White, and Borrett, 6, Whitehall Place, S.W. ; Bankers, London and County Bank, 21, Lombard Street, E.C.
Offices—3, New Broad Street, E.C.

540.—GREAT INDIAN PENINSULA EXTENSION.

Incorporated under the Companies' Act, 1862. Capital, 1,000,000l. in 50,000 shares of 20l. each. With power to borrow in addition not exceeding one-third in amount of the share capital. In abeyance.

This company is formed in the interests of the Great Indian Peninsula, by the directors and others of the shareholders of that company, for the purpose of constructing and working branches to connect the main line with important centres of trade and production, in proximity to, but not adequately served by, it, and which will operate as feeders to the main line. The company also have the power of working any coal deposits found in the neighbourhood of their railways, so as to secure fuel at a reasonable cost, and the profit on supplying other consumers of coal in Bombay and Western India.

A branch to which the operations of the Extension will be at first confined is of about 96 miles in length, from the neighbourhood of Asseerghur to Indore, in Central India, between which place and Bombay an extensive and lucrative trade has long been established. Indore is on the direct line of communication from Bombay to Agra, the seat of the Government of the North-West provinces. The distance from Bombay to Indore will be 465 miles, and from Agra to Bombay, 790 miles, being 114 miles less than from Agra to Calcutta.

The Secretary of State for India having determined not to extend the existing system of guarantee, the directors placed themselves in communication with him, with a view to obtaining for the extension company the like concessions and subventions as have been accorded to other companies, established for making railways in India without a guarantee ; and from the circumstances of the directors being also directors of the Great Indian Peninsula, harmonious and economical action is secured.

Interest at the rate of 5 per cent. per annum to be paid half-yearly, during construction, upon amounts paid upon shares from time to time.

DIRECTORS :

Chairman—WILLIAM NICOL, Esq., 41, Victoria Street, Westminster, S.W.

Acton Smee Ayrton, Esq., M.P., 33, Upper Brook Street, W.

Thomas Stock Cowie, Esq., 15, Hyde Park Square, W.

Lostock R. Reid, Esq., 122, Westbourne Terrace, W.

OFFICERS.—Sec., Thomas Rossiter Watt ; Con. Eng., George Berkeley, C.E., 24, Great George Street, Westminster, S.W.: Solicitors, White, Borrett, White, and Borrett, 6, Whitehall Place, S.W.; Bankers, London and County Bank, 21, Lombard Street, E.C. Offices—3, New Broad Street, E.C.

541.—GREAT SOUTHERN OF INDIA.

Incorporated by 21 and 22 Vic., cap. 138 (2nd August, 1858), and constituted by agreement with the East India Government. guaranteed 5 per cent. on 1,000,000l. in 20l. shares, the capital required for the first section between Negapatam and Trichinopoly, 79 miles. The capital, under arrangement with the Indian Council, may be increased to 2,000,000l., with one-third additional of extra capital on mortgage.

TRICHINOPOLY.—Application having been made to the Secretary of State for India for sanction to extend the line from Trichinopoly to a point of junction with the Madras, at or near Erode (89 miles), Sir Charles Wood (on 12th June, 1863), gave the necessary permission, and authorised the company to raise the capital required by the issue of shares, bearing guaranteed interest at the rate of 4¾ per cent. per annum, to the extent of 350,000l., and inconvertible mortgage bonds at 4½ per cent. interest (payable at the end of five or seven years) to the extent of 150,000l.

EXTENSION TO TUTICORIN.—Under sanction of the Government, surveys for an extension of the line from Caroor to Tuticorin and Tinnevelly have been completed and reported upon. The estimated length of this line will not exceed 210 miles.

MILEAGE.—The section from Trichinopoly to Caroor, 47½ miles, was opened on 3rd December, 1866 ; and from Caroor to Codumudi, 17½ miles, on the 1st July, 1867 ; the remaining distance, from Codumudi to the junction with the Madras line at Erode, 24 miles, was opened on 1st January, 1868, making the total mileage 168.

REVENUE.—The receipts for the year 1867 amounted to 58,191l., and for the year 1866 to 45,582l., showing an increase of 12,609l. The earnings per train mile amounted to 4s. 11½d., against 4s. 10¾d., and the net profit per train mile to 2s. 7¼d., against 2s. 7¾d.; being in the aggregate 30,508l. for 1867, against 24,694l. in 1866, showing an increase of 5,814l.

CAPITAL.—This account showed that 1,166,304l. had been expended to 31st December.

DIRECTORS :

Chairman—JOHN CHAPMAN, Esq., 2, Leadenhall Street, E.C.

Ex-Officio-Director—JULAND DANVERS, Esq., Government Director of the Indian Railway Companies, India Office, Whitehall, S.W.

Capt. Jas. Gilbert Johnston, 8, York Terrace, Regent's Park. N.W.

T. B. Roupell, Esq. (late Judge of Coimbatore), Loddon Court, Reading.

George Norton, Esq., (late Advocate General, Madras), Wyvol's Court, Reading, Berkshire.

C. E. Mangles, Esq., Poyle Park, Farnham.

OFFICERS.—Sec., Henry W. Notman ; Consulting Engineer, George B. Bruce, M.I.C.E.; Agent and Traffic Manager in India, Wm. Smith Betts; Engineer-in-Chief, David Logan, M.I.C.E.; Auditors. John Nelson, London, and Henry Whitworth, Manchester; Solicitors. Hoddings, Townsend, and Coy, 3, Prince's Street, Westminster, S.W.; Bankers, The Union Bank of London, 2, Prince's Street, E.C. Offices—2, Leadenhall Street, E.C.

542.—INDIAN TRAMWAY.

Established under the Limited Liability Act, for the purpose of constructing cheap lines of communication in India, feeding railways, and adapted according to local circumstances to cattle or locomotive power. The line runs from the Arconum Junction of the Madras Railway, where that line bifurcates North-West towards Bombay, and South-West towards the Western coast of India, and running due South to Coryeveram, 18 miles 65 chains. Capital, 1,000,000l., in 200,000 shares of 5l. each. First issue, 250,000l. in 50,000 shares of 5l. each. Reduced by resolution of 26th August, 1864, and confirmed 16th September, 1864—to 100,000l. in 20,000 shares. In operation, 18½ miles.

The Government, while declining to sanction the extension to the southward at present, have granted a guaranteed dividend of 3 per cent. on the capital of 100,000l., to commence on 1st January, 1868. The position of the undertaking may, therefore, be described as follows :—

1. That the company is under the guarantee of the Secretary of State for 3 per cent. per annum upon the paid up capital of 100,000l., until the extension to Cuddalore is permitted and granted (see letter from India Office, 29th November, 1867, in the reports.)

2. That in reference to that extension, when recommended by the Madras Government for the third time, by General Order, 16th May, 1867, No. 1,482, and Letter, 18th May, 1867, permission was then given by the Madras Government for the company to make arrangements with the French Government at Pondicherry for a branch from the extended line at Belpur to Pondicherry. These arrangements (subject to the extension) have been provisionally approved by the French Government and the Emperor, authorising the sum of 200,000*fr.* per annum for 20 years, being applied for subsidising the connecting line.

Note.—This extension was again recommended by the Madras Government per General Order, 19th September, 1868, No. 2,967.

3. That after the meeting on 16th December, 1867, the capital of the first issue, 100,000*l.*, was converted from shares into stock, bearing a dividend of 3 per cent., guaranteed from the Secretary of State for India in council.

It was reported in November that the directors had continued their exertions to obtain the extension of the present line to the southward and the connection with the French settlement of Pondicherry. They were in hopes of being able to report satisfactory progress, but a late communication from the Secretary of State informed them that he was awaiting the reply to a reference which he had made to the Government of India upon the general question of railway extension. Should the extension be granted the directors were confident that the shareholders would be satisfied with the result, both with regard to the negotiations with the India Office, and also with the provisional convention with the Ministers of Colonies at Paris. Since the last report the present line had been worked to the satisfaction of the Government. No casualities of any sort had occurred either from the monsoons or other causes. There had been no accidents, stoppages, or breakdowns. The line and rolling-stock were in good order and thorough repair.

It was also reported that the accounts were in accordance with instructions from the India Office, made up to 30th June 1868, both for India and London, but the balance-sheet is brought down to 30th September, 1868, in consequence of the guaranteed dividend having been received from the India Office subsequent to 30th June, and because the books had been made up in London to 30th September, 1868, in preparation for the annual ordinary general meeting, previous to the above instructions being received. After this the accounts and balance-sheet will be made up to 30th June and 31st December, as in the case of other lines guaranteed by the Secretary of State for India.

REVENUE.—This account showed that 6,199*l.* had been received from the 8th May, 1865, to the 30th June, 1868, and 4,184*l.* expended, leaving a balance of 2,015*l.*

CAPITAL.—The expenditure to 30th June, 1868, amounted to 107,907*l.*, the receipts having been as under :—

Deposit of 2*s.* per share on 5,694 shares, 7th February to May, 1862	£569	
Deposit on first call, 2*l.* per share on 18,101 registered shares	36,202	
Second call, 1*l.* 10*s.* per share on 18,101 ditto	27,151	
Final call, 1*l.* 10*s.* per share on 18,101 ditto	27,151	
Fully paid up, 5*l.* per share on 1,899 ditto	9,495=	£100,569
Government contribution for bridges	2,810	
From the Madras Government on account of the substratum of the line in conformity with the company's agreement	1,032	
Interest on investments and on calls overdue	2,123=	5,967
Balance carried to general balance.........................		1,410
		£107,947

DIRECTORS:

Chairman—Sir R. MACDONALD STEPHENSON, 72, Lancaster Gate, W.

Deputy-Chairman—GEORGE NORTON, Esq., (late Advocate-General of Madras), Wyvol's Court, Reading, Berkshire.

Major-General James Alexander, C.B., Royal Artillery.

Major-General Charles James Green, Royal Engineers.

Henry Brockett, Esq., (late Member of Council of Jamaica), Heath Lodge, Iver, Bucks.

Henry Kimber, Esq., 199, Gresham House, Old Broad Street, E.C.

OFFICERS.—Sec., M. R. Scott ; Engs., Sir Charles Fox and George Berkeley ; Auditors, J. A. Franklin and George Smith ; Solicitors, Messrs. Freshfields, 5, Bank Buildings, E.C. ; Brokers. J. and J. Whitehead, 8, Moorgate Street, E.C., and Lewis H. Haslewood, Founder's Court, Lothbury, E.C.; Bankers, the London and County Bank, 21, Lombard Street, E.C.

Offices—62, Moorgate Street, E.C.

543.—MADRAS.

Incorporated by Act of parliament in 1853. The contracts with Government comprehend about 850 miles of railway, consisting of—

1st. The main line running south-west from Madras to Beypoor on the Malabar coast, with its branches to Bangalore, and the Neilgherry Hills, making together about 515 miles.

2nd. The Bellary, or north-west, extending from the Arconum station, at 42 miles from Madras, on main line, by Cuddapa and Bellary to Moodgull, where it will form a junction with the Great Indian Peninsula coming from Bombay. Its length will be about 330 miles.

In operation—South-West line 492 miles, North-West line 185 miles, total 677 miles, including 32 to Tadputry, opened on 11th September, 1868. It is expected that an additional length of 30 miles of the North-West line will be opened by the end of May, 1869.

REVENUE.—The traffic is beginning to evince symptons of being able, in a short time, to earn more than its guarantee of 5 per cent. The work of reduction will then commence ; and, after the Indian Government has been repaid the whole of its advances in the shape of interest beyond earnings, the proprietors in the Madras will discover themselves in possesion of an excellent property. On the two systems, the comparative increase is equal to 18¼ per cent. of gross receipts of 24 in net income. The details in respect to the South-West section (492 miles) furnish the subjoined materials for congratulation :—

Half-year.	Receipts.	Per mile.	Expenses.	Net.
June 30th, 1867	£195,604	£397 11 5	£85,638	£109,966
December 31st, 1867	186,860	379 15 11	85,971	100,889
June 30th, 1868	211,332	429 10 9	90,765	120,567

The following are the results of the traffic on the North-West section for the last and two preceding half-years :—

Half-year.	Receipts.	Per mile.	Expenses.	Net.
June 30th, 1867	£45,406	£296 15 5	£14,190	£31,216
December 31st, 1867	43,123	281 17 0	13,795	29,328
30th June, 1868	73,693	481 13 1	18,005	55,688

It should be mentioned, however, that this statement shows an expenditure of 4,972l. on account of hire of rolling stock, and 66l. proportion of rent of terminal buildings, which is not taken into account in calculating the rate of working expenses or the net receipts.

The gross receipts amount to 73,693l., against 45,406l., being an increase of 28,287l., equal to 62¼ per cent, upon the half year. The net receipts are 55,688l., against 31,216l., a gain of 24,472l., or nearly 78½ per cent. over those of the corresponding half-year.

CAPITAL.—Of the 1,000,000l. of new share capital issued in February, 1868, nearly the whole has been paid in full by the proprietors in anticipation of calls.

DIRECTORS:

Chairman—JAMES WALKER, Esq.
Deputy-Chairman—J. A. ARBUTHNOT, Esq.
Ex-officio Director—JULAND DANVERS, Esq., Government Director of the India Railway Companies, India Office, Whitehall, S.W.

Alexander Mackenzie, Esq.
Lieut.-Col. D. Montgomerie.

George Norton, Esq.
Col. J. T. Smith.

OFFICERS.—Sec., Julian Byrne ; Con. Eng., John Hawkshaw, F.R.S. ; Auditors, Arthur Hall and William Hamilton Crake ; Solicitors, Messrs. Freshfield, 5, Bank Buildings, E.C. ; Bankers, The Union Bank of London, 2, Prince's Street, E.C. INDIAN ESTABLISHMENT : Agent and Man., R. B. Elwin ; Chief Eng., B. Anderson.

Offices—33, New Broad Street, E.C.

544.—OUDE AND ROHILKUND.

(FORMERLY INDIAN BRANCH).

Incorporated under Limited Liability Act. Capital, 1,000,000l. in shares of 10l. each, with power to increase to 2,000,000l. The object of this undertaking is to construct inexpensive subsidiary branches to the main trunk lines in India. Government undertakes to deliver to the company the roadways constructed and ready to receive the rails, together with land necessary for sidings and stations, for a period of 99 years, free of cost, the company to lay down rails, provide rolling stock, and construct sheds, for accommodation of passengers and goods.

OUDE AND ROHILKUND.—The extent of lines to be conceded in these provinces is as follows :—

A main line from Buxar, on the East Indian, to Mooradabad, or such other point in Rohilkund as may be determined upon .... } 430 miles.
Cawnpore Branch .... 81 „
Benares   „   .... 76 „
Fyzabad   „   .... 14 „
Nynee Tal   „   .... 71 „

672 miles.

Of the branch from Lucknow to Cawnpore, 421 miles were opened on 23rd April, 1867.
The contract entered into with the Secretary of State for India for the construction
of those lines embraces a guarantee of 5 per cent. interest on a capital of 4,000 000*l.* for
a term of 999 years, which includes the present subscribed capital of 1,000,000*l.*, in
100,000 shares of 10*l.* each, on which 2*l.* 10*s.* had been paid. Should further capital be
required to complete and stock the lines, it is also to be guaranteed 5 per cent. The
Government provide all the land free of cost. The Secretary of State reserves power
to regulate the tolls and fares, so that the net earnings to be divided as profits shall not
exceed 10 per cent. Of the net profit in excess of 5 per cent. one moiety to be applied
to repaying the guaranteed interest advanced by Government during construction, and
the other moiety towards increasing the dividend. At any time during the lease of
999 years the company may surrender the lines to the Government on giving 6 months'
notice, and receive back the whole of their capital. The Secretary of State has also the
right to purchase the lines after the expiration of 20 years from their opening, and at
the expiration of every subsequent term, or period of ten years, up to 100 years, at the
mean market value in London. of the stock during the three years immediately preceding the period when the right of purchase might be exercised. After the expiration of
100 years the Government have the right to take over the lines at cost price.

REVENUE.—The receipts for the half-year ending 31st December were 9,959*l.*, and
the expenditure 6,586*l.*, leaving a balance to profit of 3,372*l.*
The revenue account for the June half-year stated that the gross earnings were.
12,013*l.*, and the expenditure 8,830*l.*, leaving a balance to profit of 3,183*l.*
CAPITAL.—This account showed a receipt of 760,835*l.*, and an expenditure of 388,286*l.*,
leaving a balance in hand on the 31st December, 1867, of 372,529*l.*
CAPITAL.—This account showed a receipt of 1,020,075*l.*, and an expenditure of
408,318*l.*, leaving a balance in hand on the 30th June, 1868, of 611,757*l.* The receipts
were given in detail, as under :—

26,906 shares at 2*l.* 10*s.* paid		£67,265
73,094 shares converted into stock, at 10*l.* paid		730,940
100,000 new shares—first issue.		
83,013 new shares, at 1*l.* paid		83,013
183,013 total shares		£881,218
Debentures		132,000=£1,013,218
Amount raised to 31st December, 1867	£753,994	
,, since on shares converted into stock..	176,211	
,, on new shares	83,013	
	£1,013,218	
Exchange account		£619
Interest on deposits, &c.		5,842
Fines and unclaimed pay (India)		379
Miscellaneous receipts		15
Balance of accounts outstanding against the Company, including balances of		
revenue accounts		12,802
*Amount of balance	£624,560	
Less accounts outstanding as above	12,802	
Actual balance	£611,757	

£1,032,878

It was specially resolved at a general meeting on 5th August, 1868 :—" That the
directors be, and are hereby, authorised to create and issue, from time to time. with the
sanction of the Secretary of State in Council of India, debenture stock, to the extent
of 1,000,000*l.*, to be called 'Oude and Rohilkund Debenture Stock,' the sum to include
the whole or any part of the money which is owing on debenture bonds, and to attach to
the stock so created a fixed and perpetual interest, at the rate of 4 per cent. per annum,
payable half-yearly, commencing from the time or times when all debenture stock shall
be issued."
Of 100,000 new 10*l.* shares, 1*l.* paid, 84,837 have been taken up, the balance being
reserved by order of the directors.
Of the first issue of 100,000 10*l.* shares, 2*l.* 10*s.* paid, 72,802 have been paid up in full,
and consolidated into 728,020*l.* stock.

DIRECTORS:

Chairman—WILLIAM DENT, Esq., East India Director, Surbiton Park.

Managing Director—Major-General C. C. JOHNSTON, 74, Gloucester Terrace,
Hyde Park, W.

Murray Gladstone, Esq. (Gillanders, Ar-
buthnot, and Co., Calcutta), Deputy-
Chairman of the Chamber of Commerce,
Manchester.
R. W. Kennard, Esq., 37, Porchester
Terrace, Bayswater, W.

J. A. Tobin, Esq., Liverpool.
John Pender, Esq., Crumpsall House,
Crumpsall, near Manchester.
Lestock R. Reid, Esq., 122, Westbourne
Terrace, W.

OFFICERS.—Auditors, Turquand, Youngs, and Co., 16, Tokenhouse Yard, E.C., and W. B. C. Maxwell, Tunbridge Wells; Agent in India, Major-Gen. James Pattle Beadle; Eng.-in Chief in India, James Edwards Wilson, C.E. (late Superintending Engineer of the First Section of the East Indian Railway); Solicitors, Crowder, Maynard, Son, and Lawford, 57, Coleman Street, E.C.; Bankers, Bank of England and Smith, Payne, and Smiths, 1, Lombard Street, E.C.

Offices –110, Cannon Street, E.C.

545.—SCINDE.

Incorporated by Act 18 and 19 Vic., cap. 115 (2nd July, 1855), by which the company regulates and increases its capital; issues debenture and registers shares and transfers in India.

SCINDE.—From Kurrachee to Kotree, on the Indus, 109 miles. Opened 13th May, 1861.

STEAM FLOTILLA.—By 20 and 21 Vic., cap. 160 (25th August, 1857), the company is authorised to establish a Steam Flotilla on the Indus (570 miles), by a new capital of 250,000l., subject to the same stipulations and requirements as that of the Scinde. The capitals of the Scinde proper, the Steam Flotilla, the Punjaub, and the Delhi, are kept separate. Although the management is the same, the profit and loss account of each is distinct.

PUNJAUB.—From Mooltan to Lahore (222 miles), and Umritsur (32 miles). The line is connected with the Scinde by a system of steam navigation between Kotree, the upper terminus of the Scinde, and Mooltan, and places Lahore, Umritsur, and other important towns in communication with Kurrachee, the port of Scinde, the Punjaub, and neighbouring territories.

DELHI.—An extension of the Punjaub from Umritsur to the East Indian terminus at Delhi, and when finished will complete a continuous line of railway and steamboat communication from Calcutta to Kurrachee. Length, 314 miles. Capital, 5,000,000l. in 20l. shares, upon which the Secretary of State for India in Council guarantees 5 per cent. interest.

REVENUE.—The subjoined statements exhibit the details furnished from the openings of the respective lines:—

Scinde.—From 13th May, 1861, the date of the opening of the railway, to 30th June 1868.

Gross receipts .... £637,620 | Working expenses per cent....... 84·54
Working expenses................ 539,020 | Net revenue per cent............. 15·46
Net revenue .... 98,599 |

The average weekly receipts during the six months ending 30th June amounted to 2,247l., or 20l. 12s. 4d. per mile. The gross earnings per train mile were 9s. 7d.; the train miles run during the half-year having been 121,237. Contrasting the June half-year with that immediately preceding, the gross receipts show in the six months ending 30th June an increase of about 5,300l., derived entirely from the goods traffic—the passenger traffic showing no appreciable variation. As compared with the corresponding period of 1867, the half-year ending 30th June last shows an increase of about 1,094l. in the passenger traffic, and a reduction of 7,488l. in the goods traffic.

Steam Flotilla.—From the time when the first of the company's vessels commenced plying on the Indus to 31st December, 1867 :—

Gross receipts .... £404,628 | Working expenses per cent. ...... 74·09
Working expenses............... 299,788 | Net revenue per cent. .... 25·91
Net revenue...................... 104,840 |

Punjaub.—From 10th April, 1862, to 30th June, 1868 :—

Gross receipts .... £337,623 | Working expenses per cent. ...... 71·03
Working expenses............... 239,811 | Net revenue per cent. .... 28·97
Net revenue .... 97,812 |

Delhi.—The section of the Delhi, from Meerut to Umballa, a distance of 120 miles, was formally opened by the Viceroy, Sir John Lawrence, on the 14th November, 1868. Traffic operations, however, were not to commence till 1st January, 1869. On the short sections of the line already open, the traffic during the half-year ending 30th June was conducted with regularity and without accident.

CAPITAL.—The expenditure on account of the several undertakings collectively, allowing an estimate for the expenditure since the latest date to which the accounts have been made up, amounts to 9,163,600l., while the capital actually raised and paid into the Government Treasury is upwards of 9,581,073l., leaving a balance of about 417,473l. to the company's credit in the hands of the Secretary of State for India in Council.

DIRECTORS:

Chairman—WILLIAM PATRICK ANDREW, Esq., 26, Montague Square, W.

Deputy-Chairman—Sir T. HERBERT MADDOCK (late Deputy-Governor of Bengal.

Ex-Officio Director—JULAND DANVERS, Esq., Government Director of the Indian Railway Companies, India Office, Whitehall, S.W.

J. Edmund Anderdon, Esq.	Harry Borradaile, Esq. (late Bombay Civil
Colonel Sir F. L. Arthur, Bart., Queen's	Service).
Gate, Hyde Park, W.	Thomas Williams, Esq., Grove End Road,
	Regent's Park, N.W.

OFFICERS.—Acting-Sec., S. H. R. Parry; Consulting-Engineer, G. P. Bidder; Solicitors, Thomas and Hollams; Auditors, William Mackinnon and Edward Thornton, C.B. INDIAN ESTABLISHMENT:—Agent in Scinde, George Rawlinson; Chief Eng., John Brunton; Agent in the Punjaub, Lieut.-Col. Elphinstone; Auditor, George Finch; Chief Engineer, Joseph Harrison. Indus Steam Flotilla:—Agent and Superintendent, John Wood; Chief Marine Engineer, J. W. Jacobs.

Offices—Gresham House, Old Broad Street, E.C.

SOUTHERN AND CENTRAL AMERICA.

546.—ARICA AND TACNA (Peru).

This is a line of 40 miles, on the west coast of South America, connecting the port of Arica with the city of Tacna. The line was completed for the stipulated sum of 450,000l., on which a minimum of 5¾ per cent. is guaranteed by the Peruvian Government.

It was reported in November that the receipts for the six months ending 30th June amounted to $105,724, and the expenditure to $49,461, leaving a net sum of $56,461. But this was considered of slight interest as compared with the disastrous earthquake which, on the 13th August, devastated the coast of Peru, and was felt with fatal effect at Arica, where the sea swept away three-fourths of the town, including the company's station, buildings, machinery, stores of fuel, and other necessaries, besides three locomotives and more than half their rolling stock. Arrangements were being made for repairing the track as far as practicable, and it was hoped that a partial resumption of traffic might follow in the course of three or four months. The directors thought the best mode of raising money would be by the issue of debentures. They had communicated with the Liverpool shareholders, and had received proxies representing 20,000 shares in favour of raising the requisite money on loan. About four or five miles of the railway and the station and workshops at Arica had been carried away. They had been offered two American engines that were just finished to replace those that were lost. Due economy would be used in every department to restore the line and works, and to equip it for traffic as early as possible. It was stated that the line and works would be entirely restored by August next. The company had $15,500 in cash at Arica. The line, 40 miles in length, could be worked within about six miles of Arica. A formal resolution authorising the directors to raise money by the issue of debentures or bonds, on the most reasonable terms possible, to provide the necessary capital, to be repaid with interest out of the first earnings of the line, was carried unanimously.

DIRECTORS:

Chairman—JOHN PEMBERTON HEYWOOD, Esq., Liverpool.

Lewis H. Haslewood. Esq., Founder's	John Pierse Kennard, Esq., Consolidated
Court, Lothbury, E.C.	Bank, E.C.
John Hegan, Esq., 30, Moorgate Street,	Adam S. Kennard, Esq., 3, Great Stanhope
E.C.	Street, Mayfair, W.

OFFICERS.—Solicitors, Maynard, Son, and Co., 57, Coleman Street, E.C.; Bankers, The Consolidated Bank, 52, Threadneedle Street, E.C.

Offices—30, Moorgate Street, E.C.

547.—BAHIA AND SAN FRANCISCO.

A "limited" company formed under decree of the Emperor of Brazil, and laws of the Imperial Brazilian and Bahian Provincial Legislature. Incorporated with limited liability under the Joint Stock Companies' Act, 1856. The grant of the railway is in perpetuity, with a guaranteed interest of 7 per cent. per annum on the fixed capital for 90 years, viz., 5 per cent. by the Imperial Government of Brazil, and 2 per cent. by the Provincial Legislature at Bahia. Length, 77 English miles. Capital, 1,800,000l. in 90,000 shares of 20l. each. The line traverses the sugar and tobacco districts, and opens up the cotton field of the important province of the Bahia. It commences at San Salvador, the chief port of that province, and the second largest city in the empire, and terminates at or near the town of Joazeiro, on the right bank of the great river San Francisco, the navigation of which is free and uninterrupted from that town for 1,000 miles into the interior of Brazil. At present the project is limited to the first 77 miles from Bahia; and the sum of 1,800,000*l*., guaranteed by the Imperial and Provincial Governments is applicable to construction and stocking of that portion only. Opened 31st January, 1863.

REVENUE.—The net receipts for the half-year ending 31st December, 1867, provided 52,385*l*. for distribution, out of which a dividend of 2¾ per cent. absorbed 49,500*l*., and left 2,885*l*. to be carried forward. The receipts for the half-year ending 30th June amounted to 21,972*l*., being an increase of 7,389*l*., or more than 50 per cent. over the corresponding period of 1867. The earnings from passengers, parcels, horses, &c., were 5,695*l*., the increase being nearly 10 per cent. The merchandise to the interior produced 3,313*l*., *i.e.*, about 7 per cent. increase; while the merchandise from the interior had more than doubled, having earned 432*l*., against 183*l*; a continued improvement is looked for. The live stock from the interior produced 1,476*l*., an increase of 44 per cent.; while the quantity of sugar carried during the past half-year was 5,662 tons. earning 7,891*l*., *i.e.*, 5,430*l*. more than in the corresponding period of 1867. During the past six months tobacco produced only 1,322*l*., against 1,845*l*. in the previous year. The molasses traffic realised 527*l*., against 40*l*. in the first half of last year. A further large development of the molasses trade will take place in the coming season.

The normal expenditure was covered by the receipts, as will be seen by the following abstract of the revenue statement:—

Receipts.		*Expenditure.*	
Balance brought forward	£2,885	In Bahia	£23,022
Traffic	21,972	In England	1,394
Interest, exchange, and fees	2,361	Balance	65,803
Guaranteed interest	63,000		
	£90,219		£90,219

But the cash balance in London during the interval since 30th June was reduced to 55,287*l*., and did not permit the directors to recommend a higher dividend than 3 per cent. for the half-year, although the full dividend of 3½ per cent. had been earned. This deficiency of the cash balance was due to a necessary expenditure in stores and maintenance since 30th June; to a small accumulation of cash in Bahia (2,200*l*.), resulting from the traffic receipts, and to sundry debtors in Bahia and in London.

WORKING CAPITAL.—No provision was made in the concession for a working capital, and it has been found impracticable to work the line with the amount afforded by the suspense interest account. It has, therefore, been resolved to form a working capital out of the moneys belonging to the proprietors, and which, if not otherwise needed, would have been paid to them as dividend, and that such working capital be kept apart from that of the company, and remain at the disposal of the proprietors, who will be entitled to any profits that may arise from its employment, in addition to the guaranteed dividend. The directors suggested that the balance (11,803*l*.) which remained after payment of the dividend, and the balances to the credit of the suspense interest account (11,568*l*.), and the city warehouse and jetty account (5,000*l*.), forming a total of 28,371*l*., be considered and treated as the proposed working capital account, which was agreed to.

The insurance fund remains on a separate account for its own special purpose, and will be increased half-yearly by 300*l*. until it reach an amount sufficient to meet the average risks of fire.

DIRECTORS:

Chairman—T. M. WEGUELIN, Esq., M.P., 23, Eaton Square, S.W.

Ex-Officio Director—Chevalier AVALLAR BARBOZA, Representative of the Imperial Government of Brazil.

R. J. Gainsford, Esq.	Sheffield Neave, Esq.
Harvey Lewis, Esq., M.P., 24, Grosvenor Street, W.	Sir Henry Rich, Bart.
John Morgan, Esq.	F. D. Wickham, Esq.

OFFICERS.—Sec., W. Clay; Eng.-in-Chief, Charles Vignoles, F.R.S.; Auditors, J. A. Franklin and J. de Castro; Solicitors, Oliverson, Peachey, Denby, and Peachey; Bankers, Rothschild and Sons.

548.—BUENOS AYRES GREAT SOUTHERN.

From Buenos Ayres to Chascomus, length, 71 miles, single line, but between the city of Buenos Ayres and the suburb of Barracas, about two miles in distance, is double. The grant is in perpetuity, the Buenos Ayres Government guaranteeing interest at 7 per cent. per annum upon a fixed sum of 750,000*l*., the whole of the capital for 40 years. Open throughout on 14th December, 1865.

The capital consists of 600,000*l*. in shares of 20*l*. each. The debenture capital is 150,000*l*., of which about 130,000*l*. has been issued, 17,000*l*. being permanent 7 per cent. debentures, and the whole are convertible if the holder so chooses. The contractors, Messrs. Peto and Betts, held 2,500 special shares of 20l. paid, which were to be entitled to no dividend until the revenue was sufficient (after setting apart any amount appropriated to a reserve fund) to pay a dividend of 7 per cent. on the ordinary shares, and re-pay the Government any money received from them under the guarantee. The directors lately learned that these shares, which had hitherto not been in the market, were likely to be offered for sale. Taking into account the prospect of their becoming entitled to a dividend, and the inconvenience caused by the conflict of interests between the two classes of shareholders, the directors thought it would be in the interest of the company that it should purchase the shares for the purpose of extinguishing them. After some negotiation they have purchased 2,250 of the shares for the sum of 17,025l. being equal to 7l. 11s. 4d. per share.

REVENUE.— The gross earnings for the year 1866 were 63,593l.; for 1867, 85,288l.; while for 1868 they are estimated to reach 100,000l. The receipts for the half-year ending 30th June were 47,403l., the working expenses 23,377l., or 49¼ per cent., leaving a net profit of 24,026l., against 43,784l. gross receipts, 24,360l., or 55½ per cent., working expenses, and 19,242l. net profit, showing an increase in the gross receipts of 3,619l., a decrease in the working expenses of 983l., and an increase in the net profit of 4,602l. The net profits on the half-year's working were only 474l. short of the amount guaranteed by the Government. After deducting interest on debentures, &c., out of the 24,026l. profit, the payment of a dividend on account of 12s. per share, equal to 6 per cent. per annum, was declared.

The following decree was issued by the Buenos Ayres Government in October last :—

"Whereas,—1. The system of according a guarantee on the capital invested in the construction of railways has been accepted by the public authorities of the Province, by reason, it seems, that it is an inducement, and at the same time a guarantee, for the introduction of capital into the country.

"2. It is understood that a country like ours will not stop at certain sacrifices when these are made to endow it with railways built by foreign capital.

"3. That in practice the system of guarantees offers serious difficulties in the liquidation of the accounts, to which must be added that, in the present instance, the amount of the obligation is quite uncertain and variable.

"4. It is believed that the companies themselves would accept a modification of their respective contracts, and in harmony with the ideas already expressed.

"5. It would suit the Province that its obligations should be fixed and immutable, both for our Budget and for the interest of shareholders, that the obligations of Government may be discharged with the same regularity for which we have ever been distinguished, and which has tended so much to enhance the credit of Buenos Ayres in foreign markets.

"In consideration of the above the Government resolves that the delegate for the inspection of guaranteed railways, bearing in mind the laws of the concessions, the accounts of the companies, and the sums received, may arrive at an arrangement with them upon the basis of the ideas contained in this decree, submitting it opportunely to the approbation of the Government, so that, in the event of the latter authorising the same, it may be laid before the Chambers.

CAPITAL.—The expenditure on this account to 31st December, 1867, amounted to 812,806l., while the receipts to that date were as follow :—

Share capital		£649,500
Debenture bonds	£100,000	
Less deposited as security	20,000 =	80,000
Retention account		10,000
Bills payable		20,601
Interest warrants and dividends outstanding		12,722
Sundry creditors		722
Buenos Ayres balances		40,246 = £813,792

DIRECTORS :

Chairman—DAVID ROBERTSON, Esq., M.P., 56, Upper Brook Street, W., and Ladykirk, Berwick-on-Tweed.

Deputy-Chairman—G. A. H. HOLT, Esq., 36, Cambridge Terrace, Hyde Park, W.

Spencer Herapath, Esq., 4, Angel Court, L.C.
John Fair, Esq., 50, Hamilton Terrace, St. John's Wood, N.W.

Henry Wheeler, Esq., Wandsworth Common, S.
Lawrence Heyworth, Esq., Yew Tree, Liverpool.

OFFICERS.—Sec., C. O. Barker; Manager in Buenos Ayres, Edward Banfield; Auditors, John B. Wanklyn and William Cash.

Offices—4, Great Winchester Street Buildings, E.C.

549.—CENTRAL ARGENTINE.

Incorporated with limited liability under "The Companies' Act, 1862." The grant of the railway is in perpetuity, with a guaranteed interest of 7 per cent. per annum, upon a fixed outlay of 6,400*l*. per mile, for 40 years, reckoned from the date of its first beginning to run; and at the expiration of that time all obligations on the part of the Argentine Government will cease. Length, 247 English miles. Capital, 1,600,000*l*., of which, 50,000 shares of 20*l*. each have been created and issued. Calls to the extent of 16*l*. 10*s*. per share have been made, and the receipts thereon amounting to 812,527*l*.

The first section of the railway extending from the Port of Rosario, in the province of Sante Fé—70 miles—to Tortugas, was opened for public traffic on the 1st May, 1866, and the Argentine Government then officially notified their consent to the same. The second section from Tortugas to the town of Frayle-Muerto, in the province of Cordova. 52½ miles, was opened on the 1st of September. Opened to Villa Nueva, 158 miles, 1st June, 1867.

REVENUE.—The receipts on the portion of the line now open compared with previous periods as follows :—

June 30th, 1868—£30,724	.... per mile 10*s*.	8½*d*.
Dec. 31st, 1867— 22,154	.... „	7	8¾
June 30th, 1867— 12,096	.... „	5	1¼

£64,976

The subjoined extracts are from the report presented on the 30th September, and furnish satisfactory testimony of the good faith with which the Argentine Government is carrying out its engagments with the company :—"The report has reference to the progress which the board have made in carrying into effect the arrangement that was mutually entered into last year with the national Government of the Argentine Republic and the contractors, Messrs. Brassey, Wythes, and Wheelwright, with respect to raising the sum of 600,000*l*., the remaining portion of the company's capital. In their previous report the directors informed the proprietors that in the settlement of the 15,000 shares of 20*l*. each, subscribed for by Government, payment was to be made in bonds of the loan authorised by the Act of their legislature, dated 27th May, 1865, and in cash to the amount of 150,000*l*., by monthly instalments of 10,000*l*. each, in Buenos Ayres. It was intimated in the same report that the speedy completion of the line depended upon the fulfilment of the financial engagement come to with Government. The directors cannot but feel it a source of congratulation that, notwithstanding the difficulties they have had to contend with, they should now be in a position to announce the receipt of the sum of 200,000*l*. Six per cent. (new) bonds from the Government, as likewise of orders on the several custom-houses of the Republic for five of the monthly instalments above alluded to, representing 250,000*l*. hard dollars, equal, at 48*d*., to 50,000*l*. sterling. In reference to the issue of the remaining moiety of the capital (300,000*l*.), as authorised by a resolution of the general meeting, on the 25th November, 1867, the board have created debentures to the extent of 30,500*l*., which have been handed over to the contractors in part payment of the works executed and pursuant to the arrangement with them. The shipments of materials for the completion of the line are now so far advanced as to warrant the confident expectation that, assuming that the land required for the stations can be obtained in due time, the Central Argentine, comprising a length of 247 miles from the Rosario to the city of Cordova, will be completed and open for traffic at the end of 1869. No exertions on the part of the contractors will be spared towards the accomplishment of this important object ; and the directors believe that, as regards the future, an efficient and energetic management will be alone required to secure the prosperity of the undertaking. The directors have much satisfaction in further announcing that recent advices from the resident director report the receipt of bills on the national treasury for the sum of 397,533 hard dollars, equivalent to 79,506*l*. sterling, being in liquidation of the interest of 7 per cent. guaranteed by Government in the working of the railway."

DIRECTORS :

Chairman—JOHN HEGAN, Esq., 30, Moorgate Street, E.C.
Deputy-Chairman—HENRY BROCKETT, Esq., Heath Lodge, Iver, Bucks.

W. B. Buddicom, Esq., Penbeddw Hall, near Mold.
Thomas Duguid, Esq., Mossley Hill, Liverpool.
Lawrence Heyworth, Jun., Esq., Yew Tree, near Liverpool.
Edward Johnston, Esq., 6, Great St. Helen's, Bishopsgate, E.C.

Samuel Waterhouse, Esq., M.P., Hope Hall, Halifax, and 66, Pall Mall, S.W.
Adam S. Kennard, Esq., Southlands, Godstone.
Edward W. Nix, Esq., The Hall, Worth, Sussex.
William Wagstaff, Esq., Rhug, near Corwen.

RESIDENT DIRECTOR—THOMAS ARMSTRONG, Esq., Buenos Ayres.

OFFICERS. — Sec., George Woolcott, F.R.G.S. ; Eng., Edward Woods, C.E., 3, Storey's Gate, S.W. : Resident Eng., E. Harry Woods, C.E., Rosario ; Solicitors, Travers, Smith, and De Gex, 25, Throgmorton Street, E.C.; Auditors, R. P. Harding and W. T. Linford ; Bankers, The London and Westminster Bank, and The Consolidated Bank, London.

Offices—60, Gracechurch Street, E.C.

550.—CHILI AND BUENOS AYRES.

A company has been formed in Buenos Ayres for the purpose of constructing a railway from that city to the Chilean frontier. The proposed road is under the direction of a German engineer, named Otto von Armen. The route will be from Chivilcoy, Buenos Ayres, in a straight line to the Planchon Pass, in the Andes, connecting the present Western of Buenos Ayres with the Southern Chilean.

551.—COPIAPO AND CALDERA (Chili).

Incorporated by local authority, in 1849, from Port Caldera to Copiapo (1,300 feet above sea level), to supply the mining population. Length, 50½ English miles. An extension to the Corderillas, 27 miles, was opened on 30th January, 1859.

By act of the Chilian Legislature a tramway in the province of Coquimbo begins at the Cuesta of Peralta, and proceeds to the city of La Serena, with branches to all the chief mining places. From La Serena the line will be continued to the port of Coquimbo, and thence to the copper smelting works of the Mexican and South American Company at Herradura and Tongoy. Power is given to convert this into a railway to be worked by locomotive.

Another concession was obtained from the Government of Chili for continuation of the railway from Pabellon to Chanarcillo, 27 miles, opened May, 1859. The directors solicited a period of 15 years for fixing their own rates of freights and passages, instead of 10 years, and the Government acceded to the request in that respect.

552.—COQUIMBO (Chili).

This company was projected by a few English merchants in Valparaiso, in August, 1860, and in November in the same year obtained the Government sanction. The capital was immediately subscribed, chiefly in Valparaiso, the works undertaken, and these are now completed in eighteen months. The railway is single, and its length, including 8 branches, is 40 miles ; its total cost, including rolling stock, purchase of land, and all legal and other expenses, is 230,000l., or 5,750l. per mile. The line is composed of two branches. The starting point is the port of Coquimbo, and the Northern branch, which is 10 miles long, unites the port with the city of La Serena, capital of the province. The southern branch, starting also from Coquimbo, takes a southerly direction for 30 miles, penetrating into the heart of one of the richest copper mining districts of the world, the main object of the railway being to bring down the minerals to the coast, either for shipment to England and the United States, or to be worked up into copper ingots at the smelting establishments of the port. Opened 21st April, 1862, but no regular return of traffic or profits appear to be published.

553.—HONDURAS (Inter Oceanic).

The surveys of this line (200 miles) establish the superiority of the route from Puerta Cabella, on the Atlantic, to the bay of Fonseca, on the Pacific (a length of 147 miles), over the routes by Panama and Tehuantepec. This railway will shorten the distance from New York to San Francisco by 1,300 miles, or ten days' time, and attract a great proportion of the travelling from the Panama route, which had paid 12 per cent. yearly. The proposed maximum cost of the line is estimated at $10,000,000, and the net revenue $3,200,000 per annum.

A loan in aid of this undertaking was negotiated in September and October, but it has since been announced that fresh surveys will be made relative to the railway and state domains. No money will be disbursed from the subscriptions until these reports shall have been received. These surveys and the preliminary expenses are to be defrayed by the contractors.

The contractors, Messrs. Waring Brothers, made arrangements in November for the shipment of all the plant required for the first section from the harbour of Puerto Caballos, on the Atlantic coast, to the town of Santiago.

554.—MEXICAN.

Incorporated with limited liability under "The Companies' Act, 1865." From Vera Cruz to Mexico, with branch to Puebla, 300 miles. Concession in perpetuity. Subvention by the Government of Mexico, $6,000,000. Total capital, 5,400,000l., one-half of which to be raised in bonds or obligations. Share capital, 2,700,000l., in 135,000 shares of 20l. each. Of these 40,000 have been subscribed by the Mexican Government, and 35,000 (fully paid up) taken in part payment for the portion of the line already executed, but not transferable until the line is opened, or until all the calls have been made on the ordinary shares. Opened from Mexico to the Puebla Junction, a distance of 86 miles. A local traffic had been carried on between the capital and Guadaloupe (i. e. on the first few miles, 3¾ of this section) long prior to the opening for through traffic to Apixaco. The total mileage is, therefore, 133 miles, viz., 47 from Paso del Macho to Vera Cruz, and 86 above mentioned, exclusive of the tramway to Tacubaya.

REVENUE.—Of the two sections of the line opened to public traffic, the upper section from Mexico to Apixaco (86 miles) is in good working order, and furnished with adequate locomotive and carriage stock. The traffic, which had amounted in the six months ended 31st December, 1867, to 51,047l. 4s. 7d., or 22l. 16s. 7d. per mile per week, had produced 26,444l. 5s., or 23l. 13s. per mile per week in the succeeding three months, ended

31st March. The whole of this traffic, practically speaking, was derived from local sources. On the lower section, from Vera Cruz to Paso del Macho (47 miles), the traffic, which amounted in gross in the six months ended 31st December, 1867, to 29,745*l.*, on 24*l.* 6*s.* 10*d.* per mile per week, produced 17,768*l.*, or 29*l.* 1*s.* 7*d.* per mile per week in the three months ended 31st March, 1868 ; but the line remains in a very defective condition.

Under a careful review of the circumstances, the board desire to press forward, in the first instance, the completion of the Puebla branch and the reinstatement of the Vera Cruz section, together with the active prosecution of the works on the section between Paso del Macho and Fortin, so far as the means at command will admit. The directors obtained power to borrow a sum not exceeding 500,000*l.* in debenture bonds, redeemable by annual drawings extending over a long term of years, to be specially secured upon the net receipts between Mexico and Puebla. This sum will include the debenture debt now outstanding. The net receipts from the working of the section between Mexico and Apixaco amount to nearly 50,000*l.* per annum, and are estimated to produce a net result of upwards of 24*l.* per mile per week, or about 146,000*l.* per annum on the whole line, 115 miles in length, between Mexico and Puebla. The articles of association, as they now stand, authorise the directors to borrow 2,700,000*l.* on bonds, but no mention is made of any mortgage of the property of the company.

It was further reported in December that the directors had received satisfactory intelligence that all matters in question between the Government of Mexico and the company with reference to its privileges under the concession had been finally settled, and that the concession itself had been definitively confirmed in Congress. The decree of President Juarez, dated 27th November, 1867, by which the privileges and obligations of the company in its relations with the Government of Mexico were defined and set forth, was now incorporated in the public law of the State, with some modifications, which the representatives of the company considered would tend to promote a good understanding with the Government. The pecuniary obligations of the State to the company were confirmed, and the company was reassured in the possession of its sub-ventions of an annual payment for twenty-five years of 112,000*l.* ($560,000) from the Mejoras Materiales, or public improvements fund, and the assignment of a sum equal to 15 per cent. of the customs duties, by way of a subscription to the capital of the company. Those contributions were henceforward to be collected by the company itself through the medium of special obligations of the Government issued to the company for disposal, through its agents, for cash to the importers of goods and other persons chargeable with the payment of duties at the maritime and frontier custom houses. Negotiations were in progress for an advance to the company of a sum of money sufficient to complete the line to Puebla, and to discharge in cash or class A mortgage bonds all pressing liabilities of the company in England and Mexico, exclusive of those which the creditors had agreed to postpone. The repayment of the cash needed for this purpose would be collaterally secured on the deposit of class A mortgage bonds, and on an assignment of the surplus proceeds of the line between Mexico and Puebla. The traffic receipts on the Vera Cruz section, 47 miles in length, amounted for the half-year ending 30th June to 29,954*l.*, or 24*l.* 10*s.* per mile per week. The gross receipts for the half-year ending 30th June last amounted on the section from Mexico to Apixaco (86 miles) to 47,975*l.*, or 21*l.* 9*s.* per mile per week.

CAPITAL.—The expenditure, as ascertained to 31st December, 1867, amounted to 2,791,735*l.*, while the receipts were detailed as follow :—

35,000 original shares. Capital of the Vera Cruz and Orizaba, and Puebla and Mexico...		£700,000
8,112 inalienable shares, representing $811,230 received from the Mexican Government in respect of the 15 per cent. duties		162,246
47,476 ordinary shares, at 4*l.* per share :—		
Deposit £189,904		
Less not paid .... 100=	£189,804	
1st call, 3*l.* per share.................................. 142,428		
Less not paid .... 16,278=	126,150	
2nd call, 3*l.* per share 142,428		
Less not paid .... 16,758=	125,670	
3rd call, 3*l.* per share 142,428		
Less not paid .... 19,584=	122,844	
4th call (and final), 7*l.* per share 332,332		
Less not paid .... 86,729=	245,603=	£810,071
To Creditors—Loans and advances		544,864
Debenture bonds...		147,100
Contractors..		387,637
Engineers		3,984
Directors' fees		4,853
Interest on debentures...		1,428
,, Loans		145,817
,, due to shareholders		276
Sundry trade and other creditors...		1,032
		£2,910,192

DIRECTORS:

Chairman—1 ROBERT WIGRAM CRAWFORD, Esq., M.P. (Crawford, Colvin, & Co.),
71, Old Broad Street, E.C.

2 William Barron, Esq. (Barron, Forbes, and Co.), Mexico.
3 George William Campbell, Esq. (Finlay, Campbell, & Co.)
6 Henry Hucks Gibbs, Esq. (Antony Gibbs and Sons.)
8 Louis Huth, Esq. (Frederick Huth & Co.)

7 James Stewart Hodgson, Esq. (Baring, Brothers, & Co.)
5 Antonio Escandon, Esq., Mexico.
4 James Henry Crawford, Esq., Whitebarns, Buntingford.
9 Thomas Collett Sandars, Esq., Minchenden Lodge, Southgate.

OFFICERS.—Sec., William Roscoe; Consulting Eng. in England, James Samuel, 26, Great George Street, Westminster, S.W.; Resident Eng. in Mexico, Alister Fraser; Solicitors, Messrs. Freshfields, 5, Bank Buildings, E.C.; Auditors, B. H. Adams, Torrington Square, W.C., and H. H. Stansfeld, Talbot Road, Bayswater, W.; Bankers, Glyn, Mills, Currie, and Co., 67, Lombard Street, E.C.; Chief Agent in Mexico, E. T. Kirkpatrick.

Offices—18, New Broad Street, E.C.

555.—MEXICO.

On the 7th October, 1868, the Mexican Government granted a new concession to M. Emile La Sere for the re-establishment of a route across the Isthmus of Tehauntepec. M. La Sere, as president of the old Tehauntepec route, has had great experience, and the immediate commencement of work on the road by those New York capitalists whom he represents is anticipated.

The Mexican Government, on the 16th October, 1868, chartered a company, headed by Senores Abdon Morales Montenegro and Manuel B. da Cunha Reis, who are to construct a railway from the north side of the city of Mexico, via Tlalnepantla, Cuantitlan, Zumpango, Tizayuca, Tulancingo, Huanchinango, and Hico, to the river Tuxpan. From this point on the Rio Tuxpan steamboats are to connect the road with the ports of Tuxpan and Tampico. A branch road is to be built also to Pachuca. A telegraph line is also to be constructed along the road. The whole work is to be finished in five years. The concession of public lands, &c., is for sixty years.

556.—NORTHERN OF BUENOS AYRES.

Incorporated with limited liability under the Joint Stock Companies Acts. Government guarantee at 7 per cent. for 20 years on 150,000l.

In virtue of the law of the State of Buenos Ayres, and a special contract or concession, dated 25th February, 1862, the line and plant remain the property of the company in perpetuity, free from taxation. Length, 19 miles. Opened throughout 9th January, 1865.

REVENUE.—The income account for the year ending 31st December, 1867, after providing for interest on the entire loan capital, showed a balance of 8,765l., to which were added about 4,300l., due from the Buenos Ayrean Government for 1867, under their guarantee, making a total of about 13,000l., out of which the directors would have been able to recommend a dividend, but that they have been compelled to apply part of the surplus revenue to the reduction of the temporary loan of 25,000l. As the balance unpaid, viz., 10,000l., has been converted into a loan for a fixed period, the directors recommended that a general meeting be convened, upon receipt of the money due from the Buenos Ayres Government, for the purpose of taking the opinion of the shareholders as to the disposal of the balance referred to.

CAPITAL.—The expenditure to 31st December, 1867, amounted to 289,331l., the receipts having been as under:—

Guaranteed preference shares	£147,887	
Deferred shares	60,000	
Ordinary shares	25,000=	£232,887
Debentures	26,000	
Loans	4,144	
Do.	220=	30,364
		£263,251
Balance		26,079
		£289,331

The temporary loans have been paid off or exchanged for 10 per cent. debenture stock, the amount issued to 9th November having been 11,900l.

DIRECTORS:

Chairman—C. SEALE HAYNE, Esq., 3, Eaton Square, S.W.

H. D. Browne, Esq., Woodgreen Common.
Sir J. C. Lees, 26, Carlisle Terrace, Kensington, W.

G. N. Strawbridge, Esq., 12A, Copthal Court, E.C.
Edward Wright, Esq., Clare Hall, South Mimms, Herts.

OFFICERS.—Sec., E. Ayres; Auditors, H. W. Spratt and J. H. Hutchinson; Solicitors, Ashurst, Morris, and Co., 6, Old Jewry, E.C.; Bankers, The Imperial Bank, Lothbury, E.C.; Mana and Co., and London and River Plate Bank, Buenos Ayres.

Offices—16, Throgmorton Street, E.C.

557.—PANAMA.

In the year 1866 this railroad carried across from sea to sea 31,700 passengers, $63,114,113 of treasure, 67,262,679lb. of freight by weight, 2,309,201ft. of freight by measurement, and mails weighing 888,997lb. In mail matter there is very little variation, averaging about 380 tons annually. Merchand'se has steadily increased from 10,658 tons in 1856 to 93,414 tons in 1866; and coal from 8,934 tons in 1856 to 13,418 tons in 1866. Jewellery has varied from $192,718 to $844,490, but has been gradually declining in amount. The gold transported was $48,047,692 in 1856, and in 1866, $48,234,463, and in no intervening year equalled either of those amounts. Silver shows a gradual increase from $9,439,648 in 1856 to $18,653,239 in 1863, since which it has declined to $14,331,751 in 1866. The passenger traffic does not show any steady or important increase in the ten years. The income in 1866 was $2,424,977, and the expenses $1,208,364, leaving 1,216,613 net proceeds. The total tonnage transported along the road in the year was 107,598; it has almost doubled in every three years.

The company has obtained a new contract, extending their privileges for 99 years, and giving them the island of Manzanilla in fee. For this they are to pay a million of dollars down and a quarter of a million annually thereafter to the termination of the contract, which has been ratified by the congress of New Granada, and is therefore in all respects valid.

558.—PERNAMBUCO (Brazil.)

This undertaking is established by Acts of the Brazilian Legislature, and by decree of the Emperor; incorporated in England under 7 and 8 Vic., cap. 110. The company is also established under the Limited Liability Act. The grant of the railway is in perpetuity, with a guaranteed interest at 7 per cent. per annum for 90 years, viz.: 5 per cent. by the Imperial Brazilian Government, and 2 per cent. by the Provincial Legislature of Pernambuco. Capital, 1,200,000l. in 60,000 shares at 20l. each. The line is from the city and port of Pernambuco to the town of Agoa Preta in the interior—a distance of 77¾ miles. Opened 30th November, 1862.

REVENUE.—It was reported in October that the traffic had, on the whole, averaged much the same as the year previous, namely, on the year ending 30th June last there was a decrease in the receipts of 1,309l. On the eight months which had elapsed of the present year—viz., from 1st January to 31st August, there had, on the other hand, been an increase of 1,123l. The comparative stagnation was sufficiently accounted for by the general depression throughout Brazil caused by the continuance of the war. Notwithstanding which, however, but for the heavy item of exchange differences, the surplus on the year over and above all working expenses, carried to the account of the Brazilian Government, instead of 10,485l., would have been upwards of 19,000l. There was a balance of 19,641l. applicable to dividend, which allowed of an interim dividend at the rate of 3 per cent. per annum, for which were issued deferred warrants with the same option as before. There were 37,100l. of paid-off debentures available for re-issue, and as soon as they could be placed the warrants would be paid.

It was also reported in October that the bill promoted by the Government for the final decision respecting the guarantee of the additional capital, having been read in the Senate a first time, stood for the second reading for 15th July, on which day, however, a Cabinet crisis having occurred, there was a dissolution of the Ministry, and the session came abruptly to an end. But for that unlooked-for event the bill would have come on in due course, and have had the cordial support of the Government. On the dissolution of the Ministry being made known, the directors placed in the hands of the Brazilian Minister a condensed statement of the present position of the company and of the guarantee question, accompanied by a request that he would, without delay, forward it to the new Government, and call their earnest attention to it.

CAPITAL.—The expenditure on this account extends to 1,830,508l. The balance sheet to 30th June furnishes the subjoined particulars:—

Received.		Expended.	
Share capital	£1,189,740	On capital account	£1,830,508
Brazilian Government loan	400,000	Brazilian Government for guar-	
Debentures	234,890	antee to date, less the profit	
Temporary loan	15,000	on the year's working	21,166
Due by the company, including		Outstanding accounts	1,618
deferred dividend warrants ..	31,278	Suspense account	7,045
Dividend account	19,641	Stores in Brazil	23,909
		Cash, and bill receivable	6,301
	£1,890,550		£1,890,550

DIRECTORS:

Chairman—ROBERT BENSON, Esq., King's Arms Yard, E.C.

E. H. Bramah, Esq., Great George Street, S.W.
Wm. Gladstone, Esq., Old Broad Street, E.C.
W. B. Greenfield, Esq., Porchester Terrace, W.

Major General G. B. Tremenheere, Spring Grove, Isleworth, W.
The Viscount Gort, 10, Warwick Square, S.W.

CONCESSIONARIES.
Alfred de Mornay, Esq.
Edward de Mornay, Esq.

The Minister, or other Brazilian representative in London, for the time being, is a director ex-officio.

OFFICERS.—Man. and Eng., G. O. Mann, Pernambuco : Con. Eng., Charles Hutton Gregory, Delahay Street, S.W.; Sec., William Henry Bellamy ; Solicitors, Pritchard and Collette, 57, Lincoln's Inn Fields, W.C.; Auditors, George Dixon Longstaff, Upper Thames Street, E.C., and Edward Cheshire, 25, Old Broad Street, E.C.; Bankers, Robarts, and Co., Lombard Street, E.C.
Offices—15, Old Jewry Chambers, E.C.

559.—QUEBRADA.

This land, railway, and mining enterprise is established under the Limited Liability Act. Capital, 170,000l. in 10l. shares.

The object of the company was to purchase and work the Quebrada copper mines in Venezuela, also to purchase and open up a large tract of land for cultivation, containing 250,000 acres. To improve the transit from the mines to the sea, and also to open up the land, a small tramway is to be made for a distance of 27 miles.

A lease of the Quebrada mines, for a term of 999 years, together with the right of working all the mines now discovered, or that may hereafter be discovered by the company, of copper, lead, silver, and other ores, extending 36 square miles from the mouth of the adit or main level taken as the centre of the property, including the smelting-house and other buildings. has been purchased, subject to dues of 1-25th, for the sum of 15,000l. cash, and 2,000 shares fully paid up, or an equivalent number of shares partially paid, at the option of the vendor, such shares not to be transferred by the vendor or his nominees until after completion of the railway. The contractors pay to the shareholders 5 per cent. interest on the amount that may be paid for the railway until the line is opened.

A new organisation was formed in 1867, under the plan described as follows :—The capital to be 360,000l. in 72,000 shares of 5l. each. That 107,000l. be given in shares to present shareholders for the purchase of the property. That this sum be paid by the issue of three shares of 5l. each, upon which the sum of 3l. 6s. 8d. has been credited as paid, thus leaving a liability of 1l. 13s. 4d. on each new share. The capital would then stand : Amount for purchase of property, 170,000l. ; available capital for carrying on the works, 51,000 shares, at 1l. 13s. 4d., 85,000l. ; 21,000 shares, at 5l., 105,000l. ; total, 360,000l. Little or no progress, however, has yet been made with this renovated scheme.

560.—SAN PAULO.

Formed under the decrees of the Emperor of Brazil, and laws of the Imperial Brazilian and Paulo Provincial Legislatures, and incorporated, with limited liability, under the Joint Stock Companies' Act, 1856 and 1857. Guaranteed 7 per cent. from dates of payment of calls. Capital, 2,000,000l. in 100,000 shares of 20l. each. Interest payable half-yearly in London. Length, 86½ English miles. Opened 1st October, 1866.

REVENUE.—The following is a comparative statement of traffic from the opening of the line, February 16th, 1867, to 31st August, 1868:—

Month.	1867.		1868.		Increase.	
	Milreis.	Reis.	Milreis.	Reis.	Milreis.	Reis.
January	..		190,395	736	..	
February	36,485	838	71,608	640	35,122	802
March	98,109	468	*102,313	290	4,203	822
April	135,170	684	202,198	426	67,027	742
May	109,464	023	190,554	595	81,090	572
June	75,557	177	170,159	870	94,602	693
July	68,306	968	125,596	050	57,289	082
August	104,626	750	131,445	339	26,818	589
September	107,154	291	..		..	
October	142,016	990	..		..	
November	170,123	800	..		..	
December	190.408	713	..		..	

* Line partially closed from 18th February to 24th March, 1868.

The whole of the company's debentures have been taken up ; and of 200,000l. falling due on the 1st January, 1869, the board determined to reissue that amount for a period of five years, with interest at the rate of 7 per cent. per annum.

CAPITAL.—The balance sheet to 30th June, 1868, furnished the subjoined particulars:—

Receipts and liabilities.

Capital	£2,000,000	
Debentures	609,700=	£2,609,700
Liabilities—		
Loan from the Imperial Brazilian Government.................	100,000	
Interim warrants—Outstanding 30th June	25,593	
Bill payable...	5,000	
Unclaimed amounts	2,880=	133,474
Interest	18,637	
Less interest passed to contractor's account	16,443=	2,194
Transfer fees		860
Insurance recovered...		259
Interest on store account, charged to revenue.......................		1,500
Revenue account—Balance		51,349
		£2,799,338

Expenditure.

Cost of line—Expenditure chargeable to capital, to 31st December, 1867	£2,017,566	
Additional expenditure to 30th June, 1868	245=	£2,017,812
Guaranteed interest—Expended during construction		651,257
Additional expenditure		53,223
Contractors—Advances as loan £28,650		
Deducting repayments .... 20,178=	£8,471	
Materials and expenditure on construction, paid out of revenue funds...	17,201=	25,672
		£2,747,965
Balances..		51,372
		£2,799,338

DIRECTORS:

Chairman—ROBERT A. HEATH, Esq., 31, Old Jewry, E.C.

His Excellency the Brazilian Envoy Extraordinary and Minister Plenipotentiary *ex-officio.*

William Bird, Esq., Laurence Pountney Hill, E.C.	M. B. Sampson, Esq., 1, George Street, Mansion House, E.C.
Philip William Flower, Esq., 62, Moorgate Street, E.C.	Martin R. Smith, Esq., 1, Lombard Street, E.C.
John Samuel, Esq., Park Lane, W.	

One third retire in February of each year.—All eligible for re-election.

OFFICERS.—Sec., G. A. Hillier ; Eng.-in-Chief, James Brunlees, C.E., 5, Victoria Street, Westminster, S.W. ; Eng. Referee, John Hawkshaw, C.E., F.R.S.; Auditors, Mr. Alderman Thomas Dakin and E. H. Galsworthy ; Solicitor, J. B. Batten, 32, Great George Street, Westminster, S.W. ; Bankers, N. M. Rothschild and Sons, London, E.C.

Offices—111, Gresham House, Old Broad Street, E.C.

561.—VALPARAISO AND SANTIAGO (Chili).

There are 77 miles of this line in operation, but no details of traffic appear to reach this country.

The SOUTHERN is to extend from Santiago, 400 miles to the South, through one of the richest valleys in the world. In its course it will pass over numerous rivers, among which are five whose beds are nearly a mile in width. A bridge to cross one of those rivers has been built of iron in the United States, as are also the cars and machinery.

[The NICARAGUA, the PERUVIAN, and the VENEZUELA, have ceased to exist.]

UNITED STATES.

562.—ABSTRACT OF PROGRESS FOR 1868.

The development of the railroad systems in the year 1868 has been more than in any former year. Nominally there is an increase of 3,450·37 miles, and in the cost an increase in the immense sum of $193,245,232 over the totals of the previous year. Much of this aggregate is due directly to the progress made in building the Pacific, and indirectly to the impetus the near approach of their completion has given to railroad building throughout the country, but more especially in the States between the Mississippi and Missouri Rivers, and also in California. It may be assumed that 3,000 miles have been built in the year just passed. The apparent increase in cost is excessive, but it must be remembered that large amounts have been added to the construction accounts of pre-existing railroads, and in many instances the nominal cost of roads has been largely increased by the operation of consolidations and re-organisations. Of the total given above, probably $150,000,000 has been added for the 3,000 miles of new road, which considering the expensive character of the Pacific lines is not too large an estimate, being but an average of $50,000 a mile, while the Pacific roads are not built for less than an average of $80,000 per mile. Large amounts are also lying dormant on roads in progress and not yet finished. The following statement exhibits the distribution of mileage and cost to the several States and Territories :—

	Miles of road. Total.	Open.	Cost and equipment.
Maine	944	559	$19,789,521
New Hampshire	783	668	21,975,319
Vermont	643	603	24,347,149
Massachusetts	1,537	1,425	68,345,521
Rhode Island	121	121	5,006,665
Connecticut	782	641	23,064,859
New York	4,459	3,328	182,538,123
New Jersey	984	972	69,770,243
Pennsylvania	4,937	4,397	256,772,257
Delaware and E. Maryland	352	242	7,483,596
Maryland (other than above)	654	457	28,520,899
West Virginia	605	364	22,404,100
Virginia	1,909	1,464	47,540,038
North Carolina	1,617	1,096	25,687,414
South Carolina	1,338	1,076	25,131,600
Georgia	1,977	1,574	31,369,075
Florida	613	440	9,294,000
Alabama	1,604	952	28,511,726
Mississippi	900	900	24,545,303
Louisiana	837	370	14,321,201
Texas	1,837	513	14,406,000
Arkansas	687	86	4,211,000
Tennessee	1,760	1,435	43,018,916
Kentucky	1,418	812	28,799,285
Ohio	4,053	3,351	169,014,101
Michigan	2,044	1,199	44,549,043
Indiana	3,246	2,600	104,229,226
Illinois	4,561	3,439	156,958,102
Wisconsin	1,773	1,234	48,469,301
Minnesota	1,758	571	18,460,000
Iowa	3,032	1,522	61,332,000
Nebraska	449	420	21,000,000
Wyoming Ter	560	510	41,800,000
Missouri	1,837	1,353	64,014,458
Kansas	1,123	648	30,840,000
Colorado	350	....	350,000
Utah Ter	305	105	9,400,000
Nevada	390	320	25,600,000
California	2,091	468	30,336,000
Oregon	2,019	19	500,000
Total January 1st, 1869	62,917	42,272	$1,853,706,041

In these tables, it is here proper to state, the Union Pacific is assumed to have been completed to the Great Salt Lake 1,035 miles, and the Central Pacific of California a length of 458 miles. These distances were expected to be reached by January 1st, 1869. The length of the Central Branch is set down at 120 miles, and that of the Eastern Division at 405 miles, those being the distances last reported. Should the actual result of the year be more or less, the proper allowances must be made by deduction or addition as the fact may require.

The following compares the aggregates as given by us for January 1st, 1868 and 1869 :—

	Miles of Road. Total.	Open.	Cost and equipment.
1868	54,556·85	38,821·81	$1,660,460,809
1869	62,917·10	42,272·18	1,853,706,041
Increase last year	8,360·25	3,450·37	$193,245,232

The annual progress of railroad building, since in 1827 the commencement was made in the construction of the Granite at Quincy, Mass., to the present time, is shown in the following table :—

Year.	Miles.	Year.	Miles.	Year.	Miles.	Year.	Miles.
1828	3	1839	1,920	1850	7,475	1860	28,771
1829	28	1840	2,197	1851	8,589	1861	30,593
1830	41	1841	3,319	1852	11,027	1862	31,769
1831	54	1842	3,877	1853	13,497	1863	32,471
1832	131	1843	4,174	1854	15,672	1864	33,860
1833	576	1844	4,311	1855	17,398	1865	34,442
1834	762	1845	4,522	1856	19,251	1866	35,351
1835	918	1846	4,870	1857	22,625	1867	36,896
1836	1,102	1847	5,336	1858	25,090	1868	38,822
1837	1,421	1848	5,682	1859	26,755	1869	42,272
1838	1,843	1849	6,350				

City passenger railroads are not included in the above summary. These are now in general use in all considerable cities, and in numerous instances in places where population is less dense. Their economical bearings are fully recognised and their popularity is increasing. Boston, New York, Brooklyn and Philadelphia count their street railroad tracks by hundreds of miles. Probably this total is not less that 2,000 to 2,500 miles.

563.—ATLANTIC AND GREAT WESTERN.

The undertaking is the middle link of an international line of six feet gauge through the States of New York, Pennsylvania, Ohio, Indiana, and Illinois, to St. Louis. Shares, $30,000,000 in shares of $50 each ; mortgage bonds, $6,000,000 sterling, bearing interest at 7 per cent. per annum. Secured on the whole line of the Atlantic and Great Western, with branches, extensions, and equipment. The bonds are of 100l. each, with interest payable quarterly, free of income-tax, in London or New York.

TRAFFIC.—The receipts during the year, in comparison with those in 1866 and 1867 have been reported for each month as follows :—

	1868.		1867.		1866.
January	$404,467	....	$377,852	....	$475,641
February	393,251	....	380,190	....	433,279
March	408,847	....	489,555	....	385,991
April	388,654	....	407,018	....	412,521
May	355,253	....	465,102	....	464,507
June	359,184	....	333,896	....	493,243
July	343,325	....	400,550	....	466,898
August	413,484	....	461,879	....	568,589
September	477,795	....	483,177	....	533,150
October	464,376	....	483,917	....	599,670
November	454,081	....	474,134	....	474,056
December	....	....	360,641	....	388,573
	....		$5,167,371		$5,696,119

The Receiver was removed by the court on the day (15th November) on which, under the scheme of reorganisation of the company, its bonded debt commenced to pay dividends. The railway had been under the control of the Receiver for 19½ months (from the 1st of April, 1867, to the 15th November, 1868), and his last annual report showed that there had been expended out of earnings, $1,750,000. A report for the five months ended August 31st shows that about the same rate of expenditure out of earnings had been continued during that period, and that the line is now in complete order. Under the arrangement recently sanctioned by holders of all classes of its securities, the company have to provide for the year 1869, the sum of only $1,076,614, or something under 200,000l. The resumption of payment next year will commence with the divisional bonds which form the first charge on the line. These carry 7 per cent. interest, and will require for their payment $467,488. The first payment on these bonds is due April 1st, next year, and the interest commenced to accrue upon them from the 15th instant. Another charge upon their revenue is for interest on income bonds to be issued. These bonds bear 7 per cent. interest from the 15th instant, and they are issued in exchange for overdue and unpaid coupons on the bonds of the company.

The line has also been leased to the Erie for 12 years, at a rent equivalent to 30 per cent. of the gross earnings, or a minimum of $1,800,000, which sum is more than sufficient to meet the interest upon the bonds, as mitigated by the bondholders themselves.—See ADDENDA.

564.—BALTIMORE AND OHIO.

Main line, 380 miles; Washington branch, 31 miles; North Western, Virginia, 154 miles. The company now owns and controls over 600 miles, reaching from Washington to Columbus, Ohio, it having secured a 40 years' lease of the Central Ohio. It is also engaged in building a line from Washington to Point of Rocks, in order to shorten the distance to western points by 40 miles.

The company still remains in a state of transition, the shock of the late war not having yet passed off. The President, in the course of his address to the shareholders, on 9th December last, remarked: "When the history of the late war is written it will be found that the services of the Baltimore and Ohio, marked by perfect fidelity to its engagements and untiring energy—moving great armies through territories frequently raided upon—by which movements remarkable results were achieved, will prove to be among the most conspicuous rendered in aid of the Government. Such were these services, constant, weighty, of vital importance, requiring the greatest thoroughness and largest resources, that they elicited, frequently, the highest approval and commendation of the lamented Lincoln. The secretary of war throughout that perilous period, and the most illustrious generals of our armies, all knew, and appreciated, and still appreciate these invaluable services. The great historic facts connected with the continuous and important relations of the Baltimore and Ohio crush the misrepresentations of the hostile and untruthful to their deserved nothingness. As rival interests have constantly indulged in the grossest misstatements and calumnies on the subject, it is proper now to state, that for all the vast amount of the company's property, the engines and cars, the buildings, the bridges and the tracks destroyed during the war by the confederate armies, amounting to many millions of dollars, no payment has been made by the Government, nor has any compensation yet been made for large amounts of property destroyed by our federal forces for strategic purposes. The path of the Baltimore and Ohio company has been one of triumph, because its action has been based, in organising its great enterprises, upon broad and liberal principles, which, carried out, necessarily resulted in advancing mutual interests and benefitting the entire territories through which the improvements are made. With beneficent and valuable objects in view, based upon correct principles and sound policy, your gigantic enterprises have succeeded, and won general approval, whilst their reactive influences have caused the city of Baltimore to grow, legitimately and rapidly, into a mighty, prosperous and commercial community."

A form of lease, which had been previously approved by the Board of the Washington County, was unanimously adopted. Under this lease six per cent. is to be paid to the stockholders on the cost of that line, and it is to be equipped and worked exclusively by the Baltimore and Ohio.

565.—BOSTON AND MAINE.

A consolidation of four companies (authorised 1st January, 1842), namely, Boston and Portland, in Massachusetts; Boston and Maine, in New Hampshire: Maine, New Hampshire and Massachusetts, in Maine; Boston and Maine Extension in Massachusetts. Several smaller branches have been added.

	Miles.
Total length of the main line, from Boston to South Berwick Junction	74·26
Medford Branch	2·23
Methuen	3·61
Great Falls	2·95
Newburyport	26.96
Danvers	9·20=119·22.

The earnings and expenses for the years ending May 31st have been as follow:—

Earnings :	1866.		1867.		1868.
Passengers	$943,222	....	$976,683	....	$907,133
Freight	519,005	....	581,996	....	603,355
Rents	18,729	....	23,290	....	28,909
Mails	11,104	....	10,839	....	13,671
Interest and dividend	19,096	....	17,866	....	12,392
P. S. and P. R. R.	10,000	....	10,000	....	....
	$1,521,159	..	$1,620,676	....	$1,565,462
Expenses	1,017,219	..	1,085,678	....	1,129,682
Earnings less expenses	503,939	..	534,998	....	435,780
Deduct tax on dividend and surplus			27,293	....	21,786
Net profits			$507,704	....	$413,993
From which deduct two dividends of five per cent. each	415,570	....			413,470
Leaving an undivided balance of			$92,134	....	$923
Balance from previous year			882,958	....	975,093
			$975,093		$976,017

CAPITAL.—The condensed balance sheet to 31st May, 1868, gave the income and expenditure as follows:—

Received.		Expended.	
Capital stock....................	$4,076,974	Construction....................	$4,128,738
Payments on account of new capital stock..................	222,750	Equipment....................	658,019
		Property accounts—materials..	139,463
Tax bills—estimated............	37,574	Cash, notes, freight bills, and open accounts..............	150,288
Sundry balances................	49,624		
Deposit on account of Newburyport R. R. bonds..............	2,160	Boston and Maine stock, 500 shares bought as an investment of surplus....................	50,000
Amount payable on account of Newburyport bonds..........	1,490	Danvers bonds, endorsed by us, taken at par..................	73,000
Tax on dividend and surplus....	10,838		
Dividend payable July 1, 1868..	205,285	Great Falls and Conway bonds, guaranteed by Eastern in New Hampshire....................	20,000
General reserve account—being undivided earnings to date..	976,017		
		Newburyport account..........	300,000
		Danvers account................	27,330
		Land and improvements, Dover and Win.......................	19,722
		Boston passenger station.......	16,151
	$5,582,714		$5,582,714

566.—CENTRAL OF GEORGIA AND BANK.

The following statement shows the gross earnings, expenses, and net profits from 1st April, 1859:—

	Miles.	Earnings.	Expenses.	Net.
1859—60................	231	$1,159,188	$631,144	$528,044
1860—61................	231	860,460	704,751	155,709
1861—62................	231	859,598	521,390	338,208
1862—63................	231	1,120,313	469,836	650,476
1863—64................	231	2,275,354	1,916,348	359,006
1864—65................	231	3,342,017	3,056,949	285,068
1865—66................	242	1,155,397	640,478	514,919
1866—67................	242	1,136,141	623,073	513,068

The receipts for the fiscal years ending 31st March, 1867 and 1868, were as follows:—

	1867.		1868.
Passengers...............................	$429,024	....	$288,365
Freight.................................	676,509	....	694,321
Mail....................................	30,607	....	21,037
	$1,136,141	....	$1,003,723
Expenses...............................	623,073	....	511,834
Net earnings...........................	513,068	....	491,889

While the gross receipts had fallen off $132,418 as compared with the previous year, there was a saving in operating [expenses of $111,238, resulting in a reduction of net earnings of only $21,179. The operating expenses are about 51 per cent. of the gross earnings.

CAPITAL.—The following is a condensed statement of the condition of the company, on the 31st March, 1868:—

Received.		Expended.	
Capital stock....................	$4,156,000	Road and outfit................	$4,156,000
Profit and loss..................	963,188	Real estate.....................	134,858
Income from railroad..........	989,071	Banking house and lot..........	35,000
Transp. of the mails...........	10,518	Road expenses..................	873,003
Interest account...............	12,530	Incidental expenses and salaries	9,658
Dividends on stocks............	71,361	Interest on bonds..............	28,278
Rent account..................	1,537	Tax on dividend No. 48........	6,738
Bonds of this company..........	389,500	Materials on hand for road....	84,547
Dividends unpaid..............	46,838	Stock of other companies........	1,081,989
Due to other corporations and agents........................	12,438	Bonds of other companies......	66,400
		Discounted notes..............	3,023
Deposits......................	3,689	Assessment on stock...........	262
Income tax due United States..	2,244	National Bank, New York......	135
Circulation....................	129,476	Bills receivable.................	26,654
		Notes of Banks in Georgia and South Carolina................	211,817
		Cash—currency and specie.....	70,028
	$6,788,395		$6,788,395

567.—CENTRAL PACIFIC.

This line, when completed, will extend from Sacramento to the state line of Nevada. For the first seven miles the Central Pacific receives the same Government subsidy as the roads east of the Rocky Mountains, $16,000 per mile ; for the next 150 miles of more rugged country it receives $48,000 per mile, and for the remaining distance (say, 570 miles) $32,000 per mile. The people of California have shown themselves so profoundly interested in the success of the road, that the State and Municipal corporations have added to the resources of the company. The State of California has assumed the payment of the interest for twenty years upon one million and a half of the company's bonds ; a concession worth about $3,000,000 in gold.   In addition to the subsidy granted this company by the General Government, the City of San Francisco has donated, to aid in the construction of the road, four hundred thousand dollars, in city 7 per cent. thirty-year gold-paying bonds ; and the City of Sacramento has donated some thirty acres of land in that city, embracing about 1,300 feet of valuable water front on the Sacramento river, which, with the privileges connected therewith, is considered worth three hundred thousand dollars.

568.—CHESAPEAKE AND OHIO.

This line is an amalgamation of the Virginia Central and the Covington and Ohio. The Virginia Central was commenced in 1836 as a local road, and subsequently, from time to time, it was extended in a westerly direction.   It is now in successful operation from Richmond to Covington, in the State of Virginia, a distance of 205 miles. Previous to 1865 the profits of the line not only sufficed to pay dividends, but one-fourth of the line was constructed out of its surplus earnings. Since 1865 the line has been put in complete order, out of its profits, although during the war it was subjected to the ravages of the Federal and Confederate armies.

In 1855 the State of Virginia commenced the construction of a line from Covington, the terminus of the Virginia Central line, to the Ohio River, a distance of 224 miles. This was called the Covington and Ohio. The State expended on this line $3,250,000, and the counties along the line granted the right of way. Owing to the war the works were suspended in 1861. In August, 1868, the States of Virginia and West Virginia surrendered these works to the Virginia Central, on condition that the line should be completed to the Ohio River, and that the name of the Company should be changed to "The Chesapeake and Ohio." The amount of capital already expended on the entire line from Richmond to the Ohio River is nearly $12,000,000 in gold. The amount of capital required to complete the line, with a branch of 39 miles, is $13,000,000. New subscriptions to the capital stock have been received to the amount of nearly $5,000,000, for which preferred shares are issued ; and a mortgage, covering the entire property of the company, has been created for $10,000,000. Bonds are to be issued in sums of $500 and $1,000, to be secured by the mortgage. Of these bonds $2,000,000 are to be held in reserve in the hands of trustees, to pay off the debt of the Virginia Central Company, leaving bonds to the amount of $8,000,000 to be sold. One half or $4,000,000 of these bonds were disposed of in America, and the other half in Europe. The proceeds of these bonds in currency, with the new stock subscriptions will be ample to complete the line. The bonds are dated October 1st, 1868, and are due on October 1st, 18.8. They bear 7 per cent. per annum interest, payable semi-annually on the 1st days of April and October of each year. An accumulative sinking fund of 1 per cent. per annum is provided. This sinking fund is placed in the charge of trustees, selected by the bondholders. The interest, principal, and sinking fund of the bonds are payable in the gold coin of the United States of America or in British sterling money, at the rate of four shillings to the dollar. The entire debt of the Chesapeake and Ohio will be 40 per cent. of the cost of the undertaking. The mortgage debt will be under $22,000 per mile, and no floating debt will exist. The bonds are free from State or United States tax, and the property of the company is exempt from State tax until 10 per cent. has been declared on the share capital.

The gross revenue for the year ending September 30th, 1868, was $599,354
Expenses 436 648
Excess of receipts in 1868.. 162,705
Excess of receipts in 1867.. 135,647

Deducting the increase of expenditure $17,585, from the increase of receipts $44,843, there was still a gain in the result of the year's operations over those of the last year amounting to $27,057.

First mortgage bonds to the extent of 400,000 were offered on the London market, on 1st January. A sinking fund is to be offered to their purchase if at or under 110 per cent. : if above that rate, the bonds to be drawn by lot. The bonds (about one-fourth or one-third), not redeemed under the operation of the sinking fund on October 1st, 1898, will be due and payable on that day at 100 per cent.

Payments for the bonds to be made as follows :—

10 per cent. on Application.
15   ,,   ,,   Allotment.
15   ,,   ,,   Tuesday, 19th January, 1869.
15   ,,   ,,   Friday, 19th February, 1869.
16½ ,,   ,,   Friday, 19th March, 1869.
3½   ,,   ,,   1st April, being the dividend coupon then due.

£75 per £100 bond.

569.—CHICAGO, BURLINGTON, AND QUINCY.

This road consists of the line from Chicago, through Galesburg, to Burlington, 204 miles; from Galesburg to Quincy, 100 miles; from Galesburg to Peoria, 53 miles; from Yates City to Lewiston, 30 miles, and that part of the old road from the Galena Junction to Aurora, 13 miles, making a total of 400 miles.

The following is a comparative statement of the earnings of the line, 400 miles in length, for the fiscal years ending April 30th:—

	1866.	1867.	1868.
Freight	$4,204,740	$4,124,692	$4,216,911
Passengers	1,757,387	1,543,714	1,482,506
Mails, etc.	213,424	414,730	455,228
	$6,175,553	$6,083,138	$6,154,647
Expenses	3,020,164	3,093,574	3,067,165
Earnings less expenses	$3,155,388	$2,989,563	$3,087,481
Interest and exchange		623,723	43,081
Add balance to credit of income account April 30th..		588,691	1,905,496
Trustees Quincy and Chicago		....	24,571
Total		$3,641,979	$5,060,630

The amount paid for dividends during the year has been $1,667,095 ; for interest, $363,554 ; stock distribution, $2,079,800 ; expended for bonds for sinking fund, $49,500— total, $4,159,949 ; leaving balance to credit of income at the close of the year $491,968, exclusive of the amount paid into the sinking fund up to that time, viz. : $878,225. If the amount paid into the sinking fund may be deemed a proper credit to the income account, the balance of that account is $1,370,194.

CAPITAL.—The general account gives the receipts and expenditure as follows:—

Received.—Capital stock	12,544,030	Expended.—Construction	$14,507,344
Funded debt (see bond list)	5,218,750	Equipment	3,205,407
Amounts due under decree of		Due on Northern Cross	270,000
court foreclosing the mortgage		Materials on hand	440,151
on the Northern Cross not yet		Pullman Palace Car Company	
called for by the bondholders,		stock $72,300	48,200
and therefore retained by		Steam ferry and other boats ...	45,456
order of the court	270,000	Burlington depot grounds and	
Unclaimed dividends	2,853	accretions	126,137
Unpaid accounts and pay rolls..	296,850	Chicago teams for transferring	
Due agents and connecting		freight	4,500
roads	83,099	Monthly traffic accounts and bills	307,817
Sinking fund	878,225	Burlington and Missouri River	
Balance to credit of income		preferred stock	299,649
account	491,968	Due from agents and connect-	
		ing roads	64,435
		Deposits in New York, Boston,	
		and treasury	235,012
		Deposits with trustees sinking	
		fund	231,664
	$19,785,777		$19,785,777

570.—CHICAGO AND NORTH WESTERN.

Length, 1,152 miles. The earnings for the fiscal years ending May 31st have been as under:—

	1836.	1867.	1868.
Passengers	$2,510,727	$2,945,016	$3,573,031
Freight	5,393,191	6,649,589	8,266,809
Express	157,157	346,016	464,405
Mails	77,660	124,485	172,605
Miscellaneous	105,103	96,627	137.994
	$8,243,840	$10,161,735	$12,614,846
Expenses	$5,072,959	$6,724,265	$7,488,484
State and Co. taxes	249 439	266,426	289,764
United States tax on earnings	200,169	107,611	89,245
United States revenue tax	4,514	5,689	6,152
Total expenses	$5,527,083	$7,103,993	$7,873,646
Balance of earnings	2,716,756	3,057,742	4,741,199
Balance from previous year	678,929	483,988	468,224
Total	$3,335,686	$3,541,730	$2,830,586

From which the board of directors on the 13th May declared 10 per cent. dividend on both the preferred and common stocks, payable in their respective stocks, which amounted to 2,810,110

Leaving to the credit of income account, May 31st, 1868 .... $20,476,

The following is a comparative statement of the earnings from June 1st to December 31st :—

	1867.	1868.
Passenger	$2,133,092	$2,437,367
Freight	5,301,388	5,882,724
Express	312,829	195,775
Mail	98,538	98,538
Miscellaneous	80,689	81,664
Total	$7,926,538	$8,696,069

CAPITAL.—The condition of the company on the 31st May, 1868, inclusive of the dividends recently declared on the preferred and common stocks, were as follows :—

Received.—Common stock	$14,555,675
Preferred stock	16,356,287
Bonded debt	15,976,000
Chicago and Milwaukee Railway Co. bonds	1,725,400
Beloit and Madison Railroad Co. bonds	372,000
Balance of sundry accounts	226,264
Balance to credit of income account	20,476
	$49,232,104

Expended.—Old Construction Account.—Cost of Chicago and North Western and Galena and Chicago Union, as consolidated, and the cost of the Chicago and Milwaukee and Beloit and Madison, and investments in steamboats	$39,811,092
New Construction Account. — Amount expended and charged to this account since consolidation in 1864	2,777,203
New Equipment Account — Amount expended for new equipment since consolidation in 1864	4,958,899
Sundry bonds and stocks on hand and loans to other companies as per list in general balance sheet	629,179
Materials and wood on hand	1,055,728
	$49,232,104

The increase of common stock during the year was $1,323,180—issued for 10 per cent. dividend on common stock. The increase of preferred stock during the year was $1,567,162, viz. : Issued for 10 per cent. dividend on preferred stock, $1,486,930 ; for stock of the Chicago and Milwaukee, $78,400 ; for stock of Beloit and Madison $1,832.

571.—CHICAGO, ROCK ISLAND, AND PACIFIC.

The gross receipts of the Chicago and Rock Island (228¼ miles) from April 1st, 1866, to August 20th, 1866, and of the entire line (409¾ miles) from August 20th, 1866, to March 31st, 1867, were $3,574,033 ; the expenses, $1,827,851 ; and the earnings, $1,746,181.

The gross receipts for the year ending 31st March, 1868, were $4,451,974, and the expenditure $2,020,192, leaving as earnings $2,431,782. Legal expenses and taxes amounted to $163,634.

Net earnings		$2,268,147
Rent of Peoria and Bureau	$125,000	
Interest on bonds	576,240	
Dividends, April and October, 1867, 5 per cent. each and U. S. tax	957,821=	1,659,061
Surplus		$609,086
Of which there has been expended in construction repairs		82,174
Leaving a balance of		$526,912
Add balance April 1, 1867		624,753=$1,151,665

572.—CINCINNATI, HAMILTON, AND DAYTON.

Length, 60 miles. The line runs from Cincinnati, through the Great Miami Valley, to Dayton. At Dayton it connects with the Atlantic and Great Western for New York, and by the Ohio and Indiana for Pittsburg and Philadelphia. The company have leased perpetually the Dayton and Michigan, at an annual rental equal to the interest on a fraction less than $22,000 per mile. The total expenditure for construction, real estate, and equipments of the Cincinnati, Hamilton, and Dayton, amounts to about

$57,000 per mile. The two roads cost an average of $32,500 per mile. The yearly gross earnings ending March 31st have been as follow :—

1853	$321,793	1861	$615,071
1854	463,021	1862	646,205
1855	483,629	1863	877,403
1856	471,855	1864	1,083,328
1857	518,333	1865	1,241,856
1858	487,421	1866	1,361,566
1859	489,437	1867	1,301,536
1860	561,681	1868	1,332,894

The working expenses for 1868 were $748,719, in comparison with $847,594 in 1867. From the net earnings of $584,175, were deducted $225,716 for interest on lands, taxes, and other charges, the balance of $358,459 having been applied as follows :—

Dividend No. 25	$554,773	
Renewal of bridges	99,416	= $354,189

Surplus	$4,270
Add surplus from previous year	404,577
Total surplus March 31, 1868	$408,847

The receipts from operations of the Dayton and Michigan during the year were $966,603; and the expenditures, $1,040,650—an excess of expenditures over receipts of $74,046; to which add balance from previous year, $323,117—making the total amount due C. H. and D. lessees, $395,164. The receipts from operations of the Cincinnati Richmond and Chicago (including $454 from previous year,) were $183,819; and the expenditures, $196,985—leaving a balance due C., H. and D., of $13,226.

CAPITAL.—The condensed balance sheet gives the income and expenditure as under :—

Received.		Expended.	
Capital stock	$3,500,000	Construction	$3,945,669
First mortgage bonds	1,250,000	Equipment	999,198
Second mortgage bonds	500,000	Real estate	327,408
Third mortgage bonds	254,000	Wood and materials	193,821
Interest on bonds	4,483	Wood lands	12,540
Dividends unpaid	19,238	Bills receivable	9,995
Due R. R. Co.'s	66,747	Stocks and bonds	176,533
Due individuals	51,355	Due from R. R. Co 's	58,674
Due United States	3,416	Due from individuals	34,569
Pay rolls, C. H. and D., D. and		Due from P. O. department	9,206
M., and C. R. and C. R. R.	59,343	Redemption D. and M., 1st mortgage bonds	233,535
Bills payable	399,119	D. and M. lessor's account	397,164
Surplus earnings	408,847	C. R. and C.	13,226
		Cash and cash assets	104,807
	$6,516,351		$6,516,351

573.—DETROIT AND MILWAUKEE.

This company, in the prosperity of which the shareholders of the Great Western of Canada are interested, was incorporated by various Acts of the State of Michigan, from 1834 to 1860. The line, 189 miles long, extends from the city of Detroit (opposite the western terminus of the Canadian Great Western line) to the port of Grand Haven, on the eastern shore of Lake Michigan, and thence by its own ferry boats to Milwaukee, the western shore, where it connects with all the lines of the Far-West.

The property of this company having passed into the hands of its bondholders under a foreclosure of mortgage, in October, 1860, the surplus receipts were then used by order of the Court of Chancery, for the liquidation of the floating debt which was thus paid off, and since May, 1864, the company have regularly paid their bond interest.

The share capital ordinary and preference is $1,952,350, and the mortgage debt $5,313,409.

The gross earnings for the year 1867 were 361,913l., and the working expenses 203,942l., leaving a net revenue of 157,970l. The earnings for the half-year ending 30th June were 153,205l., and the working expenses, including taxes and insurance, 98,150l., leaving a net revenue of 55,055l. From the arrangements made by the deputation of the Great Western of Canada Board to relieve the finances of the Detroit and Milwaukee there was reason to expect that the company may, at an early period, be able to commence liquidating the claims for interest, so long overdue, to the Great Western of Canada.

574.—ERIE.

Length, 797 miles. On the 1st January, 1862, the whole property which formerly belonged to the New York and Erie, and its management, passed from the hands of the Supreme Court into the possession of this company, and came under the control of officers appointed by the board of directors. The company owes no floating debt, and its property consists of

Main line from Jersey City to Dunkirk ....Miles	460	
Piermont branch	18	
Newburgh branch	19	
N. W. D. Hornellsville to Attica	60	
Total length of road owned by Co.		557
The branch roads leased and operated by the company are :—		
Buffalo division, Corning to Buffalo	140	
Rochester division	18	
Canadaigua and Elmira...	66	
Hawley branch, just completed...	16	240
Whole number of miles of road owned and leased		797

The Warwick Valley road, 10 miles long, is operated by the company, but not leased, so that the whole number of miles of road operated by the company is 807. There are on the main line and branches owned by the company 190 miles of double track, and 130 miles of sidings, and on the leased roads 19 miles of double track and sidings, making the entire length of track equal to 1,137 miles of single track.

ATLANTIC AND GREAT WESTERN.—For text of lease of this undertaking by the Erie, see ADDENDA.

COLUMBUS, CHICAGO, AND INDIANA.—This line has also been leased by the Erie, the contemplated results being described as follow :—"This system provides, in connection with the Atlantic and Great Western and the Erie, the shortest route, with only one exception, between Chicago and New York, Philadelphia. and Baltimore; while it gives the shortest route between St. Louis, Louisville, and Indianapolis, and the principal cities on the Atlantic coast. It also provides the shortest route between Chicago, Indianapolis, and Louisville, thus securing an enormous amount of traffic between the Central State of Kentucky, and the Lake Michigan, and the whole Lake navigation. By the terms of an agreement entered into with adjoining lines, all the traffic betwen Chicago and Cincinnati, previously divided at competing rates between other lines, passes over the Columbus, Chicago, and Indiana, the distance being 44 miles shorter than any other route. By means of its connection with the Missouri roads, and through them with the Kansas branch of the Union Pacific, and roads leading west from Chicago, and through the Omaha branch of the Pacific roads, the largest portion of the traffic of the Great Pacific road will be secured for the United system. The lease of the Columbus, Chicago, and Indianopolis is in perpetuity, and the terms upon which the property has been secured are highly favourable to the Erie."

REVENUE.—The receipts for each month during the year 1868 were reported to have been as follow :—

January	$1,031,320	July	$1,093,043
February	901,752	August	....
March	1,136,994	September	....
April	1,263,742	October	....
May	1,163,612	November	....
June	1,089,605	December	....

The President reported as follows to the shareholders in December :—"I found the equipment of the road, both engines and cars, inadequate for its business. There is not a local station between New York and Buffalo where business men and shippers are not now greatly suffering for want of cars. In addition to these local requests, we are bound to give facilities to our western connections. They are now and have been greatly suffering from inability to furnish cars and engines to bring forward the freight. Much western trade has thereby been driven away from New York to Philadelphia and Baltimore. I propose to remedy this evil by furnishing the road with ample equipments to accommodate the public, and protect the local customers of this road. The Western connections of the company were in an unsatisfactory condition. The Michigan Central and Great Western, forming a line between Chicago and Suspension Bridge, were completely shut off from us, by want of a link of 20 miles of road, between Buffalo and Suspension Bridge. I entered into negotiations with these companies, and, as a result, the road in question is now being rapidly constructed, and by July 1 the Erie will be doing a fair share of the business of those companies between New York and Niagara Falls and Suspension Bridge, connecting at Chicago. From this source I expect to derive a revenue of from one to two millions of dollars per year. All our Western connections, excepting the Atlantic and Great Western, were narrow gauge, requiring a transhipment at Buffalo and Dunkirk of every car of through freight passing over the road, while on the competing lines of the New York Central and Pennsylvania Central there was no transhipment between Chicago and New York. The Western roads agreed to furnish the cars for the whole line between Chicago and New York, leaving it only for the Erie to provide the third rail. I could not, acting for this company, decline so important an improvement, and I was rapidly concentrating the arrangements to carry out this plan, when the recent litigations, supposed to be in the interest of competing lines, broke out. Beyond the expense of these litigations, and the annoyance and loss of time they occasioned me, I do not regret them. The charges made are without the slightest foundation in truth, as was well known to the principal instigators.

575.—HARTFORD AND NEWHAVEN.

Length of Main Line, from Newhaven Ct. to Springfield, Mass........... 61·38 miles.
Middleton branch .... 10·75 ,,
Junction to Hartford City.................................. .. .. 0·87 ,,

Total main line and branches...................................... 73·00
Length of second track, 55 miles ; sidings, &c., about 10 miles.
The earnings for the years ending August 31st, have been as follows :—

	1866.	1867.	1868.
From passengers	$909,352	$941.536	$891,091
,, freight	630,911	625,992	632,454
,, expresses	47.401	114,007	114,709
,, rents, &c.	4,138	3,798	59,079
	$1,591,804	$1,685,334	$1,697,334
Expenses	$958,321	$982,518	$1,024,935
Interest	52,480	48,285	} 190,808
Taxes, State and National	121,805	110,532	
	$1,132,607	$1,141,337	$1,215,743
Balance of earnings	$459,196	$543,996	$481,590

The income of the company from all sources during the year was as follow :—
Cash on hand, September 1, 1867 .... $166,963
Earnings of the road 1,697,334
Sales of real estate, &c.. 6,367=$1,870,664
Thus accounted for—Dividends.................................. $422,566
Interest.. 57,526
Operating and repairing road 1,008,829
Tomlinson Bridge Co., for depot grounds, New Haven 49,332
Steamboat "Orient" 3,445
Real estate in Conn... 4,975
Balance debts due the Co. 20,134
State and National taxes 133,281
Cash .... 170.573=$1,870,664

CAPITAL.—The following from the Ledger presents a general statement of the affairs of the company September 1, 1868:—

Received.		Expended.	
Capital stock....................	$3,300,000	Railway, depot grounds, build-	
Bonds	927,000	ings, &c.	$3,407,28
Contingent fund.................	314,843	Real estate, land, dwellings, &c.	131,522
Reserved fund..................	150,000	Bonds purchased	37,000
Profit and loss..............	211,590	Tomlinson Bridge stock	8,888
Dividends unpaid	7,227	Advance to Tomlinson BridgeCo.	1,760
Debts due by the company......	69,221	Equipment, engines, and cars ..	254,000
		Wood, stock, and tools on hand	189,035
		Debts due to the company, including account due from N. Y. & R. Co., and funds in the hands of agents	410,145
		Connecticut River Bridge	176,577
		Steamboat "Orient"	193,094
		Cash	170,573
	$4,979,883		$4,979,833

576.—ILLINOIS CENTRAL.

Chartered on 10th February, 1851, with authority to construct a railroad from La Salle (at which point the Illinois and Michigan Canal has its South Western terminus) north-wardly to the Mississippi River, opposite Dubuque, Iowa, and southwardly to Cairo, at the confluence of the Ohio with the Mississippi ; and also a branch from this main line to Chicago. The capital was fixed at $1,000,000, and might be increased to an amount equal to the money expended in the construction of the road and appurtenances. The company was authorised to establish its own rates of toll. The Act of incorporation also surrendered to the company all the property acquired by the State of Illinois in the course of the previous efforts made by it to construct a railroad between the same points; and all the lands donated by the United States Government under the Act of Congress, approved 20th September, 1850,

The main line extends through the whole length of the State north and south; the branch leaves the main at Centralia, and extends to Chicago, representing 706 miles of railway, 105 miles of sidings and double track, of 148 engines and 3,500 cars. The machine shops are well furnished; the facilities for building locomotives and cars are ample. A large outlay has been made at Chicago and Cairo for depôt and station accommodations. Two-thirds of the structures on the road are of iron or masonry—the cost of the property stands upon the books at $50,000 per mile, and besides the income from the railway there will be for many years a large revenue from land. The company have the right, by paying an annual rent, to run freight trains over the Peoria road, which connects the main line with the Chicago branch. The company has no other engagement involving liability, it has no interest in other lines, and has adhered strictly to the policy of taking no shares in extensions by branches or otherwise, and is free from litigation or controversy of moment. The first debt which matures is not due till 1875.

REVENUE.—The receipts for each month in the year 1868 were reported to have been as follow:—

January	$572,364		July	$576,458
February	531,224		August	704,138
March	462,317		September	873,500
April	538,077		October	901,631
May	579,560		November	609,801
June	621,685			

The financial statement for the month of November showed that in the land department 12,753 acres of land were sold during the month, for 139,981; and that the cash collected in the month amounted to $290,845. In the traffic department the receipts on the company's railways during the month amounted to $601,716, and in November, 1867, to $658,794, showing a decrease of $57,078.

The general statement presented in May gave the debtor and creditor account as follows:—

Received.—Permanent expenditures			$31,328,472
Interest and dividend account	$10,979,918		
Less avails of inverest fund	3,512,365=	7,467,552	
Net cash assets New York	1,214,292		
Do. do. Chicago	561,315=	1,775,608	
Premium paid on bonds delivered land department in anticipation		174,611	
Working stock of supplies		816,035	
			$41,562,280

Expended.—Capital stock			$23,392,300
Cancelled bond scrip			23,480
Funded debt—			
Construction bonds due 1st April, 1875, 7 per cent.	$5,090,500		
Do. do. do. 6 do.	2,499,000		
Eight per cent. bonds, due 1st March, 1865	3,000		
Optional right bonds, due 20th February, 1868	26,000		
Redemption bonds, due April 1st, 1890	2,563,000		
Sterling do. do. 1875	363,000=	10,544,500	
Bonds delivered land department	9,410,500		
Less in the hands of the trustees	1,808,500=	7,602,000	
			$41,562,280

577.—LOUISVILLE AND FRANKFORT AND LEXINGTON AND FRANKFORT.

Length, 94 miles. These companies, though distinct corporations of the State of Kentucky, are now, under the corporate name of "The Louisville Cincinnati and Lexington," partners in operating the road from Louisville to Lexington : and joint owners of the branch road which is being built from Cincinnati to La Grange, a village on the Lexington line, twenty-six miles from Louisville.

The revenue for two years ending 30th June has been as under :—

	1866-7.	1867-8.
Earnings	$510,619	$493,218
Expenses	357,101	335,971
Net	$153,217	$157,247

The aggregate earnings and cash receipts for the two years under review have been $1,003,537 ; and the expenses, $693,073—leaving as the aggregate net earnings of both roads for the years named, $310,464. Deducting from the expenses the sum of $55,184 (being decrease in amount of material used from the stock of supplies on hand), will leave the actual cash expenditures, $637,888, and the actual net cash receipts, $365,648. These have been disposed of as follows :—

Louisville and Frankfort	$122,313	
Lexington and Frankfort	52,690	
Cincinnati Branch Fund	190,644	= $365,648

CAPITAL.—The receipts and expenditure of the two companies have been as follow :—

LOUISVILLE.		LEXINGTON.	
Capital stock	$1,109,594	Capital stock	$514,646
Railroad bonds, due 1869-'78	108,000	Railroad bonds due 1869-'74	44,000
City of Louisville bonds, due '81	100,000	Cash dividends unpaid	1,477
Loan from State of Kentucky		Joint stock dividends unpaid	1,732
for right of way on perpetual		Renewal and contingent fund	35,296
credit at 6 per cent.	74,519	Stock profits	66,242
Cash dividends unclaimed	4,538	Sinking fund	10,000
Profit and loss	185,179	Profit and loss	8,266
	$1,581,831		$681,662

Expenditure.		*Expenditure.*	
Construction	$1,532,644	Construction	$654,265
Real estate	33,235	Bills receivable	1,266
Bills receivable	1,932	Bonds receivable	4,000
Stock in other companies	8,500	Stock in other companies	1,500
Cash in New York	2,699	Preferred joint stock	1,732
Cash on hand	2,810	Real estate	9,255
		E. D. Sayre, Treasurer	602
		Cash on hand	9,140
	$1,581,831		$681,662

578.—LOUISVILLE AND NASHVILLE.

A main line with two branches in Kentucky. The main stem is 185 miles in length ; the Memphis branch, 46 ; and the Lebanon branch, 37 ; Bardstown branch, 18 ; total, 307 miles. The following is a statment of the earnings of the Main Stem and branches for the year ending June 30th, 1868 :—

	Memphis.	Lebanon.	Main.
Passengers	$89,228	$83,377	$672,497
Freight	92,935	86,965	1,025,712
Express	8,020	8,672	73,023
Mails	5,100	6,395	27,990
Miscellaneous	399	485	24,510

Total Main Stem	$1,823,763
„ Lebanon branch	185,895
„ Memphis branch	195,635
„ Bardstown branch	23,051
„ Richmond branch	213
Total Main Stem and branches	$2,228,609
Running expenses	1,309,514
Net earnings (41.24 per cent.)	$919,094
Interest account	227,203
Balance	$691,891

The following is a comparative statement of the earnings, expenses, &c. :—

	1866–67.	1867–68.
Gross earning	$2,158,874	$2,228,609
Operating expenses	1,348,405	$1,309,514
Net earnings	$810,468	$919,094
Interest	182,912	227,203
Balance	$627,555	$691,891

This shows an increase in gross earnings over the previous year of $69,734, with a decrease in expenses of $38,891, making the increase in net earnings $108,625. At the date of the last annual report, June 30th, 1867, the bonded debt of the company was $2,965,000 for the main stem and branches (exclusive of the Lebanon Branch Extension). On the 30th June, 1868, it was $2,883,500—showing a

Redemption of bonds during the year of	$81,500
Added to construction during the fiscal year	28,090
Interest paid during the same time	227,203
	$336,794

CAPITAL.—The following is a consolidated statement of the resources and liabilities of the combined undertakings :—

Assets.		Liabilities.	
Main Stem	$10,196,421	Stock and stock liabilities and suspended stock Main Stem	$7,869,186
Lebanon Branch extension (south of Lebanon)	2,454,379	RichmondBranch stock account Main Stem	369,410
Richmond Branch	412,124	Bills payable Main Stem	385,639
	$13,062,925	Bills and pay rolls for June and sundries, M. S.	166,710
Resources:—		Back and July, 1868, dividends, Main Stem	321,001
Main Stem	$2,220,421	Sundry contractors and persons, Lebanon Branch extension	70,033
Lebanon Branch Ext. 3,615	= 2,224,036	Sundry contractors, Richmond Branch	24,662
		Bonded debt :—	
		Main Stem	2,883,500
		Lebanon Branch extension	1,200,000
		Profit and loss account, Main stem	1,996,818
	$15,286,932		$15,236,962

579.—MEMPHIS AND CHARLESTON.

This road is 272 miles in length, commencing at Memphis, and running thence, via Moscow and Grand Junction in Tennessee, Corinth, Mississippi, Tuscumbia, Decatur, and Huntsville, Alabama, to Stevenson, where it connects with the Nashville and Chattanooga, and through that road with the Western and Atlantic and East Tennessee and Georgia roads. At Memphis it connects with the Memphis and Ohio and Mississippi and Tennessee, at Moscow with the Somerville branch, at Grand Junction with the Mississippi Central, at Corinth with the Mobile and Ohio, at Tuscumbia with the branch to Florence, and at Decatur with the Nashville and Decatur.

The earnings for the fiscal years ending June 30, 1868, have been as follows :—

	1866.	1867.	1868.
Passengers	$852,157	$910,799	$589,824
Freight	589,916	636,886	465,845
Mail	20,506	27,799	41,700
Express	51,092	76,720	77,543
Rents, &c.	30,633	9,406	....
	$1,274,307	$1,661,612	$1,174,914
Expenses	$1,353,064	$1,114,354	....
Excess of receipts	....	$547,257	....
Excess of expenses	$78,757	....	$344,806

CAPITAL.—The condensed balance sheet to 30th June, 1868, furnished the subjoined particulars :—

Received.		Expended.	
Capital stock	$5,312,725	Construction proper	$6,200,638
State of Tennessee bonds	1,595,530	Incidental to construction	326,411
First mortgage bonds..........	1,293,000	Equipment	1,134,558
Second mortgage bonds	1,000,000	Stock in other companies......	201,100
Bills payable	111,228	Railroad hotel	6,082
Sundry liabilities.............	215,324	Road materials, &c.............	187,147
Suspense	3,733	Road expenses	830,107
Receipts for transportation....	1,174,914	Profit and loss	59,947
		Interest on bonds.............	206,792
		Interest and exchange	20,676
		Discount on bonds	490,964
		Bills receivable...............	81,650
		Coupon bonds on hand	464,000
		Sundry accounts	428,871
		Cash	67,508
	$10,706,454		$10,706,454

580.—MICHIGAN CENTRAL.

Length of road—Detroit to Chicago, 284·8 miles. Sidings, &c., 28·4 miles. Leased road—Joliet and Northern Indiana, 44·5 miles. Total length operated, 329.

The passenger, freight, and miscellaneous earnings, and per cent. of earnings, used in operating expenses since 1857, are shown in the following tabular statement :—

Year.	Passengers.	Freight.	Miscellaneous.	Per cent.
1857	$1,610,415	$1,413,492	$80,694	6·6
1858	1,321,039	1,033,748	73,969	59·6
1859	938,609	831,435	68,084	53 4
1860	803,507	962,621	66,815	53·7
1861	775,228	1,218.186	64,637	51
1862	724,915	1,559,060	77,264	45·1
1863	889,682	1,983.757	73.120	40·4
1864	1,262.415	2,073,274	98,858	47·6
1865	1,771,813	2,233,529	140,076	55·8
1866	2,061,335	2,208,591	176,563	61
1867	1,824,225	2,235,521	215,743	63

The earnings for the years ending May 31st, 1867 and 1868, were as follows :—

	1867.		1868.
Passengers	$1,824,225	....	$1,721.508
Freight	2,285,521	....	2,480,974
Mails, &c..	215,743	....	268,398
	$4,325,490		$4,470,879

Compared with the previous year the gross earnings of 1867-68 show an increase of $145,389 : with a decrease in expenses of $112,231 ; making an increase in net earnings of $257,620. The income account furnished the subjoined details :—

Received.		Expended.	
Balance from previous year	$443,450	Expenses (including local taxes)	$2,714,545
Receipts	4,480,230	Payments towards sinking fund	84,500
		Interest and exchange account..	616,170
		Divi end 5 per cent. in cash, July 1st, 1857....................	406,025
		Dividend 5 per cent. in cash, January 1st, 1868	408,860
		U. S. tax on dividends, etc.	37,817
		U. S. tax on receipts	43,518
		Balance to new account	582,243
	$4,923,680		$4,923,680

The following roads, forming an aggregate of 3,020 miles, are now parties to the line, all having put in their quota of new cars, which are being increased from time to time by each :—

Illinois Central,
St. Louis, Alton and Chicago,
Chicago, Burlington, and Quincy,
Michigan Central,
Jackson, Lansing, and Saginaw,
Great Western,

New York Central,
Hudson River,
Boston and Albany,
Housatonic,
Providence and Worcester,
Worcester and Nashaw.

The line is thus composed of roads running from the five important Mississippi points, Cairo, St. Louis, Quincy, Burlington and Dunleith to New York, Bridgeport.

Conn, Providence, Boston, Nashua, N. H., and all intermediate points, over track of uniform gauge.

CAPITAL.—The bonded debt has been decreased during the year by the conversion of bonds to stock, to the extent of $300,000 ; and the capital stock has been increased by that amount, and by the issue of $106,700 new stock, being balance unsold of amount authorised by a vote of the directors, March 13, 1867.   The bonded debt now amounts to $6,968,988 ; capital stock, $8,477,366 ; total, $15,446,354.   The sum invested in the sinking funds amounts to $1,195,728.   The company owes no floating debt of any description.   The general account exhibited the subjoined detail :—

Received.		*Expended.*	
Capital stock	$8,477,366	Construction account	$14,914,167
6 per cent. sterling bonds, payable		Cash on hand and loaned on call	354,373
Jan. 1, 1872	467,488	Materials on hand	153,732
8 per cent. sterling bonds, payable		Assets in hands of Oliver Macy,	
Sept. 1, 1869	500,000	general receiver	58,697
8 per cent. bonds, 1st mortgage,		Assets in hands of James F.	
payable Sept. 1, 1869	1,294,500	Foy, president	85,854
8 per cent. bonds, 1st mortgage,		Joliet and Northern Indiana	
payable Oct. 1, 1882	500,000	railroad stock	168,225
8 per cent. bonds, 1st mortgage,		Chicago land account	97,627
sinking funds, payable Oct. 1,		Jackson land account	24,411
1882	4,207,000	Advance to Jackson, Lansing,	
Amount due U. S. Government,		and Saginaw	105,000
3 per cent. tax on coupons	33	U. S. Government 5 per cent.	
Unpaid dividends	914	tax	2,690
Income account, balance of this		Sundry accounts	64,766
account	582,243		
	$16,029,546		$16,029,546

581.—MICHIGAN SOUTHERN AND NORTHERN INDIANA.

Length, 574 miles.   The following is a comparative statement of the earnings and expenses for the fiscal years ending 1st of March :—

	1865.	1866.	1867.	1868.
Earnings	$4,289,465	$4,686,445	$4,673,192	$4,747,219
Expenses	2,408,352	2,749,656	3,063,705	2,866,387
Net earnings	1,881,113	1,936,788	1,609,487	1,880,831

Compared with the previous year, the gross earnings show an increase of $74,026, with a decrease in operating expenses of $197.318—making the increase in net earnings $271,344.   The interest paid on the funded debt amounted to $640,516, and on guaranteed stock to $68,740.

Besides the amount of earnings invested in improvements and additions, net earnings have been applied annually by the commissioners of the sinking fund to the extinguishment of the bonded debt.   The amount thus applied from the creation of the fund is $1,310,000.

CAPITAL.—The condensed balance sheet furnishes the following details in respect to the constitution of this account :—

Received.		*Expended.*	
Capital stock—common	$10,059,400	Railroad	$14,654,881
,, guarranteed	586,800	Equipment	2,865,817
	$10,646,200	Detroit Monroe, and Toledo ..	1,291,968
		D. M. & T. stock (at par)	411,700
Funded debt (9,038,640), viz. ;		Union stock yards Chicago	100,000
Sinking fund 1st general mort-		Supplies on hand	735,436
gage bonds	6,094,000	Cash on hand	489,976
Less held by S. F.	1,310,000	Uncollected earnings	187,279
General second mortgage bonds	2,693,000	Claim against A. L. & T. R. R.	3,000
Goshen line bonds	637,000	Freight overcharges due us	13,327
Detroit, Monroe, and Toledo		Bills receivable	9,210
bonds	924,000		
Scrip outstanding	640		
February expenses	234,406		
Unclaimed interest and divi-			
dends	33,071		
Profit and loss	810,279		
	$20,762,597		$20,762,597

582.—NEW YORK CENTRAL.

This line, measured by the extent of its traffic and earnings, is the first work of the kind in the United States. Its main line extends from Albany to Buffalo, a distance of 297 miles, and it has 258 miles of side or parallel branch lines. The following is a statement of earnings from passengers, freight, and its other resources, for the years ending September 30th :—

	Passengers.		Freight.		Miscellaneous.		Total.
1853	.... $2,820,669	....	$1,835,572	....	$122,279	....	$4,787,520
1854	 3,151,514	....	2,479,821	....	287,000	....	5,918,335
1855	 3,242,229	....	3,189,603	....	131,749	....	6,563,581
1856	 3,207,378	....	5,328,041	....	171,928	....	7,707,348
1857	 3,147,637	....	4,559,276	....	320,339	....	8,027,251
1858	 2,532,647	....	3,700,270	....	295,496	....	6,528,413
1859	 2,566,370	....	3,337,148	....	297,331	....	6,200,849
1860	 2,569,265	....	4,095,934	....	292,042	....	6,957,241
1861	 2,315,933	....	4,664,449	....	328,660	....	7,309,042
1862	 2,389,724	....	6,607,381	....	359,773	....	9,356,828
1863	 2,930,341	....	7,498,509	....	468,781	....	10,897,631
1864	 3,923,152	....	8,543,371	....	531,367	....	12,997,890
1865	 4,521,454	....	8,776,027	....	678,043	....	13,975,524
1866	 4,360,248	....	9,671,920	....	564,617	....	14,596,786
1867	 4,032,023	....	9,151,751	....	795,740	....	13,979,514
	$44,889,916		$80,603,450		$5,522,867		$131,016,233

At a meeting of the directors, held 19th December, 1868, it was resolved—" Whereas this company has hitherto expended of its earnings for the purpose of constructing and equipping its road, and in the purchase of real estate and other properties, with a view to the increase of its traffic, moneys equal in amount to 80 per cent. of the capital stock of the company ; and whereas the several stockholders of the company are entitled to evidence of such expenditure, and to reimbursement of the same at some convenient future period ;—now, therefore, resolved, that a certificate, signed by the president and treasurer of this company, be issued to the stockholders severally, declaring that such stockholder is entitled to 80 per cent. of the amount of the capital stock held by him, payable rateably with the other certificates issued under this resolution, at the option of the company, out of its future earnings, with dividends thereon, at the same rates and times as dividends shall be paid on the shares of the capital stock of the company, and that such certificates may be at the option of the company convertible into stock of the company, whenever the company shall be authorised to increase its capital stock to an amount sufficient for such conversion. That such certificates be delivered to the stockholders of this company at the Union Trust, in the city of New York, on the presentation of their several certificates of stock, and that the receipt of the certificate provided for in these resolutions shall be endorsed on the stock certificate. That a dividend of 4 per cent. free of Government tax, is hereby declared, payable on 20th February next, upon the stock of this company, and also upon the interest certificates of the company this day authorised."

The following is the report of Messrs. Peckham, Stebbins, and Griswold, the committee appointed to examine the stock matters of the company :—

At a meeting of the directors of the New York Central held at the office of the company in the Exchange, in the city of Albany, on the 9th day of December, 1868. it was resolved—That although the Board of Directors of this company have full confidence in the correctness of the stock account of the company, and have no doubt as to the validity of every share outstanding, they do, nevertheless, for the greater satisfaction of the stockholders, invite the Hon. Rufus W. Peckham. of Albany, the Hon. Charles Stebbins, of Cazenovia, and the Hon. John A. Griswold, of Troy, to act as a committee to examine the stock books of the company and report thereon.

Pursuant to the foregoing resolution we have examined the stock books of the New York Central, and find that by the consolidation agreement of May, 1853, the capital stock of said company was fixed at $23,085,600, being the amount of the capital and convertible bonds of the several companies consolidated. Of these convertible bonds $18,300 were paid off and never converted, leaving the amount of capital under said consolidation agreement, $23,067,400. This amount was subsequently increased by the additions of the capital of the Buffalo and Niagara falls, the Lewiston and the Rochester and Lake Ontario roads, $932,000, making the entire capital on the 8th of August, 1859, $24,000,000. Since that time the following issue of convertible bonds, and none others, have been authorised and made by the company, viz.:—

First—An issue of $3,000,000, payable in 1864, with a convertible privilege for a certain period. None of these bonds were ever converted, but were paid in cash at maturity,

Second—An issue of $2,990,000, payable August, 1876, and convertible until August, 1869. Of the convertible bonds thus issued there have been converted into the capital stock of the company :—

In the year ending September 30th, 1863...................................... $209,000
In the year ending September 30th, 1864...................................... 177,000
In the year ending September 30th, 1865...................................... 205,000
In the year ending September 30th, 1866...................................... 210,000
In the year ending September 30th, 1867...................................... 1,736,000
In the year ending September 30th, 1868...................................... 243,000

　　　　Total $2,780,000

Thus adding to the capital stock of the company $2,780,000 ; the capital of the Athens road added, being $2,000,0 0, makes the entire capital stock of the company, as shown by its report on the 30th day of September, 1868, $28,780,000. Since the 30th of September, 1868, $15,000 more of these bonds have been converted, leaving now outstanding $195,000. In regard to any apprehension that may be entertained of an over issue of stock, we deem it proper to state that in our opinion the regulations governing the issue and transfer of the certificates of stock of this company are as perfect as such regulations can be made. They provide that all the stock registered in New York at the transfer office now kept by Duncan, Sherman, and Co., shall also be registered at another office, now the Union Trust Company, and all certificates be signed by both the transfer agent and register, in addition to the signatures of the president and treasurer of the company, and that no share of the stock shall be transferred on the books more than once in each day. The register in no case signs a certificate of stock without the surrender to and cancellation by him of a previously issued certificate for the given number of shares. A like system is in operation at the Albany office, by which all certificates of stock issued at that office are also registered and signed by the Union Trust Company in New York. For the purpose of testing the accuracy of the stock books we have examined the dividend books made and used for the payment of dividends for the last five semi-annual dividends, both at the Albany and New York offices, where alone dividends are now paid, and find that the number of shares borne upon these books in the aggregate correspond exactly with the number of shares outstanding at the time of each dividend, as shewn by the stock books of the company. From the examinations made by us we find, and therefore report, that the amount of the capital stock of the New York Central outstanding on the 16th day of December, 1868, was $28,795,000, and in our opinion it is scarcely possible that there can be any error in this statement of the amount.

583.—NEW YORK AND NEWHAVEN.

A meeting of the stockholders was held at Newhaven on the 8th August, 1866, at which the directors were authorised to issue 10,000 shares of additional stock to be disposed of at the discretion of the directors. A resolution was passed giving each person who, on the first day of September, shall be a stockholder, the privilege of taking at par, one share for every five owned by him. A resolution authorising the directors to apply moneys received from the sale of additional stock to the payment of the $912,000 seven per cent. bonds was also unanimously adopted.

The income for the years ending March 31st have been as follow :—

Earnings $1,847,291	$1,982,212	$2,068,260	$2,218,509
Expenses 1,224,694	1,349,723	1,364,243	1,077,427
Net earnings 622,596	632,489	704,016	1,141,082

After deduction of taxes, interest on coupons, canal expenses, cost of new engines, &c., there were left for dividends and permanent improvements the sum of $800,453. The resources and payments for the year were classified as under :—

Resources.		Payments.	
Cash on hand April 1st, 1867	$516,736	Dividends, July, 1867, and January, 1868, 5 per cent. each....	$600,000
Proceeds allotted stock..........	1,000	Taxes	145,212
Materials on hand, April 1st, 1867	247.024	Coupon interest	64,425
Earnings transportation	1,141,081	Final settlement Schuyler fraud	109,129
		Due from former treasurer......	88,255
		Purchase of additional real estate	80,101
		New depots, Stamford and Norwalk	44,228
		Equipment to cover depreciation	69,997
		Decrease in accounts payable ..	18,627
		Retired bonds	17,000
		Loss operating canal road	16,763
		Materials for coming season	274,934
		Cash on hand April 1st, 1868....	377,170
	$1,905,842		$1 905,842

CAPITAL.—The condensed balance sheet gives the assets and liabilities as follows:—

Received.		Expended.	
Capital stock: 60,000 shares	$6,000,000	Railroad, including the franchise, right of way, grading, masonry, bridging, fencing, superstructure, iron, stationhouses, shops, fixtures, machinery, engineering, interest, discount on bonds, &c.	$4,370,611
Bonds payable December 1st, 1866; past due...............	3,000		
Bonds payable October, 1875, interest at 6 per cent., coupons due April 1st, and October 1st, annually........	1,059,500		
Interest and dividends unpaid..	38,330	Loss by Schuyler fraud (all settled)..............	1,772,868
Accounts payable—March pay rolls and balances due connecting roads	201,088	Equipment — locomotives, cars, &c.	900,000
Profit and loss................,......	706,168	Real estate in the cities of New York and New Haven........	176,346
		Forfeited stock—allotments not taken	47,900
		Due from Wm. Bement	88,255
		Materials and supplies on hand	274,934
		Cash in bank, due from agents, &c.	377,170
	$8,008,087		$8,008,087

584.—PACIFIC OF MISSOURI.

The company was incorporated February, 12th, 1849, and organised January 31st, 1850. The surveys were commenced in June, 1850, and the formal breaking of ground took place July 4th, 1851.

At the commencement of the fiscal year 1865-6, the road was completed to Warrensburg, 218 miles from St. Louis; leaving a gap of 65 miles unfinished. On the 28th of May, 1865, trains commenced running to Holden, 232¼ miles: on the 14th of June to Kingsville, 237 miles; on the 26th of July to Pleasant Hill, 248½ miles; and on the 19th of September to Little Blue, 265 miles, where a connection was made with the track which had been laid Eastward from Independence,7·6 miles—the road having been opened and operated from Kansas City to Independence some months previous—and on the 2nd of October, 1865, the trains commenced their regular trips over the whole line of road from Kansas City to St. Louis, a distance of 283 miles. The following statement will show the earnings of the road from commencement to February 28th, 1868 :—

Year ending December 31, 1852..	$108	Year ending February 28, 1861..	$683,644
,, ,, 31, 1853..	41,323	,, ,, 28, 1862..	457,183
,, February 28, 1855..	97,176	,, ,, 28, 1863..	679.956
,, ,, 28, 1856..	330,222	,, ,, 28, 1864..	906,745
,, ,, 28, 1857..	426,285	,, ,, 28, 1865..	1,0~7,967
,, ,, 28, 1858..	668,346	,, ,, 28, 1856..	1,794,356
,, ,, 28, 1859..	674.248	,, ,, 28, 1867..	2,675 874
,, ,, 28, 1860..	648,600	,, ,, 28, 1868..	3,003,681

The expenses for the year ending February, 1868, were $2,030,626, the net earnings, $973,054, in comparison with $719,230 for the previous year.

CAPITAL.—The general financial statement of the company up to March 1st, 1868, is as follows:—

Received.		Expended.	
Capital stock	$3,614,515	Construction	$11,479,635
State bonds	7,000.000	Rolling stock and machinery ..	2,195,655
Land grant sales and rents......	219,300	Construction Missouri River ..	10 901
Total receipts from transportation	13,963,585	Office expenses and stationery..	194,473
		Contingencies..................	80,553
Mortgage construction bonds ..	1,500,000	Interest account	1,388,358
St. Louis County bonds	700,000	Discount on construction and anticipation bonds	8,860
Real estate security bonds	149,000		
Bills payable....................	649,555	Commission on purchases......	17,375
Accounts audited	156,726	Interest, discount, and commissions	1,238,933
		Land grant expenses	7,205
		Total transportation expenses.	9,660,711
		Interest on state bonds charged to transportation to January, 1859................	1,222,721
		Balance March 1, 1868	447,297
	$27,952,682		$27,952,682

585.—PHILADELPHIA AND READING.

Main line and branches, 748 miles. The following is a comparative statement of the receipts and expenses for 12 fiscal years ending 30th November :—

	Cost.	Earnings.	Expenses.	Net.
1855	$19,104,180	$4,291,889	$1,941,041	$2,350,857
1856	19,163,151	3,879,584	1,979,017	1,900,565
1857	19,262,720	3,065,522	1,601,743	1,463,769
1858	23,811,910	2,510,751	1,382,720	1,128,031
1859	24,070,835	2,724,293	1,478,477	1,245,816
1860	24,161,889	3,312,546	1,686,561	1,625,985
1861	24,481,217	2,905,838	1,282,133	1,623,705
1862	25,126,389	3,911,830	1,816,155	2,095,774
1863	25,469,544	6,252,902	2,916,159	3,336,743
1864	25,469,544	9,269,341	4,961,190	4,923,151
1865	25,469,544	11,142,519	6,330,248	4,812,271
1866	26,063,545	10,902,819	6,738,477	4,164,072
1867	....	9,106,496	6,266,434	2,840,060
1868	....	8,971,937	6,162,511	2,629,426

The gross expenses, including renewal fund, rents of lateral roads, taxes, &c., in the year 1867, were 68¾ per cent. of gross receipts, while in 1868 they were 70 per cent. of gross receipts. The resu t of the year's business, as condensed from transportation and income account, may be stated thus :—

Receipts over cost of working $2,629,426
Add balance of account, rents, &c., paid by Schuylkill Navigation, 1868 110,948

                                                              $2,740,374

From which deduct—
Interest on bonded debt......................... $375,156
Interest on bonds and mortgages 37,850
Sinking funds................................... 68,600 = 481,607

                                                              $2,258,767
Cost of renewals, &c. 409,837

Dividend fund. 1867—1868 .... $1,848,930
Amount to credit of reserve fund $2,769,255
Deduct dividend, Jan., 1868 ....$1,192,805
U. S. and State taxes .... 122,419 = 1,315,224 = 1,454,031

Total reserve fund, 1868 .... $3,302,961
Out of which has been paid, in July, 1868—
Five per cent. dividend on .... $25,048,906=$1,252,445
U. S. and State taxes on ditto .... 128,540 = 1,380,985

                                                              $1,921,975
There has been declared a dividend, payable in common stock on 25th January, 1869, of 5 per cent. on the preferred and common stock $26,301,351 .... $1,315,067
U. S. and State taxes on ditto .... 101,516 = 1,416,584

Balance of reserve fund $505,391

The prominent feature in the business of the past year was the almost entire cessation of traffic in anthracite coal for about 7 weeks in July and August, caused by differences between the proprietors of the collieries and the miners and labourers, relative to the number of hours which should comprise a day s work and the compensation therefor. This long interruption in the season of business, generally very active, caused a heavy loss of profits, as the usual staff of employées were kept in readiness for the resumption of mining operations on any day. There was a partial compensation by an unusually large traffic, at increased charges for the remaining three months, in which the coal tonnage amounted to 1,394,066 tons, showing a capacity for transportation largely in excess of any former period. Notwithstanding this interruption, the aggregate production from the three great mining districts of anthracite coal was 1,161,854 tons in excess of the previous year, thus proving that the consumption is steadily progressing.

To provide for the payment of bonds due in 1870, amounting by the last report to $2,656,000, a mortgage, dated 1st April, 1868, payable in 25 years, with interest at 7 per cent. semi-annually free from taxation, was created, secured by the entire property of the company, subject to other prior mortgage liens. An opportunity was given to 1st October last to the holders of the bonds due in 1870 to exchange them for the new bonds, after the payment of the coupon due 1st October last, and $2,255,000 were so exchanged, leaving but $401,600 of the bonds due in 1870 to be provided for. For this purpose the balance of the new bonds will be held.

586.—PITTSBURG, FORT WAYNE, AND CHICAGO.

The company is a consolidation of the Ohio and Pennsylvania, the Ohio and Indiana, and the Fort Wayne and Chicago. Length, 468 miles.

Under agreement the Pittsburg Fort Wayne and Chicago, and the Cleveland and Pittsburg are operated conjointly, the gross earningss (each company paying its own expenses), being divided into the proportion of 73½ per cent. to the former, and 26½ per cent. to the latter. The Pittsburg Fort Wayne and Chicago also receives $85,000 from the Cleveland and Pittsburg for the use of the portion of their line between Pittsburg and Rochester.

The earnings and expenses from January 1st to December 31st, 1868, compared as follows :—

	1868.	1867.
Earnings	$8,022,120	$7,242,125
Expenses	5,007,113	4,863,572
Net earnings	$3,015,002	$2,378,553

This shows an increase in the earnings of $779,994, with an increase in the expenses of $143,546, making the increase in net earnings $636,448.

At a meeting of the leading officers of the Pennsylvania and Pittsburg Fort Wayne and Chicago, held in Philadelphia, arrangements were made whereby the latter passes under the management of and is consolidated with the former corporation. By this consolidation the Pittsburg Fort Wayne and Chicago and Pittsburg Cincinnati and St. Louis are united with the Pennsylvania, which will have control of more than a thousand miles of railway, and property approximating three hundred millions of dollars.

587.—PORTLAND, SACO, AND PORTSMOUTH.

This road is 51½ miles in length, extending from Portland, Maine, to Portsmouth, N. H.

The earnings and expenses for the fiscal year ending May 31st, have been as follow :—

	1866.	1867.	1868.
Earnings	$492,739	$529,325	$518,591
Expenses	$254,429	$298,500	$328,535
Net earnings	238,310	230,824	....

CAPITAL.—The "Trial Balance" to 11th May, 1868, furnished the subjoined particulars of income and expenditure :—

Received.		Expended.	
Capital	$1,500,000	Kennebec and Portland	$100,000
Notes payable	30,000	Wharf at Portland	33,574
Dividends due	8,052	Property	3,417
Dividend. June, 1868	39,473	Portsmouth Bridge	32,000
Eastern Company	151,091	Railway	1,360,183
Boston and Maine	171,091	Improvements	87,529
Income account	6,680	United States	599
		Boston and Maine freight	65,083
		Cash	2
		Renewal	2,311
		Payments on account	26,689
		Grand Trunk	1,749
		Freight clerk	2,893
		Postmaster General	1,192
		New works at Cape Elizabeth	124,676
		Stock of materials	64,380
	1,906,389		$1,906,389

538—UNION PACIFIC.

Between the new town of Omaha, Nebraska, on the Missouri River, the Western limit of the network of American railways, and the city of Sacramento, in California, on the tide-waters of the Pacific, there is a stretch of territory, 1,721 miles across, in a few places sparsely settled by frontiersmen and other pioneers of civilisation; in others occupied by gold and silver miners; but for the most part uninhabited by any but roving bands of Indians. The travelled route through this country crosses formidable ranges of mountains and broad plains of barren land. Four years ago the only way of traversing these 1,721 miles between the Missouri and the Pacific was by mail coaches, or by mule or ox trains, the only railway on the route being a section of 31 miles, near Sacramento. In January, 1866, less than three years ago, 40 miles were laid at the Missouri end of the route, making 71 miles in all. Since that time there has been a progress made which is one of the most marked developments of American energy. The gap of 1,721 miles, upon which, in January, 1866, there were but 71 miles, had been reduced in October, 1868, to 714 miles, and at that time more than 1,000 miles of the Pacific were in operation, carrying mails, pass ngers, and goods. Of the actual number of miles then in operation, 1.007, there had been constructed by the Union Pacific, 820 miles, stretching from Omaha, on the Missouri. westward across the Rocky Mountains' summit, to Green River, and the remaining 187 miles had been built by the Central Pacific eastward from Sacramento, in California, across the Sierra Nevada range to a place called Wadsworth. As the railways now stand, the overland journey, from the Atlantic to the Pacific, may be made in about 13 days, while the journey by steamer, by way of the Isthmus of Panama, requires, at least, 20 days. While 1,007 miles are in actual operation, much more of the work has been accomplished. At the California end, while 187 miles are working, the line has been graded and the rails laid for 197 miles further eastward to Reese River, making 384 miles in all, while the line is graded for 60 miles further, and there is an expectation that the rails will be laid on this before winter compels the work to stop. The same state of affairs exist at the Missouri end of the route. The rails are laid a long distance beyond the 820 miles on which trains are now running, while the roadway is graded for 995 miles west of Omaha, nearly to Great Salt Lake in Utah, and it is expected by the time winter stops the work to have the rails laid to Bear River, one of the affluents to Salt Lake, 119 miles beyond the present terminus. This leaves 400 miles to complete in 1869. About 200 miles of this incomplete section, running around Salt Lake, will pass through a much more favourable country than many portions of the completed road. The gradients are gentle, none exceeding 15 feet to the mile. The Californian end of the road, on crossing the Sierra Nevada, has to climb to a height of 7,042 feet, within the first 100 miles from tidewater, and this involved the most difficult and expensive kind of construction, rivalling the famous Semmering Pass. The Government subsidies to the various Pacific Railways amounted, on the 1st of November, 1868, to $42,194,000 in bonds, while large amounts of the public lands, lying along the lines, have also been given to them. By the close of 1869, it is confidently expected that the work will be complete, and an unbroken line of rail extend from New York to San Francisco.

589.—VIRGINIA AND TENNESSEE.

Length, 214 miles. The earnings for the year ending June 30. 1867, were $764,147, and the running expenses $478,130, giving a net balance of $286,017, or 38 per cent. of gross earnings.

The report for the year ending September 30, 1868, shows the immediate liabilities of the road to be $461,649, with $313,000 additional, on account of interest upon past due coupons, certificates, and bonds. The assets, including open accounts, stores, and cash in hand, amount to $227,074.

The funded debt stands as follows :—

1st mortgage bonds	$494 000
2nd mortgage bonds	23,500
Enlarged bonds	990,000
Income bonds	138,500
Salt Works Branch bonds	9,500
8 per cent. bonds of the $1,000,000 so far issued	736,000
And in 8 per cent. registered certificates	61,352

The revenue for fifteen months preceding the termination of the fiscal year as now fixed was $1,108,537, and its current expenses for that period $933,710, in connection with which, however, it is but proper to remark that this charge to current expenses is rightfully entitled to a reduction, as near as can be ascertained, of at least $176,145, for payment made on account of transactions which belong to the previous fiscal years, and the current expenses would then appear to have actually been $757,564, from which it will be seen that the net revenue for this period may be stated at $350,972, a sum more than sufficient to discharge all current demands of interest, on account of the funded debt, for the same period, by an excess of over $125,000. The earnings for the months of September and October, 1868, amount respectively in round numbers to the sums of $100,000 and $94,000.

WEST INDIES.

590.—CUBA.

The different lines now finished, and in course of construction throughout the country are 27 in number, and comprise about 818 English miles, of which at least 500 are in operation. The principal line—the first constructed (from Havana to Guines, and now extending to La Union)—was commenced in November, 1835; the line from Cardenas to Macagua was started in 1838 ; and the Jucaro in 1839. All the others have been traced and commenced since 1840. The several lines are as follow :—

Havana to La Union, with two branches.
Cardenas to Macagua, Cardenas to Jucaro.
Matanzas to La Isabel, with one branch.
Regla to Guanabacoa (horse cars).
Matanzas to Bemba.
Caibarrian to S. Andres.
Cienfuegos to Sagua.
Carahatus to Quemados de los Guines.
Trinidad to Sancti Spiritus.
Macagua to Trinidad.
Mallorquin to Macagua.
Sagua la Grande.
Havana to Matanzas.
Guines to Matanzas, one branch.
Havana City.

Guanabacoa to Cojimer.
Havana to Pinar del Rio, one branch.
Havana to Mariano.
Pinar del Rio to Coloma.
Sancti Spiritus to Port las Tunas.
Nuevitas to Puerto Principe.
Cobre (copper mines) to Punta de Sal (at St. Jago).
Guantanamo.
St. Jago to Ste. Christo, branch from Ste. Christo to Maroto, branch from Maroto to Sabanilla.
San Miguel to Bagag (Puerto Principe).
Caney branch, belonging to the line from St. Jago to Sabanilla.

591.—DEMERARA.

The company was incorporated prior to 1846, for various lines, including one from Georgetown to Mahaica, length, 20 miles. The last five miles of the line were opened on 1st September, 1864.

REVENUE.—The receipts for the half-year ending December 31st amounted to 14,242l.; and after writing off 543l., one moiety of the remainder of the cost of new bridges, &c., there was a net clearance of 5,618l. to be added to the balance of 233l. from the previous half-year, making a total of 5,851l. Of this sum, the seven per cent. preference dividend, at the rate of 3½ per cent. for the half-year, absorbed 4,025l., and the usual dividend of 1¼ per cent. on the original stock amounting to 1,689l., being at the rate of 2½ per cent. per annum, left a balance of 137l. Compared with the corresponding period in 1867, the traffic for the six months ending on 30th June last shows an increase of 14,397 passengers, and in goods of 6,087 tons. After paying off the remainder of the extra outlay for renewal of bridges, &c., there is a net clearance of 5,598l. to be added to the former balance on revenue account of 137l., making 5,735l. The dividend on preference stock absorbed 4,025l.; a dividend, at the rate of 2½ per cent. per annum on the original stock, left a balance of 21l.

CAPITAL.—The general balance sheet to 30th June, 1868, furnished the subjoined particulars :—

Received.		Expended.	
Original stock	£135,100	Construction	£248,211
Preference stock	115,000	Expended on new wharf, &c., at	
Owing by the company in England	9,477	Georgetown	9,177
Balance of revenue 31st December, and revenue for half-year to 30th June	5,735	Stores and cash in Demerara	6,495
		Due to the company in England	164
		Bills receivable in hand	1,000
		Balance—Less checks not in	263
	£265,313		£265,313

DIRECTORS :

Chairman—JOHN A. TINNE, Esq., Briarley, Aigburth, Liverpool.

Deputy-Chairman—GEORGE H. CHAMBERS, Esq., 4, Mincing Lane, E.C.

Sir James R. Carmichael, Bart., 58, Threadneedle Street, E.C., and 12, Sussex Place, Regent's Park, N.W.

Jonathan Hopkinson, Esq., Wimbledon, S.W.

George H. Loxdale, Esq., Liverpool.

DIRECTORS IN DEMERARA :

Chairman—JAMES STUART, Esq.

Alexander Garnett, Esq. | Henry F. Garnett, Esq.

OFFICERS.—Secretary, V. Perronet Sells ; Manager, Frederick A. Mason.

Offices in London—4, Mincing Lane, E.C.

592.—HAVANA AND MARIANO.

Constructed to provide for the passengers and agricultural produce traffic of the western suburbs of Havana. It runs through the populated districts of Cerro, Puentes Grandes, Quemado, Viejo, and Nuevo, and directly connects the same by means of a junction at the city walls, with the street tramway now in operation with all parts of Havana. The first mortgage loan of 60,000l. was negotiated as follows :—Bonds of 100l. each, with coupons attached, at 7 per cent. interest per annum, and payable in London half-yearly. In liquidation.

DIRECTORS:

President—H. E. The MARQUIS OF MARIANO.

Vice-President—H. E. Don RAFAEL RODRIGUES TORICES.

Don Julian de Zulueta, Planter and Merchant.
Don Manuel Bornio, Merchant.
Don Manuel Pequeno, Merchant.

Don Rafael de Toca, Planter and Merchant.
Don Francisco Duranona, Planter.
Don Ramor de Herrera, Planter.

Sec., Benito Ramos Almeyda,

593.—HAVANA AND MATANZAS.

Concession granted in 1857. The line commences at Regla on the Bay of Havana, runs eastward through the island, and passing Las Minas, Campo, Florido, San Miguel, Jaruco, Baynoa, Aguacate, Ceiba, Mocha, terminates at Matanzas, traversing a distance of 54 miles.

The branch to Guanabacoa (3¼ miles) was opened in August, 1858, while the main line gradually opened from station to station, was completed to Mantanzas, on 14th June, 1861.

A sinking fund is formed for paying off the loan at par, within 15 years. Its operation commenced on the 15th of June, 1867, 25,000l. being redeemed in that year, either by purchase or public drawing, and every year afterwards until final extinction of the debt. Subscriptions for 400,000l. in bonds have been obtained at 90 during the year, and are to bear 7 per cent. interest. The object is to enable the company to purchase the Coliseo line, which runs from Matanzas to Bemba, 35 miles, and so place them in connection with the railway traffic of the island.

DIRECTORS:

President—H. E. Count de O'REILLY, Marquis of St. Felipe and Santiago, Planter.

Edward Fesser, Esq., Managing Director of Bank of Commerce, Merchant.
Don Pedro Sotolonga, Merchant.
Don Miguel Antonio Herrera, Merchant.

Don Manuel Bulnes, Planter.
Don Gabriel de Cardenas, Planter.
Don Manuel Bamos Izquierdo, Planter.
Don Jose Pedrosso, Planter.

Agents in London—Messrs. J. Henry Schröeder and Co., 145, Leadenhall Street, E.C.

594.—JAMAICA.

Length, 16 miles (with wharf at Kingston suitable for the largest vessel), and in full operation, viz. :—from Kingston to Spanish Town, the colonial seat of Government, and thence to the Angels.

The railway is now being extended from Spanish Town to Old Harbour, about 12 miles, and is expected to be opened in the Spring of 1869. The capital for the purpose, 60,000l., has been raised by the Jamaica railway company issuing their mortgage bonds, bearing six per cent. interest, with a sinking fund.

CAPITAL.—3,000 shares of 50l. each, all paid ; 1,445 shares of 50l. each, issued at 35l. discount, or 15l. per share, entitled to equal dividend. The dividends per share have been paid as under :—

June 30th, 1850....	£0	15	0	June 30th, 1856....£0 8 0	June 30th, 1862....£0 14 0
Dec. 31st, 1850....	0	10	0	Dec. 31st, 1856.... 0 9 0	Dec. 31st, 1862.... 0 16 0
June 30th, 1851....	0	13	6	June 30th, 1857.... 0 10 0	June 30th, 1863.... 0 12 0
Dec. 31st, 1851....	0	10	0	Dec. 31st, 1857.... 0 10 0	Dec. 31st, 1863.... 0 12 0
June 30th, 1852....	0	10	0	June 30th, 1858.... 0 10 0	June 30th, 1864.... Nil.
Dec. 31st, 1852....	0	10	0	Dec. 31st, 1858.... 0 7 0	Dec. 31st, 1864.... 0 18 0
June 30th, 1853....	0	10	0	June 30th, 1859.... 0 10 0	June 30th, 1865.... 0 5 0
Dec. 31st, 1853....	0	8	0	Dec. 31st, 1859.... 0 7 0	Dec. 31st, 1865.... 0 6 0
June 30th, 1854....	0	8	0	June 30th, 1860.... 0 10 0	June 30th, 1866.... 0 10 0
Dec. 31st, 1854....	0	7	0	Dec. 31st, 1860.... 0 10 0	Dec. 31st, 1866.... 0 10 0
June 30th, 1855....	0	7	0	June 30th, 1861.... 0 10 0	June 30th, 1867.... 0 10 0
Dec. 31st, 1855....	0	8	0	Dec. 31st, 1861.... 0 11 0	Dec. 31st, 1867.... 0 2 6
					June 30th, 1868.... Nil.

DIRECTORS:

John Pemberton Heywood, Esq., Liverpool and London.
Arthur Heywood, Esq., Liverpool.
Benjamin Heywood Jones, Esq., Liverpool.

T. D. Hornby, Liverpool.
William Reynolds, Esq., M.D., Liverpool.
William Smith, Esq., 63, Coleman Street, E.C.

OFFICERS.—Treasurer, John Farrer, 46, Pall Mall, King Street, Manchester; Solicitors, Harvey, Jevons, and Ryley, Liverpool.

Head Offices—46, Pall Mall, King Street, Manchester.

595,—MATANZAS AND SABANILLA (Cuba).

This line is incorporated by perpetual charter, and is 45 miles in length, running from Matanzas, through Sabanilla, in a southerly direction towards the centre of the Island, connecting the Matanzas with Havana and Cardenas, and affording direct communication with the principal sugar plantations.

The line, works, and stock have cost 460,000l. It was partly opened in 1844, and throughout in 1850; the net receipts being upwards of 50,000l. per annum. It is a single line, and kept in perfect order.

The company borrowed in the island 200,000l., at a high rate of interest. To pay off this sum bonds have been issued (being the only debt upon the line) at seven per cent. These bonds are issued in amounts of 100l. and upwards, the interest being payable half-yearly, by Messrs. Schröeder and Co., of Leadenhall Street, London. The sum of 14,000l. per annum is taken from the earnings of the line, and appropriated by annual drawings to the redemption of the bonds.

Agents—J. H. Schröeder and Co., 145, Leadenhall Street, E.C.

596.—MAURITIUS.

NORTHERN AND MIDLAND.—The whole undertaking is now complete. The traffic upon the line is reported to be highly satisfactory, and considerably in advance of the expectations which had been formed. The Northern is 36½ miles, the Midland 34 miles long. The estimated cost of the whole system was 1,300,000l. Of this sum 600,000l. has been raised by loan, on debentures of 7 per cent., in this country. A sum of 300,000l. of accumulated surplus of the colony was also applied to the cost of the railways. A further sum of 400,000l. was authorised in 1867, to be raised by loans on debentures.

AUXILIARY ASSOCIATIONS.

597,—ANGLO-AMERICAN TELEGRAPH.

Capital, 600,000l. in 10l. shares. It was reported in September that the directors had decided on a dividend on account of 10s. per share, free of income tax, to be declared out of the receipts for the three months ending 31st July. The receipts accruing to the Anglo-American and Atlantic Telegraph from the cables from 1st May to 31st July had averaged 496l. 10s. per day, one of the cables only being occupied in earning this amount from four to six hours per day. This was under the 5l. tariff. The receipts, under the new tariff for 1st September amounted to 511l., for the 2nd to 545l., for the 3rd to 526l., for the 4th to 534l., and for the 6th to 517l., showing a very fair increase in the receipts since they had reduced the tariff.

CAPITAL.—The paid-up capital 250,000l., of which 190,000l. had been paid to the contractors, leaving 55,000l. to be paid by quarterly instalments upon certificates of the company's engineer that the cable was in good working order. The remaining 5,000l. would more than cover the entire preliminary charges to the 15th September last, including engineering, travelling, and other incidental expenses.

DIRECTORS:

Chairman—SIR RICHARD A. GLASS, Ashurst, Dorking.

Deputy-Chairman—J. R. McCLEAN, Esq., M.P., C.E., 2, Park Street, Westminster, S.W.

Sir Daniel Gooch, Bart., M.P., Great Western Railway, Paddington, W.
Capt. A. T. Hamilton, 12, Bolton Row, Piccadilly, W.
Cyrus W. Field, Esq., Gramercy Park, New York.

F. A. Bevan, Esq., 54, Lombard Street, E.C.
Henry Bewley, Esq., Willow Park, Booterstown, Dublin.
J. C. Pickersgill-Cunliffe, Esq., 15, Leadenhall Street, E.C.

OFFICERS.—Sec., John C. Deane; Auditors, Joshua Dean and Francis Glass.

MEMBERS OF JOINT COMMITTEE :

Sir Richard A. Glass, Ashurst, Dorking.
The Right Hon. James Stuart-Wortley, Upper Sheen, Mortlake.
The Hon. Robert Grimston, 24, Mount Street, W.

F. A. Bevan, Esq., 54, Lombard Street, E.C.
Capt. James Gilbert Johnston, 8, York Terrace, Regent's Park.
J. C. Pickersgill-Cunliffe, 15, Leadenhall Street, E.C.

598.—THE ASHBURY RAILWAY CARRIAGE AND IRON COMPANY LIMITED.

Incorporated under "The Companies' Act, 1862," by which the liability of each shareholder is limited to the amount of his shares.

Capital, 500,000l. in 3,000 shares of 100l. each, and 10,000 shares of 20l. each.

The objects for which the company is established are to make and sell or lend on hire railway carriages and wagons, and all kinds of railway plant, fittings, machinery, and rolling stock. To carry on the business of Mechanical Engineers and General Contractors. To purchase, lease, work, and sell mines, minerals, land, and buildings. To purchase and sell as merchants, timber, coal, metals, or other materials, and to buy and sell any such materials, on commission, or as agents.

This company purchased in 1862 the business and manufactory of John Ashbury, Esq.

DIRECTORS:

Chairman—BENJAMIN WHITWORTH, Esq., Oughtrington Hall, near Lymm, Cheshire.

James Holden, Esq., Wilton Polygon, Cheetham Hill, Manchester.

Alfred Peek, Esq., Kingston House, Old Trafford, Manchester.

Thomas Vickers, Esq., Wilton Polygon, Cheetham Hill, Manchester.

John Whitehead, Junr., Esq., Elton House, near Bury.

Thomas Hodson, Esq., Upper Brook Street, Manchester.

Robert Rumney, Esq., Whalley Range, Manchester.

OFFICERS.—Sec., George Whitaker ; Assistant Sec., Auditors ; Chadwicks, Adamson, Collier, and Co., London and Manchester ; Solicitors, Sudlow and Hinde, Manchester ; Bankers, The Manchester and County Bank, Limited, Manchester.

CHIEF OFFICES AND WORKS.—Openshaw, near Manchester.
London Office—22, Great George Street, Westminster, S.W.
Glasgow Office—67, Buchanan Street.

599.—ATLANTIC TELEGRAPH.

The company was projected in 1856 by Mr. Cyrus W. Field, of New York, Messrs. John W. Brett, E. O. W. Whitehouse, and Sir C. T. Bright, Knt., of London, for the purpose of laying a telegraphic cable between Ireland and Newfoundland ; the prospectus was issued on the 6th November, 1856, and the whole of the shares were subscribed for, and the deposit of 20l. paid on each by 5th December in the same year ; the first capital of the company was 350,000l. in 350 shares of 1,000l. each. Incorporated by Act of Parliament, 1857.

After several ineffectual attempts to submerge a proper cable, and to establish telegraphic communication across the Atlantic, the great work was at length finally completed in the summer of 1866.

The traffic is now worked in conjunction with the Anglo-American, which see.

DIRECTORS:

Chairman—The Right Hon. JAMES STUART WORTLEY, East Sheen, S.W.

Deputy-Chairman—L. M. RATE, Esq., South Audley Street, W.

George P. Bidder, Esq., C.E., 24, Great George Street, Westminster, S.W.

Sir Edward Cunard, Bart., 52, Old Broad Street, E.C.

The Hon. Robert Grimston, 24, Mount Street, W.

Samuel Gurney, Esq., 20, Hanover Terrace, N.W.

Peter Coats, Esq., Paisley, N.B.

Lord Alfred Hervey, Putney House, Mortlake.

Capt. James G. Johnston, 8, York Terrace, Regent's Park, N.W.

William F. Scholfield, Esq., 127, Piccadilly, W.

HONORARY DIRECTOR:

W. H. STEPHENSON, Esq., late Official Director on this Board on behalf of Her Majesty's Government, and Ex-Chairman of the Board of Inland Revenue.

Honorary Consulting Engineer in America—GENERAL MARSHAL LEFFERTS, New York.

Secretary—WALTER HUNT, Esq.
Offices—13, St. Helen's Place, Bishopsgate Within, E.C.

600.—BRITISH-INDIAN SUBMARINE TELEGRAPH, LIMITED.

(IN CONNECTION WITH THE ANGLO-MEDITERRANEAN TELEGRAPH).

Capital, 1,200,000l. in 120,000 shares of 10l. each. The work to be completed by April, 1870.

Incorporated under the Companies' Acts, 1862 and 1867, for the purpose of constructing a Submarine Telegraph Line between Suez, Aden, and Bombay, so as to complete a direct and reliable line of telegraphic communication between Europe and India, and with a view to future extensions to China and Australia. The Telegraph Construction and Maintenance Company (Limited), the Great Eastern Steamship Company (Limited), and others interested in the proposed line, deeply impressed with the importance of the undertaking, and satisfied of its commercial value, have combined their efforts to make and lay the cable at the lowest possible cost, relying for their profit upon the success of the company, in the capital of which they will take a large share.

DIRECTORS :

Chairman—JOHN PENDER, Esq., Crumpsall House, Crumpsall, near Manchester.

Sir James Anderson.	Thomas Dyson Hornby, Esq., Brunswick
Baron Emile D'Erlanger.	Street, Liverpool.
Lieut.-Col. Glover. R.E., late Director-General of Telegraphs in India.	Philip Rawson, Esq.
	Sir Charles Wingfield, K.C.S.I., M.P., late
Lord William Hay, Chairman Anglo-Mediterranean Telegraph Company (Limited).	Chief Commissioner of Oude.

OFFICERS.—Sec. (ad interim), John T. Burt ; Managing Director, Sir James Anderson ; Engs., Latimer Clark and Henry Charles Forde ; Solicitors, Baxter, Rose, Norton, and Co., 6. Victoria Street, Westminster S.W.; and Bircham, Dalrymple, Drake, and Co.. 46, Parliament Street, Westminster, S.W.; Bankers, Glyn, Mills, Currie, and Co., 67, Lombard Street, E.C.

Offices—76, Palmerston Buildings, Old Broad Street, E.C.

601.—BRITISH AND IRISH MAGNETIC TELEGRAPH.

The company was constituted at the commencement of 1856, under the Joint Stock Limited Liability Act, 1856, in order to carry out the amalgamation of the Telegraphs of the Magnetic and British Telegraph Companies, and is possessed of the works, patents, and privileges of those companies. The lines extend throughout the United Kingdom between 510 stations, and are connected with the continental system by means of the Submarine Company's cables to France, Belgium, &c. The company is also in direct communication with the Atlantic cables.

The capital consists of 515,170l. of ordinary stock, and 121,724l. of preference at 6 per cent. The receipts for the year 1868 amounted to 162,823l., the expenses being 90,149l. The last dividend on the ordinary stock was at the rate of 12 per cent. per annum.

DIRECTORS :

Chairman—WILLIAM LANGTON, Esq., 1, Fenwick Street, Liverpool.

Deputy-Chairman—Sir JAMES R. CARMICHAEL, Bart., 58, Threadneedle Street, E.C., and 12, Sussex Place, Regent's Park, N.W.

Edward Cropper, Esq., Swaylands, Penshurst, Kent.	David Webster, Esq., Oak Cottage, Norfolk Road, St. John's Wood, N.W.
Henry Harrison, Esq., Liverpool.	Anthony Hannay, Esq. (Messrs. Kelly and
Thomas Dyson Hornby, Esq., Brunswick Street, Liverpool.	Co.), Glasgow.
V. O'B. O'Connor, Esq., 3, Beresford Place, Dublin.	John Blackie, Junr., Esq., 36, Frederick Street, Glasgow.
L. J. Mc. Donnell, Esq., Merrion Square, Dublin.	John Pender, Esq., Crumpsall House, Crumpsall, near Manchester.
William Haughton, Esq., Dublin.	William Gibb, Esq., Manchester.
Charles Kemp Dyer, Esq., Lloyd's, London, E.C.	Edward Johnston, Esq., London.
	James Holme, Esq., Liverpool.

OFFICERS.—Sec. and Gen. Man., E. B. Bright ; Treas., John Leyland ; Accountants, H. W. and J. Blackburn, Bradford ; Solicitors, Lace, Banner, Gill, and Lace, Liverpool, and Bell, Steward, and Lloyd, London ; Auditors, H. C. Beloe and John Bewley, Junr., Liverpool.

Chief Offices—Exchange Buildings, Liverpool.

Principal London Offices—57, 58, and 59, Threadneedle Street, E.C.

602.—CREDIT FONCIER OF ENGLAND, LIMITED.

This company was an extension of the Credit Foncier, and of the Credit Mobilier, which were established, the former for financial business in connection with land, the latter for general financial operations. Reconstructed on 30th July, 1866. Capital, 2,000,000l., in shares of 10l. each.

It was reported in July that the directors had effected a considerable improvement in the affairs of the company during the previous six months. The character and extent of these improvements were shown in the subjoined explanatory statements :—

Millwall Docks.—The docks of this company have been, as was stated in February, constructed in the most substantial manner, and with all the modern improvements, and they have since been opened for business, of which they h ve, already, an amount that, according to the statement of the directors of that company, is sufficient to dèfray its own expenses, and to pay the interest on all its borrowed capital

They have further assured the directors that their business continues to increase so rapidly, that they expect to be able to pay a dividend on their share capital, at an early period. The interest of the company in this undertaking consists of

Loans on mortgage debentures £130,900
Loans on preference stock, including interest 8,062
*Ordinary fully paid-up stock, representing............. 41,300=£180,262
* This stock stands in the company's books at 17,552l. 10s.

The debentures become due in October next, and will, no doubt, then be paid off.

Irrigation of France.—This company has made considerable progress towards the completion of its works during the past half-year, having finished and opened one of its most important canals, the Siagne, during this period. It is proper, however, to mention that the subscriptions for the use of the water of this canal, have not realised, during the short time the canal has been open, the calculations of the directors of that company. They continue, however, their unabated confidence in the ultimate and great success of the company, to ensure which, they add, a moderate time only is required. They report, also, that the remaining canals are almost completed, and that the estimated resources of the company are quite sufficient for the purpose. The Credit Foncier is interested in the company to the following extent, viz.:—

Debentures representing £265,000
Loans 110,470
1,537 shares of 20l. paid in full .... 30,740=£406,210

These debentures are valued in the books at 238,500l., and the shares at 23,055l.

Consolidated Land of France.—The directors concluded an arrangement with this company, by which, they hope, they have made safe the whole of the very large amount of capital at present locked up in this undertaking. They had also, in the interests of the Credit Foncier, acquired the power to realise the property of this company whenever it may appear expedient that this should be done, after the 1st July, 1869. By this arrangement, the Credit Foncier has obtained, by way of mortgage, a first charge on the greater and most valuable portion of the landed property of this company, as security for the bulk of the sum advanced to it.

It is, however, fair to explain, that to acquire these great advantages, your directors were obliged to increase their loans to that company by 60,000l., in order to protect their property by enabling them to meet other engagements. This investment, including this 60,000l., part of which only appears in this half-year's accounts, now stands, therefore, as follows, viz.:—

Loans secured by mortgage..........................£291,949
Other advances mainly secured on debentures 47,241
Debentures representing 157,208
3,659 shares 10l. paid up .... 36,590=£532,988

The debentures are valued in the books at 125,766l., and the shares at 7,318l. only.

London, Chatham, and Dover.—The securities held by the company in this railway remain, in amount, precisely as before. They have, however, become somewhat more valuable, because of the termination of the litigation in which the company had been so long involved, and because some of them, by the late parliamentary arrangement, have obtained the right to rank in a better position than formerly. They consist as follows, viz.:—

Debentures representing £190,000
Valued in the books at 171,000l.
And overdue coupons................................. 9,262
B Debenture stock 14,012
Metropolitan A stock................................ 607,700=£820,975
Valued in the books at 121,540l.

Varna and Rustchuk.—The traffic on this line is stated by its directors to be very satisfactory. They have also stated that it continues to increase so largely, that they hope, shortly, to be able to commence the payment of dividends on their share capital. They further state, that negotiations for the payment of the interest granted by the Turkish Government are still in progress, and they believe with every prospect of success, as, apart from diplomatic action by the British Government on the subject, the directors have received the assurance of their official representative at Constantinople, that remittances on this account may be shortly looked for. Should this expectation be realised, the income of the Credit Foncier would be at once largely augmented, the company holding

In shares £590,900
„ Overdue coupons .... 52,811=£643,711

These shares are valued in the company's books at 196,466l., and the overdue coupons, with accrued interest, at 26,405l.

Paris Street.—The directors had succeeded in withdrawing, without loss, the capita originally invested in this hazardous undertaking, and they have, in so doing, relieved the company from a liability of 150,000*l.*, incurred in connection with it, and which had become, during the last few months, a subject of much anxiety to them. They regretted to be obliged to add, however, that the enterprise has not yielded the profit which it was assumed that it had produced. Still, they consider it fortunate, under the circumstances, that the original capital had been recovered, with fair interest upon it.

City of Milan Improvements.—This company has made some progress during the last six months, but it must be admitted that the rental of its property still remains much below the amount expected from it, and is therefore insufficient to afford, as yet, any dividend on its share capital. The directors, however, continue to declare their confidence in the gradual increase of the rental from the Victor Emmanuel Gallery, and hope for results which will, eventually, be satisfactory to its shareholders. The Credit Foncier holds in it

On loan, including interest	£6,552	
10,933 shares of 30*l.* fully paid up	327,990=£334,542	

These shares are valued at 243,617*l.* in the books.

Belgian Public Works.—Although considerable progress has been made with the works during the past half-year, the management of the company's affairs in Brussels has not been satisfactory, and the company's interest has thereby suffered. The management, however, having been changed, the directors hope to be able to report very differently of the undertaking hereafter, believing, as they do, that it is one of great promise, and perfectly sound, and that it will ultimately yield a large and speedy return for the capital employed in it. The company's interests in it are as follows, viz.:—

7,250 A shares of 10*l.* paid up in full	£72,500
3,400 B shares entitled to one-third of the profits of the undertaking, after the repayment of the share capital, but on which nothing has been paid.—Estimated value	34,000
Temporary advance on security	10,000=£116,500

The following balance sheet, to 30th June, exhibited the financial results of the half-year's operations. It was a matter of regret to the directors, that they did not admit of the payment of a dividend; and, still more, that they necessitated the writing off, as a loss, a certain amount of capital :—

Debtor.		*Creditor.*	
Capital, 200,000 shares, at 10*l.* per share	£2,000,000	Cash at Bankers and on deposit at call	£66,283
Sundry creditors	56,719	Balance of calls	6,449
Bills payable	13,600	Loans secured on freehold properties	382,910
Debenture holders	4,190	Bills receivable	145,273
Depositors	1,030	Loans on securities, sundry debtors, &c.	138,817
Suspense account	20,000	Debentures	549,278
		Fully-paid shares and stock	560,749
		Belgian Public Works B deferred shares	34,000
		Profit and loss account—Balance at debit of this account carried down	93,397
		Assets in hands of liquidators of old company, to be delivered over on completion of its liquidation, viz.:—	
		Cash at bankers £95	
		Shares 234	
		Fully-paid stock 121,300	
		£121,629	
		Less claims thereon viz.:—	
		Debenture holders £2,400	
		Sundry creditors.. 850= 3,250=	118,379
	£2,095,539		£2,095,539

Contingent liabilities :—		*Contingent liabilities :*—	
On guarantee of city office debentures per contra £300,000		On guarantee city office debentures per contra £300,000	
Other guarantees (since paid)	£9,000	Other guarantees (since paid)	£9,000

ARTICLES OF ASSOCIATION.—At a special meeting held on 6th January, 1869, the following resolutions, proposed by the directors, were adopted, VIZ.:—"To reduce the number of the directors to a maximum of five, and a minimum of three. To give power to the general meetings to remove any, or all, of the directors, on a previous notice of twenty days. To reduce the irremuneration from 6,400*l*. to 2,000*l*. per annum, or any other sum which the meeting may determine upon. To increase the qualification of the directors from 400 to 500 shares. To abolish the titles of governor and deputy-governor, and substitute those of chairman and deputy-chairman. That the election, by the board, of any director to fill up a casual vacancy, shall be subject to confirmation at the next general meeting."

The chairman stated that an offer, which he termed a liberal one, and which he would be in a position to submit at the forthcoming meeting, had been received from the old directors to return a portion of the commissions taken by them on assumed profits. This, he thought, had better be accepted, and a stop would thus be put to the present proceedings in chancery. A resolution was passed expressing confidence in the present liquidators of the Credit Foncier and Mobilier of England (Limited), and indignation at the conduct of certain persons who wish to wind it up in the Court of Chancery, or subject to its supervision.

The report presented on 5th February stated that although the position of the company could not be considered satisfactory, it had been rendered more secure. The Millwall Docks, in which the company have 153,657*l*., including 112,357*l*. debentures and preference stock, are stated to be already earning an income that will yield a dividend upon the preference stock after paying the interest upon the debentures. The Irrigation of France, which appears for 427,557*l*., has sold to the Credit Foncier one of its most important canals—the Siagne—for 362,500*l*., to be applied in reduction of its debt, and it is believed that this will yield a much earlier return to the Credit Foncier than could otherwise have been expected. The Consolidated Land of France (late the Imperial Land of Marseilles), which appears for 554,557*l*., remains in its former position, but has entered into a provisional agreement to sell all its lands on terms that would be satisfactory to the Credit Foncier, who would have the right on the 1st of July next to realise this property on their own account—a right they will exercise should the contemplated sale not be effected in the interim. The London Chatham and Dover still stands for 826,249*l*. The Varna and Rustchuck stands for 658,484*l*., and the property, in the opinion of the directors, has been so mismanaged that they have resolved to enforce a complete change unless some negotiations that have just been opened for the sale of the line to a body of independent capitalists should result satisfactorily. The traffic available is believed, under proper administration, to be considerably in excess of the estimate originally formed of it. The City of Milan Improvements figures for 330,867*l*., and is considered now to be well managed. A small dividend may probably be paid upon it next year, but so much of the capital "was squandered and otherwise misapplied on its first formation that it cannot be expected ever to yield an adequate return." The Belgian Public Works would probably have been one of the most productive ever held by the Credit Foncier if the company had been formed with a proper amount of capital, 1,000,000*l*. having at the least been essential, whereas it was established with only 150,000*l*. paid up. Under existing circumstances, the problem as to the means by which it is to be carried through is so difficult that the Credit Foncier directors desired to take the opinion of the shareholders with regard to it. Finally, in relation to the claims made by the Credit Foncier upon their late directors, the Board recommended a compromise, which they believe can be attained, in preference to encountering the delay, risk, and expense of Chancery suits.

DIRECTORS :

Chairman—FRANCIS MOWATT, Esq., 84, Eccleston Square, S.W.

Major-Gen. G. Balfour, C.B., London. | Alexander Fairlie Cuningham, Esq., London.

OFFICERS.—Financial Sec., Henry James Barker; Auditors, Frederick Maynard, Bread Street, E.C., and W. B. Ford, 28, King Street, E.C., Accountants; Solicitors, Upton, Johnson, and Upton ; Bankers, Smith, Payne, and Smiths, The National Bank, and The Consolidated Bank, Limited.

Offices—St. Clement's House, Clement's Lane, E.C.

603.—ELECTRIC AND INTERNATIONAL TELEGRAPH.

The company has upwards of 580 stations in Great Britain and Ireland in full operation, independent of many railway stations.

The whole are in direct communication with the Foreign Telegraph system, *via* their Hague and Amsterdam Lines, so that messages can be forwarded from any of their offices in the United Kingdom to any of the 1,150 stations on the Continent of Europe, embracing all the most important cities and towns in Holland, Germany, Norway, Sweden, Italy, France, Spain, &c. Communication is also established, *via* Russia, to China. The dividend for the half-year ending 31st December was equal to 10 per cent.

per annum, and for June to 10 per cent. on the consolidated stock, and of 8 per cent. on the new stock. A surplus of 12,751l. was carried to the trust fund.

It was reported in February that the receipts for the half-year ending 31st December amounted to 202,706l., against 179,279l. in the half-year ending 31st December, 1867. The working expenses, including interest and income tax, were 102,107l. as compared with 102,548l., the net balance therefore was 100,598l. as compared with 76,730l. in December, 1867, showing an increase of 23,867l. The directors had much pleasure in recommending the usual dividend at the rate of 10 per cent. per annum upon the stock and shares, and an additional dividend of 4½ per cent. on account of back dividends, both free of income tax, making a total dividend paid for the year 1868 of 14½ per cent., of which more than 8½ per cent. was earned in the half-year. After paying this dividend there remained a surplus of 2,237l.

The company in September agreed to the purchase by Government of their property at twenty year's purchase of the net profits to 30th June, 1868. In case of difference between the company and the Government, the amount of net profits is to be settled by arbitration, either by one arbitrator mutually agreed upon, or by two arbitrators and an umpire.

CAPITAL.—The balance sheet to 30th June furnished the subjoined particulars of income, expenditure, and reserve :—

Receipts.

Consolidated stock		£1,049,875
New shares (15,000) 8l. paid	120,000=	£1,169,875
Debenture debt		7,550
Fire insurance fund		740
Balances due to sundry creditors		48,872
Trust account—		
Balance 31st December, 1867	£116,270	
Surplus 31st December, 1867	21,613	
Interest	1,361=	£139,245
Payment on account of Dunwich Cable	6,322=	132,922
Balance of Revenue account		71,245
		£1,431,206

Expenditure.

Construction of the Electric and International Telegraph	£1,033,486
Central Station and Camden Stores	39,513
Balances due from sundry debtors	110,877
Calls in arrear	240
Value of stores	49,706
Securities in hand	5,849
Trust account agreed to at the half-yearly meeting 31st July, 1858	132,922
Balance at the bankers	58,610
	£1,431,206

DIRECTORS :

Chairman—The Hon. ROBERT GRIMSTON, 24, Mount Street, Grosvenor Square, W.

Deputy-Chairman—F. N. MICKLETHWAIT, Esq., 43A, South Street, Park Lane, W.

G. P. Bidder, Esq., 24, Great George Street, Westminster, S.W.
Thomas Brassey, Esq., 56, Lowndes Square, Knightsbridge, S.W.
The Earl of Caithness, Hill Street, Berkeley Square, W.
W. F. Cooke, Esq., Aber-ya Penryn, Carnarvon.
C. W. Earle, Esq., Little Elms, Watford.

E. R. Langworthy, Esq., Manchester.
Mark Philips, Esq., Snitterfield, near Stratford-on-Avon.
Lord Alfred Paget, 56, Queen Anne Street, Cavendish Square, W.
W. H. Smith, Esq., M.P., 186, Strand, W.C.
Joseph Whitworth, Esq., Manchester.
General Wylde, C.B., 63, Onslow Square, Brompton, S.W.

OFFICERS.—Sec., H. Weaver ; Auditors, John C. Hughes, 38, Fenchurch Street, E.C., and Edwin Clarke, 5, Westminster Chambers, Victoria Street, S.W.

Head Offices—Telegraph Street, E.C.

604.—ENGLISH AND FOREIGN CREDIT.

This company was established to make advances on stocks, shares, and other approved securities, with a nominal capital of 300,000l. in shares of 15l. each. Paid-up 87,912l. 10s. First issue, 11,960 shares.

The dividend for the year ending 30th June, was equal to 6l. 13s. 4d. per cent. The accounts for the half-year ending 31st December, 1868, showed a net profit (including the balance brought forward from preceding half-year) of 7,189l. The usual dividend of 5s. per share was declared and the balance of 4,199l. carried to new account.

CAPITAL.—The balance-sheet to 30th June, exhibited in cash, in bills receivable, loans, current account, &c., 113,825l., which sum was represented as under :—

Capital	£87,912
Reserve fund	18,000
Liabilities—	
Sums due on current account	1,543
Profit and loss	6,359
Rebate to new account	10=£113,825

DIRECTORS :

Chairman—GEORGE SHEWARD, Esq., Leinster Square, Bayswater, S.W.

Vice-Chairman—THOMAS STENHOUSE, Esq., 7, East India Avenue, E.C.

Joseph Bray, Esq.. Pyrgo Park, Romford, E. James Hendrey, Esq., 78, Warwick Square, S.W. Charles E. Mangles, Esq., Poyle Park, Farnham, Surrey.

George Barnard Townsend, 3, Prince's Street, Storey's Gate, We stminster, S.W. Henry Harrison, 4, Great George Street, Westminster, S.W.

OFFICERS.—Man., John W. Batten ; Sec., David S. Derry ; Solicitor, James Brend Batten, 32, Great George Street, Westminster. S.W. ; Bankers, Consolidated Bank (Limited), Threadneedle Street, E.C., and The Alliance Bank, Bartholomew Lane, E.C. Offices—3, Winchester Buildings, Great Winchester Street, City, E.C.

605.—FRENCH ATLANTIC TELEGRAPH.

Incorporated under the Companies' Acts of 1862 and 1867, under the title of Société du Cable Trans-Atlantique Français (Limited). With a capital of 1,200,000l., or fr.30,000,000, in 60,000 shares of 20l., or fr.500, of which 10,000 are to be issued as fully paid shares.

It is expected that the whole of the work on this side of the Channel will be completed by June next, and that the Great Eastern will be ready to sail from Sheerness for Brest (the port of departure from the French coast) some time during the same month.

HONORARY COMMITTEE IN FRANCE.

His Excellency M. Drouyn de Lhuys. M. Elie de Beaumont, Senator.

Count Mallet, Senator. Vice-Admiral Trehouart, Senator.

DIRECTORS :

LONDON BOARD.

Chairman—The Right Hon. ROBERT LOWE, M.P., 34, Lowndes Square, S.W.

Edward J. Halsey, Esq. (Messrs. Fesser, Uhthoff, and Co., and Fesser and Co., Havana). Julius Reuter, Esq.

Cornelius Grinnell, Esq. (Messrs. Grinnell and Co.) William Henry Schröder, Esq. (Messrs. J. H. Schröder and Co.)

PARIS BOARD.

President—Contre Amiral LACAPELLE.

I) Marquis Eliacin de Beaumont. M. S. Boitelle, Senateur. Le Baron Ph. de Bourgoing.

M. Charles Crapelet (MM. Rattier and Co.) Le Baron Emile D'Erlanger.

OFFICERS.—General Superintendent, Sir James Anderson ; Consulting Electricians, Sir William Thomson, F.R.S., and Cromwell F. Varley, M.I.C.E. ; Technical Adviser in France, M. Bertsch, Member of the Committee of Telegraphs in France ; Engineers and Electricians, Latimer Clark, M.I.C.E. ; Henry C. Forde, M I.C.E. ; Fleeming Jenkin, F.R.S., M.I.C.E. ; Bankers in London, The Union Bank of London, Princes Street ; Bankers in Paris, Société Générale de Crédit Industriel et Commercial, MM. Emile Erlanger et Cie ; Bankers and Agents in New York, Duncan, Sherman and Co. ; Solicitors, Bischoff, Coxe, and Bompas ; Secretary, Frederick J. Griffiths. Offices in London—Bartholomew House, E.C. Offices in Paris—Rue Taitbout, 20.

606.—GENERAL CREDIT AND DISCOUNT.

Incorporated under "The Companies' Act, 1862," limiting the liability of shareholders to the amount subscribed. Re-constructed from the "General Credit and Finance," the alteration being based on a plan suggested by the directors, in effect as follows :—The liabilities to third parties were 258,075l., and the paid-up capital and reserve fund 1,675,000l., making together 1,933,075l. due to the public or the shareholders. To meet these engagements the assets amount to 2,041,100l. The directors did not represent all the assets to be perfectly good, and one item, being a loan to a foreign railway company of 151,300l., they described as in an unsatisfactory state. After consideration of the outstanding debts, and making allowance for such as might be considered doubtful, they considered any loss would be fully met by the reserve. The share capital they felt justified in considering intact ; 212,9'6l. of the 2,000,000l. of assets consisting of cash or government securities. The sum of 282,661l. in bank and mercantile bills, 224,368l. was in shares, and 786.939l. in loans secured by acceptances and collateral securities, or on railway debentures. The sum of 30,265l. represented "calls in arrear," and 55,888*l.* as "accounts current." The object of the transformation was to get rid of the liability of shareholders for the uncalled portion of capital. Under these arrangements the company possesses a subscribed capital of 2,000,000*l.,* divided into 200,000 shares of 10*l.* each, of which 1,500,000*l.* is paid up.

The average capital employed during 1863 amounted to 360,000*l.,* from the profits on which were deducted 4,884*l.,* in the shape of preliminary expenses, and 18,750*l.* divided among the proprietors, being at the rate of 10 per cent. per annum.

In 1864 the capital was extended to 1,000,000*l.,* while from the net profits there were divided 150,000*l.*; but as of this amount 31,250*l.* had been paid as back interest on new issue of shares, the sum actually realised from profits in the business may be stated at 118,780*l.,* or at the rate of 12 per cent. per annum, while 125,000*l.* were placed to reserve from premiums.

In 1865, the capital still continuing at 1,000,000*l.,* there were divided out of profits the sum of 150,000*l.,* being at the rate of 15 per cent., a further sum from profits of 50,000*l.* being added to reserve.

In 1866 the capital for the first half of the year remained at 1,000,000*l.,* while in the succeeding six months it was raised to 1,500,000*l.,* and so established an average for the year of 1,250,000*l.* On this capital there were distributed 75,000*l.* from profits, equal to 6 per cent. per annum.

In 1867, the capital being 1,500,000*l.,* the profits divided to the shareholders, as stated in the report adopted on Monday, amounted to 75,000*l.,* or 5 per cent. per annum, with 5,000*l.* to reserve.

The entire sum distributed during these five years amounted to 437,500*l.,* with 180,000*l.* to reserve, or more than one third of the entire capital, and exhibiting an average dividend of 9*l.* 12*s.* per cent.

The dividends for the year 1868 were at the rate of 5 per cent. The difficulties interposed between realisation of the company's securities in the London Chatham and Dover and the South Eastern of Portugal have not yet been removed.

The report to 31st December, 1868, exhibited an available total of 53,778*l.,* including a previous balance of 7,126*l.,* and recommended a dividend for the half-year at the rate of 5 per cent. per annum, absorbing 37,500*l.,* and the appropriation of 5,900*l.* to reserve, and 1,000*l.* in reduction of cost of freehold premises, leaving 10,278*l.* to be carried forward. Mention was made of the claim on the London Chatham and Dover for the sum of 160,050*l.,* lent on the mortgage of land at Blackfriars, and to the fact that the company, after having taken nearly two years for the task, had at length put in an answer to the bill filed against them in March, 1867. With regard to the claim on the South Eastern of Portugal (151,300*l.*) it was stated that scarcely any progress had been made in the attempt to obtain an honourable settlement from the Portuguese Government. The objects of the company are now almost exclusively directed to the securing of a first-class discount business.

CAPITAL.—The balance sheet to 31st December, 1868, furnished the subjoined debtor and creditor account:—

Dr.—200,000 shares of 10*l.* each ; 7*l.* 10*s.* paid up	£1,500,000
Contingent reserve	175,000
Reserve, invested in Government securities	5,000
Bills payable	8,543
Deposits, loans, &c.	2,491,551

PROFIT AND LOSS ACCOUNT :—
Net balance, 91,278*l.* ; from which deduct amount of interim dividend paid for 6 months ended 30th June last, at the rate of 5 per cent. per annum, free of income tax, 37,500*l.*

		53,778
		£4,233,878

Cr.—Cash at bankers and in office	£170,532		
Government securities	63,442		
Short loans, stock exchange	26,375=	£260,350	
Bank and commercial bills discounted		2,734,412	
Sundry securities and loans on securities		858,881	
Loan, South Eastern of Portugal Railway		151,300	
Do. on charge of land at Blackfriars		160,050	
Freehold premises, 7, Lothbury		56,867	
Accounts current, &c.		12,016	
		£4,233,878	

DIRECTORS:

Chairman—JOHN BRAMLEY-MOORE, Esq., Gerrard's Cross, Bucks.

William Patrick Andrew, Esq., 26, Montague Square, W.

Edward Blount, Esq. (Messrs. E. Blount and Co., Bankers, Paris).

Thomas Brassey, Jun., Esq., M.P., 4, Great George Street, Westminster, S.W.

Alexander Devaux, Esq. (Messrs. C. Devaux and Co.), 62, King William Street, E.C.

W. Mackinnon, Esq., Glasgow.

George Worms, Esq. (Messrs. G. and A. Worms.)

Sir H. D. Wolff, K.C.M.G., Rutland Gate.

OFFICERS.—Gen. Man., James Macdonald; Sub-Managers, T. F. Robinson and John R. MacDonald; Sec., R. J. Butler; Auditors, Quilter, Ball, and Co.; Bankers, Bank of England, London and Westminster Bank, 41, Lothbury, E.C., Union Bank of London, and Glyn, Mills, and Co.; Solicitors, Baxter, Rose, Norton, and Co. Offices—7, Lothbury, E.C.

607.—HUDSON'S BAY.

The Hudson's Bay Company was incorporated under a Royal Charter granted by King Charles II., in 1670, by the name of "The Governor and Company of Adventurers of England trading into Hudson's Bay," and by the Charter a vast tract of territory was vested in the company, together with the sole right of trade and commerce, and all "mines royal" within the territory.

The capital of the company was extended in 1863 to 2,000,000*l.* sterling, and divided into shares of 20*l.* each, when the assets, exclusive of the company's landed territory, extending over an area of more than 1,400,000 square miles or upwards of 896 million acres, were valued at 1,023,569*l.*, together with a cash balance of 370,000*l.*

The dividends have been at the rate of 4½ per cent. per annum.

No decision has yet been obtained in respect to the arbitration upon the claim of the company against the United States in reference to the Oregon territory, but the Canadian Parliament has taken up the subject of the incorporation of the Hudson's Bay territory with the new dominion. In preparation for this decision, an Act was passed in the last session of the Imperial Parliament enacting that power should be given to the Crown to accept the surrender of the lands and rights enjoyed by the Hudson's Bay under their charter, upon terms to be agreed between Her Majesty's Government and the company. There is a proviso that even in the event of the surrender of the company's rights being agreed to, yet that the surrender should not take effect unless the Canadian Parliament passed an address embodying the terms of the agreement, and unless the Imperial Government by an Order in Council within one month agreed to the transfer of the said powers and rights to the Canadian Dominions.

DIRECTORS:

Governor—Sir STAFFORD H. NORTHCOTE, Bart., M.P., 86, Harley Street, W. Deputy-Governor—Sir CURTIS MIRANDA LAMPSON, Bart. (C. M. Lampson and Co.), 64, Queen Street, Cheapside, E.C., and Rowfant, Crawley, Surrey.

Eden Colvile, Esq., 9, Fenchurch Buildings, E.C.

George Lyall, Esq., Headley Park, Surrey.

Daniel Meinertzhagen, Esq. (F. Huth and Co.)

James Stewart Hodgson, Esq. (Finlay, Hodgson, and Co.)

John Henry William Schröeder, Esq. (J. H. Schröeder and Co.)

Richard Potter, Esq., Standish House, Stonehouse, Gloucestershire.

Edward W. T. Hamilton, Esq., M.P., 32, Upper Brook Street, W.

Offices—4, Fenchurch Street, London, E.C. Warehouse—Lime Street, E.C.

608.—INTERNATIONAL FINANCIAL.

Incorporated under "The Companies' Act, 1862," by which the liability of each shareholder is limited to the amount of his shares. Capital, 1,500,000*l.*, in 150,000 shares of 10*l.* each.

The report for February stated that the securities had, as heretofore, been valued at the lowest market prices on 31st December last. The actual profits of the year, 1868, after deducting all charges, were 71,447*l.*, making, with the balance brought forward, 78,300*l.* Of this sum the directors wrote off 23,390*l.*, against some old items in the accounts at present unproductive, leaving the net profits available 54,911*l.* Out of this amount a dividend was declared at the rate of 5 per cent. per annum, free of income-tax; a sum of 14,392*l.* was added to the reserve fund, raising the amount to 20,000*l.*; and the balance of 3,019*l.* was carried forward to the next account. Half of the proposed dividend having been paid in July last, the dividend payable in January was at the rate of 2s. 6d. per share. The necessary measures for reducing the capital had been carried to completion, and the capital now stood at 1,500,000*l.*, in 150,000 shares of 10*l.* each, with 5*l.* per share paid thereon, in lieu of the same number of shares of 20*l.* each, representing a nominal capital of 3,000,000*l.*, with a liability of 15*l.* per share.

CAPITAL.—The balance sheet to 31st December, 1868, furnished the subjoined debtor and creditor account:—

Received.		*Expended.*	
Capital called up, viz., 5*l.* per share on 150,000 shares................£750,000		Cash at bankers, in hand, and on short loan £47,910	
Sundry creditors—		Sundry debtors—	
Being for amounts due on deposits, debentures, and sundry small accounts 187,105		For advances on securities, &c.. 214,417	
Reserve fund 5,608		Sundry investments 716,546	
Profit and loss—		Interest at the rate of 5 per cent. per annum, paid July, 1868..... 18,750	
Balance at credit of this account 54,910			
£997,624		£997,624	

DIRECTORS:

Chairman—ROBERT AMADEUS HEATH, Esq. (Heath and Co.)

John Frederick Flemmich, Esq. (Messrs. | Lachlan M. Rate, Esq., King's Arms Yard,
  Frederick Huth and Co.) | E.C.
Junius S. Morgan, Esq. (Messrs. J. S. | Baron Herman de Stern (Stern Brothers).
  Morgan and Co.)

OFFICERS.—Sec., Walter A. Michael; Auditors, Robert Palmer Harding and
Edwin H. Galsworthy; Solicitors, Bircham, Dalrymple, Drake, and Co., 46, Parliament
Street, S. W.; Bankers, Glyn, Mills, and Co., 67, Lombard Street, E.C.
  Offices—60, Threadneedle Street, E.C.

609.—LANCASTER WAGON.

Incorporated under the provisions of the Act, 1862, with liability limited to the
amount of the shares subscribed. Capital, 500,000l. in shares of 5l. each. 17,575 have
had 5l. called up, and on 5,565 the sum of 3l. per share has been paid.   Of 23,140
preference shares of 5l. each, created on 26th March, 1868, none have yet been issued.

This company is formed for the purpose of building wagons, carriages, and other
rolling stock, either for sale or to be let on hire, to railway and mining companies, coal
owners, merchants, and others engaged in the carrying trade.

CAPITAL.—The balance-sheet to 30th June, 1868, furnished the subjoined particulars:—

Debtor—Buildings to 31st December, 1867		£31,357
Plant and machinery: Expended to 31st December, 1867, per last account	£15,394	
Ditto since	140	
	£15,534	
Less charge to profit and loss for depreciation	192=	15,342
		£46,700
Due for carriages and wagons sold on deferred payment		29,380
Wagon stock for hire		8,229
Trade debts due to the company		2,810
Stocks of wagons and carriages finished and in process of construction, and of stores and materials per inventories and valuations		17,472
		£104,594
Northampton and Banbury Railway:		
Advance on security of shares	£15,000	
Interest and depreciation on stock	1,580=	16,580
Formation expenses		2,153
Profit and loss: Balance loss per last account	5,029	
Net loss half-year to June 30, 1868	1,755=	6,784= 25,518
		£130,112

* This railway is still incomplete, no farther progress having been made with the works since they
were stopped in 1866. The value of this debt as an asset of the company is still only nominal.

CREDITOR.—Shareholders' capital, viz.: First issue, 17,575 shares of 5l. each, all called up		£87,875
Second issue, 5,565 shares, 3l. per share called up		16,695
Calls paid in advance		1,640
		£106,210
Deduct: Arrears of calls, first issue	£395	
Do. second issue	240=	635
		£105,575
Loans on debentures		6,600
Bills payable		2,576
Debts due by company		5,354
Arrears of dividends		7= £130,112

DIRECTORS:

Chairman—EDWARD DENIS DE VITRE, Esq., M.D., Caton, near Lancaster.

Alexander Brogden, Esq., M.P., Light- | William Fleming, Esq., Lancaster.
  bourne House, Ulverston. | John Wignall, Esq., Fleetwood.
Charles Blades, Esq., Dalton Square, | John Sharp, Esq., Lancaster.
  Lancaster.

One-third of the directors retire in March, 1868 (to be settled by ballot), and
one-third every subsequent year at the meeting in March.

OFFICERS.—Sec., J. Oldfield; Manager, W. C. Shackleford; Solicitor, Lawrence
Holden.

Offices—Lancaster.

610.—LONDON FINANCIAL.

Capital subscribed, 2,000,000*l*.; paid-up, 1,178,487*l*.

It was reported in July that the shock railway credit received in the course of the last two years had been so great, and the recovery so much more protracted than anticipated, the directors come to the conclusion, after most careful consideration, that it would not be expedient longer to hold out a prospect of transacting new business. Hence, the Association has now, from the force of circumstances, practically merged into what may be considered an Investment Company ; and acting upon this view, they give their special attention to the reduction of expenses.

The report for the half-year ending the 31st of December stated that the total liabilities, less 12,256*l*. cash balance at bankers, now amounted to about 242,000*l*., and were secured. The liabilities would have been greatly reduced in amount, but the Board were most anxious not to sacrifice securities, considering that the property was improving, and that they had the expectation in the ensuing half-year of being in receipt of a considerable sum of money. The overdue interest claimed by the association amounted to 114,000*l*., of which there had been received in the past half-year 14,633*l*. in the shape of debenture stock. Of the remainder of such interest in arrear about 30,000*l*. was subject to a legal decision, which it was expected would shortly be given. The Association now held securities to the nominal amount of 2,290,726*l*., consisting of 246,365*l*. in debentures, 124,711*l*. in debenture stock, 223,540*l*. in Lloyd's bonds, 724,020*l*. in preference shares, and 972,090*l*. in ordinary shares.

CAPITAL.—The balance sheet to 30th June presented the following details of income and expenditure :—

Debtor.—15*l*. per share on 40,000 shares £600,000
39,525 shares for 4th call 197,625
38,699 shares for 5th call, due 10th July, 1866 193,495
37,535 shares for 6th call, due 15th May, 1867......... 187,367= £1,178,487
Liabilities : Loans and deposits, for fixed periods 159,976
Bills re-discounted.................................. 65,000
Bills payable...................................... 25,000
Debentures and interest thereon 5,550
Open accounts .... 860=   256,387= £1,434,875

Creditor.—Cash at bankers and in office................................. £15,227
Sundry debtors, for amounts owing £1,084,267
Less, balance at credit of "Special Suspense Account"......... 45,669= 1,038,597
Collaterally secured by the undermentioned debentures, bonds,
&c., of the "face" value of 1,719,455*l*., viz.:—
Railway Companies'   "Face" Value.
    Debentures £162,170
    Lloyd's bonds.................................. 193,335
    Preference shares 337,380
    Preferred shares 273,500
    Ordinary shares 625,470
    Deferred shares .... 127,600=£1,719,455
Property belonging to the Association   379,701
Railway Companies'   "Face" Value.
    Debentures................................£172,895
    Lloyd's bonds................................. 56,805
    Preference shares 74,800
    Preferred shares 5,000
    Ordinary shares 64,220
    Deferred shares 5,000
                                                    ————
                                                  £378,720
Other Companies'
    Preference shares 33,340
    Ordinary shares .... 123,200=   535,260

            Total securities £2,254,715
Rebate account   1,348
                                                                           ————
                                                                         £1,434,875

DIRECTORS :

John Borradaile, Esq., Gloucester Place, Portman Square, W.
E. Ehret Dyson, Esq., 18, Elvaston Place, London.
Thomas Powell, Esq.

James Fraser, Esq. (Messrs. J. & L. Fraser and Co.)
John Hackblock, Esq.
George Young, Esq.

OFFICERS.—Sec., John Henry Koch ; Manager, J. B. Dunn ; Eng., J. H. Tolmé
Auditors, John Ball and Robert Tucker ; Solicitors, Maynard, Son, and Co.; Bankers,
City Bank, Threadneedle Street, E.C., and Imperial Bank.
    Offices—South Sea House, Threadneedle Street, E.C.

611.—LONDON AND PROVINCIAL TELEGRAPH.

This company (limited) is established for the purpose of affording to the metropolis
and its immediate suburbs expeditious and inexpensive telegraphic communication,
To effect this, the city and its suburbs have been divided into districts, each of which
will contain one chief or central station, in addition to sub-district stations, of which
84 are in operation. The wires in operation extend to 345 miles.

An agreement has been concluded with the British and Irish Magnetic and the
Submarine Telegraph for an interchange of traffic, by which a large amount of business
is secured.

The dividend on the 10l. preference shares continues to be paid, but the expectations
of the ordinary shareholders are confined to the purchase of the property by Government.

CAPITAL.—The balance sheet to 30th June represented a receipt and expenditure of
67,804l. The capital account is constituted as follows :—

Paid up £54,550
Shares unissued, 1,090 at 5l.. 5,450
Preference shares issued .... 10,000= £70,000

DIRECTORS :

Chairman—GEORGE SHEWARD, Esq., Leinster Square, Bayswater, W.

Vice-Chairman—CHARLES KEMP DYER, Esq., Lloyd's, E.C.

Charles Reynolds, Esq., Carshalton, S. | William Austin, Esq., Farningham, Kent.
R. P. Taylor, Esq.

OFFICERS.—Sec. and Man., Charles Curtoys ; Auditors, Edward Sandell, Sise
Lane, Bucklersbury, E.C., and Henry Chatteris, Basinghall Street ; Solicitors, Johnson,
Farquhar, and Leech, Moorgate Street, E.C.

Offices—101, Cannon Street, E.C.

612.—METROPOLITAN RAILWAY CARRIAGE AND WAGON.

Capital, 300,000l. in 30,000 shares of 10l. each, with power to borrow 50,000l. This
company is established for the building or purchasing of engines, carriages, wagons, and
other rolling stock, and the disposing of, leasing, or hiring of the same to railway companies, colliery owners, freighters, and others, and it has purchased, and carries on the
business and manufactory of, the firm of Messrs. Joseph Wright and Sons, at Saltley,
near Birmingham.

DIRECTORS :

Samuel Thornton, Esq., Camp Hill, Bir-
    mingham.
William E. Everitt, Esq., Finstall, Broms-
    grove.
Thomas Phillips, Esq., Edgbaston, Bir-
    mingham.
C. L. Browning, Esq., Weoley Park, near
    Birmingham.
Joseph Wright, Esq., Surbiton, Surrey, S.W.

Edwin Gwyther, Esq., Edgbaston, Bir-
    mingham.
Daniel S. Hasluck, Esq., St. Paul's Square,
    Birmingham.
William Holliday, Esq., New Street, Bir-
    mingham.
James Watson, Esq., Edgbaston, Birming-
    ham.

OFFICERS.—Sec., F. S. Taylor ; Gen. Man., Henry Brown ; Auditor, Edwin Laundy,
Accountant, Birmingham ; Solicitors, Beale, Marigold, and Beale, Birmingham.

    Chief Office—Saltley Works, Birmingham ; London Office, 27, Great George Street,
Westminster, S.W.

613.—METROPOLITAN RAILWAY WAREHOUSING.

Incorporated under the Limited Liability Act, and in immediate connection with the
Metropolitan Railway. Capital 600,000l., in 30,000 shares of 20l. each. (with power of
increase). First issue 20,000 shares of 20l. each.

This undertaking was introduced under the auspices of the Metropolitan Railway to
supply warehouse accommodation in the metropolis, in connection with the railway
system, and to take advantage of the unoccupied ground near Farringdon Road, and
the works in progress there, for introduction into the heart of the metropolis of a block
of buildings on a scale of unusual magnitude, to combine railway communication below,
warehousing accommodation above, and a range of exhibition galleries on the upper-
most storey. In abeyance.

CAPITAL.—The statement of receipts and expenditure to 30th June presented particulars as follow:—

Received.		Expended.	
Share capital	£30,222	To 31st December, 1867	£4,257
Interest from Imperial Mercantile Credit	399	Less—interest received	628
Interest from St. John's Wood	185		£3,629
Interest on Deposit	11	Interest on share capital	891
		Office expenses	150
			£4,670
		Cash at Bankers	6,686
		Loan to Metropolitan and St. John's Wood on debenture bonds bearing interest at 5 per cent.	5,000
		Balance deposit with Imperial Mercantile Credit	14,461
	£30,818		£30,818

DIRECTORS:

Chairman—JOHN PARSON, Esq., Bitton House, Teignmouth, Devonshire.

Deputy-Chairman—GEORGE HENRY WALKER, Esq., Avon Lodge, Newbold-on-Avon, Rugby.

George Kingston Barton, Esq., M.D., 5, Windsor Terrace, Bedford.
Mr. Alderman Dakin, 2 and 3, Cree Church Lane, Leadenhall Street.
Charles Gilpin, Esq., M.P., Bedford Square.
Mr. Alderman Hale, 71, Queen Street, Cheapside.
Sir Kingsmill Key, Bart., 95, Newgate Street.
Alexander Clunes Sherriff, Esq., M.P., 10, Dean's Yard, Westminster, S.W., and Perdiswell Hall, Worcester.

OFFICERS.—Sec., John Henchman; Engs., John Fowler and Thomas Marr Johnson; Contractor for the Works, John Kelk; Auditors, B. J. Armstrong and G. W. Jones; Solicitors, Messrs. Burchell, 5, Broad Sanctuary, Westminster, S.W.

Offices—3, Old Palace Yard, Westminster, S.W.

614.—MIDLAND WAGON.

The dividends declared are at the rate of 15 per cent. per annum. The balance carried forward from 30th June last was 11,950l. The directors explained that in not dividing the whole of the profits, they desired to form a fund or rest, which would equalize the dividends in the event of any half-year's profits not showing a sufficient amount for this purpose. In availing themselves to a small extent of this balance standing to the credit of old revenue, the directors remarked that the extraordinary depression in the carriage and wagon trade of the country during the past year has but slightly affected their usual profits.

CAPITAL.—The balance sheet to 30th June furnished the following debtor and creditor account:—

Debtor.		Creditor.	
Amount due on debentures	£153,338	Rolling stock, at cost price	£492,429
Interest thereon	3,640	Freehold land and works	17,067
	£156,978	Plant, machinery, &c.	6,219
Loans on deposit and interest	20,025	Stock of materials, carriages, and wagons in course of construction	13,719
Debts due to sundry persons	11,601	Estimated value of securities	32,969
Amount due to bankers	13,155	Amount due from sundry persons, for rents due at midsummer, 1868	10,866
Amount due to shareholders, viz.:—		Arrears	11,818
On ordinary shares	120,000		£22,685
On new shares	40,000	Amount due from sundry debtors	9,728
Contingent fund	2,971		
Reserve fund for renewal of wagons, as per last report 190,399l. Amount set aside this year, 52,525l.=242,925l. Less depreciation on wagons sold during the year, written-off wagon stock, 37,788=£205,136			
Reserve fund, for depreciation on works, plant, &c.	1,000		
Balance of revenue account	23,950		
	£594,819		£594,819

DIRECTORS :

Chairman—WILLIAM OWEN, Esq., Clifton House, Rotherham.

Matthias Royce Griffin, Esq., Soho Park, Handsworth, Birmingham.
William Allen Boulnois, Esq., 6, Waterloo Place, Pall Mall, London.
Frederick Isaac Welch, Esq., The Firs, Moseley, Birmingham.
William Alexander Adams, Esq., Newbold Beeches, Leamington.

Henry Griffiths, Esq., The Mount, Edgbaston, Birmingham.
Joseph Scrivener Keep, Esq., Westmere, Edgbaston, Birmingham.
William Shakespear, Esq., Westwood House, Camp Hill, Birmingham.

OFFICERS.—Secretary, Henry Bridges; Auditors, Quilter, Ball, and Co. Offices—Birmingham.

615.—NATIONAL DISCOUNT.

Capital, 159,576l., in shares of 25l. each; paid up, 5l. per share. The dividends for the year have been at the rate of 15 per cent. per annum.

CAPITAL.—The balance sheet to 30th June furnished the following details of receipts and expenditure :—

Received.		*Expended.*	
159,576 shares of 25l. each, 5l. per share paid	£797,880	Cash, Government, and other securities	£535,374
Reserve fund	497,880	Loans at call and short date	636,902
Liabilities on deposits, loans, &c.	6,952,247	Bills discounted	7,095,115
Under acceptance	552	Premises	44,243
Premises redemption fund	1,200		
At credit of profit & loss account	61,874		
	£8,311,634		£8,311,634

TRUSTEES :

George Burnand, Esq. | Matthew Hutton Chaytor, Esq.

DIRECTORS :

Chairman—FRANCIS WILLIAM RUSSELL. Esq., M.P., 27, Lancaster Gate, W.
Deputy-Chairman—MATTHEW HUTTON CHAYTOR, Esq.

George Burnand, Esq.
Charles Richard Fenwick, Esq.
Alexander Mackenzie, Esq.
George Nicholas, Esq.

William James Thompson, Esq.
John Robert Thomson, Esq.
Henry Heyman Toulmin, Esq.
Frederick Charles Wilkins, Esq.

OFFICERS.—Sec., Richard Price; Man., Robert Pullen Webber; Solicitors, Thomas and Hollams; Bankers, The Bank of England, and Union Bank of London. Offices—33, Cornhill, E.C.

616.—NERBUDDA COAL AND IRON.

Registered under Limited Liability, with a capital of 250,000l., in shares of 20l. each. 12,500 shares with 6l. paid. Call due 14th February, 1l.

This company is formed, with the sanction of the Secretary of State for India, for the purpose of working certain mines of coal and iron at Mopani and Tendukera, in the Nerbudda Valley, and near the line of the Great Indian Peninsula. The company received from the Government a concession of the mines upon favourable terms, a nominal rental of 10l. or 100 rupees per annum being paid for the first five years, to be increased to 1,000 rupees per annum after that period, and to merge in the royalties payable after the fifth year, and afterwards a moderate royalty of 4 annas or 6d. per ton on coal sold, and 1 rupee or 2s. per ton on all iron manufactured.

The preparatory works of the company are still in progress, but it is expected to begin to supply coal in the course of the year.

CAPITAL.—The statement of receipts and expenditure, as reported in May, gave the subjoined particulars :—

Receipts.

Share Capital—12,058 shares, 6l. paid	£72,348
10 ,, 20l. ,,	200
12,068	£72,548
Less arrears of second call	£5
Ditto third ,,	20
Ditto fourth ,,	234
Ditto fifth ,,	6,219 = 6,478 = 66,070
Interest on bankers' balances	93
Profit on exchanges	152
Coal sales—sundry sales to contractors, lime, &c.	935
Transfer fees—on registration of shares	23
	£67,275

Expenditure.

Expenditure as per last balance sheet	£52,131
Block and plant	2,257
Building, new bungalow bridge, godown, &c.	718
Furniture and fixtures, England and India	16
Advertising ditto	9
General expenses, office rent, &c.	1,191
Law expenses	114
Directors' fees	£475
Secretary, clerk's salaries, &c.	405
Indian agent's salary	3,017 = 3,898
Mining expenses, shafts, borings, &c.	2,906
Investments	350
Balances: Bankers—Bombay	£404
Calcutta	197
	£602
Less due to native bankers	41
	£560
Agents and manager	1,233
Bankers and petty cash	2,938
	£4,731
Bills receivable	300
	£5,031
Less bills payable	1,250 = 3,781
	£67,275

DIRECTORS:

Chairman—HENRY HAYMEN, Esq., Clarendon Road, Kensington, W.

F. Egerton Cutler, Esq. (Messrs. Cutler, Palmer, and Co.)
Major-General D. Downing, 36, Gloucester Terrace, Hyde Park, W.

S. Lloyd Foster, Esq., Old Park Hall, Walsall, Staffordshire.
Samuel John Wilde, Esq., Hadley Green, Barnet, S.E.

Two Directors retire every year, but are eligible and always re-elected.

OFFICERS.—Sec., Herbert Heath; Manager, W. H. Simpson; Auditors, J. Waddell and Co., Public Accountants, New Poultry Chambers, E.C.: Bankers in London, The Imperial Bank, Lothbury, E.C., in India, The Chartered Mercantile Bank of India, London, and China; Solicitors, Wilkins, Blyth, and Marsland, 10, Swithins Lane, E.C.

Offices—35A, Moorgate Street, E.C.

617.—RAILWAY CARRIAGE.

Capital, 150,000l. in 15,000 shares at 10l. each, and preference share capital, 75,000l. in 15,000 shares of 5l. each. Established for the purpose of constructing, repairing, selling, hiring, and letting of plant, wagons, carriages, and rolling stock for railways, tramways, and ordinary roads. For the making, selling and letting of girders, roofs, machinery, and all kinds of ironwork, and for the working of railways and tramways.

DIRECTORS:

Chairman—RICHARD WILLIAM JOHNSON, Esq., Bricklehampton Hall, Pershore.

Deputy-Chairman—ALEXANDER CLUNES SHERRIFF, Esq., M.P., Perdiswell Hall, near Worcester, and 10, Dean's Yard, Westminster, S.W.

William Edward Hilliard, Esq., Cowley House, Uxbridge.
John Kershaw, Esq., 24, Duke Street, Westminster, S.W.

George Allen Everitt, Esq., Kingston Metal Works, Birmingham.

OFFICERS.—Sec., Herbert Wheeler; Man., William Stableford; Solicitors, Dale and Stretton, 3, Gray's Inn Square, W.C.

Offices—Oldbury, near Birmingham; and 6, Storey's Gate, Great George Street, Westminster, S.W.

618.—STAFFORDSHIRE ROLLING STOCK.

Capital, 50,000l., in 5,000 shares of 10l. each. Established for the purpose of constructing, purchasing, maintaining, and leasing carriages and wagons to railway companies, collieries, and commercial firms in the United Kingdom and elsewhere; and for the purchase of an established local company of the same description, having a paid-up capital of nearly 10,000l.

DIRECTORS :

Chairman—GEORGE FAGG, Esq., Highbury, N.

D. Fraser Luckie, Esq., Ashley Place, Westminster, S. W.
J. Evan Tibbs, Threadneedle Street, E.C., and Bylock Hall, Middlesex.

William Watkin, Esq., Amblecote Hall, Stourbridge.
Samuel Brooks, Esq., Hagley Road, Stourbridge.

OFFICERS—Sec., William Ketley ; Auditor, Charles Tackness, Lime Street Square, E.C. ; Solicitor, John Scott, King William Street, E.C.

Offices—48, Lombard Street, E.C.

619.—STAFFORDSHIRE WHEEL AND AXLE COMPANY, LIMITED.

Capital, 400,000*l.* in 20,000 shares of 20*l.* each, established for the manufacture of wrought and cast-iron railway carriage, wagon, and contractor's wheels and axles, and other iron-work used in the construction of railway rolling stock; also, of hammered uses, forgings, and smith work of every description, either for marine, locomotive, stationary, or other engineering purposes.

DIRECTORS :

Edmund Broughton, Esq., Handsworth, near Birmingham.
Charles Lloyd Browning, Esq., Weoley Park, Birmingham.
William Edward Everitt, Esq., Kingston Metal Works, Birmingham.
William Holliday, Esq., Birmingham.

Ralph Heaton, Esq., Harborne, near Birmingham.
Joshua Horton, Esq., Handsworth, near Birmingham.
Frederick Isaac Welch, Esq., Moseley, near Birmingham.

OFFICERS.—Sec., R. Henry Ryland ; Auditors, Roberts, Malins, and Colman, Accountants, Birmingham ; Solicitors, Sanders and Smith, Dudley.

Offices and Works—Spring Hill, Birmingham ; London Office, 113, Cannon St., E.C.

620.—SUBMARINE TELEGRAPH.

Between Great Britain and the continent of Europe, in connection with the British and Irish Magnetic Telegraph. This company was projected in 1857, as a "*Société en commandite,*" and the promoters succeeded in obtaining concessions of exclusive telegraphic communications with France and Belgium for the space of ten years. The original concession granted by the French Government, and which would have expired in 1862, has recently been extended 30 years, dating from January, 1859. The company possesses six distinct means of telegraphic communication by submarine cables between England and the continent of Europe. The routes are as follow :—From Dover to Calais ; from Dover to Ostend; from Folkestone to Boulogne ; from Dover to La Paune (for Hamburg, &c.) ; from Cromer to Tonning (Denmark) ; from Jersey to Coutances (France).

Dividend on the ordinary stock at the rate of 5 per cent. Arrangements for purchase by Government under the Act of 1868.

CAPITAL.—The receipts and expenditure on this account to 30th June, 1868, have been as under :—

Debtor.		Creditor.	
Capital........................	£265,000	Sum expended on capital account........................	381,695
Debenture bonds...............	84,635		
Seven per cent. preference stock	35,000	Debenture bonds paid off in excess of the sum provided by the redemption fund..............	550
Redemption fund	4,353		
Interest on debenture bonds	1,851	Sundry debtors.................	6,27
Dividend on 7 per cent. preference stock	1,225	Repairs to cables...............	183
Sundry creditors	2,929	Proportion of receipts	13,837
Interest on preference stock unpaid	4		
Dividends unpaid	693		
Proposed dividends	6,625		
Balance to new account	230		
	£402,547		£402,547

DIRECTORS :

Chairman—Sir JAMES ROBERT CARMICHAEL, Bart., 58, Threadneedle Street, E.C., and 12, Sussex Place, Regent's Park, N.W.

Francis Edwards, Esq.
Captain Grant, R.A.
Samuel Gurney, Esq.
Henry Moor, Esq.

Hon. Ashley Ponsonby.
Charles Saunderson, Esq.
A. J. Otway, Esq., M.P., 9, Harley Street, W.

OFFICERS.—Sec., Stephen Mc.Donnell Clare ; Acting Eng., James Robert France ;
Auditors, Mr. Alderman Dakin, George Copeland Capper, and Wm. R. Cole.
Offices—58, Threadneedle Street, E.C.

621.—TELEGRAPH CONSTRUCTION AND MAINTENANCE.

Established under Limited Liability, with a capital of 1,000,000l. in shares of 20l. each.
The dividends have been at the rate of 10 per cent.

DIRECTORS:

Chairman—Sir DANIEL GOOCH, Bart., M.P., C.E., Maida Hill, W.

Managing Director—Captain SHERARD OSBORN, C.B., R.N., 119, Gloucester
Terrace, Hyde Park, W.

Alexander H. Campbell, Esq., 43, Lowndes Square, Knightsbridge, S.W.
Ralph Elliot, Esq. (Glass, Elliot, and Co.), 31, Chester Square.
Captain Lord John Hay, M.P., R.N., Apsley House, Piccadilly, W.

John Pender, Esq., Crumpsall House, Crumpsall, near Manchester.
Philip Rawson, Esq., Woodhurst, Crawley, Sussex.
John Smith, Esq. (Smith, Fleming, & Co.), 18, Leadenhall Street.

Secretary—William Shuter, Esq.

Offices—54, Old Broad Street, E.C.

622.—TELEGRAPH TO INDIA.

This enterprise is leased to the Telegraph Construction and Maintenance Company (Limited).

The report presented on 5th February, 1869, gave the details of a provisional agreement entered into for leasing the land line in Egypt to the proposed British-Indian Submarine.

DIRECTORS:

Chairman—Sir R. MACDONALD STEPHENSON, 72, Lancaster Gate, Hyde Park, W.

Philip Patten Blyth, Esq. (late of Mauritius), 53, Wimpole Street, Cavendish Square, W.
The Hon. James Byng, Shipbourne Lodge, Tunbridge, Kent.

William Dent, Esq. (late of the Hon. East India Company's Civil Service, Bengal).
Admiral Sir W. H. Hall, K.C.B. (Director of the Peninsular & Oriental Company).
John Farley Leith, Esq. (late of Calcutta), 79, Gloucester Terrace, Hyde Park, W.

OFFICERS.—Sec., William Mayo ; Auditor, J. A. Franklin ; Engs., Sir Charles T. Bright and Latimer Clark ; Solicitors, Messrs. Freshfields ; Bankers, The London and County Bank.
Offices—62, Moorgate Street, E.C.

623.—THAMES SUBWAY.

Incorporated by 29 and 30 Vic., cap. 177 (16th July, 1866), for making and maintaining a subway, under the river Thames, from Deptford to the Isle of Dogs. Length, 582 yards, with various roads and approaches. Capital, 255,000l., in 10l. shares, and 33,000l. on loan. It is stated that the whole of the shares have been subscribed for ; that the costs of the Act were very moderate, the total liabilities incurred, including parliamentary, engineering, and all preliminary expenses, not exceeding 1,600l. ; while the total expenses have been 2,000l.

Meetings in February or March, and in August or September.

No. of Directors—5 : minimum, 3 ; quorum, 3 and 2. *Qualification,* 300l.

DIRECTORS:

John Gladstone Devonport, Esq.
James Edward M'Connell, Esq.

Hutton Vignoles, Esq.
Piers Frederick Legh, Esq.

624.—UNITED KINGDOM TELEGRAPH.

This company is incorporated by special Act of Parliament, and registered under the Joint Stock Companies Acts, Limited Liability. Capital, 250,000l. in 50,000 shares of 5l. each. The company also issues perpetual bonds paying the interest at 7½ per cent. per annum in frank stamps, franking messages as postage stamps frank letters.

The works are now in direct communication, by submarine telegraph, with Denmark, Norway, Sweden, and the southern coasts of Russia.

A dividend at the rate of 2 per cent. per annum was declared on the ordinary stock in August last. The mileage of line owned by the company extends to 1,677, and of wire to 10,001. This company is also subjected to future arrangements under the Government Act of 1868.

CAPITAL.—The balance sheet to 30th June, 1868, presented the subjoined detail of income and expenditure :—

Debtor.

Share capital £137,480
Preference shares, 10 per cent. 5,060
    Do.   6   ,, ... 7,895
    Do. New 10 ,, ... 100,000
Perpetual bonds £48,744
Ten years' bonds .... 500= 49,244
Debentures.. 21,503
Debenture 6 per cent. loan.......................... 19,032
Sundry creditors—Bills payable £1,173
              Sundry balances .... 9,985= 11,159
Dividends as per profit and loss account 6,864
Balance of profit and loss account .... 137=£358,376

Creditor.

Total cost of construction, &c., of the United Kingdom
    Electric Telegraph, December 31st, 1867 .... £336,198
Additional as per details in report..................... 3,723=£339,922
Fixtures and furniture at central office and stations...... 4,445
Stock of materials on hand .... 5,691= 10,137
Leasehold property... 892
Cash at Bankers' and in hand 3,947
Sundry balances .... 3,476=£358,376

DIRECTORS:

Chairman—ALEXANDER ANGUS CROLL, Esq., C.E., Coleman Street, E.C.

Deputy-Chairman—Admiral Sir HENRY J. LEEKE, K.C.B., K.H.

Lord Alfred Spencer Churchill, Rutland Gate, Hyde Park, W.
Colonel William Elsey, H.E.I.C.S., The Green, Ealing, W.
The Hon. Ralph Harbord, Gunton Park, Norwich.
Professor D. E. Hughes.

Robt. Bryce Hay, Esq., Huntingdon Lodge, Spring Grove, Isleworth.
Edward Greaves, Esq., Avonside, Warwick.
Edward W. H. Schenley, Esq., 14, Prince's Gate, W.
George Virtue, Esq., Oatlands Park, Walton-on-Thames.

Man. and Sec., W. Andrews.
Central Offices—237, Gresham House, Old Broad Street, E.C.

ADDENDA.

AUSTRIA.

TRAFFIC.—The receipts on the South Austrian lines from the 1st January to the 31st of December, 1868, amounted on 1,172 miles to 2,794,057l., and for the same period of 1867 on 1,090 miles, to 2,302,297l., showing an increase of 82 miles, and of 491,760l., or 21.3 per cent. The total traffic receipts on the Upper Italy railways, including the Venetian lines, amounted on 1,480 miles of railway, for the year 1868, to 2,162,615l., and on 1,400 miles, for the year 1867, to 2,090,159l., showing an increase of 72,456l. The aggregate receipts on both lines, 2,652 miles in length, amounted for the year 1868, to 4,956,672l., or 1,896l. per mile; and for the year 1867, on 2,490 miles of railway, to 4,392,456l., or 1,764l. per mile, showing an increase of 564,216l,, or 105l. per mile.

FRANCE.

TRAFFIC.—The traffic receipts on the *Paris and Mediterranean* for the year 1868 amounted on the old and new lines, 2,423 miles in length, to 8,655,367l., and on 2,330 miles for the year 1867 to 8,363,266l., showing an increase of 292,101l. The receipts on the *Paris and Orleans* amounted for the year 1868 on the old and new lines, 2,091 miles in length, to 4,309,767l., and on 1.851 miles for the year 1867 to 4,213,372l., showing an increase of 96,395l. The receipts on the old and new lines of the *Eastern of France,* 1,671 miles in length, amounted to 4,261,483l., and for the year 1867, on 1,650 miles, to 4,198,220l., showing an increase of 63,263l. The receipts on the old and new lines of the *Northern of France,* 887 miles in length, amounted to 3,635,675l., and for the year 1867, on the same mileage, to 3,733,000l., showing a decrease of 97,325l. The receipts on the old and new lines of the *Western of France,* 1.342 miles in length, amounted to

3,285,120*l*., and for the year 1867, on 1,305 miles in length, to 3,380,255*l*., showing a decrease of 95,135*l*.; and on the old and new lines of the *Southern of France*, 1,006 miles in length, to 1,886,589*l*., and for the year 1867, on the same mileage, to 1,760,484*l*., showing an increase of 126,105*l*. The total receipts on the six principal railways in France for the year amounted, on 9,420 miles, to 26,034,001*l*., and for the year 1867, on 9,029 miles in length, to 25,648,597*l*., showing an increase of 391 miles and of 385,404*l*. The traffic receipts on the *Paris and Mediterranean* for the year 1868 averaged 3,572*l*. per mile; on the railways of the Northern of France, 4,099*l*. per mile; on the Paris and Orleans, 2,061*l*. per mile: on the Eastern of France, 2,550*l*. per mile; on the Western of France, 2,448*l*. per mile; and on the Southern of France, 1,875*l*. per mile. The average receipts on the whole amounted to 2,764*l*. per mile in 1868, against 2,842*l*. per mile in 1867.

ATLANTIC AND GREAT WESTERN—LEASE TO ERIE.

This Indenture, made this seventh day of December, 1868, between the Atlantic and Great Western, party of the first part, and the Erie, party of the second part :

Witnesseth, that for the period of twelve years from this date, the party of the first part hath leased and rented, and by these presents doth demise, lease, and let unto the party of the second part, its successors and assigns, the railroad of the party of the first part, and all the land of the party of the first part, from and including Salamanca in the State of New York, to and including the present terminus at Dayton, in the State of Ohio, and at all points in any State or States between the termini of said railroad, and all branches or leased lines of railroad which now are or may hereafter be in operation, including all equipment and property of every name and kind belonging to or in anywise appertaining unto said railroad and branches.

And also so much of the franchises and privileges of the party of the first part as may be necessary, or as are usually exercised in and about the operation of a railroad, or may be necessary for the construction, repair, and improvement, or for the operation of such railroad, or any extension of the same, or any branch or branches thereof, and to collect, demand, and receive all tolls and emoluments thereof during said term ; and all such franchises as are usually exercised by railroad companies in protecting and securing to itself the full use and enjoyment of such railroad either in the States of New York, Pennsylvania, or Ohio.

The party of the first part reserves to itself the franchises of being a corporation and of keeping up its organization, and the right to defend and maintain suits, and to take all requisite steps for the protection of its rights as a corporation, and of its shareholders.

Said party of the second part paying, or causing to be paid, as and for rent of the aforesaid railroad property and premises, thirty per cent. of the gross earnings of said line and branches, as now, or hereafter in operation, and as hereby demised, such payments to be made quarterly on the fifteenth days of April, July, October, and January, at the office of the party of the second part in the city of New York.

And the party of the second part agrees that it will use all reasonable efforts to develope and increase thereby both the local and through business of the said demised railroad and branches.

And whereas, by a decree or order of the Court of Commons Pleas, in the county of Trumbull and State of Ohio, made in November, 1868, in the case of Samuel Gurney and others, against the Atlantic and Great Western and others, the same decree or order in the same action being also made by the Supreme Court at Special Term of the State of New York, held at Buffalo, on the 22nd day of October, 1868 ; the same decree having also been made in the State of Pennsylvania ; by which said orders and decrees it is provided that the debts of the Receiver in said action, as per schedule hereto annexed, must be paid before a delivery of the said railroad and its property can be made by said Receiver over unto the officers of the said Atlantic and Great Western ; and whereas the party of the second part has advanced and paid said moneys as provided in said decree.

Now, therefore, the said party of the second is by these presents placed in the stead of the said receiver, with the same rights to protect itself for the moneys thus advanced to pay the said receiver's debts, as the said receiver now has or could have, with all the rights, privileges, and privities of the said receiver to secure the said debts now paid by the party of the second part ; and the said party of the second part hereby has a prior right, and a mortgage lien upon the said demised property and franchises of the party of the first part, to secure the party of the second part for the cash advance above mentioned.

Provided always, that if the rent above reserved, or any part thereof, shall remain unpaid for sixty days after any day of payment when the same ought to be paid as herein agreed, then and from thenceforth it shall be lawful for the parties of the first part, their successors and assigns, having first repaid the moneys advanced by the said Erie as above specified into and upon the said demised premises and property of every kind, and every part thereof, absolutely to re-enter and remove all persons therefrom, and the same to have again, repossess, and enjoy as in their former state ; anything herein contained to the contrary notwithstanding.

And thereupon this indenture, and all the provisions herein contained and the estate herein created, are by these declared to be and the same shall be henceforth forfeited, and shall cease and determine, except so far as to enable the parties of the first part to collect the rent due or unpaid up to the time this indenture is so forfeited and determined ; and also any damages the said party of the first part may sustain by reason of the failure of the party of the second part to perform this lease or any of its covenants : and the said parties of the first part may thereupon forthwith actually re-enter and take and keep actual possession of the said demised premises and property, and each and every part thereof, without delay or legal process.

The said parties of the second part, and their successors, agree to pay, bear, and discharge all taxes and assessments of every name and kind which may be lawfully levied, assessed, or imposed on said demised premises and property, or on the use or occupation thereof, or on the income the party of the second part may receive or derive therefrom, and have the parties of the first part harmless therefrom, and the demised premises and property from sale or forfeiture for the non-payment thereof. The said parties of the second part will hereafter, at their own expense, maintain and keep in operating condition the said railroad, and everything therewith connected or which properly belongs to the said railroad of the party of the first part, using the same in a legal and proper manner, and doing all the acts for the preservation of the franchises, rights, property, and interest of the said Atlantic and Great Western which good faith, fair dealing, and the laws require.

And the said parties of the second part, their successors and assigns, hereby agree that at the expiration or other sooner determination of the term hereby granted, they will surrender said railway with all the depots, stations, shops, grounds, buildings, structures, appurtenances, engines, machinery, equipments, and all other property hereby demised to them under and by virtue of this indenture, in as good state and condition as when they received the same; but the party of the second part is not bound to surrender or return any property to which the title of the party of the first part may have terminated, unless said title shall have been again invested in the party of the first part at its own expense.

And it is mutually agreed by the parties hereto, that if any difference of opinion shall arise as to the true intent and meaning of this contract, or as to any difference which may arise under it in any manner legitimately connected herewith, that all such questions, disputes and differences shall be referred to three arbitrators, one to be chosen by the party of the first part, one by the party of the second part, and a third by the two chosen as aforesaid, and the decision of a majority of said arbitrators, given in writing and signed by two of the said arbitrators, shall be binding and final upon the parties hereto.

Possession of the demised premises is to be delivered to the party of the second part on the final execution of this agreement.

The London Board of Directors notified in February that the lease of the line to the Erie having been made, their functions came to an end. The agreement for the lease was made in America, and they have, therefore, had no opportunity of acting. They simply forwarded to the bondholders a copy of it, together with copies of the supplemental leases, mentioning at the same time that a lease of the Columbus Chicago and Indiana Central was also received, but that a telegram, since arrived, states that it has not been ratified by the shareholders of that company. Finally, the Board remark :—
"These documents speak for themselves, and every bondholder may judge from them of the actual position of affairs respecting which the directors do not wish to express any opinion, lest it should prejudice questions in dispute between the Atlantic and Great Western and Erie. They only think it right to add that they do not doubt that the president, Mr. Stebbins, the American Board, and Mr. M'Henry, who have struggled with great energy with many difficulties and discouragements, have made what they consider the best arrangements practicable under the circumstances."

Of the agreements with the Erie, the supplemental lease, of which the following is an abstract, is the most important. The first merely provides for the transfer of the Atlantic and Great Western, and all its branches, for a rent of 30 per cent. of the gross earnings :—

"This agreement, made this 7th day of December, 1868, between the Atlantic and Great Western of the first part, the Erie of the second part, and James M'Henry of the third part, witnesseth :—That, whereas by lease this day executed between the parties of the first and second part, the party of the first part for the term of twelve years did demise unto the party of the second part the Atlantic and Great Western, its property, &c., for the specific provisions of which said lease reference is thereunto had. And whereas 30 per cent. of the gross earnings of said road are agreed to be given as rent without any mention of particular amount, now, therefore, in consideration of the premises of said contract above mentioned, the three parties hereunto have mutually agreed as follows :—

"1. The Erie agree that the annual rent shall not be less than $1,800,000 per annum, to be paid quarterly.

"2. If in any year the cost of operating the road shall be less than 70 per cent, such actual per centage shall be taken as the basis for the ensuing year.

"3. If in any year the 30 per cent. shall not amount to $1,800,000, the deficiency shall be charged to the Atlantic and Great Western, and deducted from the excess over $1,800,000, and such advance to constitute a lien upon the Atlantic and Great Western, its personal property and franchises, until repaid from earnings in future years.

"4. The Erie are to furnish the Atlantic and Great Western suitable offices in New York, stationery, &c., and to pay the President a salary of $5,000 for attending to the business and keeping up the organisation of the company.

"5. The Erie are to advance to Atlantic and Great Western on account of the rent to fall due during the year 1859, $800,000, to be used in payment of debts underlying debentures.

"6. The rent in the aforementioned lease to be paid by the Erie to the Atlantic and Great Western shall commence from the date possession of the said demised property is fully vested in the Erie.

"7. Rates and fares to be the same for both companies, and to be divided equally per mile, and the Erie to render monthly to Atlantic and Great Western accurate accounts of the traffic it may carry over its line or any part thereof."

GREAT WESTERN OF CANADA.

The following memorandum was issued in the course of January, 1869 :—

After a protracted negotiation, the directors of the Great Western of Canada have the satisfaction of informing the shareholders, that they have received a communication from the Government stating that definite terms had been arrived at, for the settlement of the provincial advance, made to this company in 1853-55, as well as for the accumulated interest thereon which has now become a claim of the Dominion of Canada.

The arrangement as concluded, the Government is willing to submit to the consideration of the Canadian Parliament.

The outline of the settlement is that the Government will receive payment of the principal sum of 573,687*l*. 15*s*. in full by four annual instalments, with interest at 4 per cent. per annum, and in addition thereto the old interest in arrear is to be calculated at the same annual rate as the dividend earned and payable to the shareholders. Thus the Government will be placed, as regards the arrears of interest, on an equal footing with the shareholders, since the company ceased in 1860 to make its half-yearly payments of interest to the Government of 6 per cent. per annum.

Payment to be made as follows :—100,000*l*. (which includes the commuted arrears of interest), to be paid on February 10th, 1869, and the balance of the capital in four equal annual instalments, which meantime, will bear interest from February 1st, 1869, at the rate of 4 per cent. per annum.

It is estimated that by this arrangement a saving will be effected in interest on the Government advance already charged against revenue of about 165,000*l*., and moreover, the balance of the loan remaining at 4 per cent. interest, instead as heretofore at 6 per cent., will afford a further relief for the remainder of the term of about 27,800*l*.

This arrangement is not so advantageous as was hoped for, but the basis is of so reasonable a character that the board of directors under all the circumstances have no hesitation in recommending it for the adoption of the shareholders.

This arrangement was sanctioned by a general meeting of shareholders, held on 22nd January, 1869.

CHANGES, &c., SINCE GOING TO PRESS.

No.	Page.	
11	5	*Add* M.P. to Mr. Hughes's name.
14	8	For "David Rutledge, Esq.," *read* David Ruttledge, Esq.
15	9	For "Offices, 5, Queen's Square, Westminster, S.W." *read* Offices, Aylesbury
27	15	*Add* Esq. to Henry Grissell.
30	17	*Delete* William Ewart, Esq., from list of Directors,
35	20	*Delete* G. H. Whalley, Esq., M.P., from list of Directors.
41	22	*Delete* H. C. Lacy, Esq., from list of Directors.
49	27	Mr. De Winton has ceased to be Deputy-Chairman, retaining, however, his seat at the Board.
,,	,,	*Delete* "Loco. Supts. Andrew Baxter and Thomas Simpson," and Auditor "Wm. Edwards."
,,	,,	For "Resident Eng., T. D. Roberts," *read* Resident Eng. and Loco. Supt.
,,	,,	For Alfred Augustus James, "18, King Street," *read* 1, Tokenhouse Yard.
,,	,,	For "London and County," *read* London and County Bank, Lombard Street, E.C.
,,	,,	For "A. H. Philpotts, Esq.," *read* A. H. Phillpotts, Esq.
51	28	*Add* M.P. to Mr. Mitchell's name.
65	38	For "Robert Roby, Esq.," *read* Robert Boby, Esq.
73 74	52 53	}For "Earl of Uxbridge," *read* Marquis of Anglesey.
79	55	For "Eng., Edwin Clark," *read* Eng., Edwin Clarke.
81	56	For "Henry H. M'Niele, Esq.," *read* Henry H. M'Neile, Esq.
95	64	*Delete* Mr. Shaw, Col. Beamish, and Sir John Benson from list of Directors,
,,	,,	*Add* Henry Conybeare, Esq., 20, Duke Street, Westminster, S.W., and Isaac Kenderdine, Esq., Regent's Park, N.W.
,,	,,	Mr. Sedgwick's address should be Doddington Grove, Kennington, S.E.
130	85	Sir James Power has ceased to be M.P.
158	99	6th line from commencement, for "to Ulverston in 1864," *read* to Ulverston in 1854.
166	112	Thos. Rolls, Esq., should not be M.P.
185	140	*Add* Sec., R. D. Newill, Wellington : Solicitor, J. Brend Batten, 32, Great George Street, Westminster, S.W.
171	135	In list of Officers, for "Frederick Cleetsom," *read* Frederick Cleetson.
,,	,,	In list of Officers, for "G. N. Tyrrel," *read* G. N. Tyrrell.
190	144	In list of Directors, for "Jamas," *read* James Banks Stanhope, Esq.
200	150	In list of Officers, for "Solicitor, William Haggarty," *read* Solicitor, William Heggerty.
201	151	For "Sir R. B. Harvey, Esq.," *read* Sir R. B. Harvey, Bart.
232	193	*Delete* George Hall Lawrence, Esq. from list of Directors.
233	200	*Delete* H. C. Lacy, Esq., from list of Directors.
250	207	W. S. Roden, Esq., M.P., has been appointed Chairman.
292	230	In list of Officers, for "T. W. Theobald," *read* J. W. Theobald.
292	238	In list of Directors, for "J. J. William Fredericks, Esq.," *read* J. J. William Fredericks, Esq.
303	260	*Delete* Henry Charles Lacy, Esq. from list of Directors.
311	265	In list of Directors, for "Charles Wareing, Esq.," *read* Charles Waring, Esq.
,,	,,	In list of Directors, for "William Wareing, Esq.," *read* William Waring, Esq.
320	271	*Delete* Henry Lacy, Esq. from list of Directors.
340	280	*Delete* Edward Henry Bramah, Esq. from list of Directors.
337	279	In list of Officers, for "John Scath," *read* John Seath.
348	284	*Delete* Charles Bell, Esq., M.P., from list of Directors.
349	284	In list of Directors, for "John," *read* James Babbage, Esq.
384	310	*Add* "Esq." to Jno. Fairhurst and M. F. Blakiston.
390	314	*Add* "Esq." to John Richards Homfray.
413	325	In list of Directors, for "J. J. William Fredericks, Esq.," *read* J. J. William Fredricks, Esq.
465	351	*Delete* James E. Coleman from List of Officers.
475	357	*Add* to list of Directors, The Hon. Francis Scott, Sendhurst Grange, Woking Station, Surrey.
489	363	Mr. Bruce's address is 13, Hertford Street, May Fair, W.
490	364	In list of Directors, for "Seymour Toulon, Esq.," *read* Seymour Teulon, Esq.
497	369	*Delete* Charles Bell, Esq., M.P., from list of Directors.

APPENDIX.

I.—GENERAL LEGISLATION.

1.—REGULATION OF RAILWAYS.—1868.

An Act to Amend the Law relating to Railways.—31 and 32 Vic., cap. 119.—31st July, 1868.

Be it enacted by the Queen's most Excellent Majesty, by and with the advice and consent of the Lord's Spiritual and Temporal, and Commons, in this present Parliament assembled, and by the authority of the same, as follows:—

PRELIMINARY.

1. *Short title.*—This Act may be cited as the Regulation of Railways Act, 1868.
2. *Interpretation of terms.*—In this Act the term "railway" means the whole or any portion of a railway or tramway, whether worked by steam or otherwise:
The term "company" means a company incorporated, either before or after the passing of this Act, for the purpose of constructing, maintaining, or working a railway in the United Kingdom (either alone or in conjunction with any other purpose), and includes, except when otherwise expressed, any individual or individuals not incorporated who are owners or lessees of a railway in the United Kingdom, or parties to an agreement for working a railway in the United Kingdom:
The term "person" includes a body corporate.

I.—ACCOUNTS, AUDIT, &c.

3. *Uniform Accounts, &c., to be kept.*—Every incorporated company, seven days at least before each ordinary half-yearly meeting held after the 31st December, 1868, shall prepare and print, according to the forms contained in the first schedule to this Act, a statement of accounts and balance sheet for the last preceding half-year, and the other statements and certificates required by the same schedule, and an estimate of the proposed expenditure out of capital for the next ensuing half-year, and such statement of accounts and balance sheet shall be the statement of accounts and balance sheet which are submitted to the auditors of the company. Every company which makes default in complying with this section shall be liable to a penalty not exceeding 5l. for every day during which such default continues. The Board of Trade, with the consent of a company, may alter the said forms as regards such company for the purpose of adapting them to the circumstances of such company, or of better carrying into effect the objects of this section.

4. *Accounts, &c., to be signed, and printed copies distributed.*—Every statement of accounts, balance sheet, and estimate of expenditure, prepared as required by this Act, shall be signed by the chairman or deputy-chairman of the directors and by the accountant or other officer in charge of the accounts of the company, and shall be preserved at the company's principal office. A printed copy thereof shall be forwarded to the Board of Trade, and at all times after the date at which it is required to be printed be given, on application, to every person who holds any ordinary or preference share or stock in the company, or any mortgage, debenture, or debenture stock of the company; and every such person may at all reasonable times, without fee or charge, peruse the original in the possession of the company. Any company which acts in contravention of this section shall be liable for each offence to a penalty not exceeding 50l.

5. *Penalty for falsifying Accounts, &c.*—If any statement, balance sheet, estimate, or report which is required by this Act is false in any particular to the knowledge of any person who signs the same, such person shall be liable, on conviction thereof on indictment, to fine and imprisonment, or on summary conviction thereof to a penalty not exceeding 50l.

6. *Examination of affairs by Inspectors.*—The Board of Trade may appoint one or more competent inspectors to examine into the affairs of an incorporated company and the condition of its undertaking, or any part thereof, and to report thereon, upon any one of the applications following; that is to say,
1. Upon application made in pursuance of a resolution passed at a meeting of directors:
2. Upon application by the holders of not less than two-fifths part of the aggregate amount of the ordinary shares or stock of the company for the time being issued :

3. Upon application by the holders of not less than one-half of the aggregate amount of the mortgages, debentures, and debenture stock (if any) of the company for the time being issued :

4. Upon application by the holders of not less than two-fifths of the aggregate amount of of the guaranteed or preference shares or stock of the company for the time being issued, provided that the preference capital issued amounts to not less than one-third of the whole share capital of the company.

7. *Application to be supported by evidence.*—The application shall be made in writing, signed by the applicants, and shall be supported by such evidence as the Board of Trade may require, for the purpose of showing that the applicants have good reason for requiring such examination to be made : the Board of Trade may also, before appointing any inspector or inspectors, require the applicants to give security for payment of the costs of the inquiry.

8. *Inspection of Company's Books and Property.*—It shall be the duty of the directors, officers' and agents of the company to produce, for the examination of the inspectors, all books and documents relating to the affairs of the company in their custody or power, and to afford to the inspectors all reasonable facilities for the inspection of the property and undertaking of the company. Any inspector may examine upon oath the officers and agents of the company in relation to its business, and may administer such oath accordingly. Any person who, when so examined on oath, makes any false statement, knowing the same to be false, shall be guilty of perjury.

If any director, officer, or agent refuses to produce any book or document hereby directed to be produced, or to afford the facilities for inspection hereby required to be afforded, or if any officer or agent refuses to answer any question relating to the affairs of the company, he shall incur a penalty of 5*l.* for every day during which the refusal continues.

9. *Result of examination, how dealt with.*—Upon the conclusion of the examination the inspectors shall report their opinion to the Board of Trade and to the company, and the company shall print the same, and deliver a copy thereof to the Board of Trade, and, on application, to any person who holds any ordinary or preference share or stock, or any mortgage, debenture, or debenture stock of the company. All expenses of and incidental to any such examination as aforesaid shall be defrayed by the persons upon whose application the inspectors were appointed, unless the Board of Trade shall direct the same or any portion thereof to be paid by the company, which they are hereby authorised to do.

10. *Power of Company to appoint Inspectors.*—Any company may, by resolution at an extraordinary meeting, appoint inspectors for the purpose of examining into the affairs of the company and the condition of the company's undertaking. The inspectors so appointed shall have the same powers and perform the same duties as inspectors appointed by the Board of Trade, and shall make their report in such manner and to such persons as the company in general meeting direct ; and the directors, officers, and agents of the company shall incur the same penalties, in case of any refusal to produce any book or document by this Act required to be produced to such inspectors, or to afford the facilities for inspection by this Act required to be afforded, or to answer any question, as they would have incurred if such inspectors had been appointed by the Board of Trade.

11. *Auditor not necessarily a Shareholder.*—Whenever, after the passing of this Act, section one hundred and two of the company's Clauses Consolidation Act, 1845, is incorporated in a certificate or special Act relating to a railway company, it shall be construed as if the words " where no qualification shall be prescribed by the special Act every auditor shall have at " least one share in the undertaking," were omitted therefrom ; and so much of every certificate and special Act relating to a railway company, and in force at the passing of this Act, as incorporates that portion of the said section, and so much of any special Act relating to a railway company, and so in force, as contains a like provision, is hereby repealed.

12. *Auditors of Company, and appointment of Auditor by Board of Trade.*—With respect to the auditors of the company the following provisions shall have effect:

1. The Board of Trade may, upon application made in pursuance of a resolution passed at a meeting of the directors or at a general meeting of the company, appoint an auditor in addition to the auditors of such company, and it shall not be necessary for any such auditor to be a shareholder in the company :

2. The company shall pay to such auditor appointed by the Board of Trade, such reasonable remuneration as the Board of Trade may prescribe :

3. The auditor so appointed shall have the same duties and powers as the auditors of the company, and shall report to the company :

4. Where, in consequence of such appointment of an auditor or otherwise, there are three or more auditors, the company may declare a dividend if the majority of such auditors certify in manner required by section thirty of the Railway Companies Act, 1867, and the Railway Companies (Scotland) Act, 1867, respectively :

5. Where there is a difference of opinion among such auditors, the auditor who so differs shall issue to the shareholders, at the cost of the company, such statement respecting the grounds on which he differs from his colleagues, and respecting the financial condition and prospects of the company, as he thinks material for the infomation of the shareholders.

13. *Issue of preferred and deferred Ordinary Stock.*—Any company which in the year immediately preceding has paid a dividend on their ordinary stock of not less than 3*l.* per cent. per annum may, pursuant to the resolution of an extraordinary general meeting, divide their paid-up ordinary stock into two classes, to be and to be called the one preferred ordinary stock, and the other deferred ordinary stock, and issue the same subject and according to the following provisions, and with the following consequences (that is to say),

1. Preferred and deferred ordinary stock shall be issued only in substitution for equal amounts of paid-up ordinary stock, and by way of division of portions of ordinary stock into two equal parts :

2. Such division may be made at any time, on the request in writing of the holder of paid-up ordinary stock, but not otherwise ; and such request may apply to the whole of the ordinary stock of such holder, or to any portion thereof divisible into twentieth parts :

3. Preferred ordinary stock and deferred ordinary stock shall not be issued except in sums of 10*l.* or multiples of 10*l.* :

4. The certificates for any ordinary stock divided into preferred and deferred ordinary stock shall before such division be delivered up to the company, and shall be cancelled by them, and certificates for preferred ordinary stock and deferred ordinary stock shall be issued gratis in exchange by the company :

5. If in any case there is any part of the ordinary stock held by a stockholder comprised in one certificate which he does not desire to be divided, or which is incapable of division, under the provisions of this Act, the company shall issue to him gratis a certificate for that amount as ordinary stock :

6. As between preferred ordinary stock and deferred ordinary stock, preferred ordinary stock shall bear a fixed maximum dividend at the rate of 6 per cent. per annum :

7. In respect of dividend to the extent of the maximum aforesaid, preferred ordinary stock shall at the time of its creation, and at all times afterwards, have priority over deferred ordinary stock created or to be created, and shall rank *pari passu* with the undivided ordinary stock and the ordinary shares of the company created or to be created ; and in respect of dividend, preferred ordinary stock shall at all times and to all intents rank after all preference and guaranteed stock and shares of the company created or to be created :

8. In each year after all holders of preferred ordinary stock for the time being issued have received in full the maximum dividend aforesaid, all holders of deferred ordinary stock for the time being issued shall, in respect of all dividend exceeding that maximum paid by the company in that year on ordinary stock and shares, rank *pari passu* with the holders of undivided ordinary stock and of ordinary shares of the company for the time being issued :

9. If, nevertheless, in any year ending on the 31st of December there are not profits available for payment to all the holders of preferred ordinary stock of the maximum dividend aforesaid, no part of the dificiency shall be made good out of the profits of any subsequent year, or out of any other funds of the company :

10. Preferred ordinary stock and deferred ordinary stock from time to time shall confer such right of voting at meetings of the company, and shall confer and have all such other rights, qualifications, privileges, liabilities, and incidents, as from time to time attached and are incident to undivided ordinary stock of the company :

11. The terms and conditions on which any preferred ordinary stock or deferred ordinary stock is issued shall be stated on the certificate thereof:

12. Preferred ordinary stock and deferred ordinary stock shall respectively be held on the same trusts, and subject to the same charges and liabilities, as those on and subject to which the ordinary stock in substitution for which the same are issued was held immediately before the substitution, and so as to give effect to any testamentary or other disposition of or affecting such ordinary stock.

II.—OBLIGATIONS AND LIABILITY OF COMPANIES AS CARRIERS.

14. *Liability of Company during Sea Transit.*—Where a company by through booking contracts to carry any animals, luggage, or goods from place to place partly by railway and partly by sea, or partly by canal and partly by sea, a condition exempting the company from liability for any loss or damage which may arise during the carriage of such animals, luggage, or goods by sea from the Act of God, the King's enemies, fire, accidents from machinery, boilers, and steam, and all and every other dangers and accidents of the seas, rivers, and navigation, of whatever nature and kind soever, shall, if published in a conspicuous manner in the office where such through booking is effected, and if printed in a legible manner on the receipt or freight note which the company gives for such animals, luggage, or goods, be valid as part of the contract between the consignor of such animals, luggage, or goods and the company in the same manner as if the company had signed and delivered to the consignor a bill of lading containing such condition. For the purposes of this section the word " company " cludes the owners, lessees, or managers of any canal or other inland navigation.

15. *Fares to be posted in Stations.*—On and after the 1st of January 1869 every company shall cause to be exhibited in a conspicuous place in the booking office of each station on their line a list or lists painted, printed, or written in legible characters, containing the fares of passengers by the trains included in the time tables of the company from that station to every place for which passenger tickets are there issued.

16. *Provision for securing equality of treatment where railway company works Steam Vessels.*—Where a company is authorised to build, or buy, or hire, and to use, maintain, and work, or to enter into arrangements for using, maintaining, or working, steam vessels for the purpose of carrying on a communication between any towns or ports, and to take tolls in respect of such steam vessels, then and in every such case tolls shall be at all times charged to all persons equally and after the same rate in respect of passengers conveyed in a like vessel passing between the same places under like circumstances ; and no reduction or advance in tolls shall be made in favour of or against any person using the steam vessels in consequence of his having travelled or being about to travel on the whole or any part of the company's railway, or not having travelled or not being about to travel on any part thereof, or in favour of or against any person using the railway in consequence of his having used or being about to use, or his not having used or not being about to use, the steam vessels; and where an aggregate sum is charged by the company for conveyance of a passenger by a steam vessel and on the railway, the ticket shall have the amount of toll charged for conveyance by the steam vessel distinguished from the amount charged for conveyance on the railway.

The provisions of the Railway and Canal Traffic Act, 1854, so far as the same are applicable, shall extend to the steam vessels and to the traffic carried on thereby.

17. *Company bound to furnish particulars of charges for goods.*—Where any charge shall have been made by a company in respect of the conveyance of goods over their railway, on application in writing within one week after payment of the said charge made to the secretary of the company by the person by whom or on whose account the same has been paid, the company shall within 14 days render an account to the person so applying for the same, distinguishing how much of the said charge is for the conveyance of the said goods on the railway, including therein tolls for the use of the railway, for the use of carriages and for locomotive power, and how much of such charge is for loading and unloading, covering, collection, delivery, and for other expenses, but without particularising the several items of which the last-mentioned portion of the charge may consist.

18. *Charge when two railways worked by one Company.*—Where two railways are worked by one company, then in the calculation of tolls and charges for any distances in respect of traffic (whether passengers, animals, goods, carriages, or vehicles) conveyed on both railways, the distances traversed shall be reckoned continuously on such railways as if they were one railway.

19. *Proceedings in case of non-consumption of smoke.*—Where proceedings are taken against a company using a locomotive steam engine on a railway on account of the same not consuming its own smoke, then if it appears to the justices before whom the complaint is heard that the engine is constructed on the principle of consuming its own smoke, but that it failed to consume its own smoke, as far as practicable, at the time charged in the complaint through the default of the company, or of any servant in the employment of the company, such company shall be deemed guilty of an offence under the Railways Clauses Consolidation Act, 1845, section 114.

20. *Smoking compartments for all classes.*—All railway companies, except the Metropolitan, shall, from and after the 1st day of October next, in every passenger train where there are more carriages than one of each class, provide smoking compartments for each class of passengers, unless exempted by the Board of Trade.

21. *Railway companies to be liable to penalties in case they shall provide trains for prize fights.*—Any railway company that shall knowingly let for hire or otherwise provide any special train for the purpose of conveying parties to or to be present at any prize fight, or who shall stop any ordinary train to convenience or accommodate any parties attending a prize fight at any place not an ordinary station on their line, shall be liable to a penalty, to be recovered in a summary way before two justices of the county in which such prize fight shall be held or shall be attempted to be held, of such sum not exceeding 500*l.*, and not less than 200*l.*, as such justices shall determine, one-half of such penalty to be paid to the party at whose suit the summons shall be issued, and the other half to be paid to the treasurer of the county in which such prize fight shall be held or shall be attempted to be held in aid of the county rate; and service of the summons under which the penalty is sought to be enforced on the secretary of the company at his office ten days before the day of hearing shall be sufficient to give the justices before whom the case shall come jurisdiction to hear and determine the case.

III.—PROVISIONS FOR SAFETY OF PASSENGERS.

22. *Communication between passengers and the company's servants.*—After the 1st day of April, 1869, every company shall provide, and maintain in good working order, in every train worked by it which carries passengers, and travels more than 20 miles without stopping, such efficient means of communication between the passengers and the servants of the company in charge of the train as the Board of Trade may approve. If any company makes default in complying with this section it shall be liable to a penalty not exceeding 10*l.* for each case of default. Any passenger who makes use of the said means of communication without reasonable and sufficient cause shall be liable for each offence to a penalty not exceeding 5*l.*

23. *Penalty for trespasses on railways.*—If any person shall be or pass upon any railway, except for the purpose of crossing the same at any authorised crossing, after having received warning by the company which works such railway, or by any of their agents or servants, not to go or pass thereon, every person so offending shall forfeit and pay any sum not exceeding 40*s.* for every such offence.

24. *Trees dangerous to railways may be removed.*—If any tree standing near to a railway shall be in danger of falling on the railway so as to obstruct the traffic, it shall be lawful for any two justices on the complaint of the company which works such railway to cause such tree to be removed or otherwise dealt with as such justices may order, and the justices making such order may award compensation to be paid by the company making such complaint to the owner of the tree so ordered to be removed or otherwise dealt with as such justices shall think proper, and the amount of such compensation shall be recoverable in like manner as compensation recoverable before justices under "The Railways Clauses Consolida-

IV.—COMPENSATION FOR ACCIDENTS.

25. *Arbitration of damages.*—Where a person has been injured or killed by an accident on a railway, the Board of Trade, upon application in writing made jointly by the company from whom compensation is claimed and the person if he is injured, or his representatives if he is killed, may, if they think fit, appoint an arbitrator, who shall determine the compensation (if any) to be paid by the company.

26. *Examination by medical man.*—Whenever any person injured by an accident on a railway claims compensation on account of the injury, any judge of the court in which proceedings to recover such compensation are taken, or any person who by the consent of the parties or otherwise has power to fix the amount of compensation, may order that the person injured be examined by some duly qualified medical practitioner named in the order, and not being a witness on either side, and may make such order with respect to the costs of such examination as he may think fit.

V.—LIGHT RAILWAYS.

27. *Order for construction and working of railway as a Light Railway.*—The Board of Trade may by licence authorise a company applying for it to construct and work or to work as a light railway the whole or any part of a railway which the company has power to construct or work.

Before granting the licence the Board of Trade shall cause due notice of the application to be given, and shall consider all objections and representations received by them, and shall make such inquiry as they think necessary.

28. *Conditions and regulations for Light Railway.*—A light railway shall be constructed and worked subject to such conditions and regulations as the Board of Trade may from time to time impose or make: Provided, that (1.) the regulations respecting the weight of locomotive engines, carriages, and vehicles to be used on such railway shall not authorise a greater weight than eight tons to be brought upon the rails by any one pair of wheels; (2.) the regulations respecting the speed of trains shall not authorise a rate of speed exceeding at any time 25 miles an hour.

If the company or any person fails to comply with or acts in contravention of such conditions and regulations, or directs any one so to fail or act, such company and person shall respectively be liable to a penalty for each offence not exceeding 20*l.*, and to a like penalty for every day during which the offence continues; and every such person on conviction on indictment for any offence relating to the weight of engines, carriages, or vehicles, or the speed of trains, shall be also liable to imprisonment, with or without hard labour, for any term not exceeding two years.

29. *Publication of regulations.*—The conditions and regulations of the Board of Trade relating to light railways shall be published and kept published by the company in manner directed with respect to bye-laws by section 110 of "The Railways Clauses Consolidation Act, 1845," and the company shall be liable to a penalty not exceeding 5*l.* for every day during which such conditions and regulations are not so published.

VI.—ARBITRATIONS BY BOARD OF TRADE.

30 *Arbitrator appointed by Board of Trade.*—Whenever the Board of Trade are required to make any award or to decide any difference in any case in which a company is one of the parties, they may appoint an arbitrator to act for them, and his award or decision shall be deemed to be the award or decision of the Board of Trade.

If the arbitrator dies, or in the judgment of the Board of Trade becomes incapable or unfit, the Board of Trade may appoint another arbitrator.

31. *Remuneration of Arbitrator.*—The Board of Trade may fix the remuneration of any arbitrator or umpire appointed by them in pursuance of this or any other Act in any case where a company is one of the parties, and may, if they think fit, frame a scale of remuneration for arbitrators or umpires so appointed by them, and no arbitrator or umpire so appointed by them shall be entitled to any larger remuneration than the amount fixed by the Board of Trade.

32. *Cost, &c., of Arbitrations.*—The provisions of sections 18 to 29, both inclusive, of the Railway Companies' Arbitration Act, 1859, shall, so far as is consistent with the tenor thereof, apply to an arbitrator appointed by the Board of Trade, and to his arbitration and award, notwithstanding that one of the parties between whom he is appointed to arbitrate may not be a railway company; and in construing those sections for the purpose of this Act the word "Companies" shall be construed to mean the parties to the arbitration.

33. *Costs, charges, &c., to be taxed and settled by Masters of the Court of Queen's Bench.*—All disputed questions as to any costs, charges, and expenses of and incident to any arbitration or award made under the provisions of "The Lands Clauses Consolidation Act, 1845," or of any special Act of Parliament incorporating the same, whether the question in dispute arise as to compensation to be made for lands required to be purchased and actually taken by any railway company, or in respect of the injurious affecting of other lands not taken, or otherwise in relation thereto, shall, if either party so requires, be taxed and settled as between the parties by one of the Masters of the Court of Queen's Bench; and it shall be lawful for such Master to receive and take in respect of each folio in length of every bill of costs so settled a fee of 1s. and no more, and such fee shall be taken in money and not in stamps, and may be retained by the said Master for his own use and benefit.

VII.—MISCELLANEOUS.

34 *Printed copies of Shareholders' Address Book.*—Every incorporated company shall print correct copies of the shareholders' address book of the company corrected up to the 1st day of December in every year, and affix an asterisk against the names of those qualified to act as directors.

After the expiration of one fortnight from the aforesaid date the company shall, on application, supply such printed copies at a price not exceeding 5s. for each copy to every person who holds any ordinary or preference shares or stock in the company, or any mortgage debenture or debenture stock of the company.

Any company which acts in contravention of this section shall be liable for each offence to a penalty not exceeding 20l.

35. *Meeting preliminary to application for Act or Certificate.*—When a bill is introduced into either House of Parliament conferring on an incorporated company additional powers, or when an incorporated company applies to the Board of Trade for a certificate conferring on it additional powers, the following provisions shall have effect; namely,

1. Before the bill is read a second time in the House of Parliament into which it is first introduced, or before the application is made to the Board of Trade (as the case may be) shall be submitted to a meeting of the proprietors of such company at a meeting held specially for that purpose :

2. Such meeting shall be called by advertisement inserted once in each of two consecutive weeks in a morning newspaper published in London, Edinburgh, or Dublin (as the case may be), and in a newspaper of the county or counties in which the principal office or offices of the company is or are situate, and also by a circular addressed to each proprietor at his registered or last known or usual address, and sent by post or delivered at such address not less than 10 days before the holding of such meeting, enclosing a blank form of proxy, with proper instructions for the use of the same ; and the same form of proxy and the same instructions shall be sent to every such proprietor, and shall be addressed to each proprietor on the back of the form of proxy ; but no such form of proxy shall be stamped before it is sent out, nor shall the funds of the company be used for the stamping of any proxies, nor shall any intimation be sent as to any person to whom the proxy may be given or addressed ; and no other circular or form of proxy relating to such meeting shall be sent to any proprietor from the office of the company, or by any director or officer of the company so describing himself :

3. Such meeting shall be held on a day not earlier than seven days after the last insertion of such advertisement, and may be held on the same day as an ordinary general meeting of the company :

4. At such meeting the bill or draft certificate shall be submitted to the proprietors, and shall not be proceeded with unless approved of by proprietors present in person or by proxy, holding at least three-fourths of the paid-up capital of the company represented at such meeting, such proprietors being qualified to vote at all ordinary meetings of the company in right of such capital ; the votes of proprietors of any paid-up shares or stock, other than debenture stock, not qualified to vote at ordinary meetings, whose interests may be effected by the proposed act or certificate, if tendered at the meeting, shall be recorded separately :

5. There shall be laid before Parliament or the Board of Trade (as the case may require) a statement of the number of votes if a poll was taken, and the number of votes recorded separately.

36. *Special Trains exclusively for Post-Office.*—Whenever in pursuance of any notice under the Act of the session of the first and second years of the reign of Her present Majesty, chapter 98, " to provide for the conveyance of mails by railways," or otherwise, the mails or post letter bags are conveyed and forwarded by a company on their railway by a special train, the Postmaster-General may by the same or any other notice in writing require that the whole of such special train shall be appropriated to the service of the post-office exclusively of all other traffic except such as he may sanction, and the remuneration to be paid for such service shall be settled as prescribed by the sixth section of that Act.

37. *Service of Requisitions, &c., by Postmaster-General.*—All requisitions, notices, and documents which relate to a company, if purporting to be signed by the Postmaster General or some secretary or assistant secretary to the post-office, or by some officer appointed for the purpose by the Postmaster-General, shall, until the contrary is proved, be deemed to have been so signed, and to have been given or made by the Postmaster-General, and the provisions of the Act of the session of the first and second years of the reign of Her present Majesty, chapter 98, " to provide for the conveyance of mails by railways," requiring any notice, requisition, or document to be under the hand of the Postmaster-General, are hereby repealed.

38. *Extension of scope of Railway Companies' Powers Act,* 1864.—The Railway Companies Powers Act, 1864, shall take effect and apply in the following cases in the same manner as if they were specified in section 3 of that Act ; that is to say—

Where a company desire to make new provisions, or to alter any of the provisions of their Special Act, or of the " Companies Clauses Consolidation Act, 1845," so far as it is incorporated therewith, with respect to all or any of the matters following ; namely—

a. The general meetings of the company, and the exercise of the right of voting by the shareholders.

b. The appointment, number, and rotation of directors.

c. The powers of directors.

d. The proceedings and liabilities of directors.

e. The appointment and duties of auditors.

39. *Service of Requisitions, &c.*—All requisitions, orders, regulations, appointments, certificates, licenses, notices, and documents which relate to a company, if purporting to be signed by some secretary or assistant secretary of or by some officer appointed for the purpose by the Board of Trade, shall, until the contrary is proved, be deemed to have been so signed, and to have been given or made by the Board of Trade. They may be served by the Board of Trade on any company in the manner in which notices may be served under the Companies Clauses Consolidation Act, 1845 ; and all notices, returns, and other documents required to be made, delivered, or sent by a company to the Board of Trade shall be left at the office of, or transmitted through the post addressed to, the Board of Trade.

40. *Recovery, &c., of Penalties.*—Every penalty imposed by this Act shall be recovered and applied in the same manner as penalties imposed by the Railways Clauses Consolidation Act, 1845, and the Railways Clauses Consolidation (Scotland) Act, 1845 (as the case may require), are for the time being recoverable and applicable.

41. *Company may apply to Common Law Judge at Westminster to hear cases of Compensation under 8 and 9 Vic., cap. 18.*—Whenever, in the case of any lands purchased or taken otherwise than by agreement for the purposes of any public railway, any question of compensation in respect thereof, or any question of compensation in respect of lands injuriously affected by the execution of the works of any public railway, is under the provisions of " The Lands Clauses Consolidation Act, 1845," to be settled by the verdict of a jury empanelled and summoned as in that Act mentioned, the company or the party entitled to the compensation may, at any time before the issuing by the company to the sheriff as by that Act directed, apply to a judge of any one of the superior courts of common law at Westminster, who shall, if he think fit, make an order for the trial of the question in one of the superior courts upon such terms and in such manner as to him shall seem fit ; and the question between the parties shall be stated in an issue to be settled in case of difference by the judge, or as he shall direct, and such issue may be entered for trial and tried accordingly in the same manner as any issue joined in an ordinary action at such place as the judge shall direct ; and the proceedings in respect of such issue shall be under and subject to the control and jurisdiction of the court as in ordinary actions therein, but so nevertheless that the jury shall, where the issue relates to the value of lands to be purchased, and also to compensation claimed for injury done or to be done to lands held therewith, deliver their verdict separately in manner provided by the 49th section of " The Lands Clauses Consolidation Act, 1845."

42. *Company may obtain Judge's Order instead of issuing Warrant.*—Whenever a company is called upon or liable under the provisions of " The Lands Clauses Consolidation Act, 1845," to issue their warrant to the sheriff in the case of any disputed compensation, and the company shall obtain a judge's order as in the last preceding section mentioned, the obtaining of such an order and notice thereof to the opposite party shall be a satisfaction of the company's duty in respect of the issue of the warrant.

43. *Power of Verdict of Jury and Judgment of the Court.*—The verdict of the jury and judgment of the court upon any issue authorised by this Act shall, as regards costs and every other matter incident to or consequent thereon, have the same operation and be entitled to the same effect as if that verdict and judgment had been the verdict of a jury and judgment of a sheriff upon an inquiry conducted upon a warrant to the sheriff issued by the company under " The Lands Clauses Consolidation Act, 1845."

44. *Interpretation of certain expressions.*—In so far as any expression used in any of the three preceding sections of this Act has any special meaning assigned to it by " The Lands Clauses Consolidation Act, 1845," each such expression shall in this Act have the meaning so assigned to it.

45. *Fees to Masters for determining Questions of Disputed Compensation.*—Wherever under the provisions of the Lands Clauses Consolidation Act, 1845, or of any Act incorporating, altering, or amending the same, the costs of any proceedings for determining a question of disputed compensation are settled by one of the masters of the Court of Queen's Bench in England or Ireland, it shall be lawful for such masters to receive and take in respect of each folio in length of every bill of costs so settled a fee of 1s. and no more ; and such fee shall be taken in money and not in stamps, and may be retained by the said masters for their own use and benefit.

46. *Extension of Time.*—Where notice in writing of a proposed application under " The Railways (Extension of Time) Act, 1868," for extension of the time limited for any of the purposes mentioned in that Act, is received by the Board of Trade before the expiration of such time, or if the time has expired during the present session of Parliament before the 1st day of September 1868, and the application is duly made within the period prescribed by the said Act, then a warrant of the Board of Trade extending the time, although issued after the expiration thereof, shall have effect from the date of such expiration as if it had been previously issued.

47. *As to Repeal of Enactments in Second Schedule.*—The enactment described in the second schedule to this Act are hereby repealed.

But this repeal shall not affect—

1. The validity or invalidity of anything duly done or suffered under any enactment repealed by this section:

2. Any right acquired or accrued or liability incurred or any remedy in respect thereof.

SCHEDULES.

FORMS OF ACCOUNT REFERRED TO IN SEC. 3 OF THIS ACT.

_____RAILWAY.   HALF-YEAR ENDING_____18

[No. 1.]   STATEMENT OF CAPITAL AUTHORISED AND CREATED BY COMPANY.

ACTS OF PARLIAMENT, or certificates of the Board of Trade.	CAPITAL AUTHORISED.			CAPITAL CREATED OR SANCTIONED.			BALANCE.		
	Stock and Shares.	Loans	Total.	Stock and Shares.	Loans	Total.	Stock and Shares.	Loans	Total.
1. *[Except where*	£	£	£	£	£	£	£	£	£
2. *capital powers*									
3. *are comprised in a consoli-*									
4. *dation Act, each Act or*									
5. *certificate authorising capi-*									
&c. *tal to be stated here separate-*									
ly in order of date.]									
Total									

[No. 2.]   STATEMENT OF STOCK AND SHARE CAPITAL CREATED, SHOWING THE PROPORTION RECEIVED.

DESCRIPTION.	Amount created.	Amount received.	Calls in arrear.	Amount uncalled.	Amount unissued.
[State each class of stock or shares in order of date of creation, showing the premium or discount, if any, at which it was issued, the preferential or fixed dividends, if any, to which it is entitled, and any other condition attached to it.]	£	£	£	£	£
Total					

[No. 3.]   CAPITAL RAISED BY LOANS AND DEBENTURE STOCK.

	RAISED BY LOANS.									RAISED BY ISSUE OF DEBENTURE STOCKS.			Total raised by loans and by Debenture Stocks.
	At per Cent.	At per Cent.	At per Cent.	At per Cent.	At per Cent.	At per Cent.	At per Cent.	At per Cent.	At per Cent.	At per Cent.	At per Cent.	Total Debenture Stocks.	
Existing at Ditto at	£	£	£	£	£	£	£	£	£	£	£	£ s. d.	£ s. d.
Increase.... Decrease....													

Total amount authorised to be raised by loans and by debenture stocks in respect of capital created, as per Statement No. 1................... ....
Total amount raised by loans and by debenture stock as above ....
Balance being available borrowing powers at   186   ......|

[No. 4.]　　*Dr.*　　RECEIPTS AND EXPENDITURE ON CAPITAL ACCOUNT.　　*Cr.*

	Amount Expended to	Amount Expended during Half-year	Total.		Amount Received to	Amount Received during Half-year	Total.
	£　s.　d.	£　s.　d.	£　s.　d.		£　s.　d.	£　s.　d.	£　s.　d.
To expenditure On lines open for traffic (No. 5.) .... On lines in course of construction (No. 5.) Working stock (No. 5.) Subscriptions to other railways (No. 5.) Docks, steamboats, and other special items (No. 5.)				By receipts— Shares and stock, per account (No. 2.) .... Loans, per account (No. 3.) .... Debenture stock, per account (No. 3.) .... Sundries in detail · ·...			
To Balance　..							

[No. 5.]　　DETAILS OF CAPITAL EXPENDITURE FOR HALF-YEAR ENDING　　186 .

Lines open for traffic—
　Particulars—
Lines in course of construction—
　Particulars— } *[Showing, under separate heads, amount paid for land (purchase and compensation), construction of way and stations, including rails, chairs, sleepers, &c., engineering and surveying, law charges, parliamentary expenses, interest, commission, &c.]*

Working stock—
　Particulars—Showing each description of stock..　..　..　..　..

Subscriptions to other railways—
　Particulars—Stating lines ..,　..　..　..　..　..　..　..　..

Docks, Steamboats, and other special items—
　Particulars..　..　..　..　..　..　..　..　..　..　..　..　..

　　Total expenditure for half-year, as per account No. 4.　..　..

[No. 6.]　　RETURN OF WORKING STOCK.

	LOCOMOTIVE.		COACHING.					MERCHANDISE AND MINERAL.							
	Engines.	Tenders.	First Class.	Second Class.	Third Class.			Goods Wagons.	Goods Wagons covered.	Coke Trucks.	Cattle Trucks.	Timber Trucks.			
Stock on the　　18 Do. on the　　18															
Increase during the Half-year ..　..　.. Decrease ditto　ditto..															

[No. 7.]   ESTIMATE OF FURTHER EXPENDITURE ON CAPITAL ACCOUNT

	FURTHER EXPENDITURE.		
	During the Half-year ending .	In subsequent Half-years.	Total.
Lines open for traffic			
Particulars, showing principal items			
Lines in course of construction..			
Details of each line.			
Working stock..			
Particulars.			
Subscription to other railways			
Specifying lines.			
Docks, steamboats, and other special items.. ..			
Particulars.			
Works not yet commenced and in abeyance.. ..			
(In detail.)			
Other items (in detail.)			
Total estimated further expenditure of capital			

[No. 8.]   CAPITAL POWERS and other ASSETS available to meet further EXPENDITURE, as per No. 7.

Share and loan capital authorised or created but not yet received		
Any other assets in detail		
Total..		

[No. 9.]   *Dr.*   REVENUE ACCOUNT.   *Cr.*

Half-year ended .	*Expenditure.*	£ s. d.	Half-year ended	*Receipts.*	£ s. d.	£ s. d.
	To maintenance of way, works, and stations, see abstract .. .. A			By passengers		
				" Parcels, horses, Carriages, &c...		
	" Locomotive power see abstract .. B			" Mails		
	" Carriage and wagon repairs see abstract C			" Merchandise ..		
				" Live stock		
	" Traffic expenses see abstract .. D			" Minerals		
	" General charges see abstract .. E			" Special and miscellaneous receipts—		
	" Law charges					
	" Parliamentary expenses			Such as navigations, steamboats, rents, transfer fees,&c.		
	" Compensation (accidents and losses)					
	" Rates and taxes. .			*Details.*		
	" Government duty					
	" Special and miscellaneous expenses (if any)					
	" Balance carried to net revenue account					
	£				£	

No. 10.] *Dr.* NET REVENUE ACCOUNT. *Cr.*

Half-year ended		£ s. d.	Half-year ended		£
·	To interest on mortgage and debenture loans " Interest on debenture stock .. .. " Interest on calls in advance .. .. .. " Interest on temporary loans .. .. " Interest on Lloyd's Bonds .. .. " Interest on banking balances .. .. .. " General interest account (if in debit) .. " Rents of leased lines, guarantees, &c... .. Details .. .. .. " Special and miscellaneous payments (if any) .. .. Details. " Balance, being payment available for dividend .. .. .. [See No. 13.]		·	By balance brought from last half-year's account .. .. " Ditto revenue account No. 9 .. .. " Dividends on shares in other companies " Bankers and general interest account (if in credit) .. .. .. " Special and miscellaneous receipts (if any) .. .. Detail to be given	
	£				

[No. 11.] PROPOSED APPROPRIATION OF BALANCE AVAILABLE FOR DIVIDEND.

Half-year ended	
·	Balance available for dividend, as per account No. 10 .. .. £ Preference stock ⎫ to be stated in order ⎧ £ Ditto ⎬ of creation, with rate ⎨ Ditto ⎭ of dividend. ⎩ Ordinary stock (being at the rate per cent.) Balance to next half-year .. .. .. £

[No. 12.] ABSTRACTS.

A. MAINTENANCE OF WAY, WORKS, &C.				B. LOCOMOTIVE POWER.			
Half-year ended		£ s. d.	£ s. d.	Half-year ended		£ s. d.	£ s. d.
·	Salaries, office expenses, and general superintendence .. Maintenance and renewal of permanent way .. .. Wages .. .. .. Materials .. .. .. Repairs of roads, bridges, signals, and works .. .. .. Repairs of stations and buildings.. .. Special expenditure (if any) .. .. .. *Miles Maintained.* Double .. .. .. Single .. .. .. Total				·	Salaries, office expenses, and general superintendence .. *Running expenses:—* Wages connected with the working of Locomotive engines.. .. Coal and coke .. Water .. .. .. Oil, tallow, and other stores.. .. *Repairs & renewals:* Wages .. .. .. Materials .. .. .. Special expenditure..			
	Total..				£		

[No. 12.]   Abstracts —*Continued.*

C. Repairs and Renewals of Carriages and Wagons.

Half-year ended		£ s. d.	£ s. d.
	Carriages:—		
	Salaries, office expenses, and general superintendence ..		
	Wages..		
	Materials		
	Wagons:—		
	Salaries, office expenses, and general superintendence..		
	Wages..		
	Materials		
	Total		

D. Traffic Expenses.

Half-year ended		£ s. d.
	Salaries and wages, &c.	
	Fuel, lighting, water, and general stores	
	Clothing..	
	Printing, stationery, & tickets	
	Horses, Harness, vans, provender, &c...	
	Wagon covers, ropes, &c.. ..	
	Joint station expenses	
	Miscellaneous expenses	
	Special expenditure (if any) ..	

E. General Charges.

Half-year ended		£ s. d
	Directors	
	Auditors & public accountant (if any)	
	Salaries of Secretary, General Manager, Accountant, and Clerks..	
	Office expenses ditto ditto	

E. General Charges.

Half-year ended		£ s. d.
	Advertising	
	Fire insurance	
	Electric telegraph expenses ..	
	Railway clearing house expenses..	
	Special expenditure (if any) ..	

[No. 13.]   *Dr.*   **General Balance Sheet.**   *Cr.*

	£ s. d.	
To capital account, balance at credit thereof as per account No. 4.. ..		By cash at bankers—Current account
" Net revenue account, balance at credit thereof, as per account No. 10..		" Cash on deposit at interest .. ..
" Unpaid dividends and interest ..		" Cash invested in consols and government securities .. .. ..
" Guaranteed dividends and interest payable or accruing and provided for		" Cash invested in shares of other railway companies not charged as capital expenditure .. .. ..
" Temporary loans		" General stores—stock of materials on hand .. ..
" Lloyd's bonds and other obligations not included in loan capital statement No. 3		" Traffic accounts due to the company .. ..
" Balance due to bankers..		" Amounts due by other companies
" Debts due to other companies....		" Do. do. clearing house..
" Amount due to clearing house ..		" Do. do post office .. ..
" Sundry outstanding accounts ..		" Sundry outstanding accounts ..
" Fire insurance fund on stations, works, and buildings		" Suspense accounts (if any) to be enumerated .. ..
" Insurance fund on steamboats ..		" Special items .. ..
" Special items		
£		£

[No. 14.]   **Mileage Statement.**

Half-year ended		Miles authorized.	Miles constructed.	Miles constructing or to be constructed.	Miles worked by Engines.
	Lines owned by company				
	Do. partly owned ..				
	Do. leased or rented.				
	Total				
	Do. worked				
	Foreign lines worked over				
	Total				

[No. 15.]   STATEMENT OF TRAIN MILEAGE.

Half-Year ended		
	Passenger Trains	
	Goods and Mineral Trains	
	TOTAL	

(Signed)_____ *Chairman or Deputy Chairman of Company.*

_____ *Secretary or Accountant of Company.*

CERTIFICATE RESPECTING THE PERMANENT WAY, &c.

I hereby certify that the whole of the Company's Permanent Way, Stations, Buildings, Canals, and other Works have during the past half-year been maintained in good working condition and repair.

Engineer.

Date_____18 .

CERTIFCATE RESPECTING THE ROLLING STOCK.

I hereby certify that the whole of the company's plant, engines, tenders, carriages, wagons, machinery, and tools, also the marine engines of the steam vessels, have during the past half-year been maintained in good working order and repair.

Chief Engineer, or
Locomotive Superintendent.

Date_____18 .

AUDITOR'S CERTIFICATE.
As prescribed by Act 30 and 31 Victoria, Cap. 37, to follow.

SECOND SCHEDULE.

Date and 'Chapter of Act.	Title of Act.
3 & 4 Vict., c. 97.. (in part.)	An Act for regulating railways .. .. in part; namely,— Section twenty.
5 & 6 Vict., c. 55.. (in part.)	An Act for the better regulation of railways, and for the conveyance of troops.. .. .. } in part; namely,— Section nineteen.
7 & 8 Vict., c. 85.. (in part.)	An Act to attach certain conditions to the construction of future railways authorized or to be authorized by any Act of the present or succeeding } in part; namely,— Sessions of Parliament, and for other purposes in ralation to railways.. .. .. Section twenty-three.

2.—TELEGRAPH PURCHASE ACT—1868.

This Act, which received the royal assent on 29th July, 1868, carries out, in twenty-four sections, and sets forth the recital in the preamble that the means of communication within the United Kingdom are insufficient, that many districts are without it, and that it would be attended with great advantage to the State as well as to merchants and traders, and to the public generally, were a cheaper, more widely extended, and more expeditious system of telegraphy established, and to that end the Postmaster-General is empowered to work telegraphs in connection with the administration of the post-office.   The uniform rate, subject to regulation, of messages throughout the United Kingdom, and without regard to distance, is to be at a rate not exceeding 1s. for the first 20 words and not exceeding 3d. for each additional five words or part of five words.   The Postmaster-General is authorised, with the consent of the Treasury, " out of any moneys which may be from time to time appropriated by Act of Parliament, and put at his disposal for that purpose, to purchase for the purposes of this Act the whole or such parts as he shall think fit of the undertaking of any company." Telegraph companies are empowered to sell their undertaking, under certain conditions specified, with a provision as to the appointments of their servants by the Government, or compensation by way of annuity.   The Postmaster-General is to enter into contracts with certain railway companies mentioned in the Act, and very specific directions are given as to such acquisition.   The Postmaster-General is to transmit to their destination all messages of a railway company in any way relating to the business of the company in the United Kingdom free of charge.   All matters of difference between the Postmaster-General and railway companies are to be settled by arbitration.   The sums to be received by the directors of Reuter's Telegam Company are to be applied in the first instance to the payment of the debts and liabilities of the company. There are provisions in the statute to enable the Postmaster to acquire the right of way over canals. Special agreements may be made with newspaper proprietors and with the occupiers of newsrooms, club, or exchange-rooms, to transmit messages at a rate not exceeding 1s. for every 100 words between nine o'clock a.m. and six o'clock p.m., and a special use of a wire to be obtained under regulations, without undue priority or preference ; messages having priority are to be specially marked, and all telegraphic messages are to be paid by means of stamps, and such stamps are to be kept for sale to the public at offices under the control of-the Postmaster-General, to be appointed for that purpose. It is constituted a misdemeanour in any person having official duties to disclose or to intercept messages. Copies of all contracts and agreements made under the Act are to be laid before Parliament. In the schedule annexed to the Act 13 agreements with railways and telegraph companies are referred to, subject to the approbation of Parliament, and it declares it to be expedient that agreements should be made with other railways set forth, including the metropolitan districts. Three months' notice is to be given by the Postmaster-General to the companies. By the statute the Postmaster-General, with the approbation of the Treasury, can purchase the undertakings of telegraph companies, but no purchase or agreement to purchase is to be binding, unless the same has been laid for one month on the table of both Houses of Parliament without disapproval. The concluding enactment is to the effect that if no Act be passed in the next session of Parliament placing at the disposal of the Postmaster-General such moneys as may be requisite for carrying into effect the objects and purposes of the Act, then the agreements made to be void, and the Postmaster to pay the expenses incurred.

II.—SPECIAL LEGISLATION.

1.—SESSION 1868—ITS RESULTS.

The railway schemes lodged in the private bill office during the past eight years, on the part of established companies, or by parties seeking to incorporate new undertakings, with their progress through the legislature, have been as under :—

Bills.	1862.	1863.	1864.	1865.	1866.	1867.	1868.
Lodged	230	258	327	406	398	151	102
Withdrawn	46	66	58	67	123	46	20
Rejected	34	42	60	63	65	10	9
Royal Assents	150	150	209	276	210	95	73

ROYAL ASSENTS.

Abergavenny and Monmouth, July 13.
Acton and Brentford, June 25.
Athenry and Ennis Junction, July 13.
Barry, July 13.
Belfast Central, July 31.
Bishop Stortford, Dunmow, and Braintree, July 31.
Brecon and Merthyr Tydvil Junction, July 13.
Bristol and Exeter, June 25
Bristol and North Somerset, July 31.
Buckfastleigh, Totnes, and South Devon, May 29.
Burry Port and Gwendreath Valley, May 29.
Caledonian, July 13.
Cambrian (Revived Line to Dolgelly), July 31.
Carnarvon and Llanberis, May 29.
Cheshire Lines, May 29.
Chichester and Midhurst, July 31.
Clonmel, Lismore, and Dungarvon, July 13.
Cork and Kinsale Junction, July 31.
Cork and Macroom (Direct), July 31.
Devon and Cornwall, July 31.
Devon Valley, May 29.
Dingwall and Skye, May 29.
Downpatrick, Dundrum, and Newcastle June 25.
Dublin, Wicklow, and Wexford, June 25.

East London, July 31.
Fareham and Netley, July 31.
Glasgow and South Western, June 25.
Great Eastern, July 31.
Great Marlow, July 13.
Great Northern, June 25.
Great Western (Dividends), June 25.
Great Western, July 13.
Greenock and Ayrshire, July 13.
Holywell, July 13.
Ilfracombe, June 25.
Isle of Wight (Newport Junction), July 31.
Kington and Eardisley, July 13.
Lancashire Union, July 13.
Lancashire and Yorkshire, June 25.
Lancashire and Yorkshire and Lancashire Union, July 13.
London and Blackwall, July 13.
London, Brighton, and South Coast, July 13.
London and North Western, July 13.
London and North Western and Knighton, Central Wales, and Central Wales Extension, June 25.
London and South Western, June 25.
Mersey, July 31.
Metropolitan, July 13.
Metropolitan District, July 13.

Metropolitan and St. John's Wood, July 16.
Midland, June 25.
Midland and London and North Western, June 25.
Newquay and Cornwall Junction, May 29.
North British (Forth River), June 25.
North British (General Powers), July 13.
North London, May 29.
North and South Western Junction, June 25.
Pontypool, Caerleon, and Newport, July 13.
Potteries, Shrewsbury, and North Wales, June 25.
Rathkeale and Newcastle Junction, July 31.
St. Ives and West Cornwall Junction, July 13.
South Eastern, July 31.

South Eastern and Chatham and Dover (London, Lewes, and Brighton Abandonment), July 13.
Stourbridge, July 13.
Teign Valley, July 13.
Tottenham and Hampstead Junction, July 13.
Uxbridge and Rickmansworth, June 25.
Vale of Towy, June 25.
Waterford and Kilkenny, July 13.
Waterford and Limerick, July 13.
Waterloo and Whitehall, July 31.
Weedon and Daventry, July 31.
West Riding and Grimsby, June 25.
Wolverhampton and Walsall, July 13.

WITHDRAWN.

Afon Valley.
Bodmin and Wadebridge.
Crystal Palace and South London Junction.
Dublin and Drogheda.
Eastern Metropolitan.
Great Eastern (Management).
Great Northern and Western (Abandonment).
Islington.
Limerick and North Kerry Junction.
Liverpool and Birkenhead.
London, Thames Haven, and Kent Coast Junction.
Midland Counties and South Wales.

Monmouthshire and Great Western Junction.
Newport and Usk.
Newry and Armagh.
North and South Wiltshire.
Ross and Monmouth and Forest of Dean.
South Eastern and Brighton Working Union
—withdrawn from committee as such, but passed as South Eastern (Division of Stock).
Stokes Bay, Isle of Wight, &c. (Amalgamation).
Stonehouse and Nailsworth.
Worcester, Dean Forest, and Monmouth.

REJECTED.

Cambrian (Division of System)—in committee.
Central Cornwall—on standing orders.
Isle of Wight and Cowes and Newport Junction—in committee.
Isle of Wight Central—in committee.
Shropshire Union—in committee.

Sirhowy—on standing orders.
Somerset and Dorset—in committee.
Surrey and Sussex Junction—on standing orders.
Vale of Crickhowell—in committee.

2.—NEW CAPITAL, &c.

By a Parliamentary return, furnished after the close of the session, the amount of new capital authorised was detailed as under :—

Company.	Shares.	Loans.	Total.
Belfast Central	£190,000	£63,300	£253,300
Caledonian	1,200,000	400,000	1,600,000
Cork and Kinsale	....	15,000	15,000
Cork and Macroom	....	10,000	10,000
Great Marlow	18,000	6,000	24,000
Great Northern	120,000	40,000	160,000
Great Western	40,000	13,300	53,300
Greenock and Ayrshire	150,000	50,000	200,000
Holywell	10,000	3,300	13,300
Isle of Wight and Cowes	60,000	20,000	80,000
Lancashire and Yorkshire	50,000	....	50,000
Lancashire Union	530,000	176,600	706,600
London and North Western	405,000	135,000	540,000
London and Brighton	1,000,000	333,333	1,333,333
Midland and London and North Western (jointly)	70,000	23,200	93,200
Midland	3,750,000	1,250,000	5,000,000
North and South Western	30,000	10,000	40,000
Tottenham and Hampstead	100,000	33,333	133,333
Waterford and Kilkenny	....	20,000	20,000
Waterford and Limerick	50,000	16,600	66,600
Weedon and Daventry	30,000	10,000	40,000
Wolverhampton and Walsall	20,000	6,600	26,000
Total, 1868	£7,823,000	£16,355,566	£10,458,566
1865	£36,003,700	£12,285,443	£48,289,143
1866	33,056,453	10,874,731	43,931,184
1867	10,441,770	1,663,900	12,105,670

III.—AGREEMENTS.

1.—BRIGHTON—EAST LONDON.

An Agreement entered into the 1st day of May, 1868, between the London, Brighton, and South Coast of the one part, and the East London of the other part.

Whereas the East London was incorporated by the "East London Act. 1865," and authorised to construct, amongst other railways, the railways described in the Act as Railway No. 1 (main line), a railway to commence in the parish of St. Matthew, Bethnal Green, in the county of Middlesex, by a junction with the authorised line of the Great Eastern, and to terminate in the parish of St. Paul, Deptford, in the county of Surrey, by a junction with the main line of the London Brighton and South Coast, Railway No. 3 (Brighton up line junction); a railway to commence in the parish of St. Paul, Deptford, in the county of Surrey, by a junction with Railway No. 1, and to terminate in the same parish by a junction with the main line of the London Brighton and South Coast, Railway No. 4 (South London junction); a railway to commence in the parish of St. Paul, Deptford, in the county of Surrey, by a junction with Railway No. 4, and to terminate in the same parish by a junction with the branch then in course of construction of the London Brighton and South Coast leading from White Post Lane to the Deptford line of that company; and by the 35th section of the said Act it is provided that in the construction of the railways the company shall, with respect to the railways, sidings, and property of the Brighton, conform to and observe the following regulations and restrictions; that is to say: 1st. They shall form the communications of railways No. 1 and No. 3 with the London Brighton and South Coast by means of junctions with the local up and down lines of that railway. 2nd. They shall carry the railway No. 3 over the South London by means of a bridge with a single span of not less than 46 feet wide, and with a clear headway throughout the whole width of the bridge of not less than 14 feet. They shall at their own cost construct the bridge for carrying railway No. 1 under the Deptford branch line, so as to leave for the use of the Brighton the clear width of 26 feet between the parapet walls of such bridge. 3rd. They shall not enter upon, take, use or interfere, either temporarily or permanently, with any part of the coke ovens or sidings of the Brighton situate at or near to the New Cross station of that company, except so far as may be necessary for the construction of the junctions by the Act authorised. 4th. They shall construct the railway No. 3 by the Act authorised over such sidings by means of a viaduct, and so as to leave thereunder in every part thereof a clear headway of 14 feet, and also so as to preserve to the Brighton the full and complete use of such sidings. And whereas it is now considered desirable and advantageous by both the companies, parties hereto, that some modification should be made in the plans for constructing some of the said railways of the East London and the junctions thereof with the railways of the Brighton: Now, therefore, it is agreed by and between the Brighton and the East London as follows:

1. The East London shall use their best endeavours to obtain in the present session an Act of Parliament to authorise, so far as such authority may be necessary, the deviations and alterations and also the abandonment of the railways and parts of railways before mentioned, and the confirmation of this agreement, and upon such Act being obtained shall forthwith carry out and give effect to the said Act and the terms and conditions of these presents.

2. The Railway No. 1 (main line) authorised by the East London Act, 1865, and shown on the plan hereunto annexed by a continuous black line marked "E. L. Railway No. 1" as authorised, shall be deviated to the course and position shown on the same plan by a continuous red line, and marked as "E. L. R. No. 1;" and such deviated line shall be a double line if required by the East London within three calendar months from the passing of the said intended Act, and shall form a junction with the railway described in the London Brighton and South Coast (Additional Powers) Act, 1865, as "Second Junction Railway," at the point marked on the said plan "Junction E," and not otherwise or elsewhere.

3. The East London shall have at all times full and free right to run over, work, and use with their engines, carriages, and servants, for the purposes of their traffic of every description, so much of the said Brighton Second Junction as lies between the said point marked in the said plan "Junction E" and the authorised junction of the said Brighton Second Junction with the down local line of the Brighton as shown on the said plan and marked "Junction H."

4. The Railway No. 3 (Brighton up line junction) authorised by the East London Act, 1865, and also shown on the plan hereunto annexed by a continuous black line, and marked "E. L. Ry. No. 3 as authorised," shall be deviated to the course and position shown on the said plan by a continuous red line, and marked as "E. L. Ry. No. 3," and shall be a double line if required by the East London within three calendar months from the passing of the

said intended Act, and shall form a junction with the railway described in the London Brighton and South Coast (Additional Powers) Act, 1865, as " Third Junction Railway," at the point marked on the said plan " Junction F," and not otherwise or elsewhere.

5. The East London shall have at all times full and free right to run over, work, and use with their engines, carriages, and servants, and for the purposes of their traffic of every description, so much of the said Brighton Third Junction as lies between the said point marked on the said plan " Junction F," and the authorised junction of the said Brighton Third Junction with the up local line of the Brighton as shown on the said plan and marked " Junction I."

6. The Railway No. 4 (South London Junction) also authorised by the East London Act, 1865, and shown on the plan hereunto annexed by a continuous black line, and marked " E. L. Railway No. 4 as authorised," shall be deviated to the course and position shown on the said plan by continuous red lines, and marked as " E. L. Railway No. 4," and shall be a double line, and form a junction with the railway of the Brighton secondly described in the London, Brighton, and South Coast (Extension, &c.) Act, 1863, at the point marked on the said plan " Junction G," and not otherwise or elsewhere.

7. The said parts of the said East London railways, viz., of No. 1 (main line), No. 3 (Brighton up line junction), and No. 4 (South London Junction), for which the said deviated lines respectively are intended to be substituted, and the junctions of those lines respectively with the railways of the Brighton as authorised by the East London Act, 1865, shall be absolutely abandoned, and shall not be constructed.

7A. The East London may obtain powers for and construct their New Cross station lin⸱ shown in blue on the plan hereinbefore referred to, and the Brighton will allow access for passengers between that line and the local platforms of their New Cross passenger station by means of the subway (marked K. K. on plan) now existing under that station ; and the needful approaches to and from the platforms of either company, or such other works as may be necessary for effecting this purpose, so far as the same shall be on the land of the Brighton, shall be constructed by that company at the cost of the East London, who shall deposit with the Brighton the amount of such cost, to be estimated by the Brighton company's engineer, before the Brighton shall be required to commence such works.

8. The deviated Railway No. 3 between the points marked A. and B. on the said plan shall be constructed wholly on viaduct, with arches of not less than 30 feet span, and with a clear headway throughout each arch of not less than 14 feet from the level of the rails of the existing and authorised lines of the Brighton, and between the points marked on the said plan with the letters C and D the said deviated railway No. 3 shall be constructed wholly of viaduct, and the last-mentioned portion of railway so to be constructed of viaduct shall be constructed by the Brighton, and all costs and expenses of and incidental to the construction thereof shall be paid by the East London to the Brighton, and before the Brighton shall be required to commence the construction of such portion of railway the estimated cost thereof, to be fixed by the Brighton company's engineer, shall be deposited with the Brighton, by the East London.

9. The Brighton shall sell, and the East London shall purchase, so much and such parts of the easternmost piece of land coloured brown on the said plan hereunto annexed as shall not be required by the Brighton for the construction of the said Brighton Junction No. 2, and as lies on the east side of that railway, and as shall be required for the construction according to the terms and conditions of these presents of the said East London deviated railway No. 1, and as shall be severed thereby ; and also an easement or right to construct and maintain the East London deviated railway No. 3 according to these presents over the pieces of land coloured brown and red on the said plan hereunto annexed, reserving to the Brighton the use of the soil under the arches of the viaduct where the said East London deviated railway No. 3 shall be carried by viaduct over the same pieces of land.

10. The junctions between the said East London deviated railway Nos. 1, 3, and 4 and the said railways of the Brighton, and all works on the property of the Brighton, including signals necessary for the formation and working of such junctions respectively, shall, as soon as the other parts of the said railways are completed, be constructed by the Brighton ; and the East London shall pay to the Brighton all the expenses incurred by the Brighton in and about such works and signals and junctions, and incidental thereto respectively : and before the Brighton shall be required to commence the construction of any of such works, signals, or junctions, the estimated cost thereof, to be fixed by the Brighton company's engineer, shall be deposited with the Brighton by the East London.

11. The East London deviated railway No. 3 shall be carried over Cold Blow Lane by a bridge or arch of not less span and clear headway than the bridge or arch erected by the Brighton carrying the railway of the Brighton described in " The London Brighton and South Coast (Additional Powers) Act, 1865," as Third Junction Railway over the same lane, and the East London shall not otherwise lessen the width of the said lane or obstruct the same.

12. Except as herein or in the said intended Act expressly provided for, nothing herein or in the said intended Act contained shall prejudice or affect section 35 of " The East London Railway Act, 1865," or sections 36 to 41, both inclusive, of the same Act, and all such sections respectively shall be applicable to the deviated railways and works hereby provided for in the same manner as if those sections respectively had been herein and in the said intended Act repeated as part of this agreement and of the said intended Act ; and, except as aforesaid, neither this agreement nor the said intended Act shall prejudice or affect such sections respectively or the said Brighton company.

13. Sections 9 to 12, both inclusive, of the Railway Clauses Act, 1863, relative to junctions, shall, subject to the provisions of this agreement and of the said intended Act, apply to the junctions hereby provided for of the East London lines with the lines of the Brighton.

14. Unless and until the Brighton shall erect signals specially for the regulation of the junction of the two deviated lines of the East London railway No. 4 in the plan hereunto annexed with the railway of the Brighton secondly described in the London Brighton and South Coast (Extensions, &c.) Act, 1863, the East London shall, half-yearly, on the 30th day of June and the 31st day of December, pay to the Brighton two-thirds of the costs and expenses of the maintenance, repair, working, and management of the signals and works of the Brighton by which such junctions hall be regulated.

15. The terms and conditions to which the East London shall be subject in respect of the running powers by this agreement granted to them, and the tolls or other consideration to be paid by them to the Brighton for the same, and all questions and differences which may arise between the Brighton and the East London as to the construction or effect of these presents, or any clause thereof, or the performance or non-observance of any of the provisions hereof, or any matters connected therewith or consequent thereon or incidental thereto, shall be referred to Mr. Thomas Elliott Harrison, of Great George Street, Westminster, civil engineer, or, failing him, to an engineer to be appointed by the Board of Trade upon the application in writing of either the East London or the Brighton ; and the decision of the said Thomas Elliott Harrison, or of such other arbitrator, shall be binding and conclusive upon the said companies respectively, and the costs and expenses of the arbitration and award shall be in the discretion of the arbitrator.   In witness whereof the said companies, parties hereto, have hereunto caused their respective common seals to be affixed the day and year first above written.

2.—CITY OF GLASGOW UNION—NORTH BRITISH—GLASGOW AND SOUTH WESTERN.

Minute of Agreement between the City of Glasgow Union of the first part, the Glasgow and South Western of the second part, the North British of the third part, and Messrs. Thomas Brassey, John Kelk, and Charles Waring, of the City of London, contractors, of the fourth part.

1. The first party shall forthwith, under the powers conferred on them by "The City of Glasgow Union Railway Act, 1867," attach the fixed and permanent preferential dividend of 5l. per cent per annum provided for by that Act to the 30,000 shares in the capital of their company created under the Union Act of 1864.

2. The second party shall, subject to the approval of their shareholders, at a special meeting to be called forthwith, subscribe for, take up, and pay from time to time the amount of calls due upon 14,000 shares, representing 140,000l. of the preference stock, specified in the first article hereof, taking transfers from time to time from the fourth party of shares held by them to the extent of 14,000 of such shares, but no interest shall be payable on such calls. The whole of the said 140,000l. shall be expended on the Dunlop-street Station, and shall not be diverted to any other purpose whatever.

3. The second party, subject to the approval of their shareholders at the said special meeting, bind and oblige themselves to unite with the first party, but at the expense of the first party, in an application to Parliament in the next session, and in future sessions of Parliament until an Act be obtained, for authority to the second party to guarantee and shall forthwith thereafter guarantee a dividend of 5 per cent. on so much of the said 30,000 shares of preference stock specified in the first article hereof as over and above the said 14,000 shares to be subscribed for by them, has already been or may yet be expended in the construction of the proposed Dunlop-street Station, in terms of and as provided by memorandum of agreement between the Glasgow and South Western and City of Glasgow Union Companies, of date 18th and 27th March, 1868 (hereinafter called the Dunlop-street Station agreement).

4. Whereas it is stipulated in the agreement last mentioned, that the cumulo rent to be paid by the second party for the Dunlop-street Station, either by themselves or along with any other company or companies using the station, shall be calculated at the rate or 5l. per cent. per annum on the cost of the said station ; and it is also stipulated in said agreement that the first party should, in the next session of Parliament, and if necessary in the following session or sessions, apply to Parliament for a bill to authorise the second party to guarantee a dividend of 5 per cent. on at least so much of the preference stock to be created under the Union Act of 1867, sections 18 to 23, as might be expended in the construction of the Dunlop-street Station ; but it was by said agreement declared that whatever sums the second party should be called on to pay under the said guarantee should be imputed as payments *pro tanto* of the rent of the Dunlop-street Station ; and whereas the stipulations contained in articles 2 and 3 hereof are intended to come and shall come in lieu and in place of the guarantee stipulated in the Dunlop-street Station agreement : and whereas, in respect of such stipulations, it has been agreed that in lieu of dividend on the said preference shares to be subscribed for and taken by the second party, the rent payable by the second party for the Dunlop-street Station shall be reduced in amount by the sum of 7,000l. per annum, being a sum equal in amount to the preferential dividend on the 14,000 preference shares to be taken and held by them in terms of article 2 hereof, and also by whatever sums they may be called on to pay under the guarantee stipulated in article 3 hereof, the meaning and intention of

parties being that the said subscription of 140,000l., and the guarantee of dividend on additional stock, should be regarded and dealt with as capital sums advanced by the second party towards the cost of the Dunlop-street Station, and as coming in lieu of the payment of rent calculated on a corresponding amount at the rate of 5l. per cent. per annum, as stipulated in the Dunlop-street Station agreement : therefore, it is hereby declared that the rent payable by the second party for the Dunlop-street Station shall, notwithstanding the Dunlop-street Station agreement, and so long as they are the sole tenants in the stations, be 5 per cent. per annum on the cost thereof, to be ascertained as provided by article 2 of the Dunlop-street Station agreement, after deducting the said sum of 7,000l. per annum, and also after deducting whatever sums the second party may pay under their said guarantee stipulated for in article 3 hereof ; the balance, if any, after all these deductions are made, being the only liability of the second party for rent for Dunlop-street Station, whether in questions with any of the parties hereto or with the creditors of the first party or otherwise ; and in the event of any other tenant or tenants being admitted into Dunlop-street Station, the amount of rent charged to such tenant or tenants shall be applied in the first place, and preferably to all claims, mortgages, and engagements of the first party, in further reducing or in extinguishing, as the case may be, the rent payable by the second party, and in repaying to them annually, so far as the same may extend, the said sum of 7,000l., being interest on money advanced by them, and any balance that may remain thereafter shall be paid over to the first party. Provided always, as it is hereby provided and declared, that until the Dunlop-street Station is completed and placed at the disposal of the second party, the first party shall pay to the second party interest at the rate of 5l. per cent. per annum on the said 140,000l. from the respective dates of payment thereof, which interest shall in the option of the second party, be imputed as payments pro tanto of the rent of the Dunlop street Station. It is further stipulated and agreed that clauses shall be inserted in the said Bill to carry the above provisions into effect, so far as Parliamentary sanction is requisite, and, if necessary, to confirm this agreement, and until the said bill is passed with such clauses, no money shall be borrowed or debentures granted by the first party without the consent of the second party.

5. The ground acquired by the first party from the College of Glasgow other than that which has been already apportioned to the Edinburgh and Glasgow, shall be apportioned for the occupancy of the second and third parties, in manner delineated and shewn on the plan signed as relative hereto, by James Reid Stewart, John Stirling, and Sir Andrew Orr, and the rent payable by each company on their respective proportions of the whole of such land acquired from the college shall be 5 per cent. on the value of the ground which may be occupied by each, in the relative proportion which such value bears to the cost of the whole ground ; such relative value to be fixed by arbitration, under the Railway Companies Arbitration Act, 1859. And it is understood and agreed that the College Station may be used for passengers as well as for goods. Any passenger station, whether erected by the North British on the portion of the said ground already allocated to them (which they are hereby empowered to do), or by the Union Company on the remainder of said ground being open to the second party on the terms specified in the agreement scheduled to the bill of 1865.

6. The first party shall make application to Parliament in next session, and future sessions if necessary, for authority to constitute, and on obtaining such authority, shall constitute 100,000l. of the preference stock, to be created under article 1, into a separate stock, to be called College Station Stock, which College Station Stock shall have a real lien and security for payment of the dividends accruing thereon, in and over the rents of the said College Station, payable respectively by the second and third parties, preferably to all other debts, liabilities, debentures, and engagements of the first party.

. The second and third parties bind and oblige themselves, subject to the approval of their respective shareholders at special meetings to be forthwith called for the purpose, to unite with the first party, but at the first party's expense, in an application to Parliament in the next session, and in future sessions of Parliament till the same be obtained, for authority to the second and third parties jointly and as between themselves in equal proportions to guarantee and shall forthwith thereafter guarantee the interest of the debenture debt of the first party to the extent of 200,000l., and bind and oblige themselves respectively at the said special meetings to ask the authority of their shareholders to their directors entering into agreements in the view of such application. The stipulation in this article shall be accepted of by the third party as implement of the obligations on the second party to guarantee the interest on the debenture debt of the first party, contained in agreement between the first, second, and third parties, dated 19th and 20th February, 1867 (hereinafter called the Leeds Agreement).

8. Whereas the third party are bound in terms of the Heads of Agreement scheduled to and confirmed by the "City of Glasgow Union Railway Act, 1865," to subscribe 300,000l. of the capital of the City of Glasgow Union, whereof only 200,000l. has been as yet subscribed by the individuals who represent their interest on the register of that company, and whereas by the Leeds Agreement the third party are bound, not later than 1st May last, to subscribe and pay the calls on the further sum of 100,000l., making up the full amount of the said subscription of 300,000l. Therefore the third party shall take transfers from the fourth party for such further sum of 100,000l. of ordinary shares in the undertaking of the first party.

9. The first parties bind themselves to give, and the fourth party agree to take, the contract of the works of the Dunlop-street Station at the prices fixed in a schedule signed, as relative hereto, by Thomas Brassey and James Reid Stewart, the payments in respect of such contract to be made in cash from month to month on the usual certificate of the engineer of the first party, and under the usual deduction of 10 per cent., in terms of the existing contracts for sections 1 and 2 of the through line.

10. The first party bind themselves to give, and the fourth parties agree to take the contract for the third section of the works of the through line of the City Union from East Nile-street to Sword-street, at the prices fixed in a schedule signed, as relative hereto, by Thomas Brassey and James Reid Stewart, the payments in respect of the said contract, as well as of the works of the first contract of the through line, in so far as the same extends from Bridgegate-street to East Nile-street, to be made in manner following; that is to say, 50 per cent. of the whole amount due in respect of such works each month, as certified by the engineer of the first party, to be paid in cash, and 50 per cent. to be paid in debentures of the first party for three years, to be guaranteed by the second and third parties in manner provided in Article 7, and bearing interest at 5 per cent., such debentures of the first party to be delivered to the fourth parties so soon as the first party shall be entitled to issue the same, but not later than 1st September, 1869 ; and failing delivery of such debentures by that date, 40 per cent to be paid in cash within three months from that date, and the remaining 10 per cent. to be retained on terms analogous to those in the existing contracts for sections 1 and 2 of the through line ; and it is further agreed that if debentures are delivered for the whole amount of 50 per cent., interest corresponding to the 10 per cent, retainable under the contracts shall be paid back to or shall be retained by the first party for the period during which such 10 per cent. is retainable under the said existing contracts. Interest at the rate of 5 per cent. to be paid by the first party on 40 per cent. of the said amount so due until the said debentures are so delivered by the first party, or the said 40 per cent. paid in cash, as above-mentioned.

11. It is understood and agreed that clause 7 of the said Leeds Agreement shall not be held to apply to railway No. 4 of the undertaking of the first party, but the first party shall be bound to construct the same at the request of the second party.

12. All other agreements between all or any of the parties hereto so far as they respectively are concerned, in so far as not altered, modified, or rescinded by these presents, are hereby reserved entire and confirmed: and in particular, all rights of the North British under the heads of agreement, scheduled to and confirmed by the Union Act of 1865, in reference to the stations of the Union company, are hereby reserved entire.

13. This agreement is entered into subject to the same being approved by the shareholders of the first, second, and third parties respectively.

14. All disputes and differences in regard to the true intent and meaning of these presents, or in regard to any matter or thing connected therewith, shall be referred to arbitration, under "The Railway Companies Arbitration Act, 1859." In witness whereof, &c.

Minute of Agreement between the City of Glasgow Union of the first part, and the North British of the second part.

The parties hereto, under reservation of the obligations and conditions of previous agreements between them in relation to the premises, in so far as subsisting and not inconsistent with the provisions hereof, have agreed, and do hereby agree, and bind and oblige themselves in manner following, that is to say :—

1. The lines of railway forming part of the Deviation Railway authorised by " The City of Glasgow Union Act, 1867," and therein firstly described, and of the railway authorised by " The Edinburgh and Glasgow (Coatbridge Branch) Act, 1865," and therein firstly described, with all station accommodation, conveniences, and accessory works, shall between the points A A and B B respectively laid down upon a plan signed, in reference to these presents, by James Reid Stewart, chairman of the City of Glasgow Union, and John Stirling, chairman of the North British, and including the diversion of Hunter-street, be formed and constructed by the first parties hereto, as shewn upon the said plan, at the joint expense of the parties hereto, which expense shall include the cost of all works, lands, and buildings required for and connected therewith, to be fixed and ascertained as hereinafter provided ; and, when so constructed, such lines shall constitute part of the undertaking of the said first parties.

2. The division of Hunter-street and Barrack-street within the powers of the companies parties hernto, be executed in such manner as shall encroach to the least possible extent upon the station ground of the second parties.

3. The first parties, for behoof of the second parties, shall acquire, at the cost and expense of the second parties, such ground as they may require east of Sword-street, and which may be within the Parliamentary powers of the first parties.

4. The North British shall have right in perpetuity to run over and use the said lines of railway and whole station accommodation, conveniences, and works described in the first article hereof, between the said points A A and B B, exempt from tolls, rates, and charge of every description for all traffic passing to or from the proposed railway number 1 of the " Edinburgh and Glasgow (Coatbridge Branch) Act, 1865," as altered and varied by subsequent Acts, or any part thereof, or over the same or any part thereof from or to points beyond such railway, but such exemption from tolls, rates, and charges shall not extend and apply to traffic passing from or to their system *via* Sighthill, subject always to such rules and regulations as may be mutually agreed upon, or as in case of difference may be fixed by the Board of Trade.

5. During the first ten years from the opening of the said lines described in the first article hereof, the second parties shall contribute and pay to the said first parties one half of the cost of maintenance, renewals, and working charges, upon the said lines of railway, stations, and other works, to be constructed at the joint expenses of the parties hereto, and after the expiry of that period, such proportion of the cost of maintenance, renewals, and working charges thereof as may be fixed by arbitration.

6. The amount payable by the second parties under this agreement for the various works, the construction of which is hereby devolved on the first parties, and for the land and buildings to be acquired, and other expenses connected therewith, shall be paid to the first party month by month as the expenditure proceeds, according to accounts to be rendered by the first party, and shall, in case of difference, be determined by arbitration as after provided for.

7. The second parties shall be entitled to lay down and join with the said lines of railway described in the first article hereof, and with the sidings connected or to be connected therewith, such, and so many sidings or branches as they may find necessary for facilitating the carriage of their traffic to or from the ground acquired or which may be acquired by them fer station purposes, and the position of such junctions shall in case of difference be determined by arbitration, and the second parties shall not be liable to the first parties for any compensation in respect of land to be occupied by the junctions of such sidings and branches with the said lines or sidings of the first parties.

8. Inasmuch as the earth and other materials to be taken from the cutting, to be made in forming the lines and other works described in the first article hereof, will be required in the construction of the said Coatbridge railway of the second parties, the first parties bind and oblige themselves to deposit the said earth and other materials from the said cutting at such places on the line of the said Coatbridge railway, and in such manner as the engineer of the second parties shall from time to time direct, any extra cost or charge incurred thereby by or to the first parties to be repaid them by the second parties ; such extra cost in case of difference to be settled by arbitration.

9. The second parties shall have right, free of any charge by or payment to the first parties, to erect and maintain telegraph posts and wires, and to lay water and gas pipes along that portion of the line of railway specified and referred to in the first article hereof.

10. If any difference shall arise between the parties hereto with respect to any question hereby referred to arbitration, or as to the true intent and meaning of this agreement, or the carrying out of the same, such difference shall be settled and determined by THOMAS ELLIOT HARRISON, Newcastle-upon-Tyne, whom failing, JOHN HAWKSHAW, Civil Engineer, London.

11. This agreement is entered into, subject to the same being approved by the shareholders of the respective companies.—In witness whereof, &c.

3.—GREAT WESTERN—SOUTH WALES UNION.

Agreement entered into this 14th day of May 1868, *between the Bristol and South Wales Union of the one part, and the Great Western of the other part.*

Whereas the Union company were by the Bristol and South Wales Union Act, 1857, being their Act of incorporation, authorised to construct and have constructed a line of railway from Bristol to the New Passage Ferry in the county of Gloucester, and from the north western side of the New Passage Ferry in the parish of Portskewett to the South Wales railway in the county of Monmouth, being the railways which are first and secondly mentioned in the Union Company's Act of incorporation, and which are hereinafter referred to as the Union railway : And whereas since the opening of the Union railway for public traffic the same has been worked by the Great Western under an agreement between that company and the Union company, dated 17th February 1864, but the Ferry which the Union company under their said Act of incorporation were authorised to purchase and work in connection with the Union railway has not been worked by the Great Western : And whereas the Union company were by their said Act of incorporation authorised to raise by ordinary shares a capital of 300,000l., and to borrow on mortgage or bond 98,000l. : And whereas by the Union company's Act of 1861 the Union company were authorised, in lieu of any shares which might have been surrendered, cancelled, or forfeited, or which might remain unissued, to create and issue new shares of the amounts and in accordance with the provisions of the said last mentioned Act, and the Union company were empowered to attach to such new shares any preferential, perpetual, or terminable dividend, and such other privileges as the Union company might think fit, subject to the provisions and restrictions contained in the same Act : And whereas the Union company by their Act of 1862 were authorised to make the Extension railway and works by that Act authorised : And whereas the times limited for the compulsory purchase of land and execution of works under the said Act of 1862 were by the Union company's Act of 1864 respectively extended, but no land has been purchased and no works have been executed under the said last mentioned Acts, or either if them, save and except that notices to treat have been given for and an award made as regards five acres of land or thereabouts near Lawrence Hill Station, and the compulsory powers for the purchase of land under the Act of 1864 expired on the 17th day of July, 1867 : And whereas the undertaking of the Union company is not subject to any rentcharges, and their debenture or bond debt amounts to 98,000l., and their ordinary shares, fully paid, amounts to 168,225l., and they have issued irredeemable preference shares, bearing interest at 5l. per cent., to the extent of 131,775l. : And whereas the Union company and the Great Western have entered into the agreement hereinafter contained : Now these presents witness that for the considerations herein appearing it is hereby mutually agreed as follows :—

1. Subject to the approval of Parliament, the Union company, their railways and undertakings, including the said Ferry, and their superfluous lands, and their buildings, wharves, piers, stores, plant, and all their property, shall, on and after the 1st day of August, 1868, be merged into or amalgamated with the Great Western, and shall thenceforth form part

and parcel of the undertaking of the Great Western ; and the debenture or bond debt of the Union company shall, on and after that date and subject as after mentioned, be assumed and discharged by the Great Western ; and, subject as after mentioned, the capital, preference and ordinary, of the Union company, shall on and after that date, form part of the capital of the Great Western ; and on such amalgamation or merger all the rights, powers, privileges, authorities, and indemnities of the Union company whatsoever may be exercised and enjoyed, and all their duties and liabilities with respect to their undertaking shall and may be borne, by the Great Western, except as hereinafter excepted.

2. Subject as aforesaid, the Union company as on and from the said 1st day of August, 1868, shall be dissolved and cease to exist, except for the purpose of winding up their affairs, and the Union company shall, at their own cost, obtain power to abandon and shall abandon the extension authorised by their Act of 1862, and shall out of their own funds settle and discharge all claims arising from or in consequence of the said extension or the abandonment thereof.

3. From the 1st day of January, 1867 to the 31st day of December, 1867, both inclusive, the Great Western shall be deemed to have had the entire control and management of the undertaking and property of the Union company, but exclusive of the revenues of their Ferry and their superfluous lands and surplus property ; and on and from the 1st day of January, 1868 until the 1st day of August 1868, the Union railway shall continue to be worked by the Great Western, and during the last mentioned period the Great Western shall also work the Ferry ; and during the respective periods aforesaid the costs, charges, and expenses connected with such working, including costs of maintaining the railway, the ferry boats, and the piers on either side of the Severn, and all other costs, charges, and expenses connected with the railway and ferry, and, except as hereinafter provided, all liabilities and obligations whatsoever of the Union company under their several Acts or otherwise with respect to the working of their railway, ferry, and undertaking, shall be borne and paid by the Great Western, but the Great Western are not to be liable in any way for the said piers or ferry boats, or for the costs of maintaining and working them, until they begin to work the ferry, or are in possession of the said boats, which possession is to be given and working to commence on the 1st day of January, 1868 as aforesaid ; and the Great Western are not to be liable in any way for or in respect of the railways authorised by the Union company's Act of 1862, or for the construction thereof, or for any liabilities, penalties, or forfeitures in respect of the non-construction of the said authorised railways.

4. From the 1st day of January, 1867, until the 31st day of December, 1867, both inclusive, the entire gross earnings of the Union company's railway and stations (but exclusive of the rent and revenues of the ferry, and of the income arising from the supurfluous land and surplus property of the Union company) shall be received by the Great Western, and in consideration thereof, and in lieu of the sums now payable by the Great Wentern to the Union company under the agreement of the 17th day of February 1864, before referred to, or otherwise, the Great Western shall, during such period, pay the interest accruing due for that year on the Union company's debenture or bond debt of 98,000l., and the guaranteed interest for the same time at 5 per cent. on 114,800l. of the preferential capital of the Union company.

5. On and from the 1st day of January, 1868 until the said 1st day of August, 1868 the entire gross earnings of the Union company's railway, stations, and ferry (but exclusive of the income arising from their superfluous land and surplus property) shall be received by the Great Western, and in consideration thereof, and in lieu of the sums now payable by the Great Western to the Union company under the agreement of the 17th day of February, 1864, before referred to, or otherwise, the Great Western shall, during such period, pay the following sums, viz., the interest accruing on and from the 1st day of January, 1868 on the Union company's debenture or bond debt of 98,000l., and the guaranteed interest at 5 per cent. on 117,857l. of the preferential capital of the Union company ; and the Union company shall provide for the renewal of such of their debentures or bond debt as become due prior to the said 1st August, 1868, but all renewals or reborrowing up to the said 1st August, 1868 shall not be at a higher rate of interest than 5 per cent. per annum ; and on and from the last-mentioned date all liability in respect of such debenture and bond debt shall be assumed by the Great Western, and they shall pay the interest thereon from that date, and they may, if they think fit (according to their statutory powers), charge that debt as and when portions thereof are from time to time paid off and reborrowed either on the undertaking of the Great Western generally, or on the Union company's railway, stations, and ferry separately, or on both ; but nothing in this agreement shall authorise a charge on the Union company's railway, stations, and ferry separately, or otherwise, after the amalgamation, of a debenture or bond debt greater than that which the Union company are at the time of the amalgamation authorised to raise by mortgages, debentures, or bonds.

6. On or before the 1st day of August, 1868 the Union company shall cancel 11,325l. of their irredeemable preference shares, and the Great Western may re-issue such shares at any time or times after the 1st day of February, 1870 for the purposes of the railways, works, and ferry of the Union company.

7. The preference capital of the Union company, not exceeding the amounts hereinafter specified, shall bear and continue to bear a guaranteed preferential interest at the rate of 5l. per cent. per annum as follows :—

For the period from the 1st day of August, 1868, till the 31st day of January, 1869, the sum of 118,350l.;

For the period from the 1st day of February, 1869, till the 31st day of January, 1870, the sum of 119,600l.;

For the period from the 1st day of February, 1870, and thereafter in perpetuity, except as hereinafter provided, the sum of 120,450l.;

but if and when the Great Western re-issue the balance of the said preference capital of 11,325*l*., all that capital, not exceeding in the aggregate the sum of 131,775*l*, shall bear and continue to bear the above guaranteed preferential rate of interest, and such interest shall be payable to the holders of such capital half-yearly, on the 1st day of February and the 1st day of August in each and every year, out of the joint revenues of the Great Western, in priority to all dividends for the time being payable on the ordinary shares and stock of that company, and to be collaterally secured, as hereinafter provided for, on the earnings of the Union company's railway, stations, and ferry.

8. The Great Western shall also during the period aforesaid, viz., between the 1st day of January, 1868, and the 1st day of February, 1870, pay to the Union company, for the purpose of winding up their affairs, the following sums:—

For the period between the 1st day of January, 1868, and the 1st day of August, 1868, inclusive, 490*l*.;

For the period between the 1st day of August, 1868, and the 31st day of December, 1868, inclusive, 350*l*.;

For the year commencing 1st January, 1869, 1,682*l*.;

Far the month ending 1st February, 1870, 141*l*.

9. On and after the 1st day of February, 1870, the guaranteed preferential capital of the Union company, not exceeding 131,775*l*., shall be converted into Great Western preference stock, bearing the said guaranteed interest of 5 per cent., payable as provided in Article 7, and such stock shall be designated as follows:—Great Western (South Wales Union) guaranteed five per cent. preference stock.

10. If at any time after the 1st day of August, 1868, the guaranteed preferential interest of 5 per cent. on the preference capital of the Union, or any part thereof, is not paid as and when the same ought to be paid, then the whole or the part thereof not paid (as the case may be) shall be paid out of the gross earnings of the Union company's railway, stations, and ferry, subject only to the payment thereout of the interest on the Union company's debenture or bond debt of 98,000*l*. assumed by the Great Western; and in case the said guaranteed preferential interest, or any part thereof, is at any time in arrear and unpaid, then any holders of the preference capital of the Union company to the amount of 10,000*l*. or upwards may require the Great Western to produce to them at all reasonable times full and sufficient accounts of the traffic carried over the railway and ferry of the Union company, and showing the proportion of receipts due to the said railway of the Union company, and they shall at all reasonable times and in a reasonable manner allow the said holders of the said preference capital to the amount aforesaid to inspect and examine the said accounts, and all vouchers and documents relative thereto, and take copies of or extracts from so much of such accounts, vouchers, and documents as relates to the Union company's interest in such traffic, and they shall have all proper facilities in that behalf allowed to them by the Great Western; and the expenses of and connected with such examination and inspection, and of the making of any such copies or extracts shall be paid and borne by the Great Western, subject to a reference to arbitration (in case of difference) respecting the amount thereof, and with authority for any court of law or equity before which any question arising under this provision, or otherwise relating to the Union company, is brought, to direct that those expenses, or any part thereof, shall not be borne by the Great Western.

11. The ordinary share capital of the Union company, amounting to the said sum of 168,225*l*., shall, on or from the 1st day of February, 1870, be converted into stock, and the holders thereof shall from and after that date be paid dividends at the same rate per cent. as is paid to the holders of Great Western original ordinary stock until the said Great Western original ordinary stock has been consolidated with the other sectional ordinary stocks of the Great Western, or either of them, and after such consolidation they shall be paid the same amount of dividend as is paid in respect of the Great Western original ordinary stock so consolidated; for example, if the Great Western original stock is consolidated at 100*l*. of such stock for 120*l*. of consolidated stock, the holders of Union stock shall be entitled to the same amount of dividend for each 100*l*. of their stock as is paid in respect of each 120*l*. of consolidated stock; but the holders of the Union company's ordinary stock shall not have a voice in or be entitled to interfere in any way with any consolidation of the Great Western original ordinary stock with any other sectional ordinary stock of the Great Western.

12. When and so soon as the ordinary stocks of the four sections of the company, namely, Great Western original, Great Western South Wales, Great Western Oxford, and Great Western Newport, shall be consolidated into one stock, then the Great Western (South Wales Union) ordinary stock shall be likewise consolidated with that stock, and the holders of Great Western (South Wales Union) ordinary stock shall, as provided for in Article 11 of this agreement, be entitled to the same *pro rata* proportion of the consolidated stock as the holders of the Great Western original ordinary stock shal receive of such consolidated stock.

13. The Union company shall, on or after the 1st day of January, 1868, on the request in writing of the Great Western, transfer or cause to be transferred, all their, the Union company's, steamboats and other boats and vessels, and the appurtenances thereto belonging, freed and discharged of and from all mortgages, bonds, or other incumbrances, to the Great Western, or, as they direct, for a nominal consideration, and on the said 1st day of January, 1868, they shall for the purposes of this agreement put the Great Western in full and undisturbed possession of the said steamboats and other boats and vessels and their appurtenances.

14. Except as otherwise agreed upon between the Great Western and the Union company, all the Union company's debts, liabilities, and obligations shall be discharged by the Union company before the 1st day of August, 1868: Provided always, that if the Great Western shall, either before or after the 1st day of August, 1868, be required to discharge and shall discharge any debts or liabilities of the Union company, they may deduct any amount so

paid by them (the Great Western), with interest thereon, and all costs, charges, and expenses which they may have incurred or be liable for in consequence thereof, out of any money in their hands belonging to the Union company, or out of any dividends or interest payable to that company or the shareholders thereof, or, after the amalgamation, out of any dividends or interest payable to the holders of the Union company's shares and stock by the Great Western.

15. The Union company shall not issue any other shares, or any debentures, bonds, or other securities, or increase their capital liability, without the previous consent in writing of the Great Western, but they may issue debentures or bonds as aforesaid to replace others falling due prior to the said 1st day of August, 1868.

16. The Union company shall not do any act which will injuriously affect this agreement or the Great Western, their rights and interests, without the previous consent in writing of that company.

17. The Union company shall obtain the consent of the Lord High Admiral of the United Kingdom of Great Britain and Ireland, or the commissioners for executing the office of Lord High Admiral, to the steam ferry being merged in the Great Western, provided such consent be necessary under the provisions of the 46th section of the Bristol and South Wales Union Act, 1857.

18. All or any disputes or differences which may arise between the companies, parties hereto, touching the true intent and construction of these presents, or touching any of the incidents or consequences thereof, or touching any breach or alleged breach thereof, or any claim or demand by reason of any such breach or alleged breach, or touching anything to be done, omitted, or suffered in pursuance of these presents, or otherwise touching these presents or any of the subject matters thereof, or anything relating thereto, and any matter by these presents directed to be referred to arbitration, shall be referred to and determined by arbitration in accordance with the provisions of the Railway Companies Arbitration Act, 1859, by an arbitrator to be appointed by the Board of Trade, and these presents shall accordingly be an agreement for and a reference to arbitration under that Act.

In witness whereof the Union company and the Great Western have hereunto set their respective common seals the day and year first above written.

————

4.—LONDON AND NORTH WESTERN—MANCHESTER, SHEFFIELD, AND LINCOLNSHIRE.

Heads of an Agreement made the 13th of April, 1867, between the London and North Western of the one part, and the Manchester, Sheffield, and Lincolnshire of the other part.

It is hereby agreed as follows:

1. That the tolls to be charged in perpetuity to the North Western in exercising the running powers granted under the Garston and Liverpool Act of 1861 shall be a mileage proportion of the rates and fares (after deduction of the usual clearing house terminals and working expenses at 27 per cent. on local and through traffic) of the rates and fares to be fixed from time to time by the London and North Western.

2. That the Sheffield shall provide separate station accommodation for the North Western in the stations of the Sheffield at Sheffield, and intermediate places between Manchester and Sheffield, to be used by the North Western as fully and freely as if their own stations; the North Western to have the right to place their own servants at such stations; the rent or other consideration to be paid for such accommodation to be agreed upon or settled by arbitration in manner hereinafter provided.

3. The North Western to have the option of providing their own stations at Sheffield and elsewhere, the Sheffield to afford all reasonable facilities for that purpose.

4. The North Western to have the right to run from Ardwick or Guide Bridge, or both.

5. If and so long as the North Western do not exercise the said running powers, the Sheffield to send at least one-third of the traffic between Sheffield and Liverpool over the North Western line between Liverpool and Manchester either by the Garston line or, at the option of the North Western, over the old Liverpool and Manchester line: through booking and through facilities to the North Western stations in Liverpool to be afforded by the London and North Western for the traffic interchangeable with such stations.

6. The bill of the North Western between Chapel-in-the-Frith and Sheffield to be postponed until next year, the Sheffield undertaking not to oppose it themselves in the Commons, but to be at liberty to do so in the House of Lords if this arrangement is not carried out, and to use their influence with the landowners and the Midland not to oppose it in the Commons.

7. All necessary Parliamentary powers to be obtained to carry out this agreement, the Sheffield giving every support in their power to assist in obtaining the same.

8. When this agreement is sanctioned by Parliament the new line to Sheffield to be altogether abandoned, and the London and North Western to undertake not to promote themselves, or to assist any other company in promoting, or directly or indirectly supporting any bill for a similar purpose and with similar objects in future.

9. If either party think it necessary, the above heads to be carried out by agreement, and, if necessary, to be settled by Mr. J. H. Lloyd or Mr. Bullar.

10. Any difference arising out of this agreement to be determined by arbitration in manner provided by the Railway Companies Arbitration Act, 1859.

5.—LONDON AND NORTH WESTERN—MIDLAND.

Heads of Arrangement between the London and North Western and the Midland.

1. The agreement between the two companies for the joint ownership of the Ashby and Nuneaton lines and use of the Midland to Derby, scheduled to the London and North Western, Ashby and Nuneaton Lines, Act of 1867, not extending to goods station accommodation at Derby, the Midland now undertake to provide land for goods accommodation for the London and North Western at Derby, shown on plan signed by William John Beale on behalf of the Midland, and James Blenkinsop on behalf of the London and North Western, on land belonging to the Midland situate immediately to the south of their main passenger station at Derby; the London and North Western to pay to the Midland the actual cost to them of such land, the amount of such cost to be settled by arbitration in case of need, and the land conveyed to the London and North Western.

The London and North shall, for their passenger traffic to and from Derby, use the passenger station of the Midland at Derby, and no other, and for goods traffic the land so to be provided by the Midland as above mentioned, with any necessary additions which may be required, and for access thereto; the North Western to be at liberty to use the land they now possess in Derby for merchandise, cattle, and minerals, coloured blue on the said plan.

Such part of the bill now promoted in Parliament by the London and North Western, intituled " The London and North Western Railway Bill, 1868," as relates to a new line and station into Derby, to be withdrawn, the London and North Western engaging not again to promote or assist in the promotion of any line for that or similar objects.

2. With reference to the South Staffordshire, and the powers conferred on the Midland to use the same, and the stations and conveniences connected therewith, under the powers of the Midland (Additional Powers) Act, 1867, it is now agreed that, in addition to a mileage rate for goods, the Midland shall also pay to the London and North Western for the use of stations, wharfs, warehouses, and other conveniences for goods traffic such further sum as, in case of disagreement, shall be settled by arbitration; the London and North Western undertaking, in addition to the accommodation to which the Midland are now entitled, to provide for the Midland at stations on the South Staffordshire line, where practicable, separate accommodation for Midland goods traffic, with their own clerks and servants, the amount and position thereof to be in like manner settled by arbitration in case the parties do not agree.

3. In the case of the running powers granted to the London and North Western under the London and North Western Railway (Ashby and Nuneaton Lines) Act, 1867, if the London and North Western shall require goods accommodation at stations on the Midland line, the Midland shall in like manner, as provided under the last head, be entitled to an additional payment in respect of such accommodation over and above the mileage rate for goods.

4. With reference to the use by the London and North Western of certain lines and works at Burton-on-Trent belonging to the Midland, in respect of which use the London and North Western are now bound to pay five per cent. per annum on one half the cost of such lines and works, it is now agreed that the London and North Western shall be entitled in account to one half the net tolls which the Midland shall receive from the North Staffordshire or any other company (or person) in respect of any use by such company (or person) of the lines and works at Burton above referred to.

5. With respect to the use by the Midland of the London and North Western station in New-street, Birmingham, it is agreed that the Midland shall be entitled, on payment of a reasonable rent, to a separate office for outward parcels in a convenient position on the New-street front of the station, and the Midland shall be at liberty to deal with their parcels traffic (outwards and inwards) by their own servants and clerks; in other respects the use by the Midland of the New-street station to continue as they have hitherto enjoyed it under the agreement of 11th February, 1847, which is set out in the schedule hereto, and is hereby confirmed, the Midland using the same and no other passenger station (other than that which they now possess or may construct on or adjacent to their own line), and the working expenses to be revised from time to time as at present: the London and North Western to have the use in perpetuity of the Midland portion of the Rugby station as at present on the same terms as at present; the Midland having also the use in perpetuity of such part of the Rugby station belonging to the London and North Western as they use at present on the same terms as at present, for which purpose the existing agreements between the companies relative to the Rugby station shall be considered permanent and be confirmed.

6. These heads of arrangement to be sealed by both companies, and a more formal agreement to be prepared at the request of either party; the same, in case of disagreement, to be settled by the Attorney-General for the time being, or some barrister named by him.

7. All questions as to the mode of carrying these heads of arrangement, or the agreement founded upon them, into effect, to be settled by arbitration according to the provisions of the Railway Companies Arbitration Act, 1859.

8. Either company to be at liberty to apply to Parliament for the confirmation of these heads, and the other company shall concur therein.

JAS. BLENKINSOP.

W. J. BEALE.

SCHEDULE REFERRED TO IN THE FOREGOING AGREEMENT:—

Proposals for the Commutation of the Existing Arrangement between the Midland and the London and North Western as to the Line between Birmingham and Bristol.

It is proposed that in lieu of the liability under which the London and North Western are at present to half the loss on the guarantee of the Midland to the Birmingham and Bristol shareholders for ten years the following arrangement shall be substituted :

The Midland to have the use henceforth for their passenger traffic of the new central station of the London and North Western in Birmingham, and of the line and approaches thereto, with the use of rooms for clerks' offices, on payment of the yearly sum of 100*l*., paying also (as at present) for the use of porters and clerks, and such other services as they may require for their traffic, the London and North Western continuing to find and supply the same.

The Midland to pay also a yearly sum for their proportion of the expense of maintaining the permanent way from the Lawley-street viaduct to the new station, calculated in the proportion which their traffic bears to the other traffic using the same.

The Midland to be entitled to such accommodation as shall be requisite for the due despatch of their traffic, including sufficient platform room and use of sidings ; and any difference of opinion on this point shall be referred to Mr. Robert Stephenson, or some other person to be agreed upon.

In consideration of the above arrangement the London and North Western are to be entirely released from all present and future obligation on account of the guarantee above referred to.

It is understood that this arrangement does not extend to goods traffic, except that the Midland are to be at liberty, without further payment, to pass goods trains across the London and North Western on the south side of the Lawley-street viaduct to the present Gloucester line of the Midland, so that the same be done according to plans to be approved of by Mr. Robert Stephenson, and subject in all respects to the bye-laws and regulations of the London and North Western.

It is understood that the Midland shall not make any arrangement for the transfer of the agreement, except with the consent of the London and North Western.
Dated 11th February, 1847.

6.—LONDON AND NORTH WESTERN—MIDLAND—SETTLE AND CARLISLE.

Heads of Agreement between the Midland and London and North Western Railway Companies, dated 11th November, 1868.

1. The Midland to have equal rights with the London and North Western of user and control of the Lancaster and Carlisle between Ingleton and Carlisle, with joint management by a joint committee, with a standing arbitrator, with full power to the Midland to fix their own rates and fares.

2. Local traffic to be protected, but an arrangement, so far as practicable, to be made for the traffic between Low Gill and Ingleton inclusive, to be worked by the Midland. The Midland also to be allowed to carry local passenger traffic between Low Gill and Carlisle, and from the receipts of the traffic so carried the Midland to be allowed 15 per cent. for working expenses, the residue being paid over to the London and North Western. The local rates and fares to be fixed by the London and North Western, and to be the same for both companies.

3. That the payment to be made by the Midland for the use of the Lancaster and Carlisle shall be a mileage proportion (after deduction of the usual Clearing-house terminals and working expenses at the rate of 27 per cent.) of the rates and fares, to be fixed from time to time by the Midland, but such payment shall never be less than 40,000*l*. in any one year during the term of this agreement.

4. The London and North Western to provide station accommodation for the Midland in their intermediate stations between Carlisle and Ingleton for passenger traffic, to be used as fully and freely as they are used by the London and North Western ; the Midland to have the right, at their own expense, of placing their own booking-clerks at such stations, such use of stations to be covered by the mileage paid by the Midland. The London and North Western also to provide proper and sufficient accommodation for the goods traffic of the Midland at such intermediate stations, with power to place their own clerks and agents at their own cost, the rent or other consideration to be paid by the Midland for such accommodation, to be agreed upon or settled by arbitration in manner hereinafter provided.

5. Power for the Midland to use the present passenger station at Carlisle, as provided in the Settle and Carlisle Act of 1866, with access thereto from the Lancaster and Carlisle.

6. The London and North Western to afford the Midland all reasonable facilities for working its trains between Carlisle and Ingleton—viz., sidings and other conveniences, in common with the London and North Western, which shall be considered as included in the mileage payments, and water supply to be provided on terms to be settled, in case of difference, by arbitration.

7. An application to be made to Parliament in the session of 1869 to sanction this agree-

ment, and to abandon the construction of the Settle and Carlisle, both companies giving every support in their power in order to obtain the same.

8. The cost of the application to Parliament for the Act to be paid by the two companies in equal proportions.

9. The foregoing heads to be carried out by formal agreement, at the request of either company, to be settled, in case of difference, by some gentleman to be agreed on, or, in case of need, to be named by the Attorney-General for the time being.

10. The Midland to keep, and render monthly to the London and North Western, accurate accounts of the traffic carried over the line between Ingleton and Carlisle, or any part thereof.

11. Any difference arising out of this agreement to be determined by arbitration, in manner provided by the Companies Arbitration Act, 1859.

12. This agreement to be for a period of fifty years, and to come into operation within one month after the passing of the Act, but during the remainder of the year 1869 the rates and fares shall be agreed upon.

13. This agreement to be void, unless sanctioned by Parliament in the session of 1869, together with the abandonment af the Settle and Carlisle.

14. Nothing in this agreement contained shall in any way alter or vary, lessen or increase he rights or liabilities of the companies parties to the English and Scotch agreement.

Se of the Midland.
Seal of the London and North Western.

IV.—GENERAL INFORMATION.

1.—WEST CORK.—REPORT OF THE COMMITTEE OF INVESTIGATION.

The committee of investigation appointed by the shareholders in this company at their meeting held 8th October, 1866, " To investigate the affairs of the company," have been greatly delayed in the prosecution of their enquiry by the absence of reliable data either from the minutes and books of account, or from authentic documents upon which to frame a report, which they could present with confidence as showing the true position of the company. This delay has, however, sufficed to bring under their notice every claim, as they believe, materially affecting the company.

The line of railway as authorised, comprises 33¼ miles, viz.:—17 miles 27 chains from Bandon to Dunmanway, which is now open for traffic, and 15 miles 71 chains from Dunmanway to Skibbereen; of which only the earthwork for about four miles at the furthest end have been constructed, and is ready for the reception of the permanent way.

The company have at present powers to raise capital as follows :—

	In Shares.	On Loans.
Under Act 23 and 24 Vic., c. 203 (1860)	£200,000	£66,600
28 and 29 ,, 232 (1865)	120,000	40,000
	£320,000	£106,600

The amount of capital which has been issued is shown by the appended balance sheet prepared by Mr. Pullein, the accountant appointed by the committee.

The board, as originally constituted, obtained subscriptions for 1,530 original shares, on which they received in cash 5,420l., and expended in parliamentary costs and attempts to carry out a contract 5,103l. They also incurred liabilities for about 4,000l.

In this state of things in April, 1863, a contract was arranged with Messrs. Wheatley Kirk and S. J. Paris for the completion of the line on the following terms, viz.:—Messrs. Wheatley Kirk & Co., in consideration of a Lloyd's Bond for 5,000l., agreed to pay the outstanding liabilities, and to relieve the directors from the bond given to the Crown, and to complete the line for the then existing share and debenture capital, including a subscription of 20,000l. from the Cork and Bandon Company, and with additional share and debenture capital, the Act for which was subsequently obtained in 1865.

A contract for permanent way materials was entered into in June, 1863, between the company (with the assent of Wheatley Kirk, & Co.) and the British and Foreign Plant Company for the supply of rails, chairs, sleepers, &c., to be paid for in the company's acceptances at six month, with liberty for the company to renew the same for two years, adding interest with the collateral security of Lloyd's bonds for the amount of the acceptances, and the company agreed to consent to a judgment being entered up for the amount of the acceptances.

Sir C. P. Roney and Messrs. Holland, Sedgwick, and Corry, were elected directors in the place of members of the old board previous to the confirmation of the above agreements.

The committee regret that they are compelled to state that the payments to the contractors appear to have been made with much irregularity, and to an extent greatly in excess of what they were entitled to receive.

In pursuance of the Act 23 and 24 Vic., The Cork and Bandon agreed to raise 20,000*l.* by means of preference shares of their company, to enable them to subscribe for a like amount of ordinary shares of the West Cork; but the Cork and Bandon have not yet paid their subscription.

A contract was entered into with Messrs. Brown, Marshalls, and Co., for the supply of rolling stock, for which the company gave acceptances which are now outstanding to the amount of 12,642*l.* 16*s.* 5*d.*, and upon which they have obtained a judgment against the company.

In December, 1865, the company being unable to meet the acceptances due to the British and Foreign Plant Company, the board gave consent to a judgment for the amount under which the Plant Company seized all the unused materials which they had themselves supplied, and also the rolling stock which had been supplied shortly before by Messrs. Brown, Marshalls, and Co.; and the good were assigned to them by the Sheriff at the estimated value of 15,757*l.* 10*s.* 6*d.*

The rolling stock of the company, which consisted of one first-class, four composite, and six third-class carriages, four break-vans, two horse-boxes, four carriage-trucks, thirty covered and ten open-goods wagons were supplied by Messrs. Brown, Marshalls, and Co., and were assigned by the sheriff, as previously stated, to the British and Foreign Plant Company under their judgment. This rolling stock has, since the seizure and sale, been rented by the company from the British and Foreign Plant Company, the rent being payable out of the traffic returns.

The line is completed, and open for traffic between Bandon and Dunmanway. Your committee have received very satisfactory reports as to the manner in which it is constructed, but the stations are imperfect, one only having been placed in a satisfactory condition. Of the remaining portions of the line, viz.—16 miles between Dunmanway and Skibbereen, about four miles of earthwork have been partially completed at the farthest end. Land to the amount of about 7,000*l.* is unpaid for on this portion of the line. Mr. Brydone who went over this portion of the line at the request of the committee, reports that the works might be completed, except certain overbridges which are not considered indispensable, for 30,000*l.* cash, if the land and permanent way materials, now under seizure, could be arranged for by payment in shares.

The traffic is at present very inefficiently worked, owing to the obstructive policy of the Cork and Bandon. It has averaged about 80*l.* per week since the opening. But your committee are assured that a very large accession would be derived if reasonable facilities were allowed, as a large proportion of passengers and goods are conveyed by road alongside the line to avoid the delays and changes of carriages at the junction. They are also assured that the extension to Skibbereen would not only add greatly to the traffic over the completed portion, but would, in itself, be remunerative on the estimated cost.

As the powers limited by the existing Act for completion of the work will expire in July next, your committee concurred with the directors in promoting a bill for an extension of the time, and to enable the company to make such arrangements with regard to capital as shall render it possible to raise the required funds. In order to do this your committee believe it indispensable that a priority of preferential dividend should be conferred upon the 5,998 shares hitherto unissued, and that power should be obtained to raise on mortgage, the amount required to pay for the uncompleted land purchases, which already rank as claims on the company, and for the stations which are essential to the working of the existing line. Clauses to this effect are comprised in the bill, which will be submitted to your approval on the 6th of June next, and your committee strongly recommend its adoption.

The want of local superintendence is very apparent, and your committee, having been in communication with Sir J. Arnott and other gentlemen in the County of Cork, are persuaded that it will be very desirable that the management should be transferred to Cork, and that Sir J. Arnott and Messrs. William H. Massey, Timothy Mahony, and J. P. Ronayne under whom the Cork and Macroom has attained already a highly satisfactory position, should be appointed as local directors in conjunction with three directors in England, to be chosen by the shareholders.

If this arrangement, and the objects proposed by the bill before Parliament can be effected, your committee have every hope that the company may yet be raised out of the deplorable state into which its affairs have been brought by past mismanagement.

Your committee append the statement of accounts drawn up by their accountant, and extracts from his report explanatory of some of the items. His task has been one of much difficulty owing to the incomplete state of the accounts in the earlier period, and the total absence of entries during the last 18 months

JOHN EVERITT,

WILLIAM GRAY,

FRANCIS THOMAS MACKRETH.

PRO-FORMA BALANCE SHEET, DECEMBER 31, 1866.

Received.

To Capital : 20,000 ordinary shares of 10l. each	£200,0⸱0	
6,002 preference ditto	60,020	=260,020
To debentures : first issue	66,600	
Second ditto	39,900	=106,500
To Lloyd's bonds		8,100
To sundry creditors : viz., for—		
Permanent way, &c.	52,242	
Rolling stock	12,624	
Interest on debentures, &c.	7,375	
Land, Bandon to Dunmanway	3,982	
Land, Dunmanway tp Skibbereen	7,000	
Sundries	2,126	= 85,350
To liabilities : Lloyd's bonds issued as collateral security to the British and Foreign		
Plant Co.	25,000	
Bills payable, accepted for the accommodation of W. Kirk and Co.	8,500	= 33,500
		£459,970

Expended.

By contract works		£309,867
By Wheatley Kirk and Co.		120,982

This item will be diminished and the preceding one increased by the amount of the final certificate not yet received. As security for the amount overpaid, the company have registered in the names of Mr. Corry and the secretary the following shares, which had been debited to W. Kirk and Co., viz :—

13,116 ordinary shares	£131,160	
800 preference shares	8,000	
	£139,160	
By cash at bankers		64
By debtors for calls (believed to be almost entirely, if not quite irrecoverable)		2,022
By debtors claiming to have sets off		529
By Act of Incorporation and other preliminary expenses		10,782
By sundry expenses, viz :—		
Interest	£9,765	
Directors' remuneration and qualification	2,625	
Law and parliamentary expenses	1,689	
Printing, advertising, rent, &c.	1,640	= 15,720
		£459 970

EDMUND PULLEIN, Accountant.

EXTRACTS FROM THE ACCOUNTANT'S REPORT.

Share Capital.—The first item is the share capital, which represents the amount of the shares actually issued. This may, however, be largely reduced by the amount of certain shares issued to the contractors, Messrs. Kirk and Co., and held in trust for them and the company ; but the question may be more conveniently noticed when I come to treat of the account of that firm. The whole authorised amount of ordinary shares has been issued, but there are 5,998 preference shares which have never been issued.

Debentures.—The next item is the debentures, the whole authorised amount of which ha been issued, with the exception of 100l. The rate of interest they bear is 5 per cent. on 102,450l., and 6 per cent. on 4,050l.

Liabilities.—The liabilities which form the next item are entered short, not being expected, for the following reasons, to become claims against the company. The British and Foreign Plant company admit that the bonds issued to them were only given as collateral security, and that they are bound to return them when they can obtain them from their bankers, with whom they are at present deposited. The bills payable are entered short, under the impression that no legal claim can be made against the company in respect of them, it being now held by the Courts as, I believe, that acceptances given by a railway company are not valid. It appears from the minute book that there have been several renewals of the bills for 8,500l., originally accepted for Kirk and Co., but neither the original nor the renewed bills are entered in the bill book, and the notices of them in the minute book are not sufficiently complete to enable the renewals to be traced.

Contract works.—This account has been kept in the company's books on a wrong principle, it having been debited with the amounts from time to time paid to the contractors instead of being debited with the amount certified by the engineer. I have therefore, in my draft ledger accounts, written back the amount so debited, and have debited the account and credited Kirk and Co. with the amount certified by the engineer. The amounts stated in the engineer's certificates are calculated on the basis that the whole of the share capital and debentures, amounting to 426,000l., was to be absorbed in the construction of the line. This is understood to be about three times the amount which would have been required if the formation of the line had been paid for in cash instead of in shares and debentures, which is confirmed by the engineer's original estimate. I have written off 61,590l. for the estimated value of the plant sold by the sheriff, in February, 1866, under the Plant company's execution, having arrived at that amount in the following manner :—The Plant company supplied the plant required for the whole 33 miles of railway, for which in the engineer's certificate the contractors are credited with 135,547l. 12s. 1d., or about 4,106l. per mile. Now the Plant company could only take under their execution such plant as was not fixed to the soil, and as only about 18 miles have been completed,¶I assume that the plant provided for the remaining 15 miles has been sold. This would amount to 61,590*l*., and I have therefore credited the contract works account with 9,437*l*. 10*s*. 6*d*., the proceeds of the plant sold, and with 52,152*l*. 9*s*. 6*d*. for the estimated loss, making together the sum of 61,590*l*. The rolling stock was sold at the same time, the cost being 12,306*l*., the proceeds 6,320*l*., and the loss 5,986*l*.

W. Kirk and Co.—The next item is the large balance which I make out to the debit of Kirk and Co., subject to reduction by the amount of the engineers' final certificate not yet received. This balance is the result of the company paying the contractors for the permanent way materials (at the certified amount of about three times their value), although they were at the same time accepting the drafts of the Plant company for each delivery of plant, handing them Lloyd's bonds as collateral security for the acceptances and consenting to judgment being entered up against them by the Plant company. The Board do not appear to have contemplated the possibility of the contractors failing, but to have regarded their engagements to the Plant company merely as a liability undertaken for the accommodation of the contractors, which could not result in a claim being made against them. It is suggested that they retained the 5,998 preference shares as a security against this liability, but these would be quite inadequate even if the line had been completed, and were much more so when the works were little more than half-finished. Be this as it may, when judgment is entered up by the Plant company we are compelled to credit them with the amount in the books, and are entitled to debit Kirk and Co. therewith, more especially as they do not seem to have incurred any liability to the Plant company. The undertaking of the company to allow judgment to be entered up against them does not seem to have been carried into effect till December, 1865. On its fulfilment being required by the Plant company, Kirk and Co. (December 7th, 1865), consented to deposit 10,000 of the ordinary shares as security, and on December 29th they consented to deposit 1,500 more as security for a sum of 5,000*l*., obtained for them from the Plant company to enable the line to be opened.

Revenue.—I have been unable to prepare a statement of revenue account from want of information.

2.—CALEDONIAN—INTERDICT AGAINST PAYMENT OF DIVIDEND.

Application for the purpose of arresting payment of the dividend declared for the half-year ending 31st July was made to the Court of Session on 26th September, on the terms subjoined, at the instance of Mr. Alexander Glen, Glasgow, against the company :—

" 1. To interdict, prohibit, and discharge the respondents from declaring or paying any dividend or dividends on any of the ordinary stocks or shares of the said company for the half-year ending 31st July, 1868, and from carrying any sum to the credit of the revenue of the half-year ending 31st January, 1869.

" 2. To interdict, prohibit, and discharge the respondents from applying the sums of money raised, in virtue of the powers conferred by the Edinburgh Station Act, 1866, and the Lanarkshire and Mid-Lothian Branches Act, 1866, or any part of said sums, so far as still in the hands of the said company, in or towards payment of any dividend or dividends on the stocks or shares of the said company, and from applying said sums of money, or any part thereof, otherwise than for the purposes specified in the said Acts respectively, and from issuing any further stock or shares of the said company in virtue of the powers conferred by the said Acts or either of them, and from raising any further money thereby, or to do otherwise in the premises as to your lordships shall seem proper."

Among the statement of facts the following were given :—"The company, as appears from general balance sheet annexed to the accounts for the half-year ending 31st July, 1868, had at that date sundry liabilities to the amount of 204,116*l*., and there was due to bankers 121,969*l*.; these liabilities amounted together to 326,086*l*.'

The company was at the said date, and still is, insolvent ; and in consequence of the proposal to pay a dividend on the ordinary stocks or shares of the company as above set forth, and to compel the respondents to abstain from further illegal and unauthorised actions, the present application has been rendered necessary.

The pleas in law in the case were as follow :—

" 1. The assets of the company for the half-year ending 31st July, 1868, not being certified by the auditors in terms of the Companies' (Scotland) Act, 1867, the complainer is entitled to interdict as craved.

" 2. It is illegal and *ultra vires* of the respondents to divide as profit premiums obtained, and at the same time to charge against capital loss sustained, on the issue of stocks or shares.

" 3. In respect of proposed debit to capital, and of the undercharge to revenue on account of plant, as above set forth, the complainer is entitled to interdict as craved.

" 4. No profits available for payment of dividend on ordinary stock having been earned, the complainer in entitled to interdict.

" 5. The respondents having applied the capital raised under the Balerno branch and other Acts of the company to purposes not authorised by the said Acts, but in contravention thereof ; and there being no occasion or intention at present to apply the unissued capital above mentioned for the purposes of the Acts authorising the issue thereof, the complainer is entitled to interdict as craved.

" 6. In the present circumstances of the company, as above condescended on, the respondents are not entitled to declare or pay any dividend on the ordinary stocks or shares of the company for the half-year ending 31st July, 1868, or to carry any sum to the credit of revenue for the next half-year; and the complainer is entitled to interdict as craved."

Lord Benbohme granted the interdict, and appointed answers to be sent in within eight days. These answers, in substance, were as follow :—That it was incompetent for the complainer to open up the accounts of the company, adjusted and approved of by the shareholders in terms of the Act of Parliament before he became a shareholder; that the shareholder, who in March, 1868, assigned to him the only interest which the complainer has in the company, having acquiesced in the proceedings of the shareholders, it is incompetent for the complainer now to upset these proceedings by way of interdict ; that the application is incompetent in respect of the provisions of the Companies' (Scotland) Act, 1867.

The case was argued before Lord Kinloch on 9th October, and his Lordship delivered the following judgment on the 12th :—

Edinburgh 12th October, 1868.—The Lord Ordinary, having heard parties' procurators, and made avizandum, and considered the proceedings, passes the note, but recalls the interdict formerly granted ; prohibits the clerk from issuing a certificate of the recall till Thursday next, the 15th current, at three o'clock ; and, if a reclaiming note against this interlocutor shall have been then presented, till the same shall have been disposed of.—W. PENNY.

Note.—There is a twofold interdict now sought—1st, an interdict against the company paying any dividend on their ordinary stock for the half-year ending 31st July, 1868 ; 2nd, an interdict against the issue of any further shares under certain Acts of Parliament, or the application of the funds arising on the issue of such shares to any other purpose than those specified in these Acts.

The interdict is applied for at the instance of a holder of Caledonian (General Terminus) guaranteed stock, to the extent of 500*l.*

I. In regard to the application for interdict against payment of a dividend on the ordinary stock, it is primarily to be noticed that the procedure prescribed in this matter by the 30th section of the Company's (Scotland) Act, 1867, has been followed out by the company. That statute enacts that "no dividend shall be declared by a company until the auditors have certified that the half-yearly accounts proposed to be issued contain a full and true statement of the financial condition of the company, and that the dividend proposed to be declared on any shares is *bonâ fide* due thereon, after charging the revenue of half-year with all expenses which ought to be paid thereout, in the judgment of the auditors." In the present case "the directors recommend a dividend on the ordinary stock at the rate of 1½ per cent. per annum, less dividend on that portion of the stock charged against premium account," involving payment of a sum of 28,083*l.* The auditors, in reference to this proposal, certify that they "have carefully examined the books and vouchers of the company for the half-year ending 31st July last, which we find correct ;" and further, "care has been taken to bring into the accounts all claims affecting revenue ; and we are satisfied that the stock on hand, and the traffic and other balances, are fairly represented. In conclusion, we certify that the half-yearly accounts proposed to be issued contain a full and true statement of the financial condition of the company as shown in the books, and that the dividend proposed to be declared on the ordinary stock of the company (exclusive of the stock raised under the Cleland and Mid-Calder branches, and other Acts in 1865, proposed to be paid as heretofore out of premium account, in accordance with the resolution of the shareholders) is *bonâ fide* due thereon, after charging the revenue of half-year with all expenses which in our judgment ought to be paid thereout."

It is next necessary to notice the effect which the statute gives to this report by the auditors. The statute adapts itself to two cases. The one is, where the directors differ from the judgment of the auditors ; in which case "such difference shall, if the directors desire it, be stated in the report to the shareholders ; and the company in general meeting may decide thereon, subject to all the provisions of the law then existing, and such decision shall, for the purposes of dividend, be final and binding." There was, in the present case, no difference between the directors and auditors ; and this alternative did not therefore arise.

The other alternative is thus stated in the statute—"But if no such difference is stated, or if no decision is given on any such difference, *the judgment of the auditors shall be final and binding.*"

It was maintained by the respondents that this statutory provision excluded the objection now stated to the payment of the dividend ; for the dividend proposed to be paid is exactly what the report of the auditors has sanctioned. The Lord Ordinary finds it difficult to avoid a conclusion to this effect. Undoubtedly the report of the auditors is not to all intents conclusive. It does not absolutely fix everything as the auditors state. *Its effect is limited to the payment of the dividend.* As to this, the statute bears expressly, "the judgment of the auditors shall be final and binding"—in other words, it shall be held, without appeal from their decision, that the dividend proposed is one which, in the circumstances, it is right and fitting the company should pay. It is difficult to put on these words any other meaning than one. It appears to the Lord Ordinary that this statutory provision was intended to preclude the very thing which the complainer is now seeking to urge—a suspension of the dividend until inquiry is made into a vast variety of debateable matters, got up by a recusant shareholder, it may be on very unscrupulous averments. The statute provided a short, and for all practical purposes a satisfactory, method for determining whether a proposed dividend is to be paid or not. The accounts of the company may still be fully open to inquiry and objection, and, if need be, rectification. But, as regards the dividend, it is meanwhile to be paid—" the judgment of the auditors," says the statute, "shall be final and binding."

The complainer met this view by an argument which was undoubtedly relevant——viz., that the certificate of the auditors was not the statutory certificate; and was therefore to be entirely thrown aside.   The ground upon which this was maintained was that the auditors merely certify that the accounts contain "a full and true statement of the financial condition of the company, *as shown by the books ;"* whereas they should not, as the complainer contends, make any reference to the books, but certify the condition of the company absolutely and unqualifiedly.   And he did not hesitate to say (it was indeed necessary for his argument) that the reference to the books was a purposely inserted qualification ; and that, *within the knowledge of the auditors,* the true state of affairs was not shown in the books, and was altogether different from what their certificate imported.

The Lord Ordinary could give no weight to this argument, which implied neither more nor less than a charge of gross and deliberate fraud against the auditors, such as could not, to say the least, be assumed without the most pregnant evidence.   He considers that he must read the certificate as importing to the full what the statute required, so far as within the possible cognisance of the auditors.   As auditors, they could of course only report on the documents before them.   The books of the company were naturally the primary subject of examination.   But the auditors were not limited to these.   They were entitled tn call for all manner of vouchers in the company's possession ; and if these had the effect of in anywise qualifying the statements in the books, the auditors were bound to set this fourth as a sacred part of their duty.   To suppose the auditors in the present case not to have done so, is to impute to them a breach of duty and flagrant dishonesty which no man is entitled lightly to charge on another.   Their own statemedt is, " We have carefully examined the books and vouchers of the company for the half-year ending 31st July last, which we find correct." When they proceed to state that the accounts prepared for the shareholders set forth the true condition of the company as shown in the books, the Lord Ordinary understands them to certify the accuracy of the accounts absolutely and positively, so far as within their widest means of information ; and auditors cannot be asked to do more.   In the operative part of the certificate, the statement is express and unqualified, that the dividend proposed to be declared on the ordinary stock " is *bonâ fide* due thereon, after charging the revenue of the half-year with all expenses which in our judgment ought to be paid thereout."   The Lord Ordinary cannot discover sufficient grounds on which to take from the certificate its statutory character or its statutory finality.

It is to state the argument lower, but still in a way sufficient to maintain the refusal of the interdict, to say that, at the very least, the certificate of the auditors could only be impugned on strong and overwhelming grounds, instantly verified.   It would not be sufficient that the complainer brought into dispute the accuracy in point of fact of their statements, by a mere denial on his part, unsupported by evidence.   Nor will it be enough merely to raise doubts of their accuracy on vague and inconclusive implications.   It will be further insufficient to stir a debate on points of speculation and opinion, on which there may reasonably exist a difference of opinion between persons equally well informed and authoritative.   It is notorious that there are a great many such points in regard to the administration of railway companies.   There is nothing less settled, by fixed and binding rule, than what part of the expenditure should be debited to capital and what to revenue.   It was, doubtless, with this circumstance fully in view that the legislature reposed so much of discretion in the auditors in regard to the matter of dividend.   They are to report whether the proposed dividend is right and fitting, " after charging the revenue of the half-year with all the expenses which ought to be paid thereout in the judgment of the auditors ;" and "the judgment of the auditors shall be final and binding."

It appears to the Lord Ordinary that, assuming the competency of impugning the report of the auditors, the complainer has not set fourth any grounds sufficient to warrant him in setting aside their certificate, and preventing payment of the proposed dividend.

1. The chief topic of discussion was a sum of 112,436*l.,* said to be composed of charges which ought to have been stated against revenue in the half-year ending 31st January, 1866, and which have never yet been so stated.   The complainer contended that this sum must still be paid out of the revenue before there can be any dividend ; and the amount is sufficient to exhaust the present dividend several times over.   But, assuming that a sum of this amount was some years ago omitted to be charged against revenue (which the complainer gives the strongest reasons for holding), it is one of the nice questions of railway law how in after years such omission is to be rectified ; and the Lord Ordinary is not prepared to take the rough-and-ready plan of ordering it to be deducted from any year's revenue that may come in question.   The fact may be undoubted that this charge was omitted to be made against revenue in the account of 31st January, 1866 ; and it does not follow by any means that the rectification of this omission is *de plano* to insert the charge in the account of 31st July, 1868. There is also to be kept in view the fact that in February and March, 1868, the shareholders, in general meeting, sanctioned the recommendation of a committee of inquiry, to the effect that this very sum should be charged to captal, on which footing things have been since that time proceeding.   It may no doubt be made a question whether this could legally be done by the shareholders.   But the Lord Ordinary is not prepared to decide on the spot this question in the negative, to the effect of stopping payment of the dividend.   Besides, he cannot overlook the circumstance that the very plea of the complainer was set forth as a ground for stopping payment of the previous half-year's dividend, and is at this moment under discussion in the court on a passed Note, but refused interdict.   It may not be incompetent to renew the plea with reference to a new dividend.   But the Lord Ordinary feels somewhat indisposed to cut short the discussion in the other case by an anticipatory decision in the present.

2. Another topic of discussion largely handled before the Lord Ordinary regarded what was called the premium fund.   It appears that, in regard to certain lines authorised by

Parliament, the company arranged to give the shareholders the unusual benefit of a dividend before the line was completed and opened for traffic. They were enabled to do this by selling the shares at a premium; the premium just being procured by means of this unwonted boon, and the amount of premium received was devoted to the payment of this anticipatory dividend. There is presented here a transaction about whose character and competency a great deal might be said in any lecture on railway law. But the Lord Ordinary finds difficulty in making the transaction bear on the present question of dividend. The complainer says that the premiums in question should have gone to increase capital, and not have been employed in paying dividend; and he may, perhaps, be right in this, but it does not seem a sound logical inference which he goes on to make, that *because* premiums were wrongfully introduced into revenue in this case, therefore, when other shares were sold at a discount, the *discount* should be charged against revenue, which would be equally wrongful. In regard to the accounts approved of by the auditors, and made the foundation of the proposed dividend, the Lord Ordinary understands that the premium fund is not introduced into these accounts as part of the receipts to be disposed of; and as little is there comprehended the dividend on these peculiarly situated shares, which is paid by means of this fund. It is the ordinary dividend, *exclusive of what arises on these shares*, and the ordinary dividend as payable out of the other funds of the company, which is alone dealt with. Accordingly, what is said, as already quoted, is this:—"The directors recommend a dividend on the ordinary stock at the rate of 1½ per cent per annum *less* dividend on that portion of the stock charged against premium account." And what the auditors certify is, "that the dividend proposed to be declared on the ordinary stock of the company, *exclusive* of the stock raised under the Cleland and Mid-Calder branches and other Acts in 1865, proposed to be paid as heretofore out of premium account in accordance with the resolution of the shareholders, is *bona fide* due thereon after charging the revenue of the half-year with all expenses which, in our judgment, ought to be paid thereout." The whole matter of the premium fund seems therefore fitly laid aside from the present discussion.

3. It was contended by the complainer that a large amount of parliamentary expenses incurred in former years had never been charged to revenue, and ought to have been put to the debit of the present half-year's account. But in regard to this matter, the parties are at direct variance in point of fact: the respondents contending that all the parliamentary expenses of former years had been arranged for, either *eo nomine*, or under a general arrangement of outstanding charges. The Lord Ordinary had no sufficient materials for determining this discussion in matter of fact in favour of the complainer.

4. It was further maintained by the complainer, that a great deal too little had been charged against revenue for the half-year in question, in respect of deterioration of plant. But this is just one of these speculative points in railway administration on which the Lord Ordinary could not decide, and on which the Legislature peculiarly intended to trust to the discretion of the auditors. With regard to a sum of 32,546*l.*, said to have been charged against capital in respect of plant, without the sanction of the shareholders, the parties are at direct issue on the fact.

5. Finally, the complainer maintains that the company is insolvent, and should pay no dividend—he might add, shut up their shop. It is scarcely necessary to notice a wild plea of this sort. It proceeds on a mere confusion in accounting. The complainer estimates as nothing, and only fit to be struck out of the account, what is called "Balances per capital statement, 262,122*l.*," because this on its face is a super-expenditure of capital, above the receipts from shares and loans. But there stands to answer this, the *unraised* capital in shares and loans, to a greatly larger amount, which, of course, cannot be thrown out of view in any general estimate of the company's affairs.

There are several of the points now touched on which may well deserve further investigation; and in this view the Lord Ordinary has passed the note. He considers the complainer entitled to have the points inquired into, not merely as a general matter of accounting, *but with special reference to their bearing on this particular dividend*, which can only be done under the passed note. But he thinks that in regard to none of them is there anything made so clear and tangible as would warrant him in interdicting the dividend, in the face of the certificate of the auditors, supposing this unlimitedly open to him.

II. The Lord Ordinary has but a few words to add in regard to the second branch of the application for interdict. This applies to the particular shares authorised to be raised by the two Acts of Parliament, specially set forth in the prayer of the note. It is said that the directors have intimated an intention of applying to Parliament for authority to abandon the lines in question; and an interdict is sought against their raising any additional stock under these Acts, or, at least, applying the money so procured in any other way than the Acts respectively authorise. The Lord Ordinary thinks it a sufficient answer—first, that a mere intended abandonment does not warrant the company to desist from their statutory operations (as to which they have obligations as well as privileges), so long as the desired authority has not been obtained: second, that it is not to be assumed, and has not been shown by evidence, that the directors will employ any money raised by issuing these shares in any other than the statutory way. It is impossible, in a legal proceeding like the present, to proceed on general surmises from alleged irregularities in former proceedings. It would be a shorter process to apply on this ground for an interdict against all further administration of any kind whatever.

The Lord Ordinary would only say in conclusion, that, in determining this question of interdict, he has, according to the invariable practice of the court, taken into special consideration the mode in which the interests of both parties would be affected by a judgment one way or other. By refusing the interdict, no substantial prejudice is done to the com plainer. He has been offered caution against whatever consequences his small holding may sustain by the interdict not being granted ; and, it is presumed, only declines this caution because he thinks it unnecessary. But, if the company were interdicted from paying a dividend on the ordinary stock, on the ground taken up by the complainer that the revenue is insufficient for the purposes, then not merely the shareholders would be deprived of their dividend, but the most serious consequences might arise to the credit of the company, and its position in the share market. If the law, indeed, imperatively demanded this interdict, such considerations would go for nothing. But so long as this remains even in doubt, they are considerations of the highest moment on the question of judicial discretion.

The complainer asked that, if the Lord Ordinary's view was unfavourable to his demand, he should be enabled to take the opinion of the Inner House, without any alteration taking place on the existing state of things. Considering that the court now meets within three days, the Lord Ordinary viewed this as reasonable. Indeed, he looks on it as for the interest of the company itself that, in place of a constant appeal every half-year to the Lord Ordinary on the bills, the case for one reason or another not getting further, the opinion of the Inner House should at once be obtained.   W. P.

Affidavit by Mr. Clark, C.E.

Mr. D. K. Clark, the engineer employed by the committee of investigation to report upon the rolling stock of the company, having been applied to for his opinion whether the plant charged to capital in the last half-year's accounts at 32,546l. was really additional plant chargeable against capital, or merely plant in replacement of worn-out plant chargeable to revenue, and also as to the sufficiency of the charges in the accounts for repair and renewal of plant, has made the following affidavit :—

In the Supreme Court of Scotland.

At Bow-street Police-Court (at London), the 8th day of October, in the year of our Lord 1868, in presence of James Vaughan, Esq., one of the Magistrates of the Police-courts of the Metropolis.

Compeared Daniel Kinnear Clark, civil engineer, No. 11, Adam-street, Adelphi, who being solemnly sworn, depones that he has carefully read and considered the report by the directors of the Caledonian to the shareholders of the said company, with the accounts annexed thereto, for the half-year ending 31st July, 1868, and has docqueted a copy thereof as relative thereto. That about the end of the year 1867 he made a thorough examination of the rolling stock belonging to the said company, and made a report thereon to a committee of investigation of the affairs of the said company, dated 1st January, 1868, a copy of which is docqueted as relative hereto, and that he is in a position to judge how much of the sum of 32,546l. charged for plant in the second page of the said report and accounts is correctly charged or proposed to be charged against the capital of the said company. That he is of opinion that at least the sum of 20,000l., part of the said sum of 32,546l., has been incurred for plant which was required to replace plant worn out, and that to that extent the said sum of 32,546l. is erroneously charged, or proposed to be charged, to capital, and ought to be charged to the revenue of the said company for the half-year ending 31st July, 1868. That the sum of 10,580l. charged in the said accounts against the balance of revenue brought forward from the half-year ending 31st January, 1868, is an insufficient addition to be made to the charge of 5d. per train mile run, which has already been made against the revenue of the said last-mentioned half-year for the proper repair and renewal of the rolling stock of the said company in respect of the said period. That the said additional charge raises the allowance to 5·64d. per train mile run, but in the deponent's report to the said committee of investigation he estimated that an expenditure of from 6d. to 6½d. per train mile run would be required each half-year during the next five years for the repair and renewal of the rolling stock ; and on further consideration of the subject, and on examining and comparing the expenditure for repair and renewal of rolling stock on the Caledonian with the expenditure on other lines, the deponent is still of opinion that an expenditure of at least 6½d. per train mile has been and will be necessary each half-year for that period of time for such repair and renewal. That, in confirmation of this opinion, the deponent finds that the average cost of repairing and renewing locomotive engines on soundly managed lines of great traffic in the United Kingdom amounts to about 135l. per engine per half-year ; but the charge made against revenue for the repair and renewal of the engines of the Caledonian for the half-year 31st July last is only 97l. per engine, showing a deficiency for that half-year on engines alone of 38l. per engine, which is equal to the sum of 20,000l. The deponent has no doubt that a sum of 1½d. per train mile run, over and above the 5d. charged in the half-years ending 31st January and 31st July, 1868, is absolutely necessary for the repair and renewal of the rolling stock during these periods. That the said 1½d. per train mile for the half-year ending 31st July, 1868, amounts to 24,000l., which the deponent is clearly of opinion ought, along with the charge of 5d. already made, to be debited to the revenue of the said half-year. That, in confirmation of all the foregoing statements, the deponent, in the course of his said examination of the company's rolling stock, found that there were then from 90 to 100 engines belonging to the company which were so completely worn out as to be unfit for further service, and that it was intended to replace them by new engines. All which is truth as the deponent shall answer to God.   D. K. CLARK.

Mr. Clark also explained that the mode of calculating train mileage has been changed by the company since last year, the principle formerly adopted having been to take engine mileage, but that now adopted being train mileage. The effect of this is to make no allowance for tear and wear of engines engaged in piloting and shunting duty, and by reducing the divisor to give apparently a greater expenditure by the company per train mile.

The case was argued before the first division of the Court of Session on 20th and 21st October.

Mr. Gifford, in support of the note, contended that he was not precluded from going into the merits of the questions by the terms of section 30 of the Companies Act 1867, which makes the auditors' report final and binding as to the payment of dividends. He argued that the certificate in this case was not in the statutory form, inasmuch as it merely certified that the accounts contained "a full and true statement of the financial condition of the company, as shown by the books," instead of certifying absolutely. Although the auditors said, in a previous passage, that they had examined the books and vouchers, and found them correct, that applied only to those of the previous half-year. Further, it was decided in Bloxam v. Metropolitan Railway Company (3d L. R. Ch. Ap. 337), that this section of the Act of 1867 does apply to a case such as this, so as to exclude inquiry. He then proceeded to argue that a sum of 112,436l. had been omitted from the charges against revenue in January 1866, and must be paid out of revenue before any dividend could be paid; and that the "premium fund," formed out of premiums on certain new shares sold by the company, and partly applied as revenue, ought to have been dealt with as capital, and must be replaced before payment of any dividend. He insisted that the sums contained in the "premium fund," and expended on repairs, on parliamentary expenses, &c., and which had been charged against capital instead of revenue, must be replaced before a dividend could be legally paid. He then argued that, as 200,000l. had been raised for the Callander and Oban railway, and only 100,000l. had been paid, a balance of 100,000l. must have been misapplied. Further, the company had declared its intention to misappropriate sums which it was authorised to raise under other Acts of Parliament.

Without calling for the respondents' counsel,

The Lord President said that there were a great many questions raised under this suspension, of a very important character, which the Court could not attempt to understand at the present stage. The note had been passed, and what was asked at present was an interim interdict against the payment of dividends. Now, upon the one hand, he could not take it upon him to say what effect the granting of an interim interdict would have upon the affairs of the company; while, upon the other hand, the complainer had no personal interest whatever in getting such interim interdict. He had been offered caution to protect him against the effect of anything that might be done in the meantime, which caution he did not think it necessary to accept. If he did not take the caution which had been offered, it must be because he had perfect confidence in the company being able to pay his dividends. He could not, therefore, be exposed, by the refusal of interim interdict, to any inconvenience, or ultimate damage; while the company might be seriously injured by the granting of the interim interdict. These seemed to him conclusive grounds against interfering with the Lord Ordinary's interlocutor recalling the interim interdict.

Lord Deas concurred with the Lord President. The note had been passed, and that would secure the discussion of all the questions raised under it. Before the complainer could get interim interdict, he must show that he would sustain personal loss if it were not granted. It would not do to say merely that the public, or that other shareholders would suffer loss by the refusal of interim interdict. The complainer had been offered caution against personal loss, and they must deal with the question precisely as if he had obtained caution. In the circumstances of the case, interim interdict could do the complainer no good, and it might do the whole of the shareholders irretrievable harm.

Lord Ardmillan concurred. The Lord Ordinary had passed the note, which would bring all the questions up for the decision of the court. The demand for interim interdict was made in the face of the certificate of the auditors; and it would be a strong step, and inconsistent with the practice of the court, to grant interim interdict as craved.

Lord Kinloch said that he had stated his opinion in his interlocutor.

Mr Young asked that the judgment of the court should only refuse the reclaiming note, without adhering to the Lord Ordinary's interlocutor otherwise, because it was still open to the company to reclaim against the part of the interlocutor passing the note.

The Court refused interim interdict, and adhered to the Lord Ordinary's interlocutor, it being stated that it was only an adherence so far as it was referred to in Mr. Glen's reclaiming note.

3.—DEBENTURE DEBTS OF PRINCIPAL COMPANIES.

BELFAST AND COUNTY DOWN.

At 5 per cent.		£57,887
4¾ ,,		20,614
4½ ,,		70,438
4¼ ,,		17,518
4 ,,		208=£166,666

BELFAST AND NORTHERN COUNTIES.

At 4¾ per cent.		£38,150
4½ ,,		136,040
4⅜ ,,		5,000
4¼ ,,		103,319
4 ,,		7,260=£289,769
Debenture Stock, 4 per cent.		110=£289,879

BLYTH AND TYNE.

At 5 per cent.	....	£19,270	
4½ ,,		37,166	
4¼ ,,		12,730	
4 ,,		18,780=	£87,946

BRISTOL AND EXETER.

	At 4 per cent.	At 4¼ per cent.	At 4½ per cent.	At 4¾ per cent.	At 5 per cent.	Total.
31st Dec., 1867	£325,198	£62,255	£210,361	£197,300	£122,543	£917,657
Since paid off	39,938	13,955	32,000	....	....	139,893
	£231,260	£48,300	£178,361	£197,300	£122,543	£777,764
Since issued	48,931	64,505	....	....	....	113,436
30th June, 1868..........	£280,191	£112,805	£178,361	£197,300	£122,543	£891,200

Average rate of Interest, £4 8s. 8½d., or 4·435 per cent.

AMOUNT REMAINING ISSUABLE:—

Authorised by Shareholders and Justice's Certificate, as above	£969,811
Amount of debentures issued, as above...........................	891,200
Balance at present issuable......................................	£78,611
Hereafter issuable, as above	51,500
Total remaining borrowing powers	£130,111

CALEDONIAN.

Rate per cent.	31st Jan., 1868.	Paid off.	Borrowed or Renewed.	31st July, 1868.
At 4½	£1,321,611	£40,100	£100	£1,281,611
4¼	607,615	334,749	....	272,866
4	3,340,523	144,168	553,884	3,750,239
3¾	14.452	5,000	....	9,452
3½	53,467	667	2,650	55,450
	£5.337,669	£524,685	£556,634	£5,369,618

Average rate, £4 2s. 6¼d. per cent. per annum.

COCKERMOUTH, KESWICK, AND PENRITH.

	4¼ per cent.	4½ per cent.	Total.
To 31st January, 1868...........	£45,000	£32,000	£77,000
,, 31st July, 1868...............	....	4,350	4,350
	£45,000	£36,350	£81,350
Deduct, paid off	....	4,450	4,450
	£45,000	£31,900	76,900

CORNWALL.

Authorised by Act 9 and 10 Vic., cap. 335	£375,020	
Do. by Act 24 and 25 Vic., cap. 215	82,980=	£458,000

Rate per cent.	31st Dec., 1867.	Paid off.	Renewed or Borrowed.	30th June, 1868.
At 4	£6,025	£800	....	£5,225
4¼	159,504	87.152	....	72,351
4½	115,044	2,160	£70,242	183,126
4¾	87,064	....	....	87,064
5	80,307	....	....	80,307
	£447,944	£90,112	£70,242	£428.074

DEESIDE.

	Deeside.	Extension.
At 4 per cent.	£21,855	£17,780
4½ ,, ...	21,545	6,510
Total	£43,400	£24,30C

DUBLIN AND BELFAST JUNCTION.

At 4½ per cent.	£85,250	
4¾ ,,	2,000	
5 ,,	140,260=	£227,510
Debenture Stock, at 4 per cent................................	1,100	
,, 4¼ ,, ...	3,545=	£4,645=£232,155

DUBLIN AND DROGHEDA.

At 4 per cent.	£1,300	
4¼ „	62,370	
4½ „	153,238	
4¾ „	22,890	
5 „	12,900	=£252,698

EDINBURGH AND BATHGATE.

At 5 per cent.	£25,000	
4½ „	16,400	
4¼ „	10,000	
4 „	6,300	
4½ „	6,250	=£63,950

FURNESS.

At 4 per cent.	£9,900	
4¼ „	151,495	
4½ „	327,295	
4¾ „	114,716	=£603,406
Balance at Issue		4,860

Average rate per cent., 4*l.* 9*s.* 6*d.*

GLASGOW AND SOUTH WESTERN.

Average, £4 2*s.* 2*d*, per cent.	31st Jan., 1868.	Added.	Paid off.	31st July, 1868.
At 5 per cent.	£4,000	....	....	£4,000
4½ „	351,858	....	£2,345	349,513
4¼ „	87,700	....	66,100	21,600
4 „	942,568	£57,070	....	999,638
3¾ „	40,980	220	....	41,200
3⅝ „	25,000	....	....	25,000
3½ „	500	11,900	....	12,400
Total mortgage loan	£1,452,606	£69,190	£68,445	1,453,351
Funded Debt	51,893			51,893
Amount issued	1,504,499			1,505,244
Unissued				16,255
Total loan or funded debt, as exercised under parliamentary powers				£1,521,500

GREAT EASTERN.

Per cent.	Dec. 31st, 1867.	Increase.	Total.	Decrease.	30th June, 1868.
4	£108,989	....	£108,989	£44,610	£64,379
4¼	913,593	....	913,593	501,914	411,679
4⅜	10,000	....	10,000	....	10,000
4½	1,393,584	....	1,393,584	477,674	915,910
4¾	475,148	....	475,148	43,150	431,998
5	1,922,538	£1,235,183	3,157,721	48,800	3,108,921
5¼	1,000	....	1,000	....	1,000
5½	24,000	....	24,000	....	24,000
6	102,000	....	102,000	100,000	2,000
	£4,950,853	£1,235,183	£6,186,036	£1,216,148	£4,969,888

Redeemable debenture stock, at 5 per cent. per annum		208,800
		£5,178,688
Debenture stock, at 4 per cent. per annum		832,673
Ditto 4½ ditto		79,606
		£6,090,968
Total amount received on account of 5 per cent. redeemable debenture stock, 1867	£388,975	
Less—Amount in respect of which bonds are issued—as above	208,800	
		180,175
		£6,271,144
Borrowing powers		9,529,441
Available borrowing powers to exercise		£3,258,296
Add—Borrowing powers authorised under the following Acts:—		
Eastern Counties (Epping Lines) Act, 1862		33,330
Great Eastern (Additional Powers) Act, 1866		25,300
„ „ (Alexandra Park Branches) Act, 1866		37,000
		£3,353,926

GREAT NORTHERN.

Description.	31st Dec., 1867.	Due in half-year.	Borrowed & Renewed.	Paid.	30th June, 1868.
5 per cent. Mortgage Loans	£230,360	£5,700	....	£5,700	£224,660
4½ ,, ,, ,,	583,595	69,767	....	69,767	513,828
4¼ ,, ,, ,,	411,390	103,070	34,480	72,590	369,280
4 ,, ,, ,,	54,039	142,149	136,400	5,749	184,690
3½ ,, ,, ,,	40,000	....	....	....	40,000
Total Mortgage Loans	£1,319,384	£320,686	£166,880	£153,806	£1,332,458
Debenture Stock	2,847,731	....	£13,074	....	2,853,729
Total	£4,167,115	....	....	....	£4,186,187
Debenture Capital unissued	....				3,005
Total Debenture Capital authorised to be raised					£4,189,192

GREAT SOUTHERN AND WESTERN.

At 5 per cent...	£42,800
,, 4¾ ,, ...	23,854
,, 4½ ,, ...	176,519
,, 4⅜ ,, ...	10,000
,, 4¼ ,, ...	65,760
,, 4 ,, ...	17,998

GREAT WESTERN.

	Jan. 31st, 1868.	July 31st, 1868.
At 6 per cent. (temporary)	£200,000	....
5 ,, ...	4,206,136	£4,951,412
4¾ ,, ...	1,304,628	1,263,192
4½ ,, ...	4,613,079	4,166,039
4⅜ ,, ...	10,000	10,000
4¼ ,, ...	2,773,863	2,278,447
4 ,, ...	226,613	198,895
3½ ,, ...	3,000	3,000
Amount, January 31st, 1868	£13,337,374	
Decrease	466,336	
Amount, July 31st, 1868	£12,870.988	£12,870,988

GREAT WESTERN AND BRENTFORD.

Per cent.	31st Dec., 1867.	Paid off.	Issued Half-year.	30th June, 1868.
At 5	£21,508	....	£7,650	£29,158
4¾	9,110	£5,000	....	4,110
4½	19,750	6,110	500	14,150
4¼	4,680	500	....	4,180
In hand....	....	....	....	3,450
	£55,048	£11,610	£8,150	£55,048

HIGHLAND.

At 5 per cent..................................	£37,417
,, 4½ ,, ...	467,697
,, 4¼ ,, ...	5,100
,, 4 ,, ...	190,419=£700,634

LANCASHIRE AND YORKSHIRE.

By Loans.	Raised by Loans.							
	At 4¾.	At 4½.	At 4⅜.	At 4¼.	At 4⅛.	At 4.	At 3¾.	At 3.
June 30, 1868..	£399,720	£1,868,770	£96,150	£880,211	£49,800	£1,653,091	£59,792	£40,900
Dec. 31, 1867..	399,720	1,931,770	96,150	1,024,022	105,800	1,460,410	16,140	74,500
Increase	..	..	..	..	..	192,681	43,652	..
Decrease....	..	63,000	..	143,811	56,000	..	..	33,600

Lancashire and Yorkshire Continued.

	Total.	Debenture Stock.			Total.
		At 4 per cent.	At 3½ per cent.	Total Debenture Stocks.	
June 30th, 1868	£5,048,435	£503,021	£1,000	£504,021	£5,552,457
Dec. 31st, 1867	5,108,513	491,321	1,000	492,321	5,600,835
Increase	..	11,700	..	11,700	..
Decrease	60,078	..	..	..	48,378
Authorised to be raised by Loans and by Debenture Stocks, in respect of capital created, as per Statement No. 1					6,073,353
Raised by Loans and by Debenture Stocks, as above					5,552,457
Balance, being available Borrowing Powers at June 30th, 1868					£520,895

LONDON AND BLACKWALL.

At 5 per cent...	£195,690
,, 4¾ ,, ...	57,000
,, 4½ ,, ...	240,640
,, 4¼ ,, ...	44,900
,, 4 ,, ...	14,000 =£552,230

LONDON AND NORTH WESTERN.

By Loans.	Debentures.							
	At 3.	At 3½.	At 3¾.	At 4.	At 4¼.	At 4½.	At 4¾.	At 5.
Existing on 31st December, 1867..	£700	£3,121	£5,600	£1,898,750	£2,354,175	£6,883,633	£803,594	£179,681
Debt of various companies, since converted *	..	..	..	22,800	126,650	267,210	..	..
Total 31st Dec. 1867	700	3,121	£5,600	£1,921,550	£2,480,825	£7,150,843	£803,594	£179,681
,, 30th June, 1868	700	11,621	12,050	2,252,420	2,878,961	6,677,014	769,644	167,881
Increase	..	£8,500	£6,450	£330,870	£398,136	..	..	..
Decrease	..	..	..	..	..	£473,829	£33,950	£11,800

* Debt of the South Staffordshire, South Leicestershire, Bangor and Carnarvon, and Vale of Clwyd.

	Total Debentures	Debenture Stocks.			Raised on Debentures and by Debenture Stocks.
		At 3½.	At 4.	Debenture Stocks.	
31st December, 1867	£12,129,254	£310,830	£2,002,094	£2,312,924	£14,442,177
Subsidiaries	416,660	..	..	..	416,660
Total	£12,545,914	£310,830	£2,002,094	£2,312,924	£14,858,837
30th June, 1868	12,770,291	310,830	2,024,693	2,335,523	15,105,814
Increase......................	£224,377	..	£22,599	£22,599	£246,976
Authorised to be raised on debentures and by debenture stocks, in respect of capital created, as per Statement No. 1					£15,117,549
Raised to 30th June, 1868, on debentures and by debenture stocks as above					15,105,814
Margin of borrowing powers in respect of capital created					£11,734

LONDON AND SOUTH WESTERN.

Per cent.	31st Dec., 1867.	Paid off.	Borrowed.	30th June, 1868.
At 5	£563,350	£65,000	..	£498,350
4¾	365,877	176,110	..	189,767
4½	1,213,721	137,760	£600	1,076,561
4¼	564,230	5,500	124,700	683,430
4	839,973	128,357	137,010	848,626
	£3,547,151	£512,727	£262,310	£3,296,734
	250,417	262,310	..	..
	£3,296,734	£250,417	..	..

LONDON, BRIGHTON, AND SOUTH COAST.

Mortgage Bonds.	31st Dec., 1867.	Due during Half-year	Renewed.	Borrowed	Repaid.	30th June, 1868.
At 5	£1,063,062	..	£72,400	£87,640	..	£1,223,102
4¾	104,600	..	..	2,500	..	107,100
4½	582,650	£87,500	75,000	11,400	£22,300	581,550
4¼	256,550	90,000	..	..	15,000	166,550
4	737,370	28,600	..	..	21,400	708,770
Total	£2,744,232	£206,100	£147,400	£101,540	£58,700	£2,787,072
Debenture Stock ..	1,305,744	..	..	..	..	1,305,744
Total	£4,049,976	206,100	£147,400	£101,540	£58,700	£4,092,816

Average rate per cent, £4 11s. 9d.—Debenture Stock, £4 8s.

LONDON, CHATHAM, AND DOVER.

Principal.		Annual Interest.
£1,427,000	General Undertaking	£76,165
190,000	Western Extension	9,961
1,442,000	Metropolitan Extensions	82,454
460,000	City Lines	25,202
356,000	Eastern Section	18,080
250,000	Common Fund..	12,500
173,000	Victoria Improvements	9,428
£4,298,000		£233,790

MANCHESTER, SHEFFIELD, AND LINCOLNSHIRE.

Per cent.	31st Dec., 1867.	Borrowed.	Paid off.	30th June, 1868.
At 3¾	£1,000	....	....	£1,000
,, 4	113,280	£300	£10,450	103,130
,, 4¼	659,010	2,380	156,769	504,621
,, 4⅜	40,000	....	20,000	20,000
,, 4½	1,051,222	348,956	144,310	1,255,868
,, 4¾	1,013,830	117,300	175,190	955,940
,, 5	617,534	....	11,000	606,534
	£3,495,878	£468,936	517,719	£3,447,095
Decrease for the half-year to June 30, 1868.	48,783			
	£3,447,095			

MARYPORT AND CARLISLE.

At 4½	....	£67,931
,, 4¼	....	37,345
,, 4	....	68,879=£174,155

MIDLAND.

Per cent.	31st Dec., 1867.	Falling due.	Borrowed and renewed.	30th June, 1868.
At 5	£82,562	....	....	£82,562
,, 4¾	679,559	....	....	679,559
,, 4⅝	5,300	....	....	5,300
,, 4½	2,667,574	£77,750	£299,456	2,889,281
,, 4¼	775,025	175,231	14,275	614,069
,, 4	1,473,874	248,768	191,686	1,416,792
,, 3¾	15,260	13,500	2,770	4,530
,, 3½	6,000	200	....	5,800
,, 3	43,000	3,000	....	40,000
	£5,748,157	£518,450	£508,188	5,737,895

Margin on June 30th, 1868, for further issue of debentures within the authorised borrowing powers, 3,885*l.*

MIDLAND GREAT WESTERN.

At 5 per cent.	....	£363,481
4¾ ,,	....	1,600
4½ ,,	....	290,630
4¼ ,,	....	10,500
4 ,,	....	4,800=£671,011

NORTH BRITISH.

	At 3½.	At 3¾.	At 4.	At 4¼.	At 4½.	At 4¾	At 5.	Total.
As at 31st July, 1868..	..	..	£815,150	£740,192	£1,571,289	£216,543	£1,246,839	£4,590,015
Loans under Financial Act, 1867	..	..	300	5,460	748,110	..	6,300	760,170
As at 31st July, 1867..	£300	£1,000	£1,624,820	£204,321	£1,085,487	£277,693	£1,418,366	£4,611,988

Average rate of interest, £4 10s. per cent.

NORTH EASTERN.

Per cent.	31st Dec., 1867.	Falling due.	Renewed.	Paid off.	Borrowed	30th June, 1868.	Total.
At 5	£729,315	£42,050	....	£31,250	....	£687,265	
,, 4¾	1,155,108	....	....	....	....	1,155,108	
,, 4½ ..*.....	4,412,955	339,854	£8,960	170,429	....	4,082,061	
,, 4¼	1,717,926	280,286	262,210	115,681	£130,651	1,830,501	
,, 4	1,472,851	341,779	274,989	120,449	177,389	1,583,452	
,, 3¾	500	500	....	500	....	....	
,, 3½	59,000	30,000	40,000	10,000	....	69,000	
,, 3	21,400	1,200	....	1,200	....	20,200	
	£9,569,057	£1,035,669	£586,160	£449,509	£308,041	£9,427,588	£9,427,588

HULL & SELBY.

Per cent.	31st Dec., 1867.	Falling due.	Renewed.	Paid off.	Borrowed	30th June, 1868.	Total.
At 5	£19,500	....	.	....	....	£19,500	
,, 4¾	50,010	....	....	....	....	50,010	
,, 4½	106,262	£4,650	....	£150	....	101,612	
,, 4¼	16,412	862	£1,000	862	£16,725	33,275	
,, 4	14,400	900	3,700	700	7,000	24,200	
,, 3¾	5,000	5,000	....	5,000	....	....	
	£211,584	£11,412	£4,700	£6,712	£23,725	£228,597	228,597

GREAT NORTH OF ENGLAND.

Per cent.	31st Dec., 1867.	Falling due.	Renewed.	Paid off.	Borrowed	30th June, 1868.	Total.
At 4½	£9,607	....	....	....	....	£9,607	
,, 4¼	5,750	£4,750	£1,700	....	£1,000	3,700	
,, 4	200	....	3,050	....	4,500	7,750	
	£15,557	£4,750	£4,750		£5,500	£21,057	21,057

GREAT NORTH OF ENGLAND PURCHASE DEBENTURES.
Amount outstanding 31st Dec., 1867 ....£538,780
Paid off during half-year.. 21,742 = £517,037

Total, June 30th, 1868 ....£ 10,194,280

NORTH LONDON.

31st December, 1867.		30th June, 1868.	
At 5 per cent.	£75,000	At 5 per cent.	£75,000
4¾ ,, ...	159,300	4¾ ,, ...	151 300
4½ ,, ...	432,061	4½ ,, ...	428,991
4¼ ,, ...	65,700	4¼ ,, ...	70,350
4 ,, ...	1,800	4 ,, ...	3,800
	£733,891		£729,441

Average rate of interest, 4·58 per cent.   Average rate of interest, 4·57 per cent.

DEBENTURE STOCK.

At 4 per cent.	£7,075	At 4 per cent.	£7,075
4½ ,, ...	..	4½ ,, ...	25
	£7,075		£7,100

NORTH STAFFORDSHIRE.

Per cent.	31st Dec., 1867.	Renewed.	Paid off.	30th June, 1868.
At 5	£290,650	....	....	£290,650
4¾	443,023	£3,270	£5,370	440,923
4½	568,069	154,729	131,117	591,681
4¼	226,762	4,300	25,500	205,562
4	12,770	....	300	12,470
	£1,541,274	£162,299	£162,287	£1,541,286

Average rate of interest, £4 12s. 7d. per cent.

SOUTH DEVON.

Per cent.	31st Dec., 1867.	Paid in half-year.	Renewed or borrowed.	30th June, 1868.
At 5	£204,905	£250	....	£204,655
4¾	17,830	150	....	17,680
4½	243,565	50,200	£72,225	265,590
4¼	52,800	20,300	....	32,500
4	12,450	3,650	....	8,800
	£531,550	£74,550	£72,225	£529,225

SOUTH EASTERN.

Per cent.	31st Jan., 1868.	Received.	Paid off.	31st July, 1868.
At 5	£1,529,126	....	£90,000	£1,439,126
4¾	426,803	£120,000	133,000	413,803
4½	1,649,144	384,938	372,451	1,661,631
4¼	464,789	....	107,420	357,369
4	255,985	80,500	50,515	285,970
	£4,325,847	£585,438	£753,386	£4,157,899
South Eastern 5 per cent. debenture certificates (1868)	....	141,302	....	141,302
South Eastern 5 per cent. debenture stock (1867)................	478,500	21,500	....	500,000
Do. 4½ per cent. do.	....	1,500	....	1,500
Do. 4 per cent. do.	67,980	....	....	67,980
	£4,872,327	£749,740	£753,386	£4,868,681
			Unexercised....	60,062
				£4,928,743

Average rate of interest, £4 13s. 7¼d. per cent.

SOUTH YORKSHIRE.

Per cent.	31st Dec., 1867.	Falling due.	Borrowed or renewed.	30th June, 1868.
At 5	£191,850	£400	....	£191,450
4¾	311,982	26,070	£6,500	292,412
4⅝	....	....	2,000	2,000
4½	479,490	131,506	227,671	575,655
4⅜	2,300	2,300	....	....
4¼	128,185	87,080	13,975	55,080
4	23,468	5,400	....	18,068
	£1,137,275	£252,756	£250,146	£1,134,665
Exercised powers of borrowing				114,938
Total authorised powers of borrowing..				£1,249,603

STAINES AND WOKINGHAM.

Per cent.	31st Dec., 1867.	Renewed or Re-borrowed.	30th June, 1868.
At 5	£31,335	£10,785	£36,335
4¾	7,415	4,050	7,765
4½	51,050	1,860	44,350
Unissued	....	....	1,550
Total	£89,800	£16,695	£90,000

TAFF VALE.

Average rate of Debenture Interest, 30th June, 1868, £4 8s. 0d. per cent.	31st Dec., 1867.	Paid off.	Re-issue.	30th June, 1868.
5 per cent. Mortgage Loans	£48,510	....	....	£48,510
4¾ ,, ,, ,, ...	56,700	....	....	56,700
4½ ,, ,, ,, ...	87,864	....	£8,500	87,364
4¼ ,, ,, ,, ...	97,640	£8,000	9,100	98,740
,, ' ,, ,, ...	116,469	13,500	3,900	106,869
	£398,183	£21,500	£21,500	£398,183
,, Irredeemable Stock	38,817	....		38,817
Total	£437,000	£21,500	£21,500	£437,000

4.—DIVIDENDS OF PRINCIPAL COMPANIES FROM THE EARLIEST PERIODS.

BELFAST AND NORTHERN COUNTIES.

1849—Nov.........£0 18 0	1856—May £3 10 0	1862—Dec. £2 5 0
1850—May 1 0 0	Nov. 3 10 0	1863—June........ 2 0 0
Nov. 1 10 0	1857—May 2 10 0	Dec. 2 0 0
1851—May 1 0 0	Nov. 2 10 0	1864—June........ 1 10 0
Nov. 1 2 0	1858—May 2 5 0	Dec. 2 0 0
1852—May 1 2 0	Nov. 2 0 0	1865—June........ 1 15 0
Nov. 1 7 0	1859—May 2 5 0	Dec. 2 5 0
1853—May 1 16 3	Nov. 2 0 0	1866—June........ 2 0 0
Nov. 2 4 0	1860—May 2 0 0	Dec. 2 10 0
1854—May 2 4 0	Nov. 2 5 0	1867—June........ 2 10 0
Nov. 2 0 0	1861—June 2 5 0	Dec. 2 10 0
1855—May 2 10 0	Dec. 2 5 0	1868—June........ 2 10 0
Nov. 2 15 0	1862—June........ 2 5 0	

BLYTH AND TYNE.

1853—Dec. £4 0 0	1858—Dec. £4 5 0	1863—Dec. £4 15 0
1854—June........ 4 10 0	1859—June........ 4 10 0	1864—June........ 4 15 0
Dec. 4 10 0	Dec. 4 15 0	Dec. 4 15 0
1855—June........ 4 10 0	1860—June........ 4 15 0	1865—June........ 4 15 0
Dec. 4 10 0	Dec. 5 0 0	Dec. 5 0 0
1856—June........ 4 10 0	1861—June........ 4 15 0	1866—June........ 5 0 0
Dec. 4 0 0	Dec. 4 15 0	Dec. 5 0 0
1857—June........ 3 5 0	1862—June........ 4 15 0	1867—June........ 5 0 0
Dec. 3 10 0	Dec. 4 15 0	Dec. 5 0 0
1858—June........ 4 0 0	1863—June........ 4 15 0	1868—June........ 5 0 0

BRISTOL AND EXETER.

1842—Dec. £2 0 0	1851—Dec. £2 5 0	1860—June........£3 0 0
1843—June........ 2 0 0	1852—June........ 2 5 0	Dec. 2 15 0
Dec. 2 0 0	Dec. 2 5 0	1861—June........ 2 2 6
1844—June........ 2 0 0	1853—June........ 2 5 0	Dec. 2 10 0
Dec. 2 0 0	Dec. 2 5 0	1862—June........ 1 10 0
1845—June........ 2 0 0	1854—June........ 2 5 0	Dec. 2 10 0
Dec. 2 0 0	Dec. 2 5 0	1863—June........ 2 0 0
1846—June........ 2 0 0	1855—June........ 2 5 0	Dec. 2 10 0
Dec. 2 5 0	Dec. 2 5 0	1864—June........ 2 5 0
1847—June........ 2 5 0	1856—June........ 2 5 0	Dec. 2 15 0
Dec. 2 5 0	Dec. 2 10 0	1865—June........ 2 5 0
1848—June........ 2 5 0	1857—June........ 2 10 0	Dec. 2 15 0
Dec. 1 17 6	Dec. 2 10 0	1866—June........ 2 5 0
1849—June........ 1 15 0	1858—June........ 2 10 0	Dec. 2 5 0
Dec. 1 15 0	Dec. 2 10 0	1867—June........ 2 0 0
1850—June........ 1 8 0	1859—June........ 2 15 0	Dec. 2 7 6
Dec. 1 15 0	Dec. 3 0 0	1868—June,....... 1 17 6
1851—June........ 2 0 0		

CALEDONIAN.

1849—Jan. £1 10 0	1856—Jan. £1 0 0	1862—July £2 10 0
July .... Nil.	July 0 10 0	1863—Jan. 3 0 0
1850—Jan. .... Nil.	1857—Jan. 1 15 0	July 2 12 6
July .... Nil.	July 1 15 0	1864—Jan. 3 2 6
1851—Jan. .... Nil.	1858—Jan. 2 10 0	July 3 5 0
July .... Nil.	July 1 15 0	1865—Jan. 3 12 6
1852—Jan. 0 5 0	1859—Jan. 2 0 0	July 4 7 6
July 0 6 0	July 1 17 6	1866—Jan. 3 15 0
1853—Jan. 1 5 0	1860—Jan. 2 10 0	July 3 12 6
July 1 0 0	July 2 2 6	1867—Jan. 3 5 0
1854—Jan. 1 10 0	1861—Jan. 2 15 0	July 2 12 6
July 1 10 0	July 2 10 0	1868—Jan. 1 5 0
1855—Jan. 1 10 0	1862—Jan. 2 15 0	July 0 15 0
July 1 10 0		

DUBLIN AND BELFAST JUNCTION.

Period	£ s d	Period	£ s d	Period	£ s d
1850—June	£1 2 0	1856—Dec.	£2 10 0	1862—Dec.	£2 0 0
Dec.	1 2 0	1857—June	2 0 0	1863—June	2 0 0
1851—June	1 2 0	Dec.	2 0 0	Dec.	2 0 0
Dec.	1 13 4	1858—June	2 0 0	1864—June	1 12 6
1852—June	1 13 4	Dec.	2 0 0	Dec.	1 15 0
Dec.	2 9 0	1859—June	2 0 0	1865—June	1 15 0
1853—June	2 10 0	Dec.	2 2 6	Dec.	2 5 0
Dec.	2 10 0	1860—June	2 2 6	1866—June	2 0 0
1854—June	2 10 0	Dec.	2 2 6	Dec.	2 0 0
Dec.	2 10 0	1861—June	2 2 6	1867—June	2 0 0
1855—June	2 10 0	Dec.	2 2 6	Dec.	2 0 0
Dec.	2 10 0	1862—June	2 2 6	1868—June	2 0 0
1856—June	2 10 0				

DUBLIN AND DROGHEDA.

Period	£ s d	Period	£ s d	Period	£ s d
1850—June	£0 16 0	1856—Dec.	£2 5 0	1862—Dec.	£2 10 0
Dec.	1 0 0	1857—June	2 5 0	1863—June	2 0 0
1851—June	0 15 0	Dec.	2 5 0	Dec.	2 0 0
Dec.	1 0 0	1858—June	2 5 0	1864—June	2 0 0
1852—June	1 1 4	Dec.	2 5 0	Dec.	2 0 0
Dec.	1 17 0	1859—June	2 7 6	1865—June	2 5 0
1853—June	1 13 4	Dec.	2 10 0	Dec.	2 10 0
Dec.	2 5 0	1860—June	2 10 0	1866—June	2 5 0
1854—June	2 0 0	Dec.	2 10 0	Dec.	2 5 0
Dec.	2 0 0	1861—June	2 10 0	1867—June	2 7 6
1855—June	2 0 0	Dec.	2 10 0	Dec.	2 7 6
Dec.	2 5 0	1862—June	2 10 0	1868—June	2 10 0
1856—June	2 5 0				

FURNESS.

Period	£ s d	Period	£ s d	Period	£ s d
1847—Feb.	£2 0 0	1854—June	£3 0 0	1861—Dec.	£4 0 0
Aug.	2 0 0	Dec.	3 0 0	1862—June	4 0 0
1848—March	1 0 0	1855—June	3 0 0	Dec.	4 0 0
Aug.	Nil.	Dec.	3 0 0	1863—June	4 0 0
1849—Feb.	Nil.	1856—June	4 0 0	Dec.	4 10 0
Aug.	1 0 0	Dec.	4 0 0	1864—June	5 0 0
1850—Feb.	1 0 0	1857—June	4 0 0	Dec.	5 0 0
June	1 0 0	Dec.	4 0 0	1865—June	5 0 0
Dec.	1 5 0	1858—June	3 10 0	Dec.	5 0 0
1851—June	1 10 0	Dec.	3 0 0	1866—June	5 0 0
Dec.	1 10 0	1859—June	3 10 0	Dec.	5 0 0
1852—June	1 15 0	Dec.	3 0 0	1867—June	4 0 0
Dec.	1 15 0	1860—June	3 10 0	Dec.	4 0 0
1853—June	2 0 0	Dec.	4 0 0	1868—June	4 0 0
Dec.	2 10 0	1861—June	4 0 0		

GLASGOW AND SOUTH WESTERN.

Period	£ s d	Period	£ s d	Period	£ s d
Glasgow, Paisley and Ayr.		1849—July	Nil.	1859—July	£2 10 0
1841—Jan.	£1 5 0	1850—Jan.	£1 5 0	1860—Jan.	2 10 0
July	1 5 0	July	1 5 0	July	2 12 6
1842—Jan.	1 15 0	1851—Jan.	1 2 6	1861—Jan.	2 15 0
July	1 15 0	July	1 0 0	July	2 10 0
1843—Jan.	1 5 0	1852—Jan.	1 0 0	1862—Jan.	2 15 0
July	1 5 0	July	1 0 0	July	2 10 0
1844—Jan.	2 0 0	1853—Jan.	1 0 0	1863—Jan.	2 10 0
July	2 5 0	July	1 10 0	July	2 10 0
1845—Jan.	2 10 0	1854—Jan.	1 5 0	1864—Jan.	2 10 0
July	3 0 0	July	1 15 0	July	2 17 6
1846—Jan.	3 10 0	1855—Jan.	1 12 6	1865—Jan.	2 17 6
July	3 10 0	July	1 17 6	July	3 0 0
1847—Jan.	3 10 0	1856—Jan.	1 15 0	1866—Jan.	3 10 0
July	3 10 0	July	2 0 0	July	3 10 0
		1857—Jan.	2 10 0	1867—Jan.	3 2 6
Glasgow & South Western.		July	2 10 0	July	2 15 0
1848—Jan.	3 0 0	1858—Jan.	2 5 0	1868—Jan.	2 10 0
July	2 0 0	July	2 0 0	July	2 5 0
1849—Jan.	1 0 0	1859—Jan.	2 5 0		

GREAT EASTERN.

Eastern Counties.		*Eastern Counties (cont.)*		*Great Eastern.*	
1841—Dec. £0 17 0		1856—Dec. £1 5 0		1854—June........£1 0 0	
1842—June........ 0 17 6		1857—June........ 1 5 0		Dec. 1 10 0	
Dec. 0 12 0		Dec. 1 17 6		1855—June........ 1 5 0	
1843—June........ 0 17 6		1858—June........ 1 3 9		Dec. 1 15 0	
Dec. 0 12 6		Dec. 1 12 6		1856—June........ 1 5 0	
1844—June........ 0 12 6		1859—June........ 1 1 3		Dec. 2 0 0	
Dec......... 1 5 0		Dec. 1 13 9		1857—June........ 1 10 0	
1845—June....... 1 0 0		1860—June........ 1 1 3		Dec. 2 0 0	
Dec. 3 0 0		Dec. 1 3 9		1858—June........ 1 7 6	
1846—June....... 3 0 0		1861—June........ 0 16 3		Dec. 1 16 6	
Dec. 3 5 0		Dec. 1 10 0		1859 -June........ 1 4 0	
1847—June....... 2 10 0		1862—June....... 1 0 0		Dec. 1 17 6	
Dec. 2 0 0		*Norfolk.*		1860—June........ 1 10 0	
1848—June....... 2 0 0		1845—Dec. 2 10 0		Dec. 1 17 6	
Dec. .... Nil.		1846—June........ 3 0 0		1861—June........ 1 10 0	
1849—June....... 0 10 0		Dec. 3 10 0		Dec. 3 0 0	
Dec......... 0 15 0		1847—June........ 3 0 0		1862—June........ 2 10 0	
1850—June....... 0 10 0		Dec. 2 10 0		*Great Eastern.*	
Dec......... Nil.		1848—June........ 2 0 0		1862—Dec. 1 5 0	
1851 -June....... Nil.		Dec. .... Nil.		1863—June........ 0 12 6	
Dec. 1 0 0		1849—June........ 0 10 0		Dec. 1 5 0	
1852—June....... 1 0 0		Dec. 0 15 0		1864—June........ 0 12 6	
Dec. 1 10 0		1850—June........ 0 10 0		Dec. 1 5 0	
1853—June....... 1 5 0		Dec......... Nil.		1865—June........ Nil.	
Dec. 1 15 0		1851—June........ Nil.		Dec. .... Nil.	
1854—June....... 0 17 6		Dec. 1 0 0		1866—June........ Nil.	
Dec. 1 15 0		1852—June........ 1 0 0		Dec. .... Nil.	
1855—June....... 1 2 6		Dec. 1 10 0		1867—June........ Nil.	
Dec. 1 2 6		1853—June........ 1 5 0		Dec. .... Nil.	
1856—June....... 0 10 0		Dec. 1 15 0		1868—June........ Nil.	

GREAT NORTHERN.

1851—June........£0 15 0		1857—June..... £0 6 0		1863—June........£2 2 6	
Dec. 1 5 0		Dec. 2 15 3		Dec 4 7 6	
1852 -June........ 1 0 0		1858—June........ 1 13 9		1864—June........ 2 15 0	
Dec. 1 5 0		Dec. 3 1 3		Dec. 4 7 6	
1853—June........ 1 5 0		1859—June........ 1 13 9		1865—June........ 2 15 0	
Dec. 2 7 6		Dec. 3 10 0		Dec. 4 7 6	
1854—June........ 1 7 6		1860—June........ 2 5 0		1866—Juue........ 2 10 0	
Dec. 2 17 6		Dec. 3 3 9		Dec. 4 0 0	
1855—June........ 1 2 6		1861—June........ 1 17 6		1867—June........ 2 5 0	
Dec. 3 0 0		Dec. 3 17 6		Dec. 3 15 0	
1856—June........ 1 15 0		1862—June........ 2 5 0		1868—June........ 2 2 6	
Dec. .... Nil.		Dec. 4 5 0			

GREAT NORTH OF SCOTLAND.

Annual.					
1855 ....£1 5 0		1860—July £3 10 0		1864—July £2 10 0	
1856 .... 1 5 0		1861—Jan. 3 5 0		1865—Jan. .... Nil.	
1857 .... 4 10 0		July 3 10 0		July .... Nil.	
1858 .... 4 11 0		1862—Jan. 3 15 0		1866—Jan. .... Nil.	
Half-yearly.		July 3 10 0		July .... Nil.	
1858—July 2 10 0		1863—Jan. 3 10 0		1867—Jan. .... Nil.	
1859—Jan. 3 0 0		July 3 10 0		July .... Nil.	
		1864—Jan. 2 10 0		1868—Jan. .... Nil.	

GREAT SOUTHERN AND WESTERN (IRELAND).

1850—June........£1 10 0		1856 -Dec. £3 0 0		1863—June........£2 2 6	
Dec. 1 15 0		1857—June........ 2 10 0		Dec. 2 5 0	
1851—June....... 1 12 6		Dec. 2 10 0		1864—June........ 2 5 0	
Dec. 1 16 1		1858—June........ 2 10 0		Dec. 2 5 0	
1852—June....... 2 0 0		Dec. 2 10 0		1865—June........ 2 5 0	
Dec. 2 5 0		1859—June........ 2 10 0		Dec. 2 10 0	
1853—June....... 2 5 0		Dec. 2 10 0		1866—June........ 2 10 0	
Dec. 2 5 0		1860—June........ 2 10 0		Dec. 2 5 0	
1854—June....... 2 0 0		Dec. 2 10 0		1867—June........ 2 10 0	
Dec. 2 0 0		1861—June........ 2 10 0		Dec. 2 5 0	
1855—June....... 2 10 0		Dec. 2 10 0		1868—June........ 2 10 0	
Dec. 2 10 0		1862—June........ 2 10 0			
1856—June....... 3 0 0		Dec, ... 2 10 0			

GREAT WESTERN.

1840—Dec. £1 10 0	1861—June........ £1 2 6	1866—July £0 17 0
1841—June........ 1 10 0	Dec. 1 10 0	1867—Jan. 0 3 9
Dec. 3 0 0	1862—June........ 0 5 0	July 0 5 0
1842—June........ 3 0 0	Dec. 1 10 0	1868—Jan. 0 7 6
Dec. 3 10 0	1863—July 1 0 0	July 0 5 0
1843—June........ 2 10 0	1864—Jan. 1 10 0	*South Wales.*
Dec. 3 0 0	July 1 10 0	1851—Dec. 0 15 0
1844—June........ 3 10 0	1865—Jan. 1 12 6	1852—June........ Nil.
Dec. 4 0 0	July 1 0 0	Dec. 1 0 0
1845—June........ 4 0 0	1866—June 1 0 0	1853—June........ 1 0 0
Dec. 4 0 0	July 1 0 0	Dec. 1 10 0
1846—June........ 4 0 0	1867—Jan. 0 10 0	1854—June........ Nil.
Dec. 4 0 0	July 0 12 6	Dec. 1 10 0
1847—June........ 4 0 0	1868—Jan. 0 15 0	1855—June........ 1 10 0
Dec. 3 10 0	July 0 12 6	Dec. 1 10 0
1848—June........ 3 10 0	*West Midland (Oxford).*	1856—June........ 1 15 0
Dec. 3 0 0	1861—Dec. 0 7 6	Dec. 2 0 0
1849—June........ 2 0 0	1862—June........ Nil.	1857—June........ 1 12 6
Dec. 2 0 0	Dec. 0 15 0	Dec. 1 15 0
1850—June........ 2 0 0	1863—June........ 0 2 6	1858—June........ 1 10 0
Dec. 2 0 0	1864—Jan. 0 17 6	Dec. 1 5 0
1851—June........ 2 0 0	July 1 2 6	1859—June........ 1 2 6
Dec. 2 19 0	1865—Jan. 1 0 0	Dec. 1 7 6
1852—June........ 2 0 0	July 0 13 3	1860—June........ 1 0 0
Dec. 2 0 0	1866—Jan. 0 9 3	Dec. 1 10 0
1853—June........ 2 0 0	July 0 17 0	1861—June........ 1 7 6
Dec. 2 0 0	1867—Jan. 0 2 6	Dec. 1 10 0
1854—June........ 1 10 0	July 0 2 6	1862—June........ 1 12 6
Dec. 1 10 0	1868—Jan. 0 6 3	Dec. 1 12 6
1855—June........ 1 0 0	July 0 2 6	1863—June........ 1 15 0
Dec. 1 5 0	*West Midland (Newport).*	1864—Jan. 1 10 0
1856—June.... 1 5 0	1861—Dec. 0 5 0	July 1 12 6
Dec. 1 10 0	1862—June........ Nil.	1865—Jan. 1 12 6
1857—June........ 0 10 0	Dec. 0 5 0	July 1 12 6
Dec. 1 0 0	1863—June........ Nil.	1866—Jan. 1 12 6
1858—June........ Nil.	1864—Jan. 0 15 0	July 1 12 6
Dec. 1 5 0	July 0 12 6	1867—Jan. 1 12 6
1859—June........ 1 0 0	1865—Jan. 0 17 6	July 1 12 6
Dec. 1 15 0	July 0 8 9	1868—Jan. 1 12 6
1860—June........ 1 10 0	1866—Jan. 0 8 9	July 1 15 0
Dec. 1 15 0		

HIGHLAND.

Inverness and Aberdeen.	1863—May £2 0 0	*Highland.*
1859—May £1 5 0	Nov. 2 12 6	1865—Aug. £1 0 0
Nov. 1 15 0	1864—May 2 0 0	1866—Feb. 0 10 0
1860—May 2 0 0	Nov. 2 0 0	Aug. 0 10 0
Nov. 2 0 0	1865—May 2 0 0	1867—Feb. 0 10 0
1861—May 1 15 0	*Inverness and Perth.*	Aug. 1 0 0
Nov. 2 2 6	1864—May 1 10 0	1868—Feb. 1 10 0
1862—May 1 15 0	Nov. 1 15 0	Aug. 1 10 0
Nov. 2 10 0	1865—May 2 0 0	

LONDON AND BRIGHTON.

1842—June........£1 0 0	1851—June........£1 16 0	1860—June........£2 10 0
Dec. 2 0 0	Dec. 3 0 0	Dec. 3 10 0
1843—June........ Nil.	1852—June........ 1 17 0	1861—June........ 2 10 0
Dec. 2 0 0	Dec. 2 17 0	Dec. 3 10 0
1844—June........ 1 4 0	1853—June........ 1 16 0	1862—June........ 2 10 0
Dec. 3 0 0	Dec. 3 4 0	Dec. 3 10 0
1845—June........ 2 0 0	1854—June........ 2 6 0	1863—June........ 2 10 0
Dec. 3 10 0	Dec. 3 4 0	Dec. 2 10 0
1846—June........ 2 10 0	1855—June........ 2 2 0	1864—June........ 2 10 0
Dec. 3 10 0	Dec. 2 18 0	Dec. 3 0 0
1847—June........ 2 0 0	1856—June........ 2 10 0	1865—June........ 2 10 0
Dec. 2 0 0	Dec. 3 10 0	Dec. 3 5 0
1848—June........ 1 6 0	1857—June........ 2 10 0	1866—June........ 2 0 0
Dec. 2 6 0	Dec. 3 10 0	Dec. 2 0 0
1849—June........ 1 9 0	1858—June........ 2 10 0	1867—June .... Nil.
Dec. 2 8 0	Dec. 3 10 0	Dec. .... Nil.
1850—June........ 1 10 0	1859—June........ 2 10 0	1868—June........ Nil.
Dec. 2 17 0	Dec. 3 10 0	

LANCASHIRE AND YORKSHIRE.

Manchester and Leeds.
1841—Dec. £3 0 0
1842—June........ 2 15 0
Dec. 2 15 0
1843—June........ 2 15 0
Dec. 3 10 0
1844—June........ 3 10 0
Dec. 4 0 0
1845—June........ 4 0 0
Dec. 4 0 0
1846—June........ 3 10 0
Dec. 3 10 0
East Lancashire.
1849—Dec. 1 0 0
1850—June........ 0 10 0
Dec. 1 0 0
1851—June........ 1 0 0
Dec. 1 5 0
1852—June........ 1 0 0
Dec. 1 10 0
1853—June........ 1 10 0
Dec. 1 15 0
1854—June........ 1 15 0
Dec. 2 0 0
1855—June........ 1 15 0
Dec. 1 15 0

1856—June........£2 0 0
Dec. 2 10 0
1857—June........ 2 10 0
Dec. 2 2 6
1858—June........ 1 17 6
Dec. 2 0 0
Lancashire and Yorkshire.
1847—June........ 3 10 0
Dec. 3 10 0
1848—June........ 3 0 0
Dec. 2 10 0
1849—June........ 2 0 0
Dec. 1 10 0
1850—June........ 1 0 0
Dec. 1 0 0
1851—June........ 1 0 0
Dec. 1 10 0
1852—June........ 1 10 0
Dec. 1 12 6
1853—June........ 1 15 0
Dec. 1 15 0
1854—June........ 1 15 0
Dec. 2 0 0
1855—June........ 2 0 0
Dec. 2 2 6

1856—June........£2 5 0
Dec. 2 10 0
1857—June........ 2 10 0
Dec. 2 2 6
1858—June........ 1 17 6
Dec. 2 0 0
1859—June........ 2 5 0
Dec. 2 10 0
1860—June........ 2 15 0
Dec. 3 0 0
1861—June........ 2 15 0
Dec. 2 10 0
1862—June........ 1 17 6
Dec. 2 0 0
1863—June........ 2 2 6
Dec. 2 7 6
1864—June........ 2 17 6
Dec. 3 0 0
1865—June........ 2 15 0
Dec. 3 2 6
1866—June........ 3 7 6
Dec. 3 7 6
1867—June........ 3 5 0
Dec. 3 5 0
1868—June........ 3 7 6

LONDON AND NORTH WESTERN.

London and Birmingham.
1838—Dec. £3 17 6
1839—June........ 3 17 6
Dec. 4 8 9
1840—June........ 4 8 9
Dec. 4 8 9
1841—June........ 4 14 6
Dec. 5 5 6
1842—June........ 5 11 0
Dec. 5 11 0
1843—June........ 5 0 0
Dec. 5 0 0
1844—June........ 5 0 0
Dec. 5 0 0
1845—June........ 5 0 0
Dec. 5 0 0
Liverpool and Manchester.
1841—Dec. 5 0 0
1842—June........ 5 0 0
Dec. 5 0 0
1843—June........ 5 0 0
Dec. 5 0 0
1844—June........ 5 0 0
Dec. 4 10 0
1845—June........ 5 0 0
Grand Junction.
1841—Dec. 6 0 0
1842—June........ 5 0 0
Dec. 5 0 0
1843—June........ 5 0 0

1843—Dec. £5 0 0
1844—June........ 5 0 0
Dec. 5 0 0
1845—June........ 5 0 0
Dec. 5 0 0
Manchester & Birmingham.
1842—Dec. 2 10 0
1843—June........ 1 17 6
Dec. 2 5 0
1844—June........ 2 10 0
Dec. 2 10 0
1845—June........ 2 10 0
Dec. 4 0 0
London and North Western.
1846—June........ 5 0 0
Dec. 5 0 0
1847—June........ 4 10 0
Dec. 4 0 0
1848—June........ 3 10 0
Dec. 3 10 0
1849—June........ 3 10 0
Dec. 2 10 0
1850—June........ 2 10 0
Dec. 2 10 0
1851—June........ 2 15 0
Dec. 3 0 0
1852—June........ 2 15 0
Dec. 2 10 0
1853—June........ 2 10 0
Dec. 2 10 0

1854—June........£2 10 0
Dec. 2 10 0
1855—June........ 2 7 6
Dec. 2 12 6
1856—June........ 2 10 0
Dec. 3 0 0
1857—June........ 2 10 0
Dec. 2 10 0
1858—June........ 1 17 6
Dec. 2 2 6
1859—June........ 2 2 6
Dec. 2 12 6
1860—June........ 2 10 0
Dec. 2 12 6
1861—June........ 1 17 6
Dec. 2 7 6
1862—June........ 1 17 6
Dec. 2 15 0
1863—June........ 2 2 6
Dec. 3 0 0
1864—June........ 2 17 6
Dec. 3 10 0
1865—June........ 3 0 0
Dec. 3 12 6
1866—June........ 3 0 0
Dec. 3 7 6
1867—June........ 2 12 6
Dec. 3 7 6
1868—June........ 2 12 6

MANCHESTER, SHEFFIELD, AND LINCOLNSHIRE.

1846—Dec. £2 10 0
1847—June........ 2 10 0
Dec. 2 10 0
1848—June........ 2 10 0
Dec. .... Nil.
1849—June........ Nil.
Dec. .... Nil.
1850—June........ Nil.
Dec. .... Nil.
1851—June........ Nil.
Dec. .... Nil.
1852—June........ Nil.
Dec. .... Nil.
1853—June........ Nil.
Dec. .... Nil.

1854—June........ Nil.
Dec. £0 2 6
1855—June........ Nil.
Dec. 0 5 0
1856—June........ 0 5 0
Dec. 0 10 0
1857—June........ 0 10 0
Dec. 0 10 0
1858—June........ Nil.
Dec. .... Nil.
1859—June........ 0 4 0
Dec. 0 10 0
1860—June........ 0 10 0
Dec. 0 15 0
1861—June........ 0 7 6

1861—Dec. £0 12 6
1862—June........ Nil.
Dec. .... Nil.
1863—June........ Nil.
Dec. 0 15 0
1864—June........ 1 7 6
Dec. 1 5 0
1865—June........ 0 10 0
Dec. 1 15 0
1866—June........ 1 0 0
Dec. 1 10 0
1867—June........ 0 10 0
Dec. 1 0 0
1868—June........ Nil.

LONDON AND SOUTH WESTERN.

Year	Period	£	s	d	Year	Period	£	s	d	Year	Period	£	s	d
1839	June	£1	10	0	1849	June	£1	12	6	1859	June	£2	5	6
	Dec.	1	10	6		Dec.	1	12	6		Dec.	2	12	6
1840	June	2	0	0	1850	June	1	10	0	1860	June	2	2	6
	Dec.	3	0	0		Dec.	2	0	0		Dec.	2	12	6
1841	June	3	0	0	1851	June	1	15	0	1861	June	2	0	0
	Dec.	3	0	0		Dec.	2	12	6		Dec.	2	15	0
1842	June	3	0	0	1852	June	1	12	6	1862	June	2	0	0
	Dec.	3	5	0		Dec.	2	0	0		Dec.	3	0	0
1843	June	3	0	0	1853	June	1	15	0	1863	June	2	5	0
	Dec.	3	10	0		Dec.	2	10	0		Dec.	2	15	0
1844	June	3	5	0	1854	June	2	2	6	1864	June	2	5	0
	Dec.	4	0	0		Dec.	2	10	0		Dec.	2	15	0
1845	June	3	15	0	1855	June	2	3	9	1865	June	2	5	0
	Dec.	4	5	0		Dec.	2	16	3		Dec.	2	15	0
1846	June	3	15	0	1856	June	2	15	0	1866	June	2	0	0
	Dec.	4	5	3		Dec.	3	5	0		Dec.	2	5	0
1847	June	3	15	0	1857	June	2	7	6	1867	June	1	17	6
	Dec.	4	0	0		Dec.	2	12	6		Dec.	2	12	6
1848	June	3	0	0	1858	June	2	2	6	1868	June	2	0	0
	Dec.	2	10	0		Dec.	2	17	6					

MARYPORT AND CARLISLE.

Year	Period	£	s	d	Year	Period	£	s	d	Year	Period	£	s	d
1845	Dec.	£2	0	0	1853	Dec.	£2	0	0	1861	June	£3	10	0
1846	June		Nil.		1854	June	1	10	0		Dec.	3	10	0
	Dec.		Nil.			Dec.	2	0	0	1862	June	3	0	0
1847	June	1	10	0	1855	June	1	10	0		Dec.	3	10	0
	Dec.	1	10	0		Dec.	2	0	0	1863	June	4	0	0
1848	June		Nil.		1856	June	2	0	0		Dec.	4	10	0
	Dec.		Nil.			Dec.	2	10	0	1864	June	5	0	0
1849	June		Nil.		1857	June	2	10	0		Dec.	5	10	0
	Dec.		Nil.			Dec.	2	10	0	1865	June	4	10	0
1850	June		Nil.		1858	June	2	0	0		Dec.	5	0	0
	Dec.	1	10	0		Dec.	2	5	0	1866	June	4	15	0
1851	June	1	10	0	1859	June	2	10	0		Dec.	4	15	0
	Dec.	2	0	0		Dec.	3	5	0	1867	June	3	15	0
1852	June	1	10	0	1860	June	3	5	0		Dec.	3	15	0
	Dec.	2	0	0		Dec.	3	10	0	1868	June	3	15	0
1853	June	1	10	0										

METROPOLITAN.

Year	Period	£	s	d	Year	Period	£	s	d	Year	Period	£	s	d
1863	June	£2	10	0	1865	June	£3	10	0	1867	June	£3	10	0
	Dec.	2	10	0		Dec.	3	10	0		Dec.	3	10	0
1864	June	2	15	0	1866	June	3	10	0	1868	June	3	10	0
	Dec.	3	10	0		Dec.	3	10	0					

MIDLAND.

Bristol and Gloucester.

Year	Period	£	s	d
1838	June	£2	10	0
	Dec.	2	10	0
1839	June	1	5	0
	Dec.	1	5	0
1840	June	2	10	0
	Dec.	2	10	0
1841	June	2	10	0
	Dec.	2	10	0
1842	June	2	0	0
	Dec.	2	0	0
1843	June	2	10	0
	Dec.	2	10	0
1844	June	2	15	0
	Dec.	2	0	0
1845	June	1	14	0
	Dec.	3	0	0
1846	June	3	0	0

Merged into the Midland at 6 per cent.

Birmingham and Derby.

Year	Period	£	s	d
1840	June	1	0	0
	Dec.	0	15	0

Year	Period	£	s	d
1841	June	1	2	6
	Dec.	1	2	6
1842	June	0	12	0
	Dec.	1	0	0
1843	June	0	5	0
	Dec.	1	8	0
1844	June	1	6	8

Midland Counties.

Year	Period	£	s	d
1841	June	2	10	0
	Dec.	2	0	0
1842	June	1	10	0
	Dec.	1	10	0
1843	June	1	4	0
	Dec.	2	4	0
1844	June	2	2	6

North Midland.

Year	Period	£	s	d
1841	June	£2	0	0
	Dec.	1	10	0
1842	June	1	0	0
	Dec.	1	12	6
1843	June	1	10	0
	Dec.	2	0	0
1844	June	2	2	0

Birmingham and Gloucester.

Year	Period	£	s	d
1841	June	0	15	0
	Dec.	0	15	0
1842	June	0	12	6
	Dec.	0	12	6
1843	June	0	12	0
	Dec.	1	10	0
1844	June	1	5	0
	Dec.	2	0	0
1845	June	2	0	0
	Dec.	3	0	0
1846	June	3	0	0

Merged into the Midland at 6 per cent.

Leeds and Bradford.

Year	Period	£	s	d
1846	Dec.	2	10	0
1847	June	2	10	0
	Dec.	2	10	0
1848	June	2	10	0
	Dec.	2	10	0
1849	June	5	0	0

Leased to Midland at 10 per cent.

MIDLAND—Continued.

Midland.	£	s	d		£	s	d		£	s	d
1844—Dec.	3	0	0	1852—Dec.	1	12	6	1860—Dec.	3	10	0
1845—June	3	0	0	1853—June	1	12	6	1861—June	3	2	6
Dec.	3	13	0	Dec.	1	12	6	Dec.	3	10	0
1846—June	3	10	0	1854—June	1	15	0	1862—June	2	15	0
Dec.	3	10	0	Dec.	1	17	6	Dec.	3	5	0
1847—June	3	10	0	1855—June	1	15	0	1863—June	2	17	6
Dec.	3	10	0	Dec.	1	17	6	Dec.	3	10	0
1848—June	3	0	0	1856—June	2	0	0	1864—June	3	10	0
Dec.	2	10	0	Dec.	2	2	6	Dec.	3	17	6
1849—June	1	10	0	1857—June	2	2	6	1865—June	3	5	0
Dec.	1	5	0	Dec.	2	10	0	Dec.	3	10	0
1850—June	0	16	0	1858—June	2	2	6	1866—June	3	0	0
Dec.	1	5	0	Dec.	2	15	0	Dec.	3	2	6
1851—June	1	5	0	1859—June	2	12	6	1867—June	2	15	0
Dec.	1	7	6	Dec.	3	0	0	Dec.	2	15	0
1852—June	1	10	0	1860—June	3	5	0	1868—June	2	15	0

MIDLAND GREAT WESTERN.

	£	s	d		£	s	d		£	s	d
1847—Dec.	2	0	0	1854—Dec.	2	10	0	1861—Dec.	2	10	0
1848—June	2	0	0	1855—June	2	10	0	1862—June	2	10	0
Dec.	2	0	0	Dec.	2	10	0	Dec.	2	10	0
1849—June	2	0	0	1856—June	2	10	0	1863—June	2	5	0
Dec.	2	0	0	Dec.	2	10	0	Dec.	2	5	0
1850—June	Nil.			1857—June	2	10	0	1864—June	2	0	0
Dec.	Nil.			Dec.	2	10	0	Dec.	1	0	0
1851—June	Nil.			1858—June	2	10	0	1865—June	1	2	6
Dec.	2	0	0	Dec.	2	10	0	Dec.	1	5	0
1852—June	2	0	0	1859—June	2	10	0	1866—June	1	5	0
Dec.	2	10	0	Dec.	2	10	0	Dec.	1	5	0
1853—June	2	10	0	1860—June	2	10	0	1867—June	1	5	0
Dec.	2	10	0	Dec.	2	10	0	Dec.	1	7	6
1854—June	2	10	0	1861—June	2	10	0	1868—June	1	5	0

MONMOUTHSHIRE.

	£	s	d		£	s	d		£	s	d
1849—March	2	10	0	1855—Dec.	1	10	0	1862—June	2	15	0
Sept.	2	10	0	1856—June	2	0	0	Dec,	2	15	0
1850—March	2	10	0	Dec.	2	10	0	1863—June	2	15	0
June	Nil.			1857—June	2	10	0	Dec.	3	0	0
Dec.	2	10	0	Dec.	2	10	0	1864—June	3	5	0
1851—June	2	0	0	1858—June	1	15	0	Dec.	3	5	0
Dec.	2	0	0	Dec.	2	10	0	1865—June	3	5	0
1852—June	2	0	0	1859—June	2	10	0	Dec.	3	5	0
Dec.	2	10	0	Dec.	2	10	0	1866—June	3	0	0
1853—June	3	0	0	1860—June	2	10	0	Dec.	2	15	0
Dec.	3	0	0	Dec.	3	0	0	1867—June	2	10	0
1854—June	2	10	0	1861—June	2	15	0	Dec.	2	10	0
Dec.	2	0	0	Dec.	3	0	0	1868—June	2	0	0
1855—June	Nil.										

NORTH BRITISH.

Monkland.	£	s	d		£	s	d		£	s	d
1852—Dec.	1	15	0	1863—June	2	5	0	1849—July	2	0	0
1853—June	1	15	0	Dec.	2	5	0	1850—Jan.	1	10	0
Dec.	2	0	0	1864—June	2	10	0	July	1	5	0
1854—June	2	5	0	Dec.	2	10	0	1851—Jan.	1	10	0
Dec.	2	7	6	1865—June	2	10	0	July	1	10	0
1855—June	2	15	0	Merged in the North British				1852—Jan.	1	10	0
Dec.	3	5	0	at 6 per cent.				July	1	10	0
1856—June	3	5	0	*Edinburgh and Glasgow.*				1853—Jan.	1	10	0
Dec.	3	10	0	1842—July	2	10	0	July	1	10	0
1857—June	4	0	0	1843—Jan.	2	10	0	1854—Jan.	1	10	0
Dec.	4	0	0	July	2	5	0	July	1	10	0
1858—June	3	10	0	1844—Jan.	2	10	0	1855—Jan.	1	10	0
Dec.	4	0	0	July	2	5	0	July	1	10	0
1859—June	4	0	0	1845—Jan.	2	10	0	1856—Jan.	1	0	0
Dec.	4	0	0	July	3	0	0	July	1	0	0
1860—June	3	0	0	1846—Jan.	3	0	0	1857—Jan.	1	5	0
Dec.	3	5	0	July	3	0	0	July	1	10	0
1861—June	2	15	0	1847—Jan.	4	0	0	1858—Jan.	1	12	6
Dec.	2	15	0	July	3	0	0	July	1	10	0
1862—June	2	15	0	1848—Jan.	Nil.			1859—Jan.	1	12	6
Dec.	2	15	0	July	3	0	0	July	1	12	6
				1849—Jan.	3	0	0	1860—Jan.	1	12	6

NORTH BRITISH—*Continued.*

```
1860—July ........£2  0  0 | 1849—Jan. ........£2  0  0 | 1859—Jan. ........£1  7  6
1861—Jan. ........ 2  2  6 |    July ........ 1 10  0 |    July ........ 1 10  0
   July ........ 2  2  6 | 1850—Jan. ........ 1  0  0 | 1860—Jan. ........ 1 10  0
1862—Jan. ........ 2  2  6 |    July ........ Nil.     |    July ........ 1 10  0
   July ........ 1 10  0 | 1851—Jan. ........ Nil.     | 1861—Jan. ........ 1 12  6
1863—Jan. ........ 1 10  0 |    July ........ Nil.     |    July ........ 1 10  0
   July ........ 1 10  0 | 1852—Jan. ........ Nil.     | 1862—Jan. ........ 1 10  0
1864—Jan. ........ 2  0  0 |    July ........ Nil.     |    July ........ 0 10  0
   July ........ 2  5  0 | 1853—Jan. ........ Nil.     | 1863—Jan. ........ 0  7  6
1865—Jan. ........ 2 10  0 |    July ........ Nil.     |    July ........ 0 12  0
   July ........ 2 12  6 | 1854—Jan. ........ 0  7  6 | 1864—Jan. ........ 0 17  6
1866—Jan. ........ 2  5  0 |    July ........ Nil.     |    July ........ 1  0  0
   July ........ Nil.     | 1855—Jan. ........ Nil.     | 1865—Jan. ........ 1  6  3
1867—Jan. ........ Nil.     |    July ........ Nil.     |    July ........ 1 10  0
   July ........ Nil.     | 1856—Jan. ........ Nil.     | 1866—Jan. ........ 1 10  0
1868—Jan. ........ Nil.     |    July ........ 1  5  0 |    July ........ Nil.
   July ........ Nil.     | 1857—Jan. ........ 1  5  0 | 1867—Jan. ........ Nil.
   North British.          |    July ........ 1  7  6 |    July ........ Nil.
1847—July ........ 2 10  0 | 1858—Jan. ........ 1  7  6 | 1868—Jan. ........ Nil.
1848—Jan. ........ 2 10  0 |    July ........ 1  7  6 |    July ........ Nil.
   July ........ 2 10  0 |                           |
```

NORTH AND SOUTH WESTERN JUNCTION.

```
1853—Dec. ........£3 10  0 | 1858—Dec. ........£1 12  6 | 1863—Dec. ........£3  0  0
1854—June........ 1  0  0 | 1859—June........ 1 15  0 | 1864—June........ 3  0  0
   Dec. ........ 2  0  0 |    Dec. ........ 2  5  0 |    Dec. ........ 3  0  0
1855—June........ 1 10  0 | 1860—June........ 2 10  0 | 1865—June........ 2 10  0
   Dec. ........ 2 10  0 |    Dec. ........ 2 15  0 |    Dec. ........ 2 15  0
1856—June........ 2 10  0 | 1861—June........ 2 10  0 | 1866—June........ 3  0  0
   Dec. ........ 2 15  0 |    Dec. ........ 2 15  0 |    Dec. ........ 3  0  0
1857—June........ 2  0  0 | 1862—June........ 2 10  0 | 1867—June........ 2 10  0
   Dec. ........ 1  5  0 |    Dec ........ 3  0  0 |    Dec. ........ 2 15  0
1858—June........ 1  0  0 | 1863—June........ 2 10  0 | 1868—June........ 2 10  0
```

NORTH EASTERN.

```
York and North Midland.    | 1858—June........£1 10  0 | 1846—June........£4 10  0
1839—Dec. ........£3 10  0 |    Dec. ........ 2  0  0 |    Dec. ........ 4 10  0
1840—June........ 3 10  0 | 1859—June........ 1 12  6 | 1847—June........ 4 10  0
   Dec. ........ 3 10  0 |    Dec. ........ 2  5  0 | York, Newcastle, & Berwick.
1841—June........ 4 10  0 | 1860—June........ 2  2  6 | 1847—June........ 4 10  0
   Dec. ........ 5  0  0 |    Dec. ........ 2 10  0 | 1848—June........ 4  0  0
1842—June........ 5  0  0 | 1861—June........ 2  5  0 |    Dec. ........ 3  0  0
   Dec. ........ 5  0  0 |    Dec. ........ 2  5  0 | 1849—June ........ Nil.
1843—June........ 5  0  0 | 1862—June........ 1 10  0 |    Dec. ........ 1  7  6
   Dec. ........ 5  0  0 |    Dec. ... .... 2  5  0 | 1850—June........ 1  5  0
1844—June........ 5  0  0 | 1863—June........ 1 10  0 |    Dec. ........ 1 15  0
   Dec. ........ 5  0  0 |    Dec. ........ 2 10  0 | 1851—June........ 1 10  0
1845—June........ 5  0  0 | 1864—June........ 2  7  6 |    Dec. ........ 1 10  0
   Dec. ........ 5  0  0 |    Dec. ........ 2 17  6 | 1852—June........ 1  7  6
1846—June........ 5  0  0 | 1865—June........ 2 10  0 |    Dec. ........ 1 10  0
   Dec. ........ 5  0  0 |    Dec. ........ 3  2  6 | 1853—June........ 1 10  0
1847—June........ 5  0  0 | 1866—June........ 2 10  0 |    Dec. ........ 2  0  0
   Dec. ........ 5  0  0 |    Dec. ........ 2 15  0 | 1854—June........ 1 17  6
1848—June........ 4  0  0 | 1867—June........ 2  2  6 |    Dec. ........ 2  0  0
   Dec. ........ 6  0  0 |    Dec. ........ 2 15  0 | 1855—June........ 1 15  0
1849—June ........ Nil.     | 1868—June........ 1 17  6 |    Dec. ........ 2  5  0
   Dec. ........ 1  0  0 | Great North of England.   | 1856—June........ 2  0  0
1850—June........ 0  5  0 | 1841—June........ 1  0  6 |    Dec. ........ 2  7  6
   Dec. ........ 1  0  0 |    Dec. ........ 2 10  0 | 1857—June........ 2 10  0
1851—June........ 0 10  0 | 1842—June........ 1  5  0 |    Dec. ........ 2 10  0
   Dec. ........ 1  0  0 |    Dec. ........ 1  5  0 | 1858—June........ 2  2  6
1852—June........ 0 10  0 | 1843—June........ 1  5  0 |    Dec. ........ 2  7  6
   Dec. ........ 1 10  0 |    Dec. ........ 1 12  6 | 1859—June........ 2  2  6
1853—June........ 0 15  0 | 1844—June........ 1 12  6 |    Dec. ........ 2 12  6
   Dec. ........ 1 10  0 |    Dec. ........ 3  0  0 | 1860—June........ 2 12  6
1854—June........ 1  2  6 | 1845—June........ 3  0  0 |    Dec. ........ 2 17  6
   Dec. ........ 1  7  6 |    Dec. ........ 5  0  0 | 1861—June........ 2 12  6
1855—June........ 1  0  0 | Leased to York, Newcastle,|    Dec. ........ 2 10  0
   Dec. ........ 1 12  6 | and Berwick, at 10 per cent.| 1862—June........ 2  2  6
1856—June........ 1  5  0 | Newcastle and Darlington. |    Dec. ........ 2 10  0
   Dec. ........ 1 17  6 | 1844—Dec. ........ 4  0  0 | 1863—June........ 2  2  6
1857—June........ 2  0  0 | 1845—June........ 4  0  0 |    Dec. ........ 2 15  0
   Dec. ........ 2  0  0 |    Dec. ........ 4 10  0 | 1864—June........ 2 15  0
```

NORTH EASTERN—*Continued.*

1864—Dec. £3 2 6	1843—June........ £2 0 0	1863—Dec. £3 12 6
1865—June........ 2 15 0	Dec. 2 0 0	1864—June........ 3 10 0
Dec. 3 5 0	1844—June........ 2 10 0	Dec. 4 0 0
1866—June........ 2 15 0	Dec. 2 10 0	1865—June........ 3 15 0
Dec. 3 0 0	1845—June........ 2 10 0	Dec. 4 5 0
1867—June........ 2 10 0	Dec. 2 10 0	1866—June........ 3 15 0
Dec. 3 0 0	1846—June........ 2 15 0	Dec. 3 17 6
1868—June........ 2 5 0	Dec. 2 15 0	1867—June........ 3 7 6
Leeds Northern.	1847—June........ 3 0 0	Dec. 4 2 0
1857—June........ 1 0 0	Dec. 3 0 0	1868—June........ 3 0 6
Dec. 1 5 0	1848—June........ 3 0 0	*Stockton and Darlington.*
1858—June........ 0 16 3	Dec. 3 0 0	1854—June........ 3 15 0
Dec. 1 3 9	1849—June........ 2 5 0	Dec. 4 10 0
1859—June........ 0 17 6	Dec. 2 5 0	1855—June........ 4 10 0
Dec. 1 7 6	1850—June........ 2 0 0	Dec. 4 10 0
1860—June........ 1 7 6	Dec. 2 0 0	1856—June........ 4 10 0
Dec. 1 10 0	1851—June........ 2 0 0	Dec. 5 0 0
1861—June........ 1 8 9	Dec. 2 0 0	1857—June........ 5 0 0
Dec. 1 7 6	1852—June........ 2 0 0	Dec. 5 0 0
1862—June........ 0 18 9	Dec. 2 0 0	1858—June........ 4 5 0
Dec. 1 7 6	1853—June........ 2 0 0	Dec. 4 15 0
1863—June........ 0 18 9	Dec. 2 0 0	1859—June........ 4 15 0
Dec. 1 10 0	1854—June........ 2 5 0	Dec. 4 10 0
1864—June........ 1 11 3	Dec. 2 15 0	1860—June........ 4 10 0
Dec. 1 18 9	1855—June........ 2 10 0	Dec. 4 15 0
1865—June........ 1 12 6	Dec. 2 10 0	1861—June........ 4 10 0
Dec. 2 1 3	1856—June........ 2 10 0	Dec. 4 5 0
1866—June........ 1 12 6	Dec. 3 0 0	1862—June........ 3 15 0
Dec. 1 15 0	1857—June........ 2 10 0	Dec. 4 0 0
1867—June........ 1 5 0	Dec. 5 0 0	1863—June........ 3 15 0
Dec. 1 15 0	1858—June........ 2 7 6	Dec. 4 0 0
1868—June........ 1 1 3	Dec. 3 0 0	1864—June........ 4 0 0
Newcastle and Carlisle.	1859—June........ 2 15 0	Dec. 4 10 0
1839—June........ 3 0 0	Dec. 3 10 0	1865—June........ 4 2 6
Dec. 3 0 0	1860—June........ 3 2 6	Dec. 4 12 6
1840—June........ 3 0 0	Dec. 3 17 6	1866—June........ 4 2 6
Dec. 3 0 0	1861—June........ 3 2 6	Dec. 4 5 0
1841—June........ 2 10 0	Dec. 3 10 0	1867—June........ 3 12 6
Dec. 2 10 0	1862—June........ 3 0 0	Dec. 4 2 6
1842—June........ 2 0 0	Dec. 3 10 0	1868—June........ 3 5 0
Dec. 2 0 0	1863—June........ 3 0 0	

NORTH LONDON.

1851—Dec. £1 1 0	1857—Dec. £2 5 0	1863—June.........£3 0 0
1852—June........ 1 0 0	1858—June........ 2 10 0	Dec. 3 10 0
Dec. 1 10 0	Dec. 2 10 0	1864—June......... 3 0 0
1853—June........ 1 15 0	1859—June........ 2 10 0	Dec. 3 0 0
Dec. 2 10 0	Dec. 2 15 0	1865—June........ 3 0 0
1854—June........ 2 10 0	1860—June........ 2 10 0	Dec. 3 0 0
Dec. 2 0 0	Dec. 2 15 0	1866—June........ 3 0 0
1855—June........ 2 0 0	1861—June........ 2 10 0	Dec. 2 15 0
Dec. 2 0 0	Dec. ....,..... 2 15 0	1867—June........ 2 15 0
1856—June........ 2 5 0	1862—June........ 2 10 0	Dec. 3 0 0
Dec. 2 10 0	Dec. 3 0 0	1868—June........ 3 0 0
1857—June........ 2 5 0		

NORTH STAFFORDSHIRE.

1848—June........£1 16 3	1855—Dec. £2 0 0	1862—June.........£1 10 0
Dec. .... Nil.	1856—June........ 1 15 0	Dec. 1 15 0
1849—June........ 0 17 6	Dec. 1 15 0	1863—June........ 1 15 0
Dec. .... Nil.	1857—June........ 2 0 0	Dec. 2 0 0
1850—June........ Nil.	Dec. 2 0 0	1864—June........ 2 0 0
Dec. 1 0 0	1858—June........ 1 0 0	Dec. 2 5 0
1851—June........ 0 14 3	Dec. 1 5 0	1865—June........ 1 15 0
Dec. 0 17 6	1859—June........ 1 10 0	Dec. 2 2 6
1852—June........ 0 17 6	Dec. 2 0 0	1866—June........ 2 0 0
1853—June........ 1 10 0	1860—June........ 2 0 0	Dec. 2 0 0
Dec. 1 10 0	Dec. 2 0 0	1867—June........ 1 10 0
1854—June........ 1 12 6	1861—June........ 1 15 0	Dec. 1 15 0
Dec. 1 15 0	Dec. 1 10 0	1868—June........ 1 5 0
1855—June........ Nil.		

SOUTH DEVON.

Date	£ s d	Date	£ s d	Date	£ s d
1853—June	£0 8 0	1858—Dec.	£0 15 0	1863—Dec.	£0 18 9
Dec.	0 14 0	1859—June	0 12 6	1864—June	0 16 3
1854—June	0 11 0	Dec.	0 16 6	Dec.	1 12 6
Dec.	0 15 0	1860—June	0 13 0	1865—June	1 1 3
1855—June	0 11 0	Dec.	1 0 0	Dec.	1 12 6
Dec.	0 13 0	1861—June	0 13 9	1866—June	0 17 6
1856—June	0 14 0	Dec.	0 13 9	Dec.	1 15 0
Dec.	1 5 0	1862—June	0 6 6	1867—June	0 12 6
1857—June	0 16 1¼	Dec.	0 14 0	Dec.	1 10 0
Dec.	0 16 6	1863—June	0 9 0	1868—June	0 15 0
1858—June	0 10 0				

SOUTH EASTERN.

Date	£ s d	Date	£ s d	Date	£ s d
1844—July	£1 11 3	1853—Jan.	£1 16 8	1861—July	£2 1 8
1845—Jan.	2 6 3	July	1 6 8	1862—Jan.	2 10 0
July	2 10 0	1854—Jan.	2 0 0	July	2 2 6
1846—Jan.	2 12 6	July	1 8 4	1863—Jan.	3 0 0
July	2 12 6	1855—Jan.	1 13 4	July	2 5 0
1847—Jan.	3 3 0	July	1 8 4	1864—Jan.	2 18 4
July	3 3 0	1856—Jan.	2 4 2	July	2 2 6
1848—Jan.	3 3 0	July	1 11 8	1865—Jan.	2 17 6
July	3 3 0	1857—Jan.	2 10 0	July	1 5 0
1849—Jan.	2 8 0	July	1 10 0	1866—Jan.	2 5 0
July	1 11 3	1858—Jan.	2 6 8	July	1 8 9
1850—Jan.	1 10 0	July	1 10 0	1867—Jan.	1 10 0
July	1 10 0	1859—Jan.	2 10 0	July	1 0 0
1851—Jan.	1 13 4	July	2 0 0	1868—Jan.	2 0 0
July	1 6 8	1860—Jan.	3 0 0	July	1 2 6
1852—Jan.	1 15 0	July	2 6 8		
July	1 5 0	1861—Jan.	3 0 0		

TAFF VALE.

Date	£ s d	Date	£ s d	Date	£ s d
1850—June	£3 0 0	1856—Dec.	£4 0 0	1862—Dec.	£4 10 0
Dec.	3 4 0	1857—June	4 0 0	1863—June	4 10 0
1851—June	3 12 0	Dec.	4 0 0	Dec.	5 0 0
Dec.	3 12 0	1858—June	3 15 0	1864—June	5 0 0
1852—June	3 12 0	Dec.	3 15 0	Dec.	5 0 0
Dec.	3 12 0	1859—June	4 0 0	1865—June	5 0 0
1853—June	3 11 5	Dec.	4 0 0	Dec.	4 10 0
Dec.	3 12 6	1860—June	4 0 0	1866—June	4 10 0
1854—June	3 15 0	Dec.	4 10 0	Dec.	5 0 0
Dec.	3 15 0	1861—June	4 5 0	1867—June	4 0 0
1855—June	3 15 0	Dec.	4 5 0	Dec.	4 10 0
Dec.	3 15 0	1862—June	4 10 0	1868—June	4 5 0
1856—June	4 0 0				

ULSTER.

Date	£ s d	Date	£ s d	Date	£ s d
1840—Feb.	£0 12 6	1850—Feb.	£1 4 3	1859—June	£2 10 0
Aug.	0 17 6	Aug.	1 18 6	1859—Dec.	2 15 0
1841—Feb.	0 13 4	1851—Feb.	2 0 7	1860—June	2 10 0
Aug.	0 18 0	Aug.	2 2 10	Dec.	2 15 0
1842—Feb.	0 16 0	1852—Feb.	2 5 0	1861—June	2 10 0
Aug.	1 16 0	Aug.	2 3 0	Dec.	2 15 0
1843—Feb.	1 16 0	1853—Feb.	2 11 0	1862—June	2 10 0
Aug.	2 1 7	Aug.	2 13 0	Dec.	2 10 0
1844—Feb.	2 10 4	1854—Feb.	2 16 6	1863—June	2 10 0
Aug.	2 10 8	Aug.	3 1 0	Dec.	2 10 0
1845—Feb.	2 15 0	1855—Feb.	2 7 6	1864—June	2 5 0
Aug.	2 16 3	June	2 5 11	Dec.	2 5 0
1846—Feb.	2 11 6	Dec.	3 0 4	1865—June	2 0 0
Aug.	2 10 0	1856—June	2 13 0	Dec.	2 5 0
1847—Feb.	2 10 0	Dec.	3 0 0	1866—June	1 16 0
Aug.	3 0 0	1857—June	3 0 0	Dec.	2 0 0
1848—Feb.	2 4 1	Dec.	3 0 0	1867—June	2 0 0
Aug.	1 8 9	1858—June	2 15 0	Dec.	2 0 0
1849—Feb.	1 5 4	Dec.	2 15 0	1868—June	2 5 0
Aug.	1 6 9				

WATERFORD AND LIMERICK.

1856—June.......	Nil.	1860—Dec.	£1 0 0	1864—Dec.	£0 10 6
Dec.........	£0 10 0	1861—June........	0 10 0	1865—June........	0 2 6
1857—June.......	Nil.	Dec.	1 0 0	Dec.	0 10 0
Dec.	Nil.	1862—June........	0 10 0	1866—June........	0 2 6
1858—June.......	Nil.	Dec.	0 15 0	Dec.	0 10 0
Dec.	0 10 0	1863—June........	0 10 0	1867—June........	0 5 0
1859—June.......	0 10 0	Dec.	0 10 0	Dec.	Nil.
Dec.........	1 0 0	1864—June........	0 5 0	1868—June........	Nil.
1860—June.......	0 10 0				

WHITEHAVEN, CLEATOR, AND EGREMONT.

1857—June........	£3 0 0	1861—June........	£5 0 0	1865—June........	£5 0 0
Dec.	3 10 0	Dec.	5 0 0	Dec.	5 0 0
1858—June.......	3 10 0	1862—June........	5 0 0	1866—June........	5 0 0
Dec.	3 10 0	Dec.	5 0 0	Dec.	4 0 0
1859—June.......	4 0 0	1863—June........	7 10 0	1867—June........	4 10 0
Dec.	4 0 0	Dec.	6 0 0	Dec.	5 0 0
1860—June.......	5 0 0	1864—June........	7 0 0	1868—June........	5 0 0
Dec.	5 0 0	Dec.	6 0 0		

5.—BILLS LODGED FOR SESSION 1869.

The subjoined list comprises in detail the whole of the Bills lodged, in compliance with the Standing Orders of the House of Commons, in the Private Bill Office, on 23rd December last:—

GENERAL ACT.

Consolidated Annuities.— Consolidation and commutation of mortgages, bonds, and debenture stocks of railway companies into terminable and perpetual annuities, or into general railway debenture stock redeemable or irredeemable—appointment and incorporation of board, issue, and incidents of certificates.

SPECIAL ACTS.

Athenry and Tuam.—Further powers; amendment of Acts.

Birkenhead and Liverpool—Incorporation of company for making a railway from the Birkenhead, under the Mersey, to Liverpool; extension to the Birkenhead on the Birkenhead side, and to the Liverpool Central Station, Garston and Liverpool, and the Line of Docks railways on the Liverpool side of the Mersey; running powers over parts of the Birkenhead and over Garston and Liverpool and Liverpool Central Station, and powers to Great Western, London and North Western, Great Northern, Manchester Sheffield and Lincolnshire, and Midland.

Bouldnor, Yarmouth, and Freshwater.—Incorporation of company with power to make railway and pier in the Isle of Wight.

Brighton and Metropolitan.—Incorporation of company for making a railway from London Chatham and Dover, at Dulwich, to Brighton; powers over the London Chatham and Dover.

Bristol and North Somerset.—Arrangement of company's affairs; provisions affecting creditors, shareholders, and others; winding up and dissolution of the company, and sale of their undertaking and property; amendment of Acts, and of agreements with the Great Western.

Bristol Harbour.—Extension of time; purchase of additional lands; enlargement of wharf depot; arrangements with Great Western; interference with roads and other powers; additonal capital; provisions as to payment of dividends; incorporation of the two companies for purposes of Harbour Railway; further powers to, and agreements with, corporation of Bristol; repeal of parts of Bristol HarbourlRailway Act, 1866; alteration of tolls; provision as to Bristol and Exeter traffic to, from, and over the Harbour Railway, and amendment of Acts.

Buckfastleigh, Totnes, and South Devon.—Power to create preference shares, and to cancel existing shares, and to divide shares; further powers as to borrowing; amendment of Acts.

Caledonian.—Abandonment of certain authorised railways; capital for Muirkirk branch to have lien over revenue thereof; sanction of acquisition of certain land in Glasgow, and power to hold and dispose of same; power to take land at Alyth for station purposes; alteration of application of moneys, and of mode of raising certain capital; confirmation of accounts; amalgamation with Crieff and Methven Junction, and dissolution of that company; power to make further contribution to and hold additional shares in Busby; agreements with that company, the Solway Junction, the subscribers of the Muirkirk branch capital, and the proprietor of Hailes Quarry; amendment and repeal of provisions of Acts of Caledonian and Glasgow and South Western, and other Acts.

Caledonian, Glasgow and South Western, and Crofthead and Kilmarnock Extension.—Conferring upon Glasgow and South Western joint interest with Caledonian in the latter company's lease of Glasgow Barrhead and Neilson Direct, and in their extension of that railway to Crofthead, and in a portion of their Southside station at Glasgow; transfer to those companies jointly of Crofthead and Kilmarnock Extension and dissolution of Crofthead and

Kilmarnock Extension; abandonment of Glasgow and South Western's Kilmarnock Direct line, and of parts of Crofthead and Kilmarnock Extension; construction of railway in lieu thereof; conferring upon Caledonian joint interest with Glasgow and South Western in lands acquired for Kilmarnock Direct; sale of superfluous lands; revival and enlargement of powers of compulsory purchase of lands for improvement of Glasgow Barrhead and Neilston Direct, and extension thereof to Crofthead; provisions as to capital, use of joint line from Southside station to Kilmarnock, land taken from the estate of Lainshawe, tolls, rates, and charges, joint committees, agreements, and other matters; amendment of Acts.

Callington and Calstock.—Incorporation of company, construction of railways, gauge, acquisition of Tamar Kit Hill and Callington, and incline at Calstock to the Tamar; agreements with reference thereto; amendment of Acts.

Clapham and London Bridge.—Incorporation of company for construction of railway from Clapham Common to London Bridge.

Crystal Palace and South London Junction.—Power to make new railway; power to raise further sums and provisions in reference thereto; providing for working of railway and settlement of disputes between company and London Chatham and Dover; amendment of Acts.

Devon and Cornwall.—Formation of Bude and Torrington extensions into separate undertaking or undertakings; incorporation of separate company, and vesting in that company Bude and Torrington extensions, and powers, rights, privileges, and obligations relating thereto; exemption of separate company from the general liabilities of Devon and Cornwall; provision for repayment to Devon and Cornwall of expenses incurred by them in reference to Bude and Torrington extensions; altering or rescinding heads of arrangement between Devon and Cornwall and South Western, with reference to Bude and Torrington extensions; powers to separate company, and to the Devon and Cornwall, and to the South Western to enter into arrangements; amendment or repeal of Acts and other purposes.

Dublin and Drogheda.—Junction railway at Dublin; additional lands; power to London and North Western to contribute; amendment of Acts.

Dublin and Meath.—Confirmation of agreement between the Dublin and Meath and the Midland Great Western, and traffic arrangements between above-named companies and Dublin and Drogheda; alteration of Acts.

Dublin and Ulster.—Amalgamation of Ulster, Dublin and Belfast, and Dublin and Drogheda.

Dundalk and Greenore.—Further time for the completion of railways and the joint works authorised by the Newry and Greenore Act, 1863; to abandon railway (No. 2) authorised by the Dundalk and Greenore Act, 1867; and for other purposes.

☞ *Eastern Metropolitan Underground.*—Incorporation of company; construction of railways to connect the Great Eastern, the North London, the East London (Thames Tunnel), East London (Eastern Extension), (authorised lines), and the Metropolitan (authorised lines); arrangements with the said several companies, the corporation of the city of London, the Commissioners of sewers for the city of London, the Metropolitan Board of Works, gas and water companies; amendment of Acts, &c.

East Norfolk.—Extension of time for completion'; further money powers.

Elham Valley.—Extension of time for purchase of lands and completion of railways; amendment of Act, &c.

Ellesmere and Glyn Valley.—Abandonment of part of authorised railway and of other works; extension of time for completion of works not abandoned, and for compulsory purchase of lands; alteration of gauge; deviation in levels; power to transfer powers, or sell or lease undertaking; powers to other companies and persons; alteration of rates; reduction of capital; amendment of Acts; release of deposit and security for same, and other purposes.

Enniskillen, Bundoran, and Sligo.—For effecting an arrangement with respect to the mortgages and other debts of the railway; and for other purposes.

Fermoy and Lismore.—Further powers; amendment of Acts.

Festiniog.—Repeal, &c., of Acts relating to company; application of general Acts to the company and their undertaking; regulation, &c., of capital; provisions as to general meetings, directors, auditors, and officers of the company; widening and alteration of existing railway; new branch lines; gauge of railways; abandonment and sale of parts of existing railway; power to take take water of certain streams and to construct acqueducts; compulsory purchase of lands and outstanding interests in land; power to company to carry passengers and use locomotive engines; tolls; commutation, &c., by agreement, of certain tolls payable under Companies' Act of 1832; alteration of exemption from tolls on Traeth-Mawr Embankment; further money powers; capitalisation of expenditure on capital account out of revenue; amendment of Acts.

Furness.—Abandonment of portions of railways authorised by "the Whitehaven and Furness Junction Act, 1865," and "the Furness Act, 1865," and the pier authorised by "the Furness Act, 1866;" power to construct new railway to Windermere Lake; additional lands; powers to purchase, &c., Furness Abbey Hotel, and to sell and lease the same; power to subscribe towards, make agreements with, and appoint directors of hotel companies; power to enter into agreements, &c., with the Windermere United Steam Yacht Company Limited), and to appoint directors of that company; confirmation of purchase and appropriation of lands, and application of funds and sale and disposition of lands; powers to raise further capital, and provisions as to capital; amendment of Acts and other purposes.

Garstang and Knot End.—Extension of time for compulsory purchase of lands and completion of works ; increase of capital ; amendment of Acts, &c.

Glasgow and South Western.—To vest the Glasgow, Paisley, and Johnstone canal in the company, and to enable that company to guarantee the payment of dividends upon a portion of the share capital of the Greenock and Ayrshire ; and for other purposes.

Glasgow (City) Union.—Deviation lines ; extension of deviation of Glasgow, Paisley, and Ardrossan Canal ; purchase of lands ; abandonment of portions of lines and works authorised by the City of Glasgow Union Act, 1865, and the City of Glasgow Union Act, 1867 ; powers for vesting certain lines jointly in the company and the North British ; provisions as to rent of passenger station in Glasgow ; powers to Glasgow and South Western to guarantee dividends ; powers to Glasgow and South Western and North British to guarantee interest of mortgage debt ; provisions as to creation of College Station shares with certain preferences attached thereto ; constitution of ground annual or rent-charge on College ground ; provisions as to surplus lands and mortgages thereon ; amendment of Acts.

Great Eastern.—Purchase of land in divers places ; provisions with respect to superfluous lands ; abandonment of certain railways, and release of contracts, penalties, &c. ; provisions relating to Great Eastern Metropolitan undertaking and to the company's share and loan capital in reference thereto, and to the general undertaking ; interest during construction ; powers for protection of buildings near the railway ; defining capital ; with respect to byelaws, directors, and committees ; compensation for injury ; interest on deposits in savings' banks ; stopping up footway at Lynn, &c. ; rates, &c. ; rights and privileges ; powers to company and to various other companies for various purposes ; amendment of Acts.

Great Eastern.—Extension of company's powers to run steamboats to Hamburg and Harburgh ; amendment of Acts.

Great Northern and Western.—Power to raise further capital ; power to run over portions of railways of the Midland Great Western and of the Great Southern and Western ; power to company to enter into working and traffic agreements with those companies ; amendment of Acts.

Great Western.—Siding at Swansea ; railway from near Dolgelly to Pen-Maen-Pool ; level crossing on Bala and Dolgelly at Drws-y-Nant ; additional lands near Barmouth and Leominster ; extension of time for construction of branch railways to and near Halesowen ; extension of time for purchase of lands and construction of branch railways near Cardiff and in the Ely Valley ; extension of time for sale of certain lands acquired by the company and power to sell or lease same, or any part thereof, for building or other purposes ; agreements with Cambrian and Bala and Dolgelly ; confirmation of agreements with Metropolitan and Milford ; confirmation of agreements with the Wellington and Drayton and the Nantwich and Market Drayton respectively for amalgamation ; confirmation of agreement with Stourbridge ; arrangements with Midland, London and North Western, Hereford Hay and Brecon, and Mid-Wales respectively as to the use of the company's Barton station, Hereford ; lease, or transfer of Tenbury and Bewdley ; agreement with Commissioners of Woods and Forests ; power to apply corporate funds for the purposes of additional station and other accommodation on the railways of the Wenlock, Bala and Dolgelly, Corwen and Bala, Llangollen and Corwen, and Vale of Llangollen ; application of corporate funds to purposes of Act ; consolidation of guaranteed and preference shares and stocks ; powers to holders of Chipping Norton four per cent. stock to exchange same for other stock ; conversion of Stratford Canal annuities and creation of debenture stock for above purposes ; exercise of borrowing powers of Stourbridge, Stourbridge Extension, Wellington and Severn Junction, Wellington and Drayton, Nantwich and Market Drayton, Leominster and Kington, East Somerset, Corwen and Bala, Vale of Llangollen, Llangollen and Corwen, and Tenbury and Bewdley by company ; exercise of borrowing powers authorised by the Acts relating to the Hammersmith and City by the company and the Metropolitan ; power to the Bala and Dolgelly and the Cambrian to apply their capital to the purposes of the railway to Pen-Maen-Pool and the additional lands at Barmouth ; power to the London and North Western to apply their Corporate funds to the acquisition of the additional lands near Leominster ; closing of transfer books ; amendment of Acts.

Haddenham, Willingham, and Longstanton.—Incorporation of company ; construction of railway from the Ely Haddenham and Sutton, at Haddenham, to the Great Eastern, at Longstanton ; arrangements with Ely Haddenham and Sutton and Great Eastern ; powers to run over and use and levy tolls on railways of those companies ; powers to the Ely Haddenham and Sutton to subscribe to and to raise moneys ; amendment of Acts.

Harrow, Edgware, and London.—Incorporation of company for extending Edgware Highgate and London to Harrow.

Hereford, Hay, and Brecon.—Renewal of debentures ; conversion of debenture and other debts into debenture stock ; variation of priorities of debenture holders ; running powers over a portion of the Mid-Wales, over the Neath and Brecon, and over the railways of the Brecon and Merthyr Tydvil Junction ; working and traffic agreements with the London and North Western, the Great Western, and the Midland ; proposed railway at Hereford ; additional land at Hereford ; amendment of Act, &c.

Hounslow and Metropolitan.—Extension of time for compulsory purchase of lands and construction of works ; repeal or amendment of Act.

Hyde Park and City.—Incorporation of company ; construction of railway from near the west end of Oxford-street to Cheapside, in the city of London ; special provisions as to construction of shafts, deviation from lines and levels, underpinning houses, &c. ; purchase of easements, &c.; amendment or repeal of 92nd section of the Lands Clauses Consolidation Act, 1845; provisions affecting the Corporation of the City of London, the Commissioners of Sewers of the city of London, Metropolitan Board of Works, and vestries or district boards, and powers to those bodies to contribute funds; amendment or repeal of Acts and other purposes.

Islington.—Incorporation of a company to make and maintain a railway from Colebrooke Row, Islington, to New Union Street, in the city of London; compulsory purchase of lands; power to levy tolls.

Kent Coast.—Provisions as to debentures and debenture stock; amendment of Acts.

King's Lynn.—Alteration of name; abandonment of railway; new dock approach; powers to corporation of King's Lynn, and to Great Eastern, to Midland, and to Great Northern; amendment of Act.

Lancashire and Yorkshire.—Extension of time for purchase of lands and completion of certain authorised branch railways in the West Riding; abandonment of authorised railway in same Riding; power to Lancashire and Yorkshire, and London and North Western, to create debenture stock, for certain purposes affecting joint undertakings; conversion into stock of shares in North Union, and the Preston and Wyre; amendment of Acts.

Launceston and South Devon.—Alteration and enlargement of powers of company for raising money; amalgamation with South Devon; dissolution of company; amendment of Acts.

London, Chatham, and Dover—Widening of bridges over Fleet-lanes; power to construct roads and discontinue level crossings at Penge and Teynham; extension of time for completion of certain works authorised by the London Chatham and Dover (New Lines) Act, 1864; provisions as to the user of the Victoria Station and Pimlico railway; powers to agree as to such user with other companies; provisions as to the distribution and application of the net receipts, funds, and stocks of the company; provisions as to working, use, and management of the Kent Coast, Sevenoaks Maidstone and Tunbidge, and Crystal Palace and South London Junction; running powers and facilities over those railways respectively; amendment of Acts.

London and North Western (New Works and Additional Powers).—New railways, new roads, alteration and stopping up of roads and footpaths, and additional lands in the counties of Lancaster, Chester, Salop, Derby, Leicester, Northampton, Warwick, Oxford, Middlesex, Anglesea, Carnarvon, and Carmarthen, and in Dublin, with certain joint powers to the Llanelly, the Carnarvon and Llanberis, the Manchester Sheffield and Lincolnshire, and the Great Western; extension of time for completion of works in the counties of Salop and Flint; abandonment of portions of railways and road in counties of Lancaster and Chester; further powers as to superfluous lands; bye-laws as to docks at Widnes; vesting of undertakings of Brynmawr and Blaenavon and Cannock Mineral; vesting in company of portion of railway near Builth of Mid-Wales; issue of Company's securities in lieu of securities of affiliated companies; appointment of directors of Portpatrick; further powers to company, Great Western, and Llanelly for making bye-laws; joint ownership of further portion of Rhymney and alteration of existing provisions as to joint ownership with that company; agreements with Great Western and Hereford Hay and Brecon, and with London Brighton and South Coast, Great Eastern, Mold and Denbigh Junction, and Carnarvon and Llanberis; further provision as to management of North Union; regulation of powers of company as to capital and borrowing; amendment of Acts.

London and South Western (Bideford to Great Torrington, Extension of time).—Further extension of time for purchase of lands, &c., for and for completion of authorised railway from Bideford to Great Torrington; amendment of Acts.

London and South Western (Further Powers).—Purchase of lands in Basingstoke parish, Hants, and in Merton parish, Surrey, and widening and alteration of railway bridges south of Basingstoke station, and approach to Lower Merton station; alteration of goods and other rates; substitution of debenture or other stock for South Western (Portsmouth) annuities and for South Western (Andover) annuities; further money powers; extension of time for purchase of lands for and completion of lines authorised by South Western (Poole and Bournemouth Junction) Act, 1866; amendment of Acts.

Liverpool and Birkenhead Ferry Junction.—Incorporation of company; construction of railways; establishment of ferry; compulsory purchase of lands; tolls; traffic facilities; running powers; working and other arrangements and agreements with certain companies and corporations; powers to certain railway companies to subscribe and to raise money; amendment of Acts, and other purposes.

Llanelly.—New lines in Carmarthen and Llanelly: maintenance of junction railway in Swansea; abandonment of portion of authorised railway in Swansea; extension of time and other powers as to Mumbles Extension; purchase of additional lands; running powers over Pembroke and Tenby, and facilities affecting Carmarthen and Cardigan, Great Western, and Manchester and Milford; requiring Carmarthen and Cardigan to double part of their line; arrangements with Llanelly Harbour Commissioners; amendment of Acts.

Llynvi and Ogmore.—Relinquishment of railways; extension of time for exercising powers of former Acts; variation of security for completion of railways, repeal of restrictions upon borrowing powers; additional borrowing powers; debenture stock; application of moneys; amendment of Acts.

Manchester City.—Incorporation of company ; construction of railway from Manchester to Didsbury ; compulsory purchase of lands ; power to levy tolls; special gauge, and other purposes.

Manchester, Sheffield, and Lincolnshire (Additional Lands at Grimsby).—Purchase of lands by compulsion or agreement at Great Grimsby ; amendment of Acts and other purposes.

Manchester, Sheffield, and Lincolnshire and Midland (Joint Lines).—Transfer of the powers of the Manchester and Stockport to the above companies, and dissolution of company ; release of deposit in Court of Chancery under the Manchester and Stockport Act, 1866; extension of time for purchasing lands for and making the Manchester and Stockport ; power for Midland to become joint owners of the Marple New Mills and Hayfield and Newton and Compstall branches of the Manchester Sheffield and Lincolnshire, and to run over and use a portion of the Manchester Sheffield and Lincolnsire and London-road (Manchester) passenger station ; construction of short branch railway ; amendment of Acts and other purposes.

Manchester and Stockport.—Extension of time for the compulsory purchase of lands and construction of works.

Mendip Mineral.—Incorporation of company ; construction of railway from the East Somerset, at Doulting, to Mells ; arrangements with the Great Western and East Somerset ; amendment of Acts.

Metropolitan.—Alteration of Gower-street station ; extension of time for purchase of lands and execution of sundry works ; additional capital ; agreement with the Great Western ; amendment of Acts and enlargement of powers.

Metropolitan District.—Additional lands ; creation of preference stock ; charging of surplus land ; amendment of Acts.

Metropolitan (Southern District).—Railways from Elephant and Castle to Waterloo and Whitehall, and from that railway to Thames Embankment (North) and to Scotland-yard ; incorporation of company ; powers as to Waterloo and Whitehall ; extending time for purchase of lands and completion of that railway, and repeal of restrictions as to same ; abandonment of parts of that railway ; dissolution of Waterloo and Whitehall ; amendment of Acts.

Midland (Additional Powers).—Branch and junction railways in the counties of Derby and Leicester ; revival of powers and extension of time for purchase of lands and construction of works in the county of the city of Bristol, the West and North Ridings of the county of York, and the counties of Derby, Somerset, Gloucester, Leicester, Nottingham, Westmorland, and Cumberland ; use of Great Western station and lines at Bristol, and portion of Shrewsbury and Hereford, near Hereford ; agreements with Great Eastern and Tottenham and Hampstead Junction as to working of railway of latter company ; further provisions as to superfluous lands ; additional capital ; further provisions as to capital and borrowing powers ; amendment of Acts and other purposes.

Midland and London and North Western (Lancaster and Carlisle and Settle and Carlisle, &c.)—Power to Midland and London and North Western to make agreements with respect to the Lancaster and Carlisle and traffic thereon, and other traffic ; abandonment of Settle and Carlisle ; provisions as to capital of Midland ; repeal or amendment of Acts.

Midland Great Western.—Further powers ; amendment of Acts.

Mid-Wales.—Confirmation of scheme of arrangement between the company and their creditors ; right of voting conferred on preference shareholders in company ; revival or extension of time for compulsory purchase of land and construction of works ; working and other agreements with Neath and Brecon ; abandonment of railways ; power to run over and use certain railways and portions of railways ; arrangements with Brecon and Merthyr and Neath and Brecon as to joint station at Brecon ; additional capital ; facilities in favour of company granted by the Great Western (Vale of Neath Amalgamation) Act, 1866, to be extended to Swansea Harbour railway, and the appointment of agents at stations thereon and on Vale of Neath ; recision or alteration of award between company and Brecon and Merthyr ; amendment of Acts.

Navan and Kingscourt.—Extension to Carrickmacross ; extension of time for completion of works ; powers to Dublin and Meath ; additional capital ; amendment of Acts.

Neath and Brecon and Swansea Vale and Neath and Brecon Junction.—Arrangements as to, and readjustment of, share and loan capital ; conversion of debenture and other debts into stock ; definition of rights and priorities ; deferring claims of debenture-holders and other creditors ; provision for future management of the undertakings ; vesting rolling stock, &c., in trustees ; amalgamation of companies and repeal of agreements as to lease and working ; extension of time to complete railways ; traffic arrangements ; amendment or repeal of Acts.

North British.—Abandonment of various railways and works ; powers to purchase lands for station purposes ; provisions as to superfluous lands ; conversion, redemption, &c., of deferred dividend warrants ; constituting separate undertakings ; provision as to weekly deposit in bank made permanent ; provisions as to shore and shipping dues at Tay Port ; reduction, application, and increase of capital ; director's qualification, tolls, &c., rights and privileges ; power for Clyde Navigation Trustees to subscribe to certain railways ; provisions as to dues at Balloch Pier ; establishment of provident fund ; amendment of Acts.

North Eastern.—Deviation and abandonment of part of authorised Gilling and Pickering, and of part of Port Clarence branch ; extension of time as to other authorised railways ; alteration of Middlesborough dock tolls ; further powers for recovery of tolls, and bye-laws for Newcastle high level bridge; further provisions with reference to Wearmouth and Hartlepool Docks; amendment of Acts and other purposes.

North London.—Extension of time for construction of works; additional land; diversion of Preston's Road, Poplar; widening of bridge over York Road; repeal or amendment of Acts.

Port of London and Billingsgate.—Incorporation of company; construction of railways from London Chatham and Dover, at Snow-hill, to the river Thames, at Blackfriars, and thence to Brewer's Quay, Tower Dock, and to the Metropolitan District at Blackfriars and Tower-hill; River Wall, or Embankment, from Northern Thames Embankment, at Blackfriars, to Brewer's Quay; public carriage-road, from Adelaide Place, London Bridge, Lower Thames Street, to near the Custom House; enlargement of Billingsgate Market and widening of Lower Thames Street; new sewer from northern low level sewer at Blackfriars to northern low level sewer at Tower-hill; reclamation of part of bed or shore of river Thames; vesting in corporation of London of sites purchased for enlargement, &c., of Billingsgate Market; tolls, agreements with, subscriptions and guarantees by, and other provisions affecting the corporation of London, Metropolitan Board of Works, and the railway companies having Metropolitan termini; amendment of Acts.

Richmond and Reeth.—Incorporation of company; construction of railway; acquisition of lands, compulsorily or otherwise; authorisation of tolls and charges; creation and raising of capital and money; working arrangements with the North Eastern; incorporation of Acts; amendment of Acts and other purposes.

Rother Valley.—Incorporation of company; construction of railways; junction with South Eastern; traffic arrangements with and other provisions affecting the South Eastern; amendment of Acts.

Sandwich and Adisham.—Incorporation of company; railways from Sandwich to Adisham; compulsory purchase of lands; tolls; working arrangements with South Eastern and the London Chatham and Dover; running powers over portion of railways of those companies; amendment of Acts, and for other purposes.

Scinde.—Amalgamation of undertakings of company; further money powers; regulation of capital and borrowing powers; agreements with and other provisions affecting Secretary of State in Council of India; modification of existing leases and agreements; alteration of name; period for closing registers of transfers; amendment of Acts.

Severn and Wye.—Conversion of tramways into railways; extension of railways; alterations of tolls; additional capital; arrangements with Great Western.

South Devon.—Consolidation and conversion of shares and stocks and of mortgage or debenture debts of the company and of the Launceston and South Devon and the Dartmouth and Torbay; alteration and enlargement of powers of the company as to raising money and creation of annuities and debenture stock and rent-charge stock; further provision as to recovery of tolls and as to Exmouth Ferry; alteration and amendment of Acts.

Southend and Shoeburyness.—Incorporation of company for making railway from Southend to Shoeburyness.

Southsea.—Abandonment of railways; repeal of Act.

Stony Stratford.—Railway from Stony Stratford to Wolverton; incorporation of company; construction of railway; power to make arrangement as to traffic with the London and North Western.

Tendring Hundred.—Powers affecting Great Eastern; running powers and facilities; postponement of creditors' claims; preference capital; amendment of Acts.

Wainfleet and Firsby.—Incorporation of company; construction of railway from the East Lincolnshire line of the Great Northern at Firsby to Wainfleet; arrangements with the Great Northern; amendment of Acts.

Waterford, New Ross, and Wexford Junction.—Deviation of railways and construction of new railways, &c.; purchase of lands; levying tolls; relinquishment of works; further capital powers; change of name; working arrangements; amendment of Acts and further purposes.

Watlington and Princes Risborough.—Incorporation of company; construction of railways from Princes Risborough to Watlington; powers to lay down additional rails on, and to run over, and to levy and alter tolls on portion of the Wycombe (Thame Extension) of the Great Western; amendment of Acts.

Watton and Swaffham.—Extension of Thetford and Watton to Swaffham, by new company, or by Thetford and Watton; power to use part of East Anglian at Swaffham, and other powers affecting the Great Eastern.

West Somerset Mineral.—Power to lease undertaking; further capital; amendment of Acts.

Wrexham, Mold, and Connah's Quay.—Re-arrangement of capital and mortgage debt of Wrexham Mold and Connah's Quay; division of undertaking and separate accounts in respect thereof; further loan capital in priority over existing mortgages; power to create rent-charges; purchase of rolling stock and vesting of same in trustees; renewal of mortgages or conversion into debenture stock; additional capital; staying actions and suits, and discharge of receiver; alteration of voting at meetings, and qualification and appointment of directors; additional land; amendment of Acts.

Whitland and Taff Vale.—Incorporation of company; arrangements with other companies, &c.

Worthing.—Incorporation of company; station at Worthing; railway from London Brighton and South Coast, near the Cliftonville station, to near Preston; running powers and user of parts of Brighton and stations; powers of subscription, contribution, or guarantee: construction, maintenance, and working of traffic and other arrangements to, with, against, and between respectively the new company, the Local Board of Health for the district of Worthing, the West Worthing Improvement Commissioners, and the Brighton; levy rates, tolls, and duties; facilities for traffic: amendment of Acts, &c.

The following list contains those notices issued in November which have since fallen through in consequence of the bills referred to not having been deposited on 23rd December last:—

Bishop's Castle.—Alteration and re-arrangement of capital; creation of special debenture stock; conversion of mortgages into debenture stock; rent-charges for land; suspension of actions against company; revival of powers as to portion of main line; extension of time for purchase of lands and construction of works; powers over Shrewsbury and Hereford and Cambrian; amendment of Acts.

Brean Down.—Extension of time for completion of harbour, and for purchase of land for docks; further money powers; amendment of Acts.

Denbigh, Ruthin, and Corwen.—Power to raise money as a first charge for special purposes; deferring claims of mortgagees and other creditors; suspension of legal proceedings; regulation of capital and priorities of shareholders and others; amendment of Acts and other purposes.

English and Continental Intercommunication.—Steam vessels between England and the Continent; new sea-wall pier or breakwater, wharf, walls and jetties at Dover; graving dock, railways, and station at Dover; traffic arrangemements with South Eastern and London Chatham and Dover; exemption from harbour rates, &c.

Landowners' Association.—For the construction of branch railways and other works; incorporation of company; powers to purchase and hold lands, to construct, work, and manage railways and other works, to levy tolls, to raise capital; special provisions for acquisition of lands; powers to landowners and other persons, having limited interests in lands, to subscribe and hold shares, and to guarantee interest, and to charge the inheritance with subscriptions and guarantees, as a prior charge; provisions for compelling such persons to guarantee interest, and to charge the inheritance with guarantee, as a prior charge; powers to persons guaranteeing to participate in profits of company; powers to appoint committees; incorporation of Acts; amendment or repeal of Acts and other powers and provisions.

London and South Western (Bideford to Great Torrington, Abandonment, &c.)—Abandonment of portion of authorised railway from Bideford to Great Torrington; construction of railway in substitution for part of abandoned railway; amendment of Acts.

London and South Western (Poole and Bournemouth Junction Abandonment).—Abandonment of lines authorised by the South Western (Poole and Bournemouth Junction) Act, 1866; amendment of Acts.

Metropolitan and Islington.—Incorporation of company for making a railway from Metropolitan to the Canonbury Road, Islington; powers to Metropolitan; amendment of Acts.

Sutton, Mepal, and Somersham.—Incorporation of company; construction of railway from the Ely Haddenham and Sutton, at Sutton, to the Great Eastern, at Somersham; arrangements with Ely Haddenham and Sutton and Great Eastern; powers to run over and use and levy and alter tolls on railways of those companies; powers to the Ely Haddenham and Sutton to subscribe and to raise moneys; amendment of Acts.

Wellington and Drayton.—Increase of capital.

6.—FOUR YEARS' STATISTICS.

Compiled from Returns to the Board of Trade, by Mr. Cleghorn, Secretary to the North Eastern.

	1864.	1865.	1866.	1867.	Comparison of 1867 with 1866.
Capital authorised at 31st December—					
Share..............	£390,413,137	£432,889,245	£466,151,633	£481,447,440	Increase £15,295,807
Loan..............	130,109,197	143,402,418	154,412,773	161,405,968	6,993,195
Total..........	£520,522,334	£576,291,663	£620,564,406	£642,853,408	£22,289,002
Paid up at 31st December—					
Share—Ordinary	£214,947,054	£219,598,196	£223,245,629	£233,023,854	Increase £4,778,225
Preference	104,647,626	124,263,475	134,455,098	143,209,357	8,754,259
Loan—Debentures	93,075,392	97,821,097	105,065,863	110,392,559	5,326,696
Debenture stock	13,049,541	13,795,375	14,105,594	15,637,117	1,531,523
Total..........	£425,719,613	£455,478,143	£481,872,184	£502,262,887	£20,390,703, or 4·23 ⅌ cent.
Open for traffic at 31st December—					
....	12,789 miles.	13,289 miles.	13,854 miles.	14,247 miles.	Increase 393 miles, or 2·83 ⅌ cent.
Passengers—First class	27,701,415	29,653,205	31,265,419	31,725,708	Increase 460,289, or 1·47 ⅌ cent.
Second class	65,269,169	70,783,241	80,303,089	77,700,297	Decrease 2,602,792, or 3·24 ⅌ cent.
Third cl. & parliamentary	135,301,581	151,416,249	162,725,160	178,212,108	Increase 15,536,948, or 9·54 ⅌ cent.
Total..........	229,272,165	251,862,715	274,293,668	287,688,113	Net Inc. 13,394,445, or 4·88 ⅌ cent.
Periodical tickets not included ...	76,499	97,147	110,227	119,791	
Receipts from passengers..........	£13,915,600	£14,724,802	£15,423,765	£15,909,705	Increase £485,940, or 3·15 ⅌ cent.
Average	1s. 2¼d. per pass.	1s. 2d. per pass.	1s. 1¼d. per pass	1s. 1½d. per pass.	
Luggage, parcels, horses, carriages, &c.	1,210,099	1,279,384	1,398,443	1,453,571	Increase £55,128, or 3·94 ⅌ cent.
Mails..........	558,341	567,865	573,717	572,358	Decrease 1,359, or 0·23 ⅌ cent.
Total receipts	£15,684,040	£16,572,051	£17,395,925	£17,935,634	Increase £53,709, or 3·1 ⅌ cent.
General merchandise	34,914,913 tons.	36,787,638 tons.	38,649,938 tons.	46,474,037 tons.	Inc. 7,824,099 tons, or 20·24 ⅌ cent.
Receipts from ditto	£11,343,691	£12,158,239	£12,961,195	£13,055,880	Increase £94,695, or 0·73 ⅌ cent.
Average	6s. 6d. per ton.	6s. 7½d. per ton.	6s. 8½d. per ton.	5s. 7½d. per ton.	
Minerals..........	75,445,781 tons.	77,805,786 tons.	85,483,444 tons.	98,633,791 tons.	Inc. 13,150,347 tons, or 15·38 ⅌ cent.
Receipts from ditto..........	£6,302,883	£6,469,502	£7,074,923	£7,640,878	Increase £565,955, or 8 ⅌ cent.
Average	1s. 8d. per ton.	1s. 8d. per ton.	1s. 7¾d. per ton.	1s. 6½d. per ton.	
Live stock carried	13,673,786 heads.	14,530,937 heads.	15,081,822 heads.	15,724,058 heads.	Increase 642,236, or 4·25 ⅌ cent.
Receipts from ditto	£684,945	£690,321	£732,311	£847,597	Increase £115,286, or 15·74 ⅌ cent.
Average	1s. 0d. per head.	11¼d. per head.	11¼d. per head.	1s. 0¼d. per head.	
Total receipts	£34,015,564	£35,890,113	£38,164,354	£39,479,999	Increase £1,315,645, or 3·44 ⅌ cent.

FOUR YEARS' STATISTICS—*Continued.*

	1864.	1865.	1866.	1867.	Comparison of 1867 and 1866.
Expenses, including taxes, duty, &c. ..	£16,000,308 47·03 per cent. total receipts.	£17,149,073 48 per cent. total receipts.	£18,811,673 49·27 per cent. total receipts.	£19,848,952 50·27 per cent. total receipts.	Increase £1,037,279, or 5·51 ℔ cent.
Number of trains run—					
Passenger	3,106,651	3,448,509	3,741,086	3,924,624	Increase.. 183,538, or 4·09 ℔ cent.
Goods, mineral, &c.	1,863,318	2,108,198	2,305,133	2,403,866	Increase.. 98,733, or 4·28 ℔ cent.
Total	4,969,969	5,556,707	6,046,219	6,328,490	Increase.. 282,271, or 4·66 ℔ cent.
Number of miles run by trains—					
Passenger	66,555,219	71,206,818	73,383,356	74,886,409	Increase.. 1,503,053, or 2·04 ℔ cent.
Average	$21\frac{1}{2}$ per train.	$20\frac{3}{4}$ per train.	19·61 per train.	19·08 per train.	
Goods, mineral, &c.	62,575,724	68,320,309	69,424,497	73,656,418	Increase.. 4,231,921, or 6·09 ℔ cent.
Average	$33\frac{1}{2}$ per train.	$32\frac{1}{2}$ per train.	30 per train.	30·64 per train.	
Total	129,130,943	139,527,127	142,807,853	148,542,827	Increase.. 5,734,974, or 4·01 ℔ cent.
Average	26 per train.	25 per train.	23·61 per train.	23·47 per train.	
Average per passenger train	£5 0 $11\frac{3}{4}$	£4 16 $1\frac{1}{4}$	£4 13 0	£4 11 $4\frac{3}{4}$	
Do. per goods, minerals, &c.	9 16 9	9 3 3	9 0 $2\frac{1}{4}$	8 19 $2\frac{3}{4}$	
Do. per mile per passenger train ..	0 4 $8\frac{1}{2}$	0 4 $7\frac{3}{4}$	0 4 9	0 4 $9\frac{1}{4}$	
Do. per mile per goods, &c.	0 5 $10\frac{1}{4}$	0 5 $7\frac{3}{4}$	0 6 0	0 5 10	
Rolling stock—Locomotive engines	7,203	7,414	8,125	8,619	Increase 494
Passenger carriages..........	16,985	17,997	19,228	19,773	,, ... 545
Vehicles attached to trains ..	6,506	6,853	7,276	7,581	,, ... 305
Wagons of all descriptions ..	212,916	226,407	242,947	247,048	,, ... 4,101
Total	243,610	258,671	277,576	283,021	Increase 5,445
* Accidents to passengers—					
Killed from causes beyond their own control	15 or 1 in every $15\frac{1}{4}$ millions carried.	23 or 1 in every 11 millions carried.	15 or 1 in every 18 millions carried.	19 or 1 in every 15 millions carried.	
Injured........................... (N.B. This includes all kinds of injuries, many of which were comparatively trifling.)	698 or 1 in every $\frac{1}{3}$ of a million carried.	1,034 or 1 in every $\frac{1}{4}$ of a million carried.	540 or 1 in every $\frac{1}{2}$ million carried.	680 or 1 in every $\frac{1}{2}$ million carried.	
Killed from their own misconduct or want of caution	21 or 1 in every 11 millions carried.	13 or 1 in every 20 millions carried.	16 or 1 in every 17 millions carried.	17 or 1 in every 17 millions carried.	
Injured from their own misconduct or want of caution	8 or 1 in every 28 millions carried.	5 or 1 in every 50 millions carried.	7 or 1 in every 39 millions carried.	8 or 1 in every 36 millions carried.	

* Holders of Periodical Tickets not included in these averages.

NOTE.—The land held by railway companies whose lines are open is 162,325 acres, or an average of about $12\frac{1}{3}$ acres per lineal miles of railway.

7.—BANK RATES OF DISCOUNT.

The dates and duration of minimum rates of discount, from 1836 to 1868 inclusive, have been as follows:—

Year.	Date.	℔ cent.	Year.	Date.	℔ cent.
1836	July 21	4½	1858	February 11	3
,,	September 1	5	,,	December 9	2½
1838	February 15	4	1859	April 28	3½
1839	May 16	5	,,	May 5	4½
,,	June 20	5½	,,	June 2	3½
,,	August 1	6	,,	June 9	3
1840	January 23	5	,,	July 14	2½
1841	June 3	5	1860	January 19	3
1842	April 7	4	,,	January 31	4
1845	March 13	2½	,,	March 29	4½
,,	October 16	3	,,	April 12	5
,,	November 6	3½	,,	May 10	4½
1846	August 27	3	,,	May 24	4
1847	January 14	3½	,,	November 8	4½
,,	January 21	4	,,	November 13	5
,,	April 8	5	,,	November 15	6
,,	August 2	6	,,	November 29	5
,,	August 5	5½	,,	December 31	6
,,	October 1	6½	1861	January 7	7
,,	October 25	8	,,	February 14	8
,,	November 22	7	,,	March 21	7
,,	December 2	6	,,	April 4	6
,,	December 23	5	,,	April 11	5
1848	January 27	4	,,	April 16	6
,,	June 15	3½	,,	August 1	5
,,	November 22	3	,,	August 14	4½
1849	November 22	2½	,,	August 29	4
1850	December 26	3	,,	September 19	3½
1852	January 1	2½	,,	November 7	3
,,	April 22	2	1862	January 9	2½
1853	January 6	2½	,,	May 22	3
,,	January 20	3	,,	July 10	2½
,,	June 2	3½	,,	July 24	2
,,	September 1	4	,,	October 30	3
,,	September 15	4½	1863	January 15	4
,,	September 29	5	,,	January 28	5
1854	May 11	5½	,,	February 19	4
,,	August 3	5	,,	April 23	3½
1855	April 5	4½	,,	April 30	3
,,	May 3	4	,,	May 16	3½
,,	June 14	3½	,,	May 21	4
,,	September 6	4	,,	November 2	5
,,	September 13	4½	,,	November 5	6
,,	September 27	5	,,	December 2	7
,,	October 4	5½	,,	December 3	8
,,	October 18	7	,,	December 24	7
1856	May 22	6	1864	January 20	8
,,	May 29	5	,,	February 11	7
,,	June 26	4½	,,	February 25	6
,,	October 1	5	,,	April 16	7
,,	October 6	7	,,	May 2	8
,,	November 13	7	,,	May 5	9
,,	December 4	6½	,,	May 19	8
,,	December 18	6	,,	May 26	7
1857	August 2	6½	,,	June 16	6
,,	June 18	6	,,	July 25	7
,,	July 16	5½	,,	August 4	8
,,	October 8	6	,,	September 8	9
,,	October 12	7	,,	November 10	8
,,	October 19	8	,,	November 24	7
,,	November 5	9	,,	December 15	6
,,	November 9	10	1865	January 12	5½
,,	December 24	8	,,	January 26	5
1858	January 7	6	,,	March 2	4½
,,	January 14	5	,,	March 30	4
,,	January 28	4	,,	May 4	4½
,,	February 4	3½	,,	May 25	4

BANK RATES OF DISCOUNT—*Continued.*

Year.	Date.	℔ cent.	Year.	Date.	℔ cent.
1865	June 1	3½	1866	May 8	8
,,	June 15	3	,,	May 11	9
,,	July 27	3½	,,	May 12	10
,,	August 3	4	,,	August 16	8
,,	September 27	4½	,,	August 23	7
,,	October 2	5	,,	August 30	6
,,	October 5	6	,,	September 6	5
,,	October 7	7	,,	September 27	4½
,,	November 23	6	,,	November 8	4
,,	December 28	7	,,	December 20	3½
1866	January 4	8	1867	January 7	3
,,	January 6	8	,,	May 29	2½
,,	February 22	7	,,	July 24	2
,,	March 15	6	1868	November 19	2½
,,	May 3	7	,,	December 3	3

8.—FLUCTUATIONS IN PRICES—1868.

The following Table, from the London Weekly Share List, exhibits the extreme fluctuation in Prices of the principal Stocks and Shares, during the year 1868:—

STOCK.	First quotd price.	Last quotd price.	Highest price.	Lowest price.	Extm Fluctuatn
Bombay, Baroda, and Central India	£102	£103	22nd June..107	2nd Jan...102	5
Bristol and Exeter	85	75	4th Feb... 87	18th Dec... 75	12
Caledonian	71¼	75⅝	27th Feb... 87¼	18th Sept... 67⅝	19⅝
East India	109	105½	22nd June..112¾	31st Dec...105⅛	7⅝
East Lincolnshire .... (6 per cent.)	133	134	19th Feb...135	22nd Oct. ..132	3
Grand Trunk of Canada	15	15½	16th July .. 17¼	14th Jan... 14⅞	2⅜
Great Eastern	31	40¾	18th Nov. .. 44⅞	8th Jan... 27¼	17⅝
Great Indian Peninsula	106½	104½	22nd June..112	30th Dec. ..103¾	8¼
Great Luxembourg ....(20*l.*)	8⅝	10⅞	10th June.. 13	8th Jan... 8⅛	4⅞
Great Northern	166¾	106½	7th Feb...110½	10th July..101½	9
Ditto	109	107¾	6th Feb...112	7th July .. 94¼	17¾
Ditto	123½	124½	21st April..125½	7th Sept...121½	4
Great Western	44½	48	2nd May .. 55	7th Jan... 44	11
Ditto W. Midland, Oxford	27½	25	5th May .. 31½	27th Jan... 27	4½
Great Western of Canada....(20½*l.*)	16¾	15	2nd Jan. .. 16¾	7th Aug... 12⅞	3⅞
Hull and Selby ....(50*l.*)	109½	110	1st Aug...113	4th Mar...109	4
Lancashire and Yorkshire	123¼	127½	3rd Aug...131⅛	3rd Jan...122¼	8⅞
Lancaster and Carlisle	209	213	7th Feb...218½	19th Sept. ..209	9½
London and Blackwall	87½	94	3rd Dec... 94¼	28th Feb... 85½	8¾
London, Brighton, and South Coast	48¼	49¾	31st July .. 54½	1st Feb... 45⅜	9¼
London, Chatham, and Dover	18	17⅛	30th May .. 21	6th Nov... 16⅜	4⅝
London and North Western	114¼	112	27th Feb...120½	7th Nov...111	9½
London and South Western	76½	88	9th June.. 93¼	3rd Jan... 76	17¼
Madras	102½	105	5th Nov. ..109	13th Jan...101¼	7¾
M'chester, Sheffield, & Lincolnshire	45¼	46¾	23rd Oct. .. 48¼	17th July .. 40¼	8
Metropolitan	116	105	24th Jan...118¾	21st Dec...101	17¾
Midland	104⅛	112¾	26th Oct. ..113⅝	6th Jan...102	11⅝
North British	33½	32	1st Aug... 37	30th Nov... 31½	5½
North Eastern—Berwick	98½	99⅝	10th Feb...106½	1st Sept... 97	9½
Ditto Leeds	59	54	14th Feb... 64	11th Sept... 53½	10½
Ditto York	92	87⅝	27th Feb... 99¼	9th Sept... 87	12¼
North London	114	123	Dec...123¾	6th Jan...114	9¾
North Staffordshire	59	55	23rd Jan... 59	2nd Dec... 53	6
Scinde	101¼	101¾	4th Nov. ..105	28th Jan... 99¾	5¼
South Austrian	13¾	16¾	3rd Dec... 17	15th Jan... 13⅜	3⅝
South Devon	42	44	3rd Aug... 46½	10th Jan... 41¼	5¼
South Eastern	67	79	18th Nov... 80¼	3rd Jan... 66½	13¾

9.—TRAFFIC RECEIPTS IN THE UNITED KINGDOM.

The subjoined table exhibits the receipts on the various lines in the United Kingdom during the half-year ending December 31st or January 31st last:—

COMPANY.	Weeks.	1868. Receipts.	1868. Miles open.	1867. Receipts.	1867. Miles open.
Belfast and Northern Counties	26	66,173	99¾	60,786	97¾
Brecon and Merthyr	26	24,493	54	25,132	48
Blyth and Tyne	26	61,497	38	68,834	38
Bristol and Exeter	26	199,369	134¼	202,327	134¼
Caledonian and North British	26	1,716,980	1397¾	1,632,752	1381
Cambrian	26	80,291	176	71,088	176
Cockermouth, Keswick, &c.	22	11,920	31½	11,931	31½
Cornwall	26	47,593	65½	48,165	65½
Dublin and Belfast	26	43,284	63	43,108	63
Dublin and Drogheda	26	52,762	75	51,022	75
Dublin and Meath	26	7,991	35	7,762	35
Dublin, Wicklow, and Wexford	26	90,818	106	88,205	106
Forth and Clyde Junction	26	9,419	30	9,193	30
Furness	26	127,938	85	132,517	85
Glasgow and South Western	26	295,607	249	291,117	249
Great Eastern	26	1,044,408	728	1,003,989	728
Great Northern	26	1,142,120	487	1,130,366	487
Great North of Scotland	25	87,783	256¾	85,721	256¾
Great Northern and Western of Ireland	26	19,449	94	19,749	83¼
Great Western	26	1,984,117	1386	1,948,531	1344
Highland	22	91,754	245¾	87,385	245¼
Hoylake	26	1,608	5½	1,723	5½
Irish North Western	26	54,465	145	53,397	145
Isle of Wight	25	10,460	12	10,861	12
Lancashire and Yorkshire	26	1,289,420	411½	1,254,824	403
Limerick and Ennis	26	5,788	24¾	5,040	24¾
Limerick and Foynes	26	4,524	26½	4,187	26¼
Llanelly	26	22,420	41¼	22,598	46¾
Llynvi and Ogmore Valley	26	20,378	30¼	19,968	30¼
London and Brighton	26	699,995	365¼	702,241	335
London, Chatham, and Dover	25	339,571	136	354,182	136
Ditto, Metropolitan Extension	26	76,654	13¼	70,698	13¼
Londonderry and Coleraine	26	10,774	36¼	10,720	36¼
London and North Western Shrewsbury and Hereford Shropshire Union	26	3,367,236	1372	3,362,735	1348½
London and South Western North Devon, &c.	26	723,991	503	729,183	503
London, Tilbury, and Southend	25	47,891	46¾	49,413	46¾
Manchester and South Junction	26	37,652	8	37,962	8
Manchester, Sheffield, and Lincolnshire	26	589,941	251½	572,001	246
Maryport and Carlisle	25	39,803	38	39,176	38
Metropolitan	26	143,840	7	113.908	4½
Metropolitan and St. John's Wood	....	....	1¾	....	....
Midland	26	1,616,567	774½	1,503,278	761½
Midland Great Western	26	148,229	260¾	146,646	260¾
Monmouthshire	26	73,594	44	78,166	44
North Eastern Newcastle and Carlisle Stockton and Darlington	26	2,004,712	1258½	1,996,079	1229
North London	26	163,958	11	156,561	11
North Staffordshire Railway and Canal	26	225,159	275	223,467	268
Pembroke and Tenby	26	12,469	27	10,149	27
Rhymney	26	28,058	23¾	27,837	22¾
Somerset and Dorset	26	30,589	66	32,966	66
South Devon	26	119,817	110½	120,433	98
South Eastern	26	739,321	346	716,793	330
Taff Vale	26	164,951	63	168,534	63
Ulster	26	....	105½	....	105½
Whitehaven, Cleator, and Egremont	26	20,402	10	20,664	10

10.—MILES OPENED IN THE UNITED KINGDOM IN 1868.

	Miles.
Aylesbury and Buckingham—Verney Junction to Aylesbury—Opened October 1st	12¼
Brecon and Merthyr—Fochriw to Pengam—Opened September 1st	6¾
Ditto — Cefn to Merthyr—Opened August 1st	2¾
Caledonian—Busby to East Kilbride—Opened September 1st	4
Festiniog and Blaenau—Duffws to Festiniog—Opened May 30th	3½
Glasgow and Paisley Joint—Ibrox to Govan—Opened December 2nd	1
Great Northern—Firsby to Spilsby—Opened May 1st	4¼
Great Southern and Western—Parsonstown to Portumna—Opened November 5th	12½
Great Western—Llandrillo to Bala—Opened April 1st	7⅓
Ditto — Bala to Dolgelly—Opened August 4th	20
Lancashire and Yorkshire—Horwich to Hindley—Opened September 1st	3⅛
London, Brighton, and South Coast—Central Croydon—Opened January 1st	⅜
Ditto — Uckfield to Groombridge—Opened August 3rd	13⅜
Ditto — Peckham Rye to Sutton—Opened October 1st	10⅜
Ditto and L. & S.W.—Streatham to Tooting and Wimbledon—October 1st	5¼
London and North Western—Llanrwst to Bettws-y-coed—Opened April 6th	3¾
Ditto — Sandbach to Northwich—Opened July 1st	8¾
Ditto — Central Wales Extension, Llanwrtyd to Llandovery Opened June 1st	10¾
London and South Western—Colyton Junction to Seaton—Opened March 16th	4¼
Manchester, Sheffield, and Lincolnshire—New Mills to Hayfield—Opened March 1st	3
Ditto — Tinsley to Rotherham—Opened Aug. 1st.	2½
Metropolitan—Praed Street to Brompton (Gloucester Road)—Opened October 1st.	2½
Ditto — Brompton (Gloucester Road) to South Kensington—Opened December 24th	½
Metropolitan and St. John's Wood—Baker Street to Swiss Cottage—Opened April 13th	1¾
Metropolitan District—South Kensington to Westminster Bridge—Opened December 24th	2¼
Midland—Redditch to Alcester—Opened May 4th	7½
Ditto — Bedford to King's Cross (Metropolitan)—Opened July 13th	49¾
Ditto — Derby to Melbourne—Opened September 1st	7
Ditto — Walton to Wakefield (Westgate)—Opened August 1st	2½
Ditto — St. Pancras to Camden Road—Opened October 1st	1
Midland Great Western—Manulla Junction to Foxford—Opened May 1st	11½
Midland and South Western Junction—Hendon to Acton—Opened for Goods, October 1st	4
North British—Edinburgh, Leith, and Granton New Branches—Opened March 2nd	3½
Ditto — Dalmeny to South Queensferry—Opened June 1st	1¼
North Eastern—Ayton Junction to Ingleby—Opened April 1st	5⅛
Ditto — Barnard Castle to Middleton—Opened June 1st	8¾
Ditto — Team Valley, Gateshead to Durham—Opened December 1st	12½
Ditto — Consett Loop—Opened June 5th	½
Sirhowy—Sirhowy to Nant-y-bwch—Opened November 2nd	1¼
South Eastern—Chislehurst to Seven Oaks—Opened March 2nd	11¼
Ditto — Seven Oaks to Tunbridge—Opened May 1st	7½
Sutherland—Bonar Bridge to Golspie—Opened April 13th	26½
Torbay and Brixham—Brixham Road to Brixham—Opened February 28th	2
Tottenham and Hampstead Junction—Opened July 1st	4½
Total miles opened in 1868	315

11.—POWERS OF ATTORNEY FOR RECEIPT OF DIVIDENDS.

The following is an extract from Schedule C to the Act 27 Vic., cap. 18 (passed 13th May, 1864), referring to the above subject :—

Letters or Powers of Attorney, Proxies, &c. (that is to say), for or upon any Letter or Power of Attorney :

For the Sale, Transfer, or Acceptance of any of the Government or Parliamentary Stocks or Funds :

If the value of such Stocks or Funds shall exceed £20......... £1 0 0
And if such value shall not exceed £20........................ 0 5 0

For the receipts of Dividends or Interest on any of the Government or Parliamentary Stocks or Funds, or of the Stocks, Funds, or Shares of or in any Joint Stock Company, or other Company or Society, whose Stocks or Funds are divided into Shares and transferable :

If the same shall be for the receipt of one payment only...... £0 1 0
And if the same shall be for a continuous receipt, or for the
receipt of more than one payment 0 5 0

12.—METHOD OF CALCULATING INTEREST AT FIVE PER CENT.

Multiply the principal by the number of days, and divide by 7,300. EXAMPLE : To find the interest at 5 per cent, on £312 for 260 days.

$$312 + 260$$
$$\overline{}$$
$$7,300 = £11 \ 2s. \ 3d.$$

The interest at 5 per cent. being found as above, interest at 3 per cent. is found by multiplying the interest so found by 3, and dividing by 5 ; at $3\frac{1}{2}$, 4, or $4\frac{1}{2}$ per cent., by multiplying by the rate required, and dividing by 5 ; and at $2\frac{1}{2}$, by taking half the interest at 5 per cent.

V.—RAILWAY DIRECTORY, &c., 1869.

1.—THE RAILWAY INTEREST IN THE NEW PARLIAMENT.

The following elaborate synopsis exhibits the number of Directors, &c., who have seats in the new Parliament, together with the places they represent, and the various Boards at which they sit. From a comparison with the summary in last year's MANUAL it appears that the number of Railway Directors in the new Parliament has decreased by 4 in the House of Peers, and 32 in the Commons, making a total decrease of 36 as compared with the last Parliament.

HOUSE OF LORDS.

Abinger, Lord.—Mont Cenis.
Ailesbury, Marquis.—Berks and Hants.
Airlie, Earl.—Alyth.
Anglesey, Marquis.—Cannock Chase Extension; Cannock Chase and Wolverhampton.
Bateman, Lord.—Leominster and Kington.
Bath, Marquis.—East Somerset.
Buccleuch and Queensberry, Duke.—Furness.
Buckingham and Chandos, Duke.—Aylesbury & Buckingham; Buckinghamshire.
Caithness, Earl.—Buckinghamshire; Caithness; Morayshire; Sutherland.
Clancarty, Earl.—Great Northern and Western; Midland Great Western.
Clanricarde, Marquis.—Parsonstown and Portumna Bridge.
Cloncurry, Lord.—Great Southern and Western.
Colville, Lord.—Great Northern.
Crofton, Lord.—Great Northern and Western.
Devon, Earl.—Bristol and Exeter; Kingsbridge; Limerick and North Kerry; Metropolitan District; Moretonhampstead and South Devon; Rathkeale and Newcastle Junction; South Wales and Great Western Direct.
Devonshire, Duke.—Clonmel, Lismore, and Dungarvan; Furness.
Dunraven, Earl.—Limerick and Foynes.
Ebury, Lord.—Hatfield and St. Albans; Rickmansworth, Amersham, and Chesham; Watford and Rickmansworth.
Erne, Earl.—Dundalk and Greenore.
Exeter, Marquis.- Stamford & Essendine.
Lichfield, Earl—Wolverhampton & Walsall.
Lifford, Viscount.—Finn Valley.
Lonsdale, Earl.—Whitehaven, Cleator, and Egremont; Workington.

Lucan, Earl.—Great Northern & Western.
Lyttleton, Lord.—Halesowen and Bromsgrove.
Middleton, Lord.—Dingwall and Skye.
Montrose, Duke.—Forth and Clyde Junction.
Normanby, Marquis. — Whitby, Redcar, and Middlesborough Union.
Northwick, Lord.—Tenbury; Tenbury and Bewdley.
Poltimore, Lord.—Devon and Somerset.
Portsmouth, Earl.—Devon and Cornwall.
Powerscourt, Viscount.—Bray and Enniskerry.
Powis, Earl.—Shropshire Union.
Ribblesdale, Lord.—Ribblesdale.
Romney, Earl.—Maidstone and Ashford.
Salisbury, Marquis.—Great Eastern; Mistley, Thorpe, and Walton; Tendring Hundred.
Seafield, Earl.—Highland.
Sondes, Lord.—Seven Oaks, Maidstone, and Tunbridge.
Stair, Earl.—Portpatrick.
Stuart de Decies, Lord.—Clonmel, Lismore, and Dungarvan.
Suffield, Lord.—East Norfolk.
Sutherland, Duke.— Highland; London and North Western; Sutherland.
Templemore, Lord.—Waterford and Passage.
Templetown, Viscount.—Belfast & Northern Counties; Carrickfergus and Larne.
Tredegar, Lord.—Monmouthshire.
Vane, Earl.—Cambrian.
Waterford, Marquis.—Waterford and Passage.
Wharncliffe, Lord.—Manchester, Sheffield, and Lincolnshire.

HOUSE OF COMMONS.

Adam, W. P. (Clackmannan.)— Devon Valley ; North British.

Akroyd, E. (Halifax.)—Halifax and Ovenden.

Anstruther, Sir R. (Fifeshire.)—Caithness.

Antrobus, E. (Wilton.)—Wiltshire.

Ayrton, A. S. (Tower Hamlets.)—Great Indian Peninsula ; Great Indian Peninsula Extension.

Bagwell, J. (Clonmel.)—Clonmel, Lismore, and Dungarvan.

Baring, T. (Huntingdon.)—Grand Trunk of Canada.

Barttelot, Col. W. B. (West Sussex.)—Surrey and Sussex Junction ; West Sussex Junction.

Beach, Sir M. E. H. (East Gloucestershire)—East Gloucestershire ; Wiltshire.

Beach, W. W. B. (North Hants.) — Wiltshire.

Beaumont, 'S. A. (Wakefield.)—Lemberg-Czernowitz.

Beaumont W. B.(SouthNorthumberland)—Hexham and Allendale.

Benyon, R. (Berkshire.)—Berks and Hants.

Bingham, Lord (Mayo Co.)—Great Northern and Western.

Bourne, Lieut.-Col. J. (Evesham.)—London and North Western.

Brassey, T., Junr. (Hastings.)—Ipswich and Felixtow ; London and North Western ; North London ; Vale of Towy ; Wenlock.

Brocklehurst, W. C. (Macclesfield.)—Macclesfield, Knutsford, and Warrington.

Brogden, A.(Wednesbury.)—Lancaster and Carlisle ; Llynvi and Ogmore ; Solway Junction ; Mont Cenis.

Brown-Westhead, J. P. (York.)—Birkenhead ; London and North Western ; Shrewsbury and Hereford ; Shropshire Union ; West London ; West London Extension.

Bruce, Lord E. A. (Marlborough.)—Berks and Hants ; Marlborough ; Midland Counties and South Wales.

Buckley, Sir E. (Newcastle-under-Lyme.)—Mowddwy.

Bury, Viscount (Berwick-on-Tweed.)—London and South Western.

Callan, P. (Dundalk.)—Irish North Western.

Cave, T. (Barnstaple.)—Neath and Brecon ; Swansea Vale and Neath and Brecon Junction.

Cavendish, Lord Fred. C. (York, West Riding, North.)—Furness.

Cecil, Lord E. H. B. G. (West Essex.)—Northern and Eastern.

Chadwick, D. (Macclesfield.)—Macclesfield, Knutsford, and Warrington.

Chaplin, H. (Mid-Lincolnshire.) — Louth and Lincoln.

Child, Sir S. (West Staffordshire.)—North Staffordshire.

Clay, J. (Hull.)—Londonderry and Enniskillen.

Clive, G. (Hereford.)—Great Northern and Western.

Clive, Lieut.-Col. G. H. W. W. (Ludlow.) Penarth.

Colthurst, Sir G. C. (Kinsale.)—Cork and Macroom Direct.

Conolly, T. (Donegal Co.) — Enniskillen, Bundoran, and Sligo.

Courtenay, Lord (East Devon.)—Rathkeale and Newcastle Junction.

Crawford, R. W. (London.)—East Indian ; Mexican.

Crossley, Sir F. (York, West Riding, North.)—Halifax and Ovenden.

Delahunty, J. (Waterford.) — Kilkenny Junction ; Waterford and Central Ireland.

Denison, C. B. (York, West Riding, East.)—Great Northern ; West - Riding and Grimsby.

Dickson, Major A. G. (Dover.) — Elham Valley.

Dillwyn, L. L. (Swansea.)—Great Western.

Duff, Lieut. R. W., R.N. (Banffshire.)—Highland.

Duncombe, Col. (York, North Riding.)—Bradford, Eccleshill, and Idle ; Great Northern ; Hatfield and St. Albans.

Egerton, E. C. (East Cheshire.) — Great Northern.

Elliot, G. (North Durham.)—Talacre.

Fellowes, E. (Huntingdonshire.)—Ramsey.

Fletcher, I. (Cockermouth.) — Cockermouth, Keswick, and Penrith.

Forester, Major-Gen. G. C.W. (Wenlock.)—Severn Valley.

Garlies, Viscount (Wigton.)—Portpatrick.

Gilpin, C. (Northampton.)—Metropolitan ; South Eastern ; Smyrna and Cassaba.

Glyn, G. G. (Shaftesbury.)—North London.

Gooch, Sir D. (Cricklade.) — Birkenhead ; Great Western ; Shrewsbury and Hereford ; West London.

Gore, J. R. O. (North Shropshire.)—Llangollen and Corwen ; Vale of Llangollen.

Gower, Hon. E. F. L. (Bodmin.)—Bodmin.

Graves, S. R. (Liverpool.)—Dundalk and Greenore ; Lancashire Union ; London and North Western.

Gray, Sir J. (Kilkenny.)—Dublin Metropolitan Junctions ; Dublin, Rathmines, Rathgar, Roundtown, Rathfarnham, and Rathcoole.

Greene, E. (Bury St. Edmunds.)—Bury St. Edmunds and Thetford.

Gregory, W. H. (Galway Co.)—Athenry and Ennis Junction

Grosvenor, R. W. (Westminster.) — Uxbridge and Rickmansworth ; Watford and Rickmansworth.

Hay, Sir J. C. D. (Stamford.)—Girvan and Portpatrick Junction ; Portpatrick.

Henniker-Major, Hon. J. M. (East Suffolk.)—Mellis and Eye.

Hibbert, J. T. (Oldham.)—Lancaster and Carlisle ; Oldham, Ashton-under-Lyne, and Guide Bridge Junction.

Hodgkinson, G. (Newark.)—London, Chatham, and Dover.

Hodgson, W. N. (East Cumberland.)—Cockermouth, Keswick, and Penrith ; Lancaster and Carlisle ; London and North Western ; Portpatrick.

Holford, R. S. (East Gloucestershire.)—Wilts and Gloucestershire.

Hornby, W. H. (Blackburn.)—Lancashire and Yorkshire.

Howard, Hon. C. W. G. (East Cumberland.)—London and North Western.

Hughes, W. B. (Carnarvon.) — Anglesea Central.

Kavanagh, A. M. (Co. Carlow.)—Kilkenny Junction; Waterford, New Ross, and Wexford.

Kinnaird, Hon. A. F. (Perth.)—Buckinghamshire.

Kirk, W. (Newry.)—Newry and Armagh.

Knox, Major L. E. (Sligo.)—Dublin Metropolitan Junctions; Dublin, Rathmines, Rathgar, Roundtown, Rathfarnham, and Rathcoole.

Knox, Hon. Col. W. S. (Dungannon.)—Portadown, Dungannon, and Omagh.

Lancaster, J. (Wigan.)—Lancashire Union.

Lawson, Sir W. (Carlisle.)—Maryport and Carlisle.

Lee, W. (Maidstone.)—Metropolitan ; Metropolitan and St. John's Wood ; Victoria Station and Pimlico.

Lennox, Lord G. G. (Lymington.)—London, Brighton, and South Coast.

Lewis, H. (Marylebone.)—Bahia and San Francisco.

Loch, G. (Wick, &c.)—Highland ; Sutherland.

Lopes, Sir Massey (South Devon.)—South Devon.

Lowther, Lt.-Col. H. (West Cumberland.) —Lancaster and Carlisle.

Mackintosh, E. W. (Inverness, &c.)—Dingwall and Skye ; Highland.

Malcolm, J. W. (Boston.)—Callander and Oban.

Marling, S. S. (West Gloucestershire.)—Severn Junction; Wilts and Gloucestershire.

Martin, C. W. (Newport, Isle of Wight.)—Maidstone and Ashford.

Matheson, A. (Ross and Cromarty.)—Dingwall and Skye ; Highland ; Sutherland.

Maxwell, W. H. (Kirkcudbright.)—Glasgow and South Western.

Mc. Clean, J. R. (East Staffordshire.)—South Eastern of Portugal.

Merry, J. (Falkirk Burghs.)—Highland.

Mitchell, T. A. (Bridport.) — Bridport ; Dunaberg and Witepsk.

Morgan, C. O. S. (Monmouthshire.)—Monmouthshire.

Murphy, N. D. (Cork.)—Cork and Limerick Direct.

O'Beirne, J. L. (Cashel.)—Southern of Ireland.

O'Loghlen, Sir C. M. (Clare Co.)—Athenry and Ennis Junction.

Otway, A. J. (Chatham)—London, Brighton, and South Coast ; Waterloo and Whitehall.

Paget, R. H. (Mid Somerset.)—East Somerset.

Palk, Sir Lawrence (East Devon.) — Teign Valley.

Pease, J. W. (South Durham.)—North Eastern ; Stockton and Darlington.

Pim, J. (Dublin City.)—Dublin and Kingstown.

Price, R. G. (New Radnor.)—Aberdare and Central Wales Junction ; Kington and Eardisley; Lugg Valley ; Worcester, Bromyard, and Leominster.

Price, W. P. (Gloucester City.)—Gloucester

and Dean Forest ; Midland ; South Devon ; Tewkesbury and Malvern ; Tottenham and Hampstead Junction ; Danube and Black Sea.

Reed, C. (Hackney.)—Milford Haven.

Robertson, D. (Berwickshire.) — Buenos Ayres Great Southern.

Roden, W. S. (Stoke-on-Trent.)—Manchester, Buxton, Matlock, and Midlands Junction.

Russell, Sir W. (Norwich.)—East Gloucestershire.

St. Aubyn, J. (West Cornwall.)—Helston and Penryn.

Sandon, Viscount (Liverpool.)—North Staffordshire.

Sherriff, A. C. (Worcester City.) — Bala and Dolgelly ; Bourton-on-the-Water ; Kettering, Trapstone, and Huntingdon ; Metropolitan ; Metropolitan District ; Metropolitan and St. John's Wood ; Peterbro', Wisbeach, and Sutton ; Stourbridge ; Wellington and Drayton ; Worcester, Bromyard, and Leominster ; Worcester, Dean Forest, and Monmouth.

Stone, W. H. (Portsmouth.) — Bishop's Waltham.

Talbot, C. R. M. (Glamorganshire.) — Bristol and South Wales Union ; Great Western ; South Wales and Great Western Direct.

Tipping W. (Stockport.)—Brynmawr and Blaenavon ; Buckinghamshire ; London and North Western ; North London ; Danube and Black Sea.

Tite, W. (Bath.) —London and Blackwall.

Tomline, G. (Great Grimsby.)—Ipswich and Felixtow.

Torrens, W. T. McCullagh (Finsbury.)—Sidmouth and Budleigh-Salterton.

Trevor, Lord A. E. H. (Downshire.)--Ellesmere and Glyn Valley.

Turner, C. (South West Lancashire.)—Great Northern ; Manchester, Sheffield, and Lincolnshire ; Manchester, South Junction, and Altrincham ; Manchester and Stockport.

Verney, Sir H. (Buckingham.)—Aylesbury and Buckingham ; Buckinghamshire.

Vivian, H. H. (Glamorganshire.)—South Wales and Great Western Direct.

Waterhouse, S. (Pontefract.) — Bradford, Eccleshill, and Idle ; Great Northern ; Halifax and Ovenden ; Idle and Shipley ; West Riding and Grimsby ; Central Argentine.

Weguelin, T. M. (Wolverhampton.) –Bahia and San Francisco.

Wethered, T. O. (Great Marlow.)—Great Marlow.

Whatman, J. (Maidstone.) — Maidstone and Ashford ; South Eastern.

Williams, D. (Merioneth.) — Beddgelert ; Cambrian ; Carnarvonshire.

Williams, F. M. (Truro.) – Cornwall.

Willyams, E. B. (East Cornwall.)—Newquay and Cornwall Junction.

Winn, R. (North Lincolnshire.) — Trent, Ancholme, and Grimsby.

Wynn, Sir Watkin Williams (Denbighshire.)—Great Western ; Llangollen and Corwen ; Wellington and Drayton.

SUMMARY—(Railways.)

Directors in the House of Lords 48
  ,,   in the House of Commons .... 127 = 175

AUXILIARY ASSOCIATIONS.

HOUSE OF LORDS.

Caithness, Earl—Electric and International Telegraph.

HOUSE OF COMMONS.

Brassey T. Junr., (Hastings.) — General Credit and Discount.
Brogden, A. (Wednesbury.) — Lancaster Wagon.
Gilpin, C. (Northampton.)—Metropolitan Railway Warehousing.
Gooch, Sir D. (Cricklade.)—Anglo-American Telegraph ; Telegraph Construction and Maintenance.
Hamilton, E. W. T. (Salisbury)—Hudson's Bay.
Hay, Lord J. (Ripon.)—Telegraph Construction and Maintenance.
Lowe, Rt. Hon. R. (London University.)—French Atlantic Telegraph.

Northcote, Rt. Hon. Sir S. H. (North Devon.)—Hudson's Bay.
Mc. Clean, J. R. (East Staffordshire.)—Anglo-American Telegraph.
Otway, A. J. (Chatham.)—Submarine Telegraph.
Russell, F. W., National Discount.
Sherriff, A. C. (Worcester City.)—Metropolitan Railway Warehousing ; Railway Carriage.
Smith, W. H. (Westminster.)—Electric and International Telegraph.
Wingfield, Sir C. (Gravesend.) — British-Indian Submarine Telegraph.

SUMMARY—(Auxiliary Associations.)

Directors in the House of Lords 1
  ,,   in the House of Commons .... 14 = 15

2.—LIST OF DIRECTORS AND OFFICERS.

NOTE.—The figures in the list refer to the numbers attached to each Railway, and *not* to the folios of the pages of the "*Manual.*"

* All are *Directors* when not otherwise distinguished.

Abell Martin, Esq., 322
Aberdein Francis, Esq., 113
Abernethy James, Esq., M.I.C.E., Consulting Eng., 182
Abinger, Lord, 483
Abraham Thomas, Esq., 274
Absalom George, Esq., 366
Ackland, Sir P. P. F. P., Bart., 437
Acland Lawford, Esq., 134
Acton, Sir John D'Alberg, 50
Adair Benjamin C., Esq., 28
Adam Thomas, Esq., 167
Adam William Patrick, Esq., M.P., 118, 298
Adams Alexander, Esq., 68
Adams B. H., Esq., Auditor, 551
Adams J. F., Esq., Auditor, 263
Adams Thomas, Esq., Auditor, 234
Adams William, Esq., Surveyor, 294
Adamson John, Esq., M.D., 342
Adamthwaite John Esq., 305
Adcock William Thompson, Esq., Sec., 43, 382, 449, 450
Addison George Augustus, Esq., Auditor, 34, 186
Addison John, Esq., Eng., 447
Addison ohn, Esq., C.E., Sec. and Gen. Man., 256
Addison Thomas Batty, Esq., 153
Addison William John, Esq., 137

Adkins John Caleb, Esq., 383
Adlard William Gates, Esq., 445
Adney George, Esq., 283
Adron H , Esq., Sec., 231
Agar S. H., Esq., 185
Aggas William, Esq., Sec., 264
Agnew, Sir Andrew, Bart., 326
Agnew James, Esq., 81
Aikin James, Esq., 475
Aikman Andrew, Esq., 342
Ailesbury, Marquis of, 30
Ainslie Archibald, Esq., 316
Ainslie Daniel, Esq., 69, 70, 104
Ainsworth Thomas, Esq., Sec., 416
Ainsworth Thomas, Esq., Traff. Man., 218, 219, 220, 330
Airlie, The Right Hon. the Earl of, 10
Akers Henry, Esq., 132, 446
Akroyd Edward, Esq., M.P., 177
Akroyd William, Esq., 382
Alcock Henry, Esq., 307
Alexander, Major-Gen. James, C.B., 542
Algeo Robert, Esq., Eng., 11
Allan John, Esq., 264
Allaway Thomas, Esq., J.P., 353
Allen Charles, Esq., 317
Allen Joseph Roscoe, Esq. 37, 295
Allender George, Esq., 301, 303
Allison George, Esq., 431

Bartlett John Edward, Esq., Auditor, 15
Barttelott, Colonel Walter B., M.P., 385, 439
Barton Charles, Esq., 164
Barton James, Esq., Eng., 20, 123, 131
Barton Thomas, Esq., 401
Barwell Edward Harrison, Esq., 400
Barwis W. R., Esq, Auditor, 272
Basset J. F., Esq., 183
Bassett Alexander, Esq , Eng., 102
Bassett Richard, Esq., 98, 14 ', 171, 272, 365
Batchelor James S., Esq , Auditor, 318
Batchelor John, Esq., 318
Bateman, Right Hon. Lord, 214
Bath Henry James, Esq., 3:8
Bath, The Marquis of, 136
Bathgate John D., Esq., Sec., 316
Battcock George, Esq., 9ɔ
Batten James Brend, Esq., 321
Batten John Winterbottom, Esq., 60
Baxendale Joseph, Esq., 537
Baxter Andrew, Esq. Loco. Supt., 49
Baxter Robert Dudley, Esq., 372
Baxter William, Esq., Eng., 386
Bayley —, Esq., 304
Bayley G., Esq., 509
Bayley Robert Preston, Esq., 270
Baynes John A., Esq., Sec., 535
Beach, Sir M. E. H., Bart , M.P., 132, 444
Beach Wm. W. B., Esq., M.P., 444
Beale George Cotter, Esq., 95
Beale Samuel, Esq., 250, 266
Beale William Lansdoune, Esq., 271. 463
Beattie Alexander, Esq., M.D., 198, 268, 367
Beattie J., Esq., Loco. and Car. Supt., 233
Beaumont James, Esq., 537
Beaumont John, Esq., 298
Beaumont S. A., Esq., M.P., 479
Beaumont Wentworth Blackett, Esq., M.P., 187
Beausire Henry, Esq., Sec., 270
Bedford James, Esq., 214
Beech John, Esq., Eng., 355
Beecroft G. S., Esq., 59, 209
Beer Julius, Esq., 505
Beeston Alfred, Esq., 111, 273, 400
Begg John, Esq., 42
Beisley Sidney, Esq., 359
Belfield John, Esq., 110
Bell —, Esq., Auditor, 243
Bell Isaac Lowthian, Esq., 299
Bell, Rev. J. A., 267
Bell James, Esq., Eng., 298
Bell James G., Esq., Auditor, 406
Bell John Williams, Esq., Auditor, 346
Bell Robert, Esq., 58
Bell Robert, Esq., Eng., 298
Bellamy Edward, Esq., Sec., 205, 291, 301, 411, 422, 434, 489 ; Auditor, 191, 400
Bellamy William Henry, Esq., Sec., 558
Bellen George, Jun., Esq., 323
Bellis George, Esq., Eng., 62, 276
Benbow W. J., Esq , Audit Accountant, 209
Bennett Alfred, Esq., Auditor, 87
Bennett Daniel, Esq., 149
Bennett J., Esq., 43
Bennett Thomas, Esq., 18
Bennett Thomas, Esq., Accountant, 270
Benson, Sir John, 95 ; Eng., 96, 221
Benson Moses George, Esq., 428
Benson Ralph Augustus, Esq., 283, 423
Benson Robert, Esq., 61, 232, 434, 558
Benson Starling, Esq., 388

Bentley R. J., Esq., 373
Benyon Richard, Esq., M.P., 30
Berens Henry Hulse, Esq., 538
Beresford, Right Hon. Wm., 399
Berkley George, Esq., C.E., Eng., 539, 540, 542
Berry John, Esq., 290
Berryman William Chester, Esq., 136
Berwick Thomas J., Esq., Sec. and Eng., 187
Best H. P., Esq., 30
Bevan Theophilus, Esq., Auditor, 358
Bewley Samuel, Esq., Auditor, 123
Bibby John, Esq., 308, 367
Bickersteth John Pares, Esq., 33, 232, 354, 410, 433
Bickford John Solomon, Esq., 332
Bickham Spencer Henry, Esq., 115
Bidder George Parker, Esq., Eng., 234, 488, 511, 5i5
Bidder S. P., Esq., 532
Biddulph John, Esq., 224
Biddu ph, Col. Robert Myddleton, 141
Bigge John Frederick, Esq., 370
Bigge, Lieut.-Col. Thomas Edward, 75
Billson Henry, Esq., Auditor, 327
Binger J. O., Esq., Traff. Man., 232
Bingham, Right Hon. Lord, M.P., 169
Binstead, Capt. C. H., R.N., Pass. Supt., 209
Birch E., Esq., M I.C.E., Eng., 117, 348
Birch Wyrley, Esq., 401
Bird James Binfield, Esq., Auditor, 103
Bird, Major Robert Wilberforce, 356
Bird William, Esq., 560
Birkin Richard, Esq., 266
Birley Charles, Esq., 37
Birley Richard, Esq., 232, 250
Birley Thomas Langton, Esq., 37
Birley William, Esq., 153, 210
Biron Robert John, Esq., 140
Birt W., Esq., Goods Man., 165
Bishop C , Jun., Esq., Sec., 410
Bishop Frederic, Esq , 239
Bishop J., Esq., District Goods Man., 232
Blackett, Sir Edward, Bart., 370
Blacklock William T., Esq., 209
Blackmore Henry, Esq., Pass.-Supt., 209
Blackmore William, Esq., 126, 235, 345
Blagden George, Esq., 484
Blair James F., Esq., Eng., 86
Blake Charles, Esq., 14
Blake Henry Wollaston, 511, 526, 539
Blake Thomas, Esq., Auditor, 338
Blakeway R. C., Esq., Sec., 283, 428
Blakiston Douglas Yeoman, Esq., 364
Blakiston M. F., Esq , 384
Blanshard Richard, Esq., 376
Bliss William, Esq., 13
Blood John, Esq., 420
Bloomfield John Caldwell, Esq., D.L., 144
Blount, Sir E., Bart., 398
Blount William, Esq., 224
Bluett F. R., Esq., 129
Blyth B. and E., C.E., Engs., 70
Blyth Frederick, Esq., 176, 178
Blyth Henry Etheridge, Esq., 435
Blyth Philip Patten, Esq., 411
Boby Robert, Esq., 65
Bodenham Francis Lewis, Esq., 171, 449
Bodkin Robert, Esq., 14
Bogie George, Esq. Auditor, 118
Bolckow Henry W. F., Esq., 154
Bolden Henry, Esq., Eng., 22
Bolden Samuel Edward, Esq., 22, 186, 210

Bulteel Samuel William, Esq., Treas., 209
Bunn H. Lawrence, Esq., 189
Burbidge John Fowler, Esq., 312
Burbibge J. R., Esq., 295
Burbury S. H., Esq., 48, 224, 265
Burgess Edward Nathan, Esq., 369
Burke Edmund, Esq., 356
Burke Edmund, Esq., D.L., 94
Burke James B. Esq., Eng., 235, 412
Burke J. St. George, Esq , Q.C., 422
Burke, Sir Thomas J., Bart., 314
Burkill Isaac, Esq., 307
Burkitt William, Esq., 206
Burn, Major-Gen. Henry Pelham, 327
Burnaby, Major-Gen. Charles H., 308
Burnett —, Esq., Auditor, 385
Burnett Newell, Esq., 167
Burnett Robert Harvey, Esq., Eng. and
  Loco Supt., 260
Burrell John Stamp, Esq., 210
Burrell Walter Wyndham, Esq., 432
Burton W. H., Esq , Sec., 3 9
Bury, Right Hon. Viscount, M.P., 233
Bushby Thomas A., Esq , 49
Bushell William Done, Esq., 109, 226, 330
Butcher Richard, Esq., 428
Butler Augustine, Esq., D.L., 219
Butler, Hon. Henry Cavendish, D.L., 197
Butler Joseph, Esq., Sec., 184, 251
Butt Isaiah, Esq., Auditor, 346
Butterton William, Esq., Eng., 303
Buttle John W., Esq., Permanent Way
  Superintendent, 188
Buxton William, Esq., 375
Byng, Hon. James, 309, 367
Byrne James Lynch, Esq., Auditor, 127
Byrne Julian, Esq., Sec., 543
Byrne Patrick James, Esq., 131, 197
Bywater J. R., Esq., Auditor, 299

Cabry Joseph, Esq., Man., 39
Cabry Thomas, Esq., Eng., 299
Cadell Henry Esq., 42
Cahill Michael, Esq., 203, 415
Caithness, Right Hon. the Earl of, 61, 68,
  279, 386
Callan Philip, Esq., M.P., 197
Callow E. Bannister. Esq., Sec., 140
Calton John, Esq., Auditor, 164
Calverley Richard, Esq., 153
Campbell Colin Minton, Esq., 305
Campbell, Captain Farquhar, 70
Campbell George William, Esq., 554
Campbell, Sir Hugh Hume, Bart., 31
Campbell Robert, Esq., 149
Campbell Robert Orr, Esq., 298
Campbell-Davys W. D. H., Esq., 410
Camps Frederick, Esq., 142
Cane Edward, Esq., 170, 314
Cann William, Esq., Auditor, 147
Canuon John William, Esq., 14
Cape G. A., Esq., Sec., 503
Capel, Hon. R. Algernon, 180, 336, 407, 423
Capel William, Esq., 443
Capper Charles, Esq., 533
Carbutt Francis, Esq., 266, 404
Carden, Sir R. W., 339
Cardew Christopher Baldock, Esq., 229
Cardinall James, Esq., Auditor, 92
Carlisle William Thomas, Esq., 243
Carlyon Edmund, Esq., Auditor, 240
Carlyon John, Esq., 98
Carmichael, Sir James R., Bart., 192, 591
Carne J. W. N., Esq., D.C.L., 102, 226, 390
Carne Robert Charles Nicholl, Esq., 102

Carr Henry William, Esq., 343
Carr Hugh, Esq., Accountant, 256
Carr J D., Esq., 76
Carr Thomas H., Esq., Sec., 306
Carroll Joseph H., Esq., 94
Carroll William, Esq. Sec., 220
Carson James, Esq., 166
Carter F. H., Esq., C.A., Auditor, 139
Carter John, Esq , 212
Carter Richard, Esq., Auditor, 61
Cartmell Isaac, Esq., Auditor, 76
Cartwright Thomas, Esq., Traff. Man., 115
Cartwright William S., Esq., 318
Cary Joseph, Esq., 140, 180, 304, 319, 336,
  407, 423, 424, 455
Casement Edmund M'G., Esq., 81
Cash William, Esq., Auditor, 229, 548
Castle H. J., Esq., 103
Castle Michael, Esq., 52, 98, 365
Castleman Charles, Esq., 41, 147, 233
Cattle Henry, Esq., Sec. and Man., 88
Cattlow W. F , Esq., Auditor, 327
Caughey W. B., Esq., Auditor, 26
Caulfeild H. St. G., Esq., B.A., C.E., Eng.,
  287, 389
Caulfield, Colorel, J.P., 325
Cave George, Esq., 90, 277
Cave Thomas, Esq., M.P., 287, 389
Cavendish, Lord Frederick C., M.P., 158
Cawkwell William, Esq., Gen. Man., 232
Cecil, Lord Eustace, M.P., 309
Chadwick David, Esq., M.P., 248
Chadwick James, Esq., 165
Chaine James, Esq., 81
Challenor Bromley, Esq., Auditor, 4
Chamberlin H., Esq., 135
Chambers George H , Esq., 591
Chambers William, Esq., 251
Chambers, Right Hon. William, 316
Chambers William Grant, Esq., J.P., 211
Champion Alfred, Esq., 368
Chance James Timmins, Esq., 232
Chandler —, Esq., Auditor, 265
Chandler Charles, Esq., Sec., 327
Chaplin Ernest, Esq., 498
Chaplin Henry, Esq., M.P., 241
Chapman Abel, Esq., 265
Chapman C. H., Esq , Goods Man., 230
Chapman John, Esq., 152
Chapman John, Esq., Hill End, Mottram,
  247, 252, 254, 313
Chapman John , Esq., 124, Pall Mall, and
  Leadenhall Street, London, 116, 346, 541
Chapman T. Palmer, Esq., Auditor, 537
Chappell Frederick Patey, Esq., 54
Charlwood Robert, Esq., 149
Chase Robert, Esq., 257
Chawner Richard Croft, Esq., 74
Chenery Edgar, Esq , 257
Cheshire Edward, Esq., Auditor, 538, 558
Chesney, Major-General, R A., D.C.L.,
  F.R.S., F.R.G.S., 288 ; Eng., 468
Child Coles, Esq., 264
Child J. G. T., Esq., Auditor, 171, 252, 367,
  373
Child John, Esq., 343
Child, Sir Smith, Bart., M.P., 305
Childs James, Esq., 134, 302, 412
Ching John, Esq., 63, 82, 430
Chowne John Alfred, Esq., 352, 530
Christian C. L., Esq., Auditor, 198, 352
Christie Charles William. Esq., 224
Christie Hector, Esq., 335
Christie Peter, Esq., 290
Christison Alex., Esq., Pass. Supt., 99

Christopher William, Junr., Esq., 408
Chubb Harry, Esq., 301, 303
Chubb T. A., Esq., Sec., 367
Clancarty, Rt. Hon. The Earl of, 169, 270
Clanricarde, the Marquis of, K.P.,P.C., 314
Clapham Abraham, Esq., 307
Clark Charles Frederick, Esq., 447
Clark Francis, Esq., Auditor, 36
Clark James, Esq., 363
Clark Latimer, Esq., 533
Clark William, Esq., 97
Clarke Edwin, Esq., M.I.C.E., Eng., 79
Clarke F. L., Esq., 317
Clarke Frederick, Esq., Sec., 41, 233
Clarke George J., Esq., 28
Clarke George William, Esq., Sec., 248
Clarke John Creemer, Esq., 4
Clarke John Graham, Esq., J.P., 353
Clarke Joseph, Esq., 149
Clarke Joshua, Esq., 341
Clarke Seymour, Esq., Gen. Man., 163
Clarke Thomas, Esq., J.P., 93
Clarke William, Esq., Auditor, 136
Clarke William Barwick, Esq., 442
Clay James, Esq., M.P., 237
Clay Wentworth, Esq., Sec., 547
Clayton E. Edmund, Esq., Auditor, 65
Cleetsom F., Esq., Accountant, 171
Cleghorn John, Esq., Sec., 181, 299
Cleland John, Esq., 26, 120
Clerk Edmund Hugh, Esq., 136
Clerk James, Esq., 69, 70, 106
Clifford, Col. Henry Morgan, 3, 338
Clift J. E., Esq., 146, 331
Clifton, Colonel, 37
Clinch James, Esq., Auditor, 446
Clive George, Esq., M.P., 169
Clive, Lieut.-Col. the Hon. George H.W.W., M.P., 318
Clive H. B., Esq., 285
Cloncurry, Lord, 170
Close John, Esq., Sec., 431
Close Samuel H., Esq., Auditor, 124, 170
Close Thomas, Esq., 475
Clough Charles Butler, Esq., 62
Clouston Peter, Esq., 86, 163, 173
Coates Foster, Esq., Accountant, 406
Coates James, Esq., 126, 286
Coates William, Esq., J.P., 406
Cobb Edward, Esq., 308
Cobb Timothy Rhodes, Esq., 15, 61; Auditor, 303
Cobbold John Chevallier, Esq., 339, 399
Cochran James, Esq., 151
Cochran Robert, Esq., Sec., 297
Cockshott F. P., Esq., Supt. of Line, 168
Coddington W. H., Esq., Eng., 19, 21
Coey, Sir Edward, 81
Coffey David, Esq., 13
Coghlan Richard, Esq., Traff. Supt., 93
Cole, Colonel Arthur Lowry, C.B., 111
Cole Robert, Esq., 263
Coleman E. J., Esq., 201
Collard C. S., Esq., Sec., 412
Collin T., Esq., Goods Man., 209
Collins George Browne, Esq., 82
Collinson Timothy, Esq., 190
Collis C., Esq., Auditor, 263
Collis R. G., Esq., 93, 197; Auditor, 270
Collister John, Esq., C.E., Eng., 268
Collum Robert, Esq., M.D., 77
Colquhoun Isaac, Esq., 238
Colquhoun John Campbell, Esq., 162
Colthurst, Sir George C., Bart., M.P., 97
Colvill James C., Esq., 123

Colville, Rt. Hon. Lord, 168
Compton C. E., Esq., Supt., 98, 365
Comyn Richard, Esq., 359
Conder Henry, Esq., Assistant Supt. of Line, 168
Coningham W., Esq., 385
Connell James H., Esq., Sec., 93, 144
Conner Benjamin, Esq., Loco. Supt., 69
Connolly Thomas, Esq., M.P., 144
Constable Henry, Esq., 273
Conway Charles, Esq., 322
Conybeare H., Esq., M.I.C.E., Eng., 49, 95
Conyngham, Lord Francis, 151
Cook Edwin, Esq., 443
Cook Henry, Esq., Sec. and Gen. Man., 158
Cooke James S., Esq., Eng., 275
Cooke S. J., Esq., Sec., 490
Cooke Joseph, Esq., 216, 238
Cooke William Hyde, Esq., 396
Cookson Richard, Esq., Auditor, 37
Cooper C. J., Esq., Auditor, 283
Cooper Edward, Esq., 185
Cooper G. E., Esq., Sec., 134
Cooper George, Esq., 303
Cooper H. R., Esq., 156
Cooper J. B., Esq., Gen. Man., 327
Cooper John Douglas, Esq., J.P., 325
Cooper William, Esq., Auditor, 535
Copeland E. S., Esq., Auditor, 4
Copestake Samson, Esq., Auditor, 260
Copland Charles, Esq., Auditor, 93
Copperthwaite William Charles, Esq., 379
Corbet, Rev. Athelstan, 285
Corbet Henry Reginald, Esq., 285
Corbett, Captain, 207
Corbett John, Esq., 176
Cordon James, Esq., Goods Man., 305
Corrie Edgar, Esq., 92
Corry Edward, Esq., 421
Corscaden James, Esq., 238
Cossham Handel, Esq., 333
Cottam S. E., and Son, Accountants, 355
Cottingham J. G., Esq., 250
Cotton Edward J., Esq., Man., 28
Cotton and Flemyng, Engs., 93
Courtenay, Lord, M.P., 330
Cowan Alfred, Esq., 505
Cowan James, Esq., 145
Cowan John, Esq., 69, 106
Cowan Thomas, Esq., Traff. Supt., 123
Cowan William, Esq., Loco. Supt., 167
Cowan William, Esq., LL.D., Auditor, 256
Cowcill Thomas, Esq., Sec., 37
Cowie Thomas Stock, Esq., 539, 540
Cox Alfred, Esq., 523
Cox James, Junr., Esq., Auditor, 383
Craig —., Esq., Auditor, 292
Craig John, Esq., Auditor, 115
Crake William Hamilton, Esq., Auditor, 543
Cramsie John, Esq., 28
Crang John, Esq., 40
Cranstoun George Cranstoun Trotter, Esq., 31
Cranstoun John, Esq., Auditor, 397, 398
Craston John, Esq., Man., 35
Craven John, Esq., 200
Craven John Chester, Esq., Loco. and Car Supt. 229
Craven Jonathan Nowell, Esq., 200
Crawford Hugh, Esq., 106
Crawford James Henry, Esq., 77, 554
Crawford Robert Wigram, Esq., M.P., 537, 554
Crawford Thomas, Esq., J.P., 20

Creighton Robert, Esq., 76
Cresswell Charles Neve, Esq., 192
Cresy Theodore Grant, Esq., Sec., 8
Crewe Randolph, Esq., 454
Crockatt James, Esq., Sec., 278
Crofton, The Rt. Hon. Lord, 169
Croker, Capt. Edward Hare, 288
Crombie James, Esq., 167
Crompton C. E., Esq., Supt., 98
Cronskey J., Esq., 401
Cropper James, Esq., 210
Crosfield Henry, Esq., 79, 415 ; Auditor, 61, 210, 232, 301
Cross John, Esq., Sec., 509
Crossley, Sir Francis, Bart., M.P., 177
Crossley J. S., Esq., C.E., Eng., 159, 200, 266
Crosthwaite John F., Esq., Auditor, 88
Crowder Thomas M., Esq., 84
Crowdy George F., Esq., Sec., 149
Crowley Richard, Esq., 182
Cubitt Joseph, Esq., C.E., Eng., 92, 168
Cudworth James I'Anson, Esq., Loco. Supt., 367
Cudworth William, Esq., Eng., 379
Culley Robert, Esq., 123
Culverwell Joseph Pope, Esq., Sec. and Gen. Man., 124
Cuming Elias, Esq., 280
Cunningham George, Esq., Eng., 106
Cunningham Wm. C., Esq., Auditor, 28
Curling Edward, Esq., J.P., 330
Currie Geo. Wodehouse, Esq., 165, 234
Currey F. E., Esq., 87
Currey William, Esq., 87 ; Sec., 159
Curtis John, Esq., Sec., 1
Cusack Ralph S., Esq., Auditor, 270
Cutbill W. J., Esq., Sec., 483
Cutbill, Son, and De Lunge, Agents, 530
Cuthbertson W. B., Esq., 16

Dacre Joseph, Esq., 45
Daggs William, Esq., Sec., 214
Dakin, Mr. Alderman, 260, 261, 334, 527 ; Auditor, 516, 560
Dale David, Esq., Loco. Supt., 379
Dallas Alex. G., Esq., 119
Dallas, Sir Robert, Bart., 483
Dalrymple Hew, Esq., Sec., 55
Dalrymple James, Esq., 31
Dalton James, Esq., 89
Daniel J. F. R., Esq., Sec., 56
Daniell Henry, Esq., 245
Danvers Juland, Esq., 535, 537, 538, 539, 541, 543, 545
Darby Abraham, Esq., 3, 438, 450
Darby William Henry, Esq., 225, 409, 427, 452
D'Arcy, Major F., 144
Dartnell G. R., Esq., 185
Daubuz John Claude, Esq., 98, 430
Davey Arthur S., Esq., 6, 172
Davey Peter, Esq., 6, 172
Davidson Alexander, Esq., 113
Davidson Andrew, Esq., 69
Davidson Henry, Esq., 301
Davidson John D., Esq., Sec., 150
Davidson Patrick, Esq., 113
Davidson Robert, Esq., 150
Davidson Robert, Esq., Auditor, 119
Davidson Thomas, Esq., 150
Davies D., Esq., 72
Davies E. J. C., Esq., Sec., 408
Davies Evan, Esq., 333
Davies Evans Jones, Esq., Auditor, 358

Davies George Augustus Apreece, Esq., 408
Davies Isaac, Esq., Eng., 408
Davies, Rev. James, 207
Davies Thomas, Esq., 408
Davis H. W., Esq., Eng., 165
Davis Lewis, Esq., 318
Davis Neal, Esq., 169
Davis Richard, Esq., 376
Davis Thomas Henry, Esq., 396
Davis William, Esq., 397, 398
Davison Charles, Esq., 62
Davison Joseph, Esq., 39
Dawes George, Esq., 405
Dawson James, Esq., Accountant, 406
Dawson James William, Esq., 54
Dawson P. W., Esq., Sec., Appendix, p. 97
Dawson W. H., Esq., Sec., 311, 319
Dean Henry, Esq., 18
Dean Richard Ryder, Esq., 61, 79, 232, 301, 434, 537
Dean William F., Esq., 307
Deas James, Esq., Res. Eng., 298
De Castro J., Esq., Auditor, 547
Dees James, Esq., 362, 442
Delahunty James, Esq., M.P., 203, 415
Delap James B., Esq., 151
Deloitte W. W., Esq., Auditor, 227, 434
De Metz Augustus, Esq., 259
De Mornay Alfred, Esq., 558
De Mornay Edward, Esq., 558
Denison Christopher B., Esq., M.P., 168, 436
Denman, Hon. Richard, 309
Denne Robert Alured, Esq., 294
Denny Abraham, Esq., J. P., 420
Dent, Captain, R.N., Marine Supt., 232
Dent John Coucher, Esq., 445
Dent William, Esq., 510, 544
Dent William, Junr., Esq., 264, 510, 544
De Pass A. D., Esq., 198
De Rothschild, Baron M. Anthony, 485
De Rothschild, Baron Lionel N., 485
Derry W. Richard, Esq., 213
De Tivoli C., Esq., Sec., 497
Devaux —, Esq., 496
Devaux Alexander, Esq., 490
Devaux C. and Co., Agents, 492
De Vitre J. D., Esq., 537
Devitt R. J., Esq., Auditor, 130
Devon, The Right Hon. Earl of, 52, 205, 221, 261, 280, 330, 371
Devonshire, His Grace the Duke of, K.G., 87, 158
Dew W., Esq., Sec., 11
Dewar James, Esq., Auditor, 187
De Winton William, Esq., 49
Dickeson —, Esq., Sec., 521
Dickie David, Esq., Goods Traff. Man., 163
Dickinson Henry, Esq., 427
Dickson, Major Alex. George, M.P., 140
Dickson Benjamin, Esq., 19
Dickson James, Esq., 25
Dickson, Lieut.-Col. Samuel A., 221
Diggles Robert Edward, Esq., 32
Dillon John Henry, Esq., 180, 336, 423, 441
Dillon, Viscount, 361
Dillwyn Lewis L., Esq., M.P., 171
Dingley John, Esq., Sec., 213
Dinning Joseph, Esq., 187
Divett John, Esq., 280,
Dixon Edwin, Esq., 448
Dixon George Moore, Esq., 62, 276
Dixon Joshua, Esq., 230
Dixon Peter James, Esq., 76
Dixon R. S., Esq., 76

Hamer E., Esq., Traff. Man., 251
Hamilton, Colonel Sir Charles John James, Bart., C.B., 294
Hamilton F. A., Esq., 276
Hamlyn John, Esq., 60
Hamlyn Shilston Calmady, Esq., 116
Hammond Wm. Henry, Esq., 348
Hanam Robt. Chas., Esq., 92
Hanbury Philip, Esq., 237
Hand Robert Wm., Esq., Auditor, 232
Hands Richard, Esq., 101
Hardacre Richard, Esq., 335
Harden Henry, Esq., Loco. Supt., 123
Hardie William, Esq., Goods Man., 293
Harding E. W., Esq., 285
Harding James, Esq., 97
Harding R. P., Esq., Auditor, 549
Hardy George, Esq., 358
Hardy Peter, Esq., 450
Hare Humphrey John, Esq., 246 307, 435
Hare Theodore J., Esq., 209
Harenc H. B., Esq.. 221
Hargreaves John, Esq., 209
Harington, Sir Henry Byng, 538
Harkness W. Mc.N., Esq., Eng., 205
Harley F., Esq., Sec., 75
Harper Edward, Esq., Auditor, 171, 242
Harris Charles, Esq., 71
Harris Edward, Esq., Gen. Man., 463
Harris George, Esq., 71
Harris George Henry, Esq., Sec., 147
Harris George W., Esq., Sec., 157, 176, 178
Harris Thomas, Esq.. 71
Harrison Charles, Esq., 321
Harrison Frederick, Esq., 251
Harrison George, Esq., 118, 293
Harrison George, Esq., Sec. and Gen. Man. 277
Harrison G. K., Esq., 382
Harrison Henry, Esq., 337
Harrison Henry, Esq., 500
Harrison O. B. C., Esq., 430
Harrison Richard, Esq., Auditor, 331
Harrison Thomas E., Esq., Eng.. 299
Harrison William Bealey, Esq., 74
Hart Chas. F., Esq., Sec., 30, 443
Hart David, Esq., 23
Hartley Gilfred William, Esq., 256
Hartley James, Esq., 299
Hartridge William, Esq., 359, 493, 535
Harty Marcus, Esq., Res. Eng., 124
Harvey Edmund, Esq., Sec., 92 ; Auditor 30, 77
Harvey, Sir R. B., Bart., 201
Harvey Thomas S., Esq., 220 : Auditor, 416
Harvie Alexander, Esq., 38, 298
Hasell E. W., Esq., 210
Haslewood Lewis H., Esq., 546
Hastings George W., Esq., 412
Hastings, Admiral Sir Thos., K.C.B., 214
Haswell George, Esq., Auditor, 225, 409
Hattersley Edwin Greaves, Esq., 200
Hatton James, Esq., 209
Haughton James, Esq., Auditor, 170
Haughton William, Esq., 125, 170
Hawes William, Esq., 134, 302, 412
Hawkins Charles Henry, Esq., 89
Hawkins Charles Titian, Esq., Auditor, 446
Hawkins George, Esq., Traff. Man., 229
Hawkins James, Esq., 123
Hawkins, Colonel Septimus M., 399
Hawkins William Bailey, Esq.. 79
Hawkshaw John, Esq., C.E., F.R.S., Eng., 134, 308, 318, 465, 538, 543, 560

Hay A. Penrose, Esq., Auditor, 119, 386
Hay George, Esq., 279
Hay, Sir John C. D., Bart., M.P., 161, 326
Hay Thomas J., Esq., C.E., Acting Eng. 182
Hayes Michael, Esq., 94
Haymen Henry, Esq., 535
Hayne Charles Seale, Esq., 110, 365, 556
Hays R. B., Esq.. Auditor, 132
Hazard William Martin, Esq., 402
Head Francis S., Esq., 527
Head George Head, Esq., 210, 442
Head Robert Thomas, Esq , 240, 293
Head W. G., Esq., Auditor, 359
Hean David, Esq., 10
Heane Robert, Esq., Auditor, 266
Hearn Henry, Esq., Auditor. 15
Heath Robert A., Esq , 138, 560
Heaton William Barnard, Esq.. 295
Hector Thomas, Esq., Traffic Cashier, 167
Hedley Thomas, Esq., Auditor, 39
Hegan John, Esq., 546, 549
Heginbottom G., Esq , 186
Helps Arthur, Esq., 36
Hemans George Willoughby, Esq., C.E., Eng., 13, 14, 111, 122, 144, 203, 295, 296, 368, 400
Heming W. T., Esq., Auditor, 331
Hemingway Edward V., Esq,, 91
Henchman John, Esq., Sec., 260, 262
Hender Thomas, Esq., 213
Henderson George, Esq.. Auditor, 365
Hendrey James, Esq., 157, 533
Heneage Edward, Esq., 241
Henly Robert, Jun., Esq., 71
Henly Thomas Large, Esq., 71
Henniker-Major, the Hon. J.M., M.P., 257,
Henry David J., Esq., 111, 400
Henry Joseph, Esq., 236
Henry Robert, Esq., 14
Henry William, Esq., 295
Henshaw Alfred, Esq., Traff. Man., 49
Henty George, Esq., J.P., 85
Herapath Spencer, Esq., 548
Herbert, Hon. R. C., 72
Heriot William, Esq., 290
Herniman R., Esq., 437
Heron James, Esq., J.P., 26
Heseltine Edward, Esq.. 523
Hewett John Edward Stower, Esq., Sec., 338
Hewitt John, Esq., 353
Hewlett Alfred. Esq., 208
Heygate Wm. Unwin, Esq., 266
Heys John, Esq., 106
Heysham, Rev. John, 324
Heywood Arthur, Esq., 594
Heywood J. Pemberton, Esq., 309, 546, 594
Heyworth Lawrence, Jun., Esq., 548, 549
Hibbert John T., Esq., M.P., 210, 313
Hichens John, Esq., 40
Hickie John, Esq., 5
Hicks R.. Esq., Sec., 198, 352
Higgins F., Esq., Sec., 450
Higgins, Lieut.-Col. Wm. Bartholomew, 24
Higgs William, Esq., Auditor, 377
Hill Charles, Esq., 190
Hill Charles, Esq., 264
Hill John, Esq., Eng., 267
Hill P. Grenfell, Esq., Sec., 183
Hill, Hon. Rowland Clegg, 355
Hill Samuel, Esq., 20
Hill Thomas, Esq.,69, 106, 139, 303
Hill Thomas Rowley, Esq., 449
Hill Thomas William, Esq., 390

Jamieson Michael James, Esq., 67
Janson John C., Esq., Sec., 339
Jaques John, Esq., Loco. Supt., 209
Jarrett, Capt C. B., 353
Jarvis Lewis Whincop, Esq., 206, 269
Jayne John, Esq., 59, 408
Jebb Richard George, Esq., 141 ; Auditor, 355
Jeffers Patrick David, Esq., 94
Jefferson Henry, Esq., 442
Jeffreys Henry, Esq., 408
Jeffryes Samuel, Esq., Sec., 272, 533
Jeggins E., Esq., 295
Jeggins Samuel, Esq., Auditor, 295
Jenkin, Tratham and Triscot, Engs., 240, 293
Jenkins Robert Castle, Esq., 505
Jenner Robert Francis Lascelles, Esq., 22
Jeremy David, Esq., Auditor, 410
Jessop William, Esq., 107
Jobling Edward, Esq., Auditor, 442
Jobson David, Esq., 10
Johns Jasper Wilson, Esq., J.P., 23, 72, 80, 265, 268, 455
Johnson Charles John, Esq., 321
Johnson James, Esq., Eng., 305
Johnson Joseph. Esq., 258
Johnson Richard, Esq., Eng., 168
Johnson S. W., Esq., Loco. Supt., 165
Johnson T. Marr, Esq., Eng.-in-Chief, 261, 262
Johnson W. E., Esq., Sec., 108, 201, 350
Johnson William James, Esq., 187
Johnston, Capt., 197
Johnston, Major-Gen. C. C., Sec., 544
Johnston Edward, Esq., 549
Johnston George B., Esq., 81
Johnston, Capt. James Gilbert, 41, 147, 233, 434, 541
Johnston R. E., Esq., Eng., 33, 354, 433
Johnstone David, Esq., 173
Johnstone Harcourt, Esq., 299
Johnstone James, Esq., Auditor, 85
Johnstone John, Esq., 425
Johnstone William, Esq., Eng. and Man., 163
Joliffe Jonathan, Esq., 199
Jonasshon Moses John, Esq., 391
Jones Benjamin Heywood, Esq , 594
Jones Charles Henry, Esq., 266
Jones D. H., Esq., C.E., Eng., 388
Jones Edward Stewart, Esq., 259
Jones Frederick Pembroke, Esq., 34 ; Sec., 27
Jones John, Esq., 1
Jones John, Esq., 84
Jones John, Esq., Sec., 100, 452
Jones J. Williams, Esq., 23
Jones Thomas M. Hamilton, Esq., 28
Jones William Price, Esq., 100
Jopp Charles, Esq., C.E., Eng., 118
Jordan Gustavus, Esq., Auditor, 77
Jose Thomas Porter, Esq., 430
Joseph David, Esq., 333
Joseph Thomas. Esq., 333
Joyce Charles, Esq., 503
Judd, Major C. H., 235
Judge Joseph Spencer, Esq., 538

Kavanagh Arthur, Esq., M.P., 203, 418
Kay J. R., Esq., 209
Kay Thomas, Esq., Goods Man., 232, 414
Kaye Robert, Esq., 38, 167
Keane Marcus, Esq., 219
Keary Hall W., Esq., 50

Keate Henry, Esq., 276
Keeling George Baker, Esq., Sec., 353
Keeling George Wm., Esq., Res. Eng., 353
Kelly H. W., Esq., Sec., 122
Kelson Charles. Esq., 268, 511
Kempthorne John, Esq., 347
Kemshead Henry Morris, Esq., 301
Kendall Edmund, Esq., 155
Kendall George, Esq., Sec., 360
Kendall William, Esq., Loco. Supt., 39
Kenderdine Isaac, J., Esq., 95
Kennard Adam S., Esq., 546, 549
Kennard Coleridge J., Esq., 510
Kennard John Pierse, Esq., 509, 546
Kennard Robert William, Esq., 165, 309, 376, 509, 544
Kennaway William, Esq. Auditor, 147
Kennedy James, Esq., 297
Kennedy James Birch, Esq., J.P., 20 ; Auditor, 144
Kennedy, Lieut.-Col., J.P., Eng., 535
Kennell John F., Esq., Sec., 228, 234
Kenrick Timothy, Esq., 266, 400 ; Auditor, 463
Ker Hugh, Esq., 362
Kerr John, Esq., 173
Kerr Henry, Esq., 156 ; Auditor, 70, 86
Kerrich Edward, Esq., 191
Kerrison, Sir Edward, Bart., 257
Kershaw James, Esq., 115
Keyden James, Esq., Sec., 38, 67, 106, 162, 174
Keyden Theodore E., Esq., Auditor, 162
Kimber E., Esq., Auditor, 381
Kimber Henry, Esq., 542
Kime William Thomas, Esq., 241
Kincaid Joseph, Esq., 125, 127, 128
Kincaid Joseph, Esq., Eng.-in-Chief, 127, 128, 249, 300
King James, Esq., 86
King James King, Esq., 214
King Nicholas, Esq., M.D., 94
King Richard King Meade, Esq., 52, 363
King William, Esq., Sec., 210
King William Charles, Esq., 164, 171, 426
King William Thomas Poole, Esq., 52
Kingsford Henry Esq., 111
Kinloch George, Esq., 10
Kinnaird, Hon. Arthur F., M.P., 61
Kirk William, Esq., M.P., 295
Kirkman James, Esq., Sec. and Man., 253 ; Man., 313
Kirkwood Hugh, Esq., 162
Kirkwood John Townsend, Esq., 48, 224
Kirtley Matthew, Esq., Loco. Supt., 266
Kirwan Denis, Esq., D.L., 13, 14
Kitching Alfred, Esq., 299, 379
Kitson James, Esq., 224, 299
Kitson, Major, 532
Kitson William, Esq., 395
Knight Andrew Rouse Boughton, Esq., 243
Knight Charles Raleigh, Esq., 384
Knight Edward, Esq., 263
Knight George, Esq., 110
Knight John M., Esq., 77
Knight J. P., Esq., Traffic Supt., 367
Knowles Thomas, Esq., 208
Knox Edward C., Esq., 28
Knox, Major Lawrence Edward, M.P., 127, 128
Knox, Colonel The Hon. William Stewart, M.P., 325
Koch J. E. Campbell, Esq., 34, 400
Kynaston Roger, Esq., 231
Kynock John, Esq., 150

Powell, Lieut.-Col. W. T. R., 251
Power Edmond, Esq., 203, 415, 420
Power, Sir James, Bart., 130
Powerscourt, Viscount, 46
Powis, the Right Hon. the Earl of, 355
Powrie James, Esq., 12
Preston, Sir J. H., Bart., 135
Preston John Wilby, Esq., 374
Preston Richard M., Esq., 105
Price Bonamy, Esq., 510
Price James, Esq., Res. Eng., 270
Price R. E., Esq., 255
Price R. J. D., Esq., 100
Price Richard Green, Esq., M.P., 2, 207, 244, 449
Price S., Esq., Auditor, 24, 337
Price Thomas, Esq., Auditor, 408
Price Thomas, Esq., Auditor, 207
Price Wm. Philip, Esq., M.P., 164, 266, 365, 400, 404, 4;3
Prideaux Walter, Esq., Auditor, 376
Pridham George, Esq., 365
Priestman Samuel, Esq., 299
Pritchard Henry, Esq., 11
Procter Charles Edward, Esq., 248
Propert John, Esq., 77
Prowse A. P., Esq., Acct., 365
Pryce Robert Davis, Esq., 72
Pryor Francis, Esq., 332
Pulleine James, Esq., 431
Purcell George, Esq., Sec., 97, 429
Purchas S. G., Esq., Eng., 396
Purdon W., Esq., Eng., 89
Purser Edward, Esq., M.I.C.E., Eng., 490
Purves Allan, Esq., Auditor, 31
Purvis John, Esq., 342

Quelch J. G., Esq., Mineral Traff. Man., 299
Quilter William, Esq., 89, 271, 503
Quinn Peter, Esq., 297

Radcliffe Joshua, Esq., 177, 209, 242
Railton Lancelot, Esq., Sec., 394
Ramage Robert, Esq., Loco. Eng., 270
Rammell T. W., Esq., Eng., 422
Ramsay, Sir George, 10
Ramsay, Major John, 167
Ramsey R. B. Wardlaw, Esq., 316
Ramsbottom J., Esq., Mechanical Eng., 232
Ramsden James, Esq., 158
Randall Alexander, Esq., 249
Rankin Thomas Wright, Esq., 57
Ransford A., Esq., Auditor, 43
Raphael John, Esq., Auditor, 406
Ratcliff Thos. Wrake, Esq., Auditor, 228
Rate Lachlan Mackintosh, Esq., 138, 268, 479
Ravenhill John, Esq., 57
Rawcliffe John, Esq., 153
Rawnsley, Rev. Edward, 374
Rawson Philip, Esq., 523
Read Robert Arthur, Esq., Sec. and Gen. Man., 64, 363
Reay Stephen, Esq., Sec., 131, 232
Reed B. B., Esq., 475
Reed Charles, Esq., M.P., 273
Reed George, Esq., 4, 64, 363
Reed James, Esq., 358
Rees Richard J., Esq., Chief Acct., 363
Rees William, Esq., 282; Auditor, 410
Reeves Edmund, Esq., 9
Reid Lostock R., Esq., 539, 540, 544
Reilly John, Esq., 297
Reilly John Temple, Esq., J.P., D.L., 20, 123

Relph George Relph Greenhow, Esq., 90, 150
Rendall J., Esq., Auditor, 395
Rendel A. M., Esq., Eng., 537
Renton J. B., Esq., Sec., 373|
Revell W. E., Esq., Auditor, 72
Reynolds Wm., Esq., M.D., 62, 306, 619, 594
Rhodes J., Esq., Auditor, 373
Ribblesdale, Right Hon. Lord, 335
Ricardo A. and W., Agents, 488
Rich, Sir Henry, Bart., 547
Richards Charles, Esq., Sec., 225, 409
Richards E., Esq., Eng., 132
Richards Edward, Esq., 11, 338
Richards E. Vaughan, Esq., 512
Richardson Charles, Esq., Eng., 57
Richardson Joseph Strangman, Esq., 219, 416
Richardson R. T., Esq., 154
Richardson Samuel, Esq., Sec., 258
Richardson Thomas, Esq., 163
Richardson Thompson, Esq., 394
Richardson William, Esq., Auditor, 250
Richardson W. T., Esq., Sec., 154
Rigby William, Esq., 239
Rigden William, Esq., 201
Ring George Charles, Esq., 271; Auditor, 13;
Ritchie Robert, Esq., Surveyor, 291, 422
Ritson Robert, Esq., 256
Roach Henry, Esq., Sec., 430
Robartes Thomas James Agar, Esq., 98, 183
Robbins Richard, Esq., 101
Roberts Arthur T., Esq., 105, 276
Roberts David, Esq., Sec., 109; Account ant, 105
Roberts Edward, Esq., 413, 419
Roberts Hugh Beaver, Esq., 105
Roberts J., Esq., 413
Roberts J. H., Esq., Traffic Supt. 232
Roberts Samuel, Esq., 373
Roberts T. D., Esq., M.I.C.E., Eng., 49, 207
Roberts, Sir Thomas H., Bart, 460
Roberts W., Esq., Sec., 23, 49, 50, 207, 328
Roberts William, Esq., 12
Roberts Wm., Esq., Supt. of Line, 188
Robertson Alex. Inglis, Esq., 188
Robertson David, Esq., M.P., 548
Robertson George, Esq., Accountant, 390
Robertson George, Esq., W.S., 31, 118, 298
Robertson Henry, Esq., C.E., 503; Eng., 100, 225, 409, 427, 452
Robertson J., Esq., Supt., 165
Robertson James R., Esq., 301
Robertson John, Esq., 2, 100, 225, 409, 452
Robertson L. R., Esq., Auditor, 86
Robinson and Rooking, Auditors, 160
Robinson Charles H., Esq., Auditor, 415
Robinson James Edward, Esq., 447
Robinson John Frederick, Esq., 91
Robinson Joseph, Esq., 218, 219, 220, 416, 427, 438, 450
Robinson Richard, Esq., 56
Robinson Smith P., Esq., Auditor, 252
Robinson Stephen, Esq., 49, 2t7, 317
Robinson William, Esq., 190
Robson Charles, Esq., Auditor, 379
Robson John Stephenson, Esq., 341
Robson Neil, Esq., C.E., 173
Robson William, Esq., Auditor, 131
Roche Thomas Redington, Esq., 13
Rodd Francis, Esq., 82
Roddy Peter Robert, Esq., Eng., 419, 421
Roden W. S., Esq., M.P., 250
Rodenhurst William, Esq., 285

Rodger James, Esq., 86, 163, 173
Rodwell Hunter, Esq., Q.C., 65
Roe Peter, Esq., Supt., 297
Rogers John Jope, Esq., 183
Rogers Reginald, Esq.. Auditor, 98
Rogers Thomas Eales, Esq., 395
Rolle, Right Hon. Mark G. Kerr, 116
Rolls James, Esq., 166
Rolls John Allen, Esq., 3
Rolls Thomas, Esq., 166
Romney, Right Hon. Earl of, 249
Ronald John, Esq., S.S C., 31, 298
Ronald Thomas, Esq., Accountant, 156
Ronaldson Alex., Esq., 162, 163, 173, 174
Ronayne J. P., Esq., 429
Room Benjamin, Esq., Sec., 169
Roose Benjamin, Esq., 11
Roper Richard Steven, Esq., 322
Roscoe William, Esq., Sec., 554
Rose Philip, Esq., 227, 505
Rose, Sir William, K.C.B., 337
Rose William, Esq., 454
Roseley John, Esq., 343
Ross Edward, Esq., Sec., 247, 252. 313, 405
Ross John, Esq., 81
Ross John, Jun., Esq., 16
Ross, The Very Rev. the Dean of, 121
Roupell T. B.. Esq., 541
Routledge John, Esq., Loco. Supt., 227
Rowbotham H., Esq., Sec., 447
Rowcliffe Charles, Esq., 438
Rowcliffe Charles Edward, Esq., Sec. 349,438
Rowe J. G., Esq., Sec., 15
Rowlands John, Esq., 99
Rowlands John William, Esq., 99
Russell Alexander, Esq., 279
Russell Arthur, Esq., Auditor, 215
Russell John, Esq., Traff. Man., 442
Russell John, Esq., 90
Russell Richard, Esq., 219
Russell Robert, Esq., J.P., 151
Russell, Sir William, Bart., C.B., M.P., 132
Russell Thompson, Esq., 220
Rutherford James, Esq., Audit Clerk, 167
Ruttledge David, Esq., 14
Ruxton J. F., Esq., 19
Ruxton Thomas, Esq., 5, 113
Ryan Michael, Esq., J.P., 96
Ryde E , Esq., Surveyor, 308
Rye, Capt. R. T.,97
Rylands John, Esq., 248

Sacré Charles, Esq., Eng., 247, 313, 373, 405; Eng. and Loco. Supt., 252
Salisbury, Marquis of, 165, 275 399
St. Aubyn John, Esq., M.P., 183
St. Barbe George Foster, Esq., 245
St. Paul, Sir Horace, Bart., 310
Salkeld Joseph, Esq., Auditor, 210
Salkeld, Lieut.-Col., 69, 326, 362
Salt Thomas, Junr., Esq., 125, 305
Sampson M. B., Esq., 560
Samuda Jonathan, Esq., Aud.,247; Sec., 305
Samuel James, Esq., F.R.A.S., Con. Eng., 273, 554
Samuel John, Esq., 560
Sandars Thomas Collett, Esq., 117, 489, 554
Sandon, Viscount, M.P., 305
Sargent Henry, Esq., Sec., 203
Sarle Allen, Esq., Sec., 229
Satterthwaite Edward Hughes, Esq., 210
Saul Silas, Esq., Auditor. 324
Saunders Fred. George, Esq., 272, Sec., 171
Saunders George F., Esq., Sec., 227
Saunders Hugh Ward, Esq., 424

Saunders W. A. F., Esq., 210
Savage Charles Walter, Esq., 277
Savage Thomas Edward, Esq., 311
Sayer Robert B., Esq., Eng., 277
Scarbrough J. L., Esq., 349
Scarth W. T., Esq., 394
Schreober Charles A , Esq., 195
Schroeder John Henry and Co., Agents, 593, 595
Schuster Leo, Esq., 191, 385,
Sclanders William, Esq., Auditor. 150
Scott Archibald, Esq., Traff. Man., 233
Scott Hercules, Esq., 278
Scott James, Esq., 195, 385
Scott John Hindley Wright, Esq., 190
Scott M. R., Esq., Sec., 542
Scott Russell, Esq., 260
Scott, Sir Sibbald David, Bart,, 320
Seafield, Right Hon. the Earl of, 188
Seargeant L. J Esq., Sec., 98; Sec. and Gen. Man., 365
Seath John, Esq., Auditor, 202, 337
Sedgefield James Badcock, Esq., 4
Sedgefield W. J., Esq., Sec., 4
Sedgwick F. W , Esq., 95, 221, 419, 421, 429
Seebohm Frederick, Esq., 339
Self Edward, Esq., 246, 435
Senhouse Joseph Pocklington, Esq., 256
Sers Peter, Esq., 311
Severn John Percy, Esq., 214
Sewell Philip E., Esq., 77
Sexty John James, Esq., 445
Seymour G. E., Esq., 498
Seymour George Hicks, Esq., 299
Seymour Henry Danby, Esq., 55, 346, 363, 444
Shackleton Abraham, Esq., 122
Shand Alexander, Esq., 252
Shand John B., Esq., Sec., 334
Sharp, Major Jelf, 230
Sharp Richard, Esq., Auditor, 245
Sharpe William John, Esq., 152
Sharples Joseph, Esq., 339
Shaw Edmund, Esq., 282
Shaw George, Esq., 19
Shaw J., Esq., Traffic Man., 232
Shaw John, Esq., Sec., 367
Shaw Joseph, Esq., 171
Shaw Thomas, Esq., Man., 406
Shearer Bettsworth Pitt, Esq., 320
Sheldon H. J., Esq., 268
Shelford and Robinson, Engs., 294
Sheppard Samuel Gurney, Esq , 126, 265, 286
Sherlcliff William, Esq., Auditor, 447
Sherriff Alexander Clunes, Esq., M P., 17, 43, 202, 260, 261, 262, 319, 382, 426, 449, 450
Sheward George, Esq., 131, 232, 434, 500, 533
Shield Mathew, Esq., Sec., 212
Shilson Daniel, Esq., 63, 213
Short Thomas, Esq., Sec., 523
Shortland Willoughby, Esq., 205
Shum James, Esq., 399
Shute John, Esq., Auditor, 57
Sim Alexander, Esq., Auditor, 465
Sim, Colonel George, R.E.. 538
Simms John, Esq., Sec., 19
Simms Reuben, Esq., Auditor, 19, 21
Simpson C. T., Esq., 334
Simpson George, Esq., Accountant, 298
Simpson James, Esq., 198
Simpson John, Esq., 88
Simpson Lightly, Esq., 165, 234, 246, 355, 3 9, 404
Simpson Thomas, Esq , Loco. Supt., 49
Sinclair Arthur, Esq., 236

Woollcombe Thomas, Esq., 98, 213, 280, 365
Woodward George Rocke, Esq., 56
Worms George. Junr., Esq., 261
Worthington S. B., Esq., Supt. Permanent Way, 232
Worthington William, Esq., 247, 305
Wragge Alfred, Esq., Sec. and Man., 355
Wragge Frederick, Esq., Sec., 250
Wren Joseph, Esq., Auditor, 297
Wright Edward, Esq., 556
Wright Francis, Esq., 107
Wright Harry Lennard, Esq., 425
Wright John, Esq., Loco. Supt., 365
Wright John, Esq., 107 ; Engineer, 77, 249, 300
Wright Joseph, Esq., 129
Wright Richard Seaton, Esq., 286 ¹¹
Wrigley James, Esq., Auditor, 242
Wroughton, Colonel G. W., 30
Wyatt George, Esq., 6, 192 ; Auditor, 172
Wyatt Osmond A., Esq., 90, 277, 450, 455
Wyld James, Esq., 40
Wyley Francis, Esq., 101
Wyley William, Esq., 50
Wylie A. H., Esq., Auditor, 299

Wylie Andrew, Esq., 215
Wyllie James F., Esq., 69, 70, 104
Wynn, Sir Watkin Williams, Bart., M.P., 171, 225, 426
Wynne, Colonel Charles Robert, 300
Wynne, Right Hon. John, 361
Wynne Thomas, Esq., 375
Wythes George Edward, Esq., 229

Yates R., Esq., Sec., 356
Yates William, Esq., Loco. Supt., 209
Young A., Esq., Accountant, 77
Young A. W., Esq., 526
Young George, Esq., Auditor, 388
Young George, Esq., 198
Young Harry, Esq., 118
Young James, Esq., 162
Young John, Esq., 28
Young John, Esq., Auditor, 69, 72, 527
Young R., and Sons, Engs, 156
Young Richard, Esq. 165, 275, 319, 447
Young Robert, Esq., 38, 86, 298
Young Robert, Esq., Man. and Sec., 156

Zingler Maximilian, Esq., Sec., 479

3.—DIRECTORS AND OFFICERS OF AUXILIARY ASSOCIATIONS.

Adams William Alexander, Esq., 614
Anderson, Sir James, 600 ; Gen. Supt., 605
Andrew William Patrick, Esq., 606
Andrews W., Esq. Man. and Sec., 624
Armstrong B. J., Esq., Auditor, 613
Austin William, Esq., 611

Balfour, Major-General G., C.B., 602
Ball John, Esq., Auditor, 610
Barker Henry James, Esq., Sec., 602
Barton George Kingston, Esq., M.D., 613
Batten John W., Esq., Manager, 604
Beloe H. C., Esq., Auditor, 601
Bevan Francis A., Esq., 597
Bewley Henry. Esq., 597
Bewley John, Jun., Esq., Auditor, 601
Bidder G. P., Esq., 599, 603
Blackburn H. W. and J., Accountants,, 601
Blackie John, Jun., Esq., 601
Blades Charles, Esq., 609
Blount Edward, Esq., 606
Blyth Philip Patton, Esq., 622
Borradaile John, Esq., 610
Boughton Edmund. Esq., 619
Boulnois William Allen, Esq., 614
Bramley-Moore John, Esq., 606
Brassey Thomas, Esq., 603
Brassey Thomas. Jun., Esq., M.P., 606
Bray Joseph, Esq., 604
Bridges Henry, Esq., Sec., 614
Bright E. B., Esq., Sec. and Gen. Man., 601
Bright, Sir Charles T., Eng., 622
Brogden Alexander, Esq., M.P., 609
Brooks Samuel, Esq., 618
Brown Henry, Esq., Gen. Man., 612
Browning C. L., Esq., 612, 619
Burnand George, Esq., 615
Burt John T., Esq., Sec., 600
Butler R. J., Esq., Sec., 606
Byng, Hon. James, 622

Caithness, The Earl of, 603
Campbell Alexander Henry, Esq., 621
Capper George Copeland, Esq., Auditor, 620
Carmichael, Sir James R., Bart., 601, 620
Chadwicks, Adamson, Collier, & Co., Auditors, 598
Carlton William, Esq., Assistant Sec., 598
Chatteris Henry, Esq., Auditor, 611
Chaytor Matthew Hutton, Esq., 615
Churchill, Lord Alfred S., 624
Clare S. M., Esq., Sec., 620
Clark Latimer, Esq., M.I.C.E., Eng., 600, 622 ; Eng. and Electrician, 605
Clarke Edwin Esq., Auditor, 603
Coats Peter, Esq., 599
Cole Wm. R., Esq., Auditor, 620
Colville Eden, Esq., 607
Cooke W. F., Esq., 603
Croll Alexander Angus, Esq., C.E., 624
Cropper Edward., Esq, 601
Cunard, Sir Edward, Bart., 599
Cuningham A. Fairlie, Esq., 602
Curtoys Charles, Esq., Sec. and Man., 611
Cutler F. Egerton, Esq., 616

Dakin, Mr. Alderman Thomas, 633, Auditor, 620
Davenport John Gladstone, Esq., 623
Dean Joshua, Esq., Auditor, 597
Deane John C., Esq., Sec., 597
Dent William, Esq., 622
Derry David S., Esq., Sec., 604
De Stern, Baron Herman, 608
Devaux Alexander, Esq., 606
De Vitre Edward Denis, Esq., M.D., 609
Downing, Major-General, 616
Dunn John B., Esq., Sub-Manager, 610
Dyer Charles K., Esq., 601, 611
Dyson E. Ehret, Esq., 610

Earle C. W., Esq., 603
Edwards Francis, Esq., 620
Elliott Ralph, Esq., 621
Elsey, Col. William, H.E.I.C.S., 624
Everitt George Allen, Esq., 617
Everitt William E., Esq., 612, 619

Fagg George, Esq., 618
Fenwick Charles Richard, Esq., 615
Field Cyrus W., Esq., 597
Fleming William, Esq., 609
Flemmich John Fred., Esq., 608
Ford W. B., Esq., Auditor, 602
Forde Henry Charles, Esq., M.I.C.E., Eng.,
  600 ; Eng. and Electrician, 605
Foster S. L., Esq., 616
Fowler John, Esq., Eng., 613
France J. R., Esq., Acting Eng., 620
Franklin J. A., Esq., Auditor, 622
Fraser James, Esq., 610

Galsworthy Edwin H., Esq., 608
Gibb Wm., Esq., 601
Gilpin Charles, Esq., M.P., 613
Glass Francis, Esq., Auditor, 597
Glass, Sir R. A., 597
Glover, Lieut.-Col., R.E., 600
Gooch, Sir Daniel, Bart., M.P., 597, 621
Grant, Capt. J., R.A., 620
Greaves Edward, Esq., 624
Griffin Matthias Royce, Esq., 614
Griffiths Frederick J., Esq., Sec., 605
Griffiths Henry, Esq., 614
Grimston, The Hon. Robert, 597, 599, 603
Grinnell Cornelius, Esq., 605
Gurney Samuel, Esq., 599, 620
Gwyther Edwin, Esq., 612

Hackblock John. Esq., 610
Hale, Mr. Alderman, 613
Hall, Admiral W. H., R.N., K.C.B., 622
Halsey Edward J., Esq., 605
Hamilton, Capt. A. T., 597
Hamilton Edward W. T., Esq., M.P., 607
Hannay Anthony, Esq., 601
Harbord, The Hon. Ralph, 624
Harding R. Palmer, Esq., Auditor, 603
Harrison Henry, Esq., 601, 604
Hasluck Daniel S., Esq., 612
Haughton William, Esq., 601
Hay, Right Hon. Lord John, M.P., C.B.,
  R.N., 621
Hay Robert Brice, Esq., 624
Hay, Lord William, 600
Haymen Henry, Esq., 616
Heath Herbert, Esq., Sec., 616
Heath Robt. A., Esq., 608
Heaton Ralph, Esq., 619
Henchman John, Esq., Sec., 613
Hendrey James, Esq., 604
Hervey, Lord Alfred, 599
Hilliard William Edward, Esq., 617
Hodgson James Stewart, Esq., 607
Hodson Thomas, Esq., 598
Holden James, Esq., 598
Holliday William, Esq., 612, 619
Holme James, Esq., 601
Hornby Thomas D., Esq., 600, 601
Horton Joshua, Esq., 619
Hughes, Professor D. E., 624
Hughes John C. Esq., Auditor, 603
Hunt Walter, Esq., Sec., 599

Jenkin Fleeming, Esq., F.R.S., M.I.C.E.,
  Eng. and Electrician, 605.

Johnson Richard William, Esq., 617
Johnson Thomas Marr, Esq., 613
Johnston, Captain James Gilbert, 597, 599
Johnston Edward, Esq., 601
Jones S. W., Esq., Auditor, 613

Keep Joseph Scrivener, Esq., 614
Kelk John, Esq., Contractor, 613
Kershaw John, Esq., 617
Ketley William, Esq., Sec., 618
Key, Sir Kingsmill, Bart., 613
Koch J. H., Esq., Sec., 610

Lampson, Sir Curtis Miranda, Bart., 607
Langton William, Esq., 601
Langworthy E. R., Esq., 603
Laundy Edwin, Esq., Auditor, 612
Leeke, Admiral Sir Henry J., K.C.B.,
  K.H., 624
Legh Piers Frederick, Esq., 623
Leith John Farley, Esq., 622
Leyland John, Esq., Treasurer, 601
Lowe, Right Hon. Robert, M.P., 605
Luckie D. Fraser, Esq., 618
Lyall George, Esq., 607

Macdonald James, Esq., Gen. Man., 606
MacDonald John R., Esq., Sub-Manager,
  606
Mackenzie Alexander, Esq., 615
Mackinnon W., Esq., 606
McClean J.R., Esq., C.E., M.P., 597
M'Connell James Edward, Esq., 623
Mangles Charles E., Esq., 604
Maynard Frederick, Esq., Aud., 602
Mayo William, Esq., Sec., 622
McDonnell L. J., Esq., 601
Meinertzhagen Daniel, Esq., 607
Michael Walter A., Esq., Sec., 608
Micklethwait F. N., Esq., 603
Moor Henry, Esq., 620
Morgan J. S., Esq., 608
Mowatt Francis, Esq., 602

Nicholas George, Esq., 615
Northcote, Sir Stafford H. Bart., M.P., 607

O'Connor Valentine O'Brien, Esq., 601
Oldfield J., Esq., Sec., 609
Osborne, Capt. Sherard, C.B., R.N., 621
Otway A. J., Esq., M.P., 620
Owen William, Esq., 614

Paget, Lord Alfred, 603
Parson John, Esq., 613
Peek Alfred, Esq., 598
Pender John, Esq., 600, 601, 621
Philips Mark, Esq., 603
Phillips Thomas, Esq., 612
Pickersgill-Cunliffe J. C., Esq., 597
Ponsonby, Hon. Ashley, 620
Potter Richard, Esq., 607
Powell Thomas, Esq., 610
Price Richard, Esq., Sec., 615

Quilter, Ball, and Co., Auditors, 606, 614

Rate Lachlan M., Esq., 599, 608
Rawson Philip, Esq., 600, 621
Reuter Julius, Esq., 605
Reynolds Charles, Esq., 611
Roberts, Mallins, and Colman, Auditors,
  619
Robinson T. F., Esq., Sub-Manager, 606
Rumney Robert, Esq., 598

Russell Francis William, Esq., M.P., 615
Ryland R. Henry, Esq., Sec., 619

Sandell Edward, Esq., Auditor, 611
Saunderson Charles, Esq., 620
Schenley Edward W. H., Esq., 624
Scholfield William F., Esq., 599
Schröder William Henry, Esq., 605
Schröeder John Henry William, Esq., 607
Shackleford W. C., Esq., Man., 609
Shakspear William. Esq., 614
Sharp John, Esq., 609
Sherriff A. C., Esq., M.P., 613, 617
Sheward George, Esq., 604, 611
Shuter William. Esq., Sec., 621
Simpson W. H., Esq., Manager, 616
Smith J., Esq., 621
Smith W. H., Esq., M.P., 603
Stableford William, Esq., Manager, 617
Stenhouse Thomas, Esq., 604
Stephenson, Sir Macdonald, 622
Stephenson W. H., Esq., 599
Stuart-Wortley, Right Hon. James, 597, 599

Tackness Charles, Esq., Auditor, 618
Taylor F. S., Esq., Sec., 612
Taylor R. P., Esq., 611
Thompson William James, Esq., 615
Thomson, Sir William, F.R.S., Consulting Electrician, 605
Thomson John Robert, Esq., 615
Thornton Samuel, Esq., 612

Tibbs J. Evan, Esq., 618
Tolmé J. H., Esq., Eng., 610
Toulmin Henry Heyman, Esq., 615
Townsend Geo. Barnard, Esq., 604
Tucker Robert, Esq., Auditor, 610

Varley Cromwell F., Esq., M.I.C.E., Consulting Electrician, 605
Vickers Thomas, Esq., 598
Vignoles Hutton, Esq., 623
Virtue, George, Esq., 624

Waddell J. & Co., Auditors, 616
Walker George Henry, Esq., 613
Watkin William, Esq., 618
Watson James, Esq., 612
Weaver B., Esq., Sec., 603
Webber Robert Pullen, Esq., Manager, 615
Webster David, Esq., 601
Welch Frederick Isaac, Esq., 614, 619
Wheeler Herbert, Esq., Secretary, 617
Whitaker George, Esq., Secretary, 598
Whitehead John, Jun., Esq, 598
Whitworth Benjamin, Esq., 598
Whitworth Joseph, Esq., F.R.S., 603
Wignall John, Esq., 609
Wilde Samuel John, Esq., 616
Wilkins Frederick Charles, Esq., 615
Wingfield, Sir Charles, K.C.S.I., M.P., 600
Worms George, Esq., 606
Wylde, General, C.B., 603

Young George, Esq., 610

4.—COMMITTEE OF PRIVY COUNCIL FOR TRADE.

WHITEHALL GARDENS, S.W.

President—Right Honourable JOHN BRIGHT, M.P.

COMMITTEE :

The Lord Chancellor. — Chancellor of the Duchy of Lancaster.
First Lord of the Treasury. — Paymaster of the Forces.
The Principal Secretaries of State. — Master of the Mint.
Chancellor and Under Treasurer of the Exchequer. — Such Officers of State in Ireland as are Privy Councillors in England.
Speaker of the House of Commons. — Rt. Hon. Sir Edward Ryan.

Permanent Secretary, Thomas Henry Farrer, Esq.

Parliamentary Secretary, George John Shaw Lefevre, Esq., M.P.

Assistant Secretaries (Commercial Department)—Sir Louis Mallet, C.B.
　　　　　　　　　(Harbour　　　　”　　)—C. Cecil Trevor, Esq.
　　　　　　　　　(Railway　　　　”　　)—Robert G. Wyndham Herbert, Esq.
　　　　　　　　　(Marine　　　　”　　)—Thos. Gray, Esq.

Chief of Statistical Department and Comptroller of Corn Returns—Albany W. Fonblanque, Esq.

Accountant—H. R. Williams, Esq.

Assistants in the Harbour, Railway, and Statistical Departments—Walter F. Larkins, Esq., Duncan Macgregor, Esq., Richard Valpy, Esq.

Private Secretary to the President—Henry G. Calcraft, Esq.

Private Secretary to the Permanent Secretary—Jemmett Browne, Esq.

Private Secretary to the Parliamentary Secretary—Alexander E. Pearson, Esq.

Senior Clerks—G. J. Swanston, Henry R. Lack, Philip H. Hornby, Geo. H. Eveniss, William Boys, John Gaspard Fanshawe, Roger Pocklington, Henry G. Calcraft, John V. T. Doyle, Fred Bunter, W. W. Emerson Tennent, F. T. Jennings, Allen Stoneham, C. Loraine Bell, W. Pattrickson, H. A. Dobson, Thomas R. Bolton, Nicholas Lee, Joseph Gray, W. C. Monkhouse, Jemmett Browne, Esqrs.

Junior Clerks—B. J. Drage, G. N. Ough, Arthur R. Fairfield, Edward Roscoe, W. C. Bradstreet, W. D. W. Lyons, J. M. Reed, C. Pettet, W. W. Leaker, E. J. Pearson, A. E. Pearson, R. P. P. Bingham, A. E. Bateman, Ingram B. Walker, T. E. Price, J. W. Martyn, David Fitzgerald, Henry R. Bence Jones, Henry R. Newport, Arthur Henry Emberson, R. C. Heron Maxwell, Henry C. P. Graves, W. E. Napier, Samuel Waddington, John Hall Clark, John Taylor, T. W. P. Blomefield, Ashley H. Maude, Henry Noel de M. Malan, B. L. C. Travers, Esqrs.

Supplementary Clerks—Dr. Michelsen ; F. G. Hillman, R. Laws, J. L. Rowe, C. W. Brooksby, C. Scott, R. Cart, F. R. Cox, G. H. Simmonds, Esqrs.

Professional Members of Harbour and Marine Departments—Captain W. H. Walker, H.C.S., Captain G. A. Bedford, R.N.

Surveyor General of Steam Vessels—Captain R. Robertson, R.N.

Inspectors (Railway Department) — Captain Tyler, R.E., Colonel Yolland, R.E., Colonel F. H. Rich, R.E., Colonel C. S. Hutchinson, R.E.

Draftsman—Finlay M'Kenzie, Esq.

Librarian—W. M. Bucknall, Esq.

Deputy Accountant—Hugh Owen, Esq.

Bookkeeper—Robert Jackson, Esq.

Law Clerk—F. J. Hargrave Hamel, Esq.

Registrar—J. Whiting Parsley, Esq.

Translator—Carl F. A. Schwebemeyer, Esq.

Supernumerary Clerk Railway Department—Charles Lennox Peel, Esq.

Office Keeper—Henry T. Burgess.

Assistant Office Keeper—Kenneth Macdonald.

Messengers—T. Mitchell, F. Quelch, G. Scarrott, G. Holiday, T. Simmons, W. J. Parsons, C. Eltenton, H. Turner, W. C. Selby, S. Pace, G. Pallet.

Extra Messengers—Robert Fish, F. Lloyd, Chas. Watton.

Porter—Fred. Hill.

STANDARD WEIGHTS AND MEASURES DEPARTMENT—6, Old Palace Yard, S.W. Hours, 11 to 5.

DESIGNS OFFICE—1, Whitehall, S. W. Hours, 10 to 4. Designs and Transfers Registered, 11 to 3.

JOINT STOCK COMPANIES REGISTRATION OFFICE—13, Serjeant's Inn, Fleet Street, E.C.; Dublin, Henrietta Street ; Edinburgh, Exchequer Chamber ; Truro.

GENERAL REGISTER AND RECORD OFFICE OF SHIPPING AND SEAMEN—6, Adelaide Place, London Bridge, E.C. Hours of attendance, 10 to 4.

OFFICE FOR SURVEY OF STEAM SHIPS—5, East India Avenue, Leadenhall Street, E.C.

5.—RAILWAY BENEVOLENT INSTITUTION.

For the Relief of Railway Officers and Servants, their Widows, and Orphan Children, when in distressed circumstances.

Established 1858.

Under the Patronage of Her Most Gracious Majesty the Queen and His Royal Highness the Prince of Wales.

Invested Fund, £20,000.

President—GEORGE CARR GLYN, Esq.

TRUSTEES :

His Grace the DUKE OF BUCKINGHAM ; The Hon. F. G. B. PONSONBY ; SAMUEL BEALE, Esq.

BOARD OF MANAGEMENT :

Chairman—HENRY OAKLEY, Esq.

Deputy-Chairman—HARRY CHUBB, Esq.

AUDITORS :

P. W. DAWSON, Esq. .............R.C.H. | F. W. SPOONER, Esq. ....L. T. & S.
R. SAVILL, Esq. ....L. & N. W. | A. FITCH, Esq. ....G. N.

Treasurer—GEORGE GRENFELL GLYN, Esq., M.P.

Secretary—WILLIAM FREDERICK MILLS, Esq.

Offices, 123, Seymour Street, Euston Square, London, N.W.

6.—RAILWAY CLEARING HOUSE.

Seymour Street, Euston Square, N.W.

Chairman—GEORGE CARR GLYN, Esq.

Treasurer—GEORGE GRENFELL GLYN, Esq., M.P.

Secretary—P. W. DAWSON, Esq.

Auditors—JAMES Mc. CLELLAND, Esq., and HARRY CHUBB, Esq.

7.—IRISH RAILWAY CLEARING HOUSE.
(23 Vic., cap. 29.)
5, Kildare Street, Dublin.

Chairman—JOHN BARLOW, Esq.
Treasurer—THE BANK OF IRELAND.   Secretary—J. W. ELWIN, Esq.

8.—THE UNITED KINGDOM RAILWAY OFFICERS' AND SERVANTS' ASSOCIATION, AND RAILWAY PROVIDENT SOCIETY.
(Enrolled under Act of Parliament.)
For Pensions, Sum in case of Death of Member or Wife, &c.

To December 31st, 1868, upwards of **£8,000** paid for Accidents, and Accidental and Ordinary Deaths, and five annuitants have been elected to **£20** each.

TRUSTEES :
LORD ALFRED PAGET, Queen Anne Street, Cavendish Square.
JOHN ROBINSON Mc. CLEAN, Esq., M.P.
THOMAS BRASSEY, Sen., Esq., Great George Street, S.W.
WILLIAM GORDON THOMSON, Esq., Director Imperial Bank, Lothbury.
WILLIAM CONINGHAM, Esq., Brighton.
Treasurer—HENRY DYNE, Esq. S.E., Railway Station, Dover.
Bankers—The IMPERIAL BANK, Lothbury.
Secretary—Mr. W. HORATIO WESTON.
Offices 52, Gracechurch Street, City, E.C.

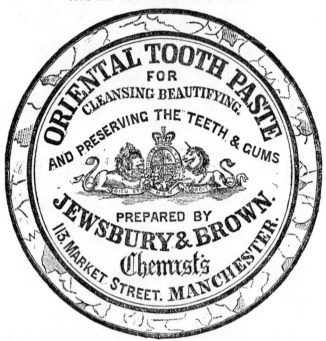

RAILWAY CARRIAGE COMPANY
(LIMITED),

OLDBURY, NEAR BIRMINGHAM,

MANUFACTURERS OF

RAILWAY CARRIAGES, WAGONS, and IRONWORK,

Of every description, either for Cash or upon Deferred Payments.

CHIEF OFFICES:

AT THE WORKS, OLDBURY, NEAR BIRMINGHAM.

LONDON OFFICES:

6, STOREY'S GATE, GREAT GEORGE ST., WESTMINSTER.

[z.-5.

THE MIDLAND WAGON COMPANY

ESTABLISHED 1853.

MANUFACTURERS OF RAILWAY CARRIAGES AND WAGONS, of every description,

For Cash, or by Deferred Payments extending over a series of years.

The Company having upwards of 10,000 COAL, COKE, IRONSTONE, and BALLAST WAGONS, have generally a number to LET.

HENRY BRIDGES, Secretary.

Midland Works, Birmingham.

[H. B.-18.

J. H. BOOBBYER, LATE STURCH AND BOOBBYER,

(Established nearly 200 years, for the supply of Goods of the best manufacture at the lowest prices).

A PRIZE MEDAL for Superior Locks was awarded to J. H. BOOBBYER at the Great Exhibition of 1851, and first-class Prize Medal for superiority of Goods exhibited by him at the Paris Universal Exhibition of 1855, from the Universal Society for Encouragement of Art and Industry.

Wholesale and Retail Ironmongery, Brass Foundry, Nail, and Tool Warehouse.

Iron, Copper, and Zinc Nails; Patent Locks of all descriptions, lever and machine-made; China, Glass, and Wood Furniture of all kinds with Patent Shifting Spindles. Dr. Arnott's Ventilator, 4s.; and the new registered Venetian Ventilator, so much admired, &c., 6s. 6d. each. Agricultural Digging Forks, Patent Spades, Daisy Rakes, and all kinds of Garden and other Tools.

PATENT SPINDLED CHINA MORTISE FURNITURE, white, 1s. per set; black, 1s. 2d.; white and gold, 1s. 8d. per set.

WHITE CHINA FINGER PLATES.....................4s. per dozen.

J. H. Boobbyer's Superior Four Lever Drawer and Cut Cupboard Lock, 2s. each, the best make; also, Mortise Locks for Room Doors. Locks of every sort made to Order, to go on place of Old Locks, at any price required, if not found on stock.

14, STANHOPE STREET, Newcastle Street, Strand,

LONDON, W.C.

[40-Lo.

THE METROPOLITAN
RAILWAY CARRIAGE AND WAGON COMPANY
(LIMITED),

SALTLEY WORKS, BIRMINGHAM,

(Successor to Messrs. Joseph Wright and Sons),

Manufacturers of Railway Carriages, Wagons, and Railway Ironwork of every description.

RAILWAY CARRIAGES and WAGONS built for Cash, or upon Deferred Payments.

A large number of Coal, Ironstone, Ballast, and other Wagons, to be Let on Hire

Manufactory & Chief Offices—SALTLEY WORKS, Birmingham; LONDON OFFICES — 27, Great George Street, Westminster, S.W

[31-Lo.

S. MOULTON & CO.,
KINGSTON INDIA RUBBER MILLS
BRADFORD, WILTSHIRE,

MANUFACTURERS of their Patent Steel Embedded and other India Rubber Springs, for Locomotives, Railway Carriages and Trucks, India Rubber Valves, Sheet Packing, Washer Rings, Hose Pipes and Tubing, Machine Banding, Waterproof Garments, Blankets, Sheeting, Elastic Hot Water Beds, Cushions, &c., &c.

[32-Lo.

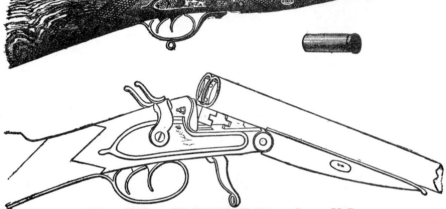

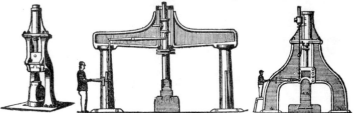

TUPPER AND COMPANY,

MANUFACTURERS OF

PATENT GALVANIZED IRON

AND

GALVANIZED TINNED IRON,

CORRUGATED AND PLAIN;

ALSO,

GALVANIZED and GALVANIZED TINNED

PATENT ROOFING TILES.

ESTIMATES AND DRAWINGS FURNISHED FOR

IRON HOUSES, CHURCHES, ROOFS, SHEDS, STORES,

&c.,

All sorts of Iron Work Galvanized.

MERCHANTS AND SHIPPERS SUPPLIED.

WORKS:

LIMEHOUSE and BIRMINGHAM.

OFFICES:

61a, MOORGATE STREET, LONDON, E.C.

[43.-Lo.

DARLINGTON WORKS, SOUTHWARK BRIDGE ROAD, LONDON.

LONDON AND SOUTH-WESTERN RAILWAY

WATERLOO TERMINUS.

SIGNAL WORKS, NEW CITY ROAD, GLASGOW.

Signal Bridge, House, Signal & Locking Apparatus

ERECTED BY

STEVENS AND SON,

ENGINEERS AND FOUNDERS,

PATENTEES AND MANUFACTURERS OF

SEMAPHORE RAILWAY SIGNALS

IN IRON, STEEL, AND WOOD,

PATENT LOCKING LEVER FRAMES,

WITH ALL THE MOST RECENT IMPROVEMENTS,

WROUGHT AND CAST IRON GIRDER BRIDGES, &c., &c.

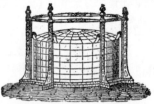

GAS ENGINEERS, &c.,

Gas Works for Towns, Mansions, Public Buildings, &c.

MANUFACTURERS OF RAILWAY SIGNAL, STATION, AND EVERY OTHER DESCRIPTION OF LAMPS.

REGISTERING TURNSTILES FOR TOLL BRIDGES, PUBLIC GARDENS, &c.

[46-Lo.

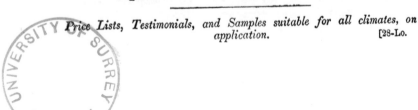